APA Handbook of Consumer Psychology

APA Handbooks in Psychology® Series

APA Addiction Syndrome Handbook—two volumes
    Howard J. Shaffer, Editor-in-Chief

APA Educational Psychology Handbook—three volumes
    Karen R. Harris, Steve Graham, and Tim Urdan, Editors-in-Chief

APA Handbook of Behavior Analysis—two volumes
    Gregory J. Madden, Editor-in-Chief

APA Handbook of Career Intervention—two volumes
    Paul J. Hartung, Mark L. Savickas, and W. Bruce Walsh, Editors-in-Chief

APA Handbook of Clinical Geropsychology—two volumes
    Peter A. Lichtenberg and Benjamin T. Mast, Editors-in-Chief

APA Handbook of Clinical Psychology—five volumes
    John C. Norcross, Gary R. VandenBos, and Donald K. Freedheim, Editors-in-Chief

APA Handbook of Community Psychology—two volumes
    Meg A. Bond, Irma Serrano-García, and Christopher B. Keys, Editors-in Chief

APA Handbook of Comparative Psychology—two volumes
    Josep Call, Editor-in-Chief

APA Handbook of Consumer Psychology—one volume
    Lynn R. Kahle, Editor-in-Chief

APA Handbook of Contemporary Family Psychology—three volumes
    Barbara H. Fiese, Editor-in-Chief

APA Handbook of Counseling Psychology—two volumes
    Nadya A. Fouad, Editor-in-Chief

APA Handbook of Dementia—one volume
    Glenn E. Smith, Editor-in-Chief

APA Handbook of Ethics in Psychology—two volumes
    Samuel J. Knapp, Editor-in-Chief

APA Handbook of Forensic Neuropsychology—one volume
    Shane S. Bush, Editor-in-Chief

APA Handbook of Forensic Psychology—two volumes
    Brian L. Cutler and Patricia A. Zapf, Editors-in-Chief

APA Handbook of Giftedness and Talent—one volume
    Steven I. Pfeiffer, Editor-in-Chief

APA Handbook of Human Systems Integration—one volume
    Deborah A. Boehm-Davis, Francis T. Durso, and John D. Lee, Editors-in-Chief

APA Handbook of Industrial and Organizational Psychology—three volumes
    Sheldon Zedeck, Editor-in-Chief

APA Handbook of Intellectual and Developmental Disabilities—two volumes
    Laraine Masters Glidden, Editor-in-Chief

APA Handbook of Men and Masculinities—one volume
    Y. Joel Wong and Stephen R. Wester, Editors-in-Chief

APA Handbook of Multicultural Psychology—two volumes
    Frederick T. L. Leong, Editor-in-Chief

APA Handbook of Nonverbal Communication—one volume
    David Matsumoto, Hyisung Hwang, and Mark Frank, Editors-in-Chief

APA Handbook of Personality and Social Psychology—four volumes
    Mario Mikulincer and Phillip R. Shaver, Editors-in-Chief
APA Handbook of Psychology and Juvenile Justice—one volume
    Kirk Heilbrun, Editor-in-Chief
APA Handbook of Psychology, Religion, and Spirituality—two volumes
    Kenneth I. Pargament, Editor-in-Chief
APA Handbook of the Psychology of Women—two volumes
    Cheryl B. Travis and Jacquelyn W. White, Editors-in-Chief
APA Handbook of Psychopathology—two volumes
    James N. Butcher, Editor-in-Chief
APA Handbook of Psychopharmacology—one volume
    Suzette M. Evans, Editor-in-Chief
APA Handbook of Research Methods in Psychology—three volumes
    Harris Cooper, Editor-in-Chief
APA Handbook of Sexuality and Psychology—two volumes
    Deborah L. Tolman and Lisa M. Diamond, Editors-in-Chief
APA Handbook of Sport and Exercise Psychology—two volumes
    Mark H. Anshel, Editor-in-Chief
APA Handbook of Testing and Assessment in Psychology—three volumes
    Kurt F. Geisinger, Editor-in-Chief
APA Handbook of Trauma Psychology—two volumes
    Steven N. Gold, Editor-in-Chief

APA Handbooks in Psychology

APA Handbook of Consumer Psychology

Lynn R. Kahle, *Editor-in-Chief*
Tina M. Lowrey and Joel Huber, *Associate Editors*

AMERICAN PSYCHOLOGICAL ASSOCIATION

Copyright © 2022 by the American Psychological Association. All rights reserved. Except as permitted under the United States Copyright Act of 1976, no part of this publication may be reproduced or distributed in any form or by any means, including, but not limited to, the process of scanning and digitization, or stored in a database or retrieval system, without the prior written permission of the publisher.

The opinions and statements published are the responsibility of the authors and editors, and such opinions and statements do not necessarily represent the policies of the American Psychological Association.

Published by
American Psychological Association
750 First Street, NE
Washington, DC 20002
https://www.apa.org

Order Department
https://www.apa.org/pubs/books
order@apa.org

In the U.K., Europe, Africa, and the Middle East, copies may be ordered from Eurospan
https://www.eurospanbookstore.com/apa
info@eurospangroup.com

Typeset in Berkeley by TIPS Technical Publishing, Inc., Carrboro, NC

Printer: Sheridan Books, Chelsea, MI
Cover Designer: Naylor Design, Washington, DC

Library of Congress Cataloging-in-Publication Data

Names: Kahle, Lynn R., editor. | Lowrey, Tina M., editor. | Huber, Joel, editor.
Title: APA handbook of consumer psychology / editor-in-chief: Lynn R. Kahle, associate editors: Tina M. Lowrey and Joel Huber.
Description: Washington, DC : American Psychological Association, [2022] | Includes bibliographical references and index.
Identifiers: LCCN 2021019779 (print) | LCCN 2021019780 (ebook) | ISBN 9781433836428 (hardcover) | ISBN 9781433838392 (ebook)
Subjects: LCSH: Consumers--Psychology. | Consumer behavior. | Consumers--Attitudes.
Classification: LCC HF5415.32 .A63 2022 (print) | LCC HF5415.32 (ebook) | DDC 658.8/342--dc23
LC record available at https://lccn.loc.gov/2021019779
LC ebook record available at https://lccn.loc.gov/2021019780

https://doi.org/10.1037/0000262-000

Printed in the United States of America

10 9 8 7 6 5 4 3 2 1

Contents

Editorial Board xi
About the Editor-in-Chief xiii
About the Associate Editors xv
Contributors xvii
A Note From the Publisher xxi
Introduction xxiii

Part I. Perspectives on Consumer Psychology. 1

Chapter 1. Consumer Psychology: Evolving Goals and Research Orientations 3
    Joel B. Cohen and William L. Wilkie

Chapter 2. The Activation and Use of Declarative and Procedural Knowledge 47
    Robert S. Wyer Jr.

Chapter 3. Intentional Behaviorism: A Research Methodology for Consumer Psychology .. 79
    Gordon R. Foxall

Chapter 4. Structural Equation Models in Consumer Research: Exploring Intuitions and Deeper Meanings of SEMs 103
    Richard P. Bagozzi

Chapter 5. Understanding the Changing Role and Functions of Marketing 143
    Kevin Lane Keller

Part II. Consumers Have Demographic and Psychographic Characteristics 163

Chapter 6. Poverty and Consumer Psychology 165
    Ronald Paul Hill

Chapter 7. Children as Consumers: A Review of 50 Years of Research in Marketing .. 185
    Deborah Roedder John and Lan Nguyen Chaplin

Chapter 8. Gender Research in Marketing, Consumer Behavior, Advertising, and Beyond: Past, Present, and Future 203
    Linda Tuncay Zayer and Kathrynn Pounders

Chapter 9. A Structural Versus Dynamic View of Personality in Consumer Behavior .. 219
    Suresh Ramanathan

Chapter 10. Consumer Values 249
    Eda Gurel-Atay

Chapter 11. Lifestyle and Sport: Emulation Marketing 267
    Pierre Valette-Florence, Tony Meenaghan, and Lynn R. Kahle

Part III. Consumers Live in a Social Psychological World 299

Chapter 12. Cultural Influences on Consumer Psychology.................... 301
    Carlos J. Torelli and Sharon Shavitt
Chapter 13. Attitude Change and Persuasion: Classic, Metacognitive, and
    Advocacy Perspectives................................... 323
    Zakary L. Tormala and Derek D. Rucker
Chapter 14. Social Relationships and Consumer Behavior 351
    Kelley Gullo Wight, Peggy J. Liu, James R. Bettman, and Gavan J. Fitzsimons
Chapter 15. Sustainability: Understanding Consumer Behavior in a Circular Economy.. 373
    Marius Claudy and Mark Peterson
Chapter 16. Marketing Ethics, Ethical Consumers, and Ethical Lapses............. 393
    Ann-Marie Kennedy and Sommer Kapitan
Chapter 17. The Role of Time in Consumer Psychology........................ 413
    Ashwani Monga, Ozum Zor, and Rafay A. Siddiqui
Chapter 18. Psychological Aspects of Economic Expectations 429
    Richard Curtin

Part IV. Businesses Use Psychology to Communicate With Consumers 449

Chapter 19. Language and Consumer Psychology 451
    Ruth Pogacar, Alican Mecit, Fei Gao, L. J. Shrum, and Tina M. Lowrey
Chapter 20. The Consumer Psychology of Traditional Media 471
    Esther Thorson
Chapter 21. Social Media: From Classic Psychological Theories to New Opportunities.. 489
    Cait Lamberton and Ashlee Humphreys
Chapter 22. Celebrity Endorsements 513
    Eda Gurel-Atay

Part V. Consumers Process Cognitions and Affect 527

Chapter 23. Omission Neglect and Consumer Judgment and Inference Based
    on Limited Evidence..................................... 529
    Frank R. Kardes, Steven S. Posavac, and Donald R. Gaffney
Chapter 24. Three Mechanisms of Mind–Body Influence: Feelings, Concepts,
    and Procedures... 551
    Spike W. S. Lee and Lorenzo Cecutti
Chapter 25. The Interplay of Affect and Cognition: A Review of How Feelings Guide
    Consumer Behavior...................................... 581
    Rashmi Adaval and Maria Galli
Chapter 26. Consumer Involvement and Engagement: From Involvement's
    Elaboration Likelihood to Engagement's Investment Propensity 609
    Linda D. Hollebeek and Rajendra K. Srivastava
Chapter 27. Neural Basis of Consumer Decision Making and Neuroforecasting 621
    Alexander Genevsky and Carolyn Yoon
Chapter 28. Consuming for Happiness..................................... 637
    Siok Kuan Tambyah and Soo Jiuan Tan

Part VI. Businesses Use Psychology to Carry Out Functions 647

Chapter 29. Omnichannel Retailing: A Consumer Perspective 649
      Peter C. Verhoef, Koert van Ittersum, P. K. Kannan, and Jeff Inman
Chapter 30. Perceived Price Differences and Consumer Behavior 673
      Kent B. Monroe
Chapter 31. The Brand Property Strength Framework: Integrating Theory
   and Research on Brand Consumer Psychology 691
      Joseph R. Priester, Monique A. Fleming, Leigh Anne Novak Donovan,
      and Chaumanix Dutton
Chapter 32. Innovation and Product Development........................... 713
      Doug Hall
Chapter 33. Human Factors Research and User-Centered Design 725
      Robert W. Proctor, Leon Zeng, and Kim-Phuong L. Vu

Index 739

Editorial Board

EDITOR-IN-CHIEF
Lynn R. Kahle, PhD, Professor Emeritus of Marketing, Department of Marketing, Lundquist College of Business, University of Oregon, Eugene, OR, United States

ASSOCIATE EDITORS
Tina M. Lowrey, PhD, Professor of Marketing, Marketing Department, HEC Paris, Jouy-en-Josas, France

Joel Huber, PhD, Alan D. Schwartz Professor Emeritus, Fuqua School of Business, Duke University, Durham, NC, United States

About the Editor-in-Chief

Lynn R. Kahle, PhD, has always believed that consuming food contributes to happiness and sustaining health. He received his PhD in social psychology from the University of Nebraska (corn-fed beef) and subsequently worked as a postdoctoral fellow at the University of Michigan Institute for Social Research (Frankenmuth chicken). He is an emeritus professor of marketing and recipient of the 2014 Thomas Stewart Distinguished Professorship at the University of Oregon Lundquist College of Business (Dungeness crab, fresh strawberries). For many years he chaired the department of marketing there (Voodoo doughnuts, pinot wine). He served as founding director of the Warsaw Sports Marketing Center (craft beer, hazelnuts). He has also taught at Hanyang University in Seoul (kimchi), Pace University in New York (pizza), Griffith University in Australia (bbq'd prawns), Copenhagen Business School in Denmark (smørrebrød), and Singapore Management University (chili crab). Dr. Kahle has enjoyed a study abroad program in Vienna, Austria (Wiener schnitzel), and won a Fulbright scholarship to work in Phnom Penh, Cambodia (Samlor korko).

He previously served as president of the Society for Consumer Psychology. He represented consumer psychology for two terms on the American Psychological Association Council of Representatives and chaired the APA Membership Board. He advocated for human rights as the president of the City of Eugene Human Rights Presidents' Council. Meetings of these groups often involved a tuna sandwich lunch.

Dr. Kahle was honored with the Lifetime Achievement Award from the American Marketing Association Consumer Behavior SIG and the Distinguished Career Contributions to the Scientific Understanding of Sports Business from the American Marketing Association Sports SIG. He received the Stotlar Award for Education from the Sport Marketing Association. Champagne is nice on occasion.

Dr. Kahle helped develop the List of Values and has subsequently conducted research on values and lifestyles. His work has been published in such places as the *Journal of Personality and Social Psychology*, *Journal of Consumer Psychology*, *Journal of Consumer Research*, and *Journal of Marketing*. He has also studied consumption in relation to religion, to sport, and to sustainability. His 15 books include *Marketplace Lifestyles in an Age of Social Media* with Pierre Valette-Florence and *Consumer Social Values*, edited with Eda Gurel-Atay. And for dessert he sometimes likes tiramisu, because it deliciously combines diverse layers into a substantial collection of integrated tastes.

About the Associate Editors

Tina M. Lowrey, PhD, is a professor of marketing at HEC Paris. Her research interests include children's consumer behavior, materialism, the application of psycholinguistic theory to marketing communications, and gift giving and ritualistic consumption. Her work has appeared in numerous journals, including the *Journal of Consumer Research*, *Journal of Consumer Psychology*, *Journal of Marketing*, *Journal of the Association for Consumer Research*, *International Journal of Research in Marketing*, and *Journal of Advertising*. She is currently serving on the *JCR* Policy Board and is on the editorial review boards of the *Journal of Consumer Psychology*, *International Journal of Research in Marketing*, and *Journal of Advertising*. She edited *Brick & Mortar Shopping in the 21st Century* and *Psycholinguistic Phenomena in Marketing Communications* (both Erlbaum). She coedited *The Routledge Companion to Consumer Behavior* (with Mike Solomon). She has chapters in *Contemporary Consumption Rituals: A Research Anthology* (which she coedited with Cele Otnes); *Handbook of Research on Identity Theory in Marketing*; *The Psychology of Entertainment Media: Blurring the Lines Between Entertainment and Persuasion*; *The Sage Handbook of Persuasion: Developments in Theory and Practice*; *Handbook of Media Effects*; *Go Figure: New Directions in Advertising Rhetoric*; *Handbook of Qualitative Research Methods in Marketing*; *Marketing Communication: Emerging Trends and Developments*; *Gender Issues and Consumer Behavior*; *Gift Giving: A Research Anthology*; and *New Developments and Approaches in Consumer Behavior Research*, among others. Dr. Lowrey has served as the Association for Consumer Research (ACR) treasurer, cochaired the first-ever virtual ACR conference in 2020 (which was supposed to be in Paris), cochaired three European and Latin American ACR conferences, and solo-chaired a Society for Consumer Psychology (SCP) boutique conference and an American Psychological Association Division 23 conference. She received a BBA in finance from the University of Houston, an MS in advertising from the University of Illinois, and her PhD in communication and social psychology from the University of Illinois. Dr. Lowrey has taught at Rider University (New Jersey) and the University of Texas at San Antonio, and is currently at HEC Paris (serving as PhD coordinator at the latter two institutions). She has visited at ESCP Paris, NYU, Tulane, University of Sydney, and Wharton. She currently teaches two doctoral seminars at HEC: research methods to PhD students in all business disciplines and consumer behavior to primarily marketing students. And, yes, she agrees with Lynn that champagne is always good, and she has not yet found any cuisine that isn't wonderful!

Joel Huber, PhD, is the Alan D. Schwartz Professor Emeritus at the Fuqua School of Business, Duke University. He received his undergraduate degree from Princeton and his MBA and PhD in 1974 from the Wharton School of the University of Pennsylvania. In addition to Fuqua, he has taught at the business schools at Penn, Columbia, and Purdue University. He was associate dean for the Daytime program at Fuqua from 1995 to 1999. He is on the review boards for numerous journals and has been an associate editor for the *Journal of Consumer Research*, *Journal of Consumer Psychology*, *Marketing Science*, and *International Journal of Research in Marketing*. From 2006 to 2009 he served as editor-in-chief for the *Journal of Marketing Research*, and from 2014 to 2020 he was the inaugural editor-in-chief for the *Journal of the Association for Consumer Research*.

Dr. Huber's research interest focuses on predicting and understanding market choice, with a continuing focus on ways to measure preference through choice-based conjoint analysis. He has worked for many years with Sawtooth Software and others to help develop new ways to determine how best to measure consumers' product desires and beliefs.

A series of grants from the U.S. Environmental Protection Agency led to studies of the value of cleaner lakes and streams and healthier drinking water. That work later evolved into a number of studies with W. Kip Viscusi and Jason Bell exploring household recycling behavior from a large national sample of households between 2005 and 2015. Research with Martin Meissner and others has used eye tracking to reveal the way people process complex repeated choice tasks.

His published papers are available on his website at https://faculty.fuqua.duke.edu/~jch8/bio/publications.htm?_ga=2.257412619.1024440125.1616942882-98465899.1570455756.

Contributors

Rashmi Adaval, PhD, Department of Marketing, University of Cincinnati, Cincinnati, OH, United States

Richard P. Bagozzi, PhD, Stephen M. Ross School of Business, University of Michigan, Ann Arbor, MI, United States

James R. Bettman, PhD, Fuqua School of Business, Duke University, Durham, NC, United States

Lorenzo Cecutti, MPhil, Rotman School of Management, University of Toronto, Toronto, Ontario, Canada

Lan Nguyen Chaplin, PhD, Department of Marketing, College of Business Administration, University of Illinois Chicago, Chicago, IL, United States

Marius Claudy, PhD, College of Business, University College Dublin, Dublin, Ireland

Joel B. Cohen, PhD, Marketing Department, University of Florida, Gainesville, FL, United States

Richard Curtin, PhD, Survey Research Center, Institute for Social Research, University of Michigan, Ann Arbor, MI, United States

Leigh Anne Novak Donovan, PhD, Lubin School of Business, Pace University, New York, NY, United States

Chaumanix Dutton, PhD, W. P. Carey School of Business, Arizona State University, Tempe, AZ, United States

Gavan J. Fitzsimons, PhD, Fuqua School of Business, Duke University, Durham, NC, United States

Monique A. Fleming, PhD, Department of Psychology, USC Dornsife College of Letters, Arts and Sciences, University of Southern California, Los Angeles, CA, United States

Gordon R. Foxall, DSocSc, PhD, Cardiff Business School, Cardiff University, Cardiff, Wales, United Kingdom; Department of Business Administration, Reykjavik University, Reykjavik, Iceland

Donald R. Gaffney, MS, Department of Marketing, Lindner College of Business, University of Cincinnati, Cincinnati, OH, United States

Maria Galli, PhD, Department of Marketing, ESADE, Sant Cugat, Spain

Fei Gao, PhD, Department of Marketing, Bentley University, Waltham, MA, United States

Alexander Genevsky, PhD, Department of Marketing Management, Rotterdam School of Management, Erasmus University, Rotterdam, The Netherlands

Eda Gurel-Atay, PhD, independent researcher, Kirkland, WA, United States

Contributors

Doug Hall, BS, Eureka! Ranch, Cincinnati, OH, United States

Ronald Paul Hill, PhD, Department of Marketing, Kogod School of Business, American University, Washington, DC, United States

Linda D. Hollebeek, PhD, Montpellier Business School - University of Montpellier, Montpellier Research in Management, Montpellier, France; Department of Business Administration, Tallinn University of Technology, Tallinn, Estonia

Joel Huber, PhD, Fuqua School of Business, Duke University, Durham, NC, United States

Ashlee Humphreys, PhD, Integrated Marketing Communications, Medill School of Journalism, Media, Integrated Marketing Communications, Northwestern University, Evanston, IL, United States

Jeff Inman, PhD, Joseph M. Katz Graduate School of Business, University of Pittsburgh, Pittsburgh, PA, United States

Deborah Roedder John, PhD, Department of Marketing, Carlson School of Management, University of Minnesota, Minneapolis, MN, United States

Lynn R. Kahle, PhD, Department of Marketing, Lundquist College of Business, University of Oregon, Eugene, OR, United States

P. K. Kannan, PhD, Robert H. Smith School of Business, University of Maryland, College Park, MD, United States; Faculty of Economics and Business, University of Groningen, Groningen, The Netherlands

Sommer Kapitan, PhD, Auckland University of Technology, Auckland, New Zealand

Frank R. Kardes, PhD, Department of Marketing, Lindner College of Business, University of Cincinnati, Cincinnati, OH, United States

Kevin Lane Keller, PhD, Tuck School of Business, Dartmouth College, Hanover, NH, United States

Ann-Marie Kennedy, PhD, Department of Management, Marketing and Entrepreneurship, University of Canterbury, Christchurch, New Zealand

Cait Lamberton, PhD, The Wharton School, Marketing Department, University of Pennsylvania, Philadelphia, PA, United States

Spike W. S. Lee, PhD, Rotman School of Management and Department of Psychology, University of Toronto, Toronto, Ontario, Canada

Peggy J. Liu, PhD, Joseph M. Katz Graduate School of Business, University of Pittsburgh, Pittsburgh, PA, United States

Tina M. Lowrey, PhD, Marketing Department, HEC Paris, Jouy-en-Josas, France

Alican Mecit, Marketing Department, HEC Paris, Jouy-en-Josas, France

Tony Meenaghan, PhD, Graduate School of Business, University College Dublin, Dublin, Ireland

Ashwani Monga, PhD, Rutgers University, Newark, NJ, United States

Kent B. Monroe, DBA, Gies College of Business, University of Illinois at Urbana-Champaign, Champaign, IL, United States

Mark Peterson, PhD, Department of Management and Marketing, University of Wyoming, Laramie, WY, United States

Ruth Pogacar, PhD, Department of Marketing, Haskayne School of Business, University of Calgary, Calgary, Alberta, Canada

Steven S. Posavac, PhD, Owen Graduate School of Management, Vanderbilt University, Nashville, TN, United States

Kathrynn Pounders, PhD, Stan Richards School of Advertising & Public Relations, Moody College of Communication, The University of Texas at Austin, TX, United States

Joseph R. Priester, PhD, Department of Marketing, Marshall School of Business, University of Southern California, Los Angeles, CA, United States

Robert W. Proctor, PhD, Department of Psychological Sciences, Purdue University, West Lafayette, IN, United States

Suresh Ramanathan, PhD, Office of the Dean, Great Lakes Institute of Management, Manamai Village, Tamil Nadu, India

Derek D. Rucker, PhD, Kellogg School of Management, Northwestern University, Evanston, IL, United States

Sharon Shavitt, PhD, Gies College of Business, University of Illinois at Urbana-Champaign, Champaign, IL, United States

L. J. Shrum, PhD, Marketing Department, HEC Paris, Jouy-en-Josas, France

Rafay A. Siddiqui, PhD, Leavey School of Business, Santa Clara University, Santa Clara, CA, United States

Rajendra K. Srivastava, PhD, Novartis Professor of Marketing Strategy and Innovation, Indian School of Business, Hyderabad and Mohali, India

Siok Kuan Tambyah, PhD, Department of Marketing, NUS Business School, National University of Singapore, Singapore

Soo Jiuan Tan, PhD, Department of Marketing, NUS Business School, National University of Singapore, Singapore

Esther Thorson, PhD, School of Journalism, College of Communication Arts and Sciences, Michigan State University, East Lansing, MI, United States

Carlos J. Torelli, PhD, Gies College of Business, University of Illinois at Urbana-Champaign, Champaign, IL, United States

Zakary L. Tormala, PhD, Graduate School of Business, Stanford University, Stanford, CA, United States

Pierre Valette-Florence, PhD, Grenoble IAE & CERAG, Université Grenoble Alpes, Saint-Martin-d'Hères, France

Koert van Ittersum, PhD, Faculty of Economics and Business, University of Groningen, Groningen, The Netherlands

Peter C. Verhoef, PhD, Department of Marketing, Faculty of Economics and Business, University of Groningen, Groningen, The Netherlands

Kim-Phuong L. Vu, PhD, Department of Psychology, California State University, Long Beach, Long Beach, CA, United States

Kelley Gullo Wight, PhD, Kelley School of Business, Indiana University, Bloomington, IN, United States

William L. Wilkie, PhD, Department of Marketing, Mendoza College of Business, University of Notre Dame, Notre Dame, IN, United States

Robert S. Wyer Jr., PhD, Department of Marketing, University of Cincinnati, Cincinnati, OH, United States

Carolyn Yoon, PhD, Stephen M. Ross School of Business, University of Michigan, Ann Arbor, MI, United States

Linda Tuncay Zayer, PhD, Quinlan School of Business, Loyola University Chicago, Chicago, IL, United States

Leon Zeng, PhD, Morningstar Inc., Chicago, IL, United States

Ozum Zor, PhD, School of Business, Rutgers University, Camden, NJ, United States

A Note From the Publisher

The *APA Handbook of Consumer Psychology* is the 33rd publication to be released in the American Psychological Association's *APA Handbooks in Psychology*® series, instituted in 2010. The series comprises both single volumes and multivolume sets focused on core subfields or on highly focused content areas and emerging subfields. A complete listing of the series titles to date can be found on pages ii–iii.

Each publication in the series is primarily formulated to address the reference interests and needs of researchers, clinicians, and practitioners in psychology. Each also addresses the needs of graduate students for well-organized and highly detailed supplementary texts, whether to "fill in" their own specialty areas or to acquire solid familiarity with other specialties and emerging trends across the breadth of psychology. Many of the sets additionally bear strong interest for professionals in pertinent complementary fields (i.e., depending on content area), be they corporate executives and human resources personnel; psychiatrists; doctors, nurses, and other health personnel; teachers and school administrators; counselors; legal professionals; and so forth.

Under the direction of small and select editorial boards consisting of top scholars in the field, with chapters authored by both senior and rising researchers and practitioners, each reference commits to a steady focus on best science and best practice. Coverage converges on what is currently known in the particular topical area (including basic historical reviews) and the identification of the most pertinent sources of information in both the core and evolving literature. Volumes and chapters alike pinpoint practical issues; probe unresolved and controversial topics; and highlight future theoretical, research, and practice trends. The editors provide guidance to the "dialogue" among chapters through internal cross-referencing that demonstrates a robust integration of topics. Readers are thus offered a clear understanding of the complex interrelationships within each field.

With content edited and authored by some of the most respected members of the largest association of psychologists in the world, the *APA Handbooks in Psychology* series is an indispensable and authoritative reference resource for researchers, instructors, practitioners, and field leaders alike.

Introduction

OVERVIEW

Consumer psychology studies the human behavior of purchase and consumption activities, as well as decisions about products, services, ideas, and experiences. It investigates a myriad of motives, social interactions, and choices that drive individual economic and consumption behaviors and processes, as well as their consequences, ranging from individual happiness to environmental conditions to societal well-being. One textbook described consumer behavior as encompassing the broad topics of "buying, having, and being" (Solomon, 2017), exposing the existential centrality of consumption. Consumption could be viewed as the manifest expression of human needs and desires. As Gloria Steinem said, "We can tell our values by looking at our checkbook stubs." Today it might be our credit card statements rather than checkbook stubs that depict our discretionary choices as consumers. Regardless, consumer psychology certainly is the foundation of expression for business and economic exchange.

Although this handbook is the first on consumer psychology in the American Psychological Association (APA) series, we hope to build on our non-APA predecessors. Haugtvedt et al. (2008) produced an excellent *Handbook of Consumer Psychology*, which we hope this volume updates. Likewise, the *Routledge International Handbook of Consumer Psychology*, by Jansson-Boyd and Zawisza (2017), also contributed an important addition to this space, on which we hope to expand. We do not dive deeply into methodology here because a recent handbook has done a thorough and admirable job on that topic (Kardes et al., 2019).

This handbook surveys what we currently know in the area of consumer psychology, including basic historical reviews. It identifies the most pertinent sources of information in both core and emerging literature. Chapters pinpoint practical issues, probe unresolved and controversial topics, and present future theoretical, research, and practice trends. The tone is meta-analytic. It lays out controversies but seeks to be balanced.

Several aspirations guided our planning for this handbook. We assume readers have a high level of curiosity and desire to have a greater understanding of consumer issues at a sophisticated level. We target the content toward a primary audience of psychologists, consumer researchers, practitioners, and graduate students. We summarize consumer knowledge relevant to advertisers, anthropologists, brand managers, communicators, economists, environmentalists, guardians of public policy, home economists, investors, marketers, social workers, and sociologists. This handbook is mostly about psychology, although we realize that other disciplines have important ideas to contribute to understanding this area (e.g., economics, sociology, anthropology). We organize around psychological constructs such as involvement and happiness, important consumer differences such as age and gender, and social processes from culture to current changes in social media. Theory about behavior guides the science of consumer psychology.

MARKETING CONCEPT

The way people conceptualize marketing has often been misunderstood. Consumer psychology does indeed dominate marketing activity, but that dominance is usually not centered on tricking or misleading consumers. Rather, the concern is satisfying consumers. Some people assume that consumer psychology first enters into marketing with advertising and promotional communication, but that assumption is usually incorrect. Often the easiest way to market a product is to involve the customer, beginning at the earliest stages. The marketer first determines what the consumer or group of customers (target market) want or need, frequently considering consumer psychology along the way. Then the marketer develops the product designed to address the identified wants or needs, as discussed by Hall (Chapter 32) and by Proctor, Zeng, and Vu (Chapter 33). After designing a prototype of the product, the marketer determines, again with psychological research, whether the new product meets the needs of the consumer from the perspective of the consumer (Chapter 26, by Hollebeek and Srivastava). Then the marketer determines strategies (Chapter 5, by Keller) for issues such as how much to charge (Chapter 30, by Monroe), how to distribute the product (Chapter 29, by Verhoef, van Ittersum, Kannan, and Inman), and how to brand the product (Chapter 31, by Priester, Fleming, Donovan, and Dutton). All of these steps should be informed by consumer psychology. According to Keller's Chapter 5, customers are attracted to firms' products when "they can offer products and services that customers value more than the price that they pay for them" (p. 144). If the product and strategy have been developed with careful attention to consumer psychology, the communication phase (Chapters 19–22, by Pogacar, Mecit, Gao, Shrum, and Lowrey; Thorson; Lamberton and Humphreys; and Gurel-Atay) is much easier. The message is not "You should buy this item because I made it" but rather "You should buy this item because it was created to satisfy your psychological needs and desires."

This idea is sufficiently central to marketing that it has been called the *marketing concept*: "The marketing concept holds that the key to success at achieving organizational goals is being more effective than competitors at delivering and communicating superior customer value to your target market" (Kotler & Keller, 2012, p. 18). The focus is always on the consumer and creating happiness or satisfaction (Chapter 28, by Tambyah and Tan).

ORGANIZATION OF THIS VOLUME

The book is divided into several sections. Part I provides critical perspectives of the field. Chapter 1, by Cohen and Wilkie, presents an evocative history of the development of consumer psychology as an area of knowledge, capturing a number of evolving research goals and orientations. Chapter 2, by Wyer, summarizes important work on how ideas about products and market purchases are activated by cues in the external environment and learned procedures. Chapter 3, by Foxall, provides one philosophy of science for psychological research. It articulates different ways psychologists measure and use hypothesized mental constructs like emotions, goals, and thoughts to increase our ability to predict and understand human behavior. Chapter 4, by Bagozzi, examines structural equation modeling, an important methodological approach to understanding how different environmental and economic variables jointly affect or are affected by the behavior of consumers. The final chapter of Part I, Chapter 5, by Keller, places consumer psychology in the context of the marketing concept and the larger discipline of marketing.

Part II emphasizes individual differences across consumers with important demographic and psychographic characteristics that apply to consumer psychology. Hill, in Chapter 6, focuses on the noteworthy concerns of people with a low income, but people with other income levels also have unique needs and concerns. Chapter 7, by John and Chaplin, investigates children by looking at that one age category, but people in other age categories, such as young adults or senior citizens, also have unique needs and concerns. Zayer and Pounders (Chapter 8) explore selected gender issues. Ramanathan (Chapter 9) describes personality research in consumer psychology. Gurel-Atay (Chapter 10) reviews social values, and Valette-Florence, Meenaghan, and Kahle (Chapter 11) discuss lifestyle and sports.

Part III examines recent advances in social psychology, investigating the psychology of consumer action in a social world. Torelli and Shavitt (Chapter 12) explore cultural influences, and Tormala and Rucker (Chapter 13) tackle the classic social psychology topic of attitude change. Wight, Liu, Bettman, and Fitzsimons (Chapter 14) detail the influence of close social relationships with family and friends. The next contributions concern the social and ethical effects of consumers' actions. Claudy and Peterson (Chapter 15) look at the sustainability effects from consumer disposal of products, and Kennedy and Kapitan (Chapter 16) present the ethical implications of the ways consumers treat each other in the marketplace. Note that other chapters (e.g., Hill, Chapter 6) also discuss important societal issues. Monga, Zor, and Siddiqui (Chapter 17) reflect on time and its psychological consequences for consumption. Consumers have expectations based on their experiences, described in the chapter by Curtin (Chapter 18). He explores the role of conscious and nonconscious influences on consumers' expectations of future economic conditions. These expectations are measured, among other places, by his widely cited and influential University of Michigan Survey of Consumer Sentiment.

Part IV explores how businesses communicate formally with consumers and how consumers communicate with each other. Pogacar, Mecit, Gao, Shrum, and Lowrey (Chapter 19) demonstrate the ways language alters both actions and beliefs. Thorson (Chapter 20) explores traditional media, and Lamberton and Humphreys (Chapter 21) consider the phenomenal growth of social media and the influence that it has on consumption, activities, and well-being. Finally, Gurel-Atay (Chapter 22) discusses use of celebrity endorsers.

Part V explores affect and cognition, especially as they relate to consumer decisions. Kardes, Posavac, and Gaffney devote Chapter 23 to omission neglect and consumer judgment and inference based on limited evidence. Lee and Cecutti (Chapter 24) consider that bodily feelings can alter emotions, beliefs, and procedures. Chapter 25, by Adaval and Galli, looks at the interplay of affect and cognition in how feelings guide consumer behavior. Hollebeek and Srivastava's Chapter 26 discusses consumer involvement. Humans are animals with neurological characteristics, and Chapter 27, by Genevsky and Yoon, explores insight on consumer psychology from neurological data. Chapter 28, by Tambyah and Tan, reaches deeply into the existential issue of happiness from consumption.

Part VI probes the psychological aspects of how businesses and organizations understand and attempt to influence consumers, organized by the various roles and functions of marketing departments. Chapter 29, on channels, by Verhoef, van Ittersum, Kannan, and

Inman, looks at the rapidly changing world of retailing to omnichannel marketing, where channels intermix between electronic sources and brick-and-mortar stores. Chapter 30, by Monroe, explores the psychological issues that companies consider in setting prices. It looks both at the level and at the form of prices offered to consumers. Chapter 31, by Priester, Fleming, Donovan, and Dutton, on branding, summarizes antecedents and consequences of seven brand properties. A brand's influence can range from relatively weak to relatively strong and enduring. The authors' framework is unique in characterizing these properties as sequentially increasing in strength. Those topics lower in the hierarchy, such as attitudes and associations, may be more easily changed in the near term, but those topics with more strength, such as brand relationships and community, are both harder to alter and exhibit greater consumer influence over time. In Chapter 32, Hall notes that organizations try to innovate offerings for an ever-changing world. Very few products or services have survived unchanged for more than a century. Innovation and creativity are not magical processes but rather ones that psychology can understand and improve. Finally, human factors research tries to design what people want and can use effectively, as discussed by Proctor, Zeng, and Vu in Chapter 33. Human factors research too relies on a psychological foundation.

FINAL THOUGHTS

We wish to acknowledge that many of the chapter authors also served as reviewers for other chapters. We deeply appreciate the patience and cooperation of the authors, in addition to their broad and deep intellectual prowess.

Of course, scientific knowledge is a moving target; thus, we acknowledge that this handbook does not cover everything about consumer psychology. It does offer a substantial examination of many of the important topics. We hope that it provides a starting point for a dialectical examination (cf. Kahle et al., 2000) of what we know about consumer psychology and how to move knowledge forward in this meaningful and vital area of human behavior.

Lynn R. Kahle
Editor-in-Chief

Tina M. Lowrey
Joel Huber
Associate Editors

REFERENCES

Haugtvedt, C. P., Herr, P. M., & Kardes, F. R. (Eds.). (2008). *Handbook of consumer psychology*. Lawrence Erlbaum.

Jansson-Boyd, C. V., & Zawisza, M. J. (Eds.). (2017). *Routledge international handbook of consumer psychology*. Routledge.

Kahle, L. R., Liu, R., Rose, G. M., & Kim, W. S. (2000). Dialectical thinking in consumer decision making. *Journal of Consumer Psychology*, 9(1), 53–58. https://doi.org/10.1207/s15327663jcp0901_5

Kardes, F. R., Herr, P. M., & Schwartz, N. (Eds.). (2019). *Handbook of research methods in consumer psychology*. Routledge. https://doi.org/10.4324/9781351137713

Kotler, P., & Keller, K. L. (2012). *Marketing management* (14th ed.). Prentice Hall.

Solomon, M. R. (2017). *Consumer behavior: Buying, having, and being* (12th ed.). Pearson.

Part I

PERSPECTIVES ON CONSUMER PSYCHOLOGY

CHAPTER 1

CONSUMER PSYCHOLOGY: EVOLVING GOALS AND RESEARCH ORIENTATIONS

Joel B. Cohen and William L. Wilkie

This chapter provides perspectives on the evolution of research on consumer behavior and consumer psychology. It is organized in three major sections:

I. Evolution of the Field: The Early Years
This first major section focuses on the early years, when consumer research was carried out in applied settings and began to grow within academic marketing. We begin with the important roles that psychologists studying advertising played, then trace the growth of the academic infrastructure for research on consumer behavior. We next highlight earlier research on larger consumer issues that receive little attention today, and we end this section with a discussion of the consumer psychology mainstream forming around cognitive and social psychology.

II. Research Exemplifying the Evolution of Consumer Psychology
The second major section of the chapter then delves into two key programs of research that exemplify the field of consumer psychology: (a) process-oriented research to explain movement toward behavior and (b) research on ways of bringing about change in preferences and behavior and helping consumers to lead better, healthier lives.

III. Facilitating Research Contributions Based on Contrasting Goals and Orientations
We conclude this chapter with a short third section identifying issues consumer psychology faces owing to the widely differing research orientations revealed in this body of work.

I. EVOLUTION OF THE FIELD: THE EARLY YEARS

Advertising and the Rise of Process-Oriented Research

Process-oriented research to explain consumer behavior found its initial home in advertising, where it was used to capture consumers' responses to ads, including comparative judgments and evaluations and the ability to recall advertising messages. Of particular note, Daniel Starch, a psychologist who taught at both the University of Wisconsin and Harvard prior to establishing a marketing research company, was a pioneer in assessing the level of attention recipients paid to an ad. Starch published several books setting forth his principles of advertising (e.g., Starch, 1923). Starch was one of the earliest to use field experiments in which coupon returns indicated the sales-making power of an advertisement. He developed procedures for tabulating ad recognition scores and, along with other psychologists who had come into the field, began to conceptualize a logical structure in which consumer response was conditioned on how easily and quickly an advertisement is read, understood, and believed. This process was seen to depend on the arresting power of the layout, headline, and illustration; simple and logical sentence structure;

and statements that carry conviction and do not challenge existing beliefs.

This research was a forerunner for several frameworks widely used in advertising. One, the AIDA model (i.e., attention/awareness, interest, desire, and action), described the steps a consumer goes through prior to making a purchase decision. Its successor, Lavidge and Steiner's (1961) hierarchy of effects model (i.e., unawareness, awareness, knowledge, liking, preference, conviction, purchase) led to other variants built upon the concept of a linear hierarchical response process (e.g., Barry, 1987; Percy & Rossiter, 1992). One segmentation-related use of such models was to imagine them as a type of funnel with progressively smaller numbers of potential purchasers moving successfully to the next step, allowing advertisers to focus on the differing needs represented for consumers at each stage. We regard this as a pivotal research contribution in consumer research, as the questions it generated on theoretical process issues (e.g., Always a fixed staging? Necessity of each step for both high and low involvement products/issues? Psychological processes occurring at each step?) are still debated today.

Motivational factors were prominent among those trained in psychology who linked effective advertising appeals to such human desires as health, appetite, sex, economy, esteem, comfort, family affection, fear, curiosity, and adventure. This research led to an emphasis on underlying drives, goals, and individual differences that has continued to this day under a number of different rubrics that are discussed in detail in other chapters. For example, when promoting newly developed cooking appliances, rather than focusing on new recipes a user can create, advertisers could move to more basic, stronger motivational levels (e.g., love, security, or belongingness), as these stronger needs can be more motivating than performance attributes or functional benefits (Reynolds & Olson, 2001). Psychologists working in advertising during this early period often attempted to capture stronger needs and emotions by telling stories connecting the person to the product, factors that have continued to receive emphasis within consumer psychology in later years (D. A. Aaker & Stayman, 1992, but see Krause & Rucker, 2020). For example, the trade press of the 1930s (most notably, Printers Ink) featured reports on the use of fear appeals in advertising, as in Lifebuoy soap stressing its prevention of body odor. Along this line, Listerine's advertising shift to fear of halitosis was hardly subtle—"Often a bridesmaid, Never a bride"—and led to a reported jump in its mouthwash sales. And nowhere were psychological appeals more in evidence in the pre-World War II years than in campaigns to sell cigarettes to women. Women smoked only roughly 5% of total U.S. cigarettes in the early 1920s, but this number grew to 18% by 1935 and reached 33% by 1965. This resulted in part from concerted ad campaigns to promote women's smoking using both sexual symbolism and body image fears lurking behind such clever instructions for women to "Reach for a Lucky instead of a Sweet" (O'Keefe & Pollay, 1996).

By the 1950s marketers increasingly turned their attention to motivation research that was qualitative in nature, designed to uncover more deep-rooted or even hidden motives of interest to psychoanalytic clinicians. Ernest Dichter held sway over this movement (famously advising Chrysler that a sedan reminded men of a wife and a convertible of a mistress and that cigarette lighters' capacity to summon fire is a symbol of man's conquest of the physical world). This movement became widely known and criticized as a danger manipulating the unknowing public in Vance Packard's (1957) best-selling book *The Hidden Persuaders* (M. R. Nelson, 2008). As more marketers became skeptical of the necessity of attempting to delve deeply into the psyches of consumers using clinical techniques (e.g., projective techniques, depth interviews) the motivation research era began to recede in popularity (Schwarzkopf & Gries, 2010).

Meanwhile, consumer research had been evolving on other fronts. Early survey research helped marketers to understand where their customers were geographically and who they were in terms of shopping, purchases, and socioeconomic characteristics. This was the forerunner of modern market segmentation, dividing the market into meaningful subcategories to target consumers more effectively and efficiently. Marketers' efforts to learn how to develop favorable attitudes, preferences, and ultimately behaviors led to a focus on mainstream social and cognitive psychology, which was crucial to the development of the modern field of consumer psychology.

Journals and Institutional Developments Spur Scholarship in the 1960s

The development of a field of knowledge requires an institutional infrastructure, and for consumer psychology, the 1960s were a key period for this development. Among the most important steps were the formation of the Consumer Psychology Division (Division 23) of the American Psychological Association (APA) and the introduction of the *Journal of Advertising Research,* both in 1960. This was followed by the *Journal of Marketing Research* in 1964, welcoming empirical research on all facets of marketing, especially from newer members of the field trained in quantitative methods, modeling, and behavioral science. Though some similar articles had appeared in prior issues of the *Journal of Marketing*, it had a broader mandate and was not focused on empirical research.

The movement was much advanced by the first books on consumer behavior (e.g., Engel et al., 1968; Howard & Sheth, 1969; Nicosia, 1966; Zaltman, 1965). In different manners, these provided needed background, frameworks, and ties to the world of consumption as an area for study. In addition, their use as textbooks was instrumental in cementing consumer behavior's role in a marketing curriculum, which made it possible for even faculty members with traditional marketing backgrounds to teach this subject. In addition, the popularity of these courses increased marketing job opportunities for those with strong social science backgrounds, which served to greatly strengthen research in the field.

Perhaps the most significant institution to this field's growth was the formation of the Association for Consumer Research (ACR), which evolved from a series of specialized conferences in the late 1960s. Most important were an invited small gathering held at Ohio State University in 1969 and then an open consumer research conference in 1970 at the University of Massachusetts. The conference was a tremendous success, far exceeding expectations in attendance, level of discussion, and excitement about the prospects for this new field. This set the stage for the official formation of ACR at the University of Maryland conference in 1971, its first official publication—a volume of conference proceedings—the election of its first president, Joel B. Cohen, and a commitment to move forward with annual meetings for researchers from academia, business, and government, all for the purpose of advancing this field of study and practice.

The *Journal of Consumer Research* (*JCR*), another key development, came into existence in 1974. It was a direct outgrowth of ACR: The journal's mission was to be highly interdisciplinary and inclusive, inviting contributions from fields such as psychology, marketing, sociology, economics, communications, and anthropology. Its orientation was academic, not managerial, welcoming topics from microlevel processes to macrolevel issues. *JCR* stood alone as an elite consumer research journal until 1992, when the *Journal of Consumer Psychology* (*JCP*) was established. Its stated purpose was to provide an outlet for researchers in consumer psychology, social and cognitive psychology, judgment and decision making, and related disciplines (including consumer and market research as well as marketing and advertising).

The advent of *JCR* and *JCP* established that this emerging field welcomed inputs from researchers in more basic disciplines as well as those identifying as marketing or consumer behavior researchers. Accommodating such breadth and diversity can bring challenges, as a journal strives to facilitate distinct types of contributions driven by competing research priorities. We discuss these challenges in the concluding section of the chapter.

Early Research on Consumers' Central Role in the Economy

It is important to note that today's relative neglect of economic and societal issues in consumer psychology runs counter to the original goals of the ACR, which was created to convene academics, business, and government thinkers to advance knowledge in this field. Consumer behavior plays an essential role in growing our economy, sustains an efficient marketplace, and contributes to the standard of life of a society. Perhaps surprisingly to many today, earlier times saw consumer psychologists involved in attempting to comprehend the nuances of consumer behavior at aggregate levels, including impacts on the larger economic system and businesses in that system. In this section we focus on two exemplars of such early efforts: the pioneering research of George Katona in the mid-20th century and the efforts of Project MAC, a welcomed inclusion of marketing faculty members into the work of the Federal Trade Commission (FTC) during the 1970s. First, though, we briefly characterize the size and scope of aggregate consumer behavior today.

The magnitude of consumer behavior in today's economic system. Much of consumer psychology's focus today is within individuals, with far less attention to aggregates. Accordingly, we underscore the enormous magnitude of the consumer aggregate. At the start of the 2020s, U.S. consumers' spending is nearing $15 trillion, with U.S. gross domestic product (GDP) nearing $22 trillion. As a generalization, consumer spending represents more than two thirds (say 70%) of GDP; thus it is a huge factor in the overall well-being of the economy (Amadeo, 2021). It can be difficult to imagine nearly $15 trillion, so here is a quick exercise: If you take each dollar bill and stretch out a line of annual consumer spending, just how far would this line extend? According to our calculations (using one dollar bill = 6 inches, 5,280 feet per mile, 238,900 miles to the Moon, 93 million miles to the Sun, U.S. annual spending late 2019 = $14.678 trillion), one year's dollar spending line would stretch from the Earth to the Sun 14 times (seven round trips), with enough remaining for 17 round trips to the Moon and yet still a cool $2.1 billion left over! And this is only the U.S. As we move internationally the aggregate consumer spending expands geometrically.

A casualty of declining attention to the study of aggregate consumer behavior is the severe understatement of the significance of the *overall* economic, cultural, societal, regulatory, and marketing systems and institutions within which consumers operate. These help determine essential characteristics of the settings within which people and companies engage in economic transactions. Governments work to both facilitate and constrain behavior in order to achieve societal benefits in growth, employment, price stability, and social welfare. Wilkie and Moore (1999) described how the Aggregate Marketing System (AGMS) is organized to serve the needs of its host society, thereby reflecting the idiosyncrasies of its (a) consumers, (b) marketers, and (c) government entities and their enveloping culture, geography, economic opportunities and constraints, and sociopolitical decisions. We now turn to a pioneering contribution linking consumer behavior to the health of the economy, the rise of consumerism, and an institutional exemplar of how progress linking public policy and consumer psychology can be made.

Pioneering contributions of George Katona, psychologist and developer of behavioral economics.

> "The Association for Consumer Research presents its Fellow in Consumer Behavior Award to George Katona for his innovative joining of Psychology and Economics for new insight into consumer behavior."
> (October 1982)

Thus read the plaque with which ACR honored George Katona with one of its very first ACR Fellow recognitions (Newman, 1983). George Katona was a singular presence intersecting economics and psychology during key formative years and as such deserves detailed coverage. Katona, by training a psychologist but working frequently in the economic realm, sought to take on important problems in his most interesting career (see Hosseini, 2011; Wärneryd, 1982).

George Katona was born in Hungary in 1901 and obtained his PhD in experimental psychology, focused on perception, in Germany. In his early career he studied Gestalt psychology with Max Wertheimer and economics with Gustav Stolper, wrote for the weekly *German Economist,* and published papers on both the psychology of perception and the psychology of the hyperinflation Germany was experiencing at the time. He immigrated to the United States in the 1930s, eventually joining the

New School for Social Research's psychology faculty. During World War II, he joined the University of Chicago's Cowles Commission for Research in Economics to study businesses' reactions to wartime government price controls, providing an exceptional opportunity for observation and measurement of both attitudes and the actions of business decision makers (Curtin, 1984).

At Cowles, Katona developed enhanced survey research methods that were sharply distinct from the economic research methods of the time. He concluded that government should support price control actions with announcements aiming to change business attitudes, relying on public opinion supportive of price control (Katona, 1945, p. 221). Rensis Lickert then invited him to join the U.S. Department of Agriculture's Division of Program Survey, where they undertook the first national survey of ownership of liquid assets, an important issue due to the massive household money savings amassed during the goods shortages of World War II. In 1946, following the war, he and Lickert, along with Angus Campbell, moved to the University of Michigan to establish their Survey Research Center, with Katona directing its Economic Behavior Program as a professor of economics and psychology. Here he pioneered new methods and uses for survey research, demonstrating clearly the key roles that consumers play in the health of the economy. In addition, and of great significance, his work developed a subfield called "Behavioral Economics" (promoting empirical economic studies as distinct from the behavioral science focus of today's behavioral economics). A summary of Katona's major contributions includes the following:

He successfully challenged the Keynesian neoclassical macroeconomic assumption that consumption is a stable function of disposable income—that the economy's direction was determined by business and government, not consumers as another factor to be considered. In contrast, Katona proposed that consumers' discretionary purchasing is a function of both their ability to spend (income) and their current willingness to spend, a psychological input that is affected by the optimism or pessimism they are feeling. He relied upon his extensive psychological training on perception, learning, experience, and aspiration to develop measures of consumers' purchasing proclivities, placing particular emphasis on his concept of "expectations" (Pratt, 1972).

Katona provided significant advances in survey research methods through his work over the years, beginning with his national survey with Rensis Lickert in the 1940s. They explained the need for representative sampling; the design of questions to cover actions, processes, motivations, and other appropriate concepts; the need for interviewers to be well trained in both questioning and in building rapport; and the inclusion of checks on coding of measures of attitudes and behavior. The Survey Research Center was a key party to advancing survey research theory, technology, and methods, both for data collection and analysis.

He helped to cement acceptance of his views by correctly forecasting the strong U.S. economy following World War II. Many economic experts were warning of returns to the prewar economic depression, and others warned of runaway price inflation due to the buildup of unspent household assets during the war years. In contrast, Katona's surveys showed that consumers were optimistic about economic growth and a positive future for themselves without price inflation (Katona, 1975, p. 104).

He developed the Index of Consumer Sentiment (ICS), finalized in the 1953 and still being conducted by the University of Michigan each month, based on telephone interviews of a U.S. household sample. The index is normalized to 100, based on 1966 results, and aims to characterize current consumer attitudes on the business climate, as well as their personal finances and spending behaviors. It is to be used in forecasting changes in the national economy, providing empirical measures of consumer expectations. In 1980, nearing the end of his career, Katona delivered a paper at the ACR Conference in which he provided a graph of ICS against actual economic activity over 25 years, showing clearly that the index declined prior to every recessionary period and resumed upward readings shortly before recoveries (Katona & Curtin, 1980). The ICS today is still highly anticipated each month by planners in business and government.

In addition to academic publishing, he issued many reports on current studies conducted by the

Survey Research Center, allowing business and government decision makers to stay current on developments. In his academic work, Katona contributed insights on many elements of the consumer experience, including the nature and role of consumer expectations, household saving, the role of anticipations, reactions to price inflation, spending on consumer durables, consumer finances, reactions to taxes, and other such topics.

In 1977, the APA recognized George Katona with its Distinguished Professional Contribution Award. George Katona's merging of economics, psychology, and social science research helped legitimize consumer research as a field of inquiry. He challenged the neoclassical field of economics, urging it to adopt behavioral science ideas and methods. In his 1980 talk at ACR he championed "problem-oriented research," underscoring limitations of the field's far greater focus on discipline-oriented research (Katona & Curtin 1980).

The rise of consumerism. "Consumerism," a powerful interest that arose in marketing academia during the second half of the 1960s, questioned the implicit role of consumers as "targets" of marketing strategies and tactics. Perhaps this reflected the tenor of the times. Social unrest was spreading across society: assassinations, civil rights, and the role of the "military–industrial complex" in the controversial Vietnam War rose to the forefront of everyday life. Thoughtful marketing academics increasingly attended to options to improve consumer outcomes and decision making, especially by vulnerable people, leading to better and healthier lives. The movement was greatly enhanced by President John F. Kennedy's 1962 famous declaration, the Consumer Bill of Rights (for a first-person account, see Lampman, 1988), which asserted four foundational propositions:

1. The Right to Safety: Consumers have the right to be protected against products/services hazardous to health and life.
2. The Right to Be Informed: Consumers have the right to be protected against fraudulent, deceitful, or misleading advertising or other practices, and to be given the facts needed for an informed choice.
3. The Right to Choose: Consumers have the right to be assured access to a variety of products and services at competitive prices. In industries where competition is not workable, regulation is substituted to ensure quality and service at fair prices.
4. The Right to Be Heard: Consumers have the right to be assured that consumer interests will receive full and sympathetic consideration in the formulation of government policy and fair and expeditious treatment in its administrative tribunals.

For marketers, this was a challenge to the notion that *caveat emptor* ("Let the buyer beware") might rule the U.S. marketplace. It provided a basis to examine the "marketing/consumer environment," with the general societal goal that such a marketplace be both "fair" and "efficient" for marketers, competitors, and consumers alike (Wilkie, 1994). The Consumer Bill of Rights was used as an organizing framework for a major compendium of research by consumer advocates (Maynes, 1988a) and an excellent overview for consumer researchers (Andreasen, 1991). The academic infrastructure for such work expanded in 1967, when the American Council on Consumer Interests began its *Journal of Consumer Affairs* (JCA).

The marketing and society stream of research flourished during this time. Remarkably, just between 1966 and 1974, some 20 societal readings books appeared, offering a variety of perspectives and evidence about marketers, consumers, responsibilities, rights, and system performance (Bartels, 1988, p. 220). Authors included high-profile public figures (e.g., Ralph Nader, John Kenneth Galbraith, Senator Warren Magnuson, FTC Commissioner Mary Gardiner Jones, John D. Rockefeller III, and the president of Pepsi-Cola), as well as numerous marketing academics, including David Aaker and George Day (1982), who edited multiple editions of their highly popular readings book, *Consumerism*.

Distinct subareas emerged in societal research in the 1970s. Some work dealt with performance and deficiencies in the marketing system, later designated as macromarketing. Also, a controversy emerged on the proper boundaries for the marketing field: Is marketing fundamentally a business topic driven by the profit motive, or something broader—a technology that can (should) be applied to social problems wherever they are found? Many approved of "broadening the concept of marketing" (Kotler & Levy, 1969), which set the stage for development of "social marketing" (Kotler & Zaltman, 1971), a subdiscipline focusing on the work of not-for-profit groups and government agencies concerned with effective intervention into social problem areas, such as health, education, or alleviation of poverty.

Project MAC: Consumer researchers advance into public policy. A major institutional development occurred in the early 1970s, when marketing academics were invited into the public policy arena under an FTC program known as the Marketing Academic Consultancy project, or "Project MAC." Although the FTC was (and is) the nation's primary regulator of marketing activities, its staff of attorneys and economists had little or no awareness of marketing or consumer research. Strong pressures on the FTC had arisen in the late 1960s, including a very negative report by "Nader's Raiders" consumerist group (Cox et al., 1969), an ensuing negative report from an American Bar Association (ABA) blue-ribbon task force (Freer, 1971), then action from President Nixon and Congress. The ABA Report's head was named new FTC Chairman, new appointments were made at top FTC levels, and the FTC budget was increased (Freer, 1971).

The impetus for Project MAC came from Commissioner Mary Gardiner Jones, who attended the first ACR Conference and decided that this new area, consumer research, was needed at the FTC (Jones, 1990). Among the key players were Murray Silverman (a new marketing PhD who joined her staff), Robert Pitofsky (the new director of the Bureau of Consumer Protection), and William Wilkie, a young marketing academic who took a leave from Purdue to pursue four key FTC projects:

- corrective advertising (a new FTC remedy form requiring firms to alert consumers that they had previously been deceived in advertising by the firm),
- cigarette health warnings (a relatively new program, as warnings had only begun recently),
- serving as a "Behavioral Science Expert" for legal and economist staff members, and
- developing a continuing presence of appropriate expertise for the FTC (Wilkie, 2014).

It was the fourth task that led to Project MAC's development. As more was learned about agency needs, it became clear that (a) successful academic researchers were likely to be interested but not to become permanent staff members and (b) a key limiting factor was (and continues to be) the absence of doctoral program background on relevant public policy. Even if motivated and with strong research skills, most academics were unlikely to understand the problem setting well enough without working within the agency for at least a brief period. The group (along with David Gardner, a marketing academic consultant who had joined the policy planning office) thus instituted Project MAC. Each year the FTC would bring two professors in-house with the proviso that agency activities be supplemented with marketing/consumer research academic community policy-focused presentations, papers, and encouraging others to join the program. Over a 10-year period, Project MAC brought 22 marketing and consumer behavior researchers into the FTC, and many others served as consultants on important projects (as described by Murphy, 1990; Wilkie, 2014; Wilkie & Gardner, 1974).

During the decade of the 1970s, the FTC was emphasizing new powers and programs. Advertising was a major target, and many new research topics emerged on topics such as

- *advertising substantiation* (advertisers must have tests supporting performance claims, see D. Cohen, 1980),
- *corrective advertising* (advertisers must inform consumers they had been deceived in prior advertising; see Wilkie et al., 1984),
- *deceptive advertising* (new dimensions developed for both charges and defenses; see D. M. Gardner, 1975),
- *comparative advertising* (TV codes lifted, fostering direct brand comparisons; see Wilkie & Farris, 1975),

- *affirmative disclosure* (many new requirements for informing consumers; see Wilkie, 1982),
- *advertising to children* (controversial restrictions proposed to limit advertising; see Mazis, 1979; Ratner, 1978), and
- *reducing advertising code barriers* (opening price advertising for eyeglasses, drugs, and other professions).

An excellent set of articles describing this period is in the *Journal of Public Policy & Marketing* (Andreasen, 1997; Bloom, 1997; Greyser, 1997; Kinnear, 1997; Mazis, 1997; Wilkie, 1997).

This period also saw a much richer level of discussion externally. Government officials spoke at research conferences, the Marketing Science Institute coordinated a number of public policy research projects, and doctoral dissertations began to directly address important questions in the public policy sphere. For example, a 1978 ACR special session on "Advertising to Children" attracted a large audience of attorneys, marketing practitioners, academics, and government officials (Mazis, 1979).

The decade also saw a considerable advance in information processing theory and research methods culminating in James Bettman's (1979) influential book, *An Information Processing Theory of Consumer Choice*. At the FTC, it became increasingly clear that remedies involving consumer information were to be preferred: Not only do these comport with economic theory (in a competitive marketplace buyers are expected to hold sufficient information to make good personal purchasing decisions, thereby guiding resource allocations within society) but it is also a less intrusive option for government in regulating businesses. Thus one opportunity (and problem) for policy makers was how to design consumer information environments to best deliver information. Alternative designs impose distinct information processing demands relative to the time, opportunity, and cognitive resources available to consumers to absorb and consider that information. In 1974, when a new national program to supply nutritional information on food packages was being considered, a flurry of research studies appeared on information load, reflecting how the information was presented and consumers' ability to process different amounts of information (e.g., Jacoby et al., 1974a, 1974b; Russo, 1974; Wilkie, 1974). More complex policy and information processing issues involving information were addressed by Bettman (1975) and Wilkie (1975) during the same time period as well as by others for some time thereafter (e.g., Hadfield et al., 1998; Moorman, 1990). For example, Russo et al. (1986) examined the potential of nutrition information posted in supermarkets (rather than simply on individual packaging) to reduce the information processing costs of comparing alternative foods. Effort-reducing displays appeared to be helpful in increasing the use of information, especially for product attributes such as high sugar that people wished to avoid. The same was found to be true for unit price information. Russo (1977) found that the value of posting unit prices on separate shelf tags in a supermarket led to consumer savings of 3%, including a 5% increase in the market shares of store brands. More generally, examining each purchase alternative in the process of evaluating results in greater familiarity and learning than when simply choosing one alternative (either as the best or good enough), which produces only a minimal effect on the acquisition and organization of product information (Johnson & Russo, 1984). This reflects different information processing mechanisms linked to strategies that consumers adopt when they simplify rather than optimize choices (Wright, 1975), a topic that was treated extensively in subsequent work (e.g., Payne et al., 1995). Other elements of information processing research are discussed later in this chapter.

For public policy, this complex area involves not only consumer processing issues but technical concerns of how to precisely measure and fairly characterize meaningful attribute levels of products or services, plus myriad legal issues, such as the freedoms accorded to a marketer in our economic market system (e.g., speech). Accordingly, the FTC launched a blue-ribbon "Consumer Information Task Force" toward the end of the decade, whose report, "Consumer Information Remedies," provided a comprehensive review of knowledge in this area as well as a set of guidelines for the FTC to follow in the future (Mazis et al., 1981).

Overall, the FTC became a powerful regulatory agency during the 1970s, with a 500% budget increase in the decade and active participation by marketing academics under Project MAC (Murphy, 1990). To illustrate Project MAC's impact, by the late 1970s, Kenneth Bernhardt, a MAC participant, was managing an FTC evaluation research office with 22 research projects and a $1 million research budget (Bernhardt, 1990). The political winds of Washington were at work during this time, at first pushing consumer research forward. In 1977, President Carter appointed consumer activists to a number of high positions in government, including at the FTC. This stimulated stronger undertakings, including hearings on banning advertising to children and on new rules to restrict marketing methods in such areas as used cars and funerals. However, these actions sparked strong backlash from the business community, which succeeded in having Congress restrict the FTC's budget and force retreats on those actions. Then, with the election of Ronald Reagan in 1980, the makeup of FTC officials again changed, and Chicago-School economists emerged to guide the FTC through the 1980s with a distinctly different agenda. In one prominent example, whereas Section 5 of the FTC Act had prohibited "unfair . . . acts or practices in or affecting commerce" Congress and the FTC moved away from prohibiting unscrupulous acts in and of themselves, ultimately changing Section 5 as follows:

> The Commission shall have no authority . . . to declare unlawful an act or practice on the grounds that such act or practice is unfair unless the act or practice causes or is likely to cause substantial injury to consumers which is not reasonably avoidable by consumers themselves and not outweighed by countervailing benefits to consumers or to competition. (15 U.S.C. § 45 n)

In the context of the FTC's "Joe Camel" case against R. J. Reynolds for allegedly creating health risks by marketing cigarettes to an underage target audience using a cartoon character and peer group acceptance as a main appeal (Calfee, 2000; J. B. Cohen, 2000), the policy change supported dismissal of the case. When it comes to consumer protection, the doctrine of "reasonable avoidance" as well as seemingly direct causality is a heavy burden for any action that is persuadable but ultimately voluntary. Accompanying such changes, the FTC perceived little need for inputs from marketing academics, and Project MAC was closed for about 10 years. It was briefly restarted in the early 1990s under President George H. W. Bush, then ended in favor of continuing consulting arrangements with local marketing academics (Murphy & Wilkie, 1990; Wilkie, 2014).

Project MAC's legacy: A rich infrastructure for consumer policy research. The MAC program participants were relatively young in their academic careers and continued to pursue societally relevant consumer research when back in an academic setting. In addition to their individual research contributions and ongoing assistance to the FTC and other federal agencies, they organized specialized public policy conferences and produced influential books (e.g., the Notre Dame Symposium, contents captured in Murphy & Wilkie, 1990). They played central roles when Thomas Kinnear established a new, policy-focused marketing journal in 1982, the *Journal of Public Policy and Marketing,* that welcomed consumer research contributions. In addition, a yearly Marketing and Public Policy Conference (MPPC) started in 1989 and continues today to bring together academic researchers, including interested consumer psychologists, and public policy officials.

In sum, academic researchers added valuable perspectives on consumer behavior for public policies aimed at sustaining a fair and effective marketplace for consumers during the 1960s, 1970s, and 1980s. Project MAC's legacy is apparent in the broad set of policy issues being pursued in this period: Gundlach and Wilkie (1990) discussed 99 distinct public policy research topics that had been studied by this field's researchers by the end of the 1980s.

Unfortunately, the end of the 1980s represented a high point in this consumer research realm, as clearly seen by a startling turn in publications in *JCR.* As David Mick (2008) pointed out, in its first

15 years (1974–1988), *JCR* published 53 articles on three key societal issues (30 on energy/conservation, eight on consumer credit/debt, 15 on consumer education/information). In its next 15 years, *JCR* published only five articles on all of these topics. And the drop was not topic-specific: For such related topics as product safety, nutrition, tobacco/alcohol/drugs, and the poor and elderly, the results are similar (Mick, 2008).

The end of Project MAC removed a bridge between marketing academia and public policy, and was likely a major factor in the research decline. In the years since, this bridge to public policy has been missed, though some individual researchers have initiated relationships with government agencies leading to published research. In 2011, the newly formed Consumer Financial Protection Bureau did seek relationships with consumer researchers, much in the spirit of Project MAC, and this did support increased research activity on consumer finance topics (e.g., Fernandes et al., 2014; Lynch, 2011).

It is also true that the addition of several journals oriented around consumers' marketplace interests and public policy (*Journal of Consumer Policy*, *Journal of Consumer Affairs*, and particularly the *Journal of Public Policy and Marketing*) increased publication opportunities for policy-oriented consumer behavior scholars on important topics such as privacy (Culnan, 2000), vulnerable consumers (see Hill & Stamey, 1990; see also Chapter 6, this volume), fast food marketing and obesity (Grier et al., 2007), labeling (Caswell et al., 2003), how comparative price advertising may misinform as well as inform consumers (Compeau & Grewal, 1998), and how inferentially misleading advertising works (Hastak & Mazis, 2011). A number of European scholars helped create a stronger integration of economics and psychology, resulting in a great deal of relevant research in the *Journal of Economic Psychology* (e.g., Dolan et al., 2008; Wood, 1998). In addition, contributions from information economics became well integrated into the consumer behavior literature (e.g., Ford et al., 1990; Ratchford, 1982; Urbany, 1986), and economists began to take a greater interest in behavioral ideas, though they were not always easy to integrate into normative economic models (e.g., Beales et al., 1981; Foxall, 1994; Katona, 1975; P. Nelson, 1970; Pappalardo, 1997). Ironically, several decades later some leading economic theorists could be said to have "capitulated" to modifying classic economic assumptions to incorporate psychological findings and concepts under the rubric of "behavioral economics" (e.g., Loewenstein, 2000; Shafir & Thaler, 2006).

The relative absence of research on consumer policy issues in this field's leading journals appears symptomatic of an ever-increasing emphasis on discipline-focused research programs that no doubt reflects consumer researchers' current priorities. Interestingly, Schwartz and Loewenstein (the first an engineer and the second a well-known professor of economics and psychology) tackled proenvironmental behavior in a recent *Journal of Public Policy and Marketing* paper (Schwartz & Loewenstein, 2017), explaining that emotion-evoking advertising often fails to produce sustained behavior change once emotions have cooled off unless behavioral commitment has been obtained. Substantive topics of such importance would benefit from greater attention and publication in the many available journals. An overlapping perspective may have stimulated David Mick (2006) and others to encourage ACR and *JCR* support for Transformative Consumer Research, which has welcomed a number of younger scholars whose goals appear to mirror those of the earlier societal consumer researchers. We discuss some of this work, focusing on relationships between consumers, their self-identities, and their possessions in the next section of the chapter, and related issues are discussed in several other chapters.

The 1970s and Beyond: The Field Turns to the Social Sciences and Emphasizes Psychology

Though some of the institutional changes that began in the 1960s (particularly the formation of ACR, the early years of *JCR*, and the addition of several journals oriented around consumers' marketplace interests and public policy mentioned earlier) spurred a brief period of growth on these topics, by far the largest sustained contributions came from the underlying social sciences, especially psychology. For example, whereas market segmentation originally relied heavily on socioeconomic status, dynamic concepts taken from sociology, anthropology, and psychology brought new ways of categorizing consumers. These included working class as well as under- and overprivileged social class members (Carey & Markus, 2016; Williams, 2002), one-earner versus dual-earner households (Rubin et al., 1990), social and reference group identity (Childers & Rao, 1992; Shavitt & Nelson, 2000), and population subcultures (e.g., youth, surfer, and motorcycle subcultures; Arnould & Thompson, 2005), along with personality traits (J. B. Cohen, 1967; Kassarjian, 1971; see Chapter 9, this volume), values (see Chapter 10), and lifestyle assessments (Wells, 1975; see Chapter 11, this volume).

Traditional marketing topics such as pricing and branding also much benefited from concepts drawn from perception, social judgment, and self-concept research along with contributions from information economics. For example, differing price policies such as price-matching provide informative signals influencing consumer perceptions and search behavior (see Chapter 30). Marketers also began to examine the expressive and symbolic significance of brands. Research here employed social identity concepts developed by social psychologists and sociologists, as well as assimilation-contrast concepts originally developed in the field of perception to guide brand image management and analysis of brand extensions (Loken & John, 1993a, 1993b; MacInnis et al., 2009; see Chapter 31, this volume).

The cognitive era dominates consumer psychology in the 1970s. The focus on motivational and goal-directed processes that attracted so much attention in the 1950s had waned by the mid-1960s. Academics began to tackle the purchase process by breaking it down into distinct stages of problem recognition, problem solving, information search, and evaluation of alternatives (Bettman, 1979; Howard & Sheth, 1969; see Chapter 23, this volume). A prime focus was on how consumers retrieved, searched for, and evaluated alternatives in order to eliminate unsatisfactory options and select one that met their needs (Bettman et al., 1998; Johnson & Meyer, 1984; Kahneman, 1992; Kardes et al., 2004) under different conditions, constraints and levels of involvement (see Chapter 26). This accompanied a major cognitive revolution engulfing psychology, featuring in-depth study of mental processes and heuristics leading to attitudes, preferences, and decisions (e.g., Alba & Hutchinson, 1987; see Chapter 2, this volume). Research on attitudes themselves—especially in the analysis and prediction of behavior as well as belief and attitude change via persuasion—had emerged in the post-World War II years as a major focus of social psychology. This carried over into consumer research via multi-attribute models, the elaboration likelihood model, and research on persuasion (Agrawal & Maheswaran, 2005; Fishbein & Ajzen, 2010; Kardes, 1988; Petty et al., 1983, 1997; see Chapter 13, this volume).

The field broadens and deepens in the 1980s. Researchers' reliance on social psychology, sociology, and anthropology that began in the 1970s deepened as they searched for insights on brands, such as their image and congruency with consumers' self-images, cross-cultural, and even evolutionary factors (J. B. Cohen & Bernard, 2013; Escalas & Bettman, 2005; Park et al., 1986; Sirgy, 1982; see Chapter 12, this volume), as well as consumers' construal of the meaning of their possessions and in aiding their integration into society (Belk, 1985; Belk et al., 1989). Topics explored in the 1970s, such as the role of others' informational and normative influences in guiding and legitimizing purchase behavior (Bearden & Rose, 1990; Burnkrant & Cousineau, 1975; Miniard & Cohen, 1983), were tied-down better as scholarship advanced.

As we neared the end of the century, the focus on highly rational models of judgment and decision making had begun to make way for approaches recognizing varying levels of cognitive engagement such as favoring satisficing versus making optimal choices given both decision importance and time available (Dhar & Nowlis 1999). Rationality had been linked to economists' perspectives on accuracy's benefits in achieving higher utilities. Psychologists, however, found that people often favored time-saving satisfactory solutions to choice dilemmas as well as behavioral consistency, self-confirmation, and self-bolstering rather than a narrower conception of economic rationality. Thus they might rely on biased cognitive processes to maintain a stable knowledge structure rather than be forced to revise it (i.e, "I have a good understanding of X" or "I like X"; see Lee & Shavitt, 2009) as well as to bolster their self-concepts, particularly when original goals seem unachievable (Festinger, 1962; Harmon-Jones et al., 2015; Zeelenberg, 1999). Reliance on using feelings to guide behavior has received particular attention (Bosmans & Baumgartner, 2005; J. B. Cohen et al., 2008; see Chapter 25, this volume). Consumers often underutilize cognitive resources in favor of faster processing, to the extent that even background stimuli and inputs below the threshold of conscious awareness can influence behavior (Bargh et al., 2012; Pham et al., 2001).

A general consensus was developing that reasoning and decision processes were not fixed but motivated by a variety of product- and person-centered factors, and that people used simplifying strategies and heuristics that were accessible and efficient in particular contexts (Bettman et al., 1998; Chernev, 2001; Johnson & Meyer, 1984; Kunda, 1990; Matta et al., 2013; Samson & Voyer, 2014). Dealing with challenges of variably motivated decision processes has now matured into a major area of scientific inquiry within consumer research and psychology alike (Dunning, 2007; Sherman et al., 2014, Touré-Tillery & Fishbach, 2018; van Osselaer & Janiszewski, 2012). This completes our quick sketch overviewing the evolution of this field, and we next illustrate how several topics deemed important from the start evolved and benefitted from newer perspectives entering the field.

II. RESEARCH EXEMPLIFYING THE EVOLUTION OF CONSUMER PSYCHOLOGY

It is not possible in this constrained space to do justice to the wide assortment of empirical work that has characterized all of consumer psychology research. However, beyond highlighting important historical eras, another major goal is to trace key aspects of the field's evolution. To do that we have identified two very different influential early paradigms that spawned considerable and significant consumer research across time. The first emanated from a focus on psychological processes, the second from a focus on efforts to manage consumer behavior in the marketplace.

Research Emanating From a Process Approach to Understanding Consumer Behavior

As mentioned earlier, the groundwork for much subsequent work on psychological processes, as well as attitudes and feelings (affect) as precursors of behavior, was laid in advertising research depicting how advertising messages and executions influence consumer behavior.

Understanding how advertising works. Persuasion was increasingly seen as a step-wise process through which advertising influenced behavior. So this will be our starting point in tracing the evolution of process research. Copy tests assessing advertising executions' impacts on increasing brand recognition and recall had long been used, but without strong evidence of success (Lodish et al., 1995). As newer theory and research from social and cognitive psychology began to make an impact, persuasion drew particular scrutiny, and the shortcomings of simply measuring message playback/recall (that characterized earlier perspectives) were identified (Mitchell & Olson, 1981; Nordhielm, 2002; Percy & Rossiter, 1992). Message learning came to be seen as part of a process whereby the information might have to be believed and integrated into more favorable cognitive responses to a product (Petty et al., 1997; Puth & Ewing, 1999). Wright (1973, 1980) formalized cognitive response theory in his analyses of persuasive processes in advertising, demonstrating that consumers didn't form attitudes simply out of learned information but rather out of their responses to that information, including counterarguments they might generate to weak message arguments, as well as how message-evoked thoughts could be captured by thought verbalizations. Sternthal et al. (1978) showed that consumers' judgments of communicators' credibility altered these cognitive responses. A separate information processing stage (originally termed "yielding") then drew added attention and gave rise to a much more complete analysis of internally generated responses under varying conditions of exposure, involvement, and processing pivotal to improved understanding of persuasion (e.g., Anand & Sternthal, 1990; Petty et al., 1983; Sternthal et al., 1978).

The framework provided by Petty and colleagues (e.g., Petty et al., 1983) has been particularly impactful (see Chapter 13) and focuses on alternative modes of processing (i.e., central vs. peripheral routes) to arrive at an overall attitude (see also Gawronski & Bodenhausen, 2014). The path taken depends on a person's motivation, opportunity, and ability to process particular information at that time, which is likely to have a major impact on the ability to counter-argue message details (Albarracín, 2002). For example, a person with very little interest or background knowledge, or who is otherwise occupied, may only process peripheral message aspects (e.g., the appearance of the spokesperson, message cues suggesting a factual basis or lack of manipulation, or even simply affect generated by exposure to message delivery). More generally, measures conceptually closer to purchase, such as liking, desire to own, or intention to purchase the brand (rather than simply responses to marketing and advertising executions) were found to be more correlated with consumers' behavior (Rucker & He, 2019).

Many marketing and advertising practitioners had come to similar conclusions, arguing for defining advertising goals in terms of creating favorable consumer attitudes (Boyd et al., 1972). They also advocated measures to provide diagnostic insight rather than simply overall liking (such as scale placement or a ranking system for preferences). Though simple measures of overall liking or preferences capture attitudinal predispositions to respond, they produce limited insight into a consumer's beliefs about or relationship with a product. These static representations say nothing about the process whereby consumers have arrived at having a predisposition to purchase and thus are not useful enough as strategy tools for increasing consumers' brand purchase proclivities. To do so, we move beyond advertising and back to early hierarchy of effects thinking about consumer purchase behavior.

Focusing on the consumer's purchase process: The hierarchy of effects framework. Working as consultants to firms desiring to better market their automobiles, a marketing research executive (Robert Lavidge) and psychology professor (Gary Steiner) teamed up to formalize thinking about the steps consumers would take in moving from unawareness of a brand to actually purchasing it. Lavidge and Steiner (1961) specified a seven-stage sequence that began with unawareness and moved through awareness, knowledge, liking, preference, and conviction to purchase. These steps could be summarized as thinking (cognitive), feeling (affective), and doing (conative), in that order, simplified as a "Think, Feel, Do" process. Subsequent research shed a great deal more light on the nature, necessity, and order of such information processing steps (Alba & Hutchinson, 1987; Wilkie, 1994). Of note, most people working with the hierarchy of effects framework used the term "feeling" in an overly broad sense, combining both evaluations and feelings at this stage. It fell to later research to distinguish the two: the first is a judgment on an evaluative dimension, the latter is an affective state comprising valence (pleasantness–unpleasantness) and arousal linked to emotions and moods (J. B. Cohen, 1990).

Reflecting the cognitive orientation of the times, this was the original hierarchical framework, and it has continued as the most popular approach taken with hierarchical models, with each step attracting the attention of consumer psychologists. For example, the first step, brand awareness, has long been seen as a major brand asset, with establishing "top of mind" awareness an important marketing and advertising objective (Keller, 1993). The accessibility of brand or other key information came to be seen as critical (J. B. Cohen & Andrade, 2018; Feldman & Lynch, 1988; Raghubir & Menon, 1998). Measuring brand awareness led researchers to confront differences between recognition (or "aided recall") and unaided recall—eliciting the brand name from memory when a product category is cued (Braun-Latour & Zaltman, 2006; Percy & Rossiter, 1992). The latter is more demanding, indicating a more robust level of brand associations in memory. Brands consumers retrieve from memory when thinking about a purchase are referred to as the "evoked set," but the ultimate choice is typically from a smaller "consideration set" (Howard & Sheth, 1969). Elicitation of these sets implies a movement further up the hierarchy than simple awareness, requiring greater familiarity, a favorable impression, or even a brand preference (Nedungadi, 1990; Unnava et al., 1996). The process of moving up the hierarchy of effects raises the question of how consumers move from awareness, through acquiring information, to reach the so-called feeling stage. This is one of the most—if not the single most—heavily researched topics in the consumer behavior literature. Its study focused initially on the relationship between product beliefs and attitude formation and later on affect as keys to understanding the constructs of liking, preference, and conviction.

Beliefs define products and help consumers categorize and evaluate them. Models of concept learning and categorization specify associative links between objects and their characteristic features and attributes, enabling us to move beyond the granular level of perception and the uniqueness of every grain of sand or snowflake to "see" a beach or a snow-capped hill, both of which can be evaluated as intact entities (e.g., Barsalou, 1983; J. B. Cohen & Basu, 1987; Wattenmaker et al., 1986). Just as we might categorize an object as a bird due to its wings, beak, and feathers, we can classify a sunscreen lotion due to its ability to absorb or reflect ultraviolet radiation and protect against sunburn (a product only aiding in skin tanning would not be categorized as a sunscreen lotion). Similarly, if identifying good objects for a picnic, we would classify them by how well they fit this objective (e.g., card table chairs better than upholstered chairs, sandwiches better than microwaveable foods).

Many issues have arisen in studying categorization, including the reasonableness of using category-defining features (i.e., a learned "must have" "can't have" rule) to place objects within categories (as discussed in the papers cited earlier). One alternative, "family resemblance," operationalized by a set of accessible category exemplars (e.g., individual instances of different types of birds or chairs) or similarity to a prototype (i.e., a more abstract central tendency of the category) is often a faster, less cognitively demanding means of categorization. When some categories—such as the category "game"—are difficult to define in terms of features/attributes (rules), using judgments of similarity to known but diverse instances of the category (chess, football, electronic games) is much more likely to be used. Many managerially relevant categorization issues are being addressed in consumer psychology, including how consumers categorize new products and products that could fit in different categories, each producing unique inferences and possibly preferences (Landwehr et al., 2011; Moreau et al., 2001), but they are beyond the scope of our review.

Of particular relevance to consumer psychology is the relationship between perceiving/categorizing a brand and the consumer's attitude toward that brand (Sujan & Dekleva, 1987). Unlike birds and other natural objects, products and brands are socially constructed entities. Within consumer culture, products and brands we can identify tend to be defined in combinations of physical and performance attributes. In fact, it may be functional and less effortful to combine these with an evaluative label such as "best," "acceptable," or "unacceptable," under which brands can be placed as soon as sufficient information is available (which likely varies by product as a function of risk of a suboptimal choice). Such evaluative categories might greatly simplify decision making, especially for everyday choices. For challenging decisions, consider people thinking about getting an MBA degree and having their own set of attributes, benefits, or goals they find important when selecting a school. Assume they have an evoked set of schools to consider and are aware of and informed to some extent about each of these (i.e., they have moved to a level in the hierarchy where they possess such beliefs). So they can associate some programs more closely with appealing location, quality curriculum, alumni network, program length, low price, high status, and so forth: The brands are differentiated along such attributes. Then there are really just two questions to ask to move from brand knowledge to a brand attitude. First we need to know the strength of association between each brand and each of the attributes the person has identified as being important (in many cases there is general consensus about how well each brand performs on each attribute, but when brands are less familiar or some characteristics produce highly subjective assessments, variance will exist in assessments of the strength of particular brand-attribute associations). Second, we need to know how strongly the person will weigh the utility/value of each attribute, reflecting their goals for this decision. One can't evaluate an MBA program simply by adding its performance across the designated attributes/benefits; they need to be weighted by the value of that benefit to the person choosing. So someone who weights location as having the utmost value (perhaps because of a spousal job) will differ in comparison to another person primarily focused on each school's reputation. These lead to people having very different attitudes toward schools, with these individually determined attitudes being predictive of their subsequent behavior, *ceteris paribus*.

In sum, this assessment of a person's attitude incorporates the movement up the hierarchy of effects. The person's knowledge about each brand is represented by two types of beliefs: (a) a belief about the strength of association between a brand and its relevant attributes, benefits, and ability to help reach a goal and (b) a belief about the value importance of each of these factors. For each brand, an attitude is determined by weighting (typically multiplying) each such attribute's strength of association by its value importance and summing across the set of relevant attributes and benefits. This model generally goes under the heading of "multi-attribute attitude models," which were initially developed in social psychology by Martin Fishbein and Milton Rosenberg (see J. B. Cohen et al., 1972 for a comparison across models) and later generalized into a theory of reasoned action (Fishbein & Ajzen, 2010) and applied to a wide range of behavior from choices that effect health to downloading music (Fishbein & Ajzen, 2010; Sirkeci & Magnusdottir, 2011). Most consumer studies used the model as a predictive tool—initially against other measures of product favorability or behavioral intentions to establish validity and occasionally against measures of behavior. Predictive success was found to vary (Ajzen & Cote, 2008) as a function of

- the correspondence of measures (e.g., overall attitudes toward people and issues are less successful in predicting specific behaviors than corresponding measures of attitudes toward taking specific actions);
- whether the attributes and benefits were individualized to capture their relevance for each person rather than a common set (for ease of measurement);
- the foreseeability of intervening and constraining events on the behavior and the feasibility of overcoming such ability and resource limitations; and
- the degree to which the behavior was under the person's control, both in terms of conflicting social pressure/norms and availability of requisite personal ability and resources.

The diagnostic capabilities of this model are far superior to the types of attitude rating/ranking scale scores as well as small sets of bipolar evaluative adjectives (good–bad, positive–negative, like–dislike) earlier used in advertising and marketing research. J. B. Cohen and Houston (1972) used survey data to provide attribute/benefit scores as well as value importance scores for a set of toothpaste brands. Such data help diagnose attribute/benefit strengths and weaknesses for the various brands (e.g., superior whitening, inferior cavity prevention), showing how they contribute to overall evaluations for people seeking different benefits (benefit segmentation). This type of data could be helpful in identifying marketplace opportunities and niches for existing or new entrants. As indicated earlier, Fishbein, Ajzen, and their colleagues (Ajzen, 1991; Ajzen & Fishbein, 1977) then extended this model to include other factors (e.g., normative beliefs, perceived personal control) to better predict a wide range of behavior (Fishbein & Ajzen, 2010).

Putting doing before feeling. Ray et al. (1973) argued that the original hierarchical ordering fit high involvement purchasing, such as an automobile, but that consumers also buy many low involvement, frequently purchased items. For these, they suggested a "think–do–feel" order is a better fit, as such products' lower stakes can enable trial purchases, with postpurchase usage providing better evaluations of the product for future purchases. This sequence thus assumes a lesser degree of evaluation-generating thought prior to purchase, with a more knowledgeable "liking" (positive or negative) judgment only after acquisition and use (Agarwal & Karahanna, 2000). Postpurchase psychological processes could lead consumers to rewrite history, perhaps making the next purchase easier and the purchaser look wise, feel good, or avoid some negative postpurchase introspection (a dissonance theory type of prediction).

An argument can be made that habitual purchases not only move assessment to the postpurchase stage but that prepurchase "thinking" may be quite limited (Neal et al., 2006; Ouellette & Wood, 1998). If behavior follows directly from an awareness that a replacement bottle of orange juice is needed and the person has already found a satisfactory brand, does its purchase really require interim steps? Indeed, consumers do make many supermarket decisions incredibly quickly, moving down the aisle, visually detecting their preferred items, and reaching and placing them in the shopping cart. Alba and Hutchinson (1987; see also Bargh et al., 2012) invoked the cognitive psychology term "automaticity" to refer to habitual actions carried out with minimal cognitive processing. Our prior notion of having evaluative categories into which brands have been placed could be one such process. When consumers act somewhat habitually, without the careful consideration often attributed to "rational decision making," it may seem incongruous to use the term "thinking" to describe the actual use of minimal thought (e.g., a boost in accessibility) prior to purchase. Future research could usefully work to better specify the nature of thoughts being generated for low involvement decisions (e.g., identification/categorization, reliance on easily accessible information). In the extreme case it can be argued that both external influences and particularly well learned information can act directly on behavior, putting actions ahead of meaningful thought or evaluations (Chartrand, 2005; Dijksterhuis et al., 2008; Janiszewski, 1993; Loftus, 1975; Nedungadi, 1990).

Putting feeling first. A body of research emerged in psychology to support the notion that more primitive preattentive cognitive processes not only can subvert normally occurring thoughtful and analytic processes but can directly influence evaluations and preferences (Batra & Ray, 1986: Janiszewski, 1993). Within the hierarchy of effects framework, prior "mere exposure" to a brand name (Zajonc, 1980) can give rise to affect as a controlling factor in preferences, which we refer to here as "putting feeling first." Actual feelings (i.e., internal affective states as in "I'm feeling bad," not to be confused with evaluative judgments or attitudes toward some object or concept) require their own focus within the hierarchy of effects framework. In 1986, Batra and Ray argued that affective responses work alongside cognitive responses to advertising messages and appear to be antecedents of higher level brand attitudes. And subsequent research by Pham et al. (2001) made the case that affective responses can not only be faster but also impart more directionally important information (e.g., regarding the valence of a newly exposed object; see also Greifender et al., 2011). Melumad et al. (2019) found that physically constrained smartphone-generated content can be more affect- than cognition-laden, thereby injecting emotion into product assessments.

Research Emanating From a Focus on Managing Marketplace Behavior

In contrast to psychological research that is directly focused on better understanding the processes governing consumers' behaviors, there is also a long history of research aimed directly at how best to influence or alter consumers' actions. This second approach, though it may also refer to processes, is distinctive because its research goal is different: It seeks to understand how to effectively change consumer behavior. Much of this research has been done with marketers' sales and profits in mind, but some has also been undertaken for prosocial purposes—to enhance consumers' well-being. We begin our coverage with research on marketers' interests in winning consumer patronage.

The 4Ps as tools to influence marketplace behavior. E. J. McCarthy (1960) advanced an influential "4Ps" paradigm that viewed controllable marketing mix variables as tools capable of altering consumers' behavior. At the time these were identified as product, price, place, and promotion. Over time, marketing scholars began to consider a wider set of variables in response to technological changes (particularly internet shopping) that enabled greater personalization as well as a broader set of promotional tools that combined to both push products through channels and pull consumers toward purchase. This included building direct relationships between sellers and buyers based on shared values (e.g., "green marketing") rather than traditional persuasion. More generally, the latter was termed "customer relationship management" (CRM), viewing value as created by an interactive process (Ballantyne et al., 2003).

Regardless of specific revisions in the 4Ps paradigm, the central idea was that these tools could be used to alter behavior. The for-profit scope was broadened by Kotler and colleagues (Kotler & Levy, 1969; Kotler & Zaltman, 1971), who argued that marketing tools have wider applicability, including to social causes (Ha & Janda 2012; Niblett, 2005). Wood (2008) delved further into this distinction, pointing out social causes can at times be asking consumers to (a) voluntarily reject or abandon a behavior they enjoy, such as smoking, or (b) engage in behavior they dislike or would prefer to avoid, such as cancer screening. In these cases, exchange is not as straightforward as in marketplace exchanges in which money is exchanged for goods and services. We see this latter point as particularly relevant, suggesting a broader view of "price" to include economic, time, physical, and especially psychological costs of the behavioral changes people are asked to make to avoid risky or societally undesirable behaviors.

Combining marketing tools with mediators of behavior and behavior change. Given its marketplace outcome emphasis, traditional usage of marketing tools to create behavior change, such as the 4Ps, largely ignored the mediators through which many interventions operate and ultimately determine whether behavioral change takes place. Identifying these and reducing them to a manageable number to comprise a conceptual framework has been a major quest of the social sciences. The long history of research on interventions in the social and health sciences, along with well-recognized deficiencies in existing theory, was recently reviewed by J. B. Cohen and Andrade (2018), who then proposed a parsimonious framework for understanding how interventions affect behavior. They asserted that most interventions work through three levers (mediators): accessibility, desirability, and feasibility. A range of tools can then be considered for each mediator.

Accessibility refers to the likelihood of a goal and action steps needed to achieve the goal actually coming to mind, both when making a decision and when enacting behavior. Proprietary research on advertising for a beverage intended to be part of a meal indicated it seldom came to consumers' minds prior to making a choice, dooming the product. Accessibility has been a key component of a number of psychological frameworks, such as when combined with diagnosticity (i.e., decision relevance) of the accessible information input (Feldman & Lynch, 1988) and when cognitive task demands are too high or extra cognitive effort is unwarranted, prompting ease of retrieval to function as a heuristic in decision making (Menon & Raghubir, 2003).

Desirability captures evaluative and affective assessments of the short- and long-term consequences of acquiring a salient object or attaining a goal. Many products provide direct satisfaction via performance utility and can also contribute to achieving broader self-oriented goals (e.g., a gym membership). Feelings experienced from purchase and use also can be immediate sources of pride and achievement. Longer term consequences can accrue from over-time value (e.g., a better quality, longer lasting product option can conflict with paying less and having those funds available for other immediate uses). Other instances of desirability conflict include immediate taste satisfaction from snacking or nicotine's positive effect on mood, each competing with longer term favorable consequences of sticking with a diet plan and living a healthier life.

Feasibility refers to the perceived likelihood of goal achievement through a given means and is based on a subjective assessment of factors enabling or impeding progress toward the goal. In mundane cases (when product acquisition is the operative goal), this is enhanced by improving time and place utility, as by a marketer improving product availability and delivery. Feasibility assessment involves two categories: resources necessary to achieve the goal, and one's ability to achieve the goal. Limited economic and time resources can lower feasibility, but marketers have tools (e.g., sales, easily available credit) to work with resource constraints. Ability issues may not be as apparent, however. A lack of knowledge or confidence can lead consumers to avoid certain financial decisions (e.g., life and health insurance, stock investments, vacation planning in an unfamiliar locale, or buying technologically sophisticated products). Similarly, consumers may not believe they have the skills or willpower needed to reach a desired goal and so avoid gym memberships, nutritional counseling, or other services available for life enhancement. And in aggregate effort cases such as energy and water conservation or blood drives, people may not believe they can accomplish much on their own. In all of these cases, change agents need to go well beyond the 4Ps to design and implement effective interventions. Fortunately, intervention-focused consumer research is likely to contribute to a more efficient marketplace, offering insights for how tools available to marketers can aid in the adoption of healthful behaviors, products, and services by consumers.

Research on the accessibility mediator. In general, a brand name, product attribute, or personal brand experience is accessible in memory because of its associative strength with likely retrieval cues (e.g., a supermarket section for "breakfast cereal," walking into a drugstore, or putting things together for a picnic). The strength and exclusivity of the retrieval cue's linkage to a specific item (e.g., a brand of breakfast cereal) stored in memory makes all the difference. With continued use, some memory traces are chronically accessible (e.g., your name and address), while nonuse makes for difficult retrieval (e.g., your fourth-grade English teacher).

A good deal has been learned about creating associations in memory that increase the likelihood of engaging in advocated behavior. Nedungadi (1990) established that increased accessibility affects the likelihood that a brand is retrieved and considered for choice. Lynch et al. (1988) found increasing use of an attribute to make a choice if it is accessible in memory and if it is perceived as more diagnostic than other accessible inputs, which can also be influenced by temporal framing (Chandran & Menon, 2004). Moreover, accessibility-based recall can exert particularly strong effects when choices are largely based on memory rather than careful deliberation during a purchase (Posavac et al., 1997). Accordingly, a breakfast cereal brand manager would like to create a "top of mind" state for a particular brand, then have it come to mind when the consumer is in the supermarket.

Keller (1987) examined this process by combining the effects of a commercial for LIFE cereal with an in-store promotion featuring a scene from the same commercial on the front of the package (both featuring a boy named "Mikey"). He began by pointing out that high levels of competing ads and brands in a crowded product category can lead to interference and confusion regarding the brand associated with Mikey; hence the name may be more accessible than the brand. Thus, even if favorable evaluations of the brand occurred during ad exposure, unless they are strongly associated with the cues available when shopping, the favorably evaluated brand may not come to mind at purchase. His research indicated that having the picture on the front of the package as a retrieval cue can increase the accessibility of memory traces originally seen in the commercial, likely leading to increased purchases.

Dick et al. (1990) examined the important role of memory-based inferences during consumer choice. When accessibility of relevant information was low, people relied more on prior overall brand evaluations, but when accessibility of relevant information was high, they used salient attribute information in memory, enabling more precise evaluations. Fazio et al. (1989) found that those having more accessible attitudes displayed greater attitude-behavior correspondence, whereas those with less relied more strongly on product shelf placement. This suggests that marketers could assess preshopping accessibility interventions against in-store product placement cues such as end-of-aisle displays. In a persuasion context, accessibility of attitudes (toward vegetarianism) was manipulated by varying how often participants expressed such attitudes. Subjects with higher accessibility were more influenced by a persuasive communication, suggesting that increasing accessibility leads to enhanced elaboration of supportive messages (Fabrigar et al., 1998).

It appears to be easier to retrieve favorable product features and more difficult to retrieve unfavorable features, suggesting that either this information was elaborated on or organized differently in memory (Wänke et al., 1997). And, since consumers likely expect that the number of positive associations (e.g., attributes, personal experiences) they can recall should be higher for a preferred brand, failing to recall more than a handful (a difficult task) might convince them that their brand assessment is not as favorable as they assumed (Schwarz, 2004). Could this be used as a competitive tactic? Accessibility's implications for brand extension research is inconclusive as to whether accessibility of a brand name, if used in a variety of categories (e.g., food blenders, hairdryers, handheld vacuums), creates benefits enough to overcome a more diffuse brand image (Meyvis & Janiszewski, 2004).

A series of papers has even linked accessibility (brought about merely by asking a survey question about purchase intentions) to a greater likelihood of purchasing such products as automobiles and personal computers (see Morwitz & Fitzsimons, 2004, for a detailed examination). One claim was that mere measurement ("How likely are you to purchase an automobile?") altered subsequent behavior. If enhanced accessibility earlier in time could have such strong effects on purchasing behavior months later, should marketers spend millions of dollars on advertising or instead invest in far less expensive survey questions? Consider the possibility that when people take intention questions seriously they may engage in behavior-focused thinking, thereby moving beyond any temporary increase in accessibility into desirability considerations.

Another research program has examined the effect of often subtle situational cues on the perception–behavior link and whether, acting without conscious awareness, increases in association strength can parallel increased accessibility in their effects (Chartrand, 2005; Cialdini, 2001; Dijksterhuis et al., 2005). Consider times when goal-directed behavior seems unconsciously guided by a familiar environment or perhaps by ingrained habits linked to it (e.g., in a supermarket, items being quickly selected, some in a relatively mindless fashion). In such contexts, virtually automatic effects on accessibility and accompanying memory associations can be critical to subsequent behavior. This helps explain marketers giving special attention to features of the environment (e.g., cleanliness, uncongested aisles, type and speed of background music, and especially product presentations). Dijksterhuis et al. (2005) presented a variety of ways that consumers are influenced by seemingly inconsequential environmental inputs (e.g., hearing German or French music in a store produced an increase in sales, respectively, of German or French wine). Similarly, a sign "Today Only!" may tap into a response associated with scarcity, while a smiling face may temporarily increase favorability and mood-influenced purchasing. These authors pointed out that observing (perception) and performing (behavior) involve largely similar neuronal brain regions, promoting relatively mindless imitation instead of more cognitively demanding mental processes.

Related psychological processes include assimilation and contrast, which displace judgments up or down from an anchoring stimulus, absent objectively valid information: seeing a speeding (vs. slow moving) car can alter speed judgments for the next car. Anchoring on a negatively (vs. positively) evaluated entity can lead to consistency biases in perception: "seeing" more (vs. less) disliked team fouls. These processes operate both through automatic and conscious influences on performance and quality assessments (Chernev, 2011). One interesting cigarette marketing speculation is whether anchoring on a dominant family brand (Marlboro) might, via contrast, displace another member of that brand family (Marlboro Light) *further* down the hazardous dimension than would be the case in the absence of such a salient category exemplar.

Some criticism has been directed at the increasing emphasis consumer psychologists have given to behavioral impacts of subtle environmental and physiological/sensory stimuli (e.g., looking up rather than down, hearing fast vs. slow music, standing rather than sitting). We see this as reflecting different research priorities: Psychological theorists prioritize adding to a body of theory to better understand each component of an underlying processes, whereas researchers focused on factors affecting "real world" consumer behavior prioritize their strength and relevance, downplaying such subtle influences.

Theorists often stress that subsequent behavior-relevant contributions often flow from better theoretical understanding. For example, because people are accustomed to looking down to process nearby stimuli and looking up to process distant stimuli (and given that the literature supports an association between head and body movement and types of thought), could looking down evoke more concrete rather than abstract thought? Could this lead to increased attention to feasibility from the outset rather than merely the desirability of, say, a financial planning goal (Van Kerckhove et al., 2015)? Assume a physiological theory suggests that standing versus sitting induces greater physical stress to the muscular system (Biswas et al., 2019). Suppose also that standing consumers consume smaller amounts of pleasant-tasting foods and beverages. Would food retailers benefit from an intervention to alleviate muscular stress? First, it is essential that a theoretical assertion is properly validated (i.e., other plausible factors are ruled out) so that one does not ignore the possibility that consumers may simply have more negative attitudes to eating while standing (from recalling negative consequences of holding multiple items or added stress from rushing through a meal) and so eat faster and less. If entirely different causes produce similar effects, mistaking the actual cause could lead to ineffective actions (e.g., trying to cope effectively with nonconsequential physiological factors).

Research on the desirability mediator. We view the perceived desirability of a product as a primary driver of one's attitude toward buying it, assuming accessibility of this judgment is high and desirability is not hampered by limitations in resources and ability (which together constitute feasibility). Desirability has been investigated under a variety of headings, including favorability, evaluation, and preferences. As discussed earlier, it may be sought after and experienced both in the short and longer term (e.g., when health and educational goals are fulfilled). Consumer research has focused on desirability accruing from performance attributes of products and brands, self-concept and personal value-associated benefits, and affect-induced feelings of satisfaction and pride (including achieving or maintaining positive moods). In addition, Shavitt and Nelson (2002) provided a broadly based conceptualization of favorability, adding to seminal work on attitude functions as well as cultural factors and research on means-end chains examined linkages between product attributes and deeper goals and personal values (e.g., Gutman, 1982; Reynolds & Olson, 2001).

Attributes as sources of product desirability. Consumers use attributes as a basis for evaluating products because they help identify the benefits consumers seek and also foster comparisons among competing brands (Puth et al., 1999). As such, marketers can view a brand as a bundle of intrinsic and extrinsic attributes and use this as a basis for product positioning strategy to influence consumers' evaluation of alternatives. Indeed, strongly associated attributes largely determine the value of a brand name and the success of brand extensions (D. C. Smith & Park, 1992). More intangible attributes, such as aesthetic properties of brands, can function similarly to tangible, highly functional attributes and influence a brand's desirability (Hoegg et al., 2010). A more complex conceptualization by Wu et al. (2017) explained how the very act of consuming a highly aesthetic product can backfire, lowering its inherent desirability. As a further illustration of complexity when assessing desirability, it turns out that at least some consumers appear to be averse to unused utility and so giving them more for their money when that would produce waste could make the offering less desirable (Bolton & Alba, 2012).

As discussed earlier, multi-attribute attitude models have occupied a significant place in consumer research, representing utility received from products and brands. As a quick summary, a brand's

strength or likelihood of possession of associated attributes and benefits is weighted by the personal value of each to determine its overall desirability/utility (J. B. Cohen et al., 1972; Lutz, 1975; Wilkie & Pessemier, 1973). Attribute strength for search attributes (e.g., color, ingredient content) can typically be assessed while shopping prior to purchase, whereas assessing strength of experience attributes (e.g., by experiencing the taste of food and beverages, the immediate performance of paper towels and lubricants) and credence attributes (e.g., to determine the benefit of vitamin potency, organic produce) require product trial or even extended purchase depending on performance ambiguity. Thus, the strength of experience and credence attributes is often belief-based (a function of advertising, social persuasion, brand familiarity, and accessibility) and subject to modification based on experience (Agarwal & Karahanna, 2000; Srinivasan & Till, 2002). When vividly conveyed by media, virtual experiences can affect attribute beliefs long before a specific purchase (e.g., as with tourism options and home improvement products).

Attributes have been broadly defined to include physical and visual features and even store names and country of origin (P. Chao, 2001). Interestingly, consumers' reactions to a brand's advertising, particularly if it serves to define the brand, can also function as a brand attribute, altering brand desirability (M. P. Gardner, 1985; Mittal, 1990). Some managers attempting to link brands with important social causes have moved beyond general environmental concerns (which have not proven to be particularly effective) to much more specific product class attributes and consequences (e.g., recyclability for disposable diapers, reducing trash from packaging and fast food restaurants; Alwitt & Pitts, 1996). For influencing organic consumption, overall desirability increases ensue from attributes such as natural, less-processed, and higher vitamin and mineral content along with longer term health benefits (S. Smith & Paladino, 2010), while environmentally friendly hotels have emphasized reductions in such attributes as energy/water consumption, towel reuse programs, and environmentally friendly cleaning products, often based on multi-attribute attitude research (Han & Kim, 2010). Since proenvironmental benefits tend to be longer term and less certain, promoting these as behavioral incentives has been a challenge (McCarty & Shrum, 2001).

Sources of product desirability from social identity. Reed (2004) referred to social identity as mental representations that become a basic part of how consumers view themselves, noting that marketers' positioning of brands to embody a particular social identity-oriented lifestyle makes them more desirable (see also Belk, 1988; Escalas & Bettman, 2013; Levy, 1959). This can lead to longer term relationships between consumers and their brands and sponsoring companies (Chugani et al., 2015; Fournier, 1998). When marketers associate a product or brand with a particular social identity (e.g., a person or group shown in an ad can be emblematic of a category that either includes the consumer, or departs significantly upward or downward, as influenced by such things as clothing, settings, and activities), a social frame of reference is created. If the frame of reference includes the consumer, it may increase the attractiveness of the brand—as a brand that "fits me well." More research is needed to determine how much of an upward departure from how the person views themselves may create added desirability (i.e., "it fits my aspirational self") or may, on the other hand, make the product less attractive (i.e., "for snobs"). Similarly, creating a negative frame of reference for eating an unhealthy food, by showing the person eating it as someone the viewer would dissociate from, may make that food less attractive, possibly leading to desirable behavior change (Catapano et al., 2019; McFerran et al., 2010).

Two interrelated issues have evolved from the joint consideration of constructs involving the self and brands and products as sources of value. The first examines the effects of different aspects of identity (e.g., ethnicity, gender, nationality, age, personality, occupation, and various social roles and reference groups) on consumption, and the second focuses on how consumption may also influence identity: We are defined in part by our possessions (Belk, 1988; Kirmani, 2009; McCracken, 1989). Do I drive a Prius because I am or aspire to be seen as an environmentalist? In the other direction, does my driving a Prius increase my self-definition or willingness to self-label as an environmentalist? Experience-based marketing can provide consumers with opportunities to label or even alter their personal identities (sometimes termed transformational value offerings; Kleine et al., 2009). Products may serve as symbols representing role stereotypes (e.g., backpacks vs. briefcases, convertibles vs. sedans). White et al. (2012) implicated interdependent (rather than independent) self-construal as contributing to preferences for identity-linked products when self-identities are threatened. Notably, Chan et al. (2012) demonstrated consumers simultaneously pursuing assimilation/affiliation and differentiation/distinctiveness goals by selecting identity-signaling brands (e.g., BMW) but with unique attributes (e.g., less popular BMW options).

Reed (2004) and Oyserman (2009), among others, have addressed limiting factors in the ability of identity-based sources of value to influence purchasing behavior. Both the relevant identity and a brand's ability to cue/activate that identity rely on accessibility, and must come together at the appropriate time. As such, situational factors are particularly important, elevating the role of place (e.g., stores associated with such personal characteristics), even though advertising may have played the major role in cementing links between identity constructs and brands. In a novel conceptualization (Hershfield et al., 2011), the authors propose that allowing people to interact with age-progressed renderings of themselves will cause them to allocate more resources to the future. Since people run the risk of outliving their money, providing this benefit could be quite important, especially given people's tendency to discount the future (Lynch et al., 2010). Bolton and Reed (2004) found that identity-related judgments were hard to correct, including by asking people to think about the same judgment from the standpoint of a different identity. More research is needed on these topics and to determine the conditions under which sources of value that define the self may have stronger effects than the presence of highly desirable attributes, both for consumer and political decisions.

Affective sources of product desirability. As indicated earlier, most psychologists (Breckler & Wiggins, 1989) distinguish between evaluation (as types of thoughts, beliefs, and judgments) and affect (as emotional responses and feelings). We have just covered evaluation in our discussion of thoughts about product attributes as a major source of desirability. With respect to affect, however, we also note that advertising conveying a positive feeling state (such as "joy of driving!" a particular car) may do more to influence the desirability of that car than does any presentation of its attributes. This can be true for many types of sensory-based information (J. Kim & Morris, 2007), especially if consumers lack enough experience/knowledge to render confident evaluations or are in a more passive, low involvement, or pleasant state of mind that is conducive to using affect heuristics or brand name familiarity (Batra & Stephens, 1994; Mackie & Worth, 1989). Here, positive feelings become an alternative source of information relative to evaluative information (Schwarz & Clore, 2007; see Chapter 25, this volume). Essentially, consumers are simplifying judgments of desirability. Instead of bringing together substantial information about a brand, they just ask "How do I feel about it?" and assume those feelings also reflect the relevant information. One problem is that feelings we bring to mind are also influenced by current experiences (e.g., from store atmospherics), and we might misattribute a positive mood to a brand being considered. Avnet et al. (2012) examined the diagnosticity of feelings in consumer judgments, concluding that their representativeness, relevance, and trustworthiness all play important roles.

As Clore and Schnall (2019) put it, "Affective reactions are important because negotiating complex environments necessitates making frequent and effortless evaluations" (p. 259). Pham et al. (2001) are among the few consumer psychologists who have examined the speed and initial impact of affective versus evaluative inputs and have speculated about affect's possible advantages due to either a more direct pathway or lower information complexity. Psychologists have spent decades studying the influence of affect (both emotions and moods) on attitudes, and we will not attempt to review or cite to this extensive literature here (see J. B. Cohen et al., 2008, for a review focused on consumer behavior). We start with the premise that most affective reactions are fleeting rather than enduring dispositions and that they do not rely on high-level processing or even awareness. Indeed the mere familiarity of a brand name (as well as the frequent pairing of a neutral stimulus with a positive word or image) seems able to increase positive affect and liking, perhaps due to a reduction in uncertainty about the stimulus. Whether such a small elevation in positive affect can have a meaningful impact on an enduring attitude or subsequent behavior is a matter of some dispute and is undoubtedly related to the context in which this occurs, including the availability of other sources of information and the importance of any subsequent action to the consumer (Ottati & Isbell, 1996). However, Andrade and Ariely (2009) pointed out how decisions based on even fleeting emotional states (precisely because they fly under the radar of recognized influences that are subject to challenge) can then become the basis for future decisions.

Positive affect can influence both desirability and the willingness to take a specified action for several reasons (Isen, 2000). Consistent with mood-congruent recall processes, thoughts, and actions already associated with positive feelings (being helpful, successful, safe, or generous) can come to mind. This may promote self-confidence, openness to variety-seeking, and willingness to consider new information, but less need for analytic thought. In addition, people often prefer to remain in positive moods and to alleviate negative moods. A negative mood can have opposite effects, so focusing on risks (what can go wrong) is likely to undermine a positive mood. Negative affect also tends to narrow one's focus, bringing forth a problem-solving state of mind. In general, such mood-based behavior is well supported, but predictions in isolation can ignore other goals and thoughts consumers will have in realistic settings and that are likely to have at least equal sway over judgments and behavior (J. B. Cohen et al., 2008).

In persuasion settings, since both positive and negative moods produce mood-congruent recall (or priming of similar affective information), evaluations of message arguments may be biased, depending on a consumer's willingness/unwillingness to engage in or suppress cognitive elaboration.

Fedorikhin and Cole (2004) suggested that the likelihood of biasing evaluations in mood-congruent directions will be stronger when consumers engage in high amounts of elaborative processing, but this may not necessarily be the case. This prediction seems to hinge on knowing the affective aspects of the information that greater amounts of elaboration would generate. But it is not clear that an affect congruency heuristic would come to dominate elaborative processing, given that something has motivated consumers to spend extra effort making an evaluative judgment.

Both extrinsic sources of mood, such as an interrupting task or intrusion, and mood occurring intrinsically (i.e., as part of the ongoing stream of behavior) can color brand attitudes. Two intrinsic sources of brand affect can arise from advertising, the first from direct presentation-mediated feelings that require no elaboration (e.g., pictures, music) and the second from judgments (e.g., factual, honest) that can become associated with the brand. Both can also contribute to increased "liking for the ad" (Batra & Stayman, 1990; Chattopadhyay & Nedungadi, 1992; MacKenzie et al., 1986). Research also shows that metacognitive experiences (i.e., consumers' feelings about whether they adequately assess a brand, as informed by their perceived fluency, ease of recalling information, or perceived confidence) can affect willingness to rely on affective heuristics versus employing higher level cognitive processes or information seeking when evaluating the brand (Briñol et al., 2004; Lee & Shavitt, 2009; Schwarz, 2004).

Consumption has been understood to be a means of regulating affect, as in raiding the refrigerator or buying something new to improve one's mood. Recent research has also shown that people seem to intuit both the effects of their behavior on affect as well as how regulating their affective states can impact different types of behavior (J. L. Aaker & Lee, 2001; Andrade & Cohen, 2007; Chen & Pham, 2019; J. B. Cohen & Andrade, 2004; Isen, 2000). Ironically, people may not perform as well on tasks that demand careful attention or may engage in more risky behavior when they are in a more carefree and happy mood, and so may regulate toward a more neutral state.

We've now completed discussing our first two mediators—accessibility and desirability—that operate in changing a consumer's behavior. We now turn to the third and final lever in the consumer's consideration: "Is this behavior actually feasible for me?"

Research on the feasibility mediator. Ecolabeling can assist in bringing about green consumption behavior through visual cues and reminders, thereby increasing accessibility, and overcome deficits in knowledge and desirability by supplying convincing positive arguments. Unfortunately, research has shown that even environmentally conscious people do not show a consistent preference for purchasing environmentally friendly products and are not necessarily willing to pay a premium for them (Peattie, 2010). Some added factor is likely to play a major role, and we now examine the feasibility mediator.

For consumers to behave in accordance with their accessible desirability assessments, they must believe they have the resources and abilities to achieve the sought-after goal, whether it is a single act (e.g., having a medical checkup) or a longer term progression of behaviors. This becomes less certain with the greater difficulty of those actions (e.g., achieving weight loss goals requires substantial over-time commitment and willpower) and when scarce resources (economic, time, psychological, and social) are needed. Conceptually, it seems important to differentiate between an activity perceived to be burdensome or costly in the broadest sense and one that is perceived to be blocked or inhibited by some physical or psychological obstacle. The former would affect desirability in a negative way, thereby lowering evaluations, and might be overcome, for example, by a marketer charging a lower price or providing an offsetting benefit. However, if people regard achieving a personal or normatively important goal as blocked or inhibited such that they do not believe that they have the means (i.e., either or both the necessary resources or ability) to reach the goal as things currently stand, that is a feasibility issue.

Those seeking to change behavior must realize they are usually dealing with a subjective perception reflecting individual circumstances rather than some type of physical blockage (e.g., the actual absence of organic food in the inner-city as a stand-in for an unpassable Wagnerian "ring of fire"). Acquiring an understanding of relevant resource and ability perceptions could start by examining verbatim responses to straightforward probe questions: "And why haven't you been to see a doctor about your high blood pressure?" with answers such as "I don't have any health insurance" and "I can't climb the stairs to her office." Creative marketing might view such perceived feasibility obstacles as changeable, in part via "product" improvements derived from internet commerce such as physician teleconferencing and improvements in smartphones that benefit tourists (H. H. Kim & Law, 2015). Even minor improvements in touchscreen and touchpad interfaces can overcome perceived deficits in feasibility (Brasel & Gips, 2014). In sum, without employing intervention tools to overcome feasibility challenges, simply bringing the behavior to mind and convincing people it is desirable are unlikely to generate the advocated behavior.

A social resource, the mere presence of others, can facilitate or impede purchase behavior, as is the case for impulsive purchasing (Luo, 2005). Providing information about others' behavior, particularly those with whom a consumer identifies, has long been a staple of social marketing (Burchell et al., 2013). For example, effective social marketing campaigns have utilized social norms: "70% of homes on Brook Place recycle their plastic waste," "Your energy consumption was considerably above your neighborhood average," or "88% of high school students who quit smoking showed no ill effects of their earlier smoking histories." Research showed increased willingness to engage in conservation behavior (e.g., reusing hotel towels) when people learned that similar others in the situation had done so, through such normative messages posted in their hotel rooms (Goldstein et al., 2008). Many proenvironmental behaviors depend on broad deployment of resources together with diffusion of key information through localized social networks (Axsen & Kurani, 2012), and this may also hold true for public health and vaccination programs. Recycling behavior increases when recycling bins are convenient as well as located next to trash cans (enhancing a perception of feasibility). Establishing norms can overcome a lack of trust that others are fully participating (e.g., observing water use restrictions).

For many choices and resulting behaviors, complexity and conflict (including having to give up something of value) combine to strain perceived feasibility and encourage delay and avoidance. This is well illustrated by Johnson and Goldstein (2003), who demonstrated the value of decision structuring when people are making organ donor decisions. Though a vast majority are favorably inclined, less than 30% had signed a donor card (likely because these decisions can be unpleasant and stressful). As a policy matter, outcomes default to the assumption that the absence of action implies that people have not agreed to such a donation upon death (so an assumed opt-out). Donation rates were significantly higher after restructuring the decision to assume an opt-in unless a person explicitly opts-out. Of note, requiring people to opt out also raises their costs (e.g., time and effort to fill out forms, emotional costs of making a difficult decision), so restructuring decisions in this way also creates a bias and ethical dilemma for policy makers. For this reason, restructuring should comport with broad acceptance of this as sound societal policy.

Another sector in which feasibility commonly surfaces as an issue for consumers involves sophisticated technology as a key component of new products and services that they may not well understand. Perceived behavioral control (the capability of achieving the desired outcome, or "self-efficacy") is a feature of numerous models of planned behavior (e.g., Ajzen, 2002). In this regard, Meuter et al. (2003) identified high levels of consumer anxiety for use of technology-mediated services as a factor contributing to lower levels of use. Mick and Fournier (1998) conducted interviews that included first-time owners of a range of technological products, to examine their perspectives and coping strategies when the promises of such products (e.g., greater freedom and control) are contradicted by challenges and accompanying stress in adjusting to them. The resource value of new high-tech products to consumers depends on the products' perceived usefulness, perceived ease-of-use, and possibly perceived enjoyment, depending on the technology in question (Dabholkar & Bagozzi, 2002). Yang and Forney (2013) also noted that consumer technology anxiety increases as newer modes of use (e.g., digital wallets, transaction-enabled mobile sites) become enabled. They identified "facilitating conditions" (e.g., better interface, processing capabilities, speed) that can function like resources; when effectively communicated, these combine with needed knowledge to increase performance expectancies, thus reducing technological anxiety as a barrier to use. Facilitating conditions were found more effective with low consumer anxiety, and hedonic benefits (perceiving fun in using) were particularly influential. In sum, facilitating resources with social networking and expert advice links, as well as other ways of lowering consumer anxiety, can be critical in increasing perceived feasibility for technology adoption.

Perceived feasibility can increase, in the first place, by providing information to improve confidence that the decision or action will help consumers to improve their own welfare. Bazerman (2001; see also Maynes, 1988b) pointed to the absence of research that would help consumers come to that understanding and make wiser purchases, noting that such research should probably begin in domains where they need the most help, rather than areas where replicable purchases or easily available data exist and that may be easier to study. That extends to clothing purchases made from home where improvements in what is termed "virtual fitting room technology" (where 3D overlays of a dress serve as a dressing room mirror) are likely to lead to more satisfied shoppers, increased sales and fewer returns (Liaw & Chen, 2013). In some cases, the lack of ability to make better choices can be overcome by improving the information presentation format, especially at the time and place where decisions are being made (Downs et al., 2015), and on information placed on packages. Crosetto et al. (2016), comparing different types of front-of-pack nutritional labels, found presentations of comprehensive, more cognitively demanding information to be more effective when people did not face time constraints, but this advantage over coarser, more salient presentations disappeared under time constraints. Other discussions of using information presentation formats on packages and labels to help consumer decision making have contributed to the public policy literature (Bettman et al., 1986; Hutton & Wilkie, 1980; Kleinmuntz & Schkade, 1993; McNeill & Wilkie, 1979; Moorman, 1996). Roe et al. (1999) found that consumers believed a product to be healthier when health and nutrient claims were presented, creating, however, a potential for harm and supporting the need for truthfulness, as a regulatory matter, if this information were likely to be helpful. The profusion of qualifying statements (which have not been evaluated by the Food and Drug Administration) for nonprescription items consumers probably consider to be "medicines" likely undermines confidence in their ability to make health-related decisions.

Perceived ability deficits are a key issue given a goal of healthy eating. In restaurants, consumers typically rely on prior experiences, food-related knowledge, and impressions of food healthiness to form beliefs about food nutrition content. Consumers ingest more than one third of their calories from food prepared outside the home, and this tends to be higher in calories, fat, saturated fat, sugar, and salt. Policy makers have searched for methods to help consumers improve their nutritional food choices. Displaying nutrition information on menus is one option: It could improve knowledge, reduce search costs, prime healthiness during a meal choice, and lead to better restaurant nutrition decisions. However, research evidence here is mixed. Seenivasan and Thomas (2016) noted that restaurant dining motivations are highly variable, depend on the occasion and venue, and that social contexts matter, all serving to make the link between more nutrition information and behavior more complex than is considered in the design of many studies.

Perceived ability is also in doubt when choosing among items sold in different sizes (e.g., packaged cookies), as the numerical expressions of quantities can have large impacts on evaluations. Consumers are less able to discriminate between options or make better choices when quantities are expressed along numerical scales (e.g., weight 500 grams vs. 1,000 grams, or size in square feet) than when they are discretely expressed (25 vs. 50 cookies, three vs. five bedrooms). This is especially true for people who are less numerically proficient, helping them overcome a bias in favor of sheer magnitude of numerical differences, such as a 500-gram difference (Bagchi & Davis, 2016; Lembregts & Van Den Berg, 2019).

Many decisions, such as choosing more economically appropriate credit cards, are made at home and can also benefit from improvements in information presentation (D'astous & Miquelon, 1991). Information presentation approaches that better inform consumers have been of considerable interest to public health officials (Hibbard & Peters, 2003). Their evidence indicates that providing an abundance of information does not necessarily translate into better consumer decision-making. Among newer presentation approaches is a distributional format for providing comparative information, serving to provide a useful reference system for the consumer (Chin & Bruine de Bruin, 2018). Without a reference system, for example, it is difficult for consumers to evaluate annual percentage rates (APRs) if only the absolute level is presented in a credit card solicitation. This decision can be improved if a reference graph of the distribution of APRs available in the credit card market can be incorporated into the consumer's evaluation of options available; these authors examined specific graph formats in relation to communication goals.

Research investigating judgments and behavior cued by deficits in feasibility may allow consumer psychologists to pinpoint factors that help people avoid behaviors that are in some manner unwise. For example, consumers' self-regulatory resources are particularly important in restraining impulse purchases and related temptations (Baumeister, 2002; Vohs & Faber, 2007). One framework posits two antagonistic systems: an "impulsive system" that leads to possibly irrational overspending versus a "reflective system" necessary to the functioning of self-control. The resources necessary for operation of the second system can be depleted by engaging in self-regulation. Since many dieters must exert self-regulatory resources not to indulge their urge to eat, having a business lunch focused on financial planning may be unwise because necessary cognitive resources may be less available.

Many types of resource interventions can make it possible for consumers to consider attractive options that appear to be blocked. For example, a lack of transportation options for many disadvantaged citizens has made it infeasible for them to plan to shop at more economical stores, a problem that can sometimes be overcome by expanded delivery options. Relatedly, lack of financial knowledge may make people susceptible to payday and other injurious loans, but this is an ability factor that can be overcome (Bolton et al., 2011). Medication safety is a significant issue for elderly consumers. Such resources as daily pill containers and easy medical dispensing methods can substitute for diminished cognitive ability. Strategies for increasing fruit and vegetable intake have used grocery-store-based resource interventions to make such behaviors more feasible (Glanz & Yaroch, 2004), and increasing display lighting has assisted consumer examination and handling of merchandise (Areni & Kim, 1994).

One of the most important aspects of goal pursuit is to encourage people to persist even if the ends they seek are far down the road. Creating subgoals as markers of success is a helpful option. J. B. Cohen and Andrade (2018) discussed research using behavioral commitment strategies to accomplish this. Some service providers ask consumers for precommitments in contracts that put money at stake when goals are not reached but where nothing was lost otherwise. One example is savings accounts with precommitments to making deposits, no possibility of early withdrawals, but significantly greater savings if the commitment is upheld. Another is a gym incentive program with a commitment contract that led to a substantial increase in gym use: If some number of days of gym attendance were missed, money would be forfeited to charity.

Technology-supplied resources showing substantial promise to improve healthful behaviors were illustrated by Ridgers et al. (2016). They noted that physical inactivity has been called a global pandemic, constituting the fourth leading cause of death worldwide, and with far too many people, especially children and adolescents, failing to meet recommended levels of activity. Fortunately, the recent proliferation of wearable activity trackers brings promise. Increasing self-monitoring and goalsetting via these trackers can help consumers correct misperceptions that their current actions meet physical activity guidelines, realize that they need to change their behavior, and receive feedback to track progress. Conversely, the devices could be discouraging for some consumers if their use increases perceptions of difficulty, and less likelihood of longer term success. Better design of feedback should overcome such problems. At time of writing, the authors could report trackers' short-term potential to increase activity levels through self-monitoring and goal setting, but longer term effects on behavior were still unclear.

Looking ahead, improvements in wireless syncing of devices to personal profiles would be a big step, especially if they can provide positive feedback. Similarly, technology for areas in which people lack ability to calibrate personal usage behavior (e.g., smart water or energy meters to display consumption in real time) are resources that could identify sources of excess consumption and give people the ability to alter their own behavior. However, providing consumers with information that, in effect, measures their performance might have unexpected consequences. Etkin (2016) offered some evidence that providing information about the time people spend in activities like walking and reading can undermine their intrinsic motivation and even decrease their subjective well-being.

Psychologists have employed construal level theory to explain how the perceived psychological distance between a person and a desired object can affect judgments of feasibility. Nearer (both in space and time) objects are represented more concretely, leading to judgments incorporating a greater number of product attributes as well as clearer feasibility considerations, whereas higher levels of construal produce more abstract representations and thought processes (Trope et al., 2007). Lack of clarity may also result from having less accessible and less reliable information about objects further removed from direct experience. Technological advances that help consumers visualize and better imagine future outcomes, perhaps conditioned on various paths, would make a substantial contribution. Temporal framing (e.g., a day vs. a year) may be particularly important when trying to motivate consumers to respond to risks, say in achieving or avoiding health outcomes (Chandran & Menon, 2004). Both higher level and longer term construals could lead consumers to "take their eyes off the ball" with respect to downplaying both ability and resource aspects of implementing decisions, thereby lowering subsequent compliance. At the brand choice level, lower levels of construal probably involve direct comparison of aligned attributes, while higher levels of construal likely broaden the basis for choice. Guiding consumers to higher levels of construal may lead them to think about the "why" of a consumer decision rather than focusing on the "how" (e.g., purchase plans) and about identity-related benefits rather than instrumental benefits (Kivetz & Tyler, 2007). Psychological distance (in its spatial, temporal, social, and probabilistic/hypothetical senses) is likely to shape consumers' mental construal of the context in which judgments and choices are made (Liberman et al., 2007).

Perceived deficits in the ability to see a task through to completion pose a significant feasibility problem when designing interventions to bring improvements in health behavior change. Models such as the health belief model address these deficits, providing suggestions for bringing about change (J. B. Cohen & Andrade, 2018; Elder et al., 1999). Earlier desirability-focused approaches emphasized forceful communication of risk and strengthening of motivation, but this is insufficient if people's level of self-confidence (i.e., self-efficacy) in their skills and personal traits is too low and they do not expect that their efforts will be successful. Similar factors are relevant for attempting to convince consumers that particular options can help them achieve a variety of goals (e.g., developing knowledge, health maintenance, money management, career skills, risk avoidance; see Thaler & Sunstein, 2008). Wang et al. (2013) examined the role of self-efficacy in consumers' adoption of self-service technologies. In their comprehensive review of the role of self-efficacy and self-concept beliefs on achievement Pajares & Schunk (2005) found the former to facilitate beneficial cognitive strategies. Self-efficacy beliefs also produce differences in attributions made for success and failure (e.g., to external constraints and barriers vs. temporary state or long-term ability internal factors): When counseling at an individual level, it is best to understand why consumers believe previous attempts to achieve such goals have failed. As indicated earlier, setting shorter term, realistic subgoals can serve as markers of success and help overcome perceived deficits in ability, as can greater attention to skills training at the outset. Finally, marketers, particularly in retailing, have been innovative in developing feasibility-enhancing support systems that make it easier for consumers to select, acquire, and consume products (e.g., internet-based information systems, technical support services, direct to home shipping, package reformulation for convenience).

Online agents are a relatively recent resource addition for helping consumers overcome concerns about their ability to make wise decisions about products and services. Gershoff et al. (2003) discussed the design of "intelligent" online recommendation systems. Here sets of computer programs assist people in searching and accessing online information, filtering irrelevant information, and integrating relevant information into an overall assessment. These become "autonomous" when a search engine can actively execute self-generated instructions without relying on users and "self-learning" when it uses the search records of users to enhance its own ability through monitoring and learning (C.-Y. Chao et al., 2016).

Much has been written about the effects of smart agents (e.g., virtual try-on and fitting room technology to help apparel shoppers obtain customized physical fits without going to the time and expense of using in-store services) on consumers' marketplace outcomes. It is generally agreed that one benefit is lowered search costs (Alba et al., 1997), but further effects of more efficient search, such as on price sensitivity, are not tied down (e.g., Diehl et al., 2003; Lynch & Ariely, 2000). It is fair to say that this resource improves the fit of options to consumers' preferences, while reducing consumer effort (Diehl, 2005). Evidence also shows increases in purchase intentions from customers' greater exploratory behaviors and satisfaction with the process (Beck & Crie, 2018; J. Kim & Forsythe, 2008).

III. FACILITATING RESEARCH CONTRIBUTIONS BASED ON CONTRASTING GOALS AND ORIENTATIONS

The body of work we have reviewed is quite diverse, and we hope that our review has made it clear that the field of consumer psychology reflects and has greatly benefited from the influence of multiple disciplines and approaches. We close the chapter by trying to identify, with greater specificity, how the main research *orientations* of these researchers differ and why we believe this diversity should be facilitated.

Differences in research orientations have existed in latent fashion almost from the beginning. Some research is heavily theory focused, often emphasizing rigorous theory testing methodology drawn from psychology. Other research is focused on marketplace behavior, some emphasizing methodology designed to provide more complete or richer descriptions drawn from sociology and anthropology, while other marketplace-focused research is designed to assist marketers in choosing between relevant options using eclectic manipulations and measurement. These divisions were sharpened when increasing numbers of persons with advanced psychology or social science training joined academic marketing departments. Here they began their study of consumer behavior and tutored future marketing scholars with the theories, paradigms, methods, and priorities they brought in from their home fields (MacInnis & Folkes, 2010).

Turf wars have resulted when different factions competed for editorial control of journals publishing consumer behavior research, owing partially to disagreements over what constituted good or valuable research. For example, it is generally understood that psychology largely departed from the broader social science emphasis on careful description of phenomena as conditioned by context in favor of emulating "hard science" theory development, typically at a more micro level. Arguing over which was the "right" approach is a fool's errand for a field with as diverse an agenda as ours. Nevertheless, part of the field's history consists of skirmishes and slights brought about by dismissive critiques, often behind the scenes and even given cover by the blind reviewing processes of journals. We believe that evidence is mounting that these conflicting and sometimes competing (e.g., for recognition and journal space) orientations might actually weaken the field by driving away either important descriptive and applied research or research likely to make a more fundamental contribution to psychological theory, though its immediate relevance to consumer psychology has not yet been shown.

In our opinion the first step in coping with this challenge is to acknowledge that core differences in research orientations and goals do exist, in the hope that (a) studies are carried out and papers are written that accurately reflect their underlying intention rather than efforts to please audiences via compromises and (b) well-intentioned gatekeepers do not make erroneous assumptions in applying publication standards geared to their own predilections and even unrecognized biases. When this happens, less appropriate publication criteria can produce controversial judgments and disparaging commentaries and revision requests.

Because domains of research not exclusively linked to psychology are covered in the *Handbook of Consumer Psychology*, we cautiously adopt the "consumer psychology" nomenclature when referring to theory but intend to use that denotation in the broadest sense when referring to theoretical research. For the sake of parsimony, we group research goals and orientations into the following three categories:

- MD: marketplace-driven consumer psychology,
- CT: consumer theory-driven consumer psychology, and
- PT: psychological theory-driven consumer psychology.

MD consumer psychology is said to start with a marketplace issue or phenomenon in contexts that involve the search, acquisition, consumption and experience, sharing (e.g., word of mouth), and disposal of goods and services (see editorials by Deighton, 2005; Inman et al., 2018). We would actually expand the category to reflect consumption (i.e., marketplace) issues of importance to society that impact health, overall quality of life and consumer welfare and protection. It is disappointing to us that the high point of this research may have occurred over 30 years ago and most such topics are largely ignored in our consumer research journals. Mainstream psychology has tended to gravitate toward building and testing theory rather than initially gathering descriptive information, as is more common in most social sciences and issue-centered areas of psychology (such as health, educational, political, forensic, and counseling psychology). However, there is no apparent reason that consumer psychology should eschew acquiring "on the ground" facts both for their own sake and upon which better theory can be built.

Research in this category has the clear goal of striving for an advance in marketplace/consumption knowledge. When the research involves experiments the emphasis should be on representing realistic conditions in which the behavior takes place and measuring it with as much accuracy as possible. Similarly, manipulations should correspond to actual or proposed "treatments" (e.g., a proposed change in labeling) that may be guided by theory, but it should not depart from reality in an attempt to represent some exogenous theoretical construct . . . if the focus is on capturing the behavior of interest, that goal must dominate research design decisions, and such designs are not likely to provide a sufficiently valid representation of theoretical constructs to rule out alternative explanations. For these reasons we believe that the review process should respect the goals of the research and not advise greater emphasis on theory. Accordingly, authors should refrain from speculative accounts of their research that provide unexamined theoretical explanations for their findings. For some, theory is seen as the sine qua non of scholarship, with "tight methodology" dominating more descriptive research methods (e.g., relying on measurement from surveys, self-reports, and observation). However laudable these may be, research in MD should be judged on its contribution to shedding light on a marketplace or consumption issue of interest. We need much more of these contributions than the field is now providing.

CT consumer psychology is intended to develop conceptual knowledge to improve understanding of why, when, and how observed consumer behavior comes about. This constitutes the mainstream of the field, and so we start by trying to define it so we can assess it appropriately when we see it. We will turn to theory-driven research with a broader goal next. Here, research is often spawned because existing explanations for consumers' behavior, including those derived from more general psychological theory, seem inadequate, incomplete, or unparsimonious. Thus the research goal is to augment, enhance, or replace existing theory because it fails to adequately take into account key aspects of consumer behavior stemming from the physical settings and stimuli, information environment and context-specific motivations facing and guiding consumers. In evaluating research within CT it should not be sufficient for research to produce a rigorous replication/nonreplication of a general psychological finding without a more specific consumer psychology contribution since outcomes may vary considerably. Similarly, a study in this category need not break new ground in any other area of psychology as long as our understanding of consumer behavior is enriched. These assessments are subjective of course, but it would be unfair not to praise research that established that some unique characteristic of the consumer behavior context played a much stronger or weaker role than would be expected more generally. Research in CT should be contextually grounded in order for any consumer behavior generalizations to be warranted.

While it is fairly straightforward to define and distinguish PT from both of the other categories, the goal here does raise an ironic challenge that such research may not truly belong in consumer psychology at all. After all there are many psychology journals that can provide a home for such papers, depending on the exact topic. And in each of the major fields there are likely to be a number of well-regarded journals that are rated along a hierarchy. So some in our field have argued that these papers should go in one of those journals unless it makes a specific contribution to consumer psychology, as consumer psychologists generally have fewer publishing options. This argument may have become more personal with the growing number of psychologists who have chosen to work in marketing departments and wish to establish a strong reputation in the field of consumer psychology.

As we have done before, let us distinguish between contributions to CT consumer psychology and PT consumer psychology. The goal in the latter case is to develop and improve psychological theory more generally, either for its own sake or under the assumption that this will also benefit consumer psychology at some point. Examples include improving theoretical understanding of how people organize information in memory and use it for various kinds of judgments and actions under resource-limiting conditions, apart from how frequently these are likely to be encountered by consumers. In PT, study conditions are not chosen because they represent contexts of particular relevance to consumer behavior but because they reflect factors thought to invoke or suppress different psychological mechanisms. In addition, this research approach is more likely to adopt designs that deprive people of realistic and normally available options or informational resources because these are viewed as undesirable confounds, making the research even less relevant to typical consumer contexts.

So when this CT fit is troublesome (e.g., important aspects of the consumer context are ignored, oversimplified, or misrepresented), our journals are challenged: Is publication of this paper appropriate? There is no easy answer. If the paper is of particularly high quality, an emphasis on rigor may lead some to recommend publication for that reason alone ("How could we not publish the paper?"). One can reason/rationalize that subsequent contributions from improved psychological theory may aid development of better aligned theory in consumer psychology, and our review has identified many contributions from mainstream psychology that have had precisely this impact.

We think the bottom line in this section is that all three categories of research have proven their worth for consumer psychology, and that each should be assessed with criteria appropriate to that particular category. However, it is also the case that questions about scarce publication opportunities, especially in our leading journals, are legitimate and are being raised. As noted, this may create added difficulties for psychological theory-driven research that fails to address the consumer context in any meaningful way: Do their strengths overcome the desire to expand our knowledge of consumer behavior and more aggregate effects within society as well as the widely accepted goal of developing stronger and more comprehensive consumer psychology theory?

REFERENCES

Aaker, D. A., & Day, G. S. (1982). *Consumerism: Search for the public interest* (4th ed.). The Free Press.

Aaker, D. A., & Stayman, D. M. (1992). Implementing the concept of transformational advertising. *Psychology and Marketing*, *9*(3), 237–253. https://doi.org/10.1002/mar.4220090306

Aaker, J. L., & Lee, A. Y. (2001). "I" seek pleasures and "we" avoid pains: The role of self-regulatory goals in information processing and persuasion. *Journal of Consumer Research*, *28*(1), 33–49.

Agarwal, R., & Karahanna, E. (2000). Time flies when you're having fun: Cognitive absorption and beliefs about information technology usage. *Management Information Systems Quarterly*, *24*(4), 665–694. https://doi.org/10.2307/3250951

Agrawal, N., & Maheswaran, D. (2005). The effects of self-construal and commitment on persuasion. *Journal of Consumer Research*, *31*(4), 841–849. https://doi.org/10.1086/426620

Ajzen, I. (1991). The theory of planned behavior. *Organizational Behavior and Human Decision Processes*, *50*(2), 179–211. https://doi.org/10.1016/0749-5978(91)90020-T

Ajzen, I. (2002). Perceived behavioral control, self-efficacy, locus of control, and the theory of planned behavior. *Journal of Applied Social Psychology*, *32*(4), 665–683. https://doi.org/10.1111/j.1559-1816.2002.tb00236.x

Ajzen, I., & Cote, N. G. (2008). Attitudes and the prediction of behavior. In W. D. Crano & R. Prislin (Eds.), *Attitudes and attitude change* (pp. 289–311). Taylor & Francis Group.

Ajzen, I., & Fishbein, M. (1977). Attitude-behavior relations: A theoretical analysis and review of empirical research. *Psychological Bulletin*, *84*(5), 888–918. https://doi.org/10.1037/0033-2909.84.5.888

Alba, J., Lynch, J. G., Jr., Weitz, B., Janiszewski, C., Lutz, R., Sawyer, A., & Wood, S. (1997). Interactive home shopping: Consumer, retailer, and manufacturer incentives to participate in electronic marketplaces. *Journal of Marketing*, *61*(3), 38–53. https://doi.org/10.1177/002224299706100303

Alba, J. W., & Hutchinson, J. W. (1987). Dimensions of consumer expertise. *Journal of Consumer Research*, *13*(4), 411–454. https://doi.org/10.1086/209080

Albarracín, D. (2002). Cognition in persuasion: An analysis of information processing in response to persuasive communications. *Advances in Experimental Social Psychology*, *34*, 61–130. https://doi.org/10.1016/S0065-2601(02)80004-1

Alwitt, L. F., & Pitts, R. E. (1996). Predicting purchase intentions for an environmentally sensitive product. *Journal of Consumer Psychology*, *5*(1), 49–64. https://doi.org/10.1207/s15327663jcp0501_03

Amadeo, K. (2021). Consumer spending increases 12% in Q2 2021. *The Balance*. https://www.thebalance.com/consumer-spending-trends-and-current-statistics-3305916

American Bar Association. (1989). Report of the American Bar Association Section of Antitrust Law Special Committee to Study the Role of the Federal Trade Commission. In P. E. Murphy & W. L. Wilkie (Eds.), *Marketing and advertising regulation: The Federal Trade Commission in the 1990s* (pp. 412–462). University of Notre Dame Press.

Anand, P., & Sternthal, B. (1990). Ease of message processing as a moderator of repetition effects in advertising. *Journal of Marketing Research*, *27*(3), 345–353. https://doi.org/10.1177/002224379002700308

Andrade, E. B., & Ariely, D. (2009). The enduring impact of transient emotions on decision making. *Organizational Behavior and Human Decision Processes*, *109*(1), 1–8. https://doi.org/10.1016/j.obhdp.2009.02.003

Andrade, E. B. & Cohen, J.B. (2007). Affect-based evaluation and regulation as mediators of behavior: The role of affect in risk taking, helping and eating patterns. In K. D. Vohs, R. F. Baumeister, & G. Loewenstein (Eds.), *Do emotions help or hurt decision making? A hedgefoxian perspective* (pp. 35–68). Russell Sage.

Andreasen, A. R. (1991). Consumer behavior research and social policy. In T. S. Robertson & H. H. Kassarjian (Eds.), *Handbook of consumer behavior* (pp. 459–506). Prentice Hall.

Andreasen, A. R. (1997). From ghetto marketing to social marketing: Bringing social relevance to mainstream marketing. *Journal of Public Policy & Marketing*, *16*(1), 129–131. https://doi.org/10.1177/074391569701600112

Areni, C. S., & Kim, D. (1994). The influence of in-store lighting on consumers' examination of merchandise in a wine store. *International Journal of Research in Marketing*, *11*(2), 117–125. https://doi.org/10.1016/0167-8116(94)90023-X

Arnould, E. J., & Thompson, C. J. (2005). Consumer culture theory (CCT): Twenty years of research. *Journal of Consumer Research*, *31*(4), 868–882. https://doi.org/10.1086/426626

Avnet, T., Pham, M. T., & Stephen, A. T. (2012). Consumers' trust in feelings as information. *Journal of Consumer Research*, *39*(4), 720–735.

Axsen, J., & Kurani, K. S. (2012). Social influence, consumer behavior, and low-carbon energy transitions. *Annual Review of Environment and Resources*, *37*(1), 311–340. https://doi.org/10.1146/annurev-environ-062111-145049

Bagchi, R., & Davis, D. F. (2016, August). The role of numerosity in judgments and decision-making. *Current Opinion in Psychology*, *10*, 89–93. https://doi.org/10.1016/j.copsyc.2015.12.010

Ballantyne, D., Christopher, M., & Payne, A. (2003). Relationship marketing: Looking back, looking forward. *Marketing Theory*, *3*(1), 159–166. https://doi.org/10.1177/1470593103003001009

Bargh, J. A., Schwader, K. L., Hailey, S. E., Dyer, R. L., & Boothby, E. J. (2012). Automaticity in social-cognitive processes. *Trends in Cognitive Sciences*, *16*(12), 593–605. https://doi.org/10.1016/j.tics.2012.10.002

Barry, T. E. (1987). The development of the hierarchy of effects: An historical perspective. *Current Issues and Research in Advertising*, *10*(1–2), 251–295.

Barsalou, L. W. (1983). Ad hoc categories. *Memory & Cognition*, *11*(3), 211–227. https://doi.org/10.3758/BF03196968

Bartels, R. (1988). *The history of marketing thought* (3rd ed.). Publishing Horizons.

Batra, R., & Ray, M. L. (1986). Affective responses mediating acceptance of advertising. *Journal of Consumer Research*, *13*(2), 234–249. https://doi.org/10.1086/209063

Batra, R., & Stayman, D. M. (1990). The role of mood in advertising effectiveness. *Journal of Consumer Research*, *17*(2), 203–214. https://doi.org/10.1086/208550

Batra, R., & Stephens, D. (1994). Attitudinal effects of ad-evoked moods and emotions: The moderating role of motivation. *Psychology & Marketing*, *11*(3), 199–215. https://doi.org/10.1002/mar.4220110302

Baumeister, R. F. (2002). Yielding to temptation: Self-control failure, impulsive purchasing, and consumer behavior. *Journal of Consumer Research*, *28*(4), 670–676. https://doi.org/10.1086/338209

Bazerman, M. H. (2001). Consumer research for consumers. *Journal of Consumer Research*, *27*(4), 499–504. https://doi.org/10.1086/319624

Beales, H., Craswell, R., & Salop, S. (1981). Information remedies for consumer protection. *American Economic Review*, *71*(2), 410–413.

Bearden, W. O., & Rose, R. L. (1990). Attention to social comparison information: An individual difference factor affecting consumer conformity. *Journal of Consumer Research*, *16*(4), 461–471. https://doi.org/10.1086/209231

Beck, M., & Crie, D. (2018). I virtually try it…I want it! Virtual fitting room: A tool to increase on-line and off-line exploratory behavior, patronage and purchase intentions. *Journal of Retailing and Consumer Services*, *40*, 279–286. https://doi.org/10.1016/j.jretconser.2016.08.006

Belk, R. W. (1985). Materialism: Trait aspects of living in the material world. *Journal of Consumer Research*, *12*(3), 265–280. https://doi.org/10.1086/208515

Belk, R. W. (1988). Possessions and the extended self. *Journal of Consumer Research*, *15*(2), 139–168. https://doi.org/10.1086/209154

Belk, R. W., Wallendorf, M., & Sherry, J. F., Jr. (1989). The sacred and the profane in consumer behavior: Theodicy on the odyssey. *Journal of Consumer Research*, *16*(1), 1–38. https://doi.org/10.1086/209191

Benbasat, I., & Wang, W. (2005). Trust in and adoption of online recommendation agents. *Journal of the Association for Information Systems*, *6*(3), 72–101. https://doi.org/10.17705/1jais.00065

Bernhardt, K. L. (1990). The FTC in 1978: Some observations from a marketing academic. In P. E. Murphy & W. L. Wilkie (Eds.), *Marketing and advertising regulation: The Federal Trade Commission in the 1990s* (pp. 114–119). University of Notre Dame Press.

Bettman, J. R. (1975). Issues in designing consumer information environments. *Journal of Consumer Research*, *2*(3), 169–177. https://doi.org/10.1086/208629

Bettman, J. R. (1979). *An information processing theory of consumer choice*. Addison-Wesley.

Bettman, J. R., Luce, M. F., & Payne, J. W. (1998). Constructive consumer choice processes. *Journal of Consumer Research*, *25*(3), 187–217. https://doi.org/10.1086/209535

Bettman, J. R., Payne, J. W., & Staelin, R. (1986). Cognitive considerations in designing effective labels for presenting risk information. *Journal of Public Policy & Marketing*, *5*(1), 1–28. https://doi.org/10.1177/074391568600500101

Biswas, D., Szocs, C., & Abell, A. (2019). Extending the boundaries of sensory marketing and examining the sixth sensory system: Effects of vestibular sensations for sitting versus standing postures on food taste perception. *Journal of Consumer Research*, *46*(4), 708–724. https://doi.org/10.1093/jcr/ucz018

Bloom, P. N. (1997). Field of marketing and public policy: Introduction and overview. *Journal of Public Policy & Marketing*, *16*(1), 126–128. https://doi.org/10.1177/074391569701600111

Bolton, L. E., & Alba, J. W. (2012). When less is more: Consumer aversion to unused utility. *Journal of Consumer Psychology*, *22*(3), 369–383. https://doi.org/10.1016/j.jcps.2011.09.002

Bolton, L. E., Bloom, P. N. & Cohen, J. B. (2011). Using loan plus lender literacy information to combat one-sided marketing of debt consolidation loans. *Journal of Marketing Research*, *48*, 51–59. https://doi.org/10.1509/jmkr.48.SPL.S51

Bolton, L. E., & Reed, A. I. I., II. (2004). Sticky priors: The perseverance of identity effects on judgment. *Journal of Marketing Research*, *41*(4), 397–410. https://doi.org/10.1509/jmkr.41.4.397.47019

Bosmans, A., & Baumgartner, H. (2005). Goal-relevant emotional information: When extraneous affect leads to persuasion and when it does not. *Journal of Consumer Research*, *32*(3), 424–434. https://doi.org/10.1086/497554

Boyd, H. W., Jr., Ray, M. L., & Strong, E. C. (1972). An attitudinal framework for advertising strategy. *Journal of Marketing*, *36*(2), 27–33. https://doi.org/10.1177/002224297203600206

Brasel, S. A., & Gips, J. (2014). Tablets, touchscreens, and touchpads: How varying touch interfaces trigger psychological ownership and endowment. *Journal of Consumer Psychology*, *24*(2), 226–233. https://doi.org/10.1016/j.jcps.2013.10.003

Braun-Latour, K. A., & Zaltman, G. (2006). Memory change: An intimate measure of persuasion. *Journal of Advertising Research*, *46*(1), 57–72. https://doi.org/10.2501/S0021849906060077

Breckler, S. J., & Wiggins, E. C. (1989). Affect versus evaluation in the structure of attitudes. *Journal of Experimental Social Psychology*, *25*(3), 253–271. https://doi.org/10.1016/0022-1031(89)90022-X

Briñol, P., Petty, R. E., & Tormala, Z. L. (2004). Self-validation of cognitive responses to advertisements. *Journal of Consumer Research*, *30*(4), 559–573. https://doi.org/10.1086/380289

Burchell, K., Rettie, R., & Patel, K. (2013). Marketing social norms: Social marketing and the "social norm approach." *Journal of Consumer Behaviour*, *12*(1), 1–9. https://doi.org/10.1002/cb.1395

Burnkrant, R. E., & Cousineau, A. (1975). Informational and normative social influence in buyer behavior. *Journal of Consumer Research*, *2*(3), 206–215. https://doi.org/10.1086/208633

Calfee, J. (2000). The historical significance of Joe Camel. *Journal of Public Policy & Marketing*, *19*(2), 168–182. https://doi.org/10.1509/jppm.19.2.168.17132

Carey, R. M., & Markus, H. R. (2016). Understanding consumer psychology in working-class contexts. *Journal of Consumer Psychology*, *26*(4), 568–582. https://doi.org/10.1016/j.jcps.2016.08.004

Caswell, J. A., Ning, Y., Liu, F., & Mojduszka, E. M. (2003). The impact of new labeling regulations on the use of voluntary nutrient-content and health claims by food manufacturers. *Journal of Public Policy & Marketing*, 22(2), 147–158. https://doi.org/10.1509/jppm.22.2.147.17637

Catapano, R., Tormala, Z. L., & Rucker, D. D. (2019). Perspective taking and self-persuasion: Why "putting yourself in their shoes" reduces openness to attitude change. *Psychological Science*, 30(3), 424–435. https://doi.org/10.1177/0956797618822697

Chan, C., Berger, J., & Van Boven, L. (2012). Identifiable but not identical: Combining social identity and uniqueness motives in choice. *Journal of Consumer Research*, 39(3), 561–573. https://doi.org/10.1086/664804

Chandran, S., & Menon, G. (2004). When a day means more than a year: Effects of temporal framing on judgments of health risks. *Journal of Consumer Research*, 31(2), 375–389. https://doi.org/10.1086/422116

Chao, C.-Y., Chang, T.-C., Wu, H.-C., Lin, Y.-S., & Chen, P.-C. (2016). The interrelationship between intelligent agents' characteristics and users' intention in a search engine by making beliefs and perceived risks mediators. *Computers in Human Behavior*, 64, 117–125. https://doi.org/10.1016/j.chb.2016.06.031

Chao, P. (2001). The moderating effects of country of assembly, country of parts, and country of design on hybrid product evaluations. *Journal of Advertising*, 30(4), 67–81. https://doi.org/10.1080/00913367.2001.10673652

Chartrand, T. L. (2005). The role of unconscious awareness in consumer behavior. *Journal of Consumer Psychology*, 15(3), 203–210. https://doi.org/10.1207/s15327663jcp1503_4

Chattopadhyay, A., & Nedungadi, P. (1992). Does attitude toward the ad endure? The moderating effects of attention and delay. *Journal of Consumer Research*, 19(1), 26–33. https://doi.org/10.1086/209283

Chen, C. Y., & Pham, M. T. (2019). Affect regulation and consumer behavior. *Consumer Psychology Review*, 2(1), 114–144. https://doi.org/10.1002/arcp.1050

Chernev, A. (2001). The impact of common features on consumer preferences: A case of confirmatory reasoning. *Journal of Consumer Research*, 27(4), 475–488. https://doi.org/10.1086/319622

Chernev, A. (2011). Semantic anchoring in sequential evaluations of vices and virtues. *Journal of Consumer Research*, 37(5), 761–774. https://doi.org/10.1086/656731

Childers, T. L., & Rao, A. R. (1992). The influence of familial and peer-based reference groups on consumer decisions. *Journal of Consumer Research*, 19(2), 198–211. https://doi.org/10.1086/209296

Chin, A., & Bruine de Bruin, W. (2019). Helping consumers to evaluate annual percentage rates (APR) on credit cards. *Journal of Experimental Psychology: Applied*, 25(1), 77–87. https://doi.org/10.1037/xap0000197

Chugani, S. K., Irwin, J. R., & Redden, J. P. (2015). Happily ever after: The effect of identity-consistency on product satiation. *Journal of Consumer Research*, 42(4), 564–577. https://doi.org/10.1093/jcr/ucv040

Cialdini, R. B. (2001). The science of persuasion. *Scientific American*, 284(2), 76–81.

Clore, G. L., & Schnall, S. (2019). The influence of affect on attitude. In D. Albarracin & B. T. Johnson (Eds.), *The handbook of attitudes: Vol. 1. Basic principles* (2nd ed., pp. 259–290). Routledge.

Cohen, D. (1980). The FTC's advertising substantiation program. *Journal of Marketing*, 44(1), 26–35. https://doi.org/10.1177/002224298004400104

Cohen, J. B. (1967). An interpersonal orientation to the study of consumer behavior. *Journal of Marketing Research*, 4(3), 270–278. https://doi.org/10.1177/002224376700400305

Cohen, J. B. (1990). Attitude, affect and consumer behavior. In B. S. Moore & A. M. Isen (Eds.), *Affect and social behavior* (pp. 152–206). Cambridge University Press.

Cohen, J. B. (2000). Playing to win: Marketing and public policy at odds over Joe Camel. *Journal of Public Policy & Marketing*, 19(2), 155–167. https://doi.org/10.1509/jppm.19.2.155.17123

Cohen, J. B., & Andrade, E. B. (2004). Affective intuition and task-contingent affect regulation. *Journal of Consumer Research*, 31(2), 358–367. https://doi.org/10.1086/422114

Cohen, J. B., & Andrade, E. B. (2018). The ADF framework: A parsimonious model for developing successful behavior change interventions. *Journal of Marketing Behavior*, 3(2), 81–119. https://doi.org/10.1561/107.00000046

Cohen, J. B., & Basu, K. (1987). Alternative models of categorization: Toward a contingent processing framework. *Journal of Consumer Research*, 13(4), 455–472. https://doi.org/10.1086/209081

Cohen, J. B., & Bernard, H. R. (2013). Evolutionary psychology and consumer behavior: A constructive critique. *Journal of Consumer Psychology*, 23(3), 387–399. https://doi.org/10.1016/j.jcps.2013.03.006

Cohen, J. B., Fishbein, M., & Ahtola, O. T. (1972). The nature and uses of expectancy-value models in consumer attitude research. *Journal of Marketing Research*, 9(4), 456–460. https://doi.org/10.1177/002224377200900420

Cohen, J. B., & Houston, M. J. (1972). Cognitive consequences of brand loyalty. *Journal of Marketing Research, 9*(1), 97–99.

Cohen, J. B., Pham, M. T., & Andrade, E. (2008). The nature and role of affect in consumer behavior. In C. P. Haugtvedt, P. M. Herr, & F. R. Kardes (Eds.), *Handbook of consumer psychology* (pp. 297–348). Taylor & Francis Group/Lawrence Erlbaum Associates.

Compeau, L. D., & Grewal, D. (1998). Comparative price advertising: An integrative review. *Journal of Public Policy & Marketing, 17*(2), 257–273. https://doi.org/10.1177/074391569801700209

Cox, E. F., Fellmeth, R. C., & Schultz, J. E. (1969). *The Nader Report on the Federal Trade Commission*. Richard W. Baron.

Crosetto, P., Muller, L., & Ruffieux, B. (2016). Helping consumers with a front-of-pack label: Numbers or colors? Experimental comparison between guideline daily amount and traffic light in a diet-building exercise. *Journal of Economic Psychology, 55*, 30–50. https://doi.org/10.1016/j.joep.2016.03.006

Culnan, M. J. (2000). Protecting privacy online: Is self-regulation working? *Journal of Public Policy & Marketing, 19*(1), 20–26. https://doi.org/10.1509/jppm.19.1.20.16944

Curtin, R. T. (1984). Curtin on Katona. In H. W. Spiegel & W. J. Samuels (Eds.), *Contemporary economists in perspective, Part 1* (pp. 495–522). JAI Press.

Dabholkar, P. A., & Bagozzi, R. P. (2002). An attitudinal model of technology-based self-service: Moderating effects of consumer traits and situational factors. *Journal of the Academy of Marketing Science, 30*(3), 184–201. https://doi.org/10.1177/0092070302303001

D'astous, A., & Miquelon, D. (1991). Helping consumers choose a credit card. *Journal of Consumer Affairs, 25*(2), 278–294. https://doi.org/10.1111/j.1745-6606.1991.tb00006.x

Deighton, J. (2005). From the editor-elect. *Journal of Consumer Research, 32*(1), 1–5. https://doi.org/10.1086/430647

Dhar, R., & Nowlis, S. M. (1999). The effect of time pressure on consumer choice deferral. *Journal of Consumer Research, 25*(4), 369–384. https://doi.org/10.1086/209545

Diehl, K. (2005). When two rights make a wrong: Searching too much in ordered environments. *Journal of Marketing Research, 42*(3), 313–322. https://doi.org/10.1509/jmkr.2005.42.3.313

Diehl, K., Kornish, L. J., & Lynch, J. G., Jr. (2003). Smart agents: When lower search costs for quality information increase price sensitivity. *Journal of Consumer Research, 30*(1), 56–71. https://doi.org/10.1086/374698

Dijksterhuis, A., Smith, P. K., van Baaren, R. B., & Wigboldus, D. H. J. (2005). The unconscious consumer: Effects of environment on consumer behavior. *Journal of Consumer Psychology, 15*(3), 193–202. https://doi.org/10.1207/s15327663jcp1503_3

Dolan, P., Peasgood, T., & White, M. (2008). Do we really know what makes us happy? A review of the economic literature on the factors associated with subjective well-being. *Journal of Economic Psychology, 29*(1), 94–122. https://doi.org/10.1016/j.joep.2007.09.001

Downs, J. S., Wisdom, J., & Loewenstein, G. (2015). Helping consumers use nutrition information: Effects of format and presentation. *American Journal of Health Economics, 1*(3), 326–344. https://doi.org/10.1162/AJHE_a_00020

Dunning, D. (2007). Self-image motives and consumer behavior: How sacrosanct self-beliefs sway preferences in the marketplace. *Journal of Consumer Psychology, 17*(4), 237–249. https://doi.org/10.1016/S1057-7408(07)70033-5

Elder, J. P., Ayala, G. X., & Harris, S. (1999). Theories and intervention approaches to health-behavior change in primary care. *American Journal of Preventive Medicine, 17*(4), 275–284. https://doi.org/10.1016/S0749-3797(99)00094-X

Engel, J. F., Kollat, D. T., & Blackwell, R. D. (1968). *Consumer behavior*. Holt, Rinehart and Winston.

Escalas, J. E., & Bettman, J. R. (2005). Self-construal, reference groups, and brand meaning. *Journal of Consumer Research, 32*(3), 378–389. https://doi.org/10.1086/497549

Escalas, J. E., & Bettman, J. R. (2013). The brand is "me": Exploring the effect of self-brand connections on processing brand information as self-information. In A. A. Ruvio & R. W. Belk (Eds.), *The Routledge companion to identity and consumption* (pp. 366–374). Routledge.

Etkin, J. (2016). The hidden cost of personal quantification. *Journal of Consumer Research, 42*(6), 967–984. https://doi.org/10.1093/jcr/ucv095

Fabrigar, L. R., Priester, J. R., Petty, R. E., & Wegner, D. T. (1998). The impact of attitude accessibility on elaboration of persuasive messages. *Personality and Social Psychology Bulletin, 24*(4), 339–352. https://doi.org/10.1177/0146167298244001

Fazio, R. H., Powell, M. C., & Williams, C. J. (1989). The role of attitude accessibility in the attitude-to-behavior process. *Journal of Consumer Research, 16*(3), 280–288. https://doi.org/10.1086/209214

Fedorikhin, A., & Cole, C. A. (2004). Mood effects on attitudes, perceived risk and choice: Moderators and mediators. *Journal of Consumer Psychology, 14*(1–2), 2–12. https://doi.org/10.1207/s15327663jcp1401&2_2

Feldman, J. M., & Lynch, J. G. (1988). Self-generated validity and other effects of measuring belief, attitude, intention, and behavior. *Journal of Applied Psychology*, 73(3), 421–435. https://doi.org/10.1037/0021-9010.73.3.421

Fernandes, D., Lynch, J. G., Jr., & Netemeyer, R. G. (2014). Financial literacy, financial education, and downstream financial behaviors. *Management Science*, 60(8), 1861–1883. https://doi.org/10.1287/mnsc.2013.1849

Festinger, L. (1962). *A theory of cognitive dissonance*. Stanford University Press.

Fishbein, M., & Ajzen, I. (2010). *Predicting and changing behavior: The reasoned action approach*. Psychology Press.

Ford, G. T., Smith, D. B., & Swasy, J. L. (1990). Consumer skepticism of advertising claims: Testing hypotheses from economics of information. *Journal of Consumer Research*, 16(4), 433–441. https://doi.org/10.1086/209228

Fournier, S. (1998). Consumers and their brands: Developing relationship theory in consumer research. *Journal of Consumer Research*, 24(4), 343–353. https://doi.org/10.1086/209515

Foxall, G. R. (1994). Behavior analysis and consumer psychology. *Journal of Economic Psychology*, 15(1), 5–91. https://doi.org/10.1016/0167-4870(94)90032-9

Freer, R. E. (1971). The Federal Trade Commission—A study in survival. *Business Lawyer*, 26(5), 1505–1526.

Gardner, D. M. (1975). Deception in advertising: A conceptual approach. *Journal of Marketing*, 39, 40–46.

Gardner, M. P. (1985). Mood states and consumer behavior: A critical review. *Journal of Consumer Research*, 12(3), 281–300. https://doi.org/10.1086/208516

Gawronski, B., & Bodenhausen, G. V. (2014). The associative–propositional evaluation model. In J. W. Sherman, B. Gawronski, & Y. Trope (Eds.), *Dual-process theories of the social mind* (pp. 188–203). Guilford Press.

Gershoff, A. D., Mukherjee, A., & Mukhopadhyay, A. (2003). Consumer acceptance of online agent advice: Extremity and positivity effects. *Journal of Consumer Psychology*, 13(1–2), 161–170. https://doi.org/10.1207/153276603768344870

Glanz, K., & Yaroch, A. L. (2004). Strategies for increasing fruit and vegetable intake in grocery stores and communities: Policy, pricing, and environmental change. *Preventive Medicine*, 39(Suppl. 2), 75–80. https://doi.org/10.1016/j.ypmed.2004.01.004

Goldstein, N. J., Cialdini, R. B., & Griskevicius, V. (2008). A room with a viewpoint: Using social norms to motivate environmental conservation in hotels. *Journal of Consumer Research*, 35(3), 472–482. https://doi.org/10.1086/586910

Greifeneder, R., Bless, H., & Pham, M. T. (2011). When do people rely on affective and cognitive feelings in judgment? A review. *Personality and Social Psychology Review*, 15(2), 107–141. https://doi.org/10.1177/1088868310367640

Greyser, S. A. (1997). Consumer research and the public policy process: Then and now. *Journal of Public Policy & Marketing*, 16(1), 137–138. https://doi.org/10.1177/074391569701600114

Grier, S. A., Mensinger, J., Huang, S. H., Kumanyika, S. K., & Stettler, N. (2007). Fast-food marketing and children's fast-food consumption: Exploring parents' influences in an ethnically diverse sample. *Journal of Public Policy & Marketing*, 26(2), 221–235. https://doi.org/10.1509/jppm.26.2.221

Gundlach, G. T., & Wilkie, W. L. (1990). The marketing literature in public policy: 1970–1988. In P. E. Murphy & W. L. Wilkie (Eds.), *Marketing and advertising regulation: The Federal Trade Commission in the 1990s* (pp. 329–344). University of Notre Dame Press.

Gutman, J. (1982). A means-end chain model based on consumer categorization processes. *Journal of Marketing*, 46(2), 60–72. https://doi.org/10.2307/3203341

Ha, H.-Y., & Janda, S. (2012). Predicting consumer intentions to purchase energy-efficient products. *Journal of Consumer Marketing*, 29(7), 461–469. https://doi.org/10.1108/07363761211274974

Hadfield, G. K., Howse, R., & Trebilcock, M. J. (1998). Information-based principles for rethinking consumer protection policy. *Journal of Consumer Policy*, 21(2), 131–169. https://doi.org/10.1023/A:1006863016924

Han, H., & Kim, Y. (2010). An investigation of green hotel customers' decision formation: Developing an extended model of the theory of planned behavior. *International Journal of Hospitality Management*, 29(4), 659–668. https://doi.org/10.1016/j.ijhm.2010.01.001

Harmon-Jones, E., Harmon-Jones, C., & Levy, N. (2015). An action-based model of cognitive-dissonance processes. *Current Directions in Psychological Science*, 24(3), 184–189. https://doi.org/10.1177/0963721414566449

Hastak, M., & Mazis, M. B. (2011). Deception by implication: A typology of truthful but misleading advertising and labeling claims. *Journal of Public Policy & Marketing*, 30(2), 157–167. https://doi.org/10.1509/jppm.30.2.157

Hershfield, H. E., Goldstein, D. G., Sharpe, W. F., Fox, J., Yeykelis, L., Carstensen, L. L., & Bailenson, J. N. (2011). Increasing saving behavior through age-progressed renderings of the future self. *Journal of Marketing Research*, 48(SPL), S23–S37. https://doi.org/10.1509/jmkr.48.SPL.S23

Hershfield, H. E., Sussman, A. B., O'Brien, R. L., & Bryan, C. J. (2015). Leveraging psychological insights to encourage the responsible use of consumer debt. *Perspectives on Psychological Science, 10*(6), 749–752. https://doi.org/10.1177/1745691615598514

Hibbard, J. H., & Peters, E. (2003). Supporting informed consumer health care decisions: Data presentation approaches that facilitate the use of information in choice. *Annual Review of Public Health, 24*(1) 413–433. https://doi.org/10.1146/annurev.publhealth.24.100901.141005

Hill, R. P., & Stamey, M. (1990). The homeless in America: An examination of possessions and consumption behaviors. *Journal of Consumer Research, 17*(3), 303–321. https://doi.org/10.1086/208559

Hoegg, J., Alba, J. W., & Dahl, D. W. (2010). The good, the bad, and the ugly: Influence of aesthetics on product feature judgments. *Journal of Consumer Psychology, 20*(4), 419–430. https://doi.org/10.1016/j.jcps.2010.07.002

Hosseini, H. (2011). George Katona: A founding father of old behavioral economics. *Journal of Socio-Economics, 40*(6), 977–984. https://doi.org/10.1016/j.socec.2011.04.002

Howard, J. A., & Sheth, J. N. (1969). *The theory of buyer behavior*. Wiley.

Hutton, R. B., & Wilkie, W. L. (1980). Life cycle cost: A new form of consumer information. *Journal of Consumer Research, 6*(4), 349–360. https://doi.org/10.1086/208778

Inman, J. J., Campbell, M. C., Kirmani, A., & Price, L. L. (2018). Our vision for the *Journal of Consumer Research*: It's all about the consumer. *Journal of Consumer Research, 11*(5), 955–959. https://doi.org/10.1093/jcr/ucx123

Isen, A. M. (2000). Some perspectives on positive affect and self-regulation. *Psychological Inquiry, 11*(3), 184–187.

Jacoby, J., Speller, D. E., & Kohn, C. A. (1974a). Brand choice behavior as a function of information load. *Journal of Marketing Research, 11*(1), 63–69. https://doi.org/10.1177/002224377401100106

Jacoby, J., Speller, D. E., & Kohn, C. A. (1974b). Brand choice behavior as a function of information load: Replication and extension. *Journal of Consumer Research, 1*(1), 33–42. https://doi.org/10.1086/208579

Janiszewski, C. (1993). Preattentive mere exposure effects. *Journal of Consumer Research, 20*(3), 376–392. https://doi.org/10.1086/209356

Johnson, E. J., & Goldstein, D. (2003). Medicine. Do defaults save lives? *Science, 302*(5649), 1338–1339. https://doi.org/10.1126/science.1091721

Johnson, E. J., & Meyer, R. J. (1984). Compensatory choice models of noncompensatory processes: The effect of varying context. *Journal of Consumer Research, 11*(1), 528–541. https://doi.org/10.1086/208989

Johnson, E. J., & Russo, J. E. (1984). Product familiarity and learning new information. *Journal of Consumer Research, 11*(1), 542–550. https://doi.org/10.1086/208990

Jones, M. G. (1990). Marketing academics at the FTC: Reflections and recommendations. In P. E. Murphy & W. L. Wilkie (Eds.), *Marketing and advertising regulation: The Federal Trade Commission in the 1990s* (pp. 216–220). University of Notre Dame Press.

Kahneman, D. (1992). Reference points, anchors, norms, and mixed feelings. *Organizational Behavior and Human Decision Processes, 51*(2), 296–312. https://doi.org/10.1016/0749-5978(92)90015-Y

Kardes, F. R. (1988). Spontaneous inference processes in advertising: The effects of conclusion omission and involvement on persuasion. *Journal of Consumer Research, 15*(2), 225–233. https://doi.org/10.1086/209159

Kardes, F. R., Posavac, S. S., & Cronley, M. L. (2004). Consumer inference: A review of processes, bases, and judgment contexts. *Journal of Consumer Psychology, 14*(3), 230–256. https://doi.org/10.1207/s15327663jcp1403_6

Kassarjian, H. H. (1971). Personality and consumer behavior: A review. *Journal of Marketing Research, 8*(4), 409–418. https://doi.org/10.1177/002224377100800401

Katona, G. (1945). *Price control and business*. Principia Press.

Katona, G. (1975). *Psychological economics*. Elsevier.

Katona, G., & Curtin, R. (1980). Problem-oriented rather than discipline-oriented research. In J. C. Olson (Ed.), *NA - Advances in consumer research* (Vol. 7, pp. 44–45). Association for Consumer Research.

Keller, K. L. (1987). Memory factors in advertising: The effect of advertising retrieval cues on brand evaluations. *Journal of Consumer Research, 14*(3), 316–333. https://doi.org/10.1086/209116

Keller, K. L. (1993). Conceptualizing, measuring, and managing customer-based brand equity. *Journal of Marketing, 57*(1), 1–22. https://doi.org/10.2307/1252054

Kim, H. H., & Law, R. (2015). Smartphones in tourism and hospitality marketing: A literature review. *Journal of Travel & Tourism Marketing, 32*(6), 692–711. https://doi.org/10.1080/10548408.2014.943458

Kim, J., & Forsythe, S. (2008). Adoption of virtual try-on technology for online apparel shopping. *Journal of Interactive Marketing, 22*(2), 45–59. https://doi.org/10.1002/dir.20113

Kim, J., & Morris, J. D. (2007). The power of affective response and cognitive structure in product-trial attitude formation. *Journal of Advertising, 36*(1), 95–106. https://doi.org/10.2753/JOA0091-3367360107

Kinnear, T. (1997). An historic perspective on the quantity and quality of marketing and public policy research. *Journal of Public Policy & Marketing, 16*(1), 144–146. https://doi.org/10.1177/074391569701600116

Kirmani, A. (2009). The self and the brand. *Journal of Consumer Psychology, 19*(3), 271–275. https://doi.org/10.1016/j.jcps.2009.05.011

Kleine, R. E., III, Kleine, S. S., & Brunswick, G. J. (2009). Transformational consumption choices: building an understanding by integrating social identity and multi-attribute attitude theories. *Journal of Consumer Behavior, 8*(1), 54–70. https://doi.org/10.1002/cb.273

Kleinmuntz, D. N., & Schkade, D. A. (1993). Information displays and decision processes. *Psychological Science, 4*(4), 221–227. https://doi.org/10.1111/j.1467-9280.1993.tb00265.x

Kotler, P., & Levy, S. J. (1969). Broadening the concept of marketing. *Journal of Marketing, 33*(1), 10–15. https://doi.org/10.1177/002224296903300103

Kotler, P., & Zaltman, G. (1971). Social marketing: An approach to planned social change. *Journal of Marketing, 35*(3), 3–12. https://doi.org/10.1177/002224297103500302

Krause, R. J., & Rucker, D. D. (2020). Strategic storytelling: When narratives help versus hurt the persuasive power of facts. *Personality and Social Psychology Bulletin, 46*(2), 216–227. https://doi.org/10.1177/0146167219853845

Kunda, Z. (1990). The case for motivated reasoning. *Psychological Bulletin, 108*(3), 480–498. https://doi.org/10.1037/0033-2909.108.3.480

Lampman, R. J. (1988). JFK's four consumer rights: A retrospective view. In E. S. Maynes (Ed.), *The frontier of research in the consumer interest* (pp. 19–33). American Council on Consumer Interests.

Landwehr, J. R., McGill, A. L., & Herrmann, A. (2011). It's got the look: The effect of friendly and aggressive "facial" expressions on product liking and sales. *Journal of Marketing, 75*(3), 132–146. https://doi.org/10.1509/jmkg.75.3.132

Lavidge, R. J., & Steiner, G. A. (1961). A model for predictive measurements of advertising effectiveness. *Journal of Marketing, 25*(6), 59–62. https://doi.org/10.2307/1248516

Lee, K., & Shavitt, S. (2009). Can McDonald's food ever be considered healthful? Metacognitive experiences affect the perceived understanding of a brand. *Journal of Marketing Research, 46*(2), 222–233. https://doi.org/10.1509/jmkr.46.2.222

Lembregts, C., & Van Den Bergh, B. (2019). Making each unit count: The role of discretizing units in quantity expressions. *Journal of Consumer Research, 45*(5), 1051–1067. https://doi.org/10.1093/jcr/ucy036

Levy, S. J. (1959). Symbols for sale. *Harvard Business Review, 37*, 117–124.

Liaw, G.-F., & Chen, C.-H. (2013). The impact of virtual fitting room technology on consumers' online purchase intention. *Management and Administrative Sciences Review, 2*(1), 23–35.

Liberman, N., Trope, Y., & Stephan, E. (2007). Psychological distance. In A. W. Kruglanski & E. T. Higgins (Eds.), *Social psychology: Handbook of basic principles* (pp. 353–381). Guilford Press.

Lodish, L. M., Abraham, M., Kalmenson, S., Livelsberger, J., Lubetkin, B., Richardson, B., & Stevens, M. E. (1995). How T.V. advertising works: A meta-analysis of 389 real world split cable T.V. advertising experiments. *Journal of Marketing Research, 32*(2), 125–139. https://doi.org/10.1177/002224379503200201

Loewenstein, G. (2000). Emotions in economic theory and economic behavior. *American Economic Review, 90*(2), 426–432. https://doi.org/10.1257/aer.90.2.426

Loftus, E. F. (1975). Leading questions and the eyewitness report. *Cognitive Psychology, 7*(4), 560–572. https://doi.org/10.1016/0010-0285(75)90023-7

Loken, B., & John, D. R. (1993a). Diluting brand beliefs: When do brand extensions have a negative impact? *Journal of Marketing, 57*(3), 71–84. https://doi.org/10.1177/002224299305700305

Loken, B., & John, D. R. (1993b). When do brand extensions have a negative impact? *Journal of Marketing, 57*(3), 71–84. https://doi.org/10.1177/002224299305700305

Luo, X. (2005). How does shopping with others influence impulsive purchasing? *Journal of Consumer Psychology, 15*(4), 288–294. https://doi.org/10.1207/s15327663jcp1504_3

Lutz, R. J. (1975). Changing brand attitudes through modification of cognitive structure. *Journal of Consumer Research, 1*(4), 49–59. https://doi.org/10.1086/208607

Lynch, J. G., Jr. (2011). Introduction to the special interdisciplinary issue on consumer financial decision making. *Journal of Marketing Research, 48*(SPL), Siv–Sviii. https://doi.org/10.1509/jmkr.48.SPL.Siv

Lynch, J. G., Jr., & Ariely, D. (2000). Wine online: Search costs affect competition on price, quality, and distribution. *Marketing Science, 19*(1), 83–103. https://doi.org/10.1287/mksc.19.1.83.15183

Lynch, J. G., Jr., Marmorstein, H., & Weigold, M. F. (1988). Choices from sets including remembered brands: Use of recalled attributes and prior overall evaluations. *Journal of Consumer Research, 15*(2), 169–184.

Lynch, J. G., Nettemeyer, R., Spiller, S. A., & Zammit, A. (2010). A generalizable scale of propensity to plan: The long and the short of planning for time and money. *Journal of Consumer Research, 37*(1), 108–128. https://doi.org/10.1086/649907

MacInnis, D. J., & Folkes, V. S. (2010). The disciplinary status of consumer behavior: A sociology of science perspective on key controversies. *Journal of Consumer Research, 36*(6), 899–914. https://doi.org/10.1086/644610

MacInnis, D. J., Park, C. W., & Priester, J. R. (Eds.). (2009). *Handbook of brand relationships*. Routledge.

MacKenzie, S. B., Lutz, R. J., & Belch, G. E. (1986). The role of attitude toward the ad as a mediator of advertising effectiveness: A test of competing explanations. *Journal of Marketing Research, 23*(2), 130–143. https://doi.org/10.1177/002224378602300205

Mackie, D. M., & Worth, L. T. (1989). Processing deficits and the mediation of positive affect in persuasion. *Journal of Personality and Social Psychology, 57*(1), 27–40. https://doi.org/10.1037/0022-3514.57.1.27

Mata, A., Ferreira, M. B., & Sherman, S. J. (2013). Flexibility in motivated reasoning: Strategic shifts of reasoning modes in covariation judgment. *Social Cognition, 31*(4), 465–481. https://doi.org/10.1521/soco_2012_1004

Maynes, E. S. (Ed.). (1988a). *The frontier of research in the consumer interest*. American Council on Consumer Interests.

Maynes, E. S. (Ed.). (1988b). *Research in the consumer interest: The frontier*. American Council on Consumer Interests.

Mazis, M. B. (1979). Overview of the "can and should the FTC restrict advertising to children?" workshop. In W. W. Wilkie (Ed.), *NA - Advances in consumer research* (Vol. 6, pp. 3–6). Association for Consumer Research.

Mazis, M. B. (1997). Marketing and public policy: Prospects for the future. *Journal of Public Policy & Marketing, 16*(1), 139–143. https://doi.org/10.1177/074391569701600115

Mazis, M. B., Staelin, R., Beales, H., & Salop, S. C. (1981). A framework for evaluating consumer regulation. *Journal of Marketing, 45*(1), 11–21. https://doi.org/10.1177/002224298104500102

McCarthy, E. J. (1960). *Basic marketing: A managerial approach*. R. D. Irwin.

McCarty, J. A., & Shrum, L. J. (2001). The influence of individualism, collectivism, and locus of control on environmental beliefs and behavior. *Journal of Public Policy & Marketing, 20*(1), 93–104. https://doi.org/10.1509/jppm.20.1.93.17291

McCracken, G. (1989). Who is the celebrity endorser? Cultural foundations of the endorsement process. *Journal of Consumer Research, 16*(3), 310–321. https://doi.org/10.1086/209217

McFerran, B., Dahl, D. W., Fitzsimons, G. J., & Morales, A. C. (2010). I'll have what she's having: Effects of social influence and body type on the food choices of others. *Journal of Consumer Research, 36*(6), 915–929. https://doi.org/10.1086/644611

McNeill, D. L., & Wilkie, W. L. (1979). Public policy and consumer information: Impact of the new energy labels. *Journal of Consumer Research, 6*(1), 1–11. https://doi.org/10.1086/208743

Melumad, S., Inman, J. J., & Pham, M. T. (2019). Selectively emotional: How smartphone use changes user-generated content. *Journal of Marketing Research, 56*(2), 259–275. https://doi.org/10.1177/0022243718815429

Menon, G., & Raghubir, P. (2003). Ease-of-retrieval as an automatic input in judgments: A mere-accessibility framework? *Journal of Consumer Research, 30*(2), 230–243. https://doi.org/10.1086/376804

Meuter, M. L., Ostrom, A. L., Bitner, M. J., & Roundtree, R. (2003). The influence of technology anxiety on consumer use and experiences with self-service technologies. *Journal of Business Research, 56*(11), 899–906. https://doi.org/10.1016/S0148-2963(01)00276-4

Meyvis, T., & Janiszewski, C. (2004). When are broader brands stronger brands? An accessibility perspective on the success of brand extensions. *Journal of Consumer Research, 31*(2), 346–357. https://doi.org/10.1086/422113

Mick, D. G. (2006). Presidential address: Meaning and mattering through transformative consumer research. In C. Pechmann & L. Price (Eds.), *NA - Advances in consumer research* (Vol. 33, pp. 1–4). Association for Consumer Research.

Mick, D. G. (2008). Introduction: The moment and place for a special issue. *Journal of Consumer Research, 35*(3), 377–379. https://doi.org/10.1086/591482

Mick, D. G., & Fournier, S. (1998). Paradoxes of technology: Consumer cognizance, emotions, and coping strategies. *Journal of Consumer Research, 25*(2), 123–143. https://doi.org/10.1086/209531

Miniard, P. W., & Cohen, J. B. (1983). Modeling personal and normative influences on behavior. *Journal of Consumer Research, 10*(2), 169–180. https://doi.org/10.1086/208957

Mitchell, A. A., & Olson, J. C. (1981). Are product attribute beliefs the only mediator of advertising effects on brand attitude? *Journal of Marketing Research, 18*(3), 318–332. https://doi.org/10.1177/002224378101800306

Mittal, B. (1990). The relative roles of brand beliefs and attitude toward the ad as mediators of brand attitude: A second look. *Journal of Marketing Research, 27*(2), 209–219. https://doi.org/10.2307/3172847

Moorman, C. (1990). The effects of stimulus and consumer characteristics on the utilization of nutrition information. *Journal of Consumer Research, 17*(3), 362–374. https://doi.org/10.1086/208563

Moorman, C. (1996). A quasi experiment to assess the consumer and informational determinants of nutrition information processing activities: The case of the nutrition labeling and education act. *Journal of Public Policy & Marketing, 15*(1), 28–44. https://doi.org/10.1177/074391569601500103

Moreau, C. P., Markman, A. B., & Lehmann, D. R. (2001). What is it? Categorization flexibility and consumers' responses to really new products. *Journal of Consumer Research, 27*(4), 489–498. https://doi.org/10.1086/319623

Morwitz, V. G., & Fitzsimons, G. J. (2004). The mere-measurement effect: Why does measuring intentions change actual behavior? *Journal of Consumer Psychology, 14*(1–2), 64–74. https://doi.org/10.1207/s15327663jcp1401&2_8

Murphy, P. E. (1990). Past FTC participation by marketing academics. In P. E. Murphy & W. L. Wilkie (Eds.), *Marketing and advertising regulation: The Federal Trade Commission in the 1990s* (pp. 205–215). University of Notre Dame Press.

Murphy, P. E., & Wilkie, W. L. (Eds.). (1990). *Marketing and advertising regulation: The Federal Trade Commission in the 1990s*. University of Notre Dame Press.

Neal, D. T., Wood, W., & Quinn, J. M. (2006). Habits—A repeat performance. *Current Directions in Psychological Science, 15*(4), 198–202. https://doi.org/10.1111/j.1467-8721.2006.00435.x

Nedungadi, P. (1990). Recall and consumer consideration sets: Influencing choice without altering brand evaluations. *Journal of Consumer Research, 17*(3), 263–276. https://doi.org/10.1086/208556

Nelson, M. R. (2008). The hidden persuaders: Then and now. *Journal of Advertising, 37*(1), 113–126. https://doi.org/10.2753/JOA0091-3367370109

Nelson, P. (1970). Information and consumer behavior. *Journal of Political Economy, 78*(2), 311–329. https://doi.org/10.1086/259630

Newman, J. W. (1983). Presentation of the ACR "Fellow in Consumer Behavior Award" to Sidney J. Levy, George Katona, and Robert Ferber. In R. P. Bagozzi & A. M. Tybout (Eds.), *NA - Advances in consumer research* (Vol. 10, pp. 6–8). Association for Consumer Research.

Niblett, G. R. (2005). Stretching the limits of social marketing partnerships, upstream and downstream: Setting the context for the 10th Innovations in Social Marketing Conference. *Social Marketing Quarterly, 11*(3–4), 9–15. https://doi.org/10.1080/15245000500308898

Nicosia, F. M. (1966). *Consumer decision processes: Marketing and advertising implications*. Prentice-Hall.

Nordhielm, C. L. (2002). The influence of level of processing on advertising repetition effects. *Journal of Consumer Research, 29*(3), 371–382. https://doi.org/10.1086/344428

O'Keefe, A. M., & Pollay, R. W. (1996). Deadly targeting of women in promoting cigarettes. *Journal of the American Medical Women's Association, 51*(1–2), 67–69.

Ottati, V. C., & Isbell, L. M. (1996). Effects of mood during exposure to target information on subsequently reported judgments: An on-line model of misattribution and correction. *Journal of Personality and Social Psychology, 71*(1), 39–53. https://doi.org/10.1037/0022-3514.71.1.39

Ouellette, J. A., & Wood, W. (1998). Habit and intention in everyday life: The multiple processes by which past behavior predicts future behavior. *Psychological Bulletin, 124*(1), 54–74. https://doi.org/10.1037/0033-2909.124.1.54

Oyserman, D. (2009). Identity-based motivation and consumer behavior. *Journal of Consumer Psychology, 19*(3), 276–279. https://doi.org/10.1016/j.jcps.2009.06.001

Pajares, F., & Schunk, D. H. (2005). Self-efficacy and self-concept beliefs: jointly contributing to the quality of human life. In H. W. Marsh, R. G. Craven, & D. M. McInerney (Eds.), *New frontiers for self research* (pp. 95–121). Information Age Publishing.

Pappalardo, J. K. (1997). The role of consumer research in evaluating deception: An economist's perspective. *Antitrust Law Journal, 65*(3), 793–812.

Park, C. W., Jaworski, B. J., & MacInnis, D. J. (1986). Strategic brand concept-image management. *Journal of Marketing, 50*(4), 135–145. https://doi.org/10.1177/002224298605000401

Payne, J. W., Bettman, J. R., Johnson, E. J., & Luce, M. F. (1995). An information processing perspective on choice. *Psychology of Learning and Motivation, 32*, 137–175. https://doi.org/10.1016/S0079-7421(08)60309-6

Peattie, K. (2010). Green consumption: Behavior and norms. *Annual Review of Environment and Resources, 35*(1), 195–228. https://doi.org/10.1146/annurev-environ-032609-094328

Percy, L., & Rossiter, J. R. (1992). A model of brand awareness and brand attitude advertising strategies. *Psychology and Marketing, 9*(4), 263–274. https://doi.org/10.1002/mar.4220090402

Petty, R. E., Cacioppo, J. T., & Schumann, D. (1983). Central and peripheral routes to advertising effectiveness: The moderating role of involvement. *Journal of Consumer Research*, *10*(2), 135–146. https://doi.org/10.1086/208954

Petty, R. E., Wegener, D. T., & Fabrigar, L. R. (1997). Attitudes and attitude change. *Annual Review of Psychology*, *48*(1), 609–647. https://doi.org/10.1146/annurev.psych.48.1.609

Pham, M. T., Cohen, J. B., Pracejus, J. W., & Hughes, G. D. (2001). Affect monitoring and the primacy of feelings in judgment. *Journal of Consumer Research*, *28*(2), 167–188. https://doi.org/10.1086/322896

Posavac, S. S., Sanbonmatsu, D. M., & Fazio, R. H. (1997). Considering the best choice: Effects of the salience and accessibility of alternatives on attitude—decision consistency. *Journal of Personality and Social Psychology*, *72*(2), 253–261. https://doi.org/10.1037/0022-3514.72.2.253

Pratt, R. (1972). Marketing applications of behavioral economics. In B. Strumpel, J. M. Morgan, & E. Zahn (Eds.), *Human behavior in economic affairs: Essays in honor of George Katona*. Jossey-Bass.

Puth, G., Mostert, P., & Ewing, M. (1999). Consumer perceptions of mentioned product and brand attributes in magazine advertising. *Journal of Product and Brand Management*, *8*(1), 38–50. https://doi.org/10.1108/10610429910257977

Raghubir, P., & Menon, G. (1998). AIDS and me, never the twain shall meet: The effects of information accessibility on judgments of risk and advertising effectiveness. *Journal of Consumer Research*, *25*(1), 52–63. https://doi.org/10.1086/209526

Ratchford, B. T. (1982). Cost-benefit models for explaining consumer choice and information seeking behavior. *Management Science*, *28*(2), 197–212. https://doi.org/10.1287/mnsc.28.2.197

Ratner, E. M. (1978). *FTC staff report on television advertising to children*. Bureau of Consumer Protection, Federal Trade Commission.

Ray, M. L., Sawyer, A. G., Rothschild, M. L., Heeler, R. M., Strong, E. C., & Reed, J. B. (1973). Marketing communications and the hierarchy of effects. In P. Clark (Ed.), *New models for mass communication research* (pp. 147–176). Sage Publishing.

Reed, A. I. I., II. (2004). Activating the self-importance of consumer selves: Exploring identity salience effects on judgments. *Journal of Consumer Research*, *31*(2), 286–295. https://doi.org/10.1086/422108

Reynolds, T. T., & Olson, J. C. (Eds.). (2001). *Understanding consumer decision making: The means-end approach to marketing and advertising strategy*. Lawrence Erlbaum Associates.

Ridgers, N. D., McNarry, M. A., & Mackintosh, K. A. (2016). Feasibility and effectiveness of using wearable activity trackers in youth: A systematic review. *JMIR Mhealth and Uhealth*, *4*(4), e129 1–12. https://doi.org/10.2196/mhealth.6540

Roe, B., Levy, A. S., & Derby, B. M. (1999). The impact of health claims on consumer search and product evaluation outcomes: Results from FDA experimental data. *Journal of Public Policy & Marketing*, *18*(1), 89–105. https://doi.org/10.1177/074391569901800110

Rubin, R. M., Riney, B. J., & Molina, D. J. (1990). Expenditure pattern differentials between one-earner and dual-earner households: 1972–1973 and 1984. *Journal of Consumer Research*, *17*(1), 43–52. https://doi.org/10.1086/208535

Rucker, D. D., & He, S. (2019). The role of attitudes in advertising. In D. Albarracín & B. Johnson (Eds.), *The handbook of attitudes* (2nd ed., Vol. 2, pp. 268–295). Routledge.

Russo, J. E. (1974). More information is better: A reevaluation of Jacoby, Speller, and Kohn. *Journal of Consumer Research*, *1*(3), 68–72. https://doi.org/10.1086/208601

Russo, J. E. (1977). The value of unit price information. *Journal of Marketing Research*, *14*(2), 193–201. https://doi.org/10.1177/002224377701400207

Russo, J. E., Staelin, R., Nolan, C. A., Russell, G. J., & Metcalf, B. L. (1986). Nutrition information in the supermarket. *Journal of Consumer Research*, *13*(1), 48–70. https://doi.org/10.1086/209047

Samson, A., & Voyer, B. G. (2014). Emergency purchasing situations: Implications for consumer decision-making. *Journal of Economic Psychology*, *44*, 21–33. https://doi.org/10.1016/j.joep.2014.05.004

Schwartz, D., & Loewenstein, G. (2017). The chill of the moment: Emotions and pro-environmental behavior. *Journal of Public Policy & Marketing*, *36*(2), 255–268. https://doi.org/10.1509/jppm.16.132

Schwarz, N. (2004). Metacognitive experiences in consumer judgment and decision making. *Journal of Consumer Psychology*, *14*(4), 332–348. https://doi.org/10.1207/s15327663jcp1404_2

Schwarz, N., & Clore, G. L. (2007). Feelings and phenomenal experiences. In A. W. Kruglanski & E. T. Higgins (Eds.), *Social psychology: Handbook of basic principles* (pp. 385–407). Guilford Press.

Schwarzkopf, S., & Gries, R. (Eds.). (2010). *Ernest Dichter and motivation research*. Palgrave Macmillan. https://doi.org/10.1057/9780230293946_1

Seenivasan, S., & Thomas, D. (2016). Negative consequences of nutrition information disclosure on consumption behavior in quick-casual restaurants. *Journal of Economic Psychology*, *55*, 51–60. https://doi.org/10.1016/j.joep.2016.02.009

Shafir, E., & Thaler, R. H. (2006). Invest now, drink later, spend never: On the mental accounting of delayed consumption. *Journal of Economic Psychology, 27*(5), 694–712. https://doi.org/10.1016/j.joep.2006.05.008

Shavitt, S., & Nelson, M. (2002). The role of attitude functions in persuasion and social judgment. In J. P. Dillard & M. Pfau (Eds.), The persuasion handbook: *Developments in theory and practice* (137–153). Sage Publications.

Shavitt, S., & Nelson, M. R. (2000). The social-identity function in person perception: Communicated meanings of product preferences. In G. Maio & J. M. Olson (Eds.), *Why we evaluate: Functions of attitudes* (pp. 37–57). Erlbaum.

Sherman, J. W., Gawronski, B., & Trope, Y. (2014). *Dual-process theories of the social mind.* Guilford Press.

Sirgy, J. M. (1982). Self-concept in consumer behavior: A critical review. *Journal of Consumer Research, 9*(3), 287–300. https://doi.org/10.1086/208924

Sirkeci, I., & Magnusdottir, L. B. (2011). Understanding illegal music downloading in the UK: A multi-attribute model. *Journal of Research in Interactive Marketing, 5*(1), 90–110. https://doi.org/10.1108/17505931111121543

Smith, D. C. & Park, C. W. (1992). The effects of brand extensions on market share and advertising efficiency. *Journal of Marketing Research, 29*(3), 296–313. https://doi.org/10.2307/3172741

Smith, S., & Paladino, A. (2010). Eating clean and green? Investigating consumer motivations towards the purchase of organic food. *Australasian Marketing Journal, 18*(2), 93–104. https://doi.org/10.1016/j.ausmj.2010.01.001

Srinivasan, S. S., & Till, B. D. (2002). Evaluation of search, experience and credence attributes: Role of brand name and product trial. *Journal of Product and Brand Management, 11*(7), 417–431. https://doi.org/10.1108/10610420210451616

Starch, D. (1923). *Principles of advertising.* A. W. Shaw.

Sternthal, B., Dholakia, R., & Leavitt, C. (1978). The persuasive effect of source credibility: Tests of cognitive response. *Journal of Consumer Research, 4*(4), 252–260. https://doi.org/10.1086/208704

Sujan, M., & Dekleva, C. (1987). Product categorization and inference making: Some implications for comparative advertising. *Journal of Consumer Research, 14*(3), 372–378. https://doi.org/10.1086/209120

Thaler, R. H., & Sunstein, C. R. (2008). *Nudge: Improving decisions about health, wealth, and happiness.* Yale University Press.

Touré-Tillery, M., & Fishbach, A. (2018). Three sources of motivation. *Consumer Psychology Review, 1*(1), 123–134. https://doi.org/10.1002/arcp.1007

Trope, Y., Liberman, N., & Wakslak, C. (2007). Construal levels and psychological distance: Effects on representation, prediction, evaluation, and behavior. *Journal of Consumer Psychology, 17*(2), 83–95. https://doi.org/10.1016/S1057-7408(07)70013-X

Unfair Methods of Competition Unlawful; Prevention by Commission. 15 U.S.C. § 45 (2006).

Unnava, H. R., Agarwal, S., & Haugtvedt, C. P. (1996). Interactive effects of presentation modality and message-generated imagery on recall of advertising. *Journal of Consumer Research, 23*(1), 81–88. https://doi.org/10.1086/209468

Urbany, J. E. (1986). An experimental examination of the economics of information. *Journal of Consumer Research, 13*(2), 257–271. https://doi.org/10.1086/209065

Van Kerckhove, A., Geuens, M., & Vermeir, I. (2015). The floor is nearer than the sky: How looking up or down affects construal level. *Journal of Consumer Research, 41*(6), 1358–1371. https://doi.org/10.1086/679309

van Osselaer, S. M. J., & Janiszewski, C. (2012). A goal-based model of product evaluation and choice. *Journal of Consumer Research, 39*(2), 260–292. https://doi.org/10.1086/662643

Vohs, K. D., & Faber, R. J. (2007). Spent resources: Self-regulatory resource availability affects impulse buying. *Journal of Consumer Research, 33*(4), 537–547. https://doi.org/10.1086/510228

Wang, C., Harris, J., & Patterson, P. (2013). The roles of habit, self-efficacy, and satisfaction in driving continued use of self-service technologies: A longitudinal study. *Journal of Service Research, 16*(3), 400–414. https://doi.org/10.1177/1094670512473200

Wänke, M., Bohner, G., & Jurkowitsch, A. (1997). There are many reasons to drive a BMW: Does imagined ease of argument generation influence attitudes? *Journal of Consumer Research, 24*(2), 170–177. https://doi.org/10.1086/209502

Wärneryd, K.-E. (1982). The life and work of George Katona. *Journal of Economic Psychology, 2*(1), 1–31. https://doi.org/10.1016/0167-4870(82)90008-3

Wattenmaker, W. D., Dewey, G. I., Murphy, T. D., & Medin, D. L. (1986). Linear separability and concept learning: Context, relational properties, and concept naturalness. *Cognitive Psychology, 18*(2), 158–194. https://doi.org/10.1016/0010-0285(86)90011-3

Wells, W. D. (1975). Psychographics: A critical review. *Journal of Marketing Research, 12*(2), 196–213. https://doi.org/10.1177/002224377501200210

White, K., Argo, J. J., & Sengupta, J. (2012). Dissociative versus associative responses to social identity threat: The role of consumer self-construal. *Journal*

Wilkie, W. L. (1974). Analysis of effects of information load. *Journal of Marketing Research, 11*(4), 462–466. https://doi.org/10.1177/002224377401100414

Wilkie, W. L. (1975). *Assessment of consumer information processing research in relation to public policy needs.* United States Government Printing Office.

Wilkie, W. L. (1982). Affirmative disclosure: Perspectives on FTC orders. *Journal of Public Policy & Marketing, 1*(1), 95–110. https://doi.org/10.1177/074391568200100108

Wilkie, W. L. (1994). *Consumer behavior* (3rd ed.). John Wiley & Sons.

Wilkie, W. L. (1997). Developing research on public policy and marketing. *Journal of Public Policy & Marketing, 16*(1), 132–136. https://doi.org/10.1177/074391569701600113

Wilkie, W. L. (2014). My memorable experiences as a marketing academic at the Federal Trade Commission. *Journal of Public Policy & Marketing, 33*(2), 194–201. https://doi.org/10.1509/jppm.14.FTC.003

Wilkie, W. L., & Farris, P. W. (1975). Comparison advertising: Problems and potential. *Journal of Marketing, 39*(4), 7–15. https://doi.org/10.1177/002224297503900402

Wilkie, W. L., & Gardner, D. M. (1974). The role of marketing research in public policy decision making. *Journal of Marketing, 38*(1), 38–47.

Wilkie, W. L., McNeill, D. L., & Mazis, M. B. (1984). Marketing's "scarlet letter": The theory and practice of corrective advertising. *Journal of Marketing, 48*(2), 11–31.

Wilkie, W. L., & Moore, E. S. (1999). Marketing's contributions to society. *Journal of Marketing, 63*(4 Suppl.), 198–218. https://doi.org/10.1177/00222429990634s118

Wilkie, W. L., & Pessemier, E. A. (1973). Issues in marketing's use of multi-attribute attitude models. *Journal of Marketing Research, 10*(4), 428–441. https://doi.org/10.1177/002224377301000411

Williams, T. G. (2002). Social class influences on purchase evaluation criteria. *Journal of Consumer Marketing, 19*(3), 249–276. https://doi.org/10.1108/07363760210426067

Wood, M. (1998). Socio-economic status, delay of gratification, and impulse buying. *Journal of Economic Psychology, 19*(3), 295–320. https://doi.org/10.1016/S0167-4870(98)00009-9

Wood, M. (2008). Applying commercial marketing theory to social marketing: A tale of 4Ps (and a B). *Social Marketing Quarterly, 14*(1), 76–85. https://doi.org/10.1080/15245000701856877

Wright, P. (1975). Consumer choice strategies: Simplifying vs. optimizing. *Journal of Marketing Research, 12*(1), 60–67. https://doi.org/10.1177/002224377501200109

Wright, P. (1980). Message-evoked thoughts: Persuasion research using thought verbalizations. *Journal of Consumer Research, 7*(2), 151–175. https://doi.org/10.1086/208804

Wright, P. L. (1973). The cognitive processes mediating acceptance of advertising. *Journal of Marketing Research, 10*(1), 53–62. https://doi.org/10.1177/002224377301000108

Wu, F., Samper, A., Morales, A. C., & Fitzsimons, G. J. (2017). It's too pretty to use! When and how enhanced product aesthetics discourage usage and lower consumption enjoyment. *Journal of Consumer Research, 44*(3), 651–672. https://doi.org/10.1093/jcr/ucx057

Yang, K., & Forney, J. C. (2013). The moderating role of consumer technology anxiety in mobile shopping adoption: Differential effects of facilitating conditions and social influences. *Journal of Electronic Commerce Research, 14*(4), 334–347.

Zajonc, R. B. (1980). Feeling and thinking: Preferences need no inferences. *American Psychologist, 35*(2), 151–175. https://doi.org/10.1037/0003-066X.35.2.151

Zaltman, G. (1965). *Marketing: Contributions from the behavioral sciences.* Harcourt, Brace.

Zeelenberg, M. (1999). Anticipated regret, expected feedback and behavioral decision making. *Journal of Behavioral Decision Making, 12*(2), 93–106. https://doi.org/10.1002/(SICI)1099-0771(199906)12:2<93::AID-BDM311>3.0.CO;2-S

CHAPTER 2

THE ACTIVATION AND USE OF DECLARATIVE AND PROCEDURAL KNOWLEDGE

Robert S. Wyer Jr.

Although people often acquire a large amount of knowledge about an object or event, they rarely if ever consider all of this knowledge when making a judgment or behavioral decision. Rather, they recall and use only a small subset of their knowledge that happens to come to mind easily at the time. Objectively irrelevant situational factors can influence the subset of concepts and knowledge that happen to be accessible in memory and, consequently, the criteria used as a basis for judgments.

This phenomenon was called to social psychologists' attention by both Taylor and Fiske (1978), who found that people are primarily influenced by stimuli that are salient to them at the time of judgment, and Higgins et al. (1977; see also Srull & Wyer, 1979), who found that unobtrusively exposing participants to a trait concept increased their likelihood of using this concept to interpret a person's behavior in a later, unrelated situation. Although these "priming" effects seemed surprising at the time, they are now accepted as a standard methodological tool for understanding the cognitive and motivational determinants of judgments and behavior (Wyer, 2019). Indeed, these procedures are often applied without considering the assumptions on which they are based.

The effects of knowledge activation are evident at many stages of information processing, including comprehension, memory retrieval, inference and decision making, and output generation. Theory and research bearing on these effects (Förster & Liberman, 2007; Wyer, 2008) initially focused on the effects of semantic knowledge. However, many phenomena that have recently been identified suggest that early conceptualizations of the processes that underlie the effects of knowledge accessibility must be expanded. These phenomena surround the influence of embodied cognition (Barsalou, 2008; Barsalou et al., 2003; Niedenthal et al., 2005); the impact of affect, emotion, and other subjective experiences on behavior in unrelated domains (C. Y. Chen & Pham, 2019; Schwarz & Clore, 1996, 2007); and the impact of previous experiences on overt behavior that occurs without awareness (Bargh, 1997, 2017).

Research on these phenomena is reviewed in this chapter. First, however, I describe the basic principles that are assumed to govern the effects of knowledge activation and the conceptualizations that have been used to account for these effects.

BASIC PROCESSES

Types of Knowledge

Two types of knowledge are often distinguished. *Declarative* knowledge comprises all of the concepts and cognitions that people can potentially draw upon for use in comprehending new information or in making judgments and behavioral decisions. This knowledge provides the basis for comprehending new information, inferences, and behavioral decisions, whereas *procedural* knowledge refers to the cognitive processes that operate on this content in order to generate these inferences and decisions. Procedural knowledge comes into play in the marketplace, influencing the processes that underlie compulsive consumption or, alternatively, self-control. The distinction between declarative and procedural knowledge is not as clear as it might seem. Some procedures are stored as part of declarative knowledge and can be retrieved and used as a basis for behavior decisions much as one might consult a recipe for use in baking a cake (Wyer et al., 2002; see also Kruglanski et al., 2002; Schank & Abelson, 1977). However, other procedures are applied automatically without conscious deliberation, serving in effect as conditioned responses to concepts or cognitions that are activated in memory. These latter procedures and how they come into play are elaborated presently.

As the preceding example suggests, knowledge is stored in conceptual *units*. A unit of knowledge can consist of a single concept along with the criteria for applying it. It can also be a configuration of concepts that refers to a single object, a group of objects, a single event, or a sequence of events. It could also be a proposition concerning the relations among objects and events (e.g., an implicit theory) or a goal and the means of attaining it.

The formation of a unit of knowledge is normally the product of cognitive operations that are performed on new or previously acquired information. If the processing of new information leads a representation to be formed of its referent, this representation becomes a unit of knowledge about the referent that is stored in memory and later retrieved as a whole. Judgments or behavioral decisions also become units of knowledge about it. Several features of these knowledge units are worth noting:

1. Units of knowledge can be either categorical or schematic. *Categorical* representations consist of features that are unrelated except through their association with their referent. Thus, a "salesperson" might be represented as someone who "greets customers," "answers questions," "is considerate," and "is friendly." In contrast, a *schematic* representation is composed of features that are in a specifiable a priori relation to one another. A human face, for example, is a spatially organized schema, and a restaurant visit (e.g., entering, ordering, eating) is a temporally ordered schema.
2. Knowledge representations vary in generality. Thus, they can pertain to a specific object or event (Barack Obama, yesterday's lunch at McDonald's) or a general one (U.S. Presidents, eating at a fast-food restaurant).
3. Units of knowledge can be coded either verbally or in other sense modalities (e.g., visual, olfactory, auditory). Information is normally represented in the modality in which it is acquired. When an object or event occurs at a particular time and place, a verbal description of it spontaneously elicits a visual image (Wyer & Radvansky, 1999; for evidence, see Wyer, 2004). In contrast, a nonverbal (visual or auditory) stimulus might be represented in its original modality without being recoded verbally.
4. One type of nonverbal knowledge consists of a configuration of internal bodily responses that are experienced as positive or negative "feelings" or, in some cases, an "emotion."
5. A special type of knowledge pertains to a goal along with the means of attaining it (Kruglanski et al., 2002; Wyer & Srull, 1989). Although such representations, or *plan-goal schema* (Schank & Abelson, 1977; Kruglanski et al., 2002), are descriptive, they constitute procedures that can be consulted and used as bases for deciding how to attain a goal to which the representation is relevant. These goal-related representations are discussed in more detail presently.

Theories of Mental Representation and Knowledge Activation

Conceptualizations of the organization of knowledge in memory are inherently metaphorical and should be evaluated in terms of their utility and not their accuracy in describing the physiology of the brain. For example, they typically assume that units of knowledge are stored at particular locations. However, although connectionist models (e.g., Ehret et al., 2015; E. R. Smith & DeCoster, 1998,

1999) assume that memories are distributed rather than localized in a particular place, these models are inherently metaphorical as well.

Theories of mental representation make different assumptions about the manner in which knowledge is activated. Although these theories and their implications are discussed elsewhere (Carlston & Smith, 1996; Wyer, 2007), the most dominant formulations are worth summarizing briefly.

Associative network models. The most widely applied conceptualization of knowledge activation assumes that units of knowledge are stored in memory at specific locations and that the relations between these units are denoted by associative pathways (for examples, see Collins & Loftus, 1975; Wyer & Carlston, 1979). The *spreading activation* model (Collins & Loftus, 1975; Wyer & Carlston, 1979) assumes that when one unit of knowledge is activated (i.e., comes to mind), excitation spreads from this unit to other units along the pathways connecting them and that when the excitation that accumulates at the latter location reaches a given threshold level, the knowledge unit at this location is also activated. When a unit of knowledge is no longer thought about, it is deactivated. However, the excitation at this location takes time to dissipate. Consequently, as long as residual excitation exists, the knowledge is more accessible in memory and more likely to be reactivated by excitation transmitted from another source.

Retrieval cue models. A quite different conceptualization of declarative knowledge activation (e.g., Hintzman, 1986; Norman & Bobrow, 1979) requires no assumptions about the organization of knowledge in memory. Rather, it assumes that each unit of knowledge has its own memory trace and is activated by compiling a set of features (retrieval cues) that are contained in it. The retrieval cues activate all traces that contain them, and the representation that results is the set of features that these traces have in common. For example, if a person is searching for a Chinese restaurant, "Chinese" and "restaurant" in combination might activate a subset of traces that contain these features, along with others that the traces have in common. As the number of traces that share a given set of retrieval cues increases, fewer features are likely to be common to these traces and the more abstract the memorial representation is likely to be. However, the compilation of a set of features that uniquely describes a specific event might lead this event to be recalled. As a result, an experience that one has not thought about in years may be spontaneously recalled as the result of fortuitously compiling a set of retrieval cues that pertain specifically to it (Norman & Bobrow, 1979).

Hybrid models. A third general conceptualization, which incorporates the implications of both spreading activation and retrieval cue models, was proposed by Wyer and Srull (1989) in the context of a more general formulation of social information processing. They assumed that knowledge is stored in content-addressable "referent bins." A bin can contain many different types of knowledge about its referent (e.g., single concepts, stereotypes, visual images, personal experiences), which are deposited in the bin in the order they are formed. Each bin is identified by a set of features that are strongly associated with its referent. Once a bin is identified on the basis of a subset of these features, a probabilistic top-down search is performed for goal-relevant information, and if this information is identified, a copy of it is retrieved. Then, when processing is complete, this copy is returned to the top of the bin from which it is drawn. Consequently, it is more likely to be retrieved later when a new search is performed.

Symbolic symbol systems. The aforementioned conceptualizations, which are normally applied to the accessibility of semantic knowledge, are too restrictive to account for many of the phenomena identified in recent research of the sort reviewed later in this chapter. A conceptualization proposed by Barsalou (1999, 2008) avoids this restriction. According to this conceptualization, knowledge pertaining to a particular referent is represented in memory in multiple modalities and can include semantic meanings and metaphorical meanings of the concept, visual images, behavioral dispositions, subjective reactions, and bodily sensations, each of which functions as a symbol that can be used to construct a new representation of the referent in memory. Moreover, any of these symbols, if activated, can increase the accessibility of any other. This is difficult to explain on the basis of more traditional conceptions of mental representation.

Schemas. Two additional conceptualizations are restricted to specific types of knowledge. One conceptualization assumes that individuals process information *schematically*. As noted earlier, people, as a result of learning, acquire prototypic representations of individual stimuli, situations, and events and use them to interpret specific experiences that they encounter. That is, they respond to configurations of individual stimulus features as a whole without identifying all of the individual features that compose it even though some features specified in the schema are missing. The impact of schemas on comprehension was compellingly demonstrated by John Bransford and his colleagues (Bransford et al., 1972; Bransford & Johnson, 1972), who showed that apparently anomalous information (e.g., "The haystack was important because the cloth would rip") becomes easily understood and remembered when it is preceded by a stimulus word (e.g., "parachute") that activates a schema that could be used to interpret it. Moreover, when people interpret information in terms of a schema, features of the schema that are not specified in the information may be spontaneously added to the representation that is formed and later recalled as actually having been mentioned (Barclay, 1973; see also Loftus & Palmer, 1974; Spiro, 1977).

Implicit theories. An extension of schema theory assumes that information is organized in memory in terms of *implicit theories*, or normative principles concerning the relations among persons, objects, and events. These principles, which could consist of a single proposition or a number of related ones, can be used to interpret specific experiences and to infer their antecedents and consequences. Simple theories have the form of *implicational molecules* (Wyer & Carlston, 1979). For example, the principle that people with similar attitudes and values as one another might be represented by the molecule [P likes O; P likes (dislikes) X; O likes (dislikes) X], and the principle that price is an indication of quality might be reflected in the molecule [X is expensive (cheap); X is of high (poor) quality]. The application of these molecules to a new experience is theoretically governed by a "completion principle"; that is, if a new experience exemplifies all but one of the propositions composing a molecule, an instantiation of the remaining principle is spontaneously inferred. Thus, a consumer might not only infer the quality of a product from information about its price but also infer its price from information about its quality. The effects of many cognitive heuristics (Tversky & Kahneman, 1974) can be conceptualized in terms of the application of such molecules (see Wyer & Carlston, 1979; Wyer & Srull, 1989).

The effects of more complex implicit theories have been identified by M. Ross (1989), who found that women's memory of their emotional reactions during their most recent menstrual period were based more on their implicit theory about how they typically felt during their menstrual cycle rather than on the emotions they actually reported experiencing at the time. (For examples of the role of implicit theories in consumer behavior, see Jain et al., 2009; Mukhopadhyay & Johar, 2005.)

The representation of procedural knowledge. The aforementioned conceptualizations specify the way in which declarative knowledge is represented in memory and retrieved for use as bases for interpreting and making inferences about new information. However, none of these conceptualizations specifies the manner in which this knowledge and inferences based upon it are transformed into overt behavior. A conceptualization that potentially provides this specification was proposed by John Anderson (1983) in research on the acquisition of cognitive skills. I elaborate this conceptualization later in the context of discussing the priming of overt behavior.

Ease of Activation

The aforementioned conceptualizations assume that the accessibility of knowledge in memory determines the likelihood that it is used as a basis for judgments and decisions. However, knowledge accessibility can have an impact on judgments in its own right. As Winkielman and Cacioppo (2001) showed (see also Winkielman et al., 2003), the ease with which information is processed can elicit positive affect, and this affect can have an impact on judgments to which it is relevant (Reber et al., 2004). This implies that independently of its implications, the more quickly and easily knowledge about a stimulus comes to mind, the more favorably the stimulus will be judged.

This possibility was confirmed in consumer behavior research (A. Y. Lee & Labroo, 2004). Participants were exposed to a series of four pictures, the last of which was a picture of a target product. In some conditions, the first three pictures described the situational context in which the target was likely to be used. In other conditions, the pictures were unrelated to this context. Portraying the context in which the target product was used led the product to be identified more quickly and easily on the basis of its picture and to be evaluated more favorably.

By the same token, if information about a stimulus is difficult to access, the stimulus may be evaluated more negatively. Several studies (Schwarz, Bless, et al., 1991; for a review, see Schwarz, 2004) indicated that the subjective difficulty of generating reasons in support of a proposition decreases beliefs in its validity. This effect occurs independently of the actual number of reasons that are generated. Consequently, people evaluate a product less favorably after generating many reasons why the product is desirable (which is subjectively difficult) than after generating few reasons (Menon & Raghubir, 2003). Simply imagining the generation of many or few reasons can have a similar effect (Wänke et al., 1997). As noted previously, however, the conditions in which people search extensively for judgment-relevant information may be more the exception than the rule.

GENERAL EFFECTS OF DECLARATIVE KNOWLEDGE ACTIVATION

A general question surrounding the effects of primed concepts and knowledge on judgments concerns the stage of processing at which these effects are localized. People who scan a magazine, for example, might find that a particular advertisement captures their attention. They might then comprehend the information contained in the ad and construe its implications for the product being advertised, either elaborating on the information's favorable implications or questioning its validity on the basis of their previously acquired knowledge about the type of product being evaluated. Finally, they might integrate the implications of the information to form a subjective evaluation of the product and transform this evaluation into an overt response or behavioral decision. In short, the effectiveness of the ad information may be mediated by attention, comprehension, a construal of its positive and negative implications, an integration of these implications, and a transformation of these implications into an overt behavior.

The effects of knowledge accessibility are potentially implicated at each of these stages. To avoid unnecessary redundancy with material covered in previous reviews of the effects at these stages (Wyer, 2008), I provide just a few representative examples of the effects that occur at two stages of processing—comprehension and inference—and generally forego a discussion of the effects that occur at other stages. I then discuss the activation of the cognitive procedures that are used to generate judgments and decisions and, in this context, review research and theory on the priming of affect, subjective experience, and bodily feedback. Finally, in the last section of the chapter, I turn to a discussion of the role of knowledge accessibility on the generation of overt behavior that occurs automatically, without conscious awareness.

Comprehension Processes

The effects of knowledge activation on comprehension can be summarized in a series of general principles. The first, which applies to the accessibility and use of knowledge in general, was recognized by Taylor and Fiske's (1978) observation that people are "cognitive misers"; that is, they base their judgments on whatever stimuli happen to be salient to them at the time:

> **Principle 1.** People typically do not engage in any more extensive

processing than is necessary in order to attain the objective they are pursuing. When several knowledge representations might be applicable, the first representation that comes to mind is the one that is used.

The second principle has more specific implications:

> **Principle 2.** The accessibility of a unit of knowledge in memory increases with both the recency with which the unit has been activated and used in the past and the frequency with which it has been used. The effect of recency decreases over time, whereas the effect of frequency decays relatively more slowly.

An early demonstration of the effect of knowledge accessibility on comprehension (Higgins et al., 1977) not only confirmed this effect but placed constraints on its occurrence. Participants were unobtrusively exposed to either favorable trait adjectives (e.g., "adventurous," "self-confident") or unfavorable adjectives (e.g., "foolhardy," "conceited"), after which they read a story about a man whose behaviors could be interpreted in terms of both sets of adjectives (e.g., "wanted to cross the Atlantic in a sailboat," "was well aware of his ability to do things well"). Participants apparently interpreted the man's behaviors in terms of the trait adjectives that had been primed and consequently evaluated the man more favorably in the first condition than in the second. However, priming favorable or unfavorable concepts that that were inapplicable for interpreting the aforementioned behaviors (e.g., "kind" vs. "unkind") had no effect on evaluations. Although this contingency seems obvious, it anticipates Feldman and Lynch's (1988) later observation that primed concepts must be applicable as well as accessible in order to have an impact.

A second early study confirmed the effect of frequency as well as recency of activation (Srull & Wyer, 1979). Participants performed a sentence construction task in which words associated with hostility were used either 20% or 80% of the time.

Then, either immediately or several days later, they read a paragraph describing behaviors of a target person that were ambiguous with respect to this attribute. Not surprisingly, judgments of the target's hostility increased with the number of times that the concept had been used in the earlier, "priming" task but decreased with the time interval between the priming task and the impression formation task.

Of particular importance is evidence that although the effect of recency of priming initially predominates over the effect of frequency, the effect of frequency predominates after a period of time has elapsed (Higgins et al., 1985). The enduring effects of frequency have more general implications. For example, it might explain the persisting effect of brand loyalty on purchase decisions despite recent exposure to more attractive alternatives. More generally, concepts and knowledge that are used frequently in the social and cultural environment in which one finds oneself can become chronically accessible, producing general cultural differences in knowledge activation and use (Chiu & Hong, 2013; Markus & Kitayama, 1991; Triandis, 1995).

A third principle also concerns the duration of priming effects:

> **Principle 3.** Once people have interpreted information in terms of recently activated concepts and knowledge, the effect of this interpretation on later judgments and decisions persists over time.

This principle recognizes that once information has been interpreted in terms of activated concepts and knowledge, this interpretation is stored in memory and can later be recalled and used as a basis for later judgments and decisions independently of the conditions that led the interpretation to be made. For example, when persons have judged recycling to be important in the context of other, relatively unimportant social issues, they later retrieve and use this judgment as a basis for their decision to help out on a recycling project (Sherman et al., 1978). Moreover, this effect increases over time (Carlston, 1980; Srull & Wyer, 1980). Srull and Wyer (1980), for example, found that when participants had been exposed to information about a target person immediately after being primed with hostility-related concepts, the effect of this priming on later judgments of the target's hostility was greater when the judgments were made after a delay of 24 hours than when they were made shortly after the information was presented.

In fact, once specific features of information have been encoded in terms of more abstract concepts, the information may become more difficult to retrieve. Thus, people find it more difficult to recognize a face after they have described it verbally (Schooler & Engstler-Schooler, 1990). Analogously, people who have described a movie verbally find it more difficult to recognize details of what protagonists said and did (Adaval & Wyer, 2004). In the consumer domain, this suggests that consumers might be less able to recall specific features of a product if they have described it to someone as "good" than if they have not generated this verbal communication.

Unconscious priming effects. The most provocative studies reported during this period were conducted by John Bargh (e.g., Bargh & Pietromonaco, 1982). They demonstrated that exposing individuals to trait concepts can affect their interpretation of information even when they are not consciously aware that the concepts have been activated. This finding is consistent with implications of the spreading activation model described. That is, although the excitation from a primed concept can accumulate at a memory location, it may not be of sufficient magnitude to call the concept at this location into consciousness. Nevertheless, this excitation can increase the concept's accessibility and increase the likelihood of applying it to stimuli to which it is applicable.

But even when people are aware of the concepts that have been activated by priming, they may not be conscious of the reason the concepts come to mind. In fact, when persons *are* aware that their interpretation of information has been influenced by an objectively irrelevant factor, they may correct for this influence and so priming has no impact (Lombardi et al., 1987; Martin et al., 1990).

Assimilation and contrast. For the comprehension of information to be influenced by primed trait concepts, its possible interpretation must overlap the range of meanings that the concepts can take. If this is not the case, the concepts might be used as a standard of comparison, leading to contrast effects. In a study by Herr (1986), for example, exposing participants to names of persons who were known to be moderately hostile (e.g., Muhammad Ali, Howard Stern) had a positive effect on their interpretation of a target person's behaviors that were ambiguous with respect to hostility. However, exposing participants to names of persons who were known to be extremely hostile (e.g., Adolf Hitler, Joseph Stalin) led them to interpret the behaviors as less hostile than they otherwise would.

Whether a primed concept is used as a standard of comparison in interpreting information can depend on whether the information is semantically ambiguous (Wyer & Schwartz, 1969). For example, consumers often receive information about a product that describes not only its attributes but also its price. Although attribute descriptions might be subject to interpretation, price information is numerical and its implications are clear. Consequently, it is more likely to be used as a comparative standard. This can occur without awareness. For example, people judge the price of a target product to be lower if they have been subliminally exposed to high numbers while performing an ostensibly irrelevant task (Adaval & Monroe, 2002).

Inference Processes

Different subsets of previously acquired knowledge about a referent can have different implications. In such cases, performing a task that requires a particular subset of judgment-relevant knowledge can increase the likelihood that this subset is applied in making judgments and decisions in a later situation. A study by L. Ross et al. (1977) provided an example. Participants read a clinical case study that was ostensibly taken from a psychology textbook and then were asked to explain why the protagonist after leaving therapy might have either committed suicide or donated a substantial sum of money to the Peace Corps. Later, they were asked to estimate the likelihood that the protagonist had actually performed a number of different behaviors, including the one they had explained. Participants were well aware that no one actually knew what the protagonist had actually done. People, in generating explanations of a hypothetical event, selectively draw upon concepts and knowledge that would support the outcome they are asked to consider. This knowledge, once accessible in memory, is used as a basis for their later predictions. An experiment by Sherman et al. (1981) had similar implications.

Research of a quite different type (Mussweiler, 2003) provided another example. When consumers consider whether a product has a high value along a particular dimension (e.g., whether the average price of a sweater is greater than $300), they selectively retrieve features of a product that might conceivably have this value, and these features, once activated, influence the judgments they make of products they encounter later. Thus, people are willing to pay more for a sweater when they have previously thought about whether the average price of sweaters is greater or less than a high value than when they have considered whether the average price is greater or less than a low value (Adaval & Wyer, 2011). Moreover, the effects generalize not only to other types of clothing but also to high-tech products (e.g., a DVD player). The features activated in the course of evaluating a sweater are largely hedonic (e.g., attractiveness, aesthetic appeal), and hedonic criteria are applicable to both other types of clothing and high-tech products. (When the attributes activated by considering a product are inapplicable to other products, this generalization does not occur.) Although the paradigm employed in this research seems rather artificial, similar effects are evident outside the laboratory. Nunes and Boatright (2004), for example, found that shoppers at a beachfront were willing to pay more for DVDs if the sweaters being sold at a neighboring booth were high priced than if they were not.

Beliefs and probabilistic inferences. The selective retrieval of judgment-relevant information can also influence beliefs. When people are asked to report their beliefs in a proposition, they typically retrieve knowledge from memory that bears on its validity. In some cases, this knowledge could be a memory trace of the proposition that was acquired at an earlier time. If such a trace is unavailable, however, people may retrieve a logically related proposition to the target and construe its implications. Both situations are worth considering.

Direct effects of accessible knowledge on beliefs. The information that directly bears on a proposition's validity can come from a particular source. As Tulving (1983) pointed out, however, the source of information is often forgotten whereas the information itself is retained. In such instances, perceptions of the proposition's validity can depend largely on its familiarity and, therefore, the ease with which it comes to mind (Schwarz, 2004). Participants in a study by Hasher et al. (1977), for example, reported their beliefs in a series of propositions at two points in time. Some propositions in the second set were identical to those in the first set, but others were novel. Participants reported stronger beliefs in the repeated propositions than in the new ones. A quite different study by Jacoby et al. (1989) had similar implications.

This phenomenon presumably underlies the "sleeper effect" (Gruder et al., 1978; see also Kumkale & Albarracín, 2004), that is, the tendency for information from a noncredible source to have an increasing effect over time once the source is forgotten or dissociated from the information itself. In the consumer domain, this suggests that information about a brand that is conveyed in an irritating commercial might elicit negative affect initially but have a positive influence on beliefs about the product once the source of the information has been forgotten.

The effect of repetition on knowledge accessibility and its consequent influence on judgments was graphically demonstrated in research by L. J. Shrum (2001; Shrum & Lee, 2012) on the impact of television on perceptions of social reality. That is, individuals who frequently watch television overestimate the incidence of events in the world that are overrepresented on television (i.e., the incidence of doctors, lawyers, and policemen; indications of an affluent lifestyle; and the incidence of violent crime; Shrum, 2001). The effect of watching television on judgments decreases when people are reminded of their viewing habits (Shrum et al., 1998). Nevertheless, frequent exposure to the events seen on television become assimilated into their general world knowledge and unconsciously influence individuals' personal values and materialism (Shrum et al., 2005).

Indirect effects of knowledge accessibility on beliefs. When individuals are asked to infer the likelihood of an event and do not have direct information bearing on this possibility, they often retrieve and use previously acquired knowledge that has logical implications for their judgment. However, because they are unlikely to conduct an exhaustive search of memory for judgments and knowledge (Taylor & Fiske, 1978), they base their judgment on the subset of knowledge that comes to mind most quickly and easily. Thus, answering questions that activate different subsets of previously acquired knowledge can influence one's beliefs to which this knowledge pertains (Salancik, 1974; Salancik & Conway, 1974).

In some cases, a single, "informational" proposition can provide a basis for one's beliefs. Wyer and Hartwick (1980) found that exposing participants to a desirable implication of drinking coffee ("coffee makes you alert") or a negative implication ("coffee gives you insomnia") in an initial questionnaire was sufficient to affect the belief that drinking coffee was desirable in an unrelated questionnaire they completed later.

A more formal statement of this process is provided by McGuire's (1960, 1981) syllogistic model of belief organization (see also Wyer, 1974; Wyer & Goldberg, 1970). This conceptualization can provide an accurate quantitative description of the relations among beliefs in two syllogistically related propositions (Wyer, 1970, 1975)[1] and thus of the impact of priming beliefs in one proposition on beliefs in the other. The conceptualization suggests that people's beliefs and evaluations can be influenced by asking them questions that activate particular subsets of knowledge that have implications for these beliefs.

Effects of Stereotype Activation

Person stereotypes. The effects of activated concepts and knowledge on the processing of information are evident in many situations in which information is presented sequentially. For example, people often infer a person's membership in a stereotyped social category before they receive specific information about the person's behavior. These inferences may be based on the person's name or characteristics of the individual's appearance (e.g., sex, age, ethnicity). In such instances, the category might spontaneously activate a subset of attributes that are associated with it, and these attributes could influence their processing of behavioral information that is presented later. Bodenhausen and his colleagues (Bodenhausen & Wyer, 1985; Bodenhausen & Lichtenstein, 1987), for example, showed that assigning a target person a name that identified him as Hispanic (a group that was associated with aggressiveness) led participants to judge the person as guilty of an aggressive crime despite information that called his guilt into question.

The effects of stereotype activation can depend on the consistency of a target's behavior with stereotype-based expectations. Participants in a study by Lambert and Wyer (1990) were told that either a priest or a salesperson had embezzled money and were asked to judge the person's morality. When participants perceived priests in general to be homogeneous with respect to morality, they used their stereotype as a standard of comparison in evaluating the target and judged him to be less moral than the salesperson who had manifested the same behavior. When participants believed that priests vary with respect to morality, however, they judged the priest who had embezzled to be more moral than a salesperson who done so.

Other factors can lead stereotypes to have boomerang effects. Bellezza et al. (2014), for example, discovered that individuals whose behavior deviated from social-role-based expectations were attributed higher status than those whose behavior conformed to expectations. This finding has implications for perception of the endorsers used in advertisements. Y. Chen and Wyer (2020) found that men, who typically occupy an agentic, achievement-oriented social role, are expected not to smile whereas women, who typically fill a warm, nurturing role,

---

[1] If beliefs are defined in units of subjective probability, $P(C) = P(A)P(C/A) + P(\sim A)P(C/\sim A)$, where $P(C)$ and $P(A)$ are beliefs that C and A are true, respectively, and $P(C/A)$ and $P(C/\sim A)$ are beliefs that C is true if A is and is not true, respectively.

are expected to do so. Thus, endorsers whose facial expressions deviate from these role-based expectations (i.e., smiling men and nonsmiling women) are attributed higher social status than endorsers whose facial expressions are stereotype-consistent. Moreover, these attributes influence their willingness to purchase a prestige-related product in an ostensibly unrelated context.

Product stereotypes. Stereotypes are not restricted to persons. In the consumer domain, people can have stereotypes of brands and the companies that manufacture them. The stereotype of a brand, for example, could influence judgments of a brand extension. Lambert and Wyer's (1990) findings suggested that a parent brand's reputation is likely to have a positive influence on an objectively inferior brand extension if consumers perceive the products manufactured by the parent to be highly variable in quality. If consumers perceive the quality of products associated with the parent brand to be consistently high or low, however, their stereotype of the brand is more apt to have a negative, contrast effect on judgments of the extension.

A product's country of origin is another common stereotype. In a study by Hong and Kang (2006), Korean participants were primed with concepts associated with either industriousness or hostility. Then, as part of a different study, they were asked to evaluate either high-tech products or low-tech products (e.g., articles of clothing) that were made in Germany, in Japan, or in an unspecified country. Associating low-tech products with either Germany or Japan increased the participants' evaluations of them when industriousness had been primed but decreased these evaluations when hostility had been primed. Priming hostility reminded participants of Germany's and Japan's behavior in World War II and activated negative attitudes toward them that generalized to the products they produced. In contrast, associating expensive, high-tech products with these countries increased participants' evaluations of the products regardless of which attribute had been primed. Participants' beliefs that the countries typically manufacture superior high-tech products apparently overrode the effects of these stereotype-based attitudes.

The activation of country-of-origin stereotypes can not only have direct effects on product evaluations but also influence the processing of specific product attributes. Hong and Wyer (1989), for example, found that when participants had received information about a product without any a priori objective in mind, the product's country of origin stimulated them to think more carefully about the attribute information that followed, leading these attributes to have greater effect on product evaluations than they otherwise would. A later study (Hong & Wyer, 1990) showed that when a product's country of origin was presented in the context of other product information, it was simply treated as one of several product attributes. When it was presented in isolation, however, participants formed an initial impression of the product on the basis of it. As a result, the country of origin not only had more impact on evaluations in its own right but also affected the interpretation that was given to specific attribute information. Thus, perceptions of attributes whose evaluative implications were ambiguous were biased toward the favorableness of the product's country of origin whereas the implications of unambiguously favorable or unfavorable attributes were interpreted as more extreme. (For other effects of country of origin on the processing of product information, see Li & Wyer, 1994.)

PROCEDURES, GOALS, AND MINDSETS

The processes that underlie the activation and use of previously acquired knowledge are generally independent of the particular type of knowledge that is activated. One type of declarative knowledge, however, deserves further attention. As noted earlier, the concepts that compose a unit of knowledge can pertain not only to objects and attributes but also to events or a sequences of events. Moreover, a sequence of events could pertain either to a specific experience (last night's dinner at Biaggi's) or to a prototypic one (the events that occur at a restaurant). These representations, which often culminate in a particular end state, not only can be used to interpret an experience one observes and to describe the experience to others but also can be proscriptive, describing a sequence of steps that could be performed in order to attain the end state. To this extent, the sequence might function as a plan-goal schema that could be used to determine the means of attaining the goal to which it pertains. (A representation of making tea, for example, might be consulted in deciding the steps involved in doing so, much as one might consult a recipe in deciding how to bake a cake.)

As Kruglanski et al. (2002; see also Wyer & Srull, 1989) noted, the cognitive representation of goals and the means of attaining them is complex. For one thing, a goal can often be attained in more than one way. Thus, more than one plan-goal schema may be associated with the same goal, a condition denoted by Kruglanski et al. as *equifinality*. Second, some of the steps in a plan for attaining one goal could also be contained in a plan for attaining a quite different goal (*multifinality*). Thus, for example, the process of making comparative judgments may be part of both a procedure for deciding which of two animals is more ferocious and a procedure for deciding which of two products is of higher quality.

Finally, goals and the means of attaining them can be defined at several levels of abstraction. Thus, "going over class notes" and "working on homework problems" may be both exemplars of "studying"; similarly, "deciding which animal is larger" and "deciding which product to buy" might both exemplify "making comparative judgments."

Note, however, that the components of a plan are not themselves behaviors. Rather, they are semantic concepts that refer to *subgoals,* the attainment of which can facilitate the attainment of the superordinate goal to which they are relevant. In our example, a person with a goal of "passing an exam" may activate the subgoal concept "studying" that is part of a plan for attaining it. A decision to attain this subgoal might activate a plan consisting of more specific subgoals, and so on. Subgoal concepts that are activated at very concrete levels may stimulate cognitive or motor behavior. I describe these processes in the last section of this chapter.

To the extent that goals exist as concepts in memory, their activation is presumably governed by processes similar to those that govern the activation of other semantic concepts. Nevertheless, several consequences of goal activation may be unique. Förster et al. (2007) provided an extensive review and analysis of research and theory on the effects of goal priming, identifying several distinctions between these effects and the effects of priming semantic concepts more generally. For example, although semantic concepts decrease in accessibility over time (Srull & Wyer, 1979), goal concepts can remain highly accessible until the goal to which they pertain is fulfilled (Chartrand et al., 2008). The Zeigarnik effect (better memory for uncompleted tasks than completed ones) is a well-known example.

Mindsets: Priming Effects of Multifinality

Kruglanski et al.'s (2002) conception of multifinality has obvious implications for the effects of knowledge accessibility on goal-directed behavior. Priming a goal concept might activate a plan with which it is associated and the subgoal concepts that compose this plan. However, these concepts could also be part of a plan for attaining a quite different goal and thus could influence the procedure that is employed in attaining the latter goal under conditions in which the goal is pursued.

This possibility can account for the effect of *behavioral mindsets* of the sort postulated by Wyer and Xu (2010; see also Wyer et al., 2012, 2013). That is, individuals who perform a task in pursuit of one goal presumably engage in behavior associated with the attainment of this goal. However, a more general behavioral concept that is activated by this behavior might be part of a procedure for attaining a quite different goal, increasing the likelihood that this procedure is activated and applied if the latter goal is pursued at a later point in time. This can occur without awareness of the reason this particular procedure was selected. Several examples of relevance to consumer behavior have been reported.

Situationally activated mindsets.
Implemental and deliberative mindsets. The best-known examples of behavioral mindsets were identified by Gollwitzer and his colleagues (Gollwitzer & Bayer, 1999; Gollwitzer et al., 1990). They noted that decision making involves both cognitive

deliberation and implementation. Deliberative processes involve the evaluation of alternative strategies for attaining a goal whereas implemental processes involve the conscious application of a particular strategy while ignoring other possible strategies. Activating these behavioral dispositions in one situation can increase the likelihood of applying them in a second, unrelated situation. Therefore, an implemental mindset can lead persons to focus on the positive consequences of a choice alternative without thinking about the possibility of negative ones (Bayer & Gollwitzer, 2005) and without being distracted by goal-irrelevant features (Bayer et al., 2009). Consequently, it increases people's confidence in their decisions, decreases their consideration of the risk associated with these decisions (Taylor & Gollwitzer, 1995), and increases the extremity of the beliefs that they report (Henderson et al., 2008).

The effect of "shopping momentum," identified by Dhar et al. (2007), exemplifies the effect of an implemental mindset on consumer behavior. Participants at the beginning of an experimental session were given an opportunity to purchase an educational CD or, alternatively, a light bulb. They typically agreed to do so in the first case but not the second. Making these decisions activated an implemental mindset that increased the likelihood of making a similar decision later. Thus, participants who had been induced to buy the educational CD were more willing to purchase a key chain later in the experiment without deliberating on the desirability of doing so.

Comparative judgment mindsets. In many shopping situations, individuals must decide not only whether to make a purchase but also which product to buy. Xu and Wyer (2007, 2008) found that persons who were induced to make a choice between alternatives in one situation acquired a "which-to-choose" mindset that increased their likelihood of deciding which option to select in a later situation without considering the possibility of choosing nothing. This was true regardless of the type of choice they had made earlier. For example, their likelihood of making a choice was increased by deciding which option to choose in an earlier situation but also by deciding which option to reject.

Moreover, inducing participants to decide which of two wild animals they preferred or, alternatively, which animal had more of a physical attribute (e.g., "Which is heavier, a deer or a hippopotamus?") had similar effects. Furthermore, it increased the likelihood of purchasing a snack from among a set of alternatives that were on sale for half price after the experiment.

Variety-seeking. Other aspects of the choice strategy that individuals employ in an initial situation can also affect their consumption behavior. Shen and Wyer (2010) asked participants to answer four questions about animals (e.g., a dog, a lion, an elephant). In one case, the answer to all questions was the same (e.g., "Which animal is the friendliest?" "Which animal is the smallest?"). In another case, all answers differed (e.g., "Which animal is the friendliest?" "Which animal is the largest?"). Later, participants were asked to choose which type of tea they would drink on four successive days. Participants chose a greater variety of teas in the second case than in the first.

Uncertainty avoidance. In a study by Muthukrishnan et al. (2009), participants made a series of gambles. In one case, the payoff associated with each gamble was clear. In a second, the payoff associated with one of the options was uncertain, leading participants to avoid it and inducing an "uncertainty-avoidance" mindset. In an unrelated situation, participants were asked to choose between (a) a product with superior attributes that was made by an unknown company and (b) a product with relatively inferior attributes from a well-known company. Participants with an uncertainty-avoidance mindset were more likely to choose the second option than the first.

Bolstering and counterarguing. Individuals who evaluate the implications of an advertisement might sometimes elaborate on these implications without questioning their validity. At other times, they might try to refute its claims. When individuals do not have a strong a priori attitude toward the product being advertised, their use of these strategies can be influenced by a mindset that was activated in an earlier situation. In a study by Xu and Wyer (2012), participants were first asked to write down their thoughts in response to four statements with which they either agreed (e.g., "Reading is good for the mind," "University tuition should not be increased") or statements with which they disagreed (e.g., "Reading is bad for the mind," "University tuition should be increased"). This activity induced a "bolstering" mindset in the first case and a "counterarguing" mindset in the second. Consequently, participants who encountered an advertisement in an unrelated situation were more persuaded by it in the first condition than in the second. (If the advertising claims were difficult to refute, however, a counterarguing mindset sensitized participants to this difficulty and *increased* the ad's effectiveness.)

Bolstering and counterarguing mindsets can be activated spontaneously by exposing individuals to information with which they either agree or disagree on a priori grounds. In a second study by Xu and Wyer (2012), participants during a presidential election year listened to a speech on economic policy by either the candidate they favored or the candidate they opposed. Thinking about the speech spontaneously activated either a bolstering or a counterarguing mindset, depending on their liking for the candidate. Consequently, when participants later heard a speech by the CEO of Toyota, they were more persuaded by the speech in the first condition than in the second.

Action mindsets. Inducing individuals to take action in a situation as opposed to doing nothing could potentially activate an "action" mindset that affects their decisions to act in an unrelated situation. Albarracín et al. (2008) showed that priming participants with action or inaction words in a word-fragment completion task increased their likelihood of choosing an active task (drawing on a piece of paper) rather than a passive one (resting with eyes closed) in an unrelated situation. Actually engaging in action could have similar effects. For example, activating a disposition to take action can increase the likelihood of engaging in not only trivial behaviors such as doodling and eating when food is present (Albarracín et al., 2008, 2009; Laran, 2010) but also complex behaviors such as solving SAT problems (Albarracín et al., 2008), voting in a presidential election (Noguchi et al., 2011), and consumer switching behavior (Jiang, Zhan, & Rucker, 2014).

A recent application of action mindsets to consumer behavior was conducted by F. Huang and Wyer (2019). Individuals who occupy counter-stereotypic social roles (e.g., female mechanic, a male nurse) are attributed motivation to engage in considerable effort to perform well in role-consistent behavior in order to overcome stereotype-based perceptions that they are unable to do so. Exposure to such individuals primed action-related concepts that influenced the disposition to make unintended purchases in a situation that participants encountered later.

Counterfactual thinking. Counterarguing involves the generation of reasons why the information conveyed in a message is not true. A closely related cognitive process, counterfactual thinking, involves the generation of reasons why a past or anticipated event might not occur. The generation of such reasons in one situation could induce a disposition to think about alternative possibilities in a second situation, consequently increasing uncertainty about what would occur. Hirt et al. (2004) found that participants who had generated reasons why a television sitcom would not win an award were less confident of their prediction that a favored basketball team would win the NBA championship. Analogously, Kray and Galinsky (2003) found that inducing a counterfactual mindset sensitized participants to the disadvantages of pursuing an attractive goal rather than focusing on its advantages alone. (Note that these effects are similar to those of a deliberative mindset; Gollwitzer et al., 1990.)

Conformity. Conforming to others' behavior in pursuit of a goal in one situation can activate a "conformity" mindset that affects the disposition to adopt people's judgments and decisions in a later situation. In a study by Dong et al. (2015), some participants performed synchronized exercises for 10 minutes whereas other participants exercised asynchronously. Engaging in synchronous behavior increased the likelihood of choosing normatively popular options in a product evaluation questionnaire. Two aspects of these effects are of theoretical importance. First, the effects were not evident when participants incidentally performed the exercises synchronously without considering the goal of doing so. That is, a conformity mindset was not induced unless an abstract concept of "doing what others do" was activated. Second, passive observers of synchronous exercising actually conformed *less* to others' opinions in the product evaluation task than observers of asynchronous exercising, Observing synchronous behavior without actually engaging in it apparently sensitized participants to the restriction on freedom imposed by performing the behavior and induced reactance.

Global processing and level of construal. People can potentially interpret information in terms of either general, high-level constructs or concrete, situation-specific ones. These dispositions can be situationally induced. Förster and Dannenberg (2010) reported several studies in which participants were primed to think about either the global aspects of a stimulus or the detailed features that compose it (Navon, 1977). Priming the former disposition led participants to categorize stimuli more broadly when performing tasks they encountered subsequently. Thus, they generated more novel responses in a task that required the generation of unusual category exemplars (Förster & Dannenberg, 2010) and were more likely to judge stimuli as similar to one another rather than using them as standards of comparison (Förster et al., 2008).

An interesting application of this difference was identified by Liberman and Förster (2009). According to construal level theory (Trope & Liberman, 2010), individuals construe stimuli in more abstract terms when the stimuli are psychologically distant. Correspondingly, they might perceive stimuli to be more psychologically distant when the stimuli are construed abstractly or globally. Consistent with this possibility, Liberman and Förster found that inducing individuals to process information globally in an initial situation led them to estimate that a longer time would elapse before they visited a dentist, to feel less close to members of their family, and to estimate a greater geographical distance between their own country and another.

Acquisition. Mindsets can be activated by not only overt behavior but also subjective experience. Hunger provides an example. In a series of studies by Xu (2010; Xu et al., 2015), participants were interviewed either before or after eating lunch. Hungry participants reported a greater liking for food than nonhungry participants did, but did not differ in their liking for nonfood objects. In contrast, they reported a greater desire to acquire *both* food and nonfood objects than nonhungry participants did. Feeling hungry apparently activated a desire to acquire food, and concepts associated with this desire induced an "acquisition" mindset that generalized to nonfood objects as well. In a laboratory study, Xu (2010) observed that participants who had gone without eating for several hours performed a blind taste test that satiated their hunger. Performing this task reduced their desire for food relative to unsatiated participants. However, their desire to acquire both food and nonfood products persisted.

Chronic mindsets. As noted earlier, concepts and knowledge that have been used frequently over a long period of time can become chronically accessible in memory. The effects of situationally induced and chronically accessible knowledge can combine additively to influence judgments (Bargh et al., 1986). Two areas of research provide evidence of the similar effects of both chronic and situationally induced mindsets: the disposition to process information either visually or semantically and the focus on positive versus negative features of a situation.

Visual processing mindsets. When information describes an event that is socially and temporally constrained, people spontaneously form a visual image of the event in the course of comprehending it (Wyer & Radvansky, 1999). There are nevertheless both individual and situationally induced differences in the disposition to code verbal information visually (Childers et al., 1985). Studies by Jiang and his colleagues (Jiang, Adaval, et al., 2014; Jiang et al., 2009; Jiang & Wyer, 2009) exemplified these differences.

In one series of experiments, for example (Jiang et al., 2009; Wyer et al., 2008), some participants were induced to process information either visually or verbally by performing either an embedded figures task or a hidden word task. In other cases, participants' chronic dispositions were inferred from responses to Childers et al.'s (1985) style-of-processing scale. In each case, participants evaluated either a standard computer mouse or an unfamiliar trackball mouse on the basis of a set of verbally described features.

When the verbal descriptions were not accompanied by a picture of the product, participants with a disposition to form visual images (*visualizers*) could easily retrieve a visual image of the familiar mouse from memory and use it as a basis for organizing the product's features but could not form an image of the unfamiliar mouse. Consequently, they evaluated the familiar mouse more favorably than the unfamiliar one. When a picture of the mouse accompanied the verbal descriptions, however, making a visual image of the product easy to form, this difference was not evident. In contrast, participants with a disposition to process information verbally (*verbalizers*) evaluated the two products similarly regardless of their familiarity. These findings were virtually identical regardless of whether dispositions to form visual images were chronic or situationally primed.

Visual information processors, unlike verbal processors, are more sensitive to inconsistencies in the visual images that are formed from different visual perspectives (Jiang et al., 2009). Moreover, they have more extreme emotional reactions to events that elicit visual images from a near perspective than those that elicit images from a more distant one (Jiang & Wyer, 2009).

Culture-related mindsets. Higgins (1997, 1998) identified differences in individuals' disposition to focus on either positive consequences of a decision outcome (a *promotion* orientation) or, alternatively, the avoidance of negative consequences (a *prevention* orientation). These orientations can be both chronic and situationally induced. A promotion focus can be primed by calling people's attention to a discrepancy between their perception of their actual self and the self they would ideally like to have, whereas a prevention focus can be activated by calling people's attention to a discrepancy between their actual self-perception and their perception of the way others would like them to be (Higgins, 1997). However, situational factors can influence these dispositions as well. For example, disposing individuals to thoughts about hopes and aspirations or, alternatively, one's obligations and responsibilities to others can activate promotion and prevention orientations, respectively (Chiu &

Hong, 2013). Moreover, a prevention orientation can be induced by disposing people to think of themselves as members of a group rather than as independent individuals (Briley & Wyer, 2002) or by leading them to use first-person plural pronouns rather than first-person singular pronouns in a sentence-construction task (Gardner et al., 1999).

These orientations can induce a mindset that influences behavior in unrelated situations. Thus, as Briley and Wyer (2002) found, persons who are disposed to think of themselves as independent are likely to maximize the positive consequences of the decisions they make, whereas those who think of themselves as part of a group are more likely to minimize the negative consequences of their decisions. For example, suppose people are given a choice between (a) a product with values of +3 and −3 along two dimensions and (b) a product with values of +1 and −1 along these dimensions. Promotion-oriented individuals are more likely to prefer the former product and prevention-oriented persons are apt to prefer the latter.

However, these orientations can be chronic as well as situationally induced. For example, Asians are likely to have a collectivist orientation and to be chronically prevention focused, whereas North Americans are typically individualistic and have a promotion focus (Triandis, 1995). Asians whose cultural identity is salient are likely to choose the second alternative described in the preceding example, whereas Americans are more inclined to choose the first (Briley et al., 2000). These cultural identities can themselves be situationally activated. For example, bicultural Hong Kong participants' promotion or prevention orientations can be influenced by conducting an experiment in either English or Chinese (Briley et al., 2005).

AFFECT, EMOTIONS, AND BODY SENSATIONS

The effects of knowledge accessibility described thus far can usually be conceptualized in terms of the theoretical formulations of mental representation and semantic information processing summarized earlier in this chapter. However, more recent research requires a much broader conception of how knowledge is represented in memory and how this knowledge is activated. Research conducted within the framework of embodied cognition (Barsalou, 1999; Niedenthal et al., 2005), for example, suggested that judgments and behavior can be based not only on semantic knowledge but also on subjective experiences and that the latter experiences can be elicited by proprioceptive feedback from one's bodily state or movements. Traditional conceptualizations of "knowledge" are too limited to account for many of these effects. For one thing, affective reactions and emotions can affect behavioral decisions in situations that are unrelated to those that elicited them. If the reactions elicited in an earlier situation persist, they can serve as a prime, influencing the processing of information that is encountered later in unrelated situations. Examples of this research and its implications are worth summarizing.

Priming Effects of Affect and Subjective Experience

Subjective experiences, or "feelings," are typically elicited by a cluster of physiological reactions. These reactions can result from sensorimotor stimulation or from cognitions (e.g., the interpretation that is given to new or previously acquired information). In many instances, the feelings elicited are either pleasant or unpleasant. However, they may differ qualitatively as well as in valence, depending on the nature of the situation in which they occur and the interpretation given to it (Roseman et al., 1990). Moreover, people can feel warm or cold, assertive or deferential, tired or energetic, or that a task is either easy or difficult.

The most extensive body of research on the priming of subjective experience shows that positive or negative affect, if activated in one situation, can influence judgments and behavioral decisions in other, objectively unrelated situations (Schwarz & Clore, 1996, 2007; Wyer et al., 1999). That is, affect can be elicited by thoughts about a present or past experience. However, the feelings can persist once the cognitions that elicit them are no longer thought about. Consequently, because people cannot clearly distinguish among the different sources of affect they happen to be experiencing at any given time, they often misattribute the feelings elicited in a past situation to the stimuli they encounter in a later one and use them as information about their reactions to these stimuli. In short, affect elicited by a past situation can have priming effects.

This phenomenon, first identified by Schwarz and Clore (1983), has since been extensively confirmed (for reviews, see Schwarz & Clore, 1996, 2007; Wyer et al., 1999). Its implications for consumer behavior are nevertheless worth noting. Several studies show that the extraneous positive or negative affect consumers happen to be experiencing at the time they consider a product can influence their evaluations of this product (Adaval, 2001, 2003; Pham, 1998; Yeung & Wyer, 2004, 2005). For example, watching an uplifting or depressing television show might influence viewers' reactions to the product being promoted in a commercial that follows it.

For these effects to occur, judgments must be of a type that is *typically* based on affect (Pham, 1998; Adaval, 2001). Thus, if people normally judge a product on the basis of purely functional considerations, they are unlikely to consider the affect they are experiencing to be relevant to an evaluation of the product, and so the affect has little influence. Moreover, if information about a product is presented sequentially, the priming influence of affect is likely to influence the impression that consumers form of it on the basis of the first information they receive, and affective reactions that are experienced subsequently have little impact (Yeung & Wyer, 2004, 2005). Similarly, if people are given a choice of products and the products are presented sequentially, the affect they are experiencing is likely to influence evaluations of the first product they encounter but not subsequent ones (Qiu & Yeung, 2008).

However, affect can be used as information not only about a specific object but also about the situation in which the object is considered (Schwarz, Bless, & Bohner, 1991). That is, happy people often interpret the situation confronting them as favorable and do not believe it is necessary to devote much thought to it. In contrast, unhappy people are likely to infer that the present situation could be problematic and requires attention. Thus, people who feel happy at the time they read a persuasive communication are less influenced by the quality of arguments contained in it than are participants who feel sad (Bless et al., 1990).

Cai et al. (2017) examined further implications of this conceptualization. Participants who were disposed to think about the possibility of a negative life experience were told to imagine receiving some money unexpectedly and to decide whether to spend the money or save it. Happy people judged the present situation to be positive. Consequently, they inferred that the negative experience they were contemplating was unlikely to occur until sometime in the future and decided to save money in anticipation of this future event. In contrast, unhappy participants perceived the experience they were contemplating to be imminent and decided to spend money in order to offset the negative feelings it ostensibly elicited.

Priming Effects of Sensorimotor Stimulation

Affective reactions are only one type of subjective experience that can affect judgments. An impressive body of research, typically conducted within the framework of embodied cognition (for reviews, see Barsalou, 2008; Niedenthal et al., 2005), provides evidence of both direct and indirect effects of bodily sensation on information processing. These effects, which are beyond the scope of most traditional theories of mental representation and knowledge accessibility, can be conceptualized within the framework of perceptual symbol systems (Barsalou, 1999, 2008). To reiterate, this conceptualization assumes that clusters of loosely connected cognitions and behavioral elements (e.g., feelings, bodily states, semantic concepts, visual images, metaphors) are formed in memory and that activating one element in a cluster can increase the accessibility and use of any other element. Thus, not only affective and emotional reactions but also other bodily states and sensory experiences can activate behavioral dispositions and can influence judgments, decisions, and overt behavior with which they are directly or symbolically associated.

This possibility has stimulated extensive research in the area of embodied cognition (for reviews, see Niedenthal et al., 2005). However, three early studies anticipated this research. In one study (Wells & Petty, 1980), participants either nodded or shook their head while hearing a message over headphones, ostensibly to test whether the headphones would fall off. Proprioceptive feedback from their head movements, which was associated with agreement and disagreement, respectively, led them to evaluate the message more favorably in the former condition than in the latter.

Strack et al. (1988) showed that subtle manipulations of individuals' facial expressions (smiling or frowning) elicited positive and negative affective reactions, respectively, and that these reactions influenced their responses to cartoons in the manner implied by Schwarz and Clore's (1983) affect-as-information hypothesis. In an interesting extension of these findings, Shen et al. (2020) found that when unhappy participants imagine themselves engaging in an enjoyable experience, the proprioceptive reactions activated by their mental simulation (smiling) are incompatible with reactions they are already experiencing as a result of their mood. This increases their difficulty of imagining the experience and decreases their evaluations of it. Correspondingly, unhappy participants find it easy to imagine themselves engaging in an unenjoyable activity and increase their evaluation of it relative to conditions in which the simulation is not performed.

Numerous other studies provide examples of the effects of sensorimotor feedback on judgments, many of which are reviewed elsewhere in this handbook (see Chapter 24). For example, situationally manipulating people's posture can influence their judgments of their assertiveness (Stepper & Strack, 1993), bodily movements associated with approach and avoidance can influence memory for positively and negatively valenced stimuli (M. Chen & Bargh, 1999; Förster & Strack, 1997, 1998), carrying a heavy shopping bag can increase estimates of the importance of consumer welfare policies (Zhang & Li, 2012), and warm ambient temperatures can induce feelings of social closeness and a consequent disposition to conform to others' opinions (X. Huang et al., 2014). This is true even if people have no direct contact with the persons whose opinions they adopt. For example, in a field experiment conducted over a 3-year period, individuals at the racetrack were more likely to bet on the favorite on warm days than on cool ones.

Particularly provocative examples of the effects of olfactory stimulation have been identified by S. W. S. Lee and Schwarz (2012) and Liljenquist et al. (2010). For example, S. W. S. Lee and Schwarz (2012) found that exposure to a fishy smell led participants to be suspicious of others' intentions, and Liljenquist et al. (2010) showed that the exposure to clean smells increased donations to charities.

The sensory experiences that underlie responses to stimuli may be elicited spontaneously by the stimulus being judged. For example, people evaluate a cup more favorably when it is positioned in a way that makes it easy to imagine picking it up and using it (Elder & Krishna, 2012), and products are evaluated more favorably when audio descriptions of them come from a direction that matches the position of a picture of them (on the right or the left of a display; Shen & Sengupta, 2014).

The Impact of Equifinality: Goal Generalization Effects of Emotions

As implied by Kruglanski et al.'s (2002) conception of equifinality, a goal can often be attained in more than one way, depending on the situation-specific plan-goal schema that is applied. Thus, a goal might activate a plan for attaining it that is specific to this situation. If this plan is not successful, however, the goal may continue to be accessible in memory (Chartrand et al., 2008) and stimulate goal-directed behavior in a later situation based on a plan that is applicable in this context.

Although this observation does not seem too surprising, its implications have been examined in studies of the effect of incidental emotions on behavior in situations that are unrelated to the conditions that gave rise to these emotions (for reviews, see C. Y. Chen & Pham, 2019; Raghunathan et al., 2006; Wyer et al., 2019). These effects are particularly evident when the emotion is negative, stimulating a desire to reduce or eliminate the unpleasant feelings associated with it. Conceptualizations of mood repair (Andrade, 2005; Cohen et al., 2008; Isen, 1984) assume that when the negative feelings that people happen to be experiencing are undifferentiated and their source is unclear, they employ the procedure that is most easily available at the time (Shen & Wyer, 2010). Negative emotions, however, are qualitatively different, being elicited by a specific set of cognitions that are situation-specific. In this case, the procedure people used to eliminate their negative feelings may depend on the context that gives rise to them.

One conceptualization of the effects of incidental emotions (Wyer et al., 2019; see Raghunathan et al., 2006, for a similar formulation) is based in part on appraisal theories of emotion (Roseman et al., 1990; see also Han et al., 2007). It assumes that an emotion is elicited by a situation-specific appraisal of the situation at hand and activates a situation-specific plan-goal schema that is directed toward an elimination of the conditions that gave rise to it. This situation-specific objective may also activate a concept of a more general goal that it exemplifies and with which other specific plan-goal schemas are associated. If features of a later situation match those to which one of these schemas is applicable, this schema might be activated and the plan it specifies might be executed, leading to goal-directed behavior in this situation that could be inapplicable for eliminating the conditions that initially gave rise to the emotion being experienced.

This possibility is confirmed by research in which participants are induced to experience an emotion in one situation and the influence of this induction on behavior in an unrelated situation is observed. Studies of the effects of negative experiences on compensatory consumption suggested this influence (for a review, see Mandel et al., 2017). For example, when individuals are made to feel unintelligent, they show a preference for products that are used by intelligent people (Gao et al., 2009), and when people feel powerless, they are attracted to objects that are associated with power (Rucker & Galinsky, 2009). Other research has identified the incidental effects of both negative and positive emotions.

Negative emotions.

Sadness and fear. Sadness is often elicited by a sense of loss and may give rise to a desire for positive experiences that might partially compensate for this loss and make the person feel better (Raghunathan & Pham, 1999). Thus, its effects might be similar to those of mood repair motivation. Fear, on the other hand, is elicited by the prospect of a negative event and is likely to induce apprehension and avoidance behavior. Thus, if people are given a choice between (a) a low likelihood of winning a lot of money and (b) a high likelihood of winning a little money, inducing sadness is likely to increase choices of the first option, whereas inducing fear is likely to increase choices of the second.

The effects of incidental fear on consumer behavior have been identified both in the laboratory and in field studies. Inducing fear can increase the effectiveness of advertising appeals that emphasize conformity while decreasing the impact of appeals that emphasize uniqueness (Griskevicius et al., 2009). Generalized avoidance responses resulting from a naturally occurring anxiety-eliciting event (a radiation leak that resulted from a Japanese earthquake) resulted in a decrease in the number of complaints that Chinese consumers registered during the month of its occurrence (Su et al., 2018).

Anger. Anger is elicited by an action that is intentionally performed by another and has potentially negative consequences for oneself (C. A. Smith & Ellsworth, 1985). It induces a disposition to aggress against the perpetrator, and this disposition can generalize to situations in which the perpetrator is not involved. Thus, inducing feelings of anger increased the likelihood that customers complained to a restaurant about a problem they encountered in an unrelated situation (Su et al., 2018).

Jealousy. Jealousy often results from the perception that one's status in a social relationship has been usurped by another (Buss & Haselton, 2005). For example, it may be elicited by evidence that one's significant other is paying undue attention to a potential rival. To this extent, it is likely to activate a goal of regaining attention that is manifested in behavior in situations that are unrelated to the conditions that gave rise to it. For example, inducing people to experience jealousy increased the amount they were willing to pay for an ostentatious luxury product (Wang & Griskevicius, 2014). Moreover, it increased their disposition to wear bizarre-looking glasses to a formal party in which their behavior was likely to receive social disapproval (X. Huang et al., 2017).

Embarrassment. People experience embarrassment when they perform an act in front of others who are likely to consider it foolish or socially inappropriate (Blair & Roese, 2013). It can stimulate a desire to avoid these individuals, particularly if the individuals are ones on whom one wants to make a good impression. Thus, individuals typically spend more time interacting with a physically attractive member of the opposite sex than with someone of average attractiveness, but they spend *less* time interacting with such a person if they are embarrassed (Wan & Wyer, 2015).

Feelings of embarrassment, unlike other self-referent emotions (e.g., guilt or shame), are elicited only when one's inappropriate behavior is observed (Goffman, 1959). Nevertheless, the feelings experienced in the situation, and the avoidance behavior they elicit, could activate a plan-goal schema that influences their behavior in a later situation under conditions in which the schema is applicable. Wan and Wyer (2019) found that individuals whose feelings of embarrassment had been elicited by recalling a past experience were subsequently less willing than control participants to interact with a physically attractive service provider of the opposite sex. This was true even when the provider had no knowledge of the participants' feelings or the conditions that gave rise to them.

A quite different series of studies (Dong et al., 2013) showed that when individuals recall an embarrassing experience they have had and the feelings they experienced are reelicited, they prefer products that symbolically permit them either to "hide their face" (dark sunglasses) or to "save their face" (restorative facial skin cream). Moreover, actually using the facial cream (thereby symbolically saving face) eliminates people's feelings of embarrassment and restores their willingness to interact socially, whereas actually wearing the sunglasses (symbolically hiding their face) does not have this effect.

Guilt and shame. Dong et al.'s (2013) findings showed that symbolically coping with embarrassment can reduce or eliminate it. Symbolically coping with other emotions can have analogous effects. Zhong and Liljenquist (2006), for example, showed that giving participants an opportunity to wash their hands after engaging in an immoral act (symbolically "washing away their sins") eliminated the negative feelings that were elicited by it. In a particularly provocative study, S. W. S. Lee and Schwarz (2010) induced participants to tell a lie either orally or in writing. In a later product evaluation task, participants who had lied orally preferred mouthwash to hand soap whereas those who had lied in writing preferred hand soap to mouthwash. Thus, participants were motivated to "wash away" the guilt they experienced. However, their means of accomplishing this depended on its symbolic appropriateness.

Positive emotions. Although negative emotions are particularly likely to activate a disposition to engage in goal-directed behavior, positive emotions can sometimes simulate goal-directed activity as well. Pride, for example, can induce feelings of superiority and a desire to signal this superiority to others. Thus, it increases people's preferences for products that they are likely to display in public without influencing reactions to products that are used privately (Griskevicius et al., 2010).

Nostalgia is a "mixed" emotion, being elicited by reminiscing about a positive past experience that is unlikely to reoccur. These feelings can induce a desire to prolong the activity that generalizes to unrelated situations, increasing manifestations of patience in a quite unrelated context. Thus, it increases the willingness to wait for service in a restaurant, increases the preference for standard over expedited delivery of a product, and so forth (X. Huang et al., 2016).

PRODUCTIONS: PRIMING AUTOMATIC BEHAVIOR

Judgments and decisions typically lead to overt cognitive and motor behavior, and this behavior can occur without awareness of the reasons it occurred and sometimes without awareness of the behavior itself. The conceptualizations of knowledge accessibility described earlier in this chapter have a difficult time accounting for these effects. In fact, the processes that underlie the generation of overt behavior are quite different.

Several conceptualizations recognize this difference. Strack and Deutsch (2004; see also Gawronski & Bodenhausen, 2011), for example, proposed a dual processing model that distinguishes between an "impulsive" system that operates automatically and is not consciously controlled and a "reflective" system that governs deliberative goal-directed processing. The impulsive system is generally activated and governs behavior when the deliberative system is dormant. However, the conceptualization does not clearly account for how the two systems interface.

A more specific conceptualization of this interface, noted earlier, is suggested by John Anderson's (1983) conceptualization of the acquisition of cognitive skills. (For an earlier extension of this conceptualization in an analysis of "procedural priming," see E. R. Smith, 1984, 1990.) To reiterate, the frequent repetition of behavior over a period of time leads individuals to form cognitive *productions* of the form "if [X], then [Y]", or [X]→[Y] rules, where [X] is a configuration of concepts and experiential features and [Y] is a sequence of cognitive or motor behavior that is elicited automatically when the conditions specified in [X] are met. [Y] can be further decomposed into a sequence of acts, each of which is a precondition for the act that follows it; that is, [Y1]→ [Y2]→ . . . [Yn].

In extending Anderson's conceptualization, Wyer et al. (2012, 2013) assumed that the features that define [X] are responded to as a configural whole and so individuals are not always aware of all of the individual elements that compose it. Moreover, the sequence of behaviors that define [Y] is theoretically activated automatically without conscious deliberation and so individuals might not be aware of their occurrence. In combination, these assumptions suggest that some features that compose the precondition might fortuitously be accessible in memory and thus might activate a production that automatically elicits behavior that is irrelevant or even antagonistic to one's objectives at the time. To borrow an example from Wyer (2018), suppose an automobile driver has two productions, one of which, [Prospect

St., office]→[turn right], is typically applied when driving to work and the other of which, [Prospect St., Kroger's]→[turn left], is applied when going grocery shopping. Then, if the person is on his way to the supermarket but happens to be thinking about a meeting he has the following day at the time he gets to Prospect Street, he might suddenly find himself in front of his office building rather than the store.

The production construct can help to conceptualize the transformation of goal-related decisions into overt behavior. As indicated earlier, a plan-goal representation of the sort postulated by Kruglanski et al. (2002) is composed of a set of subgoal concepts, and these concepts are associated with a series of subgoals at a more specific level, and so on. At a very high level of specificity, however, a subgoal concept may be the precondition of a production that activates overt behavior automatically. For example, the goal of making tea might activate a plan that contains the subgoal concept "boil water" and this in turn might activate a plan containing more specific subgoal concepts (e.g., "fill the pot"). However, the latter concepts could activate plans composed of even more specific goal concepts, each of which is the precondition of a production that elicits behavior that is performed automatically, without cognitive deliberation. Research in several areas exemplifies the effects of such productions.

The Effects of Productions on Overt Behavior

Mimicry. A particularly common example of production-governed behavior is mimicry. The disposition to imitate others' behavior is acquired through social learning at a very early age (Bandura, 1977). However, as a consequence of this learning, the observation of another's incidental behavior may activate a predisposition to copy this behavior without awareness. Evidence of this disposition was obtained in a series of studies by Chartrand and Bargh (1999). In one study, participants performed a task with a confederate who exhibited incidental behaviors (e.g., rubbing the nose, shaking the foot) during the course of the interaction. Participants unconsciously exhibited significantly more of these behaviors when the confederate engaged in them. Moreover, this tendency was particularly pronounced among participants who had a chronic disposition to empathize.

The perception–behavior link. The utility of the production construct lies in its ability to account for conditions in which previously acquired concepts and knowledge, along with features of the immediate situation one encounters, can activate a sequence of behaviors that are performed without awareness of either the conditions that gave rise to it or the behavior itself. The possibility of a "perception–behavior link" was postulated by Dijksterhuis and Bargh (2001). However, a production conception seems equally or more applicable.

A well-known study by Bargh et al. (1996) provides an example. Participants performed a sentence-construction task that required the use of semantic concepts associated with older adults (e.g., "Bingo," "aged"), thereby activating a stereotype whose features were likely to include "does things slowly." These participants walked more slowly to the elevator after leaving the experiment than control participants did. It seems likely that features of the stereotype, along with concepts of the goal of walking to the elevator, composed the precondition of a production of the form [do things slowly, walking]→[walk slowly], therefore eliciting the behavior without consciousness that it was occurring.

This example makes salient a further implication of the conceptualization. Although any number of concepts might be accessible in working memory, the simultaneous presence of situational factors are normally required to activate a production. Features of the specific situation at hand may also be required. In a different experiment by Bargh et al. (1996), Caucasian participants were subliminally exposed to African American faces while performing an arduous perceptual task. After completing the task, they were told that due to a computer malfunction, they would have to perform the task again. These participants displayed more overt expressions of anger and irritation than control participants who had not been exposed to the faces. In another set of studies, however, Colcombe (see Wyer, 2004) discovered that performing the same priming task decreased participants' performance on a task of intellectual ability but increased both their rhythm memory and their basketball shooting ability. In combination, these studies indicate that subliminally priming African American faces activated a stereotype whose features contained "hostile," "unmotivated to succeed intellectually," "motivated to do well in sports," and "interested in music." Thus, features of the stereotype activated different productions and had quite different effects, depending on the applicability of the situational features that accompanied them.

Anchoring effects. Situational factors can activate two different productions, depending on the task at hand. Shen and Wyer (2010) found that ranking stimuli from most to least activated a disposition to consider high-valued stimuli before low-valued ones, whereas ranking from least to most had the opposite effect. Thus, when participants who had performed the ranking tasks were asked to estimate the average price of hotels in a list of 120, they made higher estimates in the first condition than in the second. When participants were asked to describe the strategy they used in making estimates, however, they typically reported that they had considered the hotels in the order they appeared in the list and were apparently unaware of the strategy they had actually employed.

Goals Versus Productions

A central feature of the production conceptualization is that although individuals may consciously engage in goal-directed activity, concepts activated by this activity can become part of the precondition of a production that elicits behavior independently of the goal that gave rise to its activation. A series of studies by Shen et al. (2012) provided evidence of this possibility and, in doing so, distinguished between the effects of deliberative goal-directed processing and automatic, production-based processing. Participants in one experiment first completed a survey that described a number of activities that were either socially desirable (helping to protect the environment) or undesirable (breaking the law). In one condition, they indicated which of two behaviors (joining or not joining in the activity) they would support. In this case, they typically responded "join" to activities that were desirable behaviors and "not join" to ones that were undesirable. In a second condition, participants indicated which of the two behaviors they would oppose. In this case, they responded "join" to undesirable activities and "not join" to desirable ones. Consequently, the desirability of the activities that participants considered and their motor response ("join" vs. "not join") were independently manipulated.

Later, participants were asked if they would join or not join a promotion for a soft drink. In the absence of cognitive load, participants reported greater willingness to join the promotion when the activities they had rated earlier were socially desirable than when they were not. When participants were put under cognitive load, however, they reported greater willingness to join the proportion when they had responded "join" in the previous task than if they had responded "not join," regardless of the implications of their responses in the earlier task. Thus, their responses under cognitive load were apparently activated by a production that elicited behavior automatically and independently of the factors that gave rise to its activation.

A second series of studies separated the effects of goal activation from the effects of production-activated behavior that was independent of a goal. Participants first recalled a past experience that made them feel either happy or sad. After doing so, they shadowed a speech that was delivered either rapidly or slowly. This activity could activate both a *goal* of speaking quickly or slowly and a behavioral *disposition* to speak quickly or slowly that was independent of any goal to which it might be relevant. Thus, positive or negative feelings presumably became associated with the goal that participants were pursuing but were irrelevant to the behavior per se. Finally, participants completed a product evaluation questionnaire. In some cases, they were told that the time to complete the questionnaire was limited, thus activating a goal of working quickly, but in other cases, this goal was not imposed. In all conditions, participants were stopped after 30 seconds and the number of questionnaire items they had completed was recorded.

When the goal of completing the questionnaire quickly was called to participants' attention, the positive or negative affect that they were experiencing while performing the speech-shadowing task influenced their perception of the desirability of working quickly and this, in turn, affected the speed with which they completed the questionnaire. When this goal was not salient, however, their rate of speaking had a positive impact on their speed of completing the questionnaire regardless of the affect with which it was associated. Thus, their behavior in this condition was governed by a production that was applied independently of goal-related considerations.

The distinction between goal-activated and production-activated effects has further implications. In a study by Chartrand and Bargh (1996), for example, participants performed a sentence-construction task that activated concepts associated with either memory or impression formation. Then, they were exposed to a series of behaviors with instructions to read the behaviors, as they would be asked questions about them later. Unexpectedly, however, they were then asked to recall the behaviors. The recall protocols of participants who had been primed with impression-related concepts were similar to those of participants who were consciously motivated to form an impression of the person described by the behaviors (Hamilton et al., 1980); that is, the behaviors they recalled were clustered in terms of the trait concepts they exemplified. This was not true of participants who were primed with memory-related concepts, however. The authors interpreted these findings as evidence that a goal was unconsciously activated by the priming task that influenced behavior on the second task without awareness. However, it seems equally plausible to assume that the concepts activated by the priming task, in combination with the behaviors themselves, activated a cognitive production that elicited behavior without awareness and independently of the goal to which the behavior was relevant.

CONCLUSION

The research involved in this chapter is not intended to be exhaustive but rather to reflect the diversity of phenomena in which knowledge activation plays a role. At the conceptual level, it calls attention to the limitations of existing conceptualizations of knowledge activation in accounting for these phenomena. Given auxiliary assumptions, the effects of behavioral mindsets might be conceptualized in terms of existing theories of declarative knowledge activation. To account for the impact of sensations and bodily feedback on judgments, however, assumptions concerning the nature of the mental representations assumed by these theories must be modified. Moreover, the effects of productions in goal-directed directed behavior are beyond the scope of these conceptualizations. The development of a conceptualization that can integrate the diverse phenomena within a general theory of information processing is a desirable objective of future work.

REFERENCES

Adaval, R. (2001). Sometimes it just feels right: The differential weighting of affect-consistent and affect-inconsistent product information. *Journal of Consumer Research*, 28(1), 1–17. https://doi.org/10.1086/321944

Adaval, R. (2003). How good gets better and bad gets worse: Understanding the impact of affect on evaluations of known brands. *Journal of Consumer Research*, 30(3), 352–367. https://doi.org/10.1086/378614

Adaval, R., & Monroe, K. B. (2002). Automatic construction and use of contextual information for product and price evaluations. *Journal of Consumer Research*, 28(4), 572–588. https://doi.org/10.1086/338212

Adaval, R., & Wyer, R. S. (2004). Communicating about a social interaction: Effects on memory for protagonists' statements and nonverbal behaviors. *Journal of Experimental Social Psychology*, 40(4), 450–465. https://doi.org/10.1016/j.jesp.2003.08.001

Adaval, R., & Wyer, R. S. (2011). Conscious and nonconscious influences of a price anchor: Effects on willingness to pay for related and unrelated products. *Journal of Marketing Research*, 48(2), 355–365. https://doi.org/10.1509/jmkr.48.2.355

Albarracín, D., Handley, I. M., Noguchi, K., McCulloch, K. C., Li, H., Leeper, J., Brown, R. D., Earl, A., & Hart, W. P. (2008). Increasing and decreasing motor and cognitive output: A model of general action and inaction goals. *Journal of Personality and Social Psychology*, 95(3), 510–523. https://doi.org/10.1037/a0012833

Albarracín, D., Wang, W., & Leeper, J. (2009). Immediate increase in food intake following exercise messages.

Obesity, 17(7), 1451–1452. https://doi.org/10.1038/oby.2009.16

Anderson, J. R. (1983). *The architecture of cognition*. Harvard University Press.

Andrade, E. B. (2005). Behavioral consequences of affect: Combining evaluative and regulatory mechanisms. *Journal of Consumer Research, 32*(3), 355–362. https://doi.org/10.1086/497546

Bandura, A. (1977). *Social learning theory*. Prentice Hall.

Barclay, J. R. (1973). The role of comprehension in remembering sentences. *Cognitive Psychology, 4*(2), 229–254. https://doi.org/10.1016/0010-0285(73)90013-3

Bargh, J. A. (1997). The automaticity of everyday life. In R. S. Wyer (Ed.), *Advances in social cognition* (Vol. 10, pp. 1–62). Erlbaum.

Bargh, J. (2017). *Before you know it: The unconscious reasons we do what we do*. Touchstone.

Bargh, J. A., Bond, R. N., Lombardi, W., & Tota, M. E. (1986). The additive nature of chronic and temporary sources of construct accessibility. *Journal of Personality and Social Psychology, 50*(5), 869–878. https://doi.org/10.1037/0022-3514.50.5.869

Bargh, J. A., Chen, M., & Burrows, L. (1996). Automaticity of social behavior: Direct effects of trait construct and stereotype activation on action. *Journal of Personality and Social Psychology, 71*(2), 230–244. https://doi.org/10.1037/0022-3514.71.2.230

Bargh, J. A., & Pietromonaco, P. (1982). Automatic information processing and social perception: The influence of trait information presented outside of conscious awareness on impression formation. *Journal of Personality and Social Psychology, 43*(3), 437–449. https://doi.org/10.1037/0022-3514.43.3.437

Barsalou, L. W. (1999). Perceptual symbol systems. *Behavioral and Brain Sciences, 22*(4), 577–660. https://doi.org/10.1017/S0140525X99002149

Barsalou, L. W. (2008). Grounded cognition. *Annual Review of Psychology, 59*(1), 617–645. https://doi.org/10.1146/annurev.psych.59.103006.093639

Barsalou, L. W., Niedenthal, P. M., Barbey, A. K., & Ruppert, J. A. (2003). Social embodiment. In B. H. Ross (Ed.), *The psychology of learning and motivation* (Vol. 43, pp. 43–92). Academic Press.

Bayer, U. C., Achtziger, A., Gollwitzer, P. M., & Moskowitz, G. B. (2009). Responding to subliminal cues: Do if-then plans facilitate action preparation and initiation without conscious intent? *Social Cognition, 27*(2), 183–201. https://doi.org/10.1521/soco.2009.27.2.183

Bayer, U. C., & Gollwitzer, P. M. (2005). Mindset effects on information search in self-evaluation. *European Journal of Social Psychology, 35*(3), 313–327. https://doi.org/10.1002/ejsp.247

Bellezza, S., Gino, F., & Keinan, A. (2014). The red sneakers effect: Inferring status and competence from signals of nonconformity. *Journal of Consumer Research, 41*(1), 35–54. https://doi.org/10.1086/674870

Blair, S., & Roese, N. J. (2013). Balancing the basket: The role of shopping basket composition in embarrassment. *Journal of Consumer Research, 40*(4), 676–691. https://doi.org/10.1086/671761

Bless, H., Bohner, G., Schwarz, N., & Strack, F. (1990). Mood and persuasion: A cognitive response analysis. *Personality and Social Psychology Bulletin, 16*(2), 331–345. https://doi.org/10.1177/0146167290162013

Bodenhausen, G. V., & Lichtenstein, M. (1987). Social stereotypes and information-processing strategies: The impact of task complexity. *Journal of Personality and Social Psychology, 52*(5), 871–880. https://doi.org/10.1037/0022-3514.52.5.871

Bodenhausen, G. V., & Wyer, R. S. (1985). Effects of stereotypes on decision making and information-processing strategies. *Journal of Personality and Social Psychology, 48*(2), 267–282. https://doi.org/10.1037/0022-3514.48.2.267

Bransford, J. D., Barclay, J. R., & Franks, J. J. (1972). Sentence memory: A constructive versus interpretative approach. *Cognitive Psychology, 3*(2), 193–209. https://doi.org/10.1016/0010-0285(72)90003-5

Bransford, J. D., & Johnson, M. K. (1972). Contextual prerequisites for understanding: Some investigations of comprehension and recall. *Journal of Verbal Learning and Verbal Behavior, 11*(6), 717–726. https://doi.org/10.1016/S0022-5371(72)80006-9

Briley, D. A., Morris, M., & Simonson, I. (2000). Reasons as carriers of culture: Dynamic versus dispositional models of cultural influence on decision making. *Journal of Consumer Research, 27*(2), 157–178. https://doi.org/10.1086/314318

Briley, D. A., Morris, M., & Simonson, I. (2005). Cultural chameleons: Biculturals, conformity motives and decision-making. *Journal of Consumer Psychology, 15*(4), 351–362. https://doi.org/10.1207/s15327663jcp1504_9

Briley, D. A., & Wyer, R. S. (2002). The effect of group membership salience on the avoidance of negative outcomes: Implications for social and consumer decisions. *Journal of Consumer Research, 29*(3), 400–415. https://doi.org/10.1086/344426

Buss, D. M., & Haselton, M. (2005). The evolution of jealousy. *Trends in Cognitive Sciences, 9*(11), 506–507. https://doi.org/10.1016/j.tics.2005.09.006

Cai, F., Yang, Z., Wyer, R. S., & Xu, A. J. (2017). The interactive effects of bitter flavor and mood on the decision to spend or save money. *Journal of Experimental Social Psychology, 70,* 48–58. https://doi.org/10.1016/j.jesp.2016.12.010

Carlston, D. E. (1980). Events, inferences and impression formation. In R. Hastie, T. Ostrom, E. Ebbesen, R. Wyer, D. Hamilton, & D. Carlston (Eds.), *Person memory: The cognitive basis of social perception* (pp. 89–119). Erlbaum.

Carlston, D. E., & Smith, E. R. (1996). Principles of mental representation. In E. T. Higgins & A. W. Kruglanski (Eds.), *Social psychology: Handbook of basic principles* (pp. 184–210). Guilford Press.

Chartrand, T. L., & Bargh, J. A. (1996). Automatic activation of impression formation and memorization goals: Nonconscious goal priming reproduces effects of explicit *task* instructions. *Journal of Personality and Social Psychology, 71*(3), 464–478. https://doi.org/10.1037/0022-3514.71.3.464

Chartrand, T. L., & Bargh, J. A. (1999). The chameleon effect: The perception-behavior link and social interaction. *Journal of Personality and Social Psychology, 76*(6), 893–910. https://doi.org/10.1037/0022-3514.76.6.893

Chartrand, T. L., Huber, J., Shiv, B., & Tanner, R. J. (2008). Nonconscious goals and consumer choice. *Journal of Consumer Research, 35*(2), 189–201. https://doi.org/10.1086/588685

Chen, M., & Bargh, J. A. (1999). Consequences of automatic evaluation: Immediate behavioral predispositions to approach or avoid the stimulus. *Personality and Social Psychology Bulletin, 25*(2), 215–224. https://doi.org/10.1177/0146167299025002007

Chen, C. Y. & Pham, M. T. (2019), Affect regulation and consumer behavior. *Consumer Psychology Review, 2*(1), 114–144. https://doi.org/10.1002/arcp.1050

Chen, Y., & Wyer, R. S., Jr. (2020). The effects of endorsers' facial expressions on status perceptions and purchase intentions. *International Journal of Research in Marketing, 37*(2), 371–385. https://doi.org/10.1016/j.ijresmar.2019.10.002

Childers, T. L., Houston, M. J., & Heckler, S. E. (1985). Measurement of individual differences in visual versus verbal information processing. *Journal of Consumer Research, 12*(2), 125–134. https://doi.org/10.1086/208501

Chiu, C. Y., & Hong, Y. Y. (2013). *Social psychology of culture.* Psychology Press. https://doi.org/10.4324/9781315782997

Cohen, J. B., Pham, M. T., & Andrade, E. B. (2008). The nature and role of affect in consumer behavior. In C. P. Haugtvedt, P. M. Herr, & F. R. Kardes (Eds.), *Handbook of consumer psychology* (pp. 297–348). Lawrence Erlbaum.

Collins, A. M., & Loftus, E. F. (1975). A spreading-activation theory of semantic processing. *Psychological Review, 82*(6), 407–428. https://doi.org/10.1037/0033-295X.82.6.407

Dhar, R., Huber, J., & Khan, U. (2007). The shopping momentum effect. *Journal of Marketing Research, 44*(3), 370–378. https://doi.org/10.1509/jmkr.44.3.370

Dijksterhuis, A., & Bargh, J. A. (2001). The perception-behavior expressway: Automatic effects of social perception on social behavior. *Advances in Experimental Social Psychology, 33,* 1–40. https://doi.org/10.1016/S0065-2601(01)80003-4

Dong, P., Dai, X., & Wyer, R. S. (2015). Actors conform, observers react: The effects of behavioral synchrony on conformity. *Journal of Personality and Social Psychology, 108*(1), 60–75. https://doi.org/10.1037/pspi0000001

Dong, P., Huang, X. I., & Wyer, R. S. (2013). The illusion of saving face: How people symbolically cope with embarrassment. *Psychological Science, 24*(10), 2005–2012. https://doi.org/10.1177/0956797613482946

Ehret, P. J., Monroe, B. M., & Read, S. J. (2015). Modeling the dynamics of evaluation: A multilevel neural network implementation of the iterative reprocessing model. *Personality and Social Psychology Review, 19*(2), 148–176. https://doi.org/10.1177/1088868314544221

Elder, R. S., & Krishna, A. (2012). The "visual depiction effect" in advertising: Facilitating embodied mental simulation through product orientation. *Journal of Consumer Research, 38*(6), 988–1003. https://doi.org/10.1086/661531

Feldman, J. M., & Lynch, J. G. (1988). Self-generated validity and other effects of measurement on belief, attitude, intention and behavior. *Journal of Applied Psychology, 73*(3), 421–435. https://doi.org/10.1037/0021-9010.73.3.421

Förster, J., & Dannenberg, L. (2010). GLOMOsys: A systems account of global versus local processing. *Psychological Inquiry, 21*(3), 175–197. https://doi.org/10.1080/1047840X.2010.487849

Förster, J., & Liberman, N. (2007). Knowledge activation. A. W. Kruglanski & E. T. Higgins (Eds.), *Social psychology: Handbook of basic principles* (2nd ed., pp. 201–231). Guilford Press.

Förster, J., Liberman, N., & Friedman, R. S. (2007). Seven principles of goal activation: A systematic approach to distinguishing goal priming from priming of non-goal constructs. *Personality and Social Psychology Review, 11*(3), 211–233. https://doi.org/10.1177/1088868307303029

Förster, J., Liberman, N., & Kuschel, S. (2008). The effect of global versus local processing styles on assimilation versus contrast in social judgment. *Journal of*

Förster, J., & Strack, F. (1997). Motor actions in retrieval of valenced information: A motor congruence effect. *Perceptual and Motor Skills*, *85*(3 Suppl.), 1419–1427. https://doi.org/10.2466/pms.1997.85.3f.1419

Förster, J., & Strack, F. (1998). Motor actions in retrieval of valenced information: II. Boundary conditions for motor congruence effects. *Perceptual and Motor Skills*, *86*(3 Suppl.), 1423–1426. https://doi.org/10.2466/pms.1998.86.3c.1423

Gao, L., Wheeler, C., & Shiv, B. (2009). The 'shaken self': Product choices as a means of restoring self-view confidence. *Journal of Consumer Research*, *36*(1), 29–38. https://doi.org/10.1086/596028

Gardner, W. L., Gabriel, S., & Lee, A. Y. (1999). "I" values freedom, but "we" value relationships: Self-construal priming mirrors cultural differences in judgment. *Psychological Science*, *10*(4), 321–326. https://doi.org/10.1111/1467-9280.00162

Gawronski, B., & Bodenhausen, G. V. (2011). The associative-popositional evaluation model: Theory, evidence and open questions. *Advances in Experimental Social Psychology*, *44*, 59–127. https://doi.org/10.1016/B978-0-12-385522-0.00002-0

Goffman, E. (1959). The moral career of the mental patient. *Psychiatry*, *22*(2), 123–142.

Gollwitzer, P. M., & Bayer, U. (1999). Deliberative versus implemental mindsets in the control of behavior. In S. Chaiken & Y. Trope (Eds.), *Dual-process theories in social psychology* (pp. 403–422). Guilford Press.

Gollwitzer, P. M., Heckhausen, H., & Steller, S. (1990). Deliberative and implemental mind-sets: Cognitive tuning toward congruous thoughts and information. *Journal of Personality and Social Psychology*, *59*(6), 1119–1127. https://doi.org/10.1037/0022-3514.59.6.1119

Griskevicius, V., Goldstein, N. J., Mortensen, C. R., Sundie, J. M., Cialdini, R. B., & Kenrick, D. T. (2009). Fear and loving in Las Vegas: Evolution, emotion, and persuasion. *Journal of Marketing Research*, *46*(3), 384–395. https://doi.org/10.1509/jmkr.46.3.384

Griskevicius, V., Shiota, M. N., & Nowlis, S. M. (2010). The many shades of rose-colored glasses: An evolutionary approach to the influence of different positive emotions. *Journal of Consumer Research*, *37*(2), 238–250.

Gruder, C. L., Cook, T. D., Hennigan, K. M., Flay, B. R., Alessis, C., & Halamaj, J. (1978). Empirical tests of the absolute sleeper effect predicted from the discounting cue hypothesis. *Journal of Personality and Social Psychology*, *36*(10), 1061–1074. https://doi.org/10.1037/0022-3514.36.10.1061

Hamilton, D. H., Katz, L. B., & Leirer, V. O. (1980). Organizational processes in impression formation. In R. Hastie, T. Ostrom, E. Ebbesen, R. Wyer, D. Hamilton, & D. Carlston (Eds.), *Person memory: The cognitive basis of social perception* (pp. 121–153). Lawrence Erlbaum Associates.

Han, S., Lerner, J. S., & Keltner, D. (2007). Feelings and consumer decision making: The appraisal-tendency framework. *Journal of Consumer Psychology*, *17*(3), 158–168. https://doi.org/10.1016/S1057-7408(07)70023-2

Hasher, L., Goldstein, D., & Toppin, T. (1977). Frequency and the conference of referential validity. *Journal of Verbal Learning and Verbal Behavior*, *16*(1), 107–112. https://doi.org/10.1016/S0022-5371(77)80012-1

Henderson, M. D., de Liver, Y., & Gollwitzer, P. M. (2008). The effects of an implemental mind-set on attitude strength. *Journal of Personality and Social Psychology*, *94*(3), 396–411. https://doi.org/10.1037/0022-3514.94.3.396

Herr, P. M. (1986). Consequences of priming: Judgment and behavior. *Journal of Personality and Social Psychology*, *51*(6), 1106–1115. https://doi.org/10.1037/0022-3514.51.6.1106

Higgins, E. T. (1997). Beyond pleasure and pain. *American Psychologist*, *52*(12), 1280–1300. https://doi.org/10.1037/0003-066X.52.12.1280

Higgins, E. T. (1998). Promotion and prevention: Regulatory focus as a motivational principle. In M. P. Zanna (Ed.), *Advances in experimental social psychology* (Vol. 30, pp. 1–46). Academic Press. https://doi.org/10.1016/S0065-2601(08)60381-0

Higgins, E. T., Bargh, J. A., & Lombardi, W. (1985). The nature of priming effects on categorization. *Journal of Experimental Psychology: Learning, Memory, and Cognition*, *11*(1), 59–69. https://doi.org/10.1037/0278-7393.11.1.59

Higgins, E. T., Rholes, W. S., & Jones, C. R. (1977). Category accessibility and impression formation. *Journal of Experimental Social Psychology*, *13*(2), 141–154. https://doi.org/10.1016/S0022-1031(77)80007-3

Hintzman, D. L. (1986). "Schema abstraction" in a multiple-trace model. *Psychological Review*, *93*(4), 411–428. https://doi.org/10.1037/0033-295X.93.4.411

Hirt, E. R., Kardes, R., & Markman, K. D. (2004). Activating a mental simulation mindset through generation of alternatives: Implications for debiasing in related and unrelated domains. *Journal of Experimental Social Psychology*, *40*(3), 374–383. https://doi.org/10.1016/j.jesp.2003.07.009

Hong, S., & Kang, D. K. (2006). Country-of-origin influences on product evaluations: The impact of animosity and perceptions of industriousness and brutality on judgments of typical and atypical products. *Journal of Consumer Psychology*, *16*(3), 232–239. https://doi.org/10.1207/s15327663jcp1603_5

Hong, S., & Wyer, R. S. (1989). Effects of country-of-origin and product-attribute information on product evaluation: An information processing perspective. *Journal of Consumer Research*, *16*(2), 175–187. https://doi.org/10.1086/209206

Hong, S., & Wyer, R. S. (1990). Country of origin, attributes, and product evaluations: The effects of time delay between information and judgments. *Journal of Consumer Research*, *17*(3), 277–288. https://doi.org/10.1086/208557

Huang, F., & Wyer, R. S. (2019). *Encountering counter-stereotypic individuals increases purchase behavior* [Unpublished manuscript]. Hong Kong Polytechnic University.

Huang, X., Dong, P., & Wyer, R. S. (2017). Competing for attention: The effects of jealousy on preference for attention-grabbing products. *Journal of Consumer Psychology*, *27*(2), 171–181. https://doi.org/10.1016/j.jcps.2016.12.001

Huang, X., Huang, Z., & Wyer, R. S. (2016). Slowing down in the good old days: The effect of nostalgia on consumer patience. *Journal of Consumer Research*, *43*(3), 372–387. https://doi.org/10.1093/jcr/ucw033

Huang, X., Zhang, M., Hui, M. K., & Wyer, R. S. (2014). Warmth and conformity: The effects of ambient temperature on product preferences and financial decisions. *Journal of Consumer Psychology*, *24*(2), 241–250. https://doi.org/10.1016/j.jcps.2013.09.009

Isen, A. M. (1984). Toward understanding the role of affect in cognition. In R. S. Wyer & T. K. Srull (Eds.), *Handbook of social cognition* (Vol. 3, pp. 179–236). Erlbaum.

Jacoby, L. L., Kelley, C. M., Brown, J., & Jasechko, J. (1989). Becoming famous overnight: Limits on the ability to avoid unconscious influences of the past. *Journal of Personality and Social Psychology*, *56*(3), 326–338. https://doi.org/10.1037/0022-3514.56.3.326

Jain, S. P., Mathur, P., & Maheswaran, D. (2009). The influence of consumers' lay theories on approach/avoidance motivation. *Journal of Marketing Research*, *46*(1), 56–65. https://doi.org/10.1509/jmkr.46.1.56

Jiang, Y., Adaval, R., Steinhart, Y., & Wyer, R. S. (2014). Imagining yourself in the scene: The interactive effects of goal-driven self-imagery and visual perspectives on consumer behavior. *Journal of Consumer Research*, *41*(2), 418–435. https://doi.org/10.1086/676966

Jiang, Y., Steinhart, Y., & Wyer, R. S. (2009). *The role of visual and semantic processing strategies in consumer information processing* [Unpublished manuscript]. Hong Kong University of Science and Technology.

Jiang, Y., & Wyer, R. S., Jr. (2009). The role of visual perspective in information processing. *Journal of Experimental Psychology*, *45*(3), 486–495. https://doi.org/10.1016/j.jesp.2008.12.006

Jiang, Y., Zhan, L., & Rucker, D. D. (2014). Power and action orientation: Power as a catalyst for consumer switching behavior. *Journal of Consumer Research*, *41*(1), 183–196. https://doi.org/10.1086/675723

Kray, L. J., & Galinsky, A. D. (2003). The debiasing effect of counterfactual mindsets: Increasing the search for disconfirmatory information in group decisions. *Organizational Behavior and Human Decision Processes*, *91*(1), 69–81. https://doi.org/10.1016/S0749-5978(02)00534-4

Kruglanski, A. W., Shah, J. Y., Fishbach, A., Friedman, R., Chun, W. Y., & Sleeth-Keppler, D. (2002). A theory of goal systems. In M. P. Zanna (Ed.), *Advances in experimental social psychology* (Vol. 34, pp. 331–378). Academic Press.

Kumkale, G. T., & Albarracín, D. (2004). The sleeper effect in persuasion: A meta-analytic review. *Psychological Bulletin*, *130*(1), 143–172. https://doi.org/10.1037/0033-2909.130.1.143

Lambert, A. J., & Wyer, R. S. (1990). Stereotypes and social judgment: The effects of typicality and group heterogeneity. *Journal of Personality and Social Psychology*, *59*(4), 676–691. https://doi.org/10.1037/0022-3514.59.4.676

Laran, J. (2010). The influence of information processing goal pursuit on postdecision affect and behavioral intentions. *Journal of Personality and Social Psychology*, *98*(1), 16–28. https://doi.org/10.1037/a0017422

Lee, A. Y., & Labroo, A. A. (2004). The effect of conceptual and perceptual fluency on brand evaluation. *Journal of Marketing Research*, *41*(2), 151–165. https://doi.org/10.1509/jmkr.41.2.151.28665

Lee, S. W. S., & Schwarz, N. (2010). Dirty hands and dirty mouths: Embodiment of the moral-purity metaphor is specific to the motor modality involved in moral transgression. *Psychological Science*, *21*(10), 1423–1425. https://doi.org/10.1177/0956797610382788

Lee, S. W. S., & Schwarz, N. (2012). Bidirectionality, mediation, and moderation of metaphorical effects: The embodiment of social suspicion and fishy smells. *Journal of Personality and Social Psychology*, *103*(5), 737–749. https://doi.org/10.1037/a0029708

Li, W. K., & Wyer, R. S. (1994). The role of country of origin in product evaluations. Informational and standard-of-comparison effects. *Journal of Consumer Psychology*, *3*(2), 187–212. https://doi.org/10.1016/S1057-7408(08)80004-6

Liberman, N., & Förster, J. (2009). The effect of psychological distance on perceptual level of construal. *Cognitive Science*, *33*(7), 1330–1341. https://doi.org/10.1111/j.1551-6709.2009.01061.x

Liljenquist, K., Zhong, C. B., & Galinsky, A. D. (2010). The smell of virtue: Clean scents promote reciprocity and charity. *Psychological Science*, *21*(3), 381–383. https://doi.org/10.1177/0956797610361426

Loftus, E. F., & Palmer, J. C. (1974). Reconstruction of automobile destruction: An example of the interaction between language and memory. *Journal of Verbal Learning and Verbal Behavior*, *13*(5), 585–589. https://doi.org/10.1016/S0022-5371(74)80011-3

Lombardi, W. J., Higgins, E. T., & Bargh, J. A. (1987). The role of consciousness in priming effects on categorization. *Personality and Social Psychology Bulletin*, *13*(3), 411–429. https://doi.org/10.1177/0146167287133009

Mandel, N., Rucker, D. D., Levav, J., & Galinsky, A. D. (2017). The compensatory consumer behavior model: How self-discrepancies drive consumer behavior. *Journal of Consumer Psychology*, *27*(1), 133–146. https://doi.org/10.1016/j.jcps.2016.05.003

Markus, H. R., & Kitayama, S. (1991). Culture and the self: Implications for cognition, emotion and motivation. *Psychological Review*, *98*(2), 224–253. https://doi.org/10.1037/0033-295X.98.2.224

Martin, L. L., Seta, J. J., & Crelia, R. A. (1990). Assimilation and contrast as a function of people's willingness and ability to expend effort in forming an impression. *Journal of Personality and Social Psychology*, *59*(1), 27–37. https://doi.org/10.1037/0022-3514.59.1.27

McGuire, W. J. (1960). A syllogistic analysis of cognitive relationships. In M. J. Rosenberg & C. I. Hovland (Eds.), *Attitude organization and change* (pp. 140–162). Yale University Press.

McGuire, W. J. (1981). The probabilogical model of cognitive structure and attitude change. In R. E. Petty, T. M. Ostrom, & T. C. Brock (Eds.), *Cognitive responses in persuasion* (pp. 291–307). Erlbaum.

Menon, G., & Raghubir, P. (2003). Ease of retrieval as an automatic input in judgments: A mere-accessibility framework. *Journal of Consumer Research*, *30*(2), 230–243. https://doi.org/10.1086/376804

Mukhopadhyay, A., & Johar, G. V. (2005). Where there is a will, is there a way? Effects of lay theories of self-efficacy on setting and keeping resolutions. *Journal of Consumer Research*, *31*(4), 779–786. https://doi.org/10.1086/426611

Mussweiler, T. (2003). Comparison processes in social judgment: Mechanisms and consequences. *Psychological Review*, *110*(3), 472–489. https://doi.org/10.1037/0033-295X.110.3.472

Muthukrishnan, A. V., Wathieu, L., & Xu, A. J. (2009). Ambiguity aversion and preference for established brands. *Management Science*, *55*(12), 1933–1941. https://doi.org/10.1287/mnsc.1090.1087

Navon, D. (1977). Forest before trees: The precedence of global features in visual perception. *Cognitive Psychology*, *9*(3), 353–383. https://doi.org/10.1016/0010-0285(77)90012-3

Niedenthal, P. M., Barsalou, L. W., Winkielman, P., Krauth-Gruber, S., & Ric, F. (2005). Embodiment in attitudes, social perception, and emotion. *Personality and Social Psychology Review*, *9*(3), 184–211. https://doi.org/10.1207/s15327957pspr0903_1

Noguchi, K., Handley, I. M., & Albarracín, D. (2011). Participating in politics resembles physical activity: General action patterns in international archives, United States archives, and experiments. *Psychological Science*, *22*(2), 235–242. https://doi.org/10.1177/0956797610393746

Norman, D. A., & Bobrow, D. G. (1979). Descriptions: An intermediate stage in memory retrieval. *Cognitive Psychology*, *11*(1), 107–123. https://doi.org/10.1016/0010-0285(79)90006-9

Nunes, J. C., & Boatright, P. (2004). Incidental prices and their effect on willingness to pay. *Journal of Marketing Research*, *41*(4), 457–466. https://doi.org/10.1509/jmkr.41.4.457.47014

Pham, M. T. (1998). Representativeness, relevance and the use of feelings in decision making. *Journal of Consumer Research*, *25*(2), 144–159. https://doi.org/10.1086/209532

Qiu, C., & Yeung, C. W. M. (2008). Does mood influence everything and finally nothing? *Journal of Consumer Research*, *34*(5), 657–669. https://doi.org/10.1086/522096

Raghunathan, R., & Pham, M. T. (1999). All negative moods are not equal: Motivational influences of anxiety and sadness on decision making. *Organizational Behavior and Human Decision Processes*, *79*(1), 56–77.

Raghunathan, R., Pham, M., & Corfman, K. P. (2006). Informational properties of anxiety and sadness, and displaced coping. *Journal of Consumer Research*, *32*(4), 596–601. https://doi.org/10.1086/500491

Reber, R., Schwarz, N., & Winkielman, P. (2004). Processing fluency and aesthetic pleasure: Is beauty in the perceiver's processing experience? *Personality and Social Psychology Review*, *8*(4), 364–382. https://doi.org/10.1207/s15327957pspr0804_3

Roseman, I. J., Spindel, M. S., & Jose, P. E. (1990). Appraisals of emotion-eliciting events: Testing a theory of discrete emotions. *Journal of Personality and Social Psychology*, *59*(5), 899–915. https://doi.org/10.1037/0022-3514.59.5.899

Ross, L., Lepper, M. R., Strack, F., & Steinmetz, J. (1977). Social explanation and social expectation: Effects of real and hypothetical explanations on subjective likelihood. *Journal of Personality and Social Psychology*, *35*(11), 817–829. https://doi.org/10.1037/0022-3514.35.11.817

Ross, M. (1989). Relation of implicit theories to the construction of personal histories. *Psychological Review*, *96*(2), 341–357. https://doi.org/10.1037/0033-295X.96.2.341

Rucker, D. D., & Galinsky, A. D. (2009). Conspicuous consumption versus utilitarian ideals: How different levels of power shape consumer behavior. *Journal of Experimental Social Psychology*, *45*(3), 549–555. https://doi.org/10.1016/j.jesp.2009.01.005

Salancik, G. R. (1974). Inferences of one's attitude from behavior recalled under linguistically manipulated cognitive sets. *Journal of Experimental Social Psychology*, *10*(5), 415–427. https://doi.org/10.1016/0022-1031(74)90010-9

Salancik, G. R., & Conway, J. (1974). Attitude inferences from salient and relevant cognitive content about behavior. *Journal of Personality and Social Psychology*, *32*(5), 829–840.

Schank, R. C., & Abelson, R. P. (1977). *Scripts, plans, goals and understanding*. Erlbaum.

Schooler, J. W., & Engstler-Schooler, T. Y. (1990). Verbal overshadowing of visual memories: Some things are better left unsaid. *Cognitive Psychology*, *22*(1), 36–71. https://doi.org/10.1016/0010-0285(90)90003-M

Schwarz, N. (2004). Metacognitive experiences in consumer judgment and decision making. *Journal of Consumer Psychology*, *14*(4), 332–348. https://doi.org/10.1207/s15327663jcp1404_2

Schwarz, N., Bless, H., & Bohner, G. (1991). Mood and persuasion: Affective states influence the processing of persuasive communications. In M. P. Zanna (Ed.), *Advances in experimental social psychology* (Vol. 24, pp. 161–199). Academic Press. https://doi.org/10.1016/S0065-2601(08)60329-9

Schwarz, N., Bless, H., Strack, F., Klumpp, G., Rittenauer-Schatka, H., & Simons, A. (1991). Ease of retrieval as information: Another look at the availability heuristic. *Journal of Personality and Social Psychology*, *61*(2), 195–202. https://doi.org/10.1037/0022-3514.61.2.195

Schwarz, N., & Clore, G. L. (1983). Mood, misattribution, and judgments of well-being: Informative and directive functions of affective states. *Journal of Personality and Social Psychology*, *45*(3), 513–523. https://doi.org/10.1037/0022-3514.45.3.513

Schwarz, N., & Clore, G. L. (1996). Feelings and phenomenal experiences. In E. T. Higgins & A. Kruglanski (Eds.), *Social psychology: A handbook of basic principles* (pp. 433–465). Guilford Press.

Schwarz, N., & Clore, G. L. (2007). Feelings and phenomenal experiences. In A. W. Kruglanski & E. T. Higgins (Eds.), *Social psychology: Handbook of basic principles* (2nd ed., pp. 385–407). Guilford Press.

Shen, H., Labroo, A., & Wyer, R. S., Jr. (2020). So difficult to smile: Why unhappy people avoid enjoyable activities. *Journal of Personality and Social Psychology*, *119*(1), 23–39. https://doi.org/10.1037/pspa0000186

Shen, H., & Sengupta, J. (2014). The crossmodal effect of attention on preferences: Facilitation versus impairment. *Journal of Consumer Psychology*, *40*(5), 885–903. https://doi.org/10.1086/673261

Shen, H., & Wyer, R. S. (2010). Cognitive and motivational influences of past behavior on variety seeking. *Journal of Consumer Psychology*, *20*(1), 33–42. https://doi.org/10.1016/j.jcps.2009.07.002

Shen, H., Wyer, R. S., & Cai, F. (2012). The generalization of deliberative and automatic behavior: The role of procedural knowledge and affective reactions. *Journal of Experimental Social Psychology*, *48*(4), 819–828. https://doi.org/10.1016/j.jesp.2012.02.005

Sherman, S. J., Ahlm, K., Berman, L., & Lynn, S. (1978). Contrast effects and the relationship to subsequent behavior. *Journal of Experimental Social Psychology*, *14*(4), 340–350. https://doi.org/10.1016/0022-1031(78)90030-6

Sherman, S. J., Skov, R. B., Hervitz, E. F., & Stock, C. B. (1981). The effects of explaining hypothetical future events: From possibility to probability to actuality and beyond. *Journal of Experimental Social Psychology*, *17*(2), 142–158. https://doi.org/10.1016/0022-1031(81)90011-1

Shrum, L. J. (2001). Processing strategy moderates the cultivation effect. *Human Communication Research*, *27*(1), 94–120. https://doi.org/10.1093/hcr/27.1.94

Shrum, L. J., Burroughs, J. E., & Rindfleisch, A. (2005). Television's cultivation of material values. *Journal of Consumer Research*, *32*(3), 473–479. https://doi.org/10.1086/497559

Shrum, L. J., & Lee, J. (2012). Television's persuasive narratives: How television influences values, attitudes and beliefs. In L. J. Shrum (Ed.), *The psychology of the entertainment media: Blurring the lines between entertainment and persuasion* (2nd ed., pp. 147–167). Routledge. https://doi.org/10.4324/9780203828588

Shrum, L. J., Wyer, R. S., & O'Guinn, T. (1998). The effects of watching television on perceptions of social reality. *Journal of Consumer Research*, *24*, 447–458. https://doi.org/10.1086/209520

Smith, C. A., & Ellsworth, P. C. (1985). Patterns of cognitive appraisal in emotion. *Journal of Personality and Social Psychology*, *48*(4), 813–838. https://doi.org/10.1037/0022-3514.48.4.813

Smith, E. R. (1984). Model of social inference processes. *Psychological Review*, *91*(3), 392–413. https://doi.org/10.1037/0033-295X.91.3.392

Smith, E. R. (1990). Content and process specificity in the effects of prior experiences. In T. K. Srull & R. S. Wyer (Eds.), *Advances in social cognition* (Vol. 3, pp. 1–59). Lawrence Erlbaum Associates.

Smith, E. R., & DeCoster, J. (1998). Knowledge acquisition, accessibility, and use in person perception and stereotyping: Simulation with a recurrent connectionist network. *Journal of Personality and Social Psychology, 74*(1), 21–35. https://doi.org/10.1037/0022-3514.74.1.21

Smith, E. R., & DeCoster, J. (1999). Associative and rule-based processing: A connectionist interpretation of dual-processing models. In S. Chaiken & Y. Trope (Eds.), *Dual-process theories in social psychology* (pp. 323–336). Guilford Press.

Spiro, R. J. (1977). Remembering information from text: The "state of schema" approach. In R. C. Anderson, R. J. Spiro, & W. E. Montague (Eds.), *Schooling and the acquisition of knowledge* (pp. 137–166). Lawrence Erlbaum Associates.

Srull, T. K., & Wyer, R. S. (1979). The role of category accessibility in the interpretation of information about persons: Some determinants and implications. *Journal of Personality and Social Psychology, 37*(10), 1660–1672. https://doi.org/10.1037/0022-3514.37.10.1660

Srull, T. K., & Wyer, R. S. (1980). Category accessibility and social perception: Some implications for the study of person memory and interpersonal judgments. *Journal of Personality and Social Psychology, 38*(6), 841–856. https://doi.org/10.1037/0022-3514.38.6.841

Stepper, S., & Strack, F. (1993). Proprioceptive determinants of emotional and nonemotional feelings. *Journal of Personality and Social Psychology, 64*(2), 211–220. https://doi.org/10.1037/0022-3514.64.2.211

Strack, F., & Deutsch, R. (2004). Reflective and impulsive determinants of social behavior. *Personality and Social Psychology Review, 8*(3), 220–247. https://doi.org/10.1207/s15327957pspr0803_1

Strack, F., Martin, L. L., & Stepper, S. (1988). Inhibiting and facilitating conditions of the human smile: A nonobtrusive test of the facial feedback hypothesis. *Journal of Personality and Social Psychology, 54*(5), 768–777. https://doi.org/10.1037/0022-3514.54.5.768

Su, L., Wan, L. C., & Wyer, R. S. (2018). The contrasting influences of incidental anger and fear on responses to a service failure. *Psychology and Marketing, 35*(9), 666–675. https://doi.org/10.1002/mar.21114

Taylor, S. E., & Fiske, S. T. (1978). Salience, attention and attribution: Top of the head phenomena. In L. Berkowitz (Ed.), *Advances in experimental social psychology* (Vol. 11, pp. 249–288). Academic Press. https://doi.org/10.1016/S0065-2601(08)60009-X

Taylor, S. E., & Gollwitzer, P. M. (1995). Effects of mind-set on positive illusions. *Journal of Personality and Social Psychology, 69*(2), 213–226. https://doi.org/10.1037/0022-3514.69.2.213

Triandis, H. C. (1995). *Individualism and collectivism*. Westview.

Trope, Y., & Liberman, N. (2010). Construal-level theory of psychological distance. *Psychological Review, 117*(2), 440–463. https://doi.org/10.1037/a0018963

Tulving, E. (1983). *Elements of episodic memory*. Oxford University Press.

Tversky, A., & Kahneman, D. (1974). Judgment under uncertainty: Heuristics and biases. *Science, 185*(4157), 1124–1131. https://doi.org/10.1126/science.185.4157.1124

Wan, L. C., & Wyer, R. S. (2015). Consumer reactions to attractive service providers: Approach or avoid? *Journal of Consumer Research, 42*(4), 578–595. https://doi.org/10.1093/jcr/ucv044

Wan, L. C., & Wyer, R. S. (2019). *What is beautiful is good but I still want to avoid it: The role of incidental emotions in social interaction* [Unpublished manuscript]. Chinese University of Hong Kong.

Wang, Y., & Griskevicius, V. (2014). Conspicuous consumption, relationships, and rivals: Women's luxury products as signals to other omen. *Journal of Consumer Research, 40*(5), 834–854. https://doi.org/10.1086/673256

Wänke, M., Bohner, G., & Jurowitsch, A. (1997). There are many reasons to drive a BMW: Does imagined ease of argument generation influence attitudes? *Journal of Consumer Research, 24*(2), 170–177. https://doi.org/10.1086/209502

Wells, G. L., & Petty, R. E. (1980). The effects of overt head movements on persuasion: Compatibility and incompatibility of responses. *Basic and Applied Social Psychology, 1*(3), 219–230. https://doi.org/10.1207/s15324834basp0103_2

Winkielman, P., & Cacioppo, J. T. (2001). Mind at ease puts a smile on the face: Psychophysiological evidence that processing facilitation elicits positive affect. *Journal of Personality and Social Psychology, 81*(6), 989–1000. https://doi.org/10.1037/0022-3514.81.6.989

Winkielman, P., Schwarz, N., Fazendeiro, T. A., & Reber, R. (2003). The hedonic marking of processing fluency: Implications for evaluative judgment. In J. Musch & K. C. Klauer (Eds.), *The psychology of evaluation: Affective processes in cognition and emotion* (pp. 189–217). Erlbaum.

Wyer, R. S. (1970). The quantitative prediction of belief and opinion change: A further test of a subjective

Wyer, R. S. (1974). *Cognitive organization and change: An information processing approach*. Taylor & Francis.

Wyer, R. S. (1975). Functional measurement analysis of a subjective probability model of cognitive functioning. *Journal of Personality and Social Psychology*, 31(1), 94–100. https://doi.org/10.1037/h0076161

Wyer, R. S. (2004). *Social comprehension and judgment: The role of situation models, narratives and implicit theories*. Erlbaum.

Wyer, R. S. (2007). Principles of mental representation. In A. Kruglanski & E. T. Higgins (Eds.), *Social psychology: Handbook of basic principles* (2nd ed., pp. 285–307). Guilford Press.

Wyer, R. S. (2008). The role of knowledge accessibility in cognition and behavior: Implications for consumer information processing. In C. Haugtvedt, P. Herr, & F. Kardes (Eds.), *Handbook of consumer psychology* (pp. 31–76). Erlbaum.

Wyer, R. S. (2018). The activation and use of declarative and procedural knowledge. In C. Haugtvedt, P. Herr, & F. Kardes (Eds.), *Handbook of consumer psychology* (2nd ed). Psychology Press.

Wyer, R. S. (2019). Theory and method in consumer information processing. In F. Kardes, P. Herr, & N. Schwarz (Eds.), *Handbook of consumer research methods* (pp. 107–131). Routledge. https://doi.org/10.4324/9781351137713-6

Wyer, R. S., Adaval, R., & Colcombe, S. J. (2002). Narrative-based representations of social knowledge: Their construction and use in comprehension, memory and judgment. In M. P. Zanna (Ed.), *Advances in experimental social psychology* (Vol. 34, pp. 131–197). Academic Press. https://doi.org/10.1016/S0065-2601(02)80005-3

Wyer, R. S., & Carlston, D. E. (1979). *Social cognition, inference and attribution*. Erlbaum.

Wyer, R. S., Clore, G. L., & Isbell, L. M. (1999). Affect and information processing. In M. P. Zanna (Ed.), *Advances in experimental social psychology* (Vol. 31, pp. 1–77). Academic Press.

Wyer, R. S., Dong, P., Huang, X., Huang, Z., & Wan, L. C. (2019). The effect of incidental emotions on judgments and behavior in unrelated situations: A review. *Journal of the Association for Consumer Research*, 4(2), 198–207. https://doi.org/10.1086/701889

Wyer, R. S., & Goldberg, L. (1970). A probabilistic analysis of the relationships among beliefs and attitudes. *Psychological Review*, 77(2), 100–120. https://doi.org/10.1037/h0028769

Wyer, R. S., & Hartwick, J. (1980). The role of information retrieval and conditional inference processes in belief formation and change. In L. Berkowitz (Ed.), *Advances in experimental social psychology* (Vol. 13, pp. 241–284). Academic Press. https://doi.org/10.1016/S0065-2601(08)60134-3

Wyer, R. S., Hung, I. W., & Jiang, Y. (2008). Visual and verbal processing strategies in comprehension and judgment. *Journal of Consumer Psychology*, 18(4), 244–257. https://doi.org/10.1016/j.jcps.2008.09.002

Wyer, R. S., & Radvansky, G. A. (1999). The comprehension and validation of social information. *Psychological Review*, 106(1), 89–118. https://doi.org/10.1037/0033-295X.106.1.89

Wyer, R. S., & Schwartz, S. (1969). Some contingencies in the effects of the source of a communication upon the evaluation of that communication. *Journal of Personality and Social Psychology*, 11(1), 1–9. https://doi.org/10.1037/h0027048

Wyer, R. S., Shen, H., & Xu, A. J. (2013). The role of procedural knowledge in the generalization of social behavior. In D. Carlston (Ed.), *Oxford handbook of social cognition* (pp. 257–281). Oxford University Press.

Wyer, R. S., & Srull, T. K. (1989). *Memory and cognition in its social context*. Erlbaum.

Wyer, R. S., & Xu, A. J. (2010). The role of behavioral mindsets in goal-directed activity: Conceptual underpinnings and empirical evidence. *Journal of Consumer Psychology*, 20(2), 107–125. https://doi.org/10.1016/j.jcps.2010.01.003

Wyer, R. S., Xu, A. J., & Shen, H. (2012). The effects of past behavior on future goal-directed activity. In M. P. Zanna & J. Olson (Eds.), *Advances in experimental social psychology* (Vol. 46, pp. 237–283). Academic Press. https://doi.org/10.1016/B978-0-12-394281-4.00014-3

Xu, A. J. (2010). *The influence of past behavior on future behavior: A mind-set perspective* [Unpublished doctoral dissertation]. University of Illinois at Urbana-Champaign.

Xu, A. J., Schwarz, N., & Wyer, R. S. (2015). Hunger promotes acquisition of nonfood objects. *Proceedings of the National Academy of Sciences of the United States of America*, 112(9), 2688–2692. https://doi.org/10.1073/pnas.1417712112

Xu, A. J., & Wyer, R. S. (2007). The effect of mindsets on consumer decision strategies. *Journal of Consumer Research*, 34(4), 556–566. https://doi.org/10.1086/519293

Xu, A. J., & Wyer, R. S. (2008). The comparative mindset: From animal comparisons to increased purchase intentions. *Psychological Science*, 19(9), 859–864. https://doi.org/10.1111/j.1467-9280.2008.02169.x

Xu, A. J., & Wyer, R. S. (2012). The role of bolstering and counterarguing mindsets in persuasion. *Journal*

(Wyer, R. S. probability model. *Journal of Personality and Social Psychology*, 16(4), 559–570. https://doi.org/10.1037/h0030064)

of *Consumer Research*, *38*(5), 920–932. https://doi.org/10.1086/661112

Yeung, C. W. M., & Wyer, R. S. (2004). Affect, appraisal and consumer judgment. *Journal of Consumer Research*, *31*(2), 412–424. https://doi.org/10.1086/422119

Yeung, C. W. M., & Wyer, R. S. (2005). Does loving a brand mean loving its products? The role of brand-elicited affect in brand extension evaluations. *Journal of Marketing Research*, *42*(4), 495–506. https://doi.org/10.1509/jmkr.2005.42.4.495

Zhang, M., & Li, X. (2012). From physical weight to psychological significance: The contribution of semantic activations. *Journal of Consumer Research*, *38*(6), 1063–1075. https://doi.org/10.1086/661768

Zhong, C. B., & Liljenquist, K. (2006). Washing away your sins: Threatened morality and physical cleansing. *Science*, *313*(5792), 1451–1452. https://doi.org/10.1126/science.1130726

CHAPTER 3

INTENTIONAL BEHAVIORISM: A RESEARCH METHODOLOGY FOR CONSUMER PSYCHOLOGY

Gordon R. Foxall

A continuing concern of scholars is the need for knowledge to be publicly available. Any attempt to hide knowledge, understandable as it may be in a commercially driven world, inhibits researchers' attempts to replicate findings, to be inspired to undertake complementary investigations, and to communicate quickly and instructively with other scientists and the general public (e.g., Ziman, 1968). The complexities involved in the distinction between "private" and "public" scientists, working respectively in industrial and academic settings, have been recognized for decades, but there are gray areas—for example, the existence of proprietary psychometric tests, scientific instruments that are not in the public domain—which inhibit the flow of knowledge. In a penetrating analysis of public knowledge that discusses not only the problem but also potential routes to its solution, Kahle and Kahle (2009) stated the position eloquently: "Exploratory research has maximum impact when conducted in a context of freedom of speech, freedom of communication, freedom to learn, and freedom to teach" (p. 137; see also Ziman, 1978). It remains, however, a difficulty that is not easily resolved—after all, the issues it embeds might impinge on national security and wealth as well as academics' capacity to pursue research with disinterested curiosity. One way in which academic researchers' freedom may be enhanced is the development of metatheoretical frameworks, domains of conceptualization and analysis in which competing theories can proliferate, multiple hypotheses are presented for empirical testing, and academic debate may be maximized. In this way, the stimulus to the public interchange of ideas, the intercommunication and cross-fertilization of contending theories, and the interfacing of research methodologies can flourish.

This chapter is intended to contribute in a modest way to this process of intellectual cooperation. Its aim is to provide a framework within which consumer psychology theories might be developed, hypotheses tested, and research results evaluated.

BACKGROUND

Philosopher John Stuart Mill (1859) famously pointed out that "he who knows only his own side of the case knows little of that" (p. 35). As consumer psychologists, we do not have the luxury of ignoring alternative explanations: We are necessarily immersed in them. The challenge is to make use of differing perspectives, paradigms, and methodologies whilst approaching a unified conception of our subject matter. This requires a philosophical perspective. Philosophy often appears abstruse and far removed from the realities of research in psychology, especially empirical work that is focused on understanding the realities of consumer behavior and the practical implications that follow. However, this chapter exemplifies the importance of taking

https://doi.org/10.1037/0000262-003
APA Handbook of Consumer Psychology, L. R. Kahle (Editor-in-Chief)
Copyright © 2022 by the American Psychological Association. All rights reserved.

a philosophical stance by exploring some of the implications of doing the most natural thing in consumer psychology—attempting to explain behavior in cognitive terms.

There are many ways of explaining consumer behavior, ranging from the positivist application of behaviorism to some areas of habitual choice to the exploration of cognitive decision making to hermeneutic and other interpretivist perspectives. Although consumer psychology from time to time considers the philosophical implications of its explanatory modes, there is little or no systematic grounding in the metatheoretical implications of our quest for knowledge. I want to point out the ramifications of even the simplest explanatory attributions we make on the basis of our everyday understanding. It is not only commonplace to ascribe observed behavior to mental events such as attitudes and intentions; it is, in the social milieu in which most consumer psychologists are embedded, the overwhelmingly natural thing to do. Yet much depends on the interpretation we attach to everyday terms and the theoretical background of our use of them in research, for there are many cognitive theories, each offering a unique interpretation of what mental terms like "desire" and "belief" refer to and how they are to be employed in the process of explanation. Some theories, for instance, assume that desires and beliefs are actually existing mental events that operate as causes of overt behavior, while others make no ontological claims but propose that the only sense in which humans, animals, and machines have minds is that their behavior can be better predicted by the attribution to them of appropriate desires and beliefs. Among applied researchers, such theoretical underpinnings as these remain implicit and even unconscious, but it is important we become aware of them and evaluate our research findings accordingly. How then do we, as consumer psychologists, come to trust the knowledge generated by our research, evaluate it, and compare it with other means of understanding? This chapter examines these questions in a specific domain: the generation of consumer knowledge and comprehension in terms of cognitive structures and processes and the degree of confidence we can place in the knowledge yielded by research conducted within this framework.

A familiar problem arises, for instance, in the case of consumers' self-reporting their past, present, and future cognitions and behaviors. Problems with self-report arise when consumers make inaccurate statements about their behavior and motivations and, especially, when they seek to predict their future actions (see, for example, Araujo et al., 2017; Lucas, 2018). Cognitive explanations are particularly vulnerable to inaccuracies of this kind, particularly when consumers report the beliefs and emotions that led to their marketplace choices. We are less concerned here with overcoming these drawbacks, which are probably ineliminable in their entirety, than with exploring alternative routes to knowledge that do not rely on self-report, notably the objective investigation of situational influences on consumer choice and the development of interpretations based upon it.

The aim of this chapter is to make explicit the inevitable presence of an underlying philosophy of research in consumer psychology; the importance of metatheoretical considerations in planning, executing, and interpreting empirical investigations; and the ways in which the philosophies of mind and psychology contribute to scientific work. The chapter also articulates a specific interdisciplinary approach to explanation in consumer psychology, *intentional behaviorism*, and emphasizes the necessity of consumer research being based on a cognitive economic psychology. But its main aim is not to advocate a particular approach per se; rather it is to articulate some of the issues involved in establishing consumer psychology knowledge and to act as a springboard for debate.

Our choice of particular techniques with which to explore the nature of consumer behavior and our interpretations of the findings they generate depend on the overarching philosophy of knowledge that guides our scholarly endeavors. We owe it to our discipline and those who use our work to understand better the underlying assumptions on which it rests and the metatheoretical basis that enables us to draw conclusions and proffer explanations. Usually, we take for granted the foundations of our research, and the existence of a widely shared paradigm encourages us in failing to make them explicit either to ourselves or others. There are times in the development of a discipline, however, when we need to take stock of our knowledge base and the presumptions on which it rests, not only to assess what we have achieved but to advance through the adoption of new perspectives and techniques. The adoption of a particular methodology carries with it epistemological assumptions and constraints of which we should be aware. A prominent case in point is the assumption that consumer psychology ought to rest on the theories and findings of cognitive psychology, and it is to this prevailing conception that this chapter draws attention.

Consumer psychology has been cognitive in orientation at least since the field was transformed by the models introduced in the 1960s by Howard and Sheth (1969) and Nicosia (1966), which have provided the paradigm for numerous textbooks and research programs ever since. Although there have been additions to the range of methodologies available to consumer researchers since then—some, like modern behaviorism, essentially antithetical to cognitivism and others, such as hermeneutics, more compatible with it—the cognitive revolution in psychology generally has made a continuing mark on the investigation of consumer behavior. We seldom pause to question the assumption that consumer action is invariably preceded and caused by cognitive activities like believing and intending or that consumer behavior must at least be consistent with prior processes of rational intellectualization. Comprehending why we hold these views, and the knowledge base on which they rest, will assist our critical judgment of the outputs of cognitive consumer psychology, of the uses to which we put them, and our planning and execution of further research.

An important recognition of the philosophy of science during the course of the 20th century has been the theory-ladenness of observation (notably by Popper, 1934/1959), the realization that the data generated in empirical research are not neutral with respect to explanations but are likely to have been selected and refined in accordance with an underlying conceptual perspective. Scientific findings might, therefore, have relevance and significance only within a particular framework of conceptualization and analysis and be irrelevant to other evaluation of methodologies. An implication of Kuhn's (1970) work on the paradigmatic nature of scientific knowledge is that scientists working during an era marked by a particular approach to normal science might well have been unaware of the basic assumptions on which their work rested, unaware of alternative explanations. Although consumer psychologists periodically have been conscious of these matters, as was the case in the 1980s, the continuing lesson is that it is all too tempting to accept the methodological imperatives adopted by one's intellectual community and to effectively ignore alternatives. Knowing the other "side of the case" is essential to intellectual progress, but being able to integrate alternate viewpoints into a single methodology is particularly fruitful. The chapter aims at this outcome.

The chapter delves first into the nature of cognitive explanation. In particular, it draws upon the approach to cognitive science advanced by the philosopher of mind and psychology Daniel Dennett (1969, 1978, 1987), who has sought to justify cognitive accounts of behavior, which rely on apparently unobservable influences in the face of the predominance of materialist and physicalist perspectives on the nature of scientific inquiry (the "mind–body problem"). Dennett's approach, based on the famous intentional stance, is critically evaluated as a means of justifying and making sense of the behavioral processes involved in consumption. Dennett argued that the behavior of a system (e.g., a consumer) is predicable by the attribution to it of the intentionality—namely the desires and beliefs—it "ought" to have, given its history and current circumstances. The resulting intentional account is idealized, that is, based on assumptions about the rationality of the system. If it is to be useful in guiding psychological research, it must be "cashed out" in terms of variables capable of being employed in empirical research. Other perspectives on cognitive explanation are also examined in light of their general capacities to make human behavior intelligible and predictable and, in particular, to explicate consumer behavior. The perspective is, as far as possible, interdisciplinary and integrative, with an emphasis on making sense of contemporary consumer choice. In this endeavor, it stresses the need to employ alternative sources of explanation, such as behaviorism and hermeneutics, even in a predominantly cognitivist view of the mainsprings of consumer action. As a result, the chapter proposes an integrative explanatory system, "intentional behaviorism," which finds an important role for both behaviorist and interpretive accounts in the cognitive explanation of consumer behavior. It develops Dennett's idea of a two-stage research strategy but draws on behaviorist and interpretivist contributions to psychology, as well as schools of economic thought including behavioral economics and neuroeconomics. The aim is not to dogmatically present a blueprint for consumer psychology but to illumine the kinds of issues and range of disciplines necessary for the informed conduct of research. Hence, the approach articulated here is critically evaluated in accordance with its ability to guide consumer research and to raise the issues that underlie methodologies of investigation.

How we know what we think we know is a perennial issue in the philosophy of knowledge that underpins scientific inquiry in all fields. The question is important because it underpins the way in which we explain consumer behavior and attempt to modify it. What is consumer behavior and what are its causes? If we wish to avoid the tricky issue of the nature of causation we might rephrase this question to explore the variables of which consumer behavior is a function. Focusing on the functional relationships that link behavior with environmental stimuli or intrapersonal cognition at least provides a pragmatic dimension for understanding how consumer behavior comes to be as it is and how it can be changed. Since cognitive psychology remains the dominant paradigm for the study of consumers, it is necessary to concentrate on it but not to the exclusion of alternative avenues to understanding. Just as multiple perspectives can complement one another in the achievement of a comprehensive account of consumer choice, so too can additional behavioral sciences, such as neurophysiology, economics, and picoeconomics, elucidate research in consumer psychology.

There are not only different paradigms in psychology but also different criteria for the intersubjective establishment of credible knowledge:
Popperian falsificationalism (Popper, 1934/1959), interpretive success (e.g., Foxall, 1995b; Schwartz-Shea, 2012; Wilson, 2019), the fruitfulness of one's research program (Lakatos, 1978), and so on. All of these have vociferous advocates and also denigrating opponents. (One of the most informative introductions to interpretive consumer research and its alternatives remains Hirschman & Holbrook, 1992; for further analysis, see Holbrook & Hirschman, 1993).

I aim to show that the growth of knowledge in consumer psychology depends on the use not only of more than one paradigm but also of more than one means of establishing the truth value of our statements based on research. My procedure is to employ one of the most developed proposals for gaining psychological knowledge, based on Dennett's "three kinds of intentional psychology," as a template and, by critically examining it, to show how a methodology of psychological research might develop in order to generate sound knowledge of consumer behavior.

INTENTIONALITY: THE ESSENCE OF COGNITIVE EXPLANATION

How can we be sure that our cognitive interpretations are firmly based? Although cognition is the lingua franca of everyday discourse and, ever since the inauguration of the Enlightenment, humans have been encouraged to see their behavior as the outcome of reasoning, the veracity of explanations in terms of desires and beliefs cannot be taken for granted. *Cognitive explanation* refers to unobservables, so-called mental variables that cannot enter directly into an empirical investigation, leading some authors to comment on their "dubious ontology" and fictional status (e.g., Posner 1990; Skinner, 1953). Before we can look into how cognitive explanation might be grounded philosophically, we should be aware of the nature of the account of behavior it offers.

Intentionality and Intensionality

Intentional explanation involves the interpretation or explanation of action as a function of desires and beliefs. If an individual has a desire, d, and the belief that a specific action, *a*, will accomplish *d*, then they will perform *a* (Rosenberg, 2016, p. 39). The desire and belief in question are reasons for the action: They are invoked in explanations of the action because they make it reasonable. These mental states, as opposed to physical stimuli, constitute reasons for the action, and they explain it by rendering it intelligible to others. (Intentional explanation is more complex than this brief summary suggests, and the belief/desire model is not accepted by all philosophers of mind, e.g. Searle, 2001.) Malle et al. (2011) provided an insightful account. (For an exposition in terms of intentional behaviorism, see Foxall, 2016d, especially Chapter 11.) This folk-psychological account of behavior provides a familiar, everyday means of predicting and making sense of our own and others' actions in terms of their intentions. But our primary interest as consumer psychologists is the philosophical basis of this particular source of elucidation. Although intentions feature strongly in many of the social-psychological models that underpin much consumer research, such as the multi-attribute theories of attitude-intention-behavior causation (e.g., Fishbein & Ajzen, 2010), the idea of intentionality has a rather more restricted meaning in the philosophy of mind.

In the philosophical context, *intentionality* refers to entities, like desires and beliefs, that are *about* something other than themselves. It deals with mental states that are transitive: For example, Stephen worries *that* the train will be late, he fears *that* he will miss the movie, and he believes *that* he should have taken the car. This *aboutness* is an important element of intentionality, which accounts in part for the uniqueness of intentional explanation. Verbs that refer to mental phenomena, such as *worries*, *fears*, and *believes*, are known in philosophy as "attitudes" (a very different usage from that with which we are familiar in the context of social psychology). Something else that demarcates this approach to explanation is that each intentional attitude is followed by a proposition, a clause that begins with *that* and which defines what it is that the attitude is about. Hence, the complete sentence "Stephen worries that the train will be late" is known as a propositional attitude (Russell, 1940).

Constructions of this kind are at the heart of social cognitive explanation and are the reason it differs so markedly from behaviorist accounts.

These intentional expressions have characteristics that make them unique sources of explanation. In the case of a nonintentional sentence such as the scientific statement "This element is mercury," it is perfectly legitimate to substitute the synonym "quicksilver" for "mercury" so that the sentence reads, "This element is quicksilver." The sentence means the same—has the same "truth value"—either way. Extensional sentences like these, which contain no intentional verb, are central to much scientific discourse, including behaviorism. In philosophical terminology, the substitutability of the propositions renders the sentences "referentially transparent." However, if we say, "Susan believes that this element is mercury," we cannot also say, "Susan believes that this element is quicksilver," without altering its truth value. Susan may not know that mercury is quicksilver, so making what in another context would be a permissible substitution is not allowable when we are dealing with intentional sentences. Such sentences are said to be "referentially opaque," and they are the very substance of both cognitive and interpretivist accounts of behavior. Hence, the distinction between extensional and intentional discourse provides the means of delineating intentional and therefore cognitive *explanation* from that presented by behaviorism. This linguistic difference has given rise to a dichotomy between the physical and the mental that is often used to differentiate the realm of natural science from that of psychology (Brentano, 1874/1995). However, intentionality is not the mark of the mental: There are psychological states, such as depression and anxiety, that have no intentional object but are rather general moods or dispositions (see Crane, 1998, 2001, 2009, 2016).

Equating intentionality with aboutness is only an approximate clue to its meaning. To understand why, we need to make one more distinction: that between intentionality and intensionality. While the second is an observation about sentences, the first concerns the aboutness of mental states, the real desires and beliefs that we are aware of qualitatively and subjectively. On this understanding, intentionality is a matter of "that capacity of the mind by which mental states refer to, or are about, or are of objects and states of affairs in the world other than themselves" (Searle, 2004, p. 28). It is an ability of the mind itself, rather than statements (sentences) about it. Therefore, "Intentionality-with-a-t is . . . that property of the mind by which it is directed at or about or of objects and states of affairs in the world independent of itself" (Searle, 2004, pp. 174–175). Intensionality is a matter of the verbal expression of intentionality in sentences (propositional attitudes) that include intentional idioms (attitudes), such as *desires* or *believes*, and propositions that refer to an intentional object. Searle (2004) continued, "Intensionality-with-an-s is opposed to *extensionality*. It is a property of certain sentences, statements, and other linguistic entities by which they fail to meet certain tests of extensionality" (p. 175; see also Searle, 1983, 1994).

Tests of Extensionality

Searle also set out two criteria for delimiting extensionality. The first, which we have already noted, is the *substitution criterion*: The truth value of a sentence is unaffected by the substitution of one term for another, providing the two terms refer to the same entity (i.e., have the same extension). In the statement "I can see the Morning Star," it is legitimate to substitute "Evening Star" for "Morning Star" because both these terms both refer to the same entity, namely, the planet Venus, which is the extension of the three expressions. Such a substitution leaves the truth value of the statement intact. "The Morning Star" is extensional with respect to substitution, or, as it is sometimes put, the sentence exhibits extensionality. But it is not possible to rewrite the sentence, "Thomas believes that that is the Morning Star" as "Thomas believes that that is the Evening Star" while preserving the truth value of the sentence. Thomas might not be aware that these two terms corefer (or are codesignatives). This sentence, which includes a verb relating to a mental state, is said to be *intensional* with respect to "The Morning Star" and therefore fails to meet the substitution criterion (Searle, 2004, pp. 175–176).

Searle's second criterion is that of *existential inference*. Objects referred to in an extensional sentence must actually exist in order for the truth of the sentence to be ascertained. The truth value of "Petra expects a visit from her lawyer" requires the existence of a person who is Petra's lawyer who is scheduled to visit her. This sentence is extensional because the real existence of its extension, Petra's lawyer, makes it possible to determine its truth value. As Searle put it, its conditions of satisfaction are met by our ascertaining whether there is an actual person who is Petra's lawyer. However, the sentence "Petra expects the tooth fairy to visit her" does not carry the inference that there must be a person, the tooth fairy, who will soon be paying her a visit. Petra can believe this whether or not it is the case, for the conditions of satisfaction of this intensional sentence do not depend upon what exists: They inhere in what Petra expects.

Intentional systems. For Searle, intentionality characterizes subjective experience, mental states and events are real entities, and desires and beliefs influence behavior. He contrasted this with intensionality which is a matter of linguistic convention. Another philosopher of mind, Daniel Dennett (1969), based his work on radically variant ontological assumptions. Eschewing mentality as a property of actual mental processing and qualitative experience, Dennett made the sole criterion of any entity's having intentionality as susceptibility to prediction through the attribution to it of desires and beliefs that are appropriate to its situation. Such predictability is, therefore, the defining mark of what he calls an *intentional system* (Dennett, 1978). The ascribed desires and beliefs need not exist in any sense other than their capacity to predict such a system that may be a person, an animal, a neural system, or a computer program. Desires and beliefs ascribed to such a system in order to predict its behavior are those it "ought" to have, given its history and circumstances. Intensional systems are sufficiently rational that their behavior is explicable by reference to what their intentionality is *about* (Dennett, 1987, pp. 240–242). This approach is Dennett's intentional stance. We should contrast this with the "contextual stance" on which radical behaviorism rests: Behavior is predictable in so far as it is shown to be environmentally determined (Foxall, 1999). This is consistent with the fundamental explanatory stance of radical behaviorism, the "three-term contingency":

$$S^D \rightarrow R \rightarrow S^{r/p},$$

where S^D is a discriminative stimulus, R is a response, and $S^{r/p}$ are the reinforcing and punishing outcomes of R. This contextual stance does not assume that the system it predicts is necessarily rational, only that its behavior is sensitive to its consequences. Both the intentional and the contextual strategies are objective, third-personal stances. Exhibit 3.1 summarizes the essential explanatory differences between radical behaviorism and cognitivism.

A fundamental division drawn by Dennett (1969) separates the personal and subpersonal levels of explanation. The personal level refers to an entire system: its behavior, desires, and beliefs. The subpersonal, by contrast, refers to the brain and nervous system. Whereas personal level activities are described in intentional terms, subpersonal entities and their behavior are the subjects of extensional language. However, it is key to Dennett's thought to recognize that a central component of his work has sought to vindicate the use of intentional language to describe and explain subpersonal systems and their behavior. As we have seen, his highly significant methodological innovation, the intentional stance, employs intentionality to predict the behavior of systems.

We shall encounter Dennett's work again, but at this juncture it is useful to contrast the two conceptions of intentionality we have discussed. In language that draws a distinct separation between Searle's and Dennett's views, Galen Strawson (2010) wrote, "*No states of nonexperiential entities are ever really about anything at all*" (p. 330, italics in original). Strawson's thesis is that while intentionality entails aboutness, aboutness of itself does not signal intentionality. So the flower dances of bees cannot be intentional even if we construe them as being about places or flowers or nectar. Searle himself argued that subjectively experienced desires and beliefs constitute what he called *underived* intentionality, whereas *derived* intentionality is what we attribute to nonmental entities like bee dances.

EXHIBIT 3.1

Radical Behaviorism Versus Cognitivism

What is distinctive about behaviorism's mode of explanation is that it presents environmental influences on behavior as operating directly, without the mediation of representations. So radical behaviorism portrays behavioral responses as a function of the extrapersonal rewarding and punishing consequences of similar behavior previously enacted. In this way, radical behaviorism avoids any suggestion of a teleological explanation: A current behavior is explained not by reference consequences that it will generate in the future but by those that have followed behavior of this kind in the past. There is no suggestion, therefore, that behavior is explicable by reference to intentionality or that intrapersonal states other than physiological changes are in any way implicated. Moreover, behavioral control by the environment is captured by extensional language, and any attempt to describe it via beliefs and desires is redundant (e.g., Skinner, 1950, 1977; for comment, see Foxall, 1999; Smith, 1994). What really matters is that

> this reasoning exclusively in terms of external parameters (stimulus and response) assumes that the processing by the system does not add anything at all to the information content of the input; that is, the performance of the system can be completely characterized externally without recourse to the internal properties of the system. (Compiani, 1996, pp. 46–47)

Cognitivism's perspective diverges acutely. Indeed, the *representation* of the environment prior to behavior is its defining characteristic, involving both basic perceptual and advanced symbolic information processing (de Gelder, 1996). As Compiani (1996) put it,

> Cognitivism recovers the richness and the extension of the internal representation and of the system's internal processes, [entailing] a greater emphasis on the processes of self-organization of the cognitive system. In this context, the contribution of the system increases and, indeed, the hierarchy advocated by behaviorism is inverted in the sense that now the system's processing ability may dominate and completely upset the information content of the stimulus. (p. 47)

Only intentional language can hope to capture this level of complexity.

Strawson, however, counted this as inconsistent with the understanding of intentionality as a characteristic of mental states. In addition to aboutness, he maintained, intentionality requires conscious experience: "The paradigm cases of underived intentionality are conscious or experiential states while the paradigm cases of derived intentionality are nonexperiential things like inscriptions, books, road signs, and computers, programmed robots, and so on" (Strawson, 2010, p. 328). The import of Strawson's view is that because intentionality requires subjective experience, it amounts to more than the ascription of mental terms to a system with the aim of predicting what it will do. Ascribing mental states to subpersonal entities like neurons may be a convenient *façon de parler*, but it is not a scientific argument.

Although I have reservations about Dennett's conception of intentionality, he also proposed a framework for the intentional explanation of behavior that is instructive. In a paper written in 1981, he distinguished "three kinds of intentional psychology" (Dennett, 1981). The first, *folk psychology*, encapsulates our everyday understanding that desires and beliefs can be enlisted in making our own and others' behavior intelligible, predicting its outcomes and making the appropriate responses. Dennett's second and third kinds of intentional psychology are *intentional systems theory* (IST) and *subpersonal cognitive psychology* (SPCP). IST is an idealized account of behavior in terms of the intentionality an individual "ought" to have given their history and current circumstances. We have already encountered this idea. IST contains constructs in the form of *abstracta* (e.g., desires and beliefs), which allow behavior to be predicted and explained. Abstracta are real in the sense in which other theoretical entities (e.g., centers of gravity and parallelograms of forces, which contribute to prediction and explanation) are real even though they do not possess the kind of reality that tables and chairs have. The idealized picture so gained is cashed out in SPCP, which relies on another category of concepts, *illata*, which are physical entities that are intentionally characterizable. Neurons, for instance, are conceptualized in neurophysiology as wholly physical, but, Dennett argued, they can also be attributed the desires and beliefs that ensure their predictability. Illata are therefore open to portrayal in terms of the physical stance, which portrays items in material terms, precisely as does physics, and those of the intentional stance, through which prediction is achieved by treating the entity as an intentional system and then making appropriate ascriptions of desires and beliefs.

The proposal of illata as concepts that on one level refer to physical entities (e.g., electrons, neurons) but on another allows them to be understood in terms of intentionality is an ingenious contribution to the philosophy of mind. Alternating between the physical stance, which uses extensional language, and the intentional stance, which renders them amenable to prediction, Dennett's idea probably approximates as closely as is currently possible a reconciliation of the explanatory divide presented by the competing claims of extensional and intentional modes of expression. The delineation of three intentional psychologies—the first empirically based in observation, the second an idealized portrayal of the intentional system, and the third an attempt to translate this view into hypotheses that can be tested in psychological research—suggests a sequential research strategy for consumer psychology. The following critique of Dennett's proposal is intended to lead to a blueprint for such a strategy conceived of as a confluence of extensional and intentional reasoning, therefore known as *intentional behaviorism*.

Critical perspectives. For all its merits, Dennett's philosophical basis for psychology is not a perfect model for intentional behaviorism. First, Dennett's scheme has no place for a formal extensional model as a prelude to IST. In intentional behaviorism, this is provided by the theoretical minimalism of the extensional model of consumer choice, which provides an empirical understanding of the environmental factors of which economic behavior is a function and thereby indicates when an intentional interpretation becomes necessary and what it has to explain. Second, Dennett's proposal commits the mereological fallacy in the third stage of his research strategy (SPCP) in which illata clearly belong to the physical stance yet are given an intentional characterization (Bennett & Hacker, 2003; see also Bennett, 2007; Bennett & Hacker, 2007). The mereological fallacy is the application to the parts of a system of attributes that properly belong only to the system as a whole. I have dealt with the mereological fallacy in this connection at length in *Perspectives* *on Consumer Choice: From Behavior to Action, From Action to Agency* (see Foxall, 2016d). Desires and beliefs are constructs that belong properly only at the personal level of exposition, which is the level of intensional explanation, and their ascription to other levels is improper. The means of overcoming this problem is to consider the sphere of applicability of intentional explanation and to confine the applicability of intentional reasoning accordingly. This invokes the criterion of intensionality. Intentional behaviorism avoids this by rigorously maintaining the separation of levels of exposition. Third, Dennett suggested rather vaguely that illata will form the variables of actual psychological theories and lead to empirical work. I want to emphasize and show how it is possible that the extensional sciences of neuroscience and behaviorology (especially as they eventuate in neuroeconomics and operant behavioral economics) are the vehicles for empirical research. However, Dennett was correct in suggesting that there has to be an empirical outcome of the intended research strategy.

Several specific criticisms of Dennett's approach are apparent. First, his essentially "externalist" program, characterized by the intentional stance, is claimed to apply to any entity for which it produces accurate predictions: nonhuman as well as human animals, subpersonal elements such as neurons or computer software. This carries the danger that it extends intentional explanation into domains where it may not be appropriate. We are justified, therefore, in questioning the grounds for the generalization of intentional explanation from the human realm, to which it is usually confined, to other spheres. Initially, its application to subpersonal entities is of interest in view of Dennett's early distinction between the personal level and the subpersonal. The use of intentional reasoning in the context of the subpersonal invites the criticism that it is a breach of the "mereological fallacy," which refers to the application to parts of a system of properties (here desires and beliefs) that properly belong to the system as a whole (Bennett & Hacker, 2003). The avoidance of this criticism requires that we confine intentional explanation to entities for which no other stance is available. This rules out neurons, and so forth, for which the physical stance suffices.

Second, the validation of Dennett's IST relies on predictive accuracy, but most of the predictions likely to be generated are trivial and could as well be made by an observant layperson. Dennett's reason for accepting intentional explanation is that the intentional stance works, that is, it succeeds in predicting the behavior of the systems to which it is applied. He gave an example in terms of consumer behavior:

> When economists, for example, consider the class of *purchases* and note the defining condition that the purchaser believes he is exchanging his money for something belonging to the seller, and desires that item more than the money he exchanges for it. (Dennett, 1998, p. 326)

Note that Dennett was here making a broader point about the nature of beliefs, but the example suffices to show his reasoning about the intentional stance more generally. He continued his exposition of belief-desire folk psychology: "All that has to be the case is that the purchaser has somehow or other come into a cognitive state that identifies a seller, a price, and an opportunity to exchange and has tipped the balance in favor of completing the transaction" (Dennett, 1998, p. 326). For Dennett (1998), the explanation he offered was far from trivial:

> It would be a decidedly nontrivial task to design a robot that could distinguish an apple seller from an apple tree, while not becoming a money-pump when confronted by eager salesmen. But if you succeeded in making a successful purchaser-robot you would ipso facto have made a robot believer, a robot desirer, because belief and desire, in this maximally bland (but maximally useful) sense is a logical requirement of purchasing behavior. (p. 326)

However, a cognitive interpretation is not inevitable. A behaviorist account in terms of learning history and current consumer behavior setting is equally valid. The predictions that follow Dennett's account are, moreover, somewhat trivial—in themselves and as compared with predictions an extensional model can generate. An extensional account, as a predecessor of the use of intentional reasoning to explain behavior, could be invaluable for the determination of the point at which an intentional explanation becomes necessary and the form it should take. It may be the case that an extensional model of consumer behavior can produce more sophisticated predictions. The incorporation of two paradigms into our research strategy would provide a degree of intercompetitiveness as a spur to scientific progress (Feyerabend, 1975). Therefore, I propose using an extensional model first to determine whether an intentional explanation is required: theoretical minimalism to establish where behaviorism breaks down and intentional explanation is necessary plus the form it should take. This is in contrast to Dennett's approach, which rules the extensional account out of court without testing it empirically.

The openness of Dennett's three-stage model to empirical evaluation is actually called into question on two counts. As we have just seen, the testing of the IST in terms of its predictive validity is suspect because only facile predictions seem likely to be generated and tested. Moreover, the predictions are formed on the basis of the observation of behavior and are then used to "predict" subsequent similar behavior. This sounds circular and a matter of postdiction rather than prediction. The effect is to disqualify an externalist view of intentionality. Moving to the idea of SPCP, it also is apparent that we cannot employ illata to move toward an empirically testable set of psychological hypotheses because illata invoke the mereological fallacy. Again, the externalist approach to the ascription of intentionality is brought into question.

Third, it apparent that the alternative to intentional externalism is to employ an internalist conception of intentionality and methodology for its ascription. However, this carries the implication that we must demonstrate the capacity of the entities that we explain intentionally to employ intensional thinking: They must show *intensional fluency*. The reason is that intensionality is the test for real intentionality. The conclusion is that intentional explanations are confined to verbal humans, excluding the animals and software to which Dennett applies the intentional stance.

THE INTENTIONAL BEHAVIORIST RESEARCH STRATEGY

The IBRS comprises three stages that incorporate both extensional and intentional explanation. The former is based initially on radical behaviorism, which explains behavior by reference to the environmental stimuli responsible for its rate of performance (Skinner, 1945, 1950, 1953). By contrast, the intentional account portrays action as the outcome of desires and beliefs on the assumption that these are the causes of behavior or at least guide it insofar as rational beings attempt to behave in ways that are consistent with their intentionality. In spite of the widespread view that behavior has been comprehensively superseded by cognitive science, it remains an active research paradigm in which advances are being made at an impressive rate. In particular, and with specific reference to consumer behavior, theoretical and empirical work is continuing apace in the realms of language (e.g., Hayes, 1989) and economic choice (Foxall, 2016c). The intentional behaviorist research strategy (Foxall, 2016d, 2017a, 2020) incorporates both. Its three stages (Figure 3.1) are theoretical minimalism (based on radical behaviorism), intentional interpretation (which is akin to Dennett's IST), and cognitive interpretation (which seeks justification for the intentional interpretation in theories of cognitive structure and function). This last is the source of testable hypotheses, especially in the fields of economic analysis whose empirical examination completes the cycle.

More specifically,

- Stage 1 involves the modeling of consumer behavior as an instrumental activity that is economically and socially beneficial to the consumer. The empirical evaluation of this model reveals the point at which no stimulus field can be identified to justify further operant analysis, as well as the shape of the required intentional and cognitive portrayals of consumer choice.

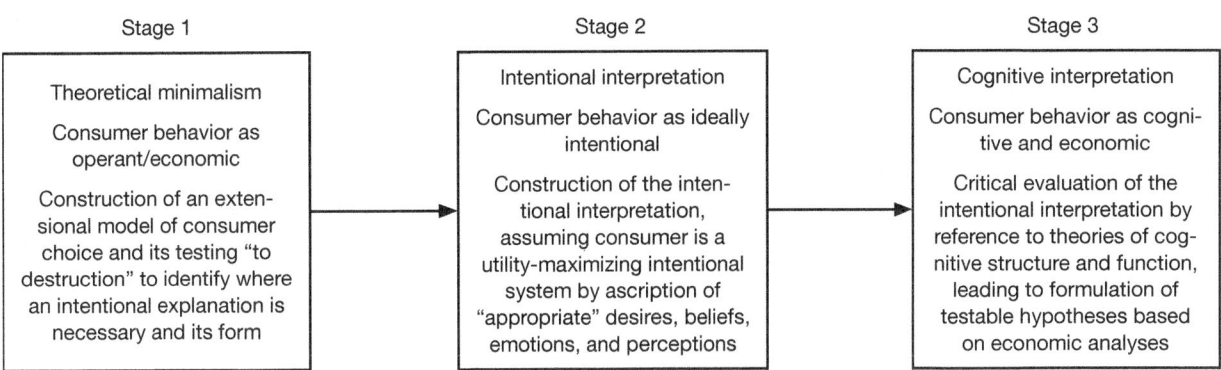

FIGURE 3.1. Intentional behaviorism: The research strategy.

- Stage 2 treats the consumer as an idealized system, that is, one that maximizes utility and, on the basis of the behavior patterns revealed during the theoretically minimalistic stage, proposes an interpretation in terms of the desires and beliefs the consumer "ought" to have, given their learning history and consumer behavior setting.
- Stage 3 evaluates this interpretation, first according to its consistency with cognitive theories of decision making and subsequently through the testing of hypotheses derived from consumer behavioral economics and neuroeconomics. Further interpretation is made available through picoeconomic analysis.

The psychological explanation aims to formulate an intentional understanding of behavior for which no stimulus field is apparent and to derive hypotheses that can be tested by the extensional sciences of neurophysiology and consumer behavior analysis. The first stage proposes an intentional interpretation of the behavior in question, basing its suggestion of contingency-representations on the general findings of the examination of the behavior through the theoretically minimalist lens of an operant analysis of consumer behavior in general. The intentional interpretation is tested by reference to its capacity to predict and its consistency with cognitive psychology. The relevant economic analysis is then employed to derive testable hypotheses for empirical research.

Stage 1: Theoretical Minimalism

The point of the first stage is to construct a theoretically minimal model of consumer behavior and to test what can be empirically evaluated. As long as this model is able to generate usable data on consumer behavior as an activity that can be explained by the rewarding and punishing consequences it produces, we consumer psychologists are able to profit from this unique paradigm, establishing what can only be known on the assumption that desires, beliefs, and other intentional variables do not enter into the determination of consumer choice. This in itself is a valuable exercise that has yielded knowledge that is theoretically valid and practically useful (Foxall, 2017b). However, an even more significant outcome of theoretical minimalism is the determination of the point at which radical behaviorism can no longer provide an explanation of certain aspects of consumer behavior for the reason that the stimulus field necessary to a radical behaviorist account can no longer be identified. This is the identification of the "bounds of behaviorism," the limitations on behaviorist explanation, and it reveals, first, that an intentional explanation is required and, second, the form it should take (i.e., the observed phenomena it must address and the questions that must be answered through their explanation).

The deployment of radical behaviorism in this regard is justified on the grounds that it is an instrumentally oriented approach to behavioral investigation and explanation: Its explication of behavior rests on the ways in which it is instrumental in generating the kinds of consequences that increase the rate of performance of the behavior (reinforcers or rewards) or diminish it (punishers). This focus on the ways in which behavior is a function not of preceding stimuli, nor of mental states that are teleologically related to actions, but of its consequences makes it a natural means of investigating economic behavior. (Radical behaviorism shares an explanatory capacity with microeconomics; see Foxall, 2016c.) The experimental analysis of behavior, on which radical behaviorism is firmly grounded, permits rigorous empirical investigation that seeks to identify and quantify the influence of environmental stimuli on behavior, unambiguously revealing the antecedent and consequential stimuli that are associated with the rate of performance. This makes it a natural paradigm for this stage of the research process.

Cognitive constructs, which are unobservables that must be represented in empirical research by proxy variables (e.g., behavioral or neurophysiological measures) would be less convincing as indicators of when and how intentional explanation becomes necessary. The vehicle for this stage of investigation is the behavioral perspective model (BPM). I consider first the nature of the extensional version of this model and the empirical research to which it has led, going on to discuss the bounds of behaviorism it identifies and the nature of the intentional model to which all this leads.

The extensional model of consumer choice. Figure 3.2 depicts the extensional model of consumer choice (BPM-E). The immediate precursor of consumer behavior is the "consumer-situation." In fact, the model essentially comprises the consumer-situation and its relationship with consumer behavior, though the putative consequences of such behavior are shown for the sake of completeness. In this version of the model, the consumer-situation comprises the consumer behavior setting as it is primed and activated by the consumer's learning history, particularly their consumption history. The consumer behavior setting represents the immediate circumstances in which the consumer is located and consists of the stimuli that prefigure reward or punishment, contingent on the performance of a particular response. These stimuli make sense only in connection with the consumer's previous history of consumption, since their ability to engender behavior stems from the consequences that similar responses have produced in the past. The rewarding (reinforcing) and punishing consequences that those prior responses have produced are of two kinds: utilitarian or functional benefits and disbenefits on one hand, informational or social benefits and disbenefits on the other. Utilitarian rewards and punishers are functional in nature, relating to the practical utilities of owning and using a product or service. Informational rewards and punishers are social and symbolic. Almost any watch provides the functional value of informing its wearer of the time (utilitarian reward), but some brands of watch (Rolex, for instance) also deliver social and symbolic values (informational reward) in the form of social status and esteem. The nonprestige brand has the disadvantage (utilitarian punishment) that it may be less reliable and long-lasting, while prestige brands are inevitably expensive. Most products and services deliver a combination of utilitarian and informational rewards and punishers.

In the extensional model then, consumer behavior is a function of the consumer-situation, which is

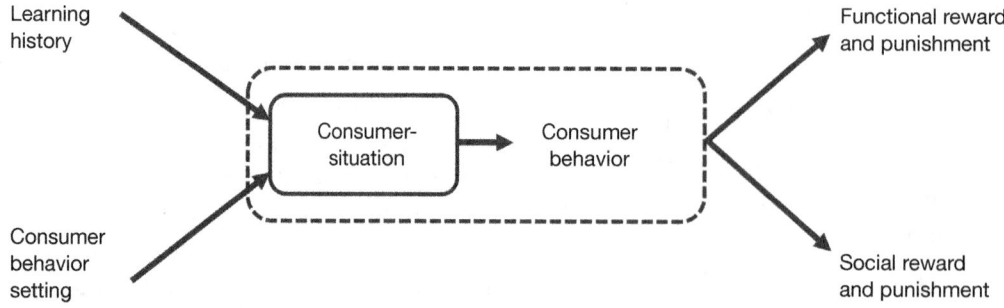

FIGURE 3.2. The extensional model of consumer choice: BPM-E. From *Intentional Behaviorism: Philosophical Foundations of Economic Psychology* (p. 182), by G. R. Foxall, 2020, Academic Press. Copyright 2020 by Elsevier. Reprinted with permission.

composed of the consumer's history of reward and punishment for the performance of behaviors that resemble those made available by the current consumer behavior setting. This learning history vitally includes the kinds of reward and punishment that the prior behavior has attracted (functional or utilitarian reward and punishment, social or informational reward and punishment), especially as these resemble the outcomes prefigured by the current consumer behavior setting contingent on the performance of specific consumer behaviors.

The *scope* of the consumer behavior setting consists in the number of responses that the setting facilitates. Relatively closed settings permit just one or perhaps a few behaviors to be performed—a gym, for example, allows a very limited range of behaviors, which are governed by the equipment available and an exercise regime that embodies strict rules. Other forms of activity are discouraged. However, an informal social gathering like a graduation party is a relatively open setting that encourages a variety of behaviors ranging from the consumption of food and drink to dancing and conversation.

Empirical research. The large volume of empirical research inspired by the extensional model has recently been described in detail (Foxall, 2017a) and will not, therefore, be rehearsed in detail here. However, it is useful to summarize some key findings. Measured as the quantity of a brand or product demanded, consumer behavior has been shown to be responsive not only to changes in price (as reflected in price elasticity of demand) but also to the quantities of utilitarian and informational reward those commodities supply to the consumer. Hence, the understanding provided by the extensional model shows how consumers respond not only to price, as emphasized by economics, but additionally to marketing variables, including brand strategies that are crucial marketing thought and practice. Another important strand of research entails the determination, on the basis of Cobb-Douglas utility function analysis, of what it is that consumers maximize: Within the constraints of their budget functions, consumers maximize not particular commodities but a bundle of utilitarian and informational reinforcement. Oliveira-Castro and Foxall (2017) employed the function

$$U_{(x1,s2)} = x_1^a x_2^b,$$

where U = utility, x_1 = quantity of utilitarian reinforcement, x_2 = quantity of informational reinforcement, and a and b are empirically obtained parameters, to examine purchases of food products (see also Oliveira-Castro et al., 2016a, 2016b). More precisely, we can say that on the basis of several investigations, consumers maximize the utility that derives from particular combinations of utilitarian and informational reinforcement subject to the constraint imposed by their budget for the goods in question. The outcome of this empirical research program has been the development of *consumer behavioral economics* as a distinct combination of microeconomics, operant psychology, and marketing science.

Bounds of Behaviorism in Consumer Psychology

Behaviorism evinces three sources of limitation: its inability to account for aspects of the continuity and discontinuity of behavior, the necessity of accounting for behavior at the personal level of exposition, and the need to delimit behavioral interpretations.

Behavioral continuity and discontinuity. Sometimes the stimuli that compose the consumer behavior setting and the consumer's learning history are not available to the researcher. The only solution is to conceptualize their behavior in intentional terms. When a consumer innovates, for example, by trying a novel brand in a produce category with which they are familiar, there is no learning history on which to draw to explain their choice, and there is no stimulus field in their current setting that can be assumed to have gained control of their behavior through a period of learning. The promotion of the new brand suggests that it is at least the equivalent of the existing brands that constitute their present consideration set, but a full explanation demands some mechanism that will elucidate how they integrate and appraise new information presented, for instance, in advertisements. It becomes necessary, therefore, to posit the cognitive processes that would account for their innovativeness. Processes of mental comparison, analogizing, symbolization, and so on, must be brought in to make sense of the consumer's behavioral discontinuity. Explaining the behavior of the consumer who trials an entirely new product, which brings a new product class into existence, must invoke symbols, mental projection, and abstract analogizing.

Personal level exposition. It is on occasion necessary to posit a personal level of exposition in order to account for consumer behavior. An instance of this arises in situations in which a consumer makes a choice between a reward that is smaller than another but which will become available sooner (the SSR), and the later appearing but larger reward (LLR). Assessing these possibilities in advance, the consumer may well state a preference for the LLR. This requires that they are able to contemplate two future products, compare and assess them, and reach a conclusion about their relative worth. This is a highly abstract proposition, one that makes substantial cognitive demands. There are no stimuli available, other than perhaps verbal information and instructions. If the situation is novel, there can by definition be no relevant consumption history on which to call for a behaviorist explanation. At a point just prior to the appearance of the SSR, its subjective value tends to increase enormously so that for the first time in the process it exceeds that of the LLR. The consumer now has to determine their course for action. They may behave impulsively at this stage, surrendering to the attractiveness of the SSR and thereby abandoning the greater reward. In this case, the consumer psychologist must resort to such cognitive variables as sensation seeking, reward sensitivity, behavioral disinhibition, attention deficit, reflection deficit, and impulsive choice in order to make their behavior intelligible.

Alternatively, however, the consumer may enlist those cognitive capacities, often known as executive functions, such as attention, behavioral flexibility, behavioral inhibition, planning, valuing future events, working memory, emotional activation, self-regulation, and metacognition in order to forestall the immediacy of the SSR and make it possible to await the LLR, even though this exists only in their imagination. They can form mental images of both the relatively concrete SSR and the practical and emotional benefits that its selection would instantly make available to them, as well as the more remote and abstract LLR, which they know will deliver greater benefits should they choose to reverse their impulsive preference. Again, their behavior is only intelligible by reference to cognitive processes.

Delimiting behavioral interpretation. When radical behaviorists are confronted with a lack of stimuli by which to conduct an analysis, their response has been to construct a behavioral interpretation that extrapolates from known instances of behavioral control to the less amenable situation. The problem is that it becomes possible to imagine possible sources of stimulus control and reward, even though there is no possibility of subjecting these speculations to experimental test. Take the case of the adoption and diffusion of new products. A behaviorist account is available for these phenomena (Foxall, 2017a), which relates consumers' decision making and actions to the contingencies of reward and punishment. However, this rests on a broad interpretation of the factors likely to operate as behavioral consequences, and the temptation is to allow such speculation to get out of hand since it cannot be subjected to a definitive experimental analysis. The behavioral interpretation must be kept in check, and this is possible via the development of an intentional interpretation that might allude to consumers' putative knowledge of the properties of a new product or service that relate to more speedy social diffusion, which Rogers (2004) summarized as relative advantage, compatibility, complexity, conspicuousness, trialability, and comprehensibility. These elements are among those that the innovator likely reflects upon when deciding whether to trial and perhaps adopt an innovation. Further intentional explanation might draw on such factors as the personality characteristics and cognitive styles of innovators (Foxall, 1995a). In this way, not only does intentional interpretation take place in its own right as part of psychological explanation, but the procedure makes a valuable contribution to behavioral interpretation by circumscribing the range of explanatory variables to realistic environment events and eschewing more farfetched speculations.

Imperatives of intentionality. The identification of the limitations of behaviorist explanation attest positively to the role that intentionality can play in consumer psychology since each of the bounds of behaviorism presents an opportunity for an alternative mode of explanation. The inability of consumer psychologists to relate behavior to a demonstrable stimulus field, for instance, is an incentive to examine the desires, beliefs, and emotions through which the consumer perceives their experience of consumption and the probable outcomes of current consumer behavior. Categories of utilitarian and informational reinforcement remain germane to understanding consumer choice, but the emphasis shifts to the way the consumer recalls and evaluates them. The consumer psychologists' perspective moves on from a view of the consumer-situation that embraces the objectively specifiable behavior setting and learning history to one that calls upon the cognitive construal of these correlates of consumer behavior and the expectations they engender. The personal level of exposition allows the consumer-situation and consumer action to be conceptualized in terms of the internal psychological processing that precedes and accompanies choice. The impact of the consumer's ability to mentally represent past and future events and their appraisal of both bring a distinct approach to consumer research. Consumer psychologists might object that they were doing this sort of thing anyway. But the import of theoretical minimalism and the identification of its limitations as well as its strengths places psychological explanation on a new level. It justifies the resort to intentional interpretation by reference to what we now know about where and why such a resort is required and the form it should take based on sound empirical grounds rather than the passive acceptance of the cognitive zeitgeist.

Psychological explanation has two elements: the formation of an intentional interpretation, which is then evaluated in terms of its consistency with a cognitive interpretation based on psychological theories of mental structure and function (Foxall, 2016a, 2016d). The cognitive interpretation is also intended to propose hypotheses for empirical examination by the extensional sciences of neurophysiology and consumer behavioral economics.

Stage 2: Intentional Interpretation

The first component of psychological explanation is *intentional interpretation* (essentially Dennett's IST), which is an account of behavior in which the consumer is treated as an intentional system whose behavior is accounted for in terms of intentionality-with-a-t.

The intentional model of consumer choice. The desires, beliefs, emotions, and perceptions that consumers hold and that influence their actions are intentional depictions of the contingencies of reward and punishment that define the intentional consumer-situation. They are accordingly known as *contingency-representations* for short. The intentional interpretation, which shares some features with Dennett's IST, portrays the consumer's psychological field as an array of interrelated contingency-representations. It is the task of the intentional model of consumer choice (BPM-I) to capture this (Foxall, 2017a). Just as the delimitation of behavioral interpretation relies on the intentional reconstruction of what consumers could reasonably know and the limitations of the range of rewards and punishers that could conceivably influence their behavior, so the intentional interpretation is informed by an extensional account of consumer choice, that gleaned in the process of theoretical minimalism. This sets limits to what can be claimed by an intentional account, as well as suggesting the essential components that the intentional interpretation must possess in order to be true to what we know of consumer behavior.

In the intentional model, the contents of the extensional model are portrayed as intentional objects. As a result, the intentional consumer-situation comprises contingency-representations of the consumer's learning history as an object of their experience and memory, as well as of the consumer behavior setting they face. In other words, it consists of desires, beliefs, emotions, and perceptions together with their objects (Crane, 2001). The consumer's past consumption experience, available to them in memory, is held to account for their current behavior, either directly or implicitly (see, e.g., Bargh, 2007; Gawronski & Payne, 2010). The stimulus field that enters into the consumer behavior setting influences choice as an array of contingency-representations, notably those of the utilitarian and informational reinforcement that is expected to accrue from the performance of particular purchase and consumption behaviors. The key component of the model is again the relationship between consumer-situation and consumer behavior, but the former has been reconceptualized in terms of contingency-representations and the latter as action. (The expected utilitarian and informational consequences are included in Figure 3.3 for the sake of completeness.)

The intentional consumer situation. The intentional consumer-situation contains the intentionality that it is appropriate to ascribe to the consumer based on their learning history and the consumer behavior setting they face (Figure 3.3). In reconstructing the desires, beliefs, emotions, and perceptions that constitute this intentionality, the knowledge of behavior generated through testing the extensional model is of central value. That consumers maximize quanta of utilitarian and informational reinforcement not only indicates consumers' overall desires but also provides clues to their attitudes toward particular products and services, which are judged in terms of the kinds of benefit they confer and the comparative evaluation of the various marketing mixes with which the consumer is confronted. Similarly, empirical research that reveals the role of essential value in consumer choice signposts consumers' attitude toward adjustments to price/quantity relationships presented by retailers. The interpretive establishment of the intentional consumer-situation also draws attention to emotional contingency-representations that can be attributed to the consumer. Patterns of pleasure, arousal, and dominance, as well as the neurophysiological changes likely to accompany them, can be confidently attributed to the structural characteristics of consumer behavior settings (i.e., patterns of utilitarian and informational rewards, and setting scope), on the basis of a large volume of empirical research (Foxall, 2011; Foxall et al., 2012).

Consumer behavior remains a function of the consumer-situation, the components of which are conceptualized intentionally. Hence, learning history exists in consumer's memory while the consumer behavior setting is an array of contingency-representations—the desires, beliefs, emotions, and perceptions through which the consumer represents the marketing mix elements presented to them and their expected functional and social outcomes.

The essential difference between an extensional and an intentional explanation emerges through further consideration of informational (social, symbolic) reward as it appears in each of these paradigms. The behaviorist explanation of verbal behavior is also relevant to this discussion. In a radical behaviorist explanation of behavior, the discriminative and rewarding stimuli in question

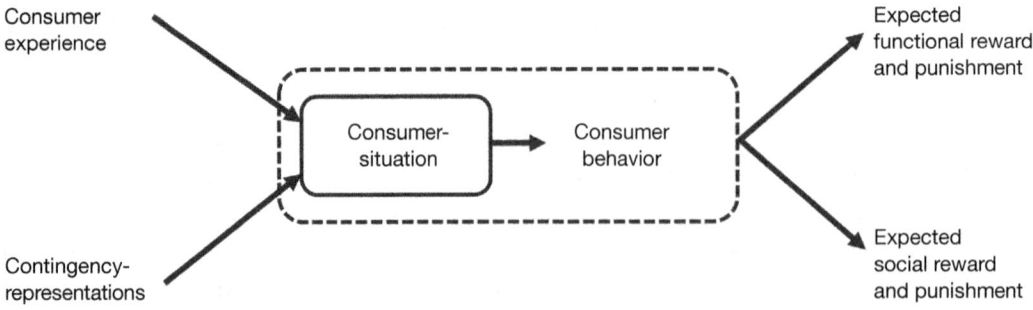

FIGURE 3.3. The intentional model of consumer choice: BPM-I. From *Intentional Behaviorism: Philosophical Foundations of Economic Psychology* (p. 191), by G. R. Foxall, 2020, Academic Press. Copyright 2020 by Elsevier. Reprinted with permission.

simply constitute discriminative stimuli, in the first case, or secondary rewards that acquire their influence over behavior through association with primary rewards, in the second. They are physical elements within the environment (including visual and auditory components of the consumer behavior setting) that develop an ability to affect behavior by being paired repeatedly with functional rewards such as food and water. The BPM-E model, founded on the strictures of radical behaviorism, is concerned only with behavior and how it may be predicted and controlled. What radical behaviorists call the "rule-governed behavior of the listener," the control of activity via verbal instructions that encapsulate the three-term contingency, consists simply, in this model, of physical, auditory stimuli that control behavior through associative learning. The "auditory blasts" that make up the verbalization of a rule are of the same essence as any other physical stimulus. The language and the explanation is entirely extensional: Verbal discriminatory stimuli and rewards can form elements of laboratory experiments entirely as functional stimuli do. This logic of explanation fits well with the depiction of the extensional consumer-situation shown in Figure 3.2.

However, when we turn to the intentional consumer-situation shown in Figure 3.3, the intentional content of verbal behavior entails that we recognize we are offering a quite distinct brand of explanation from the foregoing. As I have said, this intentional model (BPM-I) treats the consumer as a Dennettian idealized system, setting forth the intentionality appropriate to their consumption history and present circumstances. The consumer-situation is now stipulated in the language of contingency-representation: the desires, beliefs, emotions, and perceptions, which would mark the consumer who was a utility-maximizer, who seeks to secure bundles of utilitarian and informational reward consistent with not only their budget constraint as the economist specifies but their wants and expectations as the psychologist requires. Verbal instructions, such as inhere in advertisements, promotional material, and indications of price and product performance, must now be treated as having meanings that derive from the intentional language in which they are couched.

Stage 3: Cognitive Interpretation

The cognitive psychologies employed in intentional behaviorism to evaluate and substantiate the intentional interpretation lack a direct empirical component, that is, one that relates specifically to the verification of an intentional interpretation. Dennett's three kinds of intentional psychology scheme evaluates the IST level interpretation of the idealized intentional system according to its predictive success. The IST is also, ideally, confronted with empirical rigor in the research program of SPCP that seeks the variables of psychological theories in the illata that comprise physical entities, such as neurons, that are intentionally characterized. Intentional behaviorism, however, has hitherto sought to provide its justification of the intentional interpretations it generates in terms of the cognitive theories to which belong the intentional constructs in which the interpretations are couched, on the grounds that intentionality-based predictions are likely to be so vague as to be easily supported by observation and, therefore, unlikely to clinch the predictive validity of the intentional interpretation (Foxall, 2016d). Dennett also linked the IST and SPCP phases of his research strategy by means of the ready transferability of intentional idioms from the personal to the subpersonal level, a move we have a priori outlawed on the grounds that it invites the mereological fallacy. The possibility of biconditionals was, equally, judged to be an unlikely solution to the need to link the levels of exposition entailed in the explanation of human economic behavior. However, the problem of empirically embedding the intentional interpretation of intentional behaviorism persists. This chapter seeks a means of conjoining the concerns of the super-, sub-, and personal levels of exposition, which relies neither on flipping between them nor on concepts that attempt to be at once both intentional and extensional.

A predominant strand of cognitive theory explains a spectrum of behaviors from impulsive choice to delayed gratification in terms of the interaction of two types of metacognitive systems. Models based on this dichotomy can be found in various forms, but the following characteristics are common. The first kind of system, fast acting, automatic, associative, effortless, and nonconscious, acts in parallel and without the support of working memory (see, e.g., Kahneman, 2011). These metacognitive systems, often designated "S1," are responsible, if unchecked, for impulsive behaviors. The second kind, which is working-memory based, is slower, rule based, effortful, conscious and acts serially. These "S2" metacognitive systems may override the actions of S1 systems and promote a more considered pattern of behavior that is careful of the organism's longer term welfare. Some authors argue that while the cognitive functions proposed by these models share some common properties, the systems and subsystems these models variously propose are fundamentally dissimilar (e.g., Evans, 2010). Proponents of another batch of models that seemingly deal in the same subject matter couch their ideas in terms of mental or cognitive modules and, in some cases, central processing units (e.g., Fodor, 1983).[1]

Microcognitive psychology. Microcognitive psychology links the personal and subpersonal levels, though it also has implications for the superpersonal. It embodies a theory of neurocognitive behavior systems, for example, Bickel's competing neurobehavioral decision systems model (CNDS; Bickel et al., 2011; Bickel & Yi, 2008) or Stanovich's tripartite theory (Stanovich, 2009, 2011), that provide theoretical bases for linking neurophysiological functioning, decision making, and behavior/action. Although the terminology differs from model to model, microcognitive psychology proposes two or three of these neurocognitive behavior systems; at its simplest, an *impulsive or autonomous system* that is based in the limbic system and an *executive system* based in the prefrontal cortex. Either of these may be hypo- or hyperactive, and the balance between them is a determinant of the strength of the interaction of picoeconomic interests, which determines the rate at which the consumer discounts future events. (For further detail, please see Exhibit 3.2.)

Mesocognitive psychology. Mesocognitive psychology is exemplified by picoeconomics (Ainslie, 1992). As a psychology of the personal level, it presents us with the strategic interaction

---

EXHIBIT 3.2

Dual Process Cognitive Theories

Dual process theories describe opposing mental functions, the first giving rise to an immediate tendency to respond on impulse to stimuli associated with threat or opportunity to gain. (A comprehensive account is available in Foxall, 2016a, 2016b, 2016d.) This "impulsive" system is neurophysiologically based in the limbic system, principally the amygdala and ventral striatum. Functioning to provide fast evaluation of immediate actions, it tends toward hyperactivity as the incentive value of environmental cues such as drugs and other rewards. In this it depends on past conditioning and behavior, reacting to facets of situations that have previously been associated with high levels of reward by increasing the salience of economic and social goods that have been consumed on earlier occasions. All rewards, including everyday products and services, are associated with the release of dopamine in the nucleus accumbens, whether they are functional rewards such as utilitarian benefits or social rewards such as prestige and self-esteem. The insula too is implicated in the craving for drugs and other sources of emotional reward. The second system is concerned with the operation of executive functions, which provide perspective on apparent opportunities to obtain highly valenced rewards speedily by encouraging a longer term consideration of the implications of immediate consumption. This system is neurophysiologically based in the PFC. By injecting a tendency toward forethought, planning, and emotional stability, this "executive system" may enable the consumer to overcome a rush toward the kind of immediate satisfaction that results in deleterious outcomes in the longer term. The interaction of the two systems determines the rate at which the consumer discounts future rewards and hence the degree of impulsivity or self-control manifested in their behaviors. Microcognitive psychology theories are overwhelmingly concerned with the interactions of the impulsive and executive systems, and the associated neuroeconomic analyses that build upon them suggest an important means by which hypotheses that test the feasibility of the intentional interpretation can be generated and empirically evaluated (Glimcher, 2011).

---

of competing interests within the individual. The first is a short-range interest (SRI) that seeks more immediate satisfaction; it eventuates in behavior that discounts the future steeply and experientially approximates the primary mentation of which Freud spoke. The other is a long-range interest (LRI) that seeks to defer gratification if this increases the overall well-being of the individual; it leads to

---

[1] It is interesting that Brakel and Shevrin (2003) attributed dual process thinking to Freud, while Frankish (2015) argued that Dennett's distinction between two kinds of awareness in *Content and Consciousness* (Dennett, 1969) embodies a dual process model of reasoning.

behavior that discounts the future shallowly. (For further detail, please see Exhibit 3.3.)

Macrocognitive psychology. Macrocognitive psychology intertwines the personal and superpersonal levels, though it also links in the subpersonal. It embodies a theory of collective intentionality such as Searle's (1995, 2010), which establishes the origins of informational reinforcement. Collective intentionality is the creation and enforcement, by human agents, of the contingencies of reinforcement and punishment that will control their behavior/action. This procedure is part of what makes actions actions (Foxall, 2017b). In a nutshell, what makes actions actions is that the contingencies of reinforcement and punishment that govern the relevant activities' recurrence within the individual's repertoire are determined by the social activities of groups as well as by the individual themselves. Action is activity that is governed by collective or individual intentionality (Foxall, 2016d). This is the foundation of informational reinforcement and of pride (positive self-esteem) and shame (negative self-esteem) as the ultimate sources of reward and punishment of human choice (Foxall, 2016a, 2017b). (Both microcognitive psychology and consumer behavioral economics are inherent in the extensional BPM, which have already been discussed.)

CONCLUSION

It is now possible to gather the preceding arguments together in order to summarize the nature of the proposed research strategy and how it might be employed in consumer psychology.

Summary of the Research Strategy

The chapter has set out logically the stages of a research strategy for cognitive consumer research, which details the methodological sequence required to fulfill the philosophical demands of cognitive explanation. The logic is based on that suggested by Dennett, who proposed (a) how to improve on everyday folk psychology; (b) how to evaluate the intentional account of behavior generated by IST by means of an assessment of its predictive

EXHIBIT 3.3

Picoeconomics

Ainslie (1992) portrayed the competing interests engendered by a consumer's intrapersonal desires for (a) the divergent attractions of an immediate but relatively small reward and also for (b) the more substantial reward for which they must wait in terms of warring internal factions, interests which interact strategically and whose separate times of availability provoke mental conflict. The SRI provides a strong impetus toward gratification as soon as it becomes available despite its being inferior to that which will only become available with the exercise of the patience, which is required for the LRI, focused as it is on achieving a superior but delayed reward. (We have already encountered this aspect of consumer choice as a conflict between SSR and LLR.) Ross (2012) showed that these competing picoeconomic interests may be modelled as impinging on each another either contemporaneously or sequentially. If the former, the interacting subagents designated as the SRI and LRI by Ainslie can be modeled as though they possessed entirely distinct but conflicting utility functions or completely separate time preferences. The analysis of the interactions of conflicting subagents that are assumed to have separate temporal preferences, for instance, lends itself to the neuroeconomic analysis of their various subpersonal neurophysiological operations which gives rise to their particular hyperbolic time-based inclinations to act. Ross (2012, p. 720) discussed this by reference to the "competition between steeply exponentially discounting 'limbic' regions and more patient (less steeply exponentially discounting) 'cognitive' regions." This picoeconomic portrayal depends heavily on the findings of neuroeconomic experiments employing fMRI scans of humans choosing between SSR and LLR (McClure et al., 2004; see also Foxall, 2016a).

validity; and (c) the route to an intentional methodology, SPCP, in which intentional variables can enter into psychological research. In addition, the intentional behaviorist research strategy proposed (a) promotes mereological consistency by confining intentional explanation to systems as a whole rather than their parts; (b) requires intensional fluency, which takes the ability to manipulate intensional sentences properly as indicative of real intentionality; and (c) confines intentional explanation to systems that cannot be explained by nonintentional stances. The intentional behaviorism strategy also includes a theoretical minimalism level of analysis, which tests to destruction an extensional model of consumer behavior, thereby identifying the point at which cognitive explanation is required and the form it must take. This increases the precision of an intentional interpretation by showing the nature of consumer choice and its environmental determinants—as opposed to Dennett's reliance on selecting the intentionality the system "ought" to have by virtue of its history and current situation. Instead of relying on the relatively weak attempt to ground this intentional interpretation by estimating its predictive validity—a technique likely to lead to predictions of such generality as to make them difficult to falsify—intentional behaviorism advances the possibilities of establishing the consistency of the intentional interpretation with the theories and findings of cognitive psychology. This is still a largely interpretive procedure that continues to employ abstracta. But it provides cognitive consistency as an important criterion rather than the possibly spurious accuracy of fulfilled predictions that are vague. Finally, the intentional behaviorism research strategy suggests that the researcher who requires a more sensitive predictive technology for the testing out of the intentional interpretation may resort to economic analyses that enable falsifiable hypotheses to be generated and tested.

An example of the kinds of empirical research to which this paradigm may lead, which is of more general social-psychological significance, concerns the interactive understanding of the ways in which persons and situations generate and influence behavior. Situations are generally understood as constituting the noncognitive source of influence in social action. However, the idea of the intentional consumer-situation recognizes the consumer's contribution to the construal of the situation, albeit within a context of situation–trait interaction. While the expectation that situations and traits interact in the production of action is acceptable to a wide range of psychologists, Kahle (1980) elucidated the status of this approach by seeking to show *how* situations and traits interact. He hypothesized, "Motivation is enhanced when individuals have self-selected stimulus conditions and/or modified stimulus conditions to be appropriate for themselves" (Kahle, 1980, p. 50). In the context of political attitudes and behavior, Kahle and Berman (1979) reported that attitudes display causal predominance over stimulus conditions self-selection while such self-selections display causal predominance over actions. Kahle (1980) demonstrated similar relations in a laboratory investigation in which locus of control provided the person with variable and skill-chance situational influence. Internal–external locus of control (Rotter, 1966) was expected to influence the selection of a task requiring greater or less skill and greater or less chance. Kahle's (1980) study indicated that male respondents with a pronounced external orientation to situational control preferred to undertake a test of *change*, while male respondents who showed a greater internal orientation preferred a test of *skill*. The implication, which is of central significance for further empirical work employing the BPM, is that people are attracted to particular kinds of situation, and when they find themselves in compatible situations, their motivation is increased. They select stimulus conditions appropriate to their personalities unless they are prevented from doing so by controlling situational influences. The investigation of the effects of contingency representation of situations, which reflect not only consumers' personalities but their learning histories, on their selection of appropriate situations of purchase and consumption promises to enhance the understanding of person-situation interaction. The study of the effect of consumer behavior setting scope in the limitation of personal choice in this context would elucidate the relationships among preferred situational stimuli, motivation, and actual behavioral outcomes. In turn, the emphasis that the BPM places on the role of reinforcement in the persistence of behavior promises to throw light on the kinds of personality factors that shape stimulus preference.

Using the Research Strategy

Each of the stages in the comprehensive research strategy that has been described is associated with a characteristic mode of explanation (intentionality/extensionality) and a predominant style of techniques (quantitative/qualitative); see Table 3.1. Researchers with a preference for a particular explanatory mode or set of techniques may opt to pursue their investigations within a subset of the stages of the research strategy. The merits and demerits of each stage can be set forth, and the significance of the research results can be interpreted accordingly. Each of the extensional/intentional methodologies and the qualitative/qualitative research techniques provides a particular kind of explanation. The researcher is able to select the appropriate modes and techniques and, equally important, to decide how far to go in embracing alternatives to those chosen in order to validate the findings. Some researchers may wish to follow the sequence of stages as set out in Table 3.1. In this case, the intentional interpretation is established on the basis of what has been learned about consumer behavior through an extensional quantitative analysis such as that provided by BPM-E. The intentional interpretation is then evaluated, first in terms of its consonance with theories of cognitive structure and function. In itself, this is largely a matter of qualitative interpretation, though it rests on quantitative analysis by the cognitive psychologists in whose domains they fall. In addition, hypotheses derived directly from the intentional interpretation can be tested empirically by means of the economic analyses.

However, the sequential research strategy of this kind is not intended be followed in its entirety without deviation. Some researchers will be satisfied with the devising of an intentional interpretation in the absence of the thoroughgoing theoretical minimalism stage founded on a formal extensional model, basing their devising of consumers' desires and beliefs on the researcher's general knowledge of consumer behavior or on survey data. The research strategy might well terminate here, as long as the researcher is satisfied that the findings are sufficiently valid for their present requirements. Alternatively, the researcher is able to fulfill either or both of the evaluative analyses presented by the production of a cognitive interpretation or economic analyses, going beyond to the intentional interpretation stage to form an estimate of its validity, reliability, and generalizability through cognitive and economic analyses. The advantage of setting out the research strategy in its entirety, however, is that whatever stages the researcher employs, they can evaluate their findings or propose reasons why further evaluation is not necessary.

The researcher who terminates investigation at Stage 2 (intentional interpretation) or 3a (cognitive interpretation) and whose research project may not have included Stage 1 (theoretical minimalism) must be aware of the nature of the psychological knowledge to which quantitative evaluation leads. This is not to diminish qualitative and interpretivist research but merely to point out that, like quantitative research, it has limitations when pursued in isolation. As Lakatos (1978) pointed out, many philosophers have thought that

> a statement constitutes knowledge if sufficiently many people believe it sufficiently strongly. But the history of thought shows us that many people were totally committed to absurd beliefs. If the strength of beliefs were a hallmark of knowledge, we should have to rank some tales about demons, angels, devils, and of heaven and hell as knowledge. Scientists, on the other hand, are very skeptical even of their best theories. (p. 1)

This argues in favor of the comprehensive research strategy that I have outlined, in which hypotheses derived, at least in part, from qualitative reasoning

TABLE 3.1

Research Strategy Stages, Modes of Explanation, and Predominant Techniques

Stage of research strategy	Mode of explanation	Predominant techniques
1 Theoretical minimalism	Extensional	Quantitative
2 Intentional interpretation	Intentional	Qualitative/interpretive
3a Evaluation: Cognitive interpretation	Intentional/extensional	Qualitative/quantitative
3b Evaluation: Economic analysis	Extensional	Quantitative

can be tested empirically according to some rigorous criterion such as scientific falsification (Popper, 1934/1959). This does not, of course, foreshadow a time when scientific knowledge will be proven. On the contrary, it emphasizes the tentativeness of human knowledge, a situation in which neither quantitative nor qualitative inquiry can be privileged above the other.

In conclusion, the proposed research strategy, viewed in its entirety, presents a complex route to psychological knowledge. But there is no reason why researchers should feel it is incumbent on them to pursue the whole research process, moving inexorably from one stage to the next until the procedure is complete. Rather, by delineating each of the stages in a comprehensive research program, the philosophy of intentional behaviorism allows the researcher to pursue whichever of the components they find useful to their research interests. At the same time, the strategy as described indicates the kind of explanation to which research at each stage leads and makes clear what additional research stages would be required in order to undertake a full, interdisciplinary investigation. It does not instantly solve problems that were identified in the introduction, but it sets out the nature of the research that would be required to address them.

REFERENCES

Ainslie, G. (1992). *Picoeconomics: The strategic interaction of successive motivational states within the person.* Cambridge University Press.

Araujo, T., Wonneberger, A., Neijens, P., & de Vreese, C. (2017). How much time do you spend online? Understanding and improving the accuracy of self-reported measures of internet use. *Communication Methods and Measures*, *11*(3), 173–190. https://doi.org/10.1080/19312458.2017.1317337

Bargh, J. A. (Ed.). (2007). *Social psychology and the unconscious: The automaticity of higher mental processes.* Psychology Press.

Bennett, M. R. (2007). Neuroscience and philosophy. In M. Bennett, D. Dennett, P. Hacker, & J. Searle (Eds.), *Neuroscience and philosophy: Brain, mind, and language* (pp. 49–69). Columbia University Press.

Bennett, M. R., & Hacker, P. M. S. (2003). *Philosophical foundations of neuroscience.* Blackwell.

Bennett, M. R., & Hacker, P. M. S. (2007). The conceptual presuppositions of cognitive neuroscience: A reply to critics. In M. Bennett, D. Dennett, P. Hacker, & J. Searle (Eds.), *Neuroscience and philosophy: Brain, mind, and language* (pp. 127–170). Columbia University Press.

Bickel, W. K., Jarmolowicz, D. P., Mueller, E. T., & Gatchalian, K. M. (2011). The behavioral economics and neuroeconomics of reinforcer pathologies: Implications for etiology and treatment of addiction. *Current Psychiatry Reports*, *13*(5), 406–415. https://doi.org/10.1007/s11920-011-0215-1

Bickel, W. K., & Yi, R. (2008). Temporal discounting as a measure of executive function: Insights from the competing neuro-behavioral decision system hypothesis of addiction. *Advances in Health Economics and Health Services Research*, *20*, 289–309. https://doi.org/10.1016/S0731-2199(08)20012-9

Brakel, L. A., & Shevrin, H. (2003). Freud's dual process theory and the place of the a-rational. *Behavioral and Brain Sciences*, *26*(4), 527–528. https://doi.org/10.1017/S0140525X03210116

Brentano, F. (1995). *Psychology from an empirical standpoint.* Routledge. (Original work published 1874)

Compiani, M. (1996). Remarks on the paradigms of connectionism. In A. Clark & P. Millican (Eds.), *The legacy of Alan Turing: Vol II. Connectionism, concepts, and folk psychology* (pp. 45–66). Oxford University Press.

Crane, T. (1998). Intentionality as the mark of the mental. *Royal Institute of Philosophy Supplements*, *43*, 229–251. https://doi.org/10.1017/S1358246100004380

Crane, T. (2001). Intentional objects. *Ratio*, *14*(4), 336–349. https://doi.org/10.1111/1467-9329.00168

Crane, T. (2009). Intentionalism. In B. P. McLaughlin, A. Beckerman, & S. Walter (Eds.), *The Oxford handbook of philosophy of mind* (pp. 474–493). Oxford University Press.

Crane, T. (2016). *The mechanical mind* (3rd ed.). Routledge.

de Gelder, B. (1996). Modularity and logical cognitivism. In A. Clark & P. Millican (Eds.), *The legacy of Alan Turing: Vol II. Connectionism, concepts, and folk psychology* (pp. 147–168). Oxford University Press.

Dennett, D. C. (1969). *Content and consciousness.* Routledge.

Dennett, D. C. (1978). *Brainstorms.* Bradford.

Dennett, D. C. (1981). Three kinds of intentional psychology. In R. Healy (Ed.), *Reduction, time and reality* (pp. 37–51). Cambridge University Press. (Reproduced in Dennett, 1987).

Dennett, D. C. (1987). *The intentional stance.* MIT Press.

Dennett, D. C. (1998). *Brainchildren: Essays on designing minds*. MIT Press. https://doi.org/10.7551/mitpress/1663.001.0001

Evans, J. (2010). *Thinking twice: Two minds in one brain*. Oxford University Press.

Feyerabend, P. (1975). *Against method*. NLB.

Fishbein, M., & Ajzen, I. (2010). *Predicting and changing behavior: The reasoned action approach*. Psychology Press.

Fodor, J. A. (1983). *The modularity of mind*. MIT Press. https://doi.org/10.7551/mitpress/4737.001.0001

Foxall, G. R. (1995a). Cognitive styles of consumer initiators. *Technovation, 15*(5), 269–288. https://doi.org/10.1016/0166-4972(95)96600-X

Foxall, G. R. (1995b). Science and interpretation in consumer research. *European Journal of Marketing, 29*(9), 3–99. https://doi.org/10.1108/03090569510092010

Foxall, G. R. (1999). The contextual stance. *Philosophical Psychology, 12*(1), 25–46. https://doi.org/10.1080/095150899105918

Foxall, G. R. (2011). Brain, emotion, and contingency in the explanation of consumer behaviour. *International Review of Industrial and Organizational Psychology, 26*. https://doi.org/10.1002/9781119992592.ch2

Foxall, G. R. (2016a). *Addiction as consumer choice: Exploring the cognitive dimension*. Routledge. https://doi.org/10.4324/9780203794876

Foxall, G. R. (2016b). Metacognitive control of categorial neurobehavioral decision systems. *Frontiers in Psychology, 7*(170). https://doi.org/10.3389/fpsyg.2016.00170

Foxall, G. R. (2016c). Operant behavioral economics. *Managerial and Decision Economics, 37*(4–5), 215–223. https://doi.org/10.1002/mde.2712

Foxall, G. R. (2016d). *Perspectives on consumer choice: From behavior to action, from action to agency*. Palgrave Macmillan. https://doi.org/10.1057/978-1-137-50121-9

Foxall, G. R. (2017a). *Advanced introduction to consumer behavior analysis*. Edward Elgar.

Foxall, G. R. (2017b). *Context and cognition in consumer psychology: How perception and emotion guide action*. Routledge. https://doi.org/10.4324/9781315772103

Foxall, G. R. (2020). *Intentional behaviorism: Philosophical foundations of economic psychology*. Academic Press.

Foxall, G. R., Yani-de-Soriano, M., Yousafzai, S., & Javed, U. (2012). The role of neurophysiology, emotion and contingency in the explanation of consumer choice. In V. K. Wells & G. R. Foxall (Eds.), *Handbook of developments in consumer behaviour* (pp. 461–522). Edward Elgar. https://doi.org/10.4337/9781781005125.00021

Frankish, K. (2015). Dennett's dual-process theory of reasoning. In C. Muñoz-Suárez and F. De Brigard (Eds.), *Content and consciousness revisited* (pp. 73–92). Springer. https://doi.org/10.1007/978-3-319-17374-0_4

Gawronski, B., & Payne, B. K. (Eds.). (2010). *Handbook of implicit social cognition: Measurement, theory, and applications*. Guilford Press.

Glimcher, P. (2011). *Foundations of neuroeconomic analysis*. Oxford University Press.

Hayes, S. C. (Ed.). (1989). *Rule-governed behavior: Cognition, contingencies, and instructional control*. Plenum. https://doi.org/10.1007/978-1-4757-0447-1

Hirschman, E. C., & Holbrook, M. B. (1992). *Postmodern consumer research: The study of consumption as text*. Sage. https://doi.org/10.4135/9781483325941

Holbrook, M. B., & Hirschman, E. C. (1993). *The semiotics of consumption: interpreting symbolic consumer behavior in popular culture and works of art*. Muton de Gruyter. https://doi.org/10.1515/9783110854732

Howard, J. A., & Sheth, J. (1969). *The theory of buyer behavior*. Wiley.

Kahle, L. R. (1980). Stimulus condition self-selection by males in the interaction of locus of control and skill-chance situations. *Journal of Personality and Social Psychology, 38*(1), 50–56. https://doi.org/10.1037/0022-3514.38.1.50

Kahle, L. R. & Berman, J. J. (1979). Attitudes cause behaviors: A cross-lagged panel analysis. *Journal of Personality and Social Psychology, 37*(3), 315–321. https://doi.org/10.1037/0022-3514.37.3.315

Kahle, L. R., & Kahle, K. E. (2009). The silence of the lambdas: Science, technology, and public knowledge. *International Journal of Technology, Knowledge and Society, 5*(2), 137–142. https://doi.org/10.18848/1832-3669/CGP/v05i02/55988

Kahneman, D. (2011). *Thinking, fast and slow*. Allen Lane.

Kuhn, T. S. (1970). *The structure of scientific revolutions* (2nd ed.). Chicago University Press.

Lakatos, I. (1978). *The methodology of scientific research programmes*. Cambridge University Press. https://doi.org/10.1017/CBO9780511621123

Lucas, R. E. (2018). Reevaluating the strengths and weaknesses of self-report measures of subjective well-being. In E. Diener, S. Oishi, & L. Tay (Eds.), *Handbook of well-being*. DEF Publishers.

Malle, B. F., Moses, L. J., & Baldwin, D. A. (2011). *Intentions and intentionality: Foundations of social cognition*. MIT Press.

McClure, S. M., Laibson, D. L., Loewenstein, G., & Cohen, J. D. (2004). Separate neural systems value immediate and delayed monetary rewards. *Science,*

306(5695), 503–507. https://doi.org/10.1126/science.1100907

Mill, J. S. (1859). On liberty. In J. S. Mill (Ed.), *Utilitarianism, liberty and representative government* (pp. 65–170). Dent.

Nicosia, F. M. (1966). *Consumer decision processes: Marketing and advertising implications*. Prentice-Hall.

Oliveira-Castro, J. M., Cavalcanti, P., & Foxall, G. R. (2016a). What consumers maximize: Brand choice as a function of utilitarian and informational reinforcement. *Managerial and Decision Economics*, *37*(4–5), 360–371. https://doi.org/10.1002/mde.2722

Oliveira-Castro, J. M., Cavalcanti, P., & Foxall, G. R. (2016b). What do consumers maximize? The analysis of utility functions in light of the Behavioral Perspective Model. In G. R. Foxall (Ed.), *The Routledge companion to consumer behavior analysis* (pp. 202–212). Routledge.

Oliveira-Castro, J. M., & Foxall, G. R. (2017). Consumer maximization of utilitarian and informational reinforcement: Comparing two utility measures with reference to social class. *Behavior Analyst*, *40*(2), 457–474. https://doi.org/10.1007/s40614-017-0122-9

Popper, K. R. (1959). *The logic of scientific discovery* (expanded English edition). Hutchinson. (Original work published 1934)

Posner, R. A. (1990). *The problems of jurisprudence*. Harvard University Press.

Rogers, E. M. (2004). *Diffusion of innovations* (5th ed.). Free Press.

Rosenberg, A. (2016). *Philosophy of social science* (5th ed.). Westview.

Ross, D. (2012). The economic agent: Not human, but important. In U. Mäki (Ed.), *Philosophy of economics* (pp. 691–735). Elsevier. https://doi.org/10.1016/B978-0-444-51676-3.50023-3

Rotter, J. B. (1966). Generalized expectancies for internal versus external control of reinforcement. *Psychological Monographs*, *80*(1), 1–28. https://doi.org/10.1037/h0092976

Russell, B. (1940). *An inquiry into meaning and truth*. George Allen and Unwin.

Schwartz-Shea, P. (2012). *Interpretive research design: Concepts and processes*. Routledge.

Searle, J. R. (1983). *Intentionality: An essay in the philosophy of mind*. Cambridge University Press. https://doi.org/10.1017/CBO9781139173452

Searle, J. R. (1994). Intentionality (1). In S. Guttenplan (Ed.), *A companion to the philosophy of mind* (pp. 379–386). Blackwell.

Searle, J. R. (1995). *The construction of social reality*. Free Press.

Searle, J. R. (2001). *Rationality in action*. MIT Press.

Searle, J. R. (2004). *Mind*. Oxford University Press.

Searle, J. R. (2010). *Making the social world: The structure of human civilization*. Oxford University Press. https://doi.org/10.1093/acprof:osobl/9780195396171.001.0001

Skinner, B. F. (1945). The operational analysis of psychological terms. *Psychological Review*, *52*(5), 270–277. https://doi.org/10.1037/h0062535

Skinner, B. F. (1950). Are theories of learning necessary? *Psychological Review*, *57*(4), 193–216. https://doi.org/10.1037/h0054367

Skinner, B. F. (1953). *Science and human behavior*. Macmillan.

Skinner, B. F. (1977). Why I am not a cognitive psychologist. *Behaviorism*, *5*(2), 1–10.

Smith, T. L. (1994). *Behavior and its causes: Philosophical foundations of operant psychology*. Kluwer Academic Publishers.

Stanovich, K. E. (2009). Distinguishing the reflective, algorithmic, and autonomous minds: Is it time for a tri-process theory? In J. Evans & K. Frankish (Eds.), *In two minds: Dual processes and beyond* (pp. 55–88). Oxford University Press. https://doi.org/10.1093/acprof:oso/9780199230167.003.0003

Stanovich, K. E. (2011). *Rationality and the reflective mind*. Oxford University Press.

Strawson, G. (2010). *Mental reality* (2nd ed.). MIT Press.

Wilson, T. (2019). *Consumption, psychology, and practice theories: A hermeneutic perspective*. Routledge.

Ziman, J. M. (1968). *Public knowledge: An essay concerning the social dimension of science*. Cambridge University Press.

Ziman, J. M. (1978). *Reliable knowledge: An exploration of the grounds for belief in science*. Cambridge University Press.

CHAPTER 4

STRUCTURAL EQUATION MODELS IN CONSUMER RESEARCH: EXPLORING INTUITIONS AND DEEPER MEANINGS OF SEMs

Richard P. Bagozzi

Structural equation models (SEMs) are statistical procedures useful in representing constructs, especially multidimensional ones; assessing construct validity; correcting for random and systematic errors; and testing causal, functional, and associational hypotheses. As with any methodology, SEMs exhibit benefits and limitations. But SEMs are more than a methodology; rather, they are frameworks and procedures for integrating theory, hypotheses, and measurement. In this chapter, I attempt to relate SEMs to consumer psychology and other statistical procedures, and at the same time I provide some grounding in basic ideas in measurement, philosophy of mind, and philosophy of science. The latter issues are often neglected or taken for granted and not examined much in discussions of SEMs. But it can be argued that they are especially relevant for consumer psychology because of the central role played by the mind and mental concepts and their measures in consumer research.

There is frequently a tension between use of SEMs and use of traditional statistical methods, such that people sometimes see them as starkly different procedures, and indeed a de facto segregation exists in that many areas of consumer research tend to use only multiple regression or analysis of variance (ANOVA) methods, whereas other areas use primarily SEMs. To compound matters, many students technically capable of using SEMs do not take SEM courses, and many faculty members capable of teaching and using SEMs do not do so, largely because the variables and data SEMs deal with do not correspond well to the phenomena and processes found in consumer research. The result in marketing departments over the past 20 years or so has been a decline in the opportunity to learn about SEMs, observable among students in consumer research. Indeed, compared with psychology departments and organization behavior groups in business schools, where the teaching and use of SEMs flourish, marketing departments in general, and consumer behavior groups in particular, have missed opportunities to benefit from SEM methods. This has added to the gap noted earlier in the use of statistics in consumer research.

There is another, related problem worth mentioning. I recently finished a chapter prepared for the *Annual Review of Psychology*, dealing with the psychological underpinning of brands. I found the use of SEMs to be especially problematic. Published articles sometimes failed to present enough information to evaluate findings one way or another. Occasionally findings were misrepresented. In some instances, the interpretation of results was misleading and even at odds with accepted statistical practice. At the same time, opportunities to use SEMs that would have strengthened the quality of research done were sometimes missed. It is obvious

The author is very grateful to the editor and an anonymous reviewer for many helpful suggestions.
https://doi.org/10.1037/0000262-004
APA Handbook of Consumer Psychology, L. R. Kahle (Editor-in-Chief)
Copyright © 2022 by the American Psychological Association. All rights reserved.

to me that both researchers and journal evaluation processes need to reexamine how they are using and interpreting SEMs, lest the validity of research findings lose credibility and people choose not to use SEMs for the wrong reasons.

PHILOSOPHY OF MIND FOUNDATIONS

Consumer researchers use theories and develop hypotheses to explain human behavior. Unobservable hypothetical variables or processes are posited to account for observable behavior. Causal relations are the main mechanisms for study in such approaches.

Hereafter I consider a number of mind–body theories proposed by philosophers. The primary focus of this chapter concerns psychological language and discourse, but similar principles apply for consumer research grounded in economics, sociology, and anthropology, among others. Why should we be interested in mind–body theories? One of the main tasks of philosophers is to consider the conceptual and logical foundations of the nature of our minds, mental states and events, and the relationship of the mind to behavior and action. The models and theories used by consumer researchers and the findings in their studies can be shown to be based more or less on assumptions from the philosophy of mind. However, such assumptions are seldom acknowledged. To the extent that models, theories, and methods violate the logical and conceptual foundations of ideas from the philosophy of mind, findings may be invalid and policy implications unfounded. It might be maintained that much knowledge in consumer research rests on unknown and unexamined assumptions in this regard.

The Theory–Measurement Distinction

Researchers sometimes create an artificial distinction between theory and measurement and neglect to consider how the two are related. They also presume a false asymmetry as to directionality between the two. The received view claims that theory has pride of place and constrains how we should measure concepts. There is much truth to the theory–measurement dichotomy, and indeed the theory-to-measurement relation has come to be taken for granted. Mindless acceptance of such a point of view can, however, lead to formulaic and narrow approaches to consumer psychology. Not only do we see a narrowly bounded preponderance of a background-hypotheses-method-results-discussion structure underpinning most research but hypotheses are constructed to fit equally restricted methods. So a small number of main effects and interactions are hypothesized and tested with multiple regression or ANOVA in one tradition, whereas a small number of dependent and endogenous variables are predicted by a small number of exogenous variables with SEMs in another tradition. Our specialized theories lead naturally to circumscribed methods of one sort or another if we are not mindful of other ways of thinking about what we are trying to explain and how we go about explaining and testing our hypotheses. As we will see later in this chapter, the different methods alluded to prior are not so different, or at least they are special cases of a more integrative approach to measurement and hypothesis testing.

Theory can constrain measurement in the sense that how we think about phenomena influences how we measure and test them. But at the same time, it is important to be open to the possibility that how we measure and test hypotheses can influence how we come to think about the phenomena we hope to understand and explain. The theory–measurement relationship is perhaps best construed as a symmetric one. Of course, in the long run, programs of research reveal symmetries in the accretion of knowledge. But SEMs provide ways of narrowing or bridging the theory–measurement gap more formally and in a shorter span of time. That is, rather than separating theory/hypothesis formation from methods in absolute terms, SEMs can be used to integrate these two equally important facets of research in a systematic way that permits examination of posited effects, random error, and systematic error. Theory and measurement might be best viewed more as a blending of ideas and procedures rather than two separated steps. Further, the blending creates the possibility of more precise mutual influence between theory and measurement, such that the lacuna between the two is reconciled and problems in inference making and interpretation are not spuriously exacerbated.

Mind–Body Theories

We turn now to mind–body theories. Mind–body theories rest, in part, on the difference between mental and physical phenomena and whether or how the two are related. Although some theories deny that mental states or events exist and some theories limit inquiry to relations between physical states or events alone, consumer psychologists have found it useful and natural to include mental states, if not wholly, then at least partially, in their focus. Mental states or events have been used to represent things in the world of experience (e.g., perceived product quality), characteristics of consumers (e.g., materialism), and more generally consumer consciousness and self-consciousness. They have also been essential content in explaining behaviors and actions of consumers. Mind–body theories address such seemingly simple questions of whether, and if so, how and when, (a) mental states or events cause behavior or action, (b) physical phenomena influence mental states or events, and (c) mental states or events cause other mental states or events.

To be precise herein, I define *behavior* as a bodily movement a consumer makes, usually automatically or reflexively. For example, reaching for an eye-catching product as one passes a shelf in the supermarket, either to satisfy one's curiosity or perhaps purchase it impulsively, is a kind of behavior that consumer researchers might study. *Action*, by contrast, is an intentional doing, a purposive activity, where one acts on the bases of reasons (e.g., beliefs, desires, attitudes), often to achieve a goal. Action might also involve greater amounts, and qualitatively distinct forms, of consciousness and self-consciousness than behavior. Mental states or events play greater roles in explaining actions than they do in explaining behavior per se. But note that action includes behavior as a subpart of its meaning. That is, bodily movements generally accompany actions.

An important approach in psychology in the 20th century until about 1960 was behaviorism. For psychology, behaviorism advocated two policies: The field should study observable phenomena (usually behavior) and not have recourse to mental states or events to explain behavior. Classical conditioning and operant conditioning are two classic examples of psychological behaviorism, where the connection between antecedent stimulus, say, and observed behavioral response is claimed to follow a behavioral law. Mental states are largely eschewed under behaviorism in favor of examination of patterns of behavior. Sometimes researchers took a behaviorism perspective on mental events, calling them dispositions to behave in a particular manner under specific physical or behavioral circumstances, but no claim was made about the nature of internal mental states. Figure 4.1a presents a simple rendition of behaviorism as might be interpreted under a SEM lens, where, for purposes of illustration, the stimulus and response are taken to have two operationalizations each. SEMs have not been generally applied to behaviorism, and typically a single measured stimulus and a single measured behavioral response are used. But I have sketched this example to suggest that observed stimuli and responses can be used to correct for measurement error in the representation of (error-corrected) renditions of the physical variables. The parameter, γ, then represents an inferred strength of relationship between stimulus and response, corrected for measurement error. Rectangles are used to depict measurements, in this case physical measures, and ellipses represent unobservables, in this case physical phenomena corrected for error.

Contemporary consumer psychology has moved beyond behaviorism and is rooted in functionalism. Indeed since about 1970 to the present, the majority of studies performed in consumer research have followed functionalism but without necessarily acknowledging this shift. Contrary to behaviorism, where mental states or events play little or no role in explaining behavior (or action), functionalism proposes that mental states or events (e.g., cognitive processes, emotional processes) are causes of behavior (or action). Under functionalism, what makes a mental state or event what it is depends on the role it performs by itself or with other mental states or events in transforming physical phenomena (e.g., sensory stimulation in the form of priming, past behavior, or stimuli in one's environment) into behavior or action.

To take an extended example, see Figure 4.1b:

This is a 2 (regulatory orientation: promotion vs. prevention focus) × 3 (implementation intentions: control vs. promotion focus vs. prevention focus intentions) × 2 (habit: strong vs. weak) randomized experimental design (see Tam et al., 2010). Notice that behavior at the left in Figure [4.1b] consists of manipulated (primed) and measured regulatory focus (P_1), primed promotion-focus and prevention-focus implementation intentions plus a no implementation intention control (P_2), and measured snacking habits (P_3); the main dependent variable is actual snacking behavior recorded over a 2-day period (P_4) following the manipulations. Four mental properties

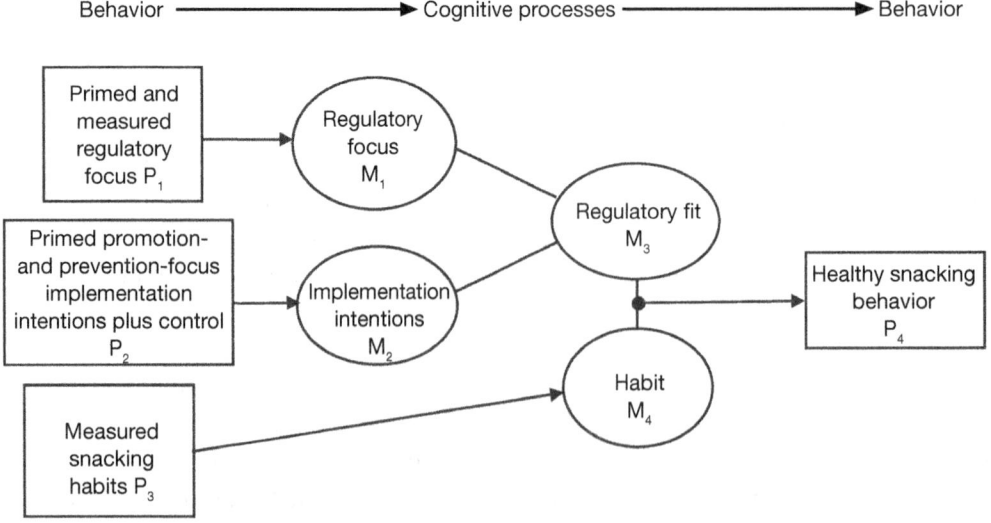

FIGURE 4.1. Two foundational approaches in psychology (behaviorism) and in psychology and consumer research (functionalism). (a) e_is are errors terms, λ_is are factor loadings expressing the degree of correspondence between observed physical states (rectangles) and latent variables (ellipses), and γ is the inferred effect of stimulus on response. (b) From "Alternative Perspectives in Philosophy of Mind and Their Relationship to Structural Equation Models in Psychology," by R. P. Bagozzi, 2011, *Psychological Inquiry*, 22(2), p. 89 (https://doi.org/10.1080/1047840X.2010.550183). Copyright 2011 by Taylor & Francis. Reprinted with permission.

function between the behavioral manipulations (P_1-P_3) and the subsequent behavior (P_4). These are the proposed mental states of regulatory focus (M_1) and implementation intentions (M_2), which together define regulatory fit (M_3), and habit (M_4) and, which is proposed to interact with M_3 to influence P_4.

In words, the results of the experiment, under planned contrasts, showed that participants with strong unhealthy snacking habits snacked healthier when they formed implementation intentions that fit their regulatory orientation (i.e., promotion-focused participants with promotion implementation intentions or prevention-focused participants with prevention implementation intentions) than when they formed implementation intentions that did not fit their regulatory orientation (i.e., promotion-focused participants with prevention implementation intentions or prevention-focused participants with promotion implementation intentions) or no implementation intentions at all. For participants with strong unhealthy snacking habits, making implementation intentions that did not fit their regulatory orientation, or not making any implementation intentions at all, resulted in similar snacking behavior. Planned contrasts also showed that participants with weak unhealthy snacking habits snacked healthier when they formed implementation intentions (either fitting or not fitting their regulatory focus) than the no implementation formed condition. For people with weak unhealthy snacking habits, forming implementation intentions that either fit or did not fit their regulatory orientation resulted in similar snacking behavior. For graphic presentation of these findings, see Figure 1 in Tam et al. (2010). (Bagozzi, 2011a, pp. 90–91)

I used an experimental example for functionalism, but the ideas would be similar for survey or quasi-experimental research under SEMs. I turn next to physicalist and dualist mind–body theories but only cover the most popular ones. For more background, see Jaworski (2011) and Bagozzi and Lee (2019).

Monist mind–body theories. Monism claims that there is only one kind of thing in the universe. Idealism, for example, asserts that everything that exists is mental. This point of view does not fit well what most consumer researchers do, and no more will be said about it here. Another monist theory is eliminativism, which claims that mental states (e.g., beliefs, values, emotions, desires, intentions) do not exist and therefore should play no role in psychological explanations. Only material or physical states exist. This theory, too, which seems to even preclude consciousness as a topic for study, has less currency for consumer researchers and will not be considered further herein, but many neuroscientists follow this point of view.

An approach that fits some research in consumer behavior is reductive physicalism, where it is maintained that "psychological categories correspond to physical categories . . . for instance what we call 'pain' is really just a physical state such as a state of the brain" (Jaworski, 2011, pp. 381–382). A variant of reductive physicalism is psychological identity theory, which claims that "mental states will be identified with states of the nervous system through empirical investigation" (Jaworski, 2011, p. 380).

To take an example, imagine consumer researchers desire to study theory of mind processes. *Theory of mind* refers to mechanisms people use to infer and reason about beliefs, feelings, intentions, and other mental events of people with whom they interact. Figure 4.2 presents a diagrammatic representation of psychological identity theory. In Panel A, theory of mind processes are manipulated by giving subjects vignettes to listen to that include stories of persons interacting with others and involving interpersonal mentalizing (the theory of mind conditions) and control vignettes consisting of stories without interpersonal mentalizing and stories with unlinked sentences. While subjects listened to the

a. Orthodox rendition

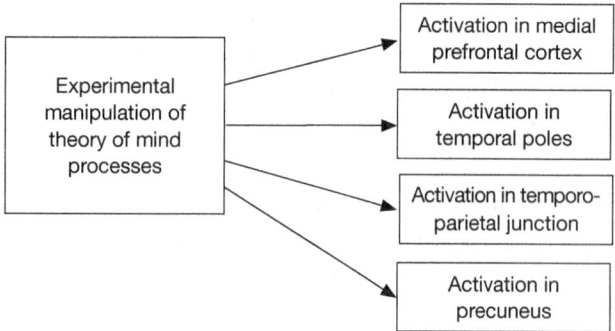

b. Modified rendition to take into account mental states rendition

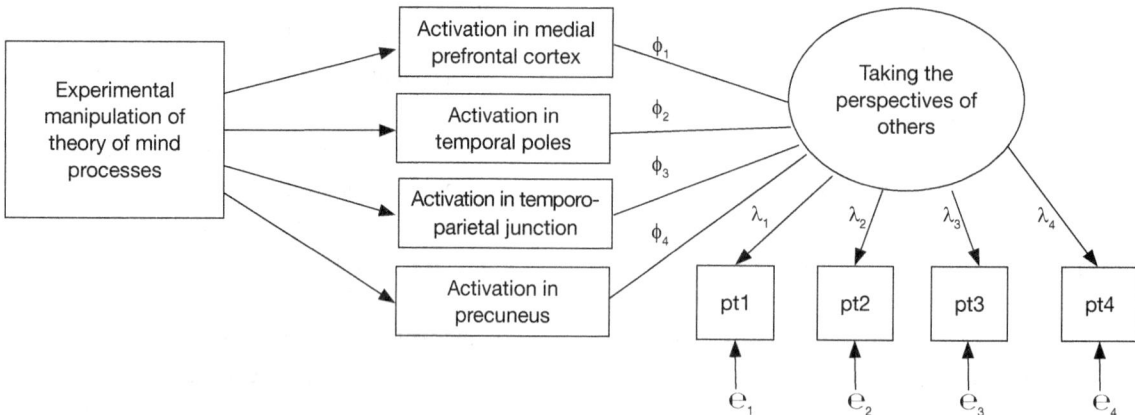

FIGURE 4.2. Psychological identity theory: Mental states are physical states. ϕs are associations between the four brain activations and perspective taking; they reflect the degree of correlation between physical states and subjective experience.

vignettes, measurements were taken of brain activation in the medial prefrontal cortex, temporal poles, temporal-parietal junction, and precuneus regions of the brain by application of functional magnetic resonance imaging (fMRI; for details of the procedure and findings, see Bagozzi et al., 2013; Dietvorst et al., 2009). Such areas of the brain have been implicated in theory of mind processing. The rendition in Figure 4.2a corresponds to an orthodox representation of psychological identity theory. Here mental states of theory of mind are induced physically, and activations of the four aforementioned brain regions are taken as physical instances of theory of mind.

Psychological identity theory seems to fit studies wherein all mental states are purported to be physical states, but unlike eliminativism it does not deny the existence of mental states but rather accepts them with an aim to reducing them to physical measurements. Some investigations of neuroscience activity might correspond to an identity theory perspective. However, much research into consumer behavior rests on the belief that mental states actually exist, and seldom can theories and tests of hypotheses in consumer research operationalize, or indeed replace, mental concepts and processes with physical ones. In addition, identity theory had been criticized for neglecting the phenomenal and subjective aspects of mental phenomena, which at times are the objects of explanation and also function on occasion as explanatory variables in consumer research. Closely related to this point is what some philosophers of mind term *qualia*, the qualitative feel for what it is like to experience a mental state. It is claimed that qualia are essential in conscious and self-conscious experience, and indeed much of consumer research appears to rest on such experiences.

Figure 4.2b is an unorthodox representation of psychological identity theory, where the particular theory of mind subjective state of taking the perspective of other people, a cognitive facet of empathy, is associated with the four physical brain states (the ϕ_is). Taking the perspective of others is represented in Figure 4.2b as a latent, unobserved, or hypothetical variable, where, for purposes of illustration, four measures (pt_i) are taken as indicators of it, the measures contain errors (e_i) that can be estimated statistically, and the degree of correspondence between measures and latent perspective taking (λ_i) can also be estimated. We call this an unorthodox representation of identity theory because an attempt is made to capture a subjective felt theory of mind response and estimate its degree of association with physical brain states claimed to define theory of mind. A more orthodox rendering of identity theory would avoid mental state or events and focus exclusively on physical ones. Although not shown in Figure 4.2, the measured activations of the brain states could be treated as reflections of error-corrected latent variables analogously to that shown for behaviorism (Figure 4.1a), but this would require multiple measures for each state.

As a final comment on reductive physicalism, it should be noted that it differs from functionalism with respect to the interpretation of mental states as qualia. Functionalism gives meaning to mental states through their bridging role between inputs (e.g., manipulation of physical stimuli) and outputs (e.g., observed behavior) and the relationships between mental states, if any. Mental states are functional states under functionalism. But the treatment of qualia is believed to be more experientially direct in the philosophy literature. It is claimed that they entail a subjective experience of how something feels and are in some sense private (e.g., tied to a first-person point of view), ineffable (i.e., not easily expressible in language), and intrinsic (i.e., a property of a mental event not defined through its relationships with other mental events but rather inhering in the focal mental event itself). Again reductive physicalism denies the experience of qualia, and to the extent that they exist or are useful in consumer research, another approach is needed, to which we now turn.

The final monist theory of mind we will consider is nonreductive physicalism,

> A family of physicalist theories that reject the *reduction* of the *special sciences* [e.g., psychology, economics, biology, sociology] to physics. Unlike *eliminative physicalists* and like *reductive physicalists*, nonreductive physicalists claim that psychological discourse has real descriptive and explanatory legitimacy. Unlike reductive physicalists, however, nonreductivists deny that this legitimacy is due to psychological categories corresponding in a straightforward way to physical categories. (Jaworski, 2011, p. 375, emphasis in original)

One version of nonreductive physicalism, anomalous monism, is due largely to philosopher Donald Davidson (2001). Davidson proposed that mental tokens (roughly particular mental states or events or their features), as opposed to mental types (general categories of mental states or events), are identical to physical states or events. This permits the postulation of mental events or states in causal relationships, grounded in physical laws, and especially for the effects of mental states (e.g., intentions) on actions, which is commonly studied in consumer research. In addition, Davidson did much to set the foundation for the roles of beliefs and desires in explanatory models, which also has found utility in consumer research for explaining decision making (Bagozzi & Dholakia, 2006a, 2006b; Dholakia et al., 2004) and real behavior (Tsai & Bagozzi, 2014). However, because Davidson did not explicitly deal with how mental events can be measured, and because anomalous monism is vulnerable to criticisms of treating mental states or events as epiphenomena (in that only physical states can cause or be caused by other physical states and not mental ones), we will not say any more about anomalous monism herein.

A central issue for nonreductive physicalism is how to express the meaning of mental phenomena. Nonreductive realization physicalism (NRP) is particularly compatible with many features of SEMs. Under NRP, mental phenomena become realized by physical phenomena, where again phenomena can refer to states or events. Figure 4.3 presents a general example. Mental state A (e.g., attitude) influences both mental state I (e.g., intention) and behavioral outcome B (e.g., purchase behavior).

Notice that each latent mental and behavioral state has multiple measures (in these cases only two measures per latent variable are presented for simplicity). This is a feature of NRP and has been termed *multiple realizability*. Although multiple realizability has been spoken of in philosophy mostly with respect to different realizations of the same mental state (e.g., felt pain) for different people, we use the term and concept here for different realizations for each mental state in a theory for each person included in a state of the theory, where multiple people are needed to estimate statistical parameters (γs, β, λs, var e_is, and var ζs). Note also that under physicalism, causal relations are assumed to occur between physical states of events, not mental ones. But Figure 4.3 shows the causal relations among mental states or events. This is not really a contradiction because all six measures depicted in Figure 4.3 are physically and empirically related to each other, but, following the convention used in the SEM literature, such empirical relations are not shown in such diagrams. That is, a_1 and a_2 are correlated measures of A, i_1 and i_2 are correlated measures of I, b_1 and b_2 are correlated measures of B, a_1 and a_2 are causally related to i_1 and i_2 and to b_1 and b_2, and i_1 and i_2 are causally related to b_1 and b_2. Commonly used inferential statistical procedures work with the observed empirical relations to estimate the parameters shown in Figure 4.3. The parameters γ_1, γ_2, and β are inferred from the empirical relations and constitute estimates of the observed causal relations reflected in the empirical data. So γ_1, γ_2, and β actually refer to causal relations among the measures (which are physical

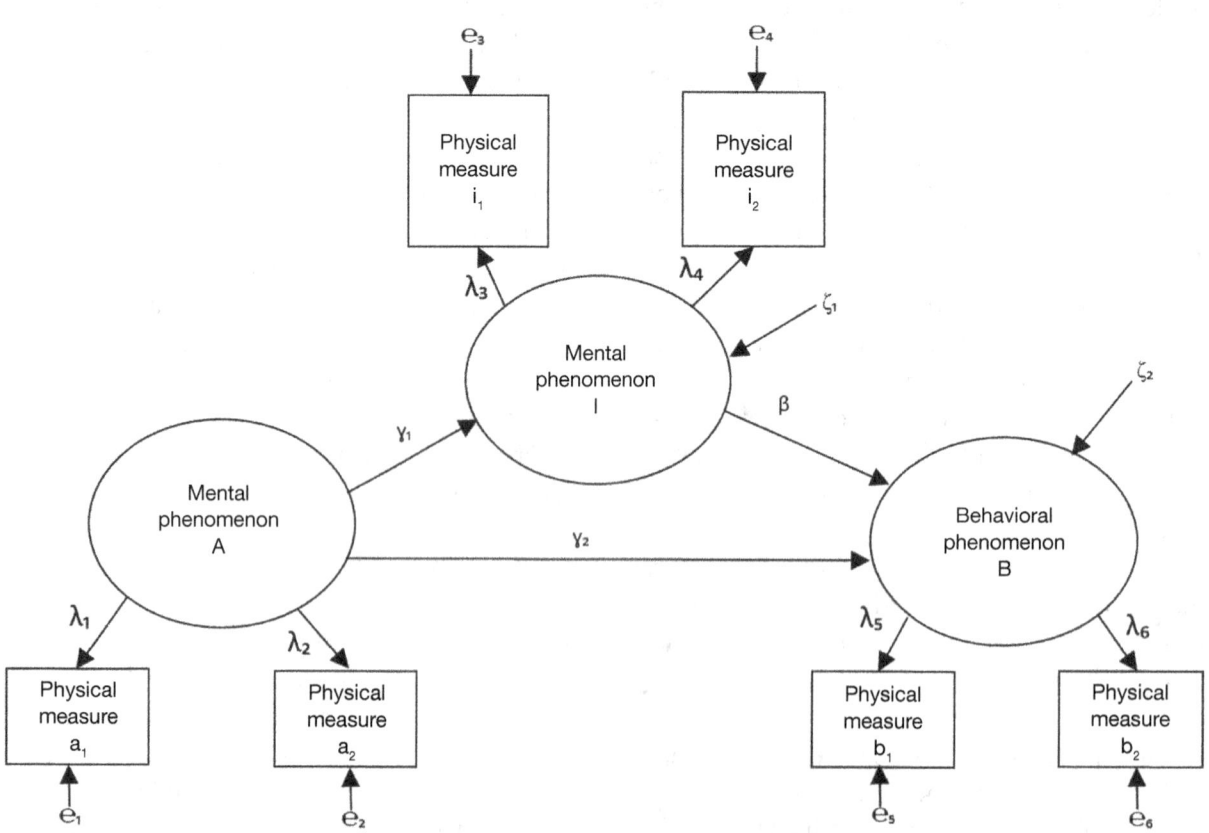

FIGURE 4.3. Nonreductive realization physicalism: Mental phenomena realized by physical phenomena.

states) after correcting for measurement errors, which attenuate the observed relations.

Another beneficial feature of NRP is that it provides support for considering higher order properties of the realization of mental states or events (see Putnam, 1988, for some philosophical foundations). We will draw upon some of these ideas, largely by extension, when we discuss higher order constructs later.

A different approach under nonreductive physicalism for providing meaning of mental phenomena is the notion of supervenience (Kim, 2000, 2005). Kim (2005) interpreted supervenience as a kind of dependence relationship:

> I take supervenience as an ontological thesis involving the idea of dependence—a sense of dependence that justifies saying that a mental property is instantiated in a giving organism at a time *because*, or *in virtue of* the fact that, one of its physical "base" properties is instantiated by the organism at that time. *Supervenience*, therefore, is not a mere claim of covariation between mental and physical properties; it includes a claim of experiential dependence of the mental on the physical. (p. 34, emphasis in original)

Although some treatments of supervenience in the philosophy of mind literature interpret the dependence of mental states on physical states in a causal sense with the physical causing the mental, Kim (2005) does not appear to have taken this perspective and instead claimed that corresponding mental state and physical state "occur precisely at the same time" (p. 42). As a consequence, and in concert with the meaning of instantiate as "to represent (an abstraction) by a concrete instance" (Merriam-Webster, n.d.), I construe the meaning of supervenience to be consistent with the representation of realization in Figure 4.3.

Philosopher Jaworski (2011) asserted that nonreductive physicalism is "the new orthodoxy in philosophy of mind" and "remains the most popular type of physicalism today" (p. 129). It seems clear that eliminativism, reductive physicalism, and nonreductive physicalism fit neuroscience interpretations of consumer psychology well. I think nonreductive physicalism, and to a lesser extent reductive physicalism, also fit consumer research even when mental states and events, and qualia, are incorporated into theories and research. Here, however, the full meaning of realization and supervenience are in need of further development, as ambiguities exist and remain unresolved. For an informative summary of current knowledge and remaining issues, see Jaworski (2011).

Dualist mind–body theories. Consumer researchers have not given much attention to the conceptual underpinnings of their concepts and the relation of concepts to measurement and methods. Despite the present popularity of nonreductive physicalism in the philosophy of mind literature, I wish to briefly mention dualist approaches. A fuller presentation of dualism was prepared for this paper but was deleted in the editing process; it is available on request for interested readers. Dualism has a long history but has fallen out of favor in philosophy. Nevertheless, in everyday life most people implicitly follow dualism, and most consumer researchers follow it as well. Hence a brief treatment is included here. Whenever we think about physical phenomena influencing mental events, mental events influencing physical phenomena, or mental events influencing each other, we typically imply a difference between the mental and physical that is not presumed by the other frameworks discussed earlier. Consumers and consumer researchers frequently draw upon intuition grounded in folk psychology to explain and interpret consumer behavior. Folk psychology is fundamentally rooted in dualistic notions but has the conceptual problems noted earlier. With the thought that someday dualism might be revitalized and a reconciliation achieved between the material and immaterial mind, I leave the discussion with mention of proposals made by Thomas Nagel (2002, 2012) for a naturalistic dualism (for perspective, see Bagozzi, 2011a; Bagozzi & Lee, 2019).

Summary. Consumer research had lacked a certain degree of self-awareness of what mental states are, how they relate to physical phenomena and other mental states, and what are conceptual and logical standards and pitfalls threatening the validity of consumer research. Many of the questions and criteria associated with such issues are brought to awareness through the use of SEMs. Much of consumer psychology, implicitly at least, follows functionalist principles. Much of it too is guided by folk psychology knowledge. Indeed sometimes it is difficult to separate functionalism from folk psychology influence in theorizing and testing hypotheses. But it is perhaps time to go beyond functionalism and naïve folk psychology to more formally address issues of how to incorporate reliability and threats to validity into our representations of theories and their tests, how to better integrate theory and method, how to conceive of mental states as simple variables but also as complex ones when desired (Bagozzi, 2022), how to measure mental states and represent the relationships in a way permitting appraisal of the conceptual tension between concept and observation, how to delineate and correct for random and systematic errors in tests of hypotheses and control for common method biases, how to examine generalizability and conduct experiments with SEMs, and more generally how to conduct, interpret, and evaluate SEM research.

A final tension to mention before turning to the topics listed in the previous paragraph is that between instrumentalism and realism. Some consumer researchers, especially more applied ones, see theories and models more as tools for predicting consumer behavior. Although SEMs can of course provide ways of implementing such aims, SEMs are especially suited for bringing about theory construction and tests of hypotheses where real properties of concepts and real causal relations can be investigated.

THREE COMPONENTS OF MEANING IN SEMs

> Science is not common sense, and its most basic ideas and frames of reference require development through complex intellectual processes which involve not only interpretations of observations but also theoretical and partly philosophical conceptualization.
> (Parsons, 1968, p. 429)

We can think of scientific research as a way of obtaining meaning from how we think about questions in the world in which we live and how we experience tests of hypotheses therein. The questions we ask concern why, how, and when phenomena of interest behave as they do, and experiences refer to interpretations of observations taken to verify, validate, or in some other way elucidate empirical meaning of phenomena of importance. Theoretical and philosophical arguments inform this process, as do methodological procedures. All these elements can be seen to assemble, articulate, and harmonize in SEMs. Early on, the integrated system of theory, method, and observations was termed the *holistic construal* (Bagozzi & Phillips, 1982).

Three kinds of meaning combine to help us make sense of the world: theoretical meaning, empirical meaning, and spurious meaning (Bagozzi, 1984, 2011b). Figure 4.4 captures the central features of sense making with these types of meaning.

Theoretical Meaning

By theoretical meaning I mean the conceptualization of variables entering a model or theory, which might be mental or physical or both, and the theory and rationale behind hypotheses linking the variables.

In order to grasp the significance of theoretical meaning, start with the focal construct, F, in Figure 4.4. The theoretical meaning of F inheres in what it is and in how, why, and when it relates to other variables, antecedents, and consequences in a larger system of hypotheses organized together in a theory. What a concept, construct, or variable is can be captured, albeit imperfectly, by its conceptualization, where it may be defined and given content to express its essence. Theoretical criteria may be applied that address its coherence, scope, specificity, well-formedness, lack of contradiction and ambiguity, logical consistency, and other semantic and syntactic criteria (Gerring, 1999; Outhwaite, 1983). Concepts may contain powers or liabilities for change and interdependencies with other concepts that further interpret its substance.

Theoretical meaning of a focal construct comes about as well (a) in its relationship to antecedents, which specify its cause, evolution, and history;

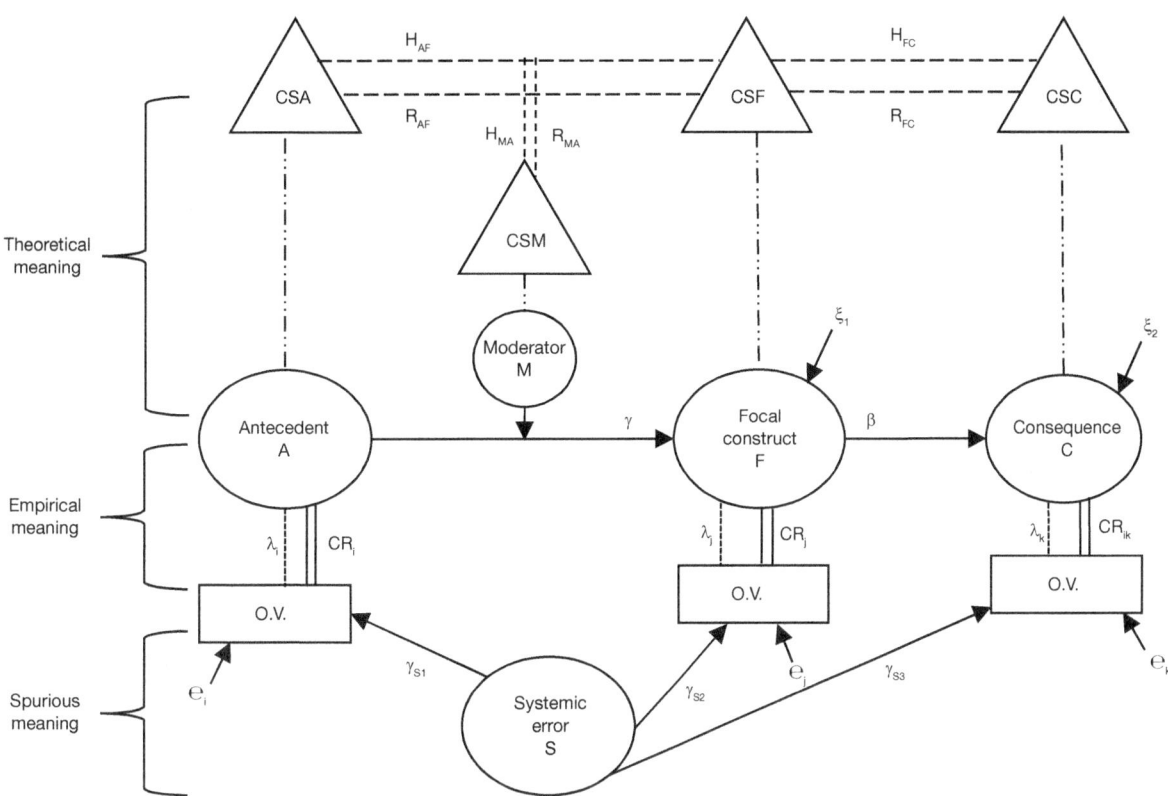

Key: O = latent variable; □ = observed variable; Δ = conceptual specification; γ, β = inferred causal paths; λ = factor loading; ══ = correspondence rule; ξ = error in latent variables; e_i = random measurement error; H = hypotheses; R = rationale for hypotheses; O.V. = observed variables (indicator, measurement)

FIGURE 4.4. Conceptual framework for structural equation models showing three senses of meaning: Theoretical, empirical, spurious (measures of moderator, M, omitted for clarity). From "Measurement and Meaning in Information Systems and Organizational Research: Methodological and Philosophical Foundations," by R. P. Bagozzi, 2011, *Management Information Systems Quarterly*, 35(2), p. 263 (https://doi.org/10.2307/23044044). Copyright 2011 by the Management Information Systems Research Center, University of Minnesota. Reprinted with permission.

(b) in its relationship to consequences that delineate what influence it has, where it is going, and what it can lead to; and (c) in its contingent dependencies and contingent effects through representation of its links to moderators. Some meaning might accrue through associations a focal construct has with other constructs (not shown in Figure 4.4). Note in the top of Figure 4.4, the meaning of focal construct, F, occurs through description of the nature of its hypothesized connections to antecedents, moderators, and consequences (H_{AF}, H_{FC}, H_{MA}) and specification of the corresponding rationales for these hypotheses (R_{AF}, R_{FC}, R_{MA}). One way of characterizing a frequently espoused objective of consumer research is scrutiny of the following questions: How and when does an antecedent, A, influence a consequence, C? It does this through its operation on a mediating variable(s), F, which stipulates how the effect of A is channeled or transformed into C (an answer to the how question), and it does this by signifying when (i.e., under what conditions) A influences C through F (an answer to the when question). Moderated mediation or mediated moderation effects, where conditional indirect effects are specified, constitute important objectives of basic and applied research in consumer psychology (Hayes, 2018).

To give an example, researchers in recent years have investigated consumer responses to perceived violations of ethical behavior by corporations. For example, corporations violate the human dignity and freedom of people when they conscript underage workers and abuse them, when they pollute or in other ways defile the environment, and when they break covenants with governments or misuse resources of local communities. One study manipulated corporate violations of environmental protections to see their effects on negative word of mouth, complaint behaviors, and boycott decisions against an offending corporation (Xie et al., 2015). To explain how perceived corporate malfeasance influenced these negative reactions toward the company, Haidt's (2012) social intuitionist model was used to specify the moral psychology emotions of contempt, righteous anger, and social disgust as mediators. These three negative moral emotions constitute what is called the *hostility triad* in the literature (Izard, 1977). Until recently, cognitive approaches based on reasoning were used to explain reactions toward offenders of moral sensibilities (Kohlberg, 1981). Against reasoned approaches to morality, Haidt (2012) proposed that people respond to moral infringements in automatic, emotional ways. Xie et al. (2015) hypothesized and found that five individual difference variables further moderated the effects of the manipulation on contempt, anger, and disgust, and these emotions, in turn, affected the decisions to take actions against the corporation. The five moderators were empathy, moral identity, social justice values, relational self-concept, and collective self-concept. In sum, consumers' responses to corporate irresponsibility were found to be explained by emotions and individual difference variables to answer how and when consumer awareness of corporate irresponsibility influences decisions to act against the corporation.

As a final comment on theoretical meaning, note that the causal parameters shown in Figure 4.4 (i.e., γ and β) are estimates from data of the hypothesized relationships. They, thus, are imperfect representations of the hypothesized effects summarized by H_{FA}, H_{MA}, and H_{FC} and substantiated theoretically by R_{FA}, H_{MA}, and R_{FC}. They also are affected by error in the measurement procedures, which in certain senses can be corrected. Therefore γ and β deviate from ideal or true representations of hypothesized effects as a function of both the quality of conceptualizations of antecedents, focal construct, consequences, and moderators, as well as error in the measurement of these variables.

Empirical Meaning

The observational content of latent variables spells out their empirical meaning. Variables in a theory achieve empirical meaning through their relationship with observations or measurements. Any variable in a theory can have one or more observations (only one observation per theoretical variable is shown in Figure 4.4 for simplicity). Notice in Figure 4.4 that two links are displayed between latent variables and observations. The first one is labeled λ, which is a factor loading and is estimated from data. It represents the empirically inferred correspondence between latent variables and observation. The value for λ will depend on the quality of operationalization in the sense of how well the specification of the latent variables accords with the specification of the observation. The value for λ will also be affected by measurement error, which we will discuss next under spurious meaning. The other link in Figure 4.4 between latent variables and observation, drawn as parallel vertical lines, is intended to depict a correspondence rule. There are a number of different correspondence rules proposed in the philosophy literature, but it is beyond the scope of this chapter to consider these (see Bagozzi, 2011b, pp. 265–266). All these rules reflect a certain degree of implied speculative meaning having to do with the theory of instrumentation, operations, or procedures applied to get data and the data themselves. Correspondence rules formally address the fit or conformity between conceptualization of latent variables and empirical definition of observations. These entail logical and observational criteria.

Spurious Meaning

Spurious meaning is a form of contamination in measurement that affects empirically estimated causal parameters (γ, β in Figure 4.4) and factor loadings (λ). It is a kind of bias that corrupts parameter estimates. The goal in forming operationalizations and conducting tests of hypotheses, such as portrayed in Figure 4.4, is to avoid or reduce such bias, estimate its nature and effects explicitly, and correct for its impact when possible for computing the key parameters in a model.

There are three distinct forms of contamination: random error, measure specificity, and systematic error. Random error in observed variables shown in Figure 4.4 are displayed as es. The errors in predictions of latest variables are shown as ζ_1 and ζ_2, respectively, for F and C. The error in observed variables, e, reflects information in an observation not explained by the corresponding hypothesized latent variable. The error in a latent variable is the residual resulting after taking into account the effects of other latent variables on the latent variable. Measurement specificity refers to a unique portion of variance associated with one particular observed variable and remaining after taking into account variance due to the proposed latent variable, random error, and systematic error. Estimation of measure specificity requires formulation of complex models with many observed variables for each latent variable and coming from different sources, and thus it is not often possible to accomplish (see Bagozzi, Yi, & Phillips, 1991, for an example).

Systematic error is a source of contamination arising from an identifiable extraneous bias. The most common systematic error is common method bias. Every method used to obtain observations has specific biases characteristic of it. When, as is most frequently done, one method is used to collect data in a study, bias in that method is usually confounded with error and can affect the level and pattern of associations among observed variables, thus infecting parameter estimates to create biases, because the parameters are functions of the associations among observed variables.

A metaphor that helps bring perspective to understand the relationships among theoretical, empirical, and spurious meanings is to consider the observed correlation between two measures, say a measure of A in Figure 4.4 and a measure of F. The observed correlation is in a sense the result of three forces: the true or actual relationship between A and F, random measurement error in the observed variables of A and F, and systematic error. Because systematic error can inflate or deflate the observed correlation of the measures, the interpretation of the measured correlation is problematic in and of itself. This is what makes doubtful the interpretation of application of methods to tests of hypotheses, to the extent that random and systematic error occur. In a sense, when limiting inquiry to approaches focusing on observed variables alone (e.g., regression, ANOVA), theoretical, empirical, and spurious meaning are confounded and inseparable from observed correlations as they stand.

Piecemeal Versus Holistic Research

Figure 4.4 represents an integrated system for conducting research that brings together conceptualization, hypothesis formation, and measurement so as to force researchers to confront the correspondence and mutual interdependencies among these facets of research in a formal way. Indeed, implications of the correspondences and interdependencies can be approximated with certain parameter estimates produced by SEM analyses. At the extremes to give perspective, consider raw empiricism and pure theory. Raw empiricism starts as an essentially exploratory and inductive technique applied to data with the aim of discovering meaningful patterns of empirical associations in the data. It is as if inquiry hones in to scrutinize observed correlations alone to unveil something new. Focus in this sense in Figure 4.4 is on the OVs and their patterned associations. Interpretation of the associations (e.g., by exploratory factor analysis or application of data mining techniques) might generate conclusions leading to naming of key variables and the nature of their relationships to each other, producing conceptual or theoretical insights. Pure theory, by contrast, operates on ideas and hypotheses with regard to theoretical meaning in Figure 4.4 but does not formally draw upon empirical meaning in its course. There is room for raw empiricism and pure theory in research, especially as starting points in programs of research. But their restricted piecemeal orientation, in comparison to a more holistic approach, risks falling short of what can be gained by attempting to fit together ideas and measurements in an organized way.

Most research in consumer psychology is neither indicative of raw empiricism nor pure theory. Rather, consumer researchers draw upon theoretical knowledge and bodies of research to test hypotheses on data. Nevertheless, our models and methods impose built-in constraints, making it difficult to implement a holistic approach, such as shown in Figure 4.4. For instance, regression-based research typically involves specification of concepts and development of hypotheses through verbal discourse, and then measurements of key variables are taken and hypotheses tested strictly at the level of observed variables. It is as if Figure 4.4 is partially carried out but with empirical meaning obscured because the relationships between theoretical variables and their measures are not specified and examined. Likewise, errors in observed variables and in predicted variables are confounded, and no attempt is made to take systematic error into account. Experimental-based research exhibits a similar outcome, due largely to the limitations in ANOVA or regression procedures for analyzing experimental data, which do not permit the execution of a system such as shown in Figure 4.4.

In what follows, we elaborate on the logic behind Figure 4.4 and discuss different issues one at a time. This is done for expository purposes; each individual presentation is taken as an essential piece of a whole program for research that in practice should be integrated. It is important to keep in mind that research involves a certain degree of conceptual, theoretical, philosophical, and empirical content. Figure 4.4 is an attempt to suggest how to do this.

MEASUREMENT

Our measures and methods are inherently fallible, and procedures exist in SEMs to discover and correct for such fallibility to a certain extent. But it is important to go beyond empirical evidence, and beyond empiricism more generally, to incorporate conceptual, theoretical, and philosophical standards into the specification, estimation of parameters, hypothesis testing, and interpretation phases of research. Measurement deals with theoretical variables and their operationalizations and does so while trying to provide information on the quality and validity of measures in a way not possible by use of classic statistical procedures (i.e., non-SEMs).

Confirmatory Factor Analysis

Common practice in economics, sociology, political science, psychology, business, and the health sciences is to develop hypotheses conceptually but to test them on observed variables, where the latter are responses to single items on a questionnaire, averages of multiple items, or such descriptive data as age and socioeconomic information. Sometimes the basis for forming averages of items is justified by first performing exploratory factor analyses to identify unidimensional scales. But the exploratory factor analyses are separated from tests of hypotheses in practice, where the averaged items so justified enter next as empirical variables in such statistical procedures as ANOVA or multiple regression.

Confirmatory factor analysis (CFA) is a procedure that specifies a model to be tested against data. The directionality of the relationship between hypothesized latent theoretical variables and manifest observed variables was left unspecified in Figure 4.4 (i.e., the factor loading link was given as a line without arrowheads).

There are two ways to specify relationships between latent variables and observed variables, where we limit consideration to factor loadings, which may differ from, or fall short of, the more conceptual specification of correspondence rules (see Figure 4.5). In the reflective indicator case, each proposed measure or indicator is modeled as a function of the latent variable plus error, with factor loading λ_i capturing the degree of (inferred empirical) correspondence between η and y_i:

$$y = \lambda_1 \eta + e_1.$$

Variance in each y is said to be partitioned into that produced by η plus error. The entire reflective indicator model with one factor, η, and four indicators can be estimated with standard SEM programs. The goodness of fit of the whole model can be summarized with a χ^2-test and various goodness-of-fit indexes as rules of thumb. Each factor loading is estimated as a regression parameter, and each error variance is estimated as well. Standardized factor loading estimates go from 0.0 to 1.0, inclusive, where the higher the number, the better the fit. One rule of thumb for what makes a satisfactory loading says it should be 0.7 or larger; in practice, especially when a large model has many factors with many loadings, researchers sometime use 0.6 or greater as a rough cutoff for item or indicator quality.

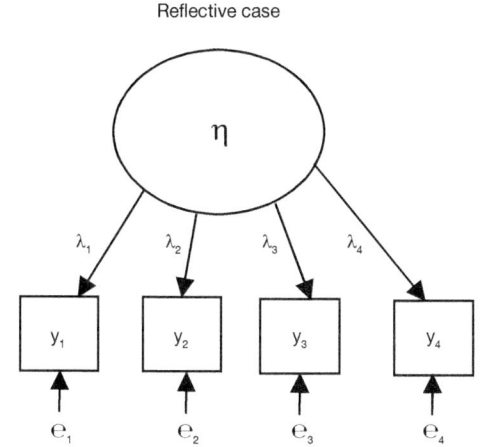
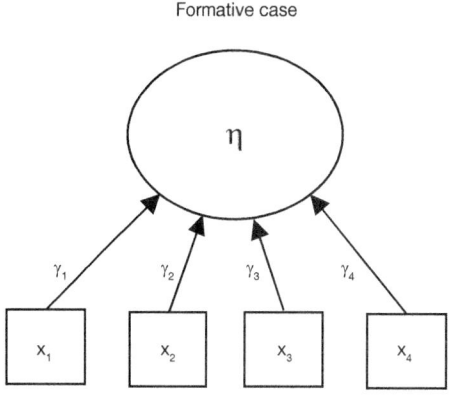

FIGURE 4.5. Two approaches to confirmatory factor analysis (single-factor model).

For the formative indicator case, a hypothesized factor is taken to be a linear function of its indicators:

$$\eta = \gamma_1 x_1 + \gamma_2 x_2 + \gamma_3 x_3 + \gamma_4 x_4.$$

The latent variable η is interpreted to be formed or shaped by its indicators. Notice that this formative model does not have an error term for the latent variable. To estimate a formative model such as this, assumptions have to be made that may or may not be plausible (e.g., error for the latent variable is zero; one gamma = 1). To obtain parameter estimates and goodness-of-fit tests for a meaningful formative indicator model, one must expand the model to include latent consequences of the focal formative factor. The top panel in Figure 4.6 presents one example. Here the latent variable, η_1, formed by x_1 through x_4, is shown to influence three latent variables, η_2 through η_4, where each has two indicators for illustration. This model can be estimated with standard SEM programs.

When should one use reflective indicators, and when should one use formative indicators?

This is a controversial topic to say the least. Some researchers assert that formative indicators should never be used in any study (Howell et al., 2007). Other researchers either deny that the problems pointed out by Howell et al. (2007) are of concern or else feel that formative models fit the meaning of some research contexts well or better than reflective models (e.g., Diamantopoulos & Siguaw, 2006; Podsakoff et al., 2003). For purposes of disclosure, I have been active in this debate and fall between the two extremes noted here, although I am closer to the former than the latter position (Bagozzi, 2007, 2011b).

Measurement procedures, such as the reflective and formative variants, purport to give empirical meaning. The reflective model shown in Figure 4.5 operationalizes η with four indicators. To the degree that each item loads satisfactorily on η and the model fits well, one can delete or add satisfactory items without changing the meaning of η. Each item is a parallel empirical realizer of the meaning of η. The proposed measures of a latent variable under a reflective model should share considerable common variance due to their similar content as reflecting the meaning of η. Each item is in one sense a redundant indicator of η. As developed later, reflective models can be used to compute reliabilities of individual items, as well as of the composite whole. They also can be used to implement models of construct validity.

The situation is quite different for formative indicators. The empirical meaning of η_1 in Panel A for Figure 4.6 is in a certain sense inherently ambiguous and depends on the number of indicators, x_1 through x_4. For example, "Omitting an indicator is omitting a part of the construct" (Bollen & Lennox, 1991, p. 308). Likewise, adding an indicator results in a new latent variable, as defined by its indicators. Adding or omitting an indicator can also change

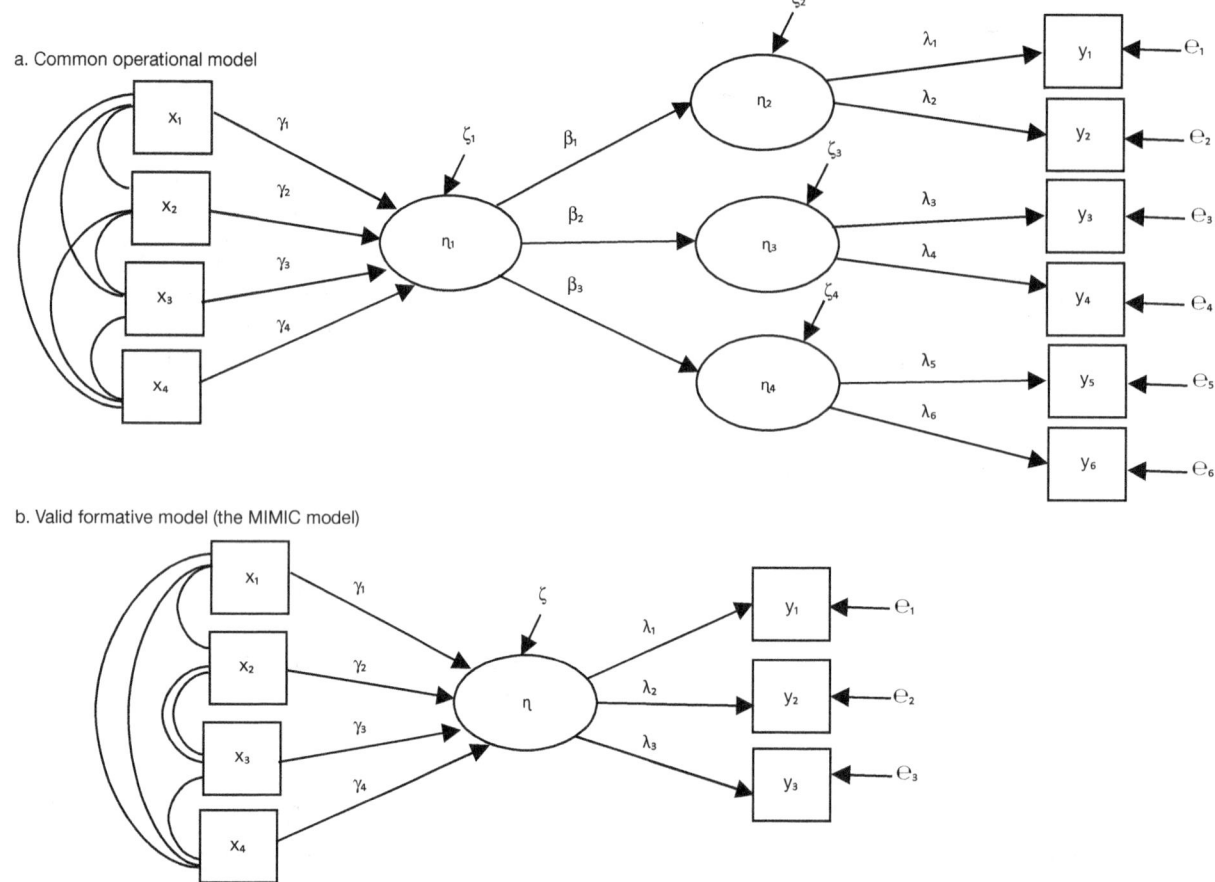

FIGURE 4.6. Two general formative indicator models. MIMIC = multiple indicator multiple cause.

the parameter values for the other indicators. This means the loadings in a formative model will change merely as a function of the number of indicators specified. Latent variables are defined by the number and strength of formative indicators. This property of formative models may be appropriate in one sense, if one wants a formative latent variable to vary in meaning as a function of its indicators. But it precludes computation of classic reliability and most kinds of construct validity, which are essential for appraising measure quality and the meaning of variables (see later discussion).

There is another problem with formative models not shared by reflective ones. The formative loadings not only depend on the number and strength of corresponding indicators but in addition are functions of the number of endogenous variables, their strength of relationship to the formative variable, and the number of measures of the endogenous variables (Bagozzi, 2007; Howell et al., 2007).

For instance, adding or deleting endogenous outcomes of η_1 in Figure 4.6a and adding or deleting indicators of η_2 through η_4 will affect the loadings of η_1 (i.e., the γs). So the measurement properties of η_1 under a formative model are not confined to its indicators, as they are under a reflective model, but also depend on the modeling of its effects. Adding or removing one or more ηs to η_2 through η_4 and varying the number of reflective indicators for the endogenous latent variables will affect the γs and thus the meaning of η_1 itself. This makes the study of η_1 unstable across investigations of η_1 and across model specifications, as well as across research contexts, and introduces ambiguity ascertaining generalizability and change in formative constructs more generally in research programs.

One can understand why Howell et al. (2007) are so categorically negative about the use of formative models. It should be stressed that the issues at hand are not solely empirical concerns.

The problem is in part a priori because ambiguity in empirical meaning for formative cases can be shown analytically to depend on how models are specified. Formative models can run satisfactorily on standard programs, leading one to presume they are meaningful, yet still exhibit equivocal and self-contradictory findings due to the aforementioned issues. A formative model that avoids the problems of indeterminacy discussed here is the multiple indicator multiple cause (MIMIC) model (Figure 4.6b; Bagozzi, 2007). Here a linear function of a set of exogenous indicators for a latent variable predict a linear combination of outcome measures, y_1 through y_3. This model is perhaps best used for predictive, rather than explanatory, purposes and fits philosophically the understanding of instrumentalism. Its employment also fits more the logic of empiricism than realism or more theory-driven goals of consumer psychologists. For additional issues concerning formative and reflective indicators, see Bagozzi (2011b).

In sum, use of formative indicator models is likely to exhibit ambiguous and biased findings, and this can occur without users being aware of this because invalid models can run satisfactorily with few diagnostics to detect the major concerns. Formative models lack commonly accepted measures of reliability and do not lend themselves to standard methods for assessing construct validity. They thus fall short in providing ways for appraising empirical meaning and spurious meaning. At the same time, both the kinds of formative models and the contexts where they might apply are limited. Finally, from a philosophy of mind perspective, the formative model does not fit any of the leading approaches well. The reflective indicator approach avoids the aforementioned problems and is recommended for most consumer research studies.

Reliability

The quality of measures of factors for reflective indicators can be assessed with measures of reliability. The reliability of an individual item of a factor, when multiple items load on it, can be computed as

$$\rho_{(item\ i)} = \frac{\lambda_i^2 \text{var(factor)}}{\lambda_i^2 \text{var(factor)} + \theta_{ii}}$$

where λ_i is the factor loading, var (factor) is the variance of the factor, and θ_{ii} is the variance of the error term for the item. Some researchers call this individual indicator reliability.

A summary measure of the quality of the set of items (also called a composite) for a factor can be computed as

$$\rho_{composite} = \frac{\left(\Sigma \lambda_i\right)^2 \text{var(factor)}}{\left(\Sigma \lambda_i\right)^2 \text{var(factor)} + \Sigma \theta_{ii}}$$

where $(\Sigma \lambda_i)^2$ refers to the sum of factor loadings on a factor, quantity squared, and $\Sigma \theta_{ii}$ is the sum of error variances for the items comprising the composite. Cronbach's alpha is a special case of $\rho_{composite}$ where $\lambda_i = 1$. Researchers should report $\rho_{composite}$ in most studies.

What are acceptable reliabilities? Most researchers regard 0.70 as the threshold of acceptability for composite reliabilities. However in large models with many factors and many factor loadings, it is not uncommon to find one or a few factors for measures with reliabilities less than 0.70, such that in practice composite reliabilities in the range of 0.60 to 0.69 are sometimes accepted as satisfactory. Individual item reliabilities ideally should be at least 0.70, but here again, sometimes a few values in the 0.60s might be deemed acceptable as a pragmatic matter. One has to balance good overall model fit in the face of a small number of less satisfactory loadings or somewhat low composite reliabilities.

A misleading practice concerning reliability should be pointed out. Researchers using multiple items to measure independent and dependent variables, mediators, or moderators often report only Cronbach's alpha as their indicator of reliability and claim as well that a satisfactory level of alpha is evidence for an acceptable scale, implying or even claiming that the scale is unidimensional. A satisfactory alpha does not imply a unidimensional scale. If the claimed items of a scale for one factor happen to measure unbeknown to the researcher two or more factors, where the factors are positively correlated, but at levels significantly less than the within-factor item correlations for the assumed factor, a high alpha might result but lack credibility. This is because the formula for alpha might be capitalizing on shared variance between items across factors to yield a high alpha and lead researchers to baselessly claim a satisfactory unidimensional scale. Cronbach's alpha applies only for unidimensional scales. It is best to first prove unidimensionality, preferably with CFA, and then for items measuring a single factor, apply Cronbach's alpha if desired. An essential assumption of Cronbach's alpha is that items to which it is applied load satisfactorily on one factor. Even proof of single-factoredness might bring little consolation because the common practice of presenting in a study a small number of items grouped together and designed to measure a variable likely leads to item placement or position biases that inflate internal consistency of items. Better would be to apply CFA and use Cronbach's alpha for appropriate items embedded in a large number of items intended to measure multiple factors and counterbalance or intersperse items across scales, if one wants to reduce such questionnaire format biases. Current practice inflates alpha and possibly suggests a factor that lacks justification or validity.

Construct Dimensionality

Researchers frequently use and present evidence for multidimensionality of constructs or factors in their studies. For example, personality variables with multiple dimensions (e.g., brand personality), multiple-factored dependent variables, and multiple independent variables are frequently included in studies. A common standard for defending such representations is to require particular findings for a CFA wherein individual parameter estimates and overall model goodness-to-fit indexes are examined to interpret how good the model and measures are. Other issues need to be addressed as discussed later.

Figure 4.7 presents an example of a multidimensional construct. Here the results are provided for a test of a four-factor model ($N = 301$) for the material self, which is defined as the construction and maintenance of a personal and social self through the acquisition, ownership, and use of material objects (Bagozzi et al., 2020). The material self-scale has four dimensions and four items measuring each dimension. Evidence for how good the scale is can be seen in the goodness-of-fit information displayed in the bottom left of Figure 4.7. The model fits well overall. Further, the factor loadings are generally high, except in one case where $\lambda = 0.62$, which is a mediocre value. Nevertheless the composite reliability for the four items that includes the 0.62 loading is quite acceptable (CR = 0.86).

An important outcome to demonstrate for multidimensional constructs or scales is that the factors are distinct. If factors correlate too highly, then it is not defensible to assert that such factors are meaningful. A common way to ascertain the distinctiveness of factors is to inspect the correlations between factors to see whether the correlations are far enough below 1.00 to justify consideration as separate factors. This can be done by one of two ways. One is to compute a confidence interval for each correlation to show that 1.00 is not included in the interval. A second way is to compare the χ^2 value for the fit of the model in Figure 4.7 to the χ^2 value of the fit of the model where the correlation between two factors of interest are constrained to 1.00. The difference in χ^2 values with one degree of freedom is a test of whether the correlation is statistically less than 1.00 or not (cf. Stoel et al., 2006). It should be noted that the correlations in a CFA model represent values corrected for measurement error; the observed correlations between measures of different factors will be lower than the estimated correlation tested for factor distinctiveness. We examined confidence intervals for all correlations shown in Figure 4.7 and performed tests for all correlation between factors, as well as average variance extracted (AVE). The findings revealed that four distinct factors indeed exist for the data under study.

Although researchers sometimes term the aforementioned procedures tests for discriminant validity, we have purposively avoided using this language and recommend that the procedures be interpreted as ways of demonstrating distinctiveness of factors. Discriminant validity has a more specific and demanding interpretation to it than factor distinctiveness under a single method. With tests of factor distinctiveness, one addresses the uniqueness of factors when all measures are obtained from a single method. For example, all items for measuring factors of a multidimensional construct might come from the same kind of self-reports by respondents

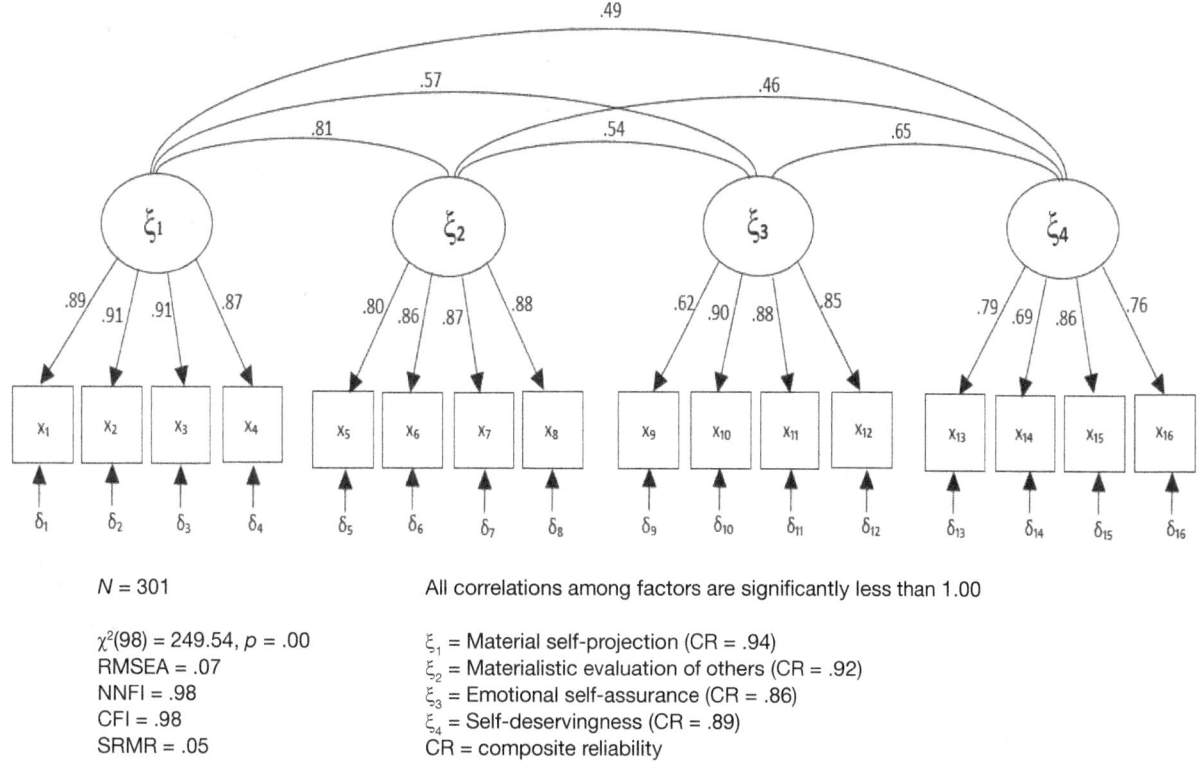

FIGURE 4.7. Four factor confirmatory factor analysis model to illustrate multidimensionality: The case of the material self.

on a questionnaire. Discriminant validity, by contrast, concerns the uniqueness of factors when all measures come from two or more different methods. For instance, for each factor in a study, such measures as self-report, peer, or expert assessments and observed outcomes or behaviors recorded objectively might be used (see Bagozzi et al., 2020).

Tests of factor distinctiveness are relatively undemanding and can be invalid because of method bias. Moreover, the validity of such tests is generally unknown because there is not enough information provided in monomethod designs to estimate validity one way or another. Because all measures in a monomethod design share common method biases, tests of factor distinctiveness will be contaminated by method biases, which will be confounded with measurement error and bias parameter estimates in unpredictable ways. Monomethod biases often inflate convergence or agreement among measures within each factor and can as well artificially exaggerate distinctiveness between measures of different factors. So, as nearly universally done in monomethod studies in consumer psychology, researchers rely on tests of distinctiveness, but such tests are often minimally informative at best and possibly invalid at worst. Construct validity is a fundamental issue that unfortunately seldom gets consideration in consumer psychology, yet it is needed to provide a satisfactory basis for assessing convergent and discriminant validity. Tests of substantive hypotheses, where measures are conflated with each other and a single, common method is used, may produce indeterminant outcomes.

Construct Validity

How well do we know what it is we are measuring in any particular study?

Reliability is a largely empirically driven criterion that examines the level of consistency and relative uniformity of correlations among proposed measures of a factor. But reliability does not directly address the quality of the relationship between a concept or construct and the indicators posited to measure it. *Construct validity* is the degree to which indicators of a latent variable measure what they are intended to measure. One can seemingly have highly reliable measures but not in fact measure what one purports to measure. During the era in psychological and social research when researchers were trying to develop stable factors based on empirical measures alone, it was not possible to provide a comprehensive answer to the question of what it was that we were measuring, because concept and measurement were effectively assumed to be one and the same. Even today, little attention is given to construct validity in consumer psychology, and it seems that validity is taken for granted or presumed to be ratified, simply because models within which measures of concepts are used give expected substantive results. When findings are not borne out, it is difficult to know whether measures were unreliable, whether the theory or its constructs were invalid, or some number of these possibilities. When findings are borne out, we might not realize that good results happen for the wrong reasons, such as the presence of method biases or the occurrence of misrepresented, or in some other way "bad," constructs.

Construct validity has two essential parts: convergent validity and discriminant validity (Bagozzi, Yi, & Phillips, 1991). Both parts apply to the research context where two or more different methods are used to measure all constructs in a study. The methods may be similar, such as sematic differential and Likert scales given to respondents to express their own self-report reactions. Or methods may be dissimilar, such as the use of self-report items, archival data, peer judgments, or expert informant appraisals to measure each variable in a study. It is obvious that reliability requires at least two, preferably three or more, items or measures to be computed. The reliability of a single measure is undefined. By a somewhat analogous logic, it might be asserted that construct validity too is undefined for the case where only a single method is used and that two or more methods are needed to address construct validity in its fullest sense. Two or more methods are needed to identify the extra parameters present in construct validity models. It therefore takes more effort and resources to do an examination of construct validity than tests of reliability and distinctiveness of factors in traditional substantive research based on monomethod approaches, and this is one reason perhaps we seldom see such investigations. Two other reasons are that researchers sometimes are unaware of what construct validity is and why it is important. Also the procedures for implementing construct validity, which are based on CFA, are more complicated than standard procedures and more difficult to interpret.

Convergent validity refers to two or more attempts by different methods to measure the same construct. The idea is that if different methods give similar results, then we have a basis for believing with some confidence that we are measuring the same thing (i.e., the construct we hope to measure). The more dissimilar the multimethods used to measure the same thing and the more in agreement the methods, the greater our confidence should be that we are measuring that thing. Thus for addressing convergent validity, the recommendation is to employ as dissimilar methods as possible. Use of different but similar methods gives weaker evidence for convergent validity than use of dissimilar methods because it is easier to get agreement. Different attempts to measure the same thing that are in agreement (convergent validity) give testimony to the validity of what we are measuring.

But convergent validity by itself is only partial grounds for believing in the validity of our measures. *Discriminant validity* answers the question: Do our measures of a construct establish that the construct is distinct from other constructs? If measures of a construct are valid and establish convergent validity, then the measures of the construct should not correlate too highly with measures of other constructs if the constructs are distinct. If the measures of a construct correlate too highly with measures of other constructs, then it may not be possible to distinguish between the constructs, and it would be incorrect to claim that the constructs are unique. Using highly dissimilar methods to test for discriminant validity would make it easier to achieve discriminant validity, so a more stringent test of discrimination would be to do so with similar but different methods.

Speaking ideally, to provide as rigorous tests as possible for establishing convergent validity and discriminant validity, it would be best in any study of construct validity to have both maximally similar and maximally dissimilar methods. Of course, this increases the number of methods to implement, as well as time and resources needed to do so, and may not always be feasible.

Convergent validity and discriminant validity were discussed earlier separately, but in reality they are related to each other and combine to define construct validity. Originally the analysis of convergent and discriminant validity was developed based on inspection of observed correlations of measures, which were organized in what was termed a game matrix (Campbell & Fiske, 1959). The MTMM matrix provided useful conceptual insights but fell short of testing convergent and discriminant validity. Today, CFA is used to give formal tests of convergent and discriminant validity. The approach provides overall goodness-of-fit tests of models and parameter estimates related to the amount of variance in measures due to proposed construct, error, and method. For a discussion of 11 different approaches for examination of construct validity, including mention of pros and cons, see Bagozzi (2011b, pp. 275–289). For illustrations of actual tests of construct validity in consumer psychology, see Bagozzi and Yi (1991, 1993) and Bagozzi, Yi, and Nassen (1998).

Figure 4.8 shows two of the most common implementations of CFA procedures for examining construct validity. Under the trait-method-error model, we show an example where three constructs (ξ_{t1}–ξ_{t3}) are measured by three methods (ξ_{m1}–ξ_{m3}). Each measure (the square boxes, x_i) can be seen to be a function of three sources of variance (shown as arrows touching the boxes). For example, $x_1 = \lambda_{11}\xi_{t1} + \lambda_{14}\xi_{m1} + \delta_1$. This says that x_1 is a linear function of the trait it is proposed to measure (ξ_{t1}), with λ_{11} revealing the degree of observed correspondence, the method used to measure ξ_{t1}, where λ_{14} is the extent that x_1 exhibits systematic error due to the method, ξ_{m1}, and random measurement error, δ_1. Convergent validity is said to be achieved when the model in Figure 4.8a fits well overall and factor loadings between measures and proposed factors (called traits in the literature) are statistically significant and high in value. The higher the value for the trait λs, the greater the correspondence between proposed factor and measure. The λs for traits are proportional to degree of convergence validity. Discriminant validity is achieved when the correlations among three trait factors are significantly below 1.00. If the correlations are too close to 1.00, evidence for discriminant validity is lacking. The lower the correlations between trait factors, the greater the discriminant validity, but of course, depending on the research context, trait factors might be validity correlated and correlated relatively highly, so the standard for discriminant validity is that each correlation between trait factor should be statistically less than 1.00. Two ways for testing this are to (a) compute confidence intervals for the trait factor correlations to show that 1.00 is not in the interval and (b) compare the model with a another model where a trait correlation is fixed to 1.00, and if the test with 1df is significant, we can conclude that the two corresponding factors are distinct and the measures achieve discriminant validity.

The trait-method-error model has a lot of intuition underpinning it, for it offers rigorous criteria for establishing construct validity according to common sense interpretations of convergent and discriminant validity. However, simulations and analyses done over the years in the literature suggested that the model sometimes is unstable, and programs are unable to provide good solutions for goodness-of-fit tests and parameter estimates. When this happens, in nearly all cases the correlated uniqueness model works well in terms of the estimation program running (Figure 4.8b). The correlated uniqueness model estimates correlated errors for each pair of measures under a method. This is less restrictive than the trait-method-error model, which posits a singular method effect for each method. The interpretation of convergent validity and discriminant validity for the correlated uniqueness model, similar to the trait-method-error model, relies on goodness-of-fit tests and parameter estimates for the λs and $\phi_{ti,j}$s. However, one difference between the models is that relationships between method factors are not modeled for the correlated uniqueness model by contrast for the

a. Trait-method-error model

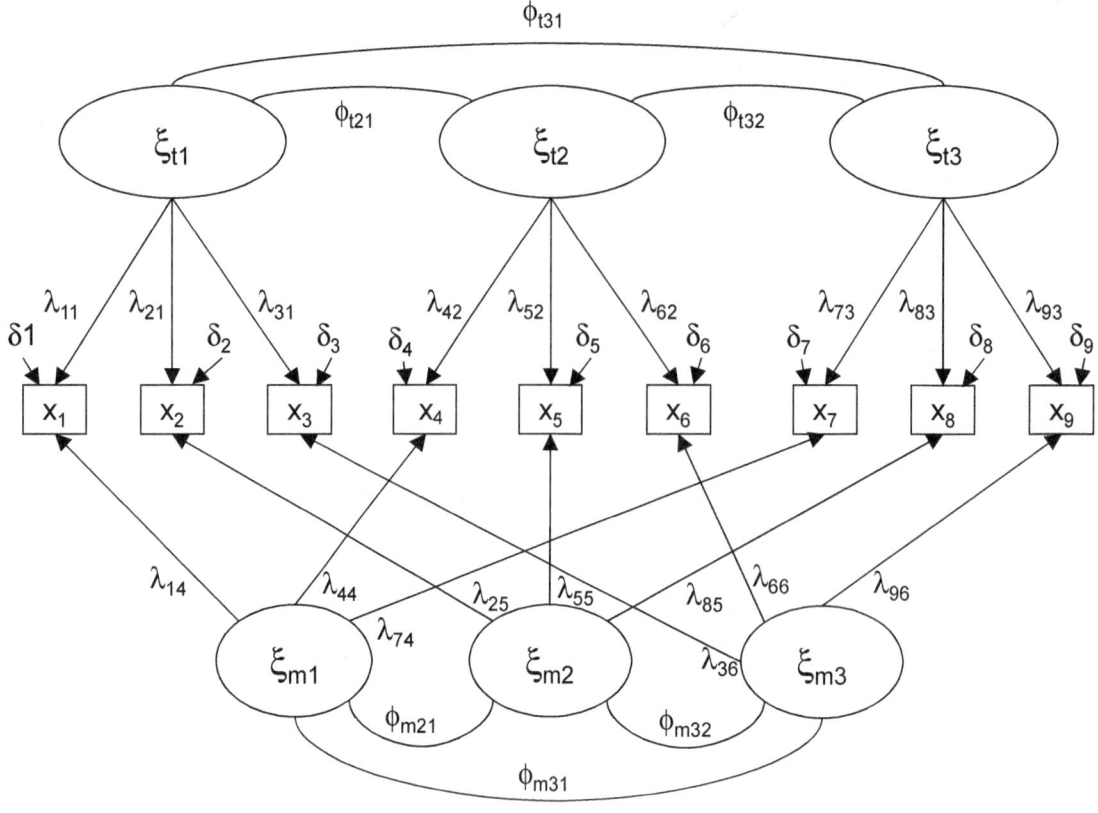

b. Correlated uniqueness model

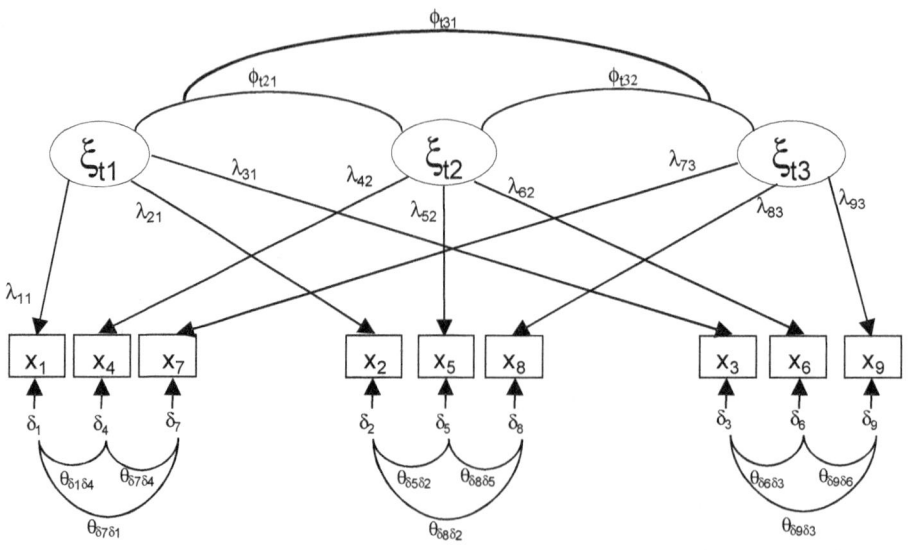

FIGURE 4.8. Two frequently used confirmatory factor analysis models for examining construct validity.

trait-method-error model. To the extent those methods are correlated, parameter estimates in the correlated uniqueness model might be biased (see Bagozzi, 2011b).

As a last comment in construct validity, it should be mentioned that the method effects in Figure 4.8 do not contain information on the nature of the bias originating from the three methods. The bias, for example, might be due to social desirability or demand characteristics that differ across the methods. To explicitly represent the source of this bias, separate measures of social desirability or demand characteristics or other sources of bias could be added to the model in Figure 4.8a, for example, as indicators of each method factor. The effects of the methods on the items would then occur as a function of these specific measures of bias, which could give insights into the sense of the bias and perhaps how to correct it in the future.

Higher Order Constructs

The latent variable factors considered up to this point were directly tied to observed variables and are called first-order factors. The empirical meaning of each factor arises through its direct connection to the observed variables proposed to measure it. The observed variables are relatively concrete measures of the factors.

Sometimes first-order factors in multifactored models share content or meaning with one or more other first-order factors, and the shared meaning can be thought to reflect more abstract sources of content. Consider the representation and measurement of the four facets of the material self, shown in Figure 4.7. This figure depicts the four factors as parallel, intercorrelated aspects of the material self, and in fact, the correlations range from moderately high to high (0.46–0.81). The scale used to measure the material self was designed to capture two dimensions: One is a social material self (material self-projection, and materialistic evaluations of others that the self makes), and the second dimension is a personal material self (emotional self-assurance and self-deservingness). The personal and social dimensions were posited as two correlated second-order factors, with the first two first-order factors loading on the second-order social material self factor and the third and fourth first-order factors loading on the second-order personal material self factor. This higher order representation of the material self was found to fit satisfactorily in a number of samples. Note that the empirical meaning of second-order factors is indirect in the sense that observed variables are one step removed, and it is through the first-order factors to their corresponding observed variables that the empirical meaning accrues to the respective second-order factors. The model in Figure 4.7 was validated in samples from five countries. Construct and nomological validity were demonstrated as well (Bagozzi et al., 2020).

Figure 4.9 represents a second-order structure for brand hate (Zarantonello et al., 2016). First-order factors for reactions of anger, contempt, and disgust toward a brand load on a second-order active brand hate factor, and first-order factors for fear, disappointment, shame, and felt dehumanization toward a brand load on a second-order passive brand-hate factor. The designations "active" and "passive" stem from characteristic action tendencies and coping styles associated with the particular first-order factor emotions.

One rationale for modeling higher order factors is that they explain the meaning of first-order factors. That is, the underlying existence of first-order factors can sometimes be captured by their shared abstract content organized in a specific structure of shared relations. A related benefit of higher order CFA models is that they provide a more parsimonious way of representing the meaning of first-order factors. Of course, there must be a basis for proposing higher order meaning. Frequently, no meaningful structure might underlay intercorrelated first-order factors, and they simply characterize different dimensions of a phenomenon that are merely associated with each other at the first-order level.

A final benefit of higher order CFA models is that they can be adapted to overcome problems of multicollinearity in certain cases. Imagine that one wishes to test the effects of three components of social identity with a brand community (affective, cognitive, and evaluative) on participation in the brand community (e.g., online and face-to-face). Under standard multiple regression procedures, the effects can be studied by regressing participation on measures of the three components of social identity. However, if the three components are too highly correlated among themselves (in particular, if the components correlate more highly among themselves than they any do with participation), this may affect the precision of beta weights for the components and yield

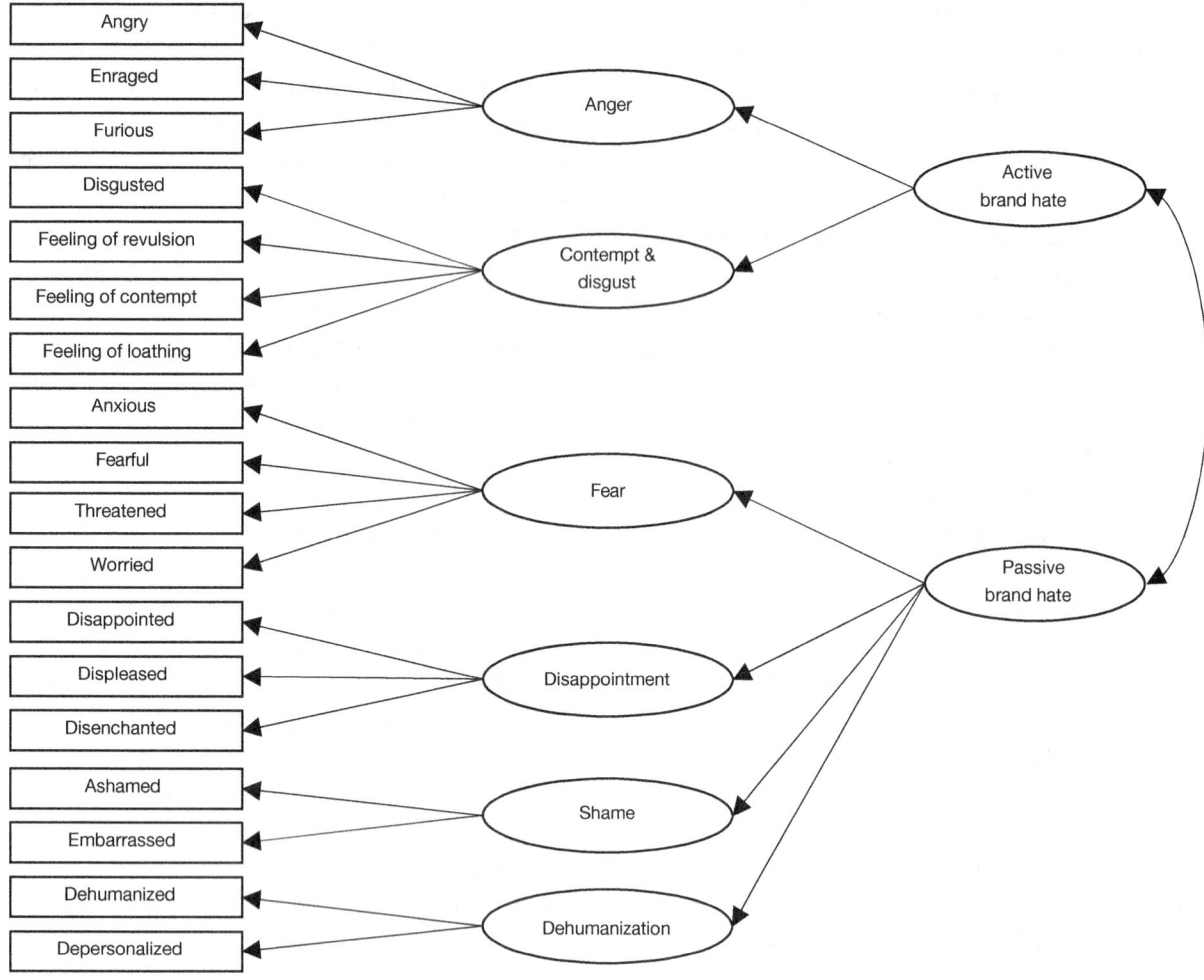

FIGURE 4.9. Example of a second-order confirmatory factor analysis for brand hate (error variances, factor loadings, and correlated second-order factor parameter omitted for simplicity). From "Brand Hate," by L. Zarantonello, S. Romani, S. Grappi, and R. P. Bagozzi, 2016, *Journal of Product & Brand Management*, 25(1), p. 18. Copyright 2016 by Emerald Publishing. Reprinted with permission.

nonsignificant predictors, when in fact predictors can have causal influence or even change the sign of predictors falsely. This is an example of a kind of multicollinearity. It occurs relatively frequently, and there is no cure within the confines of multiple regression. It is especially a problem in psychological research where cognitions, emotions, and other mental states are inherently moderately to highly correlated, because they have common causes, may affect each other, or for other reasons are highly associated. Note that even in the context of analyses by SEMs multicollinearity can be exacerbated, because these procedures correct for measurement error and therefore increase the correlations among independent variables.

What to do? When highly correlated independent variables can be considered subdimensions or components of a higher order construct, regression of a dependent variable on the higher order construct can avoid the negative consequences of multicollinearity. Consider Figure 4.10. Here three first-order factors, corresponding, say, to three facets of social identity, are shown to load on a second-order factor, ξ, and the second-order factor influences a dependent variable, η_4 (e.g., participation in a brand community). The second-order factor might be interpreted as overall social identity, as reflected in affective, cognitive, and evaluative aspects of social identity. The parameter, γ_4, captures the effect of ξ on η_4. Here multicollinearity among

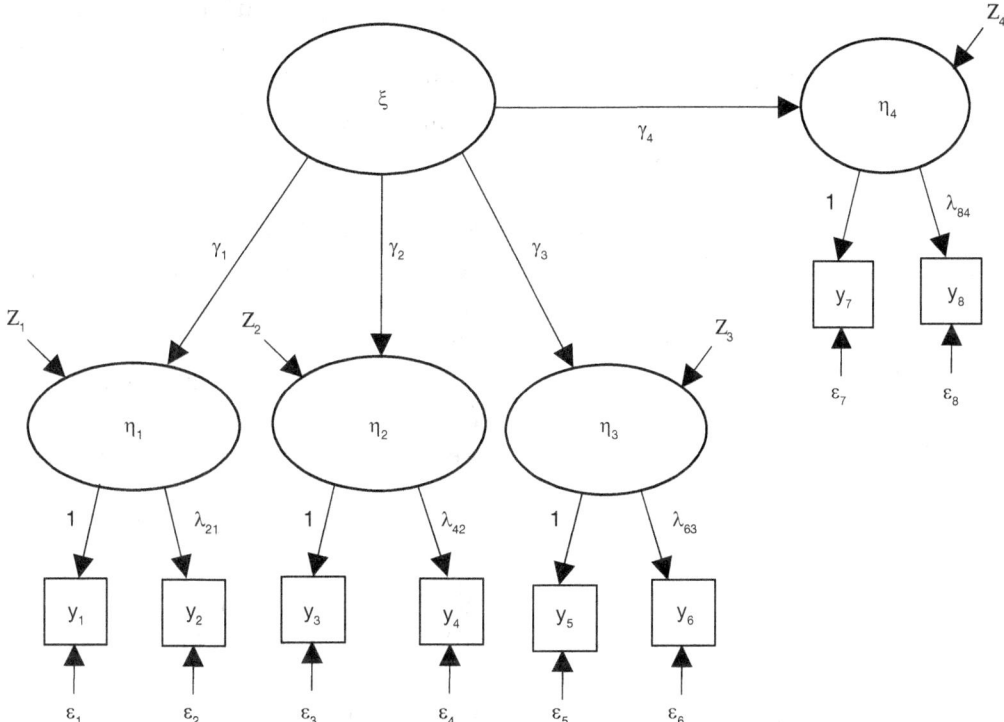

FIGURE 4.10. Use of second-order confirmatory factor analysis models to overcome the negative effects of multicollinearity.

the three independent variables does not play a role. The three parameters, γ_1 through γ_3, might reflect the relative quality of measurement of ξ by the three social identity components and, by implication, roughly the contribution to predicting η_4. However, if ξ is indicated well by its proposed components, one would not expect large differences in γ_1 through γ_3. Also it should be stressed that the use of higher order factors to circumvent multicollinearity is best done when there are conceptual, theoretical, or perhaps methodological reasons for expecting a higher order factor, to account for common variation among a set of first-order factors (see Bagozzi et al., 2012; Bagozzi & Dholakia, 2006a).

Big Ideas

"Big data is a field that treats ways to analyze, systematically extract information from, or otherwise deal with data sets that are too large or complex to be dealt with by traditional data-processing application software" (Wikipedia, n.d.). Big data relates more to inductive, exploratory analyses than to theory and deductive, hypothesis-testing approaches, although it can be used in theory-driven ways in some instances, where textual analysis, machine learning, and other procedures are applied. I mention "big data" herein tongue-in-cheek to contrast it with an emerging analogue at the other end of the spectrum, whither "big ideas" drive inquiry

By "big ideas" I mean large conceptual schemes that are organized in sequential or hierarchical structures to represent multidimensional mental phenomena useful in explaining behavior. Most theories and tests of hypotheses in consumer psychology use variables (independent, dependent, mediating, moderating) that are unidimensional and indeed defined as singular concepts and measured with singular scales as averages of items (Bagozzi, 2022). Such dependence on unitary ideas and measures fits the use of ANOVA, multiple regression, and many SEMs and indeed is paradigmatic of consumer psychology, the social sciences, and applied fields. By design, ideas are specified in solitary ways, and scales developed to measure them are formally constructed by unidimensional instruments.

To draw a contrast with the notion of big ideas, we might describe theory-driven approaches that focus on well-formed individual variables as "circumscribed or restricted perspectives." An unintended consequence of such a mindset in psychology can be seen in the history of the idea of attitudes. Beginning in the 1920s, special measurement procedures were developed to purify attitude scales so as to arrive at internally consistent measurement instruments. This was driven by the belief that an attitude was an evaluative (good–bad) response to an object or behavior and that people's evaluations could be placed along one continuum from good to bad (Ajzen, 2001; Eagly & Chaiken, 1998). This is a good example of how theory and method constrain each other. Defining attitude as a singular evaluative response and employing a procedure that yields a corresponding unidimensional scale tended to cut off possibilities of thinking about and constructing attitude in any way other than this and limited inquiry accordingly. But over the years, researchers came to realize that attitudes toward objects and behaviors can go beyond evaluations to also include distinct affective and other content, which require new ways of defining and measuring attitude as multidimensional responses. For a review of the literature in this regard and an application to attitudes toward donating bone marrow, see Bagozzi et al. (2001).

Multidimensional attitudes are not necessarily examples of big ideas but hint at the need to expand our perspectives at the level of theory and method. One of the first studies to take a big idea perspective in consumer psychology was conducted on brand love (Batra et al., 2012). Based on psychological theories of love and following a qualitative study where consumers were asked to elaborate on their love for brands, Batra et al. (2012) developed 14 concept statements defining 14 seemingly distinct aspects of brand love. These concept statements were used to generate many scale items, and then exploratory factor analysis and finally CFA were used to test a structure of responses. The scale and structure were tested in an investigation of electronic products. Figure 4.11 summarizes the higher order brand love CFA model. Here 14 distinct facets of brand love, measured as first-order factors, are shown to be organized hierarchically, such that 10 first-order factors load on three second-order factors; the second-order factors load on an overall, third-order brand love factor; and four other first-order factors also load directly on the brand love factor. The structure of brand love encompasses attitudinal, emotional, cognitive, identity, and behavioral tendencies emanating from brand love. The 14 factors can be considered realizations of brand love. Note that the wording of the 28 items measuring the 14 factors did not include mention of love. Rather the measures reflect aspects of brand love and were worded so as to capture these specific psychological states.

Note that big ideas as described are not limited to measurement of multidimensional mental phenomena organized hierarchically. Batra et al. (2012) showed that brand love mediated the effects of perceived brand quality on brand loyalty, word of mouth, and resistance to negative information about a loved brand. Warren et al. (2019) demonstrated that brand love and self-brand connections mediated the effects of brand coolness on word of mouth and willingness to pay, among other tests of nomological validity of higher order brand coolness. In these examples, the hierarchical structures for brand love and brand coolness functioned as mediating or independent variables in a larger SEM between such independent variables as product quality and such dependent variables as word of mouth and purchase intentions. The entire SEM provides a kind of nomological validity structure.

Large conceptual schemes organized in hierarchical structures to capture multidimensional mental phenomena can be interpreted as follows (Bagozzi, 2022). We can think of measurements of factors, whether physical, mental, or both, as lower level, relatively concrete observations of dimensions of a complex mental phenomenon. The lower level representations provide a basis for more abstract summaries of the meaning of these more concrete productions, organized hierarchically in multiple levels. In a sense, higher order factors emerge from the lower factors as structured abstractions of meaning cutting across the more concrete lower order meanings. Brand love is composed of 14 unique psychological properties but is more than

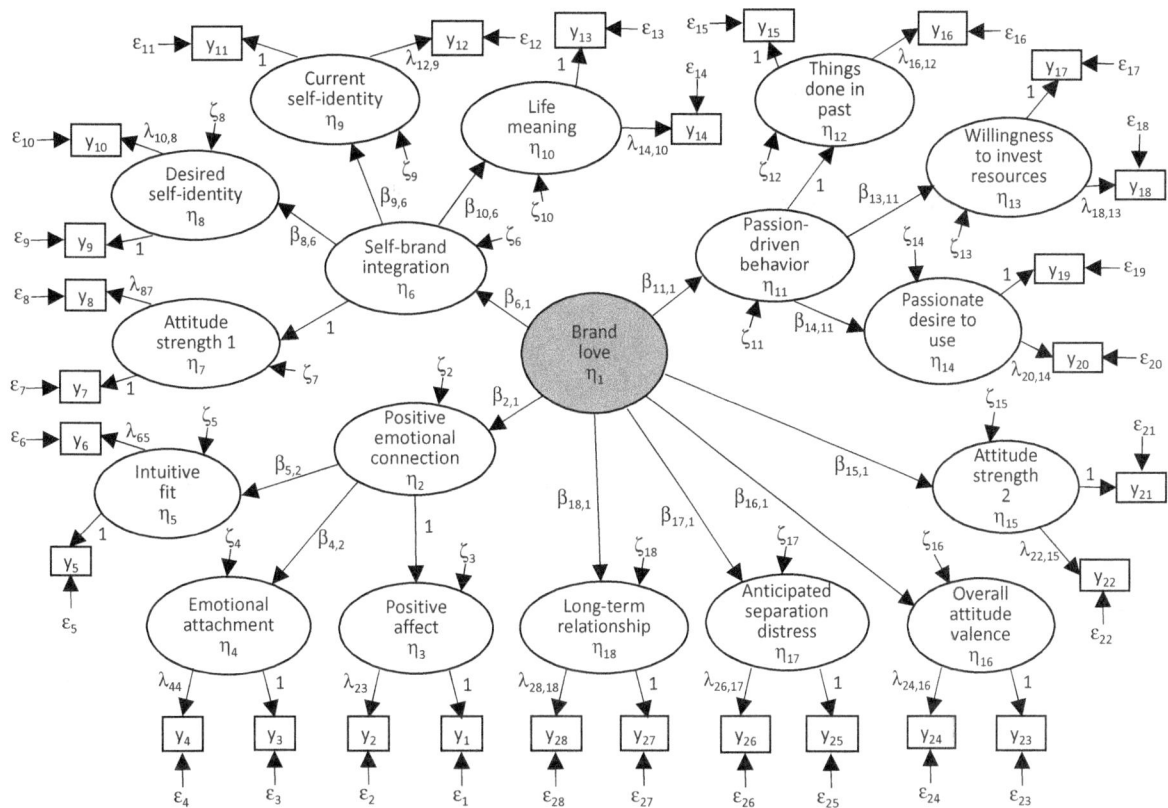

FIGURE 4.11. Higher order brand love. From "Brand Love: Development and Validation of a Practical Scale," by R. P. Bagozzi, R. Batra, and A. Ahuvia, 2017, *Marketing Letters, 28*(1), p. 7 (https://doi.org/10.1007/s11002-016-9406-1). Copyright 2017 by Springer Nature. Reprinted with permission.

the individual properties and more than the formless or unorganized collection of them. Brand love is a holistic concept emerging or going beyond its parts. Importantly, the hierarchical structure furnishes an imaginative idealization of higher level properties that are nevertheless grounded indirectly with observations through the pathway from highest order factor(s) through lower order factors and eventually to measurements. The higher level properties of a higher order CFA model applied to a conceptual system are more than the sum of simple collections of properties for first-order factors. They constitute real representations of meaning in the abstract hierarchical mental structure for persons holding such large-scale displays of personal significance. The higher order structures are subjective systems of mental states or events with phenomenological importance for the persons holding and experiencing them and can be used in explanatory frameworks.

A higher order mental structure of the sort mentioned for brand love and brand coolness has capacities and functions not easily, if at all, reducible to the parts represented by lower order factors or their measures. Rather, measures plus concepts captured by factors combine together in a formal way to create an abstract structure or configuration that we might claim has two general features. First, the higher order mental structure represents something that really exists for people in the form of measured subjective experience. Such subjective experience becomes part of a person's sense of self and their relationship with the world and people in it. The experience is felt as an integrated system of mental meanings. In this way, we might say it has ontological meaning. Second, the higher order mental structure supplies explanatory power. It functions as an independent, dependent, moderating, or mediating variable to account for behavior of phenomena of interest within a larger SEM. It can become part of our scientific frameworks for interpreting and predicting behavior.

All this is very new. Brand love and brand coolness are the only full-scale exemplars at a full level I know about to date. Brand hate and the material self are two smaller scale examples. Much remains to be explicated concerning such large conceptual schemes and their interpretations with measurement. But it is clear that classic and contemporary frameworks and methods do not address such possibilities. SEMs establish ways for thinking about implementing these new conceptual and operational principles. For a comprehensive and detailed presentation of philosophical foundations of big ideas, see Bagozzi (2022).

MULTIPLE GROUP INVESTIGATIONS

SEMs can be applied to such groups of respondents as men and women, people of different races or ethnicities, persons living in different cultures, or any other meaningful grouping of people for research purposes. Two uses of multiple group analyses are for tests of generalizability and quasi-experiments.

Generalizability

Generalizability is "the extent to which results or findings obtained from a sample are applicable to a broader population. . . . A finding that has greater generalizability also is said to have greater external validity, in that conclusions pertain to situations beyond the original study" (American Psychological Association, n.d.). In consumer research, two kinds of generalizability are of particular interest. One is what we might term *measurement generalizability*. Five questions underlie measurement generalizability and can be addressed formally with SEMs:

1. Does the same factor pattern or structure [of measures of variables] hold for two or more groups in the sense that the same number of factors exist in each group and measures load on the same factors only?
2. Given similar structure, are the factor loadings the same or invariant across groups?
3. Are the factor loadings and factor variances equal across groups and hence reliability of measures equal?
4. Do the factors covary to the same extent across groups?
5. Are the means of factors different across groups? (Bagozzi & Yi, 2012, p. 30)

The five measurement generalizability questions can provide evidence of generality of parameter estimates across groups for one or more of the issues listed and are done so by use of χ^2_d tests. The greater the number of categories of parameters found to be invariant, the greater the generalizability and external validity of the measurement model tested. The first two categories should be tested in that order initially and should hold before testing Categories 3 through 5, which can, in turn, be tested in any order. It is possible to test for equality of error variances as well.

Although evidence for generalizability is valuable for establishing the scope and validity of tests of hypotheses for measurement properties, it is important to point out that in some instances it may be of substantive or theoretical interest to reject generalizability. For example, imagine that we are investigating the nature of the material self and desire to test differences between men and women (see Figure 4.7). To see whether both the same four-factor structure of the material self and equal reliability of measures occur for men and women, we should first test the model in Figure 4.7 for men and women separately and then, given equal factor patterns, compare factor loadings and factor variances for men and women. Given equal factor patterns and equal factor loadings and factor variances, it would then be appropriate to see, for example, whether the factor means (also termed structured means) differ between men and women. Significant differences in the means of the four factors might be expected and be a focal hypothesis of interest. Men and women might differ on one or more of the four different senses of the material self or might not differ at all. Tests of differences in factor means for many phenomena in consumer psychology might be a primary purpose for hypothesis testing. But it may be equally important for researchers to verify the generality of their constructs on scales, in terms of factor structure and measure reliability, to show or discover whether their research is valid across cultures or other meaningful groupings of people. Alternatively, it may be valuable to show that certain constructs or their measures are culture-bound or are in some other way restrictive. In other words, SEMs can be used to establish boundary conditions of constructs and scales and their measures. For an example of tests of structured means, see Bergami and Bagozzi (2000).

A second kind of generalizability concerns what might be called predictive or nomological generalizability. When testing causal hypotheses, we might ask whether positive findings generalize to other samples. To test for predictive generalizability, we wish to discover whether causal paths are invariant across two or more groups of respondents. But it would not be proper to do such a test straightaway on causal paths because any differences found could be due to differences in the reliability of measures across groups, differences in the theoretical predictions, or both. These would make interpretations of differences in causal paths indeterminate. As a consequence, it is important to first perform tests of the first two questions of measurement generalizability noted earlier to prove that the same factor structure applies for the groups under study and that the measures across groups are equally reliable. Given invariant factor structures, factor loadings, and factor variances, it would then be appropriate to test for equality of causal paths. Equality of causal paths demonstrates predictive generalizability. But again as under measurement generalizability, it may be an aim of a researcher to expect systematic differences in causal paths so that it can be concluded that the different effects provide evidence for stronger consequences in one or more groups than in others. Hence, SEMs can again be used to prove evidence for boundary conditions for a theory under investigation across meaningful groups.

Quasi-Experimentation

Multiple group analyses with SEMs can be employed to advantage to conduct quasi-experiments. Here a researcher uses one or more variables as moderators to define multiple groups and investigate interaction effects. The most effective analyses of this sort should be done where variables are measured over time such that at least some independent and dependent variables are separated in time to support the claim that proposed causes precede their effects.

As an example, consider Figure 4.12. This was a study of actual contribution behaviors by members of virtual communities and was conducted over a 6-week time period (Tsai & Bagozzi, 2014). The explanatory theory was an elaboration of the model of goal-directed behavior (Bagozzi, 1992; Perugini & Bagozzi, 2001), wherein contribution behavior was a direct function of we-intentions of community members (i.e., shared decisions of members to contribute), and we-intentions, in turn, were under the influence of desires to contribute to the community. Desires served to transform reasons for contributing into a committed decision to do so and at the same time provided the key motivation for action. The reasons for contributing included social influences (subjective norms, group norms, social identity; Bagozzi & Dholakia, 2006a, 2006b; Bergami & Bagozzi, 2000), informational influences (based on attitudes toward the consequences of acting), and emotional influences (anticipated positive and negative emotions based on one's prefactual judgments concerning how one would feel if they achieved or failed to achieve shared goals to contribute to the community; Bagozzi, Baumgartner, & Pieters, 1998). Perceived behavior control acts as a covariate.

Two moderators were introduced to investigate conditions under which reasons for acting influence desires and conditions under which we-intentions lead to actual contribution behavior. The first moderator was the felt cultural orientation of respondents with respect to their self-identity. This was operationalized as individualism-collectivism. The effects of social influences on desires were predicted to be enhanced with greater felt collectivism. The effects of emotional and informational influences on desires, which are personal criteria, were expected to be intensified with greater felt individualism. The second moderator was level of experience in the group and was measured along a continuum from novice to highly experienced. The effect of we-intentions on contribution behavior was forecast to be heightened with greater experience in the group. This was a multimethod research study

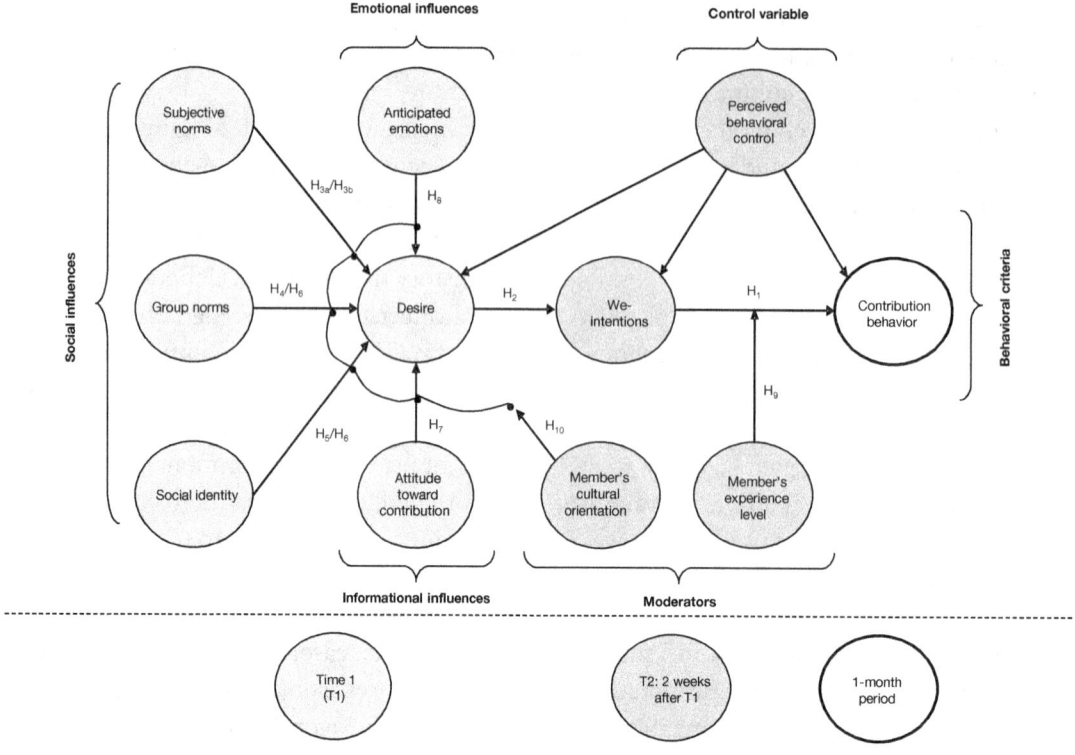

FIGURE 4.12. Use of SEMs to implement quasi-experiments. H_9 and H_{10} are interaction effects; H_1–H_8 main effects. From "Contribution Behavior in Virtual Communities: Cognitive, Emotional, and Social Influences." by H. T. Tsai and R. P. Bagozzi, 2014, *Management Information Systems Quarterly, 38*(1), p. 146 (https://doi.org/10.25300/MISQ/2014/38.1.07). Copyright 2014 by the Management Information Systems Research Center, University of Minnesota. Reprinted with permission.

combining self-report methods for most psychological variables with judgments of experts for measuring actual behavior of respondents. Method bias was estimated and ruled out as well.

Quasi-experiments lack the degree of certainty possible with true experiments, where confidence in predictions is enriched by strategic manipulation of independent variables and control of rival hypotheses is achieved through random assignment of respondents to experimental and control conditions. Nevertheless, quasi-experiments offer advantages over standard surveys and even over true experiments. One benefit over true experiments is that measurement error can be modeled explicitly in SEM implementations of quasi-experiments, with the estimated effects corrected for measurement error. True experiments analyzed with ANOVA or multiple regression do not formally take into account measurement error, although use of averaged items in scales for independent and dependent variables can reduce measurement error. SEMs offer the further possibility of taking into account and correcting for systematic error, such as discussed prior for common method biases. Another advantage of use of SEMs in quasi-experimental designs is that many interactions can be accommodated. For example, with one moderator, formed, say, by splitting at the median to form two groups, one can examine the contingent effects based on the moderator of all exogenous and endogenous variables that influence other endogenous variables. For example, in Figure 4.12, if one wished to test the moderating effects for the variables corresponding to the 10 paths shown, comparing the path model of men to the path model of women, say, would permit examination of the effects of the 10 interactions of gender with each of the 10 variables. This kind of analysis would be difficult to conduct with traditional ANOVA or regression designs. Finally, quasi-experimental SEMs permit researchers to investigate larger models in terms of sequences of effects and control for extraneous effects than is possible in most experimental designs, where the ability to incorporate many variables and complex sequences of effects is limited and must be done in piecemeal, rather than full information, ways.

The study displayed in Figure 4.12 attempts to reduce threats to validity in a number of ways. Variables were measured longitudinally over three points in time. Method bias was reduced by use of a multimethod design: self-reports by respondents and computation of actual behavior by judges who categorized the quality and quantity of contribution behaviors. In addition, the marker variable approach was applied to show that common method biases were not problems (for another example of use of the marker variable approach, see Warren et al., 2019; however, see the discussion of the pros and cons of this approach and 10 other options in Bagozzi, 2011b). In addition, as mentioned earlier, measurement error in all observed variables was modeled, and parameter estimates for all effects corrected for this error. The factor shown for anticipated emotions in Figure 4.12 was actually a second-order factor, with separate first-order factors for positive and negative anticipated emotions loading on it. This avoids negative consequences from multicollinearity on desires. This feature of SEMs cannot be done with traditional ANOVA or regression modeling. Finally, tests of mediation, to examine full versus partial mediation, were conducted to test the hypothesized sequences shown in Figure 4.12. Tests of mediation entailed formal assessment of significance of hypothesized indirect mediation paths, as well as nonhypothesized direct paths.

EXPERIMENTATION, SURVEY RESEARCH, AND CAUSALITY

Experimentation

SEMs can be used in experimental designs. The main advantage of use of SEMs, as opposed to multiple regression or ANOVA, is that measurement error can be taken into account in tests for hypotheses. Also manipulation checks can be integrated with tests of the main hypotheses (Bagozzi, 1977), and tests of mediation can be done in an integrated, as opposed to piecemeal, way (Bergami & Bagozzi, 2000). The primary disadvantage is that sample size requirements for SEMs are greater than with multiple regression or ANOVA. Whereas cell sizes of 30 or 40 subjects are often done in multiple regression and ANOVA designs, 70 or more subjects may be needed for SEMs. However, note that multiple regression and ANOVA designs are frequently underpowered with a cell size of 30 or 40 subjects in the sense of possibly yielding false positive results, and cell size of 70 or more may be needed for reasonable confidence. For a discussion and illustration of power issues with SEMs see Bagozzi and Yi (1988).

There are many issues with regard to model specification and interpretation of findings in experimental research by use of SEMs, but it is beyond the scope of this chapter to consider these. Presentations of foundational issues can be found in Bagozzi (1977); Bagozzi and Yi (1989); Bagozzi, Yi, and Singh (1991); and Kühnel (1988). Discussion of additional insights can be found in Breitsohl (2019), Curran and Hussong (2002), and Russell et al. (1998).

Multiple group analyses by SEMs can be used for the analysis of experimental data, too, but one drawback is the loss of information by splitting a moderator at the median to create two groups, should a measured moderator be employed. Of course, if interactions are found despite the split, then one can conclude lost information, if any, did not prevent detection of an interaction. The problem arises when no significant interactions occur. In such cases, we do not know whether the lost information is the cause of this outcome, whether there is no true interaction, or both. Thus, the use of multiple group analyses under SEMs is problematic when evidence for a significant interaction effect is lacking. SEMs can be used to directly test for interactions without recourse to splitting a moderator at the median. For discussions of the issues involved, see Jöreskog and Yang (1996), Marsh et al. (2004), and Mooijaart and Bentler (2010).

To consider some of the issues, we will briefly present the modeling of an interaction within the context of the theory of trying (Bagozzi & Warshaw, 1990) and a study of dieting behavior decisions, which can be generalized to other experimental cases (Bagozzi et al., 2004). Figure 4.13 shows the model where resistance to temptations to compromise a diet is shown to interact with subjective norms to influence intentions, and additional independent variables are attitudes toward successful dieting, failure to diet, and the process of dieting. The interaction between resistance to temptation and subjective norms and the main effects of the three kinds of attitudes all significantly influenced intentions.

The representation of interactions is not straightforward under SEMs. A number of nonstandard constraints have to be imposed in order to test for interactions between latent variables. For the model shown in Figure 4.13, for instance, certain nonlinearities have to be taken into account. The error variances for $\Theta_{55} = \tau_x(1)^2\Theta_{33} + \tau_x(3)^2\Theta_{11} + \Phi_{11}\Theta_{33} + \Phi_{22}\Theta_{11} + \Theta_{11}\Theta_{33}$ and $\Theta_{66} = \tau_x(2)^2\Theta_{44} + \tau_x(4)^2\Theta_{22} + \Phi_{11}\Theta_{44} + \Phi_{22}\Theta_{22} + \Theta_{22}\Theta_{44}$, where τs are intercepts. Likewise, $\lambda_{61} = \tau_x(4)\lambda_{21}$, $\lambda_{62} = \tau_x(2)\lambda_{42}$, $\lambda_{63} = \lambda_{21}\lambda_{42}$, $\Theta_{51} = \tau_x(3)\Theta_{11}$, $\Theta_{53} = \tau_x(1)\Theta_{33}$, $\Theta_{62} = \tau_x(4)\Theta_{22}$, and $\Theta_{64} = \tau_x(4)\Theta_{44}$. Finally, $\Phi_{33} = \Phi_{11}\Phi_{22} + \Phi_{22}^2$. Needless to say, programming can be a challenge. The full LISREL input program for the model in Figure 4.13 can be found in the appendix of Bagozzi et al. (2004) for the nonlinear implementation under a SEM specification. A final comment to note is that large sample sizes are required to estimate proper parameters, standard errors, and χ^2 tests. The sample size for testing the model in Figure 4.13 was 734. Weighted least squares and maximum likelihood estimation procedures can be used, as well as asymptotic distribution free methods.

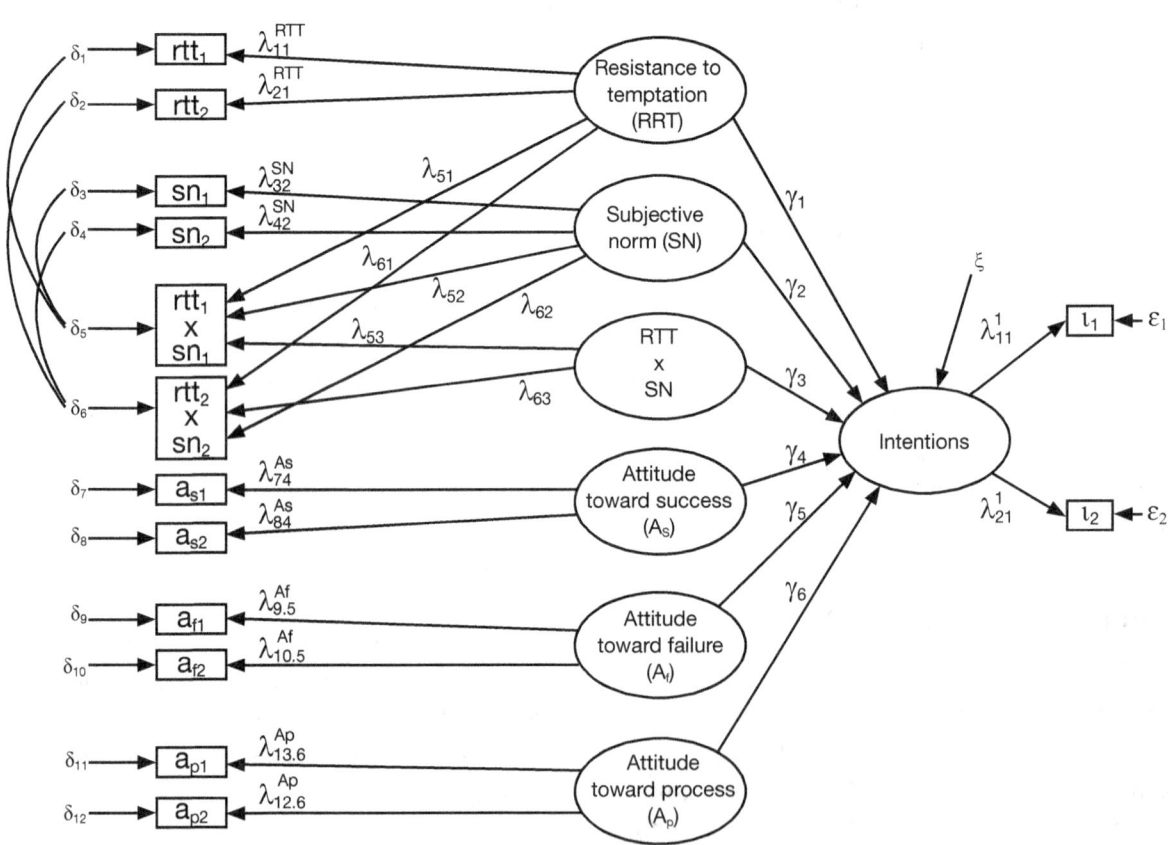

FIGURE 4.13. Path diagram for testing the effect of the interaction between subjective norm and resistance to temptation on intentions under a modified theory of reasoned action. From "Self-Control and the Self-Regulation of Dieting Decisions: The Role of Prefactual Attitudes, Subjective Norms, and Resistance to Temptation," by R. P. Bagozzi. D. J. Moore, and L. Leone, 2004, *Basic and Applied Social Psychology, 26*(2–3), p. 205 (https://doi.org/10.1080/01973533.2004.9646405). Copyright 2004 by Taylor & Francis. Reprinted with permission.

Survey Research

More than any area, SEMs are probably used most frequently in survey research. Compared with experimental and quasi-experimental research, survey research cannot claim as strong inferences as to causal relationships. Be that as it may, survey research by use of SEMs has some benefits. One advantage is that it can test large, complex models not testable under normal experimental conditions. As a leap of faith, but seldom actualized, experimental research follows a piecemeal reasoning such that external validity is traded for internal validity with the belief that by testing a small number of different relationships over time in a program of research, one eventually will validate the larger theoretical context in which experimental processes are embedded. Survey research sacrifices internal validity for external validity. Another advantage of survey research is that it can be used in a more exploratory way to discover new variables useful in explaining phenomena of interest for future experimental research and do so within a multivariate context (i.e, testing for focal effects while holding constant other effects). Still another benefit of survey research is that greater statistical power is often possible than with experiments, and generalizability can be examined in a straightforward way by comparing models for different samples of substantive interest. Finally survey research lends itself to investigation of multiple stages or steps of effects, where multiple independent effects can be scrutinized within each stage. Although claims of causality are weaker with survey than experimental research, it is possible to test for consistency of hypothesized effects with theory and to rule out certain effects and test for the nature of mediation effects.

As a brief example, see Figure 4.14. This was a longitudinal survey to test an expanded version of the model of goal-directed behavior in the field (Soscia et al., 2018). The model has 20 latent variables (17 first-order, three second-order), 22 paths, and includes some moderation effects as well (i.e., the role of felt empathy in enhancing the effects of positive and negative anticipatory emotions

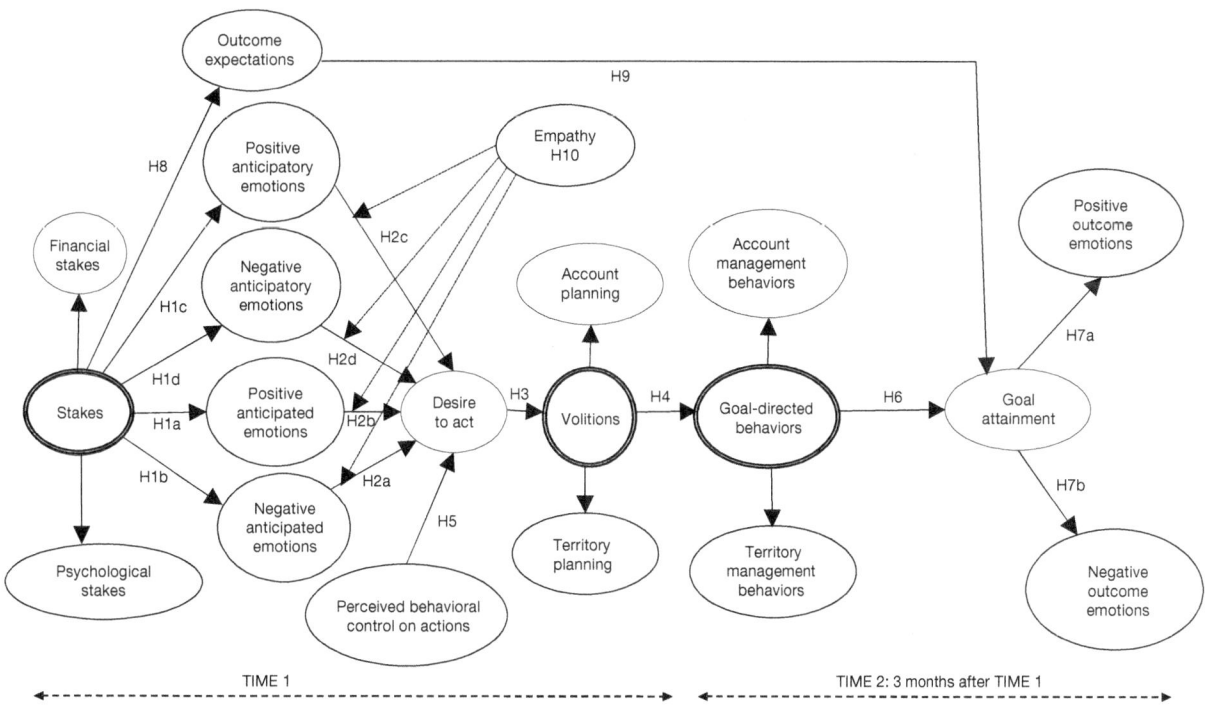

FIGURE 4.14. SEM model for longitudinal survey of an augmented model of goal-directed behavior applied to decision making by salespeople selling to individual customers. From "Cognitive and Affective Determinants of Salesforce Performance: A Two-Wave Study," by I. Soscia, R. P. Bagozzi, and P. Guenzi, 2018, *Industrial Marketing Management, 75*, p. 209 (https://doi.org/10.1016/j.indmarman.2018.06.003). Copyright 2018 by Elsevier. Reprinted with permission.

and positive and negative anticipated emotions on desires to pursue a goal). To test the model in Figure 4.14 experimentally would take many dedicated manipulations conducted in many studies. A single survey provided information on the hypotheses shown in Figure 4.14 but of course without the confidence of interpretation of causality possible with experiments.

A possibility seldom actualized is the complementary use of experimental and survey research in the same study. Because one never knows if the pieces tested in an experimental program of research will support a larger structure of relationships implied by the pieces and their organization, the addition of a survey to verify a whole model would address a kind of external validity. But the issue here is not merely one of internal versus external validity. Rather there is a need to confront two notions of causality, as we discuss next. Other complementary uses of experimentation and survey research are possible too.

Causality

The practice in consumer psychology seems to be either to not think much about what causality is or else to take it for granted that what one studies either does or does not address causality, depending on the methods and modes of analysis one uses. With regard to the latter claim, it is common to presume that when one uses experimental methods to study consumer behavior, causality is tested, whereas when one studies consumer behavior in survey contexts, causality is definitely not demonstrated. So a popular point of view is that "experiments explore the effect of things that can be *manipulated* . . . Nonmanipulable events . . . cannot be causes in experiments because we cannot deliberately vary them to see what then happens" (Shadish et al., 2002, p. 7, emphasis in original). Thus the investigation of "nonmanipulable" causes, if they exist, must be pursued by some means other than experimentation, according to this description. Presumably, survey research can be used to explore processes involving nonmanipulables. Of course, surveys can include nonmanipulable and potentially manipulable variables in any study yet temper claims as to causality. A question for future consideration is what is nonmanipulable and whether it occurs as a matter of principle or primarily as a practical matter. Even experiments are subject to threats to validity for which researchers try to anticipate and control, but nonetheless in the best designed experiments there can be ambiguities and challenges to making causal inferences that make causal claims less than certain. By contrast, certain controls (e.g., correcting for random and systematic errors, using longitudinal designs, employing multiple methods) can be included in survey research to reduce threats to validity. Therefore, from one point of view, it might be intellectually honest and best to place experimental and survey methods toward appropriate ends of a flexible and uncertain continuum, while claiming that the end points are not inherently good or bad in terms of analyzing causality but steps can be taken to close the gap. Again, it is not always a firm choice between experimentation and survey research that must be made, but in principle both approaches can complement each other.

I wish to introduce particular issues concerning causality that cut across ways of doing research and lurk beneath current and evolving paradigms in consumer psychology. One issue we already touched upon concerns the mind–body theory undergirding any specific research study. We are likely to see more fragmentation and polarity of views in the years ahead. As consumer psychology experiences more research based on neuroscience (and hormones and genetics), we are likely to have some researchers espousing strongly deterministic approaches based on causal processes for physical phenomena happening in the brain. At the same time, similar to most views of neuroscientists, some consumer psychologists will proceed from strongly reductionist points of view. So, for example, consumer psychologists following neuroscience principles will be inclined to follow eliminative or reductive physicalism mind–body points of view. This will play out in how consumer researchers both think about and test their theories. In any event, causality will probably be restricted to relationships between physical phenomena alone and confined to particular kinds of experiments.

A strictly deterministic and reductionist perspective will not sit well or fit well with consumer psychologists who place emphasis more on the mind than the brain per se to view consumer behavior as encompassing both physical and mental phenomena. Here difficult issues of causality between physical and mental states or events, and even between mental states or events, will demand more philosophical and conceptual consideration and will constrain methods of research as well. Certainly the theories and hypotheses used to investigate mental process and their relationship to physical processes will entail different assumptions and theories than those found in neuroscience-based consumer research. Hence some consumer psychologists are likely to be guided by nonreductive physicalism, others perhaps by dualism.

A pressing and very important issue that is liable to be a center of concern of researchers doing both neuroscience and more traditional functionalist or folk-psychology types of inquiry in consumer psychology is the meaning and role of consciousness, especially self-consciousness. Neuroscientists tend to deny the existence of qualia and other subjective phenomena and to eliminate such things from discussion or believe that they are reducible to physical states in the brain. Yet an emerging group of researchers has formally dealt with consciousness in neuroscience (e.g., Bagozzi & Lee, 2019). More generally, for consumer researchers interested in the notion of the self and self-regulation of behavior, self-consciousness is a real phenomenon to be studied, not to be eliminated or reduced to physical states lacking in subjective qualities. In addition, self-consciousness seems related to ideas of willpower, freedom of choice and action, and moral behavior. Causality here will involve mental states and require mind–body approaches conducive to their study. Most consumer researchers and most people in their everyday behavior use folk psychology and dualistic frameworks in interpreting their own and other people's behavior without realizing this.

A final issue related to causality concerns the distinction between consumer behavior and consumer action. Consumer behavior occurs frequently as automatic or reflexive responses to physical conditions (e.g., advertising effects), interpersonal influence, or other determinants. In such cases, consumers may be free to act or not, but very little transpires with respect to necessary and sufficient conditions behind their behavior in terms of inner processes. In one sense, such behaviors are not so much actions but reactions. By contrast, consumer actions involve more complex and identifiable causes of action. Consumers have reasons for acting (e.g., beliefs, emotions, self- and social identity issues) that relate to desires and intentions to act, and this may involve on-going or periodic monitoring and control of goal striving. Most experimental research to date in consumer psychology has focused on behavior, and less has been done investigating consumer actions. The causal processes can differ and are more complex in consumer action compared with consumer behavior. But little has been done so far to delineate the issues. Here both experimental and more naturalistic research could be fruitfully applied, such as in surveys and quasi-experiments. SEMs are well-suited for such studies.

CONCLUSION

It is apparent that SEMs are both a framework for thinking about theories and hypotheses and procedures for estimating parameters and testing hypotheses. They can be used in a holistic way to correct for normal measurement error as well as systematic error, such as method biases, while testing hypotheses. On the one hand, all parametric statistical procedures are special cases of SEMs and indeed can be estimated with available SEM programs. Multiple regression, ANOVA and multivariate analysis of covariance (MANCOVA), factor analysis, canonical correlation analyses, as well as many other statistical procedures, can be conducted with SEM programs. On the other hand, beyond their integrative properties, SEMs can do a number of things that are either impossible or very difficult to implement with classical ("first-generation") statistical methods. For example, construct validity, higher order CFA models, large-scale conceptual structural frameworks, and comprehensive survey, quasi-experimental, and experimental designs can be implemented to advantage with SEM programs.

There are many practical issues with the specification, estimation, and interpretation of SEMs that are beyond the scope of this chapter to consider. A good starting point for entertaining the many topics and questions here, with illustrations provided for the principles involved, can be found in Bagozzi and Yi (1988, 2012) and Bagozzi and Baumgartner (1994). For conceptual and logical issues, good starting points are Bagozzi (1984, 2011b, 2022); Bagozzi and Phillips (1982); Bagozzi, Yi, and Phillips (1991); Bagozzi and Edwards (1998); and Edwards and Bagozzi (2000).

Conspicuously absent from discussion in this chapter is the topic of partial least squares (PLS). PLS is seldom employed in psychology and most social sciences but has been used a lot in marketing and information sciences. Although I have used PLS and found it to give results very similar to LISREL (Bagozzi, Yi, & Singh, 1991) for certain models, a number of very serious problems of a general nature have been identified in recent years (Rönkkö et al., 2016) with PLS that suggest it should be considered with extreme caution. Some journals are even desk-rejecting papers that use PLS. Because most models that have been implemented with PLS can be implemented with SEM programs, such as AMOS and LISREL, there is little to recommend its use. There is some argument for using PLS when sample sizes are small (say, below 100), but even here the assumptions and properties of PLS may not be justified (Rönkkö et al., 2016).

SEMs are not easy to employ and interpret. The number of issues and their complexity are of an order of magnitude greater than that found for classical statistical procedures such as multiple regression and ANOVA, as currently used in consumer research. There are many pitfalls and issues of judgment and art-of-use that make SEMs particularly difficult to employ. This is the price that must be paid, perhaps, to secure the many benefits sketched in this chapter. Taking an introductory SEM course is really only a minimal first step. Postcourse experience and feedback from knowledgeable colleagues are essential, in my opinion, if the gains from its use and avoidance of hidden dangers are to happen. The effective use of SEMs in consumer psychology falls behind that found in other disciplines, and SEMs have been misused to an extent giving them a bad name in consumer research. But SEMs offer untapped opportunities across the many areas of consumer psychology.

REFERENCES

Ajzen, I. (2001). Nature and operation of attitudes. *Annual Review of Psychology*, 52(1), 27–58. https://doi.org/10.1146/annurev.psych.52.1.27

American Psychological Association. (n.d.). *APA dictionary of psychology*. https://dictionary.apa.org/

Bagozzi, R. P. (1977). Structural equation models in experimental research. *Journal of Marketing Research*, 14(2), 209–226. https://doi.org/10.1177/002224377701400209

Bagozzi, R. P. (1984). A prospectus for theory construction in marketing. *Journal of Marketing*, 48(1), 11–29. https://doi.org/10.1177/002224298404800102

Bagozzi, R. P. (1992). The self-regulation of attitudes, intentions, and behavior. *Social Psychology Quarterly*, 55(2), 178–204. https://doi.org/10.2307/2786945

Bagozzi, R. P. (2007). On the meaning of formative measurement and how it differs from reflective measurement: Comment on Howell, Breivik, and Wilcox (2007). *Psychological Methods*, 12(2), 229–237. https://doi.org/10.1037/1082-989X.12.2.229

Bagozzi, R. P. (2011a). Alternative perspectives in philosophy of mind and their relationship to structural equation models in psychology. *Psychological Inquiry*, 22(2), 88–99. https://doi.org/10.1080/1047840X.2010.550183

Bagozzi, R. P. (2011b). Measurement and meaning in information systems and organizational research: Methodological and philosophical foundations. *Management Information Systems Quarterly*, 35(2), 261–292. https://doi.org/10.2307/23044044

Bagozzi, R. P. (2022). Philosophical foundations of concepts and their representation and use in explanatory frameworks. In H. Baumgartner & B. Weijters (Eds.), *Review of marketing research*, Vol. 19 [Special issue on measurement in marketing]. Emerald Publishing.

Bagozzi, R. P., Batra, R., & Ahuvia, A. (2017). Brand love: Development and validation of a practical scale. *Marketing Letters*, 28(1), 1–14. https://doi.org/10.1007/s11002-016-9406-1

Bagozzi, R. P., & Baumgartner, H. (1994). The evaluation of structural equation models and hypothesis testing. In R. P. Bagozzi (Ed.), *Principles of marketing research* (pp. 386–422). Blackwell.

Bagozzi, R. P., Baumgartner, H., & Pieters, R. (1998). Goal-directed emotions. *Cognition and Emotion*, 12(1), 1–26. https://doi.org/10.1080/026999398379754

Bagozzi, R. P., Bergami, M., Marzocchi, G. L., & Morandin, G. (2012). Customer-organization relationships: Development and test of a theory of extended identities. *Journal of Applied Psychology*, 97(1), 63–76. https://doi.org/10.1037/a0024533

Bagozzi, R. P., & Dholakia, U. M. (2006a). Antecedents and purchase consequences of customer participation in small group brand communities. *International Journal of Research in Marketing*, 23(1), 45–61. https://doi.org/10.1016/j.ijresmar.2006.01.005

Bagozzi, R. P., & Dholakia, U. M. (2006b). Open source software user communities: A study of participation in Linux user groups. *Management Science*, 52(7), 1099–1115. https://doi.org/10.1287/mnsc.1060.0545

Bagozzi, R. P., & Edwards, J. R. (1998). A general approach for representing constructs in organizational research. *Organizational research methods*, 1(1), 45–87.

Bagozzi, R. P., Lee, K. H., & Van Loo, M. F. (2001). Decisions to donate bone marrow: The role of attitudes and subjective norms across cultures. *Psychology & Health*, 16(1), 29–56. https://doi.org/10.1080/08870440108405488

Bagozzi, R. P., & Lee, N. (2019). Philosophical foundations of neuroscience in organizational research: Functional and nonfunctional approaches. *Organizational Research Methods*, 22(1), 299–331. https://doi.org/10.1177/1094428117697042

Bagozzi, R. P., Moore, D. J., & Leone, L. (2004). Self-control and the self-regulation of dieting decisions: The role of prefactual attitudes, subjective norms, and resistance to temptation. *Basic and Applied Social Psychology*, 26(2–3), 199–213. https://doi.org/10.1080/01973533.2004.9646405

Bagozzi, R. P., & Phillips, L. W. (1982). Representing and testing organizational theories: A holistic construal. *Administrative Science Quarterly*, 27(3), 459–489. https://doi.org/10.2307/2392322

Bagozzi, R. P., Ruvio, A., & Xie, C. (2020). The material self. *International Journal of Research in Marketing*, 37(4), 661–677. https://doi.org/10.1016/j.ijresmar.2020.03.002

Bagozzi, R. P., Verbeke, W. J., Dietvorst, R. C., Belschak, F. D., van den Berg, W. E., & Rietdijk, W. J. (2013). Theory of mind and empathic explanations of Machiavellianism: A neuroscience perspective. *Journal of Management*, 39(7), 1760–1798. https://doi.org/10.1177/0149206312471393

Bagozzi, R. P., & Warshaw, P. R. (1990). Trying to consume. *Journal of Consumer Research*, 17(2), 127–140. https://doi.org/10.1086/208543

Bagozzi, R. P., & Yi, Y. (1988). On the evaluation of structural equation models. *Journal of the Academy of Marketing Science*, 16(1), 74–94. https://doi.org/10.1007/BF02723327

Bagozzi, R. P., & Yi, Y. (1989). On the use of structural equation models in experimental designs. *Journal of Marketing Research*, 26(3), 271–284. https://doi.org/10.1177/002224378902600302

Bagozzi, R. P., & Yi, Y. (1991). Multitrait-multimethod matrices in consumer research. *Journal of Consumer Research*, 17(4), 426–439. https://doi.org/10.1086/208568

Bagozzi, R. P., & Yi, Y. (1993). Multitrait–multimethod matrices in consumer research: Critique and new developments. *Journal of Consumer Psychology*, 2(2), 143–170. https://doi.org/10.1016/S1057-7408(08)80022-8

Bagozzi, R. P., & Yi, Y. (2012). Specification, evaluation, and interpretation of structural equation models. *Journal of the Academy of Marketing Science*, 40(1), 8–34. https://doi.org/10.1007/s11747-011-0278-x

Bagozzi, R. P., Yi, Y., & Nassen, K. D. (1998). Representation of measurement error in marketing variables: Review of approaches and extension to three-facet designs. *Journal of Econometrics*, 89(1–2), 393–421. https://doi.org/10.1016/S0304-4076(98)00068-2

Bagozzi, R. P., Yi, Y., & Phillips, L. W. (1991). Assessing construct validity in organizational research. *Administrative Science Quarterly*, 36(3), 421–458. https://doi.org/10.2307/2393203

Bagozzi, R. P., Yi, Y., & Singh, S. (1991). On the use of structural equation models in experimental designs: Two extensions. *International Journal of Research in Marketing*, 8(2), 125–140. https://doi.org/10.1016/0167-8116(91)90020-8

Batra, R., Ahuvia, A., & Bagozzi, R. P. (2012). Brand love. *Journal of Marketing*, 76(2), 1–16. https://doi.org/10.1509/jm.09.0339

Bergami, M., & Bagozzi, R. P. (2000). Self-categorization, affective commitment and group self-esteem as distinct aspects of social identity in the organization. *British Journal of Social Psychology*, 39(4), 555–577. https://doi.org/10.1348/014466600164633

Bollen, K., & Lennox, R. (1991). Conventional wisdom on measurement: A structural equation perspective. *Psychological Bulletin*, 110(2), 305–314. https://doi.org/10.1037/0033-2909.110.2.305

Breitsohl, H. (2019). Beyond ANOVA: An introduction to structural equation models for experimental designs. *Organizational Research Methods*, 22(3), 649–677. https://doi.org/10.1177/1094428118754988

Campbell, D. T., & Fiske, D. W. (1959). Convergent and discriminant validation by the multitrait-multimethod matrix. *Psychological Bulletin*, 56(2), 81–105. https://doi.org/10.1037/h0046016

Curran, P. J., & Hussong, A. M. (2002). Structural equation modeling of repeated measures data. In D. Moskowitz & S. Hershberger (Eds.), *Modeling intraindividual variability with repeated measures data: Methods and applications* (pp. 59–86). Lawrence Erlbaum.

Davidson, D. (2001). *Essays on actions and events* (2nd ed.). Clarendeon Press. https://doi.org/10.1093/0199246270.001.0001

Dholakia, U. M., Bagozzi, R. P., & Pearo, L. K. (2004). A social influence model of consumer participation in network-and small-group-based virtual communities. *International Journal of Research in Marketing, 21*(3), 241–263. https://doi.org/10.1016/j.ijresmar.2003.12.004

Diamantopoulos, A., & Siguaw, J. A. (2006). Formative versus reflective indicators in organizational measure development: A comparison and empirical illustration. *British Journal of Management, 17*(4), 263–282. https://doi.org/10.1111/j.1467-8551.2006.00500.x

Dietvorst, R. C., Verbeke, W. J., Bagozzi, R. P., Yoon, C., Smits, M., & Van Der Lugt, A. (2009). A sales force–specific theory-of-mind scale: Tests of its validity by classical methods and functional magnetic resonance imaging. *Journal of Marketing Research, 46*(5), 653–668. https://doi.org/10.1509/jmkr.46.5.653

Eagly, A. H., & Chaiken, S. (1998). Attitude structure and function. In D. T. Gilbert, S. T. Fiske, & G. Lindzey (Eds.), *The handbook of social psychology* (pp. 269–322). McGraw-Hill.

Edwards, J. R., & Bagozzi, R. P. (2000). On the nature and direction of relationships between constructs and measures. *Psychological Methods, 5*(2), 155–174. https://doi.org/10.1037/1082-989X.5.2.155

Gerring, J. (1999). What makes a concept good? A criterial framework for understanding concept formation in the social sciences. *Polity, 31*(3), 357–393.

Haidt, J. (2012). *The righteous mind: Why good people are divided by politics and religion.* Pantheon.

Hayes, A. F. (2018). Partial, conditional, and moderated moderated mediation: Quantification, inference, and interpretation. *Communication Monographs, 85*(1), 4–40. https://doi.org/10.1080/03637751.2017.1352100

Howell, Breivik, and Wilcox (2007). *Psychological Methods, 12*(2), 229–237. https://doi.org/10.1037/1082-989X.12.2.229

Izard, C. E. (1977). *Human emotions.* Springer.

Jaworski, W. (2011). *Philosophy of mind: A comprehensive introduction.* Wiley-Blackwell.

Jöreskog, K. G., & Yang, F. (1996). Nonlinear structural equation models: The Kenny-Judd model with interaction effects. In G. A. Marcoulides & R. E. Schumacker (Eds.), *Advanced structural equation modeling: Issues and techniques* (Vol. 3, pp. 57–88). Lawrence Erlbaum.

Kim, J. (2000). *Mind in a physical world: An essay on the mind-body problem and mental causation.* MIT Press.

Kim, J. (2005). *Physicalism, or something near enough* (Vol. 19). Princeton University Press.

Kohlberg, L. (1981). *Essays on moral development: Vol. 1. The philosophy of moral development.* Harper & Row.

Kühnel, S. M. (1988). Testing MANOVA designs with LISREL. *Sociological Methods & Research, 16*(4), 504–523. https://doi.org/10.1177/0049124188016004004

Marsh, H. W., Wen, Z., & Hau, K. T. (2004). Structural equation models of latent interactions: Evaluation of alternative estimation strategies and indicator construction. *Psychological Methods, 9*(3), 275–300. https://doi.org/10.1037/1082-989X.9.3.275

Merriam-Webster. (n.d.). *Merriam-Webster.com dictionary.* https://www.merriam-webster.com/

Mooijaart, A., & Bentler, P. M. (2010). An alternative approach for nonlinear latent variable models. *Structural Equation Modeling, 17*(3), 357–373. https://doi.org/10.1080/10705511.2010.488997

Nagel, T. (2002). *Exposure and concealment: And other essays.* Oxford University Press.

Nagel, T. (2012). *Mind and cosmos: Why the materialist neo-Darwinian conception of nature is almost certainly false.* Oxford University Press. https://doi.org/10.1093/acprof:oso/9780199919758.001.0001

Outhwaite, W. (1983). *Concept formation in social science.* Routledge & Kegan Paul.

Parsons, T. (1968). Social interaction. In D. L. Sills (Ed.), *The international encyclopedia of the social sciences* (Vol. 7, pp. 429–441). Crowell Collier and Macmillan.

Perugini, M., & Bagozzi, R. P. (2001). The role of desires and anticipated emotions in goal-directed behaviours: Broadening and deepening the theory of planned behaviour. *British Journal of Social Psychology, 40*(1), 79–98. https://doi.org/10.1348/014466601164704

Podsakoff, P. M., MacKenzie, S. B., Podsakoff, N. P., & Lee, J. Y. (2003). The mismeasure of man (agement) and its implications for leadership research. *Leadership Quarterly, 14*(6), 615–656. https://doi.org/10.1016/j.leaqua.2003.08.002

Putnam, H. (1988). *Representation and reality.* MIT Press.

Rönkkö, M., McIntosh, C. N., Antonakis, J., & Edwards, J. R. (2016). Partial least squares path modeling: Time for some serious second thoughts. *Journal of Operations Management, 47–48*(1), 9–27. https://doi.org/10.1016/j.jom.2016.05.002

Russell, D. W., Kahn, J. H., Spoth, R., & Altmaier, E. M. (1998). Analyzing data from experimental studies: A latent variable structural equation modeling approach. *Journal of Counseling Psychology*, *45*(1), 18–29. https://doi.org/10.1037/0022-0167.45.1.18

Shadish, W. R., Cook, T. D., & Campbell, D. T. (2002). *Experimental and quasi-experimental designs for generalized causal inference*. Houghton Mifflin.

Soscia, I., Bagozzi, R. P., & Guenzi, P. (2018). Cognitive and affective determinants of salesforce performance: A two-wave study. *Industrial Marketing Management*, *75*, 206–217. https://doi.org/10.1016/j.indmarman.2018.06.003

Stoel, R. D., Garre, F. G., Dolan, C., & van den Wittenboer, G. (2006). On the likelihood ratio test in structural equation modeling when parameters are subject to boundary constraints. *Psychological Methods*, *11*(4), 439–455. https://doi.org/10.1037/1082-989X.11.4.439

Tam, L., Bagozzi, R. P., & Spanjol, J. (2010). When planning is not enough: The self-regulatory effect of implementation intentions on changing snacking habits. *Health Psychology*, *29*(3), 284–292. https://doi.org/10.1037/a0019071

Tsai, H. T., & Bagozzi, R. P. (2014). Contribution behavior in virtual communities: Cognitive, emotional, and social influences. *Management Information Systems Quarterly*, *38*(1), 143–163. https://doi.org/10.25300/MISQ/2014/38.1.07

Warren, C., Batra, R., Loureiro, S. M. C., & Bagozzi, R. P. (2019). Brand coolness. *Journal of Marketing*, *83*(5), 36–56. https://doi.org/10.1177/0022242919857698

Wikipedia. (n.d.). *Big data*. https://en.wikipedia.org/wiki/Big_data

Xie, C., Bagozzi, R. P., & Grønhaug, K. (2015). The role of moral emotions and individual differences in consumer responses to corporate green and non-green actions. *Journal of the Academy of Marketing Science*, *43*(3), 333–356. https://doi.org/10.1007/s11747-014-0394-5

Zarantonello, L., Romani, S., Grappi, S., & Bagozzi, R. P. (2016). Brand hate. *Journal of Product & Brand Management*, *25*(1), 11–25. https://doi.org/10.1108/JPBM-01-2015-0799

CHAPTER 5

UNDERSTANDING THE CHANGING ROLE AND FUNCTIONS OF MARKETING

Kevin Lane Keller

This chapter offers academic insights and managerial perspectives into the question of how businesses affect the psychological response of consumers in the marketplace. To provide some background and context, we first consider some big picture issues of marketing by describing the role and scope of marketing in organizations and outlining some core marketing concepts. After highlighting some recent marketing developments, we conclude by considering how organizations develop their marketing strategies and tactics.

THE ROLE AND SCOPE OF MARKETING

Marketing can be seen everywhere and profoundly affects our day-to-day lives. Formally or informally, people and organizations engage in a vast number of different activities that could be called marketing. After offering a formal definition of marketing, we characterize the marketing imperative and its importance and the general applicability of marketing.

Marketing Definitions

Although several definitions of marketing have been put forth, they have much in common. The American Marketing Association (AMA; n.d.) defined *marketing* as "the activity, set of institutions, and processes for creating, communicating, delivering, and exchanging offerings that have value for customers, clients, partners, and society at large" (p. 5).

Similarly, the leading introductory MBA marketing textbook defined marketing as "the art and science of choosing target markets and getting, keeping, and growing customers through creating, delivering, and communicating superior customer value" (Kotler & Keller, 2016, p. 5).

These and other related definitions share several key elements—notably, customers and value. Importantly, they all embrace the concept of marketing as a means to guide organizational goals and decision making and focus on value delivery to customers and others (Doyle, 2008; Moorman & Rust, 1999). Beyond these more managerial definitions of marketing, a societal-based definition reflecting marketing's broader role within society has also been put forth: "Marketing is a societal process by which individuals and groups obtain what they need and want through creating, offering, and freely exchanging products and services of value with others" (Kotler & Keller, 2016, p. 5).

The Marketing Imperative

Importantly, as defined, marketing is more than advertising or selling. One of the most enduring and powerful concepts of marketing is *marketing myopia*, which maintains that companies are not in the business of just selling products or services. Rather, companies are in the business of supplying benefits to customers, satisfying their needs and wants, and solving their problems (Levitt, 1960).

https://doi.org/10.1037/0000262-005
APA Handbook of Consumer Psychology, L. R. Kahle (Editor-in-Chief)
Copyright © 2022 by the American Psychological Association. All rights reserved.

In other words, Union Pacific is not in the railroad business but in the transportation business to help people and businesses move themselves or objects from one place to another. Similarly, Crayola is not in the crayon business but in the business of providing colorful arts and crafts for kids to satisfy their imagination and creative instincts. Viewing marketing through this broader lens has profound implications for product development and market growth.

Because of the role it plays and the functions it performs, marketing is an essential part of any organization (Feng et al., 2015). In an increasingly competitive marketplace, where organizations compete for attention, dollars, and other scarce resources, good marketing has become an increasingly vital ingredient for business success (Weitz & Wensley, 2002; Whitler et al., 2018). Finance, operations, accounting, and other business functions will not really matter if there is not sufficient demand for products and services so the company can make a profit. Financial success often depends on the ability of marketing to effectively and efficiently generate demand (Verhoef & Leeflang, 2009). In short, there must be a top line for there to be a bottom line (Srinivasan & Hanssens, 2009).

Customers are an essential part of this equation. Fundamentally, firms exist for their customers. Firms gain customers when they can offer products and services that customers value more than the price that they pay for them. In a very fundamental way, customers underlie the value of firms. Recognizing this fact, market-savvy firms embrace customer-centricity, striving to achieve a deep understanding of all aspects of their business from a customer's perspective (Fader, 2012; Fader & Toms, 2018).

Knowledge of customers and how to build enduring productive relationships with them is a core competence of marketing (Palmatier et al., 2019). As developed in greater detail later, good marketing is no accident but a result of thoughtful, careful planning and execution (Tybout & Calder, 2010). Marketing, however, is both an "art" and a "science" (Winer & Neslin, 2014). There is also a strong creative element to marketing. Successful marketers are often imaginative in how they can bring a marketing strategy to life. As is demonstrated later, being creative and being scientific both require deep insights into consumer psychology (Haugtvedt et al., 2008).

Marketing Applications

It is also important to recognize that marketing as a discipline and the adoption of the marketing concept are applicable in a wide variety of settings. Marketing is being actively conducted for all kinds of goods, services, events, experiences, people, places, properties, organizations, information, and ideas. The basic principles reviewed in this chapter are applicable in virtually all of these settings, but, at the same time, there are often some unique issues that arise when considering specific applications.

Seeing the applicability of marketing to physical products and intangible offerings such as events and experiences is often relatively straightforward, as these entities have been prominently marketed for decades if not centuries. Whether considering Pampers diapers, Caterpillar tractors, or a Rolling Stones concert tour, the importance of marketing to help create, deliver, and communicate value and generate demand is easy to understand and appreciate. However, the scope of marketing extends much beyond that.

For example, take people and how they are being marketed as brands (Fournier & Eckhardt, 2019). A person-brand can be any individual, whether famous or not. Marketing a person-brand, like marketing any brand, requires firmly establishing awareness and the right image of the person. The desired brand identity for the person then may guide how the person looks and how the person communicates and acts.

As another example, consider geographical locations. Cities, states, regions, and nations are often marketed in terms of the uniqueness of experiences they provide tourists or businesses (Kotler et al., 2002, 2017). Governments often have active, well-funded tourist boards who tout the advantages of their location for a vacation. Other departments promote commerce and the advantages of the location as a place to locate headquarters or conduct business.

SOME CORE MARKETING CONCEPTS

Given the complexity and scope of marketing, it is not surprising that there are a number of important concepts that come into play in understanding how marketing works. Here we identify some core marketing concepts, some of which we further develop in later sections of the chapter.

The Five Cs

A central marketing concept is the "Five Cs of Marketing," defined as Customers, Companies, Competition, Collaborators, and Context. The first three are also sometimes described as the "Three Cs of Marketing," as they perhaps represent the most fundamental of all marketing concerns. Given that marketing is sometimes described in terms of the ability of companies to satisfy the needs and wants of customers better than competitors, the essential nature of the three Cs is clear.

It should be recognized, however, that customers can take many forms. Customers may be individuals or businesses (Lilien & Grewal, 2011). They may be concentrated locally or spread all over the world. Companies similarly vary widely. They may be for-profit or nonprofit. They may offer services or sell inexpensive household products or expensive durable goods. Finally, competition may be concentrated and involve two or three other firms or be very diffuse and involve numerous firms of all kinds.

Yet, at the same time, there is also agreement that collaborators and context play an important role in how companies create value for customers and satisfy their needs and wants. Collaborators represent all those organizations that partner with a firm and affect the value creation and delivery process. Collaborators include suppliers who provide the raw materials, ingredients, and other inputs necessary for the creation of value, as well as distributors who help to make products and services available for sale to customers. Understanding how to effectively and efficiently manage relationships with collaborators and marketing partners is crucially important and has benefited from research applying theories and concepts from psychology and other disciplines (A. Kumar et al., 2011; Moorman & Day, 2016; Swaminathan & Moorman, 2009; Wathne et al., 2018).

Context represents all the external forces that affect the value creation and delivery process. The marketing environment contains a number of different factors that can play an important role in marketing performance and success. They can be grouped into the following broad categories: demographic, economic, social-cultural, natural, technological, and political-legal environments.

Brands

An essential component in marketing is the *brand*, defined as "a name, term, design, symbol or any other feature that identifies one seller's good or service as distinct from those of other sellers" (Keller & Swaminathan, 2020, p. 2). Brands provide a number of benefits for consumers (Hoeffler & Keller, 2003). Fundamentally, by offering consumers a predictable experience—even if "predictably unpredictable"—they are a way to set expectations, simplify decision making, and reduce risk. Brands also often have much social and personal meaning and, as a result, they also allow consumers to signal to others or themselves who they are or who they would like to be. The brand's relationship to consumer's actual or aspirational self-identity is an important driver of consumer behavior and the source of much academic study (Keller, 1993, 2016; Tybout & Calkins, 2005).

At the same time, brands provide a number of functions for firms (Keller & Lehmann, 2006). Brands make business operations easier in terms of accounting records, inventory planning, and so forth. They also offer vital legal protection and allow firms to reap the long-term benefits of their investments in products and services. Brands can help firms secure competitive advantages in the marketplace and build a loyal customer franchise. Consumers are willing to pay more for brands they feel uniquely offer value, which in turn allows firms to enjoy price premiums and greater profitability.

For all these reasons, brands can be a firm's most valuable intangible asset (Ailawadi et al., 2003; Bahadir et al., 2008; Keller & Lehmann, 2003). For well-known firms, the value of their brands is routinely 20% to 30% of the market capitalization for the firm but can even be as much as 75% to 80% of market capitalization. Accordingly, brands must be measured and managed like any asset to ensure their long-term health and survival (Mizik, 2014; Mizik & Jacobson, 2008, 2009).

Customer Lifetime Value

Brands and consumers are inextricably linked (Ambler et al., 2002; Leone et al., 2006). Brands exist to provide value to consumers, and consumers generally find brands they value. Consumers provide value to firms, in turn, through their loyalty in purchasing brands and perhaps even paying a price premium to do so (Gupta et al., 2004, 2005). They also create value if they talk or write to others about their positive experiences. The more behaviors customers engage in that benefits firms, and the longer they do so, the more value they create for firms. Formally, customer lifetime value (CLV) can be defined as "the net present value of the stream of future profits expected over the customer's lifetime purchases" (Rust et al., 2000, 2004).

An important marketing topic, calculating CLV requires subtracting the expected costs of acquiring and retaining a customer from the resulting expected direct (and indirect) revenues, applying the appropriate discount rate. Firms can attempt to increase CLV through a variety of different strategies and tactics, such as the following (Blattberg et al., 2009):

- increased retention rate (e.g., making customers more loyal through recognition, services)
- increased spending rate (e.g., making more sales to existing customers)
- increased referral rate (e.g., getting one customer to recommend another)
- decreased marketing costs (e.g., resulting from more efficient targeting)
- decreased direct costs (e.g., resulting from more efficient selling and distribution)

CLV thus provides much valuable information and strategic insight and guidance to firms (Venkatesan & Kumar, 2004). The CLV inputs and calculations help to inform *customer relationship management* (CRM) activities, the means by which firms chose to engage their customers (V. Kumar et al., 2006; V. Kumar & Reinartz, 2018).

Finally, another related concept is the *value delivery chain* and the means by which firms actually create and provide value to customers. *Perceived value* to customers is basically all the benefits the consumer realizes versus all the costs that they incur (Doyle, 2008). Importantly, benefits come in all forms—economic, functional, psychological, and so on. Similarly, the costs incurred also come in all forms—monetary, time, energy, psychological, and so on. Firms create value with their brands when they maximize the benefits consumers realize and minimize the costs they incur.

As described in more detail later, there are a variety of qualitative and quantitative ways to measure benefits and costs of products, services, or brands. Consumers can often respond to queries as to the kinds of things that they look for in choosing or judging such entities. Identifying their importance can be harder though, and although consumers can be asked, often they find it difficult to accurately express their relative preferences.

Conjoint analysis is a multivariate statistical technique for deriving the importance or utility values that consumers attach to varying levels of a product's attributes or benefits (Green & Srinivasan, 1978, 1990). Also called trade-off analysis, it requires that consumers rank carefully selected profiles in a way to reveal their true preferences. Conjoint analysis can be particularly helpful in new product design, but it has other applications too. *Adaptive conjoint analysis* (ACA) is a hybrid data collection technique that combines self-explicated importance ratings with pair-wise trade-off tasks (Netzer et al., 2008; Toubia et al., 2003, 2008).

Segmentation, Targeting, and Positioning

Firms have to decide who they are going to compete with and how they are going to do so. One of the most important sets of decisions that a firm will make in developing their marketing strategies is segmentation, targeting, and positioning. Firms rarely attempt to sell to an entire market. Typically, they concentrate their selling on one or more focused groups of customers sharing certain characteristics (Yankelovich & Meer, 2006).

Segmentation involves dividing a market up into groups of potential or actual customers who differ in their needs and wants and the way in which they would respond to products and services and how they are marketed. *Targeting* involves choosing which of those segments offer the greatest opportunities. Finally, *positioning* involves determining how targeted customers should think or feel about a brand as compared with competitive brands.

There are many strategic ways to segment a market, as well as techniques to do so (Desarbo et al., 1995). Four major approaches are based on geographic (e.g., local, regional, national, or international), demographic (e.g., age, race, gender, education, or income), psychographic (e.g., differences in personality, lifestyle, or values), or behavioral considerations (e.g., brand awareness, knowledge, attitude, or usage). Many marketing experts advocate segmentation on the basis of benefit considerations—what consumers care about and are seeking from a brand. For example, in the toothpaste market, segments may exist for consumers who care about strong, healthy teeth; a bright, white smile; or fresh breath.

Regardless of the particular method or approach used to segment a market, an effective market segmentation scheme must satisfy the following criteria (Kotler & Keller, 2016):

- measurable: The size, purchasing power, and profiles of the segments can be measured.
- accessible: The market segments can be effectively reached and served.
- substantial: The market segments are large or profitable enough to serve.
- differentiable: The segments are conceptually distinguishable and respond differently to different marketing activities.
- actionable: Effective programs can be designed for attracting and serving the segment.

Once a market is divided into a set of mutually exclusive but exhaustive segments, firms must decide which consumer segments to target. Targeting specifies how many and which segments become the focus of a firm's marketing efforts. In deciding which segments to target, a firm considers the attractiveness of the segment in terms of CLV and other considerations and compares that to the firm's capabilities and ability to serve that segment in a unique way. In making targeting decisions, firms ask questions such as the following:

- Which customers place the greatest value on what the firm can offer?
- Which customers are the most profitable and the most loyal?
- Which customers are worth more to the firm than to competitors?

The most attractive segments to target occur when the firm feels confident about uniquely satisfying customers who would offer many financial and other benefits to the firm.

Finally, after making decisions about segmentation and targeting, a firm can decide how to position the brand to most effectively appeal to the chosen target markets (Keller et al., 2002). Formally, *brand positioning* can be defined as "the act of designing a company's offering and image to occupy a distinctive place in the minds of the target market" (Kotler & Keller, 2016, p. 275). Brand positioning is how firms want consumers to think and feel about a brand as compared with competitors. Brand positioning is a critical component of a firm's marketing strategy, as it guides resource decisions and how a firm chooses to market to its customers. Targeting and positioning go hand in hand. A firm should only target a segment that they feel they can have some competitive advantages with.

Four Ps (Product, Price, Place, and Promotion)

With the marketing strategy in place in terms of segmentation, targeting, and positioning decisions—who the firm wants to appeal to and how it wants to differentiate itself in doing so—the firm can turn to developing and implementing marketing tactics to achieve that positioning. A whole host of marketing programs and activities may be initiated by a firm to create, communicate, and deliver superior value to targeted customers. In general, in developing marketing plans, marketers make decisions in four major areas that have been colloquially referred to as the "Four Ps" of marketing:

- product: the products and services and all other related aspects of the offerings that are made available to consumers and the target market
- price: the prices by which the offerings are sold to consumers and the target market
- place: the channels of distribution or various means by which products are sold and delivered to consumers and the target market
- promotion: the marketing communications or various means by which firms choose to communicate to consumers and the target market

Although useful heuristically, it should be recognized that the four Ps are somewhat of a stylized conceptualization. There are marketing activities and programs that don't fit neatly into one of the four categories. Nevertheless, the four Ps are a useful tool to capture some fundamental marketing considerations. In developing marketing activities and programs, there are a number of important specific considerations that come into play.

For example, one important marketing distinction is between *push* and *pull* marketing activities. Push marketing activities are those marketing activities directed to intermediate members of the distribution channel—wholesalers, retailers, distributors, and others—so that they stock, promote, and sell products to consumers. Pull marketing activities, on the other hand, are those marketing activities directed toward consumers themselves (e.g., advertising, promotions, and other forms of communication) to generate demand so that these intermediaries are induced or compelled to stock, promote, and sell the product to satisfy their own customers (Tellis & Ambler, 2007).

Push strategies are more direct; pull strategies are more indirect. Most companies do both and conduct a number of activities that could fall into one or the other categories, although perhaps putting emphasis on one more than the other. As described later, integrated channel and communication strategies are critical in terms of how skillfully marketers can blend their push and pull efforts.

Growth Strategies

To achieve their missions and goals, organizations, especially publicly traded ones, need to grow. Growth can come in many forms, but one classic framework provides a useful conceptual structure. Ansoff's (1957) Product-Market Expansion Grid views growth as coming from four main sources, depending on what is sold and where, that is, whether new or current products are being sold and whether new or current markets are involved:

- market penetration: selling current products in current markets
- market development: selling current products in new markets
- product development: selling new products in current markets
- diversification: selling new products in new markets

Most firms employ variations on the first three approaches, although not all firms actively pursue significant diversification. Two primary growth strategies for many firms thus involve launching new products and entering new markets, especially those global in nature.

Successfully developing new products is a major challenge but it is critically important, and much research has explored organizational factors in new ways to increase the likelihood of new product success (Bayus, 2013; Kuppuswamy & Bayus, 2018). Achieving a deep, rich understanding of consumer attitudes and behaviors as input to the new product development process is seen as an essential ingredient (Dahl & Moreau, 2002; Hoeffler, 2003; Moreau, Lehmann, & Markman, 2001; Moreau, Markman, & Lehmann, 2001; Wood, 2016).

Much research has also explored how to expand into diverse global markets (N. Kumar & Steenkamp, 2013; Steenkamp, 2017). In a similar vein, consumer insights and how consumers may vary across markets as a result of the context and marketing environments involved is also seen as vital to developing a successful market entry strategy.

THE STATE OF MARKETING IN 2020

Although these marketing fundamentals provide a helpful foundation, modern marketing is unquestionably different in form and substance from marketing in decades past in many significant ways. The last 5 to 10 years have seen fundamental shifts across a wide range of areas. Here we highlight a few of these important trends and some of their marketing and consumer behavior implications.

Key Marketing Trends

Rapid technological developments. Perhaps the most profound trend is the rate of technological change in the world and how people work and live. With the advent of the internet, consumers now shop and communicate differently, with massive implications for how marketers distribute and sell their products. New technologies have led to an explosion of information for consumers about companies and vice-versa. The rapid diffusion and advances with mobile phones is fundamentally changing the marketing equation as consumers seek information, shop, and purchase virtually anytime and anywhere.

Fragmentation of traditional media. Traditional media, such as TV, radio, magazines, and newspapers, has splintered in many different ways, and a wide variety of choices now exist in each medium via recent developments such as satellite broadcasts and digital distribution. The emergence of new media vehicles permits much more narrow targeting (e.g., with television, Lifetime for women, HGTV for DIY home enthusiasts, and LOGO for the LGBT community). At the same time, audiences overall have shrunk as consumers increasingly move their media consumption online. Not surprisingly, traditional media has struggled to deal with streaming, DVRs, and strong online preferences. Traditional media also lacks the ability to track detailed behavior of consumers to guide marketing or share with advertisers.

Growth of digital marketing options. Accordingly, with the deep penetration of the internet in consumers' lives, digital marketing is becoming an increasingly larger component of a marketing budget. Virtually any brand now can establish a multifaceted digital communications platform consisting of websites, emails and text messages, banner and rich media ads, and SEO and search ads, as well as a host of social media options including major platforms such as Facebook, Twitter, and Instagram. These platforms offer timely, detailed information and opportunities for engagement.

Channel transformation and disintermediation. With the ability to sell directly to customers, many firms are bypassing traditional retail options to sell directly to consumers online or via company-owned outlets. As a result, the retail industry has seen long-time stalwarts, such as Sears, Macy's, JCPenney, and Kmart, struggle or disappear altogether. The additional rapid decline or demise of specialty stores (e.g., Payless shoes, Gymboree children's clothing, Forever 21 fast-fashion, and A.C. Moore arts and crafts) has also threatened the once-popular shopping meccas of the mall.

Increased competition and industry convergence. With lower barriers of entry, markets are being transformed by new forms of competition, especially in terms of direct-to-consumer market disrupters. Notable start-up firms such as Dollar Shave Club and Harry's (razors and blades), Uber (transportation), Airbnb (lodging), Casper (mattresses), WarbyParker (eyeglasses), Hulu (television), RealReal (fashions), and others have successfully entered established markets. Beyond new upstarts, other forms of competition have come from an increasing number of firms extending their brands into lateral markets, for example, when Apple entered the smartphone market. Consumers now have to decide how to contrast traditional legacy brands with these new disruptive brands as they make their choices.

Globalization and growth of developing markets. One other consequence of the explosive growth of digital forms of communication is that it is now easier to reach consumers all over the world. Combined with the ability to establish global supply chains and the means to make and distribute products all over the world, firms now have the opportunity to more effectively and efficiently enter more global markets than ever before. Due to their large populations but still maturing marketplaces, emerging or developing markets offer an attractive option to many firms.

Heightened environmental, community, social, and ethical concerns. Consumers have always been concerned with the broader implications of how firms conduct their business, but millennials and younger Gen Z consumers appear to be especially attuned to these concerns. Sustainability, diversity, and inclusion in the workforce and elsewhere and support of socially beneficial causes are just some of the areas where consumers of all ages are demanding more from businesses. Academic research has been following these same trends, and research into social marketing and corporate social responsibility (CSR) has been steadily increasing. For example, in recent years the *Journal of Marketing* devoted a special issue on "Better Marketing for a Better World" as well as publishing numerous articles on the effects of CSR on both financial and firm performance (Kang et al., 2016; Mishra & Modi, 2016; Stäbler & Fischer, 2020) as well as on consumer perceptions and attitudes (Habel et al., 2016; Olsen et al., 2014; Paharia, 2020).

Consumer and Company Implications

As a result of these shifts, it is notable how the three Cs of marketing—customers, companies and competitors—have changed, making marketing for organizations easier in some ways, but harder in others. Consider these new consumer and company realities (Keller & Swaminathan, 2020; Morgan, 2019; Morgan et al., 2009).

Increased customer empowerment. Through the internet, customers now have greater capabilities in ways that never existed. Consider what consumers can now do (Kotler & Keller, 2016):

- use the internet as a powerful information and purchasing aid
- collect fuller and richer information on products, services, brands, and companies
- search, communicate, and purchase on the move
- tap into social media to share opinions and express loyalty with others
- actively interact with companies
- digitally receive ads, coupons, and other marketing materials
- easily compare prices and seek discounts
- reject marketing they find inappropriate

Marketers must understand and account for these new consumer capabilities as they develop their marketing strategies and tactics. Yet, at the same time, it is important to recognize that empowered is not necessarily enlightened, and many consumers may still not be fully informed or engaged in product or service decision making. In fact, only some of the consumers will choose to engage with some of their brands and even then, only some of the time.

Increased company capabilities. Just as consumers are able to do things in the marketplace that they were never able to do before, the same is true of firms too. Consider what firms can now do (Kotler & Keller, 2016):

- use the internet as a powerful information and sales channel
- collect fuller and richer information about customers and competitors
- reach consumers on the move with mobile marketing
- tap into social media to amplify their brand messages
- facilitate and speed external communication among customers
- send targeted ads, coupons, samples, and information to customers
- make and sell individually differentiated goods and services
- improve purchasing, recruiting, training, and communications
- facilitate and speed up communication among employees
- improve cost efficiency

It is clear that, just as much as consumers, marketers are able to do many things that they could never do before to make their marketing more personal, more engaging, and more meaningful to their customers.

UNDERSTANDING CONSUMERS

With the structural understanding of the various facets of marketing in place, it is useful to delve into more details on some important consumer behavior issues for marketing management. Understanding how consumers respond to marketing programs and activities for a brand is critical for marketing managers. A crucial contribution of consumer researchers is the development of various concepts, frameworks, and models that can help to guide decisions by marketing managers, much of which is described elsewhere in other chapters. In this section, we highlight some important theoretical notions that can help in the development of marketing strategy and tactics (Morgan et al., 2019; Shankar & Carpenter, 2012).

Fundamentally, to design and implement the right marketing programs and activities, marketers must have a complete and accurate understanding of how consumers think, feel, and act (Homburg et al., 2000). What do consumers know about products and services? How do they shop for products and services? How do they choose among brands? Answers to these and other questions are critical for marketers to make fully informed and creative marketing decisions. After briefly considering some basic concepts with consumer knowledge, we focus some on consumer search behavior and the role of expectations in consumer decision making.

Consumer Knowledge

There are many ways to depict consumer knowledge in terms of structure and content and the cognitive representations of products, services, brands, and related concepts. Consumer brand knowledge, in particular, can be defined in terms of the personal meaning about a brand stored in memory, that is, all descriptive and evaluative brand-related information (Keller, 2003).

Researchers have studied consumer brand knowledge for decades (Alba & Hutchinson, 1987, 2000). The reality that emerges from the varied consumer research activity on branding through the years is that all different kinds of information may become linked to a brand, including the following (Keller 2003):

- awareness: category identification and needs satisfied by the brand
- attributes: descriptive features that characterize the brand name product either intrinsically (i.e., related to product performance) or extrinsically (i.e., related to brand imagery)
- benefits: personal value and meaning that consumers attach to the brand's product attributes (e.g., functional, symbolic, or experiential consequences from the brand's purchase or consumption)
- images: visual information, either concrete or abstract in nature
- thoughts: personal cognitive responses to any brand-related information
- feelings: personal affective responses to any brand-related information
- attitudes: summary judgments and overall evaluations to any brand-related information
- experiences: purchase and consumption behaviors and any other brand-related episodes

These dimensions of brand knowledge vary on all sorts of considerations beyond their content per se, for example, abstractness, valence, strength, uniqueness, and so on. An important distinction is between more rational, functional, or utilitarian knowledge and more emotional, aesthetic, or hedonic knowledge (Cohen et al., 2008; Kahle et al., 1986; Pham, 1998; Voss et al., 2003). Importantly, all of these different kinds of information may become a part of consumer memory and impact consumer response to marketing activities. By impacting consumer responses and decisions, brand knowledge affects the success of brand-building marketing efforts.

Marketers employ a wide variety of qualitative and quantitative techniques to learn about consumer knowledge (Grover & Vriens, 2006; Malhotra, 2019). Marketing research is all about generating insights. Obtaining accurate, timely, and actionable consumer insights is critical for companies so that they can sell the right products and services to the right consumers in the right way. Marketing insights provide diagnostic information about how and why companies observe certain effects in the marketplace and what that means to their marketers.

In conducting marketing research, firms must decide whether to collect their own data or use data that already exist. They must also choose a research approach (observational, focus group, survey, behavioral data, or experimental) and research instruments (questionnaire, qualitative measures, or technological devices). In addition, they must decide on a sampling plan and contact methods (by mail, by phone, in person, or online; Kotler & Keller, 2016). The marketing research or consumer insights function of firms is changing dramatically. Surveys are being downplayed due to dwindling response rates, whereas behavioral measures and A/B testing with test/control samples are being increasingly employed.

Consumer Decision Making

How consumers arrive at a decision to take an action toward a brand—make a purchase, offer a donation, or change their behavior in some way—is often an important marketing priority (Bettman, 1979, 1986). Consumer decision making can be divided up into prepurchase, purchase, and postpurchase behaviors. Marketers attempt to influence consumers across all three stages, employing a number of different marketing concepts and techniques to do so. Here, we highlight a few of the more notable ones, described in detail, along with other important concepts, in other chapters. Specifically, we consider the consumer decision journey and the role of consumer expectations along the way.

Consumer decision journey. One important distinction that is made with consumer shopping behavior is how much time, energy, and other resources consumers may expend in making a purchase decision. Many consumer purchase decisions are habitual or repeat purchases, which require little, if any, thought. At the other end of the spectrum, for important new or major purchases, consumers may engage in extended problem solving and consider a number of different alternatives in depth. In the middle of the continuum is more limited problem solving, where consumers engage in some thought but with respect to a more circumscribed set of alternatives.

Marketers have different goals with each of three different types of search behavior (Bloch et al., 1986; Maity et al., 2014; Ratchford et al., 2003, 2007). For habitual purchases, marketers try to reinforce loyalty of current customers while trying to find ways to disrupt the routinized behavior of customers loyal to competitive brands. With limited problem solving, marketers have to be sure to be one of the small set of brands that receive serious consideration. Finally, with extensive problem solving, marketers must create the right information environments and streams to make sure, as much as possible, the right information is available to the right consumers in the right times and places.

These broad characterizations of search behavior can be further refined in terms of a *consumer purchase funnel*. These can be assembled in different ways, but at their core is the basic premise that consumers can go through a series of discrete stages as they consider making a purchase. Often described in terms of hierarchy of effects models, the most basic purchase funnel consists of the simple AIDA model of Awareness-Interest-Desire-Action based on similar models in social and cognitive psychology (McGuire, 1978). These hierarchy of effects models have been expanded in various ways to consider additional stages. For example, a more detailed model might trace the flow of consumer decision making to involve consumer awareness, knowledge, consideration, preference, choice, satisfaction, loyalty, attachment, and engagement (Batra & Keller, 2016).

One of the advantages of such models is that they suggest very concrete marketing actions as a result of where consumers are in the decision process. For example, depending on how far along the consumer is in the decision process, the goals of a marketer are fairly straightforward, as follows:

1. Unaware → Aware
2. Not considered → Considered
3. Not tried → Tried
4. Negative or neutral opinion → Favorable opinion
5. No repeat → Repeat
6. Repeat → Loyalty
7. Light user → Heavy user

Hierarchy of effects models and decision funnels are "as if" depictions of the consumer decision process and useful heuristically as a stylized model. Yet, the modern reality of consumer decision making in a digital world is often very different (Srinivasan et al., 2016). Highly nonlinear, consumers skip steps, cycle back, and engage in different behaviors than before. In recognition of this new reality, marketers now refer to the *consumer decision journey* to better reflect the dynamic, more complex, and potentially nonsequential nature of consumer decision making (Court et al., 2009; Kuehnl et al., 2019).

The consumer decision journey concept recognizes that consumers may skip steps, for example, making a purchase before collecting much, if any, information and choosing a brand based on a positive review or recommendation before really even forming a preference (Lemon & Verhoef, 2016). A consumer decision journey recognizes that consumers may backtrack and form attitudes after choice or collect information after making a purchase. Finally, it recognizes that there are more discrete steps in the consumer decision process before, during, and after purchase.

In developing marketing plans to build brands and drive sales, marketing objectives need to align with the customer journey and consumer needs at different stages (Lee et al., 2018; Li & Kannan, 2014; Richardson, 2010). Some possible marketing objectives that reflect different stages of the consumer journey include the following (Batra & Keller, 2016):

- create awareness and salience
- convey detailed information
- create brand imagery and personality
- build trust
- elicit emotions
- inspire action
- shape satisfaction
- make connections

Consumer expectations. One of the realities of marketing, which is becoming even more important with greater consumer empowerment, is the centrality of consumer expectations. Consumer expectations drive how consumers interpret product or service performance and what they expect firms to do and say in the marketplace (Kopalle & Lehmann, 2001, 2006).

Consumer expectations have been shown to color how consumers process information and make decisions (Bettman et al., 1998). Influential theories, such as prospect theory (Kahneman & Tversky, 1979) or service gap models (Parasuraman et al., 1985, 1988), use expectations and frames to understand how consumers interpret and judge product and service performance and respond to how they are marketed (Boulding et al., 1993; Huber et al., 1982; Huber & Puto, 1983; Sujan et al., 1986; Winer, 1986). Consumer expectations extend beyond product or service performance to encompass social and ethical conduct. Increasingly, consumers have norms for what they believe firms should say and how they should act. Such norms can extend across a broad domain of areas inside and outside the firm (Campbell, 1999; Campbell & Kirmani, 2000; Friestad & Wright, 1994, 1995).

Firms that violate these norms can also pay the price in the marketplace in the form of negative word of mouth or even boycotts (Klein et al., 2004; Sen et al., 2001). In an increasingly transparent and often unforgiving world, the clear implication is that firms have to ensure that structures and processes are in place so that all levels of management and all employees behave with high ethical standards to the greatest degree possible. Given the challenge in recovering from social or ethical transgressions, the clear mandate is to avoid them to begin with.

That said, even with the best intentions, a firm can find itself facing a legal or ethical scandal and consumer disapproval or outright outrage. Under these circumstances, a firm must take steps to try to repair its image and restore its reputation (Cleeren et al., 2013, 2017). There are a number of insights and guidelines for crisis management and how a brand can best recover from a turn in its fortunes (Dawar & Pillutla, 2000; Gijsenberg et al., 2015; Lei et al., 2012; Van Heerde et al., 2007; Zhao et al., 2011). Being swift and sincere in responding is paramount, but the exact nature of the marketing program that does so is also critical.

Corporate social responsibility. As noted earlier, with consumers more attuned to the companies behind the brands they purchase and use and how they choose to conduct their business, firms are correspondingly engaging in even more activities and programs in the CSR arena. CSR has long been a focus of research in marketing, and a number of useful ideas have emerged through the years (Bhattacharya & Sen, 2003; Bhattacharya et al., 2011; Luo & Bhattacharya, 2006; Sen & Bhattacharya, 2001).

DEVELOPING MARKETING PROGRAMS AND TACTICS

A thorough and up-to-date understanding of consumers can lay the foundation for a marketing plan that also considers the capabilities of a firm, the competitive forces in the marketplace, and other factors. Once the marketing plans are put in place, marketing tactics and implementation enter the picture, and specific marketing programs and activities have to be designed and executed. In this section, we consider some marketing implementation essentials and how tactics are developed.

Brand Building Basics

Marketers build strong brands by creating the right brand knowledge structures with target consumers. As suggested earlier, there are a whole host of beneficial associations that may become linked to the brand—thoughts, feelings, perceptions, beliefs, images, attitudes, behaviors, and so on.

In particular, building a strong brand requires creating a brand of which consumers are sufficiently aware and with which consumers have strong, favorable, and unique brand associations (Keller, 1993). The right brand knowledge structures with consumers can result in a number of benefits to a firm, including price premiums, loyal customers, cost savings, and brand extension and licensing opportunities.

This knowledge-building process depends on all brand-related contacts, whether marketer-initiated or not. Without question, at the heart of marketers' brand building efforts are the products and services they sell and the associated pricing, distribution, and communication strategies. Decisions in other areas, however, can fundamentally impact brand equity and also play a critical role. From a marketing management perspective, there are three main sets of brand equity drivers (Keller & Swaminathan, 2020):

1. The initial choices for the brand elements or identities making up the brand (e.g., brand names, URLs, logos, symbols, characters, slogans, jingles, packages, and signage). Red Bull chose its name and logo of two bulls, its iconic smaller can, and long-time slogan ("Red Bull Gives You Wings") to reinforce its positioning as a functional energy drink that acts as an "intense mystical revitalizer."
2. The four Ps and the products and services themselves and all accompanying marketing activities and programs. Nike's marketplace success has been driven by a cohesive set of well-designed and executed marketing activities and programs that include a wide range of innovative, high performance shoes, clothing, and apparel; direct-to-consumer sales through company stores and a company-owned website as well as indirect sales through online and brick-and-mortar specialty and department stores; creative advertising and promotions through digital and traditional media; and premium pricing.
3. Other associations indirectly transferred to the brand by linking it to some other entity (e.g., a person, place, or thing). For example, Rolex sponsors elite athletes and events to reinforce its prestigious image.

Thus, although the second factor is the central driver of equity, the first and third factors are also very helpful contributors as they typically can represent much less expensive options.

Modern Approaches to Brand Building

Brand building in modern times has changed dramatically even if the basic strategic intent has not. Brands still need to be seen as relevant and differentiated by consumers to spur choice. As suggested before, however, the manner by which brands achieve this goal requires different tactics. Here, we highlight some of the developments in areas suggested by the classic four Ps of marketing.

Enhanced product and service offerings. Products and services today are augmented in many ways to provide much broader benefits and value. At the heart of a great brand is a great product or service, but having a compelling value proposition that recognizes a wide range of potential benefits and cost savings is becoming more and more essential.

For example, the Starbucks value proposition is to provide the greatest possible sensory experience for customers, from the taste and aroma of the coffee, the sight of the art on the walls, the sounds from the music being played, and the feel of the tables and chairs. In addition to these physical benefits, the Starbucks value proposition also includes the psychological benefits of relaxation, rejuvenation, and social connection, as captured by their concept of being the "third place" beyond work and home. The Samsung value proposition, on the other hand, centers on high quality and innovative products that are well-designed both functionally and aesthetically, priced to offer good value.

Marketers of technology and other products are exploring platforms and systems and the right kinds of related or supporting products or services to supplement their core product offerings. Beyond the product or service offering itself, marketers are also adding an increasing number of intangible associations that reflect considerations of how the product or service is made or delivered, who the people are behind the product or service, and other such important secondary associations (Sinclair & Keller, 2014, 2017).

Flexible, dynamic pricing. With the ability to gain detailed information on customer demand, pricing strategies have become much more complex. Firms now can adjust pricing to better reflect supply and demand pressures in many different settings but must do so in a way that is acceptable to consumers (Haws & Bearden, 2006). Also known as yield pricing, different prices can be set depending on time, capacity, or other considerations. Employing sophisticated algorithms and massive data sets, marketers effectively set a higher or lower price for any one customer depending on forecasts of their willingness to pay (Kannan & Kopalle, 2001; Yuan & Han, 2011).

Pricing strategies involve setting prices but also adjusting prices over time. Price setting is even more complex as prices often consist of a bundled set of fees, discounts for different purchase circumstances, and so forth. To help guide their decisions on how to structure prices, firms are applying consumer behavior theory and insights from behavioral economics and psychology, among other areas. Psychological concepts like prospect theory and mental accounting have been shown to provide insight into setting prices, product line pricing, and discount schedules (Kahneman & Tversky, 1979; Thaler & Sunstein, 2008; Tversky & Kahneman, 1974).

For example, behavioral economics recognizes that consumers experience loss aversion, anchor and fail to adjust properly, and are sensitive to framing (Levin et al., 1998). As a result of these other psychological forces, consumers have been found to disproportionally prefer something offered as "free" (e.g., a $10 Amazon gift card for free is preferred to a $20 Amazon gift card sold for $7), prefer positive frames (e.g., 95% lean is preferred vs. 5% fat), can prefer fewer choices than more choices in some settings (e.g., more sales arise from six jams being offered than 24 jams), and can dislike losses twice as much as they like gains (Iyengar & Lepper, 2000; Kahneman, 2011; Shampanier et al., 2007).

Omnichannel selling. With the widespread acceptance of online shopping, marketers have a variety of direct and indirect ways to sell their products. Firms can sell directly through their own online websites, catalogs, or company stores. Firms can also sell indirectly through online or offline retailers—department stores, specialty stores, discount stores, superstores, and so forth. An omnichannel approach is an integrated approach to channel strategy that aims to provide customers a holistic shopping experience regardless of whether they are shopping online via a phone, tablet, or computer or in person via a brick-and-mortar store or any other way (Ansari et al., 2008; Verhoef et al., 2015).

An omnichannel approach attempts to blend the strengths of different channels to give consumers a seamless shopping and purchase experience (Ailawadi & Farris, 2017, 2020). Consumers may choose to shop online but purchase or return products in the store itself. The goal of omnichannel selling for marketers is to make products or services available in as many relevant places as possible to create different avenues for shopping and purchase. Regardless of the particular shopping path taken, however, it is important that consumers have similarly positive experiences with the brand.

Integrated marketing communications. Given the dramatic technological developments, the modern communication environment is vastly different today than it was 2 to 3 decades ago. As noted earlier, traditional media is much more fragmented, and new media has emerged in many different forms. Marketers now talk about four distinct but related ways to communicate with consumers via paid, earned, shared, and owned media, as follows (Batra & Keller, 2016; Stephen & Galak, 2012):

1. *Paid media*: A marketer can pay to run advertising via broadcast, print, outdoor, or other traditional media or digitally via search advertising (e.g., Google Adwords); display or banner advertising; social media advertising on Facebook, Twitter, Instagram; and so forth.
2. *Earned media*: A marketer can benefit from typically "free" exposure and coverage from media outlets, third party review sites and reviews posted online.
3. *Shared media*: A marketer can benefit from any content posted to social media, social media mentions of a brand, or likes/comments in response to a social media post or blog post via Twitter, Facebook, LinkedIn, Pinterest, and Instagram.
4. *Owned media*: A marketer can use company-owned digital properties such as a company's website, a YouTube channel, or mobile apps.

All four types of media offer important benefits, and the challenge to marketers is to "mix and match" the different communication channels so that they are fully integrated and the whole is greater than the sum of the parts. Different consumers use and view each channel differently, and channels vary in the control they afford marketers to craft their message, their credibility and trustworthiness, and other considerations (Naik & Raman, 2003; Smith et al., 2006).

CONCLUSION

This chapter provided an overview of fundamental marketing and marketing management concerns. In outlining core concepts, describing new developments, and highlighting specific applications, understanding consumer psychology was essential throughout. Without question, marketers benefit from having a deep, rich understanding of consumer psychology. Yet, at the same time, researchers studying consumer psychology can benefit from understanding how marketing works and the ways marketers think and act. What decisions do they need to make? What factors do they need to consider? The aim of this chapter was to aid in the transfer of knowledge across that bridge between marketing and consumer psychology to better inform both sides. Many of the ideas and concepts introduced in this chapter are further developed and illustrated in other chapters in this handbook.

REFERENCES

Ailawadi, K., & Farris, P. (2017). Managing multi- and omni-channel distribution: Metrics and research directions. *Journal of Retailing, 93*(1), 120–135. https://doi.org/10.1016/j.jretai.2016.12.003

Ailawadi, K., & Farris, P. (2020). *Getting multi-channel distribution right*. John Wiley & Sons. https://doi.org/10.1002/9781119632894

Ailawadi, K., Lehmann, D. R., & Neslin, S. A. (2003). Revenue premium as an outcome measure of brand equity. *Journal of Marketing, 67*(4), 1–17. https://doi.org/10.1509/jmkg.67.4.1.18688

Alba, J. W., & Hutchinson, J. W. (1987). Dimensions of consumer expertise. *Journal of Consumer Research, 13*(4), 411–454. https://doi.org/10.1086/209080

Alba, J. W., & Hutchinson, J. W. (2000). Knowledge calibration: What consumers know and what they think they know. *Journal of Consumer Research, 27*(2), 123–156. https://doi.org/10.1086/314317

Ambler, T., Bhattacharya, C. B., Edell, J., Keller, K. L., Lemon, K., & Mittal, V. (2002). Relating brand and customer perspectives on marketing management. *Journal of Service Research, 5*(1), 13–25. https://doi.org/10.1177/1094670502005001003

American Marketing Association. (n.d.). *What is marketing?—The definition of marketing*. https://www.ama.org/the-definition-of-marketing-what-is-marketing/

Ansari, A., Mela, C. F., & Neslin, S. A. (2008). Customer channel migration. *Journal of Marketing Research*, 45(1), 60–76. https://doi.org/10.1509/jmkr.45.1.60

Ansoff, I. (1957). Strategies for diversification. *Harvard Business Review*, 35(5), 113–124.

Bahadir, S. C., Bharadwaj, S. G., & Srivastava, R. K. (2008). Financial value of brands in mergers and acquisitions: Is value in the eye of the beholder? *Journal of Marketing*, 72(6), 49–64. https://doi.org/10.1509/jmkg.72.6.049

Batra, R., & Keller, K. L. (2016). Integrating marketing communications: New findings, new lessons and new ideas. *Journal of Marketing*, 80(6), 122–145. https://doi.org/10.1509/jm.15.0419

Bayus, B. (2013). Crowdsourcing new product ideas over time: An analysis of the Dell IdeaStorm community. *Management Science*, 59(1), 226–244. https://doi.org/10.1287/mnsc.1120.1599

Bettman, J. R. (1979). *An information processing theory of consumer choice*. Addison-Wesley.

Bettman, J. R. (1986). Consumer psychology. *Annual Review of Psychology*, 37(1), 257–289. https://doi.org/10.1146/annurev.ps.37.020186.001353

Bettman, J. R., Luce, M. F., & Payne, J. W. (1998). Constructive consumer choice processes. *Journal of Consumer Research*, 25(3), 187–217. https://doi.org/10.1086/209535

Bhattacharya, C. B., & Sen, S. (2003). Consumer-company identification: A framework for understanding consumers' relationships with companies. *Journal of Marketing*, 67(2), 76–88. https://doi.org/10.1509/jmkg.67.2.76.18609

Bhattacharya, C. B., Sen, S., & Korschun, D. (2011). *Leveraging corporate responsibility: The stakeholder route to maximizing business and social value*. Cambridge University Press. https://doi.org/10.1017/CBO9780511920684

Blattberg, R. C., Malthouse, E. C., & Neslin, S. A. (2009). Customer lifetime value: Empirical generalizations and some conceptual questions. *Journal of Interactive Marketing*, 23(2), 157–168. https://doi.org/10.1016/j.intmar.2009.02.005

Bloch, P., Sherrell, D., & Ridgway, N. (1986). Consumer search: An extended framework. *Journal of Consumer Research*, 13(1), 119–126. https://doi.org/10.1086/209052

Boulding, W., Kalra, A., Staelin, R., & Zeithaml, V. A. (1993). A dynamic process model of service quality: From expectations to behavioral intentions. *Journal of Marketing Research*, 30(1), 7–27. https://doi.org/10.1177/002224379303000102

Campbell, M. C. (1999). Perceptions of price unfairness: Antecedents and consequences. *Journal of Marketing Research*, 36(2), 187–199. https://doi.org/10.1177/002224379903600204

Campbell, M. C., & Kirmani, A. (2000). Consumers' use of persuasion knowledge: The effects of accessibility and cognitive capacity on perceptions of an influence agent. *Journal of Consumer Research*, 27(1), 69–83. https://doi.org/10.1086/314309

Cleeren, K., Dekimpe, M. G., & van Heerde, H. J. (2013). Rising from the ashes: How brands and categories can overcome product-harm crises. *Journal of Marketing*, 77(2), 58–77. https://doi.org/10.1509/jm.10.0414

Cleeren, K., Dekimpe, M.G. & van Heerde, H.J. (2017). Marketing research on product-harm crises: A review, managerial implications, and an agenda for future research. *Journal of the Academy of Marketing Science*. 45, 593–615. https://doi.org/10.1007/s11747-017-0558-1

Cohen, J. B., Pham, M. T., & Andrade, E. B. (2008). The nature and role of affect in consumer behavior. In C. P. Haugtvedt, P. M. Herr, & F. R. Kardes (Eds.), *Marketing and consumer psychology series: Vol. 4. Handbook of consumer psychology* (p. 297–348). Taylor & Francis Group/Lawrence Erlbaum Associates.

Court, D., Elzinga, D., Mulder, S., & Vetvik, O. J. (2009). The consumer decision journey. *McKinsey Quarterly*, 3(3), 96–107.

Dahl, D. W., & Moreau, P. (2002). The influence and value of analogical thinking during new product ideation. *Journal of Marketing Research*, 39(1), 47–60. https://doi.org/10.1509/jmkr.39.1.47.18930

Dawar, N., & Pillutla, M. M. (2000). Impact of product-harm crises on brand equity: The moderating role of consumer expectations. *Journal of Marketing Research*, 37(2), 215–226. https://doi.org/10.1509/jmkr.37.2.215.18729

Desarbo, W. S., Ramaswamy, V., & Cohen, S. H. (1995). Market segmentation with choice-based conjoint analysis. *Marketing Letters*, 6(2), 137–147. https://doi.org/10.1007/BF00994929

Doyle, P. (2008). *Value-based marketing: Marketing strategies for corporate growth and shareholder value*. John Wiley & Sons.

Fader, P. S. (2012). *Customer centricity: Focus on the right customers for strategic advantage*. Wharton Digital Press.

Fader, P. S., & Toms, S. (2018). *The customer centricity playbook: Implement a winning strategy driven by customer lifetime value*. Wharton Digital Press.

Feng, H., Morgan, N. A., & Rego, L. L. (2015). Marketing department power and firm performance. *Journal of Marketing*, 79(5), 1–20. https://doi.org/10.1509/jm.13.0522

Fournier, S., & Eckhardt, G. (2019). Putting the person back in person-brands: Understanding and managing the two-bodied brand. *Journal of Marketing Research*, 56(4), 602–619. https://doi.org/10.1177/0022243719830654

Friestad, M., & Wright, P. (1994). The persuasion knowledge model: How people cope with persuasion attempts. *Journal of Consumer Research*, 21(1), 1–31. https://doi.org/10.1086/209380

Friestad, M., & Wright, P. (1995). Persuasion knowledge: Lay people's and researchers' beliefs about the psychology of advertising. *Journal of Consumer Research*, 22(1), 62–74. https://doi.org/10.1086/209435

Gijsenberg, M. J., Heerde, H. J. V., & Verhoef, P. C. (2015). Losses loom longer than gains: Modeling the impact of service crises on perceived service quality over time. *Journal of Marketing Research*, 52(5), 642–656. https://doi.org/10.1509/jmr.14.0140

Green, P. E., & Srinivasan, V. (1978). Conjoint analysis in consumer research: Issues and outlook. *Journal of Consumer Research*, 5(2), 103–123. https://doi.org/10.1086/208721

Green, P. E., & Srinivasan, V. (1990). Conjoint analysis in marketing: New developments with implications for research and practice. *Journal of Marketing*, 54(4), 3–19. https://doi.org/10.1177/002224299005400402

Grover, R., & Vriens, M. (2006). *The handbook of marketing research uses, misuses, and future advances*. Sage Publications. https://doi.org/10.4135/9781412973380

Gupta, S., & Lehmann, D. R. (2005). *Managing customers as investments: The strategic value of customers in the long run*. Wharton School Publishing.

Gupta, S., Lehmann, D. R., & Stuart, J. A. (2004). Valuing customers. *Journal of Marketing Research*, 41(1), 7–18. https://doi.org/10.1509/jmkr.41.1.7.25084

Habel, J., Schons, L. M., Alavi, S., & Wieseke, J. (2016). Warm glow or extra charge? The ambivalent effect of corporate social responsibility activities on customers' perceived price fairness. *Journal of Marketing*, 80(1), 84–105. https://doi.org/10.1509/jm.14.0389

Haugtvedt, C. P., Herr, P. M., & Kardes, F. R. (2008). Consumer memory, fluency, and familiarity. In C. P. Haugtvedt, P. M. Herr, & F. R. Kardes (Eds.), *Handbook of consumer psychology* (pp. 77–102). Routledge.

Haws, K. L., & Bearden, W. O. (2006). Dynamic pricing and consumer fairness perceptions. *Journal of Consumer Research*, 33(3), 304–311. https://doi.org/10.1086/508435

Hoeffler, S. (2003). Measuring preferences for really new products. *Journal of Marketing Research*, 40(4), 406–420. https://doi.org/10.1509/jmkr.40.4.406.19394

Hoeffler, S., & Keller, K. L. (2003). The marketing advantages of strong brands. *Journal of Brand Management*, 10(6), 421–445. https://doi.org/10.1057/palgrave.bm.2540139

Homburg, C., Workman, J. P., & Jensen, O. (2000). Fundamental changes in marketing organization: The movement toward a customer-focused organizational structure. *Journal of the Academy of Marketing Science*, 28(4), 459–478. https://doi.org/10.1177/0092070300284001

Huber, J., Payne, J. W., & Puto, C. (1982). Adding asymmetrically dominated alternatives: Violations of regularity and the similarity hypothesis. *Journal of Consumer Research*, 9(1), 90–98. https://doi.org/10.1086/208899

Huber, J., & Puto, C. (1983). Market boundaries and product choice: Illustrating attraction and substitution effects. *Journal of Consumer Research*, 10(1), 31–44. https://doi.org/10.1086/208943

Iyengar, S. S., & Lepper, M. R. (2000). When choice is demotivating: Can one desire too much of a good thing? *Journal of Personality and Social Psychology*, 79(6), 995–1006. https://doi.org/10.1037/0022-3514.79.6.995

Kahle, L. R., Beatty, S. E., & Homer, P. (1986). Alternative measurement approaches to consumer values: The list of values (LOV) and values and life style (VALS). *Journal of Consumer Research*, 13(3), 405–409. https://doi.org/10.1086/209079

Kahneman, D. (2011). *Thinking, fast and slow*. Farrar, Straus and Giroux.

Kahneman, D., & Tversky, A. (1979). Prospect theory. An analysis of decision making under risk. *Econometrica*, 47(2), 263–291. https://doi.org/10.2307/1914185

Kang, C., Germann, F., & Grewal, R. (2016). Washing away your sins? Corporate social responsibility, corporate social irresponsibility, and firm performance. *Journal of Marketing*, 80(2), 59–79. https://doi.org/10.1509/jm.15.0324

Kannan, P. K., & Kopalle, P. K. (2001). Introduction to the special issue: Marketing in the e-channel. *International Journal of Electronic Commerce*, 5(3), 63–83.

Keller, K. L. (1993). Conceptualizing, measuring, and managing customer-based brand equity. *Journal of Marketing*, 57(1), 1–22. https://doi.org/10.1177/002224299305700101

Keller, K. L. (2003). Brand synthesis: The multidimensionality of brand knowledge. *Journal of Consumer Research*, 29(4), 595–600. https://doi.org/10.1086/346254

Keller, K. L. (2016). Reflections on customer-based brand equity: Perspectives, progress, and priorities. *AMS Review*, 6(1), 1–16. https://doi.org/10.1007/s13162-016-0078-z

Keller, K. L., & Lehmann, D. (2003). How do brands create value? *Marketing Management*, 12(3), 26–31.

Keller, K. L., & Lehmann, D. R. (2006). Brands and branding: Research findings and future priorities. *Marketing Science, 25*(6), 740–759. https://doi.org/10.1287/mksc.1050.0153

Keller, K. L., Sternthal, B., & Tybout, A. (2002). Three questions you need to ask about your brand. *Harvard Business Review, 80*(9), 80–86, 125.

Keller, K. L., & Swaminathan, V. (2020). *Strategic brand management: Building, measuring, and managing brand equity*. Pearson Education.

Klein, J. G., Smith, N. C., & John, A. (2004). Why we boycott: Consumer motivations for boycott participation. *Journal of Marketing, 68*(3), 92–109. https://doi.org/10.1509/jmkg.68.3.92.34770

Kopalle, P. K., & Lehmann, D. R. (2001). Strategic management of expectations: The role of disconfirmation sensitivity and perfectionism. *Journal of Marketing Research, 38*(3), 386–394. https://doi.org/10.1509/jmkr.38.3.386.18862

Kopalle, P. K., & Lehmann, D. R. (2006). Setting quality expectations when entering a market: What should the promise be? *Marketing Science, 25*(1), 8–24. https://doi.org/10.1287/mksc.1050.0122

Kotler, P., Bowen, J. T., Makens, J., & Baloglu, S. (2017). *Marketing for hospitality and tourism*. Pearson Education.

Kotler, P., Haider, D. H., & Rein, I. J. (2002). *Marketing places: Attracting investment, industry, and tourism to cities, states, and nations*. Free Press.

Kotler, P., & Keller, K. L. (2016). *Marketing management* (15th ed.). Pearson/Prentice Hall.

Kuehnl, C., Jozic, D., & Homburg, C. (2019). Effective customer journey design: Consumers' conception, measurement, and consequences. *Journal of the Academy of Marketing Science, 47*(3), 551–568. https://doi.org/10.1007/s11747-018-00625-7

Kumar, A., Heide, J. B., & Wathne, K. H. (2011). Performance implications of mismatched governance regimes across external and internal relationships. *Journal of Marketing, 75*(2), 1–17. https://doi.org/10.1509/jm.75.2.1

Kumar, N., & Steenkamp, J.-B. E. M. (2013). *Brand breakout: How emerging market brands will go global*. Palgrave Macmillan. https://doi.org/10.1057/9781137276629

Kumar, V., Lemon, K. N., & Parasuraman, A. (2006). Managing customers for value: An overview and research agenda. *Journal of Service Research, 9*(2), 87–94. https://doi.org/10.1177/1094670506293558

Kumar, V., & Reinartz, W. (2018). *Customer relationship management concept, strategy, and tools* (3rd ed.). Springer. https://doi.org/10.1007/978-3-662-55381-7

Kuppuswamy, V., & Bayus, B. L. (2018). Crowdfunding creative ideas: The dynamics of project backers. In D. Cumming & L. Hornuf (Eds.), *The economics of crowdfunding* (pp. 151–182). https://doi.org/10.1007/978-3-319-66119-3_8

Lee, L., Inman, J. J., Argo, J. J., Böttger, T., Dholakia, U., Gilbride, T., & Tsai, C. I. (2018). From browsing to buying and beyond: The needs-adaptive shopper journey model. *Journal of the Association for Consumer Research, 3*(3), 277–293. https://doi.org/10.1086/698414

Lei, J., Dawar, N., & Gürhan-Canli, Z. (2012). Base-rate information in consumer attributions of product-harm crises. *Journal of Marketing Research, 49*(3), 336–348. https://doi.org/10.1509/jmr.10.0197

Lemon, K. N., & Verhoef, P. C. (2016). Understanding customer experience throughout the customer journey. *Journal of Marketing, 80*(6), 69–96. https://doi.org/10.1509/jm.15.0420

Leone, R., Rao, V., Keller, K. L., Luo, M., McAlister, L., & Srivatstava, R. (2006). Linking brand equity to customer equity. *Journal of Service Research, 9*(2), 125–138. https://doi.org/10.1177/1094670506293563

Levin, I. P., Schneider, S. L., & Gaeth, G. J. (1998). All frames are not created equal: A typology and critical analysis of framing effects. *Organizational Behavior and Human Decision Processes, 76*(2), 149–188. https://doi.org/10.1006/obhd.1998.2804

Levitt, T. (1960). Marketing myopia. *Harvard Business Review, 38*(4), 24–47.

Li, H. A., & Kannan, P. K. (2014). Attributing conversions in a multichannel online marketing environment: An empirical model and a field experiment. *Journal of Marketing Research, 51*(1), 40–56. https://doi.org/10.1509/jmr.13.0050

Lilien, G. L., & Grewal, R. (2011). *Handbook of business-to-business marketing*. Edward Elgar Publishing.

Luo, X., & Bhattacharya, C. B. (2006). Corporate social responsibility, customer satisfaction, and market value. *Journal of Marketing, 70*(4), 1–18. https://doi.org/10.1509/jmkg.70.4.001

Maity, M., Dass, M., & Malhotra, N. K. (2014). The antecedents and moderators of offline information search: A meta-analysis. *Journal of Retailing, 90*(2), 233–254. https://doi.org/10.1016/j.jretai.2014.03.001

Malhotra, N. K. (2019). *Marketing research: An applied orientation* (7th ed.). Pearson.

McGuire, W. J. (1978). An information-processing model of advertising effectiveness. In H. L. Davis & A. H. Silk (Eds.), *Behavioral and management science in marketing*, pp. 156–80. Wiley.

Mishra, S., & Modi, S. B. (2016). Corporate social responsibility and shareholder wealth: The role of marketing capability. *Journal of Marketing, 80*(1), 26–46. https://doi.org/10.1509/jm.15.0013

Mizik, N. (2014). Assessing the total financial performance impact of brand equity with limited time-series data. *Journal of Marketing Research, 51*(6), 691–706. https://doi.org/10.1509/jmr.13.0431

Mizik, N., & Jacobson, R. (2008). The financial value impact of perceptual brand attributes. *Journal of Marketing Research, 45*(1), 15–32. https://doi.org/10.1509/jmkr.45.1.15

Mizik, N., & Jacobson, R. (2009). Valuing branded businesses. *Journal of Marketing, 73*(6), 137–153. https://doi.org/10.1509/jmkg.73.6.137

Moorman, C., & Day, G. S. (2016). Organizing for marketing excellence. *Journal of Marketing, 80*(6), 6–35. https://doi.org/10.1509/jm.15.0423

Moorman, C., & Rust, R. T. (1999). The role of marketing. *Journal of Marketing, 63*(4 Suppl. 1), 180–197. https://doi.org/10.1177/00222429990634s117

Moreau, C. P., Lehmann, D. R., & Markman, A. B. (2001). Entrenched knowledge structures and consumer response to new products. *Journal of Marketing Research, 38*(1), 14–29. https://doi.org/10.1509/jmkr.38.1.14.18836

Moreau, C. P., Markman, A. B., & Lehmann, D. R. (2001). "What is it?" Categorization flexibility and consumers responses to really new products. *Journal of Consumer Research, 27*(4), 489–498. https://doi.org/10.1086/319623

Morgan, N. A. (2019). Researching marketing capabilities: Reflections from academia. *AMS Review, 9*(3–4), 381–385. https://doi.org/10.1007/s13162-019-00158-4

Morgan, N. A., Vorhies, D. W., & Mason, C. H. (2009). Market orientation, marketing capabilities, and firm performance. *Strategic Management Journal, 30*(8), 909–920. https://doi.org/10.1002/smj.764

Morgan, N. A., Whitler, K. A., Feng, H., & Chari, S. (2019). Research in marketing strategy. *Journal of the Academy of Marketing Science, 47*(1), 4–29. https://doi.org/10.1007/s11747-018-0598-1

Naik, P. A., & Raman, K. (2003). Understanding the impact of synergy in multimedia communications. *Journal of Marketing Research, 40*(4), 375–388. https://doi.org/10.1509/jmkr.40.4.375.19385

Netzer, O., Toubia, O., Bradlow, E. T., Dahan, E., Evgeniou, T., Feinberg, F. M., Feit, E. M., Hui, S. K., Johnson, J., Liechty, J. C., Orlin, J. B., & Rao, V. R. (2008). Beyond conjoint analysis: Advances in preference measurement. *Marketing Letters, 19*(3-4), 337–354. https://doi.org/10.1007/s11002-008-9046-1

Olsen, M. C., Slotegraaf, R. J., & Chandukala, S. R. (2014). Green claims and message frames: How green new products change brand attitude. *Journal of Marketing, 78*(5), 119–137. https://doi.org/10.1509/jm.13.0387

Paharia, N. (2020). Who receives credit or blame? The effects of made-to-order production on responses to unethical and ethical company production practices. *Journal of Marketing, 84*(1), 88–104. https://doi.org/10.1177/0022242919887161

Palmatier, R. W., Moorman, C., & Lee, J.-Y. (2019). *Handbook on customer centricity: Strategies for building a customer-centric organization*. Edward Elgar Publishing. https://doi.org/10.4337/9781788113601

Parasuraman, A., Zeithaml, V., & Berry, L. (1985). A conceptual model of service quality and its implications for future research. *Journal of Marketing, 49*(4), 41–50. https://doi.org/10.1177/002224298504900403

Parasuraman, A., Zeithaml, V. A., & Berry, L. L. (1988). SERVQUAL: A multiple item scale for measuring customer perceptions of service quality. *Journal of Retailing, 64*(1), 12–40.

Pham, M. T. (1998). Representativeness, relevance, and the use of feelings in decision making. *Journal of Consumer Research, 25*(2), 144–159. https://doi.org/10.1086/209532

Ratchford, B. T., Lee, M. S., & Talukdar, D. (2003). The impact of the internet on information search for automobiles. *Journal of Marketing Research, 40*(2), 193–209. https://doi.org/10.1509/jmkr.40.2.193.19221

Ratchford, B. T., Talukdar, D., & Lee, M. S. (2007). The impact of the internet on consumers' use of information sources for automobiles: A re-inquiry. *Journal of Consumer Research, 34*(1), 111–119. https://doi.org/10.1086/513052

Richardson, A. (2010). Using customer journey maps to improve customer experience. *Harvard Business Review, 15*(1), 2–5.

Rust, R. T., Zeithaml, V. A., & Lemon, K. N. (2000). *Driving customer equity: How customer lifetime value is reshaping corporate strategy*. Free Press.

Rust, R. T., Zeithaml, V. A., & Lemon, K. N. (2004). Customer-centered brand management. *Harvard Business Review, 82*(9), 110–118, 138.

Sen, S., & Bhattacharya, C. B. (2001). Does doing good always lead to doing better? Consumer reactions to corporate social responsibility. *Journal of Marketing Research, 38*(2), 225–243. https://doi.org/10.1509/jmkr.38.2.225.18838

Sen, S., Gürhan-Canli, Z., & Morwitz, V. (2001). Withholding consumption: A social dilemma perspective on consumer boycotts. *Journal of Consumer Research, 28*(3), 399–417. https://doi.org/10.1086/323729

Shampanier, K., Mazar, N., & Ariely, D. (2007). Zero as a special price: The true value of free products. *Marketing Science*, 26(6), 742–757. https://doi.org/10.1287/mksc.1060.0254

Shankar, V., & Carpenter, G. (2012). *Marketing strategy handbook*. Edward Elgar Publishing. https://doi.org/10.4337/9781781005224

Sinclair, R. N., & Keller, K. L. (2014). A case for brands as assets: Acquired and internally developed. *Journal of Brand Management*, 21(4), 286–302. https://doi.org/10.1057/bm.2014.8

Sinclair, R. N., & Keller, K. L. (2017). Brand value, accounting standards, and mergers and acquisitions: "The Moribund Effect." *Journal of Brand Management*, 24(2), 178–192. https://doi.org/10.1057/s41262-016-0025-1

Smith, T. M., Gopalakrishna, S., & Chatterjee, R. (2006). A three-stage model of integrated marketing communications at the marketing-sales interface. *Journal of Marketing Research*, 43(4), 564–579. https://doi.org/10.1509/jmkr.43.4.564

Srinivasan, S., & Hanssens, D. (2009). Marketing and firm value: Metrics, methods, findings, and future directions. *Journal of Marketing Research*, 46(3), 293–312. https://doi.org/10.1509/jmkr.46.3.293

Srinivasan, S., Rutz, O. J., & Pauwels, K. (2016). Paths to and off purchase: Quantifying the impact of traditional marketing and online consumer activity. *Journal of the Academy of Marketing Science*, 44(4), 440–453. https://doi.org/10.1007/s11747-015-0431-z

Stäbler, S., & Fischer, M. (2020). When does corporate social irresponsibility become news? Evidence from more than 1,000 brand transgressions across five countries. *Journal of Marketing*, 84(3), 46–67. https://doi.org/10.1177/0022242920911907

Steenkamp, J.-B. (2017). *Global brand strategy*. Palgrave Macmillan. https://doi.org/10.1057/978-1-349-94994-6

Stephen, A. T., & Galak, J. (2012). The effects of traditional and social earned media on sales: A study of a microlending marketplace. *Journal of Marketing Research*, 49(5), 624–639. https://doi.org/10.1509/jmr.09.0401

Sujan, M., Bettman, J. R., & Sujan, H. (1986). Effects of consumer expectations on information processing in selling encounters. *Journal of Marketing Research*, 23(4), 346–353. https://doi.org/10.1177/002224378602300404

Swaminathan, V., & Moorman, C. (2009). Marketing alliances, firm networks, and firm value creation. *Journal of Marketing*, 73(5), 52–69. https://doi.org/10.1509/jmkg.73.5.52

Tellis, G. J., & Ambler, T. (2007). *The Sage handbook of advertising*. Sage Publications.

Thaler, R. H., & Sunstein, C. R. (2008). *Improving decisions about health, wealth, and happiness*. Yale University Press.

Toubia, O., Evgeniou, T., & Hauser, J. R. (2008). Optimization-based and machine-learning methods for conjoint analysis: Estimation and question design. In A. Gustafsson, A. Herrmann, & F. Huber (Eds.), *Conjoint measurement: Methods and applications* (4th ed., pp. 231–257). Springer.

Toubia, O., Simester, D. I., Hauser, J. R., & Dahan, E. (2003). Fast polyhedral adaptive conjoint estimation. *Marketing Science*, 22(3), 273–303. https://doi.org/10.1287/mksc.22.3.273.17743

Tversky, A., & Kahneman, D. (1974). Judgment under uncertainty: Heuristics and biases. *Science*, 185(4157), 1124–1131. https://doi.org/10.1126/science.185.4157.1124

Tybout, A. M., & Calder, B. J. (2010). *Kellogg on marketing: The marketing faculty of the Kellogg School of Management* (2nd ed.). Wiley.

Tybout, A. M., & Calkins, T. (2005). *Kellogg on branding: The marketing faculty of the Kellogg School of Management*. Wiley.

Van Heerde, H., Helsen, K., & Dekimpe, M. G. (2007). The impact of a product-harm crisis on marketing effectiveness. *Marketing Science*, 26(2), 230–245. https://doi.org/10.1287/mksc.1060.0227

Venkatesan, R., & Kumar, V. (2004). A customer lifetime value framework for customer selection and resource allocation strategy. *Journal of Marketing*, 68(4), 106–125. https://doi.org/10.1509/jmkg.68.4.106.42728

Verhoef, P. C., Kannan, P. K., & Inman, J. J. (2015). From multi-channel retailing to omni-channel retailing. Introduction to the special issue on multi-channel retailing. *Journal of Retailing*, 91(2), 174–181. https://doi.org/10.1016/j.jretai.2015.02.005

Verhoef, P. C., & Leeflang, P. S. (2009). Understanding the marketing departments influence within the firm. *Journal of Marketing*, 73(2), 14–37. https://doi.org/10.1509/jmkg.73.2.14

Voss, K. E., Spangenberg, E. R., & Grohmann, B. (2003). Measuring the hedonic and utilitarian dimensions of consumer attitude. *Journal of Marketing Research*, 40(3), 310–320. https://doi.org/10.1509/jmkr.40.3.310.19238

Wathne, K. H., Heide, J. B., Mooi, E., & Kumar, A. (2018). Relationship governance dynamics: The roles of partner selection efforts and mutual investments. *Journal of Marketing Research*, 55(5), 704–721. https://doi.org/10.1177/0022243718801325

Weitz, B. A., & Wensley, R. (2002). *Handbook of marketing*. Sage Publications.

Whitler, K. A., Krause, R., & Lehmann, D. R. (2018). When and how board members with marketing experience facilitate firm growth. *Journal of Marketing*, 82(5), 86–105. https://doi.org/10.1509/jm.17.0195

Winer, R. S. (1986). A reference price model of brand choice for frequently purchased products. *Journal of Consumer Research*, 13(2), 250–256. https://doi.org/10.1086/209064

Winer, R. S., & Neslin, S. A. (2014). *The history of marketing science*. World Scientific Publishing Company. https://doi.org/10.1142/9128

Wood, S. (2016). The psychology of innovation. *Journal of Consumer Research*. https://academic.oup.com/jcr/pages/the_psychology_of_innovation

Yankelovich, D., & Meer, D. (2006). Rediscovering market segmentation. *Harvard Business Review*, 84(2), 122–131, 166.

Yuan, H., & Han, S. (2011). The effects of consumers' price expectations on sellers' dynamic pricing strategies. *Journal of Marketing Research*, 48(1), 48–61. https://doi.org/10.1509/jmkr.48.1.48

Zhao, Y., Zhao, Y., & Helsen, K. (2011). Consumer learning in a turbulent market environment: Modeling consumer choice dynamics after a product-harm crisis. *Journal of Marketing Research*, 48(2), 255–267. https://doi.org/10.1509/jmkr.48.2.255

# PART II

CONSUMERS HAVE DEMOGRAPHIC AND PSYCHOGRAPHIC CHARACTERISTICS

CHAPTER 6

POVERTY AND CONSUMER PSYCHOLOGY

Ronald Paul Hill

It should come as no surprise that a substantial number of consumer psychologists have shown continuous interest in impoverishment and its impact on consumption behaviors. Global and intractable poverty among certain peoples remains a vexing problem both within and across nations (United Nations Development Programme [UNDP], 2016). Approximately 11% of the world's population lives on less than $2 per day, with 42% of people residing in Sub-Saharan Africa suffering from this fate. Children are at an even higher risk, with 41 out of every 1,000 born each year dying before the age of 5 from primarily treatable diseases. The developed West has its issues as well, and portions of the United States remain mired in poverty within various subgroups. The poverty rate in the U.S. is 12.3% and about 20% for people of color (U.S. Census Bureau, n.d.). Their children are even more likely to live some portion of their lives at or below the poverty threshold, which reveals their particular vulnerability. See Table 6.1 for a global look.

IMPOVERISHED CONSUMERS AND THE MARKETPLACE

Consumer scholars have examined impoverishment, emphasizing, for the most part, racial discrimination as a primary cause. For example, Andreasen (1975, 1978) coined the term *disadvantaged consumer* and looked at conditions for African Americans in principally urban communities. His work, and that of others (e.g., Sexton, 1971), recognized the inequities that existed between primarily White and primarily Black neighborhoods and differences in access to higher quality goods and services. These distinctions continued to plague people of color for decades into the future (Andreasen, 1993), and parity still seems wishful thinking even when providers are initially accessible yet ultimately limit services based on skin color (Bone et al., 2014). Later research has captured the impact of extreme impoverishment on such markers as quality of life and satisfaction, and the results reveal that consumption opportunities below a particular baseline inhibit the ability of ordinary psychological mechanisms to operate as they do with affluent consumers (Martin & Hill, 2012).

The goal of this chapter is not, necessarily, to discuss the vast chasms that exist across humankind in access to desired or needed goods and services but to describe and advance the thinking of consumer psychologists in this regard. The term *consumer psychologist* has been used to describe researchers and scholars who have examined the domain of consumer behavior and published their work in outlets like the *Journal of Consumer Research* and the *Journal of Consumer Psychology* (Haugtvedt et al., 2008). The research discussed herein has a similar orientation, but it has broadened the domain to other publications. Thus, authors noted in this chapter, including

https://doi.org/10.1037/0000262-006
APA Handbook of Consumer Psychology, L. R. Kahle (Editor-in-Chief)
Copyright © 2022 by the American Psychological Association. All rights reserved.

TABLE 6.1

Human Deprivation Lingers in Some Indicators of Well-Being

Poverty and hunger	
Income poor	766 million (2013)
Chronic hunger	795 million (2014–2016)
Children stunted	159 million (2014)
Children underweight	90 million (2015)
Health, mortality, and education	
Children dying before age 5	6 million (2015)
Maternal mortality	303,000 (2015)
People living with HIV	36 million (2015)
Illiterate adults	758 million (2014)
Illiterate young people	114 million (2014)
Functionally illiterate in OECD countries	160 million (2009)
Children not at school at primary level	61 million (2016)
Children not learning basic skills	250 million (2014)
Access to basic social services	
Lack access to an improved water source	663 million (2015)
Lack access to an improved sanitation facility	2.4 billion (2015)
People resorting to open defecation	946 million (2015)
People living in urban slums	880 million (2015)

Note. OECD = Organisation for Economic Co-operation and Development. From *Human Development Report 2016: Human Development for Everyone* (p. 30), by the United Nations Development Programme, 2016 (http://hdr.undp.org/sites/default/files/2016_human_development_report.pdf). Copyright 2016 under the Creative Commons Attribution 3.0 IGO license. Adapted with permission.

myself, are trained within a number of disciplines such as marketing, consumer behavior, government and politics, management, sociology, and others, along with all the subdisciplines within psychology. Regardless, their multidisciplinary contributions are presented with respect for and appreciation of their perspectives. Each major section, including this one, is broken into a number of subheadings that organize this chapter. While inclusive of their work, the end product is only as comprehensive as my abilities allow.

The Important Role of the Lived Poverty Experience to Consumer Psychology

Much of the research performed by consumer psychologists uses experimental methods to understand how various phenomena occur (Rapp & Hill, 2015; see Table 6.2). While this data collection mechanism has much to offer, it also has drawbacks that make it less than optimal for the study of impoverishment. For example, manipulations of scarcity on product availability, or restrictions in access to needed goods and services, cannot reach the levels of inhibition or trigger the resulting psychological consequences of consumption in situ. Additionally, recent scholarship has shown that online panels generally do not tap into the kinds of communities where widespread poverty exists (Bryant & Hill, 2019). Scrutiny by institutional review boards (IRBs) concerning possible harm to human subjects limits experimental settings that would take away hope for future consumption opportunities. In response, the best investigations

TABLE 6.2

Methods Used in Articles Over the First 40 Years of the *Journal of Consumer Research*

Methodological approach	Total number (percentage)
Qualitative inquiry	212 (10%)
Quantitative inquiry	457 (23%)
Manipulation-based experiments	1129 (56%)
Conceptual development	172 (9%)
Analytical development	32 (2%)

Note. From "'Lordy, Lordy Look Who's 40!' The *Journal of Consumer Research* Reaches a Milestone," by J. M. Rapp and R. P. Hill, 2015, *Journal of Consumer Research*, 42(1), pp. 19–29 (https://doi.org/10.1093/jcr/ucv011). Copyright 2015 by Oxford University Press. Adapted with permission.

are community based (e.g., Viswanathan et al., 2019).

Examples abound in the literature with poverty as a primary or secondary factor in the pursuit of knowledge. For example, Saatcioglu and Ozanne (2013) looked at a trailer park and discussed the impact on material lives and psychological well-being of its inhabitants. In this case, absolute and relative poverty are a backdrop to their principal focus. The same is true of research by Hill et al. (2016), who described how men in a maximum security prison, who were primarily from impoverished neighborhoods in a large eastern city, acquired needed and desired items from formal, informal, and underground marketplaces. Finally, Viswanathan et al. (2010) helped poor women in an Indian village develop consumer skills so that they would be better able to navigate male purveyors. These and other projects have one thing in common: They include decisions to interview, work with, and capture lived consumer experiences in situ.

These articles also show the complex nature of impoverished circumstances that plays out in ordinary consumption. Take the Hill et al. (2016) research noted before. Most of the prisoners were raised in neighborhoods with high crime rates, where young people likely knew someone their age who was murdered on the streets. They often had difficult or absent parents, especially fathers, and were subjected to subpar school systems compared with their more affluent suburban neighbors. Opportunities for personal and professional growth were also meager, and many looked up to community members who found their way into marketplace access or abundance through illicit activities. They typically passed through the juvenile justice system on their way to longer if not lifetime sentences in the maximum security prison. More than half were found guilty prior to their 20th birthdays, and many had spent decades locked up. Getting what they needed or wanted had nuances reflective of their upbringing as well as their incarceration, making for an intricate tapestry of psychological reactions and coping strategies.

Local Versus Global Manifestations of Impoverishment and Their Dimensions

The term *local* refers to Western or U.S. subpopulations of impoverished consumers. As noted, the origin of such research was the product of the civil unrest and civil rights movement that brought to light the 100 years of continued discrimination against people of color following the United States Civil War. Interest by scholars and editors waned over time, with a resurgence in the 1990s. This second generation was more diffused in its focus and included investigations of homeless populations that increased significantly during the 1980s under Reagan's presidency and its subsequent neoliberalism (e.g., Hill & Stamey, 1990). The former was organized around the lack of access to goods and services, while the latter concentrated on meanings of possessions and unique strategies for acquisition and utilization (Hill, 1991). A return to this earlier interest also occurred over time (see Bone et al., 2014), with continued attention on how various people survive in their material worlds (e.g., Chakravarti, 2006).

The idea that impoverished persons are creative in their navigation of the material world was an interesting twist on consumer decision making, acquisition, utilization, and dispossession. In part, it was based on the empowerment of the poor, who fought against and denied negative societal monikers (Hill & Stamey, 1990). For instance, homeless persons living outside formal shelter systems were positioned as "hunters and gatherers" who scavenged living environments to access food, clothing, and shelter materials. They collected recyclable metals to expand their material *largess* and provide resources necessary to purchase goods. They also had unique perspectives of what a home is and how it should be construed, allowing for alternative ways of defining "homey-ness." Their efforts provided a boost to their identities as capable and independent persons who lived without support of social services in contrast to other homeless persons.

The global poor were thought of differently, in part, because they existed within the most resource constrained countries in the world (see Viswanathan et al., 2010, for an example). One article in particular sought to understand whether psychological constructs for consumers in developed nations operated differently for consumers in developing nations (Martin & Hill, 2012). This research looked at how poverty impacts life satisfaction, with consequences that should be widely expected—greater levels of poverty lead to lower levels of life satisfaction. However, the more profound findings involved *consumption adequacy*, a baseline of goods and services that are necessary to a reasonable existence. This portfolio included healthful and sufficient foods, protective and socially acceptable clothing, preventative and remedial health care, safe and secure housing, and opportunities for personal advancement such as education and employment. Without consumption adequacy, the moderating effects of self-determination theory variables do not ameliorate the persistence of intergenerational poverty conditions.

Limited Focus on Poverty and Its Rationale to Date by Consumer Psychologists

This discussion should lead to the logical conclusion that impoverished consumers are an important part of the theoretical and empirical research by consumer psychologists. One measure of their relative importance is their sheer number across the globe. While the opening remarks are telling, additional information may make the magnitude of this subpopulation more salient. If scholars continue to examine only or mostly people with advanced material standing from developed Western nations, then they will be looking at about 15% of the entire human population (Martin & Hill, 2012). The question has arisen as to whether there are significant differences in psychological processes and resulting behaviors between consumers of this elite status and the rest of humankind (Hill & Martin, 2014). In fact, much of the misinterpretation of Prahalad (2005) as an advocate for exploiting the world's poorest citizens is based on the belief that the poor in the poorest countries have the same desires as more affluent citizens in the West, and that marketing tactics should concentrate on how to create economical sizes and efficient delivery systems that make goods affordable for the pyramid base.

If this claim were to hold true, the financial calculus is simple: Assume a population of about 3.5 billion at $2.50 per day for 365 days a year and the total resource pool is $3.2 trillion! Of course, this math fails to recognize the realities of subsistence existences and how individuals best utilize such funds to merely survive. Martin and Hill (2015) also studied saving behaviors across societies and found some surprising if not counterintuitive results. While the main effect was predicted—that saving improved consumer well-being—the enhancement was greatest for the poorest consumers at the very bottom of the national economic ladder. How could this be so? If you can barely survive, how can you save? The answer defies logic until you consider the true consequences of having *no* resources. For many in developed countries, the personal and social safety nets typically keep people from starvation or living on the streets. However, the impact on those people in developing nations can be catastrophic and lead to predation. With no personal or institutional support, and the looming possibility of disaster, some saving is mandatory (Orhun & Palazzolo, 2019, have an interesting but different take on low-income saving; see also Walker et al., 2015).

The rationale for this relative neglect is multifaceted. First, most consumer scholars come from developed economies and are drawn to issues surrounding abundant marketplaces in their living environments. A quick look at the Rapp and Hill (2015) review of *Journal of Consumer Research* articles reveals that 1,595 samples were from very highly developed nations, with only 60 in other development categories (0.4%). Only three were from the low development grouping (0.02%). See Table 6.3 for examples of various study contexts. Second, the task of studying such consumers is fraught with difficulties, from how to access them to convincing bodies like IRBs that they will be protected from harm. In the first case, the dominance of experimental methods requires somehow getting these people to, and having them interact with, facilities and researchers that are foreign to them. And panels that offer low-income participants do not acquire them from deeply impoverished neighborhoods much less countries (Bryant & Hill, 2019). Further, IRBs often have protocols that come from psychology or medicine to protect the "vulnerable," making it hard to gain access.

ALTERNATIVE PERSPECTIVES OF IMPOVERISHED CONSUMERS

The preceding information is not to say that the way consumer psychologists capture impoverished consumer behavior is based on only one theoretical paradigm. For example, some scholars have used the term *vulnerability* to contextualize poverty as the consequence of individual, interpersonal, and structural problems that manifest in marketplaces (see Baker et al., 2005). Scarcity research has a much shorter history that considers how poverty is related to lack of access to goods and services, emphasizing shortages that are both temporary and longer lasting (Hamilton et al., 2019). The final paradigm is restriction, which characterizes consumption at the base of the pyramid across societies with various levels of restriction (Hill & Gaines, 2007). Whether these frames are the same, different, or overlap remains a valid question that is beyond the objectives of this chapter. Nonetheless, each are discussed in turn for fuller disclosure to readers.

TABLE 6.3

Sample of Research Into Impoverished Consumers

Lead author, year of publication	Geography	Context	Study objective
Andreasen, 1978	U.S. cities	Urban poverty	Understanding disadvantage
Baker, 2007	Small U.S. town	Natural disaster	Community response to material losses
Bone, 2014	U.S. cities	Racism	Marketer treatment of African Americans
Bryant, 2019	Eastern U.S. city	Health literacy	Food choices by poor consumers
Ekici, 2009	Turkey	Well-being	Consumer quality of life under restriction
Grier, 2007	U.S. families	Fast-food	Ethnicity and fast-food consumption
Hill, 2016	Eastern U.S. suburb	Incarceration	Service delivery in restricted environ
Martin, 2012	Global	Self-determination	Self-determination and consumption
Saatcioglu, 2013	Local community	Social exclusion	Stigma and trailer park residents
Sexton, 1971	U.S. cities	Racism	Racism in the marketplace
Viswanathan, 2010	Indian city	Gender inequity	Subsistence markets and empowerment

Consumer Vulnerability and Its Relevance to Impoverished Consumption

There are a vast number of consumer vulnerability definitions, but there has been little agreement with respect to a definition of this term (see Hill & Sharma, 2020). Some existing research uses it interchangeably with consumers' susceptibility to pitfalls or to overt or covert and misleading persuasion tactics (N. Smith & Cooper-Martin, 1997). These varied perspectives incorporate a broad range of consumers who often make significantly less-than-ideal decisions due to particular sets of circumstances. A notable exception that attempts to address this issue comes from Baker et al. (2005), who suggested that consumer vulnerability is contingent upon self-perceptions and *not* contingent upon others' perceptions. Thus, they argued that, while outsiders may perceive a given consumer as vulnerable, the focal individual is only vulnerable when they believe themselves to face significant resource deficits. This perspective raises issues as to how to integrate existing scholarship into a cohesive whole, since much prior research on vulnerability consists of observers examining resource-control deficits of targeted consumers.

Hill and Sharma (2020) sought to pull together disparate research and find common ground as well as extend the developing framework. They recognized that both observers (e.g., scholars and policy makers) and consumers make decisions as to one's vulnerability, and each has its place in our understanding of the fuller dimensions of vulnerability. Additionally, the moniker of vulnerability is dependent upon perceptions of resource access and control over these resources to negotiate the demands of marketplaces. Most interestingly, Hill and Sharma also recognized the *multiplicity* of interdependent selves that people maintain and how each one may have different levels of access and control across formal and informal markets. This belief is made tangible in the examination of how prison inmates acquired goods and services through nontraditional, underground, and gray markets. Finally, Hill and Sharma also viewed vulnerability as a dynamic process that may improve or worsen over time as the consumer, their living environment, and their accumulated selves change over time.

Clearly, vulnerability as a psychological construct has contributed to our understanding of impoverished consumer behavior. It typically takes an individualistic perspective that deeply considers the circumstances faced by particular consumers. Whether this situation is based on personal characteristics (e.g., mental illness, physical disabilities) or institutional context (e.g., lack of housing, jobs at livable wages) may be less important than how it affects marketplace access. What has received less attention is the consequences of vulnerability and how they influence coping strategies and future consumer behavior. Hill and Sharma (2020) described two primary methods of dealing with consumer poverty as defensive and nondefensive. The former are a set of behaviors that proactively address marketplace difficulties and seek equity, while the latter seem to acquiesce with existing inhibitions. What the literature fails to do is examine feeling states that mediate or moderate relationships between lack of access and coping styles.

Scarcity Research and Its Relevance to Impoverished Consumption

Two recent articles summarize and extend scarcity research. The first, by Cannon et al. (2019), presented a self-regulatory model of resource scarcity. They concentrated on two distinct routes, or what they referred to as "psychological pathways," to describe how consumers react to varied scarcity contexts. The first is a *scarcity reduction route* that leads consumers to seek innovative strategies to reduce perceived resource discrepancies, much like the impoverished women studied and empowered by Viswanathan and his colleagues (2010). The second is the *control restoration route* that involves regaining power that once existed but now is gone, as with prisoners recounted by Hill and his colleagues (2016). One of their most important contributions comes from the psychological mechanism consumers invoke to decide what strategy to follow when faced with serious scarcity, such as lack of sufficient food (Andreasen, 1993; Sexton, 1971). In this research, their choices are dependent upon the perceived mutability of situations faced. Those severely impacted will act if they feel it will improve their prospects and not otherwise.

The other article on scarcity is by Hamilton et al. (2019). She and her coauthors also gave a summary of the scarcity literature using the theme of a consumer journey. They used an interdisciplinary approach and chronicled how scarcity can impact ways that consumers interact with their material environments. Viewed as an iterative process, scarcity is defined by *product* scarcity, or lack of desired goods and services, as well as *resource* scarcity, or lack of social, cultural, and economic capital to access and utilize these same goods and services. Thus, they examined initial considerations in decision-making processes, evaluation of alternatives, final selection, and the consumption experience itself, all within the two scarcity frames and their intersections and interactions. One important conclusion is that consumers in scarcity contexts face psychological challenges that are unique to their circumstances. The authors presented a wide variety of these challenges, such as coping with stockouts and deciding between buying food or medicines, and they tried to provide a template for understanding them in total.

Together, these articles present a broad mosaic of scarcity research and how it comes together and provides substantive directions for future research. While it does encompass how impoverished consumers overlap with consumers facing scarcity, most scholars have not relied on people who are living in the most difficult of circumstances, as noted earlier, because of the ways in which individuals are recruited and examined (Bryant & Hill, 2019). Of course, both of these articles integrated poverty studies into their thinking and scholarly directions, but they are outliers in this coverage. Additionally, scarcity research yields only limited attention to *who* is vulnerable to problems of scarcity, like the urban poor and other similarly situated subpopulations, given its interest in psychological and behavioral reactions. While this concern may not make a difference when conducting investigations with random samples of people in scarcity contexts, it does make a difference to policy makers and change agents who seek meaningful ways to elevate their citizens' quality of life.

Restriction and Its Relevance to Impoverished Consumption

Of the three paradigms that might house impoverished consumer behavior, this third category is the most ambiguous and least well-known. In many respects, the initial research by Andreasen and his colleagues noted earlier (e.g., Andreasen, 1975) on disadvantage is the start of scholarly interest in restriction. For instance, disadvantage leaves impacted individuals with less opportunity to meet their needs because of fewer options and greater resource requirements. As a result, they have poorer quality and less variety of foods within their communities, and barriers to travel to and from more affluent shopping areas keep them from relative abundance available elsewhere (Andreasen, 1993). Once again, race has played a role in creating restricted contexts for consumption (Bone et al., 2014), but other demographic characteristics like gender, age, and education also are germane (e.g., Viswanathan et al., 2010). What they have in common is some personal factor that leads them to suffer a combination of resource deficits defined by scarcity.

This focus on restriction has elicited a number of articles on resulting affective states as well as behavioral consequences. An example comes from the research summary by Hill and Gaines (2007). It examines the sociological culture of poverty theory thesis from the perspective of impoverished consumers who must navigate the kinds of restrictions chronicled herein. With a wide variety of situations based on previous ethnographic research, they described how loss of social capital and friends and family, along with the spiral down into lesser availability and access to needed goods and services, causes emotional reactions such as helplessness, alienation, anger, depression, and anxiety that manifest differently than lifelong, chronic situations of poverty. These and other negative reactions have been described elsewhere in the context of a disaster event (Baker et al., 2007), the Holocaust (Klein & Hill, 2008), and subpar living conditions (Saatcioglu & Ozanne, 2013). Taken together, they reveal the devastating and often long-term consequences of what is referred to as *consumption as restriction*, described as a context defined by a lack of needed and desired goods and services.

The consequences are behavioral responses that can be self-destructive (see Ozanne et al., 1998) but are often described by scholars in positive and uplifting terms. For example, Hill and Stamey (1990) talked about how homeless persons go through tremendous emotional and physical difficulties, and they cope with them, in part, by "fighting a deviant label" and seeking ways to differentiate themselves from "sheltered" homeless and position themselves instead as independent and constructive persons. Baker et al. (2007) followed suit, presenting a number of survival and coping strategies that are adaptive and positive in the long run. On the other hand, the few exceptions include research on juvenile delinquency by Ozanne et al. (1998), and they showed how these young men think and act in ways that eventually lead to their incarcerations. Saatcioglu and Ozanne (2013) yielded a mixed bag, with some community members acting out in self-destructive ways, while others sought either harmony with their neighbors or to move up the proverbial socioeconomic food chain.

Taken together, these overlapping perspectives capture characteristics of impoverished consumption using different vantage points. Poverty is one of the primary reasons for consumer vulnerability, and it often operates in combination with other factors such as race and gender. The consumption environments experienced by the poor are often delineated by scarcity in the communities in which they exist. Finally, when restriction is the norm, it results in diverse emotional reactions and behavioral consequences that can bolster or further inhibit access to goods and services.

CAUSES OF CONSUMER IMPOVERISHMENT

There has been considerably more written about who lives in poverty, circumstances that capture their lived experiences, and resulting feeling states and behavioral reactions than about how they became impoverished in the first place. Some wish to blame the individuals themselves, while others look at structural inequities within societies. Economic downturns and cultural prohibitions play a role as well, as they restrict behavior and access to marketplaces. While not on most consumer psychologists' radars, global insecurities and forced migrations dislodge millions of people annually due to famine, war, genocide, and other forms of human tragedy. Each one of these conditions or situations may further erode the consumption adequacy and societal unrest that will exacerbate the consequences of poverty. I have chunked several together in three causes for purposes of discussion, but it is important to recognize their interrelated nature and manifestation. Each is summarized next.

Individual Traits, Social Stigmas, and Discrimination Causes

The idea that individuals are at fault for their living circumstances is at least as old as the Judeo-Christian Bible. For example, lepers, some women, and people who worshiped other gods or failed to worship the "true" God were destined to experience some form of punishment on earth. The book of Job and much of the New Testament sought to change this perspective, with varying degrees of success. Modern day examples are televangelists asserting that AIDS is God's way of punishing gay men and intravenous drug users. In a more current instance, former President Trump has characterized people of Hispanic descent as drug dealers, rapists, and murderers (Phillips, 2017). Hill (1991) examined the specific case of homeless persons, and he found a dichotomy between major portions of society, with some suggesting homelessness is caused by personal weaknesses such as laziness, alcohol and drug addiction, mental illness, and personality disorders versus others who believe it is due to structural problems like the high cost of housing and national unemployment levels. Thus, restrictions faced, as well as the often resulting lack of consumption adequacy, are a matter of personal capacities.

What is most relevant to those who study consumer psychology is the resulting social stigmas and how they are assigned and play out in the marketplace and consumption environments. As noted earlier, trailer park residents studied by Saatcioglu and Ozanne (2013) recognized the societal judgment implied by "trailer trash." Certain groups reacted with their own form of societal recognition by seeking affirmation and self-esteem through maintenance and enhancement of their properties. In a very real sense, they were co-opting status differences in the larger society and separating themselves from lower class community members. Similar distinctions were made in prison (Hill et al., 2016) and Holocaust camps (Klein & Hill, 2008) by incarcerated persons. The book by Goffman (1963) on the management of spoiled identities captured how such people face enormous restrictions in their daily lives, noting that "a person with a stigma is not quite human" (p. 15).

These traits and stigmas are clearly associated with discrimination across a wide variety of contexts. For example, the Jewish people held in Nazi prison camps faced discrimination as a result of religion, while incarcerated men in the United States are predominantly Black and view their prison time as an extension of the new Jim Crow (see Alexander, 2012). Obviously, both contexts are designed to create situations of scarcity and restriction. A very thoughtful example comes from the Bone et al. (2014) article that chronicled how African Americans navigate financial services and the discrimination they face in the selection process for loan applications. Saatcioglu and Ozanne (2013), as described, followed suit with stigma and resulting discrimination against trailer park residents who seek to raise their individual community profiles through their behaviors around community members and the ways they try to maintain their properties.

Economic, Cultural, and Structural/Political Causes

A number of researchers who advocate for impoverished consumers have often selected other, nonpersonal issues to "blame" for such circumstances. For example, problems faced by poor consumers as an outcome of economic downturns and the removal of major portions of the governmental social safety net, including subsidized housing, mental health services, and job programs, were viewed as reasons for the increase in homelessness (Hill & Stamey, 1990). In many respects, the rise of Nazi Germany was, in part, a consequence of reparations to be paid at the end of World War I and the deep economic depression that followed. Many German people were in search of someone to hold responsible, and their anger often turned to the Jewish people (Klein & Hill, 2008). A similar path was revealed in the work by Saatcioglu and Ozanne (2013), focused on persons who suffered due to economic conditions spiraling down the housing food chain, not unlike the homeless persons noted previously.

Cultural and subcultural reasons also pervade consumer psychology research and its focus on poverty. The extensive work of Viswanathan and his colleagues described earlier is particularly germane (see Viswanathan et al., 2010). Systemic discrimination that is based on caste and class pervade this research stream, with historical origins in the cultural milieu. Yet, what has been described as the "culture of poverty" (Lewis, 1966) has rarely been substantiated in a consumer behavior context. For example, Hill and Gaines (2007) examined what they referred to as "consumer culture," which permeates societies and has significant implications for individuals living in poverty. Their perspective suggests that cultural contexts are overlaid with the material environment that permeates the lives of society members. Reactions by those facing significant constraints are a variety of feeling states that may include the helplessness revealed by Lewis (1966), but other emotions may be precursors to actions that assert pride of place in societies. More recent work on socioeconomic mobility shows that such behaviors may also include aggressiveness toward service providers in the marketplace (Kwon & Yi, 2019).

Finally, the public policy and marketing literature has examined structural and political constraints that inhibit people from rising above impoverished circumstances, especially in the developing world (see Ekici & Peterson, 2009). Consider the research of Varman et al. (2012), who provided a compelling argument that neoliberal government policies in places like India lead to failures at the base of the pyramid. These results are due to conflicts between poverty alleviation goals and policies versus the profit-seeking mentality of corporate entities. As discussed earlier, this perception is called into question when scholars and policy makers examine the true intentions of Prahalad (2005) regarding service to the poorest citizens. Failures by governments and their partnerships may also be due to the lack of an intersectionality lens, which recognizes "overlapping sources of disadvantage" that capture impoverished consumers' experiences (Corus et al., 2016).

Forced Migrations, Regional Conflicts, and Environmental Disasters as Causes

There is considerable literature pertaining to immigration and difficulties faced by ethnic groups as they seek to acculturate to a different consumption environment (see Ogden et al., 2004). For instance, prosocial behaviors may be tied to national attachment by migrants (Grinstein & Nisan, 2009). However, interest here is on forced migration that occurs as a consequence of natural (e.g., drought and famine) and human (e.g., war and genocide) events that lead millions of people to flee their home nations for perceived opportunities elsewhere. The United Nations (UNDP, 2016) estimated that more than 15 million people were refugees in their latest available statistics. Refugee decisions to leave are multiple and complex, but persons who have struggled with civil unrest, regional conflicts, and environmental disasters have particularly apt reasons. Consider the number of refugees from the following areas: Arab States, over 7 million; South Asia, over 3 million; and Sub-Saharan Africa, almost 3.5 million. While not necessarily true of all refugees, many face border restrictions, poor living conditions, and ethnic and racial discrimination.

One of the deterrents to improving migrants' consumer quality of life is the ways in which they are misdescribed in the larger culture. For example, Hispanic Americans can hail from Mexico, Puerto Rico, Spain, Colombia, and a host of other nations. The same is true of Asian Americans, who are of Chinese, Japanese, Korean, Vietnamese, and other regional ethnicities. A grouping often described as homogeneous given the nature of their assimilation into U.S. culture are the peoples of African descent. Yet, recent migrants from South Africa and Zimbabwe often enter the country on work visas and have more affluent consumer lifestyles than their counterparts from Sudan or Somalia, who typically are refugees (Elo et al., 2015). This perspective suggests that consumer psychologists should consider more nuanced ways of understanding how and when migrants find a place in the material worlds of adopted countries, as well as the extent to which they are able to thrive (see Chung, 2000).

Consumer psychologists have looked at the results of natural catastrophes that dislodge local marketplaces and cause a shift in product availability and desire. Consider the work of Baker and Hill (2013) and their examination of a western U.S. township following a tornado that literally wiped out the business community and much of the residential housing. They found that, after the initial shock of the disaster passed and people were accounted for, community members coped with the "new normal" by adjusting their perspectives regarding what were acceptable as replacements for lost possessions. However, over time individuals who previously were from higher socioeconomic groups began to complain that governmental and charitable provisions did not meet standards of fair allocation since they were distributed equally rather than equitably in support of the earlier status quo. It appeared that short-term coping strategies eventually were replaced with long-term desires for relative positions among peers.

SOLUTIONS TO CONSUMER IMPOVERISHMENT

While rarely within the domain, or bandwidth, of consumer psychologists, research has had an impact on policy makers and other interested individuals who seek to solve intractable problems associated with poverty. Some of the difficulty arises from the dominant paradigm of researchers in the developed world surrounding individualism and responsibility, in which scholars focus on the self-help coping strategies that some consumers use when faced with impoverishment. For example, Hill and Stamey (1990) showed homeless persons scavenging and recycling to gain access to enough goods and services to survive. Adkins and Ozanne (2005) revealed ways in which functionally illiterate persons seek and find novel strategies for navigating marketplaces without access to the written word. Similarly, Hill et al. (2016) discussed the use of a prisoner-run underground market that allows these men to garner goods and services not available through the formal system. Yet, despite the intractable nature of long-term deprivation, there are ways for other people and entities to help resolve poverty, and they are discussed next.

The Role of Governments in Defining and Fighting Poverty

Consumer researchers have a history of looking at how governments define and respond to conditions of poverty (see Hauver et al., 1981). This early work examines how impoverishment is captured by various designations, including the U.S. poverty thresholds. Unfortunately, political decision making has little to do with lived experiences of individuals or families, relying instead on descriptions of minimum foodstuffs for mere survival. While well intentioned, when applied to people seeking to meet daily caloric and nutritional requirements, there is little or no allowance for spillage, spoilage, or differences in absorption. The ultimate decision as to how much support to provide, as well as what to provide it for (e.g., hunger and shelter, for the most part), is therefore based on a faulty premise. Additionally, the totality of support does not include any other categories of goods and services recognized by consumption adequacy as described earlier (Martin & Hill, 2012). These problems notwithstanding, U.S. and state governments have not changed such measures of poverty since the 1960s (Citro & Michael, 1995; Decancq et al., 2019).

These issues are not just associated with U.S. government definitions and uses, but they also exist across the developed world (see Farrell & Hill, 2018). At the heart of these problems seem to be a poor understanding and lack of first-hand knowledge of impoverished consumer behavior. Part of the continuing problem may also be lack of a widely accepted definition of poverty, at least within the consumer psychology literature. From a choice vantage point, their circumstances are decidedly long term, focusing on goods and services necessary for survival, and present few alternative avenues for need fulfillment (Botti et al., 2008). A possible path forward was provided by Farrell and Hill (2018), as they defined this construct:

> Poverty involves a lack of consumption adequacy by a consumer who perceives a deficit in the consistent supply of culturally-specific and nutritious foods, socially and environmentally appropriate clothing, safe and sufficient housing, curative and preventative health care, and access to developmental opportunities for personal and professional growth. (p. 784)

It is important to seriously consider opportunities for growth and development, as well as the need for critical goods and services, both now and across generations.

This definition notwithstanding, most government programs on poverty are focused on vulnerable subgroups with deficits not of their own making. Children and older adults dominate these concerns, with both cohorts lacking the cognitive and information processing skills of more typical adults (John & Cole, 1986). Poverty adds a layer of complexity to issues of young and old age, making consumer adaptation to marketplace conditions even more difficult (see Anderson et al., 2018). The Social Security Administration (SSA) revealed that among persons 65 years and older in the U.S., those living alone, divorced, or widowed are more likely to be impoverished, and the poverty rate for women is two-thirds greater than men (SSA, n.d.). Once again, programs that currently exist concentrate attention on nutrition, health care, and shelter for both subpopulations to the exclusion of other goods and services. Of course, there are different, nonconsumption issues that impact quality of life, like local crime, but they are beyond the scope of this chapter.

The Role of Nonprofits in Defining and Fighting Poverty

As articulated by President George H. W. Bush (1988), nonprofit organizations generate a "thousand points of light" into communities that seek solutions to intractable problems. An example comes from Hill (2002), who chronicled the development of a system of care for teens who were homeless and living on the streets in Portland, Oregon. He described varied perspectives of different constituencies from nonprofits to governmental entities, which ranged from compassion and concern to disregard and disrespect. Their approaches to youths mirrored these perspectives and included development of long-term trusting relationships based on a slow movement into services along with "tough love" that required strict adherence to policies and procedures. The psychological pathologies of these homeless teens were often the result of neglectful and abusive parents or caregivers, who encouraged teens to run away or forced them to leave. Deprivation exacerbated these problems, and many of the teens self-medicated using drugs and alcohol or sold their bodies on the streets. Even their best laid plans failed under a combination of adult abuse and resource deprivation.

This program development was based on the efforts of a public-private partnership that sought to integrate the efforts of government, industry, and existing nonprofits (see also Dunning, 2018). Yet, at least in the case of the homeless teens, the financial support of the system of service delivery had remained flat in the face of a growing number of needy youth. As a consequence, Hill (2002) described the role of nonprofits as triage: enough to keep the problem from getting much worse but not enough to eliminate the need altogether. Thus, while some scholars view the rise of nonprofits in multiple roles across societies as one of the lasting contributions of the 20th century (Salamon & Anheier, 1997), combined abilities across organizations in the fight against poverty have not been successful. Examples abound and include Peck (2008), who found that dramatic increases in nonprofit organizations working with impoverished citizens in the Phoenix area over a 10-year period failed to show a concomitant decrease in poverty among focal populations.

Part of this failure may be inappropriate choices for service delivery (Jindra & Jindra, 2016), along with inadequate resource levels. However, the Transformative Consumer Research Movement (TCR) suggested that another underlying and overlooked problem is intersectionality across potentially causal factors. Consider research by Corus et al. (2016), who contended that poverty and its alleviation are stymied by a failure to consider the overlapping sources of disadvantage that work together to create marketplace hardships. For instance, gender, age, race, and other factors such as education and training often exist simultaneously to cause or increase resource deficits in a consumer's material world. Corus and colleagues examined scholarship of several researchers, including Grier et al. (2007), and they found fast-food marketing communications impact both children and parents, but this influence varied across ethnic identities. Both sets of authors then looked at the intersectionality of income and race, combined with structural deficits in retail options and nutritional education programs.

The Role of Social Enterprises in Defining and Fighting Poverty

The rise of social enterprises and social entrepreneurship has added a novel dimension to possible solutions to the plight of impoverished consumers. The discussions of social enterprises are widespread (Newbert & Hill, 2014) and focus on advancing an understanding of what is meant by "social." This modifier suggests that the operation of the firm is on prosocial behavior, while at the same time seeking to be profitable over time. Thus, these entities can be described as not *purely* altruistic but instead creating value for the firm *and* society. To some consumer psychologists, this hybrid between nonprofit and for-profit organizations may seem contradictory, leading to either confusion or distrust by consumers. For example, people living in poor neighborhoods who feel exploited by bodegas and other retailers who charge high prices in relative food deserts may see other outside vendors as following suit, even if they are espousing citizen concern. When making money is linked to giving behavior, it can be suspect.

W. K. Smith et al. (2013) described these issues as tensions associated with "divergent goals, values, norms, and identities" of social versus business missions (p. 407). They fall into categories of performing, organizing, belonging, and learning. *Performing* indicts goals and incongruent expectations from stakeholders. Social benefits are typically qualitative, evolving, and without industry-wide standards, while enterprise profitability focuses concentration on standardized and numerical calculations. *Organizing* tensions are a result of different structures and processes that each component normally requires to function in their roles. For instance, the service delivery program recounted by Hill (2002) made clear deep divisions by social workers and executive directors on how to meet the needs of homeless teens within new procedures put forward by the business community. *Belonging* can lead to tensions about the true mission of the firm, reflected in one group more closely aligning with the social side, while others embrace the organization as a business. Finally, *learning* can be troublesome, especially if various members want to dig deep community roots that serve a local population instead of scaling the enterprise and seeking new growth opportunities.

One approach advanced by W. K. Smith et al. (2013) to resolve these tensions is the application of stakeholder theory. This perspective has a lengthy history in management and marketing, and it takes a normative approach to determining who are stakeholders and how they should be treated by relevant organizations (Mitchell et al., 1997). There are several ways to apply this theory to social enterprises that seek to resolve lived experiences and situations of impoverished consumers. One possibility is to recognize which constituencies of particular enterprises have the greatest impact on or are impacted upon. Examples on the business side are funders that provide resources necessary for the organization to remain active and support for the workers who are critical to its social missions. For the social side, firms learn how to recognize the psychological and physiological positions and needs of individuals they serve and how to expand consideration of health of the larger communities in which these people are embedded.

NEXT STEPS FOR CONSUMER PSYCHOLOGICAL RESEARCH ON POVERTY

This chapter closes with a look to the future regarding impoverished consumers from construct development, transdisciplinary, and practical application perspectives. In each case, opportunities exist that have remained unexplored or underdeveloped for reasons that have to do with the dominant (experimental) paradigm in the field as well as contexts often studied. This statement is not damning; instead, it is a wakeup call for scholars who are seeking relevance in a world that is inequitable by its nature. Poverty is ubiquitous and impacts every nation on earth. Yet most citizens, especially in highly developed and developing economies, are unaware of discrepancies between haves and have-nots. For example, there is a YouTube video based on research that revealed what U.S. citizens believe the income distribution is and what it should be (Wealth Inequality America, 2012). The former is inequitable, and most people desire a more just world. However, income disparities are dramatically different than the desired state (see Figure 6.1 for another view of resources and opportunities). A majority barely holds any assets at all, while the top 1% have an enormous stockpile. Clearly, more informed discussion is required.

Future Development of the Poverty Construct

The previous material strongly urges consumer psychologists to take a more holistic approach to how poverty is defined. Without repeating the definition provided, the point is to consider all aspects of consumption necessary for survival as well as options for living a better life (Farrell & Hill, 2018). While generic in its approach, this consumption adequacy seeks to position people in poverty as facing certain forms of deficit or scarcity that are meaningful and long term. One important area for the future is how poverty manifests across development categories. Consider that a cell phone in the U.S. is rapidly becoming a necessity, even if you cannot afford the usual telecommunications plans. While likely still of use in developing contexts, the day-to-day problems associated with hunger and malnutrition in parts of Sub-Saharan Africa make such needs less relevant. What may be required is a situation-specific understanding of the goods and services that make up a necessary, countrywide portfolio of products on absolute and relative levels. Barely surviving versus

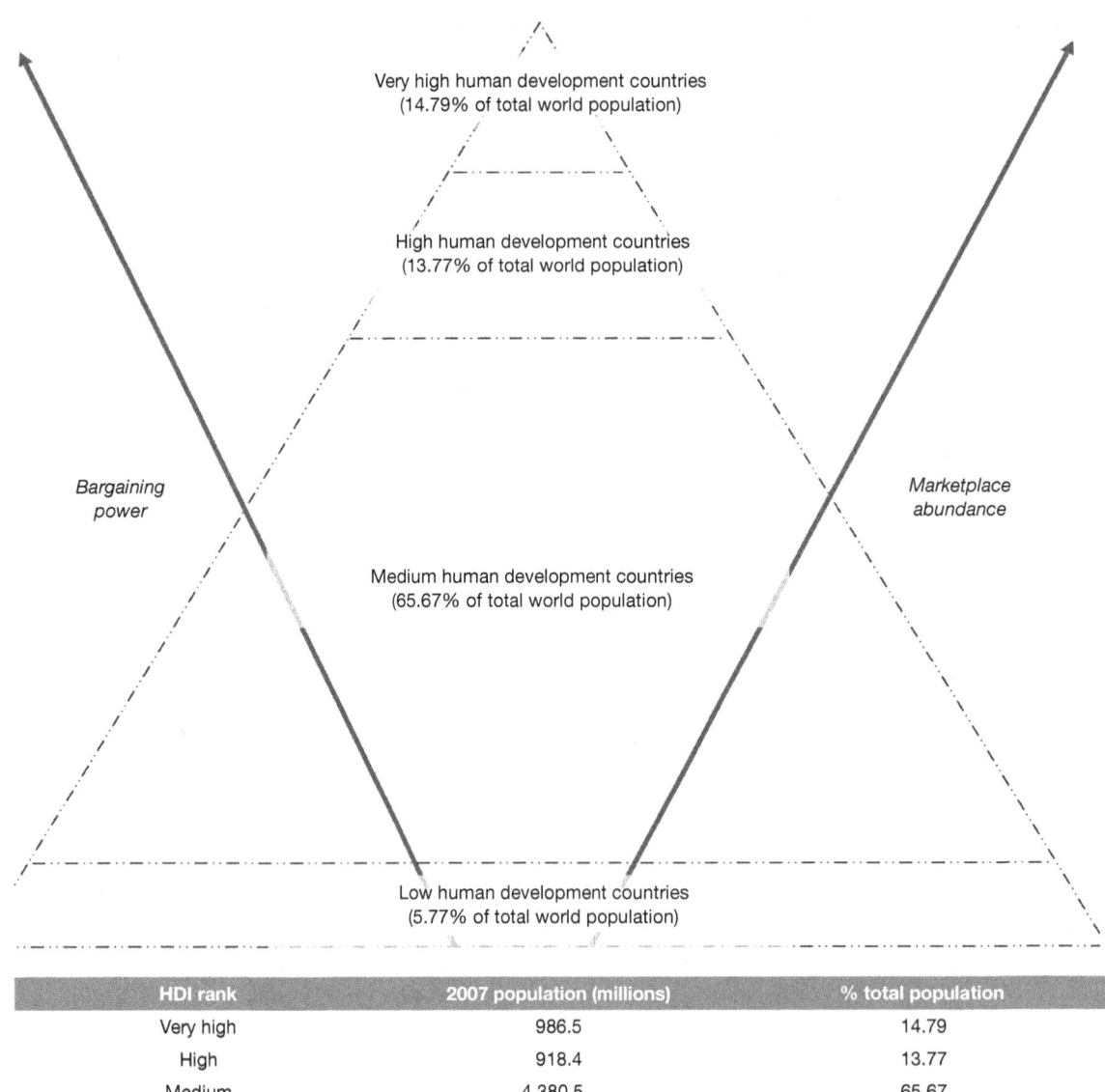

FIGURE 6.1. Human development and consumption pyramid. Bargaining power refers to increasing affluence and access to capital; marketplace abundance refers to increasing access to and control over a plethora of goods and services. HDI = Human Development Index. From "Life Satisfaction, Self-Determination, and Consumption Adequacy at the Bottom of the Pyramid," by K. D. Martin and R. P. Hill, 2012, *Journal of Consumer Research*, *38*(6) pp. 1155–1168 (https://doi.org/10.1086/661528). Copyright 2012 by Oxford University Press. Reprinted with permission.

malnutrition or even death is an important tipping point at the base of the pyramid.

Along with identifying what is missing should be a better recognition of how this impacts consumers. The field has determined that people below the consumption adequacy threshold respond with different psychological mechanisms and reactions (Martin & Hill, 2012), but the sum of their emotional responses, coping strategies, and behavioral acts remains understudied. One gap in the literature characterizes giving up in the face of deprivation, in contrast to the more popular focus on fighting against or proactively seeking new avenues for product acquisition (e.g., Baker et al., 2007; Hill et al., 2016). It is illogical to assume that every consumer suffering from material deficits seeks to resolve vagaries of their situation using novel acquisition strategies. Instead, as Goffman (1961) and Saatcioglu and Ozanne (2013) plainly described, many individuals who fail to prosper are unlikely to rise above or beyond their circumstances. While the culture of helplessness from a consumer behavior perspective is not the lived experience of all (see Hill & Gaines, 2007), research is needed to identify when emotions like despair become dominant and permanent.

Furthermore, the idea that consumer final states can be determined by looking at static measures of satisfaction is implausible. The same would be true of idiosyncratic and temporary moods. Instead, consumer psychologists and other social scientists are looking at dynamic and global indicators of quality of life and overall life satisfaction as possible outcomes of consumer behavior processes (Martin & Hill, 2012; Xiao & Li, 2011). This perspective requires scholars to think differently about what goods and services mean and do when under consideration, shopped for, bought, and consumed, especially by impoverished consumers. Additionally, consumption adequacy as a guide recognizes the full constellation of products that are coconsumed as people go about their lives. This construct implies that researchers should not examine one item or good at a time but must consider them simultaneously as they co-occur. It is likely that they operate in synergistic positive and negative ways to influence consumer quality of life.

Transdisciplinary Research on Consumption Adequacy

This term is less familiar than others such as *interdisciplinary* or *cross-disciplinary*. It is designed to suggest that what is under consideration is not an amalgamation of ideas across substantive fields and, instead, to transcend classification or their paradigmatic focus (McGregor, 2007). Consumer psychologists will probably round up the usual suspects to create this cohort, including other psychological specialties (e.g., social psychologists) and social scientists who have a natural fit (e.g., urban sociologists and cultural anthropologists). While these scholars should remain important, there are a number of disciplines that singularly or together can inform different aspects of the consumption adequacy portfolio in novel ways, along with identifying consequences of perceived deficits. A few examples are urban planners and architects to study shelter options, nutritionists and food scientists to examine food and water consumption, fashion scholars and textile experts to discuss clothing, public health workers and physicians to ponder health care and its delivery, and human rights and education researchers to look at how individuals may advance themselves within a society.

The biggest advantage of transdisciplinary research teams is the templates they bring to an understanding of poverty. In my own work in the prison and elsewhere (e.g., Nunziato & Hill, 2019), collaborations were primarily with philosophers whose perspectives were very distinct from my approach. Their look at exchange relationships were steeped in philosophical thinking that went back to the *Dialogues* of Plato (see translation by Grube, 2002). One interesting tale is of the "circle people," who were split in half and destined to spend the remainder of their lives looking for this lost, one-half self. It seems that this particular story is an apt metaphor for how materialism manifests within many societies and that the journey is never-ending. For our purposes, is it possible that impoverished consumers exist in a material world that denies their ability to feel whole compared with norms that define relative prosperity? This simple example merely scratches the surface of possibilities when referential frames are the focus rather than common theoretical perspectives.

Ultimately, scholars, researchers, policy makers, social entrepreneurs, and others must come together for the purpose of determining the dimensions of poverty as they pertain to lives of impoverished consumers. An understanding is necessary of antecedents steeped in root causes based on personal, interpersonal, and societal/structural characteristics, revealing the mosaic of factors that impact material well-being (see Hill & Sharma, 2020). Each actor would put forth the conceptual framework developed over time by their field, not to dominate the process but to provide another layer of examination to complement other approaches. How individuals and communities react to such conditions are also necessary, and these reactions are aggregated across domains to develop a transdisciplinary model of human poverty and its consequences. The responsibility for creating and funding these teams should fall on universities and their centers for study of poverty, as well as think tanks, governmental agencies at all levels, and foundations with the largess and mission to advance societal quality of life and equity among citizens.

Practical Applications and Insights

This discussion is moot unless there is real progress in how society deals with impoverished consumers. Consumer psychologists have communicated primarily with themselves (Rapp & Hill, 2015), an insularity that fails to serve consumers most in need. An important step forward is the TCR movement that originally was the brainchild of David Mick (2006). His vision involved a decided turn by the Association of Consumer Research members from their internal focus to a broader application of findings on consumer well-being. A more recent thrust was to find partners who might view TCR research of importance to activities serving various issues relevant to consumer psychologists. The topics of consideration are vast and made up of marketplace stigma, obesity and hunger, wisdom, political polarization, poverty and inequity, and many others. Together, they demonstrate the wide range of transdisciplinary domains that might be informed by consumer research.

The success of this endeavor depends on the extent to which consumer psychologists can convince governments, nongovernmental organizations, nonprofit firms, and social enterprises that they have ideas and strategies that can help solve intractable societal problems. This step is not easy. Such entities do not naturally turn to our subfield when seeking solutions, and TCR efforts are just an initial phase of contact. Grants from governments and foundations do not play a central role in the conduct of our research, so their influence is typically felt only from afar. To advance our relationships with interested parties will demand the transdisciplinary approach of the previous subsection. Many of these fields have closer connections and an understanding of moving from theory to practice and then back again. This continuous loop of productivity is a dynamic process that allows consumer psychology research to find its place among the social and natural sciences as an interdependent source of positive change.

Closing this chapter with practice is purposeful. The larger discipline of psychology has had a long history of on-the-ground level changes, especially in the clinical subdiscipline. Yet, the consumer side of the field comes primarily out of business schools and the marketing and sales functions of for-profit firms. To eventually have the status associated with other, more academic domains, marketing professors interested in consumer behavior moved away from what marketers can do to persuade consumers and toward how they respond to marketer actions. In fact, the *Journal of Consumer Research* was originally started by a multidisciplinary group of scholars who had the best interest of consumers in mind, using government as a source of respite from marketer misdeeds (see McNeill & Wilkie, 1979). For this domain to advance requires a return to application but without neglecting theoretical development. Instead, as described herein, the next phase must consider both side by side in a synergistic partnership.

REFERENCES

Adkins, N., & Ozanne, J. (2005). The low literate consumer. *Journal of Consumer Research*, 32(1), 93–105. https://doi.org/10.1086/429603

Alexander, M. (2012). *The new Jim Crow*. New Press.

Anderson, D., Strand, A., & Collins, J. (2018). The impact of electronic payments for vulnerable consumers: Evidence from social security. *Journal of Consumer Affairs*, 52(1), 35–60. https://doi.org/10.1111/joca.12140

Andreasen, A. R. (1975). *The disadvantaged consumer*. The Free Press.

Andreasen, A. R. (1978). The ghetto marketing life cycle: A case of underachievement. *Journal of Marketing Research*, 15(1), 20–28. https://doi.org/10.1177/002224377801500104

Andreasen, A. R. (1993). Revisiting the disadvantaged: Old lessons and new problems. *Journal of Public Policy & Marketing*, 12(2), 270–275. https://doi.org/10.1177/074391569101200213

Baker, S., Gentry, J., & Rittenberg, T. (2005). Building understanding of the domain of consumer vulnerability. *Journal of Macromarketing*, 25(2), 128–139. https://doi.org/10.1177/0276146705280622

Baker, S., & Hill, R. (2013). A community psychology of object meanings: Identity negotiation during disaster recovery. *Journal of Consumer Psychology*, 23(3), 275–287. https://doi.org/10.1016/j.jcps.2013.01.007

Baker, S., Hunt, D., & Rittenburg, T. (2007). Consumer vulnerability as a shared experience: Tornado recovery process in Wright, Wyoming. *Journal of Public Policy & Marketing*, 26(1), 6–19. https://doi.org/10.1509/jppm.26.1.6

Bone, S., Christensen, G., & Williams, J. (2014). Rejected, shackled, and alone: The impact of systemic restricted choice on minority consumers' construction of self. *Journal of Consumer Research*, 41(2), 451–474. https://doi.org/10.1086/676689

Botti, S., Broniarczyk, S., Häubl, G., Hill, R., Huang, Y., Kahn, B., Kopalle, P., Lehmann, D., Urbany, J., & Wansink, B. (2008). Choice under restrictions. *Marketing Letters*, 19(3), 183–199. https://doi.org/10.1007/s11002-008-9035-4

Bryant, A., & Hill, R. (2019). Poverty, consumption, and counter-intuitive behavior. *Marketing Letters*, 30(3), 233–243. https://doi.org/10.1007/s11002-019-09494-8

Bush, G. H. W. (1988). *Address accepting the presidential nomination at the Republican National Convention in New Orleans* [Speech]. The American Presidency Project. https://www.presidency.ucsb.edu/documents/address-accepting-the-presidential-nomination-the-republican-national-convention-new

Cannon, C., Goldsmith, K., & Roux, C. (2019). A self regulatory model of resource scarcity. *Journal of Consumer Psychology*, 29(1), 104–127. https://doi.org/10.1002/jcpy.1035

Chakravarti, D. (2006). Voices unheard: The psychology of consumption in poverty and development. *Journal of Consumer Psychology*, 16(4), 363–376. https://doi.org/10.1207/s15327663jcp1604_8

Chung, E. (2000). Navigating the primordial soup: Charting the lived worlds of the migrant consumer. *Journal of Consumer Marketing*, 17(1), 36–54. https://doi.org/10.1108/07363760010309537

Citro, C., & Michael, R. (1995). *Measuring poverty*. National Academy Press.

Corus, C., Saatcioglu, B., Kaufman-Scarborough, C., Blocker, C. P., Upadhyaya, S., & Appau, S. (2016). Transforming poverty-related policy with intersectionality. *Journal of Public Policy & Marketing*, 35(2), 211–222. https://doi.org/10.1509/jppm.15.141

Decancq, K., Fleurbaey, M., & Maniquet, F. (2019). Multidimensional poverty measurement with individual preferences. *Journal of Economic Inequality*, 17(1), 29–49. https://doi.org/10.1007/s10888-019-09407-9

Dunning, C. (2018). Outsourcing government: Boston and the rise of public–private partnerships. *Enterprise and Society*, 19(4), 803–815. https://doi.org/10.1017/eso.2018.93

Ekici, A., & Peterson, M. (2009). The unique relationship between quality of life and consumer trust in market-related institutions among financially constrained consumers in a developing country. *Journal of Public Policy & Marketing*, 28(1), 56–70. https://doi.org/10.1509/jppm.28.1.56

Elo, I. T., Frankenberg, E., Gansey, R., & Thomas, D. (2015). Africans in the American labor market. *Demography*, 52(5), 1513–1542. https://doi.org/10.1007/s13524-015-0417-y

Farrell, J. R., & Hill, R. (2018). Poverty research and measurement: Making the case for consumption adequacy. *Journal of Consumer Affairs*, 52(3), 770–791. https://doi.org/10.1111/joca.12183

Goffman, E. (1961). *Asylums*. Doubleday.

Goffman, E. (1963). *Stigma: Notes on the management of spoiled identity*. Prentice Hall.

Grier, S., Mensinger, J., Huang, S., Kumanyika, S., & Stettler, N. (2007). Fast-food marketing and children's fast-food consumption: Exploring parents' influences in an ethnically diverse sample. *Journal of Public Policy & Marketing*, 26(2), 221–235. https://doi.org/10.1509/jppm.26.2.221

Grinstein, A., & Nisan, U. (2009). Demarketing, minorities, and national attachment. *Journal of Marketing*, 73(2), 105–122. https://doi.org/10.1509/jmkg.73.2.105

Grube, G. (2002), *Plato: Five dialogues*. Hackett Publishing Company.

Hamilton, R., Thompson, D., Bone, S., Chaplin, L. N., Griskevicius, V., Goldsmith, K., Hill, R., John, D. R., Mittal, C., O'Guinn, T., Piff, P., Roux, C., Shah, A., & Zhu, M. (2019). The effects of scarcity on consumer decision journeys. *Journal of the Academy of Marketing Science*, 47(3), 532–550. https://doi.org/10.1007/s11747-018-0604-7

Haugtvedt, C., Herr, P., & Kardes, F. (2008). *Handbook of consumer psychology*. Lawrence Erlbaum Associates.

Hauver, J. H., Goodman, J. A., & Grainer, M. A. (1981). The federal poverty thresholds: Appearance and reality. *Journal of Consumer Research*, 8(1), 1–10. https://doi.org/10.1086/208835

Hill, R. (1991). Homeless women, special possessions, and the meaning of "home." *Journal of Consumer Research*, 18(3), 298–310. https://doi.org/10.1086/209261

Hill, R. (2002). Service provision through public-private partnerships: An ethnography of service delivery to homeless teenagers. *Journal of Service Research*, 4(4), 278–289. https://doi.org/10.1177/1094670502004004005

Hill, R., Cunningham, D., & Gentlemen, G. (2016). Dehumanization and restriction inside a maximum-security prison: Novel insights about consumer acquisition and ownership. *Journal of the Association for Consumer Research*, 1(2), 295–313. https://doi.org/10.1086/685426

Hill, R., & Gaines, J. (2007). The consumer culture of poverty: Behavioral research findings and their implications in an ethnographic context. *Journal of American Culture*, 30(1), 81–95. https://doi.org/10.1111/j.1542-734X.2007.00466.x

Hill, R., & Martin, K. (2014). Broadening the paradigm of marketing as exchange: A public policy and marketing perspective. *Journal of Public Policy & Marketing*, 33(1), 17–33. https://doi.org/10.1509/jppm.13.023

Hill, R., & Sharma, E. (2020). Consumer vulnerability. *Journal of Consumer Psychology*, 30(3), 551–570. https://doi.org/10.1002/jcpy.1161

Hill, R., & Stamey, M. (1990). The homeless in America: An examination of possessions and consumption behaviors. *Journal of Consumer Research*, 17(3), 303–321. https://doi.org/10.1086/208559

Jindra, M., & Jindra, I. (2016). Poverty and the controversial work of nonprofits. *Social Science and Public Policy*, 53(6), 634–640. https://doi.org/10.1007/s12115-016-0077-6

John, D., & Cole, C. (1986). Age differences in information processing: Understanding deficits in young and elderly consumers. *Journal of Consumer Research*, 13(3), 297–315. https://doi.org/10.1086/209070

Klein, J., & Hill, R. (2008). Rethinking macro-level theories of consumption: Research findings from Nazi concentration camps. *Journal of Macromarketing*, 28(3), 228–242. https://doi.org/10.1177/0276146708320449

Kwon, Y., & Yi, Y. (2019). The effect of perceived economic mobility on customer aggression toward service employees: A darker aspect of customer behavior. *Psychology and Marketing*, 36(11), 1120–1132. https://doi.org/10.1002/mar.21261

Lewis, O. (1966). The culture of poverty. *Scientific American*, 215(4), 19-25.

Martin, K., & Hill, R. (2012). Life satisfaction, self-determination, and consumption adequacy at the bottom of the pyramid. *Journal of Consumer Research*, 38(6), 1155–1168. https://doi.org/10.1086/661528

Martin, K., & Hill, R. (2015). Saving and well-being at the base of the pyramid: Implications for transformative financial services delivery. *Journal of Service Research*, 18(3), 405–421. https://doi.org/10.1177/1094670514563496

McGregor, S. (2007). Consumer scholarship and transdisciplinarity. *International Journal of Consumer Studies*, 31(5), 487–495. https://doi.org/10.1111/j.1470-6431.2007.00599.x

McNeill, D., & Wilkie, W. (1979). Public policy and consumer information: Impact of the new energy labels. *Journal of Consumer Research*, 6(1), 1–11. https://doi.org/10.1086/208743

Mick, D. (2006). Meaning and mattering through transformative consumer research. In C. Pechmann & L. Price (Eds.), *NA - Advances in consumer research* (Vol. 33, pp. 1–4). Association for Consumer Research.

Mitchell, R., Agle, B., & Wood, D. (1997). Toward a theory of stakeholder identification and salience: Defining the principle of who and what really counts. *Academy of Management Review*, 22(4), 853–886. https://doi.org/10.5465/amr.1997.9711022105

Newbert, S., & Hill, R. (2014). Setting the stage for paradigm development: A "small tent" approach to social entrepreneurship. *Journal of Social Entrepreneurship*, 5(3), 243–269. https://doi.org/10.1080/19420676.2014.889738

Nunziato, J., & Hill, R. (2019). Perfectionism and the place of the interior life in business: Toward an ethics of personal growth. *Business Ethics Quarterly*, 29(2), 241–268. https://doi.org/10.1017/beq.2018.26

Ogden, D., Ogden, J., & Schau, H. (2004). Exploring the impact of culture and acculturation on consumer purchase decisions: Toward a microcultural perspective. *Academy of Marketing Science Review*, 3(1), 1–22.

Orhun, A., & Palazzolo, M. (2019). Frugality is hard to afford. *Journal of Marketing Research*, 56(1), 1–17. https://doi.org/10.1177/0022243718821660

Ozanne, J., Hill, R., & Wright, N. (1998). Juvenile delinquents' use of consumption as cultural resistance: Implications for juvenile reform programs and public policy. *Journal of Public Policy & Marketing*, 17(2), 185–196. https://doi.org/10.1177/074391569801700204

Peck, L. (2008). Do antipoverty nonprofits locate where people need them? Evidence from a spatial analysis of phoenix. *Nonprofit and Voluntary Sector Quarterly*, 37(1), 138–151. https://doi.org/10.1177/0899764006298963

Phillips, A. (2017, June 16). "They're rapists," President Trump campaign launch speech two years later, annotated. *Washington Post*. https://www.washingtonpost.com/news/the-fix/wp/2017/06/16/theyre-rapists-presidents-trump-campaign-launch-speech-two-years-later-annotated/

Prahalad, C. (2005). *The fortune at the bottom of the pyramid: Eradicating poverty through profits*. Wharton School Publishing.

Rapp, J., & Hill, R. (2015). "Lordy, lordy look who's forty!" The *Journal of Consumer Research* reaches a milestone. *Journal of Consumer Research*, *42*(1), 19–29. https://doi.org/10.1093/jcr/ucv011

Saatcioglu, B., & Ozanne, J. (2013). Moral habitus and status negotiation in a marginalized working-class neighborhood. *Journal of Consumer Research*, *40*(4), 692–710. https://doi.org/10.1086/671794

Salamon, L., & Anheier, H. (1997). The civil society sector. *Society*, *34*(2), 60–65. https://doi.org/10.1007/BF02823101

Sexton, D. (1971). Comparing the cost of food to blacks and whites: A survey. *Journal of Marketing*, *35*(3), 40–46.

Smith, N., & Cooper-Martin, E. (1997). Ethics and target marketing: The role of product harm and consumer vulnerability. *Journal of Marketing*, *61*(3), 1–20. https://doi.org/10.1177/002224299706100301

Smith, W. K., Gonin, M., & Besharov, M. L. (2013). Managing social-business tensions: A review and research agenda for social enterprise. *Business Ethics Quarterly*, *23*(3), 407–442. https://doi.org/10.5840/beq201323327

Social Security Administration. (n.d.). *Marital status & poverty*. https://www.ssa.gov/policy/docs/population-profiles/marital-status-poverty.html

United Nations Development Program. (2016). *Human development report 2016: Human development for everyone*. United Nations. http://hdr.undp.org/sites/default/files/2016_human_development_report.pdf

United States Census Bureau. (n.d.). *Income and poverty in the United States: 2018*. https://www.census.gov/library/publications/2019/demo/p60-266.html

Varman, R., Skålén, P., & Belk, R. W. (2012). Conflicts at the bottom of the pyramid: Profitability, poverty alleviation, and neoliberal governmentality. *Journal of Public Policy & Marketing*, *31*(1), 19–35. https://doi.org/10.1509/jppm.10.026

Viswanathan, M., Elaydi, R., Gau, R., & Christensen, L. J. (2019). Subsistence marketplaces: Challenges and opportunities. *Journal of Public Policy & Marketing*, *38*(1), 36–41. https://doi.org/10.1177/0743915618820972

Viswanathan, M., Rosa, J., & Ruth, J. (2010). Exchanges in marketing systems: The case of subsistence consumer–merchants in Chennai, India. *Journal of Marketing*, *74*(3), 1–17. https://doi.org/10.1509/jmkg.74.3.1

Walker, C., Burton, M., Akhurst, J., & Degirmencioglu, S. (2015). Locked into the system? Critical community psychology approaches to personal debt in the context of crises of capital accumulation. *Journal of Community & Applied Social Psychology*, *25*(3), 264–275. https://doi.org/10.1002/casp.2209

Wealth Inequality America (2012). *Wealth inequality in America* [Video]. YouTube. https://www.youtube.com/watch?v=QPKKQnijnsM

Xiao, J., & Li, H. (2011). Sustainable consumption and life satisfaction. *Social Indicators Research*, *104*(2), 323–329. https://doi.org/10.1007/s11205-010-9746-9

CHAPTER 7

CHILDREN AS CONSUMERS: A REVIEW OF 50 YEARS OF RESEARCH IN MARKETING

Deborah Roedder John and Lan Nguyen Chaplin

Scholarly research on children's consumer behavior began to emerge in the 1950s and 1960s with the publication of a few studies on topics such as children's brand loyalty, influence of children in purchasing decisions, and children's knowledge of marketing and retail functions. However, it was not until the mid-1970s that children's research blossomed and gained visibility among marketing academics (John, 1999), sparked by public policy concerns about the fairness of television advertising to young children and focused on topics such as young children's understanding of advertising and its influence on children's consumption behavior. Over time, as the field matured, researchers examined a wider variety of topics, such as the development of children's consumer knowledge, cognitive and environmental influences on children's consumer behavior, and the role of marketing in teens' consumption of tobacco, alcohol, and drugs.

In this chapter, we describe the historical development of the field of children's consumer behavior from the mid-1970s to today. We identify three historical periods in the development of children's consumer research, and describe the major themes and research characteristic of each period (see Table 7.1 for a summary). The first period (1970–1985) covers the beginning of the field, focused on public policy concerns over the fairness of television advertising to young children and television advertising effects on children's preferences and choices. The second period (1980–2000) describes the broadening of the field, with a focus on understanding how children are socialized into their roles as consumers and when they develop consumer knowledge and skills. The third period (2000–2020) covers topics related to child and adolescent well-being, such as the adoption of materialistic orientations, the consumption of risky products (cigarettes, alcohol, drugs), and the development of healthy eating patterns.

Our definition of these historical periods captures major shifts in the nature and scope of research topics that were addressed in the field. As such, within any particular historical period, there are a few publications on topics other than those we highlight for the period. And, for some topics, there are articles on that topic published in multiple historical periods. For example, work addressing children's knowledge and beliefs about advertising is most concentrated in the first historical period, but several articles on this topic also appeared in other periods. Finally, the time boundaries for historical periods overlap in some cases, which reflects the fact that interest in one or more topics from one historical period overlapped with a subsequent historical period.

In selecting topics and research for each historical period, we focused on publications in top marketing journals, including the *Journal of Consumer Research*, *Journal of Marketing Research*, *Journal of Marketing*, and *Journal of Consumer Psychology*. On occasion, we include a publication from other

https://doi.org/10.1037/0000262-007
APA Handbook of Consumer Psychology, L. R. Kahle (Editor-in-Chief)
Copyright © 2022 by the American Psychological Association. All rights reserved.

TABLE 7.1

Historical Periods of Children's Consumer Research

Time period	Research era	Topics covered

1970–1985	I: TV Advertising to Children
	This era is dominated by public policy concerns about fairness of advertising to young children.
		• Children's understanding of advertising:
		   - Understanding advertising intent
		   - Recognizing bias and deception in advertising
		• Television advertising effects on children's product preferences and choices:
		   - Persuasive effects of television advertising and remedies
		   - Age differences in the effects of television advertising
		   - Effects of premium advertising

1980–2000	II: Children's Consumer Socialization
	This era broadens research into general topics about how children learn and are socialized as consumers.
		• Children's development of marketplace knowledge:
		   - Product and brand knowledge
		   - Consumption symbolism
		   - Shopping knowledge
		   - Knowledge of advertising tactics
		• Children's decision making and choice:
		   - Product evaluations, preferences, and choice
		   - Decision-making strategies
		• Family influences

2000–2020	III: Children's Consumer Well-Being
	This era is focused on questions about children's consumer well-being, happiness, and health.
		• Materialism in children and adolescents:
		   - Age differences
		   - Interpersonal influences
		• Risky consumption among adolescents:
		   - Cigarette smoking
		   - Alcohol consumption
		• Childhood obesity and healthy food choices

journals when it provides context or corroborating evidence. We exclude consideration of publications that do not include empirical data gathered from children and adolescents, such as discussions of public policy issues regarding marketing to children.

ERA I: TV ADVERTISING TO CHILDREN (1970–1985)

Interest in the area of children's consumer behavior was ignited, in large part, by concerns about the fairness of television advertising to children from consumer activists and government regulators. Arguments emerged that children were unfair targets of television advertising because they had little knowledge of advertising and did not understand the persuasive intent of the television commercials they watched. In the early 1970s, the first large-scale studies on this topic were published, which confirmed that young children under the age of 8 had little understanding of the persuasive nature of advertising, viewing it as informative, truthful, and entertaining (e.g., Blatt et al., 1972; Ward et al., 1972). Thus, young children had little in the way of "cognitive defenses" against the advertising they viewed, making them vulnerable to being unfairly persuaded by television advertising.

In 1978, the Federal Trade Commission (FTC) stepped into the controversy by proposing a trade rule regulation to (a) ban all television advertising to young children under the age of 8 and (b) ban television advertising for sugary food products to children under the age of 12 (FTC, 1978). Although ultimately withdrawn, the proposal sparked additional research on the effects of marketing on children. This research examined the effects of television advertising and marketing on children's beliefs, preferences, and choices for advertised products in general, as well as unhealthy foods such as candy and heavily sugared cereals.

In this section, we review research representative of this time period addressing children's knowledge and understanding of advertising. We also review research that examines the effect of television advertising on children, which addresses the extent to which advertising persuades children and affects their product preferences and choices.

Children's Understanding of Advertising

Two of the most important topics addressed by researchers in this area were (a) children's understanding of advertising intent and (b) children's ability to recognize bias and deception in advertising.

Understanding advertising intent. Children as young as 3 to 4 years of age can distinguish a television commercial from television program content. However, this ability to identify commercials does not necessarily translate into an understanding of the "true" difference between commercials (selling intent) and programs (entertainment). Children of this age, and even slightly older, usually describe the difference between commercials and programs using simple perceptual cues, such as commercials are short (Ward, 1972). Thus, young children know that television commercials are different than a program but do not understand the selling intent of advertising.

An understanding of advertising intent usually emerges at a later age, by the time most children are 7 to 8 years old (Macklin, 1985; Robertson & Rossiter, 1974; Ward et al., 1977). Prior to this, young children view advertising as entertainment (e.g., "commercials are funny") or as a form of unbiased information (e.g., "commercials tell you about things you can buy"). Around 7 to 8 years of age, children begin to see the persuasive intent of commercials, understanding that advertisers are trying to get people to buy something.

These age differences are well illustrated by Robertson and Rossiter (1974), who asked first-, third-, and fifth-grade boys a series of questions to determine whether they recognized the assistive (informational) intent and persuasive (selling) intent of advertising. Children were asked questions such as "Why are commercials shown on television?" and "What do commercials try to get you to do?" Children of all ages recognized assistive intent, with about 50% of children from each grade mentioning the information function of advertising. Attributions of persuasive intent, however, increased dramatically, from 52.7% of first graders (6–7 years old) to 87.1% of third graders (8–9 years old) to 99% of fifth graders (10–11 years old).

Similar age trends were reported in subsequent research using nonverbal measures to assess children's understanding of selling intent (Macklin, 1985). Children were shown a commercial and then given a set of four pictures, one portraying the selling intent of the commercial (correct choice) and three showing commercial characters and children interacting with the advertised product. When asked to select the picture that showed what the commercial was trying to do, 80% of the young children (3–5 years of age) failed to select the correct picture.

Recognizing bias and deception in advertising. By the age of 7 to 8 years, children also recognize the existence of bias and deception in advertising, no longer believing that commercials always tell the truth (Robertson & Rossiter, 1974; Ward, 1972; Ward et al., 1977). Beliefs about the truthfulness of advertising become more negative as children approach adolescence (Robertson & Rossiter, 1974; Ward, 1972; Ward et al., 1977). For example, 50% of kindergartners, 88% of third graders, and 97% of sixth graders believe that advertising never or only sometimes tells the truth (Ward et al., 1977).

A similar age progression is evident when children are asked why commercials are untruthful. Although kindergarteners are unable to articulate why commercials lie (e.g., "They just lie"), third and sixth graders connect lying to persuasive intent (e.g., "They want to sell products to make money, so they have to make the product look better than it is"; Ward et al., 1977, p. 62). With increasing age, children also develop abilities to detect instances of bias and deception in advertising. For example, Bever et al. (1975) found that most 7- to

10-year-olds could not detect specific examples of misleading advertising. However, 11- to 12-year-olds mentioned several misleading tactics used by advertisers, such as "overstatements" and "when they use visual tricks or fake things" (Bever et al., p. 119).

Television Advertising Effects on Children's Product Preferences and Choices

Concerns about the effects of television advertising on children were addressed by research in three areas: (a) persuasive effects of television advertising and possible remedies, (b) age differences in the effects of television advertising, and (c) effects of premium advertising on children's preferences and choices.

Persuasive effects of television advertising and remedies. Much of the research on television advertising effects was shaped by concerns that advertising to children is inherently unfair and deceptive, resulting in children consuming many unhealthy foods detrimental to their well-being. These concerns were laid out in the FTC's 1978 Staff Report, which also proposed several remedies, including (a) nutritional or health disclosures presented in the body of advertisements or other contexts, (b) limitations on the amount of television advertising directed to children for sugared products, (c) limitations on particular techniques or statements made in television advertising directed to children for sugared products, or (d) bans on all televised advertising directed at young children and advertising directed to older children that poses severe risks to dental health.

Although a few attempts were made to address these concerns using survey methods, the field quickly turned to experimental methods to provide stronger evidence about the effects of television advertising on children's attitudes, preferences, and choices, as well as data on the effectiveness of remedies suggested by the FTC. Early experiments addressed the basic issue of whether television advertising could persuade children and alter their attitudes and preferences for advertised products. These studies manipulated the number of advertising exposures for a product placed within a televised program and found that a single television advertisement was sufficient to increase children's preference for the advertised product but that increased repetitions of the ad within the same program had little effect unless different versions of the ads were used (Goldberg & Gorn, 1974; Gorn & Goldberg, 1977, 1980).

Moving into the 1980s, experimental work began to address a more complex set of questions, looking more closely at the impact of television advertising versus other health-related messages and programs and incorporating more realistic advertising exposure contexts and choice situations. Illustrative of this approach is a field study by Gorn and Goldberg (1982), conducted during a 2-week time period with 5- to 8-year-olds attending a summer camp. Children viewed a videotaped cartoon program each afternoon, for 14 days. For the first week, they saw a program with either (a) 4.5 minutes of commercials for highly sugared foods, such as Hershey bars, Kit Kats, and Kool-Aid, or (b) 4.5 minutes of commercials for fruits, such as oranges and apples. In the second week, they saw a program with either (a) no commercial messages (control group) or (b) 4.5 minutes of public service announcements (PSAs) on the value of moderating one's intake of sugary foods and eating a variety of foods each day. After viewing the program each day, children went to an adjacent area and were allowed to select a beverage (orange juice or Kool-Aid), and two snack foods from four options (two fruits and two candy bars).

Children who viewed the sugared food commercials chose more candy over fruit as snacks. Further, eliminating the sugared food commercials from programs was as effective as commercials advocating fruit consumption, or nutritional PSAs, in encouraging the choice of healthier fruit options. Similar findings were reported by Goldberg et al. (1978): Children exposed to commercials for highly sugared foods chose more of these foods for snacks, as opposed to children exposed to no commercials or nutritional PSAs. Overall, these results supported the position that a ban on commercials for sugary foods would be most effective in encouraging children to make healthier food choices.

Age differences in the effects of television advertising. Ample evidence accumulated that television advertising could persuade children to prefer certain products, including unhealthy options such as candy and sugared cereals. One significant question remained: Does television advertising affect children's choices in a more significant way than it does for adolescents or adults? Advertising is a persuasive medium, intended to change consumers' preferences, regardless of age. In order for children to be singled out as a vulnerable group, in need of special protection, evidence that they are uniquely and negatively affected by television advertising would strengthen the case.

Evidence to this effect was presented by Roedder et al. (1983) in a study conducted with children (9–10 years of age) and adolescents (13–14 years of age). Participants were shown a television commercial for a new chocolate candy, and afterward, their attitude toward the new product was assessed. They were also allowed to choose a prize that would be awarded to several children after the study and were given a number of options, including the advertised product and two alternatives rated more highly by both age groups (e.g., M&Ms). Both age groups had moderately favorable attitudes toward the advertised product. However, compared with adolescents, over twice as many children chose the advertised product over the other options they heavily favored. Overall, children's choices were driven by their exposure to television advertising, overwhelming their true preferences for all other choice options.

Effects of premium advertising. In addition to concerns about television advertising in general, the FTC also questioned specific types of advertising directed toward children. For example, in 1974, the FTC issued a proposed guideline requesting that the advertising industry discontinue the advertising of premium offers to children, based on the argument that advertising of premiums focused attention away from the merits of the advertised product, making evaluation of the product more difficult for children (Shimp et al., 1976).

Research addressing these concerns quickly followed, showing that premium advertising had negligible effects on retention of information about the advertised product and limited effects on preference for the advertised product (Heslop & Ryans, 1980; Shimp et al., 1976). For example, in the Shimp et al. (1976) study, first- to sixth-grade children were shown one of four different 30-second commercials for a new cereal product, which contained either no premium advertising or 10, 15, or 20 seconds of premium advertising. Immediately following, children answered questions about their recognition of specific features of the commercial, indicated their attitudes toward the advertised product and the premium, and were asked to make a choice between the advertised product and two well-known cereal brands. Findings indicated no significant differences in recognition of product information or product attitudes, and minimal effects on product preferences, across the four commercial conditions. However, subsequent research comparing premium advertising with two other execution formats (host selling, announcers) found that premium advertising was more effective than the other formats in stimulating children to choose the advertised product (Miller & Busch, 1979).

ERA II: CHILDREN'S CONSUMER SOCIALIZATION (1980–2000)

As the field of children's consumer research matured, researchers set their sights on the broader topic of consumer socialization, studying how children develop knowledge about the marketplace and are socialized to be consumers. The seeds for this focus were sown in the 1970s with the publication of several articles and a book on the topic of consumer socialization. In these publications, researchers used survey research to describe various aspects of children's and adolescents' knowledge, such as how many brands they could name and what sources of information they used to learn about products and make choices (R. L. Moore & Stephens, 1975; Moschis & Churchill, 1978; Ward et al., 1977).

In this section, we describe consumer socialization research in the 1980 to 2000 period. This research continued several themes from the 1970s but also added new topics such as decision making, product categorization, and consumption symbolism. Research in this era focused more on theoretical aspects, further incorporating relevant theories from child psychology, cognitive psychology, and decision making. In contrast to research from the prior era, which leaned heavily on survey methods with a smaller number of experiments, research in the second era featured much more experimental work, with a smaller number of survey and qualitative studies. Further, the research shifted more toward answering the "how" and "why" questions surrounding consumer socialization.

Development of Marketplace Knowledge

Some of the earliest research on young consumers described how children's basic knowledge about products, brands, advertising, shopping, and stores developed as they grew older (McNeal, 1964). For example, awareness of brand names progresses from the preschool years, where children begin to recall brand names, to the middle school years, where children can name multiple brands across multiple categories (Ward et al., 1977). In the early 1980s, researchers began to dig more deeply into how such knowledge developed during the childhood years and, particularly, how the structure of this knowledge changed over time.

Product and brand knowledge. An example of this focus can be found in research on children's product and brand knowledge. Children learn to group or categorize items at a very early age, but to do so, they typically rely on perceptual features that are visually dominant, such as shape, size, or color. As they grow older, they learn to group objects on more abstract criteria, such as taxonomic relationships (e.g., Coca-Cola and 7-Up are both soft drinks), and assign objects to categories based on underlying attributes that define the core concept of a category (e.g., sweet taste, more than color, is central to the category of soft drinks).

A study by John and Sujan (1990a) illustrates this point. Children from 4 to 10 years of age were shown triads of soft drink brands, with one item identified as the target (e.g., a can of 7-Up), the second item sharing a perceptual cue with the target (e.g., a can of Orange Crush), and the third item sharing an underlying cue of lemon-lime taste (e.g., a liter bottle of Sprite). Children were asked to identify which of the two items was "most like" the target and why. Older children (ages 9–10) used underlying cues (taste) in a ratio of about 2:1, whereas the very youngest children (ages 4–5) used perceptual cues (can) in a ratio of about 2:1 relative to underlying cues. Thus, young children's knowledge of product categories is based more on perceptual attributes, even though such attributes may not be diagnostic for identifying which brands belong to a product category (John & Sujan, 1990b).

Consumption symbolism. Children also begin to understand the social aspects of products and brands as part of the socialization process, which furthers learning about the symbolism attached to consumption objects. This knowledge allows consumers to form impressions of others, express themselves, and play a social role through consumption. In the 1970s, researchers began to acknowledge the importance of studying children's ability to understand the social value of consumption (Ward, 1974), but it was not until the early 1980s that researchers began to chart the development of children's recognition of the consumption symbolism of products.

Among the first studies was Belk et al. (1982), which examined children's ability to match personal characteristics of consumers (e.g., age, profession) with the types of houses and automobiles (e.g., size, style) they owned. For example, children were shown a pair of automobiles—one was a large traditional sedan and one was a small economy car—and were asked which of the cars would most likely be owned by a doctor. Findings revealed that children begin to make inferences about people based on products they own by second grade. As they grow older, their inferences become more consistent and more closely resemble those of adults. Additional studies corroborated this pattern. Children's ability to make stereotypical inferences about owners of products emerges by middle childhood (Belk et al., 1984; Mayer & Belk, 1982) and is almost fully developed by late childhood (Belk et al., 1984).

Shopping knowledge. Procedural knowledge regarding shopping and transacting for goods is another important area that develops as children grow older. Evidence to this effect began to emerge with descriptive studies in the 1970s, but the topic blossomed into full-fledged investigations in the 1980s. Shopping scripts, which embody the knowledge people have about procedures for purchasing and exchanging goods, were of particular interest in this period.

In general, scripts are knowledge structures that develop as individuals accumulate varied experiences and then develop generalizations about these experiences as a guide to procedures to follow to accomplish a task. Although children acquire experience as an observer or participant in the shopping process at very early ages, these experiences are not translated into shopping scripts until children are older (John & Whitney, 1986; Peracchio, 1992, 1993).

The transformation from shopping experiences to shopping scripts is illustrated by John and Whitney (1986). Children from three age groups (4–5 years, 6–7 years, and 9–10 years) were read stories about a boy or girl exchanging or returning a product to a store; included in each story was the same core content but with some variation. The amount of experience was manipulated by the number of stories read to children: low (one story), medium (three stories), and high (five stories). After hearing the stories, children were asked to describe how someone would go about returning or exchanging a product. With increasing experience, 9- to 10-year-olds abstracted the individual experiences into scripts, which featured a series of events needed to return or exchange an item and contingencies for certain situations. Results for 6- to 7-year-olds were similar, but their scripts were not as complex and did not change from the medium to high experience level. In contrast, the scripts of 4- to 5-year-olds were similar across experience levels, with a relatively high percentage of episodic events and little abstraction.

Follow-up studies showed that younger children could perform better under certain conditions (Peracchio, 1992, 1993). Their performance improved when they were given help in encoding experiences, such as presenting stories in audio-visual formats with multiple exposures and mass repetitions. Similar gains were seen when children were given prompts to help them retrieve information, including recognition versus recall tasks and more contextual questions for eliciting their scripts (e.g., "What would you do if I gave you this [broken toy] for your birthday?") instead of more general prompts (e.g., "How do you return something from the store?").

Knowledge of advertising tactics. Topics related to children's understanding of advertising were a focus of early work in the field. This interest resurfaced in the 1990s with more specific questions about children's advertising knowledge: What do children know about specific advertising tactics and appeals?

Advertising knowledge of this type, involving an understanding of what tactics and appeals are used by advertisers and why they are used, emerges much later as children approach early adolescence (Boush et al., 1994; E. S. Moore & Lutz, 2000). A study by Boush et al. (1994), conducted with sixth through eighth graders, illustrates this development. Students were asked why advertisers use particular tactics (e.g., humor, celebrity endorsers) and, for this purpose, were asked to rate each tactic on eight possible reasons (e.g., "grab your attention" and "help you learn about the product"). Results showed that knowledge about specific advertising techniques increases from sixth to eighth grade. Subsequent studies taking a more qualitative approach revealed that older children (fifth grade: E. S. Moore & Lutz, 2000; high school: Ritson & Elliott, 1999) find analyzing and discussing the creative strategies of commercials to be entertaining and a source of social interaction with their peers.

Increasing knowledge of advertising tactics is often viewed as a cognitive defense against advertising, allowing children and adolescents to respond to advertising in a more informed manner, with a lower likelihood of being misled. Early studies of advertising provided preliminary evidence to this effect (Robertson & Rossiter, 1974), but a more detailed study emerged in the 1980s challenging this view (Brucks et al., 1988). In this study, 9- to

10-year-olds were shown either (a) educational films about the selling intent of advertising and specific advertising techniques or (b) films unrelated to advertising. Several days later, students viewed and answered questions about several commercials. Before viewing commercials, half the children were given a short quiz about advertising, which served as a prompt for children to retrieve their advertising knowledge before watching the commercials. The results show that children with greater knowledge of advertising acquired from educational films did not necessarily use that knowledge when watching commercials but were most successful in applying their knowledge when prompted by the short quiz beforehand.

Decision Making and Choice

An important aspect of consumer socialization is the development of decision-making skills. Early survey research in the field described several developments. As they grow older, children develop a greater awareness of information sources, consider a wider array of information, and use more information when making decisions (R. L. Moore & Stephens, 1975; Moschis & Moore, 1979; Ward et al., 1977). In the 1980s, investigators adopted new methods of studying children's decision making and choice, delivering insights into the specific processes that children use when evaluating products and making choices.

Product evaluations, preferences, and choice. Children become more astute decision makers as they grow older, using more attribute information, focusing on more relevant attributes, and using attribute information more consistently in evaluating products (Bahn, 1986; Capon & Kuhn, 1980; Wartella et al., 1979). An illustration of these trends is provided by Capon and Kuhn (1980), who studied students in kindergarten, fourth grade, eighth grade, and college. Participants viewed several notebooks that differed in four attributes (color, shape, surface texture, side/top fasteners) and rated how much they liked each notebook. After these ratings, students were asked to rate their preferences for each attribute (e.g., for color, how much they prefer red over green notebooks). Kindergarteners were inconsistent in using their preferences for attributes, even one attribute, in their notebook ratings. Older children were more consistent, though they tended to use only a single attribute. Integration of two of more attributes was most evident among college students.

Decision-making strategies. Researchers interested in the strategies children use to gather information and make choices focused their attention on (a) identifying the age at which different decision-making strategies emerge and (b) understanding how children of different ages use different strategies to adapt to features of the decision-making task.

Emergence of decision-making strategies. One hurdle young children face in making informed choices is a repertoire of decision-making strategies and an understanding of how to use these strategies in different situations (Gregan-Paxton & John, 1995, 1997; Klayman, 1985; Wartella et al., 1979). The one strategy evident among young children is a focus on perceptual attributes, such as size or shape, with decisions often based on these attributes rather than more important attributes. Older children are able to focus more on relevant attributes and make decisions on the basis of these attributes using a variety of decision-making strategies.

Wartella et al. (1979) provided a compelling example of these trends in a study with kindergartners and third graders. Children were shown cards that contained a drawing of two or more candies, with candies varying in terms of ingredients (e.g., chocolate, raisins) and amount of each ingredient (two or five pieces). For example, one card showed "Candy E" with lots of chocolate (five pieces) and "Candy F" with a little chocolate (two pieces) and lots of raisins (five pieces) and peanuts (five pieces). Children were asked to choose a present for a friend who likes some ingredients more than others (e.g., friend who likes chocolate very much and raisins less). The candies on each card were designed so the child's strategy for choosing one of the candies was revealed by the set of choices made. The dominant strategy for kindergarteners was to choose the option with the most ingredients, regardless of attribute importance. In contrast, third graders used a variety of strategies, split between choosing the option that dominated on the most preferred attribute or the option providing the best variety of preferred attributes.

Adaptive use of decision-making strategies. With increasing age, children not only develop a repertoire of decision strategies but also learn how to use these strategies in a flexible and effective manner. Of importance is the ability to adapt strategies to the decision task, especially decisions characterized by many choice alternatives with attributes. For these more complex tasks, adults adapt by restricting attention to a smaller number of attributes and more promising alternatives, switching from decision strategies that are more difficult to use (e.g., compensatory strategies) to less cognitively demanding ones (e.g., noncompensatory strategies). Similar abilities develop in children as they move from middle childhood to early adolescence, being consistently exhibited by the time children reach 11 or 12 years of age (Gregan-Paxton & John, 1997; Klayman, 1985; Wartella et al., 1979).

An illustration of these developments is provided by Gregan-Paxton and John (1997) in a study conducted with second and fifth graders. As a reward for participating, children were allowed to select one of several colored boxes, which contained several types of prizes, such as money (e.g., penny, nickel, quarter) and candy (e.g., small or large roll of Life Savers). The boxes were mounted on a board down the left hand side in rows; the small prizes were mounted on the same board in columns and were covered by small curtains with Velcro strips. Children were allowed to remove the curtains to find out what prizes were in each box. To manipulate task complexity, four different boards were shown: 3 boxes (alternatives) × 3 prize types (dimensions), 3 × 6, 6 × 3, and 6 × 6. Further, search costs were manipulated by requiring half the children to give up one piece of candy they had received for each curtain they removed to expose a prize.

Age differences were evident in the way children adapted to more complex choices when no search costs were imposed. Older children were more efficient in gathering prize information prior to choice, searching less exhaustively and using less demanding choice strategies, especially for the more complex boards. However, when search costs were imposed, these age differences largely disappeared, as younger children also became more efficient in gathering information and simplifying their choice strategies. These findings suggest that younger children can exhibit the same type of adaptive decision making as their older counterparts, but younger children need a salient cue (search costs) to prompt them to alter their search and choice strategies.

Family Influences on Consumer Socialization

One of the earliest topics in children's consumer research was children's influence on family purchases (Ward & Wackman, 1972; Ward et al., 1977). Children's purchase requests and influence in categories such as toys, clothing, and food was studied, as well as children's influence on family purchases in categories such as vacations, restaurants, and cars. Factors affecting the degree of influence, such as the child's age and stage of decision making, were also identified. These findings established the importance of studying children's role as consumers.

In the late 1970s, researchers turned their attention in the opposite direction, studying how parents interact with and influence their children. Topics such as parental influence on children's beliefs about advertising and selling intent, media usage, decision making, and materialism received attention, studied in large-scale surveys (Moschis & Churchill, 1978; Ward et al., 1977). Moving into the 1980s, researchers continued to be interested in this topic but with a more conceptual focus. Theoretical frameworks that conceptualized the style of parenting and family communication style were now utilized to drive thinking about how parents interact with their children about consumption, media, and decision making in the marketplace.

Leading the way was research conducted on the influence of family communication patterns (R. L. Moore & Moschis, 1981; Moschis, 1985), examining four types of families: protective, pluralistic, consensual, and laissez-faire. Protective families stress obedience and social harmony, downplaying the importance of children developing their own opinions. In contrast, both pluralistic and consensual families encourage children to develop their own opinions. Pluralistic families promote open communication without requiring obedience to authority; consensual families embrace children developing their own views, combining this with a need for social harmony and family cohesiveness. Laissez-faire families are characterized by little parent–child communication. These communication patterns affect several aspects of consumer learning and decision making among children and adolescents. For example, reliance on parents versus peers as a source of consumer information differs by family type. Adolescents from pluralistic families favor parental advice more than adolescents from other types of families. On the other hand, adolescents from protective families are more receptive to information from peers. Overall, adolescents from pluralistic families know the most about consumer matters, and they also exhibit lower levels of materialism than adolescents from other types of families (R. L. Moore & Moschis, 1981).

Further insights on the role of the family were supplied by a second theoretical framework based on parental socialization types: authoritarian, rigid controlling, neglecting, permissive, and authoritative (Carlson & Grossbart, 1988; Rose, 1999). Authoritarians enforce rules in a strict way and value conformity, providing little encouragement for interaction and fostering dependency. Rigid controlling parents are similar in terms of strictness and valuing conformity, but they avoid communication less and are less anxious. In contrast to these two parenting types, permissive parents encourage verbal expression, are more nurturing, and are the least strict and value conformity less than any type other than neglecting. Authoritative parents strike a balance between permissive and authoritarian parents. They are warm, nurturing, and encourage expression like permissive parents, but they prefer strict discipline like authoritarian parents. Neglecting parents rate lowest in warmth and nurturing behaviors and avoid communication and rule enforcement.

These parental socialization types were found to also influence aspects of children's and adolescents' consumer behavior. In general, authoritative parents are more active in socialization efforts, evidenced by having more consumer goals for their children, mediating the effects of media and advertising, and being more active in communication about these topics with their children. Permissive parents show similar patterns but to a lesser extent. In contrast, neglecting parents are generally detached from these matters; authoritarian parents avoid interactions with their children and have few socialization goals (Carlson & Grossbart, 1988).

ERA III: CHILDREN'S CONSUMER WELL-BEING (2000–2020)

By the turn of the 21st century, increasing levels of childhood materialism, obesity, and consumption of risky products had caught the attention of parents, educators, and social scientists. Once again, researchers turned their attention to topics related to the well-being of children. This time, they were armed with an impressive body of knowledge of children's consumer socialization. Early research in the field had focused on concerns about television advertising to children and its effects on children's product choices, including consumption of unhealthy, heavily sugared foods. Thirty years later, these topics and more dominated research with children. In particular, several topics related to children's well-being shot to the top of the list, including tracing the development of materialism in children, decreasing childhood obesity and promoting healthy eating patterns, and deterring adolescent consumption of risky products, such as cigarettes, alcohol, and drugs.

In this section, we describe research on children's well-being from 2000 to 2020. As in the prior era, researchers continued to be interested in unpacking the process of development and understanding factors related to children's well-being. Researchers also continued to incorporate theories from child development and psychology but intertwined this interest with practical insights about proactive strategies for enhancing the well-being of children and adolescents. Also important was the development of new measurement techniques, which were especially important to capture beliefs and behaviors across a wide age range.

Materialism in Children and Adolescents

One of the most enduring concerns about children's well-being is that our culture encourages children to focus on material goods as a means of achieving personal happiness, success, and self-fulfillment, resulting in materialism. *Materialism* is "the importance a person places on possessions and their acquisition as a necessary or desirable form of conduct to reach desired end states, including happiness" (Richins & Dawson, 1992, p. 307). Early studies of consumer socialization, conducted in late 1970s and 1980s, included materialism as one of many topics in surveys. These efforts were largely descriptive in nature, uncovering factors associated with children's materialism such as family and parental influence, peer influence, media, and insecurity (for a review, see Dittmar et al., 2014).

The nature of research changed beginning in the early 2000s, as investigators began to examine more closely the mechanisms responsible for the development of materialism. An important foundation to this work was provided by studies on the development of consumption symbolism, which began in the late 1980s and developed further in the 2000s. Of particular importance were findings about the development of self–brand connections, which revealed how children and adolescents use their understanding of the social meaning of brands to define and express their self-concepts. A self–brand connection occurs when consumers incorporate a brand's personality, user characteristics, and other brand associations into their self-concepts. In studies with 8- to 18-year-olds, Chaplin and John (2005) found that as children grow older, not only do they incorporate more brands into their self-concept but the nature of their self–brand connections also changes. Younger children base their self–brand connections on ownership or perceptual features (e.g., I have this brand in my closet), whereas adolescents base their self–brand connections on symbolic meanings and social status (e.g., this brand is for athletes, like me).

Subsequent research by Chaplin and Lowrey (2010) suggests that these self–brand connections are furthered by children's increasing knowledge about consumption constellations, defined as a group of complimentary products, brands, or consumption experiences used to play a social role (e.g., cool kid). As children grow older, their consumption constellations include more products and brands, which are also more cohesive in symbolic meanings. By early adolescence, consumption constellations are well developed and rigid (e.g., brands like Apple and Adidas are for "cool" but not "quiet" kids). By late adolescence, constellations become more flexible (e.g., brands like Apple and Adidas are for "cool" kids, but some "quiet" kids might have them too).

Age differences in materialism. Early research on materialism suggested a number of factors that influence levels of materialism among children and adolescents. In the third era, researchers examined the developmental trajectory of materialism in depth, pinpointing age differences in materialism and the factors responsible for these patterns. Illustrative of this line of research is a set of studies by Chaplin and her colleagues (Chaplin et al., 2014; Chaplin & John, 2007). Participants 8 to 18 years of age were asked to build a "Happiness Collage," which represented the people and things that made them happy, and were each given a large poster board for constructing their collage. They were also each given a set of laminated cards with images they could use for their collages, with the cards mounted on five theme boards: (a) people and pets (e.g., mom, dad, teacher, pets), (b) hobbies (e.g., playing outside, going to the movies), (c) achievements (e.g., awards, good grades), (d) products and brands (e.g., new clothes, popular brands like Nike), and (e) sports (e.g., soccer, baseball). Blank cards and markers were made available in case children wanted to add something else on their collage. As children built their collages, the interviewer asked them why each item made them happy to ensure the images were interpreted as intended.

Afterward, the percentage of images belonging to "products and brands" was computed as an indicator of materialism. The results showed an inverted U-shape curve, with an increase from middle childhood (8–9 years old) to early adolescence (12–13 years old), followed by a decrease from early to late adolescence (16–18 years old).

Further, the authors found that there was an inverse relationship between these materialism patterns and self-esteem, with self-esteem decreasing between middle childhood and early adolescence and then rebounding between early and late adolescence. A subsequent study confirmed that lower levels of self-esteem cause an increase in materialism (Chaplin & John, 2007, Study 2), which is consistent with general research on materialism among adults (Kasser, 2002). These patterns of materialism and self-esteem have also been found among children living in poverty (Chaplin et al., 2014).

Interpersonal influences on materialism. Interpersonal influences are also important in understanding the development of materialism. Parents have received the most attention in this regard, even from the earliest research on materialism (R. L. Moore & Moschis, 1981; Moschis & Moore, 1979). Moving into the third era, researchers continued to study parental influence by further pinpointing how parents affect the adoption of materialistic values. A consistent finding from this stream of research is that parents who are highly materialistic have children who are also highly materialistic (Chaplin & John, 2010; Goldberg et al., 2003; Rindfleisch et al., 1997).

A number of explanations exist for this association. Early research examined the possibility of direct and indirect observation learning from parents, but later research has emphasized other mechanisms. For example, Chaplin and John (2010) found that parental influence on the level of materialism in adolescents is associated with the level of social support that parents give to their children. Parents who offer greater social support have adolescents with higher self-esteem, and as we described earlier, higher levels of self-esteem are associated with lower levels of materialism. Another possible mechanism was offered by Richins and Chaplin (2015), who found that adults who were rewarded and punished with material goods during childhood grew up to be more materialistic than their counterparts. Parental conflict and divorce, which increases family stress, has also been linked to higher levels of materialism in children (Rindfleisch et al., 1997; Roberts et al., 2005).

Peer influence on levels of materialism has received surprisingly little attention, despite the accepted view that children and adolescents are encouraged to value certain products and brands to gain the approval of peers and avoid being ostracized (Wooten, 2006). Consistent with this view, researchers have found that levels of adolescent materialism are positively associated with susceptibility to peer influence (Achenreiner, 1997) and negatively associated with peer acceptance (Chaplin & John, 2010). While most observers believe that peers exert their influence through negative means, such as ostracizing others for owning the wrong brands, it is also true that peers who offer social support can decrease levels of materialism among their friends (Chaplin & John, 2010).

Risky Consumption Among Adolescents

Adolescence is a period of many changes, and unfortunately, increased consumption of risky products is one of them (Pechmann et al., 2020). Among high school students, the majority report using alcohol (60%), followed by significant use of e-cigarettes and vaping (42%), marijuana (36%), and cigarettes (29%; Kann et al., 2018). Given the negative impact of these activities on adolescent well-being, a large volume of research exists across several disciplines, including public health, psychology, sociology, and communications.

In marketing, interest in topics related to risky consumption emerged in the early 1990s with the publication of several studies on cigarette smoking and alcohol use (Goldberg et al., 1994; Pechmann & Ratneshwar, 1994). This activity gained steam in the 2000s, focused primarily on cigarette smoking, with a small number of papers addressing alcohol and drug consumption. Next, we discuss research on cigarette smoking and alcohol as representative of the research conducted during this period.

Cigarette smoking. Much of the research in this area focused on two objectives. The first is assessing the extent to which cigarette advertising and marketing affects adolescent attitudes, beliefs, and behaviors related to cigarette smoking. The second is evaluating the effectiveness of antismoking advertising and educational interventions in reducing positive beliefs and attitudes toward cigarette smoking. Studies in both areas contribute to the overall objective of preventing and reducing cigarette smoking among adolescents, which is particularly important because nine out of 10 current adult smokers started before the age of 18 (U.S. Department of Health and Human Services, 2014) and two thirds of adolescents who smoke will become lifelong smokers (Centers for Disease Control & Prevention, 2014).

In a typical study on adolescent cigarette smoking, adolescents (12–18 years old) are exposed to a cigarette advertisement, antismoking public announcement or campaign, or other intervention program and are then asked to complete a survey that assesses their attitudes toward the materials they were exposed to, beliefs about cigarette smoking and smokers, intention to smoke or stop smoking, and background factors that may affect these beliefs and intentions (e.g., parental smoking, peer pressure). Also characteristic of many studies is inclusion of prosmoking advertising or marketing along with antismoking messages, which allows for a more realistic assessment of how effective antismoking advocacy may be with adolescents.

This approach is well illustrated by the work of Pechmann and her colleagues (Pechmann & Knight, 2002; Pechmann & Shih, 1999; Pechmann et al., 2003; Zhao & Pechmann, 2007), who have led research on adolescent cigarette smoking. Across these studies, they have shown that exposure to antismoking messages can be effective with adolescents, resulting in increased negative associations and beliefs about smoking, as well as decreasing intent to smoke. However, not all antismoking messages are equally successful (Andrews et al., 2004; Pechmann et al., 2003). Testing seven antismoking message themes, Pechmann et al. (2003) found certain themes were more effective in motivating teens to avoid smoking. When the message conveyed that cigarette smoking poses social disapproval risks, seventh and tenth graders' intentions to smoke decreased. However, messages emphasizing the health risks were not effective in decreasing teenagers' intention to smoke. Although messages with a health risk theme increased adolescents' perception of health risks associated with smoking, they did not feel vulnerable to these increased health risks, as opposed to the social disapproval risks emphasized in the effective message.

Subsequent research confirmed the limited effectiveness of communicating health risks, examining the use of warning labels on packages instead of antismoking advertisements (Andrews et al., 2014; Netemeyer et al., 2016). For example, in a study with 13- to 18-year-old smokers, Andrews et al. (2014) showed them cigarette packages with graphic warning labels and then assessed their beliefs about the health consequences of smoking, frequency of smoking, thoughts of quitting, emotions (e.g., sadness, remorse, fear), and perceived graphicness of the warnings. Surprisingly, they found that graphic warnings on cigarette packages did not directly affect adolescents' negative beliefs about smoking. However, on a more positive note, the graphic warnings did evoke fear in adolescents, which in turn increased thoughts of quitting.

Alcohol consumption. Although most of the research in this period was focused on cigarette smoking, many of the same themes emerged in studies of alcohol consumption among adolescents. First, new ways of marketing alcohol to adolescents were questioned and found to have an impact on alcohol consumption. For example, the widespread marketing of wine coolers, with sweet, fruity flavors, were found to increase the propensity for adolescent alcohol consumption (Goldberg et al., 1994). Second, despite these developments, researchers found that educational interventions could be successful in arming adolescents with knowledge about alcohol marketing, thus reducing their intent to consume these products.

For example, an educational intervention was found to have encouraging results in a study by Goldberg et al. (2006), who tested the effectiveness of a media literacy program with sixth graders. The program was designed to educate adolescents about the techniques used in advertising and to help them develop coping strategies to deal with advertising messages for alcohol products. An experimental group received this information, which was delivered in five 50-minute lessons administered by their teachers over the course of 5 days; a control group did not receive this intervention. Compared with the control group, students who received the intervention demonstrated more knowledge about alcohol advertising and developed more persuasion coping strategies. For students who had used alcohol, those in the experimental group were less likely to indicate they would drink again in the future.

Childhood Obesity and Healthy Food Choices

Childhood obesity is a growing global health concern, and encouraging patterns of healthier eating is one of the most important topics related to children's well-being. This concern is well founded. On any given day, about 34% of children and adolescents eat fast food and only 17% eat the recommended number of vegetable servings. By high school, 32% of adolescents are overweight or obese, reflecting years of poor eating habits (Pechmann et al., 2020).

Many factors have been identified that contribute to children's eating behaviors. Researchers in this era contributed to our understanding of two important influences: parents and food marketing. Parents' knowledge and beliefs about healthy eating, how they communicate that knowledge to their children, and the degree to which they model a healthy eating lifestyle with their children all contribute to children's food choices (Goldberg & Gunasti, 2007; E. S. Moore et al., 2017). In contrast, heavy exposure to unhealthy food advertisements leads children to choose less healthy food options (Dhar & Baylis, 2011; Institute of Medicine, 2006).

As a more direct means of influencing children's food consumption, researchers turned their attention to strategies to encourage children to make healthier food choices. An interesting example of this research is a field study conducted by Raju et al. (2010) in a school setting. They found school administrators were able to motivate elementary and middle school children to choose healthier options by using incentives (receive a reward for healthy choices), pledges (make a promise to eat more fruits and vegetables and to avoid eating unhealthy foods like chips and candy), and competitions (strive for a reward by eating healthy) at school.

Other studies show that subtle cues can also affect children's eating choices. For example, in a field study conducted at a middle school cafeteria, Biswas and Szocs (2019) exposed students to a cookie scent, which led to fewer purchases of unhealthy foods compared with no scent or a nonindulgent scent such as strawberry. Because the exposure to an indulgent food scent induces pleasure, it decreases subsequent desires for indulgent food. However, sensory cues can also produce unhealthy eating choices. Researchers have also shown that exposure to an overweight cartoon character can activate an overweight stereotype, resulting in children 6 to 14 years of age eating a higher amount of unhealthy treats (Campbell et al., 2016).

One strategy found to be ineffective is emphasizing the health benefits of food choices. Encouraging children to eat healthy foods by emphasizing the health benefits of certain foods can lead children to consume less of a healthy food option (Maimaran & Fishbach, 2014).

CONCLUSION

This chapter described the historical development of the field of consumer research with children and adolescents. Fifty years of consumer research with children and adolescents have yielded a remarkable body of knowledge. The field began with a focus on public policy concerns over the fairness of advertising to young children and advertising effects on youth consumption of sugary foods (1970–1985). It then shifted to understanding how child and adolescents are socialized into their roles as consumers (1980–2000). The field experienced another shift to investigating topics more closely related to child and adolescent well-being (2000–2020), which is where the field stands today. Researchers have moved from conducting large surveys of a descriptive nature to developing more creative measures to study how children's consumer values develop throughout childhood and carry over to adulthood. Today, we are more informed about how marketing messages affect children at different ages, how children are socialized into their roles as consumers, and how children's consumer behavior affects their well-being.

Moving forward, there are many opportunities to make meaningful contributions in several areas. New media and social media have supplanted traditional advertising media for the hearts and minds of children and adolescents. Yet, study of how these new ways of marketing affect children and adolescents is missing from the literature. Much of the history of children's research in our field has been aimed at assessing potential negative effects of marketing and advertising, but we lag behind other fields, such as public health and communications, in understanding the effect of new marketing techniques. With vaping and time spent on social media platforms such as TikTok, YouTube, and Snapchat by children and adolescents dangerously trending upward, it is critical that further research be conducted on ways to increase children's well-being. Our history is replete with examples of researchers who have developed and tested PSAs and educational programs, such as those developed to teach children about advertising and adolescents about cigarette advertising. Given our strong base knowledge of socialization in children and adolescents, coupled with our strong theoretical orientation and methodological prowess, we are in an ideal position to make a difference in the lives of children and adolescents.

REFERENCES

Achenreiner, G. B. (1997). Materialistic values and susceptibility to influence in children. In M. Brucks & D. J. MacInnis (Eds.), *NA - Advances in consumer research* (Vol. 24, pp. 82–88). Association for Consumer Research.

Andrews, J. C., Netemeyer, R. G., Burton, S., Moberg, D. P., & Christiansen, A. (2004). Understanding adolescent intentions to smoke: An examination of relationships among social influence, prior trial behavior, and antitobacco campaign advertising. *Journal of Marketing*, 68(3), 110–123. https://doi.org/10.1509/jmkg.68.3.110.34767

Andrews, J. C., Netemeyer, R. G., Kees, J., & Burton, S. (2014). How graphic visual health warnings affect young smokers' thoughts of quitting. *Journal of Marketing Research*, 51(2), 165–183. https://doi.org/10.1509/jmr.13.0092

Bahn, K. (1986). How and when do brand perceptions and preferences first form? A cognitive developmental investigation. *Journal of Consumer Research*, 13(3), 382–393. https://doi.org/10.1086/209077

Belk, R. W., Bahn, K. D., & Mayer, R. N. (1982). Developmental recognition of consumption symbolism. *Journal of Consumer Research*, 9(1), 4–17. https://doi.org/10.1086/208892

Belk, R. W., Mayer, R., & Driscoll, A. (1984). Children's recognition of consumption symbolism in children's products. *Journal of Consumer Research*, 10(4), 386–397. https://doi.org/10.1086/208977

Bever, T. G., Smith, M. L., Bengen, B., & Johnson, T. G. (1975). Young viewers' troubling response to TV ads. *Harvard Business Review*, 53(6), 109–120.

Biswas, D., & Szocs, C. (2019). The smell of healthy choices: Cross-modal sensory compensation effects of ambient scent food purchases. *Journal of Marketing Research*, 56(1), 123–141. https://doi.org/10.1177/0022243718820585

Blatt, J., Spencer, L., & Ward, S. (1972). A cognitive developmental study of children's reactions to television advertising. In E. A. Rubinstein, G. A. Comstock, & J. P. Murray (Eds.), *Television and social behavior: Vol. 4. Television in day-to-day life: Patterns of use* (pp. 452–467). U.S. Department of Health, Education, and Welfare.

Boush, D. M., Friestad, M., & Rose, G. M. (1994). Adolescent skepticism toward TV advertising and knowledge of advertiser tactics. *Journal of Consumer Research*, 21(1), 165–175. https://doi.org/10.1086/209390

Brucks, M., Armstrong, G. M., & Goldberg, M. E. (1988). Children's use of cognitive defenses against television advertising: A cognitive response approach. *Journal of Consumer Research*, 14(4), 471–482. https://doi.org/10.1086/209129

Campbell, M. C., Manning, K. C., Leonard, B., & Manning, H. M. (2016). Kids, cartoons, and cookies: Stereotype priming effects on children's food consumption. *Journal of Consumer Psychology*, 26(2), 257–264. https://doi.org/10.1016/j.jcps.2015.06.003

Capon, N., & Kuhn, D. (1980). A developmental study of consumer information-processing strategies. *Journal of Consumer Research*, 7(3), 225–233. https://doi.org/10.1086/208811

Carlson, L., & Grossbart, S. (1988). Parental style and consumer socialization of children. *Journal of Consumer Research*, 15(1), 77–94. https://doi.org/10.1086/209147

Centers for Disease Control and Prevention. (2014). *Surgeon General's advisory on e-cigarette use among youth: Quick facts on the risks of e-cigarettes for kids, teens, and young adults.*

Chaplin, L. N., Hill, R. P., & John, D. J. (2014). Poverty and materialism: A look at impoverished versus affluent children. *Journal of Public Policy & Marketing, 33*(1), 78–92. https://doi.org/10.1509/jppm.13.050

Chaplin, L. N., & John, D. R. (2005). The development of self–brand connections in children and adolescents. *Journal of Consumer Research, 32*(1), 119–129. https://doi.org/10.1086/426622

Chaplin, L. N., & John, D. R. (2007). Growing up in a material world: Age differences in materialism in children and adolescents. *Journal of Consumer Research, 34*(4), 480–493. https://doi.org/10.1086/518546

Chaplin, L. N., & John, D. R. (2010). Interpersonal influences on adolescent materialism: A new look at the role of parents and peers. *Journal of Consumer Psychology, 20*(2), 176–184. https://doi.org/10.1016/j.jcps.2010.02.002

Chaplin, L. N., & Lowrey, T. M. (2010). The development of consumer-based consumption constellations in children. *Journal of Consumer Research, 36*(5), 757–777. https://doi.org/10.1086/605365

Dhar, T., & Baylis, K. (2011). Fast-food consumption and the ban on advertising targeting children: The Quebec experience. *Journal of Marketing Research, 48*(5), 799–813. https://doi.org/10.1509/jmkr.48.5.799

Dittmar, H., Bond, R., Hurst, M., & Kasser, T. (2014). The relationship between materialism and personal well-being: A meta-analysis. *Journal of Personality and Social Psychology, 107*(5), 879–924. https://doi.org/10.1037/a0037409

Federal Trade Commission (1978). *Federal Trade Commission staff report on television advertising to children.*

Goldberg, M. E., & Gorn, G. J. (1974). Children's reactions to television advertising: An experimental approach. *Journal of Consumer Research, 1*(2), 69–75. https://doi.org/10.1086/208593

Goldberg, M. E., Gorn, G. J., & Gibson, W. (1978). TV messages for snack and breakfast foods: Do they influence children's preferences? *Journal of Consumer Research, 5*(2), 73–81. https://doi.org/10.1086/208717

Goldberg, M. E., Gorn, G. J., & Lavack, A. M. (1994). Product innovation and teenage alcohol consumption: The case of wine coolers. *Journal of Public Policy & Marketing, 13*(2), 218–227. https://doi.org/10.1177/074391569401300203

Goldberg, M. E., Gorn, G. J., Peracchio, L. A., & Bamossy, G. (2003). Understanding materialism among youth. *Journal of Consumer Psychology, 13*(3), 278–288. https://doi.org/10.1207/S15327663JCP1303_09

Goldberg, M. E., & Gunasti, K. (2007). Creating an environment in which youths are encouraged to eat a healthier diet. *Journal of Public Policy & Marketing, 26*(2), 162–181. https://doi.org/10.1509/jppm.26.2.162

Goldberg, M. E., Niedermeier, K. E., Bechtel, L. J., & Gorn, G. J. (2006). Heightening adolescent vigilance toward alcohol advertising to forestall alcohol use. *Journal of Public Policy & Marketing, 25*(2), 147–159. https://doi.org/10.1509/jppm.25.2.147

Gorn, G. J., & Goldberg, M. E. (1977). The impact of television advertising on children from low income families. *Journal of Consumer Research, 4*(2), 86–88. https://doi.org/10.1086/208683

Gorn, G. J., & Goldberg, M. E. (1980). Children's responses to repetitive television commercials. *Journal of Consumer Research, 6*(4), 421–424. https://doi.org/10.1086/208785

Gorn, G. J., & Goldberg, M. E. (1982). Behavioral evidence of the effects of televised food messages on children. *Journal of Consumer Research, 9*(2), 200–205. https://doi.org/10.1086/208913

Gregan-Paxton, J., & John, D. R. (1995). Are young children adaptive decision makers? A study of age differences in information search behavior. *Journal of Consumer Research, 21*(4), 567–580. https://doi.org/10.1086/209419

Gregan-Paxton, J., & John, D. R. (1997). The emergence of adaptive decision making in children. *Journal of Consumer Research, 24*(1), 43–56. https://doi.org/10.1086/209492

Heslop, L. A., & Ryans, A. B. (1980). A second look at children and the advertising of premiums. *Journal of Consumer Research, 6*(4), 414–420. https://doi.org/10.1086/208784

Institute of Medicine. (2006). *Food marketing to children and youth: Threat or opportunity?* The National Academies Press.

John, D. R. (1999). Consumer socialization of children: A retrospective look at twenty-five years of research. *Journal of Consumer Research, 26*(3), 183–213. https://doi.org/10.1086/209559

John, D. R., & Sujan, M. (1990a). Age differences in product categorization. *Journal of Consumer Research, 16*(4), 452–460. https://doi.org/10.1086/209230

John, D. R., & Sujan, M. (1990b). Children's use of perceptual cues in product categorization. *Psychology and Marketing, 7*(4), 277–294. https://doi.org/10.1002/mar.4220070404

John, D. R., & Whitney, J. C., Jr. (1986). The development of consumer knowledge in children: A cognitive structure approach. *Journal of Consumer Research, 12*(4), 406–417. https://doi.org/10.1086/208526

Kann, L., McManus, T., Harris, W. A., Shanklin, S. L., Flint, K. H., Queen, B., Lowry, R., Chyen, D., Whittle, L., Thornton, J., Lim, C., Bradford, D., Yamakawa, Y., Leon, M., Brener, N., & Ethier, K. A. (2018). Youth risk behavior surveillance—United States, 2017. *Morbidity and Mortality Weekly Report, 67*(8), 1–114. https://doi.org/10.15585/mmwr.ss6708a1

Kasser, T. (2002). *The high price of materialism.* MIT Press. https://doi.org/10.7551/mitpress/3501.001.0001

Klayman, J. (1985). Children's decision strategies and their adaptation to task characteristics. *Organizational Behavior and Human Decision Processes, 35*(2), 179–201. https://doi.org/10.1016/0749-5978(85)90034-2

Macklin, M. C. (1985). Do young children understand the selling intent of commercials? *Journal of Consumer Affairs, 19*(2), 293–304. https://doi.org/10.1111/j.1745-6606.1985.tb00357.x

Maimaran, M., & Fishbach, A. (2014). If it's useful and you know it, do you eat? Preschoolers refrain from instrumental food. *Journal of Consumer Research, 41*(3), 642–655. https://doi.org/10.1086/677224

Mayer, R., & Belk, R. (1982). Acquisition of consumption stereotypes by children. *Journal of Consumer Affairs, 16*(2), 307–321. https://doi.org/10.1111/j.1745-6606.1982.tb00177.x

McNeal, J. U. (1964). *Children as consumers.* Bureau of Business Research, University of Texas at Austin.

Miller, J. H., Jr., & Busch, P. (1979). Host selling vs. premium TV commercials: An experimental evaluation of their influence on children. *Journal of Marketing Research, 16*(3), 323–332. https://doi.org/10.1177/002224377901600304

Moore, E. S., & Lutz, R. J. (2000). Children, advertising, and product experiences: A multimethod inquiry. *Journal of Consumer Research, 27*(1), 31–48. https://doi.org/10.1086/314307

Moore, E. S., Wilkie, W. L., & Desrochers, D. M. (2017). All in the family? Parental roles in the epidemic of childhood obesity. *Journal of Consumer Research, 43*(5), 824–859.

Moore, R. L., & Moschis, G. P. (1981). The effects of family communication and mass media use on adolescent consumer learning. *Journal of Communication, 31*(4), 42–51. https://doi.org/10.1111/j.1460-2466.1981.tb00449.x

Moore, R. L., & Stephens, L. F. (1975). Some communication and demographic determinants of adolescent consumer learning. *Journal of Consumer Research, 2*(2), 80–92. https://doi.org/10.1086/208619

Moschis, G. P. (1985). The role of family communication in consumer socialization of children and adolescents. *Journal of Consumer Research, 11*(4), 898–913. https://doi.org/10.1086/209025

Moschis, G. P., & Churchill, G. A., Jr. (1978). Consumer socialization: A theoretical and empirical analysis. *Journal of Marketing Research, 15*(4), 599–609. https://doi.org/10.1177/002224377801500409

Moschis, G. P., & Moore, R. L. (1979). Decision making among the young: A socialization perspective. *Journal of Consumer Research, 6*(2), 101–112. https://doi.org/10.1086/208754

Netemeyer, R. G., Burton, S., Andrews, J. C., & Kees, J. (2016). Graphic health warnings on cigarette packages: The role of emotions in affecting adolescent smoking consideration and secondhand smoke beliefs. *Journal of Public Policy & Marketing, 35*(1), 124–143. https://doi.org/10.1509/jppm.15.008

Pechmann, C., Catlin, J. R., & Zheng, Y. (2020). Facilitating adolescent well-being: A review of the challenges and opportunities and the beneficial roles of parents, schools, neighborhoods, and policymakers. *Journal of Consumer Psychology, 30*(1), 149–177. https://doi.org/10.1002/jcpy.1136

Pechmann, C., & Knight, S. J. (2002). An experimental investigation of the joint effects of advertising and peers on adolescents' beliefs and intentions about cigarette consumption. *Journal of Consumer Research, 29*(1), 5–19. https://doi.org/10.1086/339918

Pechmann, C., & Ratneshwar, S. (1994). The effects of antismoking and cigarette advertising on young adolescents' perceptions of peers who smoke. *Journal of Consumer Research, 21*(2), 236–251. https://doi.org/10.1086/209395

Pechmann, C., & Shih, C. (1999). Smoking scenes in movies and antismoking advertisements before movies: Effects on youth. *Journal of Marketing, 63*(3), 1–13. https://doi.org/10.1177/002224299906300301

Pechmann, C., Zhao, G., Goldberg, M. E., & Reibling, E. T. (2003). What to convey in antismoking advertisements for adolescents: The use of protection motivation theory to identify effective message themes. *Journal of Marketing, 67*(2), 1–18. https://doi.org/10.1509/jmkg.67.2.1.18607

Peracchio, L. A. (1992). How do young children learn to be consumers? A script-processing approach. *Journal of Consumer Research, 18*(4), 425–440. https://doi.org/10.1086/209271

Peracchio, L. A. (1993). Young children's processing of a televised narrative: Is a picture really worth a thousand words? *Journal of Consumer Research, 20*(2), 281–293. https://doi.org/10.1086/209349

Raju, S., Rajagopal, P., & Gilbride, T. J. (2010). Marketing healthful eating to children: The effectiveness of incentives, pledges, and competitions. *Journal of*

Richins, M. L., & Chaplin, L. N. (2015). Material parenting: How the use of goods in parenting fosters materialism in the next generation. *Journal of Consumer Research*, *41*(6), 1333–1357. https://doi.org/10.1086/680087

Richins, M. L., & Dawson, S. (1992). A consumer values orientation for materialism and its measurement: Scale development and validation. *Journal of Consumer Research*, *19*(3), 303–316. https://doi.org/10.1086/209304

Rindfleisch, A., Burroughs, J. E., & Denton, F. (1997). Family structure, materialism, and compulsive consumption. *Journal of Consumer Research*, *23*(4), 312–325. https://doi.org/10.1086/209486

Ritson, M., & Elliott, R. (1999). The social uses of advertising: An ethnographic study of adolescent advertising audiences. *Journal of Consumer Research*, *26*(3), 260–277. https://doi.org/10.1086/209562

Roberts, J. A., Tanner, J. F., Jr., & Manolis, C. (2005). Materialism and the family structure-stress relation. *Journal of Consumer Psychology*, *15*(2), 183–190. https://doi.org/10.1207/s15327663jcp1502_10

Robertson, T. S., & Rossiter, J. R. (1974). Children and commercial persuasion: An attribution theory analysis. *Journal of Consumer Research*, *1*(1), 13–20. https://doi.org/10.1086/208577

Roedder, D. L., Sternthal, B., & Calder, B. J. (1983). Attitude-behavior consistency in children's responses to television advertising. *Journal of Marketing Research*, *20*(4), 337–349. https://doi.org/10.1177/002224378302000401

Rose, G. M. (1999). Consumer socialization, parental style, and developmental timetables in the United States and Japan. *Journal of Marketing*, *63*(3), 105–119. https://doi.org/10.1177/002224299906300307

Shimp, T. A., Dyer, R. F., & Divita, S. F. (1976). An experimental test of the harmful effects of premium-oriented commercials on children. *Journal of Consumer Research*, *3*(1), 1–11. https://doi.org/10.1086/208645

U.S. Department of Health & Human Services (2014). *Preventing tobacco use among youths, Surgeon General fact sheet*.

Ward, S. (1972). Children's reactions to commercials. *Journal of Advertising Research*, *12*(2), 37–45. https://www.jstor.org/stable/2489109

Ward, S. (1974). Consumer socialization. *Journal of Consumer Research*, *1*(2), 1–14. https://doi.org/10.1086/208584

Ward, S., Reale, G., & Levinson, D. (1972). Children's perceptions, explanations, and judgments of television advertising: A further explanation. In E. A. Rubinstein, G. A. Comstock, & J. P. Murray (Eds.), *Television and social behavior: Vol. 4. Television in day-to-day life: Patterns of use* (pp. 468–490). U.S. Department of Health, Education, and Welfare.

Ward, S., & Wackman, D. B. (1972). Children's purchase influence attempts and parental yielding. *Journal of Marketing Research*, *9*(3), 316–319. https://doi.org/10.1177/002224377200900312

Ward, S., Wackman, D. B., & Wartella, E. (1977). *How children learn to buy: The development of consumer information-processing skills*. Sage.

Wartella, E., Wackman, D. B., Ward, S., Shamir, J., & Alexander, A. (1979). The young child as consumer. In E. Wartella (Ed.), *Children communicating: Media and development of thought, speech, understanding*. Sage.

Wooten, D. B. (2006). From labeling possessions to possessing labels: Ridicule and socialization among adolescents. *Journal of Consumer Research*, *33*(2), 188–198. https://doi.org/10.1086/506300

Zhao, G., & Pechmann, C. (2007). The impact of regulatory focus on adolescents' response to antismoking advertising campaigns. *Journal of Marketing Research*, *44*(4), 671–687. https://doi.org/10.1509/jmkr.44.4.671

CHAPTER 8

GENDER RESEARCH IN MARKETING, CONSUMER BEHAVIOR, ADVERTISING, AND BEYOND: PAST, PRESENT, AND FUTURE

Linda Tuncay Zayer and Kathrynn Pounders

Gender has captured the attention of the masses at an unprecedented rate over the past few years, including taking center stage amid the recent social upheaval (Coleman et al., 2021). This chapter provides an overview of gender scholarship as it relates to marketing, consumer behavior, advertising, and beyond. The discussion traces its roots from related disciplines; discusses seminal works; illustrates its progression over the years, including the cultural turn; and identifies current and emerging topics.

EARLY SCHOLARSHIP

Consumer research focused on gender and the self has always integrated and relied on multiple areas, including psychology, sociology, and anthropology. Work in the 1980s and 1990s in psychology concentrated heavily on the self-concept, paving the way for researchers to examine and understand the multidimensional self. Sirgy (1982) proposed aspects of the self, such as actual self-concept, ideal self-concept, looking glass self, and sex-role concept. Later, Higgins (1987) described how the self can be separated into the actual, ideal, and ought self and introduced self-discrepancy theory, where individuals are innately motivated to be consistent with their self-concept and experience dissonance when this does not occur. The notion of self and self-concept continued to receive focus in psychology and increasing attention in consumer research as scholars noted the increasing importance of the self to consumer behavior (e.g., Schouten, 1991). Indeed, Belk (1988) developed the concept of the extended self, which states that one's possessions constitute part of one's self-concept, illustrating how consumption and the self are explicitly intertwined.

Early work on gender borrowed from the work done on the multidimensional self and self-concept. This work primarily focused on identifying differences between men and women, or the gender binary. Differences were examined in a variety of contexts, including shopping behaviors (Fischer & Arnold, 1990), information processing (Meyers-Levy & Maheswaran, 1991), and judgment (Meyers-Levy, 1988). Other work focused on the congruence of sex-role concept with brands or products (Bellizzi & Milner, 1991; Schmitt et al., 1988). This work often utilized different scales to measure masculinity and femininity (see Bem sex-role inventory: Bem, 1974; Personal Attributes Questionnaire: Spence et al., 1975). At times this work conflated the constructs of biological sex (i.e., male and female) and gender identity (i.e., masculinity and femininity).

In the 1990s, poststructural and feminist theories concerned with the basis of social positions, roles and institutions in language, and their operation in reinforcing and reproducing hierarchical gender relations emerged as a fertile framework for analyzing gender distinctions in marketing rhetoric (see Hirschman, 1993; Stern 1993). For example, Bristor and Fischer (1993) called attention to the fact that prior research had failed to differentiate between biological sex and gender identity. This paved the way for other work to move away from the conflations of sex and gender and begin to unpack sex, gender, and identity (e.g., Joy & Venkatesh, 1994; Peñaloza, 1994; Thompson, 1996).

GENDER AND THE CULTURAL TURN

While much of the early scholarship tended to focus on sex-role stereotyping and gender largely as a variable, contemporary gender scholarship conceptualizes gender as socially constructed, plural, and nonbinary. Erving Goffman's books *The Presentation of the Self in Everyday Life* (Goffman, 1959) and *Gender Advertisements* (Goffman, 1979), as well as feminist critiques of advertising and marketing in the 1980s and 1990s, laid the groundwork for future marketing, advertising, and consumer research. While some research still focuses on what is now known to be sex differences research, the 1990s and beyond took a decidedly cultural perspective on understanding gender(s).

Viewpoints from diverse fields such as sociology, anthropology, cultural studies, and humanities bring a richer understanding to the domain, particularly in regard to intersectional and transnational perspectives, although gaps still remain (see Hearn & Hein, 2015). Most notably within marketing, scholars with a consumer culture theory (Arnould & Thompson, 2005) orientation provide a wide and deep body of work that demonstrates the shift away from understanding gender in binary or essentialist terms. That is, an acknowledgment of gender fluidity, of gender to genders, masculinity to masculinities, and femininity to femininities (Butler, 2004), as well as greater recognition of LGBTQ+ issues, intersectionality, transnationality, and viewpoints informed by a macro and transformative consumer research (TCR) orientation has gained prominence. And while research continues to flourish, so too have the institutional structures to help support it, for example, through the GENMAC organization (https://genmac.co).

However, how has research since this cultural turn evolved in the past 2 decades? Maclaran et al. (2017) conceptualized the cultural turn as studying gender and individuals as "socially connected, emotional beings" (p. 294) situated within consumption markets. Much of this work is informed and shaped by the wide range of feminist scholarship. Although there were rumblings of a postfeminism world, scholarship at the turn of the century reminded the field that the work of feminist scholars was far from done (e.g., Scott, 2005). In the edited volume by Catterall et al. (2000), the authors included several important pieces that detailed the evolving relationships between feminism(s), advertising, consumer research, and marketing. The authors highlighted how, despite understandings rooted in binaries dating back to philosophers such as Plato, Hegel, Marx, and Descartes, the late 1980s and 1990s feminist scholarship brought new perspectives to understanding marketing, which was a fundamental shift from utilizing gender as a variable. Indeed, Lambiase et al. (2017) summarized how "waves" of feminism have influenced our understandings of marketing, markets, and individuals, ranging from first wave struggles of recognition of women in society to second wave rejection of markets and marketing. The third wave's attempt to broaden the agenda of feminism, bringing to light the plurality and intersectionality of feminism(s), was followed by fourth wave's postfeminism marked by greater reach through social media (Maclaran, 2015). In addition to the greater understanding these waves (a notion that is, at times, contested) brought to marketing, advertising, and consumer research, Maclaran et al. (2009) pointed out that the recognition of privilege and power inherent in feminist perspectives is not simply an issue to be examined in research contexts but in the gendered performances of marketing academics themselves. Indeed, scholarly work continues to bring to fore feminist perspectives and the critique of binary constructions of gender while articulating the complex and at times problematic history of marketing and feminism (Johnston & Taylor, 2008; Maclaran, 2012).

Bettany et al. (2010) mapped out the evolution of gender research within broader developments in the social sciences and humanities within the context of gender inequities in society, tracing the sociological roots of the term *gender* (as opposed to biological sex), or "the socially and culturally constructed aspects of the differences between men and women" (p. 7) to feminist philosopher Anne Oakley. The authors examined the array of work presented at the Gender and Consumer Behavior Conference series (subsequently changed to the Gender, Marketing, and Consumer Behavior Conference) to illustrate both the substantive as well as theoretical areas of research that pervaded the field since the establishment of the conference in 1991. In particular, they held that the late 1990s and 2000s brought with them a surge of interest in the gendering of men and masculinity, as well as research informed by queer theory, reader-response theory, and Judith Butler's theories on gender, among others. Unsurprisingly, published gender research in the field's prominent journals at this time mirrored these themes in many ways.

Next, culturally oriented gender, marketing, and consumer research is discussed with a focus on the last 20 years of research appearing in the field's prominent marketing, advertising and consumer research journals. The breadth and depth of the scholarship in this area should be noted, and the discussion provided here is not exhaustive, nor does it capture the rich scholarship outside of these fields and the important work prior to 2000 (however, see Maclaran et al., 2017; Steinfield, Littlefield, et al., 2019; Zayer et al., 2017, for additional overviews). The review of the literature begins with a focus on gender and consumption, followed by an examination of research at the intersection of gender, media, and advertising. Lastly, several contemporary areas for research that are ripe for further inquiry are outlined, including macro, intersectional, and TCR perspectives.

Gender and Consumption at the Cultural Turn

Edited volumes specific to gender, marketing, and consumer research (see, e.g., Dobscha, 2019; Otnes & Zayer, 2012) serve to highlight a range of research on timely topics ranging from consumption of advertising and social media to fatherhood and sustainability. However, across the past 2 decades, one area in particular has seen great interest by scholars: the intersections of men, masculinity, and consumption. Traditionally male-dominated spheres became a point of inquiry as men were increasingly recognized as gendered individuals. For example, Sherry et al. (2004) explored an enclave of masculinity in a retail sports-themed setting, identifying a series of traditional masculine enactments, while Modrak (2015) highlighted the rhetoric of authenticity in the urban woodsman aesthetic. However, as contestations of traditional notions of masculinity became apparent, consumer research and marketing scholars sought to unpack a myriad of factors, including social class, geography, history, ethnicity and race, sexuality, physical ability, and age, among other factors that shape masculinities and their accompanying new sensibilities in the marketplace (see, e.g., Holt & Thompson, 2004, for a discussion of a man-of-action model of masculinity). Littlefield and Ozanne (2011) drew on an ecofeminist perspective (see also Dobscha & Ozanne, 2001) to explore the socialization of masculinity within the male-dominated hunting subculture that is shaped with rituals, core values, and shared stories as well as a multiplicity of masculine expressions (Littlefield, 2010).

A series of papers around this time examined men and masculinity within the contexts of relatively new forms of consumption for men, oftentimes intertwined with consumer rituals (e.g., Chen, 2012; Frith & Gleeson, 2004; Liu, 2019; Ostberg, 2012; Otnes & McGrath, 2001; Ourahmoune, 2012; Tuncay & Otnes, 2008b; Zayer & Neier, 2011). Otnes and McGrath (2001) were the first to deeply examine men in the shared social space of shopping. Tuncay and Otnes (2008b) and Zayer and Neier (2011) built on this research, examining strategies and brand relationships of heterosexual men as they shop for once-stigmatized fashion and grooming products (see also Liu's, 2019, recent work on men's grooming). Additionally, Frith and Gleeson (2004) demonstrated how men negotiate cultural ideals of masculinity in regard to clothing but centered on an understanding of the body. Gender in ritualized contexts are not limited to explorations of men and masculinity. Ourahmoune and Özçağlar-Toulouse (2012) also investigated gender and fashion but within the rituals of weddings in

Algeria, outlining the importance of collective narratives in consumption. Additional work explored gender within the context of the everyday, including scholars Hein and O'Donohoe's (2014) study of masculinity in exchanges of banter and Valtonen and Närvänen's (2015) study that used a gender lens to explore the object–person relationships related to the bed and sleeping, while highlighting the role of the body.

A broad range of research demonstrates that while new conceptualizations of gender emerge, the stronghold of so-called traditional gender roles and family structures persists (see, e.g., Lai et al.'s, 2015, discussion of marginalized singleness and Houston's, 2004, exploration of the experiences of infertility). For instance, in Tuncay and Otnes (2008a), the authors traced the history of masculinity and consumption, pointing both to the fragmentation (and heightened commercialization) of masculinities in the 2000s, as well as the sustained relevance of hegemonic masculinity that undergirds much consumption and identity work. However, the disruption of the binary perspective—men as producer and women as consumer—has brought rich new studies to the forefront. Indeed, several works interrogated hegemonic masculinity and cultural capital within domestic or feminized spaces. For example, Klasson and Ulver (2015) illuminated how feminized masculinities are shaped into hegemonic masculinity, and Coskuner-Balli and Thompson (2013) examined subordinate capital within the context of stay-at-home fathers. Moisio et al.'s (2013) class-informed study of "Do It Yourself" (DIY) home improvement also brings to fore varying cultural capital endowments and how they shape domestic masculinity (see also themes of empowerment for female DIYers in Wolf et al., 2015). Zuzana (2011) also examined the domestic context of food and home to reveal how immigrant Romanian women in Italy use marketplace representations of the modern woman as they construct hybrid gender identities. In a similar vein, Lindridge et al. (2016) explored Nigerian female immigrants in the U.K. as they challenge and support the "patriarchal bargain" through consumption. Caldwell et al. (2007) also found a malleability and multiplicity in gender identities in their study of what they identify as contemporary young mainstream female achievers (CYMFAs) living affluent middle-class lives and enacting multiple gender identities.

Other scholarship continued to examine contested notions of gender, particularly through the lens of performativity and performance. Thompson and Üstüner (2015) introduced a discussion of gender performativity and marketplace performance loosely along the lines of structure-agency dialogue in their phenomenological study of roller derby performances in the rural United States and the ideological edgework that allows for a challenging of gender boundaries without the diminishment of legitimacy. The authors characterized gender performativity as compulsory and situated within heteronormative norms and discourses versus marketplace performativity as dealing with a liminal role that is volitional. Contributing to our understanding of what Thompson and Üstüner (2015) called "consumer-as-performer" (p. 238), Martin et al. (2006) illuminated feminine performances within the Harley motorcycle subculture, while Goulding and Saren (2009) and Blanchette (2014) explored gendered performances within the goth and neoburlesque communities. Joy et al. (2015) also used the lens of performativity in their study of gender violence in India, noting the oppressions imposed on women from different castes and classes, while Cruz et al. (2017) demonstrated how migrant men engage in marketplace performances to navigate experiences of emasculation.

Scholarship in the last 20 years has also brought to light important work with regard to LGBTQ+ communities, led by a series of studies by scholar Steven Kates on subcultural consumption (Kates, 2002), brand relationships (Kates, 2000), and how brands gain legitimacy in the gay community (Kates, 2004). Indeed, research with regard to LGBTQ+ issues continues, for instance, exploring gay symbolic consumption (Visconti, 2008), but researchers emphasize that much of the existing work is steeped in an Anglo-American history of LGBTQ+ issues and focuses on "urban, middle-class gay cis men in the West" (see Coffin et al., 2019, p. 286), neglecting other genders and intersectionalities.

Gender, Advertising, and Media Research at and Beyond the Cultural Turn

Research on gender and advertising often examines gender stereotypes and consumer responses to these stereotypes (for overviews, see Eisend, 2019; Grau & Zotos, 2016). While much of this work utilizes a quantitative orientation, testing, for example, the effectiveness of gender portrayals, other research seeks to culturally situate understandings of gender and gender portrayals.

Gender stereotypes and gendered imagery continue to be an area of focus, and several more culturally orientated studies illuminated the broad societal and ethical implications for gender relations, particularly in light of the industry's abdication (at times) of responsibility (see Gurrieri et al., 2016; Zayer & Coleman, 2015). Several studies examined gender issues from the perspective of advertising professionals as cultural intermediaries, bringing to fore broader societal discourses (Coleman et al., 2020; Gurrieri et al., 2016; Nixon & Crewe, 2004; Shao et al., 2014; Windels, 2016; Zayer & Coleman, 2015). For example, Shao et al. (2014) identified East–West tensions within the context of Chinese ad professionals' experiences in the creation of gendered ads, while Zayer and Coleman (2015) revealed how ad professionals in the U.S. draw from, reiterate, and, at times, resist discourses of gender and vulnerability in the creation of gendered portrayals. Gurrieri et al. (2016) explored depictions of violence against women in advertising and found client organizations engage in discursive strategies in justification of their work, including labeling it as "art."

Against the backdrop of cultural critiques of advertising's role in society, scholarship in the 2000s sought to gain greater insight into the area of men and masculinities as portrayed in advertising and media as well as men's responses to ads. Research highlighted how representations of traditional masculinities persist (see, e.g., Marshall et al.'s, 2014, sociohistoric tracking of portrayals of fathers in magazines) even as "new" forms of masculinity emerge (e.g. Gentry & Harrison, 2010; Hirschman, 2003; Zayer, 2010; Zayer et al., 2020). Additional scholarship by Patterson and Elliott (2002) and Schroeder and Zwick (2004) illuminated the construction of masculine identities and the male gaze in advertising and media, whereas Ostberg (2010) highlighted men's body ideals across advertising, media, and self-help resources. Zayer and Otnes (2012) identified men's meanings of masculinity, including authenticity, individuality, vulnerability, achievement, and elusiveness in response to idealized messages of masculinity, underlining the negative impact of such depictions on men's lives.

Research that focuses on gendered depictions in advertising has also frequently utilized content analysis (e.g., Eisend et al., 2014; Koerning & Granitz, 2006; Tsichla & Zotos, 2016; Vokey et al., 2013). This work has commonly focused on the portrayal of women's sex roles and femininity in advertising (Jaffe & Berger, 1994; Koerning & Granitz, 2006; Nelson & Paek, 2008), with far less focus on how men are depicted in advertising. The research on portrayals of men in advertising has largely explored the representation of hegemonic masculinity, the male body, and the gendered roles of men in advertising (Gentry & Harrison, 2010; Schroeder & Zwick, 2004; Vokey et al., 2013).

Quantitative work that examines gender stereotypes and roles in advertising largely demonstrates that depictions of traditional stereotypes are increasingly negatively perceived by consumers—especially among women. For example, Huhmann and Limbu (2016) found that the more that consumers believe an ad features gender stereotypes, the less favorable their attitude of the ad. Additionally, Åkestam (2018) demonstrated that exposure to both physical appearance and role behavior stereotypes lowers perceptions of brand and ad attitudes.

Research has also examined how exposure to models featured in ads influences self-perception in the form of self-esteem, body satisfaction, and self-image among women. Most of this work in the 2000s focused on reactions to different model body sizes, including the thin-ideal, which models have embodied since the 1980s. The bulk of this scholarship shows exposure to idealized imagery in the form of the thin-ideal is detrimental for women's self-perceptions in terms of self-esteem, self-image, and body satisfaction, while identifying a host of individual traits that impact these relationships, such as body mass index (BMI), internalization of the thin-ideal, tendency to engage in social comparison, goal orientation, and ethnicity (e.g., Bissell & Rask, 2010; Buunk & Dijkstra, 2011; Micu & Coulter, 2012; Pounders, Rice, & Mabry-Flynn, 2017; Smeesters et al., 2010).

Recently, consistent with ads increasingly featuring plus-size models, research is beginning to examine how nontraditional female models are perceived, finding mixed results. For example, Pounders and Mabry-Flynn (2019) identified a mix of positive and negative themes when exploring the response of consumers to plus-size models who appeared in mainstream magazines. Additionally, Borau and Bonnefon (2017) found women's reactions to "natural" models was dependent on their BMI.

Interestingly, there has been little work done on the physical appearance of men featured in ads and if or how this impacts their self-perceptions. One meta-analysis showed men are negatively impacted by exposure to "ideal" male models, reporting lower body esteem and body satisfaction (Barlett et al., 2008). Diedrichs and Lee (2010) examined the impact that different model body types (muscular, average-slim, average-large, or a control with no model) have on perceptions of the ad. They found the ads without a model to be significantly more effective than those with muscular models, with no significant differences in ad effectiveness between the three conditions featuring ads with male models of varying body types.

Work sometimes associated with gender and advertising has also focused on identifying sex differences in understanding response to various appeals, but it has largely examined sexual content. This body of work largely explores the reactions of cisgender men and women and demonstrates a cross-sex bias, or that consumers evaluate sexual images of the opposite sex more favorably. For example, Reichert et al. (2007) examined response to three types of sexual appeals: ads featuring women, men, or both men and women. They found that affective and attitudinal responses to opposite-sex stimuli were most favorable, followed by mixed-sex stimuli, with same-sex imagery evaluated least positively.

Researchers have also explored individual differences that may impact this established pattern of effects. Putrevu (2008) found congruence (strong or weak fit) between the sexual appeal and the featured brand consequential. Sengupta and Dahl (2008) found that men demonstrated a more favorable ad attitude to explicit sex appeals than women. Extending this work, Dahl et al. (2009) showed women to be accepting of sexual appeals in advertisements when there was a stronger fit between the advertisement and the brand, whereas men responded positively to sexual appeals regardless of their compatibility with the brand.

In addition to research that investigates physical appearance or sexual content, other contemporary research has documented representations of LGBTQ+ individuals (e.g., within mainstream advertising: Tsai, 2010; family depictions: Borgerson et al., 2006; Oakenfull & Greenlee, 2005; Oakenfull et al., 2008). Borgerson et al. (2006) investigated how gay family advertising is read and interpreted. The authors interrogated the concepts of family, revealing how ads featuring gay families are read, including the prevalence of "straightening up," whereby consumers impose family values, focus on the product, or engage in denial of overt depictions of gay families in ads (Borgerson et al., 2006, p. 968). Oakenfull and Greenlee (2005) examined consumer responses to advertising that featured "mainstream" imagery, implicit gay and lesbian imagery, and explicit gay and lesbian imagery. They found that ads featuring implicit gay and lesbian imagery are better received among heterosexual consumers, as explicit imagery is met with adverse reactions. Further, Oakenfull et al. (2008) examined how consumers' responses vary to "mainstream" ads, gay ads, lesbian ads, and ads that feature homosexual subcultural symbolism. Findings from this research demonstrated that reactions to ads are influenced by the type of homosexual imagery portrayed in the ad, as well as the sexual orientation of the consumer. Recently, Read et al. (2018) examined ads depicting same-sex couples and demonstrated how implicit attitudes are linked with cognitive processing and ad evaluations.

Looking beyond the studies of gender and advertising, several studies are located at the intersection of gender and other forms of media, including books, television shows, film, and new media. A range of research emphasizes the omnipresent and deep socializing force of gender in media, offering analyses rooted in both history as well as contemporary consumer culture. For instance, Brace-Govan's (2010) sociohistoric tracking of the representations of women's physically active bodies in sports, exercise, and beyond revealed three themes—the restrictive body, the malleable body, and the viewed body. Cappellini and Parsons (2014) tracked the representation of gender in British Italian cookbooks, and Stevens et al. (2015, p. 578) explored the intersections of glamour and performativity within the Nigella brand narrative, exposing the "masquerade" of femininity. In understanding media as text, Kjeldgaard and Nielsen (2010) focused their analysis on the interpretative strategies within countervailing gender ideals among teenage girls near Mexico City with regard to the Mexican telenovela—a site for both modernity as well as traditional womanhood. Takhar et al. (2010) also found media a site to negotiate identity, this time in the context of Bollywood films, which serve as a narrative space to navigate ethnic identity, gender, and romance for the British Sikh community. Yalkin and Veer (2018) found that Turkish soap operas act as texts that challenge religious, sexual, and gender norms and provide a space for discussions of the taboo. Zayer et al. (2012) examined representations and performances of gender, comparing themes of gender fluidity across two popular television shows, and illustrated the role of consumption in both as a means to ease tensions as well as create new tensions.

While traditional media texts continue to serve as sites for investigation, broader shifts in technology and new media consumption are taking shape, and scholars are seeking to capture the unique dynamics with regard to an understanding of gender. Interestingly, gender, marketing, and consumer research within social media and new media contexts focuses largely on women's experiences and discourses of female empowerment online (Zayer et al., 2019) or in feminized spaces (Williams et al., 2019). For example, through the lens of queer theory, Gurrieri and Cherrier (2013) examined "fatshion" blog posts to illuminate how women disrupt normalized standards of beauty. Pounders, Stowers, et al. (2017) analyzed online discussion boards for cancer support groups, bringing to light gender and identity issues of adolescent girls and young women in regard to fertility, motherhood, appearance, and romance. Examining visual and textual content of female influencers on Instagram, Drenten et al. (2020) documented sexualized labor in regard to the attention economy and monetization within social media platforms.

Recent research has moved beyond social media platforms to gaming, although their contributions move beyond the context itself. Illuminating issues related to the ethics of representation of gender, Schroeder and Borgerson (2015) provided a commentary on the "Gamergate" phenomenon and the related harassment of media analyst Anita Sarkeesian, whose work exposed tropes of women in video games. Drenten et al. (2019) further underlined gaming as a gendered pursuit, tracing the history of gender and video games and providing promising new future research directions. These studies, situated in 'new' media contexts (and many others in diverse fields such as digital humanities and computer science), will continue to inform understandings of gender in a post-Web 2.0 era. In the following sections, other promising areas for research are outlined, including macro, intersectional, and transformative perspectives that have flourished but are still ripe for further exploration.

FUTURE DIRECTIONS

Macro Issues, Transnationality, and Gender

Research taking a more macro focus, spurred in part by theoretical framings such as institutional theory, seeks to provide a holistic picture of the dynamics between consumers, markets, and marketing. For example, Sredl (2018) illuminated consumer experiences based on the shifting role of state and market ideologies through her study of family meal rituals in postsocialist Croatia, while Molander et al. (2019) conducted a critical visual analysis of images to unpack how the state ideology in Sweden serves to foster new ideals of fatherhood. Cappellini et al.

(2014) linked the hidden micropolitics of household inequalities and coping practices of Italian women within the context of the macro disruption of an economic recession. While these studies sensitize researchers to the macro dynamics at play with regard to consumption, other research also highlights the limitations encountered when examining such issues with existing frameworks or theories of gender. In this vein, Sredl (2019) underscored the importance of transnational gender theory in bringing to light oppressions uniquely felt within postsocialist contexts, and Sun (2015) emphasized the limitations of applying Western models of gender to other sociocultural contexts.

Importantly, gender research with regard to macro issues seeks to connect micro-, meso-, and macrolevels of analyses in illuminating phenomena across a range of topics. For example, Ferguson et al. (2020) illustrated how women climbers experience inequity in a consumption subculture by examining the interconnectedness of micro-, meso-, and macrolevels. Additionally, Zayer et al. (2020) bridged micro- and macrolevels of analyses in a study that spanned over three time periods and across three countries to shed light on resistance to gendered messages in advertising against the backdrop of institutional theory. Looking ahead, a more macro- or institutional-focused scholarship is expected to flourish. Indeed, Tissier-Desbordes and Visconti (2019) noted in the special issue of *Consumption Markets & Culture* on gender that consumer research scholarship will continue to emphasize the macro, political aspects of gender.

Intersectionality

Although intersectionality as a method and theoretical perspective to understanding gender is not new, a growing interest in intersectionality in marketing, advertising, and consumer research can be seen as scholars increasingly abandon the notion of unidimensionality. The intersections of identity markers (e.g., social class, age, sexuality, body) and resulting oppressions within the context of consumption and markets is a burgeoning area of research. Early work by Friend and Thompson (2003) examined intersections of ethnicity and gender in shopping, whereas Lindridge and Hogg (2006) explored age and gender within family consumption. However, it is the work of Gopaldas and Fischer (2012), Gopaldas (2013), and Gopaldas and DeRoy (2015) that has brought discussions of intersectionality and gender to the forefront of consumer research. Indeed, more recent scholarship has highlighted not merely an intersection of identities but the tensions and oppressions felt by consumers through, for example, experiences of nonbinary individuals (McKeage et al., 2018), consumption of reproductive health services (Steinfield, Coleman, et al., 2019), and intersectionality in politics (see Sanghvi's, 2019, book on gender and political marketing in the United States), as well as the "undoing" of gender (Seregina, 2019).

Transformative Consumer Research and Gender

In David Mick's "Association for Consumer Research Presidential Address" in 2005, he laid out a vision for consumer researchers moving forward in what would be called *transformative consumer research*, or "investigations that are framed by a fundamental problem or opportunity, and that strive to respect, uphold, and improve life in relation to the myriad conditions, demands, potentialities, and effects of consumption" (Mick, 2006, p. 2). Research following this orientation, and subsequently what would be referred to as transformative service research, flourished, and stand-alone TCR conferences are held biennially, featuring substantive areas such as poverty, health care, food consumption, and in 2015, the first track on gender issues. Motivated by this initial momentum, a number of publications oriented in the TCR tradition have tackled topics related to gender justice and marketing and consumer research. While other scholars emphasize the role of social marketing as a tool to fight gender inequality (see, e.g., Martam's, 2016, commentary on gender inequality in Indonesia), TCR-grounded researchers look to recognition, capabilities, and social distributive justice theories to develop a transformative gender justice framework (TGJF). Hein et al. (2016) introduced the TGJF and demonstrated its application to a case study of sex tourism, while providing guidance on how it could be applied to future examinations of gender issues.

Specifically, Hein et al. (p. 234) prompted scholars to ask the following questions: (a) Is gender identified? Why or why not? (b) How do levels of analysis interact recursively? and (c) What role do markets, policy, and marketing play? Subsequent applications of this framework focused on transformative intersectionality (Steinfield, Sanghvi, et al., 2019) and readings of power dynamics in the reproductive health market (Steinfield, Coleman, et al., 2019). Indeed, Zayer et al. (2017) provided an overview of a TCR perspective on gender within the broader literature on gender, self, and identity, while Steinfield, Littlefield, et al. (2019) provided future directions for research from a TCR perspective, including broadening the study of gender. Importantly, in light of important social movements (e.g., #MeToo and #BlackLivesMatter) and the pandemic that swept the globe, TCR informed research is more critical now than ever, as existing inequalities and disparities have been exacerbated. Coleman et al. (2021) in their editorial in the Genders, Markets, and Consumers issue of the *Journal of Association for Consumer Research* called for scholars to examine vital gendered issues such as caretaking, access to market resources, and interconnections between work, labor, and consumption in future research.

CONCLUSION

In summary, the future of gender research will bring a richer, more nuanced understanding of gender as it relates to marketing, advertising, and consumer research while building on the breadth and depth of important prior scholarship, which draws from multiple, interdisciplinary areas. The recent resurgence of interest in popular culture, politics, business, and academia with regard to gender (e.g., see recent special issues in the *Journal of Macromarketing* edited by Guerri et al., 2020, and in the *Journal of Marketing Management* edited by Dobscha & Östberg, 2021) holds promise for further research in this area—one that scholars are hopeful will also bring about positive social change in society.

REFERENCES

Åkestam, N. (2018). Caring for her: The influence of presumed influence on female consumers' attitudes towards advertising featuring gender-stereotyped portrayals. *International Journal of Advertising*, 37(6), 871–892. https://doi.org/10.1080/02650487.2017.1384198

Arnould, E., & Thompson, C. (2005). Consumer culture theory (CCT): Twenty years of research. *Journal of Consumer Research*, 31(4), 868–882. https://doi.org/10.1086/426626

Barlett, C. P., Vowels, C. L., & Saucier, D. A. (2008). Meta-analyses of the effects of media images on men's body-image concerns. *Journal of Social and Clinical Psychology*, 27(3), 279–310. https://doi.org/10.1521/jscp.2008.27.3.279

Belk, R. W. (1988). Possessions and the extended self. *Journal of Consumer Research*, 15(2), 139–168. https://doi.org/10.1086/209154

Bellizzi, J., & Milner, L. (1991). Gender positioning of a traditionally male-dominant product. *Journal of Advertising Research*, 31(3), 72–79.

Bem, S. L. (1974). The measurement of psychological androgyny. *Journal of Consulting and Clinical Psychology*, 42(2), 155–162. https://doi.org/10.1037/h0036215

Bettany, S., Dobscha, S., O'Malley, L., & Prothero, A. (2010). Moving beyond binary opposition: Exploring the tapestry of gender in consumer research and marketing. *Marketing Theory*, 10(1), 3–28. https://doi.org/10.1177/1470593109355244

Bissell, K., & Rask, A. (2010). Real women on real beauty: Self-discrepancy, internalization of the thin ideal, and perceptions of attractiveness and thinness in Dove's Campaign for Real Beauty. *International Journal of Advertising*, 29(4), 643–668. https://doi.org/10.2501/S0265048710201385

Blanchette, A. (2014). Revisiting the "passée": History rewriting in the neo-burlesque community. *Consumption Markets & Culture*, 17(2), 158–184. https://doi.org/10.1080/10253866.2013.776307

Borau, S., & Bonnefon, J. F. (2017). The advertising performance of non-ideal female models as a function of viewers' body mass index: A moderated mediation analysis of two competing affective pathways. *International Journal of Advertising*, 36(3), 457–476. https://doi.org/10.1080/02650487.2015.1135773

Borgerson, J., Schroeder, J. E., Blomberg, B., & Thorssén, E. (2006). The gay family in the ad: Consumer responses to non-traditional families in marketing communications. *Journal of Marketing Management*, 22(9–10), 955–978. https://doi.org/10.1362/026725706778935646

Brace-Govan, J. (2010). Representations of women's active embodiment and men's ritualized visibility in sport. *Marketing Theory*, 10(4), 369–396. https://doi.org/10.1177/1470593110382825

Bristor, J. M., & Fischer, E. (1993). Feminist thought: Implications for consumer research. *Journal of Consumer Research*, 19(4), 518–536.

Butler, J. (2004). *Undoing gender*. Routledge. https://doi.org/10.4324/9780203499627

Buunk, A. P., & Dijkstra, P. (2011). Does attractiveness sell? Women's attitude toward a product as a function of model attractiveness, gender priming, and social comparison orientation. *Psychology and Marketing*, 28(9), 958–973. https://doi.org/10.1002/mar.20421

Caldwell, M., Kleppe, I. A., & Henry, P. (2007). Presuming multiple gender role identities: A multi-country written and audio-visual exploration of contemporary young mainstream female achievers. *Consumption Markets & Culture*, 10(2), 95–115. https://doi.org/10.1080/10253860701256166

Cappellini, B., Marilli, A., & Parsons, E. (2014). The hidden work of coping: Gender and the micro-politics of household consumption in times of austerity. *Journal of Marketing Management*, 30(15–16), 1597–1624. https://doi.org/10.1080/0267257X.2014.929164

Cappellini, B., & Parsons, E. (2014). Constructing the culinary consumer: Transformative and reflective processes in Italian cookbooks. *Consumption Markets & Culture*, 17(1), 71–99. https://doi.org/10.1080/10253866.2012.701893

Catterall, M., Maclaran, P., & Stevens, L. (Eds.). (2000). *Marketing and feminism: Current issues and research*. Routledge.

Chen, S. (2012). The rise of 草食系男子 (soushokukei danshi) masculinity and consumption in contemporary Japan. In C. C. Otnes & L. T. Zayer (Eds.), *Gender, culture, and consumer behavior* (pp. 285–310). Routledge.

Chytkova, Z. (2011). Consumer acculturation, gender, and food: Romanian women in Italy between tradition and modernity. *Consumption Markets & Culture*, 14(3), 267–291. https://doi.org/10.1080/10253866.2011.574827

Coffin, J., Eichert, C. A., & Nolke, A. I. (2019). Towards (and beyond) LGBTQ+ studies in marketing and consumer research. In S. Dobcha (Ed.), *Handbook of research on gender and marketing* (pp. 273–293). Edward Elger Publishing. https://doi.org/10.4337/9781788115384.00017

Coleman, C., Fischer, E. & Zayer, L.T. (2021). A research agenda for (gender) troubled times: Striving for a better tomorrow. *Journal of the Association for Consumer Research*, 6(2), 205–210. https://doi.org/10.1086/713187

Coleman, C., Zayer, L.T., & Hesapçi, Ö. (2020). Institutional logics, gender, and advertising within a culture in transition: Examining strategies of Advertising professionals in turkey for managing institutional complexity. *Journal of Macromarketing*, 40(4), 510-527. https://doi.org/10.1177/0276146720948953

Coskuner-Balli, G., & Thompson, C. (2013). The status costs of subordinate cultural capital: At-home fathers' collective pursuit of cultural legitimacy through capitalizing consumption practices. *Journal of Consumer Research*, 40(1), 19–41. https://doi.org/10.1086/668640

Cruz, A., Gracia, B., & Buchanan-Oliver, M. (2017). Mobile masculinities: Performances of remasculation. *European Journal of Marketing*, 51(7/8), 1374–1395. https://doi.org/10.1108/EJM-04-2016-0199

Dahl, D. W., Sengupta, J., & Vohs, K. D. (2009). Sex in advertising: Gender differences and the role of relationship commitment. *Journal of Consumer Research*, 36(2), 215–231. https://doi.org/10.1086/597158

Diedrichs, P. C., & Lee, C. (2010). GI Joe or Average Joe? The impact of average-size and muscular male fashion models on men's and women's body image and advertisement effectiveness. *Body Image*, 7(3), 218–226. https://doi.org/10.1016/j.bodyim.2010.03.004

Dobscha, S. (2019). *Handbook of research on gender and marketing*. Edward Elgar Publishing. https://doi.org/10.4337/9781788115384

Dobscha, S., & Östberg, J. (2021). Introduction to the special issue on gender impacts: Consumption, markets, marketing, and marketing organizations. *Journal of Marketing Management*, 37(3–4), 181–187. https://doi.org/10.1080/0267257X.2021.1880163

Dobscha, S., & Ozanne, J. (2001). An ecofeminist analysis of environmentally sensitive women using qualitative methodology: The emancipatory potential of an ecological life. *Journal of Public Policy & Marketing*, 20(2), 201–214. https://doi.org/10.1509/jppm.20.2.201.17360

Drenten, J., Gurreri, L., & Tyler, M. (2020). Sexualized labour in digital culture: Instagram influencers, porn chic and the monetization of attention. *Gender, Work & Organization*, 27(1), 41–66. https://doi.org/10.1111/gwao.12354

Drenten, J., Harrison, R. L., & Pendarvis, N. J. (2019). Video gaming as a gendered pursuit. In S. Dobcha (Ed.), *Handbook of research on gender and marketing* (pp. 28–44). Edward Elger Publishing. https://doi.org/10.4337/9781788115384.00007

Eisend, M. (2019). Gender roles. *Journal of Advertising*, 48(1), 72–80. https://doi.org/10.1080/00913367.2019.1566103

Eisend, M., Plagemann, J., & Sollwedel, J. (2014). Gender roles and humor in advertising: The occurrence of stereotyping in humorous and nonhumorous advertising and its consequences for advertising effectiveness. *Journal of Advertising, 43*(3), 256–273. https://doi.org/10.1080/00913367.2013.857621

Ferguson, S., Brace-Govan, J., & Martin, D. M. (2020). Gender status bias and the marketplace. *Journal of Business Research, 107*, 211–221. https://doi.org/10.1016/j.jbusres.2018.11.047

Fischer, E., & Arnold, S. J. (1990). More than a labor of love: Gender roles and Christmas gift shopping. *Journal of Consumer Research, 17*(3), 333–345. https://doi.org/10.1086/208561

Friend, L., & Thompson, S. (2003). Identity, ethnicity and gender: Using narratives to understand their meaning in retail shopping encounters. *Consumption Markets & Culture, 6*(1), 23–41. https://doi.org/10.1080/10253860302698

Frith, H., & Gleeson, K. (2004). Clothing and embodiment: Men managing body image and appearance. *Psychology of Men & Masculinity, 5*(1), 40–48. https://doi.org/10.1037/1524-9220.5.1.40

Gentry, J., & Harrison, R. (2010). Is advertising a barrier to male movement toward gender change? *Marketing Theory, 10*(1), 74–96. https://doi.org/10.1177/1470593109355246

Goffman, E. (1959). *The presentation of the self in everyday life*. DoubleDay & Company, Inc.

Goffman, E. (1979). *Gender advertisements*. Harper & Row.

Gopaldas, A. (2013). Intersectionality 101. *Journal of Public Policy & Marketing, 32*(1 Suppl.), 90–94. https://doi.org/10.1509/jppm.12.044

Gopaldas, A., & DeRoy, G. (2015). An intersectional approach to diversity research. *Consumption Markets & Culture, 18*(4), 333–364. https://doi.org/10.1080/10253866.2015.1019872

Gopaldas, A., & Fischer, E. (2012). Beyond gender: Intersectionality, culture, and consumer behavior. In C. C. Otnes & L. T. Zayer (Eds.), *Gender, culture, and consumer behavior* (p. 394–408). Routledge.

Goulding, C., & Saren, M. (2009). Performing identity: An analysis of gender expressions at the Whitby goth festival. *Consumption Markets & Culture, 12*(1), 27–46. https://doi.org/10.1080/10253860802560813

Grau, S. L., & Zotos, Y. C. (2016). Gender stereotypes in advertising: A review of current research. *International Journal of Advertising, 35*(5), 761–770. https://doi.org/10.1080/02650487.2016.1203556

Gurrieri, L., Brace-Govan, J., & Cherrier, H. (2016). Controversial advertising: Transgressing the taboo of gender-based violence. *European Journal of Marketing, 50*(7/8), 1448–1469. https://doi.org/10.1108/EJM-09-2014-0597

Gurrieri, L., & Cherrier, H. (2013). Queering beauty: Fatshionistas in the fatosphere. *Qualitative Market Research, 16*(3), 276–295. https://doi.org/10.1108/13522751311326107

Gurrieri, L., Previte, J., & Prothero, A. (2020). Hidden in plain sight: Building visibility for critical gender perspectives exploring markets, marketing and society. *Journal of Macromarketing, 40*(4), 437–444. https://doi.org/10.1177/0276146720952530

Hearn, J., & Hein, W. (2015). Reframing gender and feminist knowledge construction in marketing and consumer research: Missing feminisms and the case of men and masculinities. *Journal of Marketing Management, 31*(15–16), 1626–1651. https://doi.org/10.1080/0267257X.2015.1068835

Hein, W., & O'Donohoe, S. (2014). Practising gender: The role of banter in young men's improvisations of masculine consumer identities. *Journal of Marketing Management, 30*(13–14), 1293–1319. https://doi.org/10.1080/0267257X.2013.852608

Hein, W., Steinfield, L., Ourahmoune, N., Coleman, C., Zayer, L. T., & Littlefield, J. (2016). Gender justice and the market: A transformative consumer research perspective. *Journal of Public Policy & Marketing, 35*(2), 223–236. https://doi.org/10.1509/jppm.15.146

Higgins, E. T. (1987). Self-discrepancy: A theory relating self and affect. *Psychological Review, 94*(3), 319–340. https://doi.org/10.1037/0033-295X.94.3.319

Hirschman, E. (1993). Ideology in consumer research, 1980 and 1990: A Marxist and feminist critique. *Journal of Consumer Research, 19*(4), 537–555. https://doi.org/10.1086/209321

Hirschman, E. (2003). Men, dogs, guns, and cars: The semiotics of rugged individualism. *Journal of Advertising, 32*(1), 9–22. https://doi.org/10.1080/00913367.2003.10601001

Holt, D. B., & Thompson, C. J. (2004). Man-of-action heroes: The pursuit of heroic masculinity in everyday consumption. *Journal of Consumer Research, 31*(2), 425–440. https://doi.org/10.1086/422120

Houston, H. R. (2004). Other mothers: Framing the cybernetic constructions of the postmodern family. *Consumption Markets & Culture, 7*(3), 191–209. https://doi.org/10.1080/1025386042000271333

Huhmann, B. A., & Limbu, Y. B. (2016). Influence of gender stereotypes on advertising offensiveness and attitude toward advertising in general. *International Journal of Advertising, 35*(5), 846–863. https://doi.org/10.1080/02650487.2016.1157912

Jaffe, L. J., & Berger, P. D. (1994). The effect of modern female sex role portrayals on advertising effectiveness. *Journal of Advertising Research, 34*(4), 32–42.

Johnston, J., & Taylor, J. (2008). Feminist consumerism and fat activists: A comparative study of grassroots activism and the Dove Real Beauty campaign. *Signs: Journal of Women in Culture and Society, 33*(4), 941–966. https://doi.org/10.1086/528849

Joy, A., Belk, R., & Bhardwaj, R. (2015). Judith Butler on performativity and precarity: Exploratory thoughts on gender and violence in India. *Journal of Marketing Management, 31*(15-16), 1739–1745. https://doi.org/10.1080/0267257X.2015.1076873

Joy, A., & Venkatesh, A. (1994). Postmodernism, feminism, and the body: The visible and the invisible in consumer research. *International Journal of Research in Marketing, 11*(4), 333–357. https://doi.org/10.1016/0167-8116(94)90011-6

Kates, S. M. (2000). Out of the closet and out on the street! Gay men and their brand relationships. *Psychology and Marketing, 17*(6), 493–513. https://doi.org/10.1002/(SICI)1520-6793(200006)17:6<493::AID-MAR4>3.0.CO;2-F

Kates, S. M. (2002). The protean quality of subcultural consumption: An ethnographic account of gay consumers. *Journal of Consumer Research, 29*(3), 383–399. https://doi.org/10.1086/344427

Kates, S. M. (2004). The dynamics of brand legitimacy: An interpretive study in the gay men's community. *Journal of Consumer Research, 31*(2), 455–464. https://doi.org/10.1086/422122

Kjeldgaard, D., & Nielsen, K. S. (2010). Glocal gender identities in market places of transition: MARIANISMO and the consumption of the telenovela Rebelde. *Marketing Theory, 10*(1), 29–44. https://doi.org/10.1177/1470593109355249

Klasson, M., & Ulver, S. (2015). Masculinising domesticity: An investigation of men's domestic foodwork. *Journal of Marketing Management, 31*(15–16), 1652–1675. https://doi.org/10.1080/0267257X.2015.1078395

Koerning, S. K., & Granitz, N. (2006). Progressive yet traditional. *Journal of Advertising, 35*(2), 81–98. https://doi.org/10.1080/00913367.2006.10639235

Lai, A. L., Lim, M., & Higgins, M. (2015). The abject single: Exploring the gendered experience of singleness in Britain. *Journal of Marketing Management, 31*(15–16), 1559–1582. https://doi.org/10.1080/0267257X.2015.1073170

Lambiase, J., Bronstein, C., & Coleman, C. (2017). Women vs. brands: Sexist advertising and gender stereotypes motivate trans-generational feminist critique. In K. Golombisky & P. Kreshel (Eds.), *Feminists, feminism, and advertising: Some restrictions apply* (pp. 29–59). Lexington Books.

Lindridge, A., & Hogg, M. K. (2006). Parental gatekeeping in diasporic Indian families: Examining the intersection of culture, gender and consumption. *Journal of Marketing Management, 22*(9–10), 979–1008. https://doi.org/10.1362/026725706778935628

Lindridge, A., Peñaloza, L., & Worlu, O. (2016). Agency and empowerment in consumption in relation to a patriarchal bargain. *European Journal of Marketing, 50*(9/10), 1652–1671. https://doi.org/10.1108/EJM-07-2011-0365

Littlefield, J. (2010). Men on the hunt: Ecofeminist insights into masculinity. *Marketing Theory, 10*(1), 97–117. https://doi.org/10.1177/1470593109355250

Littlefield, J., & Ozanne, J. (2011). Socialization into consumer culture: Hunters learning to be men. *Consumption Markets & Culture, 14*(4), 333–360. https://doi.org/10.1080/10253866.2011.604494

Liu, C. (2019). Men and their groomed body: Understanding personal grooming as both a discursive and embodied practice. *European Journal of Marketing, 53*(5), 1015–1034. https://doi.org/10.1108/EJM-04-2017-0291

Maclaran, P. (2012). Marketing and feminism in historic perspective. *Journal of Historical Research in Marketing, 4*(3), 462–469. https://doi.org/10.1108/17557501211252998

Maclaran, P. (2015). Feminism's fourth wave: A research agenda for marketing and consumer research. *Journal of Marketing Management, 31*(15–16), 1732–1738. https://doi.org/10.1080/0267257X.2015.1076497

Maclaran, P., Miller, C., Parsons, E., & Surman, E. (2009). Praxis or performance: Does critical marketing have a gender blind-spot? *Journal of Marketing Management, 25*(7–8), 713–728. https://doi.org/10.1362/026725709X471587

Maclaran, P., Otnes, C. C., & Zayer, L. T. (2017). Gender, sexuality and consumption. In M. Keller, B. Halkier, T. A. Wilska, & M. Truninger (Eds.), *Routledge handbook on consumption* (pp. 292–302). Routledge. https://doi.org/10.4324/9781315675015-29

Marshall, D., Davis, T., Hogg, M., Schneider, T., & Petersen, A. (2014). From overt provider to invisible presence: Discursive shifts in advertising portrayals of the father in *Good Housekeeping*, 1950–2010. *Journal of Marketing Management, 30*(15–16), 1654–1679. https://doi.org/10.1080/0267257X.2014.945471

Martam, I. (2016). Strategic social marketing to foster gender equality in Indonesia. *Journal of Marketing Management, 32*(11–12), 1174–1182. https://doi.org/10.1080/0267257X.2016.1193989

Martin, D., Schouten, J., & McAlexander, J. (2006). Claiming the throttle: Multiple femininities in a hyper-masculine subculture. *Consumption Markets & Culture, 9*(3), 171–205. https://doi.org/10.1080/10253860600772206

McKeage, K., Crosby, E., & Rittenburg, T. (2018). Living in a gender-binary world: Implications for a revised model of consumer vulnerability. *Journal of Macromarketing*, 38(1), 73–90. https://doi.org/10.1177/0276146717723963

Meyers-Levy, J. (1988). The influence of sex roles on judgment. *Journal of Consumer Research*, 14(4), 522–530. https://doi.org/10.1086/209133

Meyers-Levy, J., & Maheswaran, D. (1991). Exploring differences in males' and females' processing strategies. *Journal of Consumer Research*, 18(1), 63–70. https://doi.org/10.1086/209241

Mick, D. G. (2006). Presidential address: Meaning and mattering through transformative consumer research. In C. Pechmann & L. Price (Eds.), *NA - Advances in consumer research* (Vol. 33, pp. 1–4). Association for Consumer Research.

Micu, C. C., & Coulter, R. (2012). The effect of attractiveness in advertising and comparison motives on self-judgements and product evaluations: A cross-national perspective. *Journal of International Consumer Marketing*, 24(1–2), 79–99. https://doi.org/10.1080/08961530.2012.650140

Modrak, R. (2015). Learning to talk like an urban woodsman: An artistic intervention. *Consumption Markets & Culture*, 18(6), 539–558. https://doi.org/10.1080/10253866.2015.1052968

Moisio, R., Arnould, E. J., & Gentry, J. W. (2013). Productive consumption in the class-mediated construction of domestic masculinity: Do-it-yourself (DIY) home improvement in men's identity work. *Journal of Consumer Research*, 40(2), 298–316. https://doi.org/10.1086/670238

Molander, S., Kleppe, I. A., & Ostberg, J. (2019). Hero shots: Involved fathers conquering new discursive territory in consumer culture. *Consumption Markets & Culture*, 22(4), 430–453. https://doi.org/10.1080/10253866.2018.1512252

Nelson, M. R., & Paek, H. J. (2008). Nudity of female and male models in primetime TV advertising across seven countries. *International Journal of Advertising*, 27(5), 715–744. https://doi.org/10.2501/S0265048708080281

Nixon, S., & Crewe, B. (2004). Pleasure at work? Gender, consumption and work-based identities in the creative industries. *Consumption Markets & Culture*, 7(2), 129–147. https://doi.org/10.1080/1025386042000246197

Oakenfull, G. K., & Greenlee, T. B. (2005). Queer eye for a gay guy: Using market-specific symbols in advertising to attract gay consumers without alienating the mainstream. *Psychology and Marketing*, 22(5), 421–439. https://doi.org/10.1002/mar.20066

Oakenfull, G. K., McCarthy, M. S., & Greenlee, T. B. (2008). Targeting a minority without alienating the majority: Advertising to gays and lesbians in mainstream media. *Journal of Advertising Research*, 48(2), 191–198. https://doi.org/10.2501/S0021849908080239

Ostberg, J. (2010). Thou shalt sport a banana in thy pocket: Gendered body size ideals in advertising and popular culture. *Marketing Theory*, 10(1), 45–73. https://doi.org/10.1177/1470593109355255

Ostberg, J. (2012). Masculinity and fashion. In C. C. Otnes & L. T. Zayer (Eds.), *Gender, culture, and consumer behavior* (pp. 255–283). Routledge.

Otnes, C. C., & McGrath, M. A. (2001). Perceptions and realities of male shopping behavior. *Journal of Retailing*, 77(1), 111–137. https://doi.org/10.1016/S0022-4359(00)00047-6

Otnes, C. C., & Zayer, L. T. (Eds.). (2012). *Gender, culture, and consumer behavior*. Routledge. https://doi.org/10.4324/9780203127575

Ourahmoune, N. (2012). Masculinity, intimacy, and consumption. In C. C. Otnes & L. T. Zayer (Eds.), *Gender, culture, and consumer behavior* (pp. 311–335). Routledge.

Ourahmoune, N., & Özçağlar-Toulouse, N. (2012). Exogamous weddings and fashion in a rising consumer culture: Kabyle minority dynamics of structure and agency. *Marketing Theory*, 12(1), 81–99. https://doi.org/10.1177/1470593111424182

Patterson, M., & Elliott, R. (2002). Negotiating masculinities: Advertising and the inversion of the male gaze. *Consumption Markets & Culture*, 5(3), 231–249. https://doi.org/10.1080/10253860290031631

Peñaloza, L. (1994). Crossing boundaries/drawing lines: A look at the nature of gender trouble in marketing research. *International Journal of Research in Marketing*, 11(4), 359–379. https://doi.org/10.1016/0167-8116(94)90012-4

Pounders, K., & Mabry-Flynn, A. (2019). Consumer response toward plus-size models featured in the mainstream media. *Journal of Consumer Affairs*, 53(4), 1355–1379. https://doi.org/10.1111/joca.12251

Pounders, K., Rice, D. H., & Mabry-Flynn, A. (2017). Understanding how goal-striving, goal orientation, and shame influence self-perceptions after exposure to models in advertising. *Psychology and Marketing*, 34(5), 538–555. https://doi.org/10.1002/mar.21004

Pounders, K., Stowers, K., Wilcox, G., Love, B., & Mackert, M. (2017). Exploring gender and identity issues among female adolescent and young adults who connect in an anonymous platform. *Journal of Health Psychology*, 22(5), 548–560. https://doi.org/10.1177/1359105315605657

Putrevu, S. (2008). Consumer responses toward sexual and nonsexual appeals: The influence of involvement, need for cognition (NFC), and gender. *Journal of Advertising*, 37(2), 57–70. https://doi.org/10.2753/JOA0091-3367370205

Read, G., van Driel, I., & Potter, R. (2018). Same-sex couples in advertisements: An investigation of the role of implicit attitudes on cognitive processing and evaluation. *Journal of Advertising*, 47(2), 182–197. https://doi.org/10.1080/00913367.2018.1452653

Reichert, T., Latour, M., & Kim, J. Y. (2007). Assessing the influence of gender and sexual self-schema on affective responses to sexual content in advertising. *Journal of Current Issues and Research in Advertising*, 29(2), 63–77. https://doi.org/10.1080/10641734.2007.10505217

Sanghvi, M. (2019). *Gender and political marketing in the United States and the 2016 presidential election*. Palgrave Macmillan. https://doi.org/10.1007/978-1-137-60171-1

Schmitt, B., LeClerc, F., & Dube-Rioux, L. (1988). Sex typing and gender schema theory. *Journal of Consumer Research*, 15(1), 122–128. https://doi.org/10.1086/209151

Schouten, J. (1991). Selves in transition: Symbolic consumption in personal rites of passage and identity reconstruction. *Journal of Consumer Research*, 17(4), 412–425. https://doi.org/10.1086/208567

Schroeder, J., & Borgerson, J. (2015). Critical visual analysis of gender: Reactions and reflections. *Journal of Marketing Management*, 31(15–16), 1723–1731. https://doi.org/10.1080/0267257X.2015.1077883

Schroeder, J., & Zwick, D. (2004). Mirrors of masculinity: Representation and identity in advertising images. *Consumption Markets & Culture*, 7(1), 21–52. https://doi.org/10.1080/1025386042000212383

Scott, L. M. (2005). *Fresh lipstick: Redressing fashion and feminism*. Palgrave MacMillan.

Sengupta, J., & Dahl, D. (2008). Gender-related reactions to gratuitous sex appeals in advertising. *Journal of Consumer Psychology*, 18(1), 62–78. https://doi.org/10.1016/j.jcps.2007.10.010

Seregina, A. (2019). Undoing gender through performing the other. *Consumption Markets & Culture*, 22(4), 454–473. https://doi.org/10.1080/10253866.2018.1512254

Shao, Y., Desmarais, F., & Weaver, C. K. (2014). Chinese advertising practitioners' conceptualization of gender representation. *International Journal of Advertising*, 33(2), 329–350. https://doi.org/10.2501/IJA-33-2-329-350

Sherry, J. F., Jr., Kozinets, R. V., Duhachek, A., DeBerry-Spence, B., Nuttavuthisit, K., & Storm, D. (2004). Gendered behavior in a male preserve: Role playing at ESPN Zone Chicago. *Journal of Consumer Psychology*, 14(1–2), 151–158. https://doi.org/10.1207/s15327663jcp1401&2_17

Sirgy, J. M. (1982). Self-concept in consumer behavior: A critical review. *Journal of Consumer Research*, 9(3), 287–300. https://doi.org/10.1086/208924

Smeesters, D., Mussweiler, T., & Mandel, N. (2010). The effects of thin and heavy media images on overweight and underweight consumers: Social comparison processes and behavioral implications. *Journal of Consumer Research*, 36(6), 930–949. https://doi.org/10.1086/648688

Spence, J. T., Helmreich, R., & Stapp, J. (1975). Ratings of self and peers on sex role attributes and their relation to self-esteem and conceptions of masculinity and femininity. *Journal of Personality and Social Psychology*, 32(1), 29–39. https://doi.org/10.1037/h0076857

Sredl, K. (2018). Gendered market subjectivity: Autonomy, privilege, and emotional subjectivity in normalizing post-socialist neoliberal ideology. *Consumption Markets & Culture*, 21(6), 532–553. https://doi.org/10.1080/10253866.2017.1374950

Sredl, K. (2019). Gender east and west: Transnational gender theory and global marketing research. In S. Dobcha (Ed.), *Handbook of research on gender and marketing* (pp. 45–62). Edward Elger Publishing. https://doi.org/10.4337/9781788115384.00008

Steinfield, L., Coleman, C., Zayer, L. T., Ourahmoune, N., & Hein, W. (2019). Power logics of consumers' gendered (in)justices: Reading reproductive health interventions through the transformative gender justice framework. *Consumption Markets & Culture*, 22(4), 406–429. https://doi.org/10.1080/10253866.2018.1512250

Steinfield, L., Littlefield, J., Coleman, C., Hein, W., & Zayer, L. T. (2019). The TCR perspective of gender: Moving from critical theory to an activism-praxis orientation. In S. Dobcha (Ed.), *Handbook of research on gender and marketing* (pp. 186–210). Edward Elger Publishing. https://doi.org/10.4337/9781788115384.00013

Steinfield, L., Sanghvi, M., Zayer, L. T., Coleman, C., Ourahmoune, N., Harrison, R., Hein, W., & Brace-Govan, J. (2019). Transformative intersectionality: Moving business towards a critical praxis. *Journal of Business Research*, 100(July), 366–375. https://doi.org/10.1016/j.jbusres.2018.12.031

Stern, B. (1993). Feminist literary criticism and deconstruction of ads: A postmodern view of advertising and consumer responses. *Journal of Consumer Research*, 19(4), 556–566. https://doi.org/10.1086/209322

Stevens, L., Cappellini, B., & Smith, G. (2015). Nigellissima: A study of glamour, performativity, and embodiment. *Journal of Marketing Management*, 31(5–6), 577–598. https://doi.org/10.1080/0267257X.2014.1001771

Sun, Z. (2015). How advertising elicits desire and provides role models: Insights from colonialism. *Consumption Markets & Culture*, 18(4), 365–385. https://doi.org/10.1080/10253866.2015.1013469

Takhar, A., Maclaran, P., Parsons, E., & Broderick, A. (2010). Consuming Bollywood: Young Sikhs social comparisons with heroes and heroines in Indian films. *Journal of Marketing Management*, 26(11–12), 1057–1073. https://doi.org/10.1080/0267257X.2010.508978

Thompson, C. J. (1996). Caring consumers: Gendered consumption meanings and the juggling lifestyle. *Journal of Consumer Research*, 22(4), 388–407. https://doi.org/10.1086/209457

Thompson, C. J., & Üstüner, T. (2015). Women skating on the edge: Marketplace performances as ideological edgework. *Journal of Consumer Research*, 42(2), 235–265. https://doi.org/10.1093/jcr/ucv013

Tissier-Desbordes, E., & Visconti, L. (2019). Gender after gender: Fragmentation, intersectionality, and stereotyping. *Consumption Markets & Culture*, 22(4), 307–313. https://doi.org/10.1080/10253866.2018.1512238

Tsai, W.-H. S. (2010). Assimilating the queers: Representations of lesbians, gay men, bisexual, and transgender people in mainstream advertising. *Advertising & Society Review*, 11(1). https://doi.org/10.1353/ASR.0.0042

Tsichla, E., & Zotos, Y. (2016). Gender portrayals revisited: Searching for explicit and implicit stereotypes in Cypriot magazine advertisements. *International Journal of Advertising*, 35(6), 983–1007. https://doi.org/10.1080/02650487.2016.1189250

Tuncay, L., & Otnes, C. C. (2008a). Exploring the link between masculinity and consumption. In T. Lowrey (Ed.), *Brick & mortar shopping in the 21st century* (pp. 153–168). Erlbaum Associates.

Tuncay, L., & Otnes, C. C. (2008b). The use of persuasion management strategies by identity-vulnerable consumers: The case of heterosexual male shoppers. *Journal of Retailing*, 84(4), 487–499. https://doi.org/10.1016/j.jretai.2008.09.004

Valtonen, A., & Närvänen, E. (2015). Gendered reading of the body in the bed. *Journal of Marketing Management*, 31(15–16), 1583–1601. https://doi.org/10.1080/0267257X.2015.1061038

Visconti, L. M. (2008). Gays' market and social behaviors in (de)constructing symbolic boundaries. *Consumption Markets & Culture*, 11(2), 113–135. https://doi.org/10.1080/10253860802033647

Vokey, M., Tefft, B., & Tysiaczny, C. (2013). An analysis of hyper-masculinity in magazine advertisements. *Sex Roles*, 68(9–10), 562–576. https://doi.org/10.1007/s11199-013-0268-1

Williams, D., Nielsen, E. J., Morrison, M., & Morrison, T. (2019). Challenges to masculinity in a feminized digital space: Men as autonomous online agents on Pinterest. *Qualitative Market Research*, 22(2), 180–199. https://doi.org/10.1108/QMR-01-2017-0055

Windels, K. (2016). Stereotypical or just typical: How do US practitioners view the role and function of gender stereotypes in advertisements? *International Journal of Advertising*, 35(5), 864–887. https://doi.org/10.1080/02650487.2016.1160855

Wolf, M., Albinsson, P. A., & Becker, C. (2015). Do-It-Yourself projects as path toward female empowerment in a gendered market place. *Psychology and Marketing*, 32(2), 133–143. https://doi.org/10.1002/mar.20768

Yalkin, C., & Veer, E. (2018). Taboo on TV: Gender, religion, and sexual taboos in transnationally marketed Turkish soap operas. *Journal of Marketing Management*, 34(13–14), 1149–1171. https://doi.org/10.1080/0267257X.2018.1520738

Zayer, L. T. (2010). A typology of men's conceptualizations of ideal masculinity in advertising. *Advertising & Society Review*, 11(1). https://doi.org/10.1353/ASR.0.0041

Zayer, L. T., & Coleman, C. (2015). Advertising professionals' perceptions of the impact of gender portrayals on men and women: A question of ethics? *Journal of Advertising*, 44(3), 264–275. https://doi.org/10.1080/00913367.2014.975878

Zayer, L. T., Coleman, C., Hein, W., Littlefield, J., & Steinfield, L. (2017). Gender and the self: Traversing feminisms, masculinities, and intersectionality towards a transformative framework. In T. Lowrey & M. Solomon (Eds.), *The Routledge companion to consumer behavior* (pp. 147–161). Routledge. https://doi.org/10.4324/9781315526935-10

Zayer, L. T., Coleman, C., & Orjuela, J. L. R. (2019). Femvertising discourses and online consumer engagement: A case analysis of Under Armour's #IWillWhatIWant brand campaign. In J. A. Muniz Velazquez & C. Pulido (Eds.), *The Routledge handbook on positive communication* (pp. 203–212). Routledge. https://doi.org/10.4324/9781315207759-21

Zayer, L. T., McGrath, M. A., & Castro-González, P. (2020). Men and masculinities in a changing world: Delegitimizing gender ideals in advertising. *European Journal of Marketing*, 54(1), 238–260. https://doi.org/10.1108/EJM-07-2018-0502

Zayer, L. T., & Neier, S. (2011). An exploration of men's brand relationships. *Qualitative Market Research*, 14(1), 83–104. https://doi.org/10.1108/13522751111099337

Zayer, L. T., & Otnes, C. C. (2012). Climbing the ladder or chasing a dream? Men's responses to idealized portrayals of masculinity in advertising. In C. C.

Otnes & L. T. Zayer (Eds.), *Gender, culture, and consumer behavior* (pp. 87–110). Routledge.

Zayer, L. T., Sredl, K., Parmentier, M. A., & Coleman, C. (2012). Consumption and gender identity in popular media: Discourses of domesticity, authenticity, and sexuality. *Consumption Markets & Culture*, *15*(4), 333–357. https://doi.org/10.1080/10253866.2012.659437

CHAPTER 9

A STRUCTURAL VERSUS DYNAMIC VIEW OF PERSONALITY IN CONSUMER BEHAVIOR

Suresh Ramanathan

Consumers have a variety of distinguishing traits that manifest in different behaviors and responses to marketing actions. For example, traits such as price-consciousness, impulsiveness, mavenism, or need for cognition have been used to identify market segments (Ailawadi et al., 2001) among shoppers. Consumers' dispositional innovativeness, mavenism, and susceptibility to normative influence has been linked to trial probability of new packaged goods (Steenkamp & Gielens, 2003). A glance at the *Handbook of Marketing Scales* (Bearden et al., 2011) reveals an exhaustive list of scales designed to measure traits and individual differences in varied domains such as interpersonal orientation, self-concept, impulsiveness, compulsiveness, country image and affiliation, consumer opinion leadership, opinion seeking, innovativeness, and social influence.

These distinctions have evolved from a long tradition in personality psychology of identifying interindividual differences. Ever since Allport and Odbert's (1936) pathbreaking study of personality items in the English dictionary designed to yield terms that could be used to "distinguish the behavior of one human being from that of another" (p. 24), personality research largely focused its attention on unearthing interindividual differences on a variety of dimensions. Through the 1950s and 1960s, numerous researchers such as Cattell (1957, 1965) and H. J. Eysenck (1952, 1967) expanded on the theme of differential psychology, seeking to identify the genetic, physiological, emotional, cognitive, and societal underpinnings of human personality (Revelle et al., 2011). However, the task of identifying so many traits was clearly daunting. As Cattell (1965) remarked, "The trouble with measuring traits is that there are too many of them" (p. 55). Further, by the 1970s, research on personality psychology began to wane, the decline fueled by Mischel's (1968) hugely influential book, *Personality and Assessment*, where he called into question the basic assumption of trait theorists that an individual's behavior with regard to an underlying trait construct remained consistent and invariant across various contexts or situations. Instead, he argued that behavior is shaped mainly by the specific demands of a given situation and held that behavioral consistency reflecting the influence of specific traits is largely a myth. This was supported by scholars in marketing such as Kassarjian (1971), who suggested that the evidence on any relationship between traits and behavior was at best "equivocal," with most studies showing traits accounting for at most 10% of variance in behavior. Many of these studies threw in a laundry list of traits, each with its own inventory of atheoretical measures. As a result, personality theory came under withering criticism as a "study of small, non-replicable effects with no agreement about the proper structural representation of psychology" (Revelle et al., 2011, p. 14).

https://doi.org/10.1037/0000262-009
APA Handbook of Consumer Psychology, L. R. Kahle (Editor-in-Chief)
Copyright © 2022 by the American Psychological Association. All rights reserved.

The field enjoyed a resurgence in the late 1980s and 1990s as researchers began to identify commonalities in behavioral patterns across situations through factor analysis and cluster analysis techniques. Amid a variety of global trait measures developed during this time (California Q-Sort: Block & Block, 1980; Myers-Briggs Type Indicator: Myers & McCaulley, 1985), the consensus view settled on a five-factor model of personality. Thus was born the Big Five taxonomy (Goldberg, 1993; John & Srivastava, 1999) and the five-factor theory (McCrae & Costa, 1996), comprising extraversion, agreeableness, conscientiousness, openness to experience, and neuroticism. Such models describe the broad structure of stable interindividual differences and are primarily concerned with describing the "what" of personality rather than the "how" or the "why" (Revelle, 1995). Thus, questions such as "Why is an extraverted person more gregarious than an introvert?" cannot be answered.

This is where dynamic models of personality enter the picture. Born out of a philosophy that individual thoughts, feelings, and behaviors that underlie personality traits change from time to time and situation to situation rather than remain stable, dynamic models are particularly relevant in studying intra-individual differences in contrast to interindividual ones (Mischel & Shoda, 1995). While stability in traits is reflected partly in the overall average levels of various behaviors characterizing the trait, there is also information in the extent of change in these behaviors over time. Indeed, Steenkamp and Maydeu-Olivares (2015) studied 11 consumer traits among Dutch consumers over a 12-year period and found remarkable stability in almost all of them but also concluded that stability did not preclude change, with several traits showing a declining trend, most notably driven by age.

Such findings underscore the importance of studying personality from a dynamic systems perspective, with the central guiding principle being that personality is organized as a system of elements that interact with each other and the environment and evolve over time as a result of such interactions (Sosnowska et al., 2019). These elements include a variety of thoughts and feelings encompassing the person's encoding or construals of the self and situations. They also include goals, expectations, feeling states, and specific memories associated with various events that have been experienced (Mischel & Shoda, 1995). Dynamic systems acknowledge the stability of personality but also posit that there is substantial variability in behavior around the stable set point as a result of interactions with various situational elements (Cervone, 2005; Cervone & Little, 2019).

In this chapter, I examine personality through both the structural and the dynamic lenses. In the first section, I review research showing the evolution of the Big Five taxonomy and relate the underlying sublevels of traits to those relevant in the consumer domain. I then discuss models of personality that include cognitive and motivational drivers of behavior characterized by various traits. In the second section, I review literature on dynamical systems models of personality that allow for bottom-up evolution of traits from behaviors and represent personality as a self-organizing state that people settle into due to repeated instantiations of the same mental states and behaviors. In the final section, I delineate the distinctions in these approaches by examining one particular personality trait, consumer impulsiveness, through different lenses and show how the structural view of impulsiveness can be complemented by a dynamical approach, thereby providing for a more nuanced look at the trait.

STRUCTURAL MODELS OF PERSONALITY

Much of the dominant research on personality has focused on understanding the structure of stable interindividual personality differences. The effort has been in developing a taxonomy of between-person categories of personality and their underlying dimensions leading to population-level variations (McCrae & Costa, 2003; Saucier, 2003). This led to a variety of theories that dimensionalized the sources of variation in personality traits.

The Big Five and Five-Factor Personality Model

The structural approach attempts to find enduring mechanisms or qualities that define a person and distinguish them from others. Typically, this involves using factor analytic techniques to identify commonalities in the representation of dispositional features of individuals. Perhaps the most well-known and dominant theory in the literature is the five-factor taxonomy (McCrae & Costa, 1996), which posits that five dimensions are necessary and sufficient to characterize human personality: (a) extraversion, energy, or enthusiasm; (b) agreeableness, altruism, or affection; (c) conscientiousness, control, or constraint; (d) neuroticism, negative affectivity, or nervousness; and (e) openness to experience, originality, or open-mindedness. A closely related model is the Big Five (John & Srivastava, 1999), which used the lexical study approach (Allport & Odbert, 1936; Saucier & Goldberg, 1996) to identify the personality vocabulary that exists in natural language as encoded in dictionaries. Regardless of the methodology used, the general consensus in the personality literature was that the five dimensions identified by these models represented a fairly accurate description of human personality. However, critics pointed out that these models do not capture important facets of human personality, such as religiosity, honesty, and conservativeness (Paunonen & Jackson, 2000). In response, a six-factor model, HEXACO, was proposed to account for some missing characteristics (K. Lee & Ashton, 2004). This includes honesty-humility (H), emotionality (E), extraversion (X), agreeableness (A), conscientiousness (C), and openness to experience (O).

Despite the widespread adoption of the five-factor and Big Five models in the personality literature, there is very little use of this framework in the consumer behavior literature. A few scholars have attempted to link shopping motives and behavior to basic personality traits (Mooradian & Olver, 1997; Verplanken & Herabadi, 2001). In large part, the relative dearth of work on the role of personality, broadly construed, in consumer behavior, is due to the weak predictive accuracy of basic personality traits with respect to specific consumer actions. As a consequence, the field moved toward developing its own instruments to measure traits that were relevant.

Consumer Traits

A variety of scales have been used in the literature to explore individual differences in consumer responses. Some, but not all of them, are hierarchically related to the five factors discussed earlier and are the focus of this section. It is important to note that these traits may map onto more than one of the five factors, and I only report the strongest relationships as documented in the literature.

Related to openness to experience. Traits found to have a strong relationship with openness to experience include the following:

- *Need for cognition* (Cacioppo & Petty, 1982) measures individuals' inclination toward effortful cognitive activities. Individuals high in need for cognition think more than those low in the same about all information (Haugtvedt et al., 1992) and tend to have stronger attitudes that are more resistant to persuasion (Haugtvedt & Petty, 1992). There is a strong correlation between need for cognition and openness to experience (Fleischhauer et al., 2010; Sadowski & Cogburn, 1997).
- *Dispositional innovativeness* (Steenkamp & Gielens, 2003; Steenkamp et al., 1999) refers to consumers' propensity to try new offerings before others. Consistent with the definition of openness to experience, consumers who score high on the dispositional innovativeness scale are more open to change, more independent, and less dogmatic and conservative (Steenkamp et al., 1999). Steenkamp and Gielens (2003) showed that consumers with high dispositional innovativeness were more likely to try novel products and more susceptible to features and displays but were less influenced by advertising for new products.
- *Consumer exploratory tendencies* (Baumgartner & Steenkamp, 1996; Raju, 1980) measures consumers' tendencies to obtain mental stimulation by acquiring information about products or services out of curiosity. Consumers with high scores on this measure were seen to take more risks, seek more variety, display more curiosity in response to ads, and seek more information

out of curiosity (Baumgartner & Steenkamp, 1996), consistent with the conceptualization of openness to experience.

- *Need for uniqueness* (Snyder & Fromkin, 1977; Tian et al., 2001) represents the need to be different, to set oneself apart, or to be special. Consumers with a high need for uniqueness are more likely to choose products that are scarce (Snyder, 1992). They are also less likely to spread word of mouth for publicly consumed products (Cheema & Kaikati, 2010) and more likely to choose unconventional products when asked to provide reasons for their choice (Simonson & Nowlis, 2000). Need for uniqueness has been found to correlate positively with openness to experience and extraversion (Schumpe et al., 2016).
- *Regulatory focus, promotion* (Higgins, 1997) represents individuals' focus on attaining desirable outcomes and aspirations. Consumers with a promotion focus are more likely to respond positively to messages framed as gains or those that highlight positive consequences (A. Y. Lee & Aaker, 2004). They are also more likely to be responsive to free offers (e.g., Buy One Get One Free) compared with savings coupons and are more likely to add less familiar, more exotic products to their basket (Ramanathan & Dhar, 2010). Promotion focus has been found to correlate strongly with openness to experience and extraversion across multiple cultures (Higgins et al., 2008).

Each of these consumer traits is representative of the acceptance of ambiguity, autonomy of thought or behavior, willingness to take risks, and receptivity to new ideas that is characteristic of the trait of openness.

Related to conscientiousness. The trait of conscientiousness relates to self-control, task focus, responsibility, and adherence to rules and norms. Common consumer traits that are related to conscientiousness include the following:

- *Deal proneness* (Lichtenstein et al., 1993) refers to an increased propensity to respond to an offer where the price is presented positively relative to expectations. Deal proneness creates a feeling of being a smart shopper and being able to get the desired quality for a better price, signaling value-consciousness. Mowen (2000) established a strong relationship between value consciousness and conscientiousness.
- *Trait self-control* (Tangney et al., 2004) measures individuals' ability to resist a temptation from something immediately pleasurable but ultimately detrimental. Individuals who score high on this measure are less likely to experience any form of desire toward temptations because they reappraise them as detrimental to the self even before the temptation arises (Hofmann et al., 2012) and, if they do indulge themselves, are much faster to satiate on unhealthy foods compared with those who score low on the measure (Redden & Haws, 2013). Various aspects of trait self-control have been shown to correlate with conscientiousness (Bogg & Roberts, 2004; DeNeve & Cooper, 1998; Poropat, 2009).
- *Regulatory focus, prevention* (Higgins, 1997) represents individuals' focus on avoiding negative outcomes and fears. Consumers with a prevention focus are more likely to respond positively to messages framed as avoiding losses or those that highlight the absence of negative consequences (A. Y. Lee & Aaker, 2004). They are also more likely to be responsive to savings coupons and are more likely to add trusted, well-known brands to their basket (Ramanathan & Dhar, 2010). Wallace and Chen (2006) found that individuals with high levels of conscientiousness were more likely to follow safe behaviors, consistent with the definition of prevention focus.

Related to extraversion. This trait is one of the core dimensions of personality and refers to a variety of human characteristics such as gregariousness and sociability, assertiveness, energy and enthusiasm, adventurousness, positive emotions, and warmth (John & Srivastava, 1999). The following consumer traits are related to extraversion:

- *Impulsiveness* (Puri, 1996; Rook & Fisher, 1995) represents individuals' tendency to act without thinking or planning in pursuit of immediate gratification. There are many aspects to impulsiveness; however, in the context of behavioral impulsivity, spontaneous and unthinking actions are a common facet in the consumption domain. Impulsive individuals buy spontaneously, unreflectively, immediately, and kinetically (Rook & Fisher, 1995). They also tend to be more focused on their urges and desires (Rook, 1987). Extraverts tend to commit more errors by acting without thinking, consistent with this aspect of impulsiveness (Helmers et al., 1997).

- *Market mavenism* (Feick & Price, 1987) is the tendency to collect information about as many products as possible or about places to shop as a means to engage in discussions with other consumers and to provide information to others about the market. Market mavens attend to marketplace information because they expect it to serve as valuable social currency and to enhance their social standing by becoming more valuable to those with whom they interact (Feick & Price, 1987). Compared with other consumers, market mavens tend to score high on extraversion and openness to experience (Mooradian, 1996).

- *Consumer assertiveness* (Richins, 1983) is defined as a tendency for consumers to "stand up for their legitimate rights without violating the rights of others" (p. 73). This assertiveness may manifest in greater complaining behavior and make consumers less likely to respond to the persuasive purchase appeals of salespersons (Galassi & Galassi, 1977). Assertiveness relates to a subdimension of extraversion, namely, agentic extraversion, which refers to the need to dominate and pursue ambitions (Depue, 2006; Depue & Collins, 1999).

Related to agreeableness. The trait of agreeableness comprises six key facets, namely, trust, straightforwardness, altruism, compliance, modesty, and tendermindedness. Consumer traits related to this dimension are as follows:

- *Susceptibility to normative influence* (Bearden et al., 1989) refers to the need to identify with significant others by acquiring and using products or brands that would help maintain or enhance one's image in the eyes of such others and the willingness to conform to others' expectations with respect to purchase decisions. Consumers scoring high on this trait are more likely to favor brands that confer social benefits when conscious of a reference group such as friends (Orth & Kahle, 2008). They are also more responsive to messages that highlight how they could protect themselves from social disapproval, but only when the benefits are conspicuous (Wooten & Reed, 2004). Agreeableness facilitates compliance with team goals (De Dreu & Van Vianen, 2001), increased cooperation (Barrick et al., 1998), and a need for being liked (Wortman & Wood, 2011), all of which are consistent with susceptibility to normative influence.

- *Prosociality* (Baumsteiger & Siegel, 2019) refers to an individual's intentions to help others in the future. Individuals who have a high score on this trait are likely to be more generous and display greater reciprocity compared with those with low scores (Zhao et al., 2016). Prosocial traits are also highly predictive of donations to charity, both in incidence and amount donated (Manesi et al., 2019). Agreeableness is a core aspect of prosocial behavior (Ashton et al., 1998).

Related to neuroticism. This trait comprises facets such as anxiety, anger, depression, self-consciousness, impulsiveness, and vulnerability. Consumer traits that are most relevant are as follows:

- *Impulsivity* (Gray, 1987) focuses on the emotional correlates of impulsive behavior. Impulsivity driven by emotional instability results in binge eating, risky behaviors, and overspending. This dysfunctional aspect of impulsivity is strongly correlated with neuroticism (Zuckerman, 2002). Costa and McCrae (1992) observed that "because disruptive emotions interfere with adaptation, men and women high in neuroticism are also prone to have irrational ideas [and] to be less able to control their impulses" (p. 14).

Critique of individual difference measures. The proliferation of individual difference measures in the consumer behavior literature has led to what John and Srivastava (1999) characterized as a "Babel of concepts and scales" (p. 102). As a consequence, there is often no structure and no underlying psychological theory behind some of these measures. As Baumgartner (2002) noted,

> Personality research has long been a fringe player in the study of consumer behavior. Little research is directly devoted to personality issues, and if consumer personality is investigated at all, it tends to be from the narrow perspective of developing yet another individual difference measure in an already crowded field of personality scales. (p. 286)

One of the significant challenges in creating an individual difference measure is the logic of explanation. Any measure must satisfy the criterion of logical independence between the *explanans* and *explanandum*, to avoid circularity (Boag, 2018). A common problem with some individual difference measures is that they confuse relations with entities, that is, assuming that differences in what groups of people *do* translates to differences in what groups of people *are* (Boag, 2011, 2015), which is termed *reification* (Boag, 2018). This problem is further compounded when the items used in the scale measure the very same behavior that they seek to explain, leading to circularity of reasoning. For example, a scale item such as "I like a lot of variety" should not be then used to distinguish people on need for variety, because it confuses description with explanation.

The confusion arises because traits can be defined as both characteristics of an individual and dispositions or tendencies of an individual. In the former sense, a trait is a description of a class of people sharing the same qualities or features, while in the latter, it describes the likelihood of individuals to do something in a particular situation. The absence of logical independence between these two aspects of traits makes it difficult to disentangle why an individual with a particular trait does what they do. Taken to the absurd extreme, one might ask a respondent to indicate how impulsive they are on a 7-point scale and then use that measure to classify people as impulsive or nonimpulsive.

This problem with individual difference measures can be partially ameliorated by using multiple items describing various facets to the underlying characteristic that is sought to be defined. McCrae and Costa (2008) suggested that traits serve as elliptical explanations for the processes leading to a response. Taking the example of a car that breaks down, they argue that the trait of unreliability can be inferred not just from the proximal fact that it broke down but also from the features under the hood, such as shoddy workmanship, flimsy materials used to construct the car, and so on. Given that these features cannot be directly observed except by opening up the hood, the trait of unreliability serves as shorthand to define the characteristic of the car (Boag, 2018; McCrae & Costa, 2008). However, with more features being directly observed, it may be possible to directly triangulate on the underlying processes. In particular, there is utility in providing an organizing framework that links broad personality traits to individual differences in dispositions and tendencies.

Hierarchical Models of Personality

There is considerable recognition in the literature that personality traits are organized at various degrees of abstractness. Researchers such as Buss (1989), Paunonen (1998), Lastovicka (1982), and Joachimsthaler and Lastovicka (1984) have all proposed the existence of a hierarchy in personality. For example, Joachimsthaler and Lastovicka (1984) distinguished between central dispositions and secondary dispositions, suggesting that situation-specific tendencies such as information seeking and innovativeness were driven by central dispositions such as optimal stimulation level and locus of control. Mowen and Spears (1999) proposed a three-level hierarchy, where cardinal traits comprising the Big Five drove central traits such as the need for arousal (Zuckerman, 1985) or need for cognition (Cacioppo & Petty, 1982), which in turn influenced surface traits such as innovativeness (Raju, 1980; Steenkamp & Gielens, 2003;

Venkatraman & Price, 1990). The guiding principle for the hierarchy was that while cardinal traits were primary characteristics of a person, central traits were narrower and determined by the interplay between cardinal traits, the culture in which the individual lives, and the learning that the individual has experienced, while surface traits existed at the narrowest level, representing individual differences within specific situational contexts.

A more comprehensive model was proposed by Mowen (2000), incorporating four levels of traits in the hierarchy and adding a layer of comparison to referent standards in the form of values and goals to determine discrepancy from the desired state signified by the trait and hence motivate action. The model, termed the 3M—metatheoretic model of motivation and personality—marries personality theory with evolutionary psychology and control theory to create a more comprehensive theory of personality at varying levels of granularity, each guided by goals and motivations at various levels of specificity.

The 3M model consists of traits represented at four levels of abstraction. At the highest level are eight elemental traits, five of which are the Big Five and the remaining three being need for arousal, physical/bodily needs, and material needs. These additional needs are considered basic because they have an evolutionary origin. At the next level are compound traits, which are formed from the interaction of elemental traits with culturally driven processes. These include need for learning, task orientation, need for activity, need for play, competitiveness, and effectance. Compound traits differ from elemental ones in that they provide more direct guidance in performing a task. The third level consists of situational traits, which are enduring dispositions to act the same way in a particular situation as a result of interactions with basic traits with the context. For example, one could have a strong situational trait of health consciousness. The final level comprises surface traits, which are domain-specific dispositions or tendencies. For example, people may differ in their tendencies to indulge on chocolates and desserts. The model includes a comparator that looks for discrepancy from the ideal state signaled by the trait and triggers an emotional state, which then prompts action based on a cognitive appraisal of the causes for the emotion. This is based on control theory (Carver & Scheier, 1990). Another important aspect of the 3M model is that it does not assume a one-to-one mapping between elemental traits and lower level traits. In other words, a lower level trait can be multiply determined by several elemental traits.

Taking a different approach to building a descriptive model of human personality, Baumgartner (2002) advocated for a three-tiered, levels-of-analysis approach. He viewed the idea of building a comprehensive hierarchical model and then fitting specific consumer traits to it as somewhat futile and instead argued for a model that was specific to consumption situations. Adopting a three-tiered framework proposed by McAdams (2001), he suggested that consumers can be studied in terms of their dispositions, strivings, and life stories. The first level, personality traits, deals with enduring and situationally invariant dispositions that highlight differences across individuals but consistencies across situations and over time. The second level, personal concerns, is about the goals pursued by people and the means that they use to achieve them. The third level, life stories, is about the narratives constructed by people in order to integrate what they remember from the past, experience in the present, and anticipate in the future in order to develop a coherent self-identity.

While both models take a very different approach to defining how personality traits are organized, they do share one feature in common. Both explicitly acknowledge the importance of goals and strivings as an underlying feature of personality. However, while hierarchical models provide a more granular view of personality down to surface level traits, their aim is still to account for interindividual differences in behavior. They do not allow for the possibility that there might be intra-individual variation over time within the same situation or across different situations. For example, the hierarchical model has been used to show the relationship between the surface trait of compulsive buying and elemental traits such as emotional stability/neuroticism, conscientiousness, and agreeableness (Mowen & Spears, 1999). Even at the granular level, the focus is on identifying differences across individuals in the propensity to buy compulsively rather than on (a) why compulsive shoppers may be prudent with respect to other domains such as engaging in risky behaviors and (b) why compulsive shoppers may behave compulsively at one time and not at others. In fact, all structural models of personality are based on the assumption that there are stable interindividual differences that remain consistent over time. Yet, there are plenty of instances when a person is not likely to consistently enact the same behaviors even within a specific situation. The fact that motivations and emotions may themselves change over time or come into conflict with each other, thereby affecting the likelihood of enactment of a particular behavior, is not acknowledged in hierarchical models with a structural orientation. We therefore turn to a different approach to studying personality, one that acknowledges within-person variation in behavior.

DYNAMIC MODELS OF PERSONALITY

Whereas structural models of personality typically focus on interindividual variability, dynamic models address within-person (intra-individual) psychological systems and examine how they are organized and interact with each other. Given that oftentimes such interactions between persons and their environments tends to be dynamic and ever-changing, dynamic models are best suited to capture complexity rather than simple effects (Cervone, 2005; Mischel, 2004).

The guiding principles behind dynamic models of personality are the following (Cervone, 2004):

- There are multiple, interconnected processes that interact with each other in complex patterns, giving rise to a coherent whole, namely, the personality.
- People's actions are guided by their interactions with the environment or context, but they also shape or change the environment as a result of these interactions. In other words, there is bidirectionality of interaction with the environment.
- Personality is guided by basic cognitive and affective systems that give rise to specific and overt patterns of behavior.

Dynamic models thus provide a better account of both change and consistency among individuals, because they recognize the fact that every situation may evoke a different set of cognitions and affect that may or may not result in the same behavior being enacted every time; yet, on average, the person may be more likely to consistently engage in a distinctive set of behaviors. Indeed, by averaging behaviors over time, the researcher loses granularity in the patterns observed and any variation is construed statistically as an error term. There is significant information in the complex set of possible outcomes when studied over time (Cervone, 2004; Mischel & Shoda, 1995; Nowak et al., 2005). This is quite unlike the hierarchical model where there are linear pathways between a person's basic traits and the set of behaviors enacted in response to specific situations (Mowen, 2000). Next, I review three such dynamic models, the cognitive affective process system (CAPS; Mischel & Shoda, 1995), the knowledge-and-appraisal model of personality architecture (KAPA; Cervone, 2004), and the personality dynamics model (PersDyn; Sosnowska et al., 2019).

Cognitive Affective Process Model

The CAPS model (Mischel & Shoda, 1995) proposes that personality emerges from a series of situation-behavior profiles, wherein a person may respond in certain ways under some circumstances and in other ways in different situations. Mischel and Shoda (1995) took the example of two children at a summer camp, one who engages in greater verbal aggression when warned about behavior by an adult counselor but less when approached positively by a peer and the other who showed the opposite pattern. Importantly, these patterns emerged after controlling for and partialling out the average tendency, showing evidence for intra-individual variance.

The model specifies that situational features in the environment may activate a variety of cognitive and affective units such as encodings and construals, goals, affect, expectancies and beliefs, and competencies and self-regulatory mechanisms. An incoming featural input may be perceived and encoded differently by different individuals and then interact with each person's goals and motives, evoke various affective reactions, influence beliefs, and finally influence the range of behaviors possible.

According to the CAPS theory, individual differences arise from two different sources. First, individuals differ in the levels of chronic accessibility of the various cognitive-affective units. Thus, for example, individuals may differ in the degree of accessibility of values-related duties and responsibilities or in the affect generated by losses, both characteristics of regulatory focus (Higgins et al., 1997). Second, individuals may also differ in the activation of the connections among various cognitive-affective units and the organization of relationships among them (see Figure 9.2 later in the chapter). Thus, for example, individuals may differ in how they respond to an attractive dessert depending on whether a healthy garnish is on top of the dessert or to its side (Belei et al., in press). In the former case, they perceive and encode it as a mix of healthy and hedonic foods, activating conflicting goals and concomitantly lower taste perceptions compared with the latter, where they encode it unequivocally as hedonic and tasty. This gives rise to different patterns of activation of perceptions, goals, and affect for a stimulus with minimal differences in properties. The result is significant differences in behavior, with overconsumption much more likely when the garnish is on the side, compared with on top of the dessert.

Over time, the levels of activation and resultant behaviors settle into a consistent, predictable pattern wherein behaviors may vary depending on the situation but, nonetheless, display stability unless new developmental or biological changes take place in the individual or they learn something new. These developmental inputs may change the accessibility of cognitive-affective units or the activation of linkages between one unit and the other. Over time, this self-organizing network of units settles into a stable pattern, leading to the emergence of a variety of if-then behavior profiles, that is, behaviors contingent on specific situations, causing domain-specific tendencies. Repetition of these patterns over time leads to the emergence of personality traits.

While the CAPS model is remarkably specific on the psychological processes underlying the development of personality traits, it does not provide a mapping to personality variables. Where it succeeds is in providing a framework for thinking about the complex and dynamic interplay of various mediating cognitive and affective processes, underscoring the situational and temporal variability in personality.

Knowledge-and-Appraisal Model of Personality Architecture

The KAPA model (Cervone, 2004) was developed as a complement to CAPS theory. Its stated purpose was to provide a connection between personality processes, as delineated by the CAPS framework, and personality variables and dispositional tendencies, represented as a personality architecture. Further, it aims to show how this architecture contributes to an overall coherence in personality across various situations.

At the core of the KAPA model are two fundamental units of cognition: knowledge and appraisal. Knowledge represents an enduring feature of personality, while appraisal is dynamic and a function of situation and time. Features of the self, both alone and in interaction with other persons and the physical or social world, are stored as enduring representations. Some of this knowledge may be generalized, for example, "I am a friendly and social person" or "I like shopping." Other knowledge may be domain-specific and includes beliefs about the self in particular domains, for example, "I can't resist buying things that are on sale" or "I usually try to save money while shopping."

Appraisals, in contrast, are not enduring beliefs about isolated features of the self. They represent judgments of the self in relation to specific events happening in the moment. Specifically, appraisals are relational judgments that attempt to construct a meaning of a current event for the self, assessing its significance for personal well-being. By relating features of the self to the features of the specific situation, the individual tries to construct a specific real-time meaning of the situation's relevance.

The combination of enduring knowledge and situational appraisals results in a range of dispositional tendencies that serve to meet three key aspects of functioning: beliefs that people hold about the current state of the world; goals that they may have about the future state of the world; and personal standards, rules, or norms that are intrinsic to the person. Unlike the CAPS model, where different cognitive-affective units reside at only one level, the KAPA framework is flexible in defining the level at which each unit exists. For example, where the CAPS model provides for goals at only one level of abstraction, the KAPA model accommodates goals both at an enduring (knowledge) and a situational (appraisal) level. One might be generally health-conscious and recognize it as such in the enduring knowledge possessed about the self but come across a deal for ice-cream in the store that is too hard to resist, leading to an appraisal of the value of the offer that translates to an intention to act. Similarly, one may have an enduring personal standard of always being ethical but may also be tempted to pick up a $1 bill lying on the road because no one is looking (situational appraisal).

The KAPA model adds another dimension to the CAPS theory by providing a pathway from cognitions to dispositional tendencies, linking the situationally activated behaviors to underlying cognitive knowledge structures and showing how appraisals of the immediate circumstances can be reinforced by enduring self-schema but equally swayed by current concerns and needs. This leads to a complex pattern of behaviors that may or may not always be consistent with a global trait every time, leading to intra-individual variability.

While both the CAPS and KAPA models provide an explicit framework for studying within-person processes, they do not address another key dimension of dynamics, namely, the patterns of equilibria in personality. Behaviors driven by enduring traits represent the baseline, while those driven by momentary situations may represent deviations from the baseline, providing the source of variability. What is needed is a way to capture the swiftness with which the individual returns to the baseline. A new approach based on an emerging field called dynamical systems theory (Vallacher & Nowak, 2007) provides a comprehensive way to capture personality system dynamics.

Personality Dynamics

The PersDyn model (Sosnowska et al., 2019) draws from dynamical systems theory (Vallacher & Nowak, 2007) to describe the pattern of changes in personality through three key measures of the trajectory of personality states. The *personality baseline* refers to the steady state or the central point around which an individual's thoughts, feelings, goals, and behaviors fluctuate over time. It thus represents the average tendency of an individual's behavioral expressions of their traits and is consistent with the measure of average behavior captured by structural models of personality (Fleeson, 2001). Personality variability represents the extent to which a person's emotions, thoughts, and behaviors change over time, thereby capturing the influence of situational forces or temporarily active goals. Figure 9.1 shows two trajectories of experienced desires for subjects with high reward-seeking tendencies, as measured by the BAS (behavioral activation system) Reward Responsiveness Scale (Carver & White, 1994), in response to a tray filled with chocolate cake sitting in front of them (Ramanathan & Hofmann, in press). Figure 9.1a shows a trajectory with a high base level of desire and high volatility. Figure 9.1b shows a trajectory with a high base level of desire and low volatility.

The final measure is attractor strength, which refers to the ability of the system to get back to one's personality baseline. If the trajectory returns quickly to the baseline, it signals that the base level of behavior is a strong attractor. This in turn would imply a system strongly tuned to maintaining its baseline levels of behavior as an enduring state. However, if the trajectory deviates from the baseline and remains out of it for a considerable amount of time, it would signal that the person is swayed a lot by situational factors.

Thus, if someone is normally very health-conscious but deviates from a strict diet by indulging themselves, it would be important to study how soon the person gets back to the baseline and whether they deviate again. Attractor strength is thus representative of the pull of the core motivations underlying the baseline personality. A weak attractor would mean that the person is prone to a lot of deviation from their core personality.

a. High Baseline, High Volatility

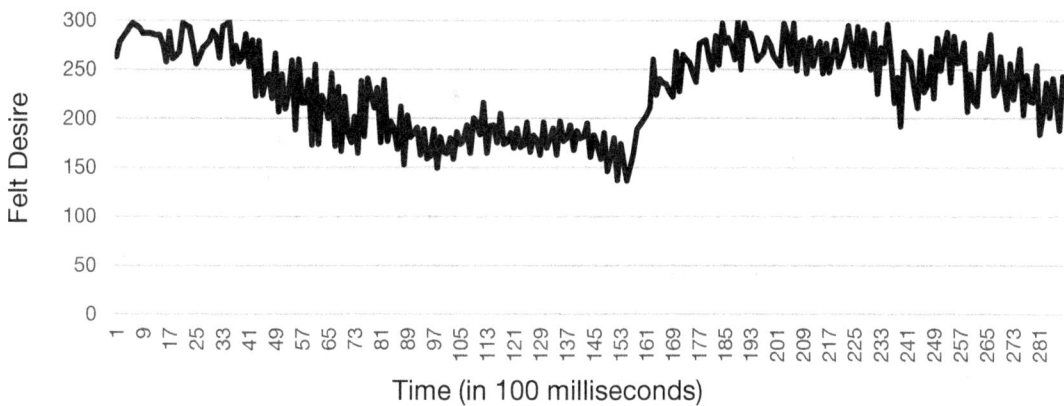

b. High Baseline, Low Volatility

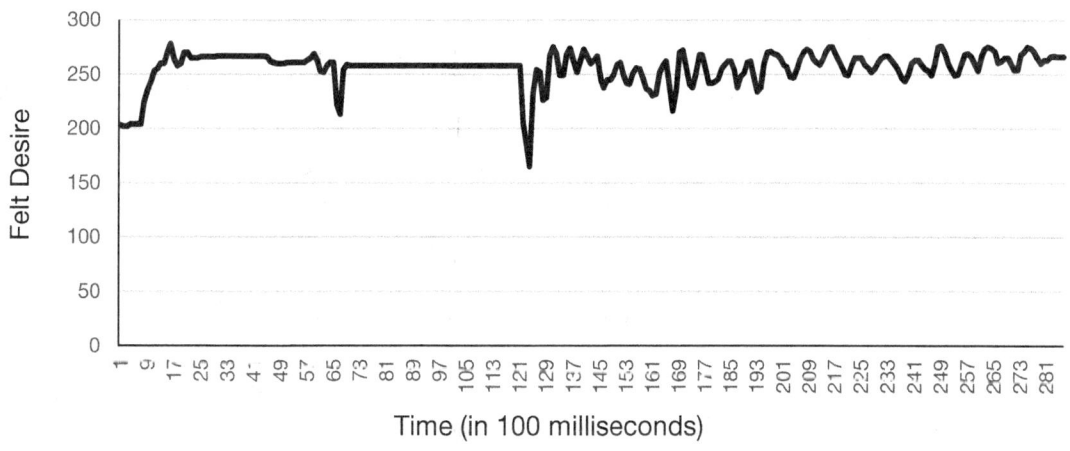

FIGURE 9.1. Trajectories of felt desire for a dessert among high behavioral activation system reward responsive individuals primed with a hedonic goal.

Attractors are trait-specific, and an individual could have a strong attractor for one trait, making it part of their core identity, and a weak attractor for another trait. This is a topic we return to later in this chapter, when we examine patterns of recurrence for impulsive versus nonimpulsive people.

Attractor states emerge due to two reasons. First, individuals may incorporate the set of states into their self-concept due to repeated instantiation of the same experiences, thereby triggering the same cognitive and affective responses, in turn leading to such thoughts, feelings, and behaviors becoming part of the automatic reflexive system. Further, by virtue of the reinforcement of these cognitions and feelings every time a behavior is enacted, the behavioral response grows stronger over time. Second, attractors may also emerge from a more conscious, deliberative process, whereby an individual chooses a set of behaviors in order to achieve a goal, thereby shaping their personality consciously. The thoughts and feelings that accompany this choice get reinforced every time the behaviors are enacted, thus causing the attractor to emerge. For example, an impulsive spendthrift may consciously set monthly targets for spending in order to bring greater control over their budget. By repeated exercise of prudence and the satisfaction of having saved money, it is possible to have an attractor state form around being prudent, thereby lowering the baseline for spending.

The preceding two sections provided two contrasting views of personality, one that highlights interindividual variation (structural model) and the other that highlights intra-individual variation (dynamic model). In the final section, I examine the construct of trait impulsiveness using both views of personality and provide a means to build a bridge between the interindividual difference approach typical of structural models of personality and the intra-individual difference approach in dynamic models.

APPLICATION: IMPULSIVENESS THROUGH DIFFERENT LENSES

One of the most common phenomena studied in the consumer literature is that of impulsive behavior. Numerous studies have examined how consumers act seemingly "mindlessly" in making shopping and consumption decisions. Phenomenological accounts (O'Guinn & Faber, 1989; Rook, 1987) have documented shoppers reporting recurrent themes of spontaneous desire and disregard for long-term consequences. For example, respondents said, "I saw the ice cream and immediately wanted some" (Rook, 1987, p. 193) and "I couldn't tell you what I bought or where I bought it. It was like I was on automatic" (O'Guinn & Faber, 1989, p. 154).

Perhaps because of its complexity as a construct, it is almost as difficult for researchers to define why people buy things or act on impulse. There is certainly no dearth of explanations, each rooted in its own derivation from specific behavioral characteristics. In particular, impulsiveness as a trait is a distinctly heterogeneous construct (Depue & Collins, 1999; Evenden, 1999; Parker et al., 1993; Zuckerman, 2005). Fineberg et al. (2014) concluded that there are at least four different facets to the construct based on various neurobiological correlates, namely, response, choice, reflection, and decision making. The International Society for Research on Impulsivity (n.d.) has similarly defined impulsivity as

> behavior without adequate thought, the tendency to act with less forethought than do most individuals of equal ability and knowledge, or a predisposition toward rapid, unplanned reactions to internal or external stimuli without regard to the negative consequences of these reactions. (para. 1)

Others have described an affective dimension to impulsivity. For example, Rook (1987) characterized impulsiveness as a characteristic where "a consumer experiences a sudden, often powerful and persistent urge to buy something immediately" (p. 191). This urge materializes as a buying stimulus that is (a) spontaneous, (b) kinetic, (c) psychologically arousing, (d) immediate, and (e) primary (Rook, 1987). This idea is supported by a large body of research suggesting that impulsive actions are driven by the reflexive system, guided by hot cognitions and lower order affect (Hofmann et al., 2009; Metcalfe & Mischel, 1999; Shiv & Fedorikhin, 1999; Strack & Deutsch, 2004).

An added complication is the fact that impulsiveness carries different meanings and implications, ranging from the garden variety form of occasional indulgence in chocolates to more serious and highly deleterious form of addictions and binge consumption. It is also seen in personality disorders such as attention-deficit/hyperactivity disorder (ADHD) and borderline personality disorder. For the purpose of this chapter, I focus on behaviors that are mainly in the consumer domain.

In the following section, I discuss impulsivity as relevant to consumer behavior through both the structural and dynamic lenses and use the motivational roots of such behavior as means to bridge the two views. I start with a structural approach, focusing on the relationship between impulsivity and the five-factor model of personality, and use a hierarchical model to delineate the pathway from broad personality traits to domain-specific tendencies. Next, I discuss the motivational antecedents of impulsivity, drawing from the CAPS model (Mischel & Shoda, 1995) to provide the bridge from the structural approach to the dynamic view of impulsivity. The dynamic view of impulsivity identifies the conditions under which attentional processes may guide these motivational antecedents, leading to differences in the ebb and flow of felt desires and resistance within individuals, which in turn affects behavioral tendencies.

Structural Models of Impulsivity

There have been numerous attempts to define the construct of impulsivity. As a very important dimension of personality that finds expression in various forms of behaviour, impulsivity has been studied at great length by personality theorists. From an interindividual perspective, researchers have tried to identify unique factors or combinations of factors that relate to the construct of impulsivity. We delineate these next.

Five-factor model and impulsivity. The personality literature has dealt extensively with trait impulsiveness. For instance, H. J. Eysenck and Eysenck (1969) proposed a two-factor theory of personality: Factor E (Extraversion) and Factor N (Neuroticism). They found that impulsivity was strongly related to the Extraversion factor, thus arguing for a link between impulsivity and sociability. In a subsequent series of studies, S. B. G. Eysenck and Eysenck (1977) defined impulsivity within a third dimension of personality, Psychoticism, and identified it along two dimensions: Venturesomeness, which is the tendency to seek pleasure despite being conscious of costs, and Sensation Seeking, which is the tendency to seek experiences and feelings. Adding to the mix is research by Costa and McCrae (1992), which posited that impulsiveness is a facet of Neuroticism, whereas Hofstee et al. (1992) located impulsiveness as a facet of Conscientiousness. From these diverse findings, it is clear that there are different dimensions to impulsivity, driven by different trait characteristics, and that each of these dimensions may relate to different aspects of personality.

Dimensions of impulsiveness. The Barratt Impulsiveness Scale (Barratt, 1959) is a commonly used measure of impulsivity. This scale has undergone several revisions, but the most recent one (Patton et al., 1995) conceptualizes impulsivity along three dimensions: attentional impulsiveness (ability or lack thereof to focus on and attend to tasks), motor impulsiveness (acting without thinking), and nonplanning impulsiveness (poor planning for tasks or for the future). Recent work by Lange et al. (2017) showed that while all three dimensions correlated negatively with Conscientiousness, only motor impulsiveness correlated positively with Extraversion, while only attentional impulsiveness correlated positively with Neuroticism.

Whiteside and Lynam (2001) created the UPPS scale, which captures four facets of impulsive behavior, based on a factor analytic assessment of several measures, including Costa and McCrae's (1992) five-factor model. These facets are Urgency, Premeditation (lack of), Perseverance (lack of), and Sensation Seeking. Two of the facets, namely, lack of Premeditation and of Perseverance, point to weaknesses in top-down processes of control and relate negatively to Conscientiousness in the conceptualization. The remaining two, Urgency and Sensation Seeking, are related to affective and motivational triggers, the former often being caused by the need to escape from negative emotions and the latter by the thrill afforded by taking risks. These tendencies are reflective of Neuroticism and Extraversion, respectively.

Other researchers have studied impulsiveness as an individual difference in trait self-control. The Brief Self-Control Scale (BSCS; Tangney et al., 2004) conceptualizes and measures impulsiveness on 13 different items in five facets of self-control: controlling thoughts, controlling emotions, controlling impulses, regulating behavior/performance, and habit breaking. These facets are largely related to Urgency, Premeditation, and Perseverance and do not account for Sensation Seeking.

In the consumer behavior literature, Puri (1996) developed the 12-item Consumer Impulsiveness Scale (CIS), which consists of two subscales, namely, the hedonic and prudent scales. The hedonic dimension comprises five items, namely, impulsive, careless, easily tempted, extravagant, and enjoys spending. The prudent dimension comprises seven items, namely, self-controlled, farsighted, responsible, restrained, rational, methodical, and a planner. Respondents indicate to what extent each of these labels are descriptive of them on a seven-point scale ranging from "Usually would describe me" to "Seldom would describe me." Limited evidence points to a relationship between the prudent dimension and Conscientiousness (Bellman, 2012) but no link between the hedonic dimension and any of the five factors.

While these measures of impulsivity tend to treat it as a domain-general construct, consistent with literature showing a generalized and common resource pool of self-control that can get depleted leading to impulsive behavior across domains (Baumeister et al., 1998), researchers have argued that not all individuals show impulsiveness across domains. One could be very diligent at work yet extremely impulsive in relationships or pursuing risky behaviors.

Hierarchical perspective. Recognizing that individuals may differ in their dispositional tendencies to act impulsively in specific domains, there have been other, more domain-specific measures of self-control that have been shown to explain behaviors in those domains to a better degree (Haws et al., 2016). These measures were developed by modifying the BSCS to make the items more germane to specific domains. For example, the Eating Self-Control scale was shown to explain significantly more variance in eating behavior compared with the BSCS, and the Spending Self-Control scale similarly explained significantly more variance in spending behavior compared with the BSCS.

In turn, Mowen (2000) showed that the surface trait of compulsive shopping relates to a situational trait, consumer impulsiveness (Puri, 1996), and a compound trait, competitiveness. While impulsiveness was predicted by the elemental traits of lack of emotional stability (neuroticism), extraversion, openness to experience, and conscientiousness, competitiveness was predicted by the elemental traits of neuroticism, need for arousal, and materialism.

The fact that a domain-general construct such as consumer impulsiveness predicts a domain-specific construct such as compulsive buying tendency is not surprising. Indeed, research on domain-specific impulsivity shows a strong correlation between domain-general measures of self-control and domain-specific tendencies in interpersonal relationships, food, work, drugs, exercise, and finances, respectively (Tsukayama et al., 2012).

What is not clear, however, is why these domain-specific tendencies emerge. Rather than simply examining interindividual differences in specific dispositional tendencies via the development of domain-specific scales of self-control, a richer discussion could emerge from considering why an individual who has high eating self-control nonetheless gives in to temptation to procrastinate at work. These intra-individual differences are rarely discussed in the consumer behavior literature.

The most significant challenge with using a structural model of impulsivity is that the trait is multidimensional. Because it has elements of most of the Big Five traits in it, impulsivity could mean very different things at the same time. When, for example, a respondent rates themselves as impulsive on a trait scale, do they mean they act rapidly without thinking? Or do they mean they prefer immediate gratification? The lack of precision in the definition also extends to the conflation of impulsiveness with lack of self-control. It is certainly possible to have a high tendency to seek rewards (a characteristic signature of impulsivity) along with a high ability to resist. Indeed, in the CIS, the hedonic and prudent dimensions are posited to be orthogonal to each other. However, the vast majority of research in the consumer behavior literature treats impulsiveness as a bipolar construct, with high levels of impulsiveness being equated to low levels of self-control.

The biggest weakness of using only trait scales to measure impulsivity is one that is common to all structural models of personality. While they are excellent at describing a behavior or class of behaviors characteristic of the general trait or domain-specific manifestations of the same, they do not shed light on the underlying cognitive and affective processes (Mischel & Shoda, 1995). The fact that there was a need to come up with domain-specific scales for self-control (Haws et al.,

2016) as a refinement of the general self-control scale (Tangney et al., 2004) signals the relatively poor correspondence between measured traits and behavior.

Some researchers, rather than using self-reported measures of impulsivity, have used actual behavior to infer differences in personality. For example, behavioral decision theorists have argued that there is a tendency among impulsive people to overweigh or amplify the significance of immediately experienced outcomes (Loewenstein & Prelec, 1992). Specifically, the impact of a constant time delay in attaining a reward diminishes as the reward becomes more remote in time. While smaller immediate gains are preferred in the case of options that are not temporally distant, larger delayed rewards are preferred in the case of options that are further away in the future (Green et al., 1997). This haphazard mode of decision making has been characterized by theorists as impulsivity, in which a choice is made on the basis of a temporary and often sudden change in preference.

Theorists in this area model such behavior with a hyperbolic function (e.g., Ainslie & Haslam, 1992). Such functions cross each other as a function of time, thus being able to account for switches in preferences. These are of the form where V is the present value of a future reward, A is its amount, D is the delay to its receipt, and k is a parameter governing the rate of decrease in value. Larger values of k signify more rapidly discounted rewards and a greater preference for smaller immediate rewards. Further, k itself can change with time. Therefore, k can be interpreted as a measure of individual differences in impulsivity (Newman et al., 1992) and the inability to delay gratification (cf. Funder & Block, 1989; Mischel et al., 1989).

While delayed discounting paradigms provide robust behavioral insights about impulsivity, they are silent about the cognitive and affective processes underlying such behavior. In particular, what motivates people to eschew the larger, delayed reward in favor of the smaller, immediate one? More generally, what are the motivational drivers of impulsiveness? What is the role of affect in this process? How and why do people repeatedly act in an impulsive manner?

Motivational drivers of impulsivity. In order to understand why some people are more impulsive than others as well as why the same people are impulsive in some situations and not in others, it becomes necessary to unpack the motivational antecedents of the trait. The CAPS model (Mischel & Shoda, 1995) provides the framework. Recall that the CAPS model suggests that an incoming cue may be perceived and encoded differently by different individuals and that these perceptions may interact with each person's goals and motives, evoke various affective reactions, influence beliefs, and finally influence the range of behaviors possible. Behavior is exquisitely sensitive to how a stimulus is attended to and perceived, guided by the individual's goals in that situation, some of which may be chronically accessible and affect downstream affective and cognitive reactions to varying degrees. Therefore, a key starting point for understanding how interindividual differences in specific tendencies toward impulsive behavior emerge lies in the nature of goals and motives activated in the situation.

Research based on neurobiology suggests that there are two distinct and independent motivational systems that lie behind impulsivity: an aversive system called the behavioral inhibition system (BIS) and an appetitive system called the behavioral activation system (BAS), both of which function relatively orthogonal to each other (Gray, 1987). Different people have different levels of activation of these two systems. Gray argued that impulsive behavior could result from either an underactive BIS or an overactive BAS and that the BAS is more likely to mediate impulsive behavior when there is a strong expectation of reward or gratification. Based on this framework, Carver and White (1994) proposed a 24-item BAS/BIS scale to measure both dimensions, with subscales for Drive, Reward Responsiveness, and Fun Seeking on the BAS scale. This scale has been used widely to measure the strength of the appetitive and inhibitory systems in individuals. However, while it gets closer to defining the motivational antecedents of impulsiveness, it does not show how these effects unfold over time. Further, a critical element that is missing in all trait models of impulsivity is the role of intra-individual variability. As Ramanathan (2002) asked,

> When and how does a one-off impulse buy or impulsive action transform itself into "it was like I was on automatic" (O'Guinn and Faber 1989)? How does a random act of impulsivity evolve into a pattern of behaviors related to each other in terms of an underlying level of gratification or hedonic value? (p. 30)

Ramanathan and Menon (2006) examined the motivational and affective antecedents of impulsiveness. Consistent with Mischel and Shoda (1995) and Metcalfe and Mischel (1999), they posited that impulsiveness is characterized by chronic accessibility of hedonic goals capable of activating "hot" or affect-laden cognitions. Due to such goals reinforcing the cognitive-affective personality structure, behaviors consistent with the goal would get prioritized and strengthen in value.

In order to test this hypothesis, Ramanathan and Menon (2006) first demonstrated that trait impulsives were characterized by high reward responsiveness. Participants completed a task called the card assortment reward responsiveness objective task (Al-Adawi et al., 1998), which measured their generalized hedonic goals. The task uses a set of cards printed with five-digit numbers, each of which uniquely has the digits 1, 2, or 3 appearing in any of the five positions just once. The respondent's task was to sort the cards over four trials into three piles based on whether one of the three distinguishing digits were present. In the first trial, the respondent sorted 60 cards. In the next three trials, the respondent sorted 100 cards within the time they took to sort the 60 cards. Trials 2 and 4 were unrewarded, and Trial 3 offered the respondent a reward of $0.20 for every five cards sorted. Then, they indicated how impulsive they were on the 12-item CIS (1 = *usually describes me*, 7 = *seldom describes me*; Puri, 1996) and the 24-item BAS/BIS scale (Carver & White, 1994). Response latencies for these measures were recorded.

Results indicated that impulsiveness was characterized by reward responsiveness, with performance on rewarded trials being higher than that on unrewarded trials among trait impulsives identified by the CIS scale but no different among trait prudents. Further, trait impulsives were faster to respond to the hedonic subscale compared with prudents but no different from prudents on filler scales. Together, these findings provided evidence for the hypothesis that impulsive individuals are reward seeking and that they have chronically accessible self-knowledge about this dispositional tendency.

While these findings are useful, they do not by themselves show that impulsive people are guided by chronically accessible goals. This was addressed in Ramanathan and Menon (2006) by means of exploiting a key property of goal accessibility. They demonstrated that impulsive consumers responded to perceived violations of their chronic hedonic goals by increasing their evaluations of products related to those goals. Participants (whose trait impulsivity measures had been collected earlier) were first asked to provide their ratings of various products, some of which were sweet or savory indulgences. Following this task, they were presented with descriptions of three situations where they faced a temptation (e.g., you are standing in line at a Starbucks, and you see these delicious muffins on display) and were asked to indicate which of three possible actions they would pursue. Each of the presented actions was designed to be about being prudent and resisting the temptation. Following the prudence induction task, participants were again presented with the pictures of products and asked to rate them. Results showed that impulsive participants increased their evaluations of the indulgent products after the prudence induction, whereas prudent participants decreased their evaluations.

If impulsive individuals have chronic hedonic goals, would they always be impulsive? Are there situations where we might observe intra-individual variability in behavior? To investigate these questions, Mukhopadhyay et al. (2008) looked at differences in behavior between chronically impulsive and nonimpulsive consumers with regard to a current temptation after recalling a previous time when they had either indulged themselves or resisted a temptation. Participants were asked to recall a recent instance when they had either given in to a temptation or resisted it and to describe the episode. Following this task, they were told to help themselves to cheeseballs while the experimenter readied another study. The number of cheeseballs eaten was counted after the session. Measures of impulsivity were taken at the end. Prudent individuals, as measured on the impulsivity scale, showed consistency in their behavior. If they had resisted a temptation on a previous occasion, they were more likely to do so on the present occasion too, while if they reported having succumbed to temptation, they were also more likely to eat the cheeseballs on the present occasion. Impulsive individuals, however, were more likely to switch. Those who recalled having given in to temptation previously resisted the temptation on the present occasion, while those who recalled resisting previously ate more cheeseballs on the present occasion. Thus, it is not the case that impulsive people are always impulsive. However, when impulsive people recalled past instances of giving in to temptation and also the reasons they had done so, they showed consistency in behavior, choosing a cake over salad. The features of the current situation and the encoding of past and present experiences guide behavior dynamically, consistent with the CAPS (Mischel & Shoda, 1995) and the KAPA (Cervone, 2004) models.

Another facet of being impulsive is the nature of emotions experienced immediately and after time has passed after an act of indulgence. Consumers experience mixed feelings of pleasure and guilt after indulging themselves (Rook, 1987). The ebb and flow of these different affective states may play a significant role in determining what happens on a subsequent occasion. Specifically, feelings of pleasure and guilt may decay at different rates for people who are impulsive versus prudent (Ramanathan & Williams, 2007). This is consistent with the KAPA model (Cervone, 2004), wherein individuals may appraise their affective experience differently based on their chronic self-knowledge about themselves. For chronically impulsive individuals, it is not functional to continue experiencing guilt at the same level of intensity after every act of indulgence. They may reappraise their guilt and reduce its felt intensity. Ramanathan and Williams (2007) examined the temporal dynamics of felt emotions and showed that both self-described impulsive and prudent individuals experienced a mix of pleasure and guilt immediately after eating an indulgent snack. However, 24 hours later, impulsive consumers, while recalling their past indulgence, reported almost the same level of pleasure but very little guilt. Prudent consumers showed a substantial amount of guilt and reduced pleasure. These emotions affected subsequent actions, with impulsive consumers more likely to reindulge compared with prudent ones. In other words, simply recalling the emotions experienced during an act of indulgence provided reasons to indulge again, similar to what was found in Mukhopadhyay et al. (2008). Once again, the KAPA model (Cervone, 2004) provides the framework to interpret these results, suggesting that fresh reappraisals of emotions previously experienced may reinforce behavior and increase consistency with chronically held motives.

The dynamic interplay among traits, emotions, cognitions, and motivations demonstrated in these studies leads us to a model where we could conceptualize personality as a dynamic system, wherein the focus is on the complex behavioral, cognitive, and affective patterns resulting from interactions between different elements of the system (i.e., self-organization of the system; Kelso, 1995), rather than on stable predispositions.

Dynamic Model of Impulsivity

The PersDyn model (Sosnowska et al., 2019) provides a framework to think about how impulsivity might present as a stable trait across individuals yet show variability across situations and time. The dynamic model of personality rests on the premise that traits are characterized by recurrent patterns of behavior with enough variability to cause occasional deviations from the baseline but an eventual return to the stable state. This return to the stable baseline is guided by a homeostatic process that regulates behavior toward an equilibrium that represents the average dispositional tendency. Such equilibrium states are called attractors. One may think of attractors as states that behaviors keep returning to over time and, equally, repellers as states that are actively avoided over time. Following Carver and Scheier (2002), one may conceptualize attractors as basins or valleys. The deeper the valley, the stronger the goal that underlies the personality trait. The occasional deviations that might occur may be imagined as a ball that needs to be moved out of the basin. It would take a lot more effort to move the ball out if the valley is deep, thus implying a stronger, more deeply entrenched trait. Equally important, a deep basin implies that the system exhibits greater stickiness or inertia, because the ball keeps bouncing within the basin, unable to exit. A weak trait, on the other hand, may be similar to a shallow basin, whereby minimal perturbation can lead to switching.

Unlike structural models of personality that assume stability of traits, the dynamic system is flexible and self-organizing (Kelso, 1995). Behavior is not determined by just the average tendency but rather by mutual influences of cognitive and affective states on each other, sometimes in such a way that patterns emerge spontaneously (Carver & Scheier, 2002). One such example of self-organization is behavior determined by the focus of attention (Lewis, 1996). Goals emerge as a consequence of what the self-organizing system focuses on by way of attention. In other words, goal pursuit is a consequence of (a) what catches the eye or other senses and (b) how attention self-organizes toward that perceptual input. People with chronic goals underlying their dispositional tendencies may thus be more prone to attending to relevant stimuli, not merely by orienting their attention to such stimuli but by actively engaging with them.

Attentional processes and impulsivity. Selective attention to stimuli is a result of three independent attentional networks: the posterior system, the anterior system, and the vigilance system (Posner & Petersen, 1990). Of particular interest to our discussion are the roles of the posterior and anterior attentional systems and their interaction with motivational states. Activation of the posterior attentional network may feed into the reward circuitry directly. The posterior system guides bottom-up processes that are characterized by sensory or motivational salience (Knudsen, 2007). Aversive stimuli (Mogg & Bradley, 1999) as well as attractive or appetitive stimuli (Mogg et al., 2003) attract attention due to activity in the limbic system of the brain. Activation of the posterior attentional network is thus likely to lead to an immediate *orientation bias* toward indulgences, characteristic of System 1 processing.

The anterior system guides top-down processes that enhance detection of stimuli at locations where people expect something of relevance or significance (Posner et al., 1980). Expectancies that are endogenously generated cause activation of this network, leading to prolonged attention toward motivationally relevant stimuli. This pattern of attention has been variously termed *attentional adhesion* (Maner et al., 2007), *disengagement bias* (Fox et al., 2001; Posner & Petersen 1990), and *maintenance bias* (Bradley et al., 2003). For example, Maner et al. (2007) found that mate-search motives caused participants with an unrestricted sociosexual orientation to sustain attention toward pictures of physically attractive members of the opposite sex. Chocoholics show similar patterns of sustained attention toward chocolate-related pictures (Smeets et al., 2009), sometimes even when these are paired with equally attractive nonchocolate foods (Kemps & Tiggemann, 2009). Such a top-down pattern of attentional bias is characteristic of System 2 processing. Together, the anterior and posterior attentional systems may thus reinforce each other, the posterior system guiding initial orientation to the tempting stimulus and the anterior system maintaining attention toward the stimulus. Recent findings by Kovach et al. (2014) showing both an initial gaze bias and a subsequent, late-stage attentional bias in the context of hypothetical food choices provided additional support for this assertion.

Based on these findings in the literature, Ramanathan and Hofmann (in press) proposed that impulsive individuals with chronic hedonic goals would be more likely to display both attentional orientation and attentional adhesion to rewarding stimuli. Further, they proposed that behavior would be influenced primarily by attentional adhesion, reflective of a self-organizing attentional process that recognizes the motivational relevance of the stimulus and generates greater engagement endogenously.

In a study demonstrating this process, Ramanathan and Hofmann (in press) used a visual dot probe task (Mogg & Bradley, 1999) to present images of highly attractive desserts side by side with neutral images, assigning a dot to appear in the location of the dessert or the neutral object at random shortly after the presentation and removal from display of the stimulus pictures. The task required the respondent to identify the location of the dot (on the side of the dessert or of the neutral image) as quickly as possible by pressing one of two keys on the keyboard. The images were presented either for a very short duration (100 ms) or for a long duration (1,250 ms). As respondents are usually faster to respond to probes that appear in the location to which they are attending compared with regions to which they are not attending, the task measures attentional bias toward a particular type of picture, for example, desserts, by evaluating the difference between response times on trials where the probe appears in the location of the desserts and those on trials where the probe appears in the opposite location. The reasoning behind the two exposure times was that the shorter exposure time would only be enough for a respondent to make a single shift of attention, thus representing an orientating bias. Longer exposure times would allow participants to make multiple shifts, and so any bias in this case would represent prolonged attentional adhesion, that is, repeated patterns of looking at the reward (see Fox et al., 2001). Following the task, respondents were ushered into an adjacent room where they were asked to wait for a second study. A tray filled with cookies was left in the room, and the experimenter recorded the number of cookies taken by the participant after the session concluded. Results showed that trait impulsives were faster to respond to the dot probe when it was in the location of the dessert compared with neutral images, both at 100 ms and 1,250 ms exposures. Importantly, it was the bias at 1,250 ms exposure that influenced the number of cookies consumed. There was no effect of the initial orientation bias. These findings underscore the importance of studying the dynamics of attentional and motivational processes in personality at a granular level.

Recurrence dynamics of impulsivity. Ramanathan and Hofmann (in press) explored the downstream effects of directed attention for impulsive versus nonimpulsive individuals. Participants' attention was manipulated by modifying the dot probe task to direct attention toward one type of stimulus (toward hedonic rewards vs. neutral). Later, they provided moment-to-moment ratings (sampled every 0.1 s) of desires and resistance toward a dessert that was placed in front, using a computer mouse to move inside a two-dimensional grid (see Figure 9.2a). The key research question was whether the trajectories for desire and resistance visited the same evaluative space repeatedly over time, which would suggest a recurrent pattern of behavior characteristic of an attractor state. For example, an individual may rate their desire toward the dessert as 8.5 at one moment, 6.4 at the next moment, and 8.3 as few moments later. Assuming that desires in a range between 8.0 and 8.5 are in the same evaluative space, the two points 8.5 and 8.3 would be counted as recurrent, while the 6.4 would not. Recurrence rate therefore is a measure of the percentage of times a trajectory converges around the same set of values. In order to eliminate chance recurrences due to the time points being too close to each other (i.e., high autocorrelation), it is customary to look for recurrence after a prespecified delay, typically at a point in time where the autocorrelation function is close to zero.

In order to determine the recurrence rate, a recurrence plot can be constructed with the original time series on one axis and the lagged time series on the other axis. A point is counted as recurrent if a point on the original time series is very similar to its counterpart on the delayed time series. The density of recurrent points on the plot is called the recurrence rate. Recurrent points that are distributed vertically as opposed to diagonally indicate that the system is stuck in a given state for a long time. Figure 9.2b shows an example of a recurrence plot for desires among impulsive people whose attention was directed toward hedonic options initially. Note that the plot shows high density initially and then becomes more random later. This corresponds to the pattern observed in Figure 9.2a, where desire remains within a narrow range of values for a period of time before exiting the state around the 25th second. This implies that the individual had a high attractor strength during their initial evaluation of the dessert. The high density also manifests in vertical lines within the plot, showing greater inertia in desires. The average length of these lines is called trap time and represents the level of stickiness or inertia in evaluations. Figure 9.2c shows the recurrence plot for resistance.

The average time impulsive individuals whose attention was initially drawn to hedonic options spent in a state of desire was significantly higher compared with other conditions, suggesting that these individuals experienced both higher recurrence and longer stickiness in desires compared with nonimpulsive individuals. A similar analysis conducted for the moment-to-moment trajectories for resistance did not show any reduction in recurrence for impulsive individuals. There was, as expected, greater recurrence of resistance for nonimpulsive individuals, but impulsive individuals did not display any attenuation of resistance, as is commonly believed to underlie an act of indulgence. Figures 9.3a and 9.3b show the recurrence patterns observed for desire and resistance among impulsive and nonimpulsive individuals. Figures 9.3c and 9.3d show trap time patterns for desire and resistance.

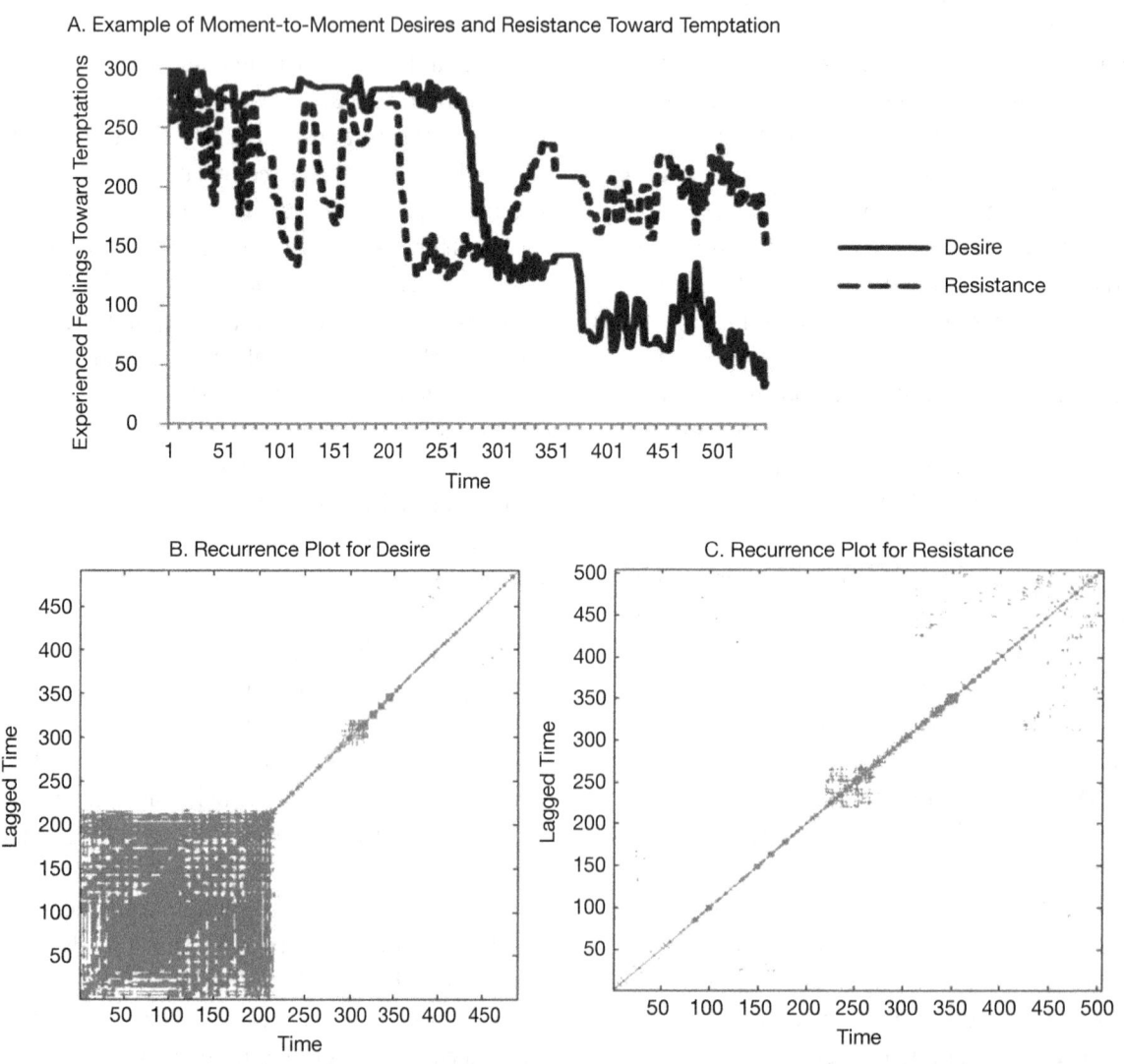

FIGURE 9.2. Recurrence dynamics of impulsivity. From "The Dynamics of Multiple Goal Pursuit: Situation and Personality as Determinants of Goal Stickiness and Switching," by S. Ramanathan, in M. R. Solomon and T. M. Lowrey (Eds.), *The Routledge Companion to Consumer Behavior* (p. 183), 2017, Taylor & Francis (https://doi.org/10.4324/9781315526935). Copyright 2017 by Taylor & Francis. Reprinted with permission.

Viewed together, these findings provide significant evidence for the PersDyn model (Sosnowska et al., 2019) as applied to impulsivity. The central idea in the PersDyn model is that it is important to study attractor strength as a measure of the coherence of the underlying trait. Impulsive individuals demonstrate both a greater recurrence rate of desires and a greater stickiness in desires when their attention is directed toward temptations. Thus, the exogenously directed attention appears to fan the flames of desires and keeps them burning longer without getting extinguished.

Ramanathan and Hofmann (in press) further explored the dynamics of desires and resistance among individuals with high versus low reward seeking tendencies, as measured by the BAS Reward Responsiveness Scale by modeling the frequency and amplitude of desires and resistance and any mutual influence from one to the other. Using a coupled oscillator model, which is employed in physics to describe the motion of two springs coupled to each other and anchored at the other end to two walls, Ramanathan and Hofmann modeled the dynamics of felt desires and resistance and the

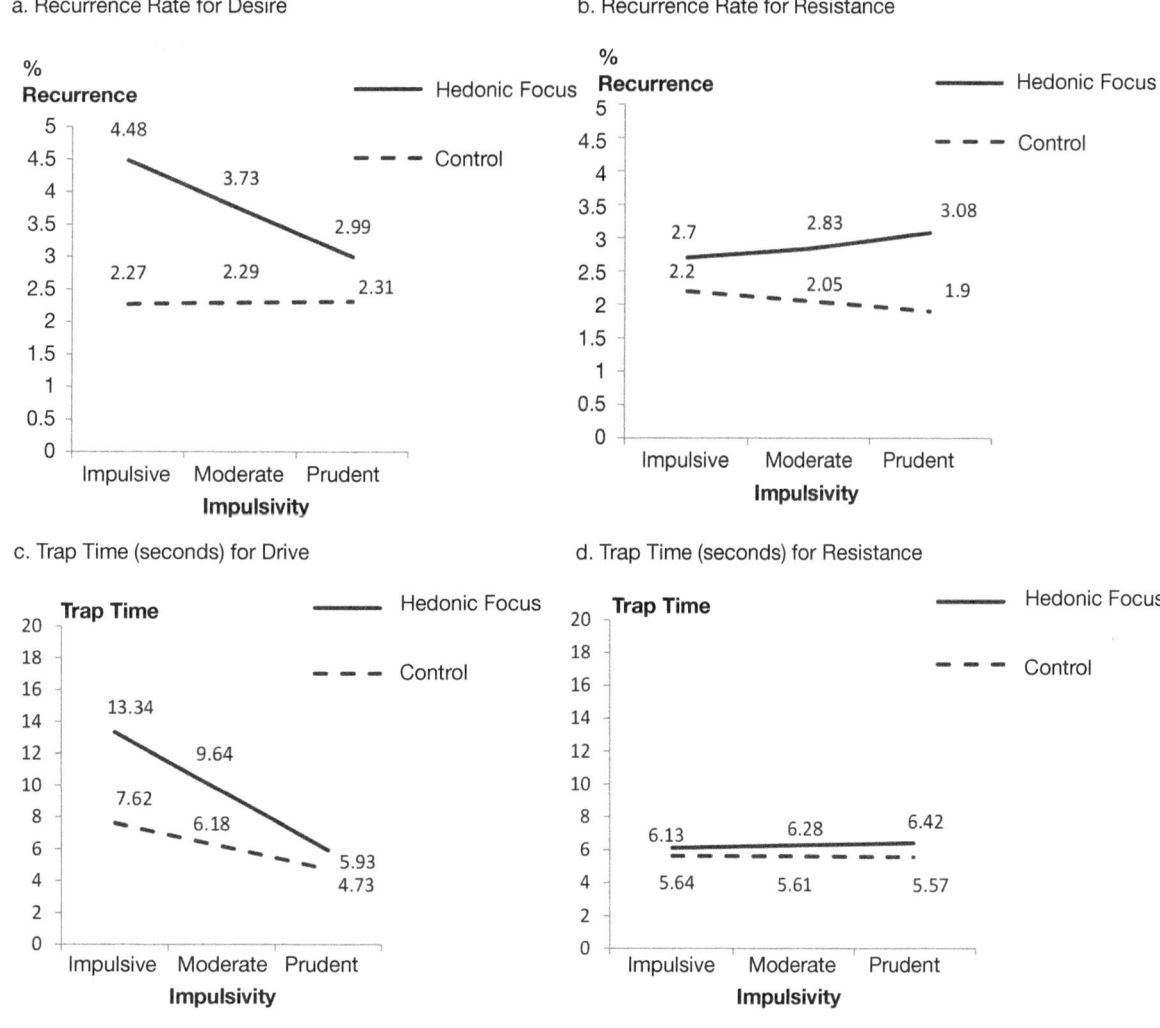

FIGURE 9.3. Recurrence plot metrics by locus of attention and level of impulsivity. From "The Dynamics of Multiple Goal Pursuit: Situation and Personality as Determinants of Goal Stickiness and Switching," by S. Ramanathan, in M. R. Solomon and T. M. Lowrey (Eds.), *The Routledge Companion to Consumer Behavior* (p. 184), 2017, Taylor & Francis (https://doi.org/10.4324/9781315526935). Copyright 2017 by Taylor & Francis. Reprinted with permission.

mutual effects of these felt emotions on each other. The two springs represented desire and resistance, and the coupling represented the influence that one motivational system had on the other. Normally, any spring, once moved from its equilibrium state, continues to oscillate at decreasing amplitudes until it returns to equilibrium. In the present analogy, the frequency with which the spring oscillates represents the speed at which the system is cycling in and out of equilibrium. The lower the frequency, the longer the system is stuck in one goal state (similar to trap time described earlier). Ramanathan and Hofmann found that when high reward seekers had their attention directed toward temptations, they exhibited a distinct pattern in their moment-to-moment dynamics of desires—they had a reduced frequency of oscillation in desires, suggestive of greater stickiness. They also showed increasing rather than decreasing amplitudes in desire (see Figure 9.4a). Importantly, Ramanathan and Hofmann also found a very interesting pattern for reward seekers who also showed higher levels of resistance—the amplitude of desire increased rather than decreased. As is seen in Figure 9.4b, the trajectory for resistance shows a temporary dampening caused by the feedback from desire but subsequently increases in amplitude.

These results provide significant support for a self-organized system of desire and resistance that influences impulsiveness and is in turn influenced by the trait, as proposed by the dynamic models of personality (Cervone, 2004; Mischel & Shoda, 1995; Sosnowska et al., 2019).

CONCLUSION

In this chapter, I presented a view of personality through different lenses, comparing and contrasting structural models from dynamic models. Structural models evolved from a need to create a taxonomy of features that could be used to describe the behavior of people. This enables us to understand broad differences among individuals and to describe the characteristics that would help differentiate one individual from another. Description of personality is, of course, an important aspect of the study of the field, especially in order to meet the taxonomical and classificatory aims of science (Boag, 2018). Classificatory constructs give a structure to entities in a given population but do not provide any explanation for why such a structure was needed or created. As Harré (1998) noted, "To say that a chimpanzee is a primate does not explain anything about its characteristics" (pp. 80–81). Yet several

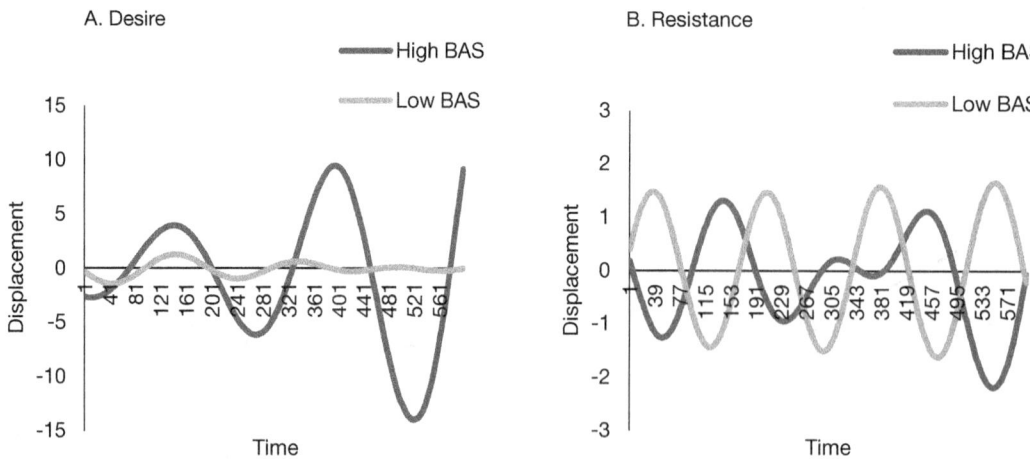

FIGURE 9.4. Dynamics of desire and resistance for high and low reward seekers in response to directed attention to hedonic stimuli. BAS = behavioral activation system. From "The Dynamics of Multiple Goal Pursuit: Situation and Personality as Determinants of Goal Stickiness and Switching," by S. Ramanathan, in M. R. Solomon and T. M. Lowrey (Eds.), *The Routledge Companion to Consumer Behavior* (p. 185), 2017, Taylor & Francis (https://doi.org/10.4324/9781315526935). Copyright 2017 by Taylor & Francis. Reprinted with permission.

structural models, including some that are commonly used in consumer psychology, attempt to infer causality from observing an effect in the form of a behavior and attributing an individual difference variable as the proximate cause.

Science also looks for explanation. Why do people have certain characteristics? What about their individual experiences and behaviors led to the development of these characteristics? How did these characteristics become enduring qualities that are chronically accessible as self-knowledge? (Cervone, 2005).

Dynamic models provide the explanatory perspective. From a consumer behavior perspective, researchers who use individual difference measures need an understanding of the field of causes and effects in which their measures operate (Mackie, 1980). This is important because many factors can produce the same changes, and the same factors can produce different changes (Boag, 2018). As I have illustrated with the studies on impulsivity, an impulsive person may respond differently to a situation depending on whether it activates or reinforces chronic hedonic goals.

Dynamic systems of personality represent an opportunity to understand individual differences from the bottom up—a means to construct the trait from its building blocks, namely, the various cognitions, affect, goals, and values that are intrinsic to the individual (Cervone, 1997, 1999). Dispositional tendencies are not simply measured via self-report scales but also explained by referencing the underlying psychological systems.

Crucially, this approach goes beyond trying to identify differences in average response tendencies (Cervone & Shoda, 1999). The key metric to focus on is not simply the average response but the pattern of response variability over time and across situations (Vansteelandt & Van Mechelen, 2004). For example, the different rates of decay for pleasure and guilt among impulsive versus nonimpulsive people (Ramanathan & Williams, 2007) show the importance of studying patterns of variability over time.

One interesting question that may be addressed by consumer behavior researchers is to determine the reasons for the development of different dispositional tendencies. Why would someone have low self-control in the domain of eating but be quite prudent when spending? What kinds of early stage developmental situations may have led to such differences in dispositions? Dynamical systems such as those discussed earlier may be able to shed light on the emergence of different dispositional tendencies.

Another question that could be potentially addressed from both the structural and the dynamic perspective is how consumers balance multiple traits. An individual could have a high need for uniqueness and also be deal-prone. Would a great deal on a less unique product be acceptable? The structural model (Mowen, 2000) relies on a feedback loop that monitors the current state relative to a reference point. In the case of two chronic traits, how would the comparator judge the outcome relative to the reference point? In the extant case, the individual would find a large discrepancy between the outcome for need for uniqueness and the reference value and would not find such a discrepancy between the outcome for the deal and the reference point. Would consumers average the two outputs of the comparator? From a dynamic perspective, it would be useful to study the affective feedback while the consumer recognizes the lack of progress on the behavioral expressions of the trait.

REFERENCES

Ailawadi, K. L., Neslin, S. A., & Gedenk, K. (2001). Pursuing the value-conscious consumer: Store brands versus national brand promotions. *Journal of Marketing, 65*(1), 71–89. https://doi.org/10.1509/jmkg.65.1.71.18132

Ainslie, G., & Haslam, N. (1992). Hyperbolic discounting. In G. Loewenstein & J. Elster (Eds.), *Choice over time* (pp. 57–92). Russell Sage Foundation.

Al-Adawi, S., Powell, J. H., & Greenwood, R. J. (1998). Motivational deficits after brain injury: A neuropsychological approach using new assessment techniques. *Neuropsychology, 12*(1), 115–124. https://doi.org/10.1037/0894-4105.12.1.115

Allport, G. W., & Odbert, H. (1936). Trait-names: A psycho-lexical study. *Psychological Review Monographs, 211*(1), 1–171.

Ashton, M. C., Paunonen, S. V., Helmes, E., & Jackson, D. N. (1998). Kin altruism, reciprocal altruism, and the Big Five personality factors. *Evolution and Human*

Behavior, *19*(4), 243–255. https://doi.org/10.1016/S1090-5138(98)00009-9

Barratt, E. S. (1959). Anxiety and impulsiveness related to psychomotor efficiency. *Perceptual and Motor Skills*, *9*(3), 191–198. https://doi.org/10.2466/PMS.9.3.191-198

Barrick, M. R., Stewart, G. L., Neubert, M. J., & Mount, M. K. (1998). Relating member ability and personality to work-team processes and team effectiveness. *Journal of Applied Psychology*, *83*(3), 377–391. https://doi.org/10.1037/0021-9010.83.3.377

Baumeister, R. F., Bratslavsky, E., Muraven, M., & Tice, D. M. (1998). Ego depletion: Is the active self a limited resource? *Journal of Personality and Social Psychology*, *74*(5), 1252–1265. https://doi.org/10.1037/0022-3514.74.5.1252

Baumgartner, H. (2002). Toward a personology of the consumer. *Journal of Consumer Research*, *29*(2), 286–292. https://doi.org/10.1086/341578

Baumgartner, H., & Steenkamp, J.-B. E. M. (1996). Exploratory consumer buying behavior: Conceptualization and measurement. *International Journal of Research in Marketing*, *13*(2), 121–137. https://doi.org/10.1016/0167-8116(95)00037-2

Baumsteiger, R., & Siegel, J. T. (2019). Measuring prosociality: The development of a prosocial behavioral intentions Scale. *Journal of Personality Assessment*, *101*(3), 305–314. https://doi.org/10.1080/00223891.2017.1411918

Bearden, W. O., Netemeyer, R. G., & Haws, K. L. (2011). *Handbook of marketing scales: Multi-item measures for marketing and consumer behavior research*. Sage Publications.

Bearden, W. O., Netemeyer, R. G., & Teel, J. E. (1989). Measurement of consumer susceptibility to interpersonal influence. *Journal of Consumer Research*, *15*(4), 473–481. https://doi.org/10.1086/209186

Belei, N. V. T., Ramanathan, S., Davis, S. W., & Menon, P. (in press). Top down, side up: Effects of food architecture on consumption of hedonic foods.

Bellman, S. B. (2012). *I would rather be happy than right: Consumer impulsivity, risky decision making, and accountability* (UMI No. 3516594) [Doctoral dissertation, University of Iowa]. ProQuest Dissertations and Theses Global.

Block, J. H., & Block, J. (1980). The role of ego-control and ego-resiliency in the organization of behavior. In W. A. Collins (Ed.), *Development of cognition, affect, and social relations: The Minnesota symposia on child psychology* (Vol. 13, pp. 39–101). Erlbaum.

Boag, S. (2011). Explanation in personality psychology: "Verbal magic" and the five-factor model. *Philosophical Psychology*, *24*(2), 223–243. https://doi.org/10.1080/09515089.2010.548319

Boag, S. (2015). Personality assessment, "construct validity," and the significance of theory. *Personality and Individual Differences*, *84*, 36–44. https://doi.org/10.1016/j.paid.2014.12.039

Boag, S. (2018). Personality dynamics, motivation, and the logic of explanation. *Review of General Psychology*, *22*(4), 427–436. https://doi.org/10.1037/gpr0000150

Bogg, T., & Roberts, B. W. (2004). Conscientiousness and health-related behaviors: A meta-analysis of the leading behavioral contributors to mortality. *Psychological Bulletin*, *130*(6), 887–919. https://doi.org/10.1037/0033-2909.130.6.887

Bradley, B. P., Mogg, K., Wright, T., & Field, M. (2003). Attentional bias in drug dependence: Vigilance for cigarette-related cues in smokers. *Psychology of Addictive Behaviors*, *17*(1), 66–72. https://doi.org/10.1037/0893-164X.17.1.66

Buss, A. H. (1989). Personality as traits. *American Psychologist*, *44*(11), 1378–1388. https://doi.org/10.1037/0003-066X.44.11.1378

Cacioppo, J. T., & Petty, R. E. (1982). The need for cognition. *Journal of Personality and Social Psychology*, *42*(1), 116–131. https://doi.org/10.1037/0022-3514.42.1.116

Carver, C. S., & Scheier, M. F. (1990). Origins and functions of positive and negative affect: A control-process view. *Psychological Review*, *97*(1), 19–35. https://doi.org/10.1037/0033-295X.97.1.19

Carver, C. S., & Scheier, M. F. (2002). Control processes and self-organization as complementary principles underlying behavior. *Personality and Social Psychology Review*, *6*(4), 304–315. https://doi.org/10.1207/S15327957PSPR0604_05

Carver, C. S., & White, T. L. (1994). Behavioral inhibition, behavioral activation, and affective responses to impending reward and punishment: The BIS/BAS Scales. *Journal of Personality and Social Psychology*, *67*(2), 319–333. https://doi.org/10.1037/0022-3514.67.2.319

Cattell, R. B. (1957). *Personality and motivation structure and measurement*. World Book Co.

Cattell, R. B. (1965). *The scientific analysis of personality*. Penguin Books.

Cervone, D. (1997). Social-cognitive mechanisms and personality coherence: Self-knowledge, situational beliefs, and cross-situational coherence in perceived self-efficacy. *Psychological Science*, *8*(1), 43–50. https://doi.org/10.1111/j.1467-9280.1997.tb00542.x

Cervone, D. (1999). Bottom-up explanation in personality psychology: The case of cross-situational coherence. In D. Cervone & Y. Shoda (Eds.), *The coherence of personality: Social-cognitive bases of consistency, variability, and organization* (pp. 303–341). Guilford Press.

Cervone, D. (2004). The architecture of personality. *Psychological Review, 111*(1), 183–204. https://doi.org/10.1037/0033-295X.111.1.183

Cervone, D. (2005). Personality architecture: Within-person structures and processes. *Annual Review of Psychology, 56*(1), 423–452. https://doi.org/10.1146/annurev.psych.56.091103.070133

Cervone, D., & Little, B. R. (2019). Personality architecture and dynamics: The new agenda and what's new about it. *Personality and Individual Differences, 136*, 12–23. https://doi.org/10.1016/j.paid.2017.07.001

Cervone, D., & Shoda, Y. (1999). *The coherence of personality: Social-cognitive bases of consistency, variability, and organization*. Guilford Press.

Cheema, A., & Kaikati, A. M. (2010). The effect of need for uniqueness on word of mouth. *Journal of Marketing Research, 47*(3), 553–563. https://doi.org/10.1509/jmkr.47.3.553

Costa, P. T., Jr., & McCrae, R. R. (1992). The five-factor model of personality and its relevance to personality disorders. *Journal of Personality Disorders, 6*(4), 343–359. https://doi.org/10.1521/pedi.1992.6.4.343

De Dreu, C. K. W., & Van Vianen, A. E. M. (2001). Managing relationship conflict and the effectiveness of organizational teams. *Journal of Organizational Behavior, 22*(3), 309–328. https://doi.org/10.1002/job.71

DeNeve, K. M., & Cooper, H. (1998). The happy personality: A meta-analysis of 137 personality traits and subjective well-being. *Psychological Bulletin, 124*(2), 197–229. https://doi.org/10.1037/0033-2909.124.2.197

Depue, R. A. (2006). Interpersonal behavior and the structure of personality: Neurobehavioral foundation of agentic extraversion and affiliation. In T. Canli (Ed.), *Biology of personality and individual differences* (pp. 60–92). Guilford Press.

Depue, R. A., & Collins, P. F. (1999). Neurobiology of the structure of personality: Dopamine, facilitation of incentive motivation, and extraversion. *Behavioral and Brain Sciences, 22*(3), 491–517. https://doi.org/10.1017/S0140525X99002046

Evenden, J. L. (1999). Varieties of impulsivity. *Psychopharmacology, 146*(4), 348–361. https://doi.org/10.1007/PL00005481

Eysenck, H. J. (1952). *The scientific study of personality*. Macmillan.

Eysenck, H. J. (1967). *The biological basis of personality*. Thomas.

Eysenck, H. J., & Eysenck, S. B. G. (1969). *Personality structure and measurement*. Routledge & Kegan Paul.

Eysenck, S. B. G., & Eysenck, H. J. (1977). The place of impulsiveness in a dimensional system of personality description. *British Journal of Social and Clinical Psychology, 16*(1), 57–68.

Feick, L. F., & Price, L. L. (1987). The market maven: A diffuser of marketplace information. *Journal of Marketing, 51*(1), 83–97. https://doi.org/10.1177/002224298705100107

Fineberg, N. A., Chamberlain, S. R., Goudriaan, A. E., Stein, D. J., Vanderschuren, L. J., Gillan, C. M., Shekar, S., Gorwood, P. A., Voon, V., Morein-Zamir, S., Denys, D., Sahakian, B. J., Moeller, F. G., Robbins, T. W., & Potenza, M. N. (2014). New developments in human neurocognition: Clinical, genetic, and brain imaging correlates of impulsivity and compulsivity. *CNS Spectrums, 19*(1), 69–89. https://doi.org/10.1017/S1092852913000801

Fleeson, W. (2001). Toward a structure- and process-integrated view of personality: Traits as density distribution of states. *Journal of Personality and Social Psychology, 80*(6), 1011–1027. https://doi.org/10.1037/0022-3514.80.6.1011

Fleischhauer, M., Enge, S., Brocke, B., Ullrich, J., Strobel, A., & Strobel, A. (2010). Same or different? Clarifying the relationship of need for cognition to personality and intelligence. *Personality and Social Psychology Bulletin, 36*(1), 82–96. https://doi.org/10.1177/0146167209351886

Fox, E., Russo, R., Bowles, R., & Dutton, K. (2001). Do threatening stimuli draw or hold visual attention in subclinical anxiety? *Journal of Experimental Psychology: General, 130*(4), 681–700. https://doi.org/10.1037/0096-3445.130.4.681

Funder, D. C., & Block, J. (1989). The role of ego-control, ego-resiliency, and IQ in delay of gratification in adolescence. *Journal of Personality and Social Psychology, 57*(6), 1041–1050. https://doi.org/10.1037/0022-3514.57.6.1041

Galassi, M. D., & Galassi, J. P. (1977). *Assert yourself! How to be your own person*. Human Sciences.

Goldberg, L. R. (1993). The structure of personality traits: Vertical and horizontal aspects. In D. C. Funder, R. D. Parke, C. Tomlinson-Keasey, & K. Widaman (Eds.), *Studying lives through time: Personality and development* (pp. 169–188). American Psychological Association. https://doi.org/10.1037/10127-024

Gray, J. A. (1987). Perspectives on anxiety and impulsivity: A commentary. *Journal of Research in Personality, 21*(4), 493–509. https://doi.org/10.1016/0092-6566(87)90036-5

Green, L., Myerson, J., & McFadden, E. (1997). Rate of temporal discounting decreases with amount of reward. *Memory & Cognition, 25*(5), 715–723. https://doi.org/10.3758/BF03211314

Harré, R. (1998). *The singular self: An introduction to the psychology of personhood*. Sage Publications, Inc.

Haugtvedt, C. P., & Petty, R. E. (1992). Personality and persuasion: Need for cognition moderates the persistence and resistance of attitude changes. *Journal of Personality and Social Psychology, 63*(2), 308–319. https://doi.org/10.1037/0022-3514.63.2.308

Haugtvedt, C. P., Petty, R. E., & Cacioppo, J. T. (1992). Need for cognition and advertising: Understanding the role of personality variables in consumer behavior. *Journal of Consumer Psychology, 1*(3), 239–260. https://doi.org/10.1016/S1057-7408(08)80038-1

Haws, K. L., Davis, S. W., & Dholakia, U. M. (2016). Control over what? Individual differences in general versus eating and spending self-control. *Journal of Public Policy & Marketing, 35*(1), 37–57. https://doi.org/10.1509/jppm.14.149

Helmers, K. F., Young, S. N., & Pihl, R. O. (1997). Extraversion and behavioral impulsivity. *Personality and Individual Differences, 23*(3), 441–452. https://doi.org/10.1016/S0191-8869(97)80010-4

Higgins, E. T. (1997). Beyond pleasure and pain. *American Psychologist, 52*(12), 1280–1300. https://doi.org/10.1037/0003-066X.52.12.1280

Higgins, E. T., Pierro, A., & Kruglanski, A. W. (2008). Re-thinking culture and personality: How self-regulatory universals create cross-cultural differences. In R. M. Sorrentino & S. Yamaguchi (Eds.), *Handbook of motivation and cognition across cultures* (pp. 161–190). Academic Press. https://doi.org/10.1016/B978-0-12-373694-9.00008-8

Higgins, E. T., Shah, J., & Friedman, R. (1997). Emotional responses to goal attainment: Strength of regulatory focus as moderator. *Journal of Personality and Social Psychology, 72*(3), 515–525. https://doi.org/10.1037/0022-3514.72.3.515

Hofmann, W., Baumeister, R. F., Förster, G., & Vohs, K. D. (2012). Everyday temptations: An experience sampling study of desire, conflict, and self-control. *Journal of Personality and Social Psychology, 102*(6), 1318–1335. https://doi.org/10.1037/a0026545

Hofmann, W., Friese, M., & Strack, F. (2009). Impulse and self-control from a dual-systems perspective. *Perspectives on Psychological Science, 4*(2), 162–176. https://doi.org/10.1111/j.1745-6924.2009.01116.x

Hofstee, W. K., de Raad, B., & Goldberg, L. R. (1992). Integration of the Big Five and circumplex approaches to trait structure. *Journal of Personality and Social Psychology, 63*(1), 146–163. https://doi.org/10.1037/0022-3514.63.1.146

International Society for Research on Impulsivity. (n.d.). *What is impulsivity?* http://www.impulsivity.org/

Joachimsthaler, E. A., & Lastovicka, J. L. (1984). Optimal stimulation level: Exploratory behavior models. *Journal of Consumer Research, 11*(3), 830–835. https://doi.org/10.1086/209018

John, O. P., & Srivastava, S. (1999). The Big Five trait taxonomy: History, measurement, and theoretical perspectives. In L. A. Pervin & O. P. John (Eds.), *Handbook of personality: Theory and research* (2nd ed., pp. 102–138). Guilford Press.

Kassarjian, H. H. (1971). Personality and consumer behavior: A review. *Journal of Marketing Research, 8*(4), 409–418. https://doi.org/10.1177/002224377100800401

Kelso, J. A. S. (1995). *Dynamic patterns: The self-organization of brain and behavior*. MIT Press.

Kemps, E., & Tiggemann, M. (2009). Attentional bias for craving-related (chocolate) food cues. *Experimental and Clinical Psychopharmacology, 17*(6), 425–433. https://doi.org/10.1037/a0017796

Knudsen, E. I. (2007). Fundamental components of attention. *Annual Review of Neuroscience, 30*(1), 57–78. https://doi.org/10.1146/annurev.neuro.30.051606.094256

Kovach, C. K., Sutterer, M. J., Rushia, S. N., Teriakidis, A., & Jenison, R. L. (2014). Two systems drive attention to rewards. *Frontiers in Psychology, 5*, 46. https://doi.org/10.3389/fpsyg.2014.00046

Lange, F., Wagner, A., Müller, A., & Eggert, F. (2017). Subscales of the Barratt Impulsiveness Scale differentially relate to the Big Five factors of personality. *Scandinavian Journal of Psychology, 58*(3), 254–259. https://doi.org/10.1111/sjop.12359

Lastovicka, J. L. (1982). On the validation of lifestyle traits: A review and illustration. *Journal of Marketing Research, 19*(1), 126–138. https://doi.org/10.1177/002224378201900112

Lee, A. Y., & Aaker, J. L. (2004). Bringing the frame into focus: The influence of regulatory fit on processing fluency and persuasion. *Journal of Personality and Social Psychology, 86*(2), 205–218. https://doi.org/10.1037/0022-3514.86.2.205

Lee, K., & Ashton, M. C. (2004). Psychometric properties of the HEXACO personality inventory. *Multivariate Behavioral Research, 39*(2), 329–358. https://doi.org/10.1207/s15327906mbr3902_8

Lewis, M. D. (1996). Self-organising cognitive appraisals. *Cognition and Emotion, 10*(1), 1–26. https://doi.org/10.1080/026999396380367

Lichtenstein, D. R., Ridgway, N. M., & Netemeyer, R. G. (1993). Price perceptions and consumer shopping behavior: A field study. *Journal of Marketing Research, 30*(2), 234–245. https://doi.org/10.1177/002224379303000208

Loewenstein, G., & Prelec, D. (1992). Anomalies in interpersonal choice: Evidence and an interpretation.

In G. Loewenstein & J. Elster (Eds.), *Choice over time* (pp. 119–145). Russell Sage Foundation.

Mackie, J. L. (1980). *The cement of the universe: A study in causation.* Clarendon Press. https://doi.org/10.1093/0198246420.001.0001

Maner, J. K., Gailliot, M. T., Rouby, D. A., & Miller, S. L. (2007). Can't take my eyes off you: Attentional adhesion to mates and rivals. *Journal of Personality and Social Psychology, 93*(3), 389–401. https://doi.org/10.1037/0022-3514.93.3.389

Manesi, Z., Van Lange, P. A. M., Van Doesum, N. J., & Pollet, T. V. (2019). What are the most powerful predictors of charitable giving to victims of typhoon Haiyan: Prosocial traits, socio-demographic variables, or eye cues? *Personality and Individual Differences, 146,* 217–225. https://doi.org/10.1016/j.paid.2018.03.024

McAdams, D. P. (2001). The psychology of life stories. *Review of General Psychology, 5*(2), 100–122. https://doi.org/10.1037/1089-2680.5.2.100

McCrae, R. R., & Costa, P. T., Jr. (1996). Toward a new generation of personality theories: Theoretical contexts for the five-factor model. In J. S. Wiggins (Ed.), *The five-factor model of personality: Theoretical perspectives* (pp. 51–87). Guilford Press.

McCrae, R. R., & Costa, P. T., Jr. (2003). *Personality in adulthood: A five-factor theory perspective* (2nd ed.). Guilford Press. https://doi.org/10.4324/9780203428412

McCrae, R. R., & Costa, P. T., Jr. (2008). The five-factor theory of personality. In O. P. John, R. W. Robins, & L. A. Pervin (Eds.), *Handbook of personality: Theory and research* (3rd ed., pp. 159–181). Guilford Press.

Metcalfe, J., & Mischel, W. (1999). A hot/cool-system analysis of delay of gratification: Dynamics of willpower. *Psychological Review, 106*(1), 3–19. https://doi.org/10.1037/0033-295X.106.1.3

Mischel, W. (1968). *Personality and assessment.* John Wiley & Sons Inc.

Mischel, W. (2004). Toward an integrative science of the person. *Annual Review of Psychology, 55*(1), 1–22. https://doi.org/10.1146/annurev.psych.55.042902.130709

Mischel, W., & Shoda, Y. (1995). A cognitive-affective system theory of personality: Reconceptualizing situations, dispositions, dynamics, and invariance in personality structure. *Psychological Review, 102*(2), 246–268. https://doi.org/10.1037/0033-295X.102.2.246

Mischel, W., Shoda, Y., & Rodriguez, M. I. (1989). Delay of gratification in children. *Science, 244*(4907), 933–938. https://doi.org/10.1126/science.2658056

Mogg, K., & Bradley, B. P. (1999). Orienting of attention to threatening facial expressions presented under conditions of restricted awareness. *Cognition and Emotion, 13*(6), 713–740. https://doi.org/10.1080/026999399379050

Mogg, K., Bradley, B. P., Field, M., & De Houwer, J. (2003). Eye movements to smoking-related pictures in smokers: Relationship between attentional biases and implicit and explicit measures of stimulus valence. *Addiction, 98*(6), 825–836. https://doi.org/10.1046/j.1360-0443.2003.00392.x

Mooradian, T. A. (1996). The five factor model and market mavenism. In K. P. Corfman & J. G. Lynch Jr. (Eds.), *NA - Advances in consumer research* (Vol. 23, pp. 260–263). Association for Consumer Research.

Mooradian, T. A., & Olver, J. M. (1997). "I can't get no satisfaction": The impact of personality and emotion on post-purchase processes. *Psychology and Marketing, 14*(4), 379–393. https://doi.org/10.1002/(SICI)1520-6793(199707)14:4<379::AID-MAR5>3.0.CO;2-6

Mowen, J. C. (2000). *The 3M model of motivation and personality: theory and empirical applications to consumer behavior.* Kluwer Academic. https://doi.org/10.1007/978-1-4757-6708-7

Mowen, J. C., & Spears, N. (1999). Understanding compulsive buying among college students: A hierarchical approach. *Journal of Consumer Psychology, 8*(4), 407–430. https://doi.org/10.1207/s15327663jcp0804_03

Mukhopadhyay, A., Sengupta, J., & Ramanathan, S. (2008). Recalling past temptations: An information-processing perspective on the dynamics of self-control. *Journal of Consumer Research, 35*(4), 586–599. https://doi.org/10.1086/591105

Myers, I. B., & McCaulley, M. (1985). *Manual: A guide to the development and use of the Meyers-Briggs Type Indicator.* Consulting Psychologists Press.

Newman, J. P., Kosson, D. S., & Patterson, C. M. (1992). Delay of gratification in psychopathic and nonpsychopathic offenders. *Journal of Abnormal Psychology, 101*(4), 630–636. https://doi.org/10.1037/0021-843X.101.4.630

Nowak, A., Vallacher, R. R., & Zochowski, M. (2005). The emergence of personality: Dynamic foundations of individual variation. *Developmental Review, 25*(3–4), 351–385. https://doi.org/10.1016/j.dr.2005.10.004

O'Guinn, T. C., & Faber, R. J. (1989). Compulsive buying: A phenomenological exploration. *Journal of Consumer Research, 16*(2), 147–157. https://doi.org/10.1086/209204

Orth, U. R., & Kahle, L. R. (2008). Intrapersonal variation in consumer susceptibility to normative influence: Toward a better understanding of brand choice decisions. *Journal of Social Psychology, 148*(4), 423–448. https://doi.org/10.3200/SOCP.148.4.423-448

Parker, J. D. A., Bagby, R. M., & Webster, C. D. (1993). Domains of the impulsivity construct: A factor analytic investigation. *Personality and Individual Differences*, *15*(3), 267–274. https://doi.org/10.1016/0191-8869(93)90216-P

Patton, J. H., Stanford, M. S., & Barratt, E. S. (1995). Factor structure of the Barratt impulsiveness scale. *Journal of Clinical Psychology*, *51*(6), 768–774. https://doi.org/10.1002/1097-4679(199511)51:6<768::AID-JCLP2270510607>3.0.CO;2-1

Paunonen, S. V. (1998). Hierarchical organization of personality and prediction of behavior. *Journal of Personality and Social Psychology*, *74*(2), 538–556. https://doi.org/10.1037/0022-3514.74.2.538

Paunonen, S. V., & Jackson, D. N. (2000). What is beyond the big five? Plenty! *Journal of Personality*, *68*(5), 821–835. https://doi.org/10.1111/1467-6494.00117

Poropat, A. E. (2009). A meta-analysis of the five-factor model of personality and academic performance. *Psychological Bulletin*, *135*(2), 322–338. https://doi.org/10.1037/a0014996

Posner, M. I., & Petersen, S. E. (1990). The attention system of the human brain. *Annual Review of Neuroscience*, *13*(1), 25–42. https://doi.org/10.1146/annurev.ne.13.030190.000325

Posner, M. I., Snyder, C. R., & Davidson, B. J. (1980). Attention and the detection of signals. *Journal of Experimental Psychology: General*, *109*(2), 160–174. https://doi.org/10.1037/0096-3445.109.2.160

Puri, R. (1996). Measuring and modifying consumer impulsiveness: A cost-benefit accessibility framework. *Journal of Consumer Psychology*, *5*(2), 87–113. https://doi.org/10.1207/s15327663jcp0502_01

Raju, P. S. (1980). Optimum stimulation level: Its relationship to personality, demographics, and exploratory behavior. *Journal of Consumer Research*, *7*(3), 272–282. https://doi.org/10.1086/208815

Ramanathan, S. (2002). *Goal-dependent automaticity in impulsive decisions* (Order No. 3061295) [Doctoral dissertation, New York University]. ProQuest Dissertations and Theses Global.

Ramanathan, S. (2017). The dynamics of goal pursuit: Situation and personality as determinants of goal stickiness and switching. In M. R. Solomon & T. M. Lowrey (Eds.), *Routledge companion to consumer behavior* (pp. 175–190). Routledge. https://doi.org/10.4324/9781315526935-12

Ramanathan, S., & Dhar, S. K. (2010). The effect of sales promotions on the size and composition of the shopping basket: Regulatory compatibility from framing and temporal restrictions. *Journal of Marketing Research*, *47*(3), 542–552. https://doi.org/10.1509/jmkr.47.3.542

Ramanathan, S., & Hofmann, W. (in press). *Sticky desires or tricky self-control? Dynamics of attentional and affective processes in response to temptations* [Working paper]. Mays Business School, Texas A&M University.

Ramanathan, S., & Menon, G. (2006). Time-varying effects of chronic hedonic goals on impulsive behavior. *Journal of Marketing Research*, *43*(4), 628–641. https://doi.org/10.1509/jmkr.43.4.628

Ramanathan, S., & Williams, P. (2007). Immediate and delayed emotional consequences of indulgence: The moderating influence of personality type on mixed emotions. *Journal of Consumer Research*, *34*(2), 212–223. https://doi.org/10.1086/519149

Redden, J. P., & Haws, K. L. (2013). Healthy satiation: The role of decreasing desire in effective self-control. *Journal of Consumer Research*, *39*(5), 1100–1114. https://doi.org/10.1086/667362

Revelle, W. (1995). Personality processes. *Annual Review of Psychology*, *46*(1), 295–328. https://doi.org/10.1146/annurev.ps.46.020195.001455

Revelle, W., Wilt, J., & Condon, D. M. (2011). Individual differences and differential psychology: A brief history and prospect. In T. Chamorro-Premuzic, S. von Stumm, & A. Furnham (Eds.), *The Wiley-Blackwell handbook of individual differences* (pp. 1–38). Wiley-Blackwell. https://doi.org/10.1002/9781444343120.ch1

Richins, M. L. (1983). An analysis of consumer interaction styles in the marketplace. *Journal of Consumer Research*, *10*(1), 73–82. https://doi.org/10.1086/208946

Rook, D. W. (1987). The buying impulse. *Journal of Consumer Research*, *14*(2), 189–199. https://doi.org/10.1086/209105

Rook, D. W., & Fisher, R. J. (1995). Normative influences on impulsive buying behavior. *Journal of Consumer Research*, *22*(3), 305–313. https://doi.org/10.1086/209452

Sadowski, C. J., & Cogburn, H. E. (1997). Need for cognition in the Big-Five factor structure. *Journal of Psychology*, *131*(3), 307–312. https://doi.org/10.1080/00223989709603517

Saucier G. (2003). An alternative multi-language structure for personality attributes. *European Journal of Personality*, *17*(3), 179–206. https://doi.org/10.1002/per.489

Saucier, G., & Goldberg, L. R. (1996). The language of personality: Lexical perspectives on the five-factor model. In J. S. Wiggins (Ed.), *The five-factor model of personality: Theoretical perspectives* (pp. 21–50). Guilford Press.

Schumpe, B. M., Herzberg, P. Y., & Erb, H.-P. (2016). Assessing the need for uniqueness: Validation of the German NfU-G scale. *Personality and Individual Differences, 90,* 231–237. https://doi.org/10.1016/j.paid.2015.11.012

Shiv, B., & Fedorikhin, A. (1999). Heart and mind in conflict: The interplay of affect and cognition in consumer decision making. *Journal of Consumer Research, 26*(3), 278–292. https://doi.org/10.1086/209563

Simonson, I., & Nowlis, S. M. (2000). The role of explanations and need for uniqueness in consumer decision making: Unconventional choices based on reasons. *Journal of Consumer Research, 27*(1), 49–68. https://doi.org/10.1086/314308

Smeets, E., Roefs, A., & Jansen, A. (2009). Experimentally induced chocolate craving leads to an attentional bias in increased distraction but not in speeded detection. *Appetite, 53*(3), 370–375. https://doi.org/10.1016/j.appet.2009.07.020

Snyder, C. R. (1992). Product scarcity by need for uniqueness interaction: A consumer catch-22 carousel? *Basic and Applied Social Psychology, 13*(1), 9–24. https://doi.org/10.1207/s15324834basp1301_3

Snyder, C. R., & Fromkin, H. L. (1977). Abnormality as a positive characteristic: The development and validation of a scale measuring need for uniqueness. *Journal of Abnormal Psychology, 86*(5), 518–527. https://doi.org/10.1037/0021-843X.86.5.518

Sosnowska, J., Kuppens, P., De Fruyt, F., & Hofmans, J. (2019). A dynamic systems approach to personality: The Personality Dynamics (PersDyn) model. *Personality and Individual Differences, 144,* 11–18. https://doi.org/10.1016/j.paid.2019.02.013

Steenkamp, J.-B. E. M., & Gielens, K. (2003). Consumer and market drivers of the trial probability of new consumer packaged goods. *Journal of Consumer Research, 30*(3), 368–384. https://doi.org/10.1086/378615

Steenkamp, J.-B. E. M., Hofstede, F., & Wedel, M. (1999). A cross-national investigation into the individual and national cultural antecedents of consumer innovativeness. *Journal of Marketing, 63*(2), 55–69. https://doi.org/10.1177/002224299906300204

Steenkamp, J.-B. E. M., & Maydeu-Olivares, A. (2015). Stability and change in consumer traits: Evidence from a 12-year longitudinal study, 2002-2013. *Journal of Marketing Research, 52*(3), 287–308. https://doi.org/10.1509/jmr.13.0592

Strack, F., & Deutsch, R. (2004). Reflective and impulsive determinants of social behavior. *Personality and Social Psychology Review, 8*(3), 220–247. https://doi.org/10.1207/s15327957pspr0803_1

Tangney, J. P., Baumeister, R. F., & Boone, A. L. (2004). High self-control predicts good adjustment, less pathology, better grades, and interpersonal success. *Journal of Personality, 72*(2), 271–324. https://doi.org/10.1111/j.0022-3506.2004.00263.x

Tian, K. T., Bearden, W. O., & Hunter, G. L. (2001). Consumers' need for uniqueness: Scale development and validation. *Journal of Consumer Research, 28*(1), 50–66. https://doi.org/10.1086/321947

Tsukayama, E., Duckworth, A. L., & Kim, B. (2012). Resisting everything except temptation: Evidence and an explanation for domain-specific impulsivity. *European Journal of Personality, 26*(3), 318–334. https://doi.org/10.1002/per.841

Vallacher, R. R., & Nowak, A. (2007). Dynamical social psychology: Finding order in the flow of human experience. In A. W. Kruglanski & E. T. Higgins (Eds.), *Social psychology: Handbook of basic principles* (2nd ed., pp. 734–758). Guilford Press.

Vansteelandt, K., & Van Mechelen, I. (2004). The personality triad in balance: Multidimensional individual differences in situation-behavior profiles. *Journal of Research in Personality, 38*(4), 367–393. https://doi.org/10.1016/j.jrp.2003.08.001

Venkatraman, M. P., & Price, L. L. (1990). Differentiating between cognitive and sensory innovativeness: Concepts, measurement, and implications. *Journal of Business Research, 20*(4), 293–315. https://doi.org/10.1016/0148-2963(90)90008-2

Verplanken, B., & Herabadi, A. (2001). Individual differences in impulse buying tendency: Feeling and no thinking. *European Journal of Personality, 15*(1 Suppl.), S71–S83. https://doi.org/10.1002/per.423

Wallace, C., & Chen, G. (2006). A multilevel integration of personality, climate, self-regulation, and performance. *Personnel Psychology, 59*(3), 529–557. https://doi.org/10.1111/j.1744-6570.2006.00046.x

Whiteside, S. P., & Lynam, D. R. (2001). The five factor model and impulsivity: Using a structural model of personality to understand impulsivity. *Personality and Individual Differences, 30*(4), 669–689. https://doi.org/10.1016/S0191-8869(00)00064-7

Wooten, D. B., & Reed, A. I. I., II. (2004). Playing it safe: Susceptibility to normative influence and protective self-presentation. *Journal of Consumer Research, 31*(3), 551–556. https://doi.org/10.1086/425089

Wortman, J., & Wood, D. (2011). The personality traits of liked people. *Journal of Research in Personality, 45*(6), 519–528. https://doi.org/10.1016/j.jrp.2011.06.006

Zhao, K., Ferguson, E., & Smillie, L. D. (2016). Prosocial personality traits differentially predict egalitarianism, generosity, and reciprocity in economic games. *Frontiers in Psychology, 7,* 1137. https://doi.org/10.3389/fpsyg.2016.01137

Zuckerman, M. (1985). Biological foundations of the sensation-seeking temperament. In J. Strelau, F. H. Farley, & A. Gale (Eds.), *The biological bases of personality and behavior: Vol. 1. Theories, measurement techniques, and development* (pp. 97–113). Hemisphere Publishing Corp/Harper & Row Publishers.

Zuckerman, M. (2002). Zuckerman-Kuhlman Personality Questionnaire (ZKPQ): An alternative five-factorial model. In B. de Raad & M. Perugini (Eds.), *Big Five assessment* (pp. 377–396). Hogrefe & Huber Publishers.

Zuckerman, M. (2005). The neurobiology of impulsive sensation seeking: Genetics, brain physiology, biochemistry, and neurology. In C. Stough (Ed.), *Neurobiology of exceptionality* (pp. 31–52). Kluwer Academic/Plenum Publishers. https://doi.org/10.1007/0-306-48649-0_2

CHAPTER 10

CONSUMER VALUES

Eda Gurel-Atay

Values are described as one of the most important constructs by many researchers in social science (Rokeach, 1973), including in consumer research (Gurel-Atay & Kahle, 2019), as they determine what is important in our lives (Steenhaut & Kenhove, 2006). Accordingly, values have been widely investigated in behavioral research across different social science disciplines, and the findings suggest that values provide the fundamental motivation for human behavior (Cheng & Fleischmann, 2010; Suh & Kahle, 2018). Indeed, people turn to their values to define who they are, to make judgments across specific situations, and to decide how to behave in certain situations (Divine & Lepisto, 2005; A. R. Lee, 2003; Rokeach, 1973).

In this chapter, I first provide a definition of values and discuss prominent value theories that are studied extensively in consumer research. Among the theories I examine are Maslow's hierarchy of needs, the means–end chain (MEC) model, and the social adaptation theory. Next, I look at the most used value measurements in consumer research: Rokeach Value Survey (RVS), Schwartz Value Scale (SVS), the List of Values (LOV), and the laddering method. Then, I examine how values change through time. Finally, I examine the use of values in consumer research (e.g., segmentation and affecting product choices) and provide ideas for future research.

DEFINITION OF VALUES

Rokeach (1968) provided one of the most cited definitions of values in literature and stated that values are "centrally held, enduring beliefs which guide actions and judgments across specific situations and beyond immediate goals to more ultimate end-states of existence" (p. 550). Schwartz (1994) defined values in a similar manner as "desirable trans-situational goals, varying in importance, that serve as guiding principles in the life of a person or other social entity" (p. 21). These definitions refer to some common elements of values as suggested by researchers previously: Values are beliefs and standards that are learned and remain relatively stable over time, they are guidelines for people to achieve their desirable end goals, they guide behaviors and judgments across specific actions and situations, and they exist in a hierarchical order by their relative importance to each other (Schwartz, 1992; Woodward & Shaffakat, 2016).

VALUE THEORIES

Because of the importance of values, several researchers attempted to develop theories regarding values. In this section, I examine the value theories often used in consumer psychology.

I would like to express my gratitude to the following colleagues who helped me with data collection, data analysis, and writing some parts of this paper: Lynn R. Kahle, Johnny Chen, and Wang-Suk Suh.
https://doi.org/10.1037/0000262-010
APA Handbook of Consumer Psychology, L. R. Kahle (Editor-in-Chief)
Copyright © 2022 by the American Psychological Association. All rights reserved.

Maslow's Hierarchy of Needs

Maslow (1943), in his prominent theory of motivations, suggested that human needs (used interchangeably with values) are arranged in a hierarchy of importance such that "the appearance of one need usually rests on the prior satisfaction of another, more pre-potent need" (p. 370). In his theory, he focused on a set of five needs: physiological needs (e.g., food, water, shelter), safety needs (e.g., job, predictability, law), love needs (e.g., belonging, affection, sexual intimacy), esteem needs (e.g., self-esteem, confidence, respect of others), and self-actualization needs (e.g., self-fulfillment, creativity, morality). He suggested that the hierarchy between the needs may not be as rigid as it seems; partial satisfaction of lower needs is sufficient to move up to upper needs. Although there may be differences across cultures, this theory of motivations reflects more universal and "common-human characteristics" (p. 390), and though there may be multiple motivations and determinants of behaviors not listed, goals of behaviors are the center principle of the theory.

Although Maslow's hierarchy has been very popular in business environments and college courses, it has been criticized often by researchers, mostly because of the difficulty to operationalize and test it empirically (Kahle et al., 1997; Soper et al., 1995). To deal with this problem, Taormina and Gao (2013) developed a scale to measure Maslow's hierarchy levels and tested the order structure of the need levels. The authors stated that "satisfaction of the lower-level need immediately below any given need in the hierarchy predicted satisfaction of the next higher-level need, yielding strong evidence for the hierarchical nature of Maslow's theory of need satisfaction" (Taormina & Gao, 2013, p. 169). They also found that satisfaction of the physiological needs was a significant predictor of the satisfaction of all other higher order needs, suggesting that the physiological needs are basic needs. Other researchers attempted to use Maslow's hierarchy to examine the relationship between different levels of needs, or values, and some other consumer research topics. Gardner and Hill (1990), for instance, found that when consumers were in positive (negative) mood states, their decision-making processes were related to higher (lower) levels of Maslow's hierarchy. Yalch and Brunel (1996) applied Maslow's hierarchy to the product design area and found that a more appealing appearance, compared with a less attractive product, was expected to satisfy the higher order needs. Oleson (2004) showed that money attitudes were most related to safety and esteem needs and least related to physiological, love, and self-actualization needs. Raymond et al. (2003) found that Korean blue-collar workers had a different hierarchical structure of values (i.e., love/belongingness as the strongest need, followed by esteem, physiological, safety, and self-actualization needs) and suggested that marketing strategies should be adapted, not standardized, across different cultures. Huneke (2005) applied a modified version of Maslow's theory to the practice of voluntary simplicity and stated that some consumers would think that their deficit needs (lower level needs of Maslow's hierarchy) were met and that they were ready to focus on pursuing their growth needs (higher level needs of Maslow's hierarchy). One of the problems with the studies focusing on Maslow's hierarchy is the lack of a standardized scale to measure Maslow's needs/values. Moreover, because all these studies are cross-sectional, and not longitudinal, it is not possible to follow people from one need level to the next with these studies (Landy, 1989). Accordingly, the order structure of the need levels—the essence of Maslow's hierarchy of needs—cannot be tested with these studies.

Means–End Chain Model

The MEC model, developed by Gutman (1982), suggests that consumers behave (e.g., buy products or services) to achieve desired end-states. These end-states, defined as values by Rokeach (1968), help consumers to identify desired and undesired consequences, creating the values–consequences linkage. Consequences, in turn, determine the product attributes to focus on in order to achieve the desired consequences (i.e., benefits), resulting in the consequences–attributes linkage. In other words, "Consumers use a cognitive chain for buying decisions that relates product attributes to benefits, which in turn contribute to fulfill personal values" (Huber et al., 2004, p. 715). Gutman (1982) also noted that consequences are affected by current situations and that consumers learn to identify the relationships between particular actions and consequences in certain situations. Olson and Reynolds (1983) modified Gutman's model by broadening the chain levels. At the bottom of the modified model, there are concrete attributes (objective, directly observable, physical characteristics of products) and abstract attributes (subjective, not directly observable, social/emotional/psychological characteristics of products). In the middle, there are functional consequences (physical outcomes of using a product) and psychosocial consequences (psychological and social outcomes of using a product). At the top of the model, there are instrumental values (modes of conduct, specific ways to achieve terminal values) and terminal values (higher end goals, desired end-states). As consumers proceed from the bottom of the model (i.e., means) to the top (i.e., ends), the level of abstraction increases.

Research on consumer MECs revealed the importance of values in product/brand choice by showing that consumers select products to facilitate the achievement of desired end states, like happiness and success. Reynolds et al. (1995) found that the strength of association between MEC elements (i.e., attributes–consequences linkage and consequences–values linkage) improved the brand persuasion of soft drink TV commercials. Mort and Rose (2004), however, showed that while attributes–consequences–values linkage held for utilitarian products, attributes–values linkage held for hedonic products. Ter Hofstede et al. (1999) suggested that linking product characteristics (attributes) to consumer characteristics (benefits and values) provides the opportunity to integrate product development and communication strategies. The authors, indeed, used the MEC model to identify cross-national market segments for yogurt throughout 11 European Union countries and offered specific strategies regarding product positioning and new product development process. Orsingher et al. (2011) applied the MEC model to the satisfaction theory, as "taking into account both attributes and goals provides an added level of knowledge of the meaning of satisfaction" (p. 744). Recently, Reynolds and Phillips (2019) combined the MEC model with neuromarketing to examine advertising effectiveness. Their analysis of 240 television ads revealed that "the strength of cognitive linkages (neuroscience) among levels of abstraction (means–end theory)" significantly correlated with the level of purchase intention of the advertised product (Reynolds & Phillips, 2019, p. 277).

The MEC model was criticized by some researchers as not providing a theoretical foundation to predict consumer behaviors (e.g., Paulssen & Bagozzi, 2005). In line with this criticism, researchers used the MEC model along with other theories to predict consumer behaviors. Bagozzi and Dabholkar (1994) combined the theory of reasoned action (Ajzen & Fishbein, 1980) with the MEC model as an explanation for recycling behavior and identified a hierarchical organization of 15 recycling goals, from the most concrete to the most abstract. Moreover, Bagozzi and Dabholkar (2000) provided an alternative conceptual foundation for the MEC model through the discursive psychology, especially to examine entities other than physical products (e.g., ideas, people). Chen et al. (2015) used the regulatory focus theory and self-construal theory to complement the MEC model to predict organic rice purchase behaviors of Taiwanese consumers.

Social Adaptation Theory

Social adaptation theory (Kahle, 1983; Kahle et al., 1980) states that social cognitions, including attitudes and values, help people to adapt to their environments by providing people with clues that signal what is important in that particular environment. In other words, "The adaptive significance of information will determine its impact" (Kahle & Homer, 1985, p. 954), meaning that information will not be used, even if it is processed, unless it is perceived as important for adaptation in a person's life. Moreover, value development and value fulfillment affect the ways individuals adapt to various life roles. For instance, people who value being well-respected most may try hard to affect other people's perceptions of them through material objects, but people who value self-respect most may try to improve themselves continuously. Accordingly, the types and brands of products they use and the reasons to use those products and brands will be different for people who endorse different values. Social adaptation theory also suggests that values form as a result of people's life experiences based on interactions with their surroundings (e.g., people, social and financial situations, environmental and cultural factors); therefore, the trends of social values over time provide an understanding of changes in people's experiences, which in turn guide future behavior.

Social adaptation theory is mostly used in advertising effectiveness studies. In an early study, for instance, Homer and Kahle (1986) showed that social adaptation helped with the assimilation of primed advertisements and accommodation of surrealistic advertisements. The authors suggested that when people were presented with priming statements in ads that were in line with their existing mental schema, including their values, those statements were easily absorbed. In contrast, when people were presented with surrealistic ads, which were unexpected, novel, and not aligned with their current schema, people spent more time to accommodate the new information, making the ad recall more likely and eventually facilitating the adaptation. More recently, Gurel-Atay and Kahle (2010) suggested that the congruence between perceived celebrity values and perceived product values would provide adaptive information to consumers and, hence, would result in more effective celebrity endorsement. Indeed, Gurel-Atay and Kahle (2010) found that people who were exposed to the high value congruence ad (i.e., celebrity values as perceived by consumers were matched with product values as perceived by consumers) spent less time examining the ad, suggesting that participants were easily and quickly able to assimilate this information into their existing mental schema. Moreover, participants who were exposed to the high value congruence ad had significantly more favorable attitudes toward the ad and brand, had higher intentions to buy the product, and were more likely to recommend the product to other people than were participants who were exposed to the low value congruence ad. These findings suggest that social adaptation theory can provide guidance to understand when and how values can affect consumer behaviors, especially in the context of marketing communication through positioning and advertising strategies.

STRUCTURE AND MEASUREMENT OF VALUES

Both quantitative and qualitative methods have been used to measure values. In this section, I review the most popular value measures used in consumer psychology.

Rokeach Value Survey

Rokeach (1968), one of the pioneers in values research, differentiated between terminal values and instrumental values. *Terminal* values are considered the ultimate goal of life that is worth striving for (Haller & Hadler, 2006); they are the end-states of existence. *Instrumental* values, on the other hand, are "desirable modes of behaviors that are instrumental to the attainment of desirable end-states" (Rokeach, 1973, p. 48). In other words, instrumental values define the ways, or paths, to attain terminal values. Rokeach (1973) listed 18 terminal values (i.e., true friendship, mature love, self-respect, happiness, inner harmony, equality, freedom, pleasure, social recognition, wisdom, salvation, family security, national security, a sense of accomplishment, a world of beauty, a world at peace, a comfortable life, and an exciting life) and 18 instrumental values (i.e., cheerfulness, ambition, love, cleanliness, self-control, capability, courage, politeness, honesty, imagination, independence, intellect, broad-mindedness, logic, obedience, helpfulness, responsibility, and forgiveness). For instance, equality (i.e., brotherhood, equal opportunity for all) represents one terminal value, and several instrumental values, such as being broad-minded or forgiving, might be instrumental in the attainment of that terminal value.

The RVS is an ordinal level scale, as people are asked to rank those terminal and instrumental values from 1 to 18. This ranking task, however, creates hardship to participants, as it is not easy to determine the importance level of 18 values. Indeed, people tend to have only a few important values, which are comparatively easy to rank order (Rokeach, 1973). When they are asked to rank more than those few values, people start to give random answers, which affects the validity and reliability of the scale (Beatty et al., 1985; Thompson et al., 1982). Moreover, an ordinal level scale does not lend itself to many statistical analysis methods (Clawson & Vinson, 1978; Johnston, 1995), which limits the use of RVS in situations that require the grouping of consumers based on values (e.g., segmentation) or using values in theory development/testing (e.g., the role of values in predicting consumer behaviors). The values included in the RVS have limited applications in consumer behavior research, as they refer to more universal situations (Beatty et al., 1985). Accordingly, even though the distinction between terminal and instrumental values is used often in consumer behavior research (e.g., Olson & Reynolds, 1983), the RVS itself is not used as is.

Schwartz Value Scale

Based on Rokeach's terminal values, Schwartz (1992) identified 10 distinct values and organized them in four dimensions: openness to change (hedonism, self-direction, and stimulation), conservation (security, tradition, and conformity), self-enhancement (achievement and power), and self-transcendence (universalism and benevolence). Openness to change refers to independent thoughts, actions, and changes while conservation refers to self-restriction, traditional practices, and stability. Similarly, self-enhancement refers to a person's own success and dominance over others while self-transcendence refers to acceptance and welfare of others (Schwartz, 1996). Schwartz (1992) suggested that these four dimensions are either compatible with each other or in conflict with each other, resulting in a circumplex structure. In this circumplex structure, values that are adjacent to each other are more similar (i.e., compatible), and values that oppose each other are more different (i.e., in conflict). For instance, self-transcendence values are compatible with conservation values and in conflict with self-enhancement values.

Each of the 10 values included in the SVS is measured by multiple items. For instance, achievement is measured through four items (i.e., ambitious, successful, capable, influential) while hedonism is measured through three items (i.e., pleasure, enjoying life, self-indulgent). In total, there are 57 items measured with a 9-point, unbalanced importance rating scale (−1: opposed to my principles; 0: not important; +7: of supreme importance). The SVS has been used by many consumer researchers in different cross-cultural settings (e.g., Burroughs & Rindfleisch, 2002; Shepherd et al., 2015). However, similar to the RVS, the huge number of items, many of which are not directly related to consumer behaviors, makes the SVS long and demanding (Gurel-Atay et al., 2019; J. A. Lee et al., 2007).

List of Values

The LOV (Kahle, 1983), theoretically based on Rokeach's terminal values and Maslow's hierarchy of needs, focuses on two important dimensions of values: motive for endorsement and locus of control. Motive for endorsement can be a current excess/abundance, or it can be a deficit. Excess values (self-respect, a sense of accomplishment, self-fulfillment, fun-enjoyment-excitement, and warm relationships with others) refer to the values people already attained, and deficit values (security, a sense of belonging, and being well-respected) refer to the values people are still lacking (Drenan, 1983; Piner, 1983). For example, people who pick warm relationships with others have the most friends of any group, and people who pick sense of accomplishment have the highest educational attainment and income (Kahle, 1983). On the other hand, people who choose being well-respected perceive that they are not well-respected, and people who choose a sense of belonging lack the support that comes from social groups. The locus of control dimension focuses on how people attain their values (Homer & Kahle, 1988). Internal values (self-respect, a sense of accomplishment, and self-fulfillment), based on internal locus of control, can be fulfilled internally without depending on others. External values (security, a sense of belonging, and being well-respected), based on external locus of control, need other people to be fulfilled. Interpersonal values (fun-enjoyment-excitement and warm relationships with others), on the other hand, require a combination of internal and external loci of control, as these values have internal and interactive motivations to fulfill with others.

The LOV is also an interval-level scale with a 9-point, unbalanced importance rating scale (1 = *important to me*; 9 = *most important to me*). Compared with the RVS and the SVS, however, the LOV includes fewer items (10 items in total; nine values to rate and one item to select the most important value), making it easy and simple to administer. Moreover, the LOV focuses on the values that are more relevant to the consumer research. Accordingly, "a cogent case has been made in the marketing and consumer behavior literature for the superiority of this instrument over its rivals" (Sudbury & Simcock, 2009, p. 29), leading it to be used extensively in consumer research (e.g., Limon et al., 2009; Minton et al., 2015; Mukhopadhyay & Yeung, 2010; Tan & Tambyah, 2016).

Laddering Method

Laddering is the associated research methodology of the MEC model (Olson & Reynolds, 1983; Reynolds & Gutman, 1988). As discussed earlier, the MEC model suggests that values affect psychological and functional consequences, which in turn affect abstract and concrete attributes. In the MEC model, as in the RVS, values are differentiated as instrumental and terminal values. Accordingly, the purpose of the laddering method is to reveal the terminal values of consumers.

Unlike the RVS, the SVS, and the LOV, the laddering method produces qualitative data. Indeed, it is an in-depth interviewing method in which people are asked the "why" question repeatedly until they link their answers to their terminal values. The interview starts at the most concrete level (i.e., concrete product attributes) and moves through the abstraction hierarchy (i.e., toward the terminal values) by asking people why a certain attribute/consequence is important. Although asking the same questions may become frustrating and make the purpose of the research obvious to participants, explaining the process to participants at the beginning of the interview can help with these problems. As an alternative or complement to quantitative methods of measuring values, laddering has been used often in consumer research (Cuny & Opaswongkarn, 2017; Phillips et al., 2010).

CHANGES IN VALUES

People continuously learn and integrate information from daily life (e.g., the culture of the society, social norms, family religion, personality traits of colleagues and friends) and form attitudes toward specific situations; in turn, this process often contributes to the determination of personal behaviors (Ajzen & Fishbein, 1975). Also, as discussed previously, social adaptation theory (Kahle, 1983) suggests that values form as a result of people's life experiences based on interactions with their surroundings (e.g., people, social and financial situations, environmental and cultural factors); therefore, the trends of social values over time provide an understanding of changes in people's experiences and behaviors. In a way, changes in social values mirror the evolution of society, which provides insight on values shaping consumer priorities and preferences.

A recent study, building on the previous three U.S. national surveys (Gurel-Atay et al., 2010; Kahle et al., 1988; Kahle & Timmer, 1983), showed a marked departure from the moderate changes in social values over time and instead demonstrated more radical shifts in values than previously observed (Gurel-Atay et al., 2018). In all of these studies, social values were measured using the LOV (Kahle & Timmer, 1983). Sequential cross-sectional national surveys were administered to representative samples of the U.S. Census to compare and contrast findings for gender, age category, ethnicity, and education across the 40-year period (1976, 1986, 2007, 2016, and 2017). The results, shown in Tables 10.1 through 10.4, revealed the following changes for each value measured with the LOV.

Self-Respect

The most substantial change in values comes from self-respect, a value that has been the primary determining factor of American culture. Self-respect had been the most favored value in America since 1976 across age categories, education levels, gender, and ethnic groups; however, its ranking dropped swiftly in 2017. The decline is made more dramatic with a

TABLE 10.1

Value Choice by Gender

Combined	1976[a]	1986[b]	2007[c]	2016	2017
	($n = 2,233$)	($n = 997$)	($n = 1,498$)	($n = 1,619$)	($n = 1,203$)
Self-respect	21.1%	23.0%	28.0%	16.0%	17.0%
Sense of accomplishment	11.4%	15.9%	10.3%	7.2%	7.7%
Being well-respected	8.8%	5.9%	8.3%	2.1%	2.6%
Security	20.6%	16.5%	12.4%	11.2%	12.1%
Warm relationships with others	16.2%	19.9%	20.9%	19.4%	14.7%
Sense of belonging	7.9%	5.1%	3.3%	16.8%	18.1%
Fun-enjoyment-excitement	4.5%	7.2%	9.3%	12.9%	15.0%
Self-fulfillment	9.6%	6.5%	8.1%	14.3%	12.9%
Male	1976[a]	1986[b]	2007[c]	2016	2017
	($n = 946$)	($n = 453$)	($n = 732$)	($n = 804$)	($n = 575$)
Self-respect	21.7%	22.4%	25.1%	14.3%	16.5%
Sense of accomplishment	14.3%	20.1%	11.7%	8.5%	8.3%
Being well-respected	8.5%	5.7%	8.6%	2.9%	2.6%
Security	20.5%	17.1%	13.9%	9.7%	10.6%
Warm relationships with others	13.1%	13.6%	17.2%	18.7%	14.1%
Sense of belonging	5.6%	3.8%	3.1%	14.3%	16.9%
Fun-enjoyment-excitement	6.9%	10.0%	11.4%	16.0%	15.1%
Self-fulfillment	9.5%	7.2%	9.0%	15.6%	15.8%
Female	1976[a]	1986[b]	2007[c]	2016	2017
	($n = 1,287$)	($n = 544$)	($n = 766$)	($n = 810$)	($n = 623$)
Self-respect	20.6%	23.5%	32.3%	17.8%	17.2%
Sense of accomplishment	9.2%	12.2%	8.9%	5.9%	7.2%
Being well-respected	9.0%	6.1%	8.0%	1.4%	2.6%
Security	20.7%	15.9%	11.0%	12.6%	13.5%
Warm relationships with others	18.5%	25.7%	22.1%	20.2%	15.3%
Sense of belonging	9.6%	6.3%	3.4%	19.3%	19.3%
Fun-enjoyment-excitement	2.7%	4.6%	7.2%	10.0%	14.7%
Self-fulfillment	9.6%	5.8%	7.2%	12.8%	10.1%

Note. 1976: $\chi^2 (7, N = 2,233) = 54.51, p < .001$; 1986: $\chi^2 (7, N = 997) = 46.838, p < .001$; 2007: $\chi^2 (7, N = 1,460) = 21.233, p < .01$; 2016: $\chi^2 (7, N = 1,612) = 33.414, p < .001$; 2017: $\chi^2 (7, N = 1,196) = 11.47, p = .119$, ns. Discrepancy in N is based on gender other than male or female indicated in 2016 and 2017.
[a]Data from Kahle and Timmer (1983). [b]Data from Kahle et al. (1988). [c]Data from Gurel-Atay et al. (2010).

TABLE 10.2

Value Choice by Age Category

Age: < 30	1976[a]	1986[b]	2007[c]	2016	2017
Self-respect	14.0%	18.9%	26.3%	10.5%	14.2%
Sense of accomplishment	15.6%	12.6%	18.6%	11.1%	7.5%
Being well-respected	4.9%	1.6%	6.6%	4.1%	4.5%
Security	15.2%	12.6%	11.4%	6.4%	5.6%
Warm relationships with others	19.9%	26.0%	14.4%	19.3%	18.3%
Sense of belonging	6.3%	7.1%	3.0%	12.5%	14.9%
Fun-enjoyment-excitement	7.8%	15.7%	13.8%	19.6%	19.8%
Self-fulfillment	18.7%	5.5%	6.0%	16.6%	15.3%
Age: 30–39	**1976[a]**	**1986[b]**	**2007[c]**	**2016**	**2017**
Self-respect	20.2%	25.0%	27.1%	14.2%	14.0%
Sense of accomplishment	11.5%	15.8%	10.4%	6.0%	7.2%
Being well-respected	8.0%	6.9%	6.0%	2.1%	3.6%
Security	20.4%	11.8%	11.6%	9.3%	14.0%
Warm relationships with others	14.8%	16.3%	19.1%	25.3%	14.5%
Sense of belonging	8.3%	3.1%	2.4%	10.3%	17.6%
Fun-enjoyment-excitement	2.7%	4.4%	15.5%	16.7%	18.1%
Self-fulfillment	5.9%	8.1%	8.0%	16.0%	10.9%
Age: 40–49	**1976[a]**	**1986[b]**	**2007[c]**	**2016**	**2017**
Self-respect	28.6%	27.5%	28.6%	15.9%	17.6%
Sense of accomplishment	11.5%	15.8%	10.3%	9.3%	13.4%
Being well-respected	12.5%	10.1%	7.6%	2.2%	2.7%
Security	20.4%	13.8%	12.0%	16.4%	12.3%
Warm relationships with others	14.8%	16.3%	17.7%	19.9%	15.0%
Sense of belonging	11.9%	4.3%	1.7%	10.2%	12.3%
Fun-enjoyment-excitement	2.7%	4.4%	13.0%	10.6%	15.5%
Self-fulfillment	5.9%	8.1%	9.6%	15.5%	11.2%
Age: 50–59	**1976[a]**	**1986[b]**	**2007[c]**	**2016**	**2017**
Self-respect	24.3%	21.6%	27.3%	19.7%	16.8%
Sense of accomplishment	9.5%	14.4%	15.5%	5.1%	6.4%
Being well-respected	12.5%	10.1%	4.6%	0.7%	1.4%
Security	21.7%	20.1%	8.7%	14.3%	16.8%
Warm relationships with others	12.7%	18.7%	5.8%	15.3%	13.6%
Sense of belonging	11.9%	4.3%	5.8%	20.1%	16.8%
Fun-enjoyment-excitement	1.8%	4.3%	9.9%	12.6%	16.4%
Self-fulfillment	5.6%	6.5%	22.5%	12.2%	11.8%

Age: > 60	1976[a]	1986[b]	2007[c]	2016	2017
Self-respect	22.4%	21.0%	30.3%	18.1%	21.3%
Sense of accomplishment	7.4%	14.1%	11.0%	6.0%	5.9%
Being well-respected	13.4%	8.5%	3.5%	1.7%	1.0%
Security	25.7%	21.8%	7.8%	11.0%	12.8%
Warm relationships with others	18.0%	23.4%	14.2%	18.5%	12.1%
Sense of belonging	6.2%	5.2%	4.3%	23.8%	25.6%
Fun-enjoyment-excitement	3.1%	3.6%	6.1%	8.3%	7.2%
Self-fulfillment	3.7%	2.4%	22.8%	12.7%	14.1%

Note. 2007: χ^2 (28, N = 1,460) = 70.831, $p < .001$; 2016: χ^2 (28, N = 1,617) = 112.591, $p < .001$; 2017: χ^2 (28, N = 1,201) = 78.132, $p < .001$. Chi-square statistics were not calculated for 1976 and 1986 due to lack of cell data for age groups.
[a]Data from Kahle and Timmer (1983). [b]Data from Kahle et al. (1988). [c]Data from Gurel-Atay et al. (2010).

TABLE 10.3

Value Choice by Ethnicity

White	1976[a]	2007[b]	2016	2017
	(*n* = 1,928)	(*n* = 1,295)	(*n* = 1,166)	(*n* = 905)
Self-respect	21.1%	28.3%	16.6%	16.9%
Sense of accomplishment	11.5%	9.3%	6.3%	7.5%
Being well-respected	8.5%	8.4%	2.2%	1.8%
Security	18.8%	12.2%	11.1%	12.3%
Warm relationships with others	16.8%	22.2%	20.1%	15.6%
Sense of belonging	8.5%	3.0%	17.2%	18.1%
Fun-enjoyment-excitement	4.8%	9.2%	12.3%	15.0%
Self-fulfillment	10.2%	7.4%	14.1%	12.8%
Black	1976[a]	2007[b]	2016	2017
	(*n* = 244)	(*n* = 64)	(*n* = 144)	(*n* = 107)
Self-respect	21.3%	35.9%	16.0%	27.1%
Sense of accomplishment	11.5%	14.1%	9.7%	9.3%
Being well-respected	10.2%	9.4%	1.4%	3.7%
Security	33.6%	14.1%	11.8%	13.1%
Warm relationships with others	11.1%	9.4%	11.8%	7.5%
Sense of belonging	4.5%	3.1%	22.9%	15.9%
Fun-enjoyment-excitement	2.5%	6.3%	9.0%	11.2%
Self-fulfillment	5.3%	7.8%	17.4%	12.1%

(*continues*)

TABLE 10.3

Value Choice by Ethnicity (*Continued*)

Hispanic	1976[a]	2007[b]	2016	2017
	(*n* = 49)	(*n* = 52)	(*n* = 148)	(*n* = 118)
Self-respect	16.3%	28.8%	10.8%	11.0%
Sense of accomplishment	10.2%	13.5%	7.4%	8.5%
Being well-respected	14.3%	7.7%	2.0%	5.9%
Security	30.6%	13.5%	11.5%	11.0%
Warm relationships with others	14.3%	13.5%	20.9%	14.4%
Sense of belonging	4.1%	7.7%	12.8%	20.3%
Fun-enjoyment-excitement	4.1%	3.8%	16.2%	14.4%
Self-fulfillment	6.1%	11.5%	18.2%	14.4%
Asian	**1976**[a]	**2007**[b]	**2016**	**2017**
	(*n* = 2)	(*n* = 26)	(*n* = 70)	(*n* = 11)
Self-respect	50.0%	15.4%	14.3%	9.1%
Sense of accomplishment	0.0%	11.5%	11.4%	0.0%
Being well-respected	0.0%	7.7%	1.4%	0.0%
Security	50.0%	11.5%	12.9%	0.0%
Warm relationships with others	0.0%	7.7%	24.3%	9.1%
Sense of belonging	0.0%	3.8%	7.1%	18.2%
Fun-enjoyment-excitement	0.0%	26.9%	14.3%	36.4%
Self-fulfillment	0.0%	15.4%	14.3%	27.3%
Other	**1976**[a]	**2007**[b]	**2016**	**2017**
	(*n* = 4)	(*n* = 19)	(*n* = 89)	(*n* = 60)
Self-respect	25.0%	26.3%	18.0%	13.3%
Sense of accomplishment	0.0%	15.8%	12.4%	8.3%
Being well-respected	0.0%	0.0%	2.2%	6.7%
Security	0.0%	10.5%	9.0%	11.7%
Warm relationships with others	75.0%	15.8%	16.9%	15.0%
Sense of belonging	0.0%	5.3%	15.7%	16.7%
Fun-enjoyment-excitement	0.0%	10.5%	20.2%	18.3%
Self-fulfillment	0.0%	15.8%	5.6%	10.0%

Note. 1976: χ^2 (35, N = 2,232) = 68.52, $p < .001$; 2007: χ^2 (28, N = 1,452) = 36.36, $p = .134$, *ns*; 2016: χ^2 (28, N = 1,617) = 40.89, $p = .055$, *ns*; 2017: χ^2 (28, N = 1,201) = 37.39, $p = .111$, *ns*.
[a]Data from Kahle and Timmer (1983). [b]Data from Gurel-Atay et al. (2010).

TABLE 10.4

Value Choice by Education

Grade school	1976[a] (n = 365)	2007[b] (n = 35)	2016 (n = 36)	2017 (n = 161)
Self-respect	21.9%	11.4%	16.7%	12.4%
Sense of accomplishment	5.2%	8.6%	13.9%	8.7%
Being well-respected	19.2%	11.4%	8.3%	2.5%
Security	26.3%	28.6%	16.7%	13.7%
Warm relationships with others	14.0%	22.9%	8.3%	12.4%
Sense of belonging	6.8%	2.9%	19.4%	23.0%
Fun-enjoyment-excitement	4.7%	11.4%	11.1%	14.3%
Self-fulfillment	1.9%	2.9%	5.6%	13.0%
High school	1976[a] (n = 1,104)	2007[b] (n = 895)	2016 (n = 737)	2017 (n = 686)
Self-respect	18.7%	31.3%	16.1%	17.9%
Sense of accomplishment	11.0%	9.4%	6.5%	7.3%
Being well-respected	9.1%	8.5%	2.3%	2.9%
Security	22.1%	11.5%	12.2%	13.4%
Warm relationships with others	16.1%	18.5%	17.6%	14.3%
Sense of belonging	11.0%	3.6%	19.0%	16.6%
Fun-enjoyment-excitement	3.6%	10.5%	13.6%	15.0%
Self-fulfillment	8.3%	6.7%	12.6%	12.5%
College	1976[a] (n = 756)	2007[b] (n = 567)	2016 (n = 844)	2017 (n = 354)
Self-respect	24.1%	25.7%	15.9%	17.2%
Sense of accomplishment	15.1%	11.8%	7.6%	8.2%
Being well-respected	2.9%	7.9%	1.7%	2.0%
Security	15.9%	12.7%	10.1%	8.8%
Warm relationships with others	17.2%	21.2%	21.4%	16.4%
Sense of belonging	4.0%	2.6%	14.8%	18.6%
Fun-enjoyment-excitement	5.7%	7.4%	12.4%	15.3%
Self-fulfillment	15.2%	10.6%	16.1%	13.6%

Note. 1976: χ^2 (35, N = 2,232) = 68.52, $p < .001$; 2007: χ^2 (14, N = 1,460) = 26.86, $p < .05$; 2016: χ^2 (14, N = 1,617) = 28.41, $p < .05$; 2017: χ^2 (14, N = 1,201) = 12.8, $p = .542$, ns.
[a]Data from Kahle and Timmer (1983). [b]Data from Gurel-Atay et al. (2010).

corresponding increase in the ranking for a sense of belonging. The data suggest a shock in the American landscape that sharply shifted the priorities of inwardly focused self-respect to one of a sense of belonging or identification with others.

Sense of Belonging

Perhaps the most dramatic change in values over the past decade has been the increase in the number of people who endorse a sense of belonging. It went from the least popular value in 1986 (5.1%) and 2007 (3.3%) to the most popular value in 2017 (18.1%). This dramatic growth occurred in every age group, especially the two oldest age groups. It occurred in all racial groups and at all educational levels. Sense of belonging has always been endorsed more by women than men in the United States, and that fact remains true. But the large increase occurred in both genders. One might argue that women have gained economically and socially relative to men during the past decade, although social indicators still show that women fall somewhat behind men in standing. Perhaps the rise of women has been accompanied by the rise in the importance of women's values. Interestingly, historically, U.S. women who endorse sense of belonging have been lower in education and income. They appear to "belong" to their families, often not working for pay outside the home. The rise in the sense of belonging to the dominant value seems today to belie the narrow stereotype of U.S. endorsers from previous decades.

Being Well-Respected

With the terminal rates at around 2% to 4% in 2017, it appears that being well-respected has become the least important value for Americans, suggesting that Americans today care less about the respect and opinions of others than the acceptance of others as being a member of the group. Interestingly, the decline of externally being well-respected parallels the decline of internal self-respect. Accordingly, the general decline in ranking across age categories, gender, education, and ethnicity, combined with similar changes in ranking for self-respect, suggests respect has been greatly deprioritized in American culture.

Sense of Accomplishment

The data show consensus in the trends for decreasing importance of a sense of accomplishment across age categories, gender, education, and ethnicity. More specifically, the importance of this value increased from 1976 to 1986, but its importance has been decreasing since then.

Self-Fulfillment

The importance of self-fulfillment has been increasing gradually over the years for almost all demographic groups. One notable exception appears when differences between age categories are examined. Although the trends for most age categories reflected the trend of the general population, more pessimism appears in the views of self-fulfillment for those aged 50 and older, whose rankings trended in the opposite direction. It is interesting to see that, for these older age groups, the importance of all three internal excess values (i.e., self-respect, self-fulfillment, and a sense of accomplishment) has been decreasing, suggesting that they depend on other people more to fulfill their values.

Fun-Enjoyment-Excitement

The importance of fun-enjoyment-excitement values has been increasing since 1976 for almost all demographic groups. The increase in the importance of this value was especially notable for Hispanics. More specifically, Hispanics experienced the most upsurge in the importance of fun-enjoyment-excitement, from 3.8% in 2007 to 16.2% in 2016 and 14.4% in 2017. Overall, these findings show that more people across both genders, all age groups, all education levels, and all races value fun-enjoyment-excitement than they did in 2007, as the percentages of people across all demographic groups who selected this value as their primary value has increased.

Warm Relationships With Others

Warm relationships with others seemed to peak in importance in 2007 for most age categories, genders, education levels, and ethnicities, but the overall trend appears to be waning over time. In the most recent survey, the sense of belonging seemed to replace the relevance of having warm relationships with others. One exception for the declining importance of warm relationships with others comes from the 50- to 59-year-old age group. The percentage of this group who selected this value as their most important value increased from 1976 (12.7%) to 1986 (18.7%), then hugely declined in 2007 (5.8%), and increased again in 2016 and 2017 (15.3% and 13.6%, respectively). A similar trend was observed for the youngest age group, too (i.e., declining in 2007 and increasing to 19.3% in 2016 and 18.3% in 2017). This finding suggests that these two age groups are more likely to look for support from families and friends.

Security

The importance of security declined over 30 years from 1976 to 2007 and has stayed steady since then in most demographic groups except the two oldest groups. This finding suggests that people's feeling of security has not changed in the last decade even in the news of more terror attacks, the financial crisis of 2008, and the emphasis put on security during presidential elections. It should be especially noted that there was no significant difference between 2016 and 2017 (before and after a presidential election) in any demographic groups (including the two oldest age groups) selecting security as their primary value.

Summary

These findings appear to support the notion that recently American society has fundamentally shifted, which is reflected in the expression of social values. Most notably, consumers have shifted away from the controllable and individual-focused excess value of self-respect to a sense of belonging, which is a more social and less controllable, externally focused deficit value. Interestingly, while another internally focused, excess value (a sense of accomplishment) also declined in importance, two other excess values, one internally focused (self-fulfillment) and one externally focused (fun-enjoyment-excitement), have become more important for consumers. The fragmentation of cable television and the explosion of social media could be both cause and effect of the shifting values. Today's consumers look ever more carefully for their own channel. However, the authors have not tested any consequential behaviors based on the value changes.

THE USE OF VALUES IN CONSUMER RESEARCH

Social values represent society's goals, ideals, and conceptions of preferred states (Kahle, 1996), and the causal sequence flows from values to attitudes to behaviors, such as brand or attribute selection (Kahle & Homer, 1985). These values are instrumental in marketing and advertising in three fundamental ways. First, how consumers behave and make decisions differs based on social values they hold firmly (Rokeach, 1973). For example, Shim and Eastlick (1998) found that self-actualizing and social affiliation values influenced attitudes toward regional shopping malls. A study conducted by groups of English and Indian people living in the United Kingdom revealed the effects of personal values on the consumption of Indian foods (White & Kokotsaki, 2004). Limon et al. (2009) found that the effects of package design on consumer brand choice differ depending on the consumer's cross-cultural values. The moderating roles of social values also vary based on product types across different cultures (i.e., Turkish, German-Turkish, and German). Shepherd et al. (2015) showed that consumers' satisfaction with America's defining values affect how they respond to different ads, packaging, brand information, marketing practices, and consumer-related policy. More specifically, American consumers who are not satisfied with America's values respond negatively to brands that reflect the dominant value of power and respond more positively to brands that reflect power's opposing value, universalism (and vice versa).

Second, consumers tend to select products that help in attaining value-related goals (Kahle & Chiagouris, 1997; Suh & Kahle, 2018). Numerous behavioral studies in the marketing context adopt "value chains" in which behaviors are determined in a sequential procedure—values-attitudes-behavior—in order to investigate "why" people reach a certain decision-making process, as well as a specific propensity to consume (e.g., Homer & Kahle, 1988; Kahle, 1996; Reynolds & Gutman, 1988). For example, Steenkamp et al. (1999) found that consumers who endorse conservation values (compared with openness to change values) tend to score lower on consumer innovativeness, suggesting that those consumers would be more reluctant to adopt new, innovative products. Suh and Kahle (2018) argued that a person who prioritizes a sense of accomplishment as the top value is more likely to focus on seeking technology products to enhance work performance than others.

Finally, consumers actively seek out others who share the same values. Social values are critical to lifestyle segmentation and target marketing (Kahle & Valette-Florence, 2012). For instance, Madrigal and Kahle (1994) investigated different vacation activity patterns based on locus of control and social values, comparing and contrasting internal (i.e., self-respect, a sense of accomplishment, and self-fulfillment) and external (i.e., sense of belonging, warm relationship with others, being well-respected, and security) values of travelers. Schewe and Meredith (2004) suggested segmenting people by cohorts based on their coming-of-age years. The coming-of-age years refer to influential events, or defining moments, that happen during late adolescent or young adult years. The authors stated that those influential events affect people's core values and subsequent attitudes, preferences, and consumption behaviors throughout their lives.

In practice, advertising is most effective when it reflects underlying cultural values that resonate with target markets (Reynolds & Olson, 2001). Accordingly, due to the central role that social values play in shaping consumer attitudes, trends in social values offer leading indicators that can inform advertising. For instance, the changes in U.S. consumers' values observed by Gurel-Atay et al. (2018) suggest that advertisers and marketers will need to rethink their posture on messaging to a new generation of consumers to align better with the global expression of social values. For advertisers, emphasizing group benefits may be more important, and emphasizing individual benefits may be less important. Consumers want to fit with their groups, and advertisers should show how products facilitate that desire. Advertisers may also want to utilize the combination of values that have been turning into more important values (i.e., a sense of belonging, fun-enjoyment-excitement, and self-fulfilling). For instance, sports-related products may be advertised with a focus on fun-enjoyment-excitement (e.g., having fun participating in and watching sports) and a sense of belonging (e.g., being a part of a team). For marketers, segmentation may be more important than ever. Different subgroups have different desires, and as the subgroup identity grows, clarity of differentiation in lifestyle choices is ever more important. Marketers need to understand and address these differences.

FUTURE RESEARCH

The impact of values on consumer behaviors and the effectiveness of marketing strategies has been extensively studied by researchers. Still, more research is needed to understand the factors affecting value development, fulfillment, and change. For instance, research has previously shown that culture is an important factor in shaping values (e.g., Hofstede, 1983). However, through globalization and the increased use of social media, the borders among cultures become less apparent. Future research should examine how these factors affect value development and value fulfillment as they are also likely to affect global customer segmentation and marketing communications across cultures.

As discussed earlier, although values are generally considered stable over time, changes in values have been happening over the years (Gurel-Atay et al., 2018). Moreover, research has shown that influential events, or defining moments, affect the core values of people (Schewe & Meredith, 2004). One influential event happening all around the world right now is the COVID-19 pandemic. It is highly possible that the fear of catching COVID-19 or losing loved ones to COVID-19 and the effects of lockdowns on mental health, employment, and spending will change the importance of values for people. For instance, the fear of COVID-19 or losing employment may lead to increases in the importance of security. The social distance measures, on the other hand, may give a huge push to an already-rising value of sense of belonging in the

United States. Researchers should examine how people's values have been changing in the United States since the last representative data collection in 2017 (Gurel-Atay et al., 2018); whether (and, if so, how) current values differ across countries as a result of different effects of COVID-19; and how these changes in values affect consumption behaviors. For instance, different value structures can be observed in countries that have been hit hard by the virus (e.g., Italy, the United States, Spain) versus the countries that have been successful with dealing with the virus (e.g., New Zealand, Australia, South Korea), hence leading to differences in consumer behaviors.

The laddering method uses a bottom-up approach to values by first focusing on consumer behaviors and then trying to reveal the underlying values. The RVS, the SVS, the LOV, or any other quantitative scales included in surveys and experiments, on the other hand, do not have a standard way of being placed in questionnaires. These value scales are placed at the front, middle, or end of studies, and where they are placed may affect the findings. For instance, when they are asked to participants first, they may prime participants' values, and this priming may lead to changes in subsequent answers and behaviors. When they are placed at the end of a study, however, participants may answer value questions as a way to reason their previous answers and behaviors. Future research should compare the impact of ordering of value scales, as it may have important consequences for both academic research and managerial implications.

REFERENCES

Ajzen, I., & Fishbein, M. (1975). A Bayesian analysis of attribution processes. *Psychological Bulletin, 82*(2), 261.

Ajzen, I., & Fishbein, M. (1980). *Understanding attitudes and predicting social behavior*. Prentice-Hall.

Bagozzi, R. P., & Dabholkar, P. A. (1994). Consumer recycling goals and their effect on decisions to recycle: A means-end chain analysis. *Psychology and Marketing, 11*(4), 313–340. https://doi.org/10.1002/mar.4220110403

Bagozzi, R. P., & Dabholkar, P. A. (2000). Discursive psychology: An alternative conceptual foundation to means–end chain theory. *Psychology & Marketing, 17*(7), 535–586.

Beatty, S. E., Kahle, L. R., Homer, P. M., & Misra, S. (1985). Alternative measurement approaches to consumer values: The list of values and the Rokeach value survey. *Psychology and Marketing, 2*(3), 181–200. https://doi.org/10.1002/mar.4220020305

Burroughs, J. E., & Rindfleisch, A. (2002). Materialism and well-being: A conflicting values perspective. *Journal of Consumer Research, 29*(3), 348–370. https://doi.org/10.1086/344429

Chen, N. H., Lee, C. H., & Huang, C. T. (2015). Why buy organic rice? Genetic algorithm-based fuzzy association mining rules for means-end chain data. *International Journal of Consumer Studies, 39*(6), 692–707. https://doi.org/10.1111/ijcs.12210

Cheng, A. S., & Fleischmann, K. R. (2010). Developing a meta-inventory of human values. *Proceedings of the American Society for Information Science and Technology, 47*(1), 1–10. https://doi.org/10.1002/meet.14504701232

Clawson, C. J., & Vinson, D. E. (1978). Human values: A historical and interdisciplinary analysis. In K. Hunt (Ed.), *NA - Advances in consumer research* (Vol. 5, pp. 396–402). Association for Consumer Research.

Cuny, C., & Opaswongkarn, T. (2017). Why do young Thai women desire white skin? Understanding conscious and nonconscious motivations of young women in Bangkok. *Psychology and Marketing, 34*(5), 556–568. https://doi.org/10.1002/mar.21005

Divine, R. L., & Lepisto, L. (2005). Analysis of the healthy lifestyle consumer. *Journal of Consumer Marketing, 22*(5), 275–283. https://doi.org/10.1108/07363760510611707

Drenan, S. (1983). Values and psychological adaptation: Personality factors. In R. Lynn (Ed.), *Social values and social change: Adaptation to life in America* (pp. 227–257). Praeger.

Gardner, M. P., & Hill, R. P. (1990). Consumers' mood states and the decision-making process. *Marketing Letters, 1*(3), 229–238. https://doi.org/10.1007/BF00640800

Gurel-Atay, E., Chen, J., Suh, W. S., & Kahle, L. R. (2018). Changes in social values in the United States—1976–2017: Is a new age of tribalism emerging? In A. Gershoff, R. Kozinets, & T. White (Eds.), *NA - Advances in consumer research* (Vol. 46, pp. 573–574). Association for Consumer Research.

Gurel-Atay, E., & Kahle, L. (2010). Celebrity endorsements and advertising effectiveness: The importance of value congruence. In M. C. Campbell, J. Inman, & R. Pieters (Eds.), *NA - Advances in consumer research* (Vol. 37, pp. 807–809). Association for Consumer Research.

Gurel-Atay, E., & Kahle, L. R. (Eds.). (2019). *Consumer social values*. Routledge. https://doi.org/10.4324/9781315283739

Gurel-Atay, E., Kahle, L. R., Lengler, J. B., & Kim, C. H. (2019). A comparing and contrasting of the list of values and the Schwartz value scale. In E. Gurel-Atay & L. R. Kahle (Eds.), *Consumer social values* (pp. 241–252). Routledge. https://doi.org/10.4324/9781315283739

Gurel-Atay, E., Xie, G. X., Chen, J., & Kahle, L. R. (2010). Changes in social values in the United States, 1976–2007: "Self-respect" is on the upswing as "a sense of belonging" becomes less important. *Journal of Advertising Research*, 50(1), 57–67. https://doi.org/10.2501/S002184991009118X

Gutman, J. (1982). A means-end chain model based on consumer categorization processes. *Journal of Marketing*, 46(2), 60–72. https://doi.org/10.1177/002224298204600207

Haller, M., & Hadler, M. (2006). How social relations and structures can produce happiness and unhappiness: An international comparative analysis. *Social Indicators Research*, 75(2), 169–216. https://doi.org/10.1007/s11205-004-6297-y

Hofstede, G. (1983). National Cultures Revisited. *Behavior Science Research*, 18(4), 285–305. https://doi.org/10.1177/106939718301800403

Homer, P. M., & Kahle, L. R. (1986). A social adaptation explanation of the effects of surrealism on advertising. *Journal of Advertising*, 15(2), 50–60. https://doi.org/10.1080/00913367.1986.10673005

Homer, P. M., & Kahle, L. R. (1988). Structural equation test of the value-attitude-behavior hierarchy. *Journal of Personality and Social Psychology*, 54(4), 638–646. https://doi.org/10.1037/0022-3514.54.4.638

Huber, F., Beckmann, S. C., & Herrmann, A. (2004). Means–end analysis: Does the affective state influence information processing style? *Psychology and Marketing*, 21(9), 715–737. https://doi.org/10.1002/mar.20026

Huneke, M. E. (2005). The face of the un-consumer: An empirical examination of the practice of voluntary simplicity in the United States. *Psychology and Marketing*, 22(7), 527–550. https://doi.org/10.1002/mar.20072

Johnston, C. S. (1995). The Rokeach value survey: Underlying structure and multidimensional scaling. *Journal of Psychology*, 129(5), 583–597. https://doi.org/10.1080/00223980.1995.9914930

Kahle, L. R. (Ed.). (1983). *Social values and social change: Adaptation to life in America*. Preaeger.

Kahle, L. R. (1996). Social values and consumer behavior: Research from the list of values. In C. Seligman, J. M. Olson, & M. P. Zanna (Eds.), *The psychology of values: The Ontario Symposium* (Vol. 8, pp. 135–152). Lawrence Erlbaum Associates.

Kahle, L. R., & Chiagouris, L. (1997). *Values, lifestyles, and psychographics*. Lawrence Erlbaum Associates.

Kahle, L. R., & Homer, P. M. (1985). Physical attractiveness of the celebrity endorser: A social adaptation perspective. *Journal of Consumer Research*, 11(4), 954–961. https://doi.org/10.1086/209029

Kahle, L. R., Homer, P. M., O'Brien, R. M., & Boush, D. M. (1997). Maslow's hierarchy and social adaptation as alternative accounts of value structures. In L. R. Kahle & L. Chiagouris (Eds.), *Values, lifestyles, and psychographics* (pp. 111–137). Lawrence Erlbaum Associates.

Kahle, L. R., Kulka, R. A., & Klingel, D. M. (1980). Low adolescent self-esteem leads to multiple interpersonal problems: A test of social-adaptation theory. *Journal of Personality and Social Psychology*, 39(3), 496–502. https://doi.org/10.1037/0022-3514.39.3.496

Kahle, L. R., Poulos, B., & Sukhdial, A. (1988). Changes in social values in the United States during the past decade. *Journal of Advertising Research*, 28(1), 35–41.

Kahle, L. R., & Timmer, S. G. (1983). A theory and a method for studying values. In L. R. Kahle (Ed.), *Social values and social change: Adaptation to life in America* (pp. 43–69). Praeger.

Kahle, L. R., & Valette-Florence, P. (2012). *Marketplace lifestyles in an age of social media: Theory and method*. M. E. Sharpe.

Landy, F. J. (1989). *Psychology of work behavior*. Thomson Brooks/Cole Publishing Co.

Lee, A. R. (2003). Stability and change in Korean values. *Social Indicators Research*, 62(1), 93–117. https://doi.org/10.1023/A:1022636931969

Lee, J. A., Soutar, G. N., & Louviere, J. (2007). Measuring values using best–worst scaling: The LOV example. *Psychology and Marketing*, 24(12), 1043–1058. https://doi.org/10.1002/mar.20197

Limon, Y., Kahle, L. R., & Orth, U. R. (2009). Package design as a communications vehicle in cross-cultural values shopping. *Journal of International Marketing*, 17(1), 30–57. https://doi.org/10.1509/jimk.17.1.30

Madrigal, R., & Kahle, L. R. (1994). Predicting vacation activity preferences on the basis of value system segmentation. *Journal of Travel Research*, 32(3), 22–28. https://doi.org/10.1177/004728759403200304

Maslow, A. H. (1943). A theory of human motivation. *Psychological Review*, 50(4), 370–396. https://doi.org/10.1037/h0054346

Minton, E. A., Kahle, L. R., & Kim, C. H. (2015). Religion and motives for sustainable behaviors: A cross-cultural comparison and contrast. *Journal of Business Research*, 68(9), 1937–1944. https://doi.org/10.1016/j.jbusres.2015.01.003

Mort, G. S., & Rose, T. (2004). The effect of product type on value linkages in the means-end chain: Implications for theory and method. *Journal of Consumer Behaviour*, 3(3), 221–234. https://doi.org/10.1002/cb.136

Mukhopadhyay, A., & Yeung, C. (2010). Building character: Effects of lay theories of self-control on the selection of products for children. *Journal of Marketing Research*, 47(2), 240–250. https://doi.org/10.1509/jmkr.47.2.240

Oleson, M. (2004). Exploring the relationship between money attitudes and Maslow's hierarchy of needs. *International Journal of Consumer Studies*, 28(1), 83–92. https://doi.org/10.1111/j.1470-6431.2004.00338.x

Olson, J. C., & Reynolds, T. J. (1983). Understanding consumers' cognitive structures: Implications for marketing strategy. In L. Percy & A. G. Woodside (Eds.), *Advertising and consumer psychology* (pp. 77–90). Lexington Books.

Orsingher, C., Marzocchi, G. L., & Valentini, S. (2011). Consumer (goal) satisfaction: A means-ends chain approach. *Psychology and Marketing*, 28(7), 730–748. https://doi.org/10.1002/mar.20409

Paulssen, M., & Bagozzi, R. P. (2005). A self-regulatory model of consideration set formation. *Psychology and Marketing*, 22(10), 785–812. https://doi.org/10.1002/mar.20085

Phillips, J. M., Reynolds, T. J., & Reynolds, K. (2010). Decision-based voter segmentation: An application for campaign message development. *European Journal of Marketing*, 44(3/4), 310–330. https://doi.org/10.1108/03090561011020444

Piner, K. E. (1983). Individual differences associated with value selection. In R. Lynn (Ed.), *Social values and social change: Adaptation to life in America* (pp. 261–274). Praeger.

Raymond, M. A., Mittelstaedt, J. D., & Hopkins, C. D. (2003). When is a hierarchy not a hierarchy? Factors associated with different perceptions of needs, with implications for standardization—Adaptation decisions in Korea. *Journal of Marketing Theory and Practice*, 11(4), 12–25. https://doi.org/10.1080/10696679.2003.11658505

Reynolds, T. J., Gengler, C. E., & Howard, D. J. (1995). A means-end analysis of brand persuasion through advertising. *International Journal of Research in Marketing*, 12(3), 257–266. https://doi.org/10.1016/0167-8116(95)00025-W

Reynolds, T. J., & Gutman, J. (1988). Laddering theory, method, analysis, and interpretation. *Journal of Advertising Research*, 28(1), 11–31.

Reynolds, T. J., & Olson, J. C. (Eds.). (2001). *Understanding consumer decision making: The means-end approach to marketing and advertising strategy*. Lawrence Erlbaum Association. https://doi.org/10.4324/9781410600844

Reynolds, T. J., & Phillips, J. M. (2019). The strata model predicting advertising effectiveness: A neural-network approach enhances predictability of consumer decision making. *Journal of Advertising Research*, 59(3), 268–280. https://doi.org/10.2501/JAR-2018-037

Rokeach, M. (1968). The role of values in public opinion research. *Public Opinion Quarterly*, 32(4), 547–559. https://doi.org/10.1086/267645

Rokeach, M. (1973). *The nature of human values*. Free Press.

Schewe, C. D., & Meredith, G. (2004). Segmenting global markets by generational cohorts: Determining motivations by age. *Journal of Consumer Behaviour*, 4(1), 51–63. https://doi.org/10.1002/cb.157

Schwartz, S. H. (1992). Universals in the content and structure of values: Theory and empirical tests in 20 countries. In M. Zanna (Ed.), *Advances in experimental social psychology* (Vol. 25, pp. 1–65). Academic Press.

Schwartz, S. H. (1994). Are there universal aspects in the structure and content of human values? *Journal of Social Issues*, 50(4), 19–45. https://doi.org/10.1111/j.1540-4560.1994.tb01196.x

Schwartz, S. H. (1996). Value priorities and behavior: Applying a theory of integrated value systems. In C. Seligman, J. M. Olson, & M. P. Zanna (Eds.), *The psychology of values: The Ontario Symposium* (Vol. 8, pp. 1–24). Lawrence Erlbaum Associates.

Shepherd, S., Chartrand, T. L., & Fitzsimons, G. J. (2015). When brands reflect our ideal world: The values and brand preferences of consumers who support versus reject society's dominant ideology. *Journal of Consumer Research*, 42(1), 76–92. https://doi.org/10.1093/jcr/ucv005

Shim, S., & Eastlick, M. A. (1998). The hierarchical influence of personal values on mall shopping attitude and behavior. *Journal of Retailing*, 74(1), 139–160. https://doi.org/10.1016/S0022-4359(99)80091-8

Soper, B., Milford, G. E., & Rosenthal, G. T. (1995). Belief when evidence does not support theory. *Psychology and Marketing*, 12(5), 415–422. https://doi.org/10.1002/mar.4220120505

Steenhaut, S., & Kenhove, P. (2006). An empirical investigation of the relationships among a consumer's personal values, ethical ideology and ethical beliefs. *Journal of Business Ethics*, 64(2), 137–155. https://doi.org/10.1007/s10551-005-5905-3

Steenkamp, J. B. E., Ter Hofstede, F., & Wedel, M. (1999). A cross-national investigation into the individual and national cultural antecedents of consumer innovativeness. *Journal of Marketing, 63*(2), 55–69. https://doi.org/10.1177/002224299906300204

Sudbury, L., & Simcock, P. (2009). Understanding older consumers through cognitive age and the list of values: A U.K.-based perspective. *Psychology and Marketing, 26*(1), 22–38. https://doi.org/10.1002/mar.20260

Suh, W., & Kahle, L. R. (2018). Social values in consumer psychology: Key determinants of human behavior. In M. R. Solomon & T. M. Lowrey (Eds.), *The Routledge companion to consumer behavior* (pp. 165–174). Routledge.

Tan, S. J., & Tambyah, S. K. (2016). Shifting values and life satisfaction: A sequential cross-sectional study of the influence of values on subjective wellbeing in Singapore. *Social Indicators Research, 127*(3), 1391–1416. https://doi.org/10.1007/s11205-015-1015-5

Taormina, R. J., & Gao, J. H. (2013). Maslow and the motivation hierarchy: Measuring satisfaction of the needs. *American Journal of Psychology, 126*(2), 155–177. https://doi.org/10.5406/amerjpsyc.126.2.0155

Ter Hofstede, F., Steenkamp, J. B. E. M., & Wedel, M. (1999). International market segmentation based on consumer-product relations. *Journal of Marketing Research, 36*(1), 1–17. https://doi.org/10.2307/3151911

Thompson, B., Levitov, J. E., & Miederhoff, P. A. (1982). Validity of the Rokeach value survey. *Educational and Psychological Measurement, 42*(3), 899–905. https://doi.org/10.1177/001316448204200325

White, H., & Kokotsaki, K. (2004). Indian food in the UK: Personal values and changing patterns of consumption. *International Journal of Consumer Studies, 28*(3), 284–294. https://doi.org/10.1111/j.1470-6431.2004.00369.x

Woodward, I., & Shaffakat, S. (2016). *Understanding values for insightfully aware leadership* (INSEAD Working Paper No. 2016/05/OBH). https://doi.org/10.2139/ssrn.2471492

Yalch, R., & Brunel, F. (1996). Need hierarchies in consumer judgments of product designs: Is it time to reconsider Maslow's theory? In K. P. Corfman & J. G. Lynch Jr. (Eds.), *NA - Advances in consumer research* (Vol. 23, pp. 405–410). Association for Consumer Research.

CHAPTER 11

LIFESTYLE AND SPORT: EMULATION MARKETING

Pierre Valette-Florence, Tony Meenaghan, and Lynn R. Kahle

Like a hammer, lifestyle research is a tool that can be used for good purposes, such as helping consumers find optimal products; for bad purposes, such as deceiving consumers to turn over their resources for a dubious product; or for anything in between. Valette-Florence (1986) proposed to define lifestyle of an individual as an interaction of three levels, wherein personal values, attitudes, activities, and consumption collectively form lifestyles. Emulation is an important mechanism of lifestyle marketing. We explore this definition later. Sports marketing has a completely different tradition from lifestyle marketing, but it shares with lifestyle marketing a focus on being a tool that uses emulation. This chapter explores these two traditions and shows their similarity. We consider the application of lifestyle logic to the field of sports and then synthesize the two approaches.

LIFESTYLE

After an introduction to the lifestyle concept and a part devoted to the historical heritage of lifestyles, this chapter presents details of the definitions of lifestyles used in marketing, the approaches using values, the approaches focusing on attitudes and activities, and the methods using analysis of products, goods, and services purchased by the consumer. Next is a presentation of the market applications of lifestyle research with a focus on values, their applications in marketing, and their use in consumer behavior. A discussion of future trends in lifestyle research closes this section.

Introduction

The 2016 U.S. presidential election had a surprising result. In spite of widespread consensus that Hillary Clinton would win, in the end Donald Trump prevailed. Several factors probably contributed to this result, including Clinton's lack of aggressive campaigning in the upper Midwest and the FBI's late claim—even later withdrawn—of suspicious emails from a former congressman whose spouse had been a Clinton advisor. Perhaps the most interesting explanation, however, came from the work of Cambridge Analytica, a right-wing consulting company tied to Stephen Bannon and Robert Mercer (Szalai, 2019). Cambridge Analytica claimed to have more than 5,000 observations, many from Facebook, on every American voter, which were pieced together into a lifestyle and social media psychographic portrait of each individual voter for the purposes of microtargeting key swing voters in swing states. Those voters presumably received a barrage of messages aimed at stirring up pro-Trump voters and suppressing pro-Clinton voters, using individualized appeals to fear and anger (Amer & Noujaim, 2019). Cambridge Analytica claimed its efforts at corralling lifestyle data into social media action plans were successful in the election of

https://doi.org/10.1037/0000262-011
APA Handbook of Consumer Psychology, L. R. Kahle (Editor-in-Chief)
Copyright © 2022 by the American Psychological Association. All rights reserved.

Trump, as well as in the British Brexit vote. Not everyone agrees with the Cambridge Analytica boast (e.g., Karpf, 2018), but we do have evidence that the rise of big data and social media has resulted in increased attention to lifestyle data (Kahle & Valette-Florence, 2012), in some cases with significant consequences, including political ones (Reynolds et al., 2016). By the 2020 U.S. presidential election, both sides used lifestyle data with similar cross-cancelling success.

The concept of lifestyles has boggled the minds of research scholars and business managers alike for some time, partly due to the limited choice of demographic and socioeconomic variables employed to explain it and partly owing to the reliance on results from motivational studies to explain a variable claiming to reveal the heart of consumer behavior. A possible conceptualization of lifestyles would be an umbrella concept including behavioral aspects (directly observable and thus measurable) and deeply rooted psychological aspects (indirectly measurable but not observable), such as personal values, beliefs, and attitudes (Hustad & Pessemier, 1974). In order to shed further light on this issue, this chapter details the historic standpoints within social sciences, followed by a thorough analysis of lifestyles as used within marketing.

Historic Heritage

The application of lifestyles within the human sciences predates their usage within the domain of marketing. From a historical point of view, the first mention of lifestyles can be traced back to the very first Greek philosophers. Aristotle (384–322 B.C.E.), in his work *Rhetoric*, discussed *ethos* (or *habitus* in Latin), which encompassed manners of being, ways of living, status, and an individual's character. The work later inspired his disciple Theophrastus (372–287 B.C.E.) to portray 30 psychological profiles of his time (*Characters* by Theophrastus). At that time, however, the depicted portraits presented rather negative connotations, even if nowadays some would still be very relevant. For instance, the "Ironical Man" is depicted as the "one who goes up to his enemies, and volunteers to chat with them, instead of showing hatred. He will praise to their faces those whom he attacked behind their backs, and will sympathize with them in their defeats" (Theophrastus, ca. 320 B.C.E./1870, Section I). It hence appears that nowadays such a man still exists and would rather be labeled as a hypocrite. Another still relevant example is that of the "Boastful Man," who is "one who will stand in the bazaar talking to foreigners of the great sums which he has at sea; he will discourse of the vastness of his money-lending business" (Theophrastus, ca. 320 B.C.E./1870, Section XXIII). A last example is that of the "Reckless Man," who seems to be

> one of these persons who collect and call crowds about them, ranting in a loud cracked voice and haranguing them; . . . but to some he gives the first chapter of his story, . . . to others a fragment; and the time which he chooses for parading his recklessness is always when there is some public gathering. (Theophrastus, ca. 320 B.C.E./1870, Section VI)

Ironically, such a portrait could find an echo in the 45th president of the United States. From a more historical standpoint, the first mention of the term *style* appeared in the work of an English philosopher, Richard Burton (1577–1640): "Stylus virum arguit" (Our style reveals us). More recent allusions to lifestyle started appearing in the portraits of Gidon and Phedon in *Characters* (1688–1694) from La Bruyère (1645–1696). French naturalist Georges Louis de Buffon (1707–1788) compared style to representation a century later: "Style is man himself."

Renowned sociologist Max Weber (1864–1920) popularized the term "lifestyle" for the first time in the 20th century (Weber, 1948). He defined it as "a means of affirmation and differentiation of social stati (*states*)" (Weber, 1922/1964), in line with the notion of "life scheme" proposed by Veblen in 1899: "The belonging to a group and the choice of an individual to differentiate the self from a group to which she or he does not belong." However, the conception of lifestyle according to the psychologist A. Adler (1919/1925, 1929) is in opposition to this view, defining lifestyle as "the system of rules of conduct developed by an individual in order to attain his or her goals in life." As used in modern marketing, the term sometimes refers to individual differences and sometimes only to behaviors.

According to this view, lifestyle is an individual's response to the external environment. The significant influence of lifestyle can be seen as a viable presence in A. Adler's writing, spanning almost half a century's work and representing the crown jewel of Adlerian psychology. The term "lifestyle" did not explicitly show up in his works until 1926 (A. Adler, 1926), except for indirect allusions to "line of direction" (*leitlinie*), "directional image" (*leitbild*), and "life plan" (*lebensplan*) in 1912 (A. Adler, 1912/1917), with the penultimate phrase having been suggested by Ludwig Klages in 1906. The principal reflections of psychologists and sociologists have arisen following these two definitions by A. Adler and Weber.

Following the works of A. Adler, social psychologists in both sociology and psychology redefined the concept of lifestyle as a reflection of personality. As opposed to Freud's emphasis on the role of impulse in personality formation and behaviors, these theorists have found a broader explanatory system integrating social influence and interpersonal relationships concurrently (Hall & Lindzey, 1970; Wells & Beard, 1973).

In the domain of sociology, few works have followed Weber's approach. Specifically, in France, the majority of published works stuck to describing lifestyles of distinct social groups, such as inhabitants of a city or suburb (Kaes, 1963), members of a profession (Boltanski, 1982), or students (Baudrillard, 1970; Bourdieu & Passeron, 1964). These approaches highlight that lifestyles are determined not only by demographic or economic criteria but also by sociopsychological criteria such as personal interest and involvement, taste, level of education, and adhesion to certain moral values.

The diversity in defining lifestyles in social sciences, as well as its characteristics regarding the different approaches by psychologists and sociologists, explains the vast array of its definitions used in marketing. These definitions are presented in the following section.

Definitions of Lifestyles Used in Marketing

From a historical standpoint, the domain of marketing can be sorted into two positions regarding lifestyles. The first is that of Lazarsfeld (1935), who explained consumer behavior through an interaction of three groups of variables: predispositions, influences in the form of social connotations, and qualifiers attributed to products. These different criteria serve as forerunners to the approach based on attitudes and activities, better known by the term AIO (activities, interests, and opinions).

Other authors, such as Gottlieb (1959), Koponen (1960), and Bernay (1971), have based their approaches on the link between personality variables and the choice of certain types of products. These studies, which adopted the name *psychographic approaches* (Kahle & Chiagouris, 2016) are just as focused around personality and its relations with socioeconomic behaviors; however, the majority of research on personalities proved to be nonconclusive (Kassarjian, 1971), explaining only a small percentage of the variation in consumer behaviors.

It is interesting to note the essentially empirical character that the studies of lifestyles have hired from these aforementioned orientations (Peltier et al., 2002). This effect is translated in marketing through the varying efforts to define lifestyles through multiple propositions. Although some remain general in nature, others have been more pragmatic and centered on the individual. Some works have also explicitly introduced the notion of social influence.

For instance, Lazer's (1963) definition is very general. It is halfway between individual description and aggregate description of behavior:

> Lifestyle is . . . the result of forces such as culture, values, and the symbolism of certain objects, moral values, and ethics. In a certain sense, the aggregate of consumer purchases and the manner in which these purchases are used reflects the lifestyle of a society. (as cited in Kahle & Valette-Florence, 2012, p. 5)

Wind and Green's (1974) definition, on the other hand, focuses more on the individual by defining the different levels of lifestyle identification. These authors identified three levels of studying lifestyles:

- Forming the most stable and anchored level are individual values and personality traits.
- The intermediate level comprises an ensemble of attitudes and activities specific to the individual. Although less stable than values, these are closer to the act of purchasing.
- Finally, the peripheral level is an assemblage of products purchased and consumed, which are the more ephemeral effects of the two previous levels.

Taking this formulation, Valette-Florence (1986) proposed to define lifestyle of an individual as an interaction of the three preceding levels, wherein personal values, attitudes, activities, and consumption collectively form lifestyles. The works of Valette-Florence and Jolibert (1990) also supported this definition, showing that the individuals having identical behavior in one of the components could, nevertheless, differentiate themselves in the two other components. The measure of lifestyle would thus be an approach sequential to each component. Thus, focusing on merely one of the different components would cause a single-faceted gathering of information.

Nevertheless, the absence of a precisely defined concept has led researchers to develop systems of measure and lifestyle descriptions that only integrate one component, rarely more. Broadly, four approaches have been mainly adopted:

- The first perspective deals with a person's system of values, particularly the primary system of values (Kahle, 1983; Rokeach, 1968; Schwartz, 1992, 1996). This approach emphasizes the organizing principles of goals.
- Another approach is centered on the study of activities and attitudes. Among these, certain studies are more articulate about attitudes toward a class of products (Haley, 1968), while other works develop a more general approach based on the ensemble of activities, interests, and opinions, hence the acronym AIO (Pessemier & Tigert, 1966; Tigert, 1973; Wells, 1968b; Wells & Tigert, 1971).
- A third is focused on study of goods and services consumed. This approach is based on the principle that a consumer's lifestyle is defined by the goods and services they buy and also by the way they consume them. Hence it can be seen as an a posteriori analysis (Wells, 1968a), which aims to determine individuals' behavioral norms by observing their purchases, their interests, and their goals. This approach starts with the consumption action and works backward.
- A more recent approach emphasizes social relationships, such as those formed via social media (Kahle & Valette-Florence, 2012). See Chapter 21 and Chapter 14 in this handbook on social media and on relationships.

Among these different studies, the development of each aspect has been varied and limited to a certain extent. In fact, though the AIO inventories are widespread, the study of values and ways of consumption regarding lifestyles has experienced limited development. The following section outlines the theoretical foundations of these approaches.

Approaches using values and marketing. From a historical perspective, the sociological approach appears to be the most prevalent in the consumer behavior and marketing research field.

In 1956, F. Adler proposed that values are an ensemble of learned or innate preferences present within each individual. The majority of social psychologists have argued for construing value as a hypothetical construction, sometimes referred to as a "meta-attitude," more closely linked to attitudes and behavior than an independent construct. This approach of treating values as a hypothetical construct was principally developed by Rokeach (1968, 1973). According to him, when individuals possess strong attitudes toward products, objects, or specific situations, they have a relatively limited number of values. This difference suggests that values and attitudes are connected in a hierarchical system in which values form the heart. Given the hierarchy of values, Rokeach hence makes a distinction between two types of values: instrumental values and terminal values. When values refer to modes of conduct, they take the name of instrumental values; however, when they refer to end-states of existence, they are referred to as terminal values. In other words, instrumental values are interpreted as ways of being or acting, whereas terminal values are objectives, either for an individual or for the society.

Rokeach (1974) operationalized a test (Rokeach Value Survey [RVS]) in order to assess individuals' value systems. Rokeach came up with 18 instrumental and 18 terminal values representing values in contemporary American society. This study also paved the way for many validations, as much at the level of its empirical implementation (J. Mitchell, 1976; Rankin & Grube, 1980) as at the level of its transcultural application (Feather, 1975, in Australia and New Guinea; M. Moore, 1975, in Israel; Penner & Anh, 1977, in Vietnam; Sinka & Sayeed, 1979, in India; Cochrane et al., 1979, and Searing, 1979, in Great Britain). This practical and operational orientation confers an interdisciplinary application to the concept of values in the marketing domain.

The List of Values (LOV; Kahle, 1983) approach will be described more later. It is also covered in Chapter 10 in this handbook on values. As with all of these values approaches, it provides marketers with an opportunity to explore the cohesion of consumer decision making from a societal and an individual perspective.

Another synthesis lies in the proposition of Schwartz (1996; Schwartz & Bilsky, 1987, 1990), who considers values as individuals' adhesion to objectives (terminal or instrumental) that facilitate the satisfaction of interests concerning different entities (individual, collective, or both), with a great importance in their everyday lives across 10 motivational domains. The innovative aspect of this proposition resides in the definition of the motivation domains, derived from the work of several researchers from diverse domains in the social sciences (e.g., Bandura, 1988; Berlyne, 1967; Deci & Ryan, 1985; Kluckhohn, 1951; Maslow, 1959; Scitovsky, 1976). Moreover, these domains, according to Schwartz (1996), exhibit one circular (quasicircumplex) structure for which the centers of interest are superposed. The interest in such a representation resides in the compatibility of two adjacent domains and in the opposite position of two opposing domains in relation to the origin. Thanks to the inventory of 56 values proposed by Schwartz, other studies have validated aspects of this structure in different cultural immersions (Cieciuch, 2014; Schwartz, 1992, 1996) or different contexts, such as environmental preservation (Grunert & Juhl, 1991). This Schwartz approach has not always performed well in outside empirical examinations (cf. Gurel-Atay et al., 2019).

Approaches focusing on attitudes and activities. This subsection puts the emphasis on attitude and activities, widely recognized within the AIO framework. From a historical point of view, this approach derives its essence from the reasoning of Merton (1949), according to whom the key to the formation of lifestyles is at the level of complex social groups, which then join together to form a society, rather than at the level of the society taken from these groups as a whole. From this viewpoint, the approaches focusing on attitudes and activities were developed around the works of Pessemier and Tigert (1966) and of Wells (1968a) in an effort to determine the lifestyles of individuals by examining their diverse activities and attitudes in the most exhaustive manner. According to Hustad and Pessemier (1974), these approaches tend to determine not only the centers of interest for the individuals, their attitudes, their activities, and some of their personality traits, but also their self-perceptions and their opinions on their respective social, political, and economic environments. Consequently, most studies of this type were developed in an essentially empirical manner, based on very long questionnaires, while lacking a clear definition of the underlying theoretical concepts being employed.

The most exhaustive approach, which is known as the AIO approach, was developed in the United States in order to study lifestyles and replaced later on to some extent by the VALS Approach (A. Mitchell, 1983), which was constructed under the same scheme but supposedly gives values a more predominant role. Globally, the AIO approach assigns a much greater importance to the environment of the individual in the process of forming lifestyles. Overall, the types of activities people choose and the things they possess all denote their belonging or desire to belong to certain groups (Grubb & Grathwohl, 1967; Laumann & House, 1970).

Studies aligning with the AIO approach therefore try to obtain a relatively complete image of an individual's lifestyle by describing individual-level values. These could be linked to various activities given the social and societal context in which they evolve, be they prevalent in interests and attitudes toward leisure or toward work and consumption. Because of the ambitious nature of these studies, they produced quite comprehensive questionnaires composed of several hundred items, sometimes up to 1,000. It is important to note that, in principle, each of these studies developed its own methodology, often proprietary and hidden from peer researchers (Kahle & Kahle, 2009), in collecting given information (Wind & Green, 1974). The VALS approach could also track differences in AIOs within a family and their evolution across societies and time.

On a practical note, almost all of the companies using a commercial AIO inventory prefer to use consumer typologies, which are admittedly simpler given the individual can be identified or positioned within a profile group by their mean distance from the center of gravity of said group. This feature has the added advantage of being directly operational for defining strategy in terms of positioning or communication. In the English-speaking world, there have been multiple adaptations of the AIO and geographic/psychographic segmentation systems by large research organizations as well as advertising agencies, including and not limited to the Lifestyle Study by DDB World Communications Group, Young & Rubicam, Grey, Universal McCann, New Wave by Ogilvy & Mather, ClusterPlus by Donnally Marketing, ACORN by CACI, RISC, PRIZM by Claritas, VALS2 by SRI, MOSAIC by Experian, and GlobalScan by Backer Spielvogel Bates (Shimp, 2010; Solomon, 2009; Weiss, 2000).

Approaches using analysis of products, goods, and services purchased by the consumer. As witnessed so far, AIO inventory origin has not only experienced development by researchers but has also been adopted by practitioners. In spite of their primacy and theoretical interest, approaches centered on values have not been as widely adopted. The same goes for similar approaches based on the analysis of goods and services purchased by the consumer.

Historically, the study of goods and services consumed is based on the principle that consumers' lifestyles are limited to the goods and services they buy, along with the way they consume these goods and services. This research method thus proceeds to hypothesize that all purchases of any given consumer—in other words, the type of products they buy—are indicators of a lifestyle. This approach can be deemed a posteriori analysis (Wells, 1968a), aiming to determine individuals' behavioral norms by observing their purchases, their interests, and their goals.

This method derives its essence from the works of Levy, who, in 1963, demonstrated that products play an important symbolic or psychological role. Contemporaneously, Kelley (1963) noted that consumers, while buying products, acquire the representative symbols of their lifestyles. D. Moore (1963) also suggested along the same lines that consumption methods are an expression of an individual's lifestyle. Thus, people buy products for their implied significance, in addition to the direct purpose served by such products.

Although limited in scope, two principal orientations can be revealed: either specific, centered around product categories elaborated during the 1970s, or more general and broader, as has emerged more recently in Asia.

Indeed, the first studies were mainly interested in specific product categories. For example, in 1969, Alpert and Gatty created a factor analysis of 80 different goods and services using a sample of 5,480 men, leading to the determination of 16 fundamental profiles such as "the car-conscious man," "the hard drinker," and "the cosmopolitan traveler" (p. 67). In practice, these studies, due to their limited topics, do not allow a broad generalization of behavior types across different product categories. However, since 1979, a new trend began where studies were generally centered on an analysis of a whole group of products purchased and consumed by individuals. This type of approach, defined in terms of consumption styles, is fully connected with an explicative perspective of consumer behavior and the research of specific segmentation criteria. Among the most important contributions, the one proposed by Uusitalo (1979a, 1979b) seems the broadest. Having access to the given information on consumer expenditure in Finnish households in 1971, furnished by the Central Bureau of Statistics, Uusitalo investigated a list of 220 products consumed by 1,908 households. Then, she isolated by factor analysis three principal consumption style: modernism, 7% (modern consumption as opposed to traditional consumption); mobility, 13% (consumption implying a displacement as opposed to consumption at home); and diversity, 11% (varied consumption as opposed to consumption restricted to products of primary necessity).

In a similar way, one interesting and novel study was conducted in 1982 by Cosmas. He interviewed 1,797 women with a questionnaire containing 250 items and 179 currently used products based on the AIO approach. He employed two types of Q factor analysis and classified the individuals according to their highest factor score among the obtained scores to decipher seven types of consumption profiles and seven lifestyles. The author then analyzed the link between lifestyles and modes of consumption. The results were rather deceptive in the sense that they indicate a very weak interaction between the two groups. Nonetheless, it is interesting to note that Cosmas's work represents the first attempt to relate two different lifestyle approaches: one measured by an AIO inventory, the other by a revelation of products consumed.

In practice, one therefore sees the interest that practitioners can reach out of these more general studies, as they allow them to classify individuals according to objective criteria measuring their consumption. As an example, the leading products or AIO clusters can be a means of better recognizing the specific ways of consumption in which the products occur. Managers may prefer to focus on product choices, but consumer researchers may prefer AIO clusters and social issues. They also can help us identify the evolutionary markers of consumption and of the clientele on a year-to-year basis.

Moving to a different continent for attention, a very sophisticated program of lifestyle research has emerged from a group of Asian marketing scholars at the National University of Singapore (e.g., Kau et al., 2004, 1998; Tambyah et al., 2009). They developed complex profiles based on lifestyle from a quality-of-life and a satisfaction or happiness perspective. They honored the academic virtues of transparency and intellectual accessibility, following the ideals of public knowledge (cf. Kahle & Kahle, 2009). They often include the LOV and other well-developed measures central to understanding lifestyle in their multidimensional profiles.

Market Applications of Lifestyle Research

Among the aforementioned approaches, the methods based on classic AIO inventory have furnished a lot of concrete illustrations. The general lifestyle typologies stemming from them have been widely used in advertising. They offer, however, a large number of other applications in commercial research, which can be classified into diverse categories, such as market-focused strategies to decide across different distribution options or a refined choice of possible market segments.

Lifestyle studies on distribution models have depicted preference for different store outlets based on specific consumer profiles. For example, Bearden et al. (1978) conducted a study concerning sale shoppers, fast food clientele, and "bazaar" shoppers. Based on a number of items measuring the degree of openness to the exterior, traditionalism, or modernism, they showed a link between consumer profiles and the degree of frequenting each category of sales point based on these items. For example, consumers who rarely patronize stores in proximity appear to be traditional individuals, introverts, and very dependent on their social surroundings to make purchasing decisions.

This analysis based on consumer lifestyles has also been validated for choosing between possible consumer segments. For example, Segnit and Broadbent (1974) studied the market of "TV dinners" and preprepared desserts in connection with the purchasing frequency of 17 dishes. They divided up the sample into three principal groups and six secondary groups. Afterward, they examined the socioeconomic characteristics as well as the lifestyles of these nine groups.

The analysis of lifestyle in the advertising domain, however, is by far the most widespread. It was principally used to create and validate campaign themes, to better target media audiences and plan their use. In the United States in the third quarter of the 20th century, certain authors initially considered psychographics as an essential tool to be used in advertising (e.g., Dunn, 1971; Simmons, 1971; Young, 1971).

Among the diverse uses of lifestyle analysis for the creation of advertisements, the example furnished by Plummer (1974a, 1974b) is a pretty illustrative one. One of the analyses allowed for the identification of beer consumers' psychographic profiles. These consumers are attracted by a virile existence and by physical effort. They also seem receptive to the myth of heroes. Based on their perception of beer being assimilated to virility, a campaign was developed portraying the daring and adventurous lifestyle of a marine (and, simultaneously, beer consumer). The consumers could thus identify themselves with the proposed image, and the result was a strong increase in sales.

Lifestyle analysis in the domain of varied media audiences was systematically practiced in the United States (Peterson, 1972). For instance, Michaels (1973) examined the lifestyle profiles of American readers of 11 types of magazines. He discovered varying levels of sensitivities without specific relationships to the object being advertised. Thus, reading agricultural magazines is generally associated with a traditional lifestyle and with bestowing a larger importance to religion (cf. Minton & Kahle, 2014, 2017; Minton et al., 2016). At the same time, readers of the American magazine *National Geographic* are generally preoccupied with artistic and ecological questions. It was therefore depicted that certain publications constitute a better support for certain types of products.

In France, numerous studies have focused on the relations between the audiences of different media or media habits and sociocultural values. Demuth and Neirac's (1976) study came up with nine groups of media consumption patterns, two of which comprise two thirds of the population: the antimedia group (34% of the population) and the group of people viewing uniquely television media (also making up 34% of the population). The correlation between these groups and 11 types of people, as identified in French society based on shared values, was studied. It was also established that belonging to the antimedia group was closely correlated to belonging to the profile type "ahead" of sociocultural currents.

As Wells (1974) noted, there are several examples of how lifestyle analysis facilitates the evaluation of media: as advertisement supports, in order to determine their adaptation to different products and types of promotional events; as factors of vehicle choice, to aid necessary positioning or repositioning in response to expectations of targeted segments; and as the messages' context, in precisely framing the scene and inherent characteristics of the message being delivered.

Values and Applications in Marketing

Beyond the AIO approach, which has mainly witnessed empirical developments, values are much more theoretically sound and offer three broad and complementary applications within the marketing field:

- The first and the oldest deals with locating, identifying, and selecting values.
- The second is centered on the study of specific types of behavior.
- The third developed the use of values by applying them in studies of lifestyles as factors of segmentation and identification of potential markets.

This distinction clarifies the complementary relations that exist among these different paths of investigation. In addition, recent developments in values (Kahle & Xie, 2008; Schwartz, 1996) can lead to new perspectives in the study of lifestyles.

According to Clawson and Vinson's (1977) article, the first two academic contributions in marketing on the values of consumers are from Copeland in 1924 and from Clawson in 1946. After the analysis of 936 advertisements appearing in American magazines in 1923, Copeland concluded that all motivations for purchase can be classified according to two dimensions. The first is linked to the type of decision being made and groups the motivations that influence individual choices by class of product, brand name, and store. The second dimension concerns *emotional* motivations, as opposed to the *rational* motivations of the previous dimension. Copeland thus identified 23 emotional motivations that originate from human emotions and instincts. In addition, these correspond, in some way, to the terminal and instrumental values proposed by Rokeach several years later. Copeland can therefore be considered as a forerunner, having proposed the first distinction between human values and product attributes.

Clawson (1946) also analyzed hundreds of advertisements, leading to a list of 128 values, of which the first six categories correspond to the six types of profiles identified by Spranger. He also added two more classes consisting of 29 physical values and seven general values. In practice, however, Clawson's study opens the way to an abysmal slope of researchers working on long lists of values having little practical use.

Indeed, by the 1960s, Rokeach brought about an evolution of values with the introduction of less specific values, giving the concept of values its character of general norm such as its most commonly accepted nomenclature today. In 1977, Vinson et al. stretched Rokeach's paradigm by considering values on only two levels. The first, conceived as global values, comprises both instrumental and terminal values simultaneously. The second refers to values having a link to attributes of desired products and to behaviors during buying transactions. Globally, these authors suggest that the most interesting applications of these studies are the analysis of the markets, the segmentation of these markets, and the planning of products and promotional strategies.

The work of Kahle and his collaborators (e.g., Suh & Kahle, 2018) has appeared as the most ubiquitous with regard to the identifying of values in lifestyle research. The corresponding methodology named LOV was developed around the works of researchers at the University of Michigan (Veroff et al., 1981). Based on the earlier studies of Maslow (1954), Rokeach (1973), and Feather (1975), this stream of research is founded on the theory of social adaptation (Kahle, 1983, 1984; Kahle et al., 1980), which considers individuals as adapting themselves to certain roles in life, partly in function with their values.

In practice, the LOV methodology consists of condensing Rokeach's terminal values into a smaller list of nine values, which are essentially oriented toward the person, as opposed to some of Rokeach's values oriented to society (Beatty et al., 1985). To be included within the LOV, values were required to relate plausibly to each of life's major roles: work, leisure, marriage, and parenting. Research on the LOV has shown that values vary widely by place (Kahle, 1986; Tan et al., 2015), time (Gurel-Atay et al., 2010; Stockard et al., 2014), and situation (Piner & Kahle, 1984). The LOV is presented in more detail in Chapter 10.

Globally, one observes that the LOV is more concise than the RVS (nine items instead of 18). It uses more generic terms and contains an orientation almost exclusive to the individual with regard to terminal values. As indicated by Valette-Florence (1988) through a comparison of the two methods at an empirical level, it is this reference to personal character that leads to the choice of one method over another. Otherwise, these two lists have strongly related conceptual structures. The LOV has a more purposive tie to the theorizing of Maslow than does the RVS (Homer & Kahle, 1988; Kahle et al., 2016), has better reliability (Beatty et al., 1985), does not confuse individual values with societal values that often have little impact on daily life (e.g., a world at peace), and is methodologically easier to use in surveys (Kahle, 1996).

It is equally important to underline Schwartz's (1996) proposition, the Schwartz Value Survey (SVS), which used between 44 and 56 items belonging to one (or more) of the 10 motivational domains, further refined to encompass 19 motivational domains (Schwartz, 2017; Schwartz et al., 2012). One noticeable feature is that values are arranged according to a circumplex structure, moving clockwise from personal focus to social focus. In addition, values are organized in a hierarchal way, with 19 single motivational domains; six main first-order facets (Universalism, Benevolence,

Self-Direction, Power, Security, and Conformity); four second-order dimensions (Openness to Change, Self-Enhancement, Conservation, and Self-Transcendence); and, at a final third-order level, broader global value orientations, formally depending on the ways one looks at the circumplex structure, either social focus, personal focus, growth (anxiety free), or self-protection (anxiety avoidance). This approach has been used with some success (e.g., Grunert and Juhl, 1991; Schwartz, 1996), especially in international research. Shortcomings of this approach have been described elsewhere (e.g., Gurel-Atay et al., 2019).

Using Values in Consumer Behavior

The development of an instrument for measuring values proposed by Rokeach and Kahle led to multiple uses of the concept of values in marketing. All in all, we can mention three principal orientations: cross-cultural studies, descriptive analyses of specific behaviors, and more explicit research of behavior.

Cross-cultural studies. These studies have sought a link between values and consumer segmentation in different cultures. Munson and McIntyre (1979) provided a good illustration of this type of approach. Their study used the RVS to uncover the differences existing between people from Thailand, from Mexico, and from the United States. The authors found that the discriminatory functions built from answers to Rokeach's test permit classifying 65% of the individuals according to their cultural baggage.

Ng et al. (1982) used Rokeach's test for differentiating human values across nine countries (Australia, Bangladesh, Hong Kong, India, Japan, Malaysia, New Zealand, New Guinea, and Taiwan). Their analyses, in spite of not making an explicit distinction between instrumental and terminal values, proved to be capable of explaining more than half of the cultural variations across the groups. Nevertheless, these studies remain descriptive in the sense that they characterize societies of different values without explaining them.

Descriptive analyses. In practice, much research can be qualified as descriptive in the sense that it does not attempt to explain the specific behaviors studied but tries more to draw up their profiles from corresponding values. For example, various works (Scott & Lamont, 1973; Vinson & Munson, 1976; Vinson et al., 1977) have shown the relationships existing between personal values and the attributes relative to automobiles.

In other domains, Grube et al. (1984) drew up the distinctive profiles of values of smokers and nonsmokers, while Pitts and Woodside (1984) demonstrated the link between values and the criteria of choosing a product and brand name for cars, deodorants, and travel. Finally, in the domain of media, Becker and Connor (1981) addressed readers' and devoted TV viewers' values in the United States, while in France, Evrard and Tissier-Desbordes (1985) studied the relation between value systems and reading in the family.

Explicit behavioral research. It is useful to identify three principal approaches. The first one treats the direct influence of values on certain types of behaviors or practices of consumption. For example, Bozinoff and Cohen (1982) examined the influence of values on the evaluation of automobiles. Their results show an interest in a linked study that includes values within situations (Kahle, 1984; Punj & Stewart, 1983). Combining both kinds of variables doubles the variance explained, in contrast to what arises if they are used separately.

The second type of approach involves a structural relation in causal models. Thus, the work of Homer and Kahle (1988) tests and validates, by means of a covariance structure analysis model, the hierarchical and simple relationship between values → attitudes → behavior with regard to natural food choice. In France, many similar works can be mentioned. Their conclusions are identical in the sense that they all lead to obtaining a significant impact on the values of consumption, whether they deal with new products (Roehrich & Valette-Florence, 1987), with domestic energy (Arellano et al., 1988), or with high-involvement products (Valette-Florence, 1988; Valette-Florence & Rapacchi, 1991). Numerous studies have followed this method and are reviewed elsewhere (Kahle, 1996; Kahle & Xie, 2008). The range of topics that scholars have investigated includes vast areas such as natural health (Thompson & Troester, 2002), sports (Kahle et al., 2001), and fashion (Rose et al., 1994).

Finally, it is appropriate to mention the originality of Gutman's (1982, 1986) conceptual approach and his collaborators (Reynolds, 1985; Reynolds & Gutman, 1984; Reynolds & Olson, 2001; Reynolds et al., 2016). Their approach gives a more qualitative explanation of the links that connect purchased products to the central values of the individuals. Their methodology consists of a means–end chain analysis, which is hierarchical and can be defined as the connections between terminal and instrumental values of individuals, the psychological or functional consequences fulfilled by using a product, and the nature of its different attributes: values → consequences → attributes.

Gutman's interest resides in the possibility of isolating the chains, which appear the most relevant for increasing awareness of or characterizing the potential of a given product to the user. Important limitations lie in the very complex implementation of this procedure and in the qualitative character of genesis and of choosing the most adequate chaining. To compensate for these problems, Valette-Florence and Rapacchi (1991) proposed a purely quantitative approach based on the joint application of the theory of graphs and the use of multiple correspondence factor analyses. The theory of graphs allows for the automated construction of hierarchical maps, while the correspondence factor analysis provides a graphic and global representation of individuals as well as different constitutive elements of chaining in a common perceptual space. In addition, this allows for the possibility of carrying out a typology of consumers according to the links they have evoked. This study, applied with success in a European context (Valette-Florence & Rapacchi, 1991), was subject to methodological improvements advocating the use of multidimensional analysis and constrained typology (Aurifeille & Valette-Florence, 1995) or the tandem use of nonlinear generalized canonical (OVERALS) and cluster analyses (Valette-Florence, 1998).

To conclude, two recent research works have put forward a renewed interest in Schwartz's values and their usefulness for characterizing human behaviors and daily life activities. Whereas the first study, by Skimina et al. (2019), brings innovative insights regarding the predictive power of values on daily life activities, the second one (Magun at al., 2016) is more in line with usual lifestyle typologies, relying on sound and powerful clustering techniques in order to segment 23 European countries. Skimina et al. do show that personal values motivate everyday activities (Goldberg, 2010), with differing results for values as traits and values as situation-specific states.

In Magun at al.'s (2016) research, using data from the European Social Survey, populations of 29 European countries were classified based on their values, which were measured with Schwartz's Portrait Values Questionnaire. Using latent class analysis, the authors identified five European value segments: Growth, Strong Social Status, Weak Social Status, Weak Personal Status, and Strong Personal Status. Interestingly, the approach gives the probabilities of the 21 values within each class, hence helping to label them accordingly. For instance, the first class (Growth) has the lowest probabilities of the value items measuring Conservation and Self-Enhancement, depicting that this particular class has the lowest commitment to these two main value orientations. Moreover, all the countries studied were diverse but well delineated in their value class composition. For instance, Nordic and Western European countries exceed Mediterranean and Postcommunist Europe in the probability of a class that combines the strongest preferences for Openness over Conservation and for Self-Transcendence over Self-Enhancement.

Future Trends in Lifestyle Research

Two major trends characterize new directions in lifestyle research. The first is the application of highly empirical models via social media outlets, such as Google and Facebook. These approaches use massive amounts of data and machine-learning artificial intelligence to craft product-specific or brand-specific algorithms that predict purchase patterns (Zuboff, 2020), similar to the Cambridge Analytica approach described at the beginning of this chapter. These algorithms are nearly always proprietary. Their popularity implies that they have been used successfully, although the academic literature lacks verification. Because the proprietary algorithms are the source of profit for their creators, we are unlikely to see public data on these studies. We do know, however, that lifestyle blogging can be effective social media (Larsen & Kahle, 2019). Some people (e.g., Zuboff, 2020) worry that this form of surveillance capitalism poses a serious threat to individual freedom.

The other trend is for academic researchers to probe more deeply into one domain of lifestyle, such as sports, sustainability (e.g., Kahle & Gurel-Atay, 2014; Minton et al., 2012), or religion (e.g., Minton & Kahle, 2014, 2017; Minton et al., 2016), and develop a body of knowledge about that lifestyle area. To illustrate, we now shift to a more careful consideration of sports consumption, which is an example of one area in which lifestyle applications abound.

SPORT AND LIFESTYLE

Many sports activities constitute aspects of lifestyle. Socialization into lifestyles often starts early in life via introduction to sports. For example, "soccer moms" may steer their children to play soccer and to absorb the "soccer lifestyle." In the process of playing soccer, the children learn many aspects of modern life, such as teamwork, cooperation, consumption, competition, setting goals, respect for authority, and fitness. These values and others provide the link between soccer and lifestyle (Rose et al., 2003). For example, fans of women's basketball place a lower emphasis on self-fulfillment than others, including fans of men's basketball (Kahle et al., 2001). The opposite pattern occurred with self-respect. Kurpis et al. (2011) showed that people who value a sense of accomplishment are more likely to participate in sports. Thus, values link with both lifestyle and sport (Aiken et al., 2015; Lee & Kahle, 2016; Stockard et al., 2014).

Fan Motives

Fans may have differing levels of commitment to sports, as illustrated by Kelman's (1974) theory. Kahle et al. (1996) investigated the motives for fans attending sporting events. Their data supported Kelman's three ascending processes of attitudinal functions derived from the three macrotheories of psychology. First, *compliance* reflects behaviorism (e.g., Skinner, 1974; Watson, 1913). The motive at this level for attending a sporting event is compliance with social rewards and avoidance of punishments. One goes to events to interact with and be bonded to friends, for example. Second, *identification* reflects more deep-seated motives, as articulated in psychoanalytic theory (e.g., Erikson, 1968; Freud, 1999). People attend events to deal with internal struggles. One goes to events to express psychosocial tensions, such as fear of being viewed as not masculine enough. Third, *internalization* reflects humanistic psychology (e.g., Maslow, 1954; Rogers, 1961). Fans attend sporting events as a method of fundamental self-expression and as a way to carry out defining characteristics, such as going to a Yankees game to show affiliation with New York. The link with values is especially evident in this third level. Efforts to understand and change fan behavior need to define which motivational level dominates for a particular fan in a particular context and then apply the appropriate theory. The utility of this conceptualization has also been shown for relationship marketing (Bee & Kahle, 2006; Kahle et al., 1997) and for cross-cultural marketing (Lu et al., 2012).

In the context of a discussion on sport and lifestyle, it is important to consider sport in the broader terms of marketing and consumer behavior. Sport represents an increasingly important domain for the application of marketing principles, whether at a global, national, or local level. Marketing principles are applied to three areas of sports-related activity: (a) the marketing of and by sports entities, which includes sports codes (e.g., American football, soccer), sports federations (e.g., NFL, FIFA), leagues (e.g., Champions League in European soccer, National Basketball Association [NBA] in the United States), teams (e.g., Dallas Cowboys, Manchester United), individual players and athletes (e.g., Peyton Manning, Cristiano Ronaldo), and events (e.g., Super Bowl, Kentucky Derby); (b) the marketing of sports-related products such as sports equipment (e.g., golf clubs, helmets, tennis rackets); and (c) marketing through sport, whereby companies and brands use sports for marketing and brand purposes, such as in advertising campaigns (e.g., Dove Men+Care, Gillette and Tiger Woods and Roger Federer) and, to an even greater extent, in sponsorships that enable brands to reach and relate to particular audiences (e.g., Nike and Michael Jordan, Chevrolet and Manchester United).

Sports fans have relationships with sports brands (Wann & James, 2018), whether such brands are sporting codes (e.g., lacrosse, rugby), sports teams, or individual players and athletes. From the fan perspective, these sports/brand relationships can span the continuum from tepid allegiance and occasional attendance through to fanaticism, namely, the psychological continuum model (Funk & James, 2001). The greater the fan allegiance to the sports brand, the more this allegiance will be reflected in the individual's life and lifestyle.

Sporting codes and teams and players and athletes are brands in their own right (Bouchet et al., 2013; Bridgewater, 2010). As such, they require effective management and marketing programs in pursuit of their ambitions (Oriard, 2007; Pritchard & Stinson, 2013). For example, soccer, rugby, and padel represent sports brands that have benefited from strong marketing campaigns on their behalf by their representative bodies, Major League Soccer (LoRé, 2019), World Rugby (World Rugby, 2020), and the International Padel Federation (Richter, 2019), respectively. Additionally, similar management and marketing campaigns can be undertaken by the sponsor in support of the sports brand (Rishe, 2019). This activity is evident in the branding and marketing input by Nike into notable sports brands such as Cristiano Ronaldo, Neymar, LeBron James, Kevin Durant, Rafael Nadal, and Tiger Woods (Enoch, 2020).

Sponsorship

Given the role of sports marketing and sponsorship in creating and managing sports brands and their images and in fostering fan relationships with particular sports brands with consequent lifestyle implications, the topic of sponsorship is more fully examined here.

This section seeks to outline the changing perceptions of sponsorship, its expanding corporate role, and the enhanced understanding of its related processes and effects. The various publics addressed by sponsorship are identified, as are the interactions between the various parties (sponsor, consumer/fan, and sponsored property). Finally, new directions for research activity to further enhance understanding of how sponsorship interacts with consumers are suggested.

Just as sponsorship has evolved over time in terms of its capacity and resultant roles, so too have the perceptions and indeed definitions of sponsorship. Although sponsorship can be seen from different perspectives (sponsor, fan, property), the most common perspective in defining sponsorship is that of the sponsor, as is evident in this widely adopted and adapted definition: "Sponsorship is an investment in cash or in kind, in an activity, in return for access to the exploitable commercial potential associated with that activity" (T. Meenaghan, 1991a, p. 10). Sponsorship can be viewed as both a medium and a meaning platform. The medium element of the platform refers to its reach, and the meaning element refers to the message that is implied through association with the sponsored entity. To maximize the value of the sponsorship investment, additional support funding is needed to supplement and expand the reach capacity of the sponsorship and additionally to articulate and influence the message element of the sponsorship in terms of how the association is perceived. Media developments have fundamentally enhanced and expanded the capabilities of the media and the meaning platform that is sponsorship.

Corporate sponsorship has been a feature of business activity for over 100 years. Sponsorship, drawing elements of its lineage from ancient Greece and Rome and the Renaissance period in postmedieval Europe, represents the corporate replacement of a supportive societal role previously undertaken by patrons and philanthropists, if not driven by an exact similarity of motive. Throughout its evolution, three key parties have been critical to the development of sponsorship, namely, sponsors, media, and properties (e.g., events, athletes) with the agency sector fulfilling the important intermediary role.

Press and radio represented the available media options in the early 20th century, but much would change with the advent of television from the late 1950s. The subsequent adoption of mass television from the early 1960s, with its increasing focus and indeed reliance on sporting and cultural programming, presented aspiring sponsors with a new and significantly more potent access route to consumer markets and lifestyles. The relatively recent advent and subsequent expansion of the internet and social media now sit alongside the attractions and capabilities of modern television and other media to provide an expanded and enhanced array of channels for sponsors. From a corporate perspective, generations of innovative and adventurous sponsors, today represented by brands such as Coca-Cola, Nike, and P&G, have responded to a rapidly changing media environment to shape the current sponsorship industry. On the property side, sponsorship rights owners such as FIFA, UEFA, the IOC, and the NFL have embraced sponsorship, not merely as a revenue stream but also for its marketing and promotional capability. Additionally, agents and agency figures have pioneered contributions to the sponsorship structures around sports and events as instanced in the case of Mark McCormack and golf (Carlson, 2003; Litsky, 2003) and that of Patrick Nally and FIFA (Blitz, 2012; Urwin & Chadwick, 2014). Together, sponsors, properties, media, and agencies have evolved the foundational structures and conventions of current sponsorship practice. Growth in the scale of the sponsorship spending industry reflects these industry changes.

In the United States, which is the largest global market, sponsorship expenditure grew from an estimated $850 million in 1985 (International Event Group [IEG], 1996) to $24.2 billion in 2018 (IEG, 2018), and global sponsorship spending grew from an estimated $2 billion in 1984 (Sponsorship Research International, 1994) to an estimated $65.8 billion in 2018 (IEG, 2018). These estimates are for sponsorship rights fees only. Working on a conservative ratio of 1:1 in terms of support spending to rights fees, the total industry spending globally for 2018 can be estimated to have exceeded $130 billion. Sports sponsorship represents the largest sector of the global sponsorship market, and this fact is reflected in the U.S. market, where sports represent 70% of total sponsorship expenditure (Gough, 2021).

Types of Sponsorship Interaction

A range of sponsorship-related interactions and relations occur in sponsorship practice, including those ones outlined here.

Sponsor–consumer interactions. This set of interactions, focusing on how sponsorship works in terms of consumers effects, are the main focus of sponsorship research in both academic and indeed practitioner research. Additionally, corporations and brands use sponsorship to connect with other stakeholder groups such as their own staff, key business associates, and other stakeholders.

Sponsor–property interactions. These interactions include topics such as sponsorship negotiations on rights and benefits sought by the respective parties as well as topics such as the resolution of disagreements about contract fulfilment. These interactions can be negative, as in instances of ambush marketing (Dalakas, Madrigal, & Burton, 2004; Klara, 2016; T. Meenaghan 1996, 1998; Nufer, 2013; Payne, 1998; Shani & Sandler 1998), or positive, as in cooperative efforts for mutual benefits (Farrelly & Quester, 2005; Farrelly et al., 2005; Motion et al., 2003; Urriolagoitia & Planellas, 2007).

Intersponsor interactions. Because most major sponsorship properties now operate on a multisponsor basis, interactions between sponsors are increasingly a feature in sponsorship practice. For example, the 2012 London Olympics had 53 different sponsors at four different levels (Guardian, 2012), whereas in 2016, Manchester United reportedly had 65 official sponsorship partners (Jones, 2016). Such crowded sponsorship environments inevitably lead to interactions between sponsors operating on the same sponsorship platform. These sponsor-to-sponsor interactions can be conflictual in nature (Crompton, 2014), but they can also be cooperative on occasion, as instanced in joint sponsor campaigns (Davies et al., 2006).

Property–fan interactions. Essentially, fans are customers of the sponsored property (e.g., sports team), albeit a rather different type of customer from traditional marketing relationships. Given the extent to which fans feel a psychological ownership of and affinity with particular properties (e.g., teams, events, athletes, players), the adoption of sponsorship by properties, as well as the choice of sponsor and the sponsor's subsequent behavior, can represent issues of real concern for fans and the larger public. Recent examples reflecting fan and indeed the larger public's displeasure include McDonald's and the Olympics Games (Baker, 2017), the London Tate Gallery and British Petroleum (Clark, 2016), and the National Portrait Gallery and the Sackler family (Badshah & Walters, 2019).

SPONSORSHIP RESEARCH

A recent bibliometric citation meta-analysis of publications on the topic of sponsorship clearly illustrates the increased scale of academic interest in this topic (Riedmueller et al., 2019). This analysis, based on the academic database Web of Science (ISI Web of Knowledge), found 949 documents by 1,681 authors in 349 journals on the topic of sponsorship. This analysis yielded interesting results in relation to the key journals used for publication, as well as the most influential articles on the topic of sponsorship. A time-series analysis covering the time period 1981 to 2016 clearly points to a significant recent increase in academic interest in this topic. Over the period 1981 to 2007, the average number of articles published on sponsorship per year was 12, while over the period 2008 to 2016, the average was 70 per year. Equally interesting is the fact that only 10 such publications on sponsorship were found over the 5-year period from 1981 to 1986. The earliest paper included in this analysis, Yogev and Kfir (1981), concerned sponsorship/patronage in the Israeli education system. "Commercial Sponsorship," published as a special monograph edition of the *European Journal of Marketing* in 1983, represented the first major review of the topic of sponsorship (J. A. Meenaghan, 1983).

To date, the sponsor–consumer interaction in terms of how sponsorship works has been the major focus of research attention. This research has largely concentrated on examining the effects of sponsorship over the various stages of the consumer adoption process, broadly similar to that sequence hitherto used in advertising research, such as the hierarchy of effects model (Barry and Howard, 1990; Lavidge & Steiner, 1961). The topic of sponsorship effects more generally has been the subject of several review articles, which have enabled cumulative understanding at various junctures over the evolution of this subject area (Cornwell, 2008; Cornwell & Kwon, 2020; Cornwell & Maignan, 1998; Demir & Söderman, 2015; Jin, 2017; Maldonado-Erazo et al., 2019; Ryan & Fahy, 2012; Walliser, 2003). For example, basking in reflected glory creates the environment to link consumer emotions to products (Dalakas, Madrigal, & Anderson, 2004).

Sponsorship as a corporate activity originally took place in a very different commercial and marketing environment than currently appertains. The Spiers and Pond sponsorship of a tour by an English cricket team to Australia in 1861 (Spiers, 2002), often identified as one of the earliest examples of sponsorship, was rationalized as an opportunity for publicity for the business. On the media front, posters and newspapers represented the available media options at that time. Thus, more elaborate ambitions for sponsorship were simply not possible, and indeed such ambitions only became realizable when the circumstances of media development subsequently facilitated their occurrence. This idea is important in considering the evolution of sponsorship understanding. The availability and capability of media restricted or enabled the role of sponsorship on behalf of brands. Against this realization, the evolving role of sponsorship can be identified as taking place over a number of phases, via a number of mechanisms.

Sponsorship as an Evolving Medium

Sponsorship as publicity. From the earliest days of sponsorship, both prior to the 20th century and for the early decades of that century, much of the logic underpinning corporate sponsorship involvement was that it represented an opportunity to generate publicity for the sponsoring product or brand. Indeed, variations on this rationalization were regularly suggested through the late 1950s and the early 1960s.

Sponsorship as pseudo-advertising. As sponsorship grew in popularity and understanding of its capabilities improved, particularly in the early days of mass television, sponsorship was often vaunted as a cheaper form of advertising relative to conventional media advertising. This view was prevalent through the 1960s and 1970s. Sponsorship was also viewed as more contextual in effect than directly impactful relative to advertising. Sponsorship allows quick exposure to a brand name or product. The following quote represents a view as to how sponsorship was conceptualized: "Few marketing and public relations exponents would argue that sponsorships actually sell products. Help to sell, yes; create a background against which to sell, yes; create an awareness of the product or service, yes; but actually sell, no" (Buckley, 1980).

Sponsorship as brand image development. Today a recognized benefit of sponsorship is that of brand image development whereby image dimensions of the sponsored property transfer to the sponsoring brand (Gwinner, 1997; Gwinner & Eaton, 1999). Although this capability was understood by both sponsors and rights holders in the late 1950s and early 1960s, this concept was not really articulated in sponsorship terms until much later. An oft-cited example of image transfer from that time is the case of Gillette, an American brand, which was regarded by many as English due to its 20-year association with cricket, the quintessentially English sport (Guardian, 2013).

Sponsorship as relationship building. As indicated earlier, the roles that sponsorship has performed have been defined by the capabilities of media existing at that time. Sponsorship research, using metrics such as brand favorability, psychological closeness to the brand, and advocacy, have been and continue to be used to indicate the extent of the consumer/fan relationship with the sponsoring brand. More recently the use of social media for activation purposes has facilitated sponsorship's use as a consumer relationship-building medium. This revised role for sponsorship is in harmony with marketing's orientation toward building and retaining customer relationships and has seen sponsorship increasingly used as a platform for sponsor fan/consumer interaction and engagement (Bee & Kahle, 2006). Event hospitality is especially important in this regard (Burton et al., 2011).

The Development of Sponsorship Understanding: How Sponsorship Works

Understanding of sponsorship, by both academia and practice, has evolved as media developments have enhanced sponsorship's capability and consequent role. Although sponsorship understanding has advanced in terms of each of the four sponsorship-related interactions discussed earlier, the main focus of academic research attention to date has concentrated on the sponsor–consumer interactions in terms of the effects of sponsorship on consumers, that is, how sponsorship "works." As with sponsorship generally, this important aspect of sponsorship has also been the focus of a number of key state-of-play contributions (Cornwell et al., 2005; Kim et al., 2015; Olson, 2010; Speed & Thompson, 2000; Walraven et al., 2012).

Published research in terms of how sponsorship "works" largely follows the linear sequential consumer adoption model. Against the backdrop of this framework, the effectiveness of sponsorship is examined in terms of cognitive, affective, and behavioral outcomes with the effects of various antecedents (e.g., sponsor/property fit, intensity of fan involvement, perceived motive) on outcomes being considered. A meta-analytical review and research synthesis based on 154 studies on sponsorship effectiveness was conducted by Kim et al. (2015). This synthesis provides a valuable snapshot of the accumulated research concentration on this topic and confirms the key relations between antecedents and outcomes.

New Directions in Sponsorship Research

Developments in media in terms of enhanced capabilities have fundamentally improved sponsorship as a platform. These media developments have enabled sponsors to focus their efforts beyond awareness and image creation to use the sponsorship platform to facilitate customer/fan engagement and interaction. In this context, two key drivers of sponsorship effectiveness have emerged in recent times, engagement and goodwill generation, each of which is now briefly discussed.

Engagement. Engagement, whether referenced as brand or consumer engagement, has long been a feature of marketing ambitions. As marketing evolved to consider the consumer/brand interaction in a relational framework, engagement emerged as a central concept in that framework. Yet there are unresolved issues regarding engagement in marketing. For example, what exactly is engagement? How is it defined? How is it operationalized? And how is it measured? An additional difficulty is that the term *engagement* is widely used at both strategic brand and at lower operational levels (as in social media campaigns). In short, engagement, although widely used, is a poorly defined and understood term in marketing (Vivek et al., 2012). It is sometimes suggested as encompassing all marketing efforts, as in customer engagement marketing, which was defined by Harmeling et al. (2016) as "a firm's deliberate effort to motivate, empower and measure customer's contributions to marketing functions" (p. 312) and sometimes in less lofty and more basic tones as meaning "likes, or shares or comments" (Abramovich, 2012, p. 1).

Further confusion is fueled when the term is inaccurately equated with other concepts, such as experiential marketing, with which it can have some overlap but which is not the same thing. Then there is the particular concern regarding the measurement of engagement and the value of the metrics applied to this task (Copano, 2012; Nate, 2018; Smith, 2019). In short, the difficulty with engagement in marketing is that "the word has become ubiquitous, yet it represents many different things to different people depending on the circumstances and campaign objectives" (Chahal, 2016, p. 1). What has given new impetus to engagement in marketing is the advent of social media and the precise capabilities of analytics that enable brands to offer personalized and interactive communications based on continually updated understandings of the targeted recipient.

In the case of sponsorship, engagement is particularly associated with sponsorship activation. The logic underpinning the usage of sponsorship for engagement purposes relates to the passionate nature of the relationships that consumers as fans have with sponsored events/activities and the capacity of brands as sponsors to be represented in that relationship space. Much of the confusion evident in the larger world of marketing as to what constitutes engagement and how it can be operationalized and indeed measured is reflected in academic discussions on engagement in a sponsorship context. Rejecting the interactions view of sponsorship engagement as enabled by social media activations (Wakefield, 2012), the case for a more substantive view of engagement is made by Cornwell (2019), who suggested that "the goal is to distinguish authentic engagement from engagement defined as the frequency of interaction as afforded by a sponsorship" (p. 54). The reality is that neither content engagement nor channel engagement (Facebook, Twitter) equate to brand engagement.

A further issue regarding engagement in sponsorship is that the discussion is too narrowly focused on the consumer/fan interaction. The reality is that sponsors "engage" with a range of stakeholder targets beyond their consumer base, including their own staff, buyers/suppliers, and other key business contacts. Client entertainment in the C suite at major events represents engagement at a significant level of potency. Until the difficulties described earlier regarding engagement are clarified and given operational specificity, engagement as a concept in sponsorship and within marketing itself will continue to focus where it can be operationalized and measured, that is, activation, even if the meaning and value of such engagement remains unclear.

Goodwill, gratitude, and reciprocity as sponsorship effectiveness drivers. The terminology surrounding marketing's interactions with consumers has traditionally involved terms such as exchange, transactional exchange, and relationship marketing. A useful framework for considering marketing relationships and, in particular, the consumer/brand relationship is social exchange theory (SET; Cropanzano & Mitchell, 2005), which regards interaction between parties as a series of social exchanges that explain the development, maintenance, and deterioration of relationships between parties. For their part, relationships bring costs and benefits, and the perceptions and decisions in relation to these costs and benefits determine the relationship quality and, therefore, decisions about its continuation or otherwise. Underpinning exchange relationships are unwritten rules concerning behavior, trust, and expectations. SET, which finds application in human relationships such as marriage, friendships, workplace relationships, and so forth, also has value in terms of considering relationships in marketing and, in particular, the consumer/brand relationship (Luo, 2002; Sierra & McQuitty, 2005). Reciprocity in a social exchange context is viewed as the energy source for the relationship within which the acceptable terms and expectations for both parties are met. In social exchange settings, giving and receiving are mutually contingent (Houston & Gassenheimer, 1987).

SET has a particular value when considering sponsorship effects and relationships, although there have been few applications to date (Adongo et al., 2019; Ikavalko, 2003; Tyrie & Ferguson, 2013). The consideration of sponsorship relationships, and in particular the sponsor–consumer/fan relationship, has in more recent times led to the usage of terms such as benefit, goodwill, gratitude, and reciprocity in discussions of how sponsorship functions (Yu et al., 2018). T. Meenaghan (2001) envisaged the sponsor, property, and consumer/fan in a triangular set of relationships, that is, sponsor to property, consumer/fan to property, and consumer/fan to sponsor. The sponsor is in an exchange relationship with the sponsored property (team, athlete, celebrity) in terms of purchasing agreed sponsorship property rights in return for monetary and other compensation. The fan, who is emotionally connected to the sponsored property (team, athlete, celebrity), is well placed to pass judgments on the sponsor and their behavior in relation to the sponsored property and to determine the extent to which their sponsor's presence and behavior is benefiting the sponsored property. The perception that benefit is being provided by the sponsor becomes the catalyst for fan goodwill and gratitude, which can manifest itself as reciprocity in terms of positive perceptions of the sponsor and improved disposition toward and perhaps purchase or repeat purchase of the sponsor's brand.

Benefit and goodwill, as key concepts in understanding sponsorship, were first mentioned by T. Meenaghan (1991b) and by McDonald (1991) in a special edition of the *European Journal of Marketing*, with the former suggesting that "sponsorship investment is likely to have a recognized beneficial effect on the sponsored activity, a fact likely to be appreciated by that activity's audience" (T. Meenaghan, 1991b, p. 8). McDonald, in the same edition, first coined the term advertising "plus" in relation to sponsorship to indicate that sponsorship not only fulfilled an important communication role but also had a beneficial effect on the sponsored activity.

McDonald (1991) further suggested that

> for some, sports sponsorship is seen as more than just desirable; it is necessary for survival. Those who follow up the sport keenly tend to have the strongest responses, but people are capable of altruism and can recognize the value to others even if they are not interested themselves. (p. 36)

McDonald (1991) went on to say, "We have found and that there is something unique that sponsorship can deliver: the 'subtle effects', the special goodwill" (p. 37). Recent research (Dreisbach et al., 2021) on fan benefits has indicated that altruistic motives are key in determining sponsorship outcomes and that activation campaigns designed for symbolic or social benefits are most effective in inducing inference of altruistic motives.

SET provides an insightful perspective with which to consider sponsor–consumer interactions where concepts such as goodwill and gratitude bring considerable value to understanding sponsorship relationships. The extent of fan goodwill is determined by the perception of benefit and the extent of fan involvement and affiliation with the sponsored property. Particularly avid fans are more aware of sponsor behavior and better positioned to judge the nature and extent of benefit provided. Thus, the concept of contingent goodwill suggests that goodwill, gratitude, and reciprocation are not automatic and unconditional but are contingent on sponsor behavior (T. Meenaghan, 2001). Goodwill in a sponsorship context has been the subject of investigation by Dees et al. (2010) and Klidas and Lambregts (2015), while gratitude as related to sponsorship has been the subject of research by Kim (2018) and Maleki et al. (2013), with Kim et al. (2010) suggesting that gratitude serves as a mediating mechanism in sponsor consumer relationships.

Reciprocity, defined as the practice of exchanging things with others for mutual benefit, serves as an umbrella for understanding concepts such as gratitude and goodwill and is appropriate for application in a sponsorship context. Reciprocity is receiving greater attention based on its ability to explain consumer response to sponsorship. (Magnusen et al., 2012; T. Meenaghan, 2001; Nufer & Bühler, 2011; Pracejus, 2004).

Traditionally, sponsorship effectiveness research has focused on determining sponsor benefits, that is, those benefits that accrue to the sponsor as a result of their sponsorship investment. As indicated earlier, these sponsor benefits focus on a range of metrics such as brand awareness, brand image, propensity to purchase, and advocacy. Such research, in focusing solely on sponsor benefits, largely ignores the fan and their relationship with the brand in this interaction.

A recent study of sponsorship effectiveness (T. Meenaghan et al., 2019) took a different approach by not just including traditional metrics reflecting sponsor benefits (e.g., propensity to purchase) but also seeking to incorporate fan perceptions of value/benefit to both the sponsored property and their experience as fans, that is, *fan/property benefits* arising from the sponsor's involvement. In examining the benefits sought by both sponsor and fan, the research results showed that where respondents were aware of the sponsor/property association, there was a 30% uplift in commercial effects, that is, benefits to the sponsor in contrast to where respondents were unaware of the association. Although these findings reflect previous research results, the results in relation to goodwill were more revealing. Research analysis showed that when respondents were aware of both the sponsor/property association (linkage) and further believed that there was "benefit to the property" and "to the fan experience" (as a result of the sponsorship), there was a 71% uplift in sponsor benefits, as measured by standard metrics such as brand awareness, image, and propensity to purchase). Thus, the perception of benefit yielded an additional 41% uplift in terms of sponsor benefits. In comparing the drivers of goodwill, perceived benefit to the sponsored property (team, athlete, celebrity) was a more powerful driver of commercial effects (i.e., sponsor benefits) than perceived benefit to the fan experience.

Conclusions About Sport

This chapter has examined the evolution of understanding in relation to how sponsorship and sports marketing influence brands and, in turn, consumers' lifestyles (e.g., Batra et al., 2001). By way of background, it sought to map the advancement of the sponsorship industry in terms of growth patterns, changing profiles of industry participants, and its evolving role and capability on behalf of business. This evolution was set against the development of media upon which sponsorship relies for activation.

In terms of future research directions relating to the sponsor–consumer interaction, significant explanatory value is likely to be derived from also adopting a consumer/fan perspective rather than solely focusing on the sponsor and the effects and benefits that they seek from their investment. The active receiver viewpoint is reflected in SET as discussed earlier and also in uses and gratifications theory as applied to media and advertising research (O'Donoghue, 2017; Ruggiero, 2000) and indeed to sponsorship (Gillooly et al., 2017; Osokin, 2019). Consumers actively seek their lifestyle and sport environments (Kahle, 1980; Kahle & Berman, 1979; Page & Kahle, 1976). In entering the world of the consumers as fans and the objects of their passions, what is available to the sponsor is the opportunity to develop a strong emotional lifestyle bond with the consumer; however, their response is contingent on their perception of the sponsor's actions and behavior. Consumers often care deeply about their lifestyles and the role of sports (teams, athletes, celebrities, etc.) in reflecting their lifestyle.

This concern in turn gives marketers an opportunity to touch consumers but also to antagonize consumers. In this context it might be appropriate to consider the words of the Nobel prize-winning Irish poet W. B. Yeats: "Tread softly because you tread on my dreams."

SYNTHESIS

We have now explored lifestyle and sports marketing, which have very different histories and traditions academically. What do lifestyle marketing and sports marketing have in common? Plenty, it turns out. Emulation is often an important process in both cases. Both types of marketing often attempt to portray an idealized existence as a marketing strategy. Both use consumer information to reframe human uncertainty about expected behavior. Both work well in many low-involvement situations.

One of the oldest topics of research in social psychology centers on conformity. Many people lack confident knowledge about nuances of how to respond to complex social situations, and they therefore emulate others for guidance. For example, Sherif (1935) asked research participants to estimate the distance light moved in an autokinetic illusion. In fact, the light was stationary, but it appeared to move, although in the conditions Sherif created, respondents had no reference against which to judge movement. When making judgments alone, respondents offered one uncertain estimate. When participating with confederates who exaggerated estimates of the light movement, experimental subjects quickly altered their estimates to conform more closely the estimates of others. Subjects used the opinions of others to develop a "correct" social judgment. Asch (1956) demonstrated an even more extreme form of conformity. He asked people to judge the relative length of lines, which his research subjects could do readily. But when he introduced confederates into the study who provided objectively wrong judgments, many people modified their estimates of the relative length of the lines to match the incorrect estimates of the confederates. In both of these studies, people relied on others to guide them in the correct way to behave in a social situation.

Social adaptation theory (Homer & Kahle, 1986; Kahle, 1984; Kahle & Beatty, 1987b; Kahle & Homer, 1985; Kahle et al., 1980, 2016) assumes that attitudinal and value cognitions, such as evaluations of products, are formulated to fit into a social context. All social contexts are somewhat ambiguous, and we often rely on others to ascertain "appropriate" roles and norms (Kahle & Beatty, 1987a; Minton et al., 2018; Orth & Kahle, 2008). We evaluate ourselves and others by how effectively we assume various roles (Eisert & Kahle, 1982), according to social comparison theory. Of course, some people pioneer new role behaviors (Kahle & Shoham, 1995; Rose et al., 2000). But frequently, people deal with the uncertainty of social context by seeking evidence about expectations from others.

One example of seeking lifestyle definition from others via sports is the phenomenon known as "basking in reflected glory" (Cialdini et al., 1976; Dalakas, Madrigal, & Anderson, 2004; Funk et al., 2016). On a Monday after the local football team wins, students are more likely to wear school insignia than on a Monday after the football team loses. People will often use a first-person pronoun, "We won," to describe a victory and a third-person pronoun, "They lost," to describe a loss. When sports provide a self-enhancing image, some people embrace it. The psychology of pronouns contains endless fascination (Lee & Kahle, 2016; Pennebaker, 2013). The important lesson from this research is that people will look to sport and lifestyle information for emulation guidance and self-definition (Mazodier et al., 2018).

Many companies, such as Nike (Knight, 2016; Strasser & Becklund, 1993), use both lifestyle and sport approaches. Nike tries to encourage a sport-oriented lifestyle in its efforts to sell shoes and clothing, which superficially have little to do with sport or lifestyle. But Nike positions itself as the company that supports performing athletes, tying itself to the lifestyle of sports and famous athletes. Although Nike represents itself as the brand of performing athletes, the top Nike endorsers, such as Michael Jordan, probably buy very few Nike products, instead receiving free products and generous endorsement fees. Nike's profit comes from selling products to people who want to emulate the endorsers while the consumers are, perhaps, walking their dogs. Ironically, Charles Barkley famously did an ad for Nike Air called "I'm not a role model." He said, "Just because I can dunk a basketball, doesn't mean I should raise your kids." Although consumers who buy Nike Air shoes may not want Charles Barkley to raise their kids, they may admire his ability to dunk a basketball enough to want their kids to learn how he does so with such ease. And to the extent that they like the Barkley persona, they may not mind if their kids borrow a few other traits by emulating Barkley.

CONCLUSION

Lifestyle and sports marketing come from very different traditions but share similar psychological mechanisms for success. Both imply that consumers can attain certain idealized images and personas through emulating others in their purchase choices. Both allow an element of fantasy to transform into commercial transactions. Both transcend rational consumption, and both deserve further research and theory development.

REFERENCES

Abramovich, G. (2012, August 29). *How brands define engagement.* Digiday. https://digiday.com/marketing/how-brands-define-engagement/

Adler, A. (1917). *The neurotic constitution* (B. Glueck & J. E. Lind, Trans.). Moffat, Yard and Company. (Original work published 1912)

Adler, A. (1925). *The practice and theory of individual psychology* (P. Radin, Trans.). Routledge and Kegan Paul. (Original work published 1919)

Adler, A. (1926). *Liebesbeziehungen und deren störungen* [Love relationships and their disorders]. Moritz Perles.

Adler, A. (1929). *The science of living.* Greenburg.

Adler, F. (1956). The value concept in sociology. *American Journal of Sociology, 62*(3), 272–279. https://doi.org/10.1086/222004

Adongo, R., Kim, S., & Elliot, S. (2019). "Give and take": A social exchange perspective on festival stakeholder relation. *Annals of Tourism Research, 75,* 42–57. https://doi.org/10.1016/j.annals.2018.12.005

Aiken, K. D., Sukhdial, A., Kahle, L. R., & Downing, J. A. (2015). Linking fan values and sponsorship effectiveness: The case of old school values. *Sport Marketing Quarterly, 24*(1), 56–66.

Alpert, L., & Gatty, R. (1969). Product positioning by behavioral lifestyles. *Journal of Marketing, 33*(2), 65–69. https://doi.org/10.1177/002224296903300215

Amer, K., & Noujaim, J. (Directors). (2019). *The great hack* [Documentary]. Netflix.

Arellano, R., Valette-Florence, P., & Jolibert, A. (1988, May 5–6). Le comportement du consommateur d'énergie domestique: Une analyse causale [The behavior of the household energy consumer: A causal analysis; Congress proceedings]. Quatrième Congrès de L'association Française du Marketing, Montpellier, France.

Asch, S. (1956). Studies of independence and conformity: I. A minority of one against a unanimous majority. *Psychological Monographs, 70*(9), 1–70. https://doi.org/10.1037/h0093718

Aurifeille, J. M., & Valette-Florence, P. (1995). Determination of the dominant means-end chains: A constrained clustering approach. *International Journal of Research in Marketing, 12*(3), 267–278. https://doi.org/10.1016/0167-8116(95)00026-X

Badshah, N., & Walters, J. (2019, March 19). National Portrait Gallery drops £1m grant from Sackler family. *The Guardian.* https://www.theguardian.com/artanddesign/2019/mar/19/national-portrait-gallery-turns-down-grant-from-sackler-family-oxycontin

Baker, R. (2017, June 17). *McDonald's cuts controversial Olympics sponsorship.* AdNews. http://www.adnews.com.au/news/mcdonald-s-cuts-controversial-olympics-sponsorship

Bandura, A. (1988). Self-regulation of motivation and action through goal systems. In V. Hamilton, G. H. Bower, & N. A. Frijda (Eds.), *Cognitive perspectives on emotion and motivation* (pp. 37–61). Kluwer Academic. https://doi.org/10.1007/978-94-009-2792-6_2

Barry, T. E., & Howard, D. J. (1990). A review and critique of the hierarchy of effects in advertising. *International Journal of Advertising, 9*(2), 121–135. https://doi.org/10.1080/02650487.1990.11107138

Batra, R., Homer, P. M., & Kahle, L. R. (2001). Values, susceptibility to interpersonal influence, and attribute importance weights: A nomological analysis. *Journal of Consumer Psychology, 11*(2), 115–128. https://doi.org/10.1207/S15327663JCP1102_04

Baudrillard, J. (1970). *La société de consommation* [The consumer society]. Gallimard.

Bearden, W., Teel, J., & Durand, R. (1978). Media usage, psychographic and demographic dimensions of retail shoppers. *Journal of Retailing, 54*(1), 65–74.

Beatty, S., Kahle, L. R., Homer, P., & Misra, S. (1985). Alternative measurement approaches to consumer values: The List of Values and the Rokeach Value Survey. *Psychology and Marketing*, 2(3), 181–200. https://doi.org/10.1002/mar.4220020305

Becker, B., & Connor, P. (1981). Personal values of the heavy user of mass media. *Journal of Advertising Research*, 21(5), 37–43.

Bee, C. C., & Kahle, L. R. (2006). Relationship marketing in sports: A functional approach. *Sport Marketing Quarterly*, 15(2), 101–110.

Berlyne, D. (1967). Arousal and reinforcement. In D. Levine (ed.), *Nebraska Symposium on Motivation 1967* (Vol. 15, pp. 1–110). University of Nebraska Press.

Bernay, E. (1971). Life style analysis as a basis for media selection. In C. Wing & D. Tigert (Eds.), *Attitude research reaches new heights* (pp. 189–195). American Marketing Association.

Blitz, R. (2012). The godfather of sports marketing. *Financial Times*. https://www.ft.com/content/1652cf54-fb40-11e0-8df6-00144feab49a

Boltanski, L. (1982). *Les cadres: La formation d'un groupe social* [The executives: The formation of a social group]. Éditions de Minuit.

Bolton, L. E., Reed, I. I. A., II, Volpp, K., & Armstrong, K. (2008). How does drug and supplemental marketing affect a healthy lifestyle? *Journal of Consumer Research*, 34(5), 713–726. https://doi.org/10.1086/521906

Bouchet, P., Hillairet, D., & Bodet, G. (2013). *Sport brands*. Routledge. https://doi.org/10.4324/9780203114667

Bourdieu, P., & Passeron, J. E. (1964). *Les héritiers: Les étudiants et la culture* [The heirs: The students and the culture]. Éditions de Minuit.

Bozinoff, L., & Cohen, R. (1982). The effects of personal values on attitude and store choice behavior. In B. J. Walker (Ed.), *An assessment of marketing thought and practice* (pp. 25–29). American Marketing Association.

Bridgewater, S. (2010). *Football brands*. Palgrave Macmillan. https://doi.org/10.1057/9780230281363

Buckley, D. (1980, Spring). Who pays the piper? *Practice Review*, 10–14

Burton, R., Tripodi, J., Owen, S., & Kahle, L. R. (2011). Hospitality: A key sponsorship service in sports marketing. In L. R. Kahle & A. Close (Eds.), *Consumer behavior knowledge for effective sports and event marketing* (pp. 209–221). Routledge.

Carlson, M. (2003, May 17). Mark McCormack: Promoter who created a worldwide sports empire. *The Guardian*. https://www.theguardian.com/news/2003/may/17/guardianobituaries.sport

Chahal, M. (2016, August 10). Is 'brand engagement' a meaningless metric? *Marketing Week*. https://www.marketingweek.com/cover-what-does-engagement-really-mean-to-marketers/

Cialdini, R. B., Borden, R. J., Thorne, A., Walker, M. R., & Sloan, L. R. (1976). Basking in reflected glory: Three (football) field studies. *Journal of Personality and Social Psychology*, 34(3), 366–375. https://doi.org/10.1037/0022-3514.34.3.366

Cieciuch, J., Davidov, E., Vecchione, M., Beierlein, C., & Schwartz, S. H. (2014). The cross-national invariance properties of a new scale to measure 19 basic human values: A test across eight countries. *Journal of Cross-Cultural Psychology*, 45(5), 764–776. https://doi.org/10.1177/0022022114527348

Clark, N. (2016, March 11). BP to end controversial sponsorship of Tate in 2017. *Independent*. https://www.independent.co.uk/arts-entertainment/art/news/bp-to-end-controversial-sponsorship-of-tate-in-2017-a6923471.html

Clawson, C. (1946). *Psychology in action*. Macmillan.

Clawson, C., & Vinson, D. (1977). Human values: A historical and interdisciplinary analysis. In K. Hunt (Ed.), *Advances in consumer research* (Vol. 5, pp. 396–402). Association for Consumer Research.

Cochrane, R., Billig, M., & Hogg, M. (1979). Politics and values in Britain: A test of Rokeach's two-value model. *British Journal of Social and Clinical Psychology*, 18(2), 159–167.

Copano, J. (2012, September 4). Engagement is the universal non-metric. Digiday. https://digiday.com/marketing/engagement-is-the-universal-non-metric/

Copeland, M. (1924). *Principles of merchandising*. A. W. Shaw Co.

Cornwell, T. B. (2008, September). State of art and science in sponsorship-linked marketing. *Journal of Advertising*, 37(3), 41–55. https://doi.org/10.2753/JOA0091-3367370304

Cornwell, T. B. (2019). Less "sponsorship as advertising" and more sponsorship-linked marketing as authentic engagement. *Journal of Advertising*, 48(1), 49–60. https://doi.org/10.1080/00913367.2019.1588809

Cornwell, T. B., & Kwon, Y. (2020). Sponsorship-linked marketing: Research surpluses and shortages. *Journal of the Academy of Marketing Science*, 48, 607–629. https://doi.org/10.1007/s11747-019-00654-w

Cornwell, T. B., & Maignan, I. (1998). An international review of sponsorship research. *Journal of Advertising*, 27(1), 1–21. https://doi.org/10.1080/00913367.1998.10673539

Cornwell, T. B., Weeks, C. S., & Roy, D. P. (2005). Sponsorship-linked marketing: Opening the black box. *Journal of Advertising*, 34(2), 21–42. https://doi.org/10.1080/00913367.2005.10639194

Crompton, J. L. (2014). Potential negative outcomes from sponsorship for a sport property. *Managing Leisure, 19*(6), 420–441. https://doi.org/10.1080/13606719.2014.912050

Cropanzano, R., & Mitchell, M. (2005). Social exchange theory: An interdisciplinary review. *Journal of Management, 31*(6), 874–900. https://doi.org/10.1177/0149206305279602

Dalakas, V., Madrigal, R., & Anderson, K. L. (2004). "We are number one": The phenomenon of Basking-in-Reflected-Glory and its implications for sports marketing. In L. R. Kahle & C. Riley (Eds.), *Sports marketing and the psychology of marketing communication* (pp. 67–80). Lawrence Erlbaum.

Dalakas, V., Madrigal, R., & Burton, R. (2004). Understanding ambush marketing: Implications of information processing. In L. R. Kahle & C. Riley (Eds.), *Sports marketing and the psychology of marketing communication* (pp. 293–304). Lawrence Erlbaum.

Davies, F., Veloutsou, C., & Costa, A. (2006). Investigating the influence of a joint sponsorship of rival teams on supporter attitudes and brand preferences. *Journal of Marketing Communications, 12*(1), 31–48. https://doi.org/10.1080/13527260500264574

Deci, E., & Ryan, R. (1985). *Intrinsic motivation and self-determination in human behavior*. Plenum. https://doi.org/10.1007/978-1-4899-2271-7

Dees, W., Hall, T., Tsuji, Y., & Bennett, G. (2010). Examining the effects of fan loyalty and goodwill on consumer perceptions of brands at an action sports event. *Journal of Sponsorship, 4*(1), 38–50. https://www.researchgate.net/publication/266602166_Examining_the_effects_of_fan_loyalty_and_goodwill_on_consumer_perceptions_of_brands_at_an_action_sports_event

Demir, R., & Söderman, S. (2015). Strategic sponsoring in professional sport: A review and conceptualization. *European Sport Management Quarterly, 15*(3), 271–300. https://doi.org/10.1080/16184742.2015.1042000

Demuth, G., & Neirac, J. N. (1976). Typologie socio-culturelle et fréquentation média-supports [Sociocultural typology and media-support frequentations]. *Revue française du marketing, 62*, 99–105.

Dreisbach, J., Woisetschläger, D. M., Backhaus, C., & Cornwell, T. B. (2021). The role of fan benefits in shaping responses to sponsorship activation. *Journal of Business Research, 124*, 780–789. https://doi.org/10.1016/j.jbusres.2018.11.041

Dunn, T. (1971). Attitude research reaches new heights. In C. W. King & D. J. Tigert (Eds.), *Attitude research reaches new heights* (pp. 202–205). American Marketing Association.

Eisert, D. C., & Kahle, L. R. (1982). Self-evaluation and social comparison of physical and role change during adolescence: A longitudinal analysis. *Child Development, 53*(1), 98–104. https://doi.org/10.2307/1129641

Enoch, B. J. (2020, July 16). *Top 15 most influential Nike sponsored athletes on social*. Sector 22. Retrieved May 20, 2021, from https://www.sector22.online/post/top-15-most-influential-nike-sponsored-athletes-on-social

Erikson, E. H. (1968). *Identity: Youth and crisis*. Norton.

Evrard, Y., & Tissier-Desbordes, E. (1985). Les systèmes de valeurs et les lectures dans la famille [The systems of values and readings in the family; Conference proceedings]. 12e séminaire international de recherche en marketing, Aix-en-Provence, France.

Farrelly, F., & Quester, P. (2005). Investigating large-scale sponsorship relationships as co-marketing alliances. *Business Horizons, 48*(1), 55–62. https://doi.org/10.1016/j.bushor.2004.10.003

Farrelly, F., Quester, P., & Greyser, S. A. (2005). Defending the co-branding benefits of sponsorship B2B partnerships: The case of ambush marketing. *Journal of Advertising Research, 45*(3), 339. https://doi.org/10.1017/S0021849905050348

Feather, N. T. (1975). *Values in education and society*. Free Press.

Freud, S. (1999). *The interpretation of dreams*. (J. Crick, Trans.). Oxford.

Funk, D. C., Alexandris, K., & McDonald, H. (2016). *Sport consumer behaviour: Marketing strategies*. Routledge. https://doi.org/10.4324/9781315691909

Funk, D. C., & James, J. (2001). The psychological continuum model: A conceptual framework for understanding an individual's psychological connection to sport. *Sport Management Review, 4*(2), 119–150.

Gillooly, L., Anagnostopoulos, C., & Chadwick, S. (2017). Social media-based sponsorship activation— A typology of content. *Sport, Business and Management, 7*(3), 293–314. https://doi.org/10.1108/SBM-04-2016-0016

Goldberg, L. R. (2010). Personality, demographics, and self-reported behavioral acts: The development of Avocational Interest Scales from estimates of the amount of time spent in interest-related activities. In C. R. Agnew, D. E. Carlston, W. G. Graziano, & J. R. Kelly (Eds.), *Then a miracle occurs: Focusing on behavior in social psychological theory and research* (pp. 205–226). Oxford University Press.

Gottlieb, M. (1959). Segmentation by personality types. In L. Stockman (Ed.), *Advancing marketing efficiency* (pp. 148–158). American Marketing Association.

Gough, C. (2021, January 11). *Sports sponsorship— Statistics & facts*. Statista. Retrieved March 11, 2021, from https://www.statista.com/topics/1382/sports-sponsorship/

Grubb, E., & Grathwohl, H. (1967). Consumer self-concept, symbolism, and market behavior: A theoretical approach. *Journal of Marketing, 31*(4), 22–27. https://doi.org/10.1177/002224296703100405

Grube, J., Weir, L., Getzlaf, S., & Rokeach, M. (1984). Own value system, value images, and cigarette smoking. *Personality and Social Psychology Bulletin, 10*(2), 306–313. https://doi.org/10.1177/0146167284102018

Grunert, S., & Juhl, H. (1991). *Values, environmental attitudes, and buying of organic foods: Their relationships in a sample of Danish teachers* [Workshop proceedings]. Workshop on Value and Lifestyle Research in Marketing, Brussels, Belgium.

Guardian. (2012, July 19). *London 2012 Olympic sponsors list: Who are they and what have they paid?* https://www.theguardian.com/sport/datablog/2012/jul/19/london-2012-olympic-sponsors-list

Guardian. (2013). *Fifty years ago the very first Gillette Cup changed cricket for ever.* https://www.theguardian.com/sport/blog/2013/may/01/fifty-years-gillette-cup-anniversary

Gurel-Atay, E., Kahle, L. R., Lengler, J. B., & Kim, C.-H. (2019). A comparison and contrasting of the List of Values and the Schwartz Value Scale. In E. Gurel-Atay & L. R. Kahle, (Eds.), *Consumer social values* (pp. 241–252). Routledge.

Gurel-Atay, E., Xie, G. X., Chen, J., & Kahle, L. R. (2010). Changes in social values in the United States, 1976-2007. *Journal of Advertising Research, 50*(1), 57–67. https://doi.org/10.2501/S002184991009118X

Gutman, J. (1982). A means-end chain model based on consumer categorization processes. *Journal of Marketing, 46*(2), 60–72. https://doi.org/10.1177/002224298204600207

Gutman, J. (1986). Analyzing consumer orientations toward beverages through means–end chain analysis. *Psychology and Marketing, 3,* 28–42. https://doi.org/10.1002/mar.4220010305

Gwinner, K. (1997). A model of image creation and image transfer in event sponsorship. *International Marketing Review, 14*(3), 145–158. https://doi.org/10.1108/02651339710170221

Gwinner, K. P., & Eaton, J. (1999). Building brand image through event sponsorship: The role of image transfer. *Journal of Advertising, 28*(4), 47–57. https://doi.org/10.1080/00913367.1999.10673595

Haley, R. (1968). Benefit segmentation: A decision-oriented tool. *Journal of Marketing, 32*(3), 30–35. https://doi.org/10.2307/1249759

Hall, S., & Lindzey, G. (1970). *Theories of personality.* Wiley.

Harmeling, C., Moffett, J., Arnold, M. J., & Carlson, B. D. (2016). Toward a theory of customer engagement marketing. *Journal of the Academy of Marketing Science, 45*(3), 312–335. https://doi.org/10.1007/s11747-016-0509-2

Homer, P. M., & Kahle, L. R. (1986). A social adaptation explanation of the effects of surrealism on advertising. *Journal of Advertising, 15*(2), 50–60. https://doi.org/10.1080/00913367.1986.10673005

Homer, P. M., & Kahle, L. R. (1988). A structural equation test of the value-attitude-behavior hierarchy. *Journal of Personality and Social Psychology, 54*(4), 638–646. https://doi.org/10.1037/0022-3514.54.4.638

Houston, F. S., & Gassenheimer, J. B. (1987). Marketing and exchange. *Journal of Marketing, 51*(4), 3–18. https://doi.org/10.1177/002224298705100402

Hustad, P., & Pessemier, E. (1974). The development and application of psychographic, life style, and associated activity and attitude measures. In W. Wells (Ed.), *Life style and psychographics* (pp. 32–70). American Marketing Association.

Ikavalko, M. (2003). *Relational exchange and commitment in art sponsorship case: Finnish National Opera and Sampo.* 7th International Conference on Arts and Cultural Management. http://ernest.hec.ca/video/pedagogie/gestion_des_arts/AIMAC/2003/resources/pdf/B/B03_Ikavalko.pdf

Inoguchi, T., & Fujii, S. (2008). The AsiaBarometer: Its aim, its scope, and its development. In V. Moller, D. Huschka, & A. Michalos (Eds.), *Barometers of quality of life around the globe: How are we doing?* (pp. 187–232). Springer.

International Event Group. (1996). *North American sponsorship spending to top $5 billion in 1996* [Press release].

International Event Group. (2018). *What sponsors want & where dollars will go in 2018?* http://www.sponsorship.com/IEG/files/f3/f3cfac41-2983-49be-8df6-3546345e27de.pdf

Jin, C. (2017). Retrospection and state of sports marketing and sponsorship research in IJSMS from 1999 to 2015. *International Journal of Sports Marketing & Sponsorship, 18*(4), 363–379. https://doi.org/10.1108/IJSMS-04-2016-0002

Jones, M. (2016, December 13). The full list of Man United's 65—Including Thai motorbikes and Nigerian soft drinks. *Sun Newspaper.* https://www.mirror.co.uk/sport/row-zed/full-list-man-uniteds-64-9173142

Kaes, R. (1963). *Vivre dans les grands ensembles* [Living in large housing estates]. Éditions ouvrières.

Kahle, L. R. (1980). Stimulus condition self-selection by males in the interaction of locus of control and skill-chance situations. *Journal of Personality and Social Psychology, 38*(1), 50–56. https://doi.org/10.1037/0022-3514.38.1.50

Kahle, L. R. (Ed.). (1983). *Social values and social change: Adaptation to life in America*. Praeger.

Kahle, L. R. (1984). *Attitudes and social adaptation: A person-situation interaction approach*. Pergamon.

Kahle, L. R. (1986). The Nine Nations of North America and the value basis of geographic segmentation. *Journal of Marketing, 50*(2), 37–47. https://doi.org/10.1177/002224298605000203

Kahle, L. R. (1996). Social values and consumer behavior: Research from the List of Values. In C. Seligman, J. M. Olson, & M. P. Zanna (Eds.), *The psychology of values: The Ontario Symposium* (Vol. 8, pp. 135–151). Lawrence Erlbaum Associates.

Kahle, L. R., & Beatty, S. E. (1987a). Cognitive consequences of legislating postpurchase behavior: Growing up with the bottle bill. *Journal of Applied Social Psychology, 17*(9), 828–843. https://doi.org/10.1111/j.1559-1816.1987.tb00342.x

Kahle, L. R., & Beatty, S. E. (1987b). The task situation and habit in the attitude-behavior relationship: A social adaptation view. *Journal of Social Behavior and Personality, 2*(2), 219–232.

Kahle, L. R., & Berman, J. J. (1979). Attitudes cause behavior: A cross-lagged panel analysis. *Journal of Personality and Social Psychology, 37*(3), 315–321. https://doi.org/10.1037/0022-3514.37.3.315

Kahle, L. R., & Chiagouris, L. (Eds.). (2016). *Values, lifestyles, and psychographics*. Routledge.

Kahle, L. R., Duncan, M., Dalakas, V., & Aiken, D. (2001). The social values of fans for men's versus women's university basketball. *Sport Marketing Quarterly, 10*(2), 156–162.

Kahle, L. R., Elton, M. P., & Kambara, K. M. (1997). Sports talk and the development of marketing relationships. *Sport Marketing Quarterly, 6*(2), 35–40.

Kahle, L. R., & Gurel-Atay, E. (2014). Introduction to the psychology of communicating sustainability. In L. R. Kahle & E. Gurel-Atay (Eds.), *Communicating sustainability for the green economy* (pp. 3–22). M. E. Sharpe.

Kahle, L. R., & Homer, P. M. (1985). Physical attractiveness of the celebrity endorser: A social adaptation perspective. *Journal of Consumer Research, 11*(4), 954–961. https://doi.org/10.1086/209029

Kahle, L. R., Homer, P. M., O'Brien, R. M., & Boush, D. (2016). Maslow's hierarchy and social adaptation as alternative accounts of value structures. In L. R. Kahle & L. Chiagouris (Eds.), *Values, lifestyles, and psychographics* (pp. 111–137). Routledge.

Kahle, L. R., & Kahle, K. E. (2009). The silence of the lambdas: Science, technology, and public knowledge. *International Journal of Technology, Knowledge and Society, 5*(2), 137–142. https://doi.org/10.18848/1832-3669/CGP/v05i02/55988

Kahle, L. R., Kambara, K. M., & Rose, G. M. (1996). A functional model of fan attendance motivations for college football. *Sport Marketing Quarterly, 5*, 51–60.

Kahle, L. R., Kulka, R. A., & Klingel, D. M. (1980). Low adolescent self-esteem leads to multiple interpersonal problems: A test of social-adaptation theory. *Journal of Personality and Social Psychology, 39*(3), 496–502. https://doi.org/10.1037/0022-3514.39.3.496

Kahle, L. R., & Shoham, A. (1995). Role-relaxed consumers: Empirical evidence. *Journal of Advertising Research, 35*(3), 59–62.

Kahle, L. R., & Valette-Florence, P. (2012). *Marketplace lifestyles in an age of social media: Theory and method*. M. E. Sharpe.

Kahle, L. R., & Xie, G. (2008). Social values in consumer psychology. In C. P. Haugtvedt, P. M. Herr, & F. R. Kardes (Eds.), *Handbook of consumer psychology* (pp. 275–285). Lawrence Erlbaum Associates.

Karpf, D. (2018). Analytic activism and its limits. *Social Media + Society, 4*(1), 1–10. https://doi.org/10.1177/2056305117750718

Kassarjian, H. (1971). Personality and consumer behavior research: A review. *Journal of Marketing Research, 8*(4), 409–418. https://doi.org/10.1177/002224377100800401

Kau, A. K., Jung, K., Tambyah, S. K., & Tan, S. J. (2004). *Understanding Singaporeans: Values, lifestyles, aspirations, and consumption behaviors*. World Scientific Publishing. https://doi.org/10.1142/5450

Kau, A. K., Tan, S. J., & Wirtz, J. (1998). *7 faces of Singaporeans: Their values, aspirations, and lifestyles*. Prentice-Hall.

Kelley, E. (1963). Discussion. In S. Greyser (Ed.), *Toward scientific marketing* (pp. 164–171). American Marketing Association.

Kelman, H. C. (1974). Attitudes are alive and well and gainfully employed in the sphere of action. *American Psychologist, 29*(5), 310–324. https://doi.org/10.1037/h0037623

Kim, Y., Lee, H. W., Magnusen, M. J., & Kim, M. (2015). Factors influencing sponsorship effectiveness: A meta-analytic review and research synthesis. *Journal of Sport Management, 29*(4), 408–425. https://doi.org/10.1123/jsm.2014-0056

Kim, Y., Smith, R. D., & James, J. D. (2010). The role of gratitude in sponsorship: The case of participant sports. *International Journal of Sports Marketing &*

Sponsorship, 12(1), 48–70. https://doi.org/10.1108/IJSMS-12-01-2010-B006

Kim, Y., Smith, R. D., & Kwak, D. H. (2018). Feelings of gratitude: A mechanism for consumer reciprocity. *European Sport Management Quarterly*, 18(3), 307–329. https://doi.org/10.1080/16184742.2017.1389973

Klages, L. (1906). Das persönliche leitbild [The personal model]. In *Graphologische monatshefte*. Ackermann.

Klara, R. (2016). How Nike brilliantly ruined Olympic marketing forever. *Adweek*. https://www.adweek.com/brand-marketing/how-nike-brilliantly-ruined-olympic-marketing-forever-172899/

Klidas, A. K., & Lambregts, K. (2015). Goodwill and commercialization in a community-based sponsorship: The case of the flower parade in the Netherlands. In D. Sharma & S. Borna (Eds.), *Proceedings of the 2007 Academy of Marketing Science (AMS) Annual Conference*. Springer. https://doi.org/10.1007/978-3-319-11806-2_93

Kluckhohn, C. (1951). Values and value orientation in the theory of action: An exploration in definition and classification. In T. Parsons & E. Shils (Eds.), *Toward a general theory of action* (pp. 388–433). Harvard University Press. https://doi.org/10.4159/harvard.9780674863507.c8

Knight, P. (2016). *Shoe dog: A memoir by the creator of Nike*. Scribner.

Koponen, A. (1960). Personality characteristics of purchasers. *Journal of Advertising Research*, 1, 6–12.

Kurpis, L., Bozman, C. S., & Kahle, L. R. (2010). Distinguishing between amateur sport participants and spectators: The List of Values approach. *International Journal of Sports Management and Marketing*, 7(3/4), 190–201. https://doi.org/10.1504/IJSMM.2010.032550

Larsen, R. H. N., & Kahle, L. R. (2019). Handmade: How Indie Girl Culture is changing the market. In E. Gurel-Atay & L. R. Kahle (Eds.), *Consumer social values* (pp. 87–106). Routledge. https://doi.org/10.4324/9781315283739-8

Laumann, E., & House, J. (1970). Living room styles and social attributes: The patterning of material artifacts in a modern urban community. *Sociology and Social Research*, 54(3), 321–342.

Lavidge, R. J., & Steiner, G. A. (1961). A model for predictive measurements of advertising effectiveness. *Journal of Marketing*, 25(6), 59–62. https://doi.org/10.1177/002224296102500611

Lazarsfeld, P. (1935). The art of asking why in marketing research. *National Marketing Review*, 1(1), 26–38.

Lazer, W. (1963). Life style concepts and marketing. In S. A. Geyser (Ed.), *Toward scientific marketing* (pp. 130–139). American Marketing Association.

Lee, C., & Kahle, L. R. (2016). The linguistics of social media: Communication of emotions and values in sport. *Sport Marketing Quarterly*, 25(4), 139–151.

Levy, S. (1963). Symbolism and lifestyle. In S. A. Greyser (Ed.), *Toward scientific marketing* (pp. 140–149). American Marketing Association.

Litsky, F. (2003, May 17). Mark H. McCormack, 72, pioneer of sports marketing. *New York Times*. https://www.nytimes.com/2003/05/17/sports/mark-h-mccormack-72-pioneer-of-sports-marketing.html

LoRé, M. (2019, April 26). *Soccer's growth in U.S. has international legends buzzing*. Forbes. https://www.forbes.com/sites/michaellore/2019/04/26/soccers-growth-in-u-s-has-international-legends-buzzing/?sh=3646eca417f1

Lu, Z., Kahle, L. R., Lee, S. M., & Lee, S-Y. (2012). Football fans' contrasting motivations: China, S. Korea, and the USA. *Asia Pacific Journal of Innovation and Entrepreneurship*, 6(1), 9–32.

Luo, X. (2002). Trust production and privacy concerns on the internet: A framework based on relationship marketing and social exchange theory. *Industrial Marketing Management*, 31(2), 111–118. https://doi.org/10.1016/S0019-8501(01)00182-1

Magnusen, M., Kim, J. W., & Kim, Y. K. (2012). A relationship marketing catalyst: The salience of reciprocity to sport organization–sport consumer relationships. *European Sport Management Quarterly*, 12(5), 501–524. https://doi.org/10.1080/16184742.2012.729070

Magun, V., Rudnev, M., & Schmidt, P. (2016). Within- and between-country value diversity in Europe: A typological approach. *European Sociological Review*, 32(2), 189–202. https://doi.org/10.1093/esr/jcv080

Maldonado-Erazo, C., Durán-Sánchez, A., Álvarez-García, J., & Del Río-Rama, M. (2019). Sports sponsorship: Scientific coverage in academic journals. *Journal of Entrepreneurship and Public Policy*, 8(1), 163–186. https://doi.org/10.1108/JEPP-03-2019-106

Maleki, R., Shojaei, V. & Boroumand, M. R. (2013). Factors influencing gratitude in sponsorship and its relationship with sport fans purchase intention. *International Journal of Sport Studies*, 3(6), 679–686.

Maslow, A. (1954). *Motivation and personality*. Harper.

Maslow, A. (1959). *New knowledge in human values*. Harper.

Mazodier, M., Henderson, C. M., & Beck, J. T. (2018). The long reach of sponsorship: How fan isolation and identification strength jointly shape sponsorship performance. *Journal of Marketing*, 82(6), 28–48, https://doi.org/10.1177/0022242918807673

McDonald, C. (1991). Sponsorship and the image of the sponsor. *European Journal of Marketing*, 25(11), 31–38. https://doi.org/10.1108/EUM0000000000630

Meenaghan, J. A. (1983). Commercial sponsorship. *European Journal of Marketing, 17*(7), 5–73. https://doi.org/10.1108/EUM0000000004825

Meenaghan, T. (1991a). The role of sponsorship in the marketing communications mix. *International Journal of Advertising, 10*(1), 35–47. https://doi.org/10.1080/02650487.1991.11104432

Meenaghan, T. (1991b). Sponsorship—legitimising the medium. *European Journal of Marketing, 25*(11), 5–10. https://doi.org/10.1108/EUM0000000000627

Meenaghan, T. (1996). Ambush marketing—A threat to corporate sponsorship. *Sloan Management Review, 38*(1), 103–113.

Meenaghan, T. (1998). Ambush marketing: corporate strategy and consumer reaction. *Psychology and Marketing, 15* (4), 305–322. https://doi.org/10.1002/(sici)1520-6793(199807)15:4<305::aid-mar2>3.0.co;2-c

Meenaghan, T. (2001). Understanding sponsorship effects. *Psychology and Marketing, 18*(2), 95–122. https://doi.org/10.1002/1520-6793(200102)18:2<95::AID-MAR1001>3.0.CO;2-H

Meenaghan, T., Macken, J., & Nolan, M. (2019). *Generating fan goodwill: The key to increased sponsorship effectiveness*. WARC. https://www.warc.com/content/paywall/article/warc-exclusive/generating-fan-goodwill-the-key-to-increased-sponsorship-effectiveness/130105

Merton, R. (1949). *Social theory and social structure*. The Free Press.

Michaels, P. (1973). Lifestyle and magazine exposure. In V. Greer (Ed.), *Conceptual and methodological foundation of marketing* (pp. 324–331). American Marketing Association.

Minton, E. A., & Kahle, L. R. (2014). *Belief systems, religion, and behavioral economics: Marketing in multicultural environments*. Business Expert Press.

Minton, E. A., & Kahle, L. R. (2017). Religion and consumer behaviour. In C. Jansson-Boyd & M. Zawisza (Eds.), *Routledge international handbook of consumer psychology* (pp. 292–311). Routledge.

Minton, E. A., Kahle, L. R., Tan, S. J., & Tambayah, S. K. (2016). Addressing criticisms of global religion research: An examination in the context of consumption behavior. *Journal for the Scientific Study of Religion, 55*(2), 365–383. https://doi.org/10.1111/jssr.12260

Minton, E. A., Lee, C., Orth, U., Kim, C. H., & Kahle, L. R. (2012). Sustainable marketing and social media: A cross-country analysis of motives for sustainable behaviors. *Journal of Advertising, 41*(4), 69–84. https://doi.org/10.1080/00913367.2012.10672458

Minton, E. A., Spielmann, N., Kahle, L. R., & Kim, C. H. (2018). The subjective norms of sustainable consumption: A cross-cultural exploration. *Journal of Business Research, 82*, 400–408. https://doi.org/10.1016/j.jbusres.2016.12.031

Mitchell, A. (1983). *The nine American lifestyles*. Macmillan.

Mitchell, J., Jr. (1976). The structure and predictive efficacy of an empirical model of the Value-Attitude System as postulated by Rokeach. *Measurement and Evaluation in Guidance, 8*(4), 229–239. https://doi.org/10.1080/00256307.1976.12022696

Moore, D. (1963). Lifestyle in mobile suburbia. In S. A. Greyser (Ed.), *Toward scientific marketing* (pp. 151–164). American Marketing Association.

Moore, M. (1975). Rating versus ranking in the Rokeach Value Survey: An Israeli comparison. *European Journal of Social Psychology, 5*(3), 405–408. https://doi.org/10.1002/ejsp.2420050313

Motion, J., Leitch, S., & Brodie, R. (2003). Equity in corporate co-branding: The case of adidas and the All Blacks. *European Journal of Marketing, 37*(7/8), 1080–1094. https://doi.org/10.1108/03090560310477672

Munson, J. M., & McIntyre, S. H. (1979). Developing practical procedures for the measurement of personal values in cross-cultural marketing. *Journal of Marketing Research, 16*(1), 48–52. https://doi.org/10.1177/002224377901600107

Nate, E. (2018). *The disastrous consequences of measuring engagement*. Martech. https://marketingland.com/the-disastrous-consequences-of-measuring-engagement-250863

Ng, S. H., Hossain, A. B. M. A., Ball, P., Bond, M. H., Hayashi, K., Lim, S. P., & Yang, K. S. (1982). Human values in nine countries. *Diversity and unity in cross-cultural psychology, 1*(17), 169–172.

Nufer, G. (2013). *Ambush marketing in sports: Theory and practice*. Routledge. https://doi.org/10.4324/9780203371282

Nufer, G., & Bühler, A. (2011). Relevant factors for successful relationships between professional sporting organisations and their sponsors. *Journal of Physical Education and Sport Management, 2*(3), 26–31.

O'Donohoe, S. (1994). Advertising uses and gratifications. *European Journal of Marketing, 28* (8/9), 52–75. https://doi.org/10.1108/03090569410145706

Olson, E. (2010). Does sponsorship work in the same way in different sponsorship contexts? *European Journal of Marketing, 44*(1/2), 180–199. https://doi.org/10.1108/03090561011008664

Oriard, M. (2007). *Brand NFL: Making and selling America's favorite sport*. University of North Carolina Press. https://doi.org/10.5149/9780807899656_oriard

Orth, U. R., & Kahle, L. R. (2008). Intrapersonal variation in consumer susceptibility to normative influence: Toward a better understanding of brand choice decisions. *Journal of Social Psychology*, *148*(4), 423–448. https://doi.org/10.3200/SOCP.148.4.423-448

Osokin, N. (2019). User engagement and gratifications of NSO supporters on Facebook: Evidence from European football. *International Journal of Sports Marketing & Sponsorship*, *20*(1), 61–80. https://doi.org/10.1108/IJSMS-11-2017-0115

Page, M. M., & Kahle, L. R. (1976). Demand characteristics in the satiation-deprivation effect on attitude conditioning. *Journal of Personality and Social Psychology*, *33*(5), 553–562. https://doi.org/10.1037/0022-3514.33.5.553

Payne, M. (1998) Ambush marketing: the undeserved advantage. *Psychology and Marketing*, *15*(4), 323–331. https://doi.org/10.1002/(SICI)1520-6793(199807)15:4<323::AID-MAR3>3.0.CO;2-A

Peltier, J. W., Schibrowski, J. A., Schultz, D. E., & Davis, J. (2002). Interactive pychographics: Cross-selling in the banking industry. *Journal of Advertising Research*, *42*(2), 7–22. https://doi.org/10.2501/JAR-42-2-7-22

Pennebaker, J. W. (2013). *The secret life of pronouns: What our words say about us*. Bloomsbury Press.

Penner, L., & Anh, T. (1977). A comparison of American and Vietnamese value systems. *Journal of Social Psychology*, *101*(2), 187–204. https://doi.org/10.1080/00224545.1977.9924007

Pessemier, E., & Tigert, D. (1966). Personality activity and attitude predictors of consumer behavior. In J. Wright & J. Goldstucker (Eds.), *New ideas for successful marketing* (pp. 332–347). American Marketing Association.

Peterson, R. (1972). Psychographics and media exposure. *Journal of Advertising Research*, *12*(3), 17–20.

Piner, K. E., & Kahle, L. R. (1984). Adapting to the stigmatizing label of mental illness: Foregone but not forgotten. *Journal of Personality and Social Psychology*, *47*(4), 805–811. https://doi.org/10.1037/0022-3514.47.4.805

Pitts, R. E., Jr., & Woodside, A. G. (Eds.). (1984). *Personal values and consumer psychology*. Lexington Books.

Plummer, J. (1974a). Applications of lifestyle research to the creation of advertising campaigns. In W. Wells (Ed.), *Life style and psychographics* (pp. 159–169). American Marketing Association.

Plummer, J. (1974b). The concept and application of lifestyle segmentation. *Journal of Marketing*, *38*(1), 33–37.

Pracejus, J. W. (2004). Seven psychological mechanisms through which sponsorship can influence consumers. In L. R. Kahle & C. Riley (Eds.), *Sports marketing and the psychology of marketing communication*. Psychology Press. https://www.routledge.com/Sports-Marketing-and-the-Psychology-of-Marketing-Communication-1st-Edition/Kahle-Riley/p/book/9781410610003

Pritchard, M. P., & Stinson, J. L. (Eds.). (2013). *Leveraging brands in sport business*. Routledge.

Punj, G., & Stewart, R. (1983). An interaction framework of consumer decision making. *Journal of Consumer Research*, *10*(2), 181–196. https://doi.org/10.1086/208958

Rankin, W., & Grube, J. (1980). A comparison of ranking and rating procedures for value system measurement. *European Journal of Social Psychology*, *10*(3), 233–246. https://doi.org/10.1002/ejsp.2420100303

Reynolds, T. J. (1985). Recent developments in means-end chain analysis. *Psychology and Marketing*, *2*, 168–180.

Reynolds, T. J., & Gutman, J. (1984). Advertising is image management: Translating image research to image strategy. *Journal of Advertising Research*, *24*(1), 27–38.

Reynolds, T. J., & Olson, J. C. (Eds.). (2001). *Understanding consumer decision making: The means-end approach to marketing and advertising strategy*. Lawrence Erlbaum Associates. https://doi.org/10.4324/9781410600844

Reynolds, T. J., Westberg, S., & Olson, J. C. (2016). A strategy framework for developing and assessing political, social issue, and corporate image advertising. In L. R. Kahle & L. Chiagouris (Eds.), *Values, lifestyles, and psychographics* (pp. 3–24). Routledge.

Richter, F. (2019, May 17). *Padel: The biggest sport you've never heard of*. Statista. https://www.statista.com/chart/18041/growth-of-padel-around-the-world/

Riedmueller, F., Ivens, B., & van Dyck, P. (2019). *Sponsorship research over three decades: A bibliometric citation analysis* [Conference proceedings]. Multidisciplinary Academic Conference 2019, Prauge, Czechia. https://books.google.ie/books?hl=en&lr=&id=4E7EDwAAQBAJ&oi=fnd&pg=PA71&dq=sponsorship+research+over+three+decades+bibliometric+citation+analysis&ots=o7horckuYF&sig=LsQGeZ0FY_AORDI-J5gVX7_mNEU&redir_esc=y#v=onepage&q=sponsorship%20research%20over%20three%20decades%20bibliometric%20citation%20analysis&f=false

Rishe, P. (2019, April 15). Tiger Woods, Nike, and MeToo: How a decade impacted the existence of an iconic partnership. *Forbes*. https://www.forbes.com/sites/prishe/2019/04/15/tiger-woods-nike-and-metoo-how-a-decade-impacted-the-existence-of-an-iconic-partnerships/?sh=2dcc6e385896

Roehrich, G., & Valette-Florence, P. (1987). À la recherche des causes individuelles de l'achat des produits nouveaux [Researching the individual causes of the purchase of new products]. *Actes du 14e séminaire international de recherche en marketing, 349–376.*

Roehrich, G., & Valette-Florence, P. (1992). Apport des chaînages cognitifs à la segmentation des marchés [Contribution of cognitive chains to market segmentation]. *Actes du colloque de l'association française du marketing, 8,* 479–498.

Rogers, C. R. (1961). *On becoming a person.* Houghton Mifflin.

Rokeach, M. (1968). *Beliefs, attitudes, and values.* Jossey-Bass.

Rokeach, M. (1973). *The nature of human values.* The Free Press.

Rokeach, M. (1974). Change and stability in American value systems. *Public Opinion Quarterly, 38*(2), 222–238. https://doi.org/10.1086/268153

Rose, G. M., Dalakas, V., & Kropp, F. (2003). Consumer socialization and parental style across cultures: Findings from Australia, Greece, and India. *Journal of Consumer Psychology, 13*(4), 366–376. https://doi.org/10.1207/S15327663JCP1304_04

Rose, G. M., Kahle, L. R., & Shoham, A. (2000). Role relaxation and organizational culture: A social values perspective. In N. M. Ashkanasy, C. P. M. Wilderom, & M. F. Peterson (Eds.), *Handbook of organizational culture & climate* (pp. 437–446). Sage.

Rose, G. M., Shoham, A., Kahle, L. R., & Batra, R. (1994). Fashion, dress, and conformity. *Journal of Applied Social Psychology, 24*(17), 1501–1519. https://doi.org/10.1111/j.1559-1816.1994.tb01560.x

Ruggiero, T. (2000, February). Uses and gratifications theory in the 21st century. *Mass Communication & Society, 3*(1), 3–37. https://doi.org/10.1207/S15327825MCS0301_02

Ryan, A., & Fahy, J. (2012). Evolving priorities in sponsorship: From media management to network management. *Journal of Marketing Management, 28*(9–10), 1132–1158. https://doi.org/10.1080/0267257X.2011.645858

Schwartz, S. H. (1992). Universals in the content and structure of values: Theoretical advance and empirical tests in 20 countries. In M. Zanna (Ed.), *Advances in experimental social psychology* (Vol. 25, pp. 1–65). Academic Press. https://doi.org/10.1016/S0065-2601(08)60281-6

Schwartz, S. H. (1996). Value priorities and behavior: Applying a theory of integrated value systems. In C. Seligman, J. M. Olson, & M. P. Zanna (Eds.), *The psychology of values: The Ontario Symposium* (Vol. 8, pp. 1–24). Erlbaum.

Schwartz, S. H. (2017). The refined theory of basic values. In S. Roccas & L. Sagiv (Eds.), *Values and behavior: Taking a cross-cultural perspective* (pp. 51–72). Springer International Publishing. https://doi.org/10.1007/978-3-319-56352-7_3

Schwartz, S. H., & Bilsky, W. (1987). Toward a universal psychological structure of human values. *Journal of Personality and Social Psychology, 53*(3), 550–562. https://doi.org/10.1037/0022-3514.53.3.550

Schwartz, S. H., & Bilsky, W. (1990). Toward a theory of the universal content and structure of values: Extensions and cross-cultural replications. *Journal of Personality and Social Psychology, 58*(5), 878–891. https://doi.org/10.1037/0022-3514.58.5.878

Schwartz, S. H., Cieciuch, J., Vecchione, M., Davidov, E., Fischer, R., Beierlein, C., Ramos, A., Verkasalo, M., Lönnqvist, J. E., Demirutku, K., Dirilen-Gumus, O., & Konty, M. (2012). Refining the theory of basic individual values. *Journal of Personality and Social Psychology, 103*(4), 663–688. https://doi.org/10.1037/a0029393

Scitovsky, T. (1976). *The joyless economy: An inquiry into human satisfaction and consumer dissatisfaction.* Oxford University Press.

Scott, J., & Lamont, L. (1973). Relating consumer values to consumer behavior: A model and method for investigation. In T. Green (Ed.), *Increasing marketing productivity* (pp. 283–288). American Marketing Association.

Searing, D. (1979). A study of values in the British House of Commons. In M. Rokeach (Ed.), *Understanding human values* (pp. 154–178). The Free Press.

Segnit, S., & Broadbent, S. (1974). *Clustering by product usage: A case history* [Congress proceedings]. The XXVth ESOMAR Congress, Amsterdam, The Netherlands.

Shani, D. & Sandler, D. (1998). Ambush marketing: Is confusion to blame for the flickering of the flame? *Psychology & Marketing, 15*(4), 367–383. https://doi.org/10.1002/(SICI)1520-6793(199807)15:4<367::AID-MAR6>3.0.CO;2-6

Sherif, M. (1935). A study of some social factors in perception. *Archives of Psychology, 187,* 60.

Shimp, T. A. (2010). *Advertising, promotion, and other aspects of integrated marketing communications* (8th ed.). South-Western Cengage Learning.

Sierra, J. J., & McQuitty, S. (2005). Service providers and customers: Social exchange theory and service loyalty. *Journal of Services Marketing, 19*(6), 392–400. https://doi.org/10.1108/08876040510620166

Simmons, W. (1971). Overall impressions on psychographics. In C. W. King & D. J. Tigert (Eds.), *Attitude research reaches new heights* (pp. 215–219). American Marketing Association.

Sinka, P., & Sayeed, O. (1979). Value systems. *International Journal of Social Work, 40,* 139–145.

Skimina, E., Cieciuch, J., Schwartz, S. H., Davidov, E., & Algesheimer, R. (2019). Behavioral signatures of values in everyday behavior in retrospective and real-time self-reports. *Frontiers in Psychology*, *10*, 281. https://doi.org/10.3389/fpsyg.2019.00281

Skinner, B. F. (1974). *About behaviorism*. Alfred A. Knopf.

Smith, D. (2019, October 9). Goodbye to likes: What should the new engagement metric be? *The Drum*. https://www.thedrum.com/opinion/2019/10/09/goodbye-likes-what-should-the-new-engagement-metric-be

Solomon, M. R. (2009). *Consumer behavior: Buying, having, being* (8th ed.). Pearson/Prentice-Hall.

Speed, R., & Thompson, P. (2000). Determinants of sports sponsorship response. *Journal of the Academy of Marketing Science*, *28*(2), 226–238. https://doi.org/10.1177/0092070300282004

Spiers, R. (2002). *Spiers and Pond and Australian cricket*. http://www.spiers.net/pond.htm

Sponsorship Research International. (1994). *Annual estimates of sponsorship expenditure*.

Stockard, J., Carpenter, G., & Kahle, L. R. (2014). Continuity and change in values in midlife: Testing the age stability hypothesis. *Experimental Aging Research*, *40*(2), 224–244. https://doi.org/10.1080/0361073X.2014.882215

Strasser, J. B., & Becklund, L. (1993). *Swoosh: The unauthorized story of Nike and the men who played there*. HarperCollins.

Suh, W. S., & Kahle, L. R. (2018). Social values in consumer psychology: Key determinants of human behavior. In M. R. Solomon & T. M. Lowrey (Eds.), *The Routledge companion to consumer behavior* (pp. 165–174). Routledge.

Szalai, R. (2019, October 9). In new memoirs, Two whistle-blowers offer details from Cambridge Analytica. *New York Times*.

Tambyah, S. K., Tan, S. J., & Kau, A. K. (2009). *The well-being of Singaporeans: Values, lifestyles, satisfaction, and quality of life*. World Scientific Publishing.

Tan, S. J., Tambayah, S. K., & Kahle, L. R. (2015). Sequential cross-sectional studies of values in Singapore and the United States. In B. Schmitt & L. Lee (Eds.), *The psychology of the Asian consumer* (pp. 103–115). Routledge.

Theophrastus. (1870). *Characters* (R. C. Jebb, Trans.). Eudaemonist. https://www.eudaemonist.com/biblion/characters/ (Original work published ca. 320 B.C.E.)

Thompson, C., & Troester, M. (2002). Consumer value systems in the age of postmodern fragmentation: The case of the natural health microculture. *Journal of Consumer Research*, *28*(4), 550–571. https://doi.org/10.1086/338213

Tigert, D. (1973). A research project in creative advertising through lifestyle analysis. In W. King & D. Tigert (Eds.), *Attitude research reaches new heights* (pp. 223–227). American Marketing Association.

Tyrie, A., & Ferguson, S. (2013). Understanding value from arts sponsorship: A social exchange theory perspective. *Arts Marketing: An International Journal*, *3*(2), 131–153. https://doi.org/10.1108/AM-10-2012-0018

Urriolagoitia, L., & Planellas, M. (2007). Sponsorship relationships as strategic alliances: A life cycle model approach. *Business Horizons*, *50*(2), 157–166. https://doi.org/10.1016/j.bushor.2006.10.001

Urwin, G., & Chadwick, S. (2014). Profile of Patrick Nally, founder, West Nally. *International Journal of Sports Marketing & Sponsorship*, *15*(4), 2–9. https://doi.org/10.1108/IJSMS-15-04-2014-B002

Uusitalo, L. (1979a). Consumption style and way of life: An empirical identification and explanation of consumption style dimensions. *Acta Oeconomiae Helsingiensis*, Series A:27. Helsinki School of Economics.

Uusitalo, L. (1979b). Identification of consumption style segments on the basis of household budget allocation. In J. C. Olson (Ed.), *Advances in consumer research* (Vol. 7, pp. 451–459). Association for Consumer Research.

Valette-Florence, P. (1986). Les démarches de styles de vie: concepts, champs d'investigation et problèmes actuels [Lifestyle approaches: Concepts, fields of investigation and current problems]. *Recherche et applications en marketing*, *1*(2), 42–58. https://doi.org/10.1177/076737018600100204

Valette-Florence, P. (1988). Analyse structurelle comparative des composantes des systèmes de valeurs selon Kahle et Rokeach [Comparative structural analysis of the components of value systems according to Kahle and Rokeach]. *Recherche et applications en marketing*, *3*(1), 15–34. https://doi.org/10.1177/076737018800300102

Valette-Florence, P. (1998). A causal analysis of means-end hierarchies in a cross-cultural context: Methodological refinements. *Journal of Business Research*, *42*(2), 161–166. https://doi.org/10.1016/S0148-2963(97)00111-2

Valette-Florence, P., & Jolibert, A. (1990). Social values, AIO, and consumption patterns: Exploratory findings. *Journal of Business Research*, *20*(2), 109–122. https://doi.org/10.1016/0148-2963(90)90055-I

Valette-Florence, P., & Rapacchi, B. (1991). Improving means-end chain analysis using graph theory and correspondence analysis. *Journal of Advertising Research*, *31*(1), 30–45.

Veblen, T. (1899). *The theory of the leisure class*. Macmillan.

Veroff, J., Douvan, E., & Kulka, R. (1981). *The inner American*. Basic Books.

Vinson, D., & Munson, J. (1976). Personal values: An approach to market segmentation. In K. Bernhardt (Ed.), *Marketing: 1776–1976 and beyond* (pp. 313–317). American Marketing Association.

Vinson, D., Scott, J., & Lamont, L. (1977). The role of personal values in marketing and consumer behavior. *Journal of Marketing*, 41(2), 44–50. https://doi.org/10.1177/002224297704100215

Vivek, S. D., Beatty, S. E., & Morgan, R. M. (2012). Customer engagement: Exploring customer relationships beyond purchase. *Journal of Marketing Theory and Practice*, 20(2), 122–146. https://doi.org/10.2753/MTP1069-6679200201

Wakefield, K L. (2012). How sponsorships work: The sponsorship engagement model. *Event Management*, 16(2), 143–155. https://doi.org/10.3727/152599512X13343565268384

Walliser, B. (2003). An international review of sponsorship research: Extension and update. *International Journal of Advertising*, 22(1), 5–40. https://doi.org/10.1080/02650487.2003.11072838

Walraven, M., Koning, R. H., & Van Bottenburg, M. (2012). The effects of sports sponsorship: A review and research agenda. *Marketing Review*, 12(1), 17–38. https://doi.org/10.1362/146934712X13286274424235

Wann, D. L., & James, J. D. (2018). *Sport fans: The psychology and social impact of fandom*. Routledge.

Watson, J. (1913). Psychology as a behaviorist views it. *Psychological Bulletin*, 20(2), 158–177.

Weber, M. (1948). *From Max Weber: Essays in sociology* (H. Gerth, Ed.; C. Mills, Trans.). Routledge and Kegan Paul.

Weber, M. (1964). *Economy and society* (A. M. Henderson & T. Parsons, Trans.). The Free Press. (Original work published 1922)

Weiss, M. J. (2000). *The clustered world: How we live, what we buy, and what it all means about who we are*. Little, Brown.

Wells, W. (1968a). Backward segmentation. In J. Arndt (Ed.), *Insights into consumer behavior* (pp. 85–100). Allyn and Bacon.

Wells, W. (1968b). Segmentation by attitude types. In R. King (Ed.), *Proceedings: Marketing and the new science of planning* (pp. 124–126). American Marketing Association.

Wells, W. (1974). Life style and psychographics: Definitions, uses, and problems. In W. Wells (Ed.), *Life Style and psychographics* (pp. 317–363). American Marketing Association.

Wells, W., & Beard, A. (1973). Personality and consumer behavior. In S. Ward & T. Robertson (Eds.), *Consumer behavior: Theoretical sources* (pp. 74–92). Prentice-Hall.

Wells, W., & Tigert, D. (1971). Activities, interests, and opinions. *Journal of Advertising Research*, 2(4), 27–35.

Wind, Y., & Green, P. (1974). Some conceptual, measurement, and analytical problems in life style research. In W. Wells (Ed.), *Life style and psychographics* (pp. 97–126). American Marketing Association.

World Rugby. (2020). *New report highlights global rise in rugby interest*. https://www.world.rugby/news/600417/new-report-highlights-global-rise-in-rugby-interest-in-2019

Yogev, A., & Kfir, D. (1981). Determinants of tracking in Israeli secondary education. Ability grouping and sponsorship in the educational system. *Megamot: Behavioral Sciences Quarterly*, 27(2), 139–153.

Young, S. (1971). Psychographic research and market relevancy. In C. W. King & D. J. Tigert (Eds.), *Attitude research reaches new heights* (pp. 220–222). American Marketing Association.

Yu, H., Gao, X., & Zhou, Y. (2018). Decomposing gratitude: Representation and integration of cognitive antecedents of gratitude in the brain. *Journal of Neuroscience*, 38(21), 4886–4898. https://doi.org/10.1523/JNEUROSCI.2944-17.2018

Zuboff, S. (2020). *The age of surveillance capitalism: The fight for a human future at the new frontier of power*. Hachette Book Group.

Part III

CONSUMERS LIVE IN A SOCIAL PSYCHOLOGICAL WORLD

CHAPTER 12

CULTURAL INFLUENCES ON CONSUMER PSYCHOLOGY

Carlos J. Torelli and Sharon Shavitt

How should a manager of a global brand decide on their marketing communication strategies—should they be tailored to the culture in each market, at great expense and effort, or can one assume that a really good strategy will work everywhere? In other words, do cultural factors matter that much in determining how consumers respond to brands, products, and advertisements?

In this chapter, we review the broad scope of cross-cultural differences examined in consumer psychology, a topic that has received extensive research attention over the last 30 years. The important roles that culture plays in understanding consumers' cognitive processes, motivations and goal striving, self-concepts and self-regulation, and persuasion and information processing have been well established. Cultural factors can help to explain or predict consumer phenomena across a range of substantive domains, including branding, advertising, sales promotion, pricing, and retailing.

Indeed, research suggests that cultural factors can have broad influences in impacting consumer motivations and thought processes that drive their decision making. Cultural factors also pattern the interpersonal aspects of life, helping us to fit in with others and know how people should be prioritized in our society. Finally, cultural factors give rise to the social structures that shape and reinforce norms and coordinate groups of people in pursuit of societal priorities.

Because of the large and expanding volume of research in this field, in this chapter we do not aim to be comprehensive. Instead, our goal is to illustrate the important role of culture in three crucial domains of consumer psychology:

1. *Self*: How the individual perceives themselves as a unit, perceives and interprets the world around them, and sets and pursues goals.
2. *Society*: How the self fits in with others and manages relationships. How other people are perceived and prioritized in relation to one other.
3. *Social coordination*: The normative processes, social structures, and material culture used to create order, coordinate behavior, and reinforce shared norms.

Before we address the role of culture in each of these domains, we begin by defining culture. Then, we review ways in which culture is generally operationalized.

DEFINING AND OPERATIONALIZING CULTURE

Cross-cultural researchers generally define culture in psychological terms, highlighting the meanings and thought patterns shared by groups of people. Hofstede (1984) memorably defined culture as "the collective programming of the mind which distinguishes the members of one group or society from

https://doi.org/10.1037/0000262-012
APA Handbook of Consumer Psychology, L. R. Kahle (Editor-in-Chief)
Copyright © 2022 by the American Psychological Association. All rights reserved.

those of another" (p. 82). Triandis (2012) likewise characterized culture as "a shared meaning system found among those who speak a particular language dialect, during a specific historical period, and in a definable geographic region" (p. 35).

Cultural meaning systems exist in the head, in the context, and in social institutions and material culture (Markus & Conner, 2013). Thus, cross-cultural differences are studied via multiple types of comparisons: between countries or regions, between ethnic groups or subcultures within a society, between contexts in which distinct cultural meanings are activated, and between individuals within a society. Geographically, the focus of many cross-cultural studies is on contrasting the behaviors of consumers in different countries, particularly Western countries compared with Asian countries (see Maheswaran & Shavitt, 2000). Some studies compare people of different ethnicities within a society, such as European American and Asian American individuals (e.g., Iyengar & Lepper, 1999).

Moreover, because culture is conceptualized as a meaning system or software of the mind (Hofstede, 1991), some of the most informative research examines how different cultural meaning systems can be triggered within the same person. Research has established that contexts can activate distinct cultural frames in the mind (e.g., Y. Y. Hong et al., 2000; Oyserman & Lee, 2007). That is, the same individual can engage in *frame-switching* (Y. Y. Hong et al., 2000), bringing to mind different cultural identities depending on exposure to distinct cultural symbols or scripts.

With these definitions and operationalizations of culture in mind, it is useful to consider what programs or meaning systems have been studied. The first place to start is with the definition or construal of the self. We address self-construal next and describe how it shapes self-related processes that take place within the individual.

THE SELF

Key Cultural Distinctions

The most fundamental cultural meaning system programmed in the mind is the definition of the self and the qualities ascribed to it (Triandis, 1989). In some cultures, people are programmed through socialization to see the self as a distinct, bounded entity in pursuit of its unique aspirations. In other cultures, people are programmed to view the self as interconnected, socially embedded, and mutually obligated to others.

This fundamental difference in cultural meaning systems is captured in the distinction between *individualism* and *collectivism*. In individualistic cultures and contexts, such as the United States and Western Europe, people tend to see themselves as independent of others and to prioritize personal goals above those of their ingroups (Hofstede, 1980). That is, they have a primarily *independent self-construal* (Markus & Kitayama, 1991). They perceive themselves as having personal agency to make their own choices, and they prioritize being independent, self-reliant, and unique in their life goals (Triandis, 1989). For instance, when asked to describe "Who am I?" absent any context, U.S. participants, compared with those in Japan, tend to describe themselves more often in terms of abstract, psychological traits and abilities (e.g., "I am creative") and less often in terms of social roles (e.g., "I am the eldest son"; Cousins, 1989). As consumers, they prioritize and cultivate those distinct qualities and the unique preferences that flow from them (Berger & Heath, 2007) and seek to demonstrate autonomy in their choices (Simpson et al., 2018; Triandis, 1995).

In collectivistic cultures and contexts, such as China, India, and Korea, on the other hand, people see themselves as members of a network of benevolent social ties. They construe the self as primarily *interdependent* with others (Markus & Kitayama, 1991), interconnected with their ingroups and mutually obligated to one other. Their priority is maintaining and building their benevolent social ties and fulfilling the obligations associated with their roles (Triandis, 1989), and they derive self-worth from accomplishing these goals (Triandis, 1995). As consumers, they prioritize choices that maintain harmony, establish consensus, and meet social and normative expectations (e.g., S. P. Han & Shavitt, 1994; H. Kim & Markus, 1999; Simpson et al., 2018).

The distinction between individualism and collectivism, and the independent and interdependent self-construals that are associated with them, represent the most commonly used classifications in consumer research (Maheswaran & Shavitt, 2000). Although more recent work has expanded beyond these classifications, as we discuss later, the field is built largely on fundamental studies of the classic distinctions between individualism and collectivism (e.g., Hofstede, 1980; Triandis, 1989, 1995) and independent and interdependent self-construals (e.g., Markus & Kitayama, 1991). The findings from these early studies largely cemented the status of the cross-cultural psychology field. As described earlier, these fundamental distinctions have been studied by comparing different nations or geographic regions, different ethnic groups within a society, and different situations that activate distinct self-construals. Across these various operationalizations of culture, similar patterns tend to emerge (see Shavitt & Barnes, 2019, 2020, for reviews).

Products, Brands, and the Self

The differences in self-view just described extend to how people view the role of brands and products in their lives. For instance, U.S. consumers see a brand as stronger to the extent that it is associated with personal brand characteristics (e.g., reliable, honest, sincere), whereas Chinese consumers see a brand as stronger to the extent that it is linked to relational characteristics (e.g., benevolent, socially responsible, helpful to the economy; C. Li et al., 2019). These cultural differences are greater to the extent that there is a stronger perceived self–brand connection, further illustrating that self-views can be represented by and reflected in perceptions of brands. Indeed, Westerners and people with an independent self-construal appear to experience stronger self-object associations, in that they link their personal possessions more strongly to the self, than do Easterners and people with an interdependent self-construal (Maddux et al., 2010). As a result, independent versus interdependent consumers tend to show a stronger *endowment effect* (Kahneman et al., 1990), displaying a greater difference in the price they demand to part with a possession versus the price they are willing to pay to acquire the same item. This may be seen as an example of independents' greater tendency to view the self in a positive and self-enhancing way, as we describe in the next section.

Cultural differences can also be observed in how strongly consumers weigh their internal reactions when making choices. People from individualistic cultures or with independent self-construals show a stronger emphasis on their own personal feelings and attitudes when choosing, letting their feelings and preferences be their guides (J. Hong & Chang, 2015; Savani et al., 2008; Wu et al., 2021). For instance, when selecting gifts for multiple recipients, American compared with Chinese givers are more likely to be guided by the preferences of their recipients, as well as by their own relative attitudes toward those recipients (Wu et al., 2021). Similarly, those with an independent self-construal are more likely to choose an apartment that promises affectively pleasant experiences, such as sunlit rooms and attractive décor (J. Hong & Chang, 2015). In contrast, people from collectivistic cultures or those with an interdependent self-construal tend to prioritize others' expectations and norms (Triandis, 1995). Thus, they tend to make decisions in a way that they can readily justify to others, for instance by choosing an apartment close to public transportation or with more square footage (J. Hong & Chang, 2015). We return to the role of justifying one's decisions later.

In sum, for people with an interdependent self-construal, personal preferences and feelings are less important as drivers of choice (see Riemer et al., 2014). It is not surprising, therefore, that independent people are more likely to give in to their impulses when shopping than are interdependent people (e.g., Kacen & Lee, 2002; Zhang & Shrum, 2009). For instance, in regions of the United States and in countries around the world that are culturally more individualistic, greater per capita beer consumption is observed (Zhang & Shrum, 2009). Purchase volume in the alcohol category reflects lower impulse control (Hoch & Loewenstein, 1991). People with an independent self-construal also tend to be more impatient overall when it comes to willingness to pay extra for expedited shipping (H. Chen et al., 2005).

In contrast, interdependent consumers, compared with independent consumers, tend to be more patient and better able to control their impulses. Thus, they are more likely to persist through the steps required to redeem coupons. Specifically, Asian (vs. European) Americans, Indians (vs. Americans), and people primed with an interdependent (vs. independent) self-construal are more likely to use coupons because they are generally more persistent at tasks, such as challenging puzzles (Lalwani & Wang, 2019). Taken together, these findings are consistent with a broader set of cultural difference in self-regulatory processes, and we return to this point later.

Goals and Self-Regulatory Processes

Cultural self-construal plays an important role in predicting the types of goals that people tend to pursue. For instance, because individualists and those with an independent self-construal tend to prioritize personal advancement, agency, and distinction from others, they tend to be motivated by attainment goals, such as the goal of achieving a particular bank balance. In contrast, because collectivists and those with an interdependent self-construal tend to prioritize the continuity of their social relationships, they tend to be motivated by maintenance goals, such as the goal of maintaining a consistent bank balance (Yang et al., 2015).

These types of goal differences can also be observed in the domain of self-presentation. Research shows that people with an independent self-construal are motivated to present themselves as self-reliant and capable in order to establish their independence (Lalwani & Shavitt, 2009; Lalwani et al., 2006). Thus, they tend to engage in *self-deceptive enhancement* (Paulhus, 1991), inflating their self-descriptions to appear unrealistically capable. In contrast, people with an interdependent self-construal are motivated to establish their social appropriateness and benevolence in order to maintain good relationships. Thus, they tend to engage in *impression management* (Paulhus, 1991) by denying any behaviors that violate societal norms (Lalwani & Shavitt, 2009; Lalwani et al., 2006). In other words, desirable self-presentation is always a relevant concern, but what appears desirable varies by culture.

Cultural patterns in the way people are socialized to self-present also affect how readily they can engage in impression management when the situation calls for it. People from collectivistic or interdependent backgrounds (e.g., Hong Kong) receive more practice in impression management and, thus, are better able than people from individualistic or independent backgrounds (e.g., the United States) to express normatively appropriate opinions, even when burdened by high cognitive load (Riemer & Shavitt, 2011). These findings suggest that being raised with distinct self-presentation goals makes pursuit of those goals more automatic or effortless.

As described earlier, cultural self-construal plays a key role in self-regulatory processes. *Self-regulation* refers to the ways that people attain their goals by overriding their impulses to gain valued benefits (e.g., Baumeister, 2002). For people with an independent self-construal, who value agentic goals and the pursuit of personal advancement, self-regulation is characterized by a *promotion focus* that emphasizes one's own personal preferences and benefits. In contrast, for people with an interdependent self-construal, who tend to value maintaining harmonious interpersonal relations with ingroups, self-regulation is characterized by a *prevention focus* geared toward protecting the group from losses or bad outcomes (e.g., Aaker & Lee, 2001; J. Hong & Lee, 2008; A. Y. Lee et al., 2000).

Cultural differences in regulatory focus are associated with a range of differences in consumer behavior patterns (see Shavitt & Barnes, 2020, for a review). For instance, they predict whether messages about maximizing potential gains or avoiding potential losses tend to be more persuasive (Aaker & Lee, 2001). Also, when considering whether to expedite shipping for online retail purchases, cultural differences in regulatory focus mean that independent consumers are more sensitive to a message framed as a promotion loss (i.e., without faster shipping, "you cannot start enjoying the novel as early as you like"), whereas interdependent consumers are more sensitive to a message framed as a prevention loss (i.e., without faster shipping, "you will have to wait longer for the novel to arrive"; H. Chen et al., 2005).

Thinking Styles

In the same way that one's cultural self-construal can emphasize that the self is either separate and distinct from others or integrated and connected to others (Oyserman & Lee, 2007), it also influences whether people view objects in their environment as separated or integrated. This difference is encapsulated in the distinction between *thinking styles* (Nisbett, 2003; Nisbett et al., 2001). Analytic and holistic thinking styles describe distinct ways that people perceive, categorize, and reason about their environment, and an important body of work has demonstrated the broad implications of these differences for consumer choice (Nisbett, 2003; Nisbett et al., 2001).

Individualistic or independent cultural contexts give rise to an *analytic thinking style*, which is characterized by perceiving objects as independent and separate from one another (Nisbett et al., 2001; Oyserman & Lee, 2007). In perceiving their environment, analytic thinkers pay attention to focal objects, distinguishing them from their context or background (Monga & John, 2007) or contrasting them against the background (Zhu & Meyers-Levy, 2009). Objects perceived in this manner tend to be categorized using defining, formal features that characterize them (e.g., hot dogs and hamburgers belong in the category of meats eaten in a bun). Analytic thinkers tend to judge the validity of arguments and the desirability of objects using either-or rules. That is, an argument is seen as either right or wrong, and a product is either good or bad. In case of apparently conflicting information, such as when evaluating a brand that has desirable attributes but a disliked endorser, analytic thinkers tend to perceive the information as inconsistent, and respond to that by choosing one side or the other (Aaker & Sengupta, 2000).

Collectivistic or interdependent cultural contexts give rise to a *holistic thinking style*. This involves perceiving objects as interrelated with their background and classifying things based on their relational or symbolic connections. Holistic thinkers are attentive to background and contextual details, and they integrate these with focal objects in the foreground (Monga & John, 2007; Oyserman & Lee, 2007). As a result, their perceptions of products can change as the background or context changes (Zhu & Meyers-Levy, 2009). Holistic thinkers are likely to compromise between propositions (Briley et al., 2000; Peng & Nisbett, 1999), entertaining seemingly contradictory arguments as being true or seeing attributes as being both favorable and unfavorable (Aaker & Sengupta, 2000). Thus, a holistic thinking style is associated with the tendency toward dialectical judgments and ambivalent attitudes (e.g., A. H. Ng & Hynie, 2014; Pang et al., 2017). In short, one's sense of the desirability of a product can be multivalent and dependent on the context in which it is encountered. Finally, rather than classifying based on shared formal features, holistic thinkers tend to categorize products based on relationships between them (e.g., hot dogs and ice cream are things you eat at a picnic) and are better able to identify such connections and relationships (Ahluwalia, 2008).

Perception: Attention to context. There are many implications of thinking styles for consumers' perceptions and judgments about products (see Shavitt & Barnes, 2020, for a review). For instance, consumers in contexts that give rise to holistic thinking are more likely to infuse their perceptions of a product with the characteristics of its context (Riemer et al., 2014), and this includes where the product is sold and how it is displayed. Thus, they perceived a mug displayed on a marble table to be more modern than the same mug on a wooden table (Zhu & Meyers-Levy, 2009). However, the reverse was true for consumers in contexts that gave rise to analytic thinking—their perceptions tended to contrast the product from its context.

A store's reputation also serves as a contextual backdrop that influences consumers differently, depending on cultural factors. Consumers primed with an interdependent (vs. independent) self-construal, who were presumably thinking holistically, were likely to judge an appliance more positively when it was presented as an offering at a high-end department store versus when the same brand, at the same price, was presented as an offering at a discount retailer (K. Lee & Shavitt, 2006).

Shelf placement can have similar effects. That is, in situations that give rise to holistic versus analytic thinking, the characteristics of products displayed alongside a target brand are more likely to be infused into perceptions of that brand (Jain et al., 2007).

Finally, consumers' responses to reference prices also show a similar pattern as a function of self-construal. In evaluating the prices of TV sets, MP3 players, and printers, C. Y. Chen (2009) found that when an independent (vs. interdependent) self-construal was made salient, participants were more influenced by internal reference prices, where the price is perceived to represent the product's inherent features, and less influenced by external reference prices, where the price is perceived to be determined by the context (e.g., competitors' prices and characteristics of the market). Taken together, then, a broad set of findings suggests that, relative to independents or people who think analytically, interdependents or people who think holistically are more attentive and responsive to a variety of contextual inputs when judging a product or its characteristics.

Categorization. Because analytic thinkers characterize based on formal features (Ji et al., 2004), they are more likely to assume that products with the same branding have similar attributes. Thus, Colgate Lasagna (an actual failed brand extension; Lowin, 2017) will be expected to taste like toothpaste. In contrast, holistic thinkers categorize objects based on relationships and shared contexts and, as a result, are accepting of more distant brand extensions (Monga & John, 2009). For instance, Monga and John (2007) found that consumers from India, compared with those from the United States, were more accepting of fictional brand extensions with low fit to their parent brand, such as Kodak filing cabinets, and that priming holistic or analytic thinking yielded similar results.

Reasoning. Another implication of holistic and analytic thinking style differences involves how readily consumers connect different attributes of a product together and use one attribute to judge another. Lalwani and Shavitt (2013) showed that holistic thinkers (consumers in India) are more likely than analytic thinkers (consumers in the United States) to believe that "you get what you pay for." They also found that people with ethnic backgrounds that are associated with holistic thinking (Asian Americans or Hispanic Americans) versus analytic thinking (European Americans) are more likely to spontaneously use the price of a product to judge its quality. The same patterns were obtained by priming people to think holistically versus analytically (Lalwani & Shavitt, 2013).

Finally, recent evidence suggests a novel consequence of analytic thinkers' greater intolerance of incongruity, reviewed earlier. Compared with holistic thinkers, analytic thinkers are more uncomfortable when having to engage in a thinking style that is incongruent with their dominant thinking style (e.g., doing a task that requires analytic thinkers to think holistically). As a result of their greater discomfort with such experiences, analytic thinkers are more likely to respond with a preference for familiar over novel consumer options (Koo et al., 2020). For instance, after engaging in an unfamiliar thinking style, analytic versus holistic thinkers are more likely to prefer familiar hotels, retail locations, and restaurant menu options.

SOCIETY: HOW THE SELF FITS IN WITH OTHERS

As the sense of self develops, so too does the sense of one's connection to others and the societal norms and structures that classify and prioritize people. In other words, being socialized in a culture gives rise not only to a sense of self but also to a sense of how that self fits into the fabric of society. This includes learning one's proper roles and responsibilities and what society expects about the ways that others are to be evaluated and treated.

Understanding these processes often means going beyond the broad cultural distinctions between individualism and collectivism, or independent and interdependent self-construals, and the thinking styles that they give rise to. Increasingly, cultural researchers are examining how notions of social hierarchy and power affect one's view of "others" in society, and the implications for consumer behavior. We turn to this subject next.

Vertical and Horizontal Individualism and Collectivism

The vertical–horizontal distinction within individualism and collectivism refers to the nature and importance of hierarchy in interpersonal relations (e.g., Singelis et al., 1995; Triandis, 1995; Triandis & Gelfand, 1998). People with a vertical orientation emphasize status enhancement more than do people with a horizontal orientation, who in turn put more emphasis on benevolence and equality. More specifically, combining this distinction with the individualism–collectivism distinction yields four distinct cultural orientations: vertical individualism (VI), horizontal individualism (HI), vertical collectivism (VC), and horizontal collectivism (HC). Individuals, as well as societies, differ in the degree to which they emphasize the cultural values associated with each orientation (Triandis, 1995; Triandis & Gelfand, 1998).

In VI societies, such as the United States or the United Kingdom, people seek to advance their personal status via competition and achievement. In HI societies, such as Sweden and Denmark, people seek to develop unique and distinct identities and demonstrate their self-reliance. In VC societies, such as Korea or India, people seek to advance the standing of their ingroups. Finally, in HC societies, such as Brazil or the Israeli kibbutz, people value sociability and interdependence with others in egalitarian relationships. Within the United States, Hispanic Americans show a greater HC tendency and lower VI tendency compared with European Americans (Torelli & Shavitt, 2010; Torelli et al., 2015).

This set of finer grained cultural categories affords relatively nuanced predictions (Shavitt et al., 2006), and research has pointed to a number of novel implications for social and consumer behavior (e.g., Lalwani et al., 2006; Torelli & Shavitt, 2010). For instance, a content analysis of over 1,200 magazine ads in multiple countries showed that ads appearing in countries that have a relatively vertical cultural orientation (e.g., Korea, the United States) emphasize status, prestige, and luxury more than do ads from countries that nurture a horizontal orientation (e.g., Denmark; Shavitt et al., 2011). Thus, they are more likely to tout their "award winning" brands and use high-prestige endorsers. In contrast, Danish ads put more emphasis on HI themes of personalization and distinctiveness from others. These differences would not be anticipated by the broader individualism–collectivism distinction.

At the individual level, this horizontal–vertical distinction also provides unique predictions about the types of brand values that appeal to consumers. For instance, consumers with a VI cultural orientation are more attracted to brands that convey values of self-enhancement and status in their advertisements, whereas those with an HC cultural orientation are attracted to brands that show a concern for others and for building a better world (Torelli et al., 2012). Similar patterns are observed as a function of national culture—with Brazilians, compared with European Americans, Canadians, and East Asians, showing greater preference for prosocial brands (Torelli & Shavitt, 2010).

In addition to emphasizing distinct values, horizontal and vertical cultures also nurture distinct concepts of certain values and goals. In particular, power is construed differently depending on one's cultural orientation and background (Torelli & Shavitt, 2010). For those with a VI orientation, power is about having and gaining personal status. Because power is understood as freedom from having to worry about what others think, high-VI people are more likely to endorse the misuse and abuse of power in order to get what they want. On the other hand, for those with an HC orientation, power is understood in the context of feeling responsible for others' well-being. Thus, power is perceived to be a tool for helping and benefiting other people (Torelli & Shavitt, 2010).

As already noted, these differences in power concepts predict responses to brand images, as well as normative expectations for the behavior of power holders. In turn, these distinct normative expectations can influence the way that people evaluate and respond to powerful service providers (e.g., doctors). For instance, in HC cultural contexts, power comes with a responsibility to be benevolent when providing service. Thus, when power was made salient (vs. baseline), the reported satisfaction of Hispanic American patients (who tend to be higher in HC) with their doctors was more affected by their perceptions that the doctor had been compassionate and reassuring (Torelli et al., 2015). This was not the case for European Americans. For them, powerholders such as doctors and business negotiators appeared more likely to be judged based on whether they behaved justly and equitably.

In line with this, perceptions of status in the workplace also show distinct patterns for U.S. workers (where status means competence and ambition) compared with Latin American workers (where status means warmth and caring). Thus, Latin Americans tend to engage in warmth-signaling behaviors in order to gain workplace status, whereas U.S. workers tend to engage in competence-signaling behaviors (Torelli et al., 2014). These and other findings make clear that how power (and status) is conceptualized and sought depends on one's cultural background and orientation (see Torelli, Leslie, et al., 2020, for a review).

Power Distance

The cultural dimension of *power distance*, originally introduced by Hofstede (1980), describes the degree to which differences in power are expected and accepted in a given culture. Although this cultural dimension partially overlaps with the horizontal–vertical distinction, there are important conceptual and structural differences between them (Shavitt et al., 2006). Conceptually, the power distance dimension refers to differences in the acceptance of hierarchies as being valid or important in one's society, whereas the vertical–horizontal distinction relates to the extent to which selves are more or less arranged along a social hierarchy. From a structural standpoint, although power distance is conceptualized as a single dimension (from high to low; Hofstede, 1980, 2001), it is highly correlated with individualism–collectivism. Thus, countries high in power distance tend to also be more collectivistic. More specifically, countries topping the list of power distance scores (e.g., China, India, Malaysia, Mexico) are countries also generally characterized as vertical collectivistic, whereas those lowest in power distance (e.g., Denmark, Sweden, Norway) are countries also characterized as horizontal individualistic (Triandis, 1995; Triandis & Gelfand, 1998). Thus, the high–low power distance dimension overlaps with the distinction between VC and HI.

Consumer researchers have investigated how power distance impacts a variety of consumer phenomena by focusing on people's endorsement of power distance beliefs (PDB; Zhang et al., 2010). People who endorse a society that is high in power distance tend to be comfortable with, and even desire, structure. As a result, they are more likely to use heuristics and engage in stereotyping. One way that such stereotyping can influence product judgments is in the tendency to use a product's price to evaluate the quality of the item. Believing that "you get what you pay for" is a common heuristic, and consumers who are high (vs. low) in PDB are more likely to make use of this heuristic to categorize products by price, resulting in ascribing higher quality to the high-priced products (Lalwani & Forcum, 2016). Other research has found that the interaction between PDB and psychological power state, or power cues, can affect people's attentional focus and their subsequent behavior. For example, D. Han et al. (2017) found that in low-PDB contexts, people high in psychological power tend to be self-focused, which leads to less charitable giving, whereas in high-PDB contexts, people high (vs. low) in psychological power tend to be more other-focused, which leads to more charitable giving.

Power distance belief also predicts the effectiveness of advertising messages. People high in PDB, given their tendency to expect and accept authority, are likely to be more persuaded by expertise and trustworthiness. For example, consumers high in PDB tend to be more persuaded by celebrity endorsements (Winterich et al., 2018) and by company-designed products over user-designed products (Paharia & Swaminathan, 2019). Consumers high in PDB also have a strong desire for status and thus show a stronger preference for status brands (Y. Kim & Zhang, 2014), national (vs. private-label) brands (Wang et al., 2020), and upward (vs. downward) brand extensions (Liu et al., 2015). When selecting gifts for multiple recipients, high-PDB consumers compared with low-PDB consumers are also more likely to prioritize the preferences of higher status over lower status recipients (Wu, et al., 2021). These patterns are consistent with the findings on vertical–horizontal cultural orientations described earlier (e.g., Torelli et al., 2012; Torelli & Shavitt, 2010).

How Cognitive Processes Are Fine-Tuned to Fit in With Others

Culturally distinct mindsets or schemas can affect information processing in ways that help a person to fit in with their society and to maintain their position in it. Evidence suggests that when power concepts are cued, people with different cultural orientations process information differently. Specifically, people who are high (vs. low) in VI tended to stereotype information when primed with power concepts that associate power with personalized status. As a result, they were better able to recognize information or attributes that were congruent with their stereotype of a well-known fast-food brand (McDonald's), such as convenient, greasy, and flavorful (Torelli & Shavitt, 2011). By contrast, people whose cultural orientation is high (vs. low) in HC tended to individuate in their information processing when primed with power concepts that associate power with helping others. That is, they showed better recall and recognition for information or attributes that were incongruent with the brand's stereotype, such as healthy and delicate (Torelli & Shavitt, 2011). These distinct information processing patterns presumably serve to address distinct goals for maintaining one's social position. For those with a VI cultural orientation, adopting a stereotyping mindset helps to defend and maintain their powerful position over others (S. T. Fiske, 1993). On the other hand, for those with an HC cultural orientation, adopting an individuating mindset helps to form distinct impressions of others in order to be in a position to meet their unique needs.

SOCIAL COORDINATION AND MATERIAL CULTURE: MOTIVATING ACTION IN PURSUIT OF SOCIETAL PRIORITIES

From an evolutionary perspective, culture emerges in part as a response to the human need for social coordination. Evolutionary psychologists argue that culture is an adaptive response to the human problems of social coordination, such as establishing cooperative alliances, defending ingroups, gaining and maintaining respect from and power over others, and providing care to offspring (Bugental, 2000; Kenrick et al., 2002). Successful coordination requires knowing what others want, feel, think, and will do. Although many social animals (e.g., bees or wolves) coordinate their actions based on a mutual understanding of roles and behavioral scripts, humans are unique in their capability to generate an infinite number of coordination devices (e.g., language, relational models, norms, rituals, moral imperatives, taboos, social structures) to solve a host of novel social coordination problems. The paradigms and devices that help humans in a society solve recurrent coordination problems are not only a central aspect of cultures but also a primary source of cultural diversity (A. P. Fiske, 2000). Thus, a comprehensive understanding of culture necessarily requires that we look beyond patterns of beliefs, self-representations, and social structures and focus on culture as knowledge that helps to coordinate collective action. This knowledge is represented and transmitted in verbal (e.g., language) and nonverbal symbols (e.g., cultural objects, social institutions; Kitayama, 2002). We discuss the findings under this cultural perspective next.

Adherence to Norms: Conformity

As stated earlier, culture is often conceived as a collective construction to solve coordination problems by providing a stable system of norms and a set of shared meanings. These norms and meanings are useful for determining how individuals interact and adjust to each other in order to reach a stable social pattern, or equilibrium (Cohen, 2001). Because there is variation in the cultural paradigms that help people in different societies to solve their coordination problems, there is a wide variation in the norms to which people conform. For instance, it is more normative in collectivistic (vs. individualistic) cultures to endorse moderation in product choices. Thus, consumers with a collectivistic mindset are more likely to choose a compromise option (i.e., a middle option in an arbitrary set, which offers moderate levels of two attribute dimensions) than those with an individualistic mindset (Briley et al., 2005). Similarly, in the individualistic West, the norm is for individuals, not groups, to engage in action. In contrast, in the collectivistic East, it is more normative to conceive of groups as agents. As a result, individualistic (i.e., Western) consumers experience greater regret in the face of an unsuccessful product decision that occurs due to a group's (vs. their own) action. That is because group decisions represent a violation of the cultural norm that individuals, and not groups, should exert action. In contrast, collectivistic (i.e., Eastern) consumers experience greater regret with the same product decision that occurs due to their own (vs. a group's) action. That is because an individual acting independently represents a norm violation (S. Ng et al., 2015).

Cultures differ not only in the norms that they promote but also in the extent to which norms should be considered as important drivers of behavior for successful coordination of social interactions. The individualism–collectivism classification illustrates alternative cultural paradigms about the importance of incorporating norms into social behaviors. Collectivistic societies, because of their emphasis on an interdependent view of the self, emphasize conforming to norms as a key driver of social behavior. In contrast, individualism, with its emphasis on an independent view of the self, emphasizes norm compliance less and instead promotes more the social expression of individuals' attitudes (Riemer et al., 2014; Triandis, 1995). Indeed, past research shows that, controlling for cultural differences in what is normative behavior, people from interdependent cultures are more susceptible to normative influence than people from independent cultures (Savani et al., 2015). The endorsement of conformity values (i.e., the motivation to restrain actions likely to upset others and violate social norms; Schwartz, 1992) is more positively correlated with a collectivistic orientation (and particularly so with a vertical collectivistic orientation) but unrelated with an individualistic orientation (Oishi et al., 1998). Furthermore, collectivistic cultures (e.g., Japan) put greater emphasis on conformity themes as a successful cultural paradigm in formal education (i.e., the stories described in school textbooks), whereas individualistic cultures (e.g.,

the United States) put greater emphasis on themes about autonomy and achievement (Imada, 2012).

Cultural differences in the tendency to conform to cultural norms between individualists and collectivists are associated with a variety of consumer behaviors. The choices of collectivistic consumers are associated with higher uniformity-seeking tendencies, made in accordance with the cultural norm, compared with those of individualistic consumers (H. Kim & Markus, 1999; Yoon et al., 2011). Collectivistic (vs. individualistic) consumers are also more likely to use appearance-enhancing products given their stronger motivation to conform to societal norms about beauty (Madan et al., 2018). Furthermore, people from collectivistic (vs. individualistic) cultures respond more negatively to firms that price products asymmetrically (i.e., increase prices when costs increase but maintain prices when costs decrease) because this common practice is inconsistent with cultural norms mandating firm benevolence (H. Chen et al., 2018).

Enforcement of Norms and Social Order: Tightness–Looseness

As discussed earlier, norms can be a powerful driver of behavior, particularly in collectivistic cultures. But why do people conform to norms? Is norm compliance a spontaneous process or the outcome of an enforcement mechanism? Norms can be enforced through somewhat informal mutual monitoring, in which deviant behaviors are held in check by different forms of shunning, or through more formal social and legal controls that impose costs on deviant behavior (Chiu & Hong, 2006). Past research suggests that cultures differ in the extent to which norms are clearly defined, as well as in the degree to which deviant behavior is tolerated. The cultural dimensions of tightness and looseness reflect these differences. *Tightness* (T) refers to cultures in which norms are clearly defined and there is little tolerance of deviant behavior, whereas *looseness* (L) relates to cultures in which norms are vague and tolerance of deviant behavior is high (Gelfand et al., 2011; Pelto, 1968; Triandis, 1995). In cultures characterized as tight, norms are clearly defined and strongly enforced. There is the shared belief that individuals must conform to group values, and tolerance for deviation is minimal. These cultures tend to be homogeneous with respect to certain attitudes and behaviors. In contrast, in "loose" cultures, norms are not clearly defined and there is ample latitude in what is considered appropriate behavior. Heterogeneity is more typical in these loose cultures, and deviations from norms are more tolerated (for a review, see R. Li et al., 2017; see also Torelli & Rodas, 2017).

The implications of the tightness–looseness dimension for consumer behavior are still under investigation. R. Li et al. (2017) proposed that a focus on this dimension would help to further explain cross-cultural differences in brand loyalty, the persuasiveness of advertising appeals, and the likelihood of adopting new products. For instance, they posit that consumers in tighter cultures will likely grow more emotionally attached to brands due to strong normative pressures, whereas those in looser cultures will be more likely to repeatedly buy brands for the sake of convenience due to their greater mobility and openness. There is some evidence consistent with this prediction, as consumers in tight (vs. loose) cultures tend to react more negatively to a company's attempt to financially compensate consumers in response to a service failure and to expect instead an apology (C. Li et al., 2012). In general, it is anticipated that advertisements in tighter cultures would emphasize what one should do, feature themes of uniformity, and be more conservative; whereas ads in looser cultures would emphasize ideals and freedom from constraints, feature themes of diversity and difference, and be more permissive (e.g., more liberal advertising including sexual themes; R. Li et al., 2017; Torelli & Rodas, 2017).

Accountability and Injunctive Norms

Monitoring is one of the key mechanisms in the enforcement of norms. *Accountability* refers to the expectation of justifying one's judgments to others (Lerner & Tetlock, 1999). When being accountable, injunctive norms, or what is believed to be appropriate in the eyes of others, provide strong justification for one's judgments and behaviors (Cialdini et al., 1991; De Cremer & Dewitte, 2002). Because people often anticipate justifying their consumption decision to others (Schlosser & Shavitt, 1999), accountability emerges as a strong moderator of cultural effects in consumption. That is, the effects of culture on consumption are often stronger when people feel accountable for their consumption decisions, as accountability prompts them to search for cultural norms perceived as widely shared justifications (Briley et al., 2000; Torelli, 2006). For instance, when evaluating a new digital camera with a poor warranty, anticipating having to explain consumption decisions to others prompts collectivistic (vs. individualistic) consumers to conform more to the norms of their intended audience (i.e., a product with a poor warranty is not dependable) and to make judgments that are more consistent with these norms, perceiving a higher risk when purchasing the product (Torelli, 2006). Similarly, Briley and colleagues (2000) demonstrated that consumers from a collectivistic culture, such as China or Japan, are more likely to settle for a compromise option (consistent with the norm of "being moderate") when justifying their choices to others than those from an individualistic culture such as the United States.

Material Representations of Culture

Culture not only exists "in the heads" of individuals as values, beliefs, and norms but is also externalized into material objects, social practices, and social institutions (Kitayama et al., 2007). For instance, the Japanese tea ceremony embodies the recognition of the beauty of nature and life that characterizes Japanese culture (Watanabe, 1974). Similarly, because arranged marriages reflecting the values of parental control, ancestral lineage, and sense of kinship have been a distinct element in Indian culture, this social practice is distinctively represented in the matchmaker (or *nayan*; Rao & Rao, 1982). More importantly, culture also manifests itself in the material world of advertisements, products, and brands.

Content and persuasiveness of ads. Advertisements are instruments for moving meanings from the culturally constituted world to products and brands (McCracken, 1986). As such, appeals in advertisements reflect the cultural orientation of a society. For example, message appeals in individualistic cultures tend to convey individuality, personal benefits, and achievement. In contrast, message appeals in collectivistic cultures tend to convey group benefits, harmony, and conformity (Shavitt & Koo, 2015). Similarly, because advertisers in the United States believe that learning about a brand is an important step that precedes liking and buying, U.S. advertisers particularly favor message appeals that focus on teaching consumers about the brand by communicating the advertised brand's attributes and advantages (Miracle, 1987; Ogilvy, 1985). This focus on building personal preferences about the attributes of objects is consistent with the individualistic values that characterize American culture. In contrast, because advertisers in Japan believe that in order for consumers to buy a particular brand, they need to be familiar with it and trust the company who sells it, message appeals in Japan tend to focus on "making friends" with the audience and showing that the company understands their feelings (Javalgi et al., 1995; Miracle, 1987). This focus on building relationships is consistent with the collectivistic values that characterize Japanese culture. Indeed, a content analysis of magazine advertisements revealed that in Korea (i.e., a collectivistic culture), compared with the United States (i.e., an individualistic culture), advertisements are more focused on family well-being, interdependence, group goals, and harmony, and they are less focused on self-improvement, ambition, personal goals, independence, and individuality (S. P. Han & Shavitt, 1994). Another content analysis showed a greater focus on individuality in U.S. magazine ads and on conformity in South Korean magazine ads (H. Kim & Markus, 1999).

Website content in individualistic and collectivistic societies also appears to show similar patterns of variation. For example, Japanese and South Korean corporate websites, compared with corporate websites in the United States and United Kingdom, have more features that foster interactions among online communities and user groups (Cho & Cheon, 2005), and features that enable peer-to-peer interaction may be more crucial to building trust and fostering business success in collectivistic cultures (Lafevre, 2013). User-generated content on discussion boards and in consumer reviews also shows patterns consistent with such cultural variation. In China, compared with the United States, postings on discussion boards are more likely to seek information from others about their opinions (Fong & Burton, 2008), a pattern that supports the tendency toward conformity.

Research also shows that, in a variety of advertising and persuasion contexts, encountering messages that match versus mismatch the goals or dominant frames associated with one's culture is more motivating and more persuasive (e.g., Briley et al., 2017; S. P. Han & Shavitt, 1994; Zhang & Gelb, 1996). That is, advertising appeals that are more prevalent are also more likely to be effective. For instance, in an early cross-national experiment with fictitious ads (S. P. Han & Shavitt, 1994), ad appeals with individualistic themes ("Solo cleans with a softness you will love") were more persuasive in the United States compared with South Korea, whereas the reverse was true for appeals with collectivistic themes ("Solo cleans with a softness your whole family will love"), particularly when the products being advertised were ones typically shared with others and thus more likely to be judged in a way that is accountable to others' views (see also Zhang & Gelb, 1996). In the context of a fictitious textbook shopping website, peer endorsements that appeared onscreen from fellow students were more persuasive for students in Hong Kong versus in Australia (Sia et al., 2009).

Moreover, when thinking about how to overcome illness, cross-national experiments show that culture influences which frames are most effective for generating optimism as well as for motivating choices that can help to overcome those challenges (Briley et al., 2017). For example, in the United States, where people are socialized to be agentic and independent, individuals adopting an initiator frame (how will I act, regardless of the situations I encounter?) were more optimistic than those adopting a responder frame (how will I react to the situations I encounter?). The converse occurred in China, where people are socialized to respond and fit into situations.

Cultural meaning of brands. Brands can also acquire cultural meanings, as consumers attribute cultural significance to certain commercial brands

(Aaker et al., 2001). Furthermore, this cultural significance can become associated with the abstract characteristics that define a cultural group. For example, some brands in the United States are associated with self-enhancement values of power (e.g., Harley-Davidson associations with strength, masculinity, and toughness that characterize the United States' vertical individualistic culture). Some brands in Venezuela (i.e., a vertical collectivistic culture) are associated with conservation values of prioritizing family bonds (Torelli, Oh, & Stoner, 2020). Brands that acquire such cultural meanings can reach the level of a cultural icon. This happens when the brand is consensually perceived to symbolize the abstract image that characterizes a certain cultural group (Torelli et al., 2010; Torelli, Oh, & Stoner, 2020). For instance, Nike's embodiment of self-enhancement values of achievement, success, and superior athletic performance contributes to its status as an American icon (Torelli, 2013). To the extent that iconic brands embody cultural ideals, they can act as identity reminders and serve as subtle cultural primes connecting consumers with a cherished cultural identity (Torelli, 2013; Torelli & Cheng, 2011).

Because iconic brands symbolize the beliefs, ideas, and values of a cultural group, consumers with a heightened need to symbolize a cultural identity will judge iconic brands as highly instrumental for fulfilling such needs. Thus, making salient a cultural identity triggers favorable attitudes toward objects that are identity congruent. For instance, when making an ethnic identity salient (e.g., Asian), consumers evaluate more favorably advertisements targeted to the ethnic ingroup (e.g., as depicted in copy and ad images; Forehand et al., 2002) than when the identity is not made salient. Because commitment to a cultural identity makes the identity more salient in different contexts, consumers who are highly identified with the identity are particularly likely to favor iconic brands (over noniconic ones) to fulfill their salient cultural identity needs and are even willing to pay more for such iconic brands. For example, Minnesotan consumers reminded (vs. not) of the importance of their Minnesotan identity were willing to pay more for a set of poker chips with the Target logo (a retailing brand iconic of Minnesota; Amaral & Torelli, 2018).

Furthermore, because a salient identity brings to mind identity-consistent decisions that do not require further reflection, the higher valuation of iconic brands occurs rather automatically and without conscious deliberation. In other words, consumers process information about an iconic brand easily and feel that it is right to favor the brand (Torelli, 2013). In turn, this feeling results in a pleasing processing experience accompanied by enhanced brand valuation (Torelli & Ahluwalia, 2012). Over time, continued reliance on iconic brands for fulfilling salient cultural identity needs can contribute to developing strong self–brand relationships (Amaral & Torelli, 2018; Escalas & Bettman, 2005). In turn, forming a strong bond with a culturally symbolic brand, due to its cultural identity meaning, can shield the brand against negative publicity when cultural identity needs are salient (Swaminathan et al., 2007).

Mixing of Cultures in a Globalized World

With globalization, the world is becoming more multicultural. This is reflected both in the mixing of cultural meanings in products and brands as well as in the integration of contrastive cultural frames within consumers' minds. Recent research illustrates the dynamic nature of cultural interactions and how consumers respond to the mixing of cultures in today's globalized marketplace.

Culture mixing in product offerings. In globalized markets, products often integrate symbols of contrastive cultures. For instance, a Starbucks store in the Forbidden City Palace of Chinese emperors or an iPhone with a "Made in China but designed in California" label are examples of how products can mix elements of contrastive cultures. We refer to such product offerings as examples of culture mixing (Hao et al., 2016; Keh et al., 2016). Unlike the association with a single culture discussed in the previous section, exposure to culture mixing simultaneously brings to mind two or more cultural representations. This draws attention to the conflict between the juxtaposed cultures, resulting in the expectation that cultures are discrete entities with relatively impermeable boundaries. For instance, compared with showing American participants culture-neutral products (e.g., a backpack or bread toaster) that carry prototypic British brand names (e.g., Williams—monocultural priming), showing them iconic Mexican products (e.g., tequila or corn tortillas) that carry the same British brand names (culture mixed product) simultaneously activates representations of Mexican and British cultures, which increases perceived differences between cultures (Torelli et al., 2011). This effect emerges not only for the target cultures (e.g., Mexican and British) but also for other cultures (e.g., Puerto Rican and Canadian).

Because experiencing conflict between identities can be aversive (Reed et al., 2012), consumers often evaluate culture mixed products less favorably than monocultural ones. For instance, research shows that Americans evaluate less favorably a culture mixed product (Sony cappuccino machines—the Sony brand is iconic of Japan, whereas cappuccino machines are iconic of Italy) than a monocultural one (Sony toaster oven—only the Japanese Sony is culturally symbolic; Torelli & Ahluwalia, 2012). This effect emerges in spite of the similar levels of moderate fit of the two products with the Sony brand. Furthermore, the less favorable evaluations of the culture mixed product are driven by the subjective experience of disfluency (i.e., feeling that the product is not "right") triggered by the simultaneous activation of two different cultural schemas. However, consumers do not always react negatively to culture mixing. Psychological and situational factors that induce openness to the novel experiences from intercultural encounters promote integrating the contrastive cultures and reducing conflict. For instance, Keh et al. (2016) demonstrated that endorsing autonomy values of stimulation and self-direction positively predicts favorable attitudes of Chinese consumers toward culturally mixed phonosemantic brand translations (i.e., translations from a Western language to Chinese that maintain the foreign sounding of the name while conveying the brand meaning in the Chinese language). Similarly, X. Chen et al. (2016) showed that openness to experience favorably impacts the creative benefits of experiencing culture mixing in the environment.

Culture mixing within the person: Bicultural identity integration. With globalization, the number of individuals who identify themselves with two (bicultural) or more cultures (multicultural) as opposed to a single culture (monocultural) is rapidly on the rise. Bicultural or multicultural individuals, who identify with and internalize more than one culture, such as immigrants, sojourners, or citizens living in multicultural societies, are those who manage different cultural identities in their day-to-day lives (Benet-Martínez et al., 2002). One distinctive characteristic of bicultural consumers is their ability to "switch" between cultural frames depending on the situation. For example, for Hong Kong Chinese students, exposure to Chinese cultural symbols (e.g., a Chinese dragon), as compared with exposure to American cultural symbols (e.g., the American flag), increases the degree to which they endorse Chinese values (Y. Y. Hong et al., 2000). This phenomenon has been demonstrated across a wide range of cultures and populations (Lau-Gesk, 2003). Furthermore, the phenomenon even extends to monocultural individuals who are exposed to the tenets of a foreign culture (e.g., European Americans living in Chinatown; Alter & Kwan, 2009). Cultural frame switching has consequences for consumer behavior, as consumers tend to favor products that are consistent with the accessible cultural frame. For instance, Mexican American consumers residing in the United States prefer songs from a Hispanic rock band as a way to connect with their Hispanic identity (Torelli et al., 2017).

Interestingly, cultural frame switching can exhibit different forms depending on whether bicultural individuals perceive their cultural identities as compatible and complementary or as oppositional and contradictory (Mok & Morris, 2013). This individual difference is called bicultural identity integration (BII; Benet-Martínez et al., 2002), which is composed of perceptions of overlap (vs. distance) and perceptions of harmony (vs. conflict) between one's two cultural identities (Benet-Martínez & Haritatos, 2005). In terms of cultural frame switching, those who are high on BII show a congruent priming effect responding to cultural cues. That is, they bring to mind the culture associated with the environmental cues. However, individuals who are low in BII exhibit a reverse priming effect, as in response to cultural cues they activate the unrelated culture (Benet-Martínez et al., 2002).

CONCLUSION

We began by posing the following question: How should a manager of a global brand decide on their marketing communication strategies? As marketing efforts become increasingly globalized, it is imperative to understand the cultural factors that affect consumer behavior. This chapter discussed how culture impacts three fundamental domains in consumer psychology: self, society, and social coordination. Our review identifies the key cultural dimensions that can be incorporated into models of consumer behavior to predict information processing and thinking styles, consumption goals and motivations, persuasiveness of advertising messages, and brand and product preferences.

We also highlighted that, in a globalized world, cultural identities and representations are not always unitary. Consumers accumulate exposure to cultures other than their own, as well as to multiple cultures in their own heritage, and thus can readily internalize two or more cultures. Moreover, products and brands can symbolize more than one culture. In this complex environment, consumers can shift their judgments and behaviors according to salient cultural frames. Although our review identifies actionable frameworks grounded on research conducted in the last decades, there is still the need for a deeper understanding of the psychological mechanisms underlying cross-cultural consumer behavior in the complex globalized markets of the 21st century.

REFERENCES

Aaker, J. L., Benet-Martínez, V., & Garolera, J. (2001). Consumption symbols as carriers of culture: A study of Japanese and Spanish brand personality constructs. *Journal of Personality and Social Psychology*, 81(3), 492–508. https://doi.org/10.1037/0022-3514.81.3.492

Aaker, J. L., & Lee, A. Y. (2001). "I" seek pleasures and "we" avoid pains: The role of self-regulatory goals in information processing and persuasion. *Journal of Consumer Research*, 28(1), 33–49. https://doi.org/10.1086/321946

Aaker, J. L., & Sengupta, J. (2000). Additivity versus attenuation: The role of culture in the resolution of information incongruity. *Journal of Consumer Psychology*, 9(2), 67–82. https://doi.org/10.1207/S15327663JCP0902_2

Ahluwalia, R. (2008). How far can a brand stretch? Understanding the role of self-construal. *Journal of Marketing Research*, 45(3), 337–350. https://doi.org/10.1509/jmkr.45.3.337

Alter, A. L., & Kwan, V. S. (2009). Cultural sharing in a global village: Evidence for extracultural cognition in European Americans. *Journal of Personality and Social Psychology*, 96(4), 742–760. https://doi.org/10.1037/a0014036

Amaral, N. B., & Torelli, C. J. (2018). Salient cultural identities and consumers' valuation of identity congruent brands: consequences for building and leveraging brand equity. *Journal of Management and Training for Industries*, 5(3), 13.

Baumeister, R. F. (2002). Yielding to temptation: Self-control failure, impulsive purchasing, and consumer behavior. *Journal of Consumer Research*, 28(4), 670–676. https://doi.org/10.1086/338209

Benet-Martínez, V., & Haritatos, J. (2005). Bicultural identity integration (BII): Components and psychosocial antecedents. *Journal of Personality*, 73(4), 1015–1050. https://doi.org/10.1111/j.1467-6494.2005.00337.x

Benet-Martínez, V., Leu, J., Lee, F., & Morris, M. W. (2002). Negotiating biculturalism: Cultural frame switching in biculturals with oppositional versus compatible cultural identities. *Journal of Cross-Cultural Psychology*, 33(5), 492–516. https://doi.org/10.1177/0022022102033005005

Berger, J., & Heath, C. (2007). Where consumers diverge from others: Identity signaling and product domains. *Journal of Consumer Research*, 34(2), 121–134. https://doi.org/10.1086/519142

Briley, D. A., Morris, M. W., & Simonson, I. (2000). Reasons as carriers of culture: Dynamic versus dispositional models of cultural influence on decision making. *Journal of Consumer Research*, 27(2), 157–178. https://doi.org/10.1086/314318

Briley, D. A., Morris, M. W., & Simonson, I. (2005). Cultural chameleons: Biculturals, conformity motives, and decision making. *Journal of Consumer Psychology*, 15(4), 351–362. https://doi.org/10.1207/s15327663jcp1504_9

Briley, D. A., Rudd, M., & Aaker, J. (2017). Cultivating optimism: How to frame your future during a health challenge. *Journal of Consumer Research*, 44(4), 895–915. https://doi.org/10.1093/jcr/ucx075

Bugental, D. B. (2000). Acquisition of the algorithms of social life: A domain-based approach. *Psychological Bulletin*, 126(2), 187–219. https://doi.org/10.1037/0033-2909.126.2.187

Chen, C. Y. (2009). Who I am and how I think: The impact of self-construal on the roles of internal and external reference prices in price evaluations. *Journal of Consumer Psychology*, 19(3), 416–426. https://doi.org/10.1016/j.jcps.2009.05.012

Chen, H., Bolton, L. E., Ng, S., Lee, D., & Wang, D. (2018). Culture, relationship norms, and dual entitlement. *Journal of Consumer Research*, 45(1), 1–20. https://doi.org/10.1093/jcr/ucx118

Chen, H., Ng, S., & Rao, A. R. (2005). Cultural differences in consumer impatience. *Journal of Marketing Research*, 42(3), 291–301. https://doi.org/10.1509/jmkr.2005.42.3.291

Chen, X., Leung, A. K. Y., Yang, D. Y. J., Chiu, C. Y., Li, Z. Q., & Cheng, S. Y. (2016). Cultural threats in culturally mixed encounters hamper creative performance for individuals with lower openness to experience. *Journal of Cross-Cultural Psychology*, 47(10), 1321–1334. https://doi.org/10.1177/0022022116641513

Chiu, C.-Y., & Hong, Y.-Y. (2006). *Social psychology of culture*. Psychology Press.

Cho, C. H., & Cheon, H. J. (2005). Cross-cultural comparisons of interactivity on corporate web sites: The United States, the United Kingdom, Japan, and South Korea. *Journal of Advertising*, 34(2), 99–115. https://doi.org/10.1080/00913367.2005.10639195

Cialdini, R. B., Kallgren, C. A., & Reno, R. R. (1991). A focus theory of normative conduct: A theoretical refinement and reevaluation of the role of norms in human behavior. In M. P. Zanna (Ed.), *Advances in experimental social psychology* (Vol. 24, pp. 201–234). Academic Press. https://doi.org/10.1016/S0065-2601(08)60330-5

Cohen, D. (2001). Cultural variation: Considerations and implications. *Psychological Bulletin*, 127(4), 451–471. https://doi.org/10.1037/0033-2909.127.4.451

Cousins, S. D. (1989). Culture and self-perception in Japan and the United States. *Journal of Personality and Social Psychology*, 56(1), 124–131. https://doi.org/10.1037/0022-3514.56.1.124

De Cremer, D., & Dewitte, S. (2002). Effect of trust and accountability in mixed-motive situations. *Journal of Social Psychology*, 142(4), 541–543. https://doi.org/10.1080/00224540209603917

Escalas, J. E., & Bettman, J. R. (2005). Self-construal, reference groups, and brand meaning. *Journal of Consumer Research*, 32(3), 378–389. https://doi.org/10.1086/497549

Fiske, A. P. (2000). Complementarity theory: Why human social capacities evolved to require cultural complements. *Personality and Social Psychology Review*, 4(1), 76–94. https://doi.org/10.1207/S15327957PSPR0401_7

Fiske, S. T. (1993). Controlling other people. The impact of power on stereotyping. *American Psychologist*, 48(6), 621–628. https://doi.org/10.1037/0003-066X.48.6.621

Fong, J., & Burton, S. (2008). A cross-cultural comparison of electronic word-of-mouth and country-of-origin effects. *Journal of Business Research*, 61(3), 233–242. https://doi.org/10.1016/j.jbusres.2007.06.015

Forehand, M. R., Deshpandé, R., & Reed, A., II. (2002). Identity salience and the influence of differential activation of the social self-schema on advertising response. *Journal of Applied Psychology*, 87(6), 1086–1099. https://doi.org/10.1037/0021-9010.87.6.1086

Gelfand, M. J., Raver, J. L., Nishii, L., Leslie, L. M., Lun, J., Lim, B. C., Duan, L., Almaliach, A., Ang, S., Arnadottir, J., Aycan, Z., Boehnke, K., Boski, P., Cabecinhas, R., Chan, D., Chhokar, J., D'Amato, A., Ferrer, M., Fischlmayr, I. C., . . . Yamaguchi, S. (2011). Differences between tight and loose cultures: A 33-nation study. *Science*, 332(6033), 1100–1104. https://doi.org/10.1126/science.1197754

Han, D., Lalwani, A. K., & Duhachek, A. (2017). Power distance belief, power, and charitable giving. *Journal of Consumer Research*, 44(1), 182–195. https://doi.org/10.1093/jcr/ucw084

Han, S. P., & Shavitt, S. (1994). Persuasion and culture: Advertising appeals in individualistic and collectivistic societies. *Journal of Experimental Social Psychology*, 30(4), 326–350. https://doi.org/10.1006/jesp.1994.1016

Hao, J., Li, D., Peng, L., Peng, S., & Torelli, C. J. (2016). Advancing our understanding of culture mixing. *Journal of Cross-Cultural Psychology*, 47(10), 1257–1267. https://doi.org/10.1177/0022022116670514

Hoch, S. J., & Loewenstein, G. F. (1991). Time-inconsistent preferences and consumer self-control. *Journal of Consumer Research*, 17(4), 492–507. https://doi.org/10.1086/208573

Hofstede, G. (1980). *Culture's consequences: International differences in work-related values*. Sage.

Hofstede, G. (1984). *Culture's consequences: International differences in work-related values* (Vol. 5). Sage.

Hofstede, G. (1991). *Organizations and cultures: Software of the mind*. McGrawHill.

Hofstede, G. (2001). *Culture's consequences: Comparing values, behaviors, institutions and organizations across nations.* Sage.

Hong, J., & Chang, H. H. (2015). "I" follow my heart and "we" rely on reasons: The impact of self-construal on reliance on feelings versus reasons in decision making. *Journal of Consumer Research, 41*(6), 1392–1411. https://doi.org/10.1086/680082

Hong, J., & Lee, A. Y. (2008). Be fit and be strong: Mastering self-regulation through regulatory fit. *Journal of Consumer Research, 34*(5), 682–695. https://doi.org/10.1086/521902

Hong, Y. Y., Morris, M. W., Chiu, C. Y., & Benet-Martínez, V. (2000). Multicultural minds. A dynamic constructivist approach to culture and cognition. *American Psychologist, 55*(7), 709–720. https://doi.org/10.1037/0003-066X.55.7.709

Imada, T. (2012). Cultural narratives of individualism and collectivism: A content analysis of textbook stories in the United States and Japan. *Journal of Cross-Cultural Psychology, 43*(4), 576–591. https://doi.org/10.1177/0022022110383312

Iyengar, S. S., & Lepper, M. R. (1999). Rethinking the value of choice: A cultural perspective on intrinsic motivation. *Journal of Personality and Social Psychology, 76*(3), 349–366. https://doi.org/10.1037/0022-3514.76.3.349

Jain, S. P., Desai, K. K., & Mao, H. (2007). The influence of chronic and situational self-construal on categorization. *Journal of Consumer Research, 34*(1), 66–76. https://doi.org/10.1086/513047

Javalgi, R. G., Cutler, B. D., & Malhotra, N. K. (1995). Print advertising at the component level: A cross-cultural comparison of the United States and Japan. *Journal of Business Research, 34*(2), 117–124. https://doi.org/10.1016/0148-2963(94)00116-V

Ji, L. J., Zhang, Z., & Nisbett, R. E. (2004). Is it culture or is it language? Examination of language effects in cross-cultural research on categorization. *Journal of Personality and Social Psychology, 87*(1), 57–65. https://doi.org/10.1037/0022-3514.87.1.57

Kacen, J. J., & Lee, J. A. (2002). The influence of culture on consumer impulsive buying behavior. *Journal of Consumer Psychology, 12*(2), 163–176. https://doi.org/10.1207/S15327663JCP1202_08

Kahneman, D., Knetsch, J. L., & Thaler, R. H. (1990). Experimental tests of the endowment effect and the Coase theorem. *Journal of Political Economy, 98*(6), 1325–1348. https://doi.org/10.1086/261737

Keh, H. T., Torelli, C. J., Chiu, C. Y., & Hao, J. (2016). Integrative responses to culture mixing in brand name translations: The roles of product self-expressiveness and self-relevance of values among bicultural Chinese consumers. *Journal of Cross-Cultural Psychology, 47*(10), 1345–1360. https://doi.org/10.1177/0022022116667843

Kenrick, D. T., Maner, J. K., Butner, J., Li, N. P., Becker, D. V., & Schaller, M. (2002). Dynamical evolutionary psychology: Mapping the domains of the new interactionist paradigm. *Personality and Social Psychology Review, 6*(4), 347–356. https://doi.org/10.1207/S15327957PSPR0604_09

Kim, H., & Markus, H. R. (1999). Deviance or uniqueness, harmony or conformity? A cultural analysis. *Journal of Personality and Social Psychology, 77*(4), 785–800. https://doi.org/10.1037/0022-3514.77.4.785

Kim, Y., & Zhang, Y. (2014). The impact of power-distance belief on consumers' preference for status brands. *Journal of Global Marketing, 27*(1), 13–29. https://doi.org/10.1080/08911762.2013.844290

Kitayama, S. (2002). Culture and basic psychological processes—Toward a system view of culture: Comment on Oyserman et al. (2002). *Psychological Bulletin, 128*(1), 89–96. https://doi.org/10.1037/0033-2909.128.1.89

Kitayama, S., Duffy, S., & Uchida, Y. (2007). Self as cultural mode of being. In S. Kitayama & D. Cohen (Eds.), *Handbook of cultural psychology* (pp. 136–174). Guilford Press.

Koo, M., Shavitt, S., Lalwani, A. K., & Chinchanachokchai, S. (2020). Engaging in a culturally mismatched thinking style increases the preference for familiar consumer options for analytic but not holistic thinkers. *International Journal of Research in Marketing, 37*(4), 837–852. https://doi.org/10.1016/j.ijresmar.2020.03.004

Lafevre, R. E. (2013). *Why eBay failed in China.* Pacific Standard. https://psmag.com/economics/why-ebay-failed-in-china-taobao-swift-guanxi-60072

Lalwani, A. K., & Forcum, L. (2016). Does a dollar get you a dollar's worth of merchandise? The impact of power distance belief on price-quality judgments. *Journal of Consumer Research, 43*(2), 317–333. https://doi.org/10.1093/jcr/ucw019

Lalwani, A. K., & Shavitt, S. (2009). The "me" I claim to be: Cultural self-construal elicits self-presentational goal pursuit. *Journal of Personality and Social Psychology, 97*(1), 88–102. https://doi.org/10.1037/a0014100

Lalwani, A. K., & Shavitt, S. (2013). You get what you pay for? Self-construal influences price-quality judgments. *Journal of Consumer Research, 40*(2), 255–267. https://doi.org/10.1086/670034

Lalwani, A. K., Shavitt, S., & Johnson, T. (2006). What is the relation between cultural orientation and socially desirable responding? *Journal of Personality and Social Psychology, 90*(1), 165–178. https://doi.org/10.1037/0022-3514.90.1.165

Lalwani, A. K., & Wang, J. J. (2019). How do consumers' cultural backgrounds and values influence their coupon proneness? A multimethod investigation. *Journal of Consumer Research*, 45(5), 1037–1050. https://doi.org/10.1093/jcr/ucy033

Lau-Gesk, L. G. (2003). Activating culture through persuasion appeals: An examination of the bicultural consumer. *Journal of Consumer Psychology*, 13(3), 301–315. https://doi.org/10.1207/S15327663JCP1303_11

Lee, A. Y., Aaker, J. L., & Gardner, W. L. (2000). The pleasures and pains of distinct self-construals: The role of interdependence in regulatory focus. *Journal of Personality and Social Psychology*, 78(6), 1122–1134. https://doi.org/10.1037/0022-3514.78.6.1122

Lee, K., & Shavitt, S. (2006). The use of cues depends on goals: Store reputation affects product judgments when social identity goals are salient. *Journal of Consumer Psychology*, 16(3), 260–271. https://doi.org/10.1207/s15327663jcp1603_8

Lerner, J. S., & Tetlock, P. E. (1999). Accounting for the effects of accountability. *Psychological Bulletin*, 125(2), 255–275. https://doi.org/10.1037/0033-2909.125.2.255

Li, C., Fock, H., & Mattila, A. S. (2012). The role of cultural tightness–looseness in the ethics of service recovery. *Journal of Global Marketing*, 25(1), 3–16. https://doi.org/10.1080/08911762.2012.697379

Li, C., Li, D., Chiu, C. Y., & Peng, S. (2019). Strong brand from consumers' perspective: A cross-cultural study. *Journal of Cross-Cultural Psychology*, 50(1), 116–129. https://doi.org/10.1177/0022022118799456

Li, R., Gordon, S., & Gelfand, M. J. (2017). Tightness–looseness: A new framework to understand consumer behavior. *Journal of Consumer Psychology*, 27(3), 377–391. https://doi.org/10.1016/j.jcps.2017.04.001

Liu, X. L., Ng, S., & Lim, E. (2015). Moving up or down: Power distance belief and the asymmetric effect of vertical brand extension. In E. W. Wan & M. Zhang (Eds). *AP - Asia-Pacific advances in consumer research* (Vol. 11, pp. 183–184). Association for Consumer Research.

Lowin, R. (2017). *Did you ever wonder what happened to Colgate Lasagna?* Food & Wine.

Madan, S., Basu, S., Ng, S., & Ching Lim, E. A. (2018). Impact of culture on the pursuit of beauty: Evidence from five countries. *Journal of International Marketing*, 26(4), 54–68. https://doi.org/10.1177/1069031X18805493

Maddux, W. W., Yang, H., Falk, C., Adam, H., Adair, W., Endo, Y., Carmon, Z., & Heine, S. J. (2010). For whom is parting with possessions more painful? Cultural differences in the endowment effect. *Psychological Science*, 21(12), 1910–1917. https://doi.org/10.1177/0956797610388818

Maheswaran, D., & Shavitt, S. (2000). Issues and new directions in global consumer psychology. *Journal of Consumer Psychology*, 9(2), 59–66. https://doi.org/10.1207/S15327663JCP0902_1

Markus, H. R., & Conner, A. (2013). *Clash! 8 cultural conflicts that make us who we are*. Hudson Street Press.

Markus, H. R., & Kitayama, S. (1991). Culture and the self: Implications for cognition, emotion, and motivation. *Psychological Review*, 98(2), 224–253. https://doi.org/10.1037/0033-295X.98.2.224

McCracken, G. (1986). Culture and consumption: A theoretical account of the structure and movement of the cultural meaning of consumer goods. *Journal of Consumer Research*, 13(1), 71–84. https://doi.org/10.1086/209048

Miracle, G. E. (1987). Feel-do-learn: An alternative sequence underlying Japanese consumer response to television commercials. In *The proceedings of the 1987 conference of the American Academy of Advertising* (pp. R73–R78). University of South Carolina.

Mok, A., & Morris, M. W. (2013). Bicultural self-defense in consumer contexts: Self-protection motives are the basis for contrast versus assimilation to cultural cues. *Journal of Consumer Psychology*, 23(2), 175–188. https://doi.org/10.1016/j.jcps.2012.06.002

Monga, A. B., & John, D. R. (2007). Cultural differences in brand extension evaluation: The influence of analytic versus holistic thinking. *Journal of Consumer Research*, 33(4), 529–536. https://doi.org/10.1086/510227

Monga, A. B., & John, D. R. (2009). Understanding cultural differences in brand extension evaluation: The influence of analytic versus holistic thinking. In D. J. MacInnis, C. W. Park, & J. R. Priester (Eds.), *Handbook of brand relationships* (pp. 247–266). M. E. Sharpe.

Ng, A. H., & Hynie, M. (2014). Cultural differences in indecisiveness: The role of naïve dialecticism. *Personality and Individual Differences*, 70, 45–50. https://doi.org/10.1016/j.paid.2014.06.022

Ng, S., Kim, H., & Rao, A. R. (2015). Sins of omission versus commission: Cross-cultural differences in brand-switching due to dissatisfaction induced by individual versus group action and inaction. *Journal of Consumer Psychology*, 25(1), 89–100. https://doi.org/10.1016/j.jcps.2014.07.003

Nisbett, R. E. (2003). *The geography of thought: How Asians and Westerners think differently . . . and why*. Free Press.

Nisbett, R. E., Peng, K., Choi, I., & Norenzayan, A. (2001). Culture and systems of thought: Holistic versus analytic cognition. *Psychological Review*,

108(2), 291–310. https://doi.org/10.1037/0033-295X.108.2.291

Ogilvy, D. (1985). *Ogilvy on advertising*. Vintage Books.

Oishi, S., Schimmack, U., Diener, E., & Suh, E. M. (1998). The measurement of values and individualism-collectivism. *Personality and Social Psychology Bulletin*, 24(11), 1177–1189. https://doi.org/10.1177/01461672982411005

Oyserman, D., & Lee, S. W.-S. (2007). Priming "culture": Culture as situated cognition. In S. Kitayama & D. Cohen (Eds.), *Handbook of cultural psychology* (Vol. 2, pp. 255–279). Guilford Press.

Paharia, N., & Swaminathan, V. (2019). Who is wary of user design? The role of power-distance beliefs in preference for user-designed products. *Journal of Marketing*, 83(3), 91–107. https://doi.org/10.1177/0022242919830412

Pang, J., Keh, H. T., Li, X., & Maheswaran, D. (2017). "Every coin has two sides": The effects of dialectical thinking and attitudinal ambivalence on psychological discomfort and consumer choice. *Journal of Consumer Psychology*, 27(2), 218–230. https://doi.org/10.1016/j.jcps.2016.10.001

Paulhus, D. L. (1991). Measurement and control of response bias. In J. P. Robinson & P. R. Shaver (Eds.), *Measures of personality and social psychological attitudes* (pp. 17–59). Academic Press Inc. https://doi.org/10.1016/B978-0-12-590241-0.50006-X

Pelto, P. J. (1968). The differences between "tight" and "loose" societies. *Trans-Action*, 5(5), 37–40. https://doi.org/10.1007/BF03180447

Peng, K., & Nisbett, R. E. (1999). Culture, dialectics, and reasoning about contradiction. *American Psychologist*, 54(9), 741–754. https://doi.org/10.1037/0003-066X.54.9.741

Rao, V. P., & Rao, V. N. (1982). *Marriage, the family, and women in India*. South Asia Books.

Reed, I. I. A., II, Forehand, M. R., Puntoni, S., & Warlop, L. (2012). Identity-based consumer behavior. *International Journal of Research in Marketing*, 29(4), 310–321. https://doi.org/10.1016/j.ijresmar.2012.08.002

Riemer, H., & Shavitt, S. (2011). Impression management in survey responding: Easier for collectivists or individualists? *Journal of Consumer Psychology*, 21(2), 157–168. https://doi.org/10.1016/j.jcps.2010.10.001

Riemer, H., Shavitt, S., Koo, M., & Markus, H. R. (2014). Preferences don't have to be personal: Expanding attitude theorizing with a cross-cultural perspective. *Psychological Review*, 121(4), 619–648. https://doi.org/10.1037/a0037666

Savani, K., Markus, H. R., & Conner, A. L. (2008). Let your preference be your guide? Preferences and choices are more tightly linked for North Americans than for Indians. *Journal of Personality and Social Psychology*, 95(4), 861–876. https://doi.org/10.1037/a0011618

Savani, K., Wadhwa, M., Uchida, Y., Ding, Y., & Naidu, N. V. R. (2015). When norms loom larger than the self: Susceptibility of preference–choice consistency to normative influence across cultures. *Organizational Behavior and Human Decision Processes*, 129, 70–79. https://doi.org/10.1016/j.obhdp.2014.09.001

Schlosser, A., & Shavitt, S. (1999). Effects of an approaching group discussion on product responses. *Journal of Consumer Psychology*, 8(4), 377–406. https://doi.org/10.1207/s15327663jcp0804_02

Schwartz, S. H. (1992). Universals in the content and structure of values: Theoretical advances and empirical tests in 20 countries. In M. P. Zanna (Ed.), *Advances in experimental social psychology* (Vol. 25, pp. 1–65). Academic Press. https://doi.org/10.1016/S0065-2601(08)60281-6

Shavitt, S., & Barnes, A. J. (2019). Cross-cultural consumer psychology. *Consumer Psychology Review*, 2(1), 70–84. https://doi.org/10.1002/arcp.1047

Shavitt, S., & Barnes, A. J. (2020). Culture and the consumer journey. *Journal of Retailing*, 96(1), 40–54. https://doi.org/10.1016/j.jretai.2019.11.009

Shavitt, S., Johnson, T. P., & Zhang, J. (2011). Horizontal and vertical cultural differences in the content of advertising appeals. *Journal of International Consumer Marketing*, 23(3–4), 297–310.

Shavitt, S., & Koo, M. (2015). Categories of Cultural Variations. In S. Ng & A. Y. Lee (Eds.), *Handbook of culture and consumer behavior* (pp. 99–118). Oxford University Press. https://doi.org/10.1093/acprof:oso/9780199388516.003.0005

Shavitt, S., Lalwani, A. K., Zhang, J., & Torelli, C. J. (2006). The horizontal/vertical distinction in cross-cultural consumer research. *Journal of Consumer Psychology*, 16(4), 325–342. https://doi.org/10.1207/s15327663jcp1604_3

Sia, C. L., Lim, K. H., Leung, K., Lee, M. K., Huang, W. W., & Benbasat, I. (2009). Web strategies to promote internet shopping: Is cultural-customization needed? *Management Information Systems Quarterly*, 33(3), 491–512. https://doi.org/10.2307/20650306

Simpson, B., White, K., & Laran, J. (2018). When public recognition for charitable giving backfires: The role of independent self-construal. *Journal of Consumer Research*, 44(6), 1257–1273. https://doi.org/10.1093/jcr/ucx101

Singelis, T. M., Triandis, H. C., Bhawuk, D. P., & Gelfand, M. J. (1995). Horizontal and vertical dimensions of individualism and collectivism: A theoretical and measurement refinement. *Cross-Cultural Research*, 29(3), 240–275. https://doi.org/10.1177/106939719502900302

Swaminathan, V., Page, K. L., & Gürhan-Canli, Z. (2007). "My" brand or "our" brand: The effects of brand relationship dimensions and self-construal on brand evaluations. *Journal of Consumer Research*, *34*(2), 248–259. https://doi.org/10.1086/518539

Torelli, C. J. (2006). Individuality or conformity? The effect of independent and interdependent self-concepts on public judgments. *Journal of Consumer Psychology*, *16*(3), 240–248. https://doi.org/10.1207/s15327663jcp1603_6

Torelli, C. J. (2013). *Globalization, culture, and branding: How to leverage cultural equity for building iconic brands in the era of globalization*. Springer. https://doi.org/10.1057/9781137331953

Torelli, C. J., & Ahluwalia, R. (2012). Extending culturally symbolic brands: A blessing or a curse? *Journal of Consumer Research*, *38*(5), 933–947. https://doi.org/10.1086/661081

Torelli, C. J., Ahluwalia, R., Cheng, S. Y., Olson, N. J., & Stoner, J. L. (2017). Redefining home: How cultural distinctiveness affects the malleability of in-group boundaries and brand preferences. *Journal of Consumer Research*, *44*(1), 44–61.

Torelli, C. J., & Cheng, S. (2011). Cultural meanings of brands and consumption: A window into the cultural psychology of globalization. *Social and Personality Psychology Compass*, *5*(5), 251–262. https://doi.org/10.1111/j.1751-9004.2011.00349.x

Torelli, C. J., Chiu, C. Y., Tam, K. P., Au, A. K., & Keh, H. T. (2011). Exclusionary reactions to foreign cultures: Effects of simultaneous exposure to cultures in globalized space. *Journal of Social Issues*, *67*(4), 716–742. https://doi.org/10.1111/j.1540-4560.2011.01724.x

Torelli, C. J., Keh, H. T., & Chiu, C.-Y. (2010). Cultural symbolism of brands. In B. Loken, R. Ahluwalia, & M. J. Houston (Eds.), *Brands and brand management: Contemporary research perspectives* (pp. 113–132). Routledge.

Torelli, C. J., Leslie, L. M., Stoner, J. L., & Puente, R. (2014). Cultural determinants of status: Implications for workplace evaluations and behaviors. *Organizational Behavior and Human Decision Processes*, *123*(1), 34–48. https://doi.org/10.1016/j.obhdp.2013.11.001

Torelli, C. J., Leslie, L. M., To, C., & Kim, S. (2020). Power and status across cultures. *Current Opinion in Psychology*, *33*, 12–17. https://doi.org/10.1016/j.copsyc.2019.05.005

Torelli, C. J., Oh, H., & Stoner, J. L. (2020). Cultural equity: Knowledge and outcomes aspects. *International Marketing Review*, *38*(1), 99–123. https://doi.org/10.1108/IMR-12-2018-0366

Torelli, C. J., Özsomer, A., Carvalho, S. W., Keh, H. T., & Maehle, N. (2012). Brand concepts as representations of human values: Do cultural congruity and compatibility between values matter? *Journal of Marketing*, *76*(4), 92–108. https://doi.org/10.1509/jm.10.0400

Torelli, C. J., & Rodas, M. A. (2017). Tightness–looseness: Implications for consumer and branding research. *Journal of Consumer Psychology*, *27*(3), 398–404. https://doi.org/10.1016/j.jcps.2017.04.003

Torelli, C. J., & Shavitt, S. (2010). Culture and concepts of power. *Journal of Personality and Social Psychology*, *99*(4), 703–723. https://doi.org/10.1037/a0019973

Torelli, C. J., & Shavitt, S. (2011). The impact of power on information processing depends on cultural orientation. *Journal of Experimental Social Psychology*, *47*(5), 959–967. https://doi.org/10.1016/j.jesp.2011.04.003

Torelli, C. J., Shavitt, S., Cho, Y. I., Holbrook, A. L., Johnson, T. P., & Weiner, S. (2015). Justice or compassion? Cultural differences in power norms affect consumer satisfaction with power-holders. *International Marketing Review*, *32*(3/4), 279–306. https://doi.org/10.1108/IMR-09-2013-0222

Triandis, H. C. (1989). The self and social behavior in differing cultural contexts. *Psychological Review*, *96*(3), 506–520. https://doi.org/10.1037/0033-295X.96.3.506

Triandis, H. C. (1995). *Individualism & collectivism*. Westview Press.

Triandis, H. C. (2012). Culture and conflict. In L. A. Samovar, R. E. Porter, & E. R. McDaniel (Eds.), *Intercultural communication: A reader* (Vol. 13, pp. 34–45). Wadsworth.

Triandis, H. C., & Gelfand, M. J. (1998). Converging measurement of horizontal and vertical individualism and collectivism. *Journal of Personality and Social Psychology*, *74*(1), 118–128. https://doi.org/10.1037/0022-3514.74.1.118

Wang, J. J., Torelli, C. J., & Lalwani, A. K. (2020). The interactive effect of power distance belief and consumers' status on preference for national (vs. private-label) brands. *Journal of Business Research*, *107*, 1–12. https://doi.org/10.1016/j.jbusres.2019.10.001

Watanabe, M. (1974). The conception of nature in Japanese culture. *Science*, *183*(4122), 279–282. https://doi.org/10.1126/science.183.4122.279

Winterich, K. P., Gangwar, M., & Grewal, R. (2018). When celebrities count: Power distance beliefs and celebrity endorsements. *Journal of Marketing*, *82*(3), 70–86. https://doi.org/10.1509/jm.16.0169

Wu, R., Steffel, M., & Shavitt, S. (2021). Buying gifts for multiple recipients: How culture affects whose desires are prioritized. *Journal of Business*

Research, *132*(C), 10–20. https://doi.org/10.1016/j.jbusres.2021.04.005

Yang, H., Stamatogiannakis, A., & Chattopadhyay, A. (2015). Pursuing attainment versus maintenance goals: The interplay of self-construal and goal type on consumer motivation. *Journal of Consumer Research*, *42*(1), 93–108. https://doi.org/10.1093/jcr/ucv008

Yoon, S. O., Suk, K., Lee, S. M., & Park, E. Y. (2011). To seek variety or uniformity: The role of culture in consumers' choice in a group setting. *Marketing Letters*, *22*(1), 49–64. https://doi.org/10.1007/s11002-010-9102-5

Zhang, Y., & Gelb, B. D. (1996). Matching advertising appeals to culture: The influence of products' use conditions. *Journal of Advertising*, *25*(3), 29–46. https://doi.org/10.1080/00913367.1996.10673505

Zhang, Y., & Shrum, L. J. (2009). The influence of self-construal on impulsive consumption. *Journal of Consumer Research*, *35*(5), 838–850. https://doi.org/10.1086/593687

Zhang, Y., Winterich, K. P., & Mittal, V. (2010). Power distance belief and impulsive buying. *Journal of Marketing Research*, *47*(5), 945–954. https://doi.org/10.1509/jmkr.47.5.945

Zhu, R., & Meyers-Levy, J. (2009). The influence of self-view on context effects: How display fixtures can affect product evaluations. *Journal of Marketing Research*, *46*(1), 37–45. https://doi.org/10.1509/jmkr.46.1.37

CHAPTER 13

ATTITUDE CHANGE AND PERSUASION: CLASSIC, METACOGNITIVE, AND ADVOCACY PERSPECTIVES

Zakary L. Tormala and Derek D. Rucker

Attitudes—the general and relatively enduring evaluations people form of other people, objects, or ideas—have been a central focus of consumer psychology research for decades. In essence, attitudes represent people's likes and dislikes, or the extent to which people hold positive or negative views of an object or entity (e.g., a product, brand, service, or political candidate). The study of attitudes is integral to consumer psychology (Haugtvedt & Kasmer, 2008; Petty et al., 1991; Tormala & Briñol, 2015), in part because attitudes are a key factor in predicting and guiding behavior (Ajzen, 2005; Bechler et al., 2021; Glasman & Albarracín, 2006). Consumers who hold positive and negative attitudes toward a product or brand, for example, tend to act in disparate ways with respect to that product or brand. Generally speaking, consumers are more likely to choose and purchase, more inclined to recommend, and more willing to pay for a product or brand if they hold a positive rather than negative attitude toward it. Given the crucial role attitudes can play in guiding behavioral outcomes, substantial research effort has been directed toward understanding attitudes, where they come from, and how they change. Within consumer psychology, particular attention has been paid to persuasion—that is, toward illuminating the effects of persuasive communications on people's attitudes.

The aim of this chapter is to provide a general overview of classic and contemporary research on attitude change and persuasion. To this end, we review three major developments that correspond with what we see as three general perspectives in attitude change and persuasion research. First, we explore what we term *classic perspectives*—the early views on persuasion that form the pillars of modern-day research in this domain. Second, we explore *metacognitive perspectives* that built on classic work to delineate how people's thoughts about their own attitudes and thought processes drive persuasion outcomes. Finally, we discuss *advocacy perspectives*—research focused on identifying the causes and consequences of generating persuasive advocacy—to review what we believe captures current momentum in persuasion research. First, though, some basic background is warranted.

THE ATTITUDE CONSTRUCT

An *attitude* captures one's evaluative assessment of a target entity. People can form and hold attitudes toward virtually anything: other people (e.g., politicians, CEOs), objects (e.g., shoes, cars), brands (e.g., Nike, Starbucks), issues (e.g., capital punishment, abortion), policies (e.g., a new tax law, workplace policy), and so on. Importantly, though, attitudes vary in ways that are critical to determining how they will influence behavior and shape people's responses to persuasive messages. First, at their core, attitudes vary according to their valence and extremity. The *valence* of an attitude is essentially its sign—whether the attitude is positive, negative, or neutral. For instance, some consumers might like Starbucks, some might dislike Starbucks, and some might be neutral or have no real leaning either way. Attitudes can also differ in their extremity. *Extremity* refers to the degree to which an attitude deviates from neutrality (Abelson, 1995). Two consumers could both like Starbucks, for example, but differ in how much they like it. One could be moderately positive and view Starbucks coffee as decent, whereas the other could be extremely positive and view the coffee as amazing. If true, we would expect different behaviors from these consumers (e.g., different consumption rates, different willingness to pay) even though they both have positive attitudes toward the brand.

Attitudes also vary in their underlying *basis*, or origin. The tripartite theory of attitudes (Bagozzi et al., 1979; Breckler, 1984; Rosenberg et al., 1960) suggests that attitudes can be rooted to different degrees in affect, cognition, and behavior. Attitudes based on affect are rooted in people's feelings (e.g., "I feel happy when I walk into a Starbucks cafe"). Attitudes based on cognition are rooted in people's beliefs (e.g., "I believe Starbucks has well-trained baristas"). Finally, attitudes based on behavior are rooted in people's past or present behavior (e.g., "I go to Starbucks every morning, so clearly I like it"). Research suggests that both the actual basis (Fabrigar & Petty, 1999) and people's perception of their attitude basis (See et al., 2008) can influence persuasion. In general, persuasive messages tend to be more effective when they match rather than mismatch the basis of the target attitude. For example, an affective appeal is more effective against affective attitudes and a cognitive appeal is more effective against cognitive attitudes (Edwards, 1990; Fabrigar & Petty, 1999; Mayer & Tormala, 2010; Teeny et al., 2021; cf. Millar & Millar, 1990).

In addition to their bases, attitudes can differ in their underlying strength. *Attitude strength* refers to an attitude's durability and impact (Krosnick & Petty, 1995). Attitudes that are *durable* are more resistant to persuasion and more naturally persistent over time. For example, compared with someone with a weak favorable attitude toward Starbucks, a consumer with a strong favorable attitude is less likely to be swayed to stop using Starbucks in favor of a local coffeehouse and more likely to continue liking Starbucks over time. Attitudes that are *impactful* exert a stronger influence on people's thoughts and behaviors. Compared with the person with a weak favorable attitude toward Starbucks, for instance, the one with a strong favorable attitude might be willing to pay more for Starbucks coffee or travel farther to get Starbucks coffee instead of going to a competitor nearby. Understanding attitude strength and the factors that give rise to it deepens our insight into how persuadable people are and how likely they are to engage in attitude-consistent behavior.

Research on attitude strength has revealed numerous aspects of people's attitudes, and people's perceptions of their attitudes, that dictate how strong or weak those attitudes will be (see Bassili, 1996; Krosnick & Petty, 1995). One classic marker of attitude strength is attitude extremity. The more extreme the attitude, the more durable and impactful it tends to be (Abelson, 1995). However, extreme attitudes can be weak and moderate attitudes can be strong if they have other properties (e.g., Litt & Tormala, 2010). To offer a few additional examples, attitude strength generally increases as attitudes become less ambivalent (Thompson et al., 1995), more accessible (i.e., Fazio, 1995), more personally important (Boninger et al., 1995), or more certain (Rucker et al., 2014; Tormala & Rucker, 2018). Attitude certainty has been especially integral to the study of persuasion in recent years, and we return to it later in the chapter.

Finally, some scholars have argued that attitudes and attitude measures can vary in the extent to which they are implicit or explicit (see Payne & Gawronski, 2010; Petty et al., 2008). *Implicit* measures are those that tap into people's automatic evaluations and associations without directly asking them to report their attitudes, whereas *explicit* measures assess more deliberative and consciously professed attitudes by asking people about their attitudes directly. Although some research has explored the effects of persuasive messages on implicit attitudes (Briñol et al., 2008; Perkins & Forehand, 2010; C. T. Smith et al., 2013), the bulk of the persuasion literature (and the consumer psychology literature more generally) has focused on people's explicit attitudes. Thus, in this chapter, we focus primarily on explicit attitudes.

PERSUASION: WHO SAYS WHAT TO WHOM AND WHEN

Although psychologists have been interested in various aspects of attitudes for nearly a century (e.g., Allport, 1935; LaPiere, 1934; Thurstone, 1928), persuasion research began in earnest about 70 years ago in an effort to understand wartime propaganda (Hovland et al., 1953). This early work focused on understanding what made persuasion more versus less effective, and it laid the foundation for persuasion research as we know it today. Of particular import and endurance, early persuasion research identified four central variables—or pillars—that continue to guide theoretical and empirical developments in this domain: source, message, audience, and context. In another form, these variables can be captured by the following expression: *Who* says *what* to *whom* and *when*?

To elaborate, a first pillar in the study of persuasion is the *source*—the person, firm, or organization (i.e., the who) that delivers a message or communication. The source could be a friend, company, politician, online influencer, or spokesperson in a commercial, to offer a few examples. A second pillar is the message itself (i.e., the what). What type of message is delivered? What kind of arguments does the message contain? The audience, or recipient of a message (i.e., the whom), represents a third pillar in persuasion research. Audience factors include demographics (e.g., age, gender, and education) as well as psychographics (e.g., personality, aspirations, and attitudes). Finally, over time, persuasion researchers began to recognize the importance of the *context* of the delivery of a persuasive message (i.e., the when), which we view as a fourth pillar. These variables offered a framework for classic perspectives in persuasion research and provide theoretical pillars that have shaped subsequent metacognitive and advocacy-focused perspectives as well. Thus, we use them as a framework for our review.

CLASSIC PERSPECTIVES

First, we use the distinctions among source, message, audience, and context factors to review classic perspectives in persuasion research, as these perspectives laid the foundation for contemporary insights in this domain.

Source Factors: Who Delivers the Message?

A great deal of research reveals that characteristics or attributes of the source of a message can have a profound effect on the persuasive impact of that message. And this effect can be independent of the message itself. Indeed, the exact same message can be more or less persuasive simply by virtue of being associated with one source or another.

One of the most studied source factors is *source credibility* (Kelman & Hovland, 1953). Credible sources are defined as those that possess *expertise* (i.e., knowledge of the topic or domain) and *trustworthiness* (i.e., motivation to provide accurate information). The expertise of a source suggests that the source has the ability to provide accurate information, whereas the trustworthiness of the source suggests the source is motivated to do so. Early research showed that high credibility sources produced more persuasion than low credibility sources (Kelman, 1958; Mills & Jellison, 1967). However, as we review in our discussion of context, subsequent research suggested that although the dominant effect of credibility is that it enhances persuasion, this effect is malleable. Increasing the credibility of a source can also decrease persuasion under some conditions (e.g., Priester & Petty, 1995, 2003).

Separate from the credibility of the source, the likability of a source can also affect persuasion. Sources can be liked because of their physical attractiveness, familiarity, or similarity to an audience. For example, M. Snyder and Rothbart (1971) found that physically attractive sources were more persuasive than physically unattractive sources. Likewise, celebrity sources have been found to be more persuasive than unfamiliar sources (Petty et al., 1983). In addition, sources that share similarities with the target, such as the same birthday, have been found to be more persuasive than those that do not (Jiang et al., 2010; see also Finch & Cialdini, 1989).

Sources with more power or authority can also be more persuasive (Festinger & Thibaut, 1951; French & Raven, 1959). This effect might operate in part through credibility, such that those who obtain positions of power or authority are perceived to have greater expertise and trustworthiness. In addition, those with power or authority might be liked, respected, or admired. Some research suggests that powerful sources induce compliance as opposed to actual attitude change (Kelman, 1958), however, which implies that source power and/or authority effects on persuasion might be more superficial and less internalized, in at least some cases.

Message Factors: What Does the Message Say?

One of the most salient aspects of a message is the position it takes. In general, a message can be proattitudinal (i.e., it argues for a position that the audience agrees with or wants to accept), counterattitudinal (i.e., it argues for a position that the audience disagrees with or wants to reject), or neutral (i.e., the audience is indifferent to the position). Early research demonstrated that people tend to be more receptive to proattitudinal information than counterattitudinal information, at least in part because people process information in a biased manner to support their existing attitudes (e.g., Lord et al., 1979; see Clark & Wegener, 2013).

Related to the message position is whether a message is one-sided or two-sided (Hovland et al., 1949). A one-sided message, per its moniker, focuses on a single position or side, such as an advertisement that puts forth all the reasons to buy a car or a public service announcement that argues with fervor against drunk driving. In contrast, a two-sided message presents arguments in favor and against a position. For example, for legal reasons, pharmaceutical companies disclose the benefits and side effects of their products. Research has shown that two-sided messages can be more persuasive because they increase the perceived trustworthiness of the message source (Crowley & Hoyer, 1994; Pechmann, 1992) and bias people's assessment of other attributes. For example, adding a minor negative or downside in an otherwise positive message can make the positive arguments seem even more favorable by comparison (Ein-Gar et al., 2012).

Of course, another important message factor is its content: what is actually said. Perhaps the most studied factor with regard to message content is whether the message contains strong (i.e., compelling or cogent) or weak (i.e., unconvincing or specious) arguments. All else equal, people tend to be more persuaded by strong compared with weak arguments (see Petty & Cacioppo, 1986). For example, Krause and Rucker (2020) found that presenting strong product facts or attributes led to more persuasion compared with presenting weak product facts or attributes. One reason that people are more persuaded by strong arguments is that they tend to trigger more favorable thoughts in recipients. Of course, for strong arguments to promote persuasion, recipients must be sufficiently motivated and able to attend to and think about those arguments. If people are unmotivated or unable to process a message, the persuasive advantage of strong arguments tends to decline (Petty & Cacioppo, 1986). For example, when facts are buried in a story, people's ability to discriminate between strong and weak ones can be hindered, which limits their persuasive impact (Krause & Rucker, 2020).

Independent of argument strength or quality, several other message factors have been shown to affect persuasion. For example, Petty and Cacioppo (1984) found that people were more persuaded when a message contained a larger number of arguments compared with a smaller number of arguments (see also Calder et al., 1974). In some cases, people treat the number of arguments as an indicator of the strength of support for a position or product, consistent with a "more is better" heuristic (Pelham et al., 1994). Message repetition can also affect persuasion. In particular, research has shown that some message repetition can increase persuasion, but too much repetition can decrease persuasion (see Cacioppo & Petty, 1979; Calder & Sternthal, 1980). One explanation for this finding is that some repetition helps people understand the strength of the arguments, but too much leads people to counterargue or dilute the message's compelling arguments with their own weaker points (Anand & Sternthal, 1987).

Audience Factors: Who Receives the Message?

As noted, audience factors include both demographics and psychographics. Moreover, audience factors can range from relatively stable to more malleable. On the more stable side, for example, some research has explored the relationship between intelligence and persuasion, finding that as intelligence increased so too did people's ability to counterargue a message, which reduced persuasion (Rhodes & Wood, 1992). On the more malleable side, prior research also attests to the importance of situational audience factors, such as one's current mood (Biggers & Pryor, 1982).

Indeed, considerable research points to the importance of the audience's emotional state in guiding persuasion processes and outcomes. For example, early research suggested that placing people in a positive mood led to greater persuasion compared with a neutral or negative mood (Biggers & Pryor, 1982; McGuire, 1985). One explanation was that mood creates a conditioned response with the stimulus (i.e., the message or attitude object), such that when people encounter the stimulus they associate it with the positive mood they had experienced. Subsequent research replicated and moderated this finding and provided insight into the multiple mechanisms driving mood effects in persuasion (see Petty et al., 1993; Wegener et al., 1995). For example, Petty et al. (1993) demonstrated that positive mood could act as a cue to persuasion or bias people's thoughts by making positive content more likely to come to mind.

Another audience factor that affects persuasion is the audience's motivation to think about the content of a persuasive message. For example, Cacioppo et al. (1983) examined the role of individual differences in participants' need for cognition—that is, the extent to which people enjoy and engage in effortful thinking (Cacioppo & Petty, 1982)—in persuasion. Petty et al. (1983) found that individuals high in need for cognition were more likely to scrutinize information presented compared with those low in need for cognition. As a result, people were more likely to be influenced by message content when they were high rather than low in need for cognition. Specifically, participants high in need for cognition showed more persuasion in response to strong relative to weak arguments, whereas participants low in need for cognition showed weaker differentiation. As we discuss next, this research helped set the stage for the development of subsequent context-focused models of persuasion.

In addition to need for cognition, a number of other audience factors can influence the persuasion process. As one example, the fluency or ease people experience as they process information can affect how persuaded they are by a message. In general, the easier people find it to process a message or think about a brand or product, the more favorable their resultant attitudes tend to be (e.g., Labroo et al., 2008; Lee & Labroo, 2004; Wänke et al., 1997). Message recipients' need for cognitive closure can also dictate the persuasive impact of a message. For example, provided they have sufficient information to form an initial opinion, high need for closure individuals have been shown to be more resistant to persuasion than their low need for closure counterparts (Kruglanski et al., 1993). Interestingly, though, increased need for closure has been associated with increased openness to persuasion tactics that deliver closure (Kardes et al., 2007). Moreover, the audience's overt physical behavior can influence their openness to persuasion. For instance, nodding one's head while processing a message can affect one's agreement with that message (e.g., Wells & Petty, 1980).

A summary of classic perspectives on source, message, and audience factors is provided in Figure 13.1. This figure also introduces a final factor that we consider next: context.

Context Factors: When and How Is the Message Processed?

As research on attitude change and persuasion proliferated in the early years, a conundrum arose: Persuasion studies began to contradict each other. For example, whereas some research revealed that distraction was bad for persuasion (Hovland et al., 1953), other research suggested the opposite (Festinger & MacCoby, 1964; for a review, see Petty

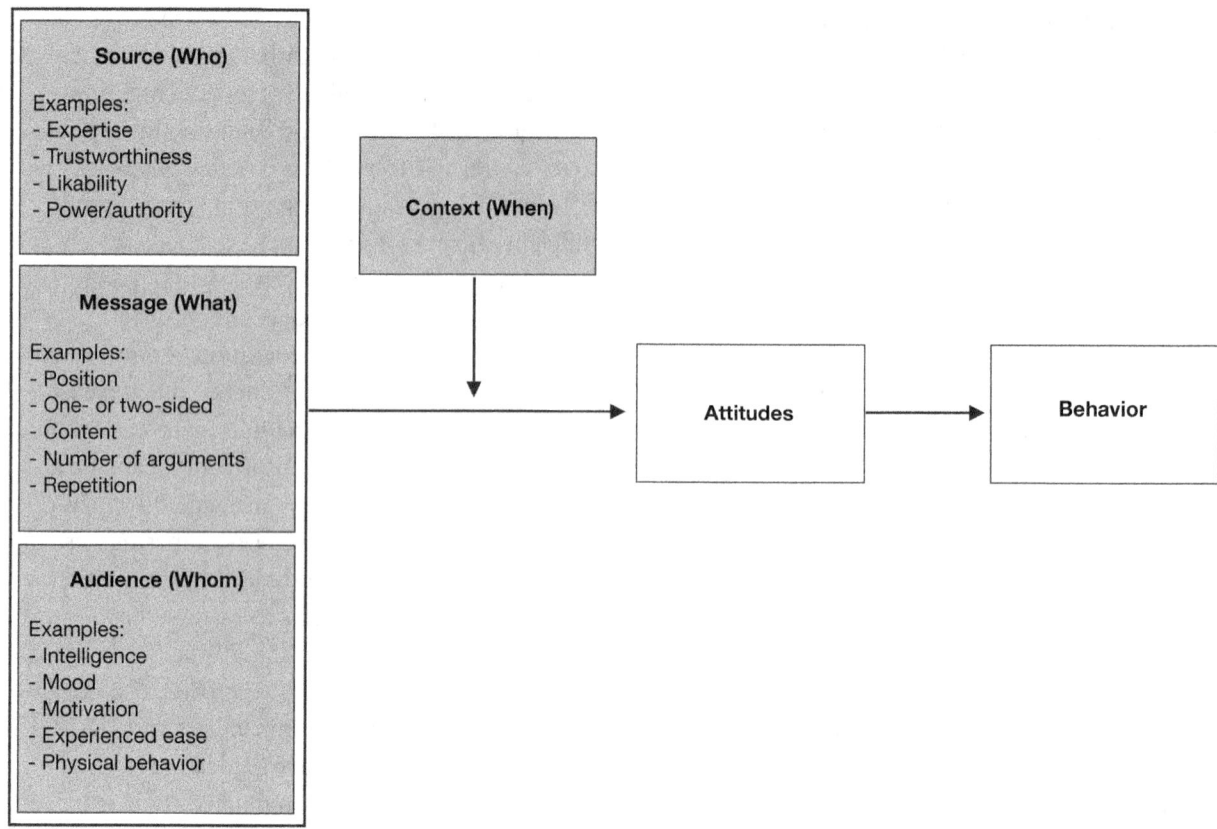

FIGURE 13.1. Classic perspectives: Source, message, audience, and context factors.

& Brock, 1981). Likewise, as noted already, the audience's need for cognition appeared to increase or decrease persuasion, depending on the circumstances. At first blush, these conflicting findings threatened the very foundation of attitude change and persuasion research. If a variable cannot be meaningfully or reliably linked to any particular outcome, how could anyone use this research to inform practice?

Fortunately, these conflicting findings set the stage for a significant development in persuasion research. Researchers moved from seeking to understand whether a variable increased or decreased persuasion to understanding when a variable increased or decreased persuasion (for an insightful discussion, see Petty et al., 1997). That is, researchers started to ask how the context in which persuasion occurred affected whether a given variable increased or decreased persuasion. Indeed, arguably the most prominent development in persuasion research over the last several decades was the arrival and articulation of the elaboration likelihood (ELM; Petty & Cacioppo, 1986) and heuristic-systematic (HSM; Chaiken et al., 1989) models of persuasion. These were multiprocess theories that delineated the critical role of contextual factors in shaping persuasion processes and outcomes.

In essence, both the ELM and HSM suggest that persuasion variables (i.e., source, message, and audience factors) can affect persuasion in different ways or through distinct processes, depending on message recipients' extent of thinking—that is, their motivation and ability to carefully process the message or issue at hand. These models contend that under low-thinking conditions (i.e., low elaboration or heuristic processing), variables affect persuasion primarily by serving as simple heuristics or cues. Under high-thinking conditions (i.e., high elaboration or systematic processing), variables affect persuasion through more deliberative or elaborative processes, such as by directing the type of thoughts that come to mind or by serving as substantive evidence (i.e., an argument). When thinking is not constrained to be low or high, variables can affect an audience's degree of thought about the message or issue at hand. Both models further contend that the process through which persuasion occurs has implications for the strength (i.e., durability and impact) of the resultant attitudes. The ELM, for example, articulates that attitudes formed or changed via high elaboration, or more thoughtful processing, are more likely to influence behavior than attitudes formed or changed via low elaboration, or more heuristic processing (for further discussion, see Petty et al., 1995).

As one example of both the importance and power of such multiprocess models, consider source credibility. As noted, early research suggested that high credibility sources increased persuasion relative to low credibility sources (Kelman, 1958; Mills & Jellison, 1967). One view of this effect was that it reflected a simple learned heuristic that people with credibility (e.g., expertise) are usually correct (see Chaiken, 1980). However, according to the ELM and HSM, heuristics are just one possible means through which source credibility can affect persuasion. Source credibility can operate through other channels as well and, as a result, it can have positive and negative effects on persuasion. For instance, Priester and Petty (1995) demonstrated that when people were not inclined to pay attention or think carefully about a message, a source lacking trustworthiness increased their motivation to process deeply. As a result of increased processing, people became more sensitive to the strength of the arguments in the message. When arguments were weak, a source low in trustworthiness elicited less persuasion than a source high in trustworthiness because increased message scrutiny (under low trust) helped people recognize that the arguments were vacuous. In contrast, when arguments were strong, a source low in trustworthiness led to more persuasion than a source high in trustworthiness because increased message scrutiny helped people recognize that the arguments were sound (see also Priester & Petty, 2003). Other research has uncovered further mechanisms through which source credibility can affect persuasion. For example, when the motivation to think is already high, source credibility appears to bias the types of thoughts that come to mind. In general, under high thought conditions, high (low) credibility sources trigger more favorable (unfavorable) message-relevant thoughts (see Chaiken & Maheswaran, 1994; Tormala, Briñol, & Petty, 2007).

Source credibility represents just one example of how the context can shape the role a given variable plays in persuasion. Other variables—including the audience's mood (Petty et al., 1993), power (Briñol, Petty, Valle, et al., 2007), feelings of ease (Briñol et al., 2013), and overt head movements (Briñol & Petty, 2003)—have similarly been shown to affect persuasion through multiple contextually dependent roles (for additional reviews, see Petty et al., 2004; Petty & Wegener, 1998).

METACOGNITIVE PERSPECTIVES

Following the classic models and extensive research investigating source, message, audience, and context factors in persuasion, considerable work in the past 2 decades has shifted to address how people reflect on persuasion processes and outcomes. That is, many researchers have turned their attention toward the role of metacognitive factors in persuasion. In essence, metacognition refers to thinking about thinking—for example, the thoughts people have about their own thoughts, attitudes, and judgments (see Petty et al., 2007). Over the past 20 years or so, persuasion researchers have been especially interested in psychological certainty, or confidence, as a central metacognitive variable. Of particular import has been the certainty people associate with their thoughts (termed *thought confidence*) and attitudes (termed *attitude certainty*). In this section, we summarize research exploring the roles of thought confidence and attitude certainty in persuasion. We organize this review around the four pillars described earlier: source effects, message effects, audience effects, and context effects. Before turning to our review, we offer some background information and a clarification.

First, work on the self-validation hypothesis (Briñol, Petty, & Tormala, 2004; Petty et al., 2002) has examined the role of thought confidence in persuasion. Thought confidence refers to the subjective sense of validity people have about their thoughts. For example, a consumer might read a product review and generate thoughts in response to that review (e.g., "The first point makes sense," "I'm not sure that second point is relevant to me"). Depending on a host of factors, these thoughts can be held with varying degrees of confidence. The consumer might be very confident of some thoughts and less confident of others or might feel globally confident or doubtful about the full set. Research on the self-validation hypothesis suggests that thoughts held with greater confidence have more impact on people's attitudes. For example, if the consumer in question has mostly positive thoughts and feels confident about them, they would likely form a positive attitude. If they have mostly negative thoughts and feel confident about them, they would be more likely to form a negative attitude. Conversely, if the consumer has positive or negative thoughts but lacks thought confidence, those thoughts would have less consequence for their ultimate attitude. Thus, the self-validation hypothesis proposes that persuasion is dependent not only on the amount and valence of people's thoughts but also on the feelings of confidence they associate with those thoughts.

In other work, researchers have focused on attitude certainty. Attitude certainty refers to the subjective sense of confidence or conviction a person has about their attitude (Rucker et al., 2014; Tormala & Rucker, 2007, 2018) or the feeling they have that their attitude is clear and correct (Petrocelli et al., 2007). Attitude certainty has a long history in attitudes research (see Gross et al., 1995), but its standing as a central variable in the persuasion process is a more recent development (for reviews, see Rucker et al., 2014; Tormala & Rucker, 2018). This rise stems in part from research on resistance to persuasion, which demonstrated that when people resisted or tried to resist persuasive messages, they sometimes became more or less certain of their attitudes than they were to begin with (e.g., Rucker & Petty, 2004; Tormala, Clarkson, & Petty, 2006; Tormala & Petty, 2002). These shifts in attitude certainty, in turn, are extremely important: The more certain people are of their attitudes, the stronger those attitudes tend to be. Indeed, even after controlling for attitude valence and extremity, high certainty attitudes tend to be more durable (e.g., resistant to change) and impactful (e.g., predictive of behavior) than their low certainty counterparts (Bassili, 1996; see Tormala & Rucker, 2018, for a review). Thus, understanding attitude certainty, where it comes from, and what it does is important for persuasion research.

As a final note, although researchers tend to use the terms *confidence* and *certainty* to capture the feelings of validity or conviction people have about their thoughts and attitudes, respectively, we view the terms as essentially synonymous. That is, for our purposes, confidence and certainty themselves have no qualitative distinction beyond normative or stylistic differences in terminology across subareas of persuasion research. However, in the context of a persuasive message, *thought* confidence and *attitude* certainty do differ in that thought confidence moderates the relationship between thoughts and attitudes, whereas attitude certainty moderates the relationship between attitudes and behavior (see Figure 13.2).

Source Effects on Certainty

Source effects have been examined with respect to both thought confidence and attitude certainty. Consider the effect of source credibility. As discussed earlier, past research suggests that, under specifiable conditions, high credibility sources (i.e., sources with expertise and trustworthiness) are more persuasive than low credibility sources. This effect stems at least partly from the fact that credible sources are perceived to have access to more valid information (e.g., Kaufman et al., 1999). However, beyond making information more persuasive, this perception of validity can also affect metacognitive certainty. Generally speaking, the more credible the source of a message, the more certain people feel about their own thoughts and attitudes after processing that message. In essence, people feel more certain when their thoughts and attitudes are based on information they perceive to be more valid. And, notably, this effect is independent of the persuasiveness of the message itself.

In studies testing the effect of source credibility on thought confidence (e.g., Briñol, Petty, & Tormala, 2004; Tormala, Briñol, & Petty, 2006, 2007), participants received persuasive messages from sources varying in expertise and trustworthiness

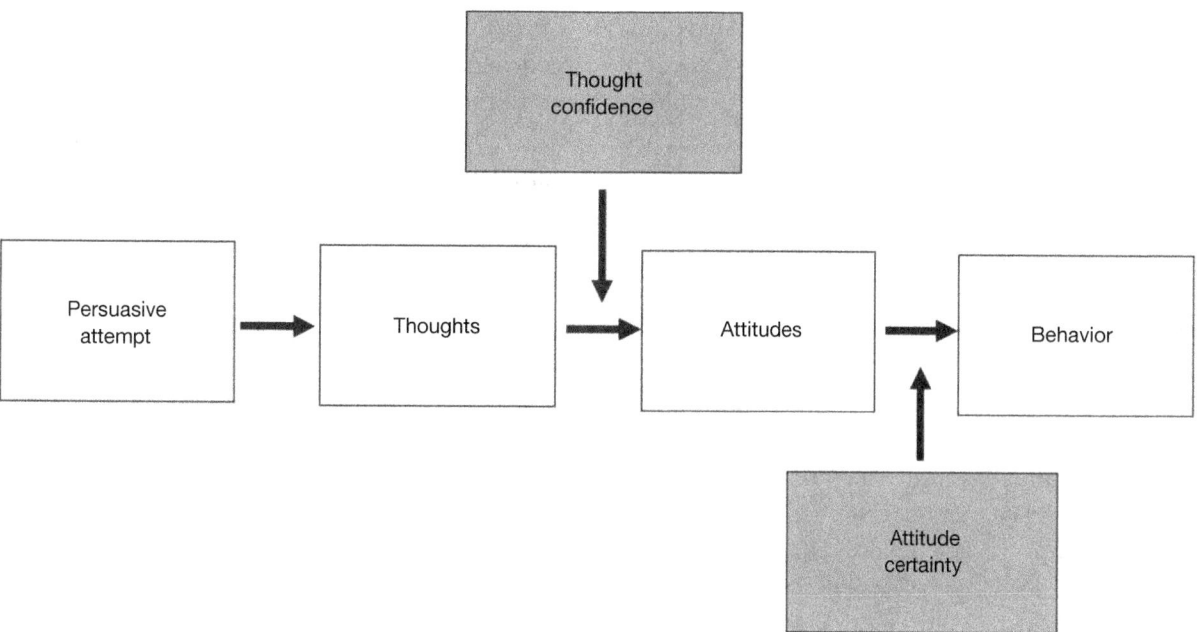

FIGURE 13.2. Metacognitive perspectives: The moderating roles of thought confidence and attitude certainty.

and subsequently reported their thoughts and attitudes. Results indicated that people generally feel more confident about their message-relevant thoughts under high rather than low credibility conditions. Importantly, though, this boost in thought confidence can either facilitate or hinder persuasion. Tormala, Briñol, and Petty (2006) found that when a message contains strong arguments, and thus elicits favorable thoughts, high credibility enhances persuasion because it increases confidence in favorable thoughts. However, when a message contains weak arguments, and thus elicits unfavorable thoughts, high credibility can backfire and undermine persuasion. This backfire effect occurs because people are less persuaded when they are confident about unfavorable thoughts. In short, source credibility can promote or undermine persuasion by making people more reliant on their thoughts, whether those thoughts are positive or negative toward the message and attitude object.

Source credibility can also affect attitude certainty. In general, people feel more certain of their attitudes following messages from high rather than low credibility sources (e.g., Clarkson et al., 2008). As with thought confidence, this effect can occur independent of the message's persuasive impact. For example, Tormala and Petty (2004a) presented participants with a message from a high or low credibility source and induced these participants to resist the message by counterarguing it. They found that participants became more certain of their attitudes—their original attitudes, which they had just defended—in the high but not the low credibility condition. In other words, resisting a message from a high credibility source increased attitude certainty, but resisting a message from a low credibility source did not. Thus, regardless of whether a message persuades its audience or not, it tends to produce greater attitude certainty when it comes from a high rather than low credibility source. This effect, in turn, boosts attitude–behavior correspondence.

In addition to source credibility, the source's numerical status—specifically, whether it is in the majority or minority on the issue at hand—can affect feelings of certainty. In a study testing the effect of numerical status on thought confidence, Horcajo et al. (2010) presented participants with a strong or weak persuasive message from a majority or minority source. Horcajo and colleagues found that participants felt more confident about their thoughts in the majority rather than minority condition, which facilitated persuasion when the message contained strong arguments (and produced favorable thoughts) but undermined persuasion when the message contained weak arguments (and produced unfavorable thoughts). As with source credibility, then, numerical status can help or hinder persuasion depending on message strength, because it affects the confidence with which people hold their underlying thoughts.

A source's numerical status can also affect attitude certainty. Tormala, DeSensi, and Petty (2007) explored the possibility that reductions in attitude certainty might play a role in minority influence. It is well-documented that although majority sources tend to be more persuasive than minority sources, there are conditions under which minority sources show increased impact (e.g., delayed attitude change; for reviews, see Tormala et al., 2009; Wood et al., 1994). Tormala, DeSensi, and Petty suggested that one potential account for this finding is that although people tend to resist minority sources in the immediate situation, they might feel uncertain of their attitudes after doing so, because dismissing a message due solely to its minority source feels illegitimate. Their findings supported this account. Participants initially resisted messages from minority sources but felt less certain about their attitudes after doing so, which opened them up to a subsequent message advocating in the same direction as the first.

Message Effects on Certainty

Although there is a dearth of research investigating message effects on thought confidence, considerable evidence reveals message effects on attitude certainty. Perhaps the most basic feature of a message is its valence—that is, whether it contains positive or negative information. Recent research suggests that people feel more certain of their attitudes toward something when they receive positive rather than negative information about it. In particular, A. I. Snyder and Tormala (2017) found that people reported more (less) attitude certainty after receiving entirely positive (negative) information about a target person. The argument was that when people receive negative information about a novel stimulus, that negativity conflicts with the default positivity people tend to have toward new entities (positivity offset; Cacioppo et al., 1997), which sparks subjective ambivalence and feelings of attitude uncertainty.

It remains to be determined whether this effect is moderated by familiarity with or knowledge about the attitude object, but the A. I. Snyder and Tormala results suggest that information valence affects attitude certainty and other properties of attitude strength.

As discussed earlier, another central feature of a message is its position—that is, the extent to which a message is pro- or counterattitudinal, or agrees or disagrees with recipients' initial attitudes. In general, people feel more certain of their attitudes after receiving proattitudinal information. As a classic illustration, consider research on attitude consensus effects. Numerous studies have revealed that people feel more certain of their attitudes after receiving high rather than low consensus feedback—for example, when they learn that a majority rather than a minority of other people share their view (e.g., Cheatham & Tormala, 2015; Petrocelli et al., 2007; Petty et al., 2002; Visser & Mirabile, 2004). In essence, high consensus feedback acts as a proattitudinal message in that it provides information that is consistent with the recipient's existing attitude. Notably, however, the effect is moderated by people's need for uniqueness: People who seek uniqueness or differentiation have been found to be more validated by low consensus feedback (e.g., learning that very few people share their views; Clarkson, Tormala, et al., 2013).

Message strength affects attitude certainty as well. For instance, in studies testing the effect of resisting persuasion on attitude certainty, Tormala and Petty (2002) found that when people counterargue and resist persuasive attacks, the stronger those attacks appear to be, the more certain people become of their attitudes. In fact, even when people resisted the exact same message, the mere perception (e.g., label or description) of it as a strong or weak influenced attitude certainty. People felt more certain if they believed a message was considered strong but not if they believed it was considered weak (Tormala & Petty, 2002, 2004b). The rationale is that when people resist persuasion, they appraise their resistance and assess its implications for the validity of their original position. If they resisted a strong message, it is perceived as more diagnostic with respect to their attitude's validity, which boosts attitude certainty (see also Rucker et al., 2014; Tormala, Clarkson, & Petty, 2006).

People also feel more certain of their attitudes when they perceive those attitudes to be based on more complete information. For instance, people report greater certainty following messages containing more rather than less information (S. M. Smith et al., 2008), even when that information does not increase their objective accuracy (e.g., Tsai et al., 2008; see also Tormala & Petty, 2007; cf. Muthukrishnan et al., 2001). Likewise, research on omission neglect reveals that people become less certain of their attitudes when they have been alerted to the fact that they might be missing pertinent information (e.g., Sanbonmatsu et al., 1992; see also Chapter 23, this volume).

One way to foster the perception of greater information in a message is to explicitly highlight the fact that both sides of an issue (or attitude object)—the positives and the negatives, the pros and cons—have been considered. Rucker et al. (2008) presented participants with messages promoting new products (e.g., ads or customer reviews) and found that participants felt more certain of their resultant attitudes when it was clear that the messages (or the sources of the messages) had considered both the pros and cons as opposed to just one side. Rucker and Petty (2004) found similar effects when participants were directed to consider both sides themselves. In essence, people are more certain of their attitudes when they believe more rather than less attitude-relevant information has been considered, and highlighting that both sides of an issue have been assessed helps promote this perception.

Of importance, however, message (or information) consistency matters too. In general, the more consistent people view the information on a topic to be, the more certain they feel about their attitude. When people receive contradictory information on a topic, it tends to lower certainty (e.g., Koriat, 2012; Maheswaran & Chaiken, 1991; S. M. Smith et al., 2008; A. I. Snyder & Tormala, 2017; Tormala & DeSensi, 2009). Therefore, the perception that both sides of an issue have been considered can raise certainty, but if that consideration uncovers enough mixed or inconsistent evidence (e.g., many pros and cons to a product or policy), it should lower certainty. Indeed, the more mixed the information on a topic, the harder it is to be confident about the accuracy of any particular point of view.

Audience Effects on Certainty

Audience effects on certainty have been studied as well. In this case, most of the research attention has been paid to audience effects on thought confidence rather than attitude certainty (but see DeMarree et al., 2020). For example, message recipients' emotional states can affect how much confidence they ascribe to their thoughts about a persuasive message. Prior work has shown that emotions can be associated with appraisals of high or low certainty (e.g., Tiedens & Linton, 2001). Briñol and colleagues further showed that people feel more confident about their thoughts when they are induced to feel high (e.g., happiness, anger) rather than low (e.g., sadness) certainty emotions (Briñol, Petty, & Barden, 2007; Petty & Briñol, 2015). This relationship also has implications for persuasion: High certainty emotions (e.g., happiness) increase thought confidence relative to low certainty emotions (e.g., sadness) and thus can facilitate or hinder persuasion depending on whether people have positive or negative thoughts. Of note, the effects of specific emotions on feelings of confidence or certainty have been proposed as a potential contributor to the complicated effects of fear, a low certainty emotion, in persuasion (Petty & Briñol, 2015; see also Maloney et al., 2011).

In addition to emotional states, cognitive states can affect feelings of certainty or uncertainty. Consider past research on ease or fluency effects in persuasion. Perhaps the best known example of metacognitive effects in attitudes and persuasion stems from prior research on the ease of retrieval effect (Schwarz et al., 1991). The ease of retrieval effect refers to the idea that when people mentally generate instances of a particular type of thought or behavior, they often form judgments that are more in line with that thought or behavior when they generate just a few instances rather than many. In a classic experiment, Schwarz et al. (1991) found that participants judged themselves to be more assertive after generating a few rather than many examples of their own assertiveness. Subsequent research applying this concept to attitudes and persuasion showed that people feel more certain, or confident, of their thoughts (Tormala, Falces et al., 2007; Tormala et al., 2002) and attitudes (Haddock et al., 1999) after generating a few rather than many arguments on a topic. Thus, experiencing ease or fluency while thinking about an issue can affect people's feelings of certainty.

Bodily movements can also contribute to people's feelings of certainty versus uncertainty (for a review, see Briñol, Petty, & Wagner, 2012). In a quintessential demonstration, Briñol and Petty (2003) found that message recipients' overt head movements affected their feelings of thought confidence, which then shaped persuasion outcomes. In particular, Briñol and Petty found that head nodding (vertical, up and down movements) increased thought confidence relative to head shaking (horizontal, side-to-side movements). As a result, head nodding increased persuasion when a message contained strong arguments (producing positive thoughts) but decreased persuasion when a message contained weak arguments (producing negative thoughts). Similar findings have been observed using other bodily movements—for example, assuming a confident posture by pushing out one's chest versus a doubtful posture by hunching over (Briñol et al., 2009).

Power can affect these feelings as well. People tend to be more confident about whatever mental content (attitudes or thoughts) is salient when they are induced to feel more versus less powerful. Studies by Briñol, Petty, Valle, et al. (2007) were consistent with the notion that participants assigned to a high-power role (boss) felt more confident about their thoughts and attitudes than did participants assigned to a low-power role (employee). Briñol, Petty, Valle, et al. theorized that when people felt confident about their thoughts, they would be more persuaded by strong compared with weak arguments, whereas when people felt confident about their attitudes, they would be less sensitive to argument quality because attitude certainty reduces message processing (e.g., Tiedens & Linton, 2001). One important contribution of Briñol, Petty, Valle, et al. (2007) is that it revealed one factor that affects whether psychological certainty is more likely to be applied to one's thoughts or one's attitude: timing. Specifically, Briñol and colleagues suggested that when people were induced to feel powerful before they received a message, power affected the certainty with which they held their initial attitudes. After all, participants had not yet processed the message, so they had yet to generate any message-related thoughts. However, when people were induced to feel powerful after receiving and processing a message, power affected their feelings of thought confidence. These feelings then shaped attitudes, presumably because people were still considering where they stood after thinking about the message.

As a final example, an audience's thoughtfulness, or perceived thoughtfulness, can affect certainty. For example, it is now well-documented that people feel more certain about their attitudes when they believe they have thought more deeply about an attitude object or issue (Barden & Petty, 2008; Wan et al., 2010). Wan et al. (2010) tested the effects on attitude certainty of regulatory depletion experienced during message processing. They found that people felt more certain when they were depleted as opposed to not depleted. This result occurred because the feeling of depletion was attributed to thorough message processing and thorough processing is generally believed to produce more accurate or correct assessments (see Barden & Tormala, 2014). However, research suggests that this relationship is malleable. For instance, Tormala et al. (2011) found that believing one has taken one's time to slowly evaluate something builds attitude certainty when the attitude object is unfamiliar (and thus warrants more careful processing) but can reduce attitude certainty when the attitude object is familiar (and thus can be more quickly assessed).

Context Effects on Certainty

Just as the effects of source, message, and audience factors on persuasion are context-dependent, the same is true for psychological certainty. Although a litany of contextual factors have been examined, two common themes warrant mention here. First, any time people are engaging in metacognitive reasoning—assessing the implications of a message or experience for their feeling of psychological certainty—the effects are more likely to emerge when people's motivation and ability to think and reflect is at least somewhat high. In fact, many of the findings described herein have been shown to be moderated by elaboration, or extent of thinking. For instance, the effect of source credibility on both thought confidence (Briñol, Petty, & Tormala, 2004) and attitude certainty (Tormala & Petty, 2004a) is elevated under high thinking conditions. Likewise, the effect of resisting a strong message on attitude certainty is more likely to emerge under deep thought (Tormala & Petty, 2004b), as are the effects of certainty-associated emotions (Briñol, Petty, & Barden, 2007), experienced ease of retrieval (Tormala et al., 2002), numerical status of the source (Horcajo et al., 2014), and head nodding (Briñol & Petty, 2003) on thought confidence. The rationale is essentially that metacognitive activity, or thinking about thinking, demands more thinking. In short, people are more likely to reflect on their own thoughts and attitudes in persuasion situations when they have the motivation and ability to do so.

In addition, as previewed by our discussion of the power research conducted by Briñol, Petty, Valle et al. (2007), it is likely that many of the findings we have reviewed are moderated by timing. In theory, certainty can be associated with any mental content—a thought or attitude, for instance—that happens to be salient when certainty is induced. If one's thoughts are most salient, certainty would be attached to those thoughts and influence the attitude that is formed on the basis of those thoughts. If one's attitude is salient, certainty would be attached to that attitude and influence attitude strength. Thus, depending on when certainty is induced—before a message while one reflects on one's existing attitude, after a message while one considers one's message-related thoughts, or maybe still later after one forms a new attitude—this induction can affect either thought confidence or attitude certainty. As additional evidence for this notion, source credibility is more likely to affect thought confidence if it is manipulated after rather than before the persuasive message (Tormala, Briñol, & Petty, 2007). Also, research manipulating source credibility before a message has shown that it affects attitude certainty (e.g., Clarkson et al., 2008). Similarly, the effect of a source's numerical status on thought confidence has been shown to be more prominent when the source information follows the message (Horcajo et al., 2010). In short, source, message, and audience factors reliably influence psychological certainty. Whether that effect manifests as thought confidence or attitude certainty may depend on when it occurs.

ADVOCACY PERSPECTIVES

The classic and metacognitive perspectives have produced countless insights into the persuasion process. We now introduce a third perspective, observable in classic and contemporary research but gaining momentum in recent years, focused on attitudinal advocacy. Within the last decade, we believe a shift has occurred whereby researchers have increasingly focused on questions pertaining to advocacy. Whereas prior perspectives placed an emphasis on understanding what promotes persuasion or on mapping out the role of metacognitive thinking in attitude formation and change, the advocacy perspective emphasizes new questions: What stimulates people to advocate? How do people advocate? What are the consequences of advocating? In other words, whereas prior research focused on identifying the antecedents and consequences of receiving persuasive messages, the advocacy perspective focuses on the antecedents and consequences of generating persuasive messages.

At its core, we view advocacy as an expression of support for or opposition to something—for instance, a statement of one's favorable or unfavorable attitude toward a particular brand, product, offer, policy, or person (e.g., job candidate or politician). In the consumer behavior context, advocacy might take the form of writing a review online for a product or restaurant, recommending a service to a friend or family member, or posting on social media, to offer a few examples. Advocacy itself can be construed in terms of the mere sharing or expression of one's attitude (i.e., letting people know what one thinks) or in terms of efforts to persuade others or change their attitudes and behaviors to move them closer to one's own (Cheatham & Tormala, 2015). As with the classic and metacognitive perspectives, work on advocacy can be organized around the four pillars of persuasion research: source, message, audience, and context effects. Broadly speaking, the advocacy literature explores who generates advocacy (source effects), how people advocate (message effects), how people are affected by advocacy (audience effects), and how contextual factors affect advocacy (context effects). In this section, we review representative findings relating to each of these critical dimensions.

Source Effects: Who Advocates?

In advocacy research, considerable attention has been directed toward delineating the factors that prompt people to advocate. Particular emphasis has been placed on charting characteristics of the advocates themselves and how those characteristics trigger advocacy. In short, what drives a source to advocate? Stated differently, who advocates? To date, researchers largely have focused on attitudinal inputs—in particular, on illuminating how people's perceptions of their attitudes can lead them to advocate on behalf of their views.

Attitude certainty. One major input that has proven to be a critical determinant of advocacy is a person's feeling of attitude certainty or uncertainty. Perhaps unsurprisingly, the dominant view and finding is that the more certain a person feels about a particular attitude or opinion, the more likely they are to advocate. However, some research points to the possibility of a negative relationship, suggesting that uncertainty is what stimulates advocacy. We review each perspective here and highlight recent work pointing to a potential reconciliation.

Certainty promotes advocacy. First, there is widespread support for the notion that certainty and advocacy are positively associated. Krosnick et al. (1993), for instance, found that attitude certainty was positively correlated with people's willingness to discuss attitude-relevant topics; Barden and Petty (2008) found that attitude certainty predicted people's willingness to vote and sign petitions; and Visser et al. (2003) found that increased attitude certainty was associated with increased willingness to donate money and write letters on behalf of one's personal opinions. More recently, Philipp-Muller et al. (2020) observed positive correlations between attitude certainty and a variety of advocacy outcomes such as wearing pins or clothing supporting their positions, placing signs in their yards, and sharing articles on social media.

Akhtar et al. (2013) found that attitude certainty also predicted persuasion intentions. In one study, participants who expressed higher certainty about their attitudes toward a vegetarian-only school lunch policy also reported a greater motivation and willingness to persuade others to their position on the issue. Akhtar et al. argued that this relationship stemmed from the association between attitude certainty and argumentation efficacy. In essence, they reasoned that people with greater attitude certainty also have elevated perceptions of their own argumentation efficacy—that is, their own ability to make a convincing case for something—and, thus, are more eager to advocate on behalf of their attitude when the opportunity arises. Consistent with this argument, research on defensive confidence suggests that people who feel confident that they can defend ideas are more willing to stand by those ideas in front of others and confront counterattitudinal information (Albarracín & Mitchell, 2004).

Other studies have offered a more nuanced look at the certainty–advocacy relationship. Rios et al. (2014), for instance, demonstrated that different types of attitude certainty (feelings of attitude correctness and attitude clarity; for elaboration, see Petrocelli et al., 2007) contribute differentially to one's advocacy approach. Rios et al. found that attitude correctness drives people's desire to win arguments and persuade others, whereas attitude clarity plays little role in this regard. Unpacking these dynamics further, Cheatham and Tormala (2015) highlighted different forms of advocacy that stem from people's different underlying motives. Of particular interest were persuasion intentions (i.e., the motivation to convince others or change their views) and sharing intentions (i.e., the motivation to express one's view, but not necessarily to persuade anyone else to adopt it). Cheatham and Tormala found that both attitude clarity and attitude correctness predicted sharing intentions, but attitude correctness was uniquely predictive of persuasion intentions. Likewise, interventions that give rise to attitude correctness (e.g., high consensus feedback) affected both sharing and persuasion intentions, whereas interventions that give rise to attitude clarity (e.g., repeated attitude expression) affected only sharing intentions. Importantly, then, attitude clarity is not impotent in the advocacy context but rather fosters a particular type of advocacy that is less focused on effecting attitude change.

In short, a great deal of evidence supports the view that attitude certainty promotes attitudinal advocacy. This evidence is bolstered by research highlighting the importance of other dimensions of attitude strength in shaping advocacy outcomes as well. As one example, consider moral conviction. Moral conviction captures the perception that one's attitude stems from one's core moral beliefs and values (e.g., Skitka, 2010) and often is tied to the belief that one's attitude is objectively correct (e.g., Goodwin & Darley, 2008; Skitka et al., 2005). A growing literature suggests that moral conviction sparks advocacy. People are more willing to sign petitions, donate, make phone calls, and wear supporting clothing, for instance, when they have high rather than low moral conviction (e.g., Philipp-Muller et al., 2020; Skitka & Bauman, 2008; Skitka et al., 2017). In addition to moral conviction, numerous other dimensions of attitude strength known to be correlated with attitude certainty (e.g., perceived knowledge, importance, direct experience) have been positively linked to advocacy-relevant outcomes (e.g., Krosnick et al., 1993; Rios et al., 2018).

Uncertainty promotes advocacy. Departing from the notion that increased certainty fosters increased advocacy behavior, a smaller body of work points to a negative relationship between these constructs. That is, some research suggests that uncertainty is what triggers advocacy. As a classic example, Festinger et al. (1956) investigated a doomsday cult confronted with the knowledge that its prophecy might be wrong. More specifically, Festinger et al. observed cult members' reactions to the fact that the world did not end on the date that their prophecy predicted it would. The researchers found that when confronted with a blow to their prophecy, and thus perhaps instilled with immense uncertainty, cult members increased their advocacy efforts and proselytized with unparalleled fervor. In other words, the cult members' actions suggested that cases might exist in which people advocate more aggressively when they feel less rather than more certain about their views.

Building on this observation and interpretation, Gal and Rucker (2010) argued that advocacy might sometimes serve a compensatory function by allowing people to affirm the very views about which they feel uncertain. They found that when people were induced to feel uncertain (as opposed to certain) about a particularly important belief, they put more effort into advocating on behalf of that belief. For instance, when participants were made to feel uncertain about their attitudes toward vegetarianism, they wrote longer messages to others in an effort to persuade others of their views. Likewise, Briñol, McCaslin, and Petty (2012) found that people expended greater effort and generated more arguments when they had doubts rather than confidence about the position for which they were advocating and their ability to persuade.

Related research suggests that feelings of self-uncertainty, which can be tied to attitude uncertainty, sometimes stimulate opinion expression. Rios et al. (2012) found that low self-esteem individuals became more open to holding and expressing minority viewpoints (i.e., attitudes with which most people disagree) following an induction of self-uncertainty. Their interpretation was that when people feel uncertain about themselves, holding and expressing minority viewpoints allows them to establish their individuality or uniqueness, which helps boost their sense of self. In general, though, people tend to be hesitant to express minority opinions unless a need for uniqueness is activated or people feel knowledgeable or certain (e.g., Rios & Chen, 2014; Rios et al., 2018).

A resolution. To summarize, although the dominant finding is that more certainty translates into greater advocacy, exceptions exist. Cheatham and Tormala (2017) theorized that both perspectives, that both certainty and uncertainty can promote advocacy, can be accommodated by a nonlinear understanding of the certainty–advocacy relationship. These researchers hypothesized that the link between attitude certainty and attitudinal advocacy is actually curvilinear, such that advocacy peaks at very high certainty, declines at moderate certainty, but shows a slight bump up as certainty drops from moderate to very low. The logic was that high certainty is associated with conviction, feelings of efficacy, and action (Akhtar et al., 2013; Tormala & Rucker, 2007), while uncertainty can trigger compensatory motives and an urge to restore or build certainty (Gal & Rucker, 2010; Rios et al., 2012; Sawicki et al., 2011). Individuals with moderate certainty are essentially caught in the middle and not particularly likely to experience any of those feelings or tendencies. Across multiple studies, Cheatham and Tormala found evidence to support this prediction. They observed a J-shaped relationship between attitude certainty and advocacy (advocacy intentions and actual advocacy behavior), whereby advocacy peaked at very high certainty, hit its nadir at moderate certainty, and showed a slight uptick at very low certainty. Thus, Cheatham and Tormala demonstrated a general increasing tendency to advocate as certainty rises, but this overall relationship masks nonlinearity that occurs at very low levels of the certainty spectrum.

Implicit theories of attitudes. Related to the discussion of attitude certainty, recent research has explored people's implicit theories of attitudes as a determinant of advocacy. As background, Petrocelli et al. (2010) found that just as people have personal theories about the fixed or malleable nature of personality traits (see Dweck, 1999; Molden & Dweck, 2006), so too do they have lay beliefs about the fixed or malleable nature of attitudes. Some people view attitudes as inherently fixed, or unchanging over time, whereas others view attitudes as relatively malleable, or variable. These theories have implications for attitude certainty: The more fixed people perceive attitudes to be, the more certain they tend to feel.

Akhtar and Wheeler (2016) explored the implications of these perceptions for advocacy. They found that because fixed (relative to malleable) theories of attitudes produce greater attitude certainty, they can exert a positive effect on advocacy intentions. The more stable people believe their attitudes are, the more certain they feel, and the more certain they feel, the more inclined to advocate they become. At the same time, fixed theories carry with them the belief that other people's attitudes are stable as well, perhaps even immutable. This perception has a negative effect on advocacy intentions. The more stable people believe others' attitudes are, the less likely they are to try to persuade them. Why advocate if others are unchangeable? In aggregate, these conflicting forces can cancel each other out, creating the appearance that implicit theories play little role in advocacy behavior. In reality, people's implicit theories of attitudes can increase or decrease their own interest in advocating depending on where their focus is. For someone with a fixed theory, who believes attitudes are inherently stable, focusing on the self can increase advocacy because it directs attention to the stability of one's own attitude, which boosts feelings of certainty. For someone with a more malleable theory, who believes attitudes are changeable, focusing on others' attitudes can foster greater advocacy because it reinforces the notion that others' attitudes can be changed.

Attitude basis. As mentioned earlier, another variable that has been important in persuasion research is the extent to which an attitude is based on affect versus cognition (e.g., Breckler, 1984; Crites et al., 1994; Zanna & Rempel, 1988). In recent work extending this distinction to advocacy, Teeny and Petty (2018) examined whether affective or cognitive attitude bases were more prominent contributors to advocacy intentions. They found that the effect depended on the type of advocacy in question—specifically, whether that advocacy was explicitly requested or more spontaneous in nature. Participants who perceived their attitudes to be more cognitive (rather than affective) were more likely to engage in requested advocacy (e.g., speaking up and making an argument if asked to do so). However, people who perceived their attitudes to be more affective (rather than cognitive) were more likely to engage in spontaneous advocacy (e.g., speaking up and making an argument if unprompted). Teeny and Petty argued that requested advocacy triggers an expectation for reasoned or thoughtful input, whereas spontaneous advocacy emphasizes current feelings or whatever pops into mind. These foci, in turn, map onto cognitive and affective attitudes, respectively. Ultimately, the key insight was that a potential source's perceived attitude basis can drive their advocacy decisions, but the direction of this effect depends on whether the advocacy in question is requested or spontaneous.

Message Effects: How Do People Advocate?

Advocacy research also has attended to message variables. How do people advocate? What kinds of messages do they send to others? In the past decade, several initial tendencies have been uncovered. For example, an early insight into this question was offered by Gal and Rucker's (2010) research, reviewed previously. Again, Gal and Rucker explored how people's persuasive efforts were shaped by incidental manipulations of confidence. They found that shaking individuals' sense of confidence in their beliefs—by having them write about their beliefs with their nondominant hand, for example—affected how people constructed subsequent persuasive messages. In particular, when people doubted their own beliefs, they appeared to exert greater effort persuading others to change their views. Specifically, individuals wrote longer messages and spent more time constructing them when they felt uncertain. Thus, (un)certainty shapes not only whether people advocate but also how much effort and vigor they put into doing so.

Consistent with the notion that certainty and advocacy can exhibit a curvilinear relationship, Cheatham and Tormala (2017) found that people's advocacy messages rose in length as they moved from moderate to high certainty or from moderate to low certainty. In addition to assessing message length, Cheatham and Tormala evaluated the actual messages people crafted. They found that high certainty advocacy was characterized by direct and forceful argumentation. Indeed, highly certain advocates' messages contained more arguments; clearer expressions of beliefs and values; and more emotional, moral, and judgmental content. By contrast, low certainty advocacy messages included more qualifiers, hedges, questions, and expressions of interest in the opposing position. In essence, although high and low certainty individuals both tended to engage in greater advocacy than their moderate certainty counterparts, the content of their advocacy differed; they appeared to advocate more forcefully (when certain) and inquisitively (when uncertain).

Dubois et al. (2016) explored the effects of power on the messages people wrote to try to persuade others. Dubois et al. found that when individuals were placed into a high-power role (e.g., manager) they tended to construct messages that focused on competence. In contrast, when they were placed into a low-power role (e.g., employee) they tended to construct messages that focused on warmth. For example, in one study participants were instructed to generate a persuasive message by selecting six arguments from a list of eighteen arguments. Participants in a high-power role selected more competence-based arguments (e.g., "The wait staff's skills and training make them experts at their jobs"), whereas those in a low-power role selected more warmth-based arguments (e.g., "The waiters are very trustworthy in providing you the right meal"). The authors argued that feelings of high (low) power nudged people toward thinking about competence (warmth), which permeated into the persuasive messages they constructed.

In the aforementioned studies, participants' intent to persuade was not compared with a no-intent-to-persuade condition. Rather, the researchers simply explored how participants attempted to persuade when instructed to do so. Recently, efforts have been made to understand how people communicate when they have an active goal to persuade as opposed to when they do not. In one of the first explorations to directly manipulate people's intent to persuade, Rocklage et al. (2018) examined how the intent to persuade an audience transformed the language of people's persuasive appeals. In one experiment, Rocklage and colleagues either had people write a review for a product (low persuasive intent) or explicitly instructed them to write a review meant to persuade others (high persuasive intent). Results indicated that when people had an intent to persuade they shifted their language to use words that conveyed more emotion (e.g., "wonderful") relative to words that used less emotion (e.g., "perfect"). The authors suggested that this result might stem from a learned association between emotion and persuasion.

In another experiment, Rocklage and colleagues asked participants to write a review (low persuasive intent) or gave participants a monetary incentive to write a review (high persuasive intent). Participants incentivized to write a review used more emotionally laden language than those simply asked to write a review.

Audience Effects: Whose Attitude Will Be Changed by One's Advocacy?

Audience factors in advocacy research can be viewed through different lenses. First, and perhaps most basic, researchers often ask how characteristics of the audience affect the success of one's advocacy efforts. That is, who is being targeted and how does that shape the advocacy outcome? This, it turns out, is the classic perspective on audience factors in persuasion, and we have reviewed it already.

Alternatively, researchers could ask how the potential audience one has affects one's likelihood of advocating. Stated differently, how do people select their targets in the first place? As fundamental as this question might seem, it is relatively unexplored in advocacy research. Recently, however, Bechler et al. (2020; see also Bechler & Tormala, 2021) conducted a series of experiments exploring target selection in persuasion. Bechler et al. investigated which type of audience people preferred to target with their messages: someone whose attitude they could shift across valence (e.g., from negative to positive) or someone whose attitude they could shift within valence (e.g., from very negative to less negative or from somewhat positive to more positive). Participants exhibited a marked preference to target others—that is, they showed elevated advocacy intentions—when they believed they could shift their audience across rather than within valence. Their explanation was that shifts across valence seem greater in magnitude and impact than objectively equivalent shifts within valence (Bechler et al., 2019; see also Bechler et al., 2021), and people naturally prefer to have more rather than less impact. Importantly, though, Bechler et al. (2020) showed that in at least some cases this perception can be incorrect and people are better off targeting others who already lean their way but can be made more extreme. We view this research as a first step toward understanding target selection in persuasion.

Interestingly, though, by far the most attention has been paid to how the source of an advocacy message can be an audience to that message as well. In other words, when people advocate to others, they often essentially advocate to themselves. This is the fundamental premise guiding a substantial body of research on *self-persuasion*. Self-persuasion has been an extremely important part of attitudes research, spanning several decades of study (see Maio & Thomas, 2007). The central theme in this work is that when people think or advocate in one direction on a topic (e.g., expressing favorable thoughts about a product or policy), their own attitudes often shift in that same direction.

Consider the classic research on role-playing effects (Janis & King, 1954). In this research, participants were randomly assigned to actively generate or passively receive counterattitudinal messages on various topics. Results indicated that actively generating the arguments created more attitude change. Since that original finding, an expansive literature has arisen suggesting that generating counterattitudinal messages can cause people to shift their attitudes in the counterattitudinal direction. Several accounts have been advanced for this effect—including that self-generated messages create cognitive dissonance, lead to biased scanning of relevant information, require greater effort, and foster value-congruent argumentation (e.g., Briñol, McCaslin, & Petty, 2012; Carlsmith et al., 1966; Catapano et al., 2019; Cialdini, 1971; Greenwald & Albert, 1968). Most germane to the current concerns, generating persuasive advocacy often has a profound effect on the advocate, suggesting that the self is an important audience to one's advocacy efforts.

Advocates do not have to generate counterattitudinal arguments to be influenced by their own thought processes. Research on the directed-thought technique (Killeya & Johnson, 1998; see also Petty et al., 2002; Xu & Wyer, 2012) suggests that inducing people to generate positive or negative thoughts can push their attitudes in a positive or negative direction, respectively. Moreover, research on resistance to persuasion suggests that asking people to list thoughts that support their own views can increase attitude stability (Briñol, Rucker, et al., 2004; Lydon et al., 1988; McGuire, 1964). Perhaps most telling, research on the mere thought effect suggests that merely thinking about an object or issue can provoke attitude change—in particular, it can cause people's attitudes to polarize (see Tesser, 1978). For example, simply instructing people to think about an issue for 180 seconds can cause them to become even more extreme in their initial direction, even when no new information or outside input is received (e.g., Tesser & Conlee, 1975). This effect appears to be driven by both attitude-congruent thought generation and the feeling of confidence people have in their own thoughts (Clarkson et al., 2011).

Finally, when people attempt to persuade others, the success or failure of their advocacy efforts can have implications for their own views. For instance, it appears that people's advocacy experiences can affect their own feelings of attitude certainty. Infante (1976) found that people became more resistant to persuasion after they themselves successfully (vs. unsuccessfully) persuaded someone else. Similarly, Prislin and colleagues (2011) found that succeeding (as opposed to failing) to persuade others boosted advocates' sense of certainty and, thus, enhanced their actual persuasive efficacy in follow-up messages. An initial advocacy success, in other words, increased attitude certainty and promoted future advocacy success.

Context Effects

Just as classic and metacognitive perspectives have emphasized the importance of contextual factors in persuasion, context is critically important to the advocacy perspective. Indeed, growing evidence suggests that the advocacy effects we have reviewed here are context dependent. In contrast to the classic and metacognitive perspectives, however, which identified major contextual themes such as the critical moderating role of people's motivation and ability to think, research on contextual factors in advocacy has been more piecemeal in nature. Many of the individual studies highlight moderators of various kinds, but we have yet to see them integrated into a coherent whole. Doing so in future work would be extremely valuable. For now, we offer a few illustrative examples of contextual moderation.

First, context has proven important in understanding the role of source factors in advocacy generation. Consider the notion that attitude certainty promotes advocacy. Akhtar et al. (2013) found that this relationship was attenuated when potential advocates were presented with weak proattitudinal arguments on a topic. The logic was that receiving weak arguments in favor of one's position increased people's confidence about their own arguments, which boosted initially uncertain individuals' willingness to advocate. In addition, research suggesting that uncertainty promotes advocacy has pinpointed at least one important moderator: self-affirmation. Both Gal and Rucker (2010) and Cheatham and Tormala (2017) found that low certainty individuals advocate to a greater extent than do moderate certainty individuals; however, this effect was attenuated when people were affirmed. Consistent with the notion that uncertain advocacy reflects a desire to either resolve or compensate for uncomfortable feelings of doubt, self-affirmation tasks appear to reduce uncertain advocacy and restore a general linear positive slope between certainty and the motivation to advocate.

Context is also critically important to audience effects. As one example, Catapano and colleagues (2019) found that the effect of counterattitudinal argument generation on self-persuasion (i.e., the classic role-playing effect) was moderated by perspective-taking instructions and in particular by whose perspective advocates were directed to take. Catapano et al. found that directing people to take the perspective of others who disagreed with them and held different ideologies (e.g., encouraging a liberal to take the perspective of a conservative) reduced attitude change following a counterargument generation task. However, taking the perspective of others who disagreed with them but held similar ideologies (e.g., encouraging a liberal to take the perspective of another liberal who happened to disagree on the target issue) increased attitude change following the same task. The reason for this result was that people generated arguments that were incongruent with their own values in the former case and congruent with their own values in the latter.

Contextual factors also moderate the mere thought effect. For instance, consistent with past research, Clarkson et al. (2011) found that increasing the amount of time people are given to think in a mere thought paradigm increased attitude polarization up to a point, after which the effect faded and attitudes began to depolarize. In one study, polarization increased as the opportunity for thought was extended from 60 to 180 seconds, but this effect reversed as the time increased from 180 to 300 seconds. The argument was that more time can make thinking easier and augment thought confidence, but too much time makes it difficult to generate new thoughts, which reduces thought confidence and undermines the effect of one's thoughts on one's attitude. Clarkson, Valente et al. (2013) found that the mere thought effect was also moderated by personal fear of invalidity. Specifically, under some conditions people with personal fear of invalidity depolarized following a mere thought task, because the thoughts that come to mind for these individuals can skew in the attitude-inconsistent direction.

To summarize, a number of instances of contextual moderation have arisen in the advocacy literature. Unlike research on classic and metacognitive factors, however, these instances have yet to cohere around a common theme or organizing framework. We see this issue as ripe for future research.

CONCLUSION

Attitudes and persuasion occupy a prominent place in consumer psychology research. Indeed, from predicting consumers' thoughts and actions to understanding how consumers respond to marketing messages, having insight into the underlying psychology of attitude formation and change is critical. Our aim in this review was to offer a broad look at traditional and modern-day work in this domain, organized around three main movements, or perspectives, in persuasion research: the classic perspective, the metacognitive perspective, and the advocacy perspective. These perspectives have been important to persuasion research in the past and will likely continue to guide research in this domain over the coming years. The field has come a long way in its understanding of attitude change and persuasion phenomena, but there remains much to learn. We hope this review offers a useful grounding in this domain and stimulates future research that further deepens our collective insight.

REFERENCES

Abelson, R. P. (1995). Attitude extremity. In R. E. Petty & J. A. Krosnick (Eds.), *Ohio State University series on attitudes and persuasion: Vol. 4. Attitude strength: Antecedents and consequences* (pp. 25–41). Lawrence Erlbaum Associates.

Ajzen, I. (2005). *Attitudes, personality, and behavior*. McGraw-Hill Education.

Akhtar, O., Paunesku, D., & Tormala, Z. L. (2013). Weak > strong: The ironic effect of argument strength on supportive advocacy. *Personality and Social Psychology Bulletin, 39*(9), 1214–1226. https://doi.org/10.1177/0146167213492430

Akhtar, O., & Wheeler, S. C. (2016). Belief in the immutability of attitudes both increases and decreases advocacy. *Journal of Personality and Social Psychology, 111*(4), 475–492. https://doi.org/10.1037/pspa0000060

Albarracín, D., & Mitchell, A. L. (2004). The role of defensive confidence in preference for proattitudinal information: How believing that one is strong can sometimes be a defensive weakness. *Personality and Social Psychology Bulletin, 30*(12), 1565–1584. https://doi.org/10.1177/0146167204271180

Allport, G. W. (1935). *Attitudes: A handbook of social psychology*. Clark University Press.

Anand, P., & Sternthal, B. (1987). Resource matching as an explanation for message persuasion. In P. Caferrata & A. M. Tybout (Eds.), *Perspectives on the affective and cognitive effects of advertising*. Lexington Books.

Bagozzi, R. P., Tybout, A. M., Craig, C. S., & Sternthal, B. (1979). The construct validity of the tripartite classification of attitudes. *Journal of Marketing Research, 16*(1), 88–95. https://doi.org/10.1177/002224377901600113

Barden, J., & Petty, R. E. (2008). The mere perception of elaboration creates attitude certainty: Exploring the thoughtfulness heuristic. *Journal of Personality and Social Psychology, 95*(3), 489–509. https://doi.org/10.1037/a0012559

Barden, J., & Tormala, Z. L. (2014). Elaboration and attitude strength: The new meta-cognitive perspective. *Social and Personality Psychology Compass, 8*(1), 17–29. https://doi.org/10.1111/spc3.12078

Bassili, J. N. (1996). Meta-judgmental versus operative indexes of psychological attributes: The case of measures of attitude strength. *Journal of Personality and Social Psychology, 71*(4), 637–653. https://doi.org/10.1037/0022-3514.71.4.637

Bechler, C. J., & Tormala, Z. L. (2021). Misdirecting persuasive efforts during the COVID-19 pandemic: The targets people choose may not be the most likely to change. *Journal of the Association for Consumer Research, 6*, 187-195. https://doi.org/10.1086/711732

Bechler, C. J., Tormala, Z. L., & Rucker, D. D. (2019). Perceiving attitude change: How qualitative shifts augment change perception. *Journal of Experimental Social Psychology, 82*, 160–175. https://doi.org/10.1016/j.jesp.2019.02.001

Bechler, C. J., Tormala, Z. L., & Rucker, D. D. (2020). Choosing persuasion targets: How expectations of qualitative change increase advocacy intentions. *Journal of Experimental Social Psychology, 86*, 103911. https://doi.org/10.1016/j.jesp.2019.103911

Bechler, C. J., Tormala, Z. L., & Rucker, D. D. (2021). The attitude–behavior relationship revisited. *Psychological Science, 32*(8), 1285–1297. https://doi.org/10.1177/0956797621995206

Biggers, T., & Pryor, B. (1982). Attitude change: A function of emotion-eliciting qualities of environment. *Personality and Social Psychology Bulletin, 8*(1), 94–99. https://doi.org/10.1177/014616728281015

Boninger, D. S., Krosnick, J. A., Berent, M. K., & Fabrigar, L. R. (1995). The causes and consequences of attitude importance. In R. E. Petty & J. A. Krosnick (Eds.), *Ohio State University series on attitudes and persuasion: Vol. 4. Attitude strength: Antecedents and consequences* (pp. 159–189). Lawrence Erlbaum Associates.

Breckler, S. J. (1984). Empirical validation of affect, behavior, and cognition as distinct components of attitude. *Journal of Personality and Social Psychology, 47*(6), 1191–1205. https://doi.org/10.1037/0022-3514.47.6.1191

Briñol, P., McCaslin, M. J., & Petty, R. E. (2012). Self-generated persuasion: Effects of the target and direction of arguments. *Journal of Personality and Social Psychology, 102*(5), 925–940. https://doi.org/10.1037/a0027231

Briñol, P., & Petty, R. E. (2003). Overt head movements and persuasion: A self-validation analysis. *Journal of Personality and Social Psychology, 84*(6), 1123–1139. https://doi.org/10.1037/0022-3514.84.6.1123

Briñol, P., Petty, R. E., & Barden, J. (2007). Happiness versus sadness as a determinant of thought confidence in persuasion: A self-validation analysis. *Journal of Personality and Social Psychology, 93*(5), 711–727. https://doi.org/10.1037/0022-3514.93.5.711

Briñol, P., Petty, R. E., Gallardo, I., & DeMarree, K. G. (2007). The effect of self-affirmation in nonthreatening persuasion domains: Timing affects the process. *Personality and Social Psychology Bulletin, 33*(11), 1533–1546. https://doi.org/10.1177/0146167207306282

Briñol, P., Petty, R. E., & McCaslin, M. J. (2008). Changing attitudes on implicit versus explicit measures: What is the difference? In R. E. Petty, R. H. Fazio, & P. Briñol (Eds.), *Attitudes: Insights from the new implicit measures* (pp. 285–326). Psychology Press.

Briñol, P., Petty, R. E., & Tormala, Z. L. (2004). Self-validation of cognitive responses to advertisements. *Journal of Consumer Research, 30*(4), 559–573. https://doi.org/10.1086/380289

Briñol, P., Petty, R. E., Valle, C., Rucker, D. D., & Becerra, A. (2007). The effects of message recipients' power before and after persuasion: A self-validation analysis. *Journal of Personality and Social Psychology, 93*(6), 1040–1053. https://doi.org/10.1037/0022-3514.93.6.1040

Briñol, P., Petty, R. E., & Wagner, B. (2009). Body posture effects on self-evaluation: A self-validation approach. *European Journal of Social Psychology, 39*(6), 1053–1064. https://doi.org/10.1002/ejsp.607

Briñol, P., Petty, R. E., & Wagner, B. C. (2012). Embodied validation: Our bodies can change and also validate our thoughts. In P. Briñol & K. DeMarree (Eds.), *Frontiers of social psychology. Social metacognition* (pp. 219–240). Psychology Press.

Briñol, P., Rucker, D., Tormala, Z. L., & Petty, R. E. (2004). Individual differences in resistance to persuasion: The role of beliefs and meta-beliefs. In E. S. Knowles & J. A. Linn (Eds.), *Resistance and persuasion* (pp. 83-104). Erlbaum.

Briñol, P., Tormala, Z. L., & Petty, R. E. (2013). Ease and persuasion: Multiple processes, meanings, and effects. In C. Unkelbach & R. Greifeneder (Eds.), *The experience of thinking: How the fluency of mental processes influences cognition and behaviour* (pp. 101–118). Psychology Press.

Cacioppo, J. T., Gardner, W. L., & Berntson, G. G. (1997). Beyond bipolar conceptualizations and measures: The case of attitudes and evaluative space. *Personality and Social Psychology Review, 1*(1), 3–25. https://doi.org/10.1207/s15327957pspr0101_2

Cacioppo, J. T., & Petty, R. E. (1979). Effects of message repetition and position on cognitive response, recall, and persuasion. *Journal of Personality and Social Psychology, 37*(1), 97–109. https://doi.org/10.1037/0022-3514.37.1.97

Cacioppo, J. T., & Petty, R. E. (1982). The need for cognition. *Journal of Personality and Social Psychology,*

42(1), 116–131. https://doi.org/10.1037/0022-3514.42.1.116

Cacioppo, J. T., Petty, R. E., & Morris, K. J. (1983). Effects of need for cognition on message evaluation, recall, and persuasion. *Journal of Personality and Social Psychology*, 45(4), 805–818. https://doi.org/10.1037/0022-3514.45.4.805

Calder, B. J., Insko, C. A., & Yandell, B. (1974). The relation of cognitive and memorial processes to persuasion in a simulated jury trial. *Journal of Applied Social Psychology*, 4(1), 62–93. https://doi.org/10.1111/j.1559-1816.1974.tb02808.x

Calder, B. J., & Sternthal, B. (1980). Television commercial wearout: An information processing view. *Journal of Marketing Research*, 17(2), 173–186. https://doi.org/10.1177/002224378001700202

Carlsmith, J. M., Collins, B. E., & Helmreich, R. L. (1966). Studies in forced compliance: I. The effect of pressure for compliance on attitude change produced by face-to-face role playing and anonymous essay writing. *Journal of Personality and Social Psychology*, 4(1), 1–13. https://doi.org/10.1037/h0023507

Catapano, R., Tormala, Z. L., & Rucker, D. D. (2019). Perspective taking and self-persuasion: Why "putting yourself in their shoes" reduces openness to attitude change. *Psychological Science*, 30(3), 424–435. https://doi.org/10.1177/0956797618822697

Chaiken, S. (1980). Heuristic versus systematic information processing and the use of source versus message cues in persuasion. *Journal of Personality and Social Psychology*, 39(5), 752–766. https://doi.org/10.1037/0022-3514.39.5.752

Chaiken, S., Liberman, A., Eagly, A. H. (1989). Heuristic and systematic processing within and beyond the persuasion context. In J. S. Uleman & J. A. Bargh (Eds.). *Unintended thought* (pp. 212–252). Guilford Press.

Chaiken, S., & Maheswaran, D. (1994). Heuristic processing can bias systematic processing: Effects of source credibility, argument ambiguity, and task importance on attitude judgment. *Journal of Personality and Social Psychology*, 66(3), 460–473. https://doi.org/10.1037/0022-3514.66.3.460

Cheatham, L., & Tormala, Z. L. (2015). Attitude certainty and attitudinal advocacy: The unique roles of clarity and correctness. *Personality and Social Psychology Bulletin*, 41(11), 1537–1550. https://doi.org/10.1177/0146167215601406

Cheatham, L. B., & Tormala, Z. L. (2017). The curvilinear relationship between attitude certainty and attitudinal advocacy. *Personality and Social Psychology Bulletin*, 43(1), 3–16. https://doi.org/10.1177/0146167216673349

Cialdini, R. B. (1971). Attitudinal advocacy in the verbal conditioner. *Journal of Personality and Social Psychology*, 17(3), 350–358. https://doi.org/10.1037/h0030590

Clark, J. K., & Wegener, D. T. (2013). Message position, information processing, and persuasion: The discrepancy motives model. In *Advances in experimental social psychology* (Vol. 47, pp. 189-232). Academic Press.

Clarkson, J. J., Tormala, Z. L., & Leone, C. (2011). A self-validation perspective on the mere thought effect. *Journal of Experimental Social Psychology*, 47(2), 449–454. https://doi.org/10.1016/j.jesp.2010.12.003

Clarkson, J. J., Tormala, Z. L., & Rucker, D. D. (2008). A new look at the consequences of attitude certainty: The amplification hypothesis. *Journal of Personality and Social Psychology*, 95(4), 810–825. https://doi.org/10.1037/a0013192

Clarkson, J. J., Tormala, Z. L., Rucker, D. D., & Dugan, R. G. (2013). The malleable influence of social consensus on attitude certainty. *Journal of Experimental Social Psychology*, 49(6), 1019–1022. https://doi.org/10.1016/j.jesp.2013.07.001

Clarkson, J. J., Valente, M. J., Leone, C., & Tormala, Z. L. (2013). Motivated reflection on attitude-inconsistent information: An exploration of the role of fear of invalidity in self-persuasion. *Personality and Social Psychology Bulletin*, 39(12), 1559–1570. https://doi.org/10.1177/0146167213497983

Crites, S. L., Jr., Fabrigar, L. R., & Petty, R. E. (1994). Measuring the affective and cognitive properties of attitudes: Conceptual and methodological issues. *Personality and Social Psychology Bulletin*, 20(6), 619–634. https://doi.org/10.1177/0146167294206001

Crowley, A. E., & Hoyer, W. D. (1994). An integrative framework for understanding two-sided persuasion. *Journal of Consumer Research*, 20(4), 561–574. https://doi.org/10.1086/209370

DeMarree, K. G., Petty, R.E. Briñol, P., & Xia, J. (2020). Documenting individual differences in the propensity to hold attitudes with certainty. *Journal of Personality and Social Psychology*, 119, 1239–1265. https://doi.org/10.1037/pspa0000241

Dubois, D., Rucker, D. D., & Galinsky, A. D. (2016). Dynamics of communicator and audience power: The persuasiveness of competence versus warmth. *Journal of Consumer Research*, 43(1), 68–85. https://doi.org/10.1093/jcr/ucw006

Dweck, C. (1999). *Self-theories: Their role in personality, motivation, and development*. Psychology Press.

Edwards, K. (1990). The interplay of affect and cognition in attitude formation and change. *Journal of Personality and Social Psychology*, 59(2), 202–216. https://doi.org/10.1037/0022-3514.59.2.202

Ein-Gar, D., Shiv, B., & Tormala, Z. L. (2012). When blemishing leads to blossoming: The positive effect of negative information. *Journal of Consumer Research*, *38*(5), 846–859. https://doi.org/10.1086/660807

Fabrigar, L. R., & Petty, R. E. (1999). The role of the affective and cognitive bases of attitudes in susceptibility to affectively and cognitively based persuasion. *Personality and Social Psychology Bulletin*, *25*(3), 363–381. https://doi.org/10.1177/0146167299025003008

Fazio, R. H. (1995). Attitudes as object-evaluation associations: Determinants, consequences, and correlates of attitude accessibility. In R. E. Petty & J. A. Krosnick (Eds.), *Ohio State University series on attitudes and persuasion, Vol. 4. Attitude strength: Antecedents and consequences* (p. 247–282). Lawrence Erlbaum Associates.

Festinger, L., & MacCoby, N. (1964). On resistance to persuasive communications. *Journal of Abnormal and Social Psychology*, *68*(4), 359–366. https://doi.org/10.1037/h0049073

Festinger, L., Riecken, H., & Schachter, S. (1956). *When prophecy fails*. University of Minnesota Press. https://doi.org/10.1037/10030-000

Festinger, L., & Thibaut, J. (1951). Interpersonal communication in small groups. *Journal of Abnormal and Social Psychology*, *46*(1), 92–99. https://doi.org/10.1037/h0054899

Finch, J. F., & Cialdini, R. B. (1989). Another indirect tactic of (self-) image management: Boosting. *Personality and Social Psychology Bulletin*, *15*(2), 222–232. https://doi.org/10.1177/0146167289152009

French, J. R., & Raven, B. (1959). The bases of social power. In D. P. Cartwright (Ed.), *Studies in social power* (pp. 150–167). Institute for Social Research, University of Michigan.

Gal, D., & Rucker, D. D. (2010). When in doubt, shout! Paradoxical influences of doubt on proselytizing. *Psychological Science*, *21*(11), 1701–1707. https://doi.org/10.1177/0956797610385953

Glasman, L. R., & Albarracín, D. (2006). Forming attitudes that predict future behavior: A meta-analysis of the attitude-behavior relation. *Psychological Bulletin*, *132*(5), 778–822. https://doi.org/10.1037/0033-2909.132.5.778

Goodwin, G. P., & Darley, J. M. (2008). The psychology of meta-ethics: Exploring objectivism. *Cognition*, *106*(3), 1339–1366. https://doi.org/10.1016/j.cognition.2007.06.007

Greenwald, A. G., & Albert, R. D. (1968). Acceptance and recall of improvised arguments. *Journal of Personality and Social Psychology*, *8*(1, Pt. 1), 31–34.

Gross, S. R., Holtz, R., & Miller, N. (1995). Attitude certainty. In R. E. Petty & J. A. Krosnick (Eds.), *Ohio State University series on attitudes and persuasion: Vol. 4. Attitude strength: Antecedents and consequences* (pp. 215–245). Lawrence Erlbaum Associates.

Haddock, G., Rothman, A. J., Reber, R., & Schwarz, N. (1999). Forming judgments of attitude certainty, intensity, and importance: The role of subjective experiences. *Personality and Social Psychology Bulletin*, *25*(7), 771–782. https://doi.org/10.1177/0146167299025007001

Haugtvedt, C. P., & Kasmer, J. A. (2008). Attitude change and persuasion. In C. P. Haugtvedt, P. M. Herr, & F. R. Kardes (Eds.), *Marketing and consumer psychology series: Vol. 4. Handbook of consumer psychology* (pp. 419–435). Taylor & Francis Group/Lawrence Erlbaum Associates.

Horcajo, J., Briñol, P., & Petty, R. E. (2014). Multiple roles for majority versus minority source status on persuasion when source status follows the message. *Social Influence*, *9*(1), 37–51. https://doi.org/10.1080/15534510.2012.743485

Horcajo, J., Petty, R. E., & Briñol, P. (2010). The effects of majority versus minority source status on persuasion: A self-validation analysis. *Journal of Personality and Social Psychology*, *99*(3), 498–512. https://doi.org/10.1037/a0018626

Hovland, C. I., Janis, I. L., & Kelley, H. H. (1953). *Communication and persuasion*. Yale University Press.

Hovland, C. I., Lumsdaine, A. A., & Sheffield, F. D. (1949). *Experiments on mass communication. (Studies in social psychology in World War II)* (Vol. 3). Princeton University Press.

Infante, D. A. (1976). Persuasion as a function of the receiver's prior success or failure as a message source. *Communication Quarterly*, *24*(3), 21–26. https://doi.org/10.1080/01463377609369224

Janis, I. L., & King, B. T. (1954). The influence of role playing on opinion change. *Journal of Abnormal and Social Psychology*, *49*(2), 211–218. https://doi.org/10.1037/h0056957

Jiang, L., Hoegg, J., Dahl, D. W., & Chattopadhyay, A. (2010). The persuasive role of incidental similarity on attitudes and purchase intentions in a sales context. *Journal of Consumer Research*, *36*(5), 778–791. https://doi.org/10.1086/605364

Kardes, F. R., Fennis, B. M., Hirt, E. R., Tormala, Z. L., & Bullington, B. (2007). The role of the need for cognitive closure in the effectiveness of the disrupt-then-reframe influence technique. *Journal of Consumer Research*, *34*(3), 377–385. https://doi.org/10.1086/518541

Kaufman, D. Q., Stasson, M. F., & Hart, J. W. (1999). Are the tabloids always wrong or is that just what we think? Need for cognition and perceptions of articles in print media. *Journal of Applied*

Social Psychology, 29(9), 1984–2000. https://doi.org/10.1111/j.1559-1816.1999.tb00160.x

Kelman, H. C. (1958). Compliance, identification, and internalization three processes of attitude change. Journal of Conflict Resolution, 2(1), 51–60. https://doi.org/10.1177/002200275800200106

Kelman, H. C., & Hovland, C. I. (1953). Reinstatement of the communicator in delayed measurement of opinion change. Journal of Abnormal and Social Psychology, 48(3), 327–335. https://doi.org/10.1037/h0061861

Killeya, L. A., & Johnson, B. T. (1998). Experimental induction of biased systematic processing: The directed-thought technique. Personality and Social Psychology Bulletin, 24(1), 17–33. https://doi.org/10.1177/0146167298241002

Koriat, A. (2012). The self-consistency model of subjective confidence. Psychological Review, 119(1), 80–113. https://doi.org/10.1037/a0025648

Krause, R. J., & Rucker, D. D. (2020). Strategic storytelling: When narratives help versus hurt the persuasive power of facts. Personality and Social Psychology Bulletin, 46(2), 216–227. https://doi.org/10.1177/0146167219853845

Krosnick, J. A., Boninger, D. S., Chuang, Y. C., Berent, M. K., & Carnot, C. G. (1993). Attitude strength: One construct or many related constructs? Journal of Personality and Social Psychology, 65(6), 1132–1151. https://doi.org/10.1037/0022-3514.65.6.1132

Krosnick, J. A., & Petty, R. E. (1995). Attitude strength: An overview. In R. E. Petty & J. A. Krosnick (Eds.), Ohio State University series on attitudes and persuasion: Vol. 4. Attitude strength: Antecedents and consequences (pp. 1–24). Lawrence Erlbaum Associates.

Kruglanski, A. W., Webster, D. M., & Klem, A. (1993). Motivated resistance and openness to persuasion in the presence or absence of prior information. Journal of Personality and Social Psychology, 65(5), 861–876. https://doi.org/10.1037/0022-3514.65.5.861

Labroo, A. A., Dhar, R., & Schwarz, N. (2008). Of frog wines and frowning watches: Semantic priming, perceptual fluency, and brand evaluation. Journal of Consumer Research, 34(6), 819–831. https://doi.org/10.1086/523290

LaPiere, R. T. (1934). Attitudes vs. actions. Social Forces, 13(2), 230–237. https://doi.org/10.2307/2570339

Lee, A. Y., & Labroo, A. A. (2004). The effect of conceptual and perceptual fluency on brand evaluation. Journal of Marketing Research, 41(2), 151–165. https://doi.org/10.1509/jmkr.41.2.151.28665

Litt, A., & Tormala, Z. L. (2010). Fragile enhancement of attitudes and intentions following difficult decisions. Journal of Consumer Research, 37(4), 584–598. https://doi.org/10.1086/653494

Lord, C. G., Ross, L., & Lepper, M. R. (1979). Biased assimilation and attitude polarization: The effects of prior theories on subsequently considered evidence. Journal of Personality and Social Psychology, 37(11), 2098–2109. https://doi.org/10.1037/0022-3514.37.11.2098

Lydon, J., Zanna, M. P., & Ross, M. (1988). Bolstering attitudes by autobiographical recall: Attitude persistence and selective memory. Personality and Social Psychology Bulletin, 14(1), 78–86. https://doi.org/10.1177/0146167288141008

Maheswaran, D., & Chaiken, S. (1991). Promoting systematic processing in low-motivation settings: Effect of incongruent information on processing and judgment. Journal of Personality and Social Psychology, 61(1), 13–25. https://doi.org/10.1037/0022-3514.61.1.13

Maio, G. R., & Thomas, G. (2007). The epistemic-teleologic model of deliberate self-persuasion. Personality and Social Psychology Review, 11(1), 46–67. https://doi.org/10.1177/1088868306294589

Maloney, E. K., Lapinski, M. K., & Witte, K. (2011). Fear appeals and persuasion: A review and update of the extended parallel process model. Social and Personality Psychology Compass, 5(4), 206–219. https://doi.org/10.1111/j.1751-9004.2011.00341.x

Mayer, N. D., & Tormala, Z. L. (2010). "Think" versus "feel" framing effects in persuasion. Personality and Social Psychology Bulletin, 36(4), 443–454. https://doi.org/10.1177/0146167210362981

McGuire, W. J. (1964). Inducing resistance to persuasion: Some contemporary approaches. Advances in Experimental Social Psychology, 1, 191–229. https://doi.org/10/cth7vv

McGuire, W. J. (1985). Attitudes and attitude change. In G. Lindzey & E. Aronson (Eds.), The handbook of social psychology (3rd ed., Vol. 2, pp. 233–346). Random House.

Millar, M. G., & Millar, K. U. (1990). Attitude change as a function of attitude type and argument type. Journal of Personality and Social Psychology, 59(2), 217–228. https://doi.org/10.1037/0022-3514.59.2.217

Mills, J., & Jellison, J. M. (1967). Effect on opinion change of how desirable the communication is to the audience the communicator addressed. Journal of Personality and Social Psychology, 6(1), 98–101. https://doi.org/10.1037/h0021217

Molden, D. C., & Dweck, C. S. (2006). Finding "meaning" in psychology: A lay theories approach to self-regulation, social perception, and social development. American Psychologist, 61(3), 192–203. https://doi.org/10.1037/0003-066X.61.3.192

Muthukrishnan, A., Pham, M. T., & Mungale, A. (2001). Does greater amount of information always bolster attitudinal resistance?

Marketing Letters, *12*(2), 131–144. https://doi.org/10.1023/A:1011113002473

Payne, B. K., & Gawronski, B. (2010). A history of implicit social cognition: Where is it coming from? Where is it now? Where is it going? In B. Gawronski & B. K. Payne (Eds.), *Handbook of implicit cognition: Measurement, theory, and application* (pp. 1–15). Guilford Press.

Pechmann, C. (1992). Predicting when two-sided ads will be more effective than one-sided ads: The role of correlational and correspondent inferences. *Journal of Marketing Research*, *29*(4), 441–453. https://doi.org/10.1177/002224379202900405

Pelham, B. W., Sumarta, T. T., & Myaskovsky, L. (1994). The easy path from many to much: The numerosity heuristic. *Cognitive Psychology*, *26*(2), 103–133. https://doi.org/10.1006/cogp.1994.1004

Perkins, A., & Forehand, M. (2010). Implicit social cognition and indirect measures in consumer behavior. In B. Gawronski & B. K. Payne (Eds.), *Handbook of implicit social cognition: Measurement, theory, and applications* (pp. 535–547). Guilford Press.

Petrocelli, J. V., Clarkson, J. J., Tormala, Z. L., & Hendrix, K. S. (2010). Perceiving stability as a means to attitude certainty: The role of implicit theories of attitudes. *Journal of Experimental Social Psychology*, *46*(6), 874–883. https://doi.org/10.1016/j.jesp.2010.07.012

Petrocelli, J. V., Tormala, Z. L., & Rucker, D. D. (2007). Unpacking attitude certainty: Attitude clarity and attitude correctness. *Journal of Personality and Social Psychology*, *92*(1), 30–41. https://doi.org/10.1037/0022-3514.92.1.30

Petty, R. E., & Briñol, P. (2015). Emotion and persuasion: Cognitive and meta-cognitive processes impact attitudes. *Cognition and Emotion*, *29*(1), 1–26. https://doi.org/10.1080/02699931.2014.967183

Petty, R. E., Briñol, P., & Tormala, Z. L. (2002). Thought confidence as a determinant of persuasion: The self-validation hypothesis. *Journal of Personality and Social Psychology*, *82*(5), 722–741. https://doi.org/10.1037/0022-3514.82.5.722

Petty, R. E., Briñol, P., Tormala, Z. L., & Wegener, D. T. (2007). The role of metacognition in social judgment. In A. W. Kruglanski & E. T. Higgins (Eds.), *Social psychology: Handbook of basic principles* (pp. 254–284). Guilford Press.

Petty, R. E., & Brock, T. C. (1981). Thought disruption and persuasion: Assessing the validity of attitude change experiments. In R. Petty, T. Ostrom, & T. Brock (Eds.), *Cognitive responses in persuasion* (pp. 55–79). Erlbaum.

Petty, R. E., & Cacioppo, J. T. (1984). The effects of involvement on responses to argument quantity and quality: Central and peripheral routes to persuasion. *Journal of Personality and Social Psychology*, *46*(1), 69–81. https://doi.org/10.1037/0022-3514.46.1.69

Petty, R. E., & Cacioppo, J. T. (1986). The elaboration likelihood model of persuasion. In *Communication and persuasion* (pp. 1–24). Springer.

Petty, R. E., Cacioppo, J. T., & Schumann, D. (1983). Central and peripheral routes to advertising effectiveness: The moderating role of involvement. *Journal of Consumer Research*, *10*(2), 135–146. https://doi.org/10.1086/208954

Petty, R. E., Fazio, R. H., & Briñol, P. (Eds.). (2008). *Attitudes: Insights from the new implicit measures*. Psychology Press. https://doi.org/10.4324/9780203809884

Petty, R. E., Haugtvedt, C. P., & Smith, S. M. (1995). Elaboration as a determinant of attitude strength: Creating attitudes that are persistent, resistant, and predictive of behavior. In R. E. Petty & J. A. Krosnick (Eds.), *Ohio State University series on attitudes and persuasion: Vol. 4. Attitude strength: Antecedents and consequences* (pp. 93–130). Lawrence Erlbaum Associates.

Petty, R. E., Rucker, D., Bizer, G., & Cacioppo, J. (2004). The elaboration likelihood model. In J. S. Seiter & R. H. Gass (Eds.), *Perspectives on persuasion, social influence and compliance gaining* (pp. 65–89). Allyn & Bacon.

Petty, R. E., Schumann, D. W., Richman, S. A., & Strathman, A. J. (1993). Positive mood and persuasion: Different roles for affect under high- and low-elaboration conditions. *Journal of Personality and Social Psychology*, *64*(1), 5–20. https://doi.org/10.1037/0022-3514.64.1.5

Petty, R. E., Unnava, R. H., & Strathman, A. J. (1991). Theories of attitude change. In T. S. Robertson & H. H. Kassarjian (Eds.), *Handbook of consumer behavior* (pp. 241–280). Prentice-Hall.

Petty, R. E., & Wegener, D. T. (1998). Matching versus mismatching attitude functions: Implications for scrutiny of persuasive messages. *Personality and Social Psychology Bulletin*, *24*(3), 227–240. https://doi.org/10.1177/0146167298243001

Petty, R. E., Wegener, D. T., & Fabrigar, L. R. (1997). Attitudes and attitude change. *Annual Review of Psychology*, *48*(1), 609–647. https://doi.org/10.1146/annurev.psych.48.1.609

Philipp-Muller, A. Z., Wallace, L. E., & Wegener, D. T. (2020). Where does moral conviction fit? A factor analytic approach examining antecedents to attitude strength. *Journal of Experimental Social Psychology*, *86*, 103900. https://doi.org/10.1016/j.jesp.2019.103900

Priester, J. R., & Petty, R. E. (1995). Source attributions and persuasion: Perceived honesty as a determinant of message scrutiny. *Personality and Social Psychology Bulletin*, *21*(6), 637–654. https://doi.org/10.1177/0146167295216010

Priester, J. R., & Petty, R. E. (2003). The influence of spokesperson trustworthiness on message elaboration, attitude strength, and advertising effectiveness. *Journal of Consumer Psychology, 13*(4), 408–421. https://doi.org/10.1207/S15327663JCP1304_08

Prislin, R., Boyle, S. M., Davenport, C., Farley, A., Jacobs, E., Michalak, J., & Xu, Y. (2011). On being influenced while trying to persuade: The feedback effect of persuasion outcomes on the persuader. *Social Psychological & Personality Science, 2*(1), 51–58. https://doi.org/10.1177/1948550610377238

Rhodes, N., & Wood, W. (1992). Self-esteem and intelligence affect influenceability: The mediating role of message reception. *Psychological Bulletin, 111*(1), 156–171. https://doi.org/10.1037/0033-2909.111.1.156

Rios, K., & Chen, Z. (2014). Experimental evidence for minorities' hesitancy in reporting their opinions: The roles of optimal distinctiveness needs and normative influence. *Personality and Social Psychology Bulletin, 40*(7), 872–883. https://doi.org/10.1177/0146167214528990

Rios, K., DeMarree, K. G., & Statzer, J. (2014). Attitude certainty and conflict style: Divergent effects of correctness and clarity. *Personality and Social Psychology Bulletin, 40*(7), 819–830. https://doi.org/10.1177/0146167214528991

Rios, K., Goldberg, M. H., & Totton, R. R. (2018). An informational influence perspective on (non) conformity: Perceived knowledgeability increases expression of minority opinions. *Communication Research, 45*(2), 241–260. https://doi.org/10.1177/0093650217699935

Rios, K., Wheeler, S. C., & Miller, D. T. (2012). Compensatory nonconformity: Self-uncertainty and low implicit self-esteem increase adoption and expression of minority opinions. *Journal of Experimental Social Psychology, 48*(6), 1300–1309. https://doi.org/10.1016/j.jesp.2012.07.005

Rocklage, M. D., Rucker, D. D., & Nordgren, L. F. (2018). Persuasion, emotion, and language: The intent to persuade transforms language via emotionality. *Psychological Science, 29*(5), 749–760. https://doi.org/10.1177/0956797617744797

Rosenberg, M. J., Hovland, C. I., McGuire, W. J., Abelson, R. P., & Brehm, J. W. (1960). *Attitude organization and change: An analysis of consistency among attitude components (Yale studies in attitude and communication)*. Yale University Press.

Rucker, D. D., & Petty, R. E. (2004). When resistance is futile: Consequences of failed counterarguing for attitude certainty. *Journal of Personality and Social Psychology, 86*(2), 219–235. https://doi.org/10.1037/0022-3514.86.2.219

Rucker, D. D., Petty, R. E., & Briñol, P. (2008). What's in a frame anyway? A meta-cognitive analysis of the impact of one versus two sided message framing on attitude certainty. *Journal of Consumer Psychology, 18*(2), 137–149. https://doi.org/10.1016/j.jcps.2008.01.008

Rucker, D. D., Tormala, Z. L., Petty, R. E., & Briñol, P. (2014). Consumer conviction and commitment: An appraisal-based framework for attitude certainty. *Journal of Consumer Psychology, 24*(1), 119–136. https://doi.org/10.1016/j.jcps.2013.07.001

Sanbonmatsu, D. M., Kardes, F. R., & Herr, P. M. (1992). The role of prior knowledge and missing information in multiattribute evaluation. *Organizational Behavior and Human Decision Processes, 51*(1), 76–91. https://doi.org/10.1016/0749-5978(92)90005-R

Sawicki, V., Wegener, D. T., Clark, J. K., Fabrigar, L. R., Smith, S. M., & Bengal, S. T. (2011). Seeking confirmation in times of doubt: Selective exposure and the motivational strength of weak attitudes. *Social Psychological & Personality Science, 2*(5), 540–546. https://doi.org/10.1177/1948550611400212

Schwarz, N., Bless, H., Strack, F., Klumpp, G., Rittenauer-Schatka, H., & Simons, A. (1991). Ease of retrieval as information: Another look at the availability heuristic. *Journal of Personality and Social Psychology, 61*(2), 195–202. https://doi.org/10.1037/0022-3514.61.2.195

See, Y. H. M., Petty, R. E., & Fabrigar, L. R. (2008). Affective and cognitive meta-bases of attitudes: Unique effects on information interest and persuasion. *Journal of Personality and Social Psychology, 94*(6), 938–955. https://doi.org/10.1037/0022-3514.94.6.938

Skitka, L. J. (2010). The psychology of moral conviction. *Social and Personality Psychology Compass, 4*(4), 267–281. https://doi.org/10.1111/j.1751-9004.2010.00254.x

Skitka, L. J., & Bauman, C. W. (2008). Moral conviction and political engagement. *Political Psychology, 29*(1), 29–54. https://doi.org/10.1111/j.1467-9221.2007.00611.x

Skitka, L. J., Bauman, C. W., & Sargis, E. G. (2005). Moral conviction: Another contributor to attitude strength or something more? *Journal of Personality and Social Psychology, 88*(6), 895–917. https://doi.org/10.1037/0022-3514.88.6.895

Skitka, L. J., Hanson, B. E., & Wisneski, D. C. (2017). Utopian hopes or dystopian fears? Exploring the motivational underpinnings of moralized political engagement. *Personality and Social Psychology Bulletin, 43*(2), 177–190. https://doi.org/10.1177/0146167216678858

Smith, C. T., De Houwer, J., & Nosek, B. A. (2013). Consider the source: Persuasion of implicit evaluations is moderated by source credibility. *Personality and*

Social Psychology Bulletin, 39(2), 193–205. https://doi.org/10.1177/0146167212472374

Smith, S. M., Fabrigar, L. R., Macdougall, B. L., & Wiesenthal, N. L. (2008). The role of amount, cognitive elaboration, and structural consistency of attitude-relevant knowledge in the formation of attitude certainty. European Journal of Social Psychology, 38(2), 280–295. https://doi.org/10.1002/ejsp.447

Snyder, A. I., & Tormala, Z. L. (2017). Valence asymmetries in attitude ambivalence. Journal of Personality and Social Psychology, 112(4), 555–576. https://doi.org/10.1037/pspa0000075

Snyder, M., & Rothbart, M. (1971). Communicator attractiveness and opinion change. Canadian Journal of Behavioural Science/Revue canadienne des sciences du comportement, 3(4), 377–387. https://doi.org/10.1037/h0082280

Teeny, J. D., & Petty, R. E. (2018). The role of perceived attitudinal bases on spontaneous and requested advocacy. Journal of Experimental Social Psychology, 76, 175–185. https://doi.org/10.1016/j.jesp.2018.02.003

Teeny, J. D., Siev, J. J., Briñol, P., & Petty, R. E. (2021). A review and conceptual framework for understanding personalized matching effects in persuasion. Journal of Consumer Psychology, 31(2) 382-414. https://doi.org/10.1002/jcpy.1198

Tesser, A. (1978). Self-generated attitude change. Advances in Experimental Social Psychology, 11, 289–338. https://doi.org/10.1016/S0065-2601(08)60010-6

Tesser, A., & Conlee, M. C. (1975). Some effects of time and thought on attitude polarization. Journal of Personality and Social Psychology, 31(2), 262–270. https://doi.org/10.1037/h0076292

Thompson, M. M., Zanna, M. P., & Griffin, D. W. (1995). Let's not be indifferent about (attitudinal) ambivalence. In R. E. Petty & J. A. Krosnick (Eds.), Ohio State University series on attitudes and persuasion: Vol. 4. Attitude strength: Antecedents and consequences (pp. 361–386). Lawrence Erlbaum Associates.

Thurstone, L. L. (1928). Attitudes can be measured. American Journal of Sociology, 33(4), 529–554. https://doi.org/10.1086/214483

Tiedens, L. Z., & Linton, S. (2001). Judgment under emotional certainty and uncertainty: The effects of specific emotions on information processing. Journal of Personality and Social Psychology, 81(6), 973–988. https://doi.org/10.1037/0022-3514.81.6.973

Tormala, Z. L., & Briñol, P. (2015). Attitude change and persuasion: Past, present, and future directions. In M. I. Norton, D. D. Rucker, & C. Lamberton (Eds.), Cambridge handbooks in psychology: The Cambridge handbook of consumer psychology (pp. 29–64). Cambridge University Press. https://doi.org/10.1017/CBO9781107706552.002

Tormala, Z. L., Briñol, P., & Petty, R. E. (2006). When credibility attacks: The reverse impact of source credibility on persuasion. Journal of Experimental Social Psychology, 42(5), 684–691. https://doi.org/10.1016/j.jesp.2005.10.005

Tormala, Z. L., Briñol, P., & Petty, R. E. (2007). Multiple roles for source credibility under high elaboration: It's all in the timing. Social Cognition, 25(4), 536–552. https://doi.org/10.1521/soco.2007.25.4.536

Tormala, Z. L., Clarkson, J. J., & Henderson, M. D. (2011). Does fast or slow evaluation foster greater certainty? Personality and Social Psychology Bulletin, 37(3), 422–434. https://doi.org/10.1177/0146167210397378

Tormala, Z. L., Clarkson, J. J., & Petty, R. E. (2006). Resisting persuasion by the skin of one's teeth: The hidden success of resisted persuasive messages. Journal of Personality and Social Psychology, 91(3), 423–435. https://doi.org/10.1037/0022-3514.91.3.423

Tormala, Z. L., & DeSensi, V. L. (2009). The effects of minority/majority source status on attitude certainty: A matching perspective. Personality and Social Psychology Bulletin, 35(1), 114–125. https://doi.org/10.1177/0146167208325677

Tormala, Z. L., DeSensi, V. L., & Petty, R. E. (2007). Resisting persuasion by illegitimate means: A meta-cognitive perspective on minority influence. Personality and Social Psychology Bulletin, 33(3), 354–367. https://doi.org/10.1177/0146167206295004

Tormala, Z. L., Falces, C., Briñol, P., & Petty, R. E. (2007). Ease of retrieval effects in social judgment: The role of unrequested cognitions. Journal of Personality and Social Psychology, 93(2), 143–157. https://doi.org/10.1037/0022-3514.93.2.143

Tormala, Z. L., & Petty, R. E. (2002). What doesn't kill me makes me stronger: The effects of resisting persuasion on attitude certainty. Journal of Personality and Social Psychology, 83(6), 1298–1313. https://doi.org/10.1037/0022-3514.83.6.1298

Tormala, Z. L., & Petty, R. E. (2004a). Resisting persuasion and attitude certainty: A meta-cognitive analysis. In E. S. Knowles & J. A. Linn (Eds.), Resistance and persuasion (pp. 65–82). Lawrence Erlbaum Associates.

Tormala, Z. L., & Petty, R. E. (2004b). Source credibility and attitude certainty: A metacognitive analysis of resistance to persuasion. Journal of Consumer Psychology, 14(4), 427–442. https://doi.org/10.1207/s15327663jcp1404_11

Tormala, Z. L., & Petty, R. E. (2007). Contextual contrast and perceived knowledge: Exploring the implications for persuasion. Journal of Experimental Social Psychology, 43(1), 17–30. https://doi.org/10.1016/j.jesp.2005.11.007

Tormala, Z. L., Petty, R. E., & Briñol, P. (2002). Ease of retrieval effects in persuasion: A self-validation analysis. *Personality and Social Psychology Bulletin*, *28*(12), 1700–1712. https://doi.org/10.1177/014616702237651

Tormala, Z. L., Petty, R. E., & DeSensi, V. L. (2009). Multiple roles for minority sources in persuasion and resistance. In R. Marin & M. Hewstone (Eds.), *Minority influence and innovation* (pp. 123–150). Psychology Press.

Tormala, Z. L., & Rucker, D. D. (2007). Attitude certainty: A review of past findings and emerging perspectives. *Social and Personality Psychology Compass*, *1*(1), 469–492. https://doi.org/10.1111/j.1751-9004.2007.00025.x

Tormala, Z. L., & Rucker, D. D. (2018). Attitude certainty: Antecedents, consequences, and new directions. *Consumer Psychology Review*, *1*(1), 72–89. https://doi.org/10.1002/arcp.1004

Tsai, C. I., Klayman, J., & Hastie, R. (2008). Effects of amount of information on judgment accuracy and confidence. *Organizational Behavior and Human Decision Processes*, *107*(2), 97–105. https://doi.org/10.1016/j.obhdp.2008.01.005

Visser, P. S., Krosnick, J. A., & Simmons, J. P. (2003). Distinguishing the cognitive and behavioral consequences of attitude and certainty: A new approach to testing the common-factor hypothesis. *Journal of Experimental Social Psychology*, *39*(2), 118–141. https://doi.org/10.1016/S0022-1031(02)00522-X

Visser, P. S., & Mirabile, R. R. (2004). Attitudes in the social context: The impact of social network composition on individual-level attitude strength. *Journal of Personality and Social Psychology*, *87*(6), 779–795. https://doi.org/10.1037/0022-3514.87.6.779

Wan, E. W., Rucker, D. D., Tormala, Z. L., & Clarkson, J. J. (2010). The effect of regulatory depletion on attitude certainty. *Journal of Marketing Research*, *47*(3), 531–541. https://doi.org/10.1509/jmkr.47.3.531

Wänke, M., Bohner, G., & Jurkowitsch, A. (1997). There are many reasons to drive a BMW: Does imagined ease of argument generation influence attitudes? *Journal of Consumer Research*, *24*(2), 170–177.

Wegener, D. T., Petty, R. E., & Smith, S. M. (1995). Positive mood can increase or decrease message scrutiny: The hedonic contingency view of mood and message processing. *Journal of Personality and Social Psychology*, *69*(1), 5–15. https://doi.org/10.1037/0022-3514.69.1.5

Wells, G. L., & Petty, R. E. (1980). The effects of over head movements on persuasion: Compatibility and incompatibility of responses. *Basic and Applied Social Psychology*, *1*(3), 219–230. https://doi.org/10.1207/s15324834basp0103_2

Wood, W., Lundgren, S., Ouellette, J. A., Busceme, S., & Blackstone, T. (1994). Minority influence: A meta-analytic review of social influence processes. *Psychological Bulletin*, *115*(3), 323–345. https://doi.org/10.1037/0033-2909.115.3.323

Xu, A. J., & Wyer, R. S., Jr. (2012). The role of bolstering and counterarguing mind-sets in persuasion. *Journal of Consumer Research*, *38*(5), 920–932. https://doi.org/10.1086/661112

Zanna, M. P., & Rempel, J. K. (1988). Attitudes: A new look at an old concept. In D. Bar-Tal & A. W. Kruglanski (Eds.), *The social psychology of knowledge* (pp. 315–334). Cambridge University Press; Editions de la Maison des Sciences de l'Homme.

CHAPTER 14

SOCIAL RELATIONSHIPS AND CONSUMER BEHAVIOR

Kelley Gullo Wight, Peggy J. Liu, James R. Bettman, and Gavan J. Fitzsimons

Social relationships permeate consumers' interactions with both the marketplace and consumption more broadly. Imagine a consumer, Sam, walking through a department store. Sam hopes to buy a birthday present for their best friend, pick up socks for their spouse, find a microwave that will be more accessible for their aging parents, pick up a bedding set for themselves and their spouse, and find something to wear at an upcoming wedding. Any individual consumer, on any given trip, may be shopping for themselves (such as the wedding outfit) or for both themselves and someone else (such as the bedding set), but they also might be buying solely for someone else for a number of reasons, including gifting, providing favors, and caretaking (P. J. Liu et al., 2019). Now imagine that Sam is not alone in the store but brought along their spouse, Joe, and called their sister, Carmen, while picking a microwave for their parents as they are splitting the cost. In this situation, the purchase decisions become joint decisions, which can further shape the decision-making process and the decisions made. Joe might be more price sensitive than Sam and expand Sam's consideration set by price-checking the products online. Or Joe might feel impatient with clothes shopping and rush Sam through picking a wedding outfit. On the other hand, Carmen might prioritize their parents' preferences and push for Sam to buy the higher quality, but more expensive, microwave. Both Joe and Carmen influence Sam's purchasing behavior whether or not they are directly involved in the decision process.

Even reminders of relationships can affect consumption behavior; after seeing an in-store advertisement featuring two best friends, Sam is reminded of their current lack of close friendships. Such reminders of a shortage of relationships can lead to a restriction in indulgent consumption because they make consumers feel undeserving (Cavanaugh, 2014), and so Sam decides not to get a treat at the department store's expensive in-house café. As these examples demonstrate, personal relationships can influence many aspects related to consumption, including consumers' goal pursuit and product choices. The resulting consumption can then also affect aspects of relationships, for example by making people feel more or less close to each other (e.g., Ruth et al., 1999). Thus, personal relationships can both directly and indirectly influence consumer behavior and vice versa. Understanding such effects is important for consumer psychologists, policy makers, and marketers.

In this chapter, we discuss the intersection of social relationships and consumer behavior. We focus our discussion on close personal consumer-to-consumer connections such as friendships, romantic relationships, and familial relationships, primarily in the form of dyads but

This chapter is based on the first author's dissertation.
https://doi.org/10.1037/0000262-014
APA Handbook of Consumer Psychology, L. R. Kahle (Editor-in-Chief)
Copyright © 2022 by the American Psychological Association. All rights reserved.

also considering groups, which are generally less researched in consumer behavior. We do not extend our discussion to nonestablished relationships (e.g., strangers, the mere social presence of others, social reference groups, or crowding) or relationships with institutional authority figures (e.g., boss–employee), professionals (e.g., doctor–patient, lawyer–client, other hired agents), salespersons, or nonhumans (e.g., with brands, firms, animals).

While social relationships influence many aspects of consumer behavior, we focus on two domains that are of high relevance for consumers, policy makers, marketers, and researchers and have received much attention in marketing's interpersonal and social influence literatures: goals and decision making. These topics are related to one another, in that one's goals shape consumption decisions, and the outcome of such decisions can affect consumers' ensuing goals. In addition, in our discussion we consider both individually held goals (e.g., for oneself to spend less) and jointly held goals (e.g., both partners aim to get physically fit to prepare for an upcoming hiking trip together) and decisions for oneself, decisions for others, and jointly made decisions.

This chapter is structured as follows. First, we propose three key theoretical relationship dimensions (closeness, competitiveness, and power) and discuss the relevant psychology and marketing literatures on each of these dimensions as well as how each dimension affects two focal consumer behavior domains (motivation and decision making). We then shift to discussing how consumer behavior actions within the context of a relationship can affect the relationship itself. Last, we highlight gaps in the current understanding of consumer relationship theory and areas for future research. We also discuss challenges in studying relationships and identify solutions for dealing with those challenges.

THREE KEY RELATIONAL DIMENSIONS

Although most research on interpersonal effects in social psychology has used closeness as the sole dimension to distinguish between relationship types (Aron et al., 1992), we contend that one's relationship with their young child, for example, is systematically different from their relationship with a friend, even though both would be categorized as "close." To more fully characterize relationships, we organize our discussion of social relationships around three key relational dimensions: closeness, competitiveness, and power.

Closeness describes how interconnected individuals are (Aron et al., 1992; Kelley et al., 1983). *Competitiveness* describes the extent to which a relationship motivates social comparison and a desire to close any gaps or perceived differences (Festinger, 1954; Garcia et al., 2013). *Power* describes who has control over outcomes within the relationship, which we further subdivide into control coming from *relationship power* (e.g., one spouse exerts more influence over the other but ownership for the outcome is shared; e.g., Brick et al., 2018) and control coming from *responsibility power* (e.g., a parent has influence over their child and has ultimate ownership for the outcomes; Steffel et al., 2016). Figure 14.1 contains a conceptual diagram of these three key relational dimensions.

We suggest that these are theoretically orthogonally related, even if some octants may be more frequently occupied than others. For example, even if most of people's close relationships tend to be noncompetitive and with similar-power individuals, we contend that people can sometimes be highly competitive with close others (e.g., sibling rivalry) or occupy different power statuses with close others (e.g., parent–young child relationships). Figure 14.2 contains a conceptual diagram of how these three key relational dimensions interrelate to form distinct types of relationships.

Although there are various other relational dimensions in relationship psychology—including attachment (e.g., Bowlby, 1964/1982), interdependence (e.g., Rusbult & Arriaga, 1997), and exchange/communal orientation (Clark & Mils, 1993)—that are relevant to consumer behavior, we focus on closeness, competitiveness, and power for two main reasons. First, research suggests that many of these dimensions are interrelated; thus, focusing on these encompassing dimensions enables us to still cover the others to some extent. Interdependence and attachment style, for example, can influence feelings of closeness (e.g., Collins &

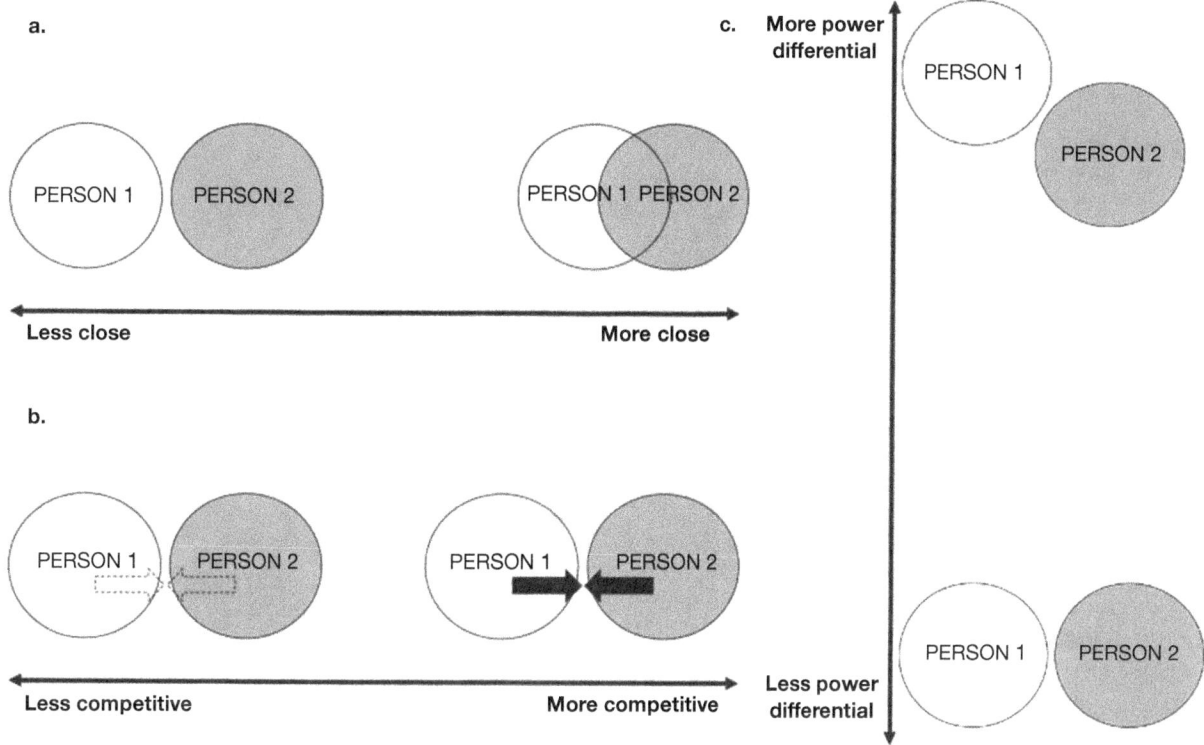

FIGURE 14.1. Conceptual depictions of three key relational dimensions. Each set of circles represents two individuals in a dyadic relationship. (a) Closeness is represented by increasingly overlapping circles. (b) Competitiveness is represented by increasingly dark arrows, which are focused on the other person. (c) Power is represented by increasing hierarchy in the vertical orientation of the circles. From *A Multi-Dimensional Approach to Social Relationships in Consumer Behavior* [Doctoral dissertation], by K. Gullo, 2020, Duke University. CC BY 3.0. Reprinted with permission.

Feeney, 2004; Kelley et al., 1983), and an exchange orientation is more likely to engender competitiveness than a communal orientation, which is associated with cooperation (Silk, 2003). Second, our goal was to develop a tractable framework that would allow research on each of the dimensions to be used to understand how qualitatively different types of relationships (e.g., one's spouse, one's child, one's friend) can affect consumer behavior outcomes. That is, we argue that nearly all social relationships can be situated along these three focal dimensions. One's relationship with their young child, for example, could prototypically be defined as high in closeness, low in competitiveness, and high in power differential, whereas one's relationship with a friend could prototypically be defined as involving midlevels of closeness, ranging from low to high competitiveness, and low in power differential. However, other relational dimensions are not as suitable for this task. Attachment style, for example, is generally viewed as an individual difference instead of varying by relationship type (as discussed in Heffernan et al., 2012).

INTERPERSONAL CLOSENESS

Interpersonal closeness is, in our view, currently the most studied relational factor in social psychology and in consumer behavior. Although various definitions exist, one excellent encompassing definition is provided by Aron et al. (1992): Closeness is the perceived overlap between the self and the other. Feelings of closeness are achieved (and reflected) through many potential paths, including reciprocal disclosure (Collins & Miller, 1994; Sedikides et al., 1999), spending time together, engaging in a variety of activities together, perceptions of mutual influence over each other's plans (Berscheid et al., 1989),

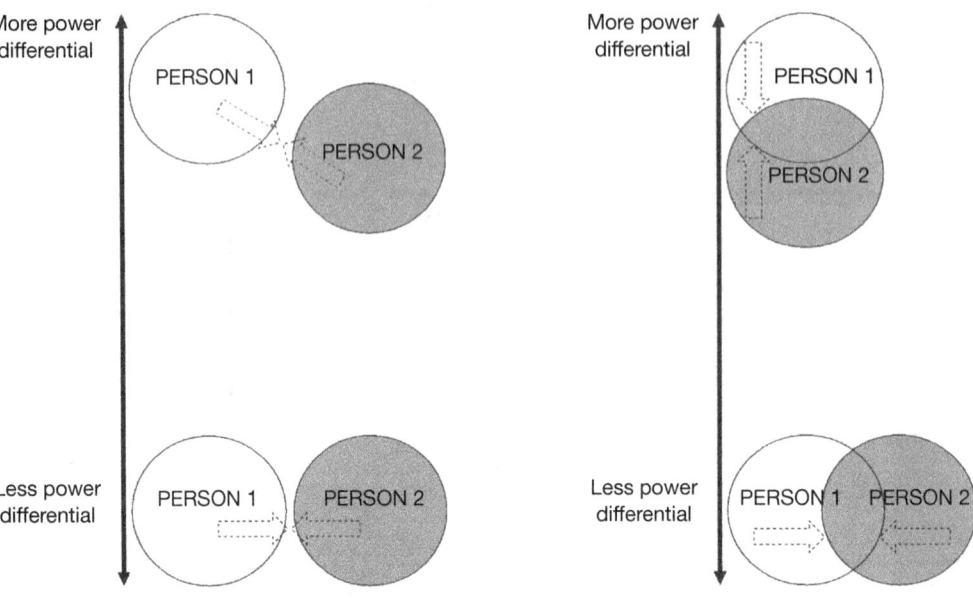

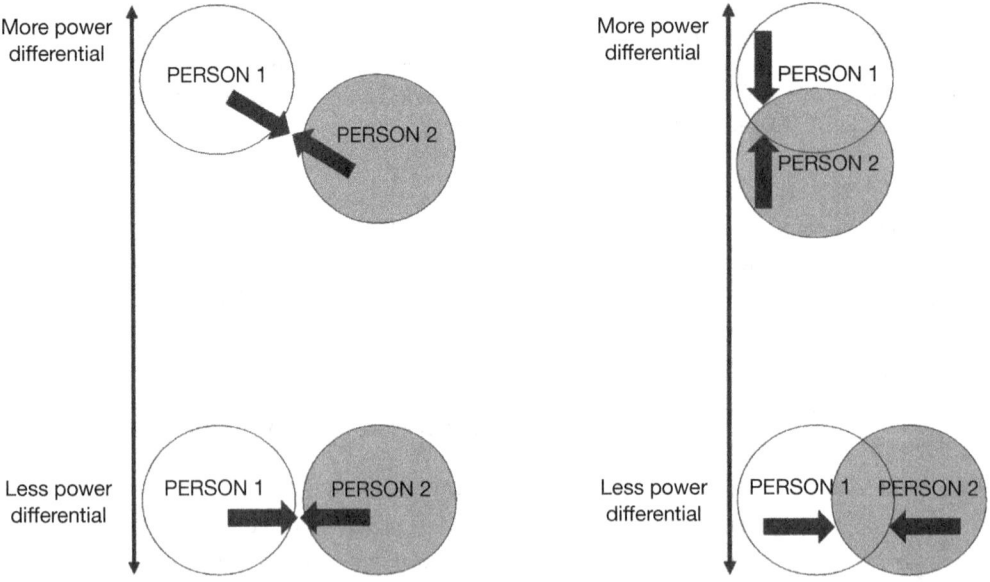

FIGURE 14.2. Conceptual depictions of how each of the three key relational dimensions interrelate to form distinct relationships. Examples of prototypical established relationships in each quadrant: (a) college roommates in different degree tracks and with varying degrees of social power within the relationship, (b) parent–child relationship over time, where the responsibility power differential decreases as the child becomes an adult, (c) teammates who compete on personal records with varying degrees of leadership roles on the team, (d) best friends or even romantic partners who compete on fitness goals with varying degrees of social power within the relationship. From *A Multi-Dimensional Approach to Social Relationships in Consumer Behavior* [Doctoral dissertation], by K. Gullo, 2020, Duke University. CC BY 3.0. Reprinted with permission.

and maintaining a relationship over time (Kelley et al., 1983).

Feeling close with another person influences how one perceives oneself and behaves toward others. As implied by the definition, people tend to think of close others as part of their own self-concept, placing themselves and close others in the same cognitive category relative to that of strangers (e.g., Bower & Gilligan, 1979). As a result, people tend to adopt, at least in part, the close other's perceived characteristics, perspectives, and resources as their own (e.g., Aron et al., 1991; Tu et al., 2016). Altogether, feeling close to others can exert a powerful influence on behavior, which we discuss in detail next.

Interpersonal Closeness and Goals

Consumer goals are a major area of study in consumer psychology because they are strong drivers of behavior. Although consumer goals research has traditionally focused on individual-level goals, recent theorizing in psychology on transactive goal dynamics (TGD; Fitzsimons et al., 2015) adopts an explicitly interpersonal perspective on goal pursuit, which we use to organize our discussion of consumer goals in close relationships.

TGD theory proposes that interpersonal relationships create an interconnected web of goals, which increases in size and strength as the relationship becomes closer and more interdependent (Fitzsimons et al., 2015). This theory delineates the types of goals created in an interpersonal context by who holds the goal and who is the target of the goal, and it is easily applied to consumption-related goal domains. *Self-oriented goals* refer to the personal goals each partner has for themselves (e.g., Sam wants to lose weight and Joe wants to buy more sustainably), whereas *partner-oriented goals* refer to goals partners hold for the other (e.g., Sam wants Joe to eat less sugar and Joe wants Sam to watch less TV). Goals become *parallel* when both partners hold the same goal, such as parallel self-oriented goals (e.g., both Sam and Joe want to lose weight) or parallel partner-oriented goals (e.g., Sam wants Joe to lose weight and Joe wants Sam to lose weight). In addition to having goals for one of the partners, TGD theory asserts that partners can have system-oriented goals for the relationship itself (e.g., saving enough money to buy a house together). Goals become *shared* when both partners hold the same goal for the same target (e.g., both Sam and Joe want Joe to lose weight or both Sam and Joe want to save enough money to buy a house; Fitzsimons et al., 2015).

Close relationships can influence goal setting, goal pursuit, and goal satiation for each type of goal (for more detailed reviews, see Fitzsimons & Finkel, 2010; Fitzsimons et al., 2015; Orehek, 2017). In *goal setting*, for example, people tend to adopt the self-oriented goals they observe close others pursuing through the process of goal contagion (Aarts et al., 2004), and this goal contagion becomes stronger as the close other is perceived to put more effort toward the goal pursuit (Dik & Aarts, 2007). Thus, if Sam from the opening example observes their spouse, Joe, pursuing a goal to buy sustainably, Sam might also adopt a sustainability goal for themselves, especially if Joe puts a lot of effort into finding sustainable options.

In terms of *goal pursuit*, extensive research on the Michelangelo phenomenon demonstrates that close others play an integral role in people achieving their self-oriented goals for their ideal self. The more that a close other affirms a person's ideal goals, such as to be a more sustainable consumer, the more successful the person is in achieving those ideals over time (for a review, see Rusbult et al., 2005). Indeed, even the presence or thought of a close other makes related goals more accessible (e.g., one's mother might activate achievement goals) and can nonconsciously trigger goal pursuit in the relevant domain (e.g., salience of one's mother may lead to pursuit of one's academic achievement goals by paying for a writing workshop; Fitzsimons & Bargh, 2003; Shah, 2003). Further, research shows that people are aware that certain close others can help them with their goal pursuit ("instrumental others"), finding that people will consciously think about such others during initial goal pursuit (Fitzsimons & Shah, 2008). Thus, Sam might think about their sister, Carmen, while at the gym because Carmen is instrumental to their fitness goals. Finally, in terms of *goal satiation,* observing a close other complete a goal can satiate one's own desire to pursue that goal (McCulloch et al., 2011).

Moreover, the very quality of one's close relationships (i.e., relationship satisfaction) influences one's ability to pursue self-oriented goals. In an experiment and a longitudinal study with romantic couples, Hofmann et al. (2015) found that momentary increases in relationship satisfaction boost perceived control, goal focus, perceived partner support, and positive affect during goal pursuit, which in combination leads to more success. However, focusing on close ties with others is not always positive. For example, engaging with one's network on social media can have harmful self-control effects. When social media users are focused on close friends (vs. weaker ties), they experience a momentary increase in self-esteem, which, in turn, reduces self-control (Wilcox & Stephen, 2013). For people with strong ties to their social network, there is a positive correlation between social media use and real-life indicators of reduced self-control, such as body mass index and credit card debt (Wilcox & Stephen, 2013).

In parallel goal pursuit, people generally perceive their close partner's individual progress to be their own (e.g., McCulloch et al., 2011; Tu et al., 2016). If Sam and Joe each have self-oriented goals to lose weight, for instance, Joe might feel like he made progress even when it is only Sam who has achieved noticeable results. Although it might be intuitive to assume that holding parallel goals would help each partner stick to theisr goal, research suggests that people are not always successful in self-control when faced with the opportunity to indulge together, despite their parallel goals. When co-indulgence is perceived as a relatively minor transgression against each other's goals, indulging together can make "partners in crime" feel closer together (Lowe & Haws, 2014). However, when the indulgence is perceived to be a relatively greater transgression, people instead feel closer when they both abstain together (Lowe & Haws, 2014). This implies that, depending on the perceived size of the transgression, people will be motivated to either co-indulge (e.g., eating cookies) or co-abstain in order to feel closer to one another.

Even when partners do not share the same goals, their individual choices affect each other's goal pursuit. For example, one study of married couples found that having only one partner with high self-control does not help the dyad make joint self-control decisions. Instead, the one high self-control partner tends to prioritize prorelationship behaviors and indulges with the other (Dzhogleva & Lamberton, 2014). Relatedly, in a working paper, Gullo and colleagues (2017) found that making goal-consistent choices for close and non-competitive others (e.g., packing a healthy lunch for one's child) can be experienced as contributing toward one's own goal progress, even when the other does not hold the same goal, thereby hindering subsequent goal pursuit.

Finally, recent research suggests that different types of close relationships can affect the approach and motivation to pursue goals by influencing regulatory focus. Among the first research in marketing to examine familial relationships and friendships as distinct types of close relationships, Fei and colleagues (2020) found that, in China, friends are associated with "interest and aspirations" (p. 544), which activates a promotion-focused mindset when friendship relationships are more accessible. In contrast, family members are often associated with "obligations and responsibilities," which activates a prevention-focused mindset when familial relationships are more accessible (Fei et al., 2020, p. 544). Returning to the opening example, this research suggests that Sam would be more likely to have a promotion-focused mindset while shopping for their best friend's birthday present. As a result, they likely would be more willing to take risks in their purchase decision and be more responsive to promotion-focused messaging. However, when Sam was buying a microwave for their parents, this research suggests that Sam would be more likely to have a prevention-focused mindset and be more sensitive to potential risks and more responsive to prevention-focused messaging.

Interpersonal Closeness and Decision Making

As previewed in the opening example, close others frequently play a role in consumers' decisions. People make choices for close others, such as gifts, and make joint-consumption decisions with close others, such as which house to purchase or even just what to eat for dinner. More peripherally, close others can influence consumers' choices for themselves. In the opening example, Joe's presence affected Sam's wedding outfit choice by making his preferences for spending less time and money on the purchase more salient. In addition, Joe could still shape Sam's decision even if he were not there (e.g., Cavanaugh, 2016; Gorlin & Dhar, 2012; Simpson et al., 2012) or via his own choices (e.g., his own wedding outfit choice). It might be important to Sam that Joe liked how they looked at the wedding, and thus Sam might have considered both of their sets of preferences and anticipated how Joe would react when choosing which outfits to try on and ultimately purchase. Thus, close social relationships can both shape individual consumer decisions and also affect how relationship-specific decision situations unfold.

Individual decisions influenced by close others. Close social relationships can affect individual decisions through several paths, for example, via both the nature and amount of shared resources (e.g., space, money) and also via social influence (e.g., observing a close other make their own choices). In terms of shared resources, a study of romantic couples revealed differences in purchases for the self depending on how financial resources were structured (Garbinsky & Gladstone, 2019). Specifically, members of romantic couples tend to make more utilitarian and less hedonic purchases for themselves, such as functional walking shoes rather than stylish shoes, when using funds from a shared account rather than from a separately held account. A primary driver of this shift in purchasing behavior is feeling the need to justify purchase decisions when financial resources are shared (Garbinsky & Gladstone, 2019). Indeed, Garbinsky et al. (2020) showed that when members of couples are lower in financial harmony, they are more likely to have some resources, such as credit cards or bank accounts, that are concealed rather than fully shared.

Another source of influence is observing the choices of close others. For instance, observing a close relationship partner's purchasing patterns over time can create similar purchasing habits for the observer, leading them automatically to select what their relationship partner usually chooses even when making the decision alone (Wood & Hayes, 2012). However, sometimes people instead choose the opposite of what they observe close others choose in order to satisfy relationship goals. When ordering last at a restaurant with a group of friends, for example, consumers are more likely to choose a less preferred menu item for the sake of introducing variety into the group (Ariely & Levav, 2000). Likewise, uniqueness concerns can cause consumers to create dissimilar custom-made products or choose less popular features for their own custom-made products (e.g., choosing a less-popular pattern for custom Vans sneakers) after observing examples from close (vs. distant) others (D'Angelo et al., 2019). P. J. Liu and colleagues (2020) offered one bridge between these divergent findings, demonstrating that consumers tend to match their friends on "ordinal" attributes (e.g., portion size, brand tier) but to differentiate on "nominal" attributes (e.g., flavor), thereby balancing uniqueness concerns with mitigating social relationship discomfort. Thus, Sam from the opening example might choose a small vanilla ice cream after watching their sister, Carmen, order a small chocolate ice cream first.

Decisions for close others. Researchers started examining the phenomenon of consumers making choices for other consumers in earnest in the last decade, often focusing on how choices for others differ from choices made for the self (e.g., Polman & Wu, 2020). There are many contexts in which consumers choose for close others; such occasions often arise as a function of being close to one another (e.g., spouses shopping for each other). P. J. Liu et al. (2019) recently offered a conceptual framework to organize this emerging literature, identifying four prototypical situations in which consumers make choices for others: gift giving, everyday pickups/favors, joint consumption, and caregiving. Because of its inherent ties with power and responsibility, we defer discussion of caregiving decisions for close others to the section of this chapter on interpersonal power.

Gift decisions for close others. Perhaps the choosing-for-others context most germane to interpersonal closeness, gift giving prototypically involves the chooser focusing on their relationship with the recipient (P. J. Liu et al., 2019; for a review, see Ward & Chan, 2015). Giving gifts is often viewed as a way to signal one's closeness with a relationship partner (Belk, 1976; Caplow, 1982). As a result, consumers tend to prioritize signaling their connection with the recipient when making a gift decision, doing so even at the expense of choosing the recipient's actual preferred gift. Indeed, even when the recipient's preferences are explicitly known, as with a gift registry, givers trying to signal their social closeness with the receiver will purposefully choose a gift not on the registry that they think demonstrates their closeness and knowledge of the receiver's preferences, often resulting in gifts less liked by the recipient (Ward & Broniarczyk, 2016). In some cases, choosing gifts that align with the inferred preferences of the recipient can even have negative downstream effects for the giver. For example, choosing a gift for a close other that is inconsistent with the giver's identity (e.g., giving a friend a mug featuring the logo of the giver's rival sports team) can threaten the giver's sense of identity (Ward & Broniarczyk, 2011).

Additionally, consumers use the perceived closeness of their relationship with the intended recipient of a gift to inform what type of gift to choose and how much to spend. For example, givers are more likely to choose experiential gifts (e.g., a massage gift card or concert tickets) for more socially close others than they are for more socially distant others because experiential gifts require more specific knowledge of the receiver's preferences and therefore pose a greater risk of sending a negative social signal from giving a gift that does not match the receiver's preferences (Goodman & Lim, 2018). Beyond the relationship with one particular recipient, givers' gift choices for a specific close other are also influenced by other people in their social network (Lowrey et al., 2004). In a qualitative study of Christmas gift exchanges over a 5-year period, consumers were observed to determine how close/important their relationship was with any given focal gift recipient by comparing their relationship with the recipient to their relationship with others in their network, thus affecting their decisions about how much to spend (Lowrey et al., 2004).

Everyday favors for close others. Everyday favors for others differ from gift giving on at least one important dimension: the social focus of the decision. Unlike deciding on a gift, the prototypical social focus of everyday favors tends to be on the recipient instead of on the relationship between the giver and receiver (P. J. Liu et al., 2019). Occasions for everyday favors commonly arise as a function of having a close relationship with another consumer. Going back to the opening example in which Sam was buying socks for Joe, it would be less likely that Sam would do such a favor if Joe were not their spouse and were instead a coworker or just a friend.

Unfortunately, some research suggests that consumers may get worse at choosing options their partners would prefer as familiarity and closeness increase, due in part to overconfidence in their knowledge of the other's preferences (Lerouge & Warlop, 2006). When consumers make snack choices, for example, they choose more variety (Choi et al., 2006) and more indulgently (Laran, 2010; Lu et al., 2016) for friends than they do for themselves. Similarly, people are more likely to choose a desirable experience for their friends (e.g., a delicious restaurant that is 2 hours away) but a more feasible experience for themselves (e.g., a restaurant of unknown quality within a 5 minute walk; Lu et al., 2013). When consumers are more uncertain of other's preferences, such as when choosing for less close others, they tend to choose products that are compromise options (e.g., a treadmill with moderate features of shock absorption and magnetic resistance), whereas they are less likely to choose compromise options for either themselves or for closer others (Chang et al., 2012).

In addition, Polman and colleagues showed that the process of making everyday decisions for others is different than it is for making the same choices for the self. For instance, when making everyday-favor consumption decisions for friends, people are more likely to have a promotion (vs. prevention) focus (Polman, 2012), seek more information and focus more on choice-alternatives (Y. Liu et al., 2018), exhibit a reverse of the choice overload effect (Polman, 2012), experience less decision fatigue (Polman & Vohs, 2016), enjoy making the decisions more (Polman & Vohs, 2016), and demonstrate lower risk-aversion, as demonstrated by a recent meta-analysis of 71 articles (Polman & Wu, 2020).

Joint-consumption decisions for close others. Consumers are also frequently in a position to make decisions for close others that they will consume together with the other, such as Sam in the opening example choosing a new bedding set that would be used by both Sam and Joe. When making joint-consumption decisions for close others, the chooser has to take both their own preferences and the close other's preferences into consideration (P. J. Liu et al., 2019; Simpson et al., 2012). In many cases, research suggests that consumers will try to balance both sets of preferences (Corfman & Lehmann, 1987; Davis, 1970; Menasco & Curry, 1989), often asking companions for their joint-consumption preferences (e.g., "Where do you want to go to dinner?"; P. J. Liu & Min, 2020).

Under certain circumstances, though, some consumers do not attempt to incorporate their coconsumer's preferences. Recent research shows that as the number of close others one is jointly consuming with and choosing for increases, some choosers start to shift toward only considering their own preferences (Wu et al., 2019). Specifically, when consumers are making a joint-consumption decision for a large group (e.g., choosing the wine to serve with a group of friends), independent-oriented (vs. interdependent-oriented) consumers tend to make choices that reflect primarily their own preferences (vs. balancing everyone's preferences; Wu et al., 2019). Likewise, consumers are more likely to choose self-benefiting joint consumption when they have a close (vs. distant) relationship with their coconsumer (Tu et al., 2016), but only if the overall consumption offers a greater total benefit. For example, when choosing an airline to fly together, this research showed that consumers are more likely to choose an airline from which they will personally benefit more from the frequent-flier points than their traveling partner will if they are close with that person (e.g., Sam traveling with Joe) than less close with that person (e.g., Sam traveling with a coworker), but only if the total frequent-flier points for the two are greater.

As Tu et al. (2016) suggested, perceptions of the relationship itself can influence joint-consumption decisions. People tend to choose more variety for joint consumption with a relationship partner, for example, when they perceive more (vs. less) time left in their committed relationship, driven by a desire to have more excitement in the relationship when perceptions of time left in the relationship are longer (Etkin, 2016). Thus, Sam from the opening examples might choose more varied date activities to do with Joe (e.g., going to dinner, watching a movie, hiking) when the perceived amount of time they have left to spend in their life together seems relatively long and might choose less varied date activities with Joe (e.g., going to dinner at different restaurants) when the relationship time seems relatively short.

INTERPERSONAL COMPETITIVENESS

Interpersonal competitiveness is a manifestation of social comparison (Festinger, 1942, 1954; Tesser et al., 1988)—that is, comparing one's own state to that of someone else—and of a motivation to perform better than the other in the focal domain, either by closing a perceived negative gap or maintaining a perceived current gain (for a review, see Garcia et al., 2013). People can feel momentarily competitive with others, such as during an auction or while playing a game, and they can have chronic feelings of competitiveness within a relationship. From the opening example, siblings Sam and Carmen might feel chronically competitive with one another in various different consumer-relevant domains, such as health or fitness goals or the number of luxury brands they own as a signal of social status, but they might not feel competitive with each other at all in other domains. On the other hand, in-laws Joe and Carmen might not feel competitive with each other in any domain. The extent to which people experience competitiveness within their social relationships is also an individual difference (e.g., the Hypercompetitive Attitude Scale; Ryckman et al., 1990); some people feel competitive in nearly all of their relationships, whereas others do not feel competitive with any relationship partner. Thus, the experience of competitiveness can vary across people, situations, and within and across one's relationships.

Garcia and colleagues (2013) outlined individual and situational factors that increase competitiveness. In their framework, *individual* factors that can increase competitiveness include individual differences, the relevance of the domain to the self (e.g., one is unlikely to feel competitive regarding fitness goals if one does not care about becoming fit), and one's relationship with the focal other (Garcia et al., 2013). Both perceptions of similarity with the focal other (Festinger, 1954; Goethals & Darley, 1987; Kilduff et al., 2010) and interpersonal closeness with the focal other (Tesser & Campbell, 1982) can induce competitiveness, because they each amplify comparison concerns. Garcia and colleagues (2013) further outlined *situational* factors that can increase competitiveness, including the incentive structure, number of competitors (competition increases as number of competitors decreases; Garcia & Tor, 2009), proximity to a meaningful standard (e.g., a performance threshold to win), and social category fault lines (e.g., Duke student vs. UNC student is a more competitive situation than Duke vs. Duke or UNC vs. UNC). Despite its relevance, the marketing literature has only recently seen an increase in research exploring interpersonal competitiveness within established relationships (as opposed to anonymous or stranger consumers competing with each other, such as in auction settings).

Interpersonal Competitiveness and Goals

Perhaps unsurprisingly given competition's inherent implications for motivation (Berger & Pope, 2011; Erev et al., 1993; Reeve et al., 1985), the extant consumer-relevant literature on interpersonal competitiveness is predominantly in the context of self-oriented goal pursuit and parallel self-oriented goal pursuit; there is a dearth of research on the role of competitiveness within other interpersonal goal orientations (e.g., partner-oriented, joint, system-oriented, or shared; Fitzsimons et al., 2015).

Motivation and interpersonal competitiveness are dynamically related in self-oriented goal pursuit. In multiphase competitions, for example, learning that one is ahead of competitors increases motivation at early stages (e.g., the beginning stages of pursuing a goal to eat healthier) but decreases motivation at later stages of goal pursuit (Huang et al., 2017). Moreover, the stage of goal pursuit and one's standing relative to others can make consumers feel more competitive with others pursuing the same goal, such as both consumers pursuing fitness goals (i.e., parallel self-oriented goals). When people are near meaningful standards in their goal pursuit, such as near a cut-off threshold (e.g., top 10) or near goal completion, they begin to feel more competitive with their fellow goal pursuers (Garcia et al., 2006; Huang et al., 2019). However, recent research finds that observing a perceived superior other complete the goal (e.g., a friend posting that they met their weight goal on a health app social network) while one is still actively pursuing it can be demotivating for continued goal pursuit (E. Chan & Briers, 2019).

Interpersonal interactions are also related to the dynamics of competitive goal pursuit. Whereas parallel-goal pursuers are friendlier and more helpful to each other at earlier stages of goal pursuit, such as during one's first few weeks of attending Weight Watchers meetings (Garcia et al., 2006; Huang et al., 2015), they are less helpful to each other at later stages of goal pursuit (Garcia et al., 2006) and are even more likely to sabotage each other (Huang et al., 2019). In one striking example, Tumbat and Belk (2011) described instances of consumer–consumer sabotage among climbers paying group guides to hike Mount Everest; climbers stole each other's equipment even at the risk of the other's injury or death on the treacherous climb.

Over time, perceived competitions in goal pursuit with one or more consumers can evolve into a rivalry relationship. A rivalry is an established competitive relationship in which competitors have shared notable competitions against each other (e.g., due to identity-relevance or intensity; Kilduff et al., 2010). Consumers are more motivated in parallel goal pursuit with a rival than a nonrival

(Kilduff, 2014) and, due to a focus on their overall legacy with the rival, are more eager and less risk-averse in their goal pursuit (Converse & Reinhard, 2016).

Interpersonal Competitiveness and Decision Making

Limited consumer research has examined the role of competitiveness in decision making within established relationships, much of it instead focusing on anonymous or nonpersonal interactions among consumers, such as in auction settings or in-store scarcity situations (e.g., Ariely & Simonson, 2003; Kristofferson et al., 2016; Norton et al., 2013; Roux et al., 2015). In general, this research finds that competitiveness in such settings leads to overpaying and aggressiveness. Although this research is important, it is less clear whether these consumer insights extend to consumers' competitiveness experiences within established relationships, such as with friends, siblings, coworkers, or a spouse, and future research in this domain is much needed.

That said, there are many anecdotal examples of consumer competitiveness in the marketplace. It is a trend among billionaires, for example, to compete with each other on extravagant purchases, such as yachts (Batty, 2016; Dobson, 2019). Thus, competitiveness with other billionaires can influence a billionaire's *individual decision* for which yacht to buy. Further, recent work by Givi and Galak (2019, 2020) in the gift-giving domain suggests competitiveness may influence *decisions for others*. When consumers have a desire to be unique, for example, they will be reluctant to give gifts that they also own (Givi & Galak, 2020). Similarly, consumers dislike giving gifts that are superior to their own possessions because they fear they will later feel envy (Givi & Galak, 2019). In both cases, Givi and Galak found that consumers will opt to give a gift they know is less preferred by the recipient in order to keep their own possessions unique and to avoid feelings of envy. Importantly, uniqueness concerns and envy are both related to competitiveness in that they involve social comparison and can motivate a subsequent shift in relative consumption behavior (i.e., uniqueness: consumption to achieve being different; envy: consumption to achieve being equitable; and competitiveness: consumption to achieve being better). This implies that competitiveness in established relationships may lead to suboptimal gift giving.

INTERPERSONAL POWER

Within relationships, the amount of influence each partner has over the other and the amount of control each partner has over outcomes in the relationship are not always equal. Researchers define interpersonal power as having relative control over another's resources, behavior, and outcomes more generally (Dépret & Fiske, 1993; Emerson, 1962; Keltner et al., 2003) while resisting influence on one's own behavior and outcomes from others (Cromwell & Olsen, 1975; Mourali & Yang, 2013). This control can come from one or more of various sources, of which we focus on two: (a) relationship power, in which one member of the group has influence over other members but ownership for the final outcomes is shared (e.g., as in a romantic couple; Brick et al., 2018), and (b) responsibility power, in which one member of the group has both control over outcomes and the ultimate ownership for the outcomes (e.g., as in the relationship between parent and young child or between adult child and an aging parent needing caretaking; Steffel et al., 2016).

In the opening examples, Joe might have relatively more power in his relationship with Sam than does Sam; Joe was able to influence Sam to behave as he wanted, leading Sam to be more price-sensitive and to rush wedding outfit shopping. As a married couple with joint ownership for the outcomes, Joe's relative influence and control is relationship power. On the other hand, Sam and their sibling, Carmen, have power in their relationship with their aging parents. Together, they control the outcomes (which microwave to buy, how much to spend) for their parents and, as caretakers, have ultimate ownership for the outcomes. Thus, their relative control with respect to their parents is responsibility power, whereas they might each have equal relationship power as siblings.

Because many consumer goals and decisions are made in the context of social relationships

(Fitzsimons et al., 2015; Simpson et al., 2012), it is important to understand how power dynamics within relationships can shape consumer behavior. Next, we consider the intersection of interpersonal power and consumer psychology, organizing the discussion around relationship power and responsibility power.

Relationship Power and Goals

Feelings of power are a strong motivator for goal pursuit. (For a review, see Guinote, 2017.) Feeling powerful, even simply from recalling a time one had control over the outcomes of a relational partner, increases approach orientation (Galinsky et al., 2003; Smith & Bargh, 2008). Thus, in the marketplace, consumers experiencing a greater feeling of power in their relationship might be more persuaded by approach-oriented ad copy (e.g., a watch that lets users "stay on time" rather than "not be late"). Additionally, people feeling powerful demonstrate better self-regulation, such as resisting the temptation of eating an additional donut (Guinote, 2017). In contrast, feeling low in power can have the opposite effects on motivation, self-regulation, and goal pursuit (Anderson & Berdahl, 2002; Galinsky et al., 2003; Smith et al., 2008).

Despite the robust findings regarding power's influence on motivation and power's inherently interpersonal nature (i.e., power to influence another person), little work has examined the effects of relationship power on interpersonal goal pursuit. In one exception, across five studies with both members of the couple, Laurin and colleagues (2016) found that the lower power partner in a romantic couple not only pursues goals on behalf of their partner (e.g., Sam avoids junk foods even though it is Joe with the dieting goal) but, over time, also adopts their partner's goals as their own (e.g., Sam now identifies with a dieting goal themself). Thus, high-power partners inadvertently influence the self-oriented goal setting and the goal-directed behavior of their low power counterparts (Laurin et al., 2016). This work provides an excellent starting point for much needed future research on how relationship power shapes goal setting and goal pursuit in social contexts.

Relationship Power and Decision Making

Although much of the extant marketing literature on power and decision making examines the effects of feeling powerful in general (rather than within an established relationship), many of the insights extend to interpersonal settings. General feelings of power make people more action-ready, such as being more likely to initiate negotiations or to switch brands (Jiang et al., 2014; Magee et al., 2007). Additionally, those in power or leadership positions tend to not pay attention to others' attitudes and opinions and thus might be less persuaded by word of mouth (Berdahl & Martorana, 2006; Fiske, 1993). On the other hand, feeling powerless leads to greater compensatory consumption of status-oriented products, such as luxury purse or watch brands (Rucker & Galinsky, 2008); greater attention to the attitudes and opinions of those in power, such as experts (Berdahl & Martorana, 2006; Fiske, 1993); and more communal orientations (Rucker et al., 2012). Combined, these findings suggest that those high in relationship power dominate decision making within the couple, perhaps without even knowing it.

Indeed, in terms of decision making for *joint consumption*, high-power partners in a relationship often get their way. When choosing which brands to consume in the household (e.g., which soda brand to buy), for example, couples with greater power differential tend to buy the brands that the high-power partner prefers (Brick et al., 2018). Lower power partners are aware of their partner's influence over decisions and so use different influence tactics (i.e., less overt tactics) to attempt to get what they want in a joint purchase decision (Kirchler, 1993).

In turn, one's relative power in a relationship affects satisfaction with the joint-consumption decisions. In a study with romantic couples, Brick and colleagues (2018) found that when couples have differing brand preferences (e.g., Coke vs. Pepsi, having low "brand compatibility"), low-power partners report lower life satisfaction. However, brand compatibility does not influence the reported life satisfaction of high-power partners because they get their way whether or not they share the same brand preferences with their partner (Brick et al., 2018). Although having power in joint decisions with a relationship partner seems to affect satisfaction over time, it is less clear whether one's power influences satisfaction with each individual joint decision in close relationships. Fisher and colleagues (2011) examined whether relative relationship power influenced joint decision satisfaction in pairs with either a weak (i.e., acquaintances) or a strong (i.e., friends) relationship. In the context of choosing between restaurants to eat at together in which each partner strongly preferred a different option, the high-power partner only reported greater satisfaction with their choice if they also had a competitive (vs. cooperative) orientation and a weak relationship with the other. Those with a cooperative orientation or in a strong relationship reported no differences in decision satisfaction (Fisher et al., 2011).

Finally, a few papers have begun to examine the impact of relationship power on other types of interpersonal decision making. In decisions for others, Rucker et al. (2011) found that those with higher power spend more on themselves than they do on their low-power counterparts, whereas those lower in power exhibit the opposite effect. In terms of others influencing individual decisions, Brick and Fitzsimons (2017) found that frustration with one's partner leads low-power partners to consume brands that are oppositional to their partner's preferences when they are without their partner. For example, if Sam is a low-power partner in their relationship with Joe, when Sam is feeling frustrated with their relationship, they might purposefully drink Starbucks coffee instead of Joe's preferred Dunkin' Donuts brand on the way to work. Thus, high-power partners can shape low-power partners' individual decisions even when they are not present.

Responsibility Power and Goals

Caregiving, such as for one's child or one's aging parents, is perhaps the most prototypical context in which a relationship is high in responsibility power (P. J. Liu et al., 2019). The motivational system behind parental care and caregiving more generally is thought to serve as the basis for other prosocial processes, such as empathy, compassion, and altruistic behavior (Buckels et al., 2015; Goetz et al., 2010; Preston, 2013). In line with this, parents tend to have virtuous partner-oriented goals for their children. For instance, they might have goals for their children to eat healthy foods (Mukhopadhyay & Yeung, 2010; Tandon et al., 2011), to spend a limited amount of time in front of the TV (Carlson & Grossbart, 1988), and to achieve future success (Li et al., 2019). Moreover, caretaking can have negative downstream consequences for one's own goal pursuit. Recent work suggested that a caretaker's own goal pursuit can be hindered after making virtuous goal-related consumption choices for their charges (e.g., a parent packing a healthy lunch for their child is then more likely to eat unhealthily themselves; Gullo et al., 2017).

Responsibility Power and Decision Making

Research on responsibility power and decision making falls mainly into the domain of *caretaking decisions for others*. In the choosing for others framework, caretaking is defined as having a social focus on the recipient but balancing one's own preferences for the recipient with the recipient's preferences (P. J. Liu et al., 2019). This balancing of preferences is true for many caretaker relationships, including parent–young child (Dix, 1991) and child–aging parent (Matthews & Rosner, 1988). When making food choices for children, for example, parents are more likely to choose lower calorie (i.e., healthier) options for their children when they are exposed to the calorie information than when the calorie information is undisclosed (Tandon et al., 2011). This suggests that parents might choose their child's more preferred option unless their own preferences for the child (e.g., the child's health) are activated and actionable.

Perceptions of resources also influence decisions that caretakers make for their charges. How parents view self-control as a resource, for example, shapes how much self-control they exert for their children when making consumption choices for them (Mukhopadhyay & Yeung, 2010). Perceptions that self-control is a limited resource or can be increased over time lead to parents making more self-control choices for their children (e.g., choosing healthier foods, watching educational TV), whereas parents who view self-control as either a large or an unchangeable resource show less restraint in their choices for their children (e.g., choosing less healthy snacks, watching entertaining TV; Mukhopadhyay & Yeung, 2010). Additionally, perceptions of financial resources can influence parental decisions for children. Drawing on evolutionary psychology, Durante and colleagues (2015) showed that parents differentially invest in money and extracurricular activities for their children in times of financial scarcity depending on which child has more reproductive value (e.g., closer to maturity, female).

Similarly, research has shown that parents can treat their children differentially when making *gift decisions* for them. Parents tend to favor the child that shares their biological sex because they identify more strongly with them, choosing to give that child more money than children of the opposite biological sex (Nikiforidis et al., 2018). Relatedly, parents also tend to choose gifts for their children that are aligned with their own identity, rather than their child's, such as a gift related to one's favorite sports team. As an extension of the self, gift giving to one's child allows for parents to bolster their own identity and live vicariously through them (e.g., Belk, 1988).

In terms of individual decisions influenced by responsibility-power relationship partners, both the caretaker and the charge can influence the other's individual choices. For example, parents use their parenting styles to influence their children's consumption habits (e.g., Carlson & Grossbart, 1988). Parents' communication with their children is also a strong determinant of how a child is socialized toward or away from obesity (Moore et al., 2017) and of materialism in adolescents (Chaplin & John, 2010). Caretaking can also affect the caretaker's subsequent choices for themselves. When in a caretaking mindset, women adopt a short-term focus and men adopt a long-term focus due to strong gender norms in parenting styles (Li et al., 2019). This shift in focus has downstream consequences for unrelated individual consumption decisions, such as whether consumers prefer a smaller immediate reward or a larger reward later.

Finally, early work on family decision making in marketing suggests that children can exert relationship power influence when making joint-consumption decisions despite the responsibility power differential between them and their parents. For example, Filiatrault and Ritchie (1980) found that children had unexpected influence over the final outcomes when making vacation choices together.

CONSUMER BEHAVIOR INFLUENCES RELATIONSHIP OUTCOMES

Thus far, we have focused our discussion on how characteristics of established relationships shape consumer behavior outcomes. In this section, we consider how consumer behaviors within the context of an established relationship can, in turn, affect the relationship itself. The research in this area has predominately explored how consumer behavior can affect relational closeness and much less has explored how consumption affects other relational dimensions. More research is needed to understand how consumption can affect competitiveness and the power dynamics within established consumer–consumer relationships.

In terms of goals, consumers feel closer to others who they perceive to be instrumental to their goal during initial goal pursuit (Fitzsimons & Shah, 2008; Huang et al., 2015); however, this boost in closeness is reduced at later stages of goal pursuit (Fitzsimons & Fishbach, 2010; Huang et al., 2015).

In terms of decision making, gift exchanges can affect feelings of closeness within the relationship (Ruth et al., 1999). Experiential gifts (e.g., massages, concerts), for example, foster greater relational closeness on the part of the recipient than material gifts (e.g., jewelry, electronics; C. Chan & Mogilner, 2017). This effect occurs because, relative to material gifts, experiential gifts elicit greater levels of emotion during consumption, which function to boost the relationship (C. Chan & Mogilner, 2017). As another example, receiving practical and convenient-to-use gifts (vs. high quality but nonpractical gifts) increases recipients' perceptions of closeness to givers (Rim et al., 2019). Ironically, gifts that reflect the giver more than the receiver can boost feelings of closeness in the relationship for both partners, even though both prefer to give and receive gifts that reflect the receiver (Aknin & Human, 2015). This can occur for several reasons, including givers' frequent mispredictions of the receiver's preferences (Galak et al., 2016) and that a giver-focused gift may function as a form of self-disclosure, which is generally thought to boost relationship closeness (Collins & Miller, 1994).

Finally, consumers are often aware that their joint-consumption decisions will affect their relationships (P. J. Liu et al., 2019), and this knowledge affects their choices. For instance, consumers sometimes intentionally choose activities to engage in with close others in order to maintain close social ties, such as playing board games as a family (Epp et al., 2014). Likewise, the consumption patterns and direction of influence vary within heterosexual couples depending on whether the relationship is in a formation or maintenance stage: Women are influenced by how healthily their male partner eats in the formation stage, but men are influenced by their female counterpart in the maintenance stage (Hasford et al., 2018). Joint consumption can also help to foster closer relationships among unacquainted consumers. Sharing extraordinary (vs. ordinary) experiences boosts relational closeness for people who are less acquainted with each other because it distracts from the social discomfort of initial interactions; this effect does not occur for established relationships because they, presumably, do not have any discomfort to distract from (Min et al., 2018).

FUTURE DIRECTIONS

Clearly, social relationships play a key role in consumer psychology, and in this chapter, we have discussed the intersection of social relationships and consumer psychology in terms of three key relational dimensions: closeness, competitiveness, and power. However, consumer research related to each of these dimensions exists in largely separate streams. Next, we discuss two key avenues for future research to further our understanding of social relationships and consumer psychology.

A Dynamic Multidimensional Perspective on Relationships

As noted, the majority of existing research on social relationships and consumer psychology considers dimension of relationships in insolation—usually closeness but also competitiveness or power.[1] However, relationships simultaneously differ on multiple dimensions, and it is not always clear how insights from any given paper can generalize to other kinds of established relationships. Considering how more than one aspect of a relationship (e.g., closeness and power) interacts to influence consumer psychology provides a number of opportunities for future research.

For example, one area worthy of exploration is how competitiveness and power jointly shape outcomes for goal pursuit and goal setting within the various interpersonal goal orientations of TGD theory (Fitzsimons et al., 2015). In particular, it is unclear how competitiveness and power might influence vicarious goal progress. Much research suggests that partners tend to assume their partner's progress as their own in parallel self-oriented goal pursuit (e.g., McCulloch et al., 2011). Might the social comparison processes of competitiveness or the self-focused nature of high-power individuals interrupt this effect? Similarly, exploring multiple relationship dimensions could further understanding of how people identify close others who are instrumental to their goal pursuit (e.g., Fitzsimons & Shah, 2008). Are high-power partners less likely to view their close relational partner as instrumental even though that partner would probably actively work to help further their goals (Laurin et al., 2016)? Can people in a competitive relationship view each other as instrumental? Or is instrumentality reserved for close, noncompetitive, and equal power relationship partners?

A dynamic approach to relational dimensions could also further research on interpersonal decision making. For instance, researchers could examine questions regarding how competitiveness influences decisions made for close others. How do consumers who feel competitive with a close relational partner navigate the conflicting motives to

---

[1] We recognize one notable exception that considered all three relational dimensions: Fisher et al.'s (2011) study of relationship strength, competitive orientation, and power on satisfaction with joint decisions.

distinguish themselves from their perceived competitor and to use perceived similarities to signal closeness? Givi and Galak (2019, 2020) offered initial insight into this question in the gift-giving domain, but more research is needed in other domains of interpersonal decision making (e.g., individual choices or joint consumption). Or how do observed choices of a close and competitive friend influence subsequent choices for the self? While some research has explored how the observed choices of strangers affect one's subsequent choices for the self (e.g., Huh et al., 2014; McFerran et al., 2010), relatively little research has explored this question in the context of close established relationships (e.g., D'Angelo et al., 2019) or considered the interplay of closeness and competitiveness. Similarly, how do high-power and low-power partners approach gift giving in a close relationship versus a more distant relationship? Exploring the multidimensional aspects of relationships and their impact on consumer behavior is an important area for future study.

Examining the Dyad and Beyond

Much traditional consumer research on social relationships has examined just one member of the relationship as the unit of analysis. Although this is appropriate in some cases (e.g., observing, but not interacting with, a close other), in other cases doing so can ignore more than half of the relationship system: It can neglect the effects of the partner's attitudes and reactions and the effects of the relationship as a whole. Taking a system-focused rather than individual-focused approach to studying social relationships (e.g., Fitzsimons et al., 2015) can provide richer insights and open many avenues for future research.

Further, with few exceptions, consumer research on social relationships has largely ignored group interactions. Although much research has been done on groups in organizational psychology, there are many important consumption-related questions yet to be explored. For example, friend groups frequently engage in consumption activities together: going out to dinner, celebrating one another's achievements, going on vacations, and so on. Understanding how group dynamics factor into both goal pursuit and decision making remains a rich and understudied area for future research.

CHALLENGES IN RESEARCHING SOCIAL RELATIONSHIPS IN CONSUMER BEHAVIOR

We recognize that there are many challenges in studying social relationships in consumer research. It is labor-, time-, and monetarily intensive to recruit dyads (not to mention groups!) as a unit of analysis. Moreover, most academic researchers primarily have in-person access to undergraduate subject pools, making it difficult to recruit members of relationships that are of relatively longer relationship length (e.g., romantic partners, friends) for in-person studies. Additionally, researchers need to learn and use the appropriate statistical models needed for handling the violation of observation independence. In this section, we point to some tools to help researchers overcome these challenges.

In recent years, many tools have become available to make relationship research more approachable, which we hope will encourage more researchers to study consumption at the level of relationships. In terms of recruitment, multiple online survey platforms (e.g., Prolific, Qualtrics Panels) currently have features that allow researchers to send surveys to both members of a couple. Such tools allow for access to relatively cheaper and quicker samples of established romantic partners than recruiting couples in-person to the lab.

In terms of statistical analysis, Kenny et al. (2006) offer a widely accepted approach to handling interdependent dyadic data. Their model, the actor–partner interdependence model (APIM), allows for isolating the effects of the actor on their outcomes, the effects of the partner's scores on the actor's outcome, and a relationship effect (the interaction of both the actor and partner). As of 2021, Kenny offers further support to researchers on his personal website (davidakenny.net), which offers an APIM package in R developed by Kenny (DyadR) and various other web tools he has developed to support dyadic analysis.

Thus, the challenges of studying the relationship level of social influences in consumer psychology are becoming less daunting. Moreover, we anticipate that the growing interest in research on social relationships and consumer psychology will mean the emergence of new tools over time. It is thus our hope that consumer researchers, policy makers, and marketers can all leverage our nascent relational framework, in combination with such tools, to better understand how qualitatively different types of relationships affect consumption behavior.

REFERENCES

Aarts, H., Gollwitzer, P. M., & Hassin, R. R. (2004). Goal contagion: Perceiving is for pursuing. *Journal of Personality and Social Psychology*, 87(1), 23–37. https://doi.org/10.1037/0022-3514.87.1.23

Aknin, L. B., & Human, L. J. (2015). Give a piece of you: Gifts that reflect givers promote closeness. *Journal of Experimental Social Psychology*, 60, 8–16. https://doi.org/10.1016/j.jesp.2015.04.006

Anderson, C., & Berdahl, J. L. (2002). The experience of power: Examining the effects of power on approach and inhibition tendencies. *Journal of Personality and Social Psychology*, 83(6), 1362–1377. https://doi.org/10.1037/0022-3514.83.6.1362

Ariely, D., & Levav, J. (2000). Sequential choice in group settings: Taking the road less traveled and less enjoyed. *Journal of Consumer Research*, 27(3), 279–290. https://doi.org/10.1086/317585

Ariely, D., & Simonson, I. (2003). Buying, bidding, playing, or competing? Value assessment and decision dynamics in online auctions. *Journal of Consumer Psychology*, 13(1–2), 113–123. https://doi.org/10.1207/S15327663JCP13-1&2_10

Aron, A., Aron, E. N., & Smollan, D. (1992). Inclusion of other in the self scale and the structure of interpersonal closeness. *Journal of Personality and Social Psychology*, 63(4), 596–612. https://doi.org/10.1037/0022-3514.63.4.596

Aron, A., Aron, E. N., Tudor, M., & Nelson, G. (1991). Close relationships as including other in the self. *Journal of Personality and Social Psychology*, 60(2), 241–253. https://doi.org/10.1037/0022-3514.60.2.241

Batty, D. (2016, October 9). Superyachts and bragging rights: Why the super-rich love their "floating homes." *The Guardian*. https://www.theguardian.com/lifeandstyle/2016/oct/09/superyachts-and-bragging-rights-why-the-super-rich-love-their-floating-homes

Belk, R. W. (1976). It's the thought that counts: A signed digraph analysis of gift-giving. *Journal of Consumer Research*, 3(3), 155–162. https://doi.org/10.1086/208662

Belk, R. W. (1988). Possessions and the extended self. *Journal of Consumer Research*, 15(2), 139–168. https://doi.org/10.1086/209154

Berdahl, J. L., & Martorana, P. (2006). Effects of power on emotion and expression during a controversial group discussion. *European Journal of Social Psychology*, 36(4), 497–509. https://doi.org/10.1002/ejsp.354

Berger, J., & Pope, D. (2011). Can losing lead to winning? *Management Science*, 57(5), 817–827. https://doi.org/10.1287/mnsc.1110.1328

Berscheid, E., Snyder, M., & Omoto, A. M. (1989). The relationship closeness inventory: Assessing the closeness of interpersonal relationships. *Journal of Personality and Social Psychology*, 57(5), 792–807. https://doi.org/10.1037/0022-3514.57.5.792

Bower, G. H., & Gilligan, S. G. (1979). Remembering information related to one's self. *Journal of Research in Personality*, 13(4), 420–432. https://doi.org/10.1016/0092-6566(79)90005-9

Bowlby, J. (1982). *Attachment and loss, Vol. 1: Attachment*. Basic Books. (Original work published 1964)

Brick, D. J., & Fitzsimons, G. J. (2017). Oppositional brand choice: Using brands to respond to relationship frustration. *Journal of Consumer Psychology*, 27(2), 257–263. https://doi.org/10.1016/j.jcps.2016.10.002

Brick, D. J., Fitzsimons, G. M., Chartrand, T. L., & Fitzsimons, G. J. (2018). Coke vs. Pepsi: Brand compatibility, relationship power, and life satisfaction. *Journal of Consumer Research*, 44(5), 991–1014. https://doi.org/10.1093/jcr/ucx079

Buckels, E. E., Beall, A. T., Hofer, M. K., Lin, E. Y., Zhou, Z., & Schaller, M. (2015). Individual differences in activation of the parental care motivational system: Assessment, prediction, and implications. *Journal of Personality and Social Psychology*, 108(3), 497–514. https://doi.org/10.1037/pspp0000023

Caplow, T. (1982). Christmas gifts and kin networks. *American Sociological Review*, 47(3), 383–392. https://doi.org/10.2307/2094994

Carlson, L., & Grossbart, S. (1988). Parental style and consumer socialization of children. *Journal of Consumer Research*, 15(1), 77–94. https://doi.org/10.1086/209147

Cavanaugh, L. A. (2014). Because I (don't) deserve it: How relationship reminders and deservingness influence consumer indulgence. *Journal of Marketing Research*, 51(2), 218–232. https://doi.org/10.1509/jmr.12.0133

Cavanaugh, L. A. (2016). Consumer behavior in close relationships. *Current Opinion in Psychology*, 10, 101–106. https://doi.org/10.1016/j.copsyc.2015.11.004

Chan, C., & Mogilner, C. (2017). Experiential gifts foster stronger social relationships than material gifts. *Journal of Consumer Research*, *43*(6), 913–931. https://doi.org/10.1093/jcr/ucw067

Chan, E., & Briers, B. (2019). It's the end of the competition: When social comparison is not always motivating for goal achievement. *Journal of Consumer Research*, *46*(2), 351–370. https://doi.org/10.1093/jcr/ucy075

Chang, C., Chuang, S., Cheng, Y., & Huang, T. (2012). The compromise effect in choosing for others. *Journal of Behavioral Decision Making*, *25*(2), 109–122. https://doi.org/10.1002/bdm.720

Chaplin, L., & John, D. (2010). Interpersonal influences on adolescent materialism: A new look at the role of parents and peers. *Journal of Consumer Psychology*, *20*(2), 176–184. https://doi.org/10.1016/j.jcps.2010.02.002

Choi, J., Kim, K. B., Choi, I., & Yi, Y. (2006). Variety-seeking tendency in choice for others: Interpersonal and intrapersonal causes. *Journal of Consumer Research*, *32*(4), 590–595. https://doi.org/10.1086/500490

Clark, M. S., & Mils, J. (1993). The difference between communal and exchange relationships: What it is and is not. *Personality and Social Psychology Bulletin*, *19*(6), 684–691. https://doi.org/10.1177/0146167293196003

Collins, N. L., & Feeney, B. C. (2004). An attachment theory perspective on closeness and intimacy. In D. J. Mashek & A. P. Aron (Eds.), *Handbook of closeness and intimacy* (pp. 163–187). Lawrence Erlbaum Associates Publishers.

Collins, N. L., & Miller, L. C. (1994). Self-disclosure and liking: A meta-analytic review. *Psychological Bulletin*, *116*(3), 457–475. https://doi.org/10.1037/0033-2909.116.3.457

Converse, B. A., & Reinhard, D. A. (2016). On rivalry and goal pursuit: Shared competitive history, legacy concerns, and strategy selection. *Journal of Personality and Social Psychology*, *110*(2), 191–213. https://doi.org/10.1037/pspa0000038

Corfman, K. P., & Lehmann, D. R. (1987). Models of cooperative group decision-making and relative influence: An experimental investigation of family purchase decisions. *Journal of Consumer Research*, *14*(1), 1–13. https://doi.org/10.1086/209088

Cromwell, R. E., & Olsen, D. H. (1975). *Power in families*. Sage.

D'Angelo, J. K., Diehl, K., & Cavanaugh, L. A. (2019). Lead by example? Custom-made examples created by close others lead consumers to make dissimilar choices. *Journal of Consumer Research*, *46*(4), 750–773. https://doi.org/10.1093/jcr/ucz019

Davis, H. L. (1970). Dimensions of marital roles in consumer decision making. *Journal of Marketing Research*, *7*(2), 168–177. https://doi.org/10.1177/002224377000700203

Dépret, E., & Fiske, S. T. (1993). Social cognition and power: Some cognitive consequences of social structure as a source of control deprivation. In G. Weary, F. Gleicher, & K. L. Marsh (Eds.), *Control motivation and social cognition* (pp. 176–202). Springer.

Dik, G., & Aarts, H. (2007). Behavioral cues to others' motivation and goal pursuits: The perception of effort facilitates goal inference and contagion. *Journal of Experimental Social Psychology*, *43*(5), 727–737. https://doi.org/10.1016/j.jesp.2006.09.002

Dix, T. (1991). The affective organization of parenting: Adaptive and maladaptive processes. *Psychological Bulletin*, *110*(1), 3–25. https://doi.org/10.1037/0033-2909.110.1.3

Dobson, J. (2019, May 12). Billionaire superyacht showdown: Who's who at the 2019 Cannes Film Festival. *Forbes*. https://www.forbes.com/sites/jimdobson/2019/05/12/billionaire-superyacht-showdown-whos-who-at-the-2019-cannes-film-festival/#5f50799f1a38

Durante, K., Griskevicius, V., Redden, J. P., & White, A. (2015). Spending on daughters versus sons in economic recessions. *Journal of Consumer Research*, *42*(3), 435–457. https://doi.org/10.1093/jcr/ucv023

Dzhogleva, H., & Lamberton, C. (2014). Should birds of a feather flock together? Understanding self-control decisions in dyads. *Journal of Consumer Research*, *41*(2), 361–380. https://doi.org/10.1086/676599

Emerson, R. M. (1962). Power-dependence relations. *American Sociological Review*, *27*(1), 31. https://doi.org/10.2307/2089716

Epp, A. M., Schau, H., & Price, L. L. (2014). The role of brands and mediating technologies in assembling long-distance family practices. *Journal of Marketing*, *78*(3), 81–101. https://doi.org/10.1509/jm.12.0196

Erev, I., Bornstein, G., & Galili, R. (1993). Constructive intergroup competition as a solution to the free rider problem: A field experiment. *Journal of Experimental Social Psychology*, *29*(6), 463–478.

Etkin, J. (2016). Choosing variety for joint consumption. *Journal of Marketing Research*, *53*(6), 1019–1033. https://doi.org/10.1509/jmr.14.0209

Fei, X., You, Y., & Yang, X. (2020). "We" are different: Exploring the diverse effects of friend and family accessibility on consumers' product preferences. *Journal of Consumer Psychology*, *30*(3), 543–550. https://doi.org/10.1002/jcpy.1152

Festinger, L. (1942). A theoretical interpretation of shifts in level of aspiration. *Psychological Review*, *49*(3), 235–250. https://doi.org/10.1037/h0055434

Festinger, L. (1954). A theory of social comparison processes. *Human Relations*, 7(2), 117–140. https://doi.org/10.1177/001872675400700202

Filiatrault, P., & Ritchie, B. J. (1980). Joint purchasing decisions: A comparison of influence structure in family and couple decision-making units. *Journal of Consumer Research*, 7(2), 131–140. https://doi.org/10.1086/208802

Fisher, R. J., Grégoire, Y., & Murray, K. B. (2011). The limited effects of power on satisfaction with joint consumption decisions. *Journal of Consumer Psychology*, 21(3), 277–289. https://doi.org/10.1016/j.jcps.2011.03.006

Fiske, S. T. (1993). Controlling other people: The impact of power on stereotyping. *American Psychologist*, 48(6), 621–628. https://doi.org/10.1037/0003-066X.48.6.621

Fitzsimons, G. M., & Finkel, E. J. (2010). Interpersonal influences on self-regulation. *Current Directions in Psychological Science*, 19(2), 101–105. https://doi.org/10.1177/0963721410364499

Fitzsimons, G. M., Finkel, E. J., & vanDellen, M. R. (2015). Transactive goal dynamics. *Psychological Review*, 122(4), 648–673. https://doi.org/10.1037/a0039654

Fitzsimons, G. M., & Fishbach, A. (2010). Shifting closeness: Interpersonal effects of personal goal progress. *Journal of Personality and Social Psychology*, 98(4), 535–549. https://doi.org/10.1037/a0018581

Fitzsimons, G. M., & Shah, J. Y. (2008). How goal instrumentality shapes relationship evaluations. *Journal of Personality and Social Psychology*, 95(2), 319–337. https://doi.org/10.1037/0022-3514.95.2.319

Galak, J., Givi, J., & Williams, E. F. (2016). Why certain gifts are great to give but not to get: A framework for understanding errors in gift giving. *Current Directions in Psychological Science*, 25(6), 380–385. https://doi.org/10.1177/0963721416656937

Galinsky, A. D., Gruenfeld, D. H., & Magee, J. C. (2003). From power to action. *Journal of Personality and Social Psychology*, 85(3), 453–466. https://doi.org/10.1037/0022-3514.85.3.453

Garbinsky, E. N., & Gladstone, J. J. (2019). The consumption consequences of couples pooling finances. *Journal of Consumer Psychology*, 29(3), 353–369. https://doi.org/10.1002/jcpy.1083

Garbinsky, E. N., Gladstone, J. J., Nikolova, H., & Olson, J. G. (2020). Love, lies, and money: Financial infidelity in romantic relationships. *Journal of Consumer Research*, 47(1), 1–24. https://doi.org/10.1093/jcr/ucz052

Garcia, S. M., & Tor, A. (2009). The N-effect: More competitors, less competition. *Psychological Science*, 20(7), 871–877. https://doi.org/10.1111/j.1467-9280.2009.02385.x

Garcia, S. M., Tor, A., & Gonzalez, R. (2006). Ranks and rivals: A theory of competition. *Personality and Social Psychology Bulletin*, 32(7), 970–982. https://doi.org/10.1177/0146167206287640

Garcia, S. M., Tor, A., & Schiff, T. M. (2013). The psychology of competition: A social comparison perspective. *Perspectives on Psychological Science*, 8(6), 634–650. https://doi.org/10.1177/1745691613504114

Givi, J., & Galak, J. (2019). Keeping the Joneses from getting ahead in the first place: Envy's influence on gift giving behavior. *Journal of Business Research*, 101, 375–388. https://doi.org/10.1016/j.jbusres.2019.04.046

Givi, J., & Galak, J. (2020). Selfish prosocial behavior: Gift-giving to feel unique. *Journal of the Association for Consumer Research*, 5(1), 34–43. https://doi.org/10.1086/706507

Goethals, G. R., & Darley, J. M. (1987). Social comparison theory: Self-evaluation and group life. In B. Mullen & G. R. Goethals (Eds.), *Theories of group behavior* (pp. 21–47). Springer.

Goetz, J. L., Keltner, D., & Simon-Thomas, E. (2010). Compassion: An evolutionary analysis and empirical review. *Psychological Bulletin*, 136(3), 351–374. https://doi.org/10.1037/a0018807

Goodman, J. K., & Lim, S. (2018). When consumers prefer to give material gifts instead of experiences: The role of social distance. *Journal of Consumer Research*, 45(2), 365–382. https://doi.org/10.1093/jcr/ucy010

Gorlin, M., & Dhar, R. (2012). Bridging the gap between joint and individual decisions: Deconstructing preferences in relationships. *Journal of Consumer Psychology*, 22(3), 320–323. https://doi.org/10.1016/j.jcps.2012.05.002

Guinote, A. (2017). How power affects people: Activating, wanting, and goal seeking. *Annual Review of Psychology*, 68(1), 353–381. https://doi.org/10.1146/annurev-psych-010416-044153

Gullo, K. (2020). *A multi-dimensional approach to social relationships in consumer behavior* [Doctoral dissertation]. Duke University. https://hdl.handle.net/10161/20959

Gullo, K., Liu, P. J., Zhou, L., & Fitzsimons, G. J. (2017). Are my dog's treats making me fat? The effects of choices made for others on subsequent choices for the self. In A. Gneezy, V. Griskevicius, & P. Williams (Eds.), *NA - Advances in consumer research* (Vol. 45, pp. 146–151). Association for Consumer Research.

Hasford, J., Kidwell, B., & Lopez-Kidwell, V. (2018). Happy wife, happy life: Food choices in romantic relationships. *Journal of Consumer Research*, 44(6), 1238–1256. https://doi.org/10.1093/jcr/ucx093

Heffernan, M. E., Fraley, C. R., Vicary, A. M., & Brumbaugh, C. (2012). Attachment features and functions in adult romantic relationships. *Journal of Social and Personal Relationships*, *29*(5), 671–693. https://doi.org/10.1177/0265407512443435

Hofmann, W., Finkel, E. J., & Fitzsimons, G. M. (2015). Close relationships and self-regulation: How relationship satisfaction facilitates momentary goal pursuit. *Journal of Personality and Social Psychology*, *109*(3), 434–452. https://doi.org/10.1037/pspi0000020

Huang, S., Broniarczyk, S. M., Zhang, Y., & Beruchashvili, M. (2015). From close to distant: The dynamics of interpersonal relationships in shared goal pursuit. *Journal of Consumer Research*, *41*(5), 1252–1266. https://doi.org/10.1086/678958

Huang, S., Etkin, J., & Jin, L. (2017). How winning changes motivation in multiphase competitions. *Journal of Personality and Social Psychology*, *112*(6), 813–837. https://doi.org/10.1037/pspa0000082

Huang, S., Lin, S. C., & Zhang, Y. (2019). When individual goal pursuit turns competitive: How we sabotage and coast. *Journal of Personality and Social Psychology*, *117*(3), 605–620. https://doi.org/10.1037/pspi0000170

Huh, Y. E., Vosgerau, J., & Morewedge, C. K. (2014). Social defaults: Observed choices become choice defaults. *Journal of Consumer Research*, *41*(3), 746–760. https://doi.org/10.1086/677315

Jiang, Y., Zhan, L., & Rucker, D. D. (2014). Power and action orientation: Power as a catalyst for consumer switching behavior. *Journal of Consumer Research*, *41*(1), 183–196. https://doi.org/10.1086/675723

Kelley, H. H., Berscheid, E., Christensen, A., Harvey, J. H., Huston, T. L., Levinger, G., McClintock, E., Peplau, L. A., & Peterson, D. R. (1983). *Close relationships*. Freeman.

Keltner, D., Gruenfeld, D. H., & Anderson, C. (2003). Power, approach, and inhibition. *Psychological Review*, *110*(2), 265–284. https://doi.org/10.1037/0033-295X.110.2.265

Kenny, D. A., Kashy, D. A., & Cook, W. L. (2006). *Dyadic data analysis*. Guilford Press.

Kilduff, G. J. (2014). Driven to win: Rivalry, motivation, and performance. *Social Psychological & Personality Science*, *5*(8), 944–952. https://doi.org/10.1177/1948550614539770

Kilduff, G. J., Elfenbein, H., & Staw, B. M. (2010). The psychology of rivalry: A relationally dependent analysis of competition. *Academy of Management Journal*, *53*(5), 943–969. https://doi.org/10.5465/amj.2010.54533171

Kirchler, E. (1993). Spouses' joint purchase decisions: Determinants of influence tactics for muddling through the process. *Journal of Economic Psychology*, *14*(2), 405–438. https://doi.org/10.1016/0167-4870(93)90009-A

Kristofferson, K., McFerran, B., Morales, A. C., & Dahl, D. W. (2017). The dark side of scarcity promotions: How exposure to limited-quantity promotions can induce aggression. *Journal of Consumer Research*, *43*(5), 683–706. https://doi.org/10.1093/jcr/ucw056

Laran, J. (2010). Goal management in sequential choices: Consumer choices for others are more indulgent than personal choices. *Journal of Consumer Research*, *37*(2), 304–314. https://doi.org/10.1086/652193

Laurin, K., Fitzsimons, G. M., Finkel, E. J., Carswell, K. L., vanDellen, M. R., Hofmann, W., Lambert, N. M., Eastwick, P. W., Fincham, F. D., & Brown, P. C. (2016). Power and the pursuit of a partner's goals. *Journal of Personality and Social Psychology*, *110*(6), 840–868. https://doi.org/10.1037/pspi0000048

Lerouge, D., & Warlop, L. (2006). Why it is so hard to predict our partner's product preferences: The effect of target familiarity on prediction accuracy. *Journal of Consumer Research*, *33*(3), 393–402. https://doi.org/10.1086/508523

Li, Y., Haws, K. L., & Griskevicius, V. (2019). Parenting motivation and consumer decision-making. *Journal of Consumer Research*, *45*(5), 1117–1137. https://doi.org/10.1093/jcr/ucy038

Liu, P. J., Dallas, S. K., & Fitzsimons, G. J. (2019). A framework for understanding consumer choices for others. *Journal of Consumer Research*, *46*(3), 407–434. https://doi.org/10.1093/jcr/ucz009

Liu, P. J., McFerran, B., & Haws, K. L. (2020). Mindful matching: Ordinal versus nominal attributes. *Journal of Marketing Research*, *57*(1), 134–155. https://doi.org/10.1177/0022243719853221

Liu, P. J., & Min, K. E. (2020). Where do you want to go for dinner? A preference expression asymmetry in joint consumption. *Journal of Marketing Research*, *57*(6), 1037–1054. https://doi.org/10.1177/0022243720949497

Liu, Y., Polman, E., Liu, Y., & Jiao, J. (2018). Choosing for others and its relation to information search. *Organizational Behavior and Human Decision Processes*, *147*, 65–75. https://doi.org/10.1016/j.obhdp.2018.05.005

Lowe, M. L., & Haws, K. L. (2014). (Im)moral support: The social outcomes of parallel self-control decisions. *Journal of Consumer Research*, *41*(2), 489–505. https://doi.org/10.1086/676688

Lowrey, T. M., Otnes, C. C., & Ruth, J. A. (2004). Social influences on dyadic giving over time: A taxonomy from the giver's perspective. *Journal of Consumer Research*, *30*(4), 547–558. https://doi.org/10.1086/380288

Lu, J., Liu, Z., & Fang, Z. (2016). Hedonic products for you, utilitarian products for me. *Judgment and Decision Making*, *11*(4), 332–341.

Lu, J., Xie, X., & Xu, J. (2013). Desirability or feasibility: Self-other decision-making differences. *Personality and Social Psychology Bulletin*, *39*(2), 144–155. https://doi.org/10.1177/0146167212470146

Magee, J. C., Galinsky, A. D., & Gruenfeld, D. H. (2007). Power, propensity to negotiate, and moving first in competitive interactions. *Personality and Social Psychology Bulletin*, *33*(2), 200–212. https://doi.org/10.1177/0146167206294413

Matthews, S. H., & Rosner, T. (1988). Shared filial responsibility: The family as the primary caregiver. *Journal of Marriage and the Family*, *50*(1), 185–195. https://doi.org/10.2307/352438

McCulloch, K. C., Fitzsimons, G. M., Chua, S. N., & Albarracín, D. (2011). Vicarious goal satiation. *Journal of Experimental Social Psychology*, *47*(3), 685–688. https://doi.org/10.1016/j.jesp.2010.12.019

McFerran, B., Dahl, D. W., Fitzsimons, G. J., & Morales, A. C. (2010). I'll have what she's having: Effects of social influence and body type on the food choices of others. *Journal of Consumer Research*, *36*(6), 915–929. https://doi.org/10.1086/644611

Menasco, M. B., & Curry, D. J. (1989). Utility and choice: An empirical study of wife/husband decision making. *Journal of Consumer Research*, *16*(1), 87–97. https://doi.org/10.1086/209196

Min, K. E., Liu, P. J., & Kim, S. (2018). Sharing extraordinary experiences fosters feelings of closeness. *Personality and Social Psychology Bulletin*, *44*(1), 107–121. https://doi.org/10.1177/0146167217733077

Moore, E. S., Wilkie, W. L., & Desrochers, D. (2017). All in the family? Parental roles in the epidemic of childhood obesity. *Journal of Consumer Research*, *43*(5), 824–859. https://doi.org/10.1093/jcr/ucw059

Mourali, M., & Yang, Z. (2013). The dual role of power in resisting social influence. *Journal of Consumer Research*, *40*(3), 539–554. https://doi.org/10.1086/671139

Mukhopadhyay, A., & Yeung, C. (2010). Building character: Effects of lay theories of self-control on the selection of products for children. *Journal of Marketing Research*, *47*(2), 240–250. https://doi.org/10.1509/jmkr.47.2.240

Nikiforidis, L., Durante, K. M., Redden, J. P., & Griskevicius, V. (2018). Do mothers spend more on daughters while fathers spend more on sons? *Journal of Consumer Psychology*, *28*(1), 149–156. https://doi.org/10.1002/jcpy.1004

Norton, D. A., Lamberton, C. P., & Naylor, R. W. (2013). The devil you (don't) know: Interpersonal ambiguity and inference making in competitive contexts. *Journal of Consumer Research*, *40*(2), 239–254. https://doi.org/10.1086/669562

Orehek, E. (2017). Goal pursuit and close relationships: A people as means perspective. In C. E. Koptez & A. Fishbach (Eds.), *The motivation-cognition interface* (pp. 131–151). Routledge.

Polman, E. (2012). Effects of self-other decision making on regulatory focus and choice overload. *Journal of Personality and Social Psychology*, *102*(5), 980–993. https://doi.org/10.1037/a0026966

Polman, E., & Vohs, K. D. (2016). Decision fatigue, choosing for others, and self-construal. *Social Psychological & Personality Science*, *7*(5), 471–478. https://doi.org/10.1177/1948550616639648

Polman, E., & Wu, K. (2020). Decision making for others involving risk: A review and meta-analysis. *Journal of Economic Psychology*, *77*, 102184. https://doi.org/10.1016/j.joep.2019.06.007

Preston, S. D. (2013). The origins of altruism in offspring care. *Psychological Bulletin*, *139*(6), 1305–1341. https://doi.org/10.1037/a0031755

Reeve, J., Olson, B. C., & Cole, S. G. (1985). Motivation and performance: Two consequences of winning and losing in competition. *Motivation and Emotion*, *9*(3), 291–298. https://doi.org/10.1007/BF00991833

Rim, S., Min, K. E., Liu, P. J., Chartrand, T. L., & Trope, Y. (2019). The gift of psychological closeness: How feasible versus desirable gifts reduce psychological distance to the giver. *Personality and Social Psychology Bulletin*, *45*(3), 360–371. https://doi.org/10.1177/0146167218784899

Roux, C., Goldsmith, K., & Bonezzi, A. (2015). On the psychology of scarcity: When reminders of resource scarcity promote selfish (and generous) behavior. *Journal of Consumer Research*, *42*(4), 615–631. https://doi.org/10.1093/jcr/ucv048

Rucker, D. D., Dubois, D., & Galinsky, A. D. (2011). Generous paupers and stingy princes: Power drives consumer spending on self versus others. *Journal of Consumer Research*, *37*(6), 1015–1029. https://doi.org/10.1086/657162

Rucker, D. D., & Galinsky, A. D. (2008). Desire to acquire: Powerlessness and compensatory consumption. *Journal of Consumer Research*, *35*(2), 257–267. https://doi.org/10.1086/588569

Rucker, D. D., Galinsky, A. D., & Dubois, D. (2012). Power and consumer behavior: How power shapes who and what consumers value. *Journal of Consumer Psychology*, *22*(3), 352–368. https://doi.org/10.1016/j.jcps.2011.06.001

Rusbult, C. E., & Arriaga, X. B. (1997). Interdependence theory. In S. Duck (Ed.), *Handbook of personal relationships: Theory, research, and interventions* (pp. 221–250). John Wiley & Sons Inc.

Rusbult, C. E., Kumashiro, M., Stocker, S. L., Kirchner, J. L., Finkel, E. J., & Coolsen, M. K. (2005). Self processes in interdependent relationships: Partner affirmation and the Michelangelo phenomenon. *Interaction Studies: Social Behaviour and Communication in Biological and Artificial Systems*, 6(3), 375–391. https://doi.org/10.1075/is.6.3.05rus

Ruth, J. A., Otnes, C. C., & Brunel, F. F. (1999). Gift receipt and the reformulation of interpersonal relationships. *Journal of Consumer Research*, 25(4), 385–402. https://doi.org/10.1086/209546

Ryckman, R. M., Hammer, M., Kaczor, L. M., & Gold, J. A. (1990). Construction of a hypercompetitive attitude scale. *Journal of Personality Assessment*, 55(3–4), 630–639. https://doi.org/10.1080/00223891.1990.9674097

Sedikides, C., Campbell, K. W., Reeder, G., & Elliot, A. J. (1999). The relationship closeness induction task. *Representative Research in Social Psychology*, 23, 1–4.

Silk, J. B. (2003). Cooperation without counting: The puzzle of friendship. In P. Hammerstein (Ed.), *Genetic and cultural evolution of cooperation* (pp. 37–45). MIT Press.

Simpson, J. A., Griskevicius, V., & Rothman, A. J. (2012). Consumer decisions in relationships. *Journal of Consumer Psychology*, 22(3), 304–314. https://doi.org/10.1016/j.jcps.2011.09.007

Smith, P. K., & Bargh, J. A. (2008). Nonconscious effects of power on basic approach and avoidance tendencies. *Social Cognition*, 26(1), 1–24. https://doi.org/10.1521/soco.2008.26.1.1

Smith, P. K., Jostmann, N. B., Galinsky, A. D., & van Dijk, W. W. (2008). Lacking power impairs executive functions. *Psychological Science*, 19(5), 441–447. https://doi.org/10.1111/j.1467-9280.2008.02107.x

Steffel, M., Williams, E. F., & Perrmann-Graham, J. (2016). Passing the buck: Delegating choices to others to avoid responsibility and blame. *Organizational Behavior and Human Decision Processes*, 135, 32–44. https://doi.org/10.1016/j.obhdp.2016.04.006

Tandon, P. S., Zhou, C., Chan, N. L., Lozano, P., Couch, S. C., Glanz, K., Krieger, J., & Saelens, B. E. (2011). The impact of menu labeling on fast-food purchases for children and parents. *American Journal of Preventive Medicine*, 41(4), 434–438. https://doi.org/10.1016/j.amepre.2011.06.033

Tesser, A., & Campbell, J. L. (1982). Self-evaluation maintenance and the perception of friends and strangers. *Journal of Personality*, 50(3), 261–279. https://doi.org/10.1111/j.1467-6494.1982.tb00750.x

Tesser, A., Millar, M., & Moore, J. (1988). Some affective consequences of social comparison and reflection processes: The pain and pleasure of being close. *Journal of Personality and Social Psychology*, 54(1), 49–61. https://doi.org/10.1037/0022-3514.54.1.49

Tu, Y., Shaw, A., & Fishbach, A. (2016). The friendly taking effect: How interpersonal closeness leads to seemingly selfish yet jointly maximizing choice. *Journal of Consumer Research*, 42(5), 669–687. https://doi.org/10.1093/jcr/ucv052

Tumbat, G., & Belk, R. W. (2011). Marketplace tensions in extraordinary experiences. *Journal of Consumer Research*, 38(1), 42–61. https://doi.org/10.1086/658220

Ward, M. K., & Broniarczyk, S. M. (2011). It's not me, it's you: How gift giving creates giver identity threat as a function of social closeness. *Journal of Consumer Research*, 38(1), 164–181. https://doi.org/10.1086/658166

Ward, M. K., & Broniarczyk, S. M. (2016). Ask and you shall (not) receive: Close friends prioritize relational signaling over recipient preferences in their gift choices. *Journal of Marketing Research*, 53(6), 1001–1018. https://doi.org/10.1509/jmr.13.0537

Ward, M. K., & Chan, C. (2015). Gift giving. In M. I. Norton, D. D. Rucker, & C. Lamberton (Eds.), *The Cambridge handbook of consumer psychology* (pp. 398–418). Cambridge University Press. https://doi.org/10.1017/CBO9781107706552.015

Wilcox, K., & Stephen, A. T. (2013). Are close friends the enemy? Online social networks, self-esteem, and self-control. *Journal of Consumer Research*, 40(1), 90–103. https://doi.org/10.1086/668794

Wood, W., & Hayes, T. (2012). Social influence on consumer decisions: Motives, modes, and consequences. *Journal of Consumer Psychology*, 22(3), 324–328. https://doi.org/10.1016/j.jcps.2012.05.003

Wu, E. C., Moore, S. G., & Fitzsimons, G. J. (2019). Wine for the table: Self-construal, group size, and choice for self and others. *Journal of Consumer Research*, 46(3), 508–527. https://doi.org/10.1093/jcr/ucy082

CHAPTER 15

SUSTAINABILITY: UNDERSTANDING CONSUMER BEHAVIOR IN A CIRCULAR ECONOMY

Marius Claudy and Mark Peterson

This chapter focuses on important issues for consumer psychology research related to sustainability behaviors of consumers in a changing economy. Specifically, we draw on the notion of a circular economy (CE) and highlight the changes such a sustainable system of production and consumption would bring for consumers regarding the acquisition, usage, and disposal of products. Furthermore, we discuss the psychological factors that can prevent as well as motivate people to engage in the consumption practices that are necessary for CEs to gain widespread acceptance and to ultimately replace unsustainable, linear systems of production.

Studying the topic of sustainable consumption must begin with clarifying the meaning of *sustainability* because the concept of sustainability can take several forms within and without marketing (Kemper & Ballantine, 2019). Prior to 1987, most individuals understood sustainability to mean the maintenance of a rate or level of performance. But in 1987, the United Nations' Brundtland Commission defined sustainable development as meeting the needs of the present without compromising the ability of future generations to meet their own needs (World Commission on Environment and Development, 1987, chap. 2, sect. 4). In the decades since 1987, a holistic definition of sustainability has arisen that refers to those concepts and practices of actors in markets (buyers, sellers, and government regulators) that benefit future generations through reduced negative impact on the resources and systems of the natural environment and a positive effect on local communities and society at large (Eagle & Dahl, 2015, p. 5). For those researching sustainability behaviors of consumers and their relevance to intergenerational justice, the holistic triple bottom line of people, planet, and profit (Elkington, 1994) is the preferred definition of sustainability (Lunde, 2018). Accordingly, the holistic, triple-bottom-line definition of sustainability for pursuing intergenerational justice is used in this chapter.

Until recently, however, the concept of sustainability was often used in an abstract sense, offering little practical guidance on how to effectively transform our currently unsustainable economic activities into sustainable ones. The concept of a CE tackles this issue and provides a clear blueprint for the design of sustainable closed-loop systems of production and consumption.

While much research has focused on the technological and political challenges that a transition toward circular production entails, far less attention has been paid to the role of consumers and consumption in a CE (e.g., Wastling et al., 2018). This chapter aims to address this paucity by highlighting the important role consumers play in enabling CEs. In doing so, we pay particular attention to the changes a CE brings for the purchase, usage, and disposal of products and highlight key

https://doi.org/10.1037/0000262-015
APA Handbook of Consumer Psychology, L. R. Kahle (Editor-in-Chief)
Copyright © 2022 by the American Psychological Association. All rights reserved.

psychological barriers firms and policy makers are likely to encounter when engaging people in the consumption of circular products and services.

CONSUMPTION IN A CIRCULAR ECONOMY

Today's take-make-dispose systems of production and consumption are unsustainable (Prothero et al., 2011). Regardless of how (eco)efficient our linear economies become, they continue to rely on virgin raw materials that eventually are burned or dumped in landfills. While plastic manufacturing accounts for 8% of oil production each year, less than a fifth of all plastic in the world is recycled (Parker, 2018). Like the endless circular flows of resources in nature, sustainable systems of production and consumption need to change so that resources are no longer wasted but instead are utilized and renewed on a continuous, indefinite basis.

In this basic notion of a *circular economy*, the aim is to maintain the value of products and materials for as long as possible (e.g., Esposito et al., 2018). The guiding principles are simple: (a) design waste out of products, (b) keep materials and products in use for as long as possible, and (c) regenerate natural systems (Ellen MacArthur Foundation, 2019b). It is important to note that the term CE constitutes an umbrella term that has summarized principles from various schools of thought, including industrial ecology (Ayres, 2008), biomimicry (Mentink, 2014), product-service systems (e.g., Morelli, 2006), or cradle-to-cradle (McDonough & Braungart, 2002). Estimates suggest that the extensive employment of CE principles in business could result in potential reductions in the use of virgin materials by 53% in the next 30 years (Ellen MacArthur Foundation, 2015, p. 12). Achieving such ambitious reductions in waste will require the large-scale transformation of existing modes of production and consumption, which requires the slowing and closing of resource loops (Wastling et al., 2018).

CE business models propose to maximize resource efficiency by slowing down resource loops. This could be done, for example, by prolonging product lifecycles for as long as possible. Product lifecycles can be extended by redesigning products so that they are more durable or can be more easily upgraded, maintained, or repaired. Along with increasing product lifecycles, firms can strive to increase the intensity of product and resource use. For example, the average power drill is used 18 minutes in its lifetime, while 80% of household products are estimated to be used less than once a month (Ellen MacArthur Foundation, 2015). Models of servitization (e.g., leasing, renting; Rothenberg, 2007), as well as access-based solutions (e.g., car-sharing schemes; Bardhi & Eckhardt, 2012), can achieve higher rates of product utilization and therefore greater usage value.

Further, CE business models aim to close resource loops and eliminate waste completely. Firms can eradicate waste by redesigning products for easy disassembly, recyclability, and recovery of materials that are then used as input factors for subsequent cycles of production. Sports apparel company Adidas, for example, aims to launch its first commercial running shoe designed for a circular lifecycle by 2021 (https://www.adidas.ca/en/futurecraft). Adidas Futurecraft shoes will be made from a single material, which will allow the company to take worn-out shoes and transform the recycled material into the next generation of shoes. While the firm still faces significant engineering challenges before it reaches 1:1 product circularity (i.e., one old shoe creates one new shoe), Adidas acknowledges that one of the most formidable challenges is to engage consumers in the CE (Wilson, 2019).

Circular business models require significant changes in consumer behavior, which provide major obstacles to the widespread adoption of CE principles by firms. For example, circular business models emphasize prolonged usage, which requires consumers to engage in maintenance, repair, and upgrading of products (Charter, 2018). Similarly, the CE replaces traditional models of ownership with sharing or access-based models of consumption. In this way, consumers will function as important suppliers of inputs of production as firms rely on consumers to maintain and return products so that materials can be recovered for the next cycle of production. Such changes in purchase, use, and disposal of products are likely to spark resistance from consumers. Yet, without consumer acceptance and active engagement in the CE, the transition toward sustainable means of production and consumption cannot succeed (e.g., Lofthouse & Prendeville, 2018; Singh & Giacosa, 2019).

The discussion covers key psychological barriers firms are likely to encounter from consumers when transitioning toward circular business models. The discussion also identifies opportunities for firms to transform barriers into ways for shifting consumer behaviors to fit CE business models.

From Linear to Circular Economies

Over the past century, technological innovation in areas such as food production, health care, and transportation have undeniably contributed to higher standards of living across the world. However, prevailing approaches to business have locked humans into a linear model of economic growth, in which "natural resources provide our factory inputs, which are then used to create mass-produced goods to be purchased and, typically, disposed after a single use" (Esposito et al., 2018, p. 5). Since the dawn of the industrial revolution, the planet has experienced not only unparalleled economic growth but also widespread destruction of biological resources. Such destruction now challenges future generations' basis for survival (Brundtland, 1987).

The industrial ecologist Robert Ayres (2008) pointed out that "the real economy is essentially a large-scale materials processing system [in which] virtually none of the materials consumed by the economy are recycled at present" (p. 292). The current linear system is characterized by a logic of economies of scale, in which volume largely determines competitiveness and in which growth is directly coupled with resource processing. As such, the system incentivizes firms to maximize the throughput of resources. Deliberately designing obsolescence into products currently rewards many firms. This is further amplified by the focus on depreciation value, which implies that accounting rules and conventions determine a product's worth, not its actual use value. Finally, the current system is characterized by limited producer responsibility for the products that firms produce and sell. Bakker et al. (2014) summarized the characteristics of our current marketing system as "design something, manufacture it as the lowest possible cost, sell it at the highest possible price and forget about it as soon as feasibly possible" (p. 31).

Not surprisingly, take-make-dispose modes of production and consumption have contributed toward a steady decline in natural resources and an exponential growth of waste and pollution—perhaps most notable in the accumulation of plastics in the Earth's oceans (Jacobo, 2019).

Advocates of the CE have therefore called for a rapid transformation of our linear systems of production and consumption into circular ones. In such a CE, the value of products and materials would be maintained for as long as possible, waste and resource use would be minimized, and when a product reaches the end of its life, it would be used again to create further value (Ellen MacArthur Foundation, 2015). In this circular system, the value of objects would depend on their use value—no longer on newness.

The CE shifts emphasis from economies of scale to quality and longevity, because growth and profits would be derived from the management and utilization of stocks (i.e., assets, capitals, products). Producers would retain responsibility for their products and materials, which they increasingly would offer in forms of access-based models, such as renting or leasing products to consumers. By reusing and recycling products and materials throughout their lifecycles, firms could decouple production from excessive use of raw materials. In other words, the CE would focus on "what is already in use along all points of a product's lifecycle, from sourcing to supply chain to consumption to the remaining unusable parts for one function and their conversion back into a new source for another purpose" (Esposito et al., 2018, p. 6).

Unlike other concepts of sustainable production and consumption, such as the degrowth movement (Demaria et al., 2013), the CE does not try to break cycles of innovation, growth, and development. Instead the CE propels them by replacing older technologies of production with newer, more sustainable ones. Circular business models should be as (or even more) profitable than current systems of production, because the reduction and elimination of waste reduces costs of production while delivering valued products and services to consumers.

"Fundamentally, a circular economy represents an 'industrial model that decouples revenues from material input' such that profits can still be obtained even without using additional natural resources" (Ellen MacArthur Foundation, 2013 p. 6). Indeed, transformative innovation in information communication technology (ICT) and industrial technologies such as intelligent decentralization (e.g., 3D printing) and allocation (e.g., artificial intelligence, internet of things [IoT]) have turned the promise of circular systems of production into realities. Such technological advances "allow better tracking of materials, more efficient collaboration and knowledge sharing, and improved forward and reverse logistics setups" and increased use of renewable energy (World Economic Forum, 2020, para. 9).

Figure 15.1 depicts a rendering of a CE. Here, one can see how inputs at the top of the center of the diagram flow down as they are transformed through manufacturing and the provision of service to consumers and users. On the left and the right sides of Figure 15.1, used elements from manufactured products (and sometimes the manufactured products themselves) are looped back up in the cycle of production and service to be transformed once again. The looped processing would continue and repeat itself over time.

However, while technological innovation and engineering have been the driving force behind the transition toward circular production, *consumption* in the CE requires significant changes in behavior, which might constitute obstacles to the widespread adoption and diffusion of CE business models. Wastling et al. (2018) contended that much research has focused on the innovation and engineering challenges of redesigning products that

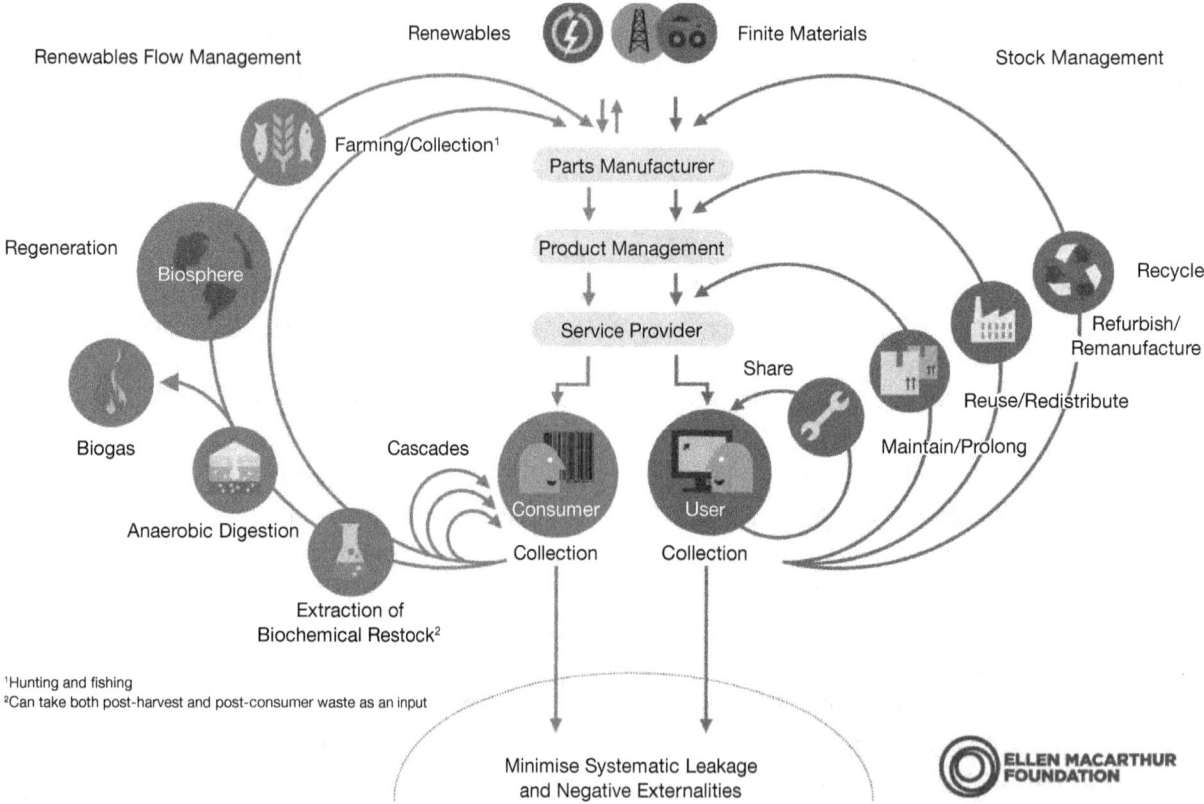

FIGURE 15.1. Schematic diagram of a circular economy. From *Circular Economy System Diagram* [Infographic], by Ellen MacArthur Foundation, 2019a, Ellen MacArthur Foundation (https://www.ellenmacarthurfoundation.org/circular-economy/concept/infographic). Copyright 2019 by Ellen MacArthur Foundation. Reprinted with permission.

enable the CE, while less emphasis has been given to the question "What is the user required to do to enable a circular economy?" (p. 4). The next sections identify some of the most significant changes the CE brings for the purchase, usage, and disposal of products. It also discusses some of the key psychological barriers that firms and policy makers are likely to encounter from consumers when adopting CE business models.

Consumption Changes in the Circular Economy

Consumption is a complex phenomenon influenced by a myriad of interrelated psychological, social, and cultural processes (e.g., Fournier, 1998; Simonson et al., 2001; Thompson et al., 2005). At the most basic level, the consumption process can be broken down into three stages: *product acquisition* (e.g., information search; evaluation and decision), *usage* (e.g., use intensity; maintenance; brand relationship), and *end of use* (i.e., disposal; upgrade). Although this constitutes a stark simplification of consumer behavior, it allows for the identification of potential psychological barriers that firms are likely to encounter from consumers at each stage of the consumption process.

Specifically, CE business models implicitly expect consumers to change their behavior in three important ways. First, consumers need to switch to products that are more durable and can be recycled. In our take-make-dispose consumption culture, product features (e.g., durability, reparability, and recyclability) often receive limited attention from consumers—as if these characteristics held only secondary importance (Prothero et al., 2011). Second, CE business models are likely to see firms switching to access-based solutions (Bardhi & Eckhardt, 2012), requiring consumers to give up ownership and instead use products on a temporary basis. Finally, CE business models can only work when consumers return or recycle products at the end of their lifecycle. All three changes are likely to encounter some form of resistance from consumers (Wastling et al., 2018).

While the number of studies on sustainable consumer behavior has grown exponentially in recent years, several metareviews on the topic provide an excellent starting point to identify the psychological factors that are most likely to influence consumers to (dis)engage with the CE. White et al.'s (2019) metareview identified and systematically structured the factors that influence and potentially help to shift consumers' behavior toward circular business models. The authors identified key drivers of sustainable consumer behavior change, including Social influences, Habits, Individual self, Feelings and cognition, and Tangibility (SHIFT). Other reviews have often focused on specific sustainability behaviors such as consumers' engagement with climate change (Gifford, 2011) or recycling (Varotto & Spagnolli, 2017) and also provide valuable insights into the psychological factors that may prevent consumers from engaging with CE business models.

It is important to note that while all studies contend that consumers' engagement is influenced by both intuitive and affective decision heuristics, as well as more effortful cognitive deliberations (Epstein, 2003; Kahneman, 2003, 2011), consumer behavior is likely to be constrained by the sociopolitical environment. Jackson (2005), for example, argued that institutional constraints, social norms, or the availability of fiscal or regulatory incentives can significantly constrain sustainable behaviors, often leaving little room for personal factors to affect behavior (Stern, 2005, p. 10786). Empirical evidence (Borrello et al., 2017; Hazen et al., 2017), as well as previous research on sustainable consumer behavior (e.g., Prothero et al., 2011), identified and discussed the most relevant psychological drivers of consumers' decisions to engage or dismiss CE products and services.

Figure 15.2 depicts the three phases of consumption and the psychological barriers associated with these behaviors. Viewed in a different way, these barriers can also be understood to be potential drivers of sustainable consumption. In other words, if consumers become more mindful about their consumption and take focus on more sustainability-oriented behaviors, factors such as habits, emotions, social norms, or efficacy can be important drivers of sustainable consumption within CEs. In this way, one can infer the importance of consumer learning about sustainability and of a consumer culture oriented to sustainability.

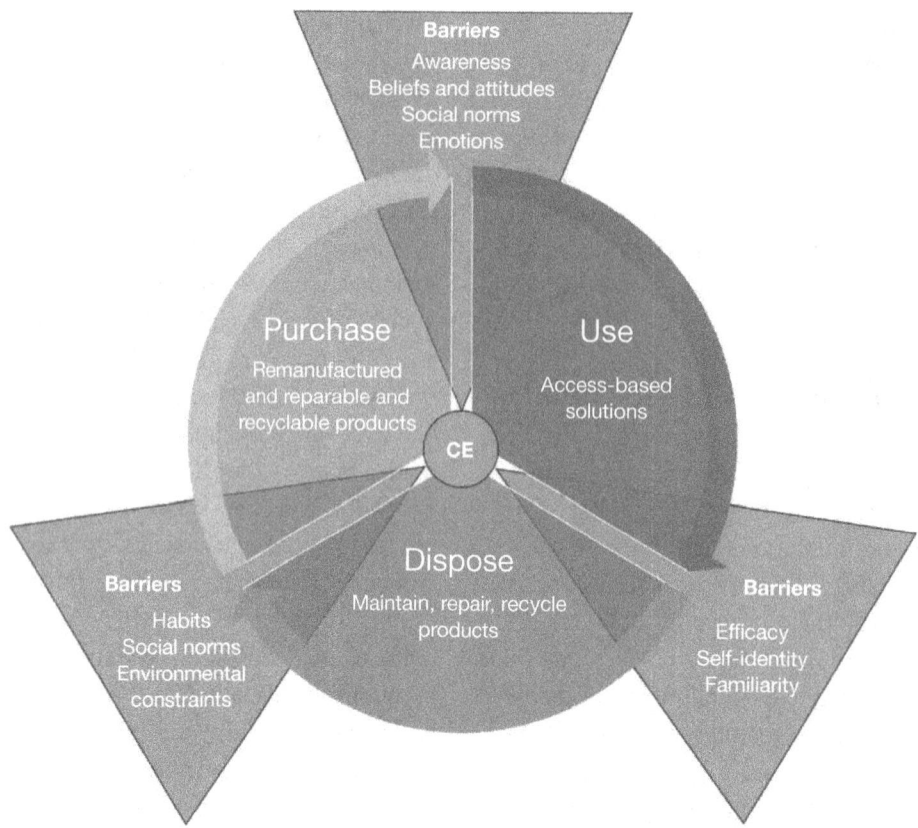

FIGURE 15.2. Behavioral changes and psychological barriers associated with sustainable consumption in a circular economy.

PRODUCT ACQUISITION: PURCHASING DURABLE, REPAIRABLE, AND RECYCLABLE GOODS

CE products constitute incremental and sometimes even radical changes for consumers. Traditionally, consumer response to innovative products has been conceptualized in a hierarchy-of-effects model (Gatignon & Robertson, 1989). Such a model conceptualizes consumers' decision making as

> the process through which an individual . . . passes from first knowledge of an innovation, to forming an attitude toward the innovation, to a decision to adopt or reject, to implementation of the new idea, and to confirmation of this decision. (Rogers, 1962, p. 163)

Indeed, the adoption of innovative CE products can be viewed as the outcome of a *cognitive* process that involves the consumer's search for, and processing of, information (Gregan-Paxton & Moreau, 2003).

Models have been employed to identify the factors that influence consumers' deliberate reasoning and subsequent decisions to purchase sustainable products and services. Some of these models include the theory of planned behavior (TPB; Ajzen, 1991), the technology acceptance model (Davis, 1989), and behavioral reasoning theory (Claudy et al., 2013; Westaby, 2005).

Knowledge and Awareness

A study commissioned by the European Commission identified the "barriers and trade-offs faced by consumers when deciding whether to engage in the CE, in particular whether to purchase a more or a less durable good" (Cerulli-Harms et al., 2018, p. 9). Based on qualitative interviews, large-scale surveys, and experimental research with over 18,000 consumers in 12 European countries, findings suggested that individuals might express positive attitudes toward CE products, but their actual engagement is low. One explanation for the attitude–behavior gap focuses on people's *knowledge* regarding the durability and reparability of products (Vermeir & Verbeke, 2006). The findings echo other studies that found that a lack of adequate information can be a critical barrier for consumers to purchase innovative eco-friendly products and services (e.g., Claudy et al., 2013; Gifford, 2011; McKenzie-Mohr, 2000). For example, providing information via eco-labels can thus be an effective means to increase awareness and knowledge.

In the case of CE, experimental findings suggest that when information was made salient, consumers "were almost three times more likely to choose products with the highest durability on offer, and more than two times more likely to choose products with the highest reparability ratings" (Cerulli-Harms et al., 2018, p. 11). Follow-up analysis disclosed that higher willingness to pay (WTP) was mainly the result of consumers associating durability and reparability attributes with higher *price/quality* ratios. The findings are in line with other studies that suggested that knowledge is likely to have a significant influence on proenvironmental behaviors (e.g., Delmas et al., 2013), but that this link can be strengthened when information is clearly related to consumers' self-values and/or self-benefits (e.g., Kahan et al., 2012; Peattie & Peattie, 2009). Indeed, simple nudges increased awareness, changed product perceptions (e.g., durability, reparability) as well as social norms, and impacted consumers' WTP for CE products across all categories (Michaud & Llerena, 2011; Trivedi et al., 2015).

One strategy to increase awareness is informing consumers via simple eco-labels, which convey information regarding the durability, content of reused materials, and/or the recyclability of CE products (e.g., Parguel et al., 2011). While some research suggests that eco-labels (e.g., color-coded energy-efficiency ratings) allow consumers to make more informed decisions (Borin et al., 2011; Taufique et al., 2017; Thøgersen 2000), studies in the domain of food consumption suggest that labels do not have a strong impact on consumers' food choices (Grunert et al., 2014). These examples highlight the important role of awareness in consumer choice. However, informing consumers may not necessarily change their behavior unless it also changes their underlying beliefs and attitudes.

Beliefs and Attitudes

Expectancy-value models such as the theory of planned behavior (Ajzen, 1991) have long formalized the relationship between consumers' beliefs, attitudes, and behavioral intentions. Empirical findings suggest that people's positive self-reported attitudes toward CE products are a strong predictor of their subsequent decisions to purchase recycled products or to repair existing products (Cerulli-Harms et al., 2018). Generally, research suggests that consumers' beliefs (regarding a product's relative advantage, compatibility, trialability, complexity, and observability) can explain differences in attitudes, as well as between 49% and 87% of variation in adoption rates (Rogers, 1962, p. 221). Indeed, when marketers make the relative advantage (i.e., durability, reparability) of CE products salient, consumers express stronger intentions to purchase. However, when marketers make the replacement of a product more convenient than repairing, maintaining, or upgrading it, many consumers tend to replace the old product and purchase a new one instead. Likewise, low prices can undermine the relative advantage of higher durability, with findings suggesting that consumers are easily swayed to purchase low-cost alternatives over more durable, higher quality options.

While beliefs about durability (and the associated price/quality ratio) appear to have a positive influence on consumers' purchase intentions and WTP for CE products in some countries, studies conducted in other cultures find different results. For example, a study conducted with Chinese consumers found that people reported negative attitudes toward remanufactured products, which increased as knowledge about the remanufacturing characteristics became more salient (e.g., Wang et al., 2013).

One possible explanation for these variations in attitudes toward CE products are the beliefs individuals hold regarding remanufactured or recycled products. While remanufactured products are by definition of the same standard and quality as new products (Thorn & Rogerson, 2002), consumers might nevertheless perceive them to be of lower quality than new ones (Hazen et al., 2017). Research in other domains also suggests that consumers hold negative beliefs toward sustainable products because they associate these products with negative attributes, such as less-pleasing aesthetics (Luchs & Kumar, 2017), low functional performance (Luchs et al., 2010), or higher prices (Chang, 2011; Gleim et al., 2013; Hughner et al., 2007).

Understanding consumers' explicit and implicit attitudes (e.g., Fazio & Olson, 2003) toward CE products is therefore an important first step toward gaining widespread support for circular business models. Further, aligning CE products with consumers' self-relevant motives (e.g., Schuitema & de Groot, 2015) by highlighting the relevant benefits associated with CE products can be a viable strategy to change attitudes and increase purchase intentions (e.g., White et al., 2019). For example, instead of highlighting sustainability credentials of CE products (e.g., durability or recyclability), manufacturers could communicate the better price/quality ratio and thus leverage consumers' self-interests more effectively (e.g., Green & Peloza 2014; Griskevicius et al., 2012).

Reasons

Consumers are reporting increasingly positive attitudes toward sustainable products, yet their preferences still widely fail to materialize into actual purchases (Shaw et al., 2016). The mismatch between consumers' expressed preferences for sustainable-product alternatives and people's actual (un)willingness to purchase is commonly referred to as the *attitude–behavior gap* (e.g., Peattie, 2001; Prothero et al., 2011). While belief-based models often fail to explain the gap between people's positive environmental attitudes and their unsustainable purchase behaviors, recent advances in reasoning theory find that models that account for people's *reasons* can explain more variance in behaviors than traditional belief-based models (Westaby, 2005; Westaby et al., 2010). Specifically, behavioral reasoning theory (BRT) offers a useful extension of models such as TPB by including context-specific reasons, which are posited to have an influence on attitude formation and decision making (Westaby, 2005). BRT contends that people can have specific *reasons for* and *reasons against* engaging in sustainable consumption, which is in line with other psychological models like decisional balance theory (Janis & Mann, 1977), cost-benefit models (Thaler, 1999), and reason theory (Westaby, 2005; Westaby & Fishbein, 1996). These opposing forces in consumers' cognitive deliberations have previously been conceptualized as "pros and cons, benefits and costs, and facilitators and constraints/obstacles/barriers" (Westaby, 2005, p. 100). For example, a person might believe that electric vehicles are better for the environment than traditional petrol or diesel cars, which would result in positive attitudes toward e-vehicles. However, they might have good reasons not to purchase an electric vehicle, such as a lack of charging stations or range anxiety. Indeed, Chatzidakis and Lee (2013) argued that

> focusing on reasons as opposed to related constructs such as beliefs [Ajzen, 1991] . . . offers advantages because they can be measured at a more context-specific level and they can also capture self-justification and defense mechanisms that are otherwise left unaccounted for, in models of buyer behavior [Westaby, 2005]. (p. 192)

Several field studies have shown that BRT offers a useful framework to uncover the underlying reasons for why people fail to engage in sustainable consumption behaviors like solar panel adoption (Claudy et al., 2013), urban bicycle-commuting (Claudy & Peterson, 2014), and car-sharing services (Claudy et al., 2015). In line with previous research around loss aversion (Gourville, 2006; Tversky & Kahneman, 1974) the studies found that reasons against often account for a large proportion of variance in people's behaviors, irrespective of their positive attitudes.

Emotions

Consumers' purchasing decisions are also influenced by affective, nondeliberative decision routes. For example, CE-related information is likely to trigger affective responses, which might subconsciously influence consumers' evaluation of CE products (Dijksterhuis et al., 2005; see also Fitzsimons et al., 2008). The influence of affect and emotions in decision making has received increasing attention from researchers and policy makers (e.g., Lerner et al., 2015). While affect generally refers to "a positive (like) or negative (dislike) evaluative feeling toward an external stimulus [e.g., CE labels]" (Slovic, 1999, p. 694), emotions refer to specific feelings (e.g., anger, sadness, or happiness). In addition, emotions are intense, short-lived, and usually have a definite cause and clear cognitive content (Bagozzi et al., 1999).

Emotions are expected to influence the decision-making process in two ways: via expected emotions and current emotions. First, consumers are likely to judge the utility of a decision outcome "by predicting one's emotional response to that outcome" (Lerner et al., 2015, p. 17). For example, an anticipated feeling of happiness for a consumer is likely to result in a more positive evaluation and hence a higher probability to purchase sustainable products (Rees et al., 2015). Second, emotions that are felt in the moment of purchase are likely to influence the decision. For example, studies suggest that consumers sometimes perceive remanufactured or recycled products as unhygienic or contaminated, which adversely impacts product evaluations and purchase intentions (e.g., Baxter et al., 2017).

These findings are in line with other research suggesting that consumers who perceived a product as contaminated (i.e., touched by other consumers) evaluated it more negatively and reported lower purchase intentions (Argo et al., 2006). More importantly, these relationships were mediated by feelings of disgust. The study added to a growing body of literature that has linked feelings to adverse behaviors in contexts such as food, disease, or moral taint (Rozin et al., 1992, 2008).

On the contrary, positive emotions are associated with greater willingness to engage in sustainable behaviors, especially when people anticipate hedonic pleasure from the behavior (Corral-Verdugo et al., 2009). For example, when people experience positive emotions (e.g., joy, pride) they tend to reduce their amount of plastic bottle usage (Peter & Honea, 2012).

Fruitful areas of future research include understanding the emotional responses that sustainable products (those that are recycled, reused, or shared) are likely to trigger, and how these emotions might influence people's evaluations and purchase intentions. Cultural effects are likely to moderate the influence of emotions on sustainability-oriented behaviors. For example, while recycled materials might trigger positive responses in Western cultures, recycled or reused products may trigger stronger negative emotions in other cultures (e.g., Wang et al., 2013).

Social Norms

A consumer's decision to purchase CE products is likely to be impacted by the behaviors and expectations of relevant others. *Social norms* refer to consumers' beliefs about what is socially appropriate and approved in a specific situation. Studies consistently provide evidence that social norms influence various sustainable behaviors and purchasing decisions, including renewable energy (Wiser, 2006), microgeneration technologies (Claudy et al., 2011), sustainable food (Dowd & Burke, 2013), transportation (Bamberg et al., 2007), and sustainable travel options (Teng et al., 2015).

The literature generally distinguishes between injunctive and descriptive norms. While *injunctive norms* refer to consumers' perceptions regarding what should be done, *descriptive norms* refer to consumers' perceptions of what relevant others are commonly doing (Cialdini et al., 1990). White et al. (2019) contended that descriptive norms in particular "can be stronger predictors of sustainable consumer behaviors than other factors such as self-interest, and people tend to underestimate how influential such norms can be" (p. 24).

In the context of innovation, the degree of observability constitutes a strong predictor of the rate of adoption and market diffusions, mainly because consumers often model their behaviors on others (Cialdini, 2007). Early adopters, opinion leaders, and other influencers generally play critical roles in making use of new products visible to others (Jansson et al., 2017; Leonard-Barton, 1985; Van Eck et al., 2011). For example, Jansson (2011) highlighted the importance of norms in the acceptance and diffusion of electric vehicles and found that increasing the social-desirability of eco-innovations via opinion leaders is likely to increase rates of adoption. Likewise, Confente et al. (2020) found that people with "green" self-identities associated higher value with products made from bioplastics, subsequently translating into higher purchase intentions. These findings echo research from other domains that suggests that social desirability and consumers' motivation to make positive impressions on relevant others is positively associated with endorsement and adoption of sustainable products and behaviors (Green & Peloza, 2014; Griskevicius et al., 2010). However, sustainability attributes are not perceived as socially desirable by all. For example, in a study of American Hummer drivers, researchers found that ecological attributes were perceived as feminine and unpatriotic by some consumers (Luedicke et al., 2010).

While researchers consistently find evidence for product consumption being intertwined with consumer identity and notions of self (e.g., Belk, 1988), a question arises about the meaning of how consumption might change when ownership is replaced with access-based solutions.

PRODUCT USAGE: UTILIZING ACCESS-BASED SOLUTIONS

Closing resource loops requires firms to maintain ownership of resources at all times, because "worn-out" goods serve as inputs of production for future generations of products. In many instances, this might be achieved more easily by moving to access-based solutions, which have been defined as "market-mediated transactions that provide customers with temporarily limited access to goods in return for an access-fee, while legal ownership remains with the service provider" (Schaefers et al., 2016, p. 3).

Access-based models, however, challenge established notions of ownership, which are likely to change the nature of how consumers utilize products as well as the relationship consumers develop with physical objects. Access-based schemes have gained traction in consumption domains, such as music (e.g., Spotify), entertainment (e.g., Netflix), travel (e.g., Airbnb), and transport (e.g., car sharing). Some researchers have proposed that consumers in developed countries have entered a postownership era (Belk, 2014, p. 1599). However, access-based forms of consumption only account for a fraction of all goods consumed. It remains to be seen whether consumers accept access-based solutions in domains such as household goods, appliances, or fashion (Albinsson & Perera, 2018, p. 201).

Theories of psychological ownership (Pierce et al., 2001) suggest that the concept of ownership goes deeper than the notions of legality and property rights and that people develop intimate relationships with their (physical) possessions, allowing them to project and express their identity and self (e.g., Brown et al., 2014; Pierce et al., 2001). The notion of psychological ownership refers to the state in which individuals feel as though the target of ownership or a piece of that target is theirs (Pierce et al., 2003). Some have argued that "consumers will not accept the strategies of a circular business model, such as sharing, collaborative consumption and access-based models because these models do not provide psychological ownership to the consumer" (Singh & Giacosa, 2019, p. 926). The following sections review the concept of psychological ownership in the context of CE in more detail and discuss the challenges that may arise for firms aiming to switch to access-based models.

Psychological Ownership

Psychological ownership refers to a consumer's mental state, in which the person feels that an object is theirs. The theory of psychological ownership sheds light on why (i.e., motives) and how (i.e., routes) individuals develop feelings of ownership (Pierce et al., 2003). Building on over a hundred years of research from various disciplines, Pierce and colleagues (2003) found that ownership is motivated by people's efficacy and reflectance, their desire to enhance self-identity, and by having a place to dwell. In turn, psychological ownership can emerge when consumers experience feelings of greater control over the ownership target, have intimate knowledge of the object, and increase their self-investment, such as time, energy, and resources (e.g., Kirk et al., 2015). While Pierce and colleagues stressed that the routes to psychological ownership can be both complementary and additive, researchers of the CE are particularly interested in whether individuals' engagement with access-based solutions can also result in feelings of ownership.

Efficacy

People's beliefs that they can control situations and circumstances to achieve desirable outcomes leads to feelings of efficacy, which can be enhanced by owning possessions: "Exploration of, and the ability to control one's environment gives rise to feelings of efficacy and pleasure, which stem from 'being the cause' and having altered the environment through one's control-actions" (Pierce et al., 2003, p. 89).

Clearly, some access-based solutions, such as the streaming of music, have provided consumers with an increased ability to control and integrate products into their daily lives (Sinclair & Tinson, 2017). Likewise, entertainment services like Netflix, Apple TV, or Amazon Prime have provided consumers not only with more choices but also with an unprecedented opportunity for discovery, individualization, and control—which are likely to positively enhance feelings of psychological ownership (e.g., Kirk & Swain, 2015).

However, in other domains (e.g., transportation access-based solutions like car sharing), ownership might be negatively related to efficacy and feelings of control (Bardhi & Eckhardt, 2012; Belk, 2014; Paundra et al., 2017). For inner-city residents, the financial stress and uncertainty for nearby parking make car ownership too burdensome for many who have public transportation readily available (Peterson & Simkins, 2019). While digitization (specifically, the ability to locate, secure, and control car-sharing solutions via mobile apps) has increased efficacy for those who use car sharing, other factors such as limited control over availability and the exact locations for picking up a car to be shared are likely to adversely influence consumers' sense of control. Consumers' desire to control possessions is thus likely to constitute a barrier to access-based solutions in other domains, such as household goods or fashion.

Self-Identity

A large body of consumer research has demonstrated the role material objects play in the development and maintenance of people's self-concept (McCracken, 1986; Price et al., 2000), as well as the formation and expressions of people's identities (e.g., Levy, 1959; Weiss & Johar, 2016). Importantly, consumers appear to identify with symbolic meanings of objects via psychological feelings of ownership. For example, individuals are less willing to part with possessions that are linked to the self because of a sense of identity loss (Winterich et al., 2017).

While Belk (2014) argued that access-based solutions can provide valuable resources for constructing and expressing identities, in other domains, ownership of products may still be perceived as more authentic and thus more important to people's extended selves. Sinclair and Tinson (2017), for example, pointed out that music streaming enhances people's ability to construct identities (e.g., creation of playlists or online profiles) and to communicate with a larger number of people (e.g., via online sharing platforms). Yet, a physical collection of vinyl records might be perceived as more closely related to one's identity. On the other hand, access-based solutions (e.g., the temporary use of designer fashion items, luxury goods, or expensive cars) might give consumers an opportunity to express themselves in ways that were previously unattainable. However, it is unclear if and how access-based forms of consumption allow consumers to construe and signal their identities the same way traditional modes of ownership models can.

Place

Finally, Pierce et al. (2003) suggested that people who develop a strong sense of identification and emotional connection with their belongings are likely to experience them as a "safe place" in their daily lives. In this way, material possessions provide people with physical and emotional security by providing familiarity in their surroundings. Importantly, the energy consumers invest in gaining familiarity and intimate knowledge of the object is likely to increase the sense of belonging to a place and others in such a place. As previously discussed, access-based solutions can provide some sense of place. Music streaming services, for example, allow consumers to structure and personalize their music experience, while algorithmically controlled recommendations might give consumers a sense of being understood. In these ways, such platforms boost the familiarity of experience. However, many access-based solutions, by definition, offer consumers only temporary usage of objects. Such temporality undermines self-efficacy, self-identity, and a sense of place for individuals. This may explain why consumers prefer ownership over access in certain domains, such as housing.

Outcomes

The discussion suggests that access-based solutions are likely to alter existing notions of psychological ownership by challenging consumers' sense of efficacy, self-identity, and place. Firms today can utilize digital platforms (e.g., mobile apps) to give consumers greater control over when, where, and how to access products and services. Such apps also serve as important ways for consumers to personalize and communicate their experiences to relevant others and, in this way, give them an opportunity to make access-based solution extensions of their identity (Belk, 1988). Digital platforms that are highly personalizable can provide consumers with feelings of intimacy and belonging, thus meeting consumers' need for place.

To summarize, the discussion suggests that closing resource loops in a CE requires consumers to embrace access-based solutions over traditional ownership models. Consumer efficacy, self-identity, and feelings of place motivate their need for ownership and can function as both drivers as well as barriers in the CE. For example, psychological ownership makes consumers feel more accountable for products, which is likely to make people use products longer and engage more frequently with product practices that extend a product's life, such as maintenance and service. On the other hand, temporary access-based solutions might diminish feelings of ownership, which can lead to behaviors that shorten a product's life. Bardhi and Eckhardt (2012), for example, found that consumers drove more recklessly when they used car-sharing services compared with driving their own car. On the contrary, Peck and Shu (2009) found that hotel guests who felt higher levels of ownership left their room cleaner.

However, research also suggests that psychological ownership makes consumers less willing to share, recycle, or resell their possessions (at reasonable prices) and instead hold on to them. The following section discusses factors that are most likely to influence consumer behavior regarding the repairing and recycling of products.

DISPOSING PRODUCTS: REPAIRING, RETURNING, AND RECYCLING

The CE requires consumers to make significant changes in the ways they dispose of products. While in a linear economy most products are thrown away, often after a single use, circular systems of production rely on consumers to repair, upgrade, or recycle products when they reach the end of their lives. In this way, consumers become suppliers of input materials for future cycles of production.

In Europe, research reports that 78% of consumers claimed to recycle unwanted goods, while 64% claimed to repair possessions when they break by bringing them back to the manufacturer, using professional repair services, and/or having them mended by friends or family members (Cerulli-Harms et al., 2018). However, findings also suggest that convenience was one of the most important barriers, as consumers were more likely to replace products if repairing products involved extra effort for consumers. Other barriers include consumers' beliefs that repairing products was too expensive and that existing products had gone out of fashion. Others simply claimed not to know where they could repair products.

Research in adjacent domains suggests that changing consumer habits is essential to increasing participation in sustainable behaviors (White et al., 2019). Consumers are creatures of habit, often automatically repeating "past behaviors with little regard to current goals and valued outcomes" (Wood & Neal, 2009, p. 1). Research has established that bad habits can be a key barrier to sustainable behaviors in domains such as transportation, energy usage, or recycling (Carrus et al., 2008). Replacing damaged or broken products often appears to be the default option, and interventions should aim to break the habit of automatic replacement and to incentivize consumers to engage more proactively with maintenance and repair services. Penalizing the disposal of products by imposing higher fines or taxes on waste (Kinnaman & Fullerton, 1995) is one tactic to shift consumers' behaviors. However, penalties can often lead to negative reactions from the public. Additionally, penalties are often difficult to implement, enforce, and monitor (Bolderdijk et al., 2013).

Providing consumers with prompts (Osbaldiston & Schott, 2012), making repair more convenient (Berry et al., 2002), and providing incentives (like rewards, discounts, or gifts; Harder & Woodard, 2007) seem to be more effective ways to encourage consumers to repair products. For example, apparel manufacturer *Nudie Jeans* (https://www.nudiejeans.com) has incorporated repair services into their (online) stores, where people can get their jeans professionally repaired and altered. The company also incentivizes consumers to take back worn-out jeans by offering discounts on new jeans when consumers hand in their old ones. Further, old pairs are either recycled or upcycled, in which case the company sells them on their website as pre-used jeans (which often sell out in hours).

While prompts and positive incentives are likely to prove useful tactics in reinforcing habits of repair and upgrade behaviors in consumers, such prompts and incentives might be less effective when it comes to recycling. Research suggests that incentives might undermine consumers' intrinsic motivations (Frey & Oberholzer-Gee, 1997) and are often unable to instill long-term behavior change after the incentive has been removed (Cairns et al., 2010).

Indeed, a recent metareview by Varotto and Spagnolli (2017) investigated the effectiveness of several psychological strategies to promote household recycling behavior. Based on a systematic review of 81 recycling-intervention studies, the authors identified and categorized several types of intervention types, including (a) *prompts and information* (i.e., provision of factual, persuasive, or reminding information), (b) provision of *feedback* (i.e., information regarding recycling performance against some predefined benchmark), (c) *commitment* (i.e., individual commitment to defined goals), (d) *incentives* (i.e., monetary rewards, refunds, gifts, prizes, discounts), (e) *environmental alterations* (i.e., making behaviors more convenient and easy to perform), and (f) *social modeling* (i.e., information that shows how others engage in the behavior).

More importantly, quantitative analysis of 47 field-intervention studies disclosed that social modeling proved to be the most effective intervention technique, followed by environmental alterations (Varotto & Spagnolli, 2017, p. 173). These results suggested that engaging consumers to participate in recycling behavior might be most effectively achieved by changing recycling norms. For example, recycling norms could be influenced by social modeling. In this way, consumers would observe the behaviors of (relevant) others, learn, and ultimately imitate these due to their desire for social approval (Bandura, 1969).

Further, making recycling easy could be done by modifying the physical environment by increasing the number, proximity, and visibility of recycling stations (e.g., Willman, 2015). Further, firms could offer free collection services or postal returns for used goods and services, making recycling as convenient as possible for consumers. Advances in artificial intelligence and the IoT technologies could further help to automate these processes by automatically informing manufacturers and consumers as soon as products malfunction or reach the end of their life.

Interestingly, Varotto and Spagnolli (2017) conducted a post hoc analysis of 187 studies that investigated the psychological factors underlying people's (non)recycling behavior. The findings disclosed that most psychological studies appear to focus on people's intrinsic motivations, information and knowledge, as well as personal beliefs and attitudes. This stands in contrast to empirical studies that suggest that the most effective behavioral levers are social influences and contextual variables, which have received comparatively little attention from researchers to date. This discrepancy between psychological studies and the effectiveness of field-intervention studies offers potentially interesting avenues for future research, particularly in the context of the CE.

CONCLUSION

Drawing on the notion of the CE, in this chapter we highlighted what a transition toward more sustainable systems of production and consumption would mean for consumers. Consumers will play a critical role in the transition toward CEs, and while much emphasis is currently given to the innovation and engineering challenges of CE products and systems, an important question remains largely unanswered: What are consumers required to do to enable CEs?

Our discussion contends that some of the biggest changes for consumers relate to the purchasing of recycled or reused products; the replacement of ownership models with access-based solutions; and the increasing need for consumers to repair, return, or recycle products when they are no longer in use. More important, we have identified and discussed some of the key psychological barriers that are associated with these behavioral changes. While many of these factors currently constitute obstacles in the transition toward CE, they also provide possible "levers" for behavioral change. For example, our discussion has shown that beliefs regarding recycled materials vary widely between individuals and cultures. Understanding consumers' beliefs and aligning CE products with consumers' self-relevance motives, for example, by communicating relevant benefits like price/quality ratios, can constitute an important first step toward behavioral change. Furthermore, we have shown that a CE places greater emphasis on access over ownership. Feelings of ownership, however, are motivated by various latent needs (e.g., self-identity or efficacy), and the question arises of how access-based solutions can be designed to meet the needs and motives of consumers (e.g., options for personalization or greater control). Finally, for a CE to succeed, people need to change the ways they currently dispose of products when they reach the end of their material life. Our current throw-away behavior is deeply habitual. However, empirical evidence in the recycling domain suggests that changing norms via social modeling as well as environmental changes has great potential to break with bad habits and to encourage consumers to recycle, take back, or repair products.

There is no doubt, at least in our minds, that moving away from our current take-make-dispose systems toward CEs is a critical step toward a more sustainable future. Research in consumer psychology will play an increasingly important role in offering guidance and advice to firms and policy makers on how to incentivize consumption practices that are congruent with circular systems of production and consumption.

REFERENCES

Ajzen, I. (1991). The theory of planned behavior. *Organizational Behavior and Human Decision Processes*, 50(2), 179–211. https://doi.org/10.1016/0749-5978(91)90020-T

Albinsson, P. A., & Perera, B. Y. (2018). Access-based consumption: From ownership to non-ownership of clothing. In *The rise of the sharing economy: Exploring the challenges and opportunities of collaborative consumption* (pp. 186–212). Praeger.

Argo, J. J., Dahl, D. W., & Morales, A. C. (2006). Consumer contamination: How consumers react to products touched by others. *Journal of Marketing*, 70(2), 81–94. https://doi.org/10.1509/jmkg.70.2.081

Ayres, R. U. (2008). Sustainability economics: Where do we stand? *Ecological Economics*, 67(2), 281–310. https://doi.org/10.1016/j.ecolecon.2007.12.009

Bagozzi, R. P., Gopinath, M., & Nyer, P. U. (1999). The role of emotions in marketing. *Journal of the Academy of Marketing Science*, 27(2), 184–206. https://doi.org/10.1177/0092070399272005

Bakker, C. M. den Hollander, E. van Hinte, & Y. Zijlstra. (2014). *Products that last: Product design for circular business models*. TU Delft.

Bamberg, S., Hunecke, M., & Blöbaum, A. (2007). Social context, personal norms and the use of public transportation: Two field studies. *Journal of Environmental Psychology*, 27(3), 190–203. https://doi.org/10.1016/j.jenvp.2007.04.001

Bandura, A. (1969). Social-learning theory of identificatory processes. In D. A. Goslin (Ed.), *Handbook of socialization theory and research* (pp. 213–262). Rand McNally.

Bardhi, F., & Eckhardt, G. M. (2012). Access-based consumption: The case of car sharing. *Journal of Consumer Research*, 39(4), 881–898. https://doi.org/10.1086/666376

Baxter, W., Aurisicchio, M., & Childs, P. (2017). Contaminated interaction: Another barrier to circular material flows. *Journal of Industrial Ecology*, 21(3), 507–516. https://doi.org/10.1111/jiec.12612

Belk, R. W. (1988). Possessions and the extended self. *Journal of Consumer Research*, *15*(2), 139–168. https://doi.org/10.1086/209154

Belk, R. W. (2014). You are what you can access: Sharing and collaborative consumption online. *Journal of Business Research*, *67*(8), 1595–1600. https://doi.org/10.1016/j.jbusres.2013.10.001

Berry, L. L., Seiders, K., & Grewal, D. (2002). Understanding service convenience. *Journal of Marketing*, *66*(3), 1–17. https://doi.org/10.1509/jmkg.66.3.1.18505

Bolderdijk, J. W., Steg, L., Geller, E. S., Lehman, P. K., & Postmes, T. (2013). Comparing the effectiveness of monetary versus moral motives in environmental campaigning. *Nature Climate Change*, *3*(4), 413–416. https://doi.org/10.1038/nclimate1767

Borin, N., Cerf, D. C., & Krishnan, R. (2011). Consumer effects of environmental impact in product labeling. *Journal of Consumer Marketing*, *28*(1), 76–86. https://doi.org/10.1108/07363761111101976

Borrello, M., Caracciolo, F., Lombardi, A., Pascucci, S., & Cembalo, L. (2017). Consumers' perspective on circular economy strategy for reducing food waste. *Sustainability*, *9*(1), 141. https://doi.org/10.3390/su9010141

Brown, G., Pierce, J. L., & Crossley, C. (2014). Toward an understanding of the development of ownership feelings. *Journal of Organizational Behavior*, *35*(3), 318–338. https://doi.org/10.1002/job.1869

Brundtland, G. H. (1987). Our common future—Call for action. *Environmental Conservation*, *14*(4), 291–294. https://doi.org/10.1017/S0376892900016805

Cairns, S., Newson, C., & Davis, A. (2010). Understanding successful workplace travel initiatives in the UK. *Transportation Research Part A: Policy and Practice*, *44*(7), 473–494. https://doi.org/10.1016/j.tra.2010.03.010

Carrus, G., Passafaro, P., & Bonnes, M. (2008). Emotions, habits and rational choices in ecological behaviours: The case of recycling and use of public transportation. *Journal of Environmental Psychology*, *28*(1), 51–62. https://doi.org/10.1016/j.jenvp.2007.09.003

Cerulli-Harms, A., Suter, J., Landzaat, W., Duke, C., Diaz, A. R., Porsch, L., Peroz, T., Kettner, S., Thorun, C., Svatikova, K., Vermeulen, J., Smit, T., Dekeulenaer, F., & Lucica, E. (2018). *Behavioral study on consumers' engagement in the circular economy*. European Commission.

Chang, C. H. (2011). The influence of corporate environmental ethics on competitive advantage: The mediation role of green innovation. *Journal of Business Ethics*, *104*(3), 361–370. https://doi.org/10.1007/s10551-011-0914-x

Charter, M. (Ed.). (2018). *Designing for the circular economy*. Routledge.

Chatzidakis, A., & Lee, M. S. W. (2013). Anti-consumption as the study of reasons against. *Journal of Macromarketing*, *33*(3), 190–203. https://doi.org/10.1177/0276146712462892

Cialdini, R. B. (2007). Descriptive social norms as underappreciated sources of social control. *Psychometrika*, *72*(2), 263–268. https://doi.org/10.1007/s11336-006-1560-6

Cialdini, R. B., Reno, R. R., & Kallgren, C. A. (1990). A focus theory of normative conduct: Recycling the concept of norms to reduce littering in public places. *Journal of Personality and Social Psychology*, *58*(6), 1015–1026. https://doi.org/10.1037/0022-3514.58.6.1015

Claudy, M. C., Garcia, R., & O'Driscoll, A. (2015). Consumer resistance to innovation—A behavioral reasoning perspective. *Journal of the Academy of Marketing Science*, *43*(4), 528–544. https://doi.org/10.1007/s11747-014-0399-0

Claudy, M. C., Michelsen, C., & O'Driscoll, A. (2011). The diffusion of microgeneration technologies—Assessing the influence of perceived product characteristics on home owners' willingness to pay. *Energy Policy*, *39*(3), 1459–1469. https://doi.org/10.1016/j.enpol.2010.12.018

Claudy, M. C., & Peterson, M. (2014). Understanding the underutilization of urban bicycle commuting: A behavioral reasoning perspective. *Journal of Public Policy & Marketing*, *33*(2), 173–187. https://doi.org/10.1509/jppm.13.087

Claudy, M. C., Peterson, M., & O'Driscoll, A. (2013). Understanding the attitude-behavior gap for renewable energy systems using behavioral reasoning theory. *Journal of Macromarketing*, *33*(4), 273–287. https://doi.org/10.1177/0276146713481605

Confente, I., Scarpi, D., & Russo, I. (2020). Marketing a new generation of bio-plastics products for a circular economy: The role of green self-identity, self-congruity, and perceived value. *Journal of Business Research*, *112*, 431–439. https://doi.org/10.1016/j.jbusres.2019.10.030

Corral-Verdugo, V., Bonnes, M., Tapia-Fonllem, C., Fraijo-Sing, B., Frías-Armenta, M., & Carrus, G. (2009). Correlates of pro-sustainability orientation: The affinity towards diversity. *Journal of Environmental Psychology*, *29*(1), 34–43. https://doi.org/10.1016/j.jenvp.2008.09.001

Davis, F. D. (1989). Perceived usefulness, perceived ease of use, and user acceptance of information technology. *Management Information Systems Quarterly*, *13*(3), 319–340. https://doi.org/10.2307/249008

Delmas, M. A., Fischlein, M., & Asensio, O. I. (2013). Information strategies and energy conservation behavior: A meta-analysis of experimental studies from 1975 to 2012. *Energy Policy*, *61*, 729–739. https://doi.org/10.1016/j.enpol.2013.05.109

Demaria, F., Schneider, F., Sekulova, F., & Martinez-Alier, J. (2013). What is degrowth? From an activist slogan to a social movement. *Environmental Values*, *22*(2), 191–215. https://doi.org/10.3197/096327113X13581561725194

Dijksterhuis, A., Smith, P. K., Van Baaren, R. B., & Wigboldus, D. H. J. (2005). The unconscious consumer: Effects of environment on consumer behavior. *Journal of Consumer Psychology*, *15*(3), 193–202. https://doi.org/10.1207/s15327663jcp1503_3

Dowd, K., & Burke, K. J. (2013). The influence of ethical values and food choice motivations on intentions to purchase sustainably sourced foods. *Appetite*, *69*, 137–144. https://doi.org/10.1016/j.appet.2013.05.024

Eagle, L., & Dahl, S. (2015). *Marketing ethics and society*. SAGE Publications.

Elkington, J. (1994). Towards the sustainable corporation: Win-win-win business strategies for sustainable development. *California Management Review*, *36*(2), 90–100. https://doi.org/10.2307/41165746

Ellen MacArthur Foundation. (2013). *Towards the circular economy Vol. 1: An economic and business rationale for an accelerated transition*. https://www.ellenmacarthurfoundation.org/publications/

Ellen MacArthur Foundation. (2015). *Towards a circular economy: Business rationale for an accelerated transition*. https://www.ellenmacarthurfoundation.org/circular-economy/concept

Ellen MacArthur Foundation. (2019a). *Circular economy system diagram* [Infographic]. https://www.ellenmacarthurfoundation.org/circular-economy/concept/infographic

Ellen MacArthur Foundation. (2019b). *Completing the picture: How the circular economy tackles climate change*. https://www.ellenmacarthurfoundation.org/publications

Epstein, S. (2003). Cognitive-experiential self-theory of personality. In T. Millon & M. J. Lerner (Eds.), *Handbook of psychology*: *Vol. 5. Personality and social psychology* (pp. 159–184). John Wiley & Sons.

Esposito, M., Tse, T., & Soufani, K. (2018). Introducing a circular economy: New thinking with new managerial and policy implications. *California Management Review*, *60*(3), 5–19. https://doi.org/10.1177/0008125618764691

Fazio, R. H., & Olson, M. A. (2003). Implicit measures in social cognition. research: Their meaning and use. *Annual Review of Psychology*, *54*(1), 297–327. https://doi.org/10.1146/annurev.psych.54.101601.145225

Fitzsimons, G. M., Chartrand, T. L., & Fitzsimons, G. J. (2008). Automatic effects of brand exposure on motivated behavior: How Apple makes you "think different." *Journal of Consumer Research*, *35*(1), 21–35. https://doi.org/10.1086/527269

Fournier, S. (1998). Consumers and their brands: Developing relationship theory in consumer research. *Journal of Consumer Research*, *24*(4), 343–353. https://doi.org/10.1086/209515

Frey, B. S., & Oberholzer-Gee, F. (1997). The cost of price incentives: An empirical analysis of motivation crowding-out. *American Economic Review*, *87*(4), 746–755.

Gatignon, H., & Robertson, T. S. (1989). Technology diffusion: An empirical test of competitive effects. *Journal of Marketing*, *53*(1), 35–49.

Gifford, R. (2011). The dragons of inaction: Psychological barriers that limit climate change mitigation and adaptation. *American Psychologist*, *66*(4), 290–302. https://doi.org/10.1037/a0023566

Gleim, M. R., Smith, J. S., Andrews, D., & Cronin, J. J., Jr. (2013). Against the green: A multi-method examination of the barriers to green consumption. *Journal of Retailing*, *89*(1), 44–61. https://doi.org/10.1016/j.jretai.2012.10.001

Gourville, J. T. (2006). Eager sellers and stony buyers: Understanding the psychology of new-product adoption. *Harvard Business Review*, *84*(6), 98–106.

Green, T., & Peloza, J. (2014). Finding the right shade of green: The effect of advertising appeal type on environmentally friendly consumption. *Journal of Advertising*, *43*(2), 128–141. https://doi.org/10.1080/00913367.2013.834805

Gregan-Paxton, J., & Moreau, P. (2003). How do consumers transfer existing knowledge? A comparison of analogy and categorization effects. *Journal of Consumer Psychology*, *13*(4), 422–430. https://doi.org/10.1207/S15327663JCP1304_09

Griskevicius, V., Cantú, S. M., & Van Vugt, M. (2012). The evolutionary bases for sustainable behavior: Implications for marketing, policy, and social entrepreneurship. *Journal of Public Policy & Marketing*, *31*(1), 115–128. https://doi.org/10.1509/jppm.11.040

Griskevicius, V., Tybur, J. M., & Van den Bergh, B. (2010). Going green to be seen: Status, reputation, and conspicuous conservation. *Journal of Personality and Social Psychology*, *98*(3), 392–404. https://doi.org/10.1037/a0017346

Grunert, K. G., Hieke, S., & Wills, J. (2014). Sustainability labels on food products: Consumer motivation, understanding and use. *Food Policy, 44*, 177–189. https://doi.org/10.1016/j.foodpol.2013.12.001

Harder, M. K., & Woodard, R. (2007). Systematic studies of shop and leisure voucher incentives for household recycling. *Resources, Conservation and Recycling, 51*(4), 732–753. https://doi.org/10.1016/j.resconrec.2006.12.001

Hazen, B. T., Mollenkopf, D. A., & Wang, Y. (2017). Remanufacturing for the circular economy: An examination of consumer switching behavior. *Business Strategy and the Environment, 26*(4), 451–464. https://doi.org/10.1002/bse.1929

Hughner, R. S., McDonagh, P., Prothero, A., Shultz, C. J., & Stanton, J. (2007). Who are organic food consumers? A compilation and review of why people purchase organic food. *Journal of Consumer Behaviour: An International Research Review, 6*(2–3), 94–110. https://doi.org/10.1002/cb.210

Jackson, T. (2005). *Motivating sustainable consumption: A review of evidence on consumer behaviour and behavioural change*. University of Surrey.

Jacobo, J. (2019). *World Ocean Day 2019: Ocean plastics problem isn't going away, but here's what you can do to help*. ABC News. https://abcnews.go.com/Technology/world-ocean-day-2019-oceans-plastics-problem/story?id=63324490

Janis, I. L., & Mann, L. (1977). *Decision making: a psychological analysis of conflict, choice and commitment*. Free Press.

Jansson, J. (2011). Consumer eco-innovation adoption: Assessing attitudinal factors and perceived product characteristics. *Business Strategy and the Environment, 20*(3), 192–210. https://doi.org/10.1002/bse.690

Jansson, J., Nordlund, A., & Westin, K. (2017). Examining drivers of sustainable consumption: The influence of norms and opinion leadership on electric vehicle adoption in Sweden. *Journal of Cleaner Production, 154*, 176–187. https://doi.org/10.1016/j.jclepro.2017.03.186

Kahan, D. M., Peters, E., Wittlin, M., Slovic, P., Ouellette, L. L., Braman, D., & Mandel, G. (2012). The polarizing impact of science literacy and numeracy on perceived climate change risks. *Nature Climate Change, 2*(10), 732–735. https://doi.org/10.1038/nclimate1547

Kahneman, D. (2003). A perspective on judgment and choice: Mapping bounded rationality. *American Psychologist, 58*(9), 697–720. https://doi.org/10.1037/0003-066X.58.9.697

Kahneman, D. (2011). *Thinking, fast and slow*. Macmillan.

Kemper, J. A., & Ballantine, P. W. (2019). What do we mean by sustainability marketing? *Journal of Marketing Management, 35*(3–4), 277–309. https://doi.org/10.1080/0267257X.2019.1573845

Kinnaman, T. C., & Fullerton, D. (1995). How a fee per-unit garbage affects aggregate recycling in a model with heterogeneous households. In L. Bovenberg & S. Cnossen (Eds.), *Public economics and the environment in an imperfect world* (pp. 135–159). Springer. https://doi.org/10.1007/978-94-011-0661-0_6

Kirk, C. P., & Swain, S. D. (2015). Interactivity and psychological ownership in consumer value co-creation. In K. Kubacki (Ed.), *Ideas in marketing: Finding the new and polishing the old* (p. 121). Springer. https://doi.org/10.1007/978-3-319-10951-0_43

Kirk, C. P., Swain, S. D., & Gaskin, J. E. (2015). I'm proud of it: Consumer technology appropriation and psychological ownership. *Journal of Marketing Theory and Practice, 23*(2), 166–184.

Leonard-Barton, D. (1985). Experts as negative opinion leaders in the diffusion of a technological innovation. *Journal of Consumer Research, 11*(4), 914–926. https://doi.org/10.1086/209026

Lerner, J. S., Li, Y., Valdesolo, P., & Kassam, K. S. (2015). Emotion and decision making. *Annual Review of Psychology, 66*(1), 799–823. https://doi.org/10.1146/annurev-psych-010213-115043

Levy, S. J. (1959). Symbols by which we buy. *Harvard Business Review, 37*, 117–124.

Lofthouse, V., & Prendeville, S. (2018). Human-centred design of products and services for the circular economy—A review. *Design Journal, 21*(4), 451–476. https://doi.org/10.1080/14606925.2018.1468169

Luchs, M. G., & Kumar, M. (2017). "Yes, but this other one looks better/works better": How do consumers respond to trade-offs between sustainability and other valued attributes? *Journal of Business Ethics, 140*(3), 567–584. https://doi.org/10.1007/s10551-015-2695-0

Luchs, M. G., Naylor, R. W., Irwin, J. R., & Raghunathan, R. (2010). The sustainability liability: Potential negative effects of ethicality on product preference. *Journal of Marketing, 74*(5), 18–31. https://doi.org/10.1509/jmkg.74.5.018

Luedicke, M. K., Thompson, C. J., & Giesler, M. (2010). Consumer identity work as moral protagonism: How myth and ideology animate a brand-mediated moral conflict. *Journal of Consumer Research, 36*(6), 1016–1032. https://doi.org/10.1086/644761

Lunde, M. B. (2018). Sustainability in marketing: A systematic review unifying 20 years of theoretical and substantive contributions (1997–2016). *AMS Review, 8*(3–4), 85–110. https://doi.org/10.1007/s13162-018-0124-0

McCracken, G. (1986). Culture and consumption: A theoretical account of the structure and movement of the cultural meaning of consumer goods. *Journal of

Consumer Research, 13(1), 71–84. https://doi.org/10.1086/209048

McDonough, W., & Braungart, M. (2002). *Cradle to cradle: Remaking the way we make things*. North Point Press.

McKenzie-Mohr, D. (2000). New ways to promote proenvironmental behavior: Promoting sustainable behavior: An introduction to community-based social marketing. *Journal of Social Issues*, 56(3), 543–554. https://doi.org/10.1111/0022-4537.00183

Mentink, B. A. S. (2014). *Circular business model innovation: A process framework and a tool for business model innovation in a circular economy* [Unpublished master's thesis]. Delft University of Technology.

Michaud, C., & Llerena, D. (2011). Green consumer behaviour: An experimental analysis of willingness to pay for remanufactured products. *Business Strategy and the Environment*, 20(6), 408–420. https://doi.org/10.1002/bse.703

Morelli, N. (2006). Developing new product service systems (PSS): Methodologies and operational tools. *Journal of Cleaner Production*, 14(17), 1495–1501. https://doi.org/10.1016/j.jclepro.2006.01.023

Osbaldiston, R., & Schott, J. P. (2012). Environmental sustainability and behavioral science: Meta-analysis of proenvironmental behavior experiments. *Environment and Behavior*, 44(2), 257–299. https://doi.org/10.1177/0013916511402673

Parker, L. (2018). Fast facts about plastic pollution. *National Geographic*. https://www.nationalgeographic.com/news/2018/05/plastics-facts-infographics-ocean-pollution/#close

Paundra, J., Rook, L., van Dalen, J., & Ketter, W. (2017). Preferences for car sharing services: Effects of instrumental attributes and psychological ownership. *Journal of Environmental Psychology*, 53, 121–130. https://doi.org/10.1016/j.jenvp.2017.07.003

Peattie, K. (2001). Towards sustainability: The third age of green marketing. *Marketing Review*, 2(2), 129–146. https://doi.org/10.1362/1469347012569869

Peattie, K., & Peattie, S. (2009). Social marketing: A pathway to consumption reduction? *Journal of Business Research*, 62(2), 260–268. https://doi.org/10.1016/j.jbusres.2008.01.033

Peck, J., & Shu, S. B. (2009). The effect of mere touch on perceived ownership. *Journal of Consumer Research*, 36(3), 434–447. https://doi.org/10.1086/598614

Peter, P. C., & Honea, H. (2012). Targeting social messages with emotions of change: The call for optimism. *Journal of Public Policy & Marketing*, 31(2), 269–283. https://doi.org/10.1509/jppm.11.098

Peterson, M., & Simkins, T. (2019). Consumers' processing of mindful commercial car sharing. *Business Strategy and the Environment*, 28(3), 457–465. https://doi.org/10.1002/bse.2221

Pierce, J. L., Kostova, T., & Dirks, K. T. (2001). Toward a theory of psychological ownership in organizations. *Academy of Management Review*, 26(2), 298–310. https://doi.org/10.5465/amr.2001.4378028

Pierce, J. L., Kostova, T., & Dirks, K. T. (2003). The state of psychological ownership: Integrating and extending a century of research. *Review of General Psychology*, 7(1), 84–107. https://doi.org/10.1037/1089-2680.7.1.84

Price, L. L., Arnould, E. J., & Folkman Curasi, C. (2000). Older consumers' disposition of special possessions. *Journal of Consumer Research*, 27(2), 179–201. https://doi.org/10.1086/314319

Prothero, A., Dobscha, S., Freund, J., Kilbourne, W. E., Luchs, M. G., Ozanne, L. K., & Thøgersen, J. (2011). Sustainable consumption: Opportunities for consumer research and public policy. *Journal of Public Policy & Marketing*, 30(1), 31–38. https://doi.org/10.1509/jppm.30.1.31

Rees, J. H., Klug, S., & Bamberg, S. (2015). Guilty conscience: Motivating pro-environmental behavior by inducing negative moral emotions. *Climatic Change*, 130(3), 439–452. https://doi.org/10.1007/s10584-014-1278-x

Rogers, E. M. (1962). *Diffusion of innovations*. Free Press of Glencoe.

Rothenberg, S. (2007). Sustainability through servicizing. *MIT Sloan Management Review*, 48(2).

Rozin, P., Haidt, J., & McCauley, C. R. (2008). Disgust. In M. Lewis, J. M. Haviland-Jones, & L. F. Barrett (Eds.), *Handbook of emotions* (pp. 757–776). Guilford Press.

Rozin, P., Markwith, M., & Nemeroff, C. (1992). Magical contagion beliefs and fear of AIDS. *Journal of Applied Social Psychology*, 22(14), 1081–1092. https://doi.org/10.1111/j.1559-1816.1992.tb00943.x

Schaefers, T., Lawson, S. J., & Kukar-Kinney, M. (2016). How the burdens of ownership promote consumer usage of access-based services. *Marketing Letters*, 27(3), 569–577. https://doi.org/10.1007/s11002-015-9366-x

Schuitema, G., & de Groot, J. I. (2015). Green consumerism: The influence of product attributes and values on purchasing intentions. *Journal of Consumer Behaviour*, 14(1), 57–69. https://doi.org/10.1002/cb.1501

Shaw, D., McMaster, R., & Newholm, T. (2016). Care and commitment in ethical consumption: An exploration of the "attitude–behaviour gap." *Journal of Business Ethics*, 136(2), 251–265. https://doi.org/10.1007/s10551-014-2442-y

Simonson, I., Carmon, Z., Dhar, R., Drolet, A., & Nowlis, S. M. (2001). Consumer research: In search of identity. *Annual Review of Psychology*, *52*(1), 249–275. https://doi.org/10.1146/annurev.psych.52.1.249

Sinclair, G., & Tinson, J. (2017). Psychological ownership and music streaming consumption. *Journal of Business Research*, *71*, 1–9. https://doi.org/10.1016/j.jbusres.2016.10.002

Singh, P., & Giacosa, E. (2019). Cognitive biases of consumers as barriers in transition towards circular economy. *Management Decision*, *57*(4), 921–936. https://doi.org/10.1108/MD-08-2018-0951

Slovic, P. (1999). Trust, emotion, sex, politics, and science: Surveying the risk-assessment battlefield. *Risk Analysis*, *19*(4), 689–701. https://doi.org/10.1111/j.1539-6924.1999.tb00439.x

Stern, P. C. (2005). Understanding individuals' environmentally significant behavior. *Environmental Law Reporter News & Analysis*, *35*(11), 10785.

Taufique, K. M. R., Vocino, A., & Polonsky, M. J. (2017). The influence of eco-label knowledge and trust on pro-environmental consumer behaviour in an emerging market. *Journal of Strategic Marketing*, *25*(7), 511–529. https://doi.org/10.1080/0965254X.2016.1240219

Teng, Y. M., Wu, K. S., & Liu, H. H. (2015). Integrating altruism and the theory of planned behavior to predict patronage intention of a green hotel. *Journal of Hospitality & Tourism Research*, *39*(3), 299–315. https://doi.org/10.1177/1096348012471383

Thaler, R. H. (1999). Mental accounting matters. *Journal of Behavioral Decision Making*,*12*(3), 183–206. https://doi.org/10.1002/(SICI)1099-0771(199909)12:3<183::AID-BDM318>3.0.CO;2-F

Thøgersen, J. (2000). Psychological determinants of paying attention to eco-labels in purchase decisions: Model development and multinational validation. *Journal of Consumer Policy*, *23*(3), 285–313. https://doi.org/10.1023/A:1007122319675

Thompson, C. J., Arnould, E. J., & Stern, B. B. (2005). Exploring the différance: A postmodern approach to paradigmatic pluralism in consumer research. In S. Brown & D. Turley (Eds.), *Consumer research: Postcards from the edge* (pp. 146–185). Routledge.

Thorn, B. K., & Rogerson, P. (2002). Take it back: Remanufacturing is a viable alternative to disposal of products that have outlived their usefulness—But only if engineers can unearth sound economic justifications. *IIE Solutions*, *34*(4), 34–40.

Trivedi, R. H., Patel, J. D., & Savalia, J. R. (2015). Pro-environmental behaviour, locus of control and willingness to pay for environmental friendly products. *Marketing Intelligence & Planning*, *33*(1), 67–89. https://doi.org/10.1108/MIP-03-2012-0028

Tversky, A., & Kahneman, D. (1974). Judgment under uncertainty: Heuristics and biases. *Science*, *185*(4157), 1124–1131. https://doi.org/10.1126/science.185.4157.1124

Van Eck, P. S., Jager, W., & Leeflang, P. S. (2011). Opinion leaders' role in innovation diffusion: A simulation study. *Journal of Product Innovation Management*, *28*(2), 187–203. https://doi.org/10.1111/j.1540-5885.2011.00791.x

Varotto, A., & A. Spagnolli. (2017). Psychological strategies to promote household recycling. A systematic review with meta-analysis of validated field interventions. *Journal of Environmental Psychology*, *51*, 168–188. https://doi.org/10.1016/j.jenvp.2017.03.011

Vermeir, I., & Verbeke, W. (2006). Sustainable food consumption: Exploring the consumer "attitude–behavioral intention" gap. *Journal of Agricultural & Environmental Ethics*, *19*(2), 169–194. https://doi.org/10.1007/s10806-005-5485-3

Wang, J., Yam, R. C., & Tang, E. P. (2013). Ecologically conscious behaviour of urban Chinese consumers: The implications to public policy in China. *Journal of Environmental Planning and Management*, *56*(7), 982–1001. https://doi.org/10.1080/09640568.2012.714750

Wastling, T., Charnley, F., & Moreno, M. (2018). Design for circular behaviour: Considering users in a circular economy. *Sustainability*, *10*(6). https://doi.org/10.3390/su10061743

Weiss, L., & Johar, G. V. (2016). Products as self-evaluation standards: When owned and unowned products have opposite effects on self-judgment. *Journal of Consumer Research*, *42*(6), 915–930. https://doi.org/10.1093/jcr/ucv097

Westaby, J. D. (2005). Behavioral reasoning theory: Identifying new linkages underlying intentions and behavior. *Organizational Behavior and Human Decision Processes*, *98*(2), 97–120. https://doi.org/10.1016/j.obhdp.2005.07.003

Westaby, J. D., & Fishbein, M. (1996). Factors underlying behavioral choice: Testing a new reasons theory approach. *Journal of Applied Social Psychology*, *26*(15), 1307–1323. https://doi.org/10.1111/j.1559-1816.1996.tb00072.x

Westaby, J. D., Probst, T. M., & Lee, B. C. (2010). Leadership decision-making: A behavioral reasoning theory analysis. *Leadership Quarterly*, *21*(3), 481–495. https://doi.org/10.1016/j.leaqua.2010.03.011

White, K., Habib, R., & Hardisty, D. J. (2019). How to SHIFT consumer behaviors to be more sustainable: A literature review and guiding framework. *Journal of Marketing*, *83*(3), 22–49. https://doi.org/10.1177/0022242919825649

Willman, K. W. (2015). Information sharing and curbside recycling: A pilot study to evaluate the value of door-to-door distribution of informational literature. *Resources, Conservation and Recycling, 104*(Pt. A), 162–171. https://doi.org/10.1016/j.resconrec.2015.08.012

Wilson, M. (2019, April 17). Exclusive: Adidas's radical new shoe could change how the world buys sneakers. *Fast Company*. https://www.fastcompany.com/90335038/exclusive-adidass-radical-new-shoe-could-change-how-the-world-buys-sneakers

Winterich, K. P., Reczek, R. W., & Irwin, J. R. (2017). Keeping the memory but not the possession: Memory preservation mitigates identity loss from product disposition. *Journal of Marketing, 81*(5), 104–120. https://doi.org/10.1509/jm.16.0311

Wiser, R. H. (2006). Using contingent valuation to explore willingness to pay for renewable energy: A comparison of collective and voluntary payment vehicles. *Ecological Economics, 62*(3–4), 419–432.

Wood, W., & Neal, D. T. (2009). The habitual consumer. *Journal of Consumer Psychology, 19*(4), 579–592. https://doi.org/10.1016/j.jcps.2009.08.003

World Commission on Environment and Development. (1987). *Our common future*. United Nations. http://www.un-documents.net/ocf-02.htm#I

World Economic Forum. (2020). *Favorable alignment of enablers*. https://reports.weforum.org/toward-the-circular-economy-accelerating-the-scale-up-across-global-supply-chains/favourable-alignment-of-enablers/

CHAPTER 16

MARKETING ETHICS, ETHICAL CONSUMERS, AND ETHICAL LAPSES

Ann-Marie Kennedy and Sommer Kapitan

Alternative, ethical consumption practices have become mainstream. In the 2010s and into the 2020s, belief-based shopping is driving market response as ethical shoppers demand social and political involvement from brands. More than two thirds of consumers now report buying or boycotting a brand based on their beliefs on social and political issues (Edelman, 2018). Information is becoming more widely accessible, media and social media regularly highlight key topics to encourage consumer choice, and more alternative products with ethical attributes are hitting the marketplace (e.g., Freestone & McGoldrick, 2008; Newholm & Shaw, 2007). This makes understanding the consumer psychology of ethical consumer decision making a more critical issue for scholars than ever before.

Yet marketers likewise face a new role in a marketplace flooded with consumer data, from which they can better extract and cater to consumer needs and wants. While marketers tend to sign on to a national or global code of ethics, these codes are nonregulated and thus there is no consequence for noncompliance. To ensure ethical marketing practice, marketers must develop their own practical wisdom, or phronēsis, to guide their marketing practice (Eagle & Kennedy, 2021; Laczniak & Murphy, 2006).

In this chapter, we examine both the consumer psychology of ethical decision making and its drivers and seek to unpack unethical marketing practices that take advantage of consumer psychology. Throughout, we show how decreasing information asymmetry and increasing consumer power have changed how consumers see their role in the marketplace and how marketers respond to rising consumer collective action. As consumers have more widespread and available access to firm, source, and manufacturing information about brands, marketers likewise have access to an ever-growing and vast pool of data about consumer habits, preferences, and digital behaviors.

We first advance a framework of ethical consumer psychology to examine the motivations, contexts, and outcomes of consumers' ethical decision making. We draw together the literature on consumer motivations for ethical decisions (internal and external), the different contexts in which these motivations come to bear (e.g., religiosity, sustainability, and prosocial consumer issues from altruism and fair trade to energy conservation and fair labor issues), and the outcomes that emerge from such ethical decision-making processes (attitudes, beliefs, and values, as well as key behaviors such as purchase, support, word of mouth, volunteering, and activism). We then review psychological tactics used by marketers and explore their ethicality. The extant literature is reviewed regarding unethical practices in personal selling, direct marketing, sales promotions, distribution, pricing, product policy,

https://doi.org/10.1037/0000262-016
APA Handbook of Consumer Psychology, L. R. Kahle (Editor-in-Chief)
Copyright © 2022 by the American Psychological Association. All rights reserved.

marketing communications, and finally, social marketing. Last, we discuss emerging issues from web 2.0 technology for children and consumer privacy. Overall we aim to explore the implications of both consumer and marketer (un)ethical behavior on both practice and scholarly work.

PART I: CONSUMER ETHICS

Socially conscious consumers were first identified in the pages of the *Journal of Consumer Research* in the 1970s (Brooker, 1976; Webster, 1975) as those who consider the public consequences of their consumption decisions or use their "purchasing power to bring about social change" (Webster, 1975, p. 188). By the 1980s, research into green consumerism captivated scholarly attention. By the 1990s, this had evolved to signal consumer willingness to purchase based on broader ethical brand positions beyond just "green" and on topics as diverse as human rights, the environment, animal testing, fair trade, and labor relations (e.g., Freestone & McGoldrick, 2008; Newholm & Shaw, 2007; Roberts, 1996; Shaw & Clarke, 1999; Thøgersen, 1999). Key to this view, consumers purchase based on their ethical values, which are "the criteria that individuals use to select and justify behavior" (Freestone & McGoldrick, 2008, p. 447). Importantly, ethical values can be both individual values and social, shared values around topics of ethical concern.

The evolution of scholarly examination of ethical consumer factors only increased into the 2000s, yet the focus remained on niche and alternative consumption projects from voluntary simplicity (e.g., Etzioni, 2004) and down-shifting to anticonsumption, proenvironmental, and fair trade shoppers (e.g., Thøgersen, 1999). By the 2010s, the gap in attitudes and behaviors for ethical and green consumers remained a focus of study, though more and more researchers examined the vast complexity and heterogeneity of the marketplace (e.g., Carrington et al., 2014; Freestone & McGoldrick, 2008). What was earlier treated and seen as an alternative practice of ethical consumption has been appropriated by a wider and broader set of divergent consumers, as belief-driven buyers shape market reaction and consumer spending patterns (Edelman, 2018; Freestone & McGoldrick, 2008). This is reflected in purchase patterns as well: Sustainable and socially conscious product sales increased 20% from 2014 (Nielsen, 2018), 4 times more than conventional products' sales, and are forecast to increase 5% to 8% more by 2021.

Decreasing information asymmetry and increasing adoption of moral consumption as an identity project have helped make ethical shopping mainstream. Two clear streams of literature on ethical consumption chart how "shopping for a better world" has moved ethical consumption from an identity project of alternative consumers into a prevailing consumer mindset. Scholars have tended to cluster their work around models of ethical consumer decision making (e.g., Freestone & McGoldrick, 2008) or to focus on the construction of an ethical consumer identity that might inoculate consumers against commodity consumption (e.g., Cherrier & Murray, 2007; Schor, 1998). This chapter shows how these streams inform one another via the framework we advance to underpin ethical consumer psychology (see Figure 16.1).

As affluent societies began to relieve individuals' basic needs, particularly in the post-World War II consumer culture, consumers were freed to consider the consequences of their consumption and move beyond materialistic values (e.g., Freestone & McGoldrick, 2008; Newholm & Shaw, 2007). This increased the status value of such prosocial consumption choices and products while allowing space for consideration of the negative impacts on people and the environment of some consumption decisions. Yet responsible, ethical consumption practices that involve choices about products in support of labor, the planet, or people were not universally adopted by all consumers, and they remained an alternative ideology. Judgment and decision-making scholars pointed in particular to the marketplace imbalances of information asymmetry. The market and brands long had more power and information, which meant ethical consumers were at a disadvantage (Pearce, 1999) or overwhelmed by the difficulty and effort of parsing information to make ethical decisions (e.g., Ehrich & Irwin, 2005). The rise of the consumer-shaped internet and social media and the rapid penetration

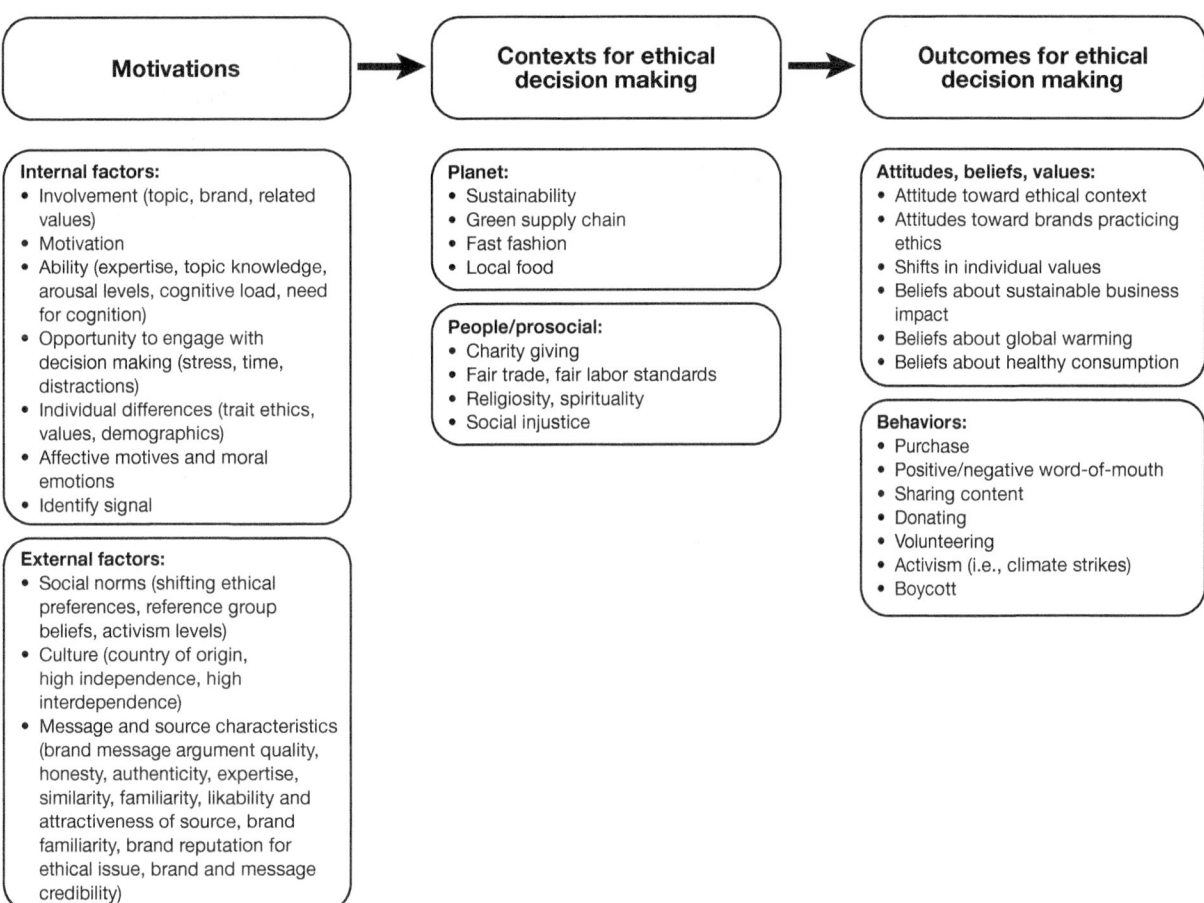

FIGURE 16.1. A framework of ethical consumer psychology.

of digital devices, however, have increased the availability and spread of information and shifted that asymmetry (e.g., Newholm & Shaw, 2007). Consumers now have more access to more data about companies, manufacturing, waste streams, and sourcing of materials and labor than ever before. As a result, a shift in consumer values has moved many shoppers from a materialistic, individualistic outlook toward "a more socially and environmentally proactive outlook" (Freestone & McGoldrick, 2008, p. 445). One might argue that this access to information and ability to both know about others and share about oneself may drive both the status of prosocial goods and those social groups who are consumers of them, as well as increase status shaming for those who do not.

The digital era has likewise, especially via social media, lent a sense of collective social action to ethical shopper behaviors that are a vehicle for moral self-expression and that signal status and belonging as part of a group of concerned consumers (e.g., Griskevicius et al., 2010). The resulting processes have shifted the consumer into a more powerful position and made ethical consumption a cultural phenomenon, particularly in terms of sustainability, fast fashion, fair trade, social injustice, and fair labor standards. Practitioners are adamant that brand strategies that engage with social, political, and ethical topics are useful when targeting millennials and Gen Z (Smiley, 2019). Yet older consumers have long been key buying groups who purchase and boycott based on moral responsibility. Older buyers continue to form a potentially potent and significant force when marketers consider the spending power of those aged 50+, along with their increased time to read, research, and become involved in ethical shopping (e.g., Carrigan et al., 2004).

Motivations for Ethical Consumption and Action by Consumers

The rise in ethical consumer values coincides with the rise in the availability of information about brands and their ethical (or lack of ethical) attributes. Likewise, ethical consumption patterns follow the penetration of social media in which others in a consumer's social network consistently demonstrate their own ethical consumption choices and the viral nature of key topics that circulate via social media create awareness and concern among consumers (Aldoory & Grunig, 2012). Phipps et al. (2013) used social cognitive theory to point to the role of environmental opportunity and learned behavior from social others as external drivers of key sustainable behaviors. These external factors do not stand alone, however. External models and facilitators of ethical consumption such as green buying can become internalized via a process of reciprocal determinism that impacts personal attitudes and motivations to create initial and habit-forming behaviors that bolster external reinforcements. Social influence, habit formation, and individual reflection and characteristics are also key to the psychological factors underpinning ethical consumer behaviors that are proenvironmental and prosocial (White et al., 2019, 2020).

The process of linking from consumer values to the offerings a consumer purchases is thus dependent on both internal and external factors (e.g., Phipps et al., 2013; White et al., 2019). These internal and external factors reinforce one another to create key outcomes for ethical decision making, as shown in Figure 16.1. The framework of ethical consumer psychology (see Figure 16.1) that has become apparent in this review underscores how consumer motivations, activated and built via certain contexts, lead to key outcomes from shifted attitudes and product preferences to boycotting or spreading positive word of mouth about a brand's ethical attributes.

Consumer affinity for the ethical cause is a key internal motivation and moderator of consumer responses to ethical marketing and ethical offering attributes (e.g., Bolton & Mattila, 2015; Chernev & Blair, 2015). As Carrington et al. (2014) showed, involvement stems from prioritizing ethical concerns and structuring purchases, support, and actions around issues of primary importance. The embedding of such issues into daily life for those who espouse the strongest ethical values, however, means that secondary ethical concerns can be compromised or traded off as they are less integrated into shopping plans.

Ethical consumers must therefore be highly motivated to be conscientious and form plans before shopping or consumption routines are enacted. Any lack of commitment or willingness to integrate a particular ethical concern into buying routines is an underlying mechanism in the gap between intentions and behaviors for the rising number of consumers who claim to espouse ethical values (Carrington et al., 2014). Part of this intention gap, however, might be explained by the way an ethical brand image can create a "halo effect." Once an ethically conscious consumer is convinced a brand is ethical on a given cause, they tend to evaluate it more positively on many attribute dimensions, including issues of secondary ethical concern, whether true or not for the brand (Bolton & Mattila, 2015; Chernev & Blair, 2015). This ethical halo may allow some brands to satisfy consumers and slip into the shopping baskets of those shopping based on nonprimary ethical concerns, those ethical standpoints that are not yet integrated into daily selection and purchase habits. However, those with weaker ethical drives and experiences may associate ethical brands with negative product attributes, relinquishing the halo effect as both their attitude and behavior do not provide strong convictions for ethical product purchase.

Ability and opportunity still clearly play a role in motivation for ethical consumption outcomes, however, regardless of level of concern for an ethical topic. Individuals react to personal costs and rewards and show differential price sensitivity for ethical products (e.g., Auger et al., 2003)—it is financially easier and less involving to buy a waste-free shampoo bar or eco hand soap than an electric vehicle. Individuals also can be willfully ignorant or simply lack knowledge of ethical information, which helps avoid having to factor in a response to labor practices or sourcing into a hedonic consumption decision such as buying new home furnishings (Ehrich & Irwin, 2005). Emotional management factors from avoidance of guilt and sadness to creating empathy and gratitude in this way often reduce how consumers respond to cause-related and ethical marketing (Ehrich & Irwin, 2005; J. Kim & Johnson, 2013; Xie et al., 2015). Likewise, hedonic consumer behaviors that drive enjoyment might reduce purchase of ethical products and services (Adomaviciute, 2013).

External factors in ethical decision making from the feedback loop of social cognitive theory (e.g., Phipps et al., 2013) include shifting social norms, brand messaging, and the physical and sociocultural environment. Societal norms help generate general beliefs about what is desirable, expressed often via media and advertising as well as through socialization processes (e.g., Feather, 1992; Kahle et al., 1988). Social norms have been shown to act as stronger pulls for ethical values than individual norms (e.g., Freestone & McGoldrick, 2008; Tsarenko et al., 2013). Projection of a positive image of self, particularly to admired others and role models, is strongly associated with ethical consumption practices from buying hybrid electric vehicles to cruelty-free hand soap, fair trade coffee, and packaging-free shampoo bars (e.g., Griskevicius et al., 2010; Lee, 2008; Pickett-Baker & Ozaki, 2008). An individual's perception of being socially attuned is only enhanced and fed by external influences, which can be more impactful than ethical consumer values alone in driving outcomes (e.g., Freestone & McGoldrick, 2008; Tsarenko et al., 2013). In this way, positive social values serve both individual and collective interests—a consumer who genuinely values ethical consumption to protect the planet may also have a self-interest in being "seen to be green" (Griskevicius et al., 2010) while avoiding being "seen to be wasteful." A consumer sharing a photo on social media of their first purchase of a packaging-free shampoo bar, for instance, may garner a significant number of "likes" on their photo. Such social approval thus reinforces the values that led the consumer to make an ethical purchase in the first place. This reinforcement encourages repeat actions and leads to habit formation. In the absence of social approval, an ethical action is therefore less likely to become habitual.

Familiarity, availability, and promotional positioning of retail options can also further influence adoption of ethical outcomes and practices by consumers (Kennedy et al., 2016; Tsarenko et al., 2013). As Kennedy et al. (2016) showed, the initial purchase of a retail eco brand widely available in New Zealand supermarkets created an image of a paragon of health for self, society, and planet that encouraged consumers to make repeat purchases. Once they had purchased the eco brand often enough—displaying the eco hand soap and dish soap near their sinks and giving chemical-free, natural soaps as gifts at baby showers—consumers reported they saw themselves as more ethical decision makers (Kennedy et al., 2016). Messaging and promotional factors can also motivate ethical decisions, as message frames, number and type of claims, and even emphasizing the dire nature and importance of the ethical issue influence choice (Du et al., 2010; Olsen et al., 2014).

Cultural orientation has a large impact on whether consumers buy products with ethical attributes for more than just personal benefit. That choice of societal benefit against personal benefit means ethical decision makers are motivated in part by cultural determinants. Researchers have linked consumers' responses to ethical and cause-related marketing to cultural measures from communal versus exchange orientation in the marketplace (Bolton & Mattila, 2015) to levels of collectivism or interdependence (Cho et al., 2013; J. Kim & Johnson, 2013; Robinson et al., 2012). Cultural orientations have bearing on how ethical decision makers navigate their personal versus social values. For instance, interdependent consumers—who tend to privilege the opinions, views, and needs of social others—have both higher purchase intentions and more positive attitudes to brands that focus on social benefits in their marketing campaigns (Robinson et al., 2012). Cultural orientation also generates different emotional responses. Independent buyers in the United States, for instance, respond more positively to ethical marketing campaigns with a self-focused emotion (e.g., pride), while interdependent buyers in Korea are more greatly influenced by other-focused emotions such as guilt (J. Kim & Johnson, 2013). Taken together, social influence and marketing messaging account for a large share of the external motivations that contribute to the rise of consumers who consider ethical values in their decision making (Edelman, 2018; Nielsen, 2018).

Contexts for Ethical Consumer Psychology

Can ethical consumption be decontextualized? Figure 16.1 lists key contexts for ethical decision making, such as fast fashion, fair labor standards, and fair trade. The literature shows evidence that consumers consistently practice ethical choices only in key consumption settings (e.g., cage-free eggs, fair trade coffee; Belk et al., 2005). How these key consumption contexts are developed via media and social media remain pressing questions for scholars and practitioners alike.

Current worldwide trends indicate a renewed focus on single-use plastics, as a rise in bans of plastic bags at retail sites and bans of plastic straws in hospitality show (Bloomberg, 2020). "Single-use" was named the word of the year in 2018, and "climate strike" was the word of the year in 2019, with "nonbinary" gender definitions close behind (Collins, 2020). How do these concepts become viral, and what has made each of these rich issues such a compelling factor for research into shifts in consumer ethical behavior?

Given the rapid uptake of social media channels to fuel conversation and awareness, build data exchange, and facilitate purchase behavior, consumer psychologists would be encouraged to look to the lens of media and communication theory. This would help marketing scholars better encapsulate the sway of these devices and platforms in building changes in behavior. For instance, Grunig's situational theory on all-issue publics, single-issue publics, and hot-issue publics versus apathetic nonpublics (e.g., Aldoory & Grunig, 2012) are important to consumer psychology because influencing these target audiences via media channels now involves key consumer actions (as illustrated in Figure 16.1). Agenda setting (e.g., Dearing & Rogers, 1996) now occurs as a much more fluid and dynamic attempt to build attention and social action. Agenda setting is now led from not merely the media but via brand influence direct to consumers online and social influencers whom consumers come to trust (e.g., Kapitan & Silvera, 2016). In this chapter, we point to the process of social cognitive learning and the role of social signaling and status in driving uptake of ethical behaviors (Griskevicius et al., 2010; Phipps et al., 2013). Yet it becomes meaningful to consider when and how an ethical topic reaches the tipping point from alternative consumption practice (e.g., Cherrier & Murray, 2007; Schor, 1998) to common parlance, usage, and practice. Communication theory could be key to future studies in better encapsulating the consumer psychology of ethical decision making. The process and method that diffuses a marginalized ideology into a generalized consumer behavior will thus be paramount for consumer psychology.

Consumer Ethical Beliefs, Attitudes, and Behaviors

An ethical consumer choice, as Figure 16.1's framework shows, can generate both positive behaviors, such as purchasing and spreading positive word of mouth about brands deemed ethical, and transformative behaviors, such as boycotts and venting outrage online (e.g., Belk et al., 2005). The most important predictor of future ethical behavior stems from past ethical behavior, rendering the establishment of an initial ethical outcome, habit, or action as an essential part of ethical consumer psychology (e.g., Belk et al., 2005; Carrington et al., 2014; Phipps et al., 2013; White et al., 2019).

Ethically aligned purchase behavior is most likely when associated with intentional, planned actions based on primary ethical values (Carrington et al., 2014). Ethical decision making that occurs as part of rapid, premeditated habit tends to stem from deep embedment of ethical issues into daily life, such as selecting and placing a known brand of organic tofu into a shopping basket without glancing much at the rest of the store shelf (Carrington et al., 2014). For an ethical shopper who prizes organic production and animal rights, this ethical decision making occurs without effort or conflict. The values and purchase decisions were negotiated prior to arrival at the point of purchase or consumption. These habits are most likely to occur when internal factors align with external factors in a context that is most important to a consumer and in a setting that allows a consumer to exercise their ethical values. This is part of the feedback loop that creates a reinforcing cycle of environmental, personal, and behavioral determinants key to ethical outcomes (Phipps et al., 2013).

The intention-behavior gap in ethical consumer decision making occurs when consumers do not act in line with their stated values (e.g., Auger & Devinney, 2007). Decisions that are misaligned with ethical concerns important to a given consumer tend to occur when habits are not yet formed, leaving effortful decision making to the point of purchase, or during spontaneous shopping (Carrington et al., 2014).

For those who deem ethical values as an important enough part of identity to guide decision making and purchase choices, consumption can be a form of voting for ethical brands. As trust in traditional institutions wanes worldwide (Edelman, 2018; Shaw et al., 2006), the market increasingly becomes a site of consumer engagement, with brands held to account. Consumer power stems in part from the perception that any action, no matter how small, taken in support of ethical values has efficacy and impact (Shaw et al., 2006). Those who exhibit the most perceived self-efficacy for their ethical actions likewise have higher commitment to their ethical consumption goals. Interestingly, this can occur whether consumers have stronger ego (self) or altruistic (social) values in their approach to ethical actions. Both horizontal collectivists and vertical individualists have the highest perceptions of efficacy in ethical purchases, as they are most likely to perceive that the ethical decisions they make can have a greater effect on themselves or others (e.g., Cho et al., 2013).

Collective social action that was once viewed as a sign of alternative consumer groups such as anticonsumers, downshifters, and voluntary simplifiers (e.g., Cherrier & Murray, 2007; Schor, 1998) is now part of the lexicon and discussions among shoppers on Instagram and Facebook (e.g., White et al., 2019). Positive word of mouth, especially around social influencers in the digital age who demonstrate their ethical consumer purchases or actions online, is creating new conversations around the efficacy of single actions multiplying into a vote for or against a brand through purchasing decisions (e.g., Aldoory & Grunig, 2012). A consumer purchase of goods with ethical attributes or from companies that have ethical supply chains is seen as just as powerful a statement to brands as boycotts and buyouts. In this view of consumer empowerment, any action based on ethical values can be part of the collective action and seen as taking part in social responsibility (Sen et al., 2001; Shaw et al., 2006). Consumers who boycott brands (e.g., BP and Shell following oil spills, Chick-fil-A following antigay statements and funding of anti-LGBTQIA+ groups) and those who actively evangelize buying such items as fair trade products are sending brands a message via their consumption actions (e.g., Connolly & Prothero, 2003). This sense of collective action and self-efficacy for individual choices illustrates the growing sense of consumer power that fuels and reinforces ethical decision making.

However, while consumers may be increasingly seeking ethical consumption experiences, marketers may be seeking the opposite. External cues and motivators, as shown in Figure 16.1, can become tactics to spur desired consumer outcomes. Information asymmetry for consumers has shifted in the digital era, with more information about brand attributes, ethical origins, and sourcing available to shoppers than ever before. Yet that same informational desert that before left marketers uncertain of how to capture and measure consumer response has delivered big data into the hands of marketers. Brands that understand the motivations and key contexts that spur consumer action can now use consumer data, from geolocations and clicks to shopping history and social and political preferences, to drive profit, revenue growth, and brand equity in a highly competitive marketplace. Decreasing information asymmetry that has driven a rise in ethical consideration for consumers can likewise drive an uptick in questionable, less ethical marketer practice.

PART II: MARKETERS' PSYCHOLOGICAL TACTICS AND THEIR ETHICALITY

Ethical marketing relates to "practices that emphasize transparent, trustworthy, and responsible personal &/or organizational marketing policies and actions that exhibit integrity as well as fairness to consumers and other stakeholders" (Murphy et al., 2005, p. xvii). The American Marketing Association (2020) provides a code of ethics that aims to ensure marketers are aware of and uphold such ethical marketing and is based on the values of honesty, responsibility, fairness, respect, transparency, and citizenship. Such self-regulated codes are a response to the negative image that marketers tend to amass for unethical behavior, which sheds an untrustworthy light on the profession. High profile cases such as Cambridge Analytica show the potent role of consumer data in tempting the profession—marketers harvested social media data from millions of Facebook profiles, without user consent, to create more effective targeted political advertising (K. Collins & Dance, 2018). Unethical marketing leads to a lack of trust, loyalty, satisfaction, and purchase intention in consumers (Leonidou et al., 2013). Yet many unethical practices are par for the course for marketers and require them to develop their own phronēsis (practical wisdom or ethics in practice; Eagle & Kennedy, 2021) to recognize and remedy (Laczniak & Murphy, 2006).

As such, this second section of the chapter helps to develop a marketer's phronēsis by outlining common unethical marketing behavior that takes advantage of consumer psychology, to push the motivations both external and internal that will propel desired consumer outcomes. The chapter does not cover unethical marketing in a business-to-business context—see Murphy et al. (2005) for an overview—or broader level holistic aspects such as supply chain issues. We then move on to discuss emerging areas of marketing that create ethical issues based on the fundamental information asymmetry that yields rich data for marketers to harvest via web 2.0 use and consumer privacy in a connected world. Marketing areas related to consumer psychology that can cause ethical concerns span advertising, personal selling, direct marketing, sales promotions, distribution, pricing, product policy, and social marketing (marketing for behavior change; see Table 16.1).

Ethical Issues in Marketing

Aggressive sales techniques can bully vulnerable consumers, such as the elderly, to purchase due to coercion (Murphy et al., 2005), which can outrage both the person being bullied and others on their behalf. As some elderly people have less processing ability for uncovering misleading or untruthful claims, especially in a high-pressure selling situation, they may be prone to overselling as well (Ramsey et al., 2007). Even without high-pressure selling techniques, aggressive sales techniques toward vulnerable consumers are still questionable. The famous case of Nestlé aggressively marketing their infant formula to third-world consumers with lower levels of marketing literacy had disastrous consequences. Nestlé used salespeople dressed as nurses to hand out free samples of infant formula, and breastfeeding mothers were unaware that their milk would dry up by the time they had finished the samples or that they needed to boil water for the formula, leading to infant malnutrition and deaths (Davidson, 2009; Post & Baer, 1978).

Because direct marketing often takes place without the possibility to view the product in person and have an instant exchange, fraudulent practices such as nonfulfillment of orders and product misrepresentation can prey on consumers' trust in the marketing system and their marketer interaction scripts built up through social learning (Avery & Ferraro, 2000; Smith 1995). Negative option sales, where consumers must opt-out of purchases, further take advantage of the usual scripts that consumers use to interpret market interactions.

Bait-and-switch implies that a consumer tries to purchase a sale item that, on purchase, is not available. Instead, a higher priced item is offered and price comparisons are discouraged (Lindsey-Mullikin & Petty, 2011). This, along with push promotions using newer location-based technologies such as RFID, GPS, and Bluetooth—often without the permission of consumers—causes ethical issues with sales promotions. Such new technology is effective because it breaks through clutter to gain consumer attention. It asks consumers to engage with it (e.g., share, like, retweet) instead of passively receiving the messages, which improves the likelihood that the promotion will be successful

TABLE 16.1

Ethical Issues in Marketing Practice

Marketing area	Ethical marketing issues using consumer psychology	
Personal selling	• Misrepresentation • Coercion • Overselling	• High-pressure selling • Taking advantage of vulnerable consumers
Direct marketing	• Misrepresentation of products • Violations of privacy	• Fraudulent behavior • Negative option sales
Sales promotions	• Bait-and-switch • Misleading sales promotions	• Push promotions
Distribution	• Restricted availability—false shortages	
Pricing	• Misleading pricing • Artificially high price discounted—retailer high-low pricing • Price gouging • Price discrimination	• Downsizing • Predatory pricing • Price skimming with planned obsolescence • Nondisclosure of extra pricing • Nondisclosed dynamic pricing
Product	• Unsafe products • Harmful products • Misrepresentation of product • Planned obsolescence • Slack packaging • Deceptive labeling • Bottom-of-the-pyramid/low-income product development of nonessentials	• Greenwashing • Counterfeit • Manufacture disease in the pharmaceutical industry • Free samples of pharmaceuticals to low-income consumers
Advertising	• Puffery/deceptive/misleading claims • Advertising to vulnerable consumer groups • Manipulative advertising • Use of misappropriated Indigenous culture • Stereotyping/dehumanizing/discrimination • Use of fear appeals or plays on insecurities • Advertising insignificant differences between competition	• Materialism/overconsumption/addiction inducement • Greenwashing • Nondisclosed product placement/endorsement • Stealth marketing • Ambush marketing • Online privacy
Social marketing	• Paternalism • Victim blaming • Stigmatization • Coercion	• Rewards • Nudging/behavioral economics/social engineering • Interference with personal rights

Note. Data from Connors (2009), Davidson (2009), Eagle and Dahl (2015), Gaski (1999), Kennedy and Santos (2019), Laczniak and Murphy (1993), Murphy et al. (2005), Nill and Schibrowsky (2007), Schlegelmilch and Öberseder (2010), Smith (1995), Smith and Quelch (1993), and Tsalikis and Fritzsche (2013).

(Nyilasy & Reid, 2009). Thus, according to the persuasion knowledge model, the novelty of the promotion does not yet elicit a negative response or coping strategy against these types of marketing attempts at persuasion (Friestad & Wright, 1994).

Distribution issues that directly relate to consumer psychology include restricted availability, where false shortages encourage consumer feelings of scarcity and hoarding behavior (Stiff et al., 1975). Many deceptive or misleading pricing approaches lead consumers to discontinue their price comparison search early, as they assume they have found the best price and the cheapest retailer (Lindsey-Mullikin & Petty, 2011). However, unfair practices, such as price gouging, discrimination, and skimming coupled with planned obsolescence, as well as predatory pricing, play on restrictions to consumer choice and those less able to search for alternatives.

Ethical issues relating to products include their safety, for when products are deemed to be safe and then may unexpectedly cause harm (e.g., a plug socket or a crib) or for products or services that are known to cause harm (e.g., tobacco and vape products). Beyond this, product misrepresentations occur in areas such as slack packaging or deceptive labeling. *Slack packaging* is where the package is made to look bigger than the content to mislead the consumer into thinking the whole package is full (e.g., potato chips; Ameer, 2013). *Deceptive labeling* including the words "healthy" or "low fat" (for a product that is, for example, high in sugar) can incur psychological outcomes such as the health halo effect, where the consumer assumes the product is good for them (Chandon, 2013) based on heuristics. This deceptive labeling can carry on to environmental sustainability where products have green-colored branding and feature the word "natural" but are greenwashing or merely adopting the slogans and words without being supported by actual company and brand practice.

While products should be developed for low-income and bottom-of-the-pyramid consumers (e.g., sachets of laundry detergent) with lower levels of marketing literacy, unethical practices include product development of nonessential items (e.g., sachets of makeup) where demand is driven through aspirational advertising (Davidson, 2009). Lastly, the pharmaceutical industry takes advantage of consumer psychology and motivations when they manufacture disease (i.e., make everyday mild things seem to be a problem, e.g., erectile dysfunction, tight muscles, shyness) where direct marketing is legal (Connors, 2009). Free samples of drugs breed trust and brand loyalty from consumers, which may not be warranted (Connors, 2009).

Ethical issues with social marketing stem from the paternalistic nature of the area, assuming that the social marketer knows better than the consumer and ignoring their autonomy and freedom of rights (Brenkert, 2002). Social marketing that asks people to take control of their own behavior change can create victim blaming and stigma around different issues along with guilt (e.g., for obesity; Carter et al., 2011). Providing rewards or coercion to change behaviors can work in the short term; however, long-term change that is not intrinsically motivated is unlikely to stick (Eagle et al., 2015). Lastly, any manipulation of consumers to change their behaviors that they are unaware of (e.g., behavioral economics, social engineering, nudging) is seen as unethical (Buchanan et al., 1994; Kennedy, 2016).

The more that advertising embellishes the performance of a product or service, the more it reduces consumers' ability to make rational judgments. Such puffery is deceptive in that it can mislead consumers to predict higher levels of product performance or quality than is realistic (Murphy et al., 2005). This is especially unethical when aimed at vulnerable consumer groups who have less marketing knowledge or have processing difficulties. Bottom-of-the-pyramid consumers and children are among those who may be more likely to believe that puffery is true because they are less advertising literate and as such have not developed mental defenses against such persuasive communications (Moses & Baldwin, 2005). Greenwashing has a similar effect, when a consumer believes that a product is more environmentally friendly than it really is (Davis, 1992).

Incorporating Indigenous culture into marketing communications not only causes offense and potential harm to the Indigenous group (Kennedy & Laczniak, 2014) but can also lead consumers into associations with the offending brand that are erroneous. Such associations can lead consumers to assume that a brand is owned by the Indigenous group and to support it over competitors. On top of this, marketing communications that present Indigenous groups, cultures, genders, or any group of people using stereotypes, with discriminatory practices, or in a dehumanizing way (e.g., with the female body) further confirm and support such negative viewpoints in everyday life. Especially in social marketing, using fear appeals to drive behavior change is seen as unethical as it overrides a consumer's ability to make a rational decision, instead using Type 1 heuristic processing in a somewhat coercive way (Carter et al., 2011). The same argument is apparent with advertising insignificant differences in products based on emotional appeals and branding (Murphy et al., 2005). It has long been held that advertising drives materialism, overconsumption, and, in as much as it advertises addictive products, addiction as well (Pollay, 1986). In each of these cases, disposition theory would suggest that consumers who enjoy the marketing communication, regardless of the ethicality of its content, will have more positive affect for the brand (Raney, 2004), and even the use of unethical aspects for shock appeal is successful, as it gains attention in a cluttered marketing environment, according to the hierarchy of effects model (Eagle & Dahl, 2015). However, as marketing and advertising literacy increases and consumers have more easy access to information about brands, the likelihood of this is questioned for all but vulnerable consumers (Davidson, 2009).

Ambush marketing is where a company places advertising around an event, as if they were the main sponsor of the event (O'Sullivan & Murphy, 1998). Following classical conditioning, the brand tries to associate themselves with an event that they did not officially sponsor. For instance, they may advertise on billboards outside the stadium where a sports event is being held or heavily advertise during the televised event. Kodak did this during one Olympics where Fuji was the official sponsor of the Olympics that year, but Kodak was the official film of the U.S. team (Payne, 1991). The consumer psychology related to such an event means that the offending organization gains more attention and goodwill than they would otherwise (McKelvey, 1994).

Stealth marketing is known also as buzz, covert, shill, undercover, below the radar, or masked marketing (Balter & Butman, 2006; Petty & Andrews, 2008; Swanepoel et al., 2009). It refers to the "use of surreptitious marketing practices that fail to disclose or reveal the true relationship with the company that produces or sponsors the marketing message" (Martin & Smith, 2008, p. 45). In an online context it uses e-word of mouth to spread the message through not only "influencers" but also regular people (Ahuja et al., 2007). Whether online or offline, it uses the covert operative's existing social network to increase brand awareness exponentially, which, according to contagion theory, is spread infectiously, rather than through rational choice (Marsden, 1998; Swanepoel et al., 2009). It preys on psychological aspects of consumer behavior including opinion leadership and word of mouth. Such marketing is unethical because consumers haven't given consent to interact with the marketer, it exploits existing social relationships, it is an intrusion into their privacy, and it takes advantage of goodwill toward others (Martin & Smith, 2008). These mean that the consumer's usual protective cognitive technique of skepticism toward marketing is circumvented (Brown & Krishna, 2004). For example, mobile phone maker Sony Ericsson hired fake tourists and had them ask passers-by to take photos of them with their new phone's camera, while the Tremor network of teens and Vocalpoint network of moms for Proctor and Gamble receive free samples to give out and advocate for, should they choose to (Walker, 2004). Paid tweets and retweets of marketing messages also work through repetitive exposure to brand material increasing intention to purchase (Gunn, 2001; Van Buskirk, 2010). Such practices of nondisclosure of sponsored content by vloggers and bloggers have led to specific guidelines (such as inclusion of "#ad" on a post) by the Federal Trade Commission (FTC) in the United States, the Advertising Standards Authority in the United Kingdom, and others (Paul, 2009). However, enforcement is lax and untested, and rules and practice continue to outpace regulation, which means current standards do not halt the rampant practice of nondisclosure in the digital world.

Emerging Ethical Areas

New media issues in ethical marketing relate to company/consumer interaction via web 2.0 platforms such as social media, data privacy, and more subtle use of marketing online—especially with children (Eagle & Dahl, 2015). The interactive nature of web 2.0 platforms delve deeper into the consumer psyche, especially for younger consumers. Anthropomorphic marketing, especially online, decreases persuasion avoidance and can bring about decreased risk perception (S. Kim & McGill, 2011), stronger emotional responses (Delbaere et al., 2011), increased brand liking, and thus increased purchase intention (Eagle & Dahl, 2015). For instance, children's lower levels of marketing literacy and defenses against marketing persuasion (Moses & Baldwin, 2005), teamed with a favorite character using a product online, can influence them to see that product as very desirable (Auty & Lewis, 2004). A character using a product within an immersive online game such as Fortnite can further increase persuasion (Mallinckrodt & Mizerski, 2007), as children are unable to recognize this as marketing (Kennedy et al., 2019). Children are powerless against online marketing controlled contexts, which leads marketers to become their opinion leaders and guides to marketing literacy and allows them to shape and socialize a child's identity and consumption goals (Kennedy et al., 2019).

The FTC is charged with protecting consumers' personal information (FTC, 2010; 15 U.S.C. § 45); however, identifying exactly what is meant by "personal information" is somewhat problematic. Information collected on consumers in an online context includes their browsing history, purchase history, social media use, interactions with websites and others online, and even their location. However, only information that is personally identifiable (PII) is covered by current policy—and many marketers such as banks rely on aggregate information to segment and target audiences for new financial products or new offerings uniquely tailored to their needs. PII is information that specifically identifies the person, such as their name, address, email, and phone number, and may or may not include their personal directory data—from their cell phones, for example—such as their photos, videos, contacts, calendar, calls, and texts (Digital Advertising Alliance, 2013). If data is "de-identified" then it is also exempt from privacy policies (FTC, 2012). It is common and today now a standard practice for companies to purchase either PII or non-PII data to combine with their own data collection for maximum marketing efficiency, especially for targeted advertising (Network Advertising Initiative, 2015). The blurring between what constitutes PII and non-PII data continues to grow (FTC, 2010), along with conflict over the inclusion of non-PII data at all in policy discussions. Specifically, the industry feels that consumers are unconcerned over the use of their non-PII data and thus marketers should be free to use and collect such data as they wish (FTC, 2012).

In the digital era, consumers have gained an unprecedented ease of access to myriad tools and apps, including information about brands via searches that are not deeply complex. Yet the exchange of consumer data for access to such digital services means that consumers are again at a deep disadvantage compared with marketers (see Figure 16.2). Unfortunately, marketing activities are not covered by most existing ethics principles

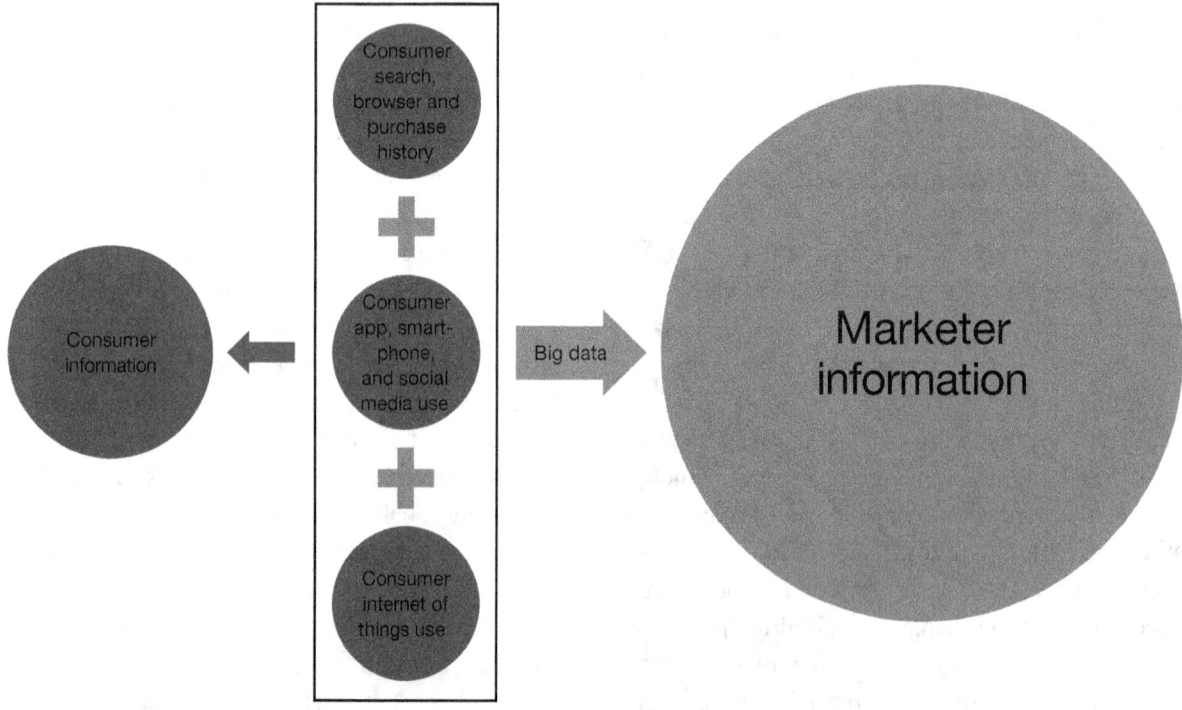

FIGURE 16.2. Information asymmetry in a connected marketplace.

and "companies may infer consent" (White House Report, 2012, p. 111) because a consumer can identify the marketer and give them feedback and thus end their relationship with them if unsatisfied.

Such assumptions are erroneous when considering the vital role that companies such as Facebook, TikTok, or Google play in many people's lives and the negative implications for consumers if they did withdraw from their services. It does not take into account that such a "take it or leave it" approach is biased toward the marketer because the consumer has no real options of alternative services (FTC, 2012) and may be forced to use those services for work and travel purposes (e.g., with Facebook work groups, Gmail, or map navigation services via Google maps).

Apart from the lack of control over marketer use of personal data as a first party to it, current policy also neglects control over a third party's use of personal data. Such third parties include data brokers who collect information from a multitude of places, both online and offline, to create commercial marketing products. Products include email addresses for client solicitation; reports on consumer interests for targeting; and analytics on a person's likely response to advertising, predicted purchase intent, or even social influence (FTC, 2014a). Even more alarmingly, data brokers may locate a consumer online, through websites consumers log in to, and place a cookie or web bug on that site that allows marketers to then track and advertise to that consumer (FTC, 2014a). By using cookies, web bugs, history sniffing, and device fingerprinting, data brokers can track and record IP addresses, identities, access times, access browsers, online and social media behavior, search engine terms, purchases, and advertising interactions and link consumer data to PII such as their names and email addresses (FTC, 2000, 2016).

Such tracking can also be conducted across consumer devices (FTC, 2017), mobile shopping applications (FTC, 2014b), mobile applications in general (Digital Advertising Alliance, 2013), and objects that connect to the internet (FTC, 2015). Cross-device tracking links a consumer's behavior across their personal devices, such as their computer, mobile phone, and laptop or tablet. In concert with offline purchases and interactions with the company, a consumer profile can be created (Rich, 2015) to target advertising from approved companies or third parties that consumers may not be aware of (Turow & Moy, 2015). Additionally, such "smart" consumer products as watches, TVs, home heating and lights, personal digital assistants via smart speakers and cars, and so forth present additional avenues for collection of consumer data surrounding home habits, physical locations, and conditions (FTC, 2015). Mobile applications have access to both personally identifiable data as well as personal directory data such as the photos, videos, contacts, calls, texts, and locations of a mobile phone. While consent would be sought for using location data and PII, if data were used for market research or product development, consent need not be sought (Digital Advertising Alliance, 2013).

Problems with such big data collection include the potential for exposure of sensitive information and the creation or perpetuation of disparities with regard to discriminatory targeting practices. For instance, offers may not be available to lower socioeconomic groups who would benefit from them, or vulnerable groups may be unfairly targeted (FTC, 2016). Among others, Twitter (*In the Matter of Twitter, Inc.*, 2011), Facebook (*In the Matter of Facebook, Inc.*, 2012), and Google (*In the Matter of Google, Inc.*, 2011) have all at times been charged by the FTC for deceptive privacy practices or unsatisfactory protection of PII.

The culmination of the collection of consumer data is the creation of a consumer profile to be sold to specific companies for marketing purposes. This can be combined with a consumer's behavior on the company's own website or social media to re-identify the data and uncover PII for marketing purposes (FTC, 2000). Internet service providers (ISPs) and large organizations such as Facebook and Google already undertake these activities legally (Feldman, 2017). The Cambridge Analytica case exemplifies the unethical nature of such behavior. By collecting data from 50 million Facebook accounts, the company gained personality information through a personality quiz on Facebook. In order to use the app, consumers had to allow it access to their Facebook profile information. Using this information and a confirmatory shortened quiz completed about the user by their friends, the company was able to create a behavioral model to predict political attitudes and sold these models to political candidates and commercial clients to sway elections (K. Collins & Dance, 2018). Facebook has subsequently changed its policies to avoid such unethical practice, but the use of online data for marketing without consent is still prolific.

Regulation and ethical policy from government- and firm-level can help drive marketing ethical reactions. Yet, what proactive rules and possible ethical criteria should govern future use and as yet unknown circumstances for the stakeholder contract that consumers enter when they step into the commercial marketplace? Simple rules can still apply to help mediate when new usages and interactions arise in the marketplace between stakeholders. Namely, marketers can turn to one of three basic frames for ethics in business. They can adopt the golden rule of treating others as they would wish to be treated; follow enlightened self-interest so that they avoid retribution for their missteps; or follow the tenets of utilitarianism, choosing actions that generate the most benefit for the most people (Kahle et al., 2000). However, these tenets can be applied to justify vastly different practices and outcomes and, in that sense, show problems in their usage. Yet, given the international nature of corporations in today's world, it is difficult for many to come to an agreement on one "right" set of principles, that is, a set of hypernorms.

One suggestion for an internationally applicable set of hypernorms was proposed by Laczniak and Kennedy (2011). To compile this global code of ethical norms, they analyzed the most subscribed sets of global codes of conduct for multinational corporations. These included the Clarkson Principles, Caux Round Table, Coalition for Environmentally Responsible Economies, Organisation for Economic Co-operation and Development Guidelines, U.N. Global Compact, Global Sullivan Principles, and the American Marketing Association code of ethics. They found a set of hypernorms that are internationally applicable and appropriate for the whole supply chain. These hypernorms are based on principles that include (a) using the stakeholder model through applying human, labor, and consumer rights principles; (b) undertaking authentic sustainability decision making that includes environmental stewardship along with respecting the host country and contributing to its development; (c) rejection of bribery and corruption through disclosure, transparency, and authentic compliance with the spirit of the host country's laws; and last, (d) ethical advocacy of the guidelines to others. The principles provide three hypernorms: stakeholder theory, comprehensive sustainability, and authentic compliance, which may provide a philosophical basis to guide both consumer and marketer decision making and ethical policy.

CONCLUSION

Ethical values can be personal, social, or both. Consumers are not always spurred by personal ethical values alone, such as caring for the planet or fair labor standards in fashion. The identity project of ethical consumers today is often bound up by the social signal of ethical consumption projects that help communicate social status (e.g., Griskevicius et al., 2010). In short, it is cool to care. Consumer connections in the social media world fuel a sense of collective social action (e.g., Connolly & Prothero, 2003; Shaw et al., 2006) as well as lend the aura of status to ethical consumer habits. Yet are social norms around ethical consumption divergent across generations and cultures? Belk et al. (2005) argued that across Europe, North America, and Australasia, people merely pay lip service to ethical ideas but reject their central importance in their own lived experiences as consumers. And are ethical consumers, which the literature notes tend to act ethically in only their primary issues of ethical concern (Carrington et al., 2014), really only single-issue or hot-issue publics (Aldoory & Grunig, 2012) that respond to a single context of ethical decision making alone? If so, how can consumer psychology elevate a single-issue ethical consumer and help embed issues of secondary ethical concern into their daily habits and shopping baskets? Do social norms and external motivators succeed in creating internal drivers for ethical decision making, or once the hot issue fades and awareness wanes, do actions in the topic no longer generate social status and fail to curate converted ethical consumers?

Though this chapter notes a rise in the general status and symbolism of ethical consumption, the literature has not yet shown how to maintain this mainstream status or how broad the contexts extend for ethical decision making beyond a single issue. In the current mainstream iteration of ethical values, consumers who adopt privileging benefits-for-others are rewarded with, at least at present, some status and benefit-for-self. This serves as a prime motivator and determinant for personal ethical actions and means that consumer psychology as a field must be emboldened by this mainstreaming of ethical behaviors to chart deeper answers to spur continued consumer ethical choices.

Yet that same information shift that has driven the psychology of ethical consumption by arming consumers with more information has also rendered them more vulnerable to unethical marketing practices (see Figure 16.2). It's a catch-22, for the ease of information availability and accessibility that has created a strong and vocal sense of collective action among consumers who, armed with information and the social signal of being seen to respond to a hot-topic issue (Aldoory & Grunig, 2012), demand more social, political, and ethical attribute positioning from brands (Edelman, 2018). Yet the other side of the catch-22 shows that at the same time, the very data, information, and social connectivity in the digital area that drives the mainstreaming of ethical consumption practices might also be its downfall. Marketers amass and collect vast swaths of data, from browsing history to clicks and past purchase behavior, that push and pull at consumer psychology as they divide and microtarget consumers for products, services, and offerings that meet (or are perceived to meet) very specific and compelling consumer needs and desires.

Overall, however, ethical marketing is essential for an efficiently functioning marketing system. This requires consumers to trust that their interactions with marketers are not deceptive, or untruthful, but open and transparent (Murphy et al., 2005). Consumers must believe that products and services are safe; that they are being treated equitably, with fairness and justice (Murphy et al., 2005); and that,

in general, they have efficacy in deciding whether or not to engage with a marketer at all. This requires marketers to use consumer psychology—from the internal motivation, ability, and opportunity of shoppers to the external pushes, as shown in Figure 16.1—ethically in an evolving digital world. Two factors have made ethical shopping more mainstream: decreasing information asymmetry for consumers and increasing adoption of moral consumption as an identity project. Armed with more information about brands and with more connections to others via digital platforms, consumers today are actively discussing, sharing, and debating their roles as buyers or boycotters of brands that support people, the planet, and a host of related ethical issues. In this way, social influence and information availability are driving consumers to some key outcomes through the framework of ethical consumer psychology (e.g., Phipps et al., 2013; White et al., 2019).

REFERENCES

Adomaviciute, K. (2013). Relationship between utilitarian and hedonic consumer behavior and socially responsible consumption. *Economics and Management*, 18(4), 754–760. https://doi.org/10.5755/j01.em.18.4.5580

Ahuja, R. D., Michels, T. A., Walker, M. M., & Weissbuch, M. (2007). Teen perceptions of disclosure in buzz marketing. *Journal of Consumer Marketing*, 24(3), 151–159. https://doi.org/10.1108/07363760710746157

Aldoory, L., & Grunig, J. E. (2012). The rise and fall of hot-issue publics: Relationships that develop from media coverage of events and crises. *International Journal of Strategic Communication*, 6(1), 93–108. https://doi.org/10.1080/1553118X.2011.634866

Ameer, I. (2013). Ethical marketing decisions: Review, contribution and impact on recent research. *International Journal of Research Studies in Management*, 2(1), 1–10. https://doi.org/10.5861/ijrsm.2012.207

American Marketing Association. (2020). *Codes of conduct: AMA statement of ethics.* https://www.ama.org/codes-of-conduct/

Auger, P., Burke, P., Devinney, T., & Louviere, J. J. (2003). What will consumers pay for social product features? *Journal of Business Ethics*, 42(3), 281–304. https://doi.org/10.1023/A:1022212816261

Auger, P., & Devinney, T. (2007). Do what consumers say matter? The misalignment of preferences with unconstrained ethical intentions. *Journal of Business Ethics, 76*(4), 361–383. https://doi.org/10.1007/s10551-006-9287-y

Auty, S., & Lewis, C. (2004). Exploring children's choice: The reminder effect of product placement. *Psychology and Marketing, 21*(9), 697–713. https://doi.org/10.1002/mar.20025

Avery, R. J., & Ferraro, R. (2000). Verisimilitude or advertising? Brand appearances on prime-time television. *Journal of Consumer Affairs, 34*(2), 217–244. https://doi.org/10.1111/j.1745-6606.2000.tb00092.x

Balter, D., & Butman, J. (2006). Clutter cutter. *Marketing Management, 15*(4), 49–50.

Belk, R., Devinney, T., & Eckhardt, G. (2005). Consumer ethics across cultures. *Consumption Markets & Culture, 8*(3), 275–289. https://doi.org/10.1080/10253860500160411

Bloomberg. (2020). 'Catching up with the rest of the world:' China sets ban on single-use plastic. *Fortune*. https://fortune.com/2020/01/20/china-single-use-plastic-ban/

Bolton, L. E., & Mattila, A. S. (2015). How does corporate social responsibility affect consumer response to service failure in buyer-seller relationships? *Journal of Retailing, 91*(1), 140–153. https://doi.org/10.1016/j.jretai.2014.10.001

Brenkert, G. G. (2002). Ethical challenges of social marketing. *Journal of Public Policy & Marketing, 21*(1), 14–25. https://doi.org/10.1509/jppm.21.1.14.17601

Brooker, G. (1976). The self-actualizing socially-conscious consumer. *Journal of Consumer Research, 3*(2), 107–113. https://doi.org/10.1086/208658

Brown, C. L., & Krishna, A. (2004). The skeptical shopper: A metacognitive account for the effects of default options on choice. *Journal of Consumer Research, 31*(3), 529–539. https://doi.org/10.1086/425087

Buchanan, D. R., Reddy, S., & Hossain, Z. (1994). Social marketing: A critical appraisal. *Health Promotion International, 9*(1), 49–57. https://doi.org/10.1093/heapro/9.1.49

Carrigan, M., Szmigin, I., & Wright, J. (2004). Shopping for a better world? An interpretive study of the potential for ethical consumption within the older market. *Journal of Consumer Marketing, 21*(6), 401–417. https://doi.org/10.1108/07363760410558672

Carrington, M. J., Neville, B. A., & Whitwell, G. J. (2014). Lost in translation: Exploring the ethical consumer intention-behavior gap. *Journal of Business Research, 67*(1), 2759–2767. https://doi.org/10.1016/j.jbusres.2012.09.022

Carter, S. M., Rychetnik, L., Lloyd, B., Kerridge, I. H., Baur, L., Bauman, A., Hooker, C., & Zask, A. (2011). Evidence, ethics, and values: A framework for health promotion. *American Journal of Public Health, 101*(3), 465–472. https://doi.org/10.2105/AJPH.2010.195545

Chandon, P. (2013). How package design and packaged-based marketing claims lead to overeating. *Applied Economic Perspectives and Policy, 35*(1), 7–31. https://doi.org/10.1093/aepp/pps028

Chernev, A., & Blair, S. (2015). Doing well by doing good: The benevolent halo of corporate social responsibility. *Journal of Consumer Research, 41*(6), 1412–1425. https://doi.org/10.1086/680089

Cherrier, H., & Murray, J. B. (2007). Reflexive dispossession and the self: Constructing a processual theory of identity. *Consumption Markets & Culture, 10*(1), 1–29. https://doi.org/10.1080/10253860601116452

Cho, Y., Thyroff, A., Raper, M. I., Park, S., & Lee, H. J. (2013). To be or not to be green: Exploring individualism and collectivism as antecedents of environmental behavior. *Journal of Business Research, 66*(8), 1052–1059. https://doi.org/10.1016/j.jbusres.2012.08.020

Collins. (2020). *The Collins word of the year 2019 is....* https://www.collinsdictionary.com/woty

Collins, K., & Dance, G. J. X. (2018, March 20). How researchers learned to use Facebook "likes" to sway your thinking. *New York Times*. https://nyti.ms/2u5YSDs

Connolly, J., & Prothero, A. (2003). Sustainable consumption: Consumption, communities and consumption discourse. *Consumption Markets & Culture, 6*(4), 275–291. https://doi.org/10.1080/1025386032000168311

Connors, A. L. (2009). Big bad pharma: An ethical analysis of physician-directed and consumer-directed marketing tactics. *Albany Law Review, 73*(1), 243–282.

Davidson, K. (2009). Ethical concerns at the bottom of the pyramid: Where CSR meets BOP. *Journal of International Business Ethics, 2*(1), 22–32.

Davis, J. J. (1992). Ethics and environmental marketing. *Journal of Business Ethics, 11*(2), 81–87. https://doi.org/10.1007/BF00872314

Dearing, J., & Rogers, E. (1996). *Communication concepts 6: Agenda-setting*. SAGE.

Delbaere, M., McQuarrie, E. F., & Phillips, B. J. (2011). Personification in advertising. *Journal of Advertising, 40*(1), 121–130. https://doi.org/10.2753/JOA0091-3367400108

Digital Advertising Alliance. (2013, July). *Application of self-regulatory principles to the mobile environment*. https://www.mmaglobal.com/files/whitepapers/DAA_Mobile_Guidance.pdf

Du, S., Bhattacharya, C. B., & Sen, S. (2010). Maximizing business returns to corporate social responsibility (CSR): The role of CSR communication. *International*

Journal of Management Reviews, 12(1), 8–19. https://doi.org/10.1111/j.1468-2370.2009.00276.x

Eagle, L., & Dahl, S. (2015). *Marketing ethics & society*. Sage. https://doi.org/10.4135/9781473920415

Eagle, L., Dahl, S., & Low, D. R. (2015). Ethics in social marketing. In L. Eagle & S. Dahl (Eds.), *Marketing ethics and society* (pp. 235–264). Sage. https://doi.org/10.4135/9781473920415.n11

Eagle, L., & Kennedy, A.M. (2021). Ethics in practice in social marketing. In C. Fourali & J. French (Eds.) *The Palgrave Encyclopedia of Social Marketing*. Palgrave Macmillan. https://doi.org/10.1007/978-3-030-14449-4

Edelman. (2018). *Two thirds of consumers worldwide now buy based on beliefs*. https://www.edelman.com/news-awards/two-thirds-consumers-worldwide-now-buy-beliefs

Ehrich, K. R., & Irwin, J. R. (2005). Willful ignorance in the request for product attribute information. *Journal of Marketing Research*, 42(3), 266–277. https://doi.org/10.1509/jmkr.2005.42.3.266

Etzioni, A. (2004). The post affluent society. *Review of Social Economy*, 62(3), 407–420. https://doi.org/10.1080/0034676042000253990

Feather, N. T. (1992). Values, valences, expectations, and actions. *Journal of Social Issues*, 48(2), 109–124. https://doi.org/10.1111/j.1540-4560.1992.tb00887.x

Federal Trade Commission. (2000, June). *Online profiling: A report to Congress*. https://www.ftc.gov/reports/online-profiling-federal-trade-commission-report-congress

Federal Trade Commission. (2010, December). *Protecting consumer privacy in an era of rapid change: A proposed framework for businesses and policymakers*. https://www.ftc.gov/news-events/media-resources/protecting-consumer-privacy-security/ftc-policy-work

Federal Trade Commission. (2012, May). *Protecting consumer privacy in an era of rapid change: Recommendations for business and policy makers*. https://www.ftc.gov/news-events/media-resources/protecting-consumer-privacy-security/ftc-policy-work

Federal Trade Commission. (2014a, May). *Data brokers: A call for transparency and accountability*. https://www.ftc.gov/system/files/documents/reports/data-brokers-call-transparency-accountability-report-federal-trade-commission-may-2014/140527databrokerreport.pdf

Federal Trade Commission. (2014b, August). *What's the deal? An FTC study on mobile shopping apps*. https://www.ftc.gov/system/files/documents/reports/whats-deal-federal-trade-commission-study-mobile-shopping-apps-august-2014/140801mobileshoppingapps.pdf

Federal Trade Commission. (2015, January). *Internet of things: Privacy and security in a connected world*. https://www.ftc.gov/system/files/documents/reports/federal-trade-commission-staff-report-november-2013-workshop-entitled-internet-things-privacy/150127iotrpt.pdf

Federal Trade Commission. (2016, January). *Big data: A tool for inclusion or exclusion, understanding the issues*. https://www.ftc.gov/system/files/documents/reports/big-data-tool-inclusion-or-exclusion-understanding-issues/160106big-data-rpt.pdf

Federal Trade Commission. (2017, January). *Cross-device tracking*. https://www.ftc.gov/system/files/documents/reports/cross-device-tracking-federal-trade-commission-staff-report-january-2017/ftc_cross-device_tracking_report_1-23-17.pdf

Feldman, B. (2017, March 28). "Sorry, ISPs are trying to do what?" What to know about Congress's new internet-privacy rollback. *New York Magazine*. https://nymag.com/intelligencer/2017/03/why-congress-is-dismantling-the-fccs-internet-privacy-rules.html

Freestone, O. M., & McGoldrick, P. J. (2008). Motivation of the ethical consumer. *Journal of Business Ethics*, 79(4), 445–467. https://doi.org/10.1007/s10551-007-9409-1

Friestad, M., & Wright, P. (1994). The persuasion knowledge model: How people cope with persuasion attempts. *Journal of Consumer Research*, 21(1), 1–31. https://doi.org/10.1086/209380

Gaski, J. F. (1999). Does marketing ethics really have anything to say?—A critical inventory of the literature. *Journal of Business Ethics*, 18(3), 315–334. https://doi.org/10.1023/A:1017190829683

Griskevicius, V., Tybur, J. M., & Van den Bergh, B. (2010). Going green to be seen: Status, reputation, and conspicuous conservation. *Journal of Personality and Social Psychology*, 98(3), 392–404. https://doi.org/10.1037/a0017346

Gunn, E. (2001). Product placement prize. *Advertising age*, 72, 10.

In the Matter of Facebook, Inc., Dkt. No. C-4365, 2012 (F.T.C. Aug. 10, 2012). https://www.ftc.gov/sites/default/files/documents/cases/2012/08/120810facebookcmpt.pdf

In the Matter of Google, Inc., Dkt. No. C-4336, 2011 (F.T.C. Oct. 24, 2011). https://www.ftc.gov/sites/default/files/documents/cases/2011/10/111024googlebuzzcmpt.pdf

In the Matter of Twitter, Inc., Dkt. No. C-4316, 2011 (F.T.C. Mar. 11, 2011). https://www.ftc.gov/sites/default/files/documents/cases/2011/03/110311twittercmpt.pdf

Kahle, L. R., Boush, D. M., & Phelps, M. (2000). Good morning Vietnam: An ethical analysis of Nike activities in Southeast Asia. *Sport Marketing Quarterly, 9*(1), 43–52.

Kahle, L. R., Poulos, B., & Sukhdial, A. (1988). Changes in social values in the United States during the past decade. *Journal of Advertising Research, 38*(4), 35–41.

Kapitan, S., & Silvera, D. H. (2016). From digital media influencers to celebrity endorsers: Attributions drive endorser effectiveness. *Marketing Letters, 27*(3), 553–567. https://doi.org/10.1007/s11002-015-9363-0

Kennedy, A. M. (2016). Macro-social marketing. *Journal of Macromarketing, 36*(3), 354–365. https://doi.org/10.1177/0276146715617509

Kennedy, A. M., Jones, K., & Williams, J. (2019). Children as vulnerable consumers in online environments. *Journal of Consumer Affairs, 53*(4), 1478–1506. https://doi.org/10.1111/joca.12253

Kennedy, A. M., Kapitan, S., & Soo, S. (2016). Eco-warriors: Shifting sustainable retail strategy via authentic retail brand image. *Australasian Marketing Journal, 24*(2), 125–134. https://doi.org/10.1016/j.ausmj.2016.03.001

Kennedy, A. M., & Laczniak, G. R. (2014). Indigenous intellectual property rights: Ethical insights for marketers. *Australasian Marketing Journal, 22*(4), 307–313. https://doi.org/10.1016/j.ausmj.2014.09.004

Kennedy, A. M., & Santos, N. (2019). Social fairness and social marketing. *Journal of Social Marketing, 9*(4), 522–539. https://doi.org/10.1108/JSOCM-10-2018-0120

Kim, J., & Johnson, K. K. P. (2013). The impact of moral emotions on cause-related marketing campaigns: A cross-cultural examination. *Journal of Business Ethics, 112*(1), 79–90. https://doi.org/10.1007/s10551-012-1233-6

Kim, S., & McGill, A. L. (2011). Gaming with Mr. Slot or gaming the slot machine? Power, anthropomorphism, and risk perception. *Journal of Consumer Research, 38*(1), 94–107. https://doi.org/10.1086/658148

Laczniak, G., & Kennedy, A.-M. (2011). Hyper norms: Searching for a global code of conduct. *Journal of Macromarketing, 31*(3), 245–256. https://doi.org/10.1177/0276146711405530

Laczniak, G., & Murphy, P. (1993). *Ethical marketing decisions: The higher road.* Allen and Bacon.

Laczniak, G. R., & Murphy, P. E. (2006). Normative perspectives for ethical and socially responsible marketing. *Journal of Macromarketing, 26*(2), 154–177. https://doi.org/10.1177/0276146706290924

Lee, K. (2008). Opportunities for green marketing: Young consumers. *Marketing Intelligence & Planning, 26*(6), 573–586. https://doi.org/10.1108/02634500810902839

Leonidou, L. C., Kvasova, O., Leonidou, C. N., & Chari, S. (2013). Business unethicality as an impediment to consumer trust: The moderating role of demographic and cultural characteristics. *Journal of Business Ethics, 112*(3), 397–415. https://doi.org/10.1007/s10551-012-1267-9

Lindsey-Mullikin, J., & Petty, R. D. (2011). Marketing tactics discouraging price search: Deception and competition. *Journal of Business Research, 64*(1), 67–73. https://doi.org/10.1016/j.jbusres.2009.10.003

Mallinckrodt, V., & Mizerski, D. (2007). The effects of playing an advergame on young children's perceptions, preferences, and requests. *Journal of Advertising, 36*(2), 87–100. https://doi.org/10.2753/JOA0091-3367360206

Marsden, P. S. (1998). Memetics: A new paradigm for understanding customer behavior and influence. *Marketing Intelligence & Planning, 16*(6), 363–368. https://doi.org/10.1108/EUM0000000004541

Martin, K. D., & Smith, N. C. (2008). Commercializing social interaction: The ethics of stealth marketing. *Journal of Public Policy & Marketing, 27*(1), 45–56. https://doi.org/10.1509/jppm.27.1.45

McKelvey, S. (1994, April 18). Sans legal restraint, no stopping brash, creative ambush marketers. *Brandweek, 35*(16), 20.

Moses, L. J., & Baldwin, D. A. (2005). What can the study of cognitive development reveal about children's ability to appreciate and cope with advertising? *Journal of Public Policy & Marketing, 24*(2), 186–201. https://doi.org/10.1509/jppm.2005.24.2.186

Murphy, P. E., Laczniak, G. R., Bowie, N. E., & Klein, T. A. (2005). *Ethical marketing.* Pearson Prentice Hall.

Network Advertising Initiative. (2015). *NAI mobile application code.* https://www.networkadvertising.org/mobile/NAI_MobileCode15_NLT.pdf

Newholm, T., & Shaw, D. (2007). Editorial: Studying the ethical consumer: A review of research. *Journal of Consumer Behaviour, 6*(5), 253–270. https://doi.org/10.1002/cb.225

Nielsen. (2018). *Sustainable shoppers.* https://www.nielsen.com/wp-content/uploads/sites/3/2019/04/global-sustainable-shoppers-report-2018.pdf

Nill, A., & Schibrowsky, J. A. (2007). Research on marketing ethics: A systematic review of the literature. *Journal of Macromarketing, 27*(3), 256–273. https://doi.org/10.1177/0276146707304733

Nyilasy, G., & Reid, L. N. (2009). Agency practitioner theories of how advertising works. *Journal of Advertising, 38*(3), 81–96. https://doi.org/10.2753/JOA0091-3367380306

Olsen, M. C., Slotegraaf, R. J., & Chandukala, S. R. (2014). Green claims and message frames: How green new products change brand attitude. *Journal of Marketing, 78*(5), 119–137. https://doi.org/10.1509/jm.13.0387

O'Sullivan, P., & Murphy, P. (1998). Ambush marketing: The ethical issues. *Psychology and Marketing, 15*(4), 349–366. https://doi.org/10.1002/(SICI)1520-6793(199807)15:4<349::AID-MAR5>3.0.CO;2-8

Paul, I. (2009, October 6). *New FTC blogging regulations: Forcing transparency on a culture of full disclosure*. Huffington Post Blog. http://www.huffingtonpost.com/iam-paul/new-ftc-blogging-regulati_b_311851.html

Payne, M. R. (1991, October). *Ambush marketing: Immoral or imaginative practice* [Paper presentation]. Sponsorship Europe '91 Conference, Barcelona, Spain.

Pearce, R. (1999). Social responsibility in the marketplace: Asymmetric information in food labelling. *Business Ethics: A European Review, 8*(1), 26–36. https://doi.org/10.1111/1467-8608.00122

Petty, R. D., & Andrews, J. C. (2008). Covert marketing unmasked: A legal and regulatory guide for practices that mask marketing messages. *Journal of Public Policy & Marketing, 27*(1), 7–18. https://doi.org/10.1509/jppm.27.1.7

Phipps, M., Ozanne, L. K., Luchs, M. G., Subrahmanyan, S., Kapitan, S., Catlin, J. R., Gau, R., Naylor, R. W., Rose, R. L., Simpson, B., & Weaver, T. (2013). Understanding the inherent complexity of sustainable consumption: A social cognitive theory approach. *Journal of Business Research, 66*(8), 1227–1234. https://doi.org/10.1016/j.jbusres.2012.08.016

Pickett-Baker, J., & Ozaki, R. (2008). Pro-environmental products: Marketing influence on consumer purchase decision. *Journal of Consumer Marketing, 25*(5), 281–293. https://doi.org/10.1108/07363760810890516

Pollay, R. W. (1986). The distorted mirror: Reflections on the unintended consequences of advertising. *Journal of Marketing, 50*(2), 18–36. https://doi.org/10.1177/002224298605000202

Post, J. E., & Baer, E. (1978). De-marketing infant formula-consumer products in the developing world. *Journal of Contemporary Business, 7*(4), 17–35.

Ramsey, R. P., Marshall, G. W., Johnston, M. W., & Deeter-Schmelz, D. R. (2007). Ethical ideologies and older consumer perceptions of unethical sales tactics. *Journal of Business Ethics, 70*(2), 191–207. https://doi.org/10.1007/s10551-006-9105-6

Raney, A. A. (2004). Expanding disposition theory: Reconsidering character liking, moral evaluations, and enjoyment. *Communication Theory, 14*(4), 348–369. https://doi.org/10.1111/j.1468-2885.2004.tb00319.x

Rich, J. (2015). *Beyond cookies: Privacy lessons for online advertising*. AdExchanger Industry Preview. https://www.ftc.gov/system/files/documents/public_statements/620061/150121beyondcookies.pdf

Roberts, J. (1996). Will the real socially responsible consumer please step forward? *Business Horizons, 39*(1), 79–83. https://doi.org/10.1016/S0007-6813(96)90087-7

Robinson, S. R., Irmak, C., & Jayachandran, S. (2012). Choice of cause in cause-related marketing. *Journal of Marketing, 76*(4), 126–139. https://doi.org/10.1509/jm.09.0589

Schlegelmilch, B. B., & Öberseder, M. (2010). Half a century of marketing ethics: Shifting perspectives and emerging trends. *Journal of Business Ethics, 93*(1), 1–19. https://doi.org/10.1007/s10551-009-0182-1

Schor, J. (1998). *The overspent American: Downshifting and the new consumer*. Basic Books.

Sen, S., Gürhan-Canli, Z., & Morwitz, V. (2001). Withholding consumption: A social dilemma perspective on consumer boycotts. *Journal of Consumer Research, 28*(3), 399–417. https://doi.org/10.1086/323729

Shaw, D., & Clarke, L. (1999). Belief formation in ethical consumer groups: An exploratory study. *Marketing Intelligence & Planning, 17*(2), 109–120. https://doi.org/10.1108/02634509910260968

Shaw, D., Newholm, T., & Dickinson, R. (2006). Consumption as voting: An exploration of consumer empowerment. *European Journal of Marketing, 40*(9/10), 1049–1067. https://doi.org/10.1108/03090560610681005

Smiley, M. (2019, July 26). Multicultural agency Cashmere unveils division to help brands with social good initiatives. *Ad Week*. https://www.adweek.com/agencies/multicultural-agency-cashmere-unveils-division-to-help-brands-with-social-good-initiatives/

Smith, N. C. (1995). Marketing strategies for the ethics era. *MIT Sloan Management Review, 36*(4), 85.

Smith, N. C., & Quelch, J. A. (1993). *Ethics in marketing*. Irwin.

Stiff, R., Johnson, K., & Tourk, K. A. (1975). Scarcity and hoarding: Economic and social explanations and marketing implications. In M. J. Schlinger (Ed.), *NA - Advances in consumer research* (Vol. 2, pp. 203–216). Association for Consumer Research.

Swanepoel, C., Lye, A., & Rugimbana, R. (2009). Virally inspired: A review of the theory of viral stealth marketing. *Australasian Marketing Journal, 17*(1), 9–15. https://doi.org/10.1016/j.ausmj.2009.01.005

Thøgersen, J. (1999). The ethical consumer. Moral norms and packaging choice. *Journal of Consumer Policy, 22*(4), 439–460. https://doi.org/10.1023/A:1006225711603

Tsalikis, J., & Fritzsche, D. J. (2013). Business ethics: A literature review with a focus on marketing ethics. In A. C. Michalos & D. C. Poff (Eds.), *Citation classics from the Journal of Business Ethics* (pp. 337–404). Springer. https://doi.org/10.1007/978-94-007-4126-3_17

Tsarenko, Y., Ferraro, C., Sands, S., & McLeod, C. (2013). Environmentally conscious consumption: The role of retailers and peers as external influences. *Journal of Retailing and Consumer Services, 20*(3), 302–310. https://doi.org/10.1016/j.jretconser.2013.01.006

Turow, J., & Moy, L. (2015, November 16). *FTC cross-device tracking workshop* [Workshop transcript]. https://www.ftc.gov/system/files/documents/videos/cross-device-tracking-part-2/ftc_cross-device_tracking_workshop_-_transcript_segment_2.pdf

Unfair Methods of Competition Unlawful; Prevention by Commission. 15 U.S.C. § 45 (2006).

Van Buskirk, E. (2010, July 7). Gaming the system: How marketers rig the social media machine. *Wired*. https://www.wired.com/2010/07/gaming-the-system-how-marketers-rig-the-social-media-machine/

Walker, R. (2004, December 5). The hidden (in plain sight) persuaders. *New York Times Magazine*. https://www.nytimes.com/2004/12/05/magazine/the-hidden-in-plain-sight-persuaders.html

Webster, F. E., Jr. (1975). Determining the characteristics of the socially conscious consumer. *Journal of Consumer Research, 2*(3), 188–196. https://doi.org/10.1086/208631

White, K., Habib, R., & Dahl, D. W. (2020). A review and framework for thinking about the drivers of prosocial consumer behavior. *Journal of the Association of Consumer Research, 5*(1), 2–18. https://doi.org/10.1086/706782

White, K., Habib, R., & Hardisty, D. J. (2019). How to SHIFT consumer behaviors to be more sustainable: A literature review and guiding framework. *Journal of Marketing, 83*(3), 22–49. https://doi.org/10.1177/0022242919825649

White House Report. (2012, February). *Consumer data privacy in a networked world: A framework for protecting privacy and promoting innovation in the global digital economy*. https://obamawhitehouse.archives.gov/sites/default/files/privacy-final.pdf

Xie, C., Bagozzi, R. P., & Gronhaug, K. (2015). The role of moral emotions and individual differences in consumer responses to corporate green and non-green action. *Journal of the Academy of Marketing Science, 43*(3), 333–356. https://doi.org/10.1007/s11747-014-0394-5

THE ROLE OF TIME IN CONSUMER PSYCHOLOGY

Ashwani Monga, Ozum Zor, and Rafay A. Siddiqui

Time is a marker of life. It is the moment we are in currently, the past moments etched in our memory, and the future moments that await us. Time is so fundamental that it is difficult to define. In the words of physicist Richard Feynman, "Time is what happens when nothing else happens" (Feynman et al., 2011, Section 5-2). Perhaps even the reverse could be used as a definition: Time is what happens when everything else happens. After all, time is integral to most human endeavors. In the domain of consumption, the subjective perception of time is central to how consumers think, feel, and behave. The current chapter examines consumers' time perception from three perspectives: (a) time as a distance that varies in terms of its length, (b) time as a spending currency that varies in terms of its value, and (c) time as a quantity that varies in terms of its scarcity.

To provide a sense of these three perspectives of time in consumption settings, consider the example of Susan, who is looking to buy a new phone. She can either drive to a store to purchase the new phone or order it online and wait 5 days for delivery. While she prefers not to drive, she also does not like the idea of waiting too long. What she eventually does would depend on how she perceives the 5 days between the current moment and the moment at which the product would arrive. She will purchase online if she perceives the wait time to be very short but drive to the store if she perceives it to be very long. Thus, the perceived length of time will determine Susan's choice, illustrating the first perspective that we explore in this chapter: seeing time as a distance between two moments.

Now suppose Susan opts to drive to a store. She knows that one store is very close to where she lives, whereas another one, offering a $40 discount on the phone, involves an additional hour of driving. Susan needs to decide whether to go to the nearby store or save $40 by spending the additional hour. She will go to the farther store if she perceives the value of the hour that she spends to be less than the $40 that she will save in return. Thus, the perceived value of time will determine Susan's choice, illustrating the second perspective that we explore in this chapter: seeing time as a currency that is spent to receive something in return.

Finally, the decision regarding which store to visit is not occurring in a vacuum but in the context of the time that Susan has available and the other activities that she will forgo if she allocates an additional hour toward the drive. Thus, Susan sees time as a limited quantity, the perceived scarcity of which will determine her choice. She will opt for the nearby store if she perceives her time scarcity to be high—visiting the farther store will only add to the stress and make it harder to accomplish the other activities that are vying for her time. Thus, the perceived scarcity of time will determine Susan's choice, illustrating the final perspective that we

https://doi.org/10.1037/0000262-017
APA Handbook of Consumer Psychology, L. R. Kahle (Editor-in-Chief)
Copyright © 2022 by the American Psychological Association. All rights reserved.

explore in this chapter: seeing time as a quantity that is constrained by the supply of available time and the demand from competing activities.

The three perspectives that we discuss in this chapter are not the sole ways in which the notion of time has an influence. But we focus just on these because they broadly capture the crux of the role of time in consumption. We should also note that the three perspectives are interlinked. For instance, how scarce time feels may influence how long the 5-day delivery time seems and how one values the time spent driving. That is, scarcity perceptions may influence perceptions of both length and value—these three perspectives are not mutually exclusive. But we discuss them separately because they relate to different theories, generate distinct consequences, and provide unique insights into consumption. We next discuss the theories and consumption settings that relate to (a) perceived length of the distance of time, (b) perceived value of the currency of time, and (c) perceived scarcity of the quantity of time.

TIME AS DISTANCE: PERCEPTION OF LENGTH

As mentioned earlier, time is very hard to grasp because it is such a fundamental and abstract notion. Consequently, people try to understand time through metaphors. In particular, individuals employ notions of space to understand and convey time-related concepts. This space–time mapping is evident in how we communicate aspects of time. Just as we talk about long distances, we talk about long time periods, and just as we talk about moving forward in space, we talk about moving forward in time (Boroditsky & Ramscar, 2002; Hernández, 2001; B. K. Kim et al., 2012). That is, because people grasp the physical concept of distance well, they employ it to understand time and communicate about it.

Seeing time as a short or long distance is consequential in several consumption settings, most of all in settings of intertemporal choice between a smaller-sooner reward (SS) and a larger-later reward (LL). For instance, in the technology space, it is often the case that a better product can be bought at the same price, as long as one is willing to wait. Thus, one may be able to buy a certain kind of phone today but a much better phone sometime in the future at the same price, as long as one is willing to wait for the newer version. Similarly, when choosing among shipping options for online purchases, one may be able to save money by choosing free standard shipping rather than paying for expedited shipping, as long as one is willing to wait longer for delivery. While patience in such contexts is often seen as a function of how enticing the product seems, what also matters is how consumers see the wait time. We next discuss some factors that relate to the perception of the length of time and how changes in length perception may affect consumption preferences.

Psychophysics

When the wait time for the LL reward seems shorter, consumers are more likely to choose LL over SS—they will exhibit more patience. Moreover, following psychophysical principles, consumers' subjective estimates of wait time are not sufficiently sensitive to changes in objective time (B. K. Kim et al., 2012; Zauberman et al., 2009). For example, while 1 year is objectively four times as long as 3 months, consumers may feel as if it is only slightly longer. Thus, while consumers may generally prefer to not wait at all, if they do lean toward waiting, they may not see a 1-year wait as much longer than a 3-month wait. In other words, the psychophysics of time perception determines not only impatience but also how impatience may change with time periods.

Taking the example of product shipping, one may be willing to pay for expedited shipping to receive a product right away rather than get free shipping that involves a 4-day wait, if one subjectively perceives a 4-day wait to be too long. However, once a consumer is willing to wait, a 4-day wait may not seem very different from a 7-day wait. Such changes in subjective perception of time are fundamental to models of hyperbolic discounting and to the intertemporal preferences of consumers (Zauberman et al., 2009).

Descriptions

How consumers perceive an interval of time can be a function of how it is described. Assuming that today is October 1st, a time interval described as ending on October 21st will feel shorter compared with the same interval being described as ending after a duration of 20 days. This is because, relative to duration, dates direct one to focus on the endpoint as opposed to the interval itself (LeBoeuf, 2006). Perceptions may change even when the same duration is described using different units. Consider a delivery time that is framed as 3 days rather than 72 hours. The delivery time of 72 hours may feel longer than that of 3 days, influencing consumers' shipping options (Siddiqui et al., 2018). This is because consumers often base their estimates on the magnitude of the number (72 > 3) and do not adequately attend to the unit, an effect known as the *numerosity heuristic* (Pelham et al., 1994). However, abstract mindsets can drive attention toward units, reversing numerosity to unitosity (Monga & Bagchi, 2012). Furthermore, the language used to conceptualize wait time matters as well. Thinking of wait time anthropomorphically (May & Monga, 2014) or using different phrases such as "how far" versus "how long" (May & Monga, 2020) can influence the subjective perception of wait time and, consequently, patience.

Events

The perceived length of a time interval can be influenced by the number and type of events occurring within the interval. When our day is filled with many things to do, the day starts to feel longer than empty days on which we may not have much to do. Thus, length perceptions are influenced by the number of events within the time interval (May, 2017; Zauberman et al., 2010). What also matters is the type of intervening events. For example, when thinking about how much time has passed since one's admission to college, thinking specifically about college-related events, as opposed to thinking about non-college-related events that have occurred since the time of admission, makes the elapsed time seem much longer (Zauberman et al., 2010). This effect of relevant intervening events extends to predictions about how long it may take to complete a task. Consider a consumer about to assemble Ikea furniture. When looking at the nicely packaged table that comes in a single box, the consumer might assume that it will not take long to put the table together. However, once the consumer opens the box and realizes the large number of parts that need to be put together, the estimate of how long it will take to complete the setup can increase. This is because as the number of perceived steps required to complete the task becomes salient, so does the perception of the time required to complete it (Kruger & Evans, 2004; Siddiqui et al., 2014).

Events may also vary in terms of their affective properties, which can influence the perceived length of a time interval. For instance, the end of a month may be associated with paying bills (loss) or with receiving a paycheck (gain). Ending with a loss rather than a gain makes a time interval seem shorter (Bilgin & LeBoeuf, 2010). Likewise, when events are emotionally intense, they appear to be closer. For instance, describing a personally embarrassing moment emotionally can make it seem closer (Van Boven et al., 2010). Intense affect unrelated to the target event may also influence interval length perceptions. Because arousal elongates perceptions of time, the wait time interval for a reward is judged to be much longer after individuals are exposed to sexual cues in an unrelated context (B. K. Kim & Zauberman, 2013).

How future events are viewed is also a function of how individuals see their future selves. It is known that when the perceived distance from a future event (e.g., retirement) seems long, consumers may become impulsive, attending to short run considerations while ignoring their future utility (Hoch & Loewenstein, 1991). They may be less likely to save money for the future, especially if they see their own future self as someone removed from their current self. One way to combat such present orientation, and promote savings behavior, is to make consumers feel more connected to their future selves (Bartels & Urminsky, 2015; Hershfield et al., 2011; Urminsky, 2017).

Finally, while we view events progressing in a linear fashion from the past to the present to the future, it is possible to view events in a cyclical fashion as well (Crossan et al., 2005; Graham, 1981). For instance, the cycle of seasons keeps going from fall to winter to spring to summer and then back to fall. Similarly, people may view their own daily routine, from morning to night and then back to morning, as cyclical. Having a cyclical rather than linear perception can have consequences in certain domains, such as one's perceptions of grief (Ruscher, 2012).

Construal

Construal level theory describes how consumers may adopt a relatively abstract or a relatively concrete mindset when making judgments. Abstract mindsets lead to a higher level construal of events (Trope & Liberman, 2010). For instance, thinking about Black Friday sales abstractly will make higher level features salient, such as the fun of being at the sale, while thinking concretely will make lower level features salient, such as how feasible it will be to drive to the mall for the sale. Thinking abstractly versus concretely can influence the perceived temporal distance to the sale (Trope & Liberman, 2003). Abstract mindsets make the target event seem psychologically distant, leading to a perception of greater temporal distance. Hence, if the Black Friday sale is 1 month away, then thinking abstractly (vs. concretely) will make that 1-month interval seem longer.

Spatial Orientation

As mentioned earlier, spatial distance is used to understand temporal distance. But spatial distance can even interact with temporal distance. For instance, Boroditsky and Ramscar (2002) considered the meaning of the phrase "Next Wednesday's meeting has been moved forward 2 days." The dilemma is that such a phrase could mean that the meeting is now on Monday, or it could mean that the meeting is now on Friday. Individuals' understanding of the meaning of this phrase depends on their spatial orientation. If individuals have recently been moving forward in space, such as by taking a flight, then they are more likely to think forward in time—they believe that the meeting is now 2 days later, on Friday. However, if they are still waiting for their flight and have not moved forward in space yet, then they would interpret the phrase differently—they believe that the meeting is now 2 days earlier, on Monday (Boroditsky & Ramscar, 2002). This effect of spatial information influencing our understanding of time has been shown in other contexts too. Future events seem particularly farther away in time if they are farther away in terms of spatial distance (B. K. Kim et al., 2012). For instance, if someone living in Seattle thinks about a Black Friday sale being held in San Francisco, as opposed to a mall in town, then Black Friday seems farther away in time, provided the larger spatial distance to San Francisco is salient.

TIME AS CURRENCY: PERCEPTION OF VALUE

Consumers usually acquire goods and services in exchange for a currency that they spend. While money may be the currency that comes to mind when buying a product, time is spent in many transactions as well. For instance, if one wants to have dinner at a vegan restaurant, a time investment is needed to search for such a restaurant. Hunting for bargains on Black Friday involves an expenditure of time, such as searching through multiple retail websites and waiting in line at stores. And opting for cheaper unassembled furniture involves a willingness to spend time to assemble it. The extent to which consumers are willing to spend their time in exchange for a product or some other benefit depends on how much they value the time that they have. Because time is hard to grasp by itself, the value of time relates to aspects outside of time, such as money.

Money

The adage "time is money" identifies money as a means to assess the value of time. Scholars have long advocated time and money as tradeable resources, where spending time is equivalent to spending money. This equivalence makes sense considering the similarities between the two. After all, both time and money are scarce resources that should be spent wisely. Additionally, both money and time can be spent in exchange for purchasing products and services. Consumers sometimes need to decide whether to spend their time or their money. For example, consumers can choose to spend time physically commuting to a store to pick up supplies or spend money to have the supplies delivered to one's doorstep.

Given this interchangeability between time and money, the value of time is often assessed in terms of its opportunity cost (Becker, 1965; Jacoby et al., 1976; Stigler, 1961). That is, the value of time for a consumer can be assessed by the amount of money that can be saved, or obtained, for each unit of time spent. Consequently, individuals' wage rates can influence the value that they place on their time—the more individuals earn per hour, the more they subjectively value 1 hour of their time.

Timing

While time appears to be a valuable resource akin to money, it has unique properties that make it different. Money can be deposited in a bank for later use, but time cannot be stored and has to be used in the moment when it is available. Thus, while money has a relatively stable value, the value of time can vary depending on timing. For instance, time may be worth more over a weekday than over a weekend. The value of an hour may appear low on a leisurely Sunday morning but high on a hectic Monday morning, given the accounting period to which that hour belongs (Soster et al., 2010). The value of time is considered lower on weekends and evenings because these periods represent non-work time—such time is less likely to be evaluated using the wages one might earn during work time (Becker, 1965). Beyond wage rates, time may also be valued through other favored opportunities that one might pursue with time. For instance, the value of an hour spent at a mall searching for low product prices may depend on the enjoyable activities that one might do instead, such as spending that hour at a spa. But, if price comparison shopping is something that one derives utility from, then that 1 hour spent will appear to be less of a cost. Thus, in addition to wage rates, consumers may use alternative investments of time as comparison points from which to assess the value of their time (Marmorstein et al., 1992).

The value of time may also depend on timing in another way, which is whether the time is available in the current period or in a future period. While people sometimes engage in mental accounting of time (Prelec & Loewenstein, 1998; Soster et al., 2010), they are generally not very adept at tracking time (Soman, 2001). Their views of current and future time periods may also be different. Individuals may value their current time more than their future time because they expect to have a surplus of time in the future compared with the immediate moment (Soman, 1998; Zauberman & Lynch, 2005). Thus, people may push activities to a subsequent week under the (faulty) assumption that they will have more time then. The timing also matters for time valuation in terms of whether one perceives a time deficit or a time surplus at a given moment. A time deficit increases the marginal utility of time valuation, whereas a time surplus decreases the marginal utility (Festjens & Janiszewski, 2015).

Product Attributes

A fundamental distinction between products is that some are hedonic while others are utilitarian. Hedonic products that fulfill a desire for fun and enjoyment are often a luxury to have, whereas utilitarian products that provide practical benefits are usually necessities (Dhar & Wertenbroch, 2000). Consequently, it is easier to justify purchasing utilitarian goods as opposed to hedonic goods, as the latter can lead to feelings of guilt. For instance, when faced with a choice between a video game console (hedonic) and a food processor (utilitarian), the consumer will have to construct justifiable reasons to spend money on the game console rather than the food processor. This construction of reasons is easier when one spends time to acquire products rather than money (Okada, 2005), since the ambiguous nature of time's value gives consumers more freedom to strategically devalue it when acquiring something hedonic.

The price of a product may also influence how time is valued. A classic example is the jacket and calculator problem (Tversky & Kahneman, 1981). Some participants are asked to imagine that they are looking to purchase a $125 jacket and a $15 calculator, whereas others are asked to imagine that they are looking to purchase a $15 jacket and a $125 calculator. Both groups are then offered a $5 discount on the calculator's price, provided they are willing to spend 20 minutes of their time to drive to another branch of the store. Participants are much more likely to opt for the trip if the price of the calculator is $15 rather than $125, even though they would still be saving the same $5 (Tversky & Kahneman, 1981). This illustrates that the value of the 20 minutes invested in driving to the store was not a fixed dollar amount—the value of time varied depending on how large the dollar amount saved was in relation the total price of the product. Such valuation of time may also be influenced by the expectations that consumers have about product price (Saini et al., 2010).

The amount of uncertainty involved in consumption can also influence how much consumers value their time. For instance, when faced with two options for a flight, where option A will get them to their destination at a guaranteed time and option B will get them to their destination at an earlier time but with a greater chance of a delayed arrival, most consumers opt to be risk averse and choose option A (Leclerc et al., 1995). In contrast to such aversion to risk, consumers become more risk-seeking when they spend time (rather than money) to purchase products. When purchasing a camera for instance, one might have to choose between a brand that is average on all attributes or one that is extremely good on a few attributes but quite bad on others. The latter option is the riskier one but may offer greater potential value. In such situations, consumers paying with time by doing a task (vs. paying with money) were willing to spend more time (but not money) for the riskier option (Okada & Hoch, 2004). This is because consumers are aware that they can rationalize expenditures of time better than money, underscoring the malleability in the valuation of time (Okada & Hoch, 2004). Thus, while the value of time may be related to money (e.g., one's wage rate), time and money do differ in important ways that affect consumer decisions (for a review, see Monga & Zor, 2019).

Arbitrary Cues

Time has a degree of ambiguity that often makes its valuation challenging. Previous research shows that ambiguity reinforces a reliance on more arbitrary cues in valuation (Ariely et al., 2006). This means that rather than systematically assessing the value of time, consumers will be more susceptible to relying on cues from their environment and the choice context when deciding how much time to spend (Saini & Monga, 2008). Consider the case where a consumer is searching for a new house and the real estate agent gives them three options: see 5 houses over 1 day, 10 houses over 2 days, or 15 houses over 3 days. While seeing more houses is a benefit, there is a cost of spending more time. In this situation of spending time (as opposed to money), consumers will be more likely to choose the middle option of 10 houses over 2 days. This tendency to choose the compromise option may still emerge, but be relatively lower, if one were making choices between spending different amounts of money for different real estate agents. Thus, when paying in time, which is more ambiguous than money, consumers are not sure about how much time to spend and therefore rely more on heuristics, such as the compromise option and anchoring, to make their decisions (Saini & Monga, 2008).

This reliance on heuristics makes individuals less sensitive to changes in search costs. For instance, when shopping for clothing, product search could be conducted by spending one's own time (e.g., in a store or online) or paying someone else (e.g., a concierge at a luxury store). When search costs are in time (vs. money), individuals' search behavior is relatively immune to the costs of search (Monga & Saini, 2009), adding a contingency to economic theories suggesting that higher search costs decrease search behavior (Stigler, 1961).

Mindsets

Spending time to acquire products can cause consumers to process information using a more holistic mindset and ease the justification process. Paying attention to the time costs (rather than money costs) in a purchase prompts a consumer to evaluate the purchase with regard to other alternative options rather than the product's specific attributes (Su & Gao, 2014). For example, when shopping for a smartphone, thinking in terms of time can lead to greater consideration of alternative brands as opposed to a single brand's characteristics.

Spending in time rather than money can also promote an altruistic mindset. When reminded of money, individuals can become penny-pinching and unhelpful (Vohs et al., 2006), but time can have a positive effect on altruistic behavior. Additionally, focusing on time leads to an abstract mindset. An abstract mindset causes consumers to take a higher level perspective of an action, making one focus on the big picture. This big-picture mindset then encourages more charitable donations of time (Mac-Donnell & White, 2015).

The flip side is that thinking of time in terms of money can reverse these positive effects. Prompting the economic value of time (i.e., hourly wage rate and billing time) increases willingness to forgo leisure time in favor of earning a higher amount of money (DeVoe & Pfeffer, 2007b). This economic evaluation of time decreases willingness to spend time volunteering (DeVoe & Pfeffer, 2007a, 2010) and, eventually, impairs happiness (DeVoe & House, 2012). Thus, evoking the economic value of time induces a feeling that one must spend time on activities that benefit the self rather than others.

Emotions

Thinking about a product in terms of the time that one will spend on it can also foster greater personal connection with the product. When a good is more experiential, such as a dinner at a restaurant as opposed to a pair of jeans, thinking about the product in terms of the time (rather than money) spent on it leads to more favorable attitudes toward it due to a sense of personal connection (Mogilner & Aaker, 2009). When consumers consider spending time, emotions are activated, resulting in higher donations of both time and money (Liu & Aaker, 2008).

More broadly, spending time can lead to happiness, such that one has more positive rather than negative moments in their daily life (Mogilner, 2019; Mogilner et al., 2018). Consumers have the tendency to chase happiness by leaning toward long work hours in order to have more money to purchase more material products. However, prior research shows that money does not bring happiness but that time does (Hershfield et al., 2016; Kahneman et al., 2006). When individuals value their time more than their money, they experience greater happiness (Lee-Yoon & Whillans, 2019). Accordingly, Whillans et al. (2016) showed that consumers make monetary investments to have more time, such as by choosing a direct, but expensive, flight rather than an indirect, but inexpensive, flight. And a focus on time prompts individuals to pursue activities with higher personal meaning and social connection (Mogilner, 2010; Mogilner & Aaker, 2009).

TIME AS QUANTITY: PERCEPTION OF SCARCITY

In the previous section, we discussed the role of time as a currency in consumption situations. But time is not spent solely on acquiring products. Multiple activities place simultaneous demands on time, making time an important determinant of consumer well-being. A paucity of time limits the options that consumers choose. Indeed, the oft-touted objective of achieving a work-life balance highlights how individuals must ultimately allocate the limited resource of time among the limitless activities that they want to engage in. In this section, we look at how the scarcity of time plays a role in consumption settings.

Individuals perceive time to be scarce because, in general, there are too many tasks that demand time, but there is not a sufficient supply of time to achieve them all (Perlow, 1999). To characterize time scarcity, previous work has used various terms such as time stress, time shortage, time pressure, time constraint, time crunch, time famine, and time poverty (Darian & Cohen, 1995; Hamermesh & Lee, 2007; Payne et al., 1996; Perlow, 1999; Turner & Grieco, 2000). The usage of these terms largely depends on the context, but all point to individuals having a lack of time. Having a lack of time may seem comparable to having a lack of money, because both situations emphasize the scarcity of a resource. While the former describes the scarcity of time to allocate between tasks, the latter describes the scarcity of financial resources to allocate between purchases. However, there is a critical difference. While one could recover from financial scarcity by regaining money, it is impossible to regain time that one has spent already. Thus, the scarcity of time is more binding for individuals than the scarcity of money (Hamermesh & Lee, 2007). Even the collective amount of time that a person has is bounded by one's lifespan. As Leclerc et al. (1995) mentioned, "Even the wealthy are limited to 24 hours per day. For many, time is not just a scarce resource; it is *the* scarce resource" (p. 110).

While time perception affects consumers decisions, it also has a profound impact on consumer welfare. In our everyday lives, we must balance several goals. Ideally, we would want to accomplish our work tasks and then still have enough time to spend on leisure activities and social bonding. But that is rarely the case, and consumers end up feeling deprived of time to achieve all the goals that they want to. This feeling of being time scarce can result in psychological stress, affecting happiness. Time scarcity can consequently affect consumer decisions. For instance, a time scarce consumer would consider time to be of high value and therefore be less likely to spend time waiting. In the same manner, a time scarce consumer may prioritize certain goals over others (e.g., focusing on work and forgoing a trip to the gym). Conversely, being time scarce can also make a consumer feel good, perceiving oneself as a busy person who is undertaking important tasks. We next discuss some of the theories and consumption settings that relate to the perception of time scarcity.

Nature of Tasks

Objectively, everyone has the same amount of time in a day. However, subjectively, individuals may perceive time as limited depending on their lifestyle as they need to coordinate all their tasks within 24 hours in a day and 7 days in a week. This involves structuring time around tasks involving work and nonwork. Work tasks represent the time spent at a job for the acquisition of an income that provides economic purchasing power (Feldman & Hornik, 1981). Nonwork tasks include the time spent on necessary activities (e.g., sleeping and eating), chores (e.g., house cleaning), and leisure (e.g., watching television; Feldman & Hornik, 1981). The finite nature of time imposes a constraint on individuals as they try to achieve one or more tasks.

Consumers may focus on a single task at a time (i.e., monochronic time use), or focus on multiple tasks during a single period of time (i.e., polychronic time use) while achieving work and nonwork tasks (Kaufman et al., 1991; Kaufman-Scarborough, 2017). When pursuing single tasks, time may seem scarce at times, such as when individuals get closer to completing the task (Jhang & Lynch, 2015). But time scarcity becomes even more important for multiple tasks when individuals pursue competing goals, such as spending time on a work-related project versus spending time with loved ones. As consumers perceive a greater conflict between these types of tasks, they feel increasingly time scarce (Etkin et al., 2015). Time scarcity becomes more severe as the number of competing tasks increases, as happens when one progresses through different stages in life. During college, students may feel they have enough time for both academics and extracurriculars. But as they transition into full-time work, they may face a scarcity of time to pursue multiple goals.

Others' Time

Feelings of time scarcity are influenced by the available time of those around us. When time is socially coordinated, time scarcity can be the result of a scheduling failure (Young & Lim, 2014; Young & Melin, 2019). According to this point of view, time can be treated as a network good, which increases its benefit when more people have it. Young and Lim (2014) explained this by using an example of telephones. In the early days of telephones, few households and businesses owned them because there were not many people to call. However, once phones became a mainstream communication tool, owning a phone increased its benefit. In a similar vein, the utility individuals derive from time is related to having free time to spend with others rather than having an abundance of free time for just oneself. Thus, both employed and unemployed individuals have higher well-being on weekends than weekdays, as even unemployed individuals increase their enjoyment from activities that they do with others (Young & Lim, 2014).

Relatedly, work schedules can also impact time scarcity. In the standard work schedule, where days between Monday and Friday are workdays, the weekend (i.e., Saturday and Sunday) represents collective time off from work. Individuals working in nonstandard schedules can feel higher time scarcity as they need to budget their time for work and family differently than other members of the community (Garhammer, 1995). Consequently, limitations of social coordination shape perceived time scarcity.

Demographics

Although everyone struggles with time scarcity, specific segments of consumers can be under particularly high time pressure. For instance, women have been found to feel greater time scarcity than men (Mattingly & Sayer, 2006). This can be due to added responsibilities for women, such as being responsible for more tasks in the household. Indeed, even though men also spend time on housework and child care, women still end up spending relatively more time on these tasks (Bureau of Labor Statistics, 2020). Furthermore, time scarcity gets worse for those with competing responsibilities, such as dual-career couples, employed parents, and single parents (Jacobs & Gerson, 2004).

Age also determines how consumers perceive time. Consumers are aware that they have a limited number of days remaining in their lifespan, which contributes to their feelings of time scarcity. As individuals age, they perceive their time left as limited and pursue present-oriented and emotionally meaningful goals rather than future-oriented and knowledge-related goals (Carstensen et al., 1999; Lang & Carstensen, 2002; Löckenhoff & Carstensen, 2004). In particular, as consumers progress in age, they prefer to spend time on social goals as opposed to work-oriented goals. And within these social goals, they pursue more emotionally meaningful social interactions by narrowing down their networks and spending time with family and close friends (English & Carstensen, 2014). Relatedly, older consumers develop a higher liking and recall for emotional advertisements than for rational advertisements (Williams & Drolet, 2005).

Income

Time scarcity can also be evaluated in light of the amount of money that one is earning at work. As discussed previously, consumers often assess the value of their time by relying on earnings, such as one's hourly wage rate (Becker, 1965). A high income makes time seem scarcer (DeVoe & Pfeffer, 2011; Hamermesh & Lee, 2007) because people heuristically associate high-value objects with scarcity (Dai et al., 2008; King et al., 2009; Lynn, 1992). Furthermore, the perceived economic value of time strengthens this positive relationship between income and time scarcity (DeVoe & Pfeffer, 2011). Thus, the higher one's wage rate, the scarcer time seems to be. On the flip side, the weight given to time scarcity can differentially influence wage rates. People demand higher wage rates when the method used to elicit wage rates prompts a higher weight on time scarcity (Monga et al., 2017).

Patience

Time scarcity experienced because of the burden of current tasks can also have a direct influence on patience in consumption decisions. Consider a consumer who has just ordered a Tesla and is informed that it will take 3 months for the car to arrive, but the consumer can opt to spend more money and get the car in 1 month instead. The decision of whether to wait an additional 2 months to avoid spending additional money can rest on feelings of time scarcity. The scarcer people feel their time is, the less likely they are willing to wait for product deliveries (Etkin et al., 2015). Feelings of busyness, which are associated with time scarcity, can also prompt consumers to eat healthier, because busyness can make consumers feel self-important, leading to greater self-control (J. C. Kim et al., 2019). Thus, interestingly, time scarcity can prompt impatience with regard to product delivery but also lead to healthier eating if the consumer equates time scarcity to busyness.

Deadlines

Under time pressure, consumers accelerate their decision-making process and adopt new strategies to process information (Payne et al., 1988). In particular, consumers under time scarcity may interpret themselves as using time more effectively and become less prone to task detachment. For instance, missing a deadline because of (i.e., being busy with another task) curtails a sense of failure and reduces the time that one needs for completing the missed task by increasing motivation (Wilcox et al., 2016). Such motivation may also be related to inferences about difficulty. Specifically, the deadline to complete a task could make it seem that the task is difficult. Zhu et al. (2019) found that consumers were willing to spend more money to file their tax returns when the time until the filing deadline was long rather than short, since the longer deadline made filing taxes seem more difficult. They attribute this effect to a learned association between long deadlines and difficult tasks.

A concept related to deadlines is that of consumption time windows. Expiration dates for perishable products signal to the consumer that they must finish the product within the prescribed period or risk consuming a ruined product. Intuitively, consumers should be more likely to purchase products that offer a longer time window. However, for certain types of products, shorter time windows are preferred (Siddiqui et al., 2017). For virtue products like salads, consumers prefer a shorter time window as it pushes them to consume the product at a faster rate. Since salads are beneficial to one's health, the short time window acts as a self-control device to ensure that the salads are consumed at a high rate. But self-control effects may arise even within the same time period, such as within a single day. Specifically, consumption of online information shifts from virtue to vice as the time period shifts from morning to evening (Zor et al., 2021).

Other work suggests that shorter perceived time windows may also benefit consumers by pushing them to consume enjoyable experiences. Shu and Gneezy (2010) demonstrated that longer time windows cause consumers to procrastinate on positive experiences. Thus, longer redemption windows for gift certificates result in lower redemption rates.

Well-Being

In terms of long-term consumer well-being, time scarcity can have negative consequences, particularly due to its negative effect on mental and physical health. It is known that being under the pressure of a time constraint is linked to stress (Maule & Svenson, 1993; Zuzanek, 2004). Time scarcity has been associated with mental health problems, such as increased depression and reduced well-being (Kasser & Sheldon, 2009; Roxburgh, 2004). When lacking sufficient time to complete all tasks, people may adjust their priorities. For instance, one may forgo tasks needing hours of preparation and instead focus on more urgent tasks such as daily work and child care. Tasks that are important, but not as urgent, may receive a lower priority (Zhu et al., 2018). Important tasks that get neglected may include those that pertain to one's well-being. For instance, perceived insufficiency of time fosters unhealthy eating behaviors and physical inactivity (Venn & Strazdins, 2017). Accordingly, it is highly likely that time scarcity may heighten the risk of developing obesity, high blood pressure, and hypertension (Banwell et al., 2005; Yan et al., 2003).

Even though time scarcity seems to have adverse effects on well-being, having an abundance of time also hurts well-being. With abundant leisure time, people may get bored and feel that they are wasting the precious resource of time. Conversely, feeling that one's time is scarce—filled with tasks rather than empty—can have a positive psychological effect. Hsee et al. (2010) showed that when individuals have a reason, even a specious one, to be busy, they prefer being busy rather than idle. Accordingly, the authors observed that individuals prefer walking from one location to another just to receive a different, but equally attractive, candy rather than waiting idly to receive a candy at the same location. Furthermore, individuals are happier when busy than when idle (Hsee et al., 2010). Beyond using time wisely, a busy lifestyle (i.e., long working hours and lack of leisure time) stands as a status symbol. People perceive being busy as equal to possessing desired human characteristics, such as ambition and competence, being scarce, and being in demand (Bellezza et al., 2017). Thus, time scarcity may sometimes benefit consumer well-being by increasing feelings of accomplishment and happiness, as well as perceptions of one's status in the eyes of others.

Managing Scarcity

Consumer research has identified routes through which consumers may manage their time scarcity and increase their productivity. Making plans is one such route. Previous research defines effective plans as specific directions that deal with if-then situations rather than more general "do your best" statements (Gollwitzer, 1999). Fernbach et al. (2015) described two planning strategies that consumers might use. The first strategy, efficiency planning, targets saving time by stretching it to avoid waste. For instance, efficient planning of shopping would require visiting multiple stores in one mall trip rather than visiting each store on separate trips. The second strategy, priority planning, aims to save time by giving up on less critical alternatives. For instance, priority planning of time is necessary when one is under time pressure; therefore, it requires visiting one store and sacrificing others in a mall trip. Either one of these strategies can be suitable according to the given situation and severity of time scarcity. Accordingly, to cure immediate time scarcity, priority planning yields more efficient outcomes. However, when considering a solution to time scarcity for the long run, efficiency planning is more suitable as the time savings add up over multiple occasions.

Although time scarcity can be managed by planning, consumers may exhibit a planning fallacy, such that they are overoptimistic about the time in which they will be able to finish a task (Buehler et al., 1994). Consumers are prone to this drawback when planning for the long term. Indeed, consumers often underestimate the weight of their long-term responsibilities and expect to have less time scarcity in the future than today (Zauberman & Lynch, 2005). Thus, when making plans for the long-term, consumers underestimate the time scarcity that they may face in the future.

Consumers can also manage time scarcity by setting deadlines to help manage time effectively. Deadlines help people prevent time scarcity in the future by overcoming procrastination. Externally designated deadlines (e.g., those set by a professor or supervisor) can improve task performance and prevent procrastination better than self-designated deadlines (Ariely & Wertenbroch, 2002). Deadlines ideally lead individuals to take sooner rather than later actions for achieving tasks. Task initiation is more likely when individuals perceive a deadline to be in the same temporal category as the present (e.g., same week or month) rather than a different category (e.g., different week or month; Tu & Soman, 2014). Therefore, the categorization of time itself can be a strategy to manage time scarcity.

Scheduling can be another strategy to cope with time scarcity. Consumers can structure time and organize the order of the tasks that they want to accomplish. Thus, scheduling may diminish the stress related to time scarcity and busyness (Bond & Feather, 1988). As mentioned earlier, consumers often pursue more than one task at a time. While scheduling multiple tasks, consumers may follow one of two strategies: intermittent scheduling or back-to-back scheduling (Malkoc & Tonietto, 2019; Tonietto et al., 2019). An intermittent strategy blends unscheduled time into scheduled tasks, while a back-to-back strategy separates scheduled and unscheduled time by creating a block of time for scheduled tasks and leaving another block unscheduled. When a free period of time follows a scheduled task (vs. unscheduled time), consumers find this time period insufficient and perform fewer as well as less important tasks (Tonietto et al., 2019). Thus, consumers may manage time scarcity, and improve their productivity, by choosing the appropriate scheduling strategy.

Counterintuitively, spending time itself can sometimes alleviate the feeling of scarcity, especially when time is spent in a meaningful way (Rudd et al., 2019). Mogilner et al. (2012) demonstrated that spending time to help other people makes one perceive the same duration of time longer and fuller. Eliciting certain emotions may also help consumers mitigate the feeling of time scarcity. For instance, after watching a commercial that evokes awe, individuals perceive time to be less scarce (Rudd et al., 2012).

CONCLUSION

The perception of time is central to how consumers think, feel, and behave. In this chapter, we examined time perception from three perspectives: a distance between moments, a currency to spend, and a quantity that is scarce. Within each perspective, we discussed how time perception influences important consumption decisions. For instance, shortening the perception of wait time can make consumers more patient for a larger reward, using time instead of money as a currency to purchase goods can lead to more hedonic consumption, and experiencing time scarcity can cause consumers to focus on the present and look for immediate gains. Such influences underscore the role of time in consumer well-being, as the appropriate assessment of time and its efficient allocation and utilization are vital to consumer fulfilment. Apart from its role in the acquisition of material goods, time is an inseparable component of consumers' experiences, social bonding, goal pursuit, patience, and several other consumption aspects. Time cannot be separated from consumption, just as life cannot be separated from time.

REFERENCES

Ariely, D., Loewenstein, G., & Prelec, D. (2006). Tom Sawyer and the construction of value. *Journal of Economic Behavior & Organization, 60*(1), 1–10. https://doi.org/10.1016/j.jebo.2004.10.003

Ariely, D., & Wertenbroch, K. (2002). Procrastination, deadlines, and performance: Self-control by precommitment. *Psychological Science, 13*(3), 219–224. https://doi.org/10.1111/1467-9280.00441

Banwell, C., Hinde, S., Dixon, J., & Sibthorpe, B. (2005). Reflections on expert consensus: A case study of the social trends contributing to obesity. *European Journal of Public Health, 15*(6), 564–568. https://doi.org/10.1093/eurpub/cki034

Bartels, D. M., & Urminsky, O. (2015). To know and to care: How awareness and valuation of the future jointly shape consumer spending. *Journal of Consumer Research, 41*(6), 1469–1485. https://doi.org/10.1086/680670

Becker, G. S. (1965). A theory of the allocation of time. *Economic Journal, 75*(299), 493–517. https://doi.org/10.2307/2228949

Bellezza, S., Paharia, N., & Keinan, A. (2017). Conspicuous consumption of time: When busyness and lack of leisure time become a status symbol. *Journal of Consumer Research, 44*(1), 118–138. https://doi.org/10.1093/jcr/ucw076

Bilgin, B., & LeBoeuf, R. A. (2010). Looming losses in future time perception. *Journal of Marketing Research, 47*(3), 520–530. https://doi.org/10.1509/jmkr.47.3.520

Bond, M. J., & Feather, N. T. (1988). Some correlates of structure and purpose in the use of time. *Journal of Personality and Social Psychology, 55*(2), 321–329. https://doi.org/10.1037/0022-3514.55.2.321

Boroditsky, L., & Ramscar, M. (2002). The roles of body and mind in abstract thought. *Psychological Science, 13*(2), 185–189. https://doi.org/10.1111/1467-9280.00434

Buehler, R., Griffin, D., & Ross, M. (1994). Exploring the "planning fallacy": Why people underestimate their task completion times. *Journal of Personality and Social Psychology, 67*(3), 366–381. https://doi.org/10.1037/0022-3514.67.3.366

Bureau of Labor Statistics. (2020, June 25). *American time use survey—2019 results*. https://www.bls.gov/news.release/pdf/atus.pdf

Carstensen, L. L., Isaacowitz, D. M., & Charles, S. T. (1999). Taking time seriously. A theory of socioemotional selectivity. *American Psychologist, 54*(3), 165–181. https://doi.org/10.1037/0003-066X.54.3.165

Crossan, M., Cunha, M. P. E., Vera, D., & Cunha, J. (2005). Time and organizational improvisation. *Academy of Management Review, 30*(1), 129–145. https://doi.org/10.5465/amr.2005.15281441

Dai, X., Wertenbroch, K., & Brendl, C. M. (2008). The value heuristic in judgments of relative frequency. *Psychological Science, 19*(1), 18–19. https://doi.org/10.1111/j.1467-9280.2008.02039.x

Darian, J. C., & Cohen, J. (1995). Segmenting by consumer time shortage. *Journal of Consumer Marketing, 12*(1), 32–44. https://doi.org/10.1108/07363769510146787

DeVoe, S. E., & House, J. (2012). Time, money, and happiness: How does putting a price on time affect our ability to smell the roses? *Journal of Experimental Social Psychology, 48*(2), 466–474. https://doi.org/10.1016/j.jesp.2011.11.012

DeVoe, S. E., & Pfeffer, J. (2007a). Hourly payment and volunteering: The effect of organizational practices on decisions about time use. *Academy of Management Journal, 50*(4), 783–798. https://doi.org/10.5465/amj.2007.26279171

DeVoe, S. E., & Pfeffer, J. (2007b). When time is money: The effect of hourly payment on the evaluation of time. *Organizational Behavior and Human Decision Processes, 104*(1), 1–13. https://doi.org/10.1016/j.obhdp.2006.05.003

DeVoe, S. E., & Pfeffer, J. (2010). The stingy hour: How accounting for time affects volunteering. *Personality and Social Psychology Bulletin, 36*(4), 470–483. https://doi.org/10.1177/0146167209359699

DeVoe, S. E., & Pfeffer, J. (2011). Time is tight: How higher economic value of time increases feelings of time pressure. *Journal of Applied Psychology, 96*(4), 665–676. https://doi.org/10.1037/a0022148

Dhar, R., & Wertenbroch, K. (2000). Consumer choice between hedonic and utilitarian goods. *Journal of*

Marketing Research, 37(1), 60–71. https://doi.org/10.1509/jmkr.37.1.60.18718

English, T., & Carstensen, L. L. (2014). Selective narrowing of social networks across adulthood is associated with improved emotional experience in daily life. International Journal of Behavioral Development, 38(2), 195–202. https://doi.org/10.1177/0165025413515404

Etkin, J., Evangelidis, I., & Aaker, J. (2015). Pressed for time? Goal conflict shapes how time is perceived, spent, and valued. Journal of Marketing Research, 52(3), 394–406. https://doi.org/10.1509/jmr.14.0130

Feldman, L. P., & Hornik, J. (1981). The use of time: An integrated conceptual model. Journal of Consumer Research, 7(4), 407–419. https://doi.org/10.1086/208831

Fernbach, P. M., Kan, C., & Lynch, J. G., Jr. (2015). Squeezed: Coping with constraint through efficiency and prioritization. Journal of Consumer Research, 41(5), 1204–1227. https://doi.org/10.1086/679118

Festjens, A., & Janiszewski, C. (2015). The value of time. Journal of Consumer Research, 42(2), 178–195.

Feynman, R. P., Leighton, R. B., & Sands, M. (2011). The Feynman lectures on physics: Vol. I. The new millennium edition: Mainly mechanics, radiation, and heat. Basic Books.

Garhammer, M. (1995). Changes in working hours in Germany: The resulting impact on everyday life. Time & Society, 4(2), 167–203. https://doi.org/10.1177/0961463X95004002002

Gollwitzer, P. M. (1999). Implementation intentions: Strong effects of simple plans. American Psychologist, 54(7), 493–503. https://doi.org/10.1037/0003-066X.54.7.493

Graham, R. J. (1981). The role of perception of time in consumer research. Journal of Consumer Research, 7(4), 335–342. https://doi.org/10.1086/208823

Hamermesh, D. S., & Lee, J. (2007). Stressed out on four continents: Time crunch or yuppie kvetch? Review of Economics and Statistics, 89(2), 374–383. https://doi.org/10.1162/rest.89.2.374

Hernández, L. P. (2001). Metaphor-based cluster models and conceptual interaction: The case of "time." Atlantis, 23(2), 65–81.

Hershfield, H. E., Goldstein, D. G., Sharpe, W. F., Fox, J., Yeykelis, L., Carstensen, L. L., & Bailenson, J. N. (2011). Increasing saving behavior through age-progressed renderings of the future self. Journal of Marketing Research, 48(SPL), S23–S37. https://doi.org/10.1509/jmkr.48.SPL.S23

Hershfield, H. E., Mogilner, C., & Barnea, U. (2016). People who choose time over money are happier. Social Psychological & Personality Science, 7(7), 697–706. https://doi.org/10.1177/1948550616649239

Hoch, S. J., & Loewenstein, G. F. (1991). Time-inconsistent preferences and consumer self-control. Journal of Consumer Research, 17(4), 492–507. https://doi.org/10.1086/208573

Hsee, C. K., Yang, A. X., & Wang, L. (2010). Idleness aversion and the need for justifiable busyness. Psychological Science, 21(7), 926–930. https://doi.org/10.1177/0956797610374738

Jacobs, J. A., & Gerson, K. (2004). The time divide: Work, family, and gender inequality. Harvard University Press.

Jacoby, J., Szybillo, G. J., & Berning, C. K. (1976). Time and consumer behavior: An interdisciplinary overview. Journal of Consumer Research, 2(4), 320–339. https://doi.org/10.1086/208644

Jhang, J. H., & Lynch, J. G., Jr. (2015). Pardon the interruption: Goal proximity, perceived spare time, and impatience. Journal of Consumer Research, 41(5), 1267–1283. https://doi.org/10.1086/679308

Kahneman, D., Krueger, A. B., Schkade, D., Schwarz, N., & Stone, A. A. (2006). Would you be happier if you were richer? A focusing illusion. Science, 312(5782), 1908–1910. https://doi.org/10.1126/science.1129688

Kasser, T., & Sheldon, K. M. (2009). Time affluence as a path toward personal happiness and ethical business practice: Empirical evidence from four studies. Journal of Business Ethics, 84(2), 243–255. https://doi.org/10.1007/s10551-008-9696-1

Kaufman, C. F., Lane, P. M., & Lindquist, J. D. (1991). Exploring more than 24 hours a day: A preliminary investigation of polychronic time use. Journal of Consumer Research, 18(3), 392–401. https://doi.org/10.1086/209268

Kaufman-Scarborough, C. (2017). Monochronic and polychronic time. In Y. Y. Kim (Ed.), The international encyclopedia of intercultural communication (pp. 1–5). Wiley Blackwell. https://doi.org/10.1002/9781118783665.ieicc0110

Kim, B. K., & Zauberman, G. (2013). Can Victoria's Secret change the future? A subjective time perception account of sexual-cue effects on impatience. Journal of Experimental Psychology: General, 142(2), 328–335. https://doi.org/10.1037/a0028954

Kim, B. K., Zauberman, G., & Bettman, J. R. (2012). Space, time, and intertemporal preferences. Journal of Consumer Research, 39(4), 867–880. https://doi.org/10.1086/666464

Kim, J. C., Wadhwa, M., & Chattopadhyay, A. (2019). When busy is less indulging: Impact of busy mindset on self-control behaviors. Journal of Consumer Research, 45(5), 933–952. https://doi.org/10.1093/jcr/ucy069

King, L. A., Hicks, J. A., & Abdelkhalik, J. (2009). Death, life, scarcity, and value: An alternative perspective on the meaning of death. *Psychological Science, 20*(12), 1459–1462. https://doi.org/10.1111/j.1467-9280.2009.02466.x

Kruger, J., & Evans, M. (2004). If you don't want to be late, enumerate: Unpacking reduces the planning fallacy. *Journal of Experimental Social Psychology, 40*(5), 586–598. https://doi.org/10.1016/j.jesp.2003.11.001

Lang, F. R., & Carstensen, L. L. (2002). Time counts: Future time perspective, goals, and social relationships. *Psychology and Aging, 17*(1), 125–139. https://doi.org/10.1037/0882-7974.17.1.125

LeBoeuf, R. A. (2006). Discount rates for time versus dates: The sensitivity of discounting to time-interval description. *Journal of Marketing Research, 43*(1), 59–72. https://doi.org/10.1509/jmkr.43.1.59

Leclerc, F., Schmitt, B. H., & Dube, L. (1995). Waiting time and decision making: Is time like money? *Journal of Consumer Research, 22*(1), 110–119. https://doi.org/10.1086/209439

Lee-Yoon, A., & Whillans, A. V. (2019). Making seconds count: When valuing time promotes subjective well-being. *Current Opinion in Psychology, 26*, 54–57. https://doi.org/10.1016/j.copsyc.2018.05.002

Liu, W., & Aaker, J. (2008). The happiness of giving: The time-ask effect. *Journal of Consumer Research, 35*(3), 543–557. https://doi.org/10.1086/588699

Löckenhoff, C. E., & Carstensen, L. L. (2004). Socioemotional selectivity theory, aging, and health: The increasingly delicate balance between regulating emotions and making tough choices. *Journal of Personality, 72*(6), 1395–1424. https://doi.org/10.1111/j.1467-6494.2004.00301.x

Lynn, M. (1992). The psychology of unavailability: Explaining scarcity and cost effects on value. *Basic and Applied Social Psychology, 13*(1), 3–7. https://doi.org/10.1207/s15324834basp1301_2

MacDonnell, R., & White, K. (2015). How construals of money versus time impact consumer charitable giving. *Journal of Consumer Research, 42*(4), 551–563. https://doi.org/10.1093/jcr/ucv042

Malkoc, S. A., & Tonietto, G. N. (2019). Activity versus outcome maximization in time management. *Current Opinion in Psychology, 26*, 49–53. https://doi.org/10.1016/j.copsyc.2018.04.017

Marmorstein, H., Grewal, D., & Fishe, R. P. H. (1992). The value of time spent in price-comparison shopping: Survey and experimental evidence. *Journal of Consumer Research, 19*(1), 52–61. https://doi.org/10.1086/209285

Mattingly, M. J., & Sayer, L. C. (2006). Under pressure: Gender differences in the relationship between free time and feeling rushed. *Journal of Marriage and the Family, 68*(1), 205–221. https://doi.org/10.1111/j.1741-3737.2006.00242.x

Maule, A. J., & Svenson, O. (1993). Theoretical and empirical approaches to behavioral decision making and their relation to time constraints. In O. Svenson & A. J. Maule (Eds.), *Time pressure and stress in human judgment and decision making* (pp. 3–25). Springer. https://doi.org/10.1007/978-1-4757-6846-6_1

May, F. (2017). The effect of future event markers on intertemporal choice is moderated by the reliance on emotions versus reason to make decisions. *Journal of Consumer Research, 44*(2), 313–331. https://doi.org/10.1093/jcr/ucw081

May, F., & Monga, A. (2014). When time has a will of its own, the powerless don't have the will to wait: Anthropomorphism of time can decrease patience. *Journal of Consumer Research, 40*(5), 924–942. https://doi.org/10.1086/673384

May, F., & Monga, A. (2020). *So far, so long: Frame of delay moderates the effect of delayed rewards on patience* [Working paper]. Department of Marketing, Pamplin College of Business.

Mogilner, C. (2010). The pursuit of happiness: Time, money, and social connection. *Psychological Science, 21*(9), 1348–1354. https://doi.org/10.1177/0956797610380696

Mogilner, C. (2019). It's time for happiness. *Current Opinion in Psychology, 26*, 80–84. https://doi.org/10.1016/j.copsyc.2018.07.002

Mogilner, C., & Aaker, J. (2009). "The time vs. money effect": Shifting product attitudes and decisions through personal connection. *Journal of Consumer Research, 36*(2), 277–291. https://doi.org/10.1086/597161

Mogilner, C., Chance, Z., & Norton, M. I. (2012). Giving time gives you time. *Psychological Science, 23*(10), 1233–1238. https://doi.org/10.1177/0956797612442551

Mogilner, C., Whillans, A., & Norton, M. I. (2018). Time, money, and subjective wellbeing. In E. Diener, S. Oishi, & L. Tay (Eds.), *Handbook of well-being* (pp. 515–531). DEF Publishers.

Monga, A., & Bagchi, R. (2012). Years, months, and days versus 1, 12, and 365: The influence of units versus numbers. *Journal of Consumer Research, 39*(1), 185–198. https://doi.org/10.1086/662039

Monga, A., May, F., & Bagchi, R. (2017). Eliciting time versus money: Time scarcity underlies asymmetric wage rates. *Journal of Consumer Research, 44*(4), 833–852. https://doi.org/10.1093/jcr/ucx066

Monga, A., & Saini, R. (2009). Currency of search: How spending time on search is not the same as spending money. *Journal of Retailing, 85*(3), 245–257. https://doi.org/10.1016/j.jretai.2009.04.005

Monga, A., & Zor, O. (2019). Time versus money. *Current Opinion in Psychology, 26*, 28–31. https://doi.org/10.1016/j.copsyc.2018.04.011

Okada, E. M. (2005). Justification effects on consumer choice of hedonic and utilitarian goods. *Journal of Marketing Research, 42*(1), 43–53. https://doi.org/10.1509/jmkr.42.1.43.56889

Okada, E. M., & Hoch, S. J. (2004). Spending time versus spending money. *Journal of Consumer Research, 31*(2), 313–323. https://doi.org/10.1086/422110

Payne, J. W., Bettman, J. R., & Johnson, E. J. (1988). Adaptive strategy selection in decision making. *Journal of Experimental Psychology: Learning, Memory, and Cognition, 14*(3), 534–552. https://doi.org/10.1037/0278-7393.14.3.534

Payne, J. W., Bettman, J. R., & Luce, M. F. (1996). When time is money: Decision behavior under opportunity-cost time pressure. *Organizational Behavior and Human Decision Processes, 66*(2), 131–152. https://doi.org/10.1006/obhd.1996.0044

Pelham, B. W., Sumarta, T. T., & Myaskovsky, L. (1994). The easy path from many to much: The numerosity heuristic. *Cognitive Psychology, 26*(2), 103–133. https://doi.org/10.1006/cogp.1994.1004

Perlow, L. A. (1999). The time famine: Toward a sociology of work time. *Administrative Science Quarterly, 44*(1), 57–81. https://doi.org/10.2307/2667031

Prelec, D., & Loewenstein, G. (1998). The red and the black: Mental accounting of savings and debt. *Marketing Science, 17*(1), 4–28. https://doi.org/10.1287/mksc.17.1.4

Roxburgh, S. (2004). "There just aren't enough hours in the day": The mental health consequences of time pressure. *Journal of Health and Social Behavior, 45*(2), 115–131. https://doi.org/10.1177/002214650404500201

Rudd, M., Catapano, R., & Aaker, J. (2019). Making time matter: A review of research on time and meaning. *Journal of Consumer Psychology, 29*(4), 680–702. https://doi.org/10.1002/jcpy.1087

Rudd, M., Vohs, K. D., & Aaker, J. (2012). Awe expands people's perception of time, alters decision making, and enhances well-being. *Psychological Science, 23*(10), 1130–1136. https://doi.org/10.1177/0956797612438731

Ruscher, J. B. (2012). Describing grief under cyclical versus linear conceptions of time. *Journal of Language and Social Psychology, 31*(3), 321–330. https://doi.org/10.1177/0261927X12446600

Saini, R., & Monga, A. (2008). How I decide depends on what I spend: Use of heuristics is greater for time than for money. *Journal of Consumer Research, 34*(6), 914–922. https://doi.org/10.1086/525503

Saini, R., Rao, R. S., & Monga, A. (2010). Is that deal worth my time? The interactive effect of relative and referent thinking on willingness to seek a bargain. *Journal of Marketing, 74*(1), 34–48. https://doi.org/10.1509/jmkg.74.1.34

Shu, S. B., & Gneezy, A. (2010). Procrastination of enjoyable experiences. *Journal of Marketing Research, 47*(5), 933–944. https://doi.org/10.1509/jmkr.47.5.933

Siddiqui, R. A., May, F., & Monga, A. (2014). Reversals of task duration estimates: Thinking how rather than why shrinks duration estimates for simple tasks, but elongates estimates for complex tasks. *Journal of Experimental Social Psychology, 50*, 184–189. https://doi.org/10.1016/j.jesp.2013.10.002

Siddiqui, R. A., May, F., & Monga, A. (2017). Time window as a self-control denominator: Shorter windows shift preference toward virtues and longer windows toward vices. *Journal of Consumer Research, 43*(6), 932–949.

Siddiqui, R. A., Monga, A., & Buechel, E. C. (2018). When intertemporal rewards are hedonic, larger units of wait time boost patience. *Journal of Consumer Psychology, 28*(4), 612–628. https://doi.org/10.1002/jcpy.1019

Soman, D. (1998). The illusion of delayed incentives: Evaluating future effort-money transactions. *Journal of Marketing Research, 35*(4), 427–437.

Soman, D. (2001). The mental accounting of sunk time costs: Why time is not like money. *Journal of Behavioral Decision Making, 14*(3), 169–185. https://doi.org/10.1002/bdm.370

Soster, R. L., Monga, A., & Bearden, W. O. (2010). Tracking costs of time and money: How accounting periods affect mental accounting. *Journal of Consumer Research, 37*(4), 712–721. https://doi.org/10.1086/656388

Stigler, G. J. (1961). The economics of information. *Journal of Political Economy, 69*(3), 213–225. https://doi.org/10.1086/258464

Su, L., & Gao, L. (2014). Strategy compatibility: The time versus money effect on product evaluation strategies. *Journal of Consumer Psychology, 24*(4), 549–556. https://doi.org/10.1016/j.jcps.2014.04.006

Tonietto, G. N., Malkoc, S. A., & Nowlis, S. M. (2019). When an hour feels shorter: Future boundary tasks alter consumption by contracting time. *Journal of Consumer Research, 45*(5), 1085–1102. https://doi.org/10.1093/jcr/ucy043

Trope, Y., & Liberman, N. (2003). Temporal construal. *Psychological Review, 110*(3), 403–421. https://doi.org/10.1037/0033-295X.110.3.403

Trope, Y., & Liberman, N. (2010). Construal-level theory of psychological distance. *Psychological Review, 117*(2), 440–463. https://doi.org/10.1037/a0018963

Tu, Y., & Soman, D. (2014). The categorization of time and its impact on task initiation. *Journal of Consumer Research, 41*(3), 810–822. https://doi.org/10.1086/677840

Turner, J., & Grieco, M. (2000). Gender and time poverty: The neglected social policy implications of gendered time, transport and travel. *Time & Society, 9*(1), 129–136. https://doi.org/10.1177/0961463X00009001007

Tversky, A., & Kahneman, D. (1981). The framing of decisions and the psychology of choice. *Science, 211*(4481), 453–458. https://doi.org/10.1126/science.7455683

Urminsky, O. (2017). The role of psychological connectedness to the future self in decisions over time. *Current Directions in Psychological Science, 26*(1), 34–39. https://doi.org/10.1177/0963721416668810

Van Boven, L., Kane, J., McGraw, A. P., & Dale, J. (2010). Feeling close: Emotional intensity reduces perceived psychological distance. *Journal of Personality and Social Psychology, 98*(6), 872–885. https://doi.org/10.1037/a0019262

Venn, D., & Strazdins, L. (2017). Your money or your time? How both types of scarcity matter to physical activity and healthy eating. *Social Science & Medicine, 172*, 98–106. https://doi.org/10.1016/j.socscimed.2016.10.023

Vohs, K. D., Mead, N. L., & Goode, M. R. (2006). The psychological consequences of money. *Science, 314*(5802), 1154–1156. https://doi.org/10.1126/science.1132491

Whillans, A. V., Weidman, A. C., & Dunn, E. W. (2016). Valuing time over money is associated with greater happiness. *Social Psychological & Personality Science, 7*(3), 213–222. https://doi.org/10.1177/1948550615623842

Wilcox, K., Laran, J., Stephen, A. T., & Zubcsek, P. P. (2016). How being busy can increase motivation and reduce task completion time. *Journal of Personality and Social Psychology, 110*(3), 371–384. https://doi.org/10.1037/pspa0000045

Williams, P., & Drolet, A. (2005). Age-related differences in responses to emotional advertisements. *Journal of Consumer Research, 32*(3), 343–354. https://doi.org/10.1086/497545

Yan, L. L., Liu, K., Matthews, K. A., Daviglus, M. L., Ferguson, T. F., & Kiefe, C. I. (2003). Psychosocial factors and risk of hypertension: The Coronary Artery Risk Development in Young Adults (CARDIA) study. *Journal of the American Medical Association, 290*(16), 2138–2148. https://doi.org/10.1001/jama.290.16.2138

Young, C., & Lim, C. (2014). Time as a network good: Evidence from unemployment and the standard workweek. *Sociological Science, 1*, 10–27. https://doi.org/10.15195/v1.a2

Young, C., & Melin, J. L. (2019). Time is a network good. *Current Opinion in Psychology, 26*, 23–27. https://doi.org/10.1016/j.copsyc.2018.03.009

Zauberman, G., Kim, B. K., Malkoc, S. A., & Bettman, J. R. (2009). Discounting time and time discounting: Subjective time perception and intertemporal preferences. *Journal of Marketing Research, 46*(4), 543–556. https://doi.org/10.1509/jmkr.46.4.543

Zauberman, G., Levav, J., Diehl, K., & Bhargave, R. (2010). 1995 feels so close yet so far: The effect of event markers on subjective feelings of elapsed time. *Psychological Science, 21*(1), 133–139. https://doi.org/10.1177/0956797609356420

Zauberman, G., & Lynch, J. G., Jr. (2005). Resource slack and propensity to discount delayed investments of time versus money. *Journal of Experimental Psychology: General, 134*(1), 23–37. https://doi.org/10.1037/0096-3445.134.1.23

Zhu, M., Bagchi, R., & Hock, S. J. (2019). The mere deadline effect: Why more time might sabotage goal pursuit. *Journal of Consumer Research, 45*(5), 1068–1084. https://doi.org/10.1093/jcr/ucy030

Zhu, M., Yang, Y., & Hsee, C. K. (2018). The mere urgency effect. *Journal of Consumer Research, 45*(3), 673–690. https://doi.org/10.1093/jcr/ucy008

Zor, O., Kim, K. H., & Monga, A. (2021). *Tweets we like aren't alike: Time of day influences online engagement* [Working paper]. Department of Marketing, Rutgers Business School.

Zuzanek, J. (2004). Work, leisure, time-pressure, and stress. In J. T. Haworth & A. J. Veal (Eds.), *Work and leisure* (pp. 123–144). Routledge.

CHAPTER 18

PSYCHOLOGICAL ASPECTS OF ECONOMIC EXPECTATIONS

Richard Curtin

Everyone forms expectations, from the youngest infants to the oldest adults. *Expectations* are beliefs about the future. Plato cited this definition 2,000 years ago, and to this day it remains the generally accepted meaning of the term. Economics, psychology, political science, and sociology have all used the concept of expectations to explain how people make decisions. Economics holds that rational expectations are required for optimal economic decisions. Psychology is more inclusive, holding that expectations influence how people feel and think as well as behave. Political science holds that expectations shape political orientations and influence voting and policy preferences. Sociology holds that expectations affect a society's culture and shape the dynamics of societal change. Despite the centrality of expectations across all social sciences, there is no scientific consensus on how, why, or when expectations are formed.

The most widely cited theories are the rational expectations hypothesis favored in economics (Muth, 1961) and the bounded rationality hypothesis favored in psychology (H. A. Simon, 1955). Economics assumes full rationality and unbiased expectations, while psychology assumes bounded rationality and biased expectations. The sole focus of the rational expectations hypothesis is on the resulting expectations, leaving the details unspecified about how the expectations were formed. In contrast, the bounded rationality hypothesis is justified by the notion that people can only follow rational procedures in forming expectations, with a resulting bias due to people's failure to fully utilize those rational procedures. The most commonly identified shortfalls were attributed to the use of incomplete information, incorrect interpretations of the data, or an inability to calculate expectations.

The goal of this article is to describe the psychological underpinnings of a new theory of expectations. The new theory represents a significant departure from orthodox views largely due to innovative advances in psychology and neuroscience. At its core, the new theory is based on the evolutionary purpose of expectations: People form expectations as a means to expand the overall capacity of their mental faculties. Expectations are naturally and automatically formed by people about every aspect of their environment. Forming expectations diminishes the burden of consciously processing repetitious information, allowing the conscious mind to more fully focus on new information. While expectations are initially formed by conscious deliberation, people effectively shift the maintenance and updating to the nonconscious mind, which has a capacity for information processing that is orders of magnitude greater than the conscious mind. Although nonconscious processes are unknowable by the conscious mind, the expectation itself can be recalled. When asked to explain their expectations, people usually say it is a guess, hunch, or intuition,

https://doi.org/10.1037/0000262-018
APA Handbook of Consumer Psychology, L. R. Kahle (Editor-in-Chief)
Copyright © 2022 by the American Psychological Association. All rights reserved.

since they cannot recall any details or supporting information that shaped their expectations. Such expectations have been universally discounted by scholars as neither rational nor formed by a rational process.

In addition to the importance of nonconscious cognitive processes, this chapter highlights how accurate economic expectations depend on affective influences, including how affect shapes evaluations, how mood shapes information processing, and how emotions play a positive role in forming expectations when decision risks are unknowable. Social networks also have a crucial influence on the formation of expectations, especially forming expectations about complex events. Rather than advocating for the separation of passion from reason, the new theory holds that passion and reason are required for expectations to maintain a reasonable degree of accuracy. A basic principle of the new theory is that accuracy is fundamental to the evolutionary purpose of expectations.

A new theory of expectations must be justified by adding strength where current theories have weaknesses as well as preserving the strengths of current theories. A long-standing conundrum is the accuracy paradox: Although most consumers report inaccurate knowledge of basic economic statistics about unemployment and inflation, for example, when those answers are aggregated, their expectations prove to be highly accurate predictors of the national trends in those same statistics (Curtin, 2019b). This result has long stifled research on expectations since the results defy common sense. Nonetheless, given its accuracy at the aggregate level, data from the University of Michigan's consumer sentiment surveys have been part of the Index of Leading Indicators for several decades based on their predictive performance. The inflation expectations derived from the surveys have repeatedly been shown to rival the forecasts of professional economists (Curtin, 2010; Gramlich, 1983; Mehra, 2002; Thomas, 1999). This is a challenging finding for conventional theories since professional economists have enormous advantages compared with ordinary consumers—they have easy access to the appropriate information, know how to interpret ongoing trends, and can readily calculate the resulting expectation based on sophisticated econometric programs.

The new theory of expectations was developed using the unique research design of the University of Michigan's consumer sentiment surveys, which I have directed for more than 4 decades. The surveys are unique in that they include a number of open-ended questions that ask respondents to explain in their own words the reasons for holding their expectations. I initially resisted the startling implications of my observations as the explanations offered by respondents were inconsistent with the prevailing theories in economics and psychology. What I learned over the years from a careful review of the data suggested a completely different theory that governs the formation of economic expectations. The new theory can account for the accuracy paradox as well as explain many other anomalies left unexplained by the conventional theories. My book *Consumer Expectations: Micro Foundations and Macro Impact* (Curtin, 2019b) provided a detailed description and rationale for the theory as well as the supporting empirical analyses. While the new theory was developed in the context of economic expectations, the theory is easily generalizable to how people form most expectations used in psychology, political science, and sociology. The main purpose of this chapter is to describe how recent innovations in psychology and neuroscience have enriched our understanding of expectations. Prior to this discussion, the anomalies left unexplained by the current theories are contrasted with the strengths of the new theory, including a brief overview of the key differences from the conventional views of economics and psychology.

ACCURACY PARADOX

Orthodox theories hold that expectations about future trends in income, employment, and inflation are important ingredients for making optimal economic decisions. The conventional approach holds that the task of gathering the required information is impossible for any individual to accomplish. It takes thousands of employees and sophisticated computer programs to estimate the monthly inflation and unemployment rates by the

Bureau of Labor Statistics, a task no single individual could accomplish. For consumers, the burden is easily reduced to a more manageable task by simply accessing the information from federal statistical agencies. Announcements of the latest economic statistics on income, employment, inflation, national economic growth, and the like are widely publicized in the mass media. While some people could avoid hearing these regular announcements, the vast majority of consumers have sufficient exposure to the mass media that it would be difficult to miss these announcements.

Empirical tests of consumers' knowledge of these statistics have revealed surprising and contradictory findings. It has been repeatedly found that, at the micro level, consumers do not possess accurate knowledge of these economic statistics, yet, at the macro level, they accurately predict national trends (Blinder & Krueger, 2004; Curtin, 2008, 2019b). This paradox seemed to support the biased expectations of bounded rationality at the individual level as well as the accuracy of rational expectations at the national level. Both theories cannot be simultaneously correct. Needless to say, psychologists stressed the bias at the individual level and economists stressed the accuracy at the aggregate level. A resolution to this paradox is a basic requirement of any advance in the theory of expectations.

INACCURATE EXPECTATIONS AT INDIVIDUAL LEVEL

A long list of empirical studies has documented widespread ignorance of official economic statistics (Blendon et al., 1997; Blinder & Krueger, 2004; Curtin, 2008). Most of these studies were conducted when good financial times prevailed in the overall economy. I hypothesized that if the economy faced unusual sharp negative changes, the interest of consumers about the performance of the economy on their own personal situations would be much higher, in accordance with the greater weight given to negative news championed by Kahneman and Tversky (1979). Consumers' knowledge was assessed in 2009, at the peak of the Great Recession, a time when the importance of negative changes in economic statistics could be assumed to be at a maximum. My assumption about the importance of economic news was widely supported. Indeed, news about economic conditions dominated the media to a greater extent than in many prior decades, and consumers reported their intense interest in knowing as much as possible about evolving economic conditions (PEW Research Center, 2009).

Much to my surprise, consumers' knowledge of official economic statistics at the height of the Great Recession differed only marginally from an earlier study, conducted in the 2007, when the economy was near its expansion peak (Curtin, 2008). In both 2007 and 2009, the questions were identical, as was the coding of responses, and both surveys were based on representative national sample designs. About half of all respondents said they knew the unemployment rate in both 2007 and 2009, and just one in four reported that they knew the latest data on the inflation rate and gross domestic product (GDP) growth rate (Curtin, 2019b). Among those respondents who claimed knowledge, the surprising finding was that the 2009 data showed even larger percentage point errors from the official data than in 2007! Moreover, about one third of all consumers claimed to have never heard of the consumer price index (CPI) or the GDP.

How could such widespread ignorance exist on these crucial economic performance measures? My research turned toward documenting the critical assumption that the relevant economic statistics were widely available in the mass media. To determine whether the mass media reported the quantitative statistics, I undertook a careful analysis of media reports from January 2006 to April 2007 and from January 2008 to April 2009. The goal was to determine whether the economic statistics were cited in a numerical format. Qualitative reports, such as "unemployment rose sharply," "consumer prices fell," and so forth, were ignored. The media sample included the top five TV networks and the top 22 newspapers in terms of circulation. All had digital records of their broadcasts or published news articles. Each was searched for quantitative reports on the unemployment rate, the CPI, and the growth rate in the national economy.

Quantitative figures for the unemployment rate were reported by six in 10 TV networks, the CPI by one in three networks, and numerical figures for GDP at about half the time. More importantly, there were only small and insignificant differences from 2007 to 2009. The same dismal coverage of quantitative economic statistics was found across the 22 newspapers. Just one newspaper published all of the economic statistics in quantitative form: the *Washington Post*, although the *Wall Street Journal* and the *New York Times* came close. The Associated Press and United Press International wire services included the numeric data for every release. Since most networks and newspapers receive the wire service releases, this likely indicates that many made deliberate decisions to not report quantitative figures. Internet access of government sites to obtain the latest data had at most 23,000 worldwide users during that time period, a fraction of network viewers and newspaper readers.

The clear preference of the mass media was to summarize the economic statistic in qualitative terms, and it was usually accompanied by information about how it had affected people. The preference of the media was to use visual data to best communicate the story. The emphasis was shifted to facial expressions and body language. This form of emotional or noncognitive communication has long evolutionary roots, much longer than spoken language. Moreover, neuroscientists have documented that people have a special ability to understand facial and bodily expressions as though they had personally experienced that same event (Rizzolatti & Craighero, 2004). Mirror neurons play a significant role in the social communication of expectations, which is discussed later. It should not be surprising that the media implicitly understood the impact of pictures and video as a means to more effectively communicate to their audience.

The finding that most individuals possess little or no knowledge of economic statistics is hardly new. What is new is that the mass media has been found to largely omit numerical estimates in their coverage of official economic statistics. This omission makes the lack of detailed knowledge about these key economic statistics less surprising. While this may explain half of the accuracy paradox, it does not explain why consumer expectations are accurate when aggregated. It is this issue that is next explored.

ACCURATE TIME SERIES PREDICTIONS

Economic theory holds that people should form expectations about future events that could have an impact on their own economic situation. There is nothing in economic theory that suggests consumers should form expectations about events that would have no impact, or a very minimal impact, on their own economic situation. While expectations regarding inflation and employment are clearly relevant to most consumers, it is not the national inflation or employment rate that is most relevant. It is the prices and employment opportunities that they personally face in the marketplace that are critical to their economic decisions. For example, it is well known that employment prospects differ by skills and experience as well as by education, age, and geographic locations. Conventional theories, however, test the accuracy of people's expectations by a comparison with the national average published by the Bureau of Labor Statistics. Why would a consumer form unemployment expectations that conform to the national average when their own situation differed from the average? Presumably, if everyone used the national average as a reference, most would find their expectations to provide misleading information for the own decisions by being too high or too low.

The use of national averages as the default assumption has been justified by a variety of arguments. Some admit the inappropriateness of the national data but assume that consumers would then adjust the data from that starting point to match their own situations. It makes no sense, however, that people would double their workload by first forming expectations of the national rate and then obtaining the needed information to estimate the economic conditions they actually face. These unrealistic assumptions were deftly sidestepped by the more common adoption of "representative agent" models. Under the assumption of a single representative agent, that agent naturally faces the economy-wide average. This line of reasoning acted to neutralize the more plausible assumption that people form expectations based on the economic conditions they personally face. More importantly, this assumption avoids the obvious implication that context counts when forming expectations. The context in which prices are observed, for example, has a crucial implication on how it influences inflation expectations.

The straightforward implication is that the accuracy paradox is due to the use of a single national comparative standard. If comparison standards were sensitive to differences in the economic situations faced by consumers, accuracy at the individual level would increase. Some consumers face significantly less or more favorable job prospects, just as some face higher or lower gains in prices. There is no justification in denying the heterogeneity of expectations across consumers. To be sure, as a practical matter, the multiplicity of accuracy standards makes the analysis at the individual level much more difficult to evaluate.

That same inability to assess accuracy disappears at the aggregate level. If each consumer in a representative national sample accurately reported the rate that they actually faced, an aggregation of those individual expectations should converge to the national data, with unusually high and low expectations having a similar offsetting effect as unusually high and low price changes that are averaged into the official CPI. This equivalence would hold under the rational expectations hypothesis but not under the bounded rationality hypothesis. The bounded rationality hypothesis holds that expectations are likely to be biased, and, as a result, differences across the population would not be expected to offset and thus converge to the national data.

Despite the consensus that forming expectations depends on cognitive ability, empirical tests of differences in people's cognitive abilities are hard to operationalize in population surveys. The best proxy that is commonly available is based on amount of formal education. Presumably under the bounded rationality hypothesis, consumers with less than a high school degree would form expectations that showed significantly more bias than the expectations of consumers with a graduate school degree.

Surprisingly, the most rigorous empirical test of the bias due to cognitive bounds is by estimating the rational expectation hypothesis. Quarterly observations from the University of Michigan surveys on inflation expectations over the period from 1978 to 2005 were used for this test (Curtin, 2010). Separate regressions were performed for five education subgroups as well as for the entire sample. The statistical tests for the rational expectations hypothesis are quite strict, requiring a zero constant term and an estimated parameter of 1.0 on the inflation expectation in regressions predicting the official CPI published by the federal statistical agency. Significance tests were used for the individual parameters as well as the joint hypothesis that the constant was zero and the estimated parameter equaled one. If any one of these tests failed, the rational expectations hypothesis would be rejected, giving credence to the impact of bounds on people's rationality. The results, across every education subgroup, were that in no regression were the constant terms significantly different from zero and the parameter on expected inflation significantly different from one. The degree of explained variance, however, did increase from 0.80 for the lowest educated to 0.88 for the highest educated. The results hardly support the notion that variations in the cognitive abilities of individuals have a significant impact on their inflation expectations, a critical assumption of the bounded rationality hypothesis.

This may have been an exceptional example. Other tests were performed to examine whether differences in education are related to the accuracy of unemployment expectations. These tests were conducted across 15 countries, including 14 European countries along with the United States (Curtin, 2019b). While not every country showed a significant association with expectations predicting the actual change in unemployment, the tests showed an overwhelming confirmation that education as a measure of cognition did not relate to differences in the accuracy of the prediction. Of the 15 countries, in 11 countries the lowest educated subgroup significantly predicted subsequent changes in the national unemployment rate, compared with 12 countries with accurate predictions by the highest educated subgroup. These results also go against the notion that differences in conscious cognitive abilities cause biased expectations.

The clear finding is that individual differences from national averages did not diminish the accuracy of the aggregate predictions. Expectations are formed on the basis of personally relevant data, and despite this heterogeneity across the population, the aggregate data accurately forecast national trends. While the recognition of personally tailored expectations may seem like a minor innovation, it resolves the accuracy paradox in a manner that completely transforms the theory of why, how, and when expectations are formed.

A more detailed discussion of cognitive abilities, both conscious and nonconscious, is the subject of subsequent sections. This review highlights the evolutionarily older and more developed nonconscious cognitive abilities in comparison with the relatively recent addition of the prefrontal cortex, responsible for conscious cognitive deliberation. Before turning to an examination of the psychological assumptions that are central to this new theory, the impact from the shift toward personally relevant economic expectations on the conventional theories is briefly discussed.

SIMILARITIES OF FEDERAL DATA AND TAILORED EXPECTATIONS

An examination of official data on the national unemployment rate in greater detail provides a straightforward reconciliation of the differences and commonalities suggested by the new theory of tailored expectations. Table 18.1 shows the mean unemployment rates during the past quarter century by age and education subgroups. Orthodox theories suggest that people should target the overall mean unemployment rate, which averaged 5.8% from 1992 to 2019. The average unemployment rates by age and education differed substantially and persistently over this time period. Indeed, it was more than twice as high for the youngest or the least educated than for the oldest workers and the most educated. It would be highly irrational for anyone to use the overall average unless their subgroup average differed insignificantly from the overall mean. Note, however, that the correlations among age and education subgroups were uniformly quite high, ranging from 0.92 to 0.98, meaning that most groups move in a parallel fashion over economic cycles. This implies that, despite the large differences across the population in their personal experiences, the aggregate time-series coherence remained quite high.

Not surprisingly, that same pattern has been displayed by the economic expectations collected by the University of Michigan surveys (see Table 18.2). The Sentiment Index shows consistent difference in mean levels across income, age, and education subgroups and consistently high correlations. The data suggest a straightforward reconciliation to the accuracy paradox: Inaccuracies at the individual level were due to using an incorrect standard to assess accuracy, and the accuracy at the aggregate level was aided by the high correlations over time.

TABLE 18.1

Unemployment Rates

Age	Mean	Correlations				Education	Mean	Correlations		
		20–24	25–34	35–44	45–54			Less than high school	High school	Some college
20–24	9.8					Less than high school	8.9			
25–34	5.9	0.97				High school	5.6	0.95		
35–44	4.6	0.97	0.98			Some college	4.6	0.94	0.98	
45–54	4.1	0.97	0.98	0.98		College degree	2.7	0.92	0.97	0.97
55+	4.0	0.96	0.98	0.97	0.98					

Note. Data from the U.S. the Bureau of Labor Statistics (2019).

TAILORED EXPECTATIONS: A NEW THEORY

The most important changes to the traditional procedures involve how expectations are defined, how their accuracy is judged, and how the formation costs and benefits are calculated. The shift from national data to data tailored to someone's own situation is hardly revolutionary, since it is consistent with orthodox theory. For example, consumers would be motivated to incorporate expected changes in mortgage rates, home values, and their future income when making a decision to purchase a home. Consumers would form their expectations based on the prices for houses they would consider purchasing, on mortgage rates on loans they could obtain, and on wages and employment conditions that match their skills. The use of the national standard for accuracy allowed many prior studies to incorrectly conclude that consumers are largely uninformed about a wide range of economic statistics. Actual trends in economic conditions vary considerably across populations and locations, even within states or cities. While it would be impossible for individuals to replicate the capacity of federal agencies, people do not need national data to make optimal decisions.

The conventional justification for focusing on the national data collected by federal agencies implies that before the existence of these agencies, people were unable to form accurate economic expectations. It is argued that the expectations they held prior to the establishment of these agencies must have exhibited large errors and caused nonoptimal decisions. However, the statistical agencies were created only recently: The CPI was created in 1917, the national economic accounts came into existence in the 1930s, and data on the labor force were first gathered in the early 1940s. Despite the late arrival of these "official" estimates, expectations have been essential components of economic decisions since the dawn of civilization. Indeed, economic expectations played a similar role in decisions about barter and trade thousands of years ago

TABLE 18.2

Index of Consumer Sentiment Among Subgroups*

	Education of householder				
	Less than high school	High school	Some college	College degree	Graduate studies
Means	74.5	83.3	87.9	92.7	91.5
(Standard error)	(0.82)	(0.99)	(1.01)	(1.00)	(1.04)
Correlations	0.892	0.952	0.952	0.958	0.929
	Age of householder				
	18–34	35–44	45–54	55–64	65+
Means	95.6	89.2	84.8	81.6	77.0
(Standard error)	(0.95)	(1.03)	(1.03)	(0.96)	(0.84)
Correlations	0.943	0.960	0.973	0.958	0.938
	Household income quintiles				
	Bottom fifth	Second fifth	Middle fifth	Fourth fifth	Top fifth
Means	75.7	83.3	88.4	91.7	96.5
(Standard error)	(0.81)	(0.96)	(1.05)	(1.07)	(1.10)
Correlations	0.931	0.967	0.981	0.979	0.954

Note. Data from the University of Michigan (2019).
*Correlations are between subgroup and all other subgroups.

and were widely recognized in the writing of Plato and other ancient chroniclers. What conventional theory has vastly underestimated is the ability of consumers to acquire information and form expectations based on their own circumstances, without the aid of federal statistical agencies. Note that this recognition does not diminish the importance of the tasks performed by these agencies; it only correctly recognizes that national data cannot answer all of the relevant needs faced by individual consumers.

Another implication of the new theory involves how costs and benefits shape the formation of expectations. The costs of forming expectations are usually ignored in orthodox theories, or they are simply assumed to be much less than the benefits of accurate expectations. This likely reflects the assumption that the costs of mental calculations are trivial. However, the sheer number of expectations formed by consumers means that opportunity costs of forming a specific expectation are not trivial. Humans do not have an unlimited ability for conscious cognitive deliberation. This constraint alone would mean that people could only form a very limited number of expectations. Fortunately, as detailed later, most expectations are automatically maintained by a person's much larger capacity for nonconscious information processing and learning.

More importantly, formation costs vary based on the degree of accuracy required. The typical assumption in economics is that the full array of economic statistics is updated or revised with each new data release by the federal agencies. Each updated expectation can then be recalled when required by a decision. The implicit assumption is that this process is similar to an insurance model: People undergo the cost of forming or revising an expectation to avoid greater costs when a decision arises that would benefit from using that expectation.

The new theory of expectations is driven by a revised cost–benefit comparison. The benefit is not equivalent to the degree the expectation matched the national data, as is currently done. Rather, the benefit is calculated from the net improvement in the outcome of the decision due to the use of the expectation. The benefit of expectations is derived from its impact on the decision, not on how accurately it reflects the national data. Some decisions are dependent on very accurate expectations, and other decisions require only ballpark estimates. The benefit then determines an upper limit on the costs people are willing to incur to form the expectation.

Orthodox theories hold that economic expectations are revised on a regular basis determined by the releases of new or revised data by federal statistical agencies. The conventional view is that news of these releases sparks revisions. Unfortunately, it has already been shown that the mass media do not generally include numerical estimates for these statistics. In the new theory, revisions do not depend on information provided by the mass media but are revised in an ongoing process that depends on people's own experiences and information gained from family, friends, and others in their social networks. In the new theory, revisions are not limited to once a month or quarter; they occur continually along with ongoing experiences in people's daily lives.

Conventional theories hold that expectations should be context independent, meaning that the expectation is invariant to the context in which it was elicited. Indeed, a bedrock principle of orthodox theory is that rational expectations are context independent. Context independence matches the assumption that national data uniquely define the economic statistic and represent the sole goal of the formation process. In contrast, the new theory holds that expectations are context sensitive. Numerous studies have shown that the context in which the expectation is elicited has a significant impact on its outcome. For example, countless studies have shown that expectations differ depending on whether a positive or negative context is used (Kahneman, 2011). Rather than an anomaly, most expectations are formed for a given purpose, within a given context, for a specific consumer. Context sensitivity does not represent a departure from rationality but rather an aid to crafting the right expectation for a given situation.

At this point readers may think the new theory of the formation of expectations is an even more daunting task than forming expectations according to the traditional theories. This brief description involves a considerable enlargement of the tasks required to form expectations. Expectations need to be tailored to people's situations, their accuracy must be judged by the benefits derived from improved decisions, and formation costs need to be calculated based on the decision context. The solution is surprisingly simple, once the constraints on conscious cognitive deliberation are lessened. The answer involves the fundamental purpose of expectation, which is quite different from its role in providing the likelihood that some event will occur.

EVOLUTIONARY PURPOSE OF EXPECTATIONS

Most social science disciplines limit their interest in expectations to their proximate benefit, that is, how expectations can provide an enhanced understanding of a decision or a more accurate forecast of some behavior. Each discipline proposed a unique process for forming expectations since no general theory exists that applies to the formation of all types of expectations. Some disciplines used very simple procedures; others used very sophisticated procedures. The only common element across all models is the assumed importance of conscious cognitive reasoning. Deliberative decisions require that people first gather the appropriate information, then interpret the underlying trends, and finally perform the necessary calculations to form an expectation. This set of procedures has never been questioned as it represents the basic elements of conscious cognitive deliberation. Everyone was assumed to follow a comparable process, with the result that the cognitive limitations of ordinary consumers frequently resulted in biased expectations.

None of the disciplines have recognized the more fundamental purpose of expectations, which is to maximize the efficiency and effectiveness of people's mental faculties. While expectations do represent the likelihood that some future event will occur, expectations perform a much more fundamental role in expanding the capacity of the human mind. Expectations reduce the need to repeatedly process the same information, allowing people to more fully focus their attention on new information. Information relevant for revising expectations that is not consciously processed is not ignored; it is processed by one's nonconscious cognitive capacity. These nonconscious cognitive processes are routinely responsible for gathering, interpreting, and calculating expectations. The nonconscious also enables humans to learn data patterns and revise expectations. Importantly, these same processes apply equally to the formation of all expectations.

No one needs to be taught how to form expectations. The formation of expectations begins shortly after birth and continues throughout one's life. The range and number of expectations naturally grow along with the diversity of a person's experiences. The fundamental purpose of forming expectations is to maximize the effectiveness and efficiency of their most constrained mental faculty, conscious cognitive deliberation. The capacity of conscious cognitive deliberation is quite limited when compared with nonconscious cognitive resources (Lewicki et al., 1992). Humans can only consciously process a few dozen bits of information per second, compared with just over 11,000,000 bits per second nonconsciously (Dijksterhuis, 2004; Wilson, 2002). Of all cognitive processes performed, it has been estimated that conscious cognition processes account for less than 0.10 of the total, with the vast majority of cognitive processes occurring nonconsciously. People have a natural incentive to maximize the amount of information processed nonconsciously so that they can focus their limited conscious cognitive resources on new information. The new information may be on topics that have no impact on their economic situation but simply represent their recreational interests or even bits of meaningless gossip. Whatever their special interests or how much conscious attention they devote to these other interests, people are still likely to nonconsciously process the relevant information needed to form and revise their economic expectations.

The impact of the bounds on cognition cited by psychologists has been based on conscious cognitive abilities, inexplicitly excluding the much larger capacity of nonconscious cognition. People's cognitive abilities cover all processes by which sensory input is stored, transformed, recovered, and used (Neisser, 1967). There is no justification for excluding nonconscious cognition, even if those processes cannot be consciously retrieved and carefully examined. Perhaps the most significant failure of conventional theories of expectations is the omission of the important role of nonconscious cognitive processing and learning.

Despite the dominance of the nonconscious, there is no denying that conscious cognitive deliberation represents people's most prized mental resource. Making decisions by conscious deliberation allows each element of the decision process to be identified, evaluated, and compared with alternatives. Importantly, decisions by conscious deliberation can utilize deductive logic and causal models, the most esteemed scientific methodology. Conscious decisions can be readily explained to others by citing the details of the calculations, including which data and assumptions were the most crucial in forming the expectation. Expectations formed in this manner represent critical thinking and the scientific method at its best.

There is no reason to doubt that expectations formed consciously represent the ideal methodology, but there are severe limitations to the use of conscious deliberation. Forming expectations by conscious cognitive deliberation is an effortful task. Studies have shown that even after rather minor problem-solving tasks, the effort expended means that some time must pass before the task can be repeated at the same level of performance; other studies have shown that following one effortful task, performance on a second comparable task was significantly diminished (Kahneman, 2011). Moreover, given that people hold numerous expectations, it would be an impossible task to form all expectations by conscious cognitive deliberation. The same time constraints would apply if every expectation formed nonconsciously underwent a conscious review before it was used in a decision (Kahneman, 2011). Without new information, a conscious review of an expectation formed by nonconscious processes is likely to come to the same conclusion, as it would be based on the same information.

A persistent underlying concern is that no one can be sure whether expectations formed nonconsciously were biased by nonrational factors such as emotions. That concern is surely warranted for expectations that have no personal economic consequences, but accurate or inaccurate expectations for future mortgage rates or income prospects can result in notable economic gain or pain. While expectations being rational and unbiased does not mean that they are invariably correct, it does mean that they were formed rationally based on the available information.

Economic expectations have a special advantage since people regularly obtain new information about prices and employment conditions, for example, which serves to test the accuracy of their current expectations. At the other extreme are expectations that offer little or no likelihood that their veracity can be directly observed. More generally, the longer the period between observations, the more persistent the potential bias.

While the initialization of expectations requires conscious cognitive deliberation, once established, the nonconscious mind can automatically revise expectations as new information becomes available. Importantly, the nonconscious mind can decipher underlying patterns and learn how to automatically revise expectations. Although people have no conscious awareness of the nonconscious processes, they instinctively know the outcomes. When asked to justify their expectations, people often describe it as an intuition, a gut feeling, or even a guess. Instead of a feeling or a guess, perhaps the most preferred explanation of nonconscious expectations is to cite some causal reason; these explanations are rightly called rationalizations. Nonetheless, the most important advantage is that expectations are maintained and revised without any drain on conscious cognitive deliberation.

Some scholars have argued that what cannot be observed cannot be part of science (Popper, 2003). Others have noted that the processes included in the "black box" of nonconsciousness can be described from an examination of how inputs are transformed into outputs (Curtin, 2019b). Advances in neuroscience may someday provide a means to verify the work of the nonconscious mind in forming expectations. If one of the primary functions of the human brain is to process information so judgments can be made quickly and effortlessly, it is unjustified to exclude the bulk of cognitive processes that occur nonconsciously.

AUTOMATIC INFORMATION PROCESSING AND LEARNING

Developments in neuroscience have highlighted the central role the neurotransmitter dopamine plays in forming and revising expectations by a nonconscious and automatic process. Of the three dopaminergic pathways that transmit dopamine, the mesolimbic system guides learning and behavior in response to incentives (Di Chiara, 1997). The initial formation of an expectation activates dopamine and relates the expectation to an associated stimulus. Dopamine is then hypothesized to respond to the difference between expectations and actual outcomes, referred to as the prediction error hypothesis. Dopamine reinforces expectations when the outcome is consistent with the prior expectation, and it acts to revise expectations when the outcome is inconsistent. There is no scientific consensus yet on whether dopamine causes changes in expectations or simply reflects changes that occur in other areas of the brain. Regardless of the causal status, the formation and revisions of expectations represent an innate feature of the human mind.

Expectations are formed easily and automatically by everyone at all life stages. Forming expectations is not the difficult computational task envisioned by the rational expectations or the bounded rationality hypotheses. Infants, within months of their birth, begin to form expectations about various features of their environment, reacting with surprise and dismay when what they expect doesn't occur (Onishi & Baillargeon, 2005; Spelke et al., 1992). The same reaction is displayed by adults when what they expect fails to occur. Moreover, given that people form expectations about all aspects of their environment, there is no reason to anticipate that people form expectations by a unique procedure specifically designed for each area.

Greater experience with a certain element of the economic or political environment typically causes people's expectations to become more accurate. This is true regardless of whether the expectation was formed consciously or nonconsciously. The mental ability to process information, interpret that information, and make decisions—the essential elements of cognition—are equivalent whether performed consciously or nonconsciously. A key difference is that conscious processes can employ deductive logic and casual models, but nonconscious processes use correlations and inductive logic. Experts are admired for their accurate intuitive judgments, just as anyone with expertise in any area is noted for the accuracy of their intuitive judgments. Importantly, it is widely understood that experts in one area can still hold quite naive expectations in other areas.

A common objection of economists and psychologists to the use of nonconscious decision making is that, while it is certainly possible for trivial decisions, no life-or-death decision would be made nonconsciously. That view is false. Imagine you are driving, walking, or biking to your to office or any other location you frequently visit. After arriving at work, most people cannot remember all the details of their commute. Most of the decisions are made automatically and nonconsciously. An unexpected event, say a dog running into your path, causes instant conscious awareness. If nothing unexpected occurs, most people would find it difficult to identify all the details of the trip. To be sure, new drivers must pay careful conscious attention to every detail and must place a premium on being free of any other distractions. Experience improves their driving, resulting in making most of the task guided by the nonconscious and allowing the conscious mind to listen and respond to others in the vehicle, listen to talk radio, or enjoy music.

There are numerous other examples. People nonconsciously gather information about inflation in a comparable manner. While grocery shopping, people are mainly concerned with the immediate task of buying groceries, going about filling their baskets with all the items they need. In the process, they are exposed to the prices of every item they select, to which they generally give scant conscious attention. If a price is significantly higher or lower than usual, it causes conscious awareness and prompts a decision of whether to buy more if a price is unusually low or to find an alternative if the price has steeply increased. While no conscious attention is given to most prices, that information is still processed nonconsciously. Alternatively, if you assumed that shoppers processed all prices consciously, it would make grocery shopping a much more time-consuming task. For busy people, that would have a high opportunity cost.

These mental processes require a reasonable degree of accuracy; otherwise expectations would not improve people's decisions, which is the raison d'être of expectations. It has been long known that people can learn about their environment nonconsciously. Nonconscious learning is done using frequencies, associations, and inductive reasoning. In contrast, conscious learning is capable of deductive reasoning and causal analysis, and it allows the critical inspection of every factor that was responsible for the outcome. While causal analysis is the traditionally prized scientific method, recent developments in econometrics have favored models that rely solely on correlations, a procedure psychologists have long recognized as factor models (Sargent & Sims, 1977; Stock & Watson, 2002).

NONCONSCIOUS LEARNING

More than a half century ago, Reber (1967) published a review article about people's nonconscious ability to learn, sometimes called implicit learning. The most common of these initial experiments involved artificial grammar. People demonstrated the ability to use the artificial grammar correctly but could not verbally describe the rules. This nonconscious knowledge was shown to persist over a 2-year period at a statistically significantly level (Allen & Reber, 1980). Other experiments on the nonconscious detection of covariations found that the subject could gain knowledge of how events covaried without any explicit conscious knowledge (see Lewicki, 1986, for a review). Other experiments involved "sugar factories" whose output subjects could control by varying a range of inputs. Subjects learned how to maximize outputs but had no conscious knowledge of the operating rules (Berry & Broadbent, 1988). Other experiments have involved how people nonconsciously balance risks and rewards (Bechara et al., 1997). Overall, this ability to learn nonconsciously is a key element in promoting adaptive behavior (Damasio, 1994).

Economic expectations inevitably involve numeric quantities. So it is reasonable to determine the level of mathematical ability that is required to form economic expectations. Bounded rationality is typically justified by the claim that many consumers cannot perform the necessary mathematical calculations to form unbiased expectations. The required mathematical ability, however, does not limit the formation of expectations to the conscious mind. People naturally display a very basic knowledge of numbers soon after birth in every culture. The development of a core number sense occurs before people are able to understand verbal language (Dehaene, 1997). Infants are able to perform basic arithmetic operations even before they can talk (T. J. Simon et al., 1995; Starkey et al., 1990). Soon after birth, infants display an inherent numeric sense, ranging from 0 to 3. At the age of 6 months, infants can perform basic operations like addition and subtraction. Although people have inherent knowledge of small numbers, they may be hopelessly at sea in the millions, billions, and trillions of economic statistics.

A second inherent faculty that deals with large numbers has been called the "mental number line" (Dehaene, 1997). Unlike the limited but exact quantities for small numbers, the mental number line is based on approximate magnitudes. The mental number line represents the meaning of numbers. Economists have often fretted about inconsistencies in how people react to large numbers; the mental number line ignores marginal differences, with the size of the "just noticeable" difference rising along with the size of the numbers involved. Weber's law, proposed by E. H. Weber, a founder of experimental psychology, proposed that as quantities increase, their meaning is interpreted logarithmically (Dehaene, 2003). Logarithmic scales are used to measure differences in brightness and sound, just as the meaning of very large economic quantities such as GDP are understood when transformed logarithmically and expressed as percentages. There are limitations to this inherent numerical capacity. Negative numbers, fractions, square roots, and many other mathematical operations are generally excluded from nonconscious cognitive processes.

Perhaps the basic problem with relying on knowledge generated by the nonconscious is that it represents what is widely considered among scholars to be a second class methodology. Indeed, deductive methodology and causal models are also preferred by consumers, as demonstrated by their willingness to claim such reasoning when asked to explain their economic expectations. Scholars, like most people, have been trained to be skeptical of expectations formed by accumulating frequencies and forming associations across events. That the conscious and nonconscious mind use different standards is not a deficit but an advantage. This advantage has now been recognized by advocates of big data who base their predictions not on the deductive logic of causal models but directly on predictions based on associations. Presumably, sometime in the future, scientists will determine how to reconcile these two distinct methodologies to best serve scientific advancement.

AFFECTIVE INFLUENCES ON EXPECTATIONS

Unlike traditional economic and psychological theories that hold that reason must be isolated from passion to produce unbiased expectations, affective influences and social networking act to create more accurate expectations (Curtin, 2019b). The negative impacts of emotions and social pressures have been long cited over thousands of years as the main causes of biased expectations. While this negative potential is not denied, these same factors are critical to form accurate and timely expectations. Moreover, chronically inaccurate expectations about important economic conditions faced by people would defeat the very evolutionary purpose of forming expectations.

When hearing personally relevant economic information, no consumer can process that information in an emotionally detached manner. Since the revised theory only applies to forming expectations about personally relevant information, it implies that the impact of affective states on expectations is pervasive. Economics postulated that when information is conflated with emotion, people must exert the necessary willpower to separate their own emotions from how they evaluate the economic conditions they face (see Chaiken & Trope, 1999, for an overview of dual process models). Without this separation, it was argued, expectations would be biased and lead to inferior decisions. While the necessity of dividing passion from reason has long been stressed, it turns out to be incorrect advice. Damasio (1994) found that reason and passion were both necessary elements to make rational decisions. The sole reliance on reason was what he called "Descartes' error." Without affective considerations, people cannot choose; the absence of critical information about people's preferences, including their likes and dislikes, are needed for making decisions. It should be no surprise that evolution has never acted to reduce the impact of people's affective systems as a source of rational decision making. Indeed, the impact of affective states on the formation of economic expectations is as pervasive as ever.

The most important affective states on the formation of expectations can be summarized under the headings of evaluations, moods, and emotions. Each has a significant influence on the formation of expectations in terms of how information is processed. Evaluations represent judgments about specific pieces of economic information; mood is a more general affective state, which lacks a single identifiable cause and acts as a persistent nonconscious evaluation of the environment; emotions are the most intense, arise quickly, are generally brief, and have an identifiable referent (Curtin, 2019b).

It is of some importance to note that affective states operate independently from the cognitive capacities of people. The three main components of the human brain are the brain stem and cerebellum, which regulate core bodily functions; the limbic system, which is responsible for emotion, memory, and learning; and finally the neocortex, which is responsible for higher order brain functions such as conscious rational deliberation (Massey, 2002). The frontal neocortex first developed about 150,000 years ago, whereas the brain stem, cerebellum, and limbic system evolved over millions of years. Each operates independently, and neither the limbic nor the prefrontal cortex replaced prior brain functions. The limbic system is sometimes called the "emotional brain," just as the prefrontal cortex could be referred to as the "rational brain."

There are several important characteristics of mental functioning that apply to the formation of expectations. Given the more recent development of the prefrontal cortex, there are much larger differences across people in their conscious cognitive capacities than in their emotional capacities. This benefit is due to the evolution of the limbic system over millions of years, making the nonconscious processes attributable to the limbic system more equal across populations. Indeed, emotional communication through facial and bodily expression is nearly universally understood across all cultures (Darwin, 1872). Importantly, emotional communication accounts for a good deal of the information about economic developments and is the favored communication mode of the mass media.

Another important characteristic is that the limbic system can process information much faster than the prefrontal neocortex (Curtin, 2019a). This speed advantage is well documented, as people's behavioral reactions to events begin to occur milliseconds before they become consciously aware of the situation. The superior speed in initiating behavioral responses, however, is not the most important aspect for forming expectations. Any personally relevant information perceived by the conscious mind is typically accompanied by an evaluation generated by the limbic system (Zajonc, 1984). This is the exact opposite of conventional wisdom, which dictates that evaluations are based on a conscious review of the facts. To be sure, conscious reviews can reverse automatic evaluations, although such prior evaluations by the limbic system are usually based on the same personally relevant information that would be used in conscious evaluations.

Mood influences how information is processed, regardless of whether it is done consciously or nonconsciously. Mood connotes a general affective state that cannot be attributed to any single discernible cause (Curtin, 2019b). Consumer confidence is often associated with the mood of the consumer, ranging from pessimism to optimism. When consumers are pessimistic, new information about economic conditions is more likely to be processed consciously; a pessimistic mood indicates that current economic events are troubling, and the new information thus warrants conscious processing, negative information most of all. An optimistic mood, in contrast, typically promotes nonconscious information processing, even of contrary negative information. Importantly, negative events are not ignored when an optimistic mood prevails, as that information is still processed nonconsciously.

The dynamics of the repeated cycles in consumer confidence over the past half century reflect the impact of shifting consumer moods (Curtin, 2019a). Optimistic consumers increasingly shift to nonconscious information processing of economic events, and pessimistic consumers shift toward conscious processing of economic information. As a result, the reliance on conscious and nonconscious information processing shifts along cyclical upturns and downturns. The cumulative increase in optimism due to long economic expansions not only promotes nonconscious processing but also acts to discount contrary information. During such times, consumers are often described as resilient, with the upward momentum making them rather impervious to negative news. On rare occasions, an extended economic boom can promote an "irrational exuberance" among consumers, who then ignore negative economic information to their detriment. Similarly, an exclusive focus on negative economic events can reinforce pessimism and effectively lengthen and deepen a recession. Although the potential for these extreme reactions has always existed, they are too infrequent for a rigorous empirical assessment based only on survey evidence.

Traditional theories hold that of all affective states, emotion is the main source of biased expectations. It is true that emotion can produce irrational expectations, although the blanket condemnation of emotions is unwarranted. Orthodox economic theory holds that when risks are unquantifiable, no rational action is possible. "Animal spirits" was the term used by John Maynard Keynes to describe people's ability to make decisions based on ambiguous information (Keynes, 1936). In such situations, emotions can effectively replace the cognitive faculties normally used to make decisions; these emotional resources are still referred to as animal spirits in the economics literature. Consumers regularly use their emotional resources to form expectations around turning points in economic cycles. Despite the predominance of favorable economic information at cyclical peaks, or the dominance of negative information at troughs, consumers' emotional faculties produce shifts in expectations that occur prior to the actual changes in the economy and thus act as a leading economic indicator (see Figure 18.1). These turning points in expectations occur in the absence of traditional rational assessments of current economic information and have proved to be remarkably accurate predictors of subsequent trends in GDP.

IMPACT OF SOCIAL NETWORKING ON EXPECTATIONS

Humans are fundamentally social creatures. Unlike economics, which often assumes people act independently, psychology has always assumed that social influences have a significant impact on how people form their expectations. Indeed, many voluntary and involuntary communications among people are mainly accomplished by emotional displays (Curtin, 2019b). Emotional expressions evolved over a much longer evolutionary period compared with written or spoken language. Facial and bodily expressions are comprehensible on a universal level and effectively dominate human communication. Research has shown that mirror neurons provide people with a special ability to understand and empathize with others. Mirror neurons respond in a nearly identical fashion whether the event is personally experienced or experienced by someone else (Rizzolatti & Craighero, 2004). This unique ability has a pervasive impact on the formation of expectations, but it is widely ignored by orthodox theories.

People understand that their economic situations are inextricably linked to the actions of others. Most people realize that the economic experiences of other people in their social networks may mirror changes in their own economic situation. Most people rely on members of their social networks to serve as good proxies for how their own economic situation may change. Moreover, empirical research has shown that social networks are more capable than individuals acting alone when solving complex problems (Hinsz et al., 1997).

Perhaps the most important aspect of social influences on trends in the macro economy is self-fulfilling economic expectations. Economics now accepts the notion that under certain circumstances, an "inflationary psychology" can itself cause higher inflation, and a "deflationary psychology" can itself cause falling prices. Monetary policies have directly and successfully focused on these

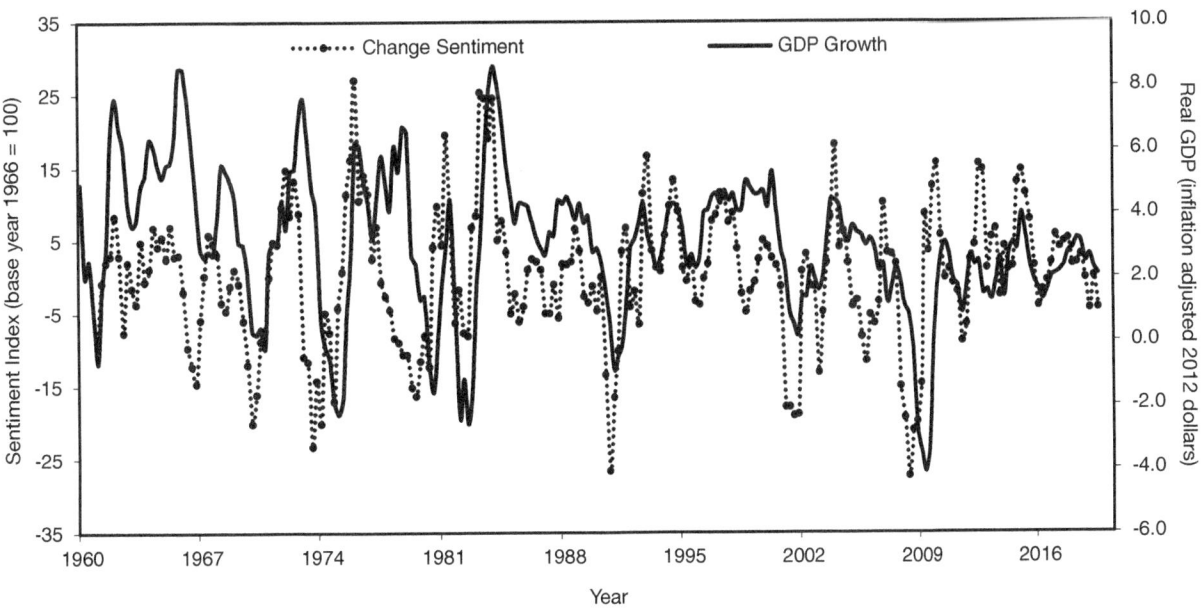

FIGURE 18.1. Annual change in consumer sentiment and annual growth in gross domestic product (GDP). Data from U.S. Bureau of Economic Analysis (2019) and the University of Michigan (2019).

threats in the past century. Self-fulfilling expectations have a much broader impact on the macro economy, which is much more common than inflationary and deflationary trends. Upturns as well as downturns in consumer sentiment are driven, to some extent, by social forces that provoke cascading optimism or pessimism across the entire population (Curtin, 2019b).

THE CONSTRUCTION OF EXPECTATIONS: SUMMARY

The primary function of expectations is to improve the efficiency and effectiveness of the human mind in the acquisition and interpretations of information. Humans have a limited capacity for conscious cognitive deliberation and a much larger capacity for nonconscious information processing and learning. The greater the share of information that can be automatically processed by the nonconscious mind, the greater the potential benefits from the use of their most constrained and prized resource, conscious cognitive deliberation. This represents the essential evolutionary purpose of expectations.

Forming expectations is an innate and automatic process. People start forming expectations soon after birth and continue to form expectations about every facet of their environment as they age. People use all of their mental faculties to form expectations, making it difficult to assign exclusive claims to conscious or nonconscious processes. The vast number of expectations formed makes it very likely that most expectations are formed by nonconscious information processing and learning. Orthodox theories of expectations that focus exclusively on conscious deliberation provide a misleading account of how expectations are formed.

All mental faculties can form accurate expectations, whether conscious or nonconscious, cognitive or affective. To be sure, each of these resources can produce biased expectations, and each expectation is subject to revision when it proves to be an inaccurate guide for decisions. The correction process occurs automatically, as it is essential for human adaptation. If it did not occur automatically, then revising economic expectations would require resources from the more limited conscious cognitive deliberation. This would defeat the evolutionary rationale for expectations. Biased economic expectations could only persist unchanged if they were never confronted with actual developments, but such purposeless expectations are unlikely to be formed since they fail to meet the basic evolutionary purpose of expectations. Such expectations are more accurately called beliefs, as they are disassociated with actual developments in the economy.

A core economic principle is that the costs of forming economic expectations must be no greater than the derived benefits. Conventional theories only partially recognize the costs of forming expectations, mainly the costs of obtaining the latest economic information. The costs of mental calculations are typically ignored. Orthodox economic theories also ignore the opportunity costs of mental calculations, apparently in the misguided belief that people's conscious capacity is sufficient to handle all potential uses. Costs are minimized when the revisions of expectations are performed by nonconscious cognitive resources. It is certainly true that some expectations formed nonconsciously could not instantly reflect sudden changes in the economic environment and therefore may need conscious attention. The implied shift to conscious cognitive processes, however, comes at a higher cost, and the benefits must be correspondingly higher.

A significant departure from orthodox theories is that the benefits of expectations are not limited to how accurately they mirror the actual economic statistics. Expectations are instrumental; they are judged by how they enhance decisions. Benefits are derived from the potential added gains from the decision for which the expectation was used. To be sure, some decisions are critically dependent on accurate economic expectations. Most decisions do not demand expectations to be accurate to the decimal point, and many decisions may only require that the expected direction of change is correct.

Expectations are context dependent; they are formed for specific decisions in a given context. The estimates of the costs and benefits are also tailored to an individual's situation and decision needs. Context dependence is not a source of bias; it simply recognizes that the context is important to the interpretation of information for a given decision. The human mind is naturally and automatically context sensitive; otherwise people's reactions would be maladaptive.

Expectations reflect cognitive as well as affective components of people's mental faculties. Affective states influence changes in forming and revising economic expectations in a variety of ways. The main areas involve evaluations, mood, and emotions. All perceptions of personally relevant economic events are automatically accompanied by an evaluation of that information. The data on brain dynamics indicate that actions are often initiated fractions of a second before conscious awareness and that people's conscious awareness is automatically accompanied by an evaluation (Bargh & Chartrand, 1999).

Moods affect how information is processed, and shifts in mood result in cyclical increases as well as declines in economic expectations. People cannot intentionally choose their mood; it represents the impact of personally relevant economic events. Optimism is associated with nonconscious processing, and pessimism with conscious information processing. A sustained optimistic mood produces a resilience that allows people to ignore contrary information, while sustained pessimism produces uncertainty and fear that focuses conscious attention on even trivial negative developments.

Emotions motivate consumers to achieve their goals. Perhaps the most significant role of emotions occurs when decision risks are unknowable. In the presence of ambiguous information about risks, no rational decision is possible. In these situations, orthodox theory provides consumers with an unrealistic recommendation: Take no action until risks are calculable. Humans have a long history of taking action without hesitation, from how their ancestors reacted to threats on the African savanna to how they now react to economic threats in the modern economy. Emotions serve the same essential function as cognition during times when risks are unknowable.

Economic expectations are inherently social. Although economists prefer the disembodied notion of markets, consumers naturally frame issues in terms of the actions and reactions of people. Information gains from social networks are an important factor in shaping consumers' expectations. Evolutionary development has enabled a potent source of communication by emotional expressions. People have an ability to understand the facial and body language of others as if they were personally having the same experiences via mirror neurons (Rizzolatti & Craighero, 2004; Ross & Dumouchel, 2004). This allows an expectation to be spread much faster across the population, especially when it portends an economic threat.

IMPLICATIONS FOR ORTHODOX THEORIES

The new theory of expectations shares a number of commonalities with the older orthodox views. The most significant is that accuracy is the goal of forming and revising expectations. Rather than a departure from rationality, the new theory offers a compelling alternate rationale for maintaining accurate economic expectations. The fundamental evolutionary rationale for expectations is that they provide humans with the ability to use all their mental faculties more efficiently and more effectively. Mental faculties evolved over past millennia to enable humans to make decisions more rapidly and more accurately. Each addition to their mental faculties provided distinct advantages; none replaced prior mental functions, as each represented a unique resource to enhance the capacity of humans to make decisions. Evolution did not favor passion as a foil to reason but favored passion as a necessary component of rational decisions, helping to align motivations, social communications, and behavioral reactions. The growth in the cognitive capacity of humans enabled them to gather evidence, interpret and learn from the evidence, and modify expectations. Importantly, their cognitive skills reflect conscious and nonconscious processes as well as reason and passion. While every element of our mental faculties helps to form and maintain expectations, the major task of maintaining the accuracy of expectations is mostly accomplished by the nonconscious. The nonconscious excels at processing, accumulating, and learning from the many bits and pieces of personally relevant economic data people encounter in their daily lives. This allows the mind to more fully concentrate its most valuable and limited ability for conscious cognitive deliberation on new information and unexpected developments.

The emphasis on nonconscious cognitive processes stands in sharp contrast to the psychologist's emphasis on the bounds of people's conscious cognitive abilities. An enlargement of cognition to include nonconscious cognitive abilities cannot fully revive the older theories, however. Nonconscious cognitive abilities are more equally shared across the population due to their much longer evolutionary development. Moreover, the primary evidence to support the importance of cognitive bounds was the finding of biased economic expectations. The presumed bias has been shown to be due to incorrectly using national data as the comparison standard rather than the conditions that consumers actually face in the marketplace. In contrast, when the data were analyzed in time-series models, consumers' inflation expectations formed accurate predictors among the lowest as well as the highest educated respondents. The same pattern was found for unemployment expectations that were examined in more than a dozen countries: The predictive accuracy of expectations among those with the lowest education matched that of those with the highest education.

There is no sense in denying that the expectations of any given individual cannot be unduly influenced by passion rather than reason. This is much less likely to occur if restricted to personally relevant economic expectations. Under the new theory, people acquire economic information naturally in their daily lives and the nonconscious automatically incorporates the information, establishes patterns, and learns how to modify expectations.

It is not surprising that the new theory about the process of forming expectations replaced conventional views about the process, nor should it be surprising that the new theory is marginally consistent with the rational expectations hypothesis, since that theory only specified an accurate outcome. The complete rejection of the bounded rationality hypothesis is just as misleading as the presumed consistency with the rational expectations hypothesis. The bounds on rationality may be due more to the lack of factual information than cognitive capacity, and rational expectations may be conditional on contextual factors rather than viewing rationality as a universal guide that shapes all expectations.

The rational expectations hypothesis is a hybrid invention that will never shed its status as a hypothesis. Orthodox economic theory only holds in the state of equilibrium, when all relationships among economic variables are in balance. It is not surprising that economics only recently added rational expectations to its models, as expectations for change are redundant in equilibrium since today's outcomes are identical to tomorrow's. In disequilibrium, however, expectations play a distinctive role in signaling potential future changes. The problem is that orthodox theory denies that rationality holds in disequilibrium. The rationality of expectations is thus a conjecture without any foundation in economic theory. Moreover, economic theory holds that there is no certain path back to equilibrium, so rational expectations cannot act as guideposts to regain equilibrium. This allows for a more comprehensive theory of how economic expectations are formed and revised to be seamlessly integrated into orthodox economic theory.

REFERENCES

Allen, R., & Reber, A. S. (1980). Very long term memory for tacit knowledge. *Cognition, 8*(2), 175–185. https://doi.org/10.1016/0010-0277(80)90011-6

Bargh, J. A., & Chartrand, T. L. (1999). The unbearable automaticity of being. *American Psychologist, 54*(7), 462–479. https://doi.org/10.1037/0003-066X.54.7.462

Bechara, A., Damasio, H., Tranel, D., & Damasio, A. R. (1997). Deciding advantageously before knowing the advantageous strategy. *Science, 275*(5304), 1293–1295. https://doi.org/10.1126/science.275.5304.1293

Berry, D. C., & Broadbent, D. (1988). Interactive tasks and the implicit-explicit distinction. *British Journal of Psychology, 79*(2), 251–272. https://doi.org/10.1111/j.2044-8295.1988.tb02286.x

Blendon, R. J., Benson, J. M., Brodie, M., Morin, R., Altman, D. E., Gitterman, D., Brossard, M., & James, M. (1997). Bridging the gap between the public's and economists' views of the economy. *Journal of Economic Perspectives, 11*(3), 105–118. https://doi.org/10.1257/jep.11.3.105

Blinder, A. S., & Krueger, A. B. (2004). What does the public know about economic policy, and how does it know it? *Brookings Papers on Economic Activity*, *2004*(1), 327–397. https://doi.org/10.1353/eca.2004.0012

Chaiken, S., & Trope, Y. (1999). *Dual process theories in social psychology*. Guilford Press.

Curtin, R. T. (2008). What U.S. consumers know about economic conditions. In E. Giovannini (Ed.), *Statistics, knowledge and policy 2007: Measuring and fostering the progress of societies* (pp. 153–176). OECD.

Curtin, R. T. (2010). Inflation expectations and empirical tests: Theoretical models and empirical tests. In P. Sinclair (Ed.), *Inflation expectations* (Vol. 56, pp. 34–61). Routledge International Studies in Money and Banking.

Curtin, R. T. (2019a). Consumer expectations: A new paradigm. *Business Economics*, *54*(4), 199–210. https://doi.org/10.1057/s11369-019-00148-1

Curtin, R. T. (2019b). *Consumer expectations: Micro foundations and macro impact*. Cambridge. https://doi.org/10.1017/9780511791598

Damasio, A. R. (1994). *Descartes' error*. Putnam.

Darwin, C. (1872). *The expression of the emotions in man and animal*. John Murray. https://doi.org/10.1037/10001-000

Dehaene, S. (1997). *The number sense: How the mind creates mathematics*. Oxford University Press.

Dehaene, S. (2003). The neural basis of the Weber–Fechner law: A logarithmic mental number line. *Trends in Cognitive Sciences*, *7*(3), 145–147. https://doi.org/10.1016/S1364-6613(03)00055-X

Di Chiara, G. (1997). Alcohol and dopamine. *Alcohol Health and Research World*, *21*(20), 108–114.

Dijksterhuis, A. (2004). Think different: The merits of unconscious thought in preference development and decision making. *Journal of Personality and Social Psychology*, *87*(5), 586–598. https://doi.org/10.1037/0022-3514.87.5.586

Gramlich, E. (1983). Models of inflation expectations formation. *Journal of Money, Credit and Banking*, *15*(2), 155–173. https://doi.org/10.2307/1992397

Hinsz, V. B., Tindale, R. S., & Vollrath, D. A. (1997). The emerging conceptualization of groups as information processors. *Psychological Bulletin*, *121*(1), 43–64. https://doi.org/10.1037/0033-2909.121.1.43

Kahneman, D. (2011). *Thinking, fast and slow*. Farrar, Straus and Giroux.

Kahneman, D., & Tversky, A. (1979). Prospect theory: An analysis of decisions under risk. *Econometrica*, *47*(2), 263–292. https://doi.org/10.2307/1914185

Keynes, J. M. (1936). *The general theory of employment, interest, and money*. Harcourt, Brace.

Lewicki, P. (1986). Processing information about covariations that cannot be articulated. *Journal of Experimental Psychology*, *12*(1), 135–146.

Lewicki, P., Hill, T., & Czyzewska, M. (1992). Nonconscious acquisition of information. *American Psychologist*, *47*(6), 796–801. https://doi.org/10.1037/0003-066X.47.6.796

Massey, D. S. (2002). A brief history of human society: The origin and role of emotion in social life. *American Sociological Review*, *67*(1), 1–29. https://doi.org/10.2307/3088931

Mehra, Y. P. (2002). Survey measures of expected inflation: Revisiting the issues of predictive content and rationality. *Economic Quarterly: Federal Reserve Bank of Richmond*, *88*(3), 17–36.

Muth, J. F. (1961). Rational expectations and the theory of price movements. *Econometrica*, *29*(3), 315–335. https://doi.org/10.2307/1909635

Neisser, U. (1967). *Cognitive psychology* (4th ed.). University of Illinois Press.

Onishi, K. H., & Baillargeon, R. (2005). Do 15-month-old infants understand false beliefs? *Science*, *308*(5719), 255–258. https://doi.org/10.1126/science.1107621

PEW Research Center. (2009). *Evening news viewership*.

Popper, K. (2003). *Conjectures and refutations: The growth of scientific knowledge*. Routledge.

Reber, A. S. (1967). Implicit learning of artificial grammars. *Journal of Verbal Learning and Verbal Behavior*, *6*(6), 855–863. https://doi.org/10.1016/S0022-5371(67)80149-X

Rizzolatti, G., & Craighero, L. (2004). The mirror-neuron system. *Annual Review of Neuroscience*, *27*(1), 169–192. https://doi.org/10.1146/annurev.neuro.27.070203.144230

Ross, D., & Dumouchel, P. (2004). Emotions as strategic signals. *Rationality and Society*, *16*(3), 251–286. https://doi.org/10.1177/1043463104044678

Sargent, T. J., & Sims, C. A. (1977). Business cycle modeling without pretending to have too much a priori economic theory. *New Methods in Business Cycle Research*, *1*, 145–168.

Simon, H. A. (1955). A behavioral model of rational choice. *Quarterly Journal of Economics*, *69*(1), 99–118. https://doi.org/10.2307/1884852

Simon, T. J., Hespos, S. J., & Rochat, P. (1995). Do infants understand simple arithmetic? A replication of Wynn (1992). *Cognitive Development*, *10*(2), 253–269. https://doi.org/10.1016/0885-2014(95)90011-X

Spelke, E. S., Breinlinger, K., Macomber, J., & Jacobson, K. (1992). Origins of knowledge. *Psychological Review*, *99*(4), 605–632. https://doi.org/10.1037/0033-295X.99.4.605

Starkey, P., Spelke, E. S., & Gelman, R. (1990). Numerical abstraction by human infants. *Cognition*, *36*(2), 97–127. https://doi.org/10.1016/0010-0277(90)90001-Z

Stock, J. H., & Watson, M. W. (2002). Forecasting using principal components from a large number of predictors. *Journal of the American Statistical Association*, *97*(460), 1167–1179. https://doi.org/10.1198/016214502388618960

Thomas, L. B., Jr. (1999). Survey measures of expected U.S. inflation. *Journal of Economic Perspectives*, *13*(4), 125–144. https://www.aeaweb.org/articles?id=10.1257/jep.13.4.125

University of Michigan. (2019). *Surveys of consumers: Quarterly data 1978:1–2019:4*. https://data.sca.isr.umich.edu/subset/subset.php

U.S. Bureau of Economic Analysis. (2019). *Gross domestic product*. https://www.bea.gov/data/gdp/gross-domestic-product

U.S. Bureau of Labor Statistics. (2019). *Labor force statistics from the current population survey: Unemployment rate 1992:1–2019:4*. https://www.bls.gov/cps/

Wilson, T. (2002). *Strangers to ourselves: Discovering the adaptive unconscious*. Belknap Press of Harvard University Press.

Zajonc, R. B. (1980). Feeling and thinking: Preferences need no inferences. *American Psychologist*, *35*(2), 151–175. https://doi.org/10.1037/0003-066X.35.2.151

Zajonc, R. B. (1984). On the primacy of affect. *American Psychologist*, *39*(2), 117–123. https://doi.org/10.1037/0003-066X.39.2.117

Part IV

Businesses Use Psychology to Communicate with Consumers

CHAPTER 19

LANGUAGE AND CONSUMER PSYCHOLOGY

Ruth Pogacar, Alican Mecit, Fei Gao, L. J. Shrum, and Tina M. Lowrey

The proposition that language shapes thought—termed *linguistic relativity*—is often attributed to Edward Sapir and his student Benjamin Whorf, although the general philosophical proposition was advanced by Humboldt (1836/1988) and has roots that can be traced back to Plato. According to the Sapir-Whorf hypothesis, language shapes the way people perceive the world. Although linguistic relativity is typically used to describe how people who speak different languages perceive the world differently, we take a broad view of the proposition to discuss how language influences judgments and behaviors through different psychological processes.

As an organizing framework, we have structured this discussion around the different types of psychological processes that language influences: cognitive processes, social processes, and cultural processes. Across the three process domains, we discuss the effects of different linguistic factors. For our purposes, in terms of language, cognitive processes are ones that occur primarily within a person, social processes are ones that involve interpersonal communication, and cultural processes are ones that involve cross-language effects. However, we acknowledge that these different categories are imprecise and that there is often overlap between them. Our objective is simply to provide a heuristic framework to organize the large volume of research on language effects.

The literature on language effects is vast, and a comprehensive review is beyond the scope of this chapter. Thus, we stress that our review is selective, both in terms of the representative research for various linguistic factors and effects and the coverage of the many different types of factors. Finally, we also note that our review primarily focuses on research in consumer psychology, with an emphasis on the most current findings. However, for context, we also discuss research in the basic disciplines that inform applications to consumer psychology.

COGNITIVE PROCESSES AND LANGUAGE

Language shapes individuals' cognition along multiple dimensions. Language influences what people attend to, how they perceive stimuli, what they remember, and their attitudes, reasoning processes, and behavior (R. W. Brown & Lenneberg, 1954). Not only does the substantive message transmitted by language affect people's cognition but the characteristics of language itself also affect what and how people think. Communicators often use linguistic factors (e.g., phonetic symbolism, unusual spelling, metaphor) as marketing devices to make their claims more persuasive (Pogacar, Lowrey, & Shrum, 2018). In this section, we provide a selective review of research on the effects of linguistic factors on

---

This research was supported by a research grant from the HEC Foundation of HEC Paris and Investissements d'Avenir (ANR-11-IDEX-0003/Labex Ecodec/ANR-11-LABX-0047) awarded to L. J. Shrum and Tina M. Lowrey. The authors thank Ann Kronrod for helpful comments on previous versions of this chapter.

https://doi.org/10.1037/0000262-019
APA Handbook of Consumer Psychology, L. R. Kahle (Editor-in-Chief)
Copyright © 2022 by the American Psychological Association. All rights reserved.

consumers' cognitive processes. Table 19.1 provides a summary of the findings for the factors discussed.

Phonetic Symbolism

One of the most ubiquitous linguistic factors that has been investigated in consumer contexts is phonetic symbolism (Spence, 2012). *Phonetic symbolism* is the notion that the mere sound of a word conveys meaning, independent of its definition. Most research on phonetic symbolism effects has focused on isolated phonemes (distinct units of sound), typically conveyed by different vowels and consonants. Both individual vowel and consonant sounds are associated with many different sensory perceptions. For example, higher pitched sounds are associated with concepts such as sharper, faster, smaller, lighter, higher pitch, psychologically closer, and more feminine, whereas lower pitched sounds connote the opposite (duller, slower, larger, lower pitch, psychologically distant, more masculine; Klink, 2000; Maglio et al., 2014). Consonants display similar associations. For example, fricative consonant sounds, which are formed from air friction through open articulators (e.g., "f," "v"), are associated with similar perceptions as front vowels. In contrast, plosive consonant sounds, which are formed through

TABLE 19.1

Summary of Findings: Cognitive Processes

Linguistic factor	Mechanism	Effects	References
Phonetic symbolism	Cross-modal sensory correspondence/ semantic association	Brand name preference	Baxter & Lowrey, 2014; Lowrey & Shrum, 2007
		Brand performance	Pogacar et al., 2015
		Brand/product attitude	Yorkston & Menon, 2004
		Brand/product perception, product recommendation	Guèvremont & Grohmann, 2015; Klink, 2000
		Purchase intention	Maglio et al., 2014
Sound repetition	Processing fluency, affect	Brand/product attitude, purchase intention	Argo et al., 2010
		Product choice	Davis et al., 2016
		Ad attitude	Filkukova & Klempe, 2013
Pronunciation	Processing fluency	Novelty, risk perception	Song & Schwarz, 2009
		Stock market performance	Alter & Oppenheimer, 2006
Voice: pitch and speech rate	Cross-modal sensory correspondence/ semantic association	Product perception	Lowe & Haws, 2017
		Ad attitude	Chattopadhyay et al., 2003; Gelinas-Chebat & Chebat, 1992
Unusual spelling	Attention, processing fluency, affect	Brand memory	Lowrey et al., 2003
		Brand perception	McNeel, 2017
Metaphor	Spreading activation of semantic processing	Product attitude, purchase intention	Ang & Lim, 2006; Cian et al., 2015
		Ad attitude	McQuarrie & Mick, 1999
		Product attitude, choice	Kronrod & Danziger, 2013
		Food consumption	Yang et al., 2019
		Portion size choice	Gao et al., 2020
		Stock price prediction	Morris et al., 2007

air stoppage by closed articulators (e.g., "t," "k"), are associated with similar perceptions as back vowels (French, 1977).

These simple phonetic associations influence a large array of consumer judgments, such as brand name preferences (Baxter & Lowrey, 2014; Shrum et al., 2012), product perceptions (Klink, 2000), attitudes (Yorkston & Menon, 2004), recommendations (Guèvremont & Grohmann, 2015), willingness to pay (Maglio et al., 2014), and risk assessment (Botner et al., 2020). Phonetic symbolism is most effective (i.e., most persuasive) when the sound-symbolic perceptions are congruent with the expected or preferred attributes of the associated products. For example, brand names with front vowel sounds (higher pitched), which are associated with concepts such as smaller, faster, and sharper, are preferred over brand names with back vowel sounds (lower pitched) for products such as sports cars and knives, but the opposite is true for products such as SUVs and hammers (Lowrey & Shrum, 2007). Notably, many phonetic symbolism effects appear to be robust across languages (Pogacar et al., 2017; Shrum et al., 2012), and certain sounds are even associated with better brand performance (Pogacar et al., 2015).

Sound Repetition

Some words (or phrases) have repetitive sounds. For example, alliterative words are ones in which the initial stressed sound in a syllable or word is repeated (e.g., Bed Bath and Beyond, Coca-Cola). Alliteration often has positive effects on consumer evaluations. For example, alliterative price promotions were evaluated more favorably than nonalliterative ones (e.g., 3 Theybles $30 vs. 3 Theybles $29; Davis et al., 2016), even though the nonalliterative promotion was a better deal. Similar effects have been noted for brand names that have repeated sounds across syllables (Argo et al., 2010).

Rhyme is also an example of sound repetition. Brand names often use rhyme (e.g., 7-Eleven, Lean Cuisine), which has a number of positive effects on marketing outcomes, including increased recall (Carr & Miles, 1997), more favorable product evaluation, and more positive affect (Argo et al., 2010).

Rhyme can even influence perceptions of truthfulness. For example, in one classic study, rhyming aphorisms (e.g., "woes unite foes") were rated as more truthful than equivalent but nonrhyming aphorisms (e.g., "woes unite enemies"; McGlone & Tofighbakhsh, 2000). Subsequent research demonstrated the effect in consumer contexts: Rhyming product slogans were better remembered, better liked, more persuasive, and considered more trustworthy compared with similar but nonrhyming slogans (Filkuková & Klempe, 2013).

Pronunciation

Consumers often make judgments simply on the basis of how easy a word (or brand name) is to pronounce. Easier to pronounce words are easier to process than harder to pronounce words (i.e., greater processing fluency; Schwarz, 2004), and ease of processing has a number of benefits. For example, it influences perceptions of familiarity. Because things that are familiar are usually easier to process, people often erroneously assume that things that are easier to process are more familiar (Schwarz, 2004). Familiarity in turn can influence various types of inferential judgments. For example, things that are more familiar are generally liked better (Zajonc, 1968), and people whose names are easier to pronounce are liked better than those whose names are difficult to pronounce (Laham et al., 2012). In a study on stock performance and processing fluency, stocks whose names were easier to pronounce outperformed stocks whose names were harder to pronounce (Alter & Oppenheimer, 2006).

Ease of processing and familiarity also influence judgments of both novelty and risk. Things that are easier to process are perceived as more familiar, and things that are perceived as familiar are considered less risky but also less novel. In one study, Song and Schwarz (2009) manipulated the ease/difficulty of pronunciation of a carnival ride. Participants perceived the ride with an easier to pronounce name to be less risky than a ride with a more difficult to pronounce name, but they also considered the ride with the easier to pronounce name to be more dull and less adventurous.

Voice: Pitch and Speech Rate

Voice pitch is the reflection of fundamental frequency. A long literature in linguistics and psychology suggests that voice pitch influences a number of judgments (for a review, see Dahl, 2010). For example, people generally evaluate speakers with lower pitched voices more favorably than those with higher pitched voices (Bond et al., 1987) and in particular find the former to be more calm, potent, truthful, and emphatic than the latter (Apple et al., 1979). Similar findings are observed in consumer contexts, with lower voice pitch associated with greater persuasion (Chattopadhyay et al., 2003; Gelinas-Chebat & Chebat, 1992), although in some cases these effects may depend on gender of the spokesperson (Sharf & Lehman, 1984).

Voice pitch also affects perceptions of product size. The effect is conceptually similar to phonetic symbolism effects. For example, Lowe and Haws (2017) manipulated whether a spokesperson's voice in an audio ad for a sandwich was higher or lower pitched, and then asked participants to estimate the size of the sandwich. Participants who heard the ad from the spokesperson with the lower pitched voice estimated that the sandwich would be larger than those who heard the ad from the spokesperson with the higher pitched voice. The effect occurred through a process of visual imagery in which the lower pitch evoked mental imagery of larger products.

Speakers may also differ on how fast they talk, which in turn can affect consumer judgments. Generally, faster speech rates are more persuasive than slower speech rates because people generally prefer speech rates that are slightly faster than normal speed (Chattopadhyay et al., 2003). Slightly faster than normal speakers may be considered more intelligent, knowledgeable, truthful, and persuasive (Miller et al., 1976). However, faster speech rates can also cause negative outcomes because faster speech limits the time people have to process the information, which can impair their attention and recall (Chattopadhyay et al., 2003).

Unusual Spelling

Brand names often employ unusual spellings. Examples include substituting a letter for a word (e.g., U-Haul), dropping a letter that does not affect the desired pronunciation (e.g., La-Z-Boy), using a single letter as a phonetic substitute for a word (e.g., In-N-Out Burger), or misspellings that replace certain letters in a correctly spelled word (e.g., Froot Loops; for a review, see Wong, 2013). Unusually spelled brand names are often more memorable because the oddness of the spellings attracts attention and is unexpected, which increases depth of processing, leading to better brand name recall (Lowrey et al., 2003).

Unusual spellings can also provide meaning and signal brand identity. For example, the use of a single letter as a phonetic substitute for a word (e.g., Toys R Us) or dropping the "g" from "ing"-ending words (e.g., Dunkin' Donuts) connotes casualness, and certain types of misspellings may be related to particular demographic groups (e.g., children, subcultures), which serves for targeting the specific market. However, unusual spellings can also have negative effects if the names are difficult to pronounce and thus increase processing disfluency, which can reduce cross-modal congruency (McNeel, 2017).

Metaphor

At the most basic level, *metaphor* is a type of figurative speech that uses one concept to describe another concept. Metaphors can be used for constructing brand names (e.g., Amazon, Apple), slogans (e.g., Budweiser, the king of beers), and other appeals. However, metaphor is more than just a connection between two superficially dissimilar concepts; metaphor is a cognitive mapping tool that aids understanding of complex concepts by using a source concept that is relatively concrete and easy to grasp to conceptualize a target concept, which is typically more abstract and difficult to grasp (Landau et al., 2010, 2018). In fact, this description serves as a metaphor that likens comprehension or understanding of an entity (abstract concept) to a sensorimotor state of grasping an object (concrete concept).

Consider the metaphor "love is sweet," which conceptualizes the abstract concept of love in terms of a concrete sensory taste concept of sweetness. This concept mapping guides subsequent information processing. For example, priming love through romantic stimuli increased intentions to consume sweet foods (but not nonsweet foods) but only for those who tended to think abstractly (vs. concretely; Yang et al., 2019). Similarly, priming the conceptual metaphor of fullness reduced perceptions of hunger and decreased portion size choice (Gao et al., 2020). In another study, Cian et al. (2015) used conceptual metaphor theory to test the proposition that people tend to associate rationality higher on a vertical dimension compared with emotion, and this metaphoric association influences judgments about placement on webpages. In one experiment, participants were given a blank webpage and asked to place a particular content section anywhere on the page, and the content was manipulated to be more rational (science section) or emotional (music section). Consistent with metaphor transfer effects, participants placed the science section higher on the webpage than the music section.

Metaphors can positively influence product attitudes and purchase intentions (Ang & Lim, 2006; McQuarrie & Mick, 1999). For example, metaphors are more persuasive than literal language for writing consumer reviews for hedonic products (Kronrod & Danziger, 2013). Metaphors can also influence consumers' expectations and predictions. Using agent metaphors (relating to action or movement) to describe a current day stock price trend increased expectations and predictions of a continuing future trend (Morris et al., 2007).

In summary, there are numerous linguistic factors that affect how consumers process information. In this section, we have focused on factors whose effects generally occur within-person. That is, they occur in individual responses to marketing communications. Communicators—whether they be marketers, politicians, job candidates, or product reviewers—will benefit from understanding how these linguistic factors work, the conditions that maximize their effectiveness, and the situations that limit their effectiveness. In the next section, we turn to communications that are typically social in nature; that is, involving communication between persons or referencing social relationships.

SOCIAL PROCESSES AND LANGUAGE

People regularly engage in social communications, and many of these interactions occur in consumer contexts. For example, marketing communications may reference a social relationship with the consumer (e.g., "we're in this together"). Consumers may also communicate with each other (e.g., product reviews, word of mouth) or with marketers (e.g., consumer complaints). Consumer-related communications are often influenced by norms and resulting expectations. For instance, the relationship between communicator and listener (e.g., close vs. distant) creates normative expectations. Violation of these expectations (often unexpected or unintended) can have detrimental effects on the social relationship. Similarly, communicating in ways that are normatively appropriate can enhance the social relationship. The same applies to business communications, whether they are communications between consumers or between consumers and firms.

In this section, we provide a selective review of research that investigates social communications in consumer contexts. We organize our discussion around three key areas: social referents, language tone, and contagion effects. We also discuss figurative and complex language and the influence of message generation on communicators. Table 19.2 provides a summary of the findings.

Social Referents

Language can denote people, objects, or states indirectly via referent words (e.g., "she" or "they" in place of a person's name) or symbols (e.g., a smiley-face in place of text). Next we discuss several examples relevant to consumer psychology.

Pronouns. Pronouns (e.g., "I," "you," "we") and other particles (e.g., "the," "on," "it") account for the vast majority of words people use in both written and oral communication. Although it is tempting to view them as relatively innocuous, they can actually be quite influential. The pronouns people use to communicate are more than just substitutes for proper nouns. Frequently, their use conveys assumptions about social relations, and thus

TABLE 19.2

Summary of Findings: Social Processes

Linguistic factor	Mechanisms	Effects	Reference
Pronouns	Expectations, social norms	Brand attitude	Sela et al., 2012
	Agency, empathy perceptions	Satisfaction, purchase intention, behavior	Packard et al., 2018
Emoticons	Warmth, competence perceptions	Satisfaction, purchase intention, behavior	Li et al., 2019
Assertive language	Expectations	Compliance intentions	Kronrod et al., 2012a
		Compliance intentions, behavior	Kronrod et al., 2012b
		Ad, brand attitude, monetary allocation	Zemack-Rugar et al., 2017
Asynchronous word of mouth	Self-enhancement motivation	Information sharing	Berger & Iyengar, 2013
Consensus language	Consensus group size perceptions	Behavior (click-through rate)	Lee & Kronrod, 2020
Linguistic complexity	Elaboration	Brand recall, recognition, attitude	Lowrey, 1998
Explaining language	Narrative building	Evaluation, behavioral intention	Moore, 2012
	Expectation, social norms	Recommendation, choice	Moore, 2015

understanding these assumptions and their relations to norms and expectations is crucial for facilitating social interactions.

Pronouns generally serve a self-referencing function in persuasive communications (processing information in relation to the self). In particular, pronouns are used to imply or reflect social relationships (Kacewicz et al., 2014). Pronouns also suggest the closeness of a relationship. For example, the use of "we" suggests a closer relationship than does the use of "you and I" (G. M. Fitzsimons & Kay, 2004; Simmons et al., 2005). Implying closeness can enhance persuasion but only if the receiver thinks the closeness implication is appropriate. Thus, couples might refer to themselves as "we," but one's mortgage broker is less likely to use the same intimate pronoun. If they do, it may not be well received if the closeness implication is inaccurate. Consider a study conducted by Sela et al. (2012), who asked participants to imagine they were customers of Cellcom, a phone service provider, and manipulated whether that relationship was considered a close or distant one. Then, they had participants read a persuasive communication from Cellcom intended to create more positive attitudes, but they varied pronoun usage ("we" vs. "you and Cellcom"). When the relationship between Cellcom and the customer (participant) was perceived as close, participants evaluated the brand more favorably when the marketing communication used the "we" pronoun rather than "you and Cellcom," but the reverse was true when the relationship was perceived to be a distant one.

Pronouns can also communicate important information apart from social relations. For example, marketers often discourage the use of first-person pronouns ("I") in marketer-to-consumer communications and instead encourage the use of "we" and "you" in order to emphasize the customer and downplay a focus on the self (in this case, the marketer). However, in a series of studies, Packard et al. (2018) showed that not only is this conventional wisdom misguided but the use of the first-person pronoun has distinct advantages. In particular, the usage of the first-person "I" on the part of the firm or salesperson increases perceptions that the firm or salesperson has agency and empathy for the customer. Consequently, the use of singular self-referencing ("I") increased consumer satisfaction, purchase intentions, and purchase behavior compared with the use of "we."

Emoticons. Emoticons are a form of *textual paralanguage*, which refers to written manifestations of nonverbal cues, such as symbols and images (Luangrath et al., 2017). In many ways, emoticons function similarly to pronouns in terms of interpersonal communication norms. For example, service employees who use emoticons (e.g., ☺) are perceived as warmer than those who don't, and customers are subsequently more satisfied with the service provided when emoticons are used. However, again, the violation of norms and expectations has consequences. For instance, whether service employees' use of emoticons increases customer satisfaction depends on whether the emoticons are considered appropriate to the customer–service provider relationship (Li et al., 2019). Thus, when a consumer expects a communal relationship with their service provider, emoticons are consistent with this expectation and convey the expected care (e.g., Domino's Pizza's use of emoticons on social media). However, when customers do not have communal relationship expectations, emoticon use can backfire, causing more negative evaluations of competence (e.g., Goldman Sachs's use of emoticons in its 2015 company report).

Language Tone

Grice's (1975) principle of cooperation posits that people expect their conversation partners to adhere to certain rules of conversation. These include "cooperating" so that the conversation succeeds and both participants comprehend each other's intended meanings. This expectation leads to positive consumer responses when fulfilled and negative responses when violated (P. Brown & Levinson, 1987; Forgas, 1998). However, although the benefits of tailoring conversations, and messages more generally, to meet receiver expectations is intuitive and straightforward, actually understanding what those expectations are is not always straightforward. In this section, we review research on language tone—specifically, assertive language tone—in marketing communications, with an emphasis on how alignment with expectations has facilitating and positive effects on marketing outcomes.

Assertive language refers to language that is direct, commanding, and forceful in tone. Marketers routinely use assertive language in various types of communications, such as slogans ("Just do it") and ad appeals ("Buy now!"). However, research across a number of disciplines suggests that such forceful language may reduce compliance and persuasion in many situations (Dillard & Shen, 2005; G. J. Fitzsimons & Lehmann, 2004; Quick & Considine, 2008), and these situations often involve mismatches in consumer expectations. For example, although assertive language has positive effects on compliance for hedonic products, for utilitarian products, assertive language is actually counterproductive (Kronrod et al., 2012a). The reason for the difference can be traced to the interplay between language and mood. People in positive moods expect others to address them with direct, assertive language because when people are in positive moods, they themselves tend to use more assertive language, and hedonic products are more associated with positive mood than are utilitarian products.

Assertive language can also impact persuasion apart from expectation congruity. For example, the effectiveness of assertive language can depend on whether a particular message is considered praising or scolding (Grinstein & Kronrod, 2016). Assertive language is more effective when praising, whereas nonassertive language is more effective when scolding. This occurs because assertive praising language intensifies the positive meaning, whereas nonassertive language attenuates the negativity of scolding, thereby making it more palatable. Nonassertive praise is less effective because it seems halfhearted, and assertive scolding is less effective because it seems too harsh. These findings are particularly consequential for contexts such as financial planning and medical compliance.

Assertive language is more persuasive when consumers believe the issue at hand is important. For instance, assertive environmental messages work well for consumers who already believe environmental issues are highly important (e.g., "Reducing air pollution: Everyone must use more public transportation!"), but for those who don't, less assertive messages work better (e.g., "Reducing air pollution: Everyone could use more public transportation"; Kronrod et al., 2012b). For those who think the particular message issue is unimportant, the assertive message produces psychological reactance that increases message counterarguing (Brehm, 1966).

Finally, assertive language can lead to reactance (in ways similar to intimate pronoun use) when expectations are not met or norms are violated. For example, assertive slogans like "Just do it!" vary in effectiveness, depending on consumers' relationships with brands (Zemack-Rugar et al., 2017). Consumers who perceive themselves as being in a committed relationship with the brand experience stronger compliance norms, and therefore assertive ads create greater pressure to comply for committed consumers. Committed consumers expect to feel guilty if they ignore an assertive message and therefore feel pressured to comply. This pressure increases reactance, which paradoxically reduces compliance, leading to reduced preference for assertive ads and associated brands as well as decreased spending on the brand for committed consumers.

Contagion Effects

Social contagion refers to the spread of information through people's social networks. This is primarily a function of word of mouth. *Word of mouth* refers to product- or brand-related discussions (e.g., "The latest *New Yorker* has an interesting cover"), sharing brand-related content (e.g., *New Yorker* cartoons on Twitter), recommendations (e.g., "You should read this *New Yorker* article"), and mere mentions (e.g., "I read the *New Yorker*"). According to Berger (2014), word of mouth serves five key functions: impression management, emotional regulation, information acquisition, social bonding, and persuasion. Furthermore, the medium of communication influences the degree to which these functions motivate word of mouth. People using written modes of word of mouth are more likely to mention highly interesting products and brands, compared with people engaging in spoken discussions, because of communication asynchrony (the delay between message and response; Berger & Iyengar, 2013). The delay is longer in written communications, which allows writers to carefully deliberate and thus decide on more interesting topics.

Self-enhancement—the desire to enhance others' esteem for oneself—also plays a role by prompting communicators to spend more time polishing written communications and focusing on topics that are as interesting as possible. For example, in one experiment, Berger and Iyengar (2013) manipulated whether participants wrote about a brand (instant messenger), talked about a brand (face-to-face), or talked about a brand asynchronously (told to wait at least 5 seconds before responding to their partner). Participants mentioned a larger number of interesting products and brands when they wrote about a brand than when they talked about the brand naturally. However, participants who talked asynchronously also discussed a greater number of interesting products than those in the synchronous conversations, indicating that it is the asynchrony of communication that allows people to focus on self-enhancement and thus produce more interesting word of mouth.

Consensus language—which suggests general agreement among people on a product or behavior (e.g., "everyone loves this documentary")—has important consequences for contagion. Although communication from strong ties (e.g., family, close friends) on sites like Facebook is generally more contagious (Aral & Walker, 2014), consensus language is more influential when used by weak ties (e.g., distant friends, acquaintances). For example, in one experiment, Lee and Kronrod (2020) had confederates send private Facebook messages to five strong and five weak ties, half with consensus language in the message and half without. When recipients got a message from a weak tie confederate using consensus language (e.g., "everyone is talking about . . . "), recipients were more likely to click through to the linked news article than recipients who received the same message from a strong tie confederate. However, when confederates did not employ consensus language, click-through rates did not differ for strong and weak ties. The weak ties were more influential because they suggested a larger and more diverse group in consensus.

Figurative and Complex Language

Consumers' expectations also shape their responses to language that is figurative and metaphorical ("pizza as big as the moon") versus literal ("14-inch pizza"). Norms for figurative versus literal language vary for advertiser-generated and consumer-generated content. Conversational norms dictate that advertising should use artful wordplay, whereas user-generated content is expected to reflect a sincere opinion. Further, figurative language is the norm—and therefore more effective—for hedonic than utilitarian products. Because of these different expectations, consumer reviews with more figurative language lead to more favorable attitudes for hedonic than for utilitarian products (Kronrod & Danziger, 2013).

The degree to which people are willing or able to process complex language also produces different expectations. For routine decisions, such as ordering coffee, people expect and prefer simple advertising language. However, when people are highly involved in a consumer decision (e.g., buying a car), their motivation to process information is higher, and they are more willing to engage with complex language to access the information they seek. Thus, high-involvement consumers may be more willing to engage with complex sentence structure (i.e., syntax; Lowrey, 2006). For example, although complex advertisements are not preferred for most routine communications, complex syntax leads to more favorable attitudes than simple syntax when involvement with the message is high because motivation to process ad information increases message elaboration (Lowrey, 1998).

Influence of Language on Communicators

The process of articulating a word-of-mouth message can also impact the writers of word-of-mouth transmissions because language facilitates information processing (Moore & Lafreniere, 2020). For example, people who use explaining language (explanations for why an experience occurred) demonstrate a greater understanding of their consumption experience than those who do not use explaining language because cognitive processes such as narrative building help them make sense of the events (Moore, 2012). Interestingly, understanding has different effects on hedonic and utilitarian experiences. Enhanced understanding dampened consumers' evaluations of both positive and negative hedonic experiences, but it polarized evaluations of both positive and negative utilitarian experiences.

Word-of-mouth explanations can also vary in terms of what they explain. For example, in writing product reviews, communicators might explain their actions (why they chose a product) or their reactions (how they feel about the product). The types of explanations by review writers differ for hedonic and utilitarian products. Review writers tend to provide action explanations for utilitarian products but provide reaction explanations for hedonic products (Moore, 2015). They provide these different types of explanations because consumers find explained actions more helpful for utilitarian than for hedonic products but find explained reactions more helpful for hedonic than for utilitarian products. In other words, the differences occur because review writers are trying to be helpful to their audiences.

In summary, language influences both communicators and receivers via referents, tone, and contagion. In this section, we have discussed how norms and expectations play an important role in determining the effects of language use in consumer contexts, particularly in social communication. Given that the effectiveness of the use of certain types of language conventions is driven by these expectations, and positive effects emerge when expectations are met, it is crucial that communicators understand the expectations of their audience. In the next section, we turn to the effects of language on cultural processes and, in particular, focus on the effects of cross-linguistic differences.

CULTURAL PROCESSES AND LANGUAGE

Consumer research on cross-linguistic differences can be broadly categorized in terms of two research streams. The first stream of research focuses on bilingual consumers and the extent to which they respond differently to consumption contexts involving different linguistic factors (e.g., marketing slogans that activate one of their languages). The second stream of research focuses on the effects of differences across languages in grammatical structure and writing systems on consumer judgment and decision making. Both streams of research draw on the Sapir-Whorf hypothesis of linguistic relativity and extend it to consumer contexts. According to the Sapir-Whorf thesis, languages provide different schemas through which the world is perceived and interpreted (Whorf, 1952). As a result, each culture has its idiosyncratic worldview, which influences the way individuals perceive, think, and act.

Although the debate continues about the extent to which language exerts an influence on behavior, empirical evidence suggests an interactive relation between language and behavior in several domains, including color perception (Roberson et al., 2008), time perception (Casasanto & Boroditsky, 2008), emotions (Gendron et al., 2012), and motion (Meteyard et al., 2007). As we detail in the next sections, consumer research studying cross-linguistic differences has also provided theory-consistent evidence by empirically testing the Whorfian link between language and memory structures. Table 19.3 provides a summary of the research findings.

Bilingualism

With English being the new lingua franca, and the world being more globalized than ever before, studying languages no longer pertains strictly to linguistics. More than half of the world's population speaks more than one language, making bilingual consumption contexts increasingly prevalent. The exponential increase in economic growth rates of emerging markets, coupled with sensitivity to minority groups in developed markets, has fueled interest in consumer research to understand how bilingual consumers process information and respond to bilingual consumption contexts. Consumer research on bilingualism can be categorized into two areas: a sociolinguistic or a psycholinguistic approach.

Sociolinguistic approach. Research adopting the sociolinguistic perspective has focused on the signaling functions of native (minority) languages in advertising targeted at ethnic minority groups. One prominent research area pertains to the effects

TABLE 19.3

Summary of Findings: Cultural Processes

Linguistic factor	Mechanisms	Effects	References
Code-switching	Expectations, social norms	Ad attitude, brand attitude	Koslow et al., 1994; Krishna & Ahluwalia, 2008; Luna & Peracchio, 2005
Second-language processing	Retrieval fluency	Ad recall	Luna & Peracchio, 2001, 2002, 2005
		Brand name evaluation	Zhang & Schmitt, 2004, 2007
		Emotional intensity of ad messages	Puntoni et al., 2009
		Rating scale extremity	De Langhe et al., 2011
		Emotional intensity and endowment	Karatas, 2020
		Judgment, choice	Schmitt & Zhang, 1998
		Brand recall, brand attitude	Yorkston & De Mello, 2005
Grammatical structure	Categorization	Future-related behavior	Chen, 2013
		Anthropomorphism, ad attitudes, choice	Mecit et al., 2018
		Brand attitude	Pan & Schmitt, 1996
		Brand recall	Schmitt et al., 1994; Tavassoli & Han, 2001
Writing system	Fluency, matching	Brand name evaluation	Tavassoli, 2001

of mixing languages within a communication, often referred to as *code-switching* (Luna & Peracchio, 2005; for a review, see Carroll et al., 2007). The general finding is that code-switching can have positive effects, under certain conditions. For example, consumers in a minority subculture respond favorably to code-switching in advertising because it signals solidarity with the minority group (Koslow et al., 1994). However, relying solely on the ethnic language has little effect because consumers do not attribute the use of their ethnic language to cultural sensitivity of the advertiser. Similar asymmetric effects have been observed in corporate communication contexts, although the findings depend on whether the firm is local or multinational (Krishna & Ahluwalia, 2008).

One way in which code-switching affects persuasion is by making the code-switched word more salient (Luna & Peracchio, 2005). For example, in an advertising context, inserting an English word in a Spanish slogan (e.g., "En mi *kitchen* nunca haría café con ninguna otra cafetera") or inserting a Spanish word in an English slogan (e.g., "In my *cocina* I would never make coffee with any other coffee-maker") directs attention to the code-switched term ("kitchen" and "cocina") and leads to elaboration on the schema of the code-switched language. Accordingly, code-switching affects consumer evaluations, depending on whether consumers have favorable or unfavorable associations with the language activated.

Psycholinguistic approach. Consumer research adopting the psycholinguistic approach has focused on the information processing consequences of language use on memory (Ahn & Ferle, 2008), emotions (Puntoni et al., 2009), and judgments (Karatas, 2020). Researchers adopting this approach mostly rely on the revised hierarchical model of bilingual language processing to test their predictions in consumer contexts. According to the model, bilingual individuals store words in their native and second language independently at the lexical level; however, they access the same semantic representation (Dufour & Kroll, 1995). Empirical tests of this model have demonstrated that conceptual links between the lexical representation in one's native language and the semantic representations in memory are stronger than the links between the lexical representation in one's second language and the semantic representations. Luna and Peracchio (2001) confirmed this finding in the context of advertising to bilinguals and advanced the model by showing that text-congruent images facilitate processing of second language messages. Images, therefore, can be used by advertisers to offset the effect of language asymmetries on memory.

Second-language proficiency also plays a crucial role in processing bilingual information (Zhang & Schmitt, 2004, 2007). When individuals learn words in the second language, they tend to relate the words to their equivalents in their first language. This association on the lexical level makes the activation of equivalent words in the first language necessary to represent concepts on the semantic level. The asymmetry in the strength of links connecting the first and the second languages to conceptual representations on the semantic level decreases as proficiency in the second language increases (Dufour & Kroll, 1995). In a similar vein, there are other moderators that offset the asymmetrical effects of bilingualism on memory, such as processing motivation (Luna & Peracchio, 2002) and attitude toward the language (Luna & Peracchio, 2005).

Proficiency in a second language affects not only the asymmetry in the strength of links but also the reliance on the mode of representation. In some languages, such as Chinese, words tend to be processed semantically, whereas in others, such as English, words tend to be processed phonologically (Hung & Tzeng, 1981). Consequently, consumers who are fluent in both Chinese and English favor the phonetic translation when the English name is emphasized, but favor the semantic translation when the Chinese name is emphasized. However, consumers who are bilingual but not proficient in English prefer the semantic translation in both conditions (Zhang & Schmitt, 2004). These results provide further evidence of the effect of language asymmetries on memory.

In addition to memory effects, the language triggered by the consumption context can affect bilingual consumers' perceptions of how emotional the message is. For example, marketing slogans expressed in consumers' native languages tend to be perceived as more emotional compared with messages in their second language (Puntoni et al., 2009). This effect occurs because experiences are stored as elements of an episodic memory trace, and recall leads to an echo of emotions that people have experienced during these episodes. Because words that people encounter more frequently are part of a greater number of episodic traces, messages in one's native language are more likely to lead to a stronger echo of emotions compared with messages in a second language, because people are more familiar with the words in their native language than in their second language. This general process affects judgments. For example, thinking in a second (vs. native) language diminishes the impact of affective evaluations of products, leading to a lowered sense of psychological ownership. Thus, asking consumers to make judgments in their second language in effect attenuates the endowment effect (Karatas, 2020).

This difference between one's native and second language can systematically influence how people respond to scales that probe emotional processes. Processing information in one's native language elicits more intense emotional states compared with information processed in a second language (Puntoni et al., 2009). Consequently, and somewhat counterintuitively, this results in the use of more intense (extreme) responses to emotional scale anchors (e.g., happy and sad) when responding to items using rating scales in a second language compared with scales in one's native language (De Langhe et al., 2011). Because the emotional anchors are experienced as less intense in a second language, respondents choose more extreme responses in order to convey their true emotions. This finding is particularly important for researchers who administer scales in participants' second language.

Cross-Cultural Differences and Language

A significant component of cross-cultural consumer research focuses on language effects (cross-linguistics). This research is generally based on the premise that language shapes the way people perceive and understand the world and that cross-linguistic differences can be used to trace cultural differences in reasoning styles (Logan, 1986; Whorf, 1952). In the following section, we review consumer research on cross-linguistics, which we broadly categorize into two major areas: cross-linguistic differences in grammatical structure and writing systems.

Grammatical structure. In line with the Sapir-Whorf thesis, cross-linguistic differences in grammatical structure influence consumer behavior and decision making in many areas. For example, classifiers affect consumers' categorization structures (Schmitt & Zhang, 1998) and retrieval processes (Yorkston & De Mello, 2005). *Classifiers* are words that accompany a noun and "classify" it and are relatively rare in English. For example, in Chinese, the classifier *zhi* is used for pen, pencil, and chopstick and *ke* for tree, sunflower plant, and wheat. However, in Japanese, only one classifier is used for all six objects, and in English, such classifiers are nonexistent. In a study comparing Chinese, Japanese, and English, Schmitt and Zhang (1998) demonstrated that the presence or absence of classifiers and their structures in these languages affects the way objects are categorized, which in turn influences product choice when the consideration set includes options with positively valenced classifiers. From a different perspective, yet applying the same concept, Yorkston and De Mello (2005) investigated the effects of linguistic gender marking on memory and categorization. In a study comparing Spanish speakers to English speakers, they demonstrated that for Spanish speakers, cues that are consistent with the grammatical gender of the brand name enhance brand recall.

Languages can also differ on how they reference future time. Some languages, such as English, use a strong, obligatory future tense ("I will go to the store tomorrow"), whereas other languages, such as Mandarin, do not ("I go to the store tomorrow"). Thus, future-time markings in a sentence serve to disassociate the future from the present moment, whereas lack of future-time markings results in an association between the present and the future. These simple grammatical differences can have important effects on downstream judgments. For example, the speakers of languages with obligatory future tenses (which disassociate present from future) engage in less future-oriented behavior than speakers of languages with no obligatory future tense (Chen, 2013). Hence, speakers of these languages may engage in behaviors that are not beneficial for their future selves. As a result, compared with Mandarin speakers, English speakers save less for retirement and engage in more risky behaviors (e.g., unprotected sex) that may jeopardize their well-being in the future.

Similarly, some languages differ on whether they have different pronouns for human and nonhuman entities. Some languages, such as English, distinguish between humans (he, she) and nonhumans (it), whereas other languages, such as French, do not. In French, the same pronouns (*elle, il* [she, he]) are used to refer to both humans and nonhumans. The presence (vs. absence) of a specific pronoun for nonhuman entities has interesting effects. For example, speakers of languages (French, Turkish) that do not distinguish between humans and nonhumans ("it-less" languages) anthropomorphize more than do speakers of languages that do distinguish between humans and nonhumans, such as English (Mecit et al., 2018).

Writing systems. A *writing system* refers to the way a language is coded in graphic units. Like grammar, writing systems vary greatly across languages. Linguistic research classifies languages into three major categories in terms of their writing system: languages using alphabetic characters (e.g., English, Russian), languages using syllabaries (e.g., Japanese, Cherokee), and languages using logographic characters (e.g., Chinese). In languages using alphabetic characters, every grapheme (letter) represents a subsyllabic unit of speech and has a corresponding phoneme (sound). In contrast, in languages using logographic characters, each character or symbol refers to meaningful concepts and not to a phoneme.

This loose association between the character and the sound in Chinese (vs. a close association in English) affects judgments. For example, Pan and Schmitt (1996) demonstrated that the match between sound and brand associations drives consumers' attitudes for English brands, whereas the match between script and brand associations affect consumers' attitudes for Chinese brands. They operationalized sound matching by using a male voice for a masculine product and a female voice for a feminine product (vice versa for sound mismatch). Similarly, script matching was operationalized by using a male script for a masculine product, a female script for a feminine product, and vice versa for script sound mismatch. Participants then evaluated brand names associated with either masculine (e.g., a tie) or feminine (e.g., a lipstick) product categories. Chinese speakers preferred the script-matching stimuli, whereas English speakers preferred the sound-matching stimuli. In contrast to previous research that found preference for moderate incongruity (e.g., Meyers-Levy et al., 1994), participants in both cases (Chinese and English speaking) preferred the more congruent stimuli because the process is automatic rather than deliberative.

Differences between Chinese and English writing systems also affect the way brand names are learned and remembered in these languages. In Chinese, mental representations of verbal information tend to be coded visually, whereas in English they tend to be coded phonologically. Therefore, unaided brand recall is affected depending on whether the verbal information is spoken or written (Schmitt et al., 1994). Avoiding cross-cultural confounds, another study replicated and extended these findings by comparing Korean written in the alphabetic Hangul to Korean written in the logographic Hancha (Tavassoli & Han, 2001). Because speakers of languages with logographic writing systems rely more on their visual memory compared with speakers of languages with alphabetic writing systems, the associations participants had with print colors had a greater impact on their evaluations of logographic brand names than of alphabetic brand names (Tavassoli, 2001).

INTEGRATION AND FUTURE RESEARCH

Consumers process scores of communications every day, whether in the form of marketer-to-consumer communications, such as ads, or consumer-to-consumer communications, such as product reviews and word-of-mouth transmissions. Both marketers and consumers surely give careful thought to what they want to say so that their communications are maximally effective. Clearly, what is said matters. In this chapter, we argue that it is not just what is said that matters but also *how* it is said. We have reviewed research that demonstrates how subtle variations in how an argument, or even just a brand name, is presented can have important effects on all aspects of consumer thought. We have organized our review in terms of the general levels of processing that underlie these linguistic factors and their effects: cognitive, social, and cultural. This organizing framework is arguably arbitrary and imprecise, and the different categories are often overlapping rather than independent; it is meant only as an organizing heuristic.

Although the research we have reviewed demonstrates the remarkable diversity and ubiquity of linguistic effects, there are some things they have in common. One is that the effects of the various linguistic factors are often very subtle and also often automatic. That is, consumers may be less consciously aware of the effects, and thus their responses are relatively uncontrollable (e.g., phonetic symbolism, sound repetition, pronunciation). In other cases, even when the processes are more controlled, are observable, and require elaborative thought, consumers are often unaware of the full range of effects and their underlying reasons (e.g., pronoun use, assertive language, code-switching). This lack of awareness of the effects of various factors on consumer judgments makes them potentially very effective tools for marketers. However, the effects of the linguistic factors are often not intuitive and can even backfire. Thus, their effective use requires a thorough understanding of what the factors do and how they do it. Providing this understanding is a primary objective of this review.

A second commonality that emerges is that there are clear boundary conditions for the linguistic effects. That is, sometimes linguistic factors are effective; sometimes they aren't. Although some boundary conditions may be idiosyncratic to the specific factors or idiosyncratic to the underlying processes, one common boundary condition relates to congruence, or fit, with expectations. For example, how a brand name sounds (high vs. low pitch) has symbolic connotations that influence liking for the name and the product itself. But liking is dependent upon the fit with the symbolic connotations and the expected or preferred attributes: The better the fit, the greater the liking.

The same fit effects are also noted for more complex communications, particularly interpersonal ones. For example, the choice of pronouns used in communications matters. Certain pronouns, such as "we," "I," and "us," influence perceptions of the communication and also the communicators. But again, sometimes the same pronoun ("we") is effective, sometimes not, and effectiveness is dependent upon the fit between the appropriateness of the pronoun and the perceptions of the closeness of the relationship. Emoticons often increase perceptions of warmth but only when they fit the appropriateness of the situation. Code-switching has positive persuasive effects but only when receivers' perceptions of the communicator (e.g., brand, company) fit with their expectations about the relationship.

As with any review chapter, documenting what is known about a topic also can expose what is not known, which represents future research questions. In terms of the research discussed in the cognitive processes section, one question pertains to the origins of effects such as phonetic symbolism. That is, how does this general effect arise? One possibility is that associations, such as size and sound, are learned over time. If so, then one would expect to see differential age effects during the developmental stage (i.e., not observable in young children, but the effects increase with age). One might also expect to see cultural differences in both the existence and the strength of the association. A second possibility is that the effects are innate and thus present at birth, and the effects occur through pure neural connections. This possibility may arise because certain associations (again, sound and size) may have evolutionary benefits and thus are selected for over generations (Shrum & Lowrey, 2007; for a review of possible mechanisms, see Sidhu & Pexman, 2018). Another question is whether two distinct processes govern phonetic symbolism, such as the fit between sounds and concepts (e.g., Yorkston

& Menon, 2004) versus simple sound preferences (e.g., Pogacar, Kouril, et al., 2018; Pogacar, Shrum, & Lowrey, 2018).

With respect to research falling under the social processes section, two questions emerge. The first concerns violations of expectations. As just noted, fit with expectations is generally a requirement for maximizing effectiveness (e.g., positive marketing outcomes). However, are there situations in which violations of expectations may actually have positive effects? For example, unexpected communication might also stimulate deeper processing and thus may be effective for high-involvement situations or enhancing memory. A second question is whether and how the fast-evolving pace of technology impacts consumers' communications (e.g., writing product reviews online, communicating with artificial intelligence products). Readers may have already observed a heightened tolerance for misspellings and autocorrect errors, a seemingly pathological aversion to commas (presumably arising from a texting culture), and acronyms such as "LOL" increasingly becoming part of everyday speech. Could other characteristics of technologically mediated communication also become norms? For instance, the rapid and direct style of online communication may change long-standing norms of etiquette for in-person communication. Similarly, might the shift from more personal modes of conversation (e.g., face-to-face) to less personal ones (e.g., text and email) influence the nature of our relationships? Perhaps future generations will replace a smaller number of strong social ties with larger networks of weaker ties. What might be the implications of such a shift for society?

With respect to cultural processes and language, two questions come to mind. One pertains to bilingual consumers. It is both theoretically and practically relevant to determine whether thinking in a second language affects both memory-based preferences (i.e., based on the consideration set retrieved from memory) and stimulus-based preferences (i.e., based on the choice alternatives present in the environment) of bilingual consumers. For example, for a bilingual consumer who has seen ads for perfumes in English compared with French language contexts, the word "perfume" in English might evoke a different consideration set for perfumes than the word "parfum" in French. Therefore, consumers' consideration sets can involve different perfume brands in different language contexts. Both theory and practice would benefit from a better understanding of which conditions and for which kind of consideration set this differential activation can affect preference.

On top of its practical implications for marketers, theoretically, research in this area can contribute to the debate on the extent to which language influences thought. A second question is how processing advertising messages in a second language affects consumption-related constructs. Given that languages differ widely in the way they conceptualize time (Chen, 2013), one promising question is to what extent processing messages in a second language affects consumers' time perception and their intertemporal decisions. This line of inquiry can further build on consumer cognition models and allow us to identify systematic grammar-based cross-cultural differences in intertemporal choice models.

Finally, one implication of the general findings on the effects of linguistic factors concerns the methods used to test linguistic effects. In particular, automatic text analysis tools are becoming increasingly popular because they can quickly and efficiently quantify natural language along a number of dimensions. However, current automatic text analysis tools (or natural language processing tools) mainly focus on content analysis and sentiment analysis. Given the findings we have just reviewed on the effects of various linguistic factors (e.g., phonetic symbolism, metaphor, grammatical structures), integrating these factors into text analysis tools would be greatly beneficial to researchers by providing more parameters by which to evaluate language effects.

Language is fascinating. It is something we at times take for granted (it's just how folks communicate) and at other times struggle with (how to write a persuasive communication). Learning new languages, and visiting new cultures, expands our knowledge about the forms and functions of language. Our objective in this review was to showcase the complexity and diversity of language in consumer contexts, expand knowledge about the effects of linguistic nuances, and ideally pass on our fascination to new readers, who will someday contribute to the development of answers for new research questions.

REFERENCES

Ahn, J., & Ferle, C. (2008). Enhancing recall and recognition for brand names and body copy: A mixed-language approach. *Journal of Advertising*, *37*(3), 107–117. https://doi.org/10.2753/JOA0091-3367370308

Alter, A. L., & Oppenheimer, D. M. (2006). Predicting short-term stock fluctuations by using processing fluency. *Proceedings of the National Academy of Sciences of the United States of America*, *103*(24), 9369–9372. https://doi.org/10.1073/pnas.0601071103

Ang, S. H., & Lim, E. A. C. (2006). The influence of metaphors and product type on brand personality perceptions and attitudes. *Journal of Advertising*, *35*(2), 39–53. https://doi.org/10.1080/00913367.2006.10639226

Apple, W., Streeter, L. A., & Krauss, R. M. (1979). Effects of pitch and speech rate on personal attributions. *Journal of Personality and Social Psychology*, *37*(5), 715–727. https://doi.org/10.1037/0022-3514.37.5.715

Aral, S., & Walker, D. (2014). Tie strength, embeddedness, and social influence: A large-scale networked experiment. *Management Science*, *60*(6), 1352–1370. https://doi.org/10.1287/mnsc.2014.1936

Argo, J. J., Popa, M., & Smith, M. C. (2010). The sound of brands. *Journal of Marketing*, *74*(4), 97–109. https://doi.org/10.1509/jmkg.74.4.097

Baxter, S., & Lowrey, T. M. (2014). Examining children's preference for phonetically manipulated brand names across two English accent groups. *International Journal of Research in Marketing*, *31*(1), 122–124. https://doi.org/10.1016/j.ijresmar.2013.10.005

Berger, J. (2014). Word of mouth and interpersonal communication: A review and directions for future research. *Journal of Consumer Psychology*, *24*(4), 586–607. https://doi.org/10.1016/j.jcps.2014.05.002

Berger, J., & Iyengar, R. (2013). Communication channels and word of mouth: How the medium shapes the message. *Journal of Consumer Research*, *40*(3), 567–579. https://doi.org/10.1086/671345

Bond, R. N., Welkowitz, J., Goldschmidt, H., & Wattenberg, S. (1987). Vocal frequency and person perception: Effects of perceptual salience and nonverbal sensitivity. *Journal of Psycholinguistic Research*, *16*(4), 335–350. https://doi.org/10.1007/BF01069287

Botner, K. A., Mishra, A., & Mishra, H. (2020). The influence of the phonetic elements of a name on risk assessment. *Journal of Consumer Research*, *47*(1), 128–145. https://doi.org/10.1093/jcr/ucz050

Brehm, J. W. (1966). *A theory of psychological reactance*. Academic Press.

Brown, P., & Levinson, S. C. (1987). *Politeness: Some universals in language usage* (Vol. 4). Cambridge University Press. https://doi.org/10.1017/CBO9780511813085

Brown, R. W., & Lenneberg, E. H. (1954). A study in language and cognition. *Journal of Abnormal and Social Psychology*, *49*(3), 454–462. https://doi.org/10.1037/h0057814

Carr, D., & Miles, C. (1997). Rhyme attenuates the auditory suffix effect: Alliteration does not. *Quarterly Journal of Experimental Psychology Section A*, *50*(3), 518–527. https://doi.org/10.1080/713755722

Carroll, R., Luna, D., & Peracchio, L. A. (2007). Dual language processing of marketing communications. In T. M. Lowrey (Ed.), *Psycholinguistic phenomena in marketing communications* (pp. 221–246). Lawrence Erlbaum.

Casasanto, D., & Boroditsky, L. (2008). Time in the mind: Using space to think about time. *Cognition*, *106*(2), 579–593. https://doi.org/10.1016/j.cognition.2007.03.004

Chattopadhyay, A., Dahl, D. W., Ritchie, R. J., & Shahin, K. N. (2003). Hearing voices: The impact of announcer speech characteristics on consumer response to broad cast advertising. *Journal of Consumer Psychology*, *13*(3), 198–204. https://doi.org/10.1207/S15327663JCP1303_02

Chen, M. K. (2013). The effect of language on economic behavior: Evidence from savings rates, health behaviors, and retirement assets. *American Economic Review*, *103*(2), 690–731. https://doi.org/10.1257/aer.103.2.690

Cian, L., Krishna, A., & Schwarz, N. (2015). Positioning rationality and emotion: Rationality is up and emotion is down. *Journal of Consumer Research*, *42*(4), 632–651. https://doi.org/10.1093/jcr/ucv046

Dahl, D. W. (2010). Understanding the role of spokesperson voice in broadcast advertising. In A. Krishna (Ed.), *Sensor marketing: Research on the sensuality of products* (pp. 169–182). Taylor & Francis.

Davis, D. F., Bagchi, R., & Block, L. G. (2016). Alliteration alters: Phonetic overlap in promotional messages influences evaluations and choice. *Journal of Retailing*, *92*(1), 1–12. https://doi.org/10.1016/j.jretai.2015.06.002

De Langhe, B., Puntoni, S., Fernandes, D., & van Osselaer, S. M. (2011). The anchor contraction effect in international marketing research. *Journal of*

Dillard, J. P., & Shen, L. (2005). On the nature of reactance and its role in persuasive health communication. *Communication Monographs, 72*(2), 144–168. https://doi.org/10.1080/03637750500111815

Dufour, R., & Kroll, J. F. (1995). Matching words to concepts in two languages: A test of the concept mediation model of bilingual representation. *Memory & Cognition, 23*(2), 166–180. https://doi.org/10.3758/BF03197219

Filkuková, P., & Klempe, S. H. (2013). Rhyme as reason in commercial and social advertising. *Scandinavian Journal of Psychology, 54*(5), 423–431. https://doi.org/10.1111/sjop.12069

Fitzsimons, G. J., & Lehmann, D. R. (2004). Reactance to recommendations: When unsolicited advice yields contrary responses. *Marketing Science, 23*(1), 82–94. https://doi.org/10.1287/mksc.1030.0033

Fitzsimons, G. M., & Kay, A. C. (2004). Language and interpersonal cognition: Causal effects of variations in pronoun usage on perceptions of closeness. *Personality and Social Psychology Bulletin, 30*(5), 547–557. https://doi.org/10.1177/0146167203262852

Forgas, J. P. (1998). Asking nicely? The effects of mood on responding to more or less polite requests. *Personality and Social Psychology Bulletin, 24*(2), 173–185. https://doi.org/10.1177/0146167298242006

French, P. L. (1977). Toward an explanation of phonetic symbolism. *Word, 28*(3), 305–322. https://doi.org/10.1080/00437956.1977.11435647

Gao, F., Lowrey, T. M., & Shrum, L. J. (2020). *Metaphoric transfer effect of "fullness" reduces hunger perceptions and portion size choice* [Manuscript under review].

Gelinas-Chebat, C., & Chebat, J. C. (1992). Effects of two voice characteristics on the attitudes toward advertising messages. *Journal of Social Psychology, 132*(4), 447–459. https://doi.org/10.1080/00224545.1992.9924724

Gendron, M., Lindquist, K. A., Barsalou, L., & Barrett, L. F. (2012). Emotion words shape emotion percepts. *Emotion, 12*(2), 314–325. https://doi.org/10.1037/a0026007

Grice, P. H. (1975). Logic and conversation. In P. Cole & J. L. Morgan (Eds.), *Syntax and semantics: Vol. 3. Speech acts* (pp. 41–58). Academic Press.

Grinstein, A., & Kronrod, A. (2016). Does sparing the rod spoil the child? How praising, scolding, and an assertive tone can encourage desired behaviors. *Journal of Marketing Research, 53*(3), 433–441. https://doi.org/10.1509/jmr.14.0224

Guèvremont, A., & Grohmann, B. (2015). Consonants in brand names influence brand gender perceptions. *European Journal of Marketing, 49*(1/2), 101–122. https://doi.org/10.1108/EJM-02-2013-0106

Humboldt, W. (1988). *On language: The diversity of human language structure and its influence on the mental development of mankind* (P. Heath, Trans.). Cambridge University Press. (Original work published 1836)

Hung, D. L., & Tzeng, O. J. L. (1981). Orthographic variations and visual information processing. *Psychological Bulletin, 90*(3), 377–414. https://doi.org/10.1037/0033-2909.90.3.377

Kacewicz, E., Pennebaker, J. W., Davis, M., Jeon, M., & Graesser, A. C. (2014). Pronoun use reflects standings in social hierarchies. *Journal of Language and Social Psychology, 33*(2), 125–143. https://doi.org/10.1177/0261927X13502654

Karatas, M. (2020). Making decisions in foreign languages: Weaker senses of ownership attenuate the endowment effect. *Journal of Consumer Psychology, 30*(2), 296–303. https://doi.org/10.1002/jcpy.1138

Klink, R. R. (2000). Creating brand names with meaning: The use of sound symbolism. *Marketing Letters, 11*(1), 5–20. https://doi.org/10.1023/A:1008184423824

Koslow, S., Shamdasani, P., & Touchstone, E. (1994). Exploring language effects in ethnic advertising: A sociolinguistic perspective. *Journal of Consumer Research, 20*(4), 575–585. https://doi.org/10.1086/209371

Krishna, A., & Ahluwalia, R. (2008). Language choice in advertising to bilinguals: Asymmetric effects for multinationals versus local firms. *Journal of Consumer Research, 35*(4), 692–705. https://doi.org/10.1086/592130

Kronrod, A., & Danziger, S. (2013). "Wii will rock you!" The use and effect of figurative language in consumer reviews of hedonic and utilitarian consumption. *Journal of Consumer Research, 40*(4), 726–739. https://doi.org/10.1086/671998

Kronrod, A., Grinstein, A., & Wathieu, L. (2012a). Enjoy! Hedonic consumption and compliance with assertive messages. *Journal of Consumer Research, 39*(1), 51–61. https://doi.org/10.1086/661933

Kronrod, A., Grinstein, A., & Wathieu, L. (2012b). Go green! Should environmental messages be so assertive? *Journal of Marketing, 76*(1), 95–102. https://doi.org/10.1509/jm.10.0416

Laham, S. M., Koval, P., & Alter, A. L. (2012). The name pronunciation effect: Why people like Mr. Smith more than Mr. Colquhoun. *Journal of Experimental Social Psychology, 48*(3), 752–756. https://doi.org/10.1016/j.jesp.2011.12.002

Landau, M. J., Meier, B. P., & Keefer, L. A. (2010). A metaphor-enriched social cognition. *Psychological Bulletin, 136*(6), 1045–1067. https://doi.org/10.1037/a0020970

Landau, M. J., Zhong, C. B., & Swanson, T. J. (2018). Conceptual metaphors shape consumer psychology. *Consumer Psychology Review*, *1*(1), 54–71. https://doi.org/10.1002/arcp.1002

Lee, J. K., & Kronrod, A. (2020). The strength of weak-tie consensus language. *Journal of Marketing Research*, *57*(2), 353–374. https://doi.org/10.1177/0022243720904957

Li, X., Chan, K. W., & Kim, S. (2019). Service with emoticons: How customers interpret employee use of emoticons in online service encounters. *Journal of Consumer Research*, *45*(5), 973–987. https://doi.org/10.1093/jcr/ucy016

Logan, R. (1986). *The alphabet effect*. Morrow.

Lowe, M. L., & Haws, K. L. (2017). Sounds big: The effects of acoustic pitch on product perceptions. *Journal of Marketing Research*, *54*(2), 331–346. https://doi.org/10.1509/jmr.14.0300

Lowrey, T. M. (1998). The effects of syntactic complexity on advertising persuasiveness. *Journal of Consumer Psychology*, *7*(2), 187–206. https://doi.org/10.1207/s15327663jcp0702_04

Lowrey, T. M. (2006). The relation between script complexity and commercial memorability. *Journal of Advertising*, *35*(3), 7–15. https://doi.org/10.2753/JOA0091-3367350301

Lowrey, T. M., & Shrum, L. J. (2007). Phonetic symbolism and brand name preference. *Journal of Consumer Research*, *34*(3), 406–414. https://doi.org/10.1086/518530

Lowrey, T. M., Shrum, L. J., & Dubitsky, T. M. (2003). The relation between brand-name linguistic characteristics and brand-name memory. *Journal of Advertising*, *32*(3), 7–17. https://doi.org/10.1080/00913367.2003.10639137

Luangrath, A. W., Peck, J., & Barger, V. A. (2017). Textual paralanguage and its implications for marketing communications. *Journal of Consumer Psychology*, *27*(1), 98–107. https://doi.org/10.1016/j.jcps.2016.05.002

Luna, D., & Peracchio, L. (2002). "Where there is a will...": Motivation as a moderator of language processing by bilingual consumers. *Psychology and Marketing*, *19*(7–8), 573–593. https://doi.org/10.1002/mar.10026

Luna, D., & Peracchio, L. (2005). Advertising to bilingual consumers: The impact of code-switching on persuasion. *Journal of Consumer Research*, *31*(4), 760–765. https://doi.org/10.1086/426609

Luna, D., & Peracchio, L. A. (2001). Moderators of language effects in advertising to bilinguals: A psycholinguistic approach. *Journal of Consumer Research*, *28*(2), 284–295. https://doi.org/10.1086/322903

Maglio, S. J., Rabaglia, C. D., Feder, M. A., Krehm, M., & Trope, Y. (2014). Vowel sounds in words affect mental construal and shift preferences for targets. *Journal of Experimental Psychology: General*, *143*(3), 1082–1096. https://doi.org/10.1037/a0035543

McGlone, M. S., & Tofighbakhsh, J. (2000). Birds of a feather flock conjointly (?): Rhyme as reason in aphorisms. *Psychological Science*, *11*(5), 424–428. https://doi.org/10.1111/1467-9280.00282

McNeel, A. E. (2017). *A whole new wurld? How unusual brand name spelling negatively affects sensory perceptions of new products through cognitive and affective processing* [Unpublished doctoral dissertation]. City University of New York.

McQuarrie, E. F., & Mick, D. G. (1999). Visual rhetoric in advertising: Text-interpretive, experimental, and reader response analyses. *Journal of Consumer Research*, *26*(1), 37–54. https://doi.org/10.1086/209549

Mecit, N. A., Lowrey, T. M., & Shrum, L. J. (2018). Linguistic antecedents of anthropomorphism. In A. Gershoff, R. Kozinets, & T. White (Eds.), *NA - Advances in consumer research* (Vol. 46, pp. 698–699). Association for Consumer Research.

Meteyard, L., Bahrami, B., & Vigliocco, G. (2007). Motion detection and motion verbs: Language affects low-level visual perception. *Psychological Science*, *18*(11), 1007–1013. https://doi.org/10.1111/j.1467-9280.2007.02016.x

Meyers-Levy, J., Louie, T. A., & Curren, M. T. (1994). How does the congruity of brand names affect evaluations of brand name extensions? *Journal of Applied Psychology*, *79*(1), 46–53. https://doi.org/10.1037/0021-9010.79.1.46

Miller, N., Maruyama, G., Beaber, R. J., & Valone, K. (1976). Speed of speech and persuasion. *Journal of Personality and Social Psychology*, *34*(4), 615–624. https://doi.org/10.1037/0022-3514.34.4.615

Moore, S. G. (2012). Some things are better left unsaid: How word of mouth influences the storyteller. *Journal of Consumer Research*, *38*(6), 1140–1154. https://doi.org/10.1086/661891

Moore, S. G. (2015). Attitude predictability and helpfulness in online reviews: The role of explained actions and reactions. *Journal of Consumer Research*, *42*(1), 30–44. https://doi.org/10.1093/jcr/ucv003

Moore, S. G., & Lafreniere, K. C. (2020). How online word-of-mouth impacts receivers. *Consumer Psychology Review*, *3*(1), 34–59. https://doi.org/10.1002/arcp.1055

Morris, M. W., Sheldon, O. J., Ames, D. R., & Young, M. J. (2007). Metaphors and the market: Consequences and preconditions of agent and object metaphors in stock market commentary. *Organizational Behavior and Human Decision Processes*, *102*(2),

174–192. https://doi.org/10.1016/j.obhdp.2006.03.001

Packard, G., Moore, S. G., & McFerran, B. (2018). (I'm) happy to help (you): The impact of personal pronoun use in customer–firm interactions. *Journal of Marketing Research*, 55(4), 541–555. https://doi.org/10.1509/jmr.16.0118

Pan, Y., & Schmitt, B. (1996). Language and brand attitudes: Impact of script and sound matching in Chinese and English. *Journal of Consumer Psychology*, 5(3), 263–277. https://doi.org/10.1207/s15327663jcp0503_03

Pogacar, R., Kouril, M., Carpenter, T. P., & Kellaris, J. J. (2018). Implicit and explicit preferences for brand name sounds. *Marketing Letters*, 29(2), 241–259. https://doi.org/10.1007/s11002-018-9456-7

Pogacar, R., Lowrey, T. M., & Shrum, L. J. (2018). The influence of marketing language on consumer perceptions and choice. In M. R. Solomon & T. M. Lowrey (Eds.), *The Routledge companion to consumer behavior* (pp. 263–275). Routledge.

Pogacar, R., Peterlin, A. P., Pokorn, N. K., & Pogačar, T. (2017). Sound symbolism in translation: A case study of character names in Charles Dickens's *Oliver Twist*. *Translation and Interpreting Studies*, 12(1), 137–161. https://doi.org/10.1075/tis.12.1.07pog

Pogacar, R., Plant, E., Rosulek, L. F., & Kouril, M. (2015). Sounds good: Phonetic sound patterns in top brand names. *Marketing Letters*, 26(4), 549–563. https://doi.org/10.1007/s11002-014-9288-z

Pogacar, R., Shrum, L. J., & Lowrey, T. M. (2018). The effects of linguistic devices on consumer information processing and persuasion: A language complexity × processing mode framework. *Journal of Consumer Psychology*, 28(4), 689–711. https://doi.org/10.1002/jcpy.1052

Puntoni, S., De Langhe, B., & van Osselaer, S. (2009). Bilingualism and the emotional intensity of advertising language. *Journal of Consumer Research*, 35(6), 1012–1025. https://doi.org/10.1086/595022

Quick, B. L., & Considine, J. R. (2008). Examining the use of forceful language when designing exercise persuasive messages for adults: A test of conceptualizing reactance arousal as a two-step process. *Health Communication*, 23(5), 483–491. https://doi.org/10.1080/10410230802342150

Roberson, D., Pak, H., & Hanley, J. R. (2008). Categorical perception of colour in the left and right visual field is verbally mediated: Evidence from Korean. *Cognition*, 107(2), 752–762. https://doi.org/10.1016/j.cognition.2007.09.001

Schmitt, B., Pan, Y., & Tavassoli, N. (1994). Language and consumer memory: The impact of linguistic differences between Chinese and English. *Journal of Consumer Research*, 21(3), 419–431. https://doi.org/10.1086/209408

Schmitt, B., & Zhang, S. (1998). Language structure and categorization: A study of classifiers in consumer cognition, judgment, and choice. *Journal of Consumer Research*, 25(2), 108–122. https://doi.org/10.1086/209530

Schwarz, N. (2004). Metacognitive experiences in consumer judgment and decision making. *Journal of Consumer Psychology*, 14(4), 332–348. https://doi.org/10.1207/s15327663jcp1404_2

Sela, A., Wheeler, S. C., & Sarial-Abi, G. (2012). We are not the same as you and I: Causal effects of minor language variations on consumers' attitudes toward brands. *Journal of Consumer Research*, 39(3), 644–661. https://doi.org/10.1086/664972

Sharf, D. J., & Lehman, M. E. (1984). Relationship between the speech characteristics and effectiveness of telephone interviewers. *Journal of Phonetics*, 12(3), 219–228. https://doi.org/10.1016/S0095-4470(19)30878-2

Shrum, L. J., & Lowrey, T. M. (2007). Sounds convey meaning: The implications of phonetic symbolism for brand name construction. In T. M. Lowrey (Ed.), *Psycholinguistic phenomena in marketing communications* (pp. 39–58). Erlbaum.

Shrum, L. J., Lowrey, T. M., Luna, D., Lerman, D. B., & Liu, M. (2012). Sound symbolism effects across languages: Implications for global brand names. *International Journal of Research in Marketing*, 29(3), 275–279. https://doi.org/10.1016/j.ijresmar.2012.03.002

Sidhu, D. M., & Pexman, P. M. (2018). Five mechanisms of sound symbolic association. *Psychonomic Bulletin & Review*, 25(5), 1619–1643. https://doi.org/10.3758/s13423-017-1361-1

Simmons, R. A., Gordon, P. C., & Chambless, D. L. (2005). Pronouns in marital interaction: What do "you" and "I" say about marital health? *Psychological Science*, 16(12), 932–936. https://doi.org/10.1111/j.1467-9280.2005.01639.x

Song, H., & Schwarz, N. (2009). If it's difficult to pronounce, it must be risky: Fluency, familiarity, and risk perception. *Psychological Science*, 20(2), 135–138. https://doi.org/10.1111/j.1467-9280.2009.02267.x

Spence, C. (2012). Managing sensory expectations concerning products and brands: Capitalizing on the potential of sound and shape symbolism. *Journal of Consumer Psychology*, 22(1), 37–54. https://doi.org/10.1016/j.jcps.2011.09.004

Tavassoli, N. T. (2001). Color memory and evaluations for alphabetic and logographic brand names. *Journal of Experimental Psychology: Applied*, 7(2), 104–111. https://doi.org/10.1037/1076-898X.7.2.104

Tavassoli, N. T., & Han, J. (2001). Scripted thought: Processing Korean Hancha and Hangul in a multimedia context. *Journal of Consumer Research*, 28(3), 482–493. https://doi.org/10.1086/323735

Whorf, B. L. (1952). Language, mind, and reality. *A Review of General Semantics*, 9(3), 167–188.

Wong, A. D. (2013). Brand names and unconventional spelling: A two-pronged analysis of the orthographic construction of brand identity. *Written Language and Literacy*, 16(2), 115–145. https://doi.org/10.1075/wll.16.2.01won

Yang, X., Mao, H., Jia, L., & Bublitz, M. G. (2019). A sweet romance: Divergent effects of romantic stimuli on the consumption of sweets. *Journal of Consumer Research*, 45(6), 1213–1229. https://doi.org/10.1093/jcr/ucy044

Yorkston, E., & De Mello, G. (2005). Linguistic gender marking and categorization. *Journal of Consumer Research*, 32(2), 224–234. https://doi.org/10.1086/432232

Yorkston, E., & Menon, G. (2004). A sound idea: Phonetic effects of brand names on consumer judgments. *Journal of Consumer Research*, 31(1), 43–51. https://doi.org/10.1086/383422

Zajonc, R. B. (1968). Attitudinal effects of mere exposure. *Journal of Personality and Social Psychology*, 9(2, Pt. 2), 1–27. https://doi.org/10.1037/h0025848

Zemack-Rugar, Y., Moore, S. G., & Fitzsimons, G. J. (2017). Just do it! Why committed consumers react negatively to assertive ads. *Journal of Consumer Psychology*, 27(3), 287–301. https://doi.org/10.1016/j.jcps.2017.01.002

Zhang, S., & Schmitt, B. (2004). Activating sound and meaning: The role of language proficiency in bilingual consumer environments. *Journal of Consumer Research*, 31(1), 220–228. https://doi.org/10.1086/383437

Zhang, S., & Schmitt, B. (2007). Phonology and semantics in international marketing: What brand name translations tell us about consumer cognition. In T. M. Lowrey (Ed.), *Psycholinguistic phenomena in marketing communications* (pp. 58–78). Lawrence Erlbaum.

CHAPTER 20

THE CONSUMER PSYCHOLOGY OF TRADITIONAL MEDIA

Esther Thorson

Dave Stewart predicted in 1992 that a major thrust of future research on advertising should be concerned with the question of how the media context influences responses to consumer messages. Of course, in 1992, Stewart was talking about traditional media, because there was not anything else. Stewart's question, in a nutshell, is what this chapter is about.

Traditional media include all of the one-to-many systems for conveying content to consumers. Traditional media include magazines, newspapers, mail (i.e., print), radio, television, and outdoor signage (e.g., billboards). Histories of the relationship of consumer messages and traditional media (e.g., McDonald & Scott, 2007; O'Barr, 2010; Presbrey, 2000) show that as each of these media developed (at least in the United States) decisions were made to rely on advertising to pay for creation and delivery of content, with consumers obtaining free or highly subsidized content in return for consuming the advertising. Thus print, radio, and television are examples of *platform firms*, that is, those in which the business model for the medium depends on bringing advertisers together with consumers (Evans et al., 2011; Sridhar et al., 2011). The media serve as a *platform*, that is, a multisided business that derives revenue from bringing consumer messages and consumers together.

Of course, when the modern study of advertising began in the late 1800s (Presbrey, 2000), much of the early research involved the psychology of consumers encountering media as platforms from which they received desired content in exchange for processing that content in a context is which there were many, many ads. It is important to understand this conception of how the consumer psychology of traditional media developed, because consumer messages are mostly the psychological price people pay for news, editorial and entertainment content that they desire. This chapter is therefore organized around a consumer psychology of traditional media that focuses on the processing of advertising in the sense of a trade-off between consuming something undesired as payment for consuming something desired. The coin in this realm is, of course, consumer attention.

Unfortunately, the platform-based business of traditional media is headed toward oblivion because advertisers no longer depend on the traditional media to reach consumers, thus erasing the value of bringing consumers to advertising embedded in traditional media content. Replacing traditional media are all the devices (e.g., laptops, tablets, cellphones) and content innovations (e.g., websites, blogs, social media) that are, in many ways, superior to affordances provided by traditional media. Affordances lacking in traditional media include such features as interactivity, sharing capacity, and editability. For example, people's contact with consumer messages is now detailed, individualized, and easily aggregated

https://doi.org/10.1037/0000262-020
APA Handbook of Consumer Psychology, L. R. Kahle (Editor-in-Chief)
Copyright © 2022 by the American Psychological Association. All rights reserved.

over various new media and over time in the digital realm, with sophisticated measurement that the traditional media could never provide. (See Chapter 21 on social media for further elaboration of how advertising now operates in that environment.)

As is discussed in the early sections of this chapter, the consumer psychology of traditional media developed under the constraints of the platform nature of their business model. Processing consumer messages was not the motivation to consume traditional media. In fact, avoiding consumer messages would allow consumers to derive unadulterated pleasure of consuming traditional media. Thus, it is critical to understand the role of message rejection and reactance on how people process consumer messages in traditional media. In fact, much consumer psychology theory in this domain can be understood in terms of the fact that, for the consumer, the primary or desired task is not to process ads.

We also see that attempts to understand consumer message processing in traditional media are greatly influenced by basic psychological theory, especially from the psychological literatures on learning and memory, attitudes, attention, and emotion.

Finally, this chapter joins a growing effort to understand human processing from an evolutionary view (e.g., Barkow et al., 1992; Confer et al., 2010; Saad, 2004; Saad & Gill, 2000; Shapiro & Epstein, 1998; Tooby & Cosmides, 1989; Wiederman, 1993). It starts from thinking about our human ancestors trying to persuade each other, while dealing with persuasion attempts by others. I argue that processes mediated through traditional media can be readily understood in terms of how evolution led to critical observations of human social psychology. The fundamental concept argued in evolutionary theory about brain and language is that humans desire to persuade, but they resist the attempts of others to persuade them. While the glory days of consumer messages embedded in traditional media are clearly over, I argue here that much of what has been learned about processing ads in traditional media remains relevant and even informative about consumer messages in the digital world (see Rodgers et al., 2009).

HOW CONSUMER MESSAGES RELATE TO TRADITIONAL MEDIA

This chapter was written during a massive shift in media use patterns. The shift is, of course, away from traditional media and toward digitally based media including devices like computers, iPads, and mobile devices and, more importantly, to a large variety of channels of content available on these devices, for example, social media (see Chapter 21), games, blogs, videos, streaming content, digital news, and so on. This shift is generally interpreted to imply that in the future traditional media may be almost entirely replaced by digitally based media. This leads us to ask, would complete abandonment of traditional media mean that years of research on the consumer psychology of traditional media is rendered useless? That is, will the thousands of research studies that focused on how people process television, print, radio, outdoor, and direct mail largely lose their value?

The argument developed here is that the value of consumer psychology of traditional media will remain relevant, perhaps with even some of it proving to be fundamental to understanding digital media consumer psychology. This optimistic view is based on an argument that media consumer psychology has led to creation of theories about how people respond to mediated persuasion that hold true regardless of the particular form of media carrying those messages. Consumer messages in the digital environment, although targeted to individual interests and needs, are still mostly an interruption of the processing of desired content.

Of course, many theories about the psychology of traditional media exist, and one chapter can certainly never cover all of them. Nonetheless, the approach here is to focus on a small number of highly influential theories about the psychology of encountering, attending to, trying to avoid, remembering, being persuaded by, and handling dual processing of messages about goods, services, organizations, activities, and so on. Because of the platform business structure of traditional media, people are mostly subjected to consumer messages that they would rather not experience: messages that irritate or bore them or interrupt ongoing content in which they are interested (Schumann & Thorson, 1990). Only sometimes are consumer messages welcomed, as in, for example, highly creative ads during the Super Bowl, funny attention-grabbing ads whenever and wherever they occur, ads that fool people into thinking they are not ads (e.g., infomercials or native advertising), and ads that convince people they provide important information about products that will somehow enhance their status (e.g., fashion, decorating, sports equipment advertising; ads usually embedded in a highly relevant editorial context about the topic). The psychology of advertising, at least for traditional media, involves a fairly common understanding that sitting through ads is a way of reducing the cost to people of content they desire. Individuals process ads as compensation for receiving desired editorial or programming content. Before delving into important theoretical understandings of processing mediated consumer messages, I turn briefly to some important facts and statistics about the development of traditional media caused by digital media innovation. This provides understanding of why I say traditional media are likely close to collapse, even for still-profitable broadcast television.

TRADITIONAL MEDIA DISRUPTED

eMarketer (He, 2019) reported that Americans spend an average of 12 hours and 9 minutes each day on media use. Six hours and 35 minutes go to digital media, broadcast or cable TV gets 3 hours 35 minutes, radio 1 hour 20 minutes, newspapers 11 minutes, and magazines 9 minutes. Thus television remains a competitive player, but most print media are becoming used only at very low levels.

Money spent on mediated consumer messages (from here referred to as "advertising") has tracked closely the change in time spent with media. From 2002 through 2019, TV advertising spending went from 33.4% to 30.6% of total advertising spending, newspaper from 31% to 6%, magazine from 15.3% to 5.5%, and radio from 13.3% to 7.2%, while internet-based went from 3.8% to 44.7% (Marketing Charts, 2019). Boding poorly for television, however, consumer age (He, 2019) has been responsible for its much slower disruption than the other traditional media. From 2012 to 2016, television gained 2% in time for those 65 or older, but for those 35 to 49, there was a 19% loss; those aged 25 to 34, a 34% loss; and those aged 12 to 24, a 38% loss. Without a major technological change, broadcast and cable television will join the other traditional media with virtually complete loss of advertising dollars. (It should be noted that "broadcast internet," a technology sometimes referred to as ATSC 3.0, may in coming years save broadcast television; e.g., see Wouk & Cohen, 2020.) Currently, maintenance of commercial television largely depends on the continued loyalty of live sports and local broadcast news to commercial television (Sino, 2018).

In this discussion, it should be noted that *television* is defined as content channeled via broadcast or cable, but of course there are now broader definitions of television that include direct streaming to computers, tablets, or mobile devices. An important difference, however, is that much of streaming content is paid for by the consumer and contains very little or no advertising. It should also be noted that outdoor media ad expenditures have remained undisrupted to date, although the total expenditures are so low that they remain largely irrelevant to understanding the psychology of mediated consumer messages (He, 2019).

Before the ubiquity of digital mediation and digital devices, people were still surrounded by an enormous barrage of consumer messages. The internet became a major player in advertising in the mid-1990s (Ad Age, 2003). Since then, the number of ads that people are exposed to every day is estimated to have increased significantly (Hall, 2019). Nevertheless, even before the birth of digital channels and devices, people in Western cultures were exposed to a lot of advertising.

The bottom line is that the continuation of traditional advertising-supported media is much in doubt (in other words, traditional media will no longer be supported as platform businesses). Therefore the task of a chapter on the psychology of traditional consumer media is to identify aspects of the study of traditional media that hold possibilities for understanding digitally mediated consumer messages (e.g., see earlier versions of this argument in

Schumann & Thorson, 2007; Thorson & Rodgers, 2019). Later sections of this chapter highlight the major psychological perspectives and theories that have arisen from the consumer psychology of traditional media.

THE EVOLUTIONARY PSYCHOLOGY OF PERSUASION AND MEDIATED PERSUASION

To understand the fundamentals of processing consumer-mediated persuasion, we can think of the situation in terms of the evolution of people's social interactions with each other (e.g., Mercier & Landemore, 2012). Evolutionary psychologists provide important insights into human responses to attempts to persuade them (e.g., Sperber, 2000). Of course, the earliest of such attempts were interpersonal, but presumably the psychological mechanisms that humans developed to deal with persuasion attempts over thousands of years are relevant to mediated persuasion attempts (Reeves & Nass, 1996).

An important thread in our understanding human response to persuasion attempts comes from research over the last 20 years or so that suggests humans often fail to use logically correct reasoning under many circumstances (e.g., Kahneman, 2003; Mercier & Landemore, 2012). One of the most common errors humans make is called *confirmation bias* (Nickerson, 1998). In many situations, people are more likely to accept information that is consistent with what they already believe, rather than information that is inconsistent with prior beliefs. Reasoning seems biased toward "confirming" one's own beliefs. The frequency of this finding has suggested that the primary function of human reasoning is argumentative (Mercier & Landemore, 2012). That is, cognition operates to identify ways to win arguments, rather than to evaluate them logically. From an evolutionary point of view, this makes sense. It is important to persuade people to share their resources with you, to engage in sex with you, or to come to your aid when you are attacked. Therefore, the fundamental goal in the development of brain and language is an effort to persuade others. Of course, the snag is that others are trying to persuade you at the same time you're trying to persuade them. The evolutionary perspective claims everyone's motivation is propagation of their genes into subsequent generations, and of course this is always a competitive situation. Persuading others is paramount to you, but resisting the persuasive efforts of others on you is just as important.

This evolutionary perspective suggests that both interpersonal, and, as it came into being, mediated persuasion, will meet a lot of resistance or reactance. An important guide to resistance and reactance is psychological reactance theory (PRT; J. W. Brehm, 1966). This prominent psychological theory has been extensively applied to understanding how people process and respond to advertising. For example, Fransen et al. (2015) explained how PRT delineates important strategies and motivations to resist persuasion. Given advertising in traditional media is a price, not a goal for consumers, this perspective provides an excellent overview of consumer processing of messages in traditional media (Clee & Wicklund, 1980).

REACTANCE STRATEGIES

In PRT, reactance strategies include avoiding, contesting, doing biased processing, and seeking to gain empowerment (Fransen et al., 2015). In PRT, motivations occur when humans perceive events or messages to be persuasion attempts. These perceptions include perceived threats to freedom, reluctance to change, and anxiety about being deceived. Each of these perceptions is consistent with our picture of the evolution of human response to persuasion, and each represents areas of research on the psychology of processing traditional mediated persuasive messages. I look first at the strategies and then at the perceptions, using each to elucidate the consumer psychology of processing advertising.

Avoidance

There exists a large literature on how people avoid ads (e.g., Rojas-Méndez et al., 2009; Siddarth & Chattopadhyay, 1998; Speck & Elliott, 1997). With television, they switch channels when an ad comes on or fast-forward through it. They may turn the television off. They can multitask, that is, in the digital age, look at another screen like a smartphone or a laptop or, for traditional media, listen to radio or read a magazine during television ad breaks. They can intentionally ignore ads. Advertising avoidance has become an entire subfield, with scores of studies focused on it. Avoiding persuasion possibilities is an important strategy that humans have developed to cope with the onslaught of mediated persuasion messages.

Contesting

The most common form of contesting a persuasive message is *counterarguing*, which involves coming up with reasons why the persuasion is incorrect or misleading. A typical way to measure the impact of traditional ads is to measure how much and what kind of counterarguing they induce (Anand & Sternthal, 1992; Greenwald, 1968; Xu & Wyer, 2012). One variable known to increase counterarguing is making the fact that the message is intended to persuade more obvious. One way to reduce counterarguing is to disguise advertising to make it appear as just a part of editorial content. "Advertorials" lead to far greater positive response and less counterarguing than ads that look like ads (Attaran et al., 2015; Cameron & Ju-Pak, 2000). In the online environment, advertising that looks like editorial content (called "native advertising") is more effectively persuasive when people are led to believe it is actually news content (Lee et al., 2016; Wojdynski & Evans, 2016). Advertising that appears as "product placement" in films is highly effective persuasion (Homer, 2009). Getting a brand talked about in a news story via publicity efforts leads to a more positive response to the brand than advertising for that brand (Stammerjohan et al., 2005). These strategies of disguising advertising as a persuasive message show how removal of the cue that a message is an attempted persuasion effort leads to much more acceptance, less counterarguing, and so on.

Another way to reduce reactance is to provide cues that the source of the message is not advertisers looking out for their own good (e.g., political ads, brand ads) but rather that the source desires good outcomes for the receiver. For example, there is much less reactance to public service announcements than to brand or political advertising (Gunther & Thorson, 1992).

One of the most important theories of contesting is the persuasion knowledge model (PKM) introduced by Friestad and Wright (1994) and enjoying extensive application in studies of consumer processing of ads. Ham et al. (2015) provided an extensive review of PKM research in terms of its effects on advertising persuasion. The fundamental tenet of PKM is that when people become aware that a message is an intentional effort to persuade them (e.g., it is an ad), they respond by thinking about ways the ad is trying to impact or even trick them into compliance. That is, when persuasion knowledge is stimulated by a cue, persuasive effectiveness is reduced.

Another area of contesting is *defensive stereotyping*, which can refer either to the structure of the message itself (Friestad & Wright, 1994) or to the source of the message. If the source is perceived negatively, then the value of the message itself is reduced. The advertising literature has measured this kind of response by relying on the general attitude to advertising (e.g., MacKenzie & Lutz, 1989). If people believe that advertising is a negative aspect of society (e.g., it misinforms, leads to materialism), the messages seen as ads will be treated much more negatively than when people have a positive general attitude toward advertising.

Biased Processing

Biased processing strategies can be subsumed under the assumption that the function of human reasoning is argumentative. As outlined earlier, humans are generally not looking for what is true but for information that supports their own beliefs. There are several ways this can be accomplished. One is to weight attributes that are inconsistent with one's own viewpoint lower and those that are consistent as higher. Another is to identify information inconsistent with one's own perspective as very narrow and having little effect among all the supportive information. A third is *optimism bias*, which refers to when people, to protect and justify their own beliefs or behaviors, believe that bad things are less likely to happen to them than to other people. For example, in response to an anti-alcohol ad that says drinking reduces your life expectancy, drinkers may think about how their parents drank heavily and still lived long lives.

Empowerment

A fourth strategy involves coming up with perspectives that help people perceive they can successfully resist persuasion efforts. Most relevant to responding to mediated consumer messages is attitude bolstering. *Attitude bolstering* occurs when people think about their own perspectives and how good, convincing, and correct they are. A good example of this is the fact that consumers think they are more resistant to persuasion than others (e.g., Sagarin et al., 2002). Indeed, extensive support for this idea comes from research on what is called the third-person effect (Davison, 1983). The classic questions used to measure the third-person effect are "How affected are you personally to this ad?" and "How affected do you think others are to this ad?" When the answers to these questions are compared, people consistently say others are more affected than they are. Interestingly, when the ad in question happens to be a public service message, people consistently say they are more affected by it than others are (Gunther & Thorson, 1992).

As can be seen, then, the four strategies are consistent with major findings about the social psychology of advertising avoidance. In addition to the strategies, however, motives are posited for people to employ the strategies in the first place. Recall that our evolutionary perspective emphasizes the idea that humans have generally been rewarded for persuading others to their advantage while resisting the persuasion of others to their advantage or, worse yet, to one's own disadvantage. We see that three major posited motives for persuasion resistance can be understood in terms of this perspective.

MOTIVES FOR PERSUASION RESISTANCE

Motives to resist a message are generally caused by three perceptions (Fransen et al., 2015). Each of these can be thought of in terms of human evolution. One motive is perception of a threat to freedom. The idea that humans developed cognitive systems whose primary function was argumentative (Mercier & Landemore, 2012), that is, wanting to win arguments likely associated with getting food, space, sex, and for self, means that there is a clear motivation not to have others' arguments win. When others win, an individual is likely to be left with the less desirable food and less power to obtain ends that would increase their survivability. In fact, Kirmani and Campbell (2009), in their discussion of PKM, pointed out that consumers often enter a persuasion situation specifically with the idea of winning.

Fransen et al. (2015) considered the motive to protect one's own freedom to be innate. Of course, the evolutionary perspective would suggest this motivation developed as the human brain evolved. As we saw previously in PRT, S. S. Brehm and Brehm (1981/2013) argued that humans have an innate desire for autonomy and independence. When humans see their autonomy threatened, they seek to restore it, which means they react against whatever the threat is. Cues to the presence of threat include one's being unable to hold one's own attitudes and behaviors or one's inability to become committed to a different position. Research suggests that even when a message is designed to be in an individual's best interest, the loss of freedom threat can operate—and that response is often accompanied by anger (S. S. Brehm & Brehm, 1981/2013). Further, the more a message has highly assertive cues, for example, spoken in an imperative language style, the more likely it is the stimulation of the autonomy threat perception occurs. Again, this makes sense in terms of ancient humans who recognized that when encountering an aggressive cue from others wanting them to do something, that situation likely led to danger. It should be noted that cues to the presence of persuasion efforts, of course, are also considered critical in PKM.

Fransen et al.'s (2015) second and third motives can probably be subsumed under "perceived threats." One of them is reluctance to change, a response perhaps triggered because of fear of the outcome or reduction in view of one's own self-esteem. The evolutionary perspective would reduce this also to a fundamental situation where the threatened individual does not fare well, that is, where results are a reduction of necessary resources for survival and/or increased probability of a survival threat.

The third response is fear of deception, which again concerns the likelihood that the individual is tricked into acquiescing and as a result loses critical resources. It should be noted that Fransen et al. (2015) related fear of deception to the operation of persuasion knowledge, just as in PKM. As soon as the individual realizes persuasion is involved, suspicion and skepticism are aroused. In today's world of advertising messages, the alerting occurs when the sponsor of a message is not immediately revealed but then is later identified. Undisclosed sponsorships can backfire when disclosure does occur. The perception grows that the message has ulterior motives, that is, instead of providing positives for the individual, the resources will go to the messenger instead. Interestingly, Kirmani and Campbell (2009) suggested that the fear of deception is also a major motivator for people, as they described interpersonal persuasion attempts by others (p. 299).

Overall, Fransen et al. (2015) provided an important and helpful perspective in which mediated consumer messages are often responded to with reactive strategies: avoidance, contesting, biased processing of the message itself, and empowerment responses. Here it is argued that this dominant form of processing advertising results from thinking of persuasion in terms of evolutionary psychology. We are highly motivated to argue successfully so others are persuaded by us. But there is often danger in having others' arguments persuade us. Surveys of the vast territory of studies of human processing of advertising verify the dominance of desiring not to be persuaded. As can be seen, barriers to being responsive to advertising in a variety of ways provide a useful and wide-ranging perspective on the consumer psychology of traditional media. It is also clear that advertising messages in traditional media occur because these media are in the business of acting as a platform.

It should be noted, however, that there is also a social psychology literature that examines how people do attempt to evaluate the degree of danger in responding to persuasive attempts, both mediated and interpersonal. For example, Kirmani and Campbell (2009) pointed out that with interpersonal professional communicators (salespeople), consumers may decide to look to them to provide information they feel they need to achieve their goals (e.g., getting the best automobile for the money). When consumers are reading fashion, sports, and other topic-specific magazines, they may intentionally look for guidance in the advertising (e.g., what are the best athletic shoes, the most expensive handbags). Kirmani and Campbell also suggested that consumers may be motivated to assess how knowledgeable an agent (i.e., the persuader) is. Probably most importantly, consumers may decide that the agent is likely to understand and support the consumer's goals and therefore rely on and respond to persuasion from the agent. In consumer-mediated messages, consumers may decide a particular brand, retail outlet, or medium is to be trusted and therefore become likely to follow persuasion suggestions. Therefore, it is important to note that reactance against the persuasion of others is not always the response, but rather the consumer has additional choices about judging circumstances when the persuasive message should be accepted. Again, this judgment about whom to trust and whom to fear is a concept deeply important in PKM (Kirmani & Campbell, 2009, p. 296).

This foray into instances when consumers consider the persuasion situation and decide it provides positive outcomes for self is a good introduction to the following section. After looking thoroughly at resisting advertising, we turn next to how advertising manages to work—to be liked, paid attention to, and remembered and, most importantly, how it acts to motivate purchase, earn a vote, or nudge people to change their behavior toward healthy alternatives.

UNDERSTANDING THE PSYCHOLOGY OF SUCCESSFUL CONSUMER MESSAGES IN TRADITIONAL MEDIA

An important tool for a broad understanding of the psychology of successful consumer messages is the work of Nyilasy and Reid (2009; which I have often used as an organizing principle for overviewing advertising psychology in general; e.g., Thorson

& Rodgers, 2019). Nyilasy and Reid (2009) did in-depth interviews with advertising professionals about how they think advertising works, leading to what they called advertising practitioner theory. The theory rests on three basic beliefs on which practitioners largely agree and then use to create and implement consumer messages into traditional (and presently digital) media.

First, they say that to work, advertising must "break through" the clutter of stimulation from all kinds of other inputs, both competing advertising and surrounding content, and "engage." In the present framework, this can be thought of as getting past all the strategies people are engaged in so as to protect themselves from persuasion forces—avoiding ads, counterarguing them, self-bolstering to prove that the persuader has nothing useful to offer, or employing biased processing on the messages to make them consistent with what individuals already believe.

A second practitioner belief is "mutation of effects," which simply means that over time and a number of repetitions of a consumer message, it wears out, that is, becomes less effective and goes from being accepted to being avoided and reacted against. Another way to say this is that consumer reactance reappears against a once-accepted message.

The third practitioner belief is that to get past consumer reactance barriers, consumer messages must always be "creative," that is, they must put something in the message that humans have not encountered before, something that breaks through persuasion barriers, leading it to receive welcoming attention. Most creative consumer messages fall into the category of novel or sticky, that is, they have attributes people haven't seen before in ads (think of Ridley Scott's "1984" Super Bowl ad for Apple's first personal computer; Hiltzik, 2017) or components that are very memory-strong ("I can't believe I ate the whole thing"; "Whassup?"; "Where's the beef?").

The three practitioner beliefs integrate well with the assumption that the most common response to advertising is negative, which, as we have seen, receives strong support from the consumer psychology literature. Even successful advertising wears out, again stimulating negative responses to it. Second, the practitioner beliefs point to the importance and possibility of triggering basic psychological responses like remembering (and learning), liking, paying attention to, and desiring whatever the ad is trying to persuade.

Indeed, a majority of studies in the last 75 years of the psychology of processing advertising in the traditional media can be summarized in terms of search for stimuli that influence whether people pay attention to, remember, come to like (i.e., experience attitude change about), or exhibit acquiescent responses to advertising (e.g., buying a brand, not driving while drunk, donating to causes, or starting to think that a corporation is a better social actor than originally thought). Kirmani and Campbell (2009) referred to this literature as being focused on the "agent of social influence" (p. 294), rather than the target of social influence impact, that is, the consumer. Pursuing the agent view, I look first at stimulus dimensions that have proved important to breaking through and engaging, and then return to look at types of psychological responses to ads that are important for persuasion to occur.

A METHODOLOGICAL NOTE

This is a good place to remark that the theoretical perspective developed here is primarily concerned with the psychology of processing ads "in the wild." It is the case, however, that a large portion of advertising research has relied on two methodologies that are probably often misleading about how advertising performs when encountered naturally in traditional media. The first methodology is surveying people about their responses to advertising. This requires self-report, which is, especially for low-involving stimuli and undesired stimuli like ads, notoriously misleading (e.g., Lastovicka, 1995). Buttle (1991) argued that surveys fail to provide any useful information about what people actually do with advertising. Vavreck (2007) pointed out how poorly predictive self-report of exposure to advertising is on voter turnout. Aaker and Stayman (1990) noted additional shortcomings of survey research for evaluating ad effectiveness.

A second problematic methodology is laboratory experiments. Here the central problem is that when consumers experience forced viewing of commercials, their attention to the commercials is almost always much higher than when viewing in real settings. Edwards et al. (2002) provided evidence that forced viewing increases scores on reactance measures. Venkatraman et al. (2015) showed that neurophysiologic measures perform better than experimental data in predicting ad performance in the field.

Nevertheless, having spent a large part of my career engaged with surveys and experiments, I believe they have some benefits even though they are often problematic. Experiments are helpful particularly for understanding the role of effective stimulus attributes of consumer messages, and of course experimentation is the only methodology that allows causal inference. But the fundamental perspective here is that the psychology of processing consumer messages that appear in real-world traditional media like television, radio, outdoor, or print publications must be studied in circumstances where consumers are able to exhibit their strong propensity to avoid, react against, and reject a large percent of the messages directed at them. It also should be noted that recent research suggests that responses to advertising online, even though supposedly accurately targeted toward people's needs and desires, still shows significant reactance (Cho & University of Texas at Austin, 2004; Johnson, 2013; Seyedghorban et al., 2016).

CONSUMER MESSAGE ATTRIBUTES THAT BREAK THROUGH AVOIDANCE

We turn next to features of advertising that make it more effective and processes that it can stimulate that also increase its power.

Narratives

Consumer messages can either emphasize information in something of a lecture format or they can tell a story in which the persuasion objective (e.g., to sell a brand) plays a role (Deighton et al., 1989; Wells, 1989). Narrative ads will ideally contain all the linguistic elements of a story: who, what, when, where, why, how, and the chronology of events (Kim et al., 2017). There is evidence that humans have evolved to respond to stories because they are such a natural way to organize events and make sense of them (Fisher, 1989). There are many theories of how narratives lead to more positive psychological responses to ads (e.g., J. Wang & Calder, 2009; Woodside et al., 2008). Deighton et al. (1989) demonstrated that narrative advertising seems to pull people into empathetic processing, which would explain how it decreases negativity. Green and Brock (2000) proposed that consumers are transported into a flow of pleasant experience, which in turn decreases negative thoughts such as counterarguing or skepticism. Escalas (1998, 2007) argued that embedding brands in stories leads to consumers self-identifying with the brand and in that way displaces negative responses. Findings are quite clear in all of this work that narrative ads are more effective persuaders than ads.

There are clearly common denominators in all of the theories about the power of narratives that are consistent with the evolutionary perspective. It is thought that since the beginnings of human language sophisticated enough to tell stories, narratives have had a dominant impact on cognition, feelings, attention, and relating to others. Stories help people understand their own personal experiences, emphasize their connectedness with others, and, as a result, increase trust, reducing skepticism and fear of deceit. Embedding a persuasive intent into a story is a strong way to reduce message reactance.

Integrated Messages Across Different Media

Since the mid-1990s, there has been active study of how the ads in different media interact with each other to affect people's responses to brands (e.g., Luxton et al., 2015; Schultz, 1992) or how advertising interacts with other kinds of promotional activity within a single campaign (e.g., Stammerjohan et al., 2005). For example, a brand campaign that uses a similar "look and feel," the same tagline, and the same selling appeal for its television and radio commercials and its magazine ads is hypothesized to produce greater persuasion (as measured in terms of sales, attitudes toward the brand, or whatever measure is desired) than spending the same amount of advertising dollars on a single one of the media. This approach is called integrated marketing communication (IMC; Schultz, 1992; Schultz & Schultz, 1998). Although there is much industry enthusiasm for creating "one look" campaigns, where there are common denominators in the selling message but the advertising appears in a number of different channels or the advertising is combined with various public relations activities, brand websites, or promotions like coupons or contests, there is surprisingly little research on the effectiveness of integrating persuasive voices.

Another way to say this is that coordinated messages across different media create "synergy," that increases the effect of each medium by itself (e.g., Chang & Thorson, 2004; Thorson et al., 2005). Naik and Peters (2009), although they focused only on digital media, where, of course, impact measurement is so much better, found that synergies among digital media can be calculated mathematically, allowing marketers to optimize their advertising spend across the various media in an integrated campaign. Assael (2011) argued that although IMC is considered a fundamentally correct way to go about media planning, there is still much to be learned about why and how combined media campaigns produce their superior outcomes.

In fact, there are few clear theoretical findings about why receiving the same message in slightly different forms would be better than pure repetition of ads themselves. Tavassoli and Lee (2003) suggested there is value in "encoding variability," that is, the same message coming in either different sensory channels (e.g., auditory and visual) or coming from different sources (e.g., a news story about a brand vs. an ad for the brand) in the sense that richer, more complex, and stronger memory traces are created. Haugtvedt et al. (1994) suggested that having the same message reach people with slight variations leads to slower "wearout" of the advertising. It is also likely that the processes underlying synergetic effects of IMC vary in terms of specific combinations of media. For example, Stammerjohan et al. (2005) showed that positive publicity complements advertising in predictable ways, while the effects of negative publicity seem to be mitigated through advertising that creates brand familiarity.

Like the other topics we have examined, the idea of integrating different media works online as well as in traditional media (e.g., Jensen & Jepsen, 2006; Jiang & Chia, 2010).

Disguised Advertising

We have already discussed the fact that when advertising does not look like advertising, then many of the barriers to persuasion disappear or are at least diminished. Advertising disguise, however, is an ethically challenged approach (see literature cited earlier; see also Garfield, 2014), and therefore it is listed here as an approach but not recommended. Further, there are considerable dangers to using disguised advertising, especially as consumers come to realize it is actually advertising (e.g., Adler, 2015). This is such a problem that the U.S. federal government has introduced rules on "disclosure" for disguised advertising in the digital realm (Adler, 2015). For example, "influencers" who post about products on Facebook, Instagram, or YouTube must disclose whether the brands they talk about are actually paying them.

ADVERTISING ATTRIBUTES THAT AFFECT MEMORY AND ATTENTION

The emphasis that practitioners place on breaking through and engaging reflects the importance of attentional processes. Perhaps to its detriment, early research on attention to advertising was indexed by memory for ads. In the 1940s Nielsen invented a machine that would log what radio stations people listened to, and in the 1950s the company began using TV viewing diaries to track what television shows were being watched. In the 1980s the "people meter" was created and was attached to a large sample of televisions in homes to monitor viewing. Although fairly primitive, program monitoring allowed Nielsen to know that people had watched programming that advertising appeared in and, by calling individuals 24 hours later and asking what they could remember of the advertising, get an index of how well the ad broke through and engaged. The measure was called 24-hour recall (advertisers bought this service), but it was argued to index not only memory but also attention. Krugman (1977), an early television researcher, argued that "an important index for the success of advertising was remembering seeing it and knowing what it said." For a time, there was a lot of research on what features of ads created stronger memory and presumed attention that preceded the stronger memory (e.g., Zinkhan, 1982). Pieters et al. (2002) provided evidence that ad originality and familiarity increased attention to ads. Smith et al. (2007) also argued that creativity was the major driver of attention to advertising and actually developed a scale to measure perceived ad creativity. Memory for ads was considered so important as an evaluative measure of their impact that many studies attempted to predict 24-hour recall (e.g., Stewart & Furse, 1986) and intent to purchase an advertising brand.

During the 1990s research turned away from memory as an index of advertising attention and instead began measuring attention directly. Physiological measures like the orienting response (observed in heart rate) were used to track attention across the 30 or 60 seconds of advertising (e.g., Thorson & Lang, 1992). Eye movements and fixations (Rayner et al., 2008) were used to index the attention consumers devote to different areas of magazine ads. For television, attention was measured as eyes on screen (e.g., Thorson, 1994). Some of the significant findings about attending to advertising included the fact that how much people are engaged in programming and whether they are effectively engaged impacts how much they like advertising embedded in the programming (e.g., Murry et al., 1992). Z. Wang and Lang (2012) argued that programs provide an "excitation transfer" from response to programs to ads embedded in them. De Pelsmacker et al. (2002) demonstrated that ads in the context of liked and appreciated television programs created more positive attitudes toward the ads embedded in them. How media context influences response to embedded advertising continues as most ads become digital (e.g., Goldsmith & Lafferty, 2002).

ATTITUDES TOWARD CONSUMER MESSAGES AND ADVERTISING IN GENERAL

As noted in the discussion of memory for advertising, the measure was long considered the best measure of whether ads were persuasive. Surprisingly, however, it turned out that memory was not the best predictor. Instead, one of the most influential predictors was attitude toward the ad itself (Berger & Mitchell, 1989; Bergkvist & Rossiter, 2008). Liking an ad would not seem like a good reason to remember it or be persuaded by it, but attitude-toward-the-ad studies greatly proliferated, and if any one finding is robust in the literature it is that one of the most important things a message embedded in traditional media content can do is lead consumers to like it (e.g., MacKenzie & Lutz, 1989; MacKenzie et al., 1986). This makes sense in our platform-based approach to consumer psychology of messages because sometimes, even though the situation is loaded against it, an ad is really liked. (Note the third belief of practitioners that creative messages can elicit this kind of psychological response.) Attitude toward the ad is also proving a good predictor of advertising in the digital environments (e.g., McMillan et al., 2003).

A related but important and consistent finding about the role of attitude in consumer processing of messages is that a general view that advertising is good for people and society (sample statements include "Advertising helps people discover new products they will like"; "Advertising keeps the economy moving along") is highly predictive of less ad avoidance and more ad processing (e.g., Dutta-Bergman, 2006, Mehta, 2000; Muehling, 1987). This finding is also understandable in view of the platform conception of traditional media processing because the attitude itself is inconsistent with the negative view that the only reason to watch ads is that they are the price of free or reduced cost desired programming.

EMOTIONAL THEORIES OF CONSUMER PROCESSING OF MESSAGES IN TRADITIONAL MEDIA

Early advertising emotion studies focused on what emotions were relevant and what their impacts were (see review in Thorson, 1999, and Agres et al., 1990). Dozens of taxonomies of advertising-related emotion were suggested. Holbrook and Batra (1987) tested Plutchik's (1980) eight emotional categories: joy, acceptance, fear, surprise, sadness, disgust, anger, and anticipation. (It should be noted that Plutchik's treatment of emotion was based on evolutionary theory, consistent with that taken here.) Mehrabian and Russell (1974) employed a three-dimensional emotional system that included the dimensions of pleasure–displeasure, arousal–nonarousal, and domination–nondomination. Holbrook and Batra (1987) showed that all three of these emotional dimensions predicted people's liking for ads and advertised brands. Burke and Edell (1989) employed three feelings scales, including upbeat, negative, and warm. They found that all three kinds of feelings that people experienced in response to ads were predictive of how they evaluated ads, how much they liked ads, beliefs they had about the brands, and their attitudes toward the brands. The role of positive and negative emotions, of course, are generally theorized to be the motivational system that enabled our human ancestors to survive. That is, the key to survival was to approach resources needed for survival, while avoiding stimuli that indicated threats (e.g., Kenrick & Shiota, 2008). It is thus not surprising that the role of emotional responses to advertising is one of the most significant predictors of how effective they are. Indeed, emotional response to advertising is now proving important to understand advertising performance in digital media (e.g., Eckler & Bolls, 2011; Teixeira et al., 2012; Yoo & Kim, 2005).

CONCLUSION

This chapter organized and explicated the many years of study of the psychology of consumer messages in traditional media under two broad theories. The first and most fundamental is evolutionary theory of human social psychology. This perspective emphasizes the importance to humans of persuading others to their will but avoiding being persuaded by those others to do their will. This orientation was clearly important to ensuring that one's genes were passed on. However, there are clearly circumstances where being persuaded by others also helps with that outcome. In the consumer psychology of advertising, those circumstances define when ads are successful.

The other theoretical perspective employed here is the practitioners' metatheory about what three factors lead to successful advertising: breaking through the clutter to be noticed, mutation of effects, and the role of creativity of consumer messages. These three beliefs provide a simple but powerful guide to much research on how advertising works when located in traditional media. The role of narrative, the impact of disguising advertising so it looks like editorial or entertainment content, and the role of human attention, attitudes, and emotion in the processing of ads in traditional media fit well within the perspective.

Finally, when overviewing the literature on traditional media and comparing it to the burgeoning research on digital media, it is clear that many theories and findings of the older research remain relevant. Examples of this relevance are scattered throughout the chapter.

REFERENCES

Aaker, D. A., & Stayman, D. M. (1990). Measuring audience perceptions of commercials and relating them to ad impact. *Journal of Advertising Research*, *30*(4), 7–17.

Ad Age. (2003). *History 1990s*. https://adage.com/article/adage-encyclopedia/history-1990s/98705

Adler, S. (2015, July 31). The perils of native advertising. *Huffpost*. https://www.huffpost.com/entry/the-perils-of-native-advertising_b_7913946

Agres, S., Edell, J. A., & Dubitsky, T. M. (Eds.). (1990). *Emotion in advertising: Theoretical and practical explorations* (pp. 255–268). Quorum Books.

Anand, P., & Sternthal, B. (1992). The effects of program involvement and ease of message counterarguing on advertising persuasiveness. *Journal of Consumer Psychology*, *1*(3), 225–238. https://doi.org/10.1016/S1057-7408(08)80037-X

Assael, H. (2011). From silos to synergy: A fifty-year review of cross-media research shows synergy has yet to achieve its full potential. *Journal of Advertising Research*, *51*(150th Anniversary Suppl.), 42–58. https://doi.org/10.2501/JAR-51-1-042-058

Attaran, S., Notarantonio, E. M., & Quigley, C. J., Jr. (2015). Consumer perceptions of credibility and selling intent among advertisements, advertorials, and editorials: A persuasion knowledge model approach. *Journal of Promotion Management*, *21*(6), 703–720. https://doi.org/10.1080/10496491.2015.1088919

Barkow, J. H., Cosmides, L., & Tooby, J. (Eds.). (1992). *The adapted mind: Evolutionary psychology and the generation of culture*. Oxford University Press.

Berger, I. E., & Mitchell, A. A. (1989). The effect of advertising on attitude accessibility, attitude confidence, and the attitude-behavior relationship. *Journal of Consumer Research*, 16(3), 269–279. https://doi.org/10.1086/209213

Bergkvist, L., & Rossiter, J. R. (2008). The role of ad likability in predicting an ad's campaign performance. *Journal of Advertising*, 37(2), 85–98. https://doi.org/10.2753/JOA0091-3367370207

Brehm, J. W. (1966). *A theory of psychological reactance*. Academic Press.

Brehm, S. S., & Brehm, J. W. (2013). *Psychological reactance: A theory of freedom and control*. Academic Press. (Original work published 1981)

Burke, M. C., & Edell, J. A. (1989). The impact of feelings on ad-based affect and cognition. *Journal of Marketing Research*, 26(1), 69–83. https://doi.org/10.1177/002224378902600106

Buttle, F. (1991). What do people do with advertising? *International Journal of Advertising*, 10(2), 95–110. https://doi.org/10.1080/02650487.1991.11104440

Cameron, G. T., & Ju-Pak, K. H. (2000). Information pollution? Labeling and format of advertorials. *Newspaper Research Journal*, 21(1), 65–76. https://doi.org/10.1177/073953290002100106

Chang, Y., & Thorson, E. (2004). Television and web advertising synergies. *Journal of Advertising*, 33(2), 75–84. https://doi.org/10.1080/00913367.2004.10639161

Cho, C. H., & University of Texas at Austin. (2004). Why do people avoid advertising on the internet? *Journal of Advertising*, 33(4), 89–97. https://doi.org/10.1080/00913367.2004.10639175

Clee, M. A., & Wicklund, R. A. (1980). Consumer behavior and psychological reactance. *Journal of Consumer Research*, 6(4), 389–405. https://doi.org/10.1086/208782

Confer, J. C., Easton, J. A., Fleischman, D. S., Goetz, C. D., Lewis, D. M., Perilloux, C., & Buss, D. M. (2010). Evolutionary psychology. Controversies, questions, prospects, and limitations. *American Psychologist*, 65(2), 110–126. https://doi.org/10.1037/a0018413

Davison, W. P. (1983). The third-person effect in communication. *Public Opinion Quarterly*, 47(1), 1–15. https://doi.org/10.1086/268763

Deighton, J., Romer, D., & McQueen, J. (1989). Using drama to persuade. *Journal of Consumer Research*, 16(3), 335–343. https://doi.org/10.1086/209219

De Pelsmacker, P., Geuens, M., & Anckaert, P. (2002). Media context and advertising effectiveness: The role of context appreciation and context/ad similarity. *Journal of Advertising*, 31(2), 49–61. https://doi.org/10.1080/00913367.2002.10673666

Dutta-Bergman, M. J. (2006). The demographic and psychographic antecedents of attitude toward advertising. *Journal of Advertising Research*, 46(1), 102–112. https://doi.org/10.2501/S0021849906060119

Eckler, P., & Bolls, P. (2011). Spreading the virus: Emotional tone of viral advertising and its effect on forwarding intentions and attitudes. *Journal of Interactive Advertising*, 11(2), 1–11. https://doi.org/10.1080/15252019.2011.10722180

Edwards, S. M., Li, H., & Lee, J. H. (2002). Forced exposure and psychological reactance: Antecedents and consequences of the perceived intrusiveness of pop-up ads. *Journal of Advertising*, 31(3), 83–95. https://doi.org/10.1080/00913367.2002.10673678

Escalas, J. E. (1998). Advertising narratives: What are they and how do they work. In B. Stern (Ed.), *Representing consumers: Voices, views, and visions* (pp. 267–289). Taylor & Francis.

Escalas, J. E. (2007). Self-referencing and persuasion: Narrative transportation versus analytical elaboration. *Journal of Consumer Research*, 33(4), 421–429. https://doi.org/10.1086/510216

Evans, D. S., Schmalensee, R., Noel, M. D., Chang, H. H., & Garcia-Swartz, D. D. (2011). *Platform economics: Essays on multi-sided businesses* (D. S. Evans, Ed.). Competition Policy International. https://ssrn.com/abstract=1974020

Fisher, W. R. (1989). *Human communication as narration: Toward a philosophy of reason, value, and action*. University of South Carolina Press.

Fransen, M. L., Verlegh, P. W., Kirmani, A., & Smit, E. G. (2015). A typology of consumer strategies for resisting advertising, and a review of mechanisms for countering them. *International Journal of Advertising*, 34(1), 6–16. https://doi.org/10.1080/02650487.2014.995284

Friestad, M., & Wright, P. (1994). The persuasion knowledge model: How people cope with persuasion attempts. *Journal of Consumer Research*, 21(1), 1–31. https://doi.org/10.1086/209380

Garfield, B. (2014, February 24). If native advertising is so harmless, why does it rely on misleading readers? *The Guardian*. https://www.theguardian.com/commentisfree/2014/feb/25/yahoo-opens-gemini-native-advertising

Goldsmith, R. E., & Lafferty, B. A. (2002). Consumer response to web sites and their influence on advertising effectiveness. *Internet Research*, 12(4), 318–328. https://doi.org/10.1108/10662240210438407

Green, M. C., & Brock, T. C. (2000). The role of transportation in the persuasiveness of public narratives. *Journal of Personality and Social Psychology, 79*(5), 701–721. https://doi.org/10.1037/0022-3514.79.5.701

Greenwald, A. (1968). Cognitive learning and cognitive response. In A. Greenwald, T. Brock, & T. Ostrom (Eds.), *Psychological foundations of attitudes* (pp. 147–170). Academic Press. https://doi.org/10.1016/B978-1-4832-3071-9.50012-X

Gunther, A. C., & Thorson, E. (1992). Perceived persuasive effects of product commercials and public service announcements: Third-person effects in new domains. *Communication Research, 19*(5), 574–596. https://doi.org/10.1177/009365092019005002

Hall, J. (2019, August 26). How to get your marketing to cut through the noise. *Forbes.* https://www.forbes.com/sites/johnhall/2019/08/25/how-to-get-your-marketing-to-cut-through-the-noise/#8baca5f3a84e

Ham, C. D., Nelson, M. R., & Das, S. (2015). How to measure persuasion knowledge. *International Journal of Advertising, 34*(1), 17–53. https://doi.org/10.1080/02650487.2014.994730

Haugtvedt, C. P., Schumann, D. W., Schneier, W. L., & Warren, W. L. (1994). Advertising repetition and variation strategies: Implications for understanding attitude strength. *Journal of Consumer Research, 21*(1), 176–189. https://doi.org/10.1086/209391

He, A. (2019, May 31). Average time spent with media in 2019 has plateaued. *eMarketer.* https://www.emarketer.com/content/us-time-spent-with-media-in-2019-has-plateaued-with-digital-making-up-losses-by-old-media

Hiltzik, M. (2017, January 31). Column: A reminder that Apple's "1984" ad is the only great Super Bowl commercial ever—And it's now 33 years old. *Los Angeles Times.* https://www.latimes.com/business/hiltzik/la-fi-hiltzik-1984-super-bowl-20170125-story.html

Holbrook, M. B., & Batra, R. (1987). Assessing the role of emotions as mediators of consumer responses to advertising. *Journal of Consumer Research, 14*(3), 404–420. https://doi.org/10.1086/209123

Homer, P. M. (2009). Product placements. *Journal of Advertising, 38*(3), 21–32. https://doi.org/10.2753/JOA0091-3367380302

Jensen, M. B., & Jepsen, A. L. (2006). Online marketing communications: Need for a new typology for IMC? *Journal of Website Promotion, 2*(1–2), 19–35. https://doi.org/10.1080/15533610802104083

Jiang, P., & Chia, S. L. (2010). Developing Integrated Marketing Communication (IMC) in online communities: A conceptual perspective from search, experience and credence segmentation. *International Journal of Internet Marketing and Advertising, 6*(1), 22–40. https://doi.org/10.1504/IJIMA.2010.030431

Johnson, J. P. (2013). Targeted advertising and advertising avoidance. *RAND Journal of Economics, 44*(1), 128–144. https://doi.org/10.1111/1756-2171.12014

Kahneman, D. (2003). A perspective on judgment and choice: Mapping bounded rationality. *American Psychologist, 58*(9), 697–720. https://doi.org/10.1037/0003-066X.58.9.697

Kenrick, D. T., & Shiota, M. N. (2008). Approach and avoidance motivation(s): An evolutionary perspective. In A. J. Elliot (Ed.), *Handbook of approach and avoidance motivation* (pp. 273–288). Psychology Press.

Kim, A., Ratneshwar, S., & Thorson, E. (2017). Why narrative ads work: An integrated process explanation. *Journal of Advertising, 46*(2), 283–296. https://doi.org/10.1080/00913367.2016.1268984

Kirmani, A., & Campbell, M. C. (2009). Taking the target's perspective: The persuasion knowledge model. In M. Wänke (Ed.), *Social psychology of consumer behavior* (pp. 297–316). Psychology Press.

Krugman, H. E. (1977). Memory without recall; exposure without perception. *Journal of Advertising Research, 40*(6), 49–54. https://doi.org/10.2501/JAR-40-6-49-54

Lastovicka, J. L. (1995). A methodological interpretation of experimental and survey research evidence concerning alcohol advertising effects. In S. E. Martin & P. D. Mail (Eds.), *The effects of the mass media on the use and abuse of alcohol* (pp. 69–81). U.S. Department of Health and Human Services, Public Health Service, National Institutes of Health, National Institute on Alcohol Abuse and Alcoholism.

Lee, J., Kim, S., & Ham, C. D. (2016). A double-edged sword? Predicting consumers' attitudes toward and sharing intention of native advertising on social media. *American Behavioral Scientist, 60*(12), 1425–1441. https://doi.org/10.1177/0002764216660137

Leong, S. M., Ang, S. H., & Heng, L. (1994). *Using drama to persuade: the effects of involvement and ad form on persuasion.* ACR Asia-Pacific Advances.

Luxton, S., Reid, M., & Mavondo, F. (2015). Integrated marketing communication capability and brand performance. *Journal of Advertising, 44*(1), 37–46. https://doi.org/10.1080/00913367.2014.934938

MacKenzie, S. B., & Lutz, R. J. (1989). An empirical examination of the structural antecedents of attitude toward the ad in an advertising pretesting context. *Journal of Marketing, 53*(2), 48–65. https://doi.org/10.1177/002224298905300204

MacKenzie, S. B., Lutz, R. J., & Belch, G. E. (1986). The role of attitude toward the ad as a mediator of advertising effectiveness: A test of competing explanations. *Journal of Marketing Research, 23*(2), 130–143. https://doi.org/10.1177/002224378602300205

Marketing Charts. (2019, June 24). *US online and traditional media advertising outlook, 2019–2023*. https://www.marketingcharts.com/advertising-trends-108995

McDonald, C., & Scott, J. (2007). A brief history of advertising. In G. J. Tellis & T. Ambler (Eds.), *The SAGE handbook of advertising* (pp. 17–34). SAGE. https://doi.org/10.4135/9781848607897.n2

McMillan, S. J., Hwang, J. S., & Lee, G. (2003). Effects of structural and perceptual factors on attitudes toward the website. *Journal of Advertising Research*, 43(4), 400–409. https://doi.org/10.2501/JAR-43-4-400-409

Mehrabian, A., & Russell, J. A. (1974). *An approach to environmental psychology*. MIT Press.

Mehta, A. (2000). Advertising attitudes and advertising effectiveness. *Journal of Advertising Research*, 40(3), 67–72. https://doi.org/10.2501/JAR-40-3-67-72

Mercier, H., & Landemore, H. (2012). Reasoning is for arguing: Understanding the successes and failures of deliberation. *Political Psychology*, 33(2), 243–258. https://doi.org/10.1111/j.1467-9221.2012.00873.x

Muehling, D. D. (1987). An investigation of factors underlying attitude-toward-advertising-in-general. *Journal of Advertising*, 16(1), 32–40. https://doi.org/10.1080/00913367.1987.10673058

Murry, J. P., Jr., Lastovicka, J. L., & Singh, S. N. (1992). Feeling and liking responses to television programs: An examination of two explanations for media-context effects. *Journal of Consumer Research*, 18(4), 441–451. https://doi.org/10.1086/209272

Naik, P. A., & Peters, K. (2009). A hierarchical marketing communications model of online and offline media synergies. *Journal of Interactive Marketing*, 23(4), 288–299. https://doi.org/10.1016/j.intmar.2009.07.005

Nickerson, R. S. (1998). Confirmation bias: A ubiquitous phenomenon in many guises. *Review of General Psychology*, 2(2), 175–220. https://doi.org/10.1037/1089-2680.2.2.175

Nyilasy, G., & Reid, L. N. (2009). Agency practitioner theories of how advertising works. *Journal of Advertising*, 38(3), 81–96. https://doi.org/10.2753/JOA0091-3367380306

O'Barr, W. M. (2010). A brief history of advertising in America. *Advertising & Society Review*, 11(1). https://doi.org/10.1353/ASR.0.0046

Pieters, R., Warlop, L., & Wedel, M. (2002). Breaking through the clutter: Benefits of advertisement originality and familiarity for brand attention and memory. *Management Science*, 48(6), 765–781. https://doi.org/10.1287/mnsc.48.6.765.192

Plutchik, R. (1980). A general psychoevolutionary theory of emotion. In R. Plutchik & H. Kellerman (Eds.), *Theories of emotion* (pp. 3–33). Academic Press. https://doi.org/10.1016/B978-0-12-558701-3.50007-7

Presbrey, F. (2000). The history and development of advertising. *Advertising & Society Review*, 1(1). https://doi.org/10.1353/asr.2000.0021

Rayner, K., Miller, B., & Rotello, C. M. (2008). Eye movements when looking at print advertisements: The goal of the viewer matters. *Applied Cognitive Psychology*, 22(5), 697–707. https://doi.org/10.1002/acp.1389

Reeves, B., & Nass, C. I. (1996). *The media equation: How people treat computers, television, and new media like real people and places*. Cambridge University Press.

Rodgers, S., Thorson, E., & Jin, Y. (2009). Social science theories of traditional and internet advertising. In D. W. Stacks & M. B. Salwen (Eds.), *An integrated approach to communication theory and research* (2nd ed., pp. 198–219). Routledge.

Rojas-Méndez, J. I., Davies, G., & Madran, C. (2009). Universal differences in advertising avoidance behavior: A cross-cultural study. *Journal of Business Research*, 62(10), 947–954. https://doi.org/10.1016/j.jbusres.2008.08.008

Saad, G. (2004). Applying evolutionary psychology in understanding the representation of women in advertisements. *Psychology and Marketing*, 21(8), 593–612. https://doi.org/10.1002/mar.20020

Saad, G., & Gill, T. (2000). Applications of evolutionary psychology in marketing. *Psychology and Marketing*, 17(12), 1005–1034. https://doi.org/10.1002/1520-6793(200012)17:12<1005::AID-MAR1>3.0.CO;2-H

Sagarin, B. J., Cialdini, R. B., Rice, W. E., & Serna, S. B. (2002). Dispelling the illusion of invulnerability: The motivations and mechanisms of resistance to persuasion. *Journal of Personality and Social Psychology*, 83(3), 526–541. https://doi.org/10.1037/0022-3514.83.3.526

Schultz, D. E. (1992). Integrated marketing communications. *Journal of Promotion Management*, 1(1), 99–104. https://doi.org/10.1300/J057v01n01_07

Schultz, D. E., & Schultz, H. F. (1998). Transitioning marketing communication into the twenty-first century. *Journal of Marketing Communications*, 4(1), 9–26.

Schumann, D. W., & Thorson, E. (1990). The influence of viewing context on commercial effectiveness: A selection-processing model. *Current Issues and Research in Advertising*, 12(1–2), 1–24.

Schumann, D. W., & Thorson, E. (2007). *Internet advertising theory and research*. Lawrence Erlbaum Associates.

Seyedghorban, Z., Tahernejad, H., & Matanda, M. J. (2016). Reinquiry into advertising avoidance on the internet: A conceptual replication and extension.

Shapiro, L., & Epstein, W. (1998). Evolutionary theory meets cognitive psychology: A more selective perspective. *Mind & Language*, *13*(2), 171–194. https://doi.org/10.1111/1468-0017.00072

Siddarth, S., & Chattopadhyay, A. (1998). To zap or not to zap: A study of the determinants of channel switching during commercials. *Marketing Science*, *17*(2), 124–138. https://doi.org/10.1287/mksc.17.2.124

Sino, S. (2018, October 2). The future of traditional television survival relies on live sports. *The Business of Sports*. http://www.thebusinessofsports.com/2018/10/02/the-future-of-traditional-television-survival-relies-on-live-sports/

Smith, R. E., MacKenzie, S. B., Yang, X., Buchholz, L. M., & Darley, W. K. (2007). Modeling the determinants and effects of creativity in advertising. *Marketing Science*, *26*(6), 819–833. https://doi.org/10.1287/mksc.1070.0272

Speck, P. S., & Elliott, M. T. (1997). Predictors of advertising avoidance in print and broadcast media. *Journal of Advertising*, *26*(3), 61–76. https://doi.org/10.1080/00913367.1997.10673529

Sperber, D. (2000). Metarepresentations in an evolutionary perspective. In D. Sperber (Ed.), *Metarepresentations: A multidisciplinary perspective* (pp. 117–137). Oxford University Press.

Sridhar, S., Mantrala, M. K., Naik, P. A., & Thorson, E. (2011). Dynamic marketing budgeting for platform firms: Theory, evidence, and application. *Journal of Marketing Research*, *48*(6), 929–943. https://doi.org/10.1509/jmr.10.0035

Stammerjohan, C. A., Wood, C. M., Chang, Y., & Thorson, E. (2005). An empirical investigation of the interaction between publicity, advertising, and previous brand attitudes and knowledge. *Journal of Advertising*, *34*(4), 55–67. https://doi.org/10.1080/00913367.2005.10639209

Stewart, D. W. (1992). Speculations on the future of advertising research. *Journal of Advertising*, *21*(3), 1–18. https://doi.org/10.1080/00913367.1992.10673372

Stewart, D. W., & Furse, D. H. (1986). *Effective television advertising: A study of 1000 commercials*. Lexington Books.

Tavassoli, N. T., & Lee, Y. H. (2003). The differential interaction of auditory and visual advertising elements with Chinese and English. *Journal of Marketing Research*, *40*(4), 468–480. https://doi.org/10.1509/jmkr.40.4.468.19391

Teixeira, T., Wedel, M., & Pieters, R. (2012). Emotion-induced engagement in internet video advertisements. *Journal of Marketing Research*, *49*(2), 144–159. https://doi.org/10.1509/jmr.10.0207

Thorson, E. (1994). Using eyes-on-screen as a measure of attention to television. In A. Lang (Ed.), *Measuring cognitive responses to media messages* (pp. 65–84). Lawrence Erlbaum.

Thorson, E. (1999). Emotion and advertising. In J. P. Jones (Ed.), *The advertising business* (pp. 209–218). SAGE. https://doi.org/10.4135/9781452231440.n20

Thorson, E., & Lang, A. (1992). The effects of television videographics and lecture familiarity on adult cardiac orienting responses and memory. *Communication Research*, *19*(3), 346–369. https://doi.org/10.1177/009365092019003003

Thorson, E., & Rodgers, S. (2019). *Advertising theory in the Digital Age*. In S. Rodgers & E. Thorson (Eds.), *Advertising theory* (2nd ed., pp. 3–17). Routledge. https://doi.org/10.4324/9781351208314-1

Thorson, E., Shim, J. C., & Yoon, D. (2005). Synergy effects of public service multi-media campaigns. *Korean Journal of Broadcasting and Telecommunication Studies*, *11*(7), 21–48.

Tooby, J., & Cosmides, L. (1989). Evolutionary psychology and the generation of culture, Part I: Theoretical considerations. *Ethology and Sociobiology*, *10*(1–3), 29–49. https://doi.org/10.1016/0162-3095(89)90012-5

Vavreck, L. (2007). The exaggerated effects of advertising on turnout: The dangers of self-reports. *Quarterly Journal of Political Science*, *2*(4), 325–343. https://doi.org/10.1561/100.00006005

Venkatraman, V., Dimoka, A., Pavlou, P. A., Vo, K., Hampton, W., Bollinger, B., Hershfield, H. E., Ishihara, M., & Winer, R. S. (2015). Predicting advertising success beyond traditional measures: New insights from neurophysiological methods and market response modeling. *Journal of Marketing Research*, *52*(4), 436–452. https://doi.org/10.1509/jmr.13.0593

Wang, J., & Calder, B. J. (2009). Media engagement and advertising: Transportation, matching, transference and intrusion. *Journal of Consumer Psychology*, *19*(3), 546–555. https://doi.org/10.1016/j.jcps.2009.05.005

Wang, Z., & Lang, A. (2012). Reconceptualizing excitation transfer as motivational activation changes and a test of the television program context effects. *Media Psychology*, *15*(1), 68–92. https://doi.org/10.1080/15213269.2011.649604

Wells, W. D. (1989). Lectures and dramas. In P. Cafferata & A. M. Tybout (Eds.), *Cognitive and affective responses to advertising* (pp. 13–20). Lexington Books.

Wiederman, M. W. (1993). Evolved gender differences in mate preferences: Evidence from personal advertisements. *Ethology and Sociobiology, 14*(5), 331–351. https://doi.org/10.1016/0162-3095(93)90003-Z

Wojdynski, B. W., & Evans, N. J. (2016). Going native: Effects of disclosure position and language on the recognition and evaluation of online native advertising. *Journal of Advertising, 45*(2), 157–168. https://doi.org/10.1080/00913367.2015.1115380

Woodside, A. G., Sood, S., & Miller, K. E. (2008). When consumers and brands talk: Storytelling theory and research in psychology and marketing. *Psychology and Marketing, 25*(2), 97–145. https://doi.org/10.1002/mar.20203

Wouk, C., & Cohen, S. (2020, July 24). ATSC 3.0: The next-gen TV update is coming in 2020. *Digital Trends.* https://www.digitaltrends.com/home-theater/atsc-3-0-ota-broadcast-standard-4k-dolby-atmos/

Xu, A. J., & Wyer, R. S., Jr. (2012). The role of bolstering and counterarguing mind-sets in persuasion. *Journal of Consumer Research, 38*(5), 920–932. https://doi.org/10.1086/661112

Yoo, C. Y., & Kim, K. (2005). Processing of animation in online banner advertising: The roles of cognitive and emotional responses. *Journal of Interactive Marketing, 19*(4), 18–34. https://doi.org/10.1002/dir.20047

Zinkhan, G. M. (1982). An empirical investigation of aided recall in advertising. *Current Issues and Research in Advertising, 5*(1), 137–160.

SOCIAL MEDIA: FROM CLASSIC PSYCHOLOGICAL THEORIES TO NEW OPPORTUNITIES

Cait Lamberton and Ashlee Humphreys

The Oxford English Dictionary offers a standard definition of *social media* as "websites and applications that enable users to create and share content or to participate in social networking." At first read, this definition appears self-explanatory to the contemporary reader. However, we may also pause to recognize that we would have been unable to even make sense of this definition 4 decades ago—the idea of "websites," "applications," "content," and "social networking" were part of a vanishingly small proportion of the population's cognitive structure and daily life. Social media provides consumers with a range of new psychological experiences that present scholars with new opportunities to enrich prior theory in order to better understand this experience and the effects of social media on consumer psychology. Such intuitions may justify the fragmentation in consumer psychology research in social media, which often treats each new study as though it is the first of its kind, appealing to few common theoretical bases (Lamberton & Stephen, 2016).

In the present chapter, we argue that though much is novel about the social media experience, the combination of classic psychological theory and new phenomena offers the opportunity for knowledge development. We do not purport to offer a comprehensive review or analysis of social media, as other work provides such encapsulations (Alves et al., 2016; Barger et al., 2016; Humphreys, 2016).

Rather, we begin with a snapshot of the social media landscape as it exists in mid-2020. We then consider five key components of social media systems that are most relevant to consumer psychology and identify general theories that can inform our understanding of each component. In many cases, these well-established theories, with which any consumer psychologist will be intimately familiar, can be easily applied to social media phenomena. However, because of the evolving nature of social media, much still remains to be explored—such that we can both develop frameworks dynamic enough to capture social media phenomena as they unfold over time and develop new, social-media-relevant versions of prior theoretical accounts. Thus, though we anticipate that any snapshot will become quickly outdated, these theories and extensions offer structures through which we can deepen our understanding of consumer psychology as a whole. We close with a brief discussion of the consequences of social media use, for consumers themselves, firms, policy makers, and the future of consumer psychology. While the net valence of these consequences is likely to be heterogeneous across consumers and somewhat equivocally captured in research, we hope this chapter encourages scholars to extend theory in ways that help us gain the most from social media engagement and understand its ultimate importance for consumers and consumer psychology.

https://doi.org/10.1037/0000262-021
APA Handbook of Consumer Psychology, L. R. Kahle (Editor-in-Chief)
Copyright © 2022 by the American Psychological Association. All rights reserved.

SNAPSHOT: DEFINITIONS, USES, AND FIVE KEY FACTORS

While social media platforms vary substantially, we focus most on platforms that offer parallel social and cognitive experiences to consumers. These platforms, comprising social networking sites and feeds, have three core attributes (Boyd & Ellison, 2007). We discuss these three core attributes, then turn to five key factors that can be analyzed in order to better understand the way that social media platforms affect consumer psychology.

Definition and Use

First, social media platforms allow the creation and maintenance of identity through the creation of unique user profiles. Second, they allow consumer creation and expression, as consumers can upload visual, audio, or text-based content. Third, social media sites have the eponymous social component, that is, they offer users the opportunity to interact with others in virtual social settings that are scalable beyond simple dyadic exchange.

As of late 2019, social media is dominated by a fairly small number of platforms, consistent with a mature industry (Rogers, 1995). Facebook, a social media site that allows people and organizations to create a profile using a set template and share, post, and respond to others' written, photographic, and video content, dwarfs the other primary players in the social media landscape, with almost 2,500,000,000 active users per month. WeChat, a Chinese social networking site with similar functionality to Facebook, reports approximately 1,100,000,000 monthly active users (DeGennaro, 2019). A relative newcomer, short-video sharing site TikTok reports about 800,000,000 active users as of March 2020. Twitter, with 260,000,000 users, is mirrored by Chinese counterpart Sina Weibo, with approximately 400,000,000 monthly active users. Further, Snapchat, with 360,000,000 users; LinkedIn, with 653,000,000 users; and Pinterest, with 150,500,000 users all fall into our purview as social media sites relevant to consumer psychology. Social media use is very common but not completely ubiquitous. Seventy-three percent of U.S. adults use YouTube, while 69% use Facebook (Perrin & Anderson, 2019).

There are also general classes of social media platforms and experiences that, while not as clearly branded as the aforementioned, offer psychological parallels that make them highly relevant to our discussion. For example, enterprise social media (ESM) like Slack includes "web-based platforms that allow workers to communicate messages with specific coworkers or broadcast messages to everyone in the organization" (Leonardi et al., 2013, p. 2). Branded online social media communities also allow types of online interaction similar to those in the largest independent platforms and may be either controlled by a brand directly (e.g., the SAP Community Network, community.sap.com, which includes over 2,500,000 members as of early 2020, or Sony's Playstation Community, which also connects to the brand's YouTube and Twitter channels) or emerge due to consumers' shared interests, independent of brand control (e.g., Turkopticon, a community where Amazon Mechanical Turk workers provide support and information to one another). We will also discuss distinct psychological characteristics of these classes of social media sites and examine the theories that may help us understand the way that consumers engage with each.

A few things should be noted related to social media usage patterns overall, as these patterns may provide baseline psychological insights about their role in consumer experience. First, as of 2019, consumers of different demographic groups vary in their platform use (Kemp, 2019). For example, the best available data suggests that men outnumber women slightly on Twitter and LinkedIn (Perrin & Anderson, 2019). By contrast, Pinterest (designed for photo-sharing) and Instagram lean more heavily toward female consumers. Similarly, the age profiles of various social media sites vary widely and, interestingly, have changed with time; whereas Facebook began as a site for college students, its typical heavy user group has shifted upward in age. Further, many parents restrict access to some social media sites for younger children. The psychology of such differences, in itself, may be of interest, though at present we can only speculate about the relative utility of verbal versus visual communication preference or, perhaps, more utilitarian as opposed to more hedonic uses of social media across these groups.

Second, while platforms differ across nations and cultures, the goals that consumers have when using them may share important commonalities. For example, governments may simply limit access to some platforms—but in their absence, consumers appear to find near-substitutes to meet their goals. China's censorship of Facebook and Twitter, for example, drives traffic to WeChat and Sina Weibo, which offer near-equivalents to Chinese consumers. Chinese consumers use psychological experience and use of social media as related to their cultural and historical context.

Platform use varies by country for other reasons as well. Fifty-eight percent of people over 13 in Saudi Arabia use Snapchat, compared with 35% of the same population in the United States and 25% in Canada. To the extent that Snapchat's message structure prioritizes psychological and social needs for privacy, more acutely felt in more conservative societies, we may expect such divides would be mirrored if other social media were to adopt similar design features. By contrast, LinkedIn claims its largest reach among the U.S. population, with 160,000,000 users, or 63% of the U.S. population over 18. If we accept that there may be particularly strong emphasis on professional success in this market, this high level of reach may signal individuals' need to form facilitating networks independent of offline social structures (families, civic groups, religious communities).

Third, we should also consider such usage figures with some skepticism. In the first 9 months of 2019 alone, Facebook acknowledged that it had shut down 5,400,000,000 fake accounts, and outside estimates put the number of current fakes at 400,000,000, but the firm also acknowledged that it was becoming increasingly difficult to detect false entries as they expanded, due both to their proliferation and a lack of dedicated company resources to do so (Moore & Murphy, 2019). We know little about the psychological effects of such "phantom" social media users, though past theory would suggest that even consumers aware of their existence may fail to sufficiently adjust their estimates of "social proof" provided by observed behavior (Donath, 2007), consistent with typical anchoring and adjustment effects. However, what we do know is that social media use is a routinized behavior for many, with 50% of 18- to 24-year-olds immediately accessing Facebook when they wake up (Noyes, 2020). Clearly, regardless of their actual population size, the design of social media platforms presents a cue-behavior-reward system that creates stable psychological structures and tight behavioral attachment; we discuss the potential effects of such routinization next.

Distinction and Diversity

How is social media distinct from other media, and what differences among media might be of psychological relevance? We focus on five key attributes to help distinguish between typical communications across these dominant platforms (Humphreys, 2016). These attributes are captured in Table 21.1 (Humphreys, 2016, p. 25; see also Baym, 2015).

First, consumers experience varying degrees of social presence—the experience of giving and receiving social feedback—when interacting in social media. Many forms of social media allow for more social presence than traditional media. Further, unlike traditional media, social media participants are able to manage their social presence in ways that both shape and express their identity, goals, and preferences. Unlike in traditional media, brands can also vary their degree of social presence in social media, ranging from mere observer to active participant. Second, social media offers a range of temporal structures—from synchronous to asynchronous. Within these structures, the role of the consumer changes fundamentally, such that they become "prosumers"—acting simultaneously as communicator and audience, often in the same interaction (Kotler, 1986; Toffler, 1980), and synchronously cocreating value with other consumers, platforms, and brands simply via their participation (Humphreys & Grayson, 2008). Third, social media varies in the amount of visual and auditory information, thus encouraging us to consider the relevance of theory related to media richness in addition to theory that assists us in understanding textual information shared online. Fourth, as is common to other digital

TABLE 21.1

Five Key Attributes of Social Media and Relevant Psychological Theories

Social media key attribute	Definition	Example	Relevant psychological theories and constructs
Social presence	Quality and amount of social information conveyed	Addressing consumers via Facebook Live (high social presence) versus presenting static photos (low social presence)	Identity theory Self-presentation theory Inference making
Temporal and social structure	Level of temporal copresence and arrangement with conversation partners	Using Twitter's instant message function (synchronous) as opposed to reading archived tweets (asynchronous)	Social norms Power Networks
Media richness	Amount of sensory information transferred between the sender and receiver	Text-based messaging (low media richness) versus streaming video (high media richness)	Elaboration likelihood model Curiosity Signal detection theory
Permanence	Degree to which previous messages are available to users	Posting a picture on Facebook (high permanence) versus using Snapchat (low permanence)	Individual and collective memory Privacy
Replication	Degree to which a message can be consistently reproduced	Watching an existing video on YouTube (high replicability) versus playing a social media game with anonymous players (low replicability)	Fluency Variety seeking Attribution theory

experiences, social media can range from semipermanent to highly ephemeral. Last, whereas consumers can rely on non-social-media communications to be highly replicable (e.g., a given advertisement will be the same if seen 20 times, whether presented digitally or offline), social media introduces a wide range of replicability in experience.

As noted in the rightmost column of Table 21.1, we argue that past theory may be applied to help us understand how variation across these social media attributes changes consumers' social media experience and use. Using these theories provides basic frameworks for understanding social media phenomena, but social media phenomena may also highlight ways in which current theory may be revised to understand these contexts. Rooting knowledge in basic constructs will also help consumer psychology researchers working on social media problems to avoid the fragmentation that seems to be common in digital research (Lamberton & Stephen, 2016) and, instead, allow scholars to use this domain as a means of extending, rather than constantly reinventing, our knowledge. In addition, making these theoretical connections may allow social media work to be less time-bound—given the length of journal review processes, it is possible that any given social media platform may transform radically or even disappear before a given paper makes it to print. Connecting to existing theories therefore allows social media to be a sort of laboratory to deepen our generalizable understanding of human nature, without tying our findings to a particular platform or structure.

To consider both the enduring relevance of these classic theories and the ways in which they may be extended by studying social media, we next explore each social media factor listed in Table 21.1, considering their relevance for multiple parts of the social media system (communicators, audiences, structures, and messages). These five factors are affected by the structure of the platforms and the choices that consumers make within the structure afforded by the platform.

SOCIAL PRESENCE

Our first discussion, on the effect of social presence, is split into three parts: the social presence of consumers, which affects their identity formation and expression; the social presence of firms, which affects the consumer social media experience; and the effect of social presence on the consumer's social experience in terms of interpersonal perception.

Part 1: Consumers' Social Presence Management

Social presence can vary in social media, enabling consumers to develop and present a rich self-depiction in the social media domain or, alternatively, to minimize or obscure their own social presence, such that only a partial presentation is created and seen by others. Foundational theories relevant to identity formation and self-presentation (Baumeister, 1982; Rosenberg, 1979; Schlenker, 1986; Swann, 1990; Wicklund & Gollwitzer, 1982) predict that when social media offers a rich environment, consumers will engage in this type of consumer identity work. For instance, one study found that Facebook use in young adults can be correlated with depression and attributes this finding to social comparison (Lin et al., 2016, p. 324), but other studies found that Facebook use can buffer the effects in older adults (Wadley, 2018). Further, these papers highlighted the fact that many conflicts can exist as consumers undertake these social comparison and identity-signaling processes, either due to disconnections between their actual and ideal selves or when they encounter the false selves presented by others. However, findings related to consumers' use of social media for identity construction and self-presentation have not, thus far, focused on extending prior work. Rather, they remain unconnected and often in direct conflict with one another. This apparent conflict presents an important opportunity for the extension of classic identity formation and presentation research as applied to consumers' active management of social presence.

One uncontroversial argument is that online social media participation facilitates identity formation and expression (Livingstone, 2008; Nadkarni & Hofmann, 2012; Weber & Mitchell, 2008). In fact, some research suggests that image-related utility is likely to be a larger driver of social media contribution than is intrinsic utility for many consumers (Toubia & Stephen, 2013). Because of its role in helping individuals to form and signal their identities and social groups, social media has also been shown to be of particular psychological importance during critical developmental phases. Particularly, adolescents developing self-identity can be profoundly shaped by social media experiences (Matsuba, 2006). For example, a study of mobile social media use among Chinese students suggested that social media's ability to facilitate friendship development yields downstream effects on identity formation. The stronger the friendships supported by social media, the stronger the effects on identity formation via this medium—though effects were notably stronger for female students than male students (W. Wang et al., 2020, pp. 4479–4481).

Social media also helps consumers to maintain a sense of identity by providing continual social capital during major life transitions, such as the transition to college (Ellison et al., 2007, p. 1149; Ruble, 1994). During this time, social media broadens consumers' social networks. Increased social network heterogeneity, in turn, is associated with the development of social capital and subjective well-being (Ellison et al., 2007; B. Kim & Kim, 2017). Once the self has been formed, social media also allows the provision of feedback that further affirms identity. For example, once one has presented their self in a social media context, they may perceive that their friends support them, thus bolstering their self-esteem further (W. Wang et al., 2021). Thus, social presence in social media may be said to be self-reinforcing, in the same way that classic work in self-presentation would suggest. Equally, middle-aged social media users use platforms to reconnect with old acquaintances (Quinn, 2013, 2014).

But does social presence in social media reflect full and accurate representations of self? Relatively early work on social media participation offers evidence that individuals' self-presentation in social media contexts may represent more of an ideal than an actual self (Manago et al., 2008). For example, Gentile et al. (2012) argued that the curation of one's social media sites feeds individuals' narcissism, leading to inflated views of the self. Other work argued that inauthentic self-presentation is a characteristic of the low-to-moderate self-esteem "vulnerable narcissist," whereas grandiose narcissists can use Facebook to present their true selves with greater visibility (Grieve et al., 2020). Taken together, this work questions such presentation as a valid reflection of a given consumer's decision to give high presence to their actual self-image.

On the other hand, other research suggests that psychologists may be able to take self-presentations at face value, as they do in fact represent people's personalities accurately in the aggregate (Back et al., 2010). In this research, the authors collected multiple Big Five personality reports for each participant, participants' ideal-self ratings, and observer ratings based on reviewing participants' social media sites. Analysis revealed that observers were quite accurate in their evaluations of participants' actual personalities based on their social media profiles. Further, researchers found little evidence that participants presented idealized images in terms of any personality traits. In addition, consumer researchers have found that in some cases, consumers who post identity-consistent products on social media may subsequently have less desire to purchase those products (Grewal et al., 2019). These findings suggest that product posting in social media platforms reflects an authentic underlying identity-expression goal.

Taken together, these findings highlight a number of interesting factors to consider as means of extending past theory. First, social media offers means of identity construction and expression that are not only constantly evolving but also highly intertwined. Just as prior work argued that individuals vary in offline self-presentation strategies depending on their audience (Tice et al., 1995), we propose that individuals may vary their identity formation and presentation in online settings by varying the level and accuracy of social presence they bring to any given platform. Second, we may recognize that consumers' presence management in social media may offer insights into their personalities and goals: The warring goals to "be adored" or "be known" are at play here, as they are offline (Marwick, 2013; Swann, 1990). Social media allows us to examine the degree to which we trade these goals off against one another, both within and between social media experiences, and, thus, to gain greater insight into consumers' identity and expression projects.

Part 2: Brands' Social Presence Management

As prior research has noted, brands are perceived to have personalities much like people (Aaker, 1997, p. 347). As such, brands also face a psychologically meaningful set of decisions about their level of presence on social media. Specifically, they can decide whether to have high social presence, "pull" versus "push," communicating explicitly and with full identification in social media forums, or lower presence, that is, communicating more implicitly in social media environments. These social presence decisions map onto traditional communications decisions that brands make with regard to media types, though they differ slightly when we focus only on social media platforms. First, if firms sponsor brand-based social media platforms, using what might be referred to as "owned social media," they have identified themselves explicitly and will exert greater control and stronger presence in online interactions. Alternatively, they may insert themselves into others' social media conversations via advertisement or sponsored posts, a means of capturing what may be considered "paid social media." Lastly, brands may simply create content that draws attention and allow others to make it "viral," relying on what we may call "earned social media."

How might we understand these varying levels of presence in terms of consumer psychology? First, we can draw from theory related to the control of *discourse* to understand the psychological effects of varying levels of brand social presence in social media. On one hand, a brand can use cultural discourses—"the systems of ideas and practices concerning individuals throughout history" (Humphreys, 2016, p. 237)—to create brand meaning that resonates with consumers and consumer groups (Holt, 2004). By leading social media conversations, brands may be able to prompt conformity with the brand's strategic intentions. Cultural discourses promoted in social media may prompt consumers to internalize the brand's goals, which they may replicate through actions in the offline world. This theory explains how brands could effectively persuade consumers through social media. Equally, brands may monitor cultural discourses on social media and use or co-opt them for strategic ends, working with groups online (Holt, 2016).

Second, however, we should consider the importance of classic *reactance theory* in considering responses to heavily brand-centric social media communication of the type provided by high-presence owned or paid social media. Reactance occurs when individuals feel that their freedom to behave as they wish is constrained (Brehm, 1966). Given that social media platforms are seen as free spaces on which individuals may interact as they wish, brands that appear to hijack social media for their own benefit often experience substantial backlash. For example, the attempt by McDonald's to elicit heartwarming "McDStories" on Twitter, in addition to raising the specter of inauthenticity, opened the door to a bevy of consumer comments that both rejected the request and expressed negativity toward the brand (Hill, 2012). Consumers may also respond negatively to tactics referred to as "comment baiting" or "tag baiting": presenting a post that requires individuals to take a prescribed action, for example, "Comment YES if you don't want the National Museum to close" or "Like us or miss out on a chance to save homeless animals" (Cooper, 2018).

However, we should also consider that social media may prompt us to revise universal expectations of reactance and, with it, counterargument. In fact, firm-generated content on social media can yield positive effects on sales, cross-buying, and customer profitability, especially among consumers with greater levels of social media familiarity (Kumar et al., 2016). In this work, however, the largest contribution to the effect of firm-generated content to marketing outcomes was through "receptivity," operationalized as the total number of comments, likes, and shares received by a given post (Kumar et al., 2016, p. 15), which may reflect the degree to which the post resonates with consumers' a priori goals and attitudes. Further, the authors found that these effects are magnified when combined with television and email marketing. Taken together, these data suggest that intrusiveness is less likely to generate reactance—and more likely to shape brand-positive discourse—when brand presence is high not only in social media but also across other media as well as in terms of other associated, positively valenced consumer cognitions.

Social media also offers new ways to explore social presence, in that firms can use social media to embed brand meaning directly through consumer interactions (Holt, 2016). As Fournier and Lee (2009) pointed out, brand communities generally take one of three shapes: pools (where individuals who share a common general interest are simply combined into a group, with equal voice and attention given to all members), hubs[1] (where one person or product of interest is the focus of attention for other, nonfocal members), and networks (where relationships exist between consumers and brands, consumers and consumers, and brands and brands). These authors argued that brands wishing to build stable online social media communities will benefit most if their users are grouped into a network of relationships rather than pools or hubs. The stability of networks comes in part from the fact that networks not only are dependent on the persistence of horizontal (i.e., consumer-to-consumer) or vertical (i.e., consumer-to-brand) links but can benefit from both. That is, if either horizontal or vertical links in a community network are weakened, the other type can compensate in ways that preserve the community as a whole. By contrast, if consumers in a social media pool become less connected to one another, the cohesion of the pool is threatened. Similarly, if a community that takes a hub structure experiences a weakening of individual connections to the hub brand, the utility of the community is threatened. The consideration of such allocation decisions as a means of expanding our understandings of discourse and reactance, in general, may help us extend both theories. What can we learn about the relationships between authenticity, reactance, and receptivity of messages, either from firms to consumers or consumers to

---

[1] Note that this use of the word "hub" differs from the use of the word "hub" when referring to roles that consumers may play in differently structured social networks. We further discuss the latter meaning in a following section.

consumers? And what can we contribute to our understanding of social presence effects, given the many kinds of brand community structures that emerge and evolve in social media domains?

Part 3: Interpersonal Interpretation

Social media consumers face the task of making sense of content provided by others who may vary in terms of social presence themselves. In many ways, this parallels offline channels where people negotiate issues of trust through facework (Goffman, 1956). However, this challenge differs from the offline world in multiple ways. First, in contrast to the diversity of communication scripts and nonverbal expressions that facilitate interpretation offline, social media communicators are, to some extent, more standardized and more likely to use a social media site's templates and obey its norms. Such restrictions necessarily reduce the richness that we typically experience in offline social presence, limiting the amount of information that an audience can gather from a given interaction and creating a need to fill in gaps about missing information. This requirement makes *inference-making* theory critical (Kardes et al., 2004; Marwick & Boyd, 2011, 2014) in understanding social media use. For example, whereas an offline communicator who discusses their charitable donations will infuse their conversation with differences in tone, body language, and emotion that will help the listener distinguish insincere from sincere commitment, in an online setting people have to make inferences about the sincerity of an action based on social-media format-specific cues. Second, individuals are aware that highly socially present communicators are deliberately shaping and offering a social media identity or message intended to persuade. In this sense, we may expect that the persuasion knowledge model affects consumers' interpretations of information presented on social media (Friestad & Wright, 1994). Communication scholars have also offered theories for how people interpret social information online, finding that people use available information to classify others into archetypes (Spears et al., 2001), or overextrapolate available information into broader beliefs, forming hyperpersonal connections faster than offline (Walther, 1992, 2006).

We first explore a mechanism of interpersonal social presence of communication with *costly signaling theory* (Sundie et al., 2011; Zahavi, 1975). These authors argue that the greater the costs of a signal in terms of time, money, prestige, or effort, the greater the likelihood that the statement is perceived as true and real. Most relevant to social media, this work was applied by Kristofferson et al.'s (2014) exploration of "slacktivism" and demonstrated in a larger community by John et al. (2017). In both of these pieces, researchers showed that consumers may be minimally persuaded by others' social media behavior if it requires no cost, for example, if it only comes from clicking the "like" button. However, if social media behavior is bolstered by external behaviors that affirm "liking," a consumer-as-audience-member is likely to accept such behavior as meaningful and to be persuaded by another's act.

Related work has also explored consumers' responses to others' behaviors in social media. Such work contributes to our understanding of interpersonal perceptions. For example, as noted earlier, social media has been broadly used as a means of allowing consumers to observe one another's charitable actions or other accomplishments. In many cases, interpretations of this type of presence are not positive; attempts to presumably downplay one's otherwise admirable actions, a behavior common in social media contexts, has been termed "humblebragging," formally defined as "bragging masked by a complaint" or humility (Sezer et al., 2018, p. 1). Researchers find that humblebragging tends to backfire, such that relative to straightforward bragging, individuals acting as audiences for these communications judge the communicator as less competent, less likeable, and worthy of less generosity.

Another major theory that has been shown to guide inference making in social media domains relates to *mere virtual presence* (Naylor et al., 2012). This framework builds on past research in mere presence effects as predicted by classic *social impact theory* (Latané, 1981, 1996) and as studied in a brick-and-mortar context by Argo et al. (2005). In the offline world, Argo et al. (2005) demonstrated that the mere presence of others—a noninteracting but noticed existence of an individual in a space—can trigger consumers to purchase more prestigious brands and engage in more reputation-protecting activities. In this offline work, researchers tested for the effect of factors recognized to increase social influence: the number, proximity and power of individuals in the space contiguous to the focal consumer.

In adapting this theory for the social media world, Naylor et al. (2012) suggested that it is, rather, similarity to the self that determines the effect of other social media users' impact on a given individual. For example, if a Facebook brand page displays information about individuals who are demographically different from a given person, that person is likely to infer that the brand is more inappropriate for them than if the same brand displays users who are demographically similar. Perhaps most interestingly, though, this research explores the case where consumers, as social media audience members, do not have access to full information about other users. In such cases, results suggest that consumers rely on egocentric anchoring—they project their own characteristics onto other social media users. As such, the influence of an ambiguously defined social media user is not noticeably different from the influence of an identified-similar other—unless the self of the interpreter is externally activated and, thus, becomes more accessible as an inference-making anchor (Naylor et al., 2011). Thus, it is not only the social presence of the communicator that affects consumer interpretation but also its cognitive accessibility to the self.

Further, research has considered consumers' interpretation of firm actions in social media. Classic theory would predict that to the extent that consumers interpret firms' social media participation as an attempt to prompt them to take certain actions, their persuasion knowledge would be activated (Friestad & Wright, 1994). When this occurs, firms' social media actions undergo a fundamental change of meaning, no longer conveying information as intended. For example, when a marketing attempt goes viral, in social media, it may do so either because it is widely loved, as with Kiley Jenner singing "rise and shine" to her daughter during a video tour of the Kylie Cosmetics office (Torres, 2019), or widely mocked, as with the photo-bombing #fijiwatergirl, who managed to insert herself into Golden Globes red carpet pictures (Kolirin, 2019). In the latter case, the message the firm intended to convey via this social media content may be laced with irony (a construct worthy of discussion in the social media domain in general; Warren & Mohr, 2018). As a result, its message is inverted altogether—consumers' interpretations may be completely orthogonal to the brand's original intent.

TEMPORAL AND SOCIAL STRUCTURES IN SOCIAL MEDIA

Social media platforms can adopt multiple structures, some of which are inherent to a given platform but others that can emerge organically from consumer use. We broaden *structure* here to also encompass social structure, as the two are often intertwined in social media. Temporal structure can vary depending on the structure of information flow, being relatively synchronous (condensed in time) or asynchronous (dispersed in time), and in terms of social dispersion, ranging from one-to-one to many-to-many. Considering these factors together yields Table 21.2.

For example, Facebook offers most consumers a *one-to-many* platform, where a single message can be given to multiple others simultaneously. Snapchat may be set either to offer *one-to-one* temporally condensed messaging or to bridge multiple individuals at the same time. Crowdsourcing platforms such as CrowdFlower and Kickstarter, by contrast, allow many consumers to focus their attention on a single entity or firm, usually given a fairly short-term deadline, creating a *many-to-one* structure with a high degree of temporal condensation. Platforms that encourage synchronous discussion among multiple individuals, such as Slack channels and Skype, and websites that act as temporally condensed repositories for shared information that remain relevant over time present *many-to-many* opportunities that may be less temporally condensed, as they can be referred to at later dates with little loss of value.

Depending on the structures adopted, past theory would predict that social media platforms will

TABLE 21.2

Examples of Temporal and Social Structure Integration in Social Media

Platform temporal structures	Platform social structure			
	One-to-one	**One-to-many**	**Many-to-one**	**Many-to-many**
Temporally condensed	WhatsApp	Facebook Twitter	Kiva Kickstarter CrowdFlower	Slack channels Group Skype Enterprise social media
Temporally dispersed	Email	Brand communities Bulletin boards	Blogs	User-generated help communities

vary in their appeal to consumers who hold different psychological needs and goals as well as their effects on consumer psychology. First, we may consider ideas from *social identity* theory (e.g., Tajfel et al., 1979) as relevant to the structural characteristics of different social media platforms. Specifically, this theory might lead us to predict that one-to-many and many-to-many synchronous platforms are most likely to create and enhance coherent group structures. This is likely to occur because of the power of such social media structures to immediately communicate and reinforce multiple types of norms. As these groups allow observation and response to others' behavior, it is easy for consumers to observe both injunctive norms ("rules or beliefs as to what constitutes morally-approved and disapproved conduct"; Cialdini et al., 1990, p. 1015) as well as descriptive norms, which are reflected in the actions that people generally take, that is, what constitutes typical activity in a particular setting (Goldstein et al., 2008).

To illustrate the power of ingroups developed via one-to-many platform social structures, Facebook's norms allow for the posting of cat videos. But LinkedIn's generally do not (unless cats play a key role in one's professional life). However, if a consumer receives harsh criticism of their LinkedIn cat video post, they may take two actions: They may find a subset of LinkedIn members who believe cat videos are acceptable, thus joining an ingroup in which they fit well, or they may decide to save their cat videos for another platform, thus conforming to the group norms on LinkedIn's general site. Such adoption of new norms will, in turn, reinforce a sense of ingroup membership and lead to further norm internalization. Past research has shown, for example, that observing the behavior of ingroup members alters the behavior observed (Cruwys et al., 2012) and that incidence of ingroup-consistent behaviors increases as one identifies more strongly with the group (Duffy & Nesdale, 2009).

Second, it is useful to consider the psychological effects that *power hierarchies* play in differently structured networks. One might be tempted to predict that power hierarchies are more likely to emerge in one-to-many social media platforms, as the focus on a single speaker necessarily offers them the ability to shape the perceptions and conversation of those whom they address. However, this argument overlooks the fact that in these networks, many consumers are simultaneously sharing their messages, thus reducing the power available to any single consumer. In organic synchronous one-to-many networks, therefore, power is likely to follow attention, which can shift instantaneously. Indeed, the spotlight of online fame in such platforms moves easily and quickly. Consider the experience of multiple momentary TikTok stars, whose short videos capture broad attention for vanishingly short timespans (Tett, 2020).

Interestingly, many of these platforms are structured to allow consumers to rank or rate one another or to achieve elite status, thus directly creating mechanisms by which power may be accumulated. For example, Twitter's "blue check" verification affords a level of status to authenticated Twitter users; indeed, individuals who receive this verification often comment on the elevated position afforded to them, while those who have not received a blue check may complain of unfair treatment or undeserved recognition by the platform. Such platform-conferred indicators of authority, in turn, have high potential to change consumer behavior: Research suggests that consumers who feel higher in power are more likely than lower power consumers to go against the sentiment-grain, for example, posting negative reviews even in the face of highly positive agreement (Wu et al., 2016).

We may also be tempted to expect that the democratizing nature of social media allows all participants megaphones. Some argue that social media dissolves power structures and, with them, the many behavioral pathologies that power concentration can promote (Friedman & Wyman, 2005; Jenkins, 2012). However, recent work suggests that indeed, by virtue of their transparency, highly inclusive many-to-many social media structures such as Twitter (assuming the tweeter's identity is disclosed) in fact do the most to concentrate power. In such contexts, knowledge disparities between groups of different status become more transparent. As a result, social media interaction, by raising visibility, can reinforce differences in status (H. Kim, 2018).

Third, theory relevant to networks is critical in understanding the interplay of social media structure and consumer behavior. That is, consumers are more likely to take on different positions in network structures, and with them, different communication capacities, in one-to-many social media contexts than in many-to-many or many-to-one contexts. Importantly, these different roles are likely to distinguish between consumers that actually influence one another and those that do not. Foundational research in this area, in fact, suggested that approximately 20% of a user's friends are responsible for driving their site activity (Trusov et al., 2010). Past work also suggested that these roles include "hubs," individuals who have large numbers of social ties and exert substantial influence on information diffusion, attitude formation, and behavior across their network (e.g., Goldenberg et al., 2009). However, other consumers may have different roles, for example, being highly influenced "followers," who, by influencing other similar consumers, can have enormous effects on diffusion (Watts & Dodds, 2007). Interestingly, it may be that different proportions of individuals taking these roles effectively changes the structure of a site. For example, followers have more reciprocal connections with other followers than do hubs and their immediate followers (Q. Wang et al., 2019). That is, platforms with fewer hubs are likely to resemble many-to-many platforms to a greater extent, and those that center around hubs are likely to have a more unidirectional flow of information, more like a one-to-many network.

MEDIA RICHNESS AND SENSORY PROCESSING

We should also examine theories that are most directly to media richness: the amount, complexity, and modality of information in the media. Interestingly, although one might argue that richer social media platforms are of greater value to consumers, as they contain multisensory elements with video, textual, interactive, customizable, and sensory characteristics, psychological theory would make complex predictions. In particular, the combination of media richness and high levels of interactivity may undermine consumer processing. Thus, efforts to manage the effects of social media richness present a psychologically complex double-edged sword, which should prompt us to extend prior theories in meaningful ways. Richness is therefore importantly related to the resources that consumers devote to sensory processing and motivation to understanding the message.

Likely the key theoretical contributor to understanding the psychological effects of richness in social media comes from a basic understanding of participatory *involvement* and *elaboration*. Richer media, by capturing attention and inviting interaction, are likely to promote greater involvement (e.g., Celsi & Olson, 1988). If richness raises involvement, such theory would suggest that richer social media could garner greater attention and deeper comprehension (Celsi & Olson, 1988, p. 210). Certainly, anecdotal evidence suggests that richness does appeal to consumers; mass migrations between platforms have been attributed to richer experiences of extremely similar functional features (e.g., shifts between Snapchat and Instagram "stories," which vary in richness; Meyer, 2016). However, it is unclear precisely in what way this might happen. For example, based on the elaboration likelihood model (Petty & Cacioppo, 1986), increased involvement raises the perceived relevance of related information, prompts the investment of more effort in decision making, and leads to less reliance on heuristics and biases as drivers of behavior. Richer environments may also provide the type of contextual information that reduces the likelihood of consumer offense (Liu et al., 2019), sparking deeper engagement and a stronger desire to interact. Such theories would argue, therefore, that very rich social media environments reinforce learning, interpersonal relationships, social norm sharing, and even understanding of Zoom-based lectures.

But it is also clear that consumers' cognitive acuity in social media settings can be remarkably low, such that deeply flawed information is more readily accepted than one might hope. Some of this tendency has been attributed to personality (Pennycook & Rand, 2020) or the reality that, for many consumers, online activities are more hedonic and subjectively evaluated than utilitarian and objectively evaluated (Brasel & Gips, 2015; Childers et al., 2001)—if one is simply expecting to be entertained, they may not engage their cognitive faculties deeply. Further, the demands of richness may have the opposite effect, prompting consumers to filter out content if it is irrelevant to their goals or self-identity. However, in the aggregate, such effects suggest that richer media can create real information processing challenges for consumers.

Indeed, attention is a scarce resource (Simon, 1960), and consumers likely look for signals for what to attend to in the crowded social media landscape. For this reason, perhaps the most relevant but least applied ideas for understanding the potential effects of media richness on consumer information processing relate to *signal detection theory* (Tanner & Swets, 1954). Signal detection theory, originally developed after the Second World War to understand the ability of airborne radar operators to detect submarines, clearly was not designed with social media in mind. However, as researchers have noted, the need for such vigilance in social media settings, if not of national security importance for most of us, may still have profound effects on our well-being (Canfield et al., 2016). As these authors succinctly summarized,

> Studies typically find that people are less likely to identify a signal when there is a low base rate, the cost of missing a signal is low, the cost of mistaking noise for a signal is high, or there is little difference between the signal and noise (e.g., navigating a dimly lit room). Individual factors include experience, personality, and demographics. People are less likely to identify a signal correctly when they are less experienced, more impulsive, older, or less intelligent. Environmental factors that increase stress, such as uncomfortable ambient conditions or greater workload, can reduce performance. (Canfield et al., 2016, p. 827)

Richness can also encompass complexity. For instance, scholars have examined the effect of image complexity on online behavior such as sharing or intention to purchase (Kusumasondjaja & Tjiptono, 2019; Lee & Shin 2020).

In a social media setting, we can therefore imagine why individuals may fail to detect signals as media richness—here representing the amount of information—increases. As indicated in Table 21.3, as richness increases, numerous problematic signal detection factors would also be predicted to increase as well.

This synthesis suggests that there may be cases where low-richness social media experiences can promote better processing by consumers. First, reducing the cognitive load experienced in social media through simpler interfaces, the presentation of fewer simultaneous messages, or well-calibrated search tools or filters should, based on signal detection theory, allow consumers to better detect the important information in the social media display. In addition, presenting consumers with strategically impoverished media environments can present information gaps, which, in turn, can promote

TABLE 21.3

Proposed Effects of Social Media Richness on Consumer Information Processing

Factor that decreases likelihood of signal detection for a given message	Proposed relationship with media richness	Explanation
Low base rate	Base rate decreases	As media contains more messages, the average appearance base rate for any single message becomes lower, reducing likelihood of detection.
Low cost of missing a signal	Cost decreases	The constant flow of signals suggests that a missed item can be captured on another platform or another occasion, reducing vigilance.
Small difference between signal and noise	Difference decreases	If rich messages yield mimicry, the richer a media source, the more homogeneity will emerge, making detection more difficult.
Low levels of experience	Inexperience rises	Richer media are likely to draw in a steadier stream of stimulus-seeking novices who have weaker ability to detect stimuli.
More impulsive	Impulsivity rises	High levels of sensory stimulation lend themselves to more immediate gratification, lowering vigilance.
Older	Design for older consumers increases	To the extent that richer stimuli are developed to optimize navigation and allow easy interactivity, older consumers may also be more drawn to social media.
High stress	Stress increases	Richer environments can create more stress for consumers.
High cognitive load	Cognitive load increases	Richer environments can create more cognitive load for consumers.
High distractions	Distraction increases	Richer environments can create more distraction for consumers.

curiosity and drive information acquisition (consistent with Loewenstein, 1994).

Here we see a key challenge in understanding the full psychological effect of media richness, however. No social media architecture, like no "choice architecture," is truly neutral. A social media platform's decision to exclude or filter certain messages in an effort to reduce the cognitive load created by an otherwise rich experience can be seen as a type of algorithmic control. For example, filters that preselect social media content consistent with a consumer's past behaviors or preferences would likely contribute to polarization (Barberá et al., 2015; Eady et al., 2019), creating the "echo chambers" and filter bubbles that can separate individuals, at least with regard to political issues[2] (Pariser, 2011). Indeed, the Center for Human Technologies has suggested that the algorithms used to order Facebook's feeds in ways that are presumably better tailored to consumers' interests and desires, for example, have lent themselves to major societal problems (see https://www.humanetech.com for discussions).

Thus, there is a substantial opportunity to update signal detection theory for the world of social media. Specifically, we would suggest that this theory be augmented with consideration of the goals of the consumer, a consideration of different variables associated with richness (whether related to amount, complexity, or modality of information), and the attempts of the platform or other communicators to simplify processing. Taken together, this may allow us to build a new theory of social media signal detection.

---

[2] We note that some apparently contradictory findings exist with regard to the likelihood of U.S. liberals versus conservatives to engage in bubble-extrinsic social media communications (i.e., Barberá et al., 2015, found that liberals are more likely to communicate with those of other ideologies on Twitter, whereas Eady et al., 2019, found that conservatives are more likely to follow liberal media and political sources on the same platform). Whether these different findings represent changes in behavior between publication dates or what should be concluded from a close examination of the two papers in tandem is a worthy area for further exploration.

PERMANENCE

In most consumer psychology domains, permanence is a valuable trait. Inasmuch as permanence reduces the uncertainty associated with an asset, it should increase its value, consistent with basic economic maxims. Further, to the extent that permanence increases psychological ownership of a highly self-relevant social media experience, it should also raise its value (Atasoy & Morewedge, 2018). To the extent that social media becomes part of a consumer's "digital extended self" (Belk, 2013), its permanence thus becomes a means of identity longevity for a consumer, offering them an indelible memorial to thoughts, events, interactions, and relationships. Indeed, recent research has discussed the idea that social media now takes its place alongside museums and schools as a means by which cultural memory may be shaped and stabilized (Lepore, 2015; Stone & Jay, 2019). Certainly, research exploring the exact nature of these novel memory repositories is warranted; in fact, they may offer very rich opportunities for psychologists to study collective memory in naturalistic ways (Hirst & Echterhoff, 2008). From this perspective, social media elements that remind us of our past, such as in Facebook's Memories feature, could achieve Facebook's goal of raising engagement (Hod, 2018).

However, researchers have also pointed out that part of the value of social media may lie in its ephemerality—that is, in its lack of permanence. Relevant theory to describe this value may be found in research on "liquid consumption" (Bardhi & Eckhardt, 2017), the idea that consumers value impermanence in resources (Humphreys & Gielser, 2007). According to this theory, ephemerality may have substantial benefits for consumers. This work is consistent with other research that identifies benefits of ephemerality: To the extent that ephemerality weakens psychological ownership, it may also allow greater identity fluidity (Weiss & Johar, 2013, 2016) and decrease territorialism among consumers (Kirk et al., 2018), both capacities that can benefit consumers. Further, some level of ephemerality may be of benefit at the group level. Indeed, the same researchers arguing for the importance of collective social memory also suggest the potential importance of collective social forgetting and the importance of memory malleability for identity development (Hirst, 2010; Hirst & Coman, 2018). From this perspective, the ability to delete one's past interactions, or even to set them for expiration, as Snapchat allows, may be critical in gaining social media's full benefit. By contrast, Facebook's Memories feature may be more painful than it is helpful, anchoring consumers in a regrettable or painful past. Research could further investigate the moderating effects that determine when reminders of past events are favorable or unfavorable, using other signals in one's profile or social interactions.

In short, permanence generates a great deal of psychological tension. On one hand, a review of past literature shows that multiple intrinsic psychological dispositions, the convenience of social media interactions, the value of social ties and support, and a high sense of trust and control can raise consumers' comfort with leaving a large "big data digital footprint" on social media (Muhammad et al., 2018, p. 560). To the extent that these factors exist, we might expect that permanence is valued. However, permanence may constitute a threat if consumers are concerned about privacy—but this presents consumers with a dilemma. Acquisti et al. (2013) characterized this dilemma aptly, noting the apparent conflict between consumers' desire for privacy (i.e., for their past behavior to be available only to them) and their online behavior (which creates the aforementioned memorials with virtually every interaction). In this work, the authors showed that consumers' exact valuation for online privacy is highly unstable; such valuations can be affected by many different contextual elements such as the presence or absence of rewards or guarantees of privacy. As they wrote,

> Our findings suggest a vicious (or virtuous) circle of privacy valuations of potential interest to policy makers: those who feel they have less (more) privacy tend to value privacy less (more) and become more (less) likely to accept monetary offers for their data; giving away (protecting) their data, in

turn, may make individuals feel they have less (more) privacy—and so on. (Acquisti et al., 2013, p. 252)

Such findings suggest that a desire for permanence may be similarly unstable and context-dependent. As consumers are highly unlikely to continually adjust their social media settings to reflect their momentary preferences for permanence or "forgetting" and may not, indeed, have much awareness of the long-term consequences of either, consumer psychologists have a substantial amount of work to do to fully understand this factor's importance and communicate it to social media users.

REPLICATION

The psychological effects of high replication in social media may be explained by three fairly straightforward theoretical propositions. First, social media platforms and experiences that are repeated consistently over time are likely to become highly *fluent* to consumers. To the extent that this fluency creates a positive metacognitive experience, even unnoticed repetition would lead consumers to develop a positive attitude toward a given social media platform or set of experiences (Alter & Oppenheimer, 2009; Bornstein & D'Agostino, 1992). Indeed, some research shows that interactions on such platforms can lead to a highly pleasurable "flow state," and anecdotal evidence suggests that even relatively minor changes in platform design can be met with strong aversion. Fluency theory would thus argue strongly in favor of replicability as a facilitator of positive consumer psychological experiences.

Second, there is evidence that consumers tend to *satiate* quickly when they feel they have consumed a given good (or type of experience) recently, and as a result, may *variety-seek* after they reach this point in the same way as they would in other domains (Redden & Galak, 2013). Likely, the fact that social media content offers a constant source of nonreplicable content—largely as created by other communicators—helps reduce the likelihood of satiation; consumers can seek variety fairly passively in this domain—a characteristic that may suggest that our past theories of satiation and variety-seeking might be fruitfully updated for social media.

Third, the consistent presence of behavior-based rewards in social media environments can create a compelling habit system (Duhigg, 2012; Wood & Neal, 2007). If every time a consumer logs onto their social media account, they experience a sensory, visual, or identity-based "reward," such behavior is likely to become habitual, even addictive (Shen et al., 2015). When consumers face stressful life experiences, in fact, reliance on such habits may be particularly strong (Neal et al., 2013). Many platforms have designed precisely such rewards into their social media experiences. For example, the "likes" that one's posts may garner offers a rewarding sense of self-worth, providing a constant psychological reward for engagement. As another example, a longer Snapchat "streak" (directing snaps back and forth with a friend for several days) is rewarded with "100" or a mountain emoji and may, like classic deprivation, lead to a feeling of devastation when the chain is broken (Mic, 2017). The replicability of these cue-behavior-reward aspects of the experience certainly lends itself to their stickiness.

A classic permanence-relevant theory that has been little-explored in recent social media research relates to the attribution process, specifically as discussed by Kelley (1973). In Kelley's *attribution theory*, individuals are expected to attribute an event to the inherent properties of an entity (in this case, a social media communicator or subject) to the extent that such an event is distinctive, consistent over time, consistent over modality, and achieves high consensus (e.g., all observers perceive a given action the same way). Applying this theory to social media, scholars might examine the communicator's distinctiveness, consistency over time and across modality, and ability to create social consensus.

Mizerski et al. (1979) famously applied these concepts to consumer psychology, arguing that these rules were most applicable in "extended information-processing/attribution situations" (p. 128). In such situations, to the extent that communicators (in their discussion, advertisers) allow consumers to make stronger attributions, the advertiser becomes a more valuable information source. Clearly, social media was not a salient topic when this work was done. However, we may expect that when a platform offers higher replicability, it is seen as a more trustworthy source of experience or information. Further, if this highly replicable experience is appreciated by other consumers (high in consensus) in ways unique to the platform, that platform is more likely to gain consumer loyalty. The same principle may be applied to brands that use social media to communicate with consumers—having consistent communications across diverse platforms may strengthen their communication's effects and perceptions of authenticity.

However, new questions would also arise from the application of attribution theory to social media, particularly when combined with ideas from the stereotype content model (Cuddy et al., 2008; Fiske et al., 2002). For example, consumers may prefer to use different platforms to express various aspects of the self: Whereas LinkedIn is reserved for professional communications, thus emphasizing one's "competence dimension," Facebook may offer a means of communicating one's hobbies, family connections, and rich friendships, that is, their "warmth," and Twitter may be reserved for sharing political opinions, which may be a mix of both competence and warmth, depending on one's viewpoints. Attribution theory would suggest that individuals who observe this lack of personality replication across platforms would find the communicator untrustworthy. However, we may also consider that norms related to various platforms would qualify the importance of consistency over modality—the consistency that is sought may simply be the consistent adherence to platform-specific norms, rather than consistency in content or message. Further, social media may allow us to inquire more deeply into the importance of consensus. Some work suggests that consensus may not be important in shaping consumer behavior for consumers who are particularly high in susceptibility to social influence (Sciandra et al., 2017); would this hold in all social media domains? What cues do consumers use to evaluate the adequacy of consensus in social media settings?

CONCLUSION: SOCIAL MEDIA'S CONSEQUENCES FOR CONSUMER PSYCHOLOGY

In this chapter, we have suggested multiple theories for understanding the consumer psychology of social media. Researchers, in turn, may need to further develop fundamental psychological theories in ways that help us understand the roles that these five key attributes identified will have in shaping psychological processes. By connecting the current social media research to existing theories, we hope to enrich and extend them, building a robust scientific base for understanding this new domain. But it is critical to ask: Is social media good for consumers, on balance? And how should consumer psychologists think about the consequences of consumer behavior on social media?

A substantial body of literature provides evidence that consumers with high levels of social media have lower levels of well-being. For example, social media use can become addictive or overused, leading to loneliness, anxiety, and poor sleep quality (Griffiths et al., 2014; W. Wang, Li, & Lei, 2017; W. Wang, Wang, et al., 2017). These problems appear to be particularly severe among younger adults; a U.S. sample showed that being in the highest versus lowest quartile of social media use was associated with significantly increased likelihood of depression (Lin et al., 2016). Other scholars have pointed to the negative effects of social media on identity formation and self-esteem during adolescence (Woods & Scott, 2016).

On the other hand, some research suggests that social media use may be associated with higher self-esteem (Gonzales & Hancock, 2011; Valkenburg et al., 2006). In Gonzales and Hancock's (2011) work, boosts in well-being are provided by the opportunity to share positive information or even momentarily browse social media sites. In Valkenburg et al.'s (2006) research, the positive feedback from others enhanced individuals' self-esteem. People who suffer emotional turmoil in the wake of negative life experiences can use social media to bolster their well-being (Berger & Buechel, 2012), and unsatisfied individuals can build their social capital by accessing online social networks (Ellison et al., 2007). And, as originally touted, some corners of social media enable expression of new identities, *communitas* among members of a subculture, experimentation, and support that may be unavailable offline (e.g., Turkle, 2005; Turner, 2005).

To complicate matters further, consumer research suggests that effects on self-esteem are contingent less on the magnitude of social media use than on *how* it is used. For example, Wilcox and Stephen's (2013) work argued that consumers who focus more on close friends in their social media show increased self-control as compared with those who browse more distantly related others. However, their work also casts light on whether self-esteem should be the outcome about which researchers care most: High self-esteem, in turn, is associated with higher BMI and debt, both of which are associated with lower well-being. As such, it is unclear when and why social media use will systematically raise or lower self-esteem—either directly by prompting social comparison or indirectly by triggering other behaviors that, when carried out, may undermine longer term self-esteem.

Given our foregoing discussion, we propose that a goal of future consumer psychology work in social media should be to consider the extent to which the six attributes described here may be moderators of social media's overall effect on consumers' psychological well-being. Such explorations will benefit from a systems approach (e.g., Meadows, 2009) that takes into account not only consumers or platforms in isolation but rather the entire set of interlocking goals, incentives, and processes, as well as the stakeholders in each, that may shape social media engagement's consequences. Importantly, we should recognize that consumer goals may either align or conflict with those of firms on social media; our discussion here has identified a number of these goals:

- consumer goals: to affiliate, to form and express identity, to persuade, to learn, and so forth
- brand goals: to drive awareness and shape brand perception, create engagement, and drive consumption

To the extent that consumers can achieve their goals, we would expect that their well-being may be greater. However, we do not yet understand the way that, in the aggregate, consumers' and firms' goals interact with one another across variously designed platforms—this is a major blind spot in our understanding of the psychological consequences of social media.

Finally, we should also not omit consideration of social media's implications for the development of psychology as a whole. In many ways, social media provides a psychological laboratory, offering an opportunity for both researchers and firms to observe behavior unobtrusively. Certainly, given the number of papers that rely on such data, academics have implicitly approved of such tactics. Social media has allowed many researchers to conduct psychologically important experiments using a broader array of participants, many of which have given us rich insights. However, there is growing concern about the effects of consumer surveillance. Facebook now has one of the largest repositories of consumer information, and companies like Axios can already link identity with browsing behavior and offline purchases. To the degree that this information is monetized and enclosed for profit, it may be unavailable for development of academic knowledge and prevent it from contributing to the public good.

The privacy issue may have important political implications. These political implications, in turn, may affect psychology of both individuals and groups. Specifically, as states and businesses gain access to permanent, archived private information and control the inflow and outflow of information via the media, they may gain increasing power over citizens. At the same time, consumers' desire to control prevailing narratives through their own social media use may lower their trust in government (Chen & Sun, 2019), leading to government policy changes that reinforce their preferred narrative.

In addition, the broad reach and wide replicability of misinformation in social media may have troubling political implications. Targeting and tailoring of information based on observation of consumers' past social media behaviors, community memberships, and preferences may lend itself to the delivery of polarizing information, as well as the incubation of extremism. Further, because consumers can filter out any disconfirming information on social media, they are likely to embrace echo chambers and ignore efforts to fact-check (e.g., Zollo et al., 2017). In these cases, it is precisely the lack of social presence in some social media platforms like Twitter that allows a person or state to use bots and artificial intelligence for their broad persuasive influence, with little accountability for their statements. While computer scientists have undertaken efforts to use consumers' Facebook behaviors to identify topics most at risk of being translated into misinformation by those who would seek to mislead (Del Vicario et al., 2019), psychologists may make major contributions by seeking to understand why some topics lend themselves to such distortion and others do not.

These broader issues underscore the complexity of social and digital media and highlight the importance of studying this set of phenomena and their effects from different perspectives, considering their political, social, and cultural implications for the psyche. Yet these issues also outline an important role for consumer psychology in the world of social media and call for cooperative, multimethod approaches to developing a richer understanding of this constantly changing media form.

REFERENCES

Aaker, J. L. (1997). Dimensions of brand personality. *Journal of Marketing Research*, 34(3), 347–356. https://doi.org/10.1177/002224379703400304

Acquisti, A., John, L. K., & Loewenstein, G. (2013). What is privacy worth? *Journal of Legal Studies*, 42(2), 249–274. https://doi.org/10.1086/671754

Alter, A. L., & Oppenheimer, D. M. (2009). Uniting the tribes of fluency to form a metacognitive nation. *Personality and Social Psychology Review*, 13(3), 219–235. https://doi.org/10.1177/1088868309341564

Alves, H., Fernandes, C., & Raposo, M. (2016). Social media marketing: A literature review and implications. *Psychology and Marketing*, 33(12), 1029–1038. https://doi.org/10.1002/mar.20936

Argo, J. J., Dahl, D. W., & Manchanda, R. V. (2005). The influence of a mere social presence in a retail context. *Journal of Consumer Research*, 32(2), 207–212. https://doi.org/10.1086/432230

Atasoy, O., & Morewedge, C. K. (2018). Digital goods are valued less than physical goods. *Journal of Consumer Research*, 44(6), 1343–1357. https://doi.org/10.1093/jcr/ucx102

Back, M. D., Stopfer, J. M., Vazire, S., Gaddis, S., Schmukle, S. C., Egloff, B., & Gosling, S. D. (2010). Facebook profiles reflect actual personality, not self-idealization. *Psychological Science*, 21(3), 372–374. https://doi.org/10.1177/0956797609360756

Barberá, P., Jost, J. T., Nagler, J., Tucker, J. A., & Bonneau, R. (2015). Tweeting from left to right: Is online political communication more than an echo chamber? *Psychological Science*, 26(10), 1531–1542. https://doi.org/10.1177/0956797615594620

Bardhi, F., & Eckhardt, G. M. (2017). Liquid consumption. *Journal of Consumer Research*, 44(3), 582–597. https://doi.org/10.1093/jcr/ucx050

Barger, V., Peltier, J. W., & Schultz, D. E. (2016). Social media and consumer engagement: A review and research agenda. *Journal of Research in Interactive Marketing*, 10(4), 268–287. https://doi.org/10.1108/JRIM-06-2016-0065

Baumeister, R. F. (1982). A self-presentational view of social phenomena. *Psychological Bulletin*, 91(1), 3–26. https://doi.org/10.1037/0033-2909.91.1.3

Baym, N. K. (2015). *Personal connections in the digital age*. Wiley.

Belk, R. W. (2013). Extended self in a digital world. *Journal of Consumer Research*, 40(3), 477–500. https://doi.org/10.1086/671052

Berger, J. A., & Buechel, E. (2012). Facebook therapy? Why do people share self-relevant content online? In Z. Gürhan-Canli, C. Otnes, & R. Zhu (Eds.), *NA - Advances in consumer research* (Vol. 40, pp. 203–208). Association for Consumer Research.

Bornstein, R. F., & D'Agostino, P. R. (1992). Stimulus recognition and the mere exposure effect. *Journal of Personality and Social Psychology*, 63(4), 545–552. https://doi.org/10.1037/0022-3514.63.4.545

Boyd, D., & Ellison, N. B. (2007). Social network sites: Definition, history, and scholarship. *Journal of Computer-Mediated Communication*, 13(1), 210–230. https://doi.org/10.1111/j.1083-6101.2007.00393.x

Brasel, S. A., & Gips, J. (2015). Interface psychology: Touchscreens change attribute importance, decision criteria, and behavior in online choice. *Cyberpsychology, Behavior, and Social Networking*, 18(9), 534–538. https://doi.org/10.1089/cyber.2014.0546

Brehm, J. W. (1966). *A theory of psychological reactance*. Academic Press.

Canfield, C. I., Fischhoff, B., & Davis, A. (2016). Quantifying phishing susceptibility for detection and behavior decisions. *Human Factors*, 58(8), 1158–1172. https://doi.org/10.1177/0018720816665025

Celsi, R. L., & Olson, J. C. (1988). The role of involvement in attention and comprehension processes. *Journal of Consumer Research*, *15*(2), 210–224. https://doi.org/10.1086/209158

Chen, J., & Sun, L. (2019). Media influence on citizens' government trust: A cross-sectional data analysis of China. *International Journal of Public Administration*, *42*(13), 1122–1134. https://doi.org/10.1080/01900692.2019.1575854

Childers, T. L., Carr, C. L., Peck, J., & Carson, S. (2001). Hedonic and utilitarian motivations for online retail shopping behavior. *Journal of Retailing*, *77*(4), 511–535. https://doi.org/10.1016/S0022-4359(01)00056-2

Cialdini, R. B., Reno, R. R., & Kallgren, C. A. (1990). A focus theory of normative conduct: Recycling the concept of norms to reduce littering in public places. *Journal of Personality and Social Psychology*, *58*(6), 1015–1026. https://doi.org/10.1037/0022-3514.58.6.1015

Cooper, P. (2018, December 18). The things brands do on social media that people hate. *Hootsuite*. https://blog.hootsuite.com/what-people-hate-most-about-brands-on-social-media/

Cruwys, T., Platow, M. J., Angullia, S. A., Chang, J. M., Diler, S. E., Kirchner, J. L., Lentfer, C. E., Lim, Y. J., Quarisa, A., Tor, V. W., & Wadley, A. L. (2012). Modeling of food intake is moderated by salient psychological group membership. *Appetite*, *58*(2), 754–757. https://doi.org/10.1016/j.appet.2011.12.002

Cuddy, A. J. C., Fiske, S. T., & Glick, P. (2008). Warmth and competence as universal dimensions of social perception: The stereotype content model and the BIAS map. *Advances in Experimental Social Psychology*, *40*(1), 61–149. https://doi.org/10.1016/S0065-2601(07)00002-0

DeGennaro, T. (2019, September 18). 10 most popular social media sites in China (2019 Updated). *Dragon Social*. https://www.dragonsocial.net/blog/social-media-in-china/#Weibo

Del Vicario, M., Quattrociocchi, W., Scala, A., & Zoolo, F. (2019). Polarization and fake news: Early warning of potential misinformation targets. *ACM Transactions on the Web*, *13*(2), 1–22. https://doi.org/10.1145/3316809

Donath, J. (2007). Signals in social supernets. *Journal of Computer-Mediated Communication*, *13*(1), 231–251. https://doi.org/10.1111/j.1083-6101.2007.00394.x

Duffy, A. L., & Nesdale, D. (2009). Peer groups, social identity, and children's bullying behavior. *Social Development*, *18*(1), 121–139. https://doi.org/10.1111/j.1467-9507.2008.00484.x

Duhigg, C. (2012). *The power of habit: Why we do what we do in life and business*. Penguin Random House.

Eady, G., Nagler, J., Guess, A., Zilinsky, J., & Tucker, J. A. (2019). How many people live in political bubbles on social media? Evidence from linked survey and Twitter data. *SAGE Open*, *9*(1). https://doi.org/10.1177/2158244019832705

Ellison, N. B., Steinfield, C., & Lampe, C. (2007). The benefits of Facebook "friends": Social capital and college students' use of online social network sites. *Journal of Computer-Mediated Communication*, *12*(4), 1143–1168. https://doi.org/10.1111/j.1083-6101.2007.00367.x

Fiske, S. T., Cuddy, A. J. C., Glick, P., & Xu, J. (2002). A model of (often mixed) stereotype content: Competence and warmth respectively follow from perceived status and competition. *Journal of Personality and Social Psychology*, *82*(6), 878–902. https://doi.org/10.1037/0022-3514.82.6.878

Fournier, S., & Lee, L. (2009, April). Getting brand communities right. *Harvard Business Review*. https://hbr.org/2009/04/getting-brand-communities-right

Friedman, T. L., & Wyman, O. (2005). *The world is flat*. Farrar, Straus and Giroux.

Friestad, M., & Wright, P. (1994). The persuasion knowledge model: How people cope with persuasion attempts. *Journal of Consumer Research*, *21*(1), 1–31. https://doi.org/10.1086/209380

Gentile, B., Twenge, J., Freeman, E., & Campbell, W. K. (2012). The effect of social networking websites on positive self-views: An experimental investigation. *Computers in Human Behavior*, *28*, 1929–1933. https://doi.org/10.1016/j.chb.2012.05.012

Goffman, E. (1956). *The presentation of self in everyday life*. Harmondsworth.

Goldenberg, J., Han, S., Lehmann, D. R., & Hong, J. W. (2009). The role of hubs in the adoption process. *Journal of Marketing*, *73*(2), 1–13. https://doi.org/10.1509/jmkg.73.2.1

Goldstein, N. J., Cialdini, R. B., & Griskevicius, V. (2008). A room with a viewpoint: Using social norms to motivate environmental conservation in hotels. *Journal of Consumer Research*, *35*(3), 472–482. https://doi.org/10.1086/586910

Gonzales, A. L., & Hancock, J. T. (2011). Mirror, mirror on my Facebook wall: Effects of exposure to Facebook on self-esteem. *Cyberpsychology, Behavior, and Social Networking*, *14*(1–2), 79–83. https://doi.org/10.1089/cyber.2009.0411

Grewal, L., Stephen, A. T., & Coleman, N. V. (2019). When posting about products on social media backfires: The negative effects of consumer identity signaling on product interest. *Journal of Marketing Research*, *56*(2), 197–210. https://doi.org/10.1177/0022243718821960

Grieve, R., March, E., & Watkinson, J. (2020). Inauthentic self-presentation on Facebook as a function of vulnerable narcissism and lower self-esteem. *Computers in Human Behavior, 102*, 144–150. https://doi.org/10.1016/j.chb.2019.08.020

Griffiths, M. D., Kuss, D. J., & Demetrovics, Z. (2014). Social networking addiction: An overview of preliminary findings. In K. P. Rosenberg & L. C. Feder (Eds.), *Behavioral addictions: Criteria, evidence, and treatment* (pp. 119–141). Elsevier. https://doi.org/10/gkfx

Hill, K. (2012, January 24). #McDStories: When a hashtag becomes a bashtag. *Forbes*. https://www.forbes.com/sites/kashmirhill/2012/01/24/mcdstories-when-a-hashtag-becomes-a-bashtag/#3a861a02ed25

Hirst, W. (2010). The contribution of malleability to collective memory. In P. A. Reuter-Lorenz, K. Baynes, G. R. Mangun, & E. A. Phelps (Eds.), *The cognitive neuroscience of mind* (pp. 139–154). MIT Press.

Hirst, W., & Coman, A. (2018). Building a collective memory: The case for collective forgetting. *Current Opinion in Psychology, 23*, 88–92. https://doi.org/10.1016/j.copsyc.2018.02.002

Hirst, W., & Echterhoff, G. (2008). Creating shared memories in conversation: Toward a psychology of collective memory. *Social Research, 75*(1), 183–216. https://www.jstor.org/stable/40972057

Hod, O. (2018, June 11). *All of your Facebook memories are now in one place*. Facebook. https://about.fb.com/news/2018/06/all-of-your-facebook-memories-are-now-in-one-place/

Holt, D. B. (2004). *How brands become icons*. Harvard Business Publishing Corporation.

Holt, D. B. (2016). Branding in the age of social media. *Harvard Business Review, 94*(3), 40–50. https://hbr.org/2016/03/branding-in-the-age-of-social-media

Humphreys, A. (2016). *Social media: Enduring principles*. Oxford University Press.

Humphreys, A., & Gielser, M. (2007). Access versus ownership in consumer research. In G. J. Fitzsimons & V. G. Morwitz (Eds.), *NA - Advances in consumer research* (Vol. 34, pp. 696–699). Association for Consumer Research.

Humphreys, A., & Grayson, K. (2008). The intersecting roles of consumer and producer: A critical perspective on co-production, co-creation and prosumption. *Sociology Compass, 2*(3), 963–980. https://doi.org/10.1111/j.1751-9020.2008.00112.x

Jenkins, H. (2012). *Textual poachers: Television fans and participatory culture* (2nd ed.). Routledge. https://doi.org/10.4324/9780203114339

John, L. K., Emrich, O., Gupta, S., & Norton, M. I. (2017). Does "liking" lead to loving? The impact of joining a brand's social network on marketing outcomes. *Journal of Marketing Research, 54*(1), 144–155. https://doi.org/10.1509/jmr.14.0237

Kardes, F. R., Posavac, S. S., & Cronley, M. L. (2004). Consumer inference: A review of processes, bases, and judgment contexts. *Journal of Consumer Psychology, 14*(3), 230–256. https://doi.org/10.1207/s15327663jcp1403_6

Kelley, H. H. (1973). The processes of causal attribution. *American Psychologist, 28*(2), 107–128. https://doi.org/10.1037/h0034225

Kemp, S. (2019). *The global state of digital in 2019 report*. Hootsuite. https://hootsuite.com/pages/digital-in-2019

Kim, B., & Kim, Y. (2017). College students' social media use and communication network heterogeneity: Implications for social capital and subjective well-being. *Computers in Human Behavior, 73*, 620–628. https://doi.org/10.1016/j.chb.2017.03.033

Kim, H. (2018). The mutual constitution of social media use and status hierarchies in global organizing. *Management Communication Quarterly, 32*(4), 471–503. https://doi.org/10.1177/0893318918779135

Kirk, C. P., Peck, J., & Swain, S. D. (2018). Property lines in the mind: Consumers' psychological ownership and their territorial responses. *Journal of Consumer Research, 45*(1), 148–168. https://doi.org/10.1093/jcr/ucx111

Kolirin, L. C. (2019, January 8). *Fiji water girl steals the show at the Golden Globes*. CNN. https://edition.cnn.com/2019/01/07/entertainment/fiji-water-golden-globe-scli-intl/index.html

Kotler, P. (1986). The prosumer movement: A new challenge for marketers. In R. J. Lutz (Ed.), *NA - Advances in consumer research* (Vol. 13, pp. 510–513). Association for Consumer Research.

Kristofferson, K., White, K., & Peloza, J. (2014). The nature of slacktivism: How the social observability of an initial act of token support affects subsequent prosocial action. *Journal of Consumer Research, 40*(6), 1149–1166. https://doi.org/10.1086/674137

Kumar, A., Bezawada, R., Rishika, R., Janakiraman, R., & Kannan, P. K. (2016). From social to sale: The effects of firm-generated content in social media on customer behavior. *Journal of Marketing, 80*(1), 7–25. https://doi.org/10.1509/jm.14.0249

Kusumasondjaja, S., & Tjiptono, F. (2019). Endorsement and visual complexity in food advertising on Instagram. *Internet Research, 29*(4), 659–687. https://doi.org/10.1108/IntR-11-2017-0459

Lamberton, C., & Stephen, A. T. (2016). A thematic exploration of digital, social media, and mobile marketing: Research evolution from 2000 to 2015 and an agenda for future inquiry. *Journal of Marketing, 80*(6), 146–172. https://doi.org/10.1509/jm.15.0415

Latané, B. (1981). The psychology of social impact. *American Psychologist, 36*(4), 343–356. https://doi.org/10.1037/0003-066X.36.4.343

Latané, B. (1996). Dynamic social impact: The creation of culture by communication. *Journal of Communication, 46*(4), 13–25. https://doi.org/10.1111/j.1460-2466.1996.tb01501.x

Lee, J. E., & Shin, E. (2020). The effects of apparel names and visual complexity of apparel design on consumers' apparel product attitudes: A mental imagery perspective. *Journal of Business Research, 120*, 407–417. https://doi.org/10.1016/j.jbusres.2019.08.023

Leonardi, P. M., Huysman, M., & Steinfield, C. (2013). Enterprise social media: Definition, history, and prospects for the study of social technologies in organizations. *Journal of Computer-Mediated Communication, 19*(1), 1–19. https://doi.org/10.1111/jcc4.12029

Lepore, J. (2015, January 26). Can the internet be archived? *New Yorker*. https://www.newyorker.com/magazine/2015/01/26/cobweb

Lin, L. Y., Sidani, J. E., Shensa, A., Radovic, A., Miller, E., Colditz, J. B., Hoffman, B. L., Giles, L. M., & Primack, B. A. (2016). Association between social media use and depression among U.S. young adults. *Depression and Anxiety, 33*(4), 323–331. https://doi.org/10.1002/da.22466

Liu, P. J., Lamberton, C., Bettman, J. R., & Fitzsimons, G. J. (2019). Delicate snowflakes and broken bonds: A conceptualization of consumption-based offense. *Journal of Consumer Research, 45*(6), 1164–1193. https://doi.org/10.1093/jcr/ucy051

Livingstone, S. (2008). Taking risky opportunities in youthful content creation: Teenagers' use of social networking sites for intimacy, privacy and self-expression. *New Media & Society, 10*(3), 393–411. https://doi.org/10.1177/1461444808089415

Loewenstein, G. (1994). The psychology of curiosity: A review and reinterpretation. *Psychological Bulletin, 116*(1), 75–98. https://doi.org/10.1037/0033-2909.116.1.75

Manago, A. M., Graham, M. B., Greenfield, P. M., & Salimkhan, G. (2008). Self-presentation and gender on MySpace. *Journal of Applied Developmental Psychology, 29*(6), 446–458. https://doi.org/10.1016/j.appdev.2008.07.001

Marwick, A. E. (2013). *Status update: Celebrity, publicity, and branding in the social media age*. Yale University Press.

Marwick, A. E., & Boyd, D. (2011). I tweet honestly, I tweet passionately: Twitter users, context collapse, and the imagined audience. *New Media & Society, 13*(1), 114–133. https://doi.org/10.1177/1461444810365313

Marwick, A. E., & Boyd, D. (2014). Networked privacy: How teenagers negotiate context in social media. *New Media & Society, 16*(7), 1051–1067. https://doi.org/10.1177/1461444814543995

Matsuba, M. K. (2006). Searching for self and relationships online. *Cyberpsychology & Behavior, 9*(3), 275–284. https://doi.org/10.1089/cpb.2006.9.275

Meadows, D. H. (2009). *Thinking in systems*. Earthscan.

Meyer, R. (2016, September 1). How Instagram opened a ruthless new chapter in the teen photo wars. *The Atlantic*. https://www.theatlantic.com/technology/archive/2016/09/how-one-teen-uses-instagram-and-snapchat-stories/498254/

Mic, T. L. (2017, April 14). *Teens explain the world of Snapchat's addictive streaks, where friendships live or die*. Business Insider. https://www.businessinsider.com/teens-explain-snapchat-streaks-why-theyre-so-addictive-and-important-to-friendships-2017-4

Mizerski, R. W., Golden, L. L., & Kernan, J. B. (1979). The attribution process in consumer decision making. *Journal of Consumer Research, 6*(2), 123–140. https://doi.org/10.1086/208756

Moore, E., & Murphy, H. (2019, November 19). Facebook's massive fake numbers problem. *Los Angeles Times*. https://www.latimes.com/business/technology/story/2019-11-18/facebooks-massive-fake-numbers-problem

Muhammad, S. S., Dey, B. L., & Weerakkody, V. (2018). Analysis of factors that influence customers' willingness to leave big data digital footprints on social media: A systematic review of literature. *Information Systems Frontiers, 20*(3), 559–576. https://doi.org/10.1007/s10796-017-9802-y

Nadkarni, A., & Hofmann, S. G. (2012). Why do people use Facebook?. *Personality and individual differences, 52*(3), 243–249. https://doi.org/10.1016/j.paid.2011.11.007

Naylor, R. W., Lamberton, C. P., & Norton, D. A. (2011). Seeing ourselves in others: Reviewer ambiguity, egocentric anchoring, and persuasion. *Journal of Marketing Research, 48*(3), 617–631. https://doi.org/10.1509/jmkr.48.3.617

Naylor, R. W., Lamberton, C. P., & West, P. M. (2012). Beyond the "like" button: The impact of mere virtual presence on brand evaluations and purchase intentions in social media settings. *Journal of Marketing, 76*(6), 105–120. https://doi.org/10.1509/jm.11.0105

Neal, D. T., Wood, W., & Drolet, A. (2013). How do people adhere to goals when willpower is low? The profits (and pitfalls) of strong habits. *Journal of Personality and Social Psychology, 104*(6), 959–975. https://doi.org/10.1037/a0032626

Noyes, D. (2020). *The top 20 valuable Facebook statistics—Updated May 2020*. Zephoria. https://zephoria.com/top-15-valuable-facebook-statistics/

Pariser, E. (2011). *The filter bubble*. Penguin Books.

Pennycook, G., & Rand, D. G. (2020). Who falls for fake news? The roles of bullshit receptivity, overclaiming, familiarity, and analytic thinking. *Journal of Personality*, 88(2), 185–200. https://doi.org/10.1111/jopy.12476

Perrin, A., & Anderson, M. (2019, April 10). *Share of U.S. adults using social media, including Facebook, is mostly unchanged since 2018*. Pew Research Center. https://www.pewresearch.org/fact-tank/2019/04/10/share-of-u-s-adults-using-social-media-including-facebook-is-mostly-unchanged-since-2018/

Petty, R. E., & Cacioppo, J. T. (1986). The elaboration likelihood model of persuasion. *Advances in Experimental Social Psychology*, 19, 123–205. https://doi.org/10.1016/S0065-2601(08)60214-2

Quinn, K. (2013). We haven't talked in 30 years! Relationship reconnection and internet use at midlife. *Information Communication and Society*, 16(3), 397–420. https://doi.org/10.1080/1369118X.2012.756047

Quinn, K. (2014). An ecological approach to privacy: "Doing" online privacy at midlife. *Journal of Broadcasting & Electronic Media*, 58(4), 562–580. https://doi.org/10.1080/08838151.2014.966357

Redden, J. P., & Galak, J. (2013). The subjective sense of feeling satiated. *Journal of Experimental Psychology: General*, 142(1), 209–217. https://doi.org/10.1037/a0028896

Rogers, E. M. (1995). *Diffusion of innovations* (4th ed.). Free Press.

Rosenberg, M. (1979). *Conceiving the self*. Adfo Books.

Ruble, D. N. (1994). A phase model of transitions: Cognitive and motivational consequences. *Advances in Experimental Social Psychology*, 26, 163–214. https://doi.org/10.1016/S0065-2601(08)60154-9

Schlenker, B. R. (1986). Self-identification: Toward an integration of the private and public self. In R. Baumeister (Ed.), *Public self and private self* (pp. 21–62). Springer.

Schmidt, A. L., Zollo, F., Del Vicario, M., Bessi, A., Scala, A., Galdarelli, G., Stanley, H. E., & Quattrociocchi, W. (2017). Anatomy of news consumption on Facebook. *Proceedings of the National Academy of Sciences of the United States of America*, 114(12), 3035–3039. https://doi.org/10.1073/pnas.1617052114

Sciandra, M. R., Lamberton, C., & Reczek, R. W. (2017). The wisdom of some: Do we always need high consensus to shape consumer behavior? *Journal of Public Policy & Marketing*, 36(1), 15–35. https://doi.org/10.1509/jppm.14.123

Sezer, O., Gino, F., & Norton, M. I. (2018). Humblebragging: A distinct—and ineffective—self-presentation strategy. *Journal of Personality and Social Psychology*, 114(1), 52–74. https://doi.org/10.1037/pspi0000108

Shen, L., Fishbach, A., & Hsee, C. K. (2015). The motivating-uncertainty effect: Uncertainty increases resource investment in the process of reward pursuit. *Journal of Consumer Research*, 41(5), 1301–1315. https://doi.org/10.1086/679418

Simon, H. A. (1960). *The Ford distinguished lectures: Vol. 3. The new science of management decision*. Harper & Brothers. https://doi.org/10.1037/13978-000

Spears, R., Postmes, T., Lea, M., & Watt, S. E. (2001). A SIDE view of social influence. In J. P. Forgas & K. D. Williams (Eds.), *The Sydney symposium of social psychology. Social influence: Direct and indirect processes* (pp. 331–350). Psychology Press.

Stone, C. B., & Jay, A. C. V. (2019). From the individual to the collective: The emergence of a psychological approach to collective memory. *Applied Cognitive Psychology*, 33(4), 504–515. https://doi.org/10.1002/acp.3564

Sundie, J. M., Kenrick, D. T., Griskevicius, V., Tybur, J. M., Vohs, K. D., & Beal, D. J. (2011). Peacocks, Porsches, and Thorstein Veblen: Conspicuous consumption as a sexual signaling system. *Journal of Personality and Social Psychology*, 100(4), 664–680. https://doi.org/10.1037/a0021669

Swann, W. B., Jr. (1990). To be adored or to be known? The interplay of self-enhancement and self-verification. In E. T. Higgins & R. M. Sorrentino (Eds.), *Handbook of motivation and cognition: Foundations of social behavior* (Vol. 2, pp. 408–448). Guilford Press.

Tajfel, H., & Turner, J. C. (1979). An integrative theory of intergroup conflict. In W. G. Austin & S. Worchel (Eds.), *The social psychology of intergroup relations* (pp. 33–37). Brooks/Cole.

Tanner, W. P., Jr., & Swets, J. A. (1954). A decision-making theory of visual detection. *Psychological Review*, 61(6), 401–409. https://doi.org/10.1037/h0058700

Tett, G. (2020, February 5). My daughter's TikTok triumph and the fleeting nature of internet fame. *Financial Times*. https://www.ft.com/content/9d4267b2-47a5-11ea-aee2-9ddbdc86190d

Tice, D. M., Butler, J. L., Muraven, M. B., & Stillwell, A. M. (1995). When modesty prevails: Differential favorability of self-presentation to friends and strangers. *Journal of Personality and Social Psychology*, 69(6), 1120–1138. https://doi.org/10.1037/0022-3514.69.6.1120

Toffler, A. (1980). *The third wave*. William Morrow & Co.

Torres, L. (2019, October 17). *People are memeing Kylie Jenner singing "rise and shine" to her daughter, and now even Ariana Grande is in on the action*. Insider. https://www.businessinsider.com/kylie-jenner-rise-and-shine-meme-ariana-grande-video-2019-10

Toubia, O., & Stephen, A. T. (2013). Intrinsic vs. image-related utility in social media: Why do people contribute content to Twitter? *Marketing Science, 32*(3), 368–392. https://doi.org/10.1287/mksc.2013.0773

Trusov, M., Bodapati, A. V., & Bucklin, R. E. (2010). Determining influential users in internet social networks. *Journal of Marketing Research, 47*(4), 643–658. https://doi.org/10.1509/jmkr.47.4.643

Turkle, S. (2005). *The second self: Computers and the human spirit*. MIT Press. https://doi.org/10.7551/mitpress/6115.001.0001

Turner, F. (2005). Where the counterculture met the new economy: The WELL and the origins of virtual community. *Technology and Culture, 46*(3), 485–512. https://doi.org/10.1353/tech.2005.0154

Valkenburg, P. M., Peter, J., & Schouten, A. P. (2006). Friend networking sites and their relationship to adolescents' well-being and social self-esteem. *Cyberpsychology & Behavior, 9*(5), 584–590. https://doi.org/10.1089/cpb.2006.9.584

Wadley, J. (2018, October 17). Social media buffers depression among older adults with pain. *Michigan News*. https://news.umich.edu/social-media-buffers-depression-among-older-adults-with-pain/

Walther, J. B. (1992). Interpersonal effects in computer-mediated interaction: A relational perspective. *Communication Research, 19*(1), 52–90. https://doi.org/10.1177/009365092019001003

Walther, J. B. (2006). Nonverbal dynamics in computer-mediated communication. In V. Manusov & M. L. Patterson (Eds.), *The Sage handbook of nonverbal communication* (pp. 461–480). Sage.

Wang, Q., Miao, F., Tayi, G. K., & Xie, E. (2019). What makes online content viral? The contingent effects of hub users versus non–hub users on social media platforms. *Journal of the Academy of Marketing Science, 47*(6), 1005–1026. https://doi.org/10.1007/s11747-019-00678-2

Wang, W., Li, Z., & Lei, L. (2017). The effect of mobile social media overuse on adolescents' loneliness, anxiety and sleep quality. *Medicine & Philosophy, 38*(4), 71–74.

Wang, W., Qian, G., Wang, X., Lei, L., Hu, Q., Chen, J., & Jiang, S. (2021). Mobile social media use and self-identity among Chinese adolescents: The mediating effect of friendship quality and the moderating role of gender. *Current Psychology, 40*, 4479–4487. https://doi.org/10.1007/s12144-019-00397-5

Wang, W., Wang, X., Lei, L., & Fu, X. (2017). The effect of mobile social media behavior used on adolescents' friendship quality: The mediating roles of online self-disclosure and online social support. *Psychosocial Science, 4*, 870–877.

Warren, C., & Mohr, G. S. (2019). Ironic consumption. *Journal of Consumer Research, 46*(2), 246–266. https://doi.org/10.1093/jcr/ucy065

Watts, D. J., & Dodds, P. S. (2007). Influentials, networks, and public opinion formation. *Journal of Consumer Research, 34*(4), 441–458. https://doi.org/10.1086/518527

Weber, S., & Mitchell, C. (2008). Imaging, keyboarding, and posting identities: Young people and new media technologies. In D. Buckingham (Ed.), *Youth, identity, and digital media* (pp. 25–47). MIT Press.

Weiss, L., & Johar, G. V. (2013). Egocentric categorization and product judgment: Seeing your traits in what you own (and their opposite in what you don't). *Journal of Consumer Research, 40*(1), 185–201. https://doi.org/10.1086/669330

Weiss, L., & Johar, G. V. (2016). Products as self-evaluation standards: When owned and unowned products have opposite effects on self-judgment. *Journal of Consumer Research, 42*(6), 915–930. https://doi.org/10.1093/jcr/ucv097

Wicklund, R. A., & Gollwitzer, P. M. (1982). *Symbolic self-completion*. Lawrence Erlbaum Associates.

Wilcox, K., & Stephen, A. T. (2013). Are close friends the enemy? Online social networks, self-esteem, and self-control. *Journal of Consumer Research, 40*(1), 90–103. https://doi.org/10.1086/668794

Wood, W., & Neal, D. T. (2007). A new look at habits and the habit-goal interface. *Psychological Review, 114*(4), 843–863. https://doi.org/10.1037/0033-295X.114.4.843

Woods, H. C., & Scott, H. (2016). #Sleepyteens: Social media use in adolescence is associated with poor sleep quality, anxiety, depression and low self-esteem. *Journal of Adolescence, 51*, 41–49. https://doi.org/10.1016/j.adolescence.2016.05.008

Wu, L., Mattila, A. S., Wang, C.-Y., & Hanks, L. (2016). The impact of power on service customers' willingness to post online reviews. *Journal of Service Research, 19*(2), 224–238. https://doi.org/10.1177/1094670516630623

Zahavi, A. (1975). Mate selection—A selection for a handicap. *Journal of Theoretical Biology, 53*(1), 205–214. https://doi.org/10.1016/0022-5193(75)90111-3

Zollo, F., Bessi, A., Del Vicario, M., Scala, A., Caldarelli, G., Shekhtman, L., Havlin, S., & Quattrociocchi, W. (2017). Debunking in a world of tribes. *PLOS ONE, 12*(7), e0181821. https://doi.org/10.1371/journal.pone.0181821

CHAPTER 22

CELEBRITY ENDORSEMENTS

Eda Gurel-Atay

Many companies use celebrities in advertisements to promote different kinds of products. Indeed, millions of dollars are spent on celebrity contracts each year by assuming that the benefits of using celebrities will exceed the costs. Accordingly, given the popularity and importance of celebrity endorsements, the impact of celebrity endorsements on marketing communication effectiveness has been studied extensively over the years. While some studies focused on developing the theories to explain celebrity endorsement effectiveness (e.g., McCracken, 1989), others used previously established theories to explain how and when celebrity endorsements work effectively (e.g., Petty et al., 1983). The benefits and risks associated with using celebrity endorsements have also gained attention from consumer researchers over the years (e.g., Amos et al., 2008, Fleck et al., 2012).

In this chapter, we first provide a definition of celebrity endorsements and discuss their importance and relation to consumer psychology research through the source effectiveness model (Kelman, 1961). Then, we discuss consumer psychology theories that can be used to understand the effectiveness of celebrity endorsements. Among the theories we examine are the attribution theory, meaning transfer model (MTM), the match-up hypothesis, and the social adaptation theory (SAT). Finally, we look at the benefits and risks of using celebrity endorsements and provide ideas for future research.

DEFINING CELEBRITY ENDORSEMENTS

Celebrities are people who are well-known by large groups of people; they are the "names that need no further identification" (Mills, 1956, p. 71). These celebrities include actors and actresses (e.g., Jack Nicholson), singers (e.g., Taylor Swift), sports athletes (e.g., LeBron James), politicians (e.g., Al Gore), activists (e.g., Greta Thunberg), YouTubers (e.g., Shane Dawson), and people from certain professions (e.g., Mehmet Oz), among others. A *celebrity endorser* is, on the other hand, "an individual who is known by the public for his/her achievements in areas other than the product class endorsed" (Friedman & Friedman, 1979).

A celebrity endorser is also defined as "any individual who enjoys public recognition and who uses this recognition on behalf of a consumer good by appearing with it in an advertisement" (McCracken, 1989, p. 310). Celebrity endorsers are considered as "inviters" as they convince consumers to take actions (e.g., buying the endorsed brand, supporting a social activity) by lending their image to the endorsed brand (Fleck et al., 2012; Gouranga & Brajesh, 2011).

Passages in this chapter come from the author's dissertation, "Celebrity Endorsements and Advertising Effectiveness: The Importance of Value Congruence" by E. Gurel-Atay, 2011.
https://doi.org/10.1037/0000262-022
APA Handbook of Consumer Psychology, L. R. Kahle (Editor-in-Chief)
Copyright © 2022 by the American Psychological Association. All rights reserved.

IMPORTANCE OF CELEBRITY ENDORSEMENTS TO CONSUMER PSYCHOLOGY: RELATION TO SOURCE EFFECTIVENESS

Source attributes refer to the aspects of the persons or groups presenting the persuasive appeal. These attributes are usually categorized into two groups: credibility (i.e., expertise and trustworthiness) and attractiveness (i.e., familiarity, likeability, and similarity; Hovland & Weiss, 1951; McGuire, 1969). Because these source variables play an important role to improve the persuasiveness of a message, companies try to find sources that satisfy these two criteria to present their messages to customers (K. E. Kahle & Kahle, 2006). One of the sources used frequently in marketing, specifically in advertisements, is celebrities. Accordingly, it is important to understand how credibility and attractiveness of celebrities affect celebrity endorsement effectiveness.

Credibility

Source credibility is concerned with how a person's perceptions of "the expertise or the objectivity of the source guides him/her in seeking the 'truth' of a particular persuasive communication" (Percy, 1983, p. 79). According to the source credibility model, credibility has two components. The first component, expertise, deals with how knowledgeable the source is on the subject of the advertising message, and the second component, trustworthiness, refers to the willingness of the source to discuss the subject of the advertising message honestly. It is argued that experts "are effective because communications attributed to an expert endorser produce greater agreement with the subject than the same communications attributed to a nonexpert" (Biswas et al., 2006, p. 19).

Studies conducted by social psychologists and marketing researchers over the last 60 years showed that sources with high credibility are perceived as more persuasive than sources with low credibility (McGuire, 1969). For instance, Hung (2014) suggested that credible endorsers tend to induce product trials and then stimulate a sustainable relationship between the endorsed brand and its consumers. Similarly, Biswas et al. (2006) showed that, for high-tech products, expert endorsers were more effective than celebrity endorsers in reducing customer risk perceptions. Consumers also believe that a credible endorser has more knowledge about the product, which leads consumers to pay more attention to the endorsed product (Glover, 2009). Feick and Higie (1992) provided evidence for the positive impact of expertise on the attitudes and intentions for the lower preference heterogeneity services (i.e., services that are characterized by little variation in consumers' tastes and preferences). S. W. Wang and Close-Scheinbaum (2018) conducted a recent study in the airline industry and showed that for low-involvement consumers, trustworthiness is the only important source model component, whereas for high-involvement consumers, both trustworthiness and attractiveness are important.

Attractiveness

McGuire (1969) suggested that attractiveness is composed of three interrelated aspects: familiarity (knowledge of the source), similarity (resemblance between the source and receiver of the message), and likeability (affection for the source, usually as a result of physical attractiveness; Biswas et al., 2006). Therefore, when message receivers (consumers in a marketing context) are familiar with the source, like the source, and find similarities between the source and themselves, the messages become more persuasive (McGuire, 1969).

Snyder and Rothbart (1971) found that listening to a message in the presence of a photograph of an attractive male source was more persuasive than listening to the same message in the presence of a photograph of an unattractive source or no visual cue at all. Baker and Churchill (1977) conducted an experiment in two product categories (i.e., coffee and cologne/perfume/aftershave) and found that physical attractiveness of the models used in the ads increased the affective evaluations (e.g., appealing, interesting, impressive) of the ads but not the cognitive evaluations (e.g., believable, informative). Feick and Higie (1992) provided evidence for the positive impact of similarity on the attitudes and intentions for the higher preference heterogeneity services (i.e., services that are characterized by high variation in consumers' tastes and preferences). Liu and Brock

(2011) showed that attractive celebrities had significant positive effects on consumer attention, recall of advertisement message, and purchase intentions. Malik et al. (2013) also suggested that the use of attractive (and trustworthy) celebrities led to more purchase intentions.

Some other studies, however, did not find a significant effect of attractiveness. Maddux and Rogers (1980) showed that physical attractiveness has no effect on persuasion, suggesting that under some conditions attractive sources may need to possess expertise or provide supportive argumentation to persuade the message receiver. Caballero and Solomon (1984) did not find any effect of source attractiveness in producing sales of beer (high-involvement product). They found a significant effect of attractiveness in sales of tissues, but in the opposite direction: Low attractiveness led to more sales.

USING CONSUMER PSYCHOLOGY THEORIES TO UNDERSTAND CELEBRITY ENDORSEMENTS

Consumer psychology theories are often used to understand how celebrity endorsements work to affect consumers' attitudes and behaviors. In this section, I review the most popular ones of these consumer psychology theories.

Attribution Theory

Attribution theory states that people use information to make causal inferences and to decide what to do with those inferences (Kelley, 1973). More specifically, people determine if a behavior is a result of a disposition or a stimulus based on three criteria: distinctiveness (whether or not the behavior is distinctively related to a stimulus), consistency (whether or not the behavior is consistent over time), and consensus (whether or not other people would react the same to the same stimulus). When there is high distinctiveness, high consistency, and high consensus, the behavior is attributed to the stimulus and not to a disposition.

Mowen (1980) used attribution theory to suggest that effectiveness of celebrity endorsements depends on the consumers' willingness to understand the causal reasons for a celebrity to endorse a product: If consumers think that the celebrity endorses a specific product only (i.e., high distinctiveness); the celebrity endorses the product at different times, different places, and through different media (i.e., high consistency); and other people perceive the product in a similar way to the celebrity (i.e., high consensus), then the celebrity endorsement will be more effective. Likewise, research on the motives of celebrities to endorse products/brands, in addition to the research on celebrity trustworthiness, suggests that consumers respond more favorably when they perceive celebrities' motives as not merely monetary (Tripp et al., 1994). Kapitan and Silvera (2016) also suggested that to evaluate celebrity endorsement effectiveness, it is essential to understand the "dispositional attributions consumers make about how much an endorser likes, uses, and truly values the endorsed product" (p. 554). For instance, Moore et al. (1994) showed that when people were exposed to advertisements from multiple, unpaid endorsers, they were more likely to generate positive attitudes toward the product. Similarly, Silvera and Austad (2004) found that correspondent inferences (i.e., the beliefs about the celebrity's liking and using of the product) affect the attitudes toward the endorsed product, both directly and indirectly (through attitudes toward the endorser and attitudes toward the ad).

Meaning Transfer Model

McCracken (1989) suggested that in a consumer culture, celebrities have symbolic meanings assigned to them by the society. When they endorse products, celebrities pass these shared cultural and symbolic meanings to products. Then, these meanings are transferred from products to consumers. Accordingly, this transfer of cultural meanings from celebrities to consumers takes place in three stages. In the first stage, celebrities gain meanings from their careers, cultures, and personalities. In the second stage, celebrities, ideally selected based on the congruence between the meanings they possess and the meanings the products they will endorse possess, transfer these meanings to products in a way that is clear and easy to be understood by consumers. In this stage, it is important to conceal, or at least not highlight, the meanings the celebrities possess that are not in congruent with the endorsed brand. In the last stage, the consumers drive the meanings of celebrities to themselves through the product meanings. In other words, consumers look up to celebrities who have the meanings they want to have and perceive products endorsed by those celebrities as means to achieve those meanings themselves. When consumers buy and use the endorsed products, the meanings of celebrities pass on to them and the MTM is completed.

In examining this transfer, McCracken (1989) stated, "It is necessary to characterize the whole person" (p. 313) instead of focusing on separate components of cultural meanings (e.g., gender, lifestyles, age, personality) of celebrities, as these components altogether help celebrities to represent an "interconnected set of meanings" (p. 313), which, in turn, makes celebrities useful for endorsement purposes. Indeed, endorsement campaigns succeed when the "interconnected set of meanings" of a celebrity becomes the meanings of the endorsed products.

Several researchers used the MTM to examine the effectiveness of celebrity endorsements. Batra and Homer (2004) showed, in one of the first attempts to test the MTM empirically, that cultural meanings can actually be transferred in ads from celebrities to endorsed brands, even when the celebrity traits are not emphasized verbally and explicitly. However, this transfer occurs only under certain conditions: when a social consumption context is involved (i.e., high visibility context), when "the brand image beliefs are appropriate to the consumer schema for the product category involved" (Batra & Homer, 2004, p. 318), and for purchase intentions but not for brand attitudes. Similarly, Miller and Allen (2012) showed that mere co-occurrence of a celebrity in an ad, with no explicit message, affected brand attitudes through the mediating effect of brand beliefs. Specifically, meanings possessed by celebrities transferred to a well-known clothing brand affected consumers' brand attitudes via brand beliefs. Furthermore, the transferred meaning effect becomes stronger as time passes, indicating a sleeper effect (Knoll et al., 2017).

In a qualitative study, Halonen-Knight and Hurmerinta (2010) used MTM in a real celebrity endorsement context and suggested to manage celebrity endorsements as a brand alliance, more specifically as an alliance of equals. Similarly, in a qualitative study, Jain and Roy (2016) used focus groups and projective methods to identify dimensions that would result in celebrity meaning transfer. Their results showed that, out of seven dimensions they identified (personality, credibility, physical appearance, feelings, performance, values, and cogent power), all but one (cogent power) meaning actually transferred to brands via endorsement.

As stated earlier, it is important not to emphasize the unwanted meanings of celebrities during the endorsement process if companies do not want to associate those unwanted meanings with their products. Indeed, Campbell and Warren (2012) found that negative meanings are more likely to transfer to brands from celebrities, regardless of the congruence between the celebrity and the product and even if those meanings are not emphasized during the endorsement process.

Match-Up Hypothesis and Social Adaptation Theory

One of the theories used frequently by researchers to explain the impact of celebrity endorsements is the match-up hypothesis. The match-up hypothesis suggests that "endorsers are more effective when there is a fit between the endorser and the endorsed product" (Till & Busler, 2000, p. 1). In an earlier work, Misra and Beatty (1990) defined this fit as the consistency between "the highly relevant characteristics of the spokesperson" and "the highly relevant attributes of the brand" (p. 161). Most studies approached this fit, or match-up, from an attractiveness or expertise perspective. More specifically, some researchers suggested that attractive celebrities will be more effective if they are used to promote attractiveness-related products, such as razors or perfume (L. R. Kahle & Homer, 1985; Kamins, 1990). Some other researchers focused on the expertise, or product relatedness, dimension and claimed that when there is congruence between the product type and the profession of the celebrity (as in the case of a sports athlete promoting sports shoes), advertising effectiveness will be enhanced because the celebrities are perceived as experts by consumers (Till & Busler, 2000).

L. R. Kahle and Homer (1985), by integrating the match-up hypothesis with the SAT (L. R. Kahle, 1996; L. R. Kahle and Timmer, 1983), focused on the attractiveness dimension. SAT assumes that the impact of any information depends on the adaptive significance of the information; as long as the information provides usefulness for the adaptation, or facilitates adaptation, the receiver will process it. For instance, SAT says that, if attractiveness provides the most relevant product-related information, then it should have a significant main effect on attitudes. Kamins (1990) also argued that using an attractive celebrity in the advertisement provides adaptive information because it might cause customers to think that the brand endorsed by a celebrity will enhance their attractiveness as it did for the celebrity. Indeed, he showed that an attractive celebrity had significant effects on spokesperson credibility and attitude toward the ad for an attractiveness-related product but had no effect on the same measures for an attractiveness-unrelated product.

Till and Busler (2000) examined both of the most studied match-up dimensions (attractiveness and expertise) and found a match-up effect for expertise, but not for attractiveness, for brand attitudes. Biswas et al. (2006) showed that when there is low congruence between the celebrity and product, expert endorsers are more effective than celebrity endorsers in reducing consumer risk perception for high-tech products; when the congruence between the celebrity and product is high, the differential effects of expert versus celebrity endorsers for consumer perceptions of risks disappear.

Gurel-Atay and Kahle (2009) suggested that the match-up between the celebrity and product can also be achieved through value congruence. In other words, the congruency between consumers' perceptions of celebrities' values and product values might play an important role in determining the effectiveness of celebrity endorsements. Indeed, Gurel-Atay and Kahle found that people exposed to the high value congruence ad spent less time in examining the ad, suggesting that participants were easily and quickly able to match up the celebrities and products. Moreover, participants who were exposed to the high value congruence ad had significantly more favorable attitudes toward the ad and brand, had higher intentions to buy the product, and were more likely to recommend the product to other people than were participants who were exposed to the low value congruence ad. Similarly, the congruence between the product and personality of the endorser is also important (Fleck et al., 2012; Wright, 2016).

Boyd and Shank (2004) showed that when there is a fit between the celebrity and consumer in terms of gender, consumers perceive the celebrity as more trustworthy, regardless of the product type endorsed by the celebrity; however, consumers' ratings of expertise depends on the interaction between the celebrity, consumer, and product. Specifically,

> Women rate endorsers as more expert when there is a fit between the endorser and product (e.g., when the endorser uses the product in their sport) while men rate endorsers as more expert when there is not an endorser-product match. (Boyd & Shank, 2004, p. 82)

Some researchers have found greater persuasiveness when there is incongruence between the spokesperson and product. Debevec and Iyer (1986) showed that attitudes toward the brand and purchase intentions for a feminine (masculine) product were more positive when the product was endorsed by a male (female) spokesperson. J. G. Lee and Thorson (2008) argued that different degrees of congruence might have different impacts on the effectiveness of celebrity endorsement. By using the schema congruity, "the extent to which new information conforms to consumer expectations based on previously defined category schemas in memory" (J. G. Lee and Thorson, 2008, p. 435), they argued that resolving moderate incongruity between the celebrity and product might be rewarding, worthwhile, and interesting for consumers because of the curiosity prompted by the moderate level of unexpectedness; however, their studies provided mixed results. Specifically, they found that attitude toward the brand in the moderately incongruent condition was significantly higher than the extremely incongruent condition but not significantly different from the extremely congruent condition. Purchase intentions for the moderately incongruent condition were significantly higher than in extreme conditions.

In an interesting twist, Fleck et al. (2012) showed that attitudes toward the celebrity influenced the perceptions of congruence such that people found appreciated and liked celebrities congruent with any brand. The authors also examined the two dimensions of congruence: relevance ("a celebrity can be considered as relevant if there is a clear meaning why he/she endorses the brand or product"; Fleck et al., 2012, p. 653) and expectancy ("celebrity is expected if he/she corresponds to a pattern evoked by the message of the brand"; Fleck et al., 2012, p. 653). They found that expectancy has a stronger effect on congruence than relevancy, suggesting that as long as the celebrity fits the pattern in consumers' minds regarding the brand, and regardless of the relevance (especially in terms of expertise), consumers will perceive congruence between the celebrity and the endorsed brand.

Other Models

Although the effectiveness of celebrity endorsements is mostly studied from a prospective of three approaches (source effectiveness, the MTM, and the match-up hypothesis), other theories were also suggested by researchers. Kelman (1961) claimed, by referring to the source attractiveness model, that celebrity endorsement leads to changes in consumer attitudes through an identification process, in which consumers establish an identity associated with the celebrity. In one of the earliest studies on celebrity endorsements, Friedman and Friedman (1979) showed that celebrities have significant effects on attitudes toward the product and purchase intentions when they endorse products high in psychological or social risk, such as costume jewelry. They also found that celebrities are more effective than expert or typical-consumer endorsers in advertisement recall and brand name recall, regardless of the product type. Some researchers applied associative learning theory (Collins & Loftus, 1975) to celebrity endorsement studies by claiming that celebrities and brands that represent nodes in memory are linked together over time through endorsement processes. Specifically, feelings and meanings associated with the celebrity are transferred to endorsed brands, and this transfer leads to simultaneous activation of memory nodes (Biswas et al., 2006; Till & Busler, 2000). Kamins (1989) and Kamins et al. (1989) showed that brand attitudes and purchase intentions were affected positively by celebrity appeals. They also showed that the two-sided celebrity appeal performed best, and the one-sided noncelebrity appeal performed worst in terms of attitudes toward the brand and purchase intentions. Carlson and Donavan (2008), by using the social identity theory (Tajfel & Turner, 1985), claimed that when consumers' identification with a sports athlete celebrity is high, their attitudes toward the team and their intentions to purchase the endorsed product are also high.

Based on the elaboration likelihood model (ELM), Petty et al. (1983) suggested that celebrities would be effective through the peripheral route. More specifically, the authors showed that "when an advertisement concerned a product of low involvement, the celebrity status of the product endorsers was a very potent determinant of attitudes about the product" (Petty et al., 1983, p. 143). When the advertisement included a product of high involvement, the quality of the product information, instead of the celebrity status, determined the attitudes toward the product. Kang and Herr (2006) extended the study of Petty et al. by focusing on the availability of cognitive resources. Specifically, they showed that limited cognitive resources resulted in higher impacts of source characteristics (e.g., attractiveness), regardless of the product type. On the other hand, when cognitive resources were available, source characteristics affected attitudes toward attractiveness-relevant products (e.g., razors and shampoo) but not attitudes toward attractiveness-irrelevant products (e.g., computers). Y. Lee and Koo (2016) demonstrated that when there is congruence between the celebrity and product in terms of expertise (but not in terms of attractiveness), product involvement increased the effect of this congruence on consumer responses, suggesting that the celebrity endorsement process works through the central route.

Researchers have also integrated different theories. Roy et al. (2012), based on the balance theory (Heider, 1958), integrated the match-up hypothesis and source credibility model and showed that the congruence both between celebrity and product and between celebrity and message resulted in more favorable consumer responses. Ambroise et al. (2014) combined the MTM and associative learning to study the cobranding effects between celebrity endorsers and products they endorsed. The authors suggested that by repeatedly pairing celebrities and brands, associations are created in consumers' minds. Then, through these associative networks, "when consumers think about the brand, they transfer their brand evaluation to the celebrity, and vice versa" (Ambroise et al., 2014, p. 277).

In an effort to integrate the most used celebrity endorsement theories (i.e., source credibility, source effectiveness, match-up hypothesis, and MTM) in a prescriptive framework, Schimmelpfennig and Hunt (2019) suggested using product/brand value propositions to identify which of the endorsement strategies would be most effective. More specifically, the authors suggested the following value proposition and endorsement strategy pairs: "provide best performance" with expertise, "enhance physical attractiveness" with expertise in physical attractiveness, "create positive affect in a nominal decision" with liking, "craft unique experience via endorser attributes" with image congruence, and "enable consumer to build persona" with transfer of cultural meaning (Schimmelpfennig & Hunt, 2019, p. 496).

BENEFITS OF USING CELEBRITY ENDORSEMENTS

Celebrity endorsers are used often in marketing as they provide many benefits to the endorsed brand. They cut through the clutter by getting the attention of consumers, provide a way to differentiate from competitors, and help companies to have a distinctive image in consumers' minds (Fleck et al., 2012). Research on the effectiveness of celebrity endorsements also revealed positive effects on purchase intentions (Paul & Bhakar, 2018), brand equity (Dwivedi et al., 2015), attitudes toward ad and brand (Goldsmith et al., 2000), assuring consumers about the true quality of a product (Rao & Ruekert, 1994), sales of the endorsed brand (Elberse & Verleun, 2012), and stock prices of endorsed brands (Agrawal & Kamakura, 1995).

While most studies focused on consumers' responses to celebrity endorsements (e.g., Goldsmith et al., 2000), Agrawal and Kamakura (1995) assessed the economic value, or profitability, of these endorsements. They suggested that when a celebrity endorsement contract is announced, investors evaluate the future profit impact of the contract, and these evaluations are reflected in the companies' stock returns. To test for their proposition, Agrawal and Kamakura analyzed announcements of 110 celebrity endorsement contracts between January 1980 and December 1992 by using event study methodology. Their findings showed that "on average, the impact of these announcements on stock returns is positive and suggest that celebrity endorsement contracts are generally viewed as a worthwhile investment in advertising" (Agrawal & Kamakura, 1995, p. 56). Similarly, Knowles et al. (1996) used the event study methodology to show that

> anticipation of Jordan's return to the NBA, and the related increased visibility for him, resulted in an average increase in the market-adjusted values of his client firms of almost 2 percent, or more than $1 billion in stock market value. (p. 67)

Elberse and Verleun (2012), on the other hand, focused also on sales, in addition to stock prices, and examined both the immediate impact of celebrity endorsement announcements and the long-term impact of the changes in celebrities' performance and reputation over time. With their data covering 95 firms, 178 athlete endorsers, and 341 endorsements (between January 1990 and March 2008), Elberse and Verleun found a positive impact of athlete endorsements on the endorsed brand's sales (after controlling for changes in advertising and pricing strategies) prolonged over time, but the impact on stock prices was short term. Moreover, when there was a victory on the part of the endorsing athlete, like earning a championship, both the sales and the stock price of the endorsed brand increased.

RISKS OF USING CELEBRITY ENDORSEMENTS

Although using celebrities as brand endorsers brings many benefits to companies in terms of more favorable consumer responses, higher sales, and higher equity (Knoll & Matthes, 2017), this strategy is not free of risks (Amos et al., 2008). Indeed, the marketing history is filled with failed celebrity endorsement campaigns. These campaigns fail when the congruence between the celebrity and the brand is not appropriate (e.g., Olympic figure skater Michelle Kwan endorsing Coca-Cola), when celebrities fail to adhere to their contracts and use other brands (e.g., Charlize Theron endorsing Raymond Weil Watches and wearing Dior watches), when celebrities misbehave during the endorsement contract (e.g., Michael Phelps smoking marijuana while endorsing Kellogg's cereals), or when multiple brands are endorsed by the same celebrity (e.g., David Beckham and AIA Insurance, with Beckham endorsing many other brands, like Adidas, H&M, and Gillette).

Research on the match-up hypothesis revealed the importance of congruence between the celebrity and the product/brand to achieve success through celebrity endorsements. As discussed earlier, when there is no good fit (e.g., through attractiveness, expertise, gender, values, or personality) between the celebrity and product/brand, consumers' evaluations of celebrity endorsements become less favorable (e.g., Biswas et al., 2006; Wright, 2016).

Attribution theory suggests that consumers tend to look for the causal reasons for a celebrity to endorse a product (Kelley, 1973; Mowen, 1980). For instance, Bergkvist et al. (2016) examined recent or ongoing endorsement campaigns and found that consumers had higher attitudes toward the brand when they thought the celebrity was motivated by not only money but also the product quality. Accordingly, when celebrities violated their contracts and used other brands of the same product type, consumers questioned their motivation, trustworthiness, and sincerity, which usually resulted in terminating the endorsement relationship.

Till and Shimp (1998) showed, through the associative network models, that negative information about a celebrity led to lower brand evaluations, especially when both the celebrity and the brand had small sets of associations. White et al. (2009) showed that when there was negativity regarding the celebrity, this negativity transferred to the brand. Interestingly, when there was negative information about the brand, the celebrity was not affected in a reverse transfer.

Louie et al. (2001) examined 48 events in which celebrity endorsers engaged in undesirable behaviors and found a statistically significant negative impact of such events on 128 endorsed brands' stock prices. Moreover, this negative impact was amplified when the celebrity was perceived to be blamed for the undesirable event. Gupta (2009) also examined the blame effect with a qualitative study on the public reaction to Michael Vick after his dog fighting involvement was exposed to the public. The analyses of posts on online blogs revealed that when people thought that the action was under the celebrity's control, they blamed the celebrity. When, however, people thought that the celebrity did not have control over the action and/or the consequences of the action, they evaluated the celebrity as blameless.

Tripp (1994) examined the effects of multiple product endorsements by celebrities and found that the number of products a celebrity endorses had a negative impact on consumers' perceptions of celebrity credibility, celebrity likeability, and attitude toward the ad. It is suggested that when celebrities endorse multiple products, their endorsement is perceived as motivated by money and, hence, insincere (Campbell & Warren, 2012). In the same vein, Agnihotri and Bhattacharya (2018), analyzing 149 endorsement news events in India from 2003 to 2014, found that niche celebrities create more abnormal returns than mainstream celebrities, suggesting that overusing celebrities may mitigate the effectiveness of celebrity endorsements.

When there is negativity surrounding the celebrity, should companies discontinue the endorsement relationship with the celebrity in order to avoid transferring the negativity of celebrities to the brands, as some research suggests (e.g., Campbell & Warren, 2012)? Some studies raise caveats against this strategy. For instance, Ilicic et al. (2016) warned against terminating the endorsement too soon when a celebrity becomes less favorable, as their study on celebrities' genuineness showed that effective advertising can offset the negative associations regarding the celebrity when the celebrity is perceived as genuine. Louie and Obermiller (2002) examined the consumer reactions to company decisions regarding the termination of an endorsement relationship after a negative event and they found that the level of blame on the celebrity matters. Specifically, consumers evaluated the companies better when companies discontinued the relationship with high-blamed celebrities and when companies continued the relationship with low-blamed celebrities. Hock and Raithel (2020) examined the economic effects of company reactions to negative publicity based on a study of 128 negative events. Their analyses revealed that companies have more positive abnormal returns on their stock prices "when they (1) suspend higher blame endorsers, (2) suspend endorsers whose negative publicity is related to their occupation, (3) maintain endorsers with a high product fit, and (4) do not suspend apologetic endorsers" (Hock & Raithel 2020, p. 6). S. Wang and Kim (2019) showed that when consumers strongly identified with the celebrity, they used rationalization and decoupling strategies to mitigate the impact of the negative event. Um and Kim (2016) also showed that consumers were less likely to be affected by negative publicity of celebrities when the brand commitment was high, suggesting that brands who already enjoy high commitment from their customers may not need to discontinue the endorsement relationship. Accordingly, continuing or discontinuing the endorsement relationship after a negative publicity event is not a binary decision; companies need to consider the celebrity–consumer relationship, company–consumer relationship, and the level of blame toward the celebrity, among other factors.

FUTURE RESEARCH

The celebrity endorsement strategy has been used by companies and has been studied by researchers extensively. Still, more research is needed to understand both the traditional marketing issues (e.g., celebrity endorsers for cause marketing) and contemporary issues in marketing (e.g., social media influencers).

Future Research on Traditional Marketing Issues

One of the areas that needs more research is the congruence between celebrities and other components of marketing besides products. Most research in the celebrity endorsement area focuses on the congruence between celebrities and products; however, the congruence between celebrities and consumers as well as brands is also important. Indeed, studies based on the self-congruity theory (e.g., Sirgy, 1982) and traditional similarity studies (e.g., Feick & Higie, 1992) suggest that sources that are similar to the target audience in terms of lifestyles, product usage, and demographics are more effective in generating favorable responses. Choi and Rifon (2012) studied the congruence between consumers' ideal self-image and celebrity image as perceived by consumers and found that this congruence improved the celebrity endorsement effectiveness. Albert et al. (2017), on the other hand, did not find a significant influence of celebrity–consumer fit on the outcomes. More research is needed to understand the dynamics between celebrity endorsers and consumers. Similarly, brand characteristics, in addition to product categories, should be included in celebrity endorsement research, since two brands from the same product category might be positioned completely different in consumers' minds, meaning that they might reflect different values or personalities (Herrmann & Huber, 2000). Indeed, brand personality studies (e.g., Aaker, 1997; Madrigal & Boush, 2008) showed that brands have distinct images, or personalities, in consumers' minds, and those brand images affect attitudes, behavioral intentions, and purchase behaviors. In the business world, there are several companies that produce and sell similar products but represent different values and/or personalities (e.g., Microsoft vs. Apple, Pepsi vs. Coca-Cola). Future research should examine the congruence between brand values and celebrity values, as well as the congruence between brand values and consumer values, by using real brands in experiments.

The effectiveness of celebrity endorsers for cause/social marketing and with nonprofit organizations is also understudied (Harris & Ruth, 2014). Similar to the importance of congruence between celebrity endorsers and product, the congruence between celebrity endorsers and causes is also crucial. The congruence between celebrities and causes can be achieved through the celebrity's experience with the cause, that is, experience-based fit (Park, 2016; Wheeler, 2009), or through the images and core values represented by the celebrity and the cause, that is, symbolic-based fit (de los Salmones et al., 2013). Indeed, social marketing issues can be considered as either internally related to consumers (as in the case of quitting smoking, using condoms, or self-examination for breast cancer) or externally related to consumers (as in the case of donating to cancer research, recycling, or helping poor people). Accordingly, it can be expected that celebrities who represent internally oriented values, images, or personalities (e.g., self-fulfillment, ambitious, a sense of achievement) can be more effective in promoting internally related social issues than promoting externally related social issues and vice versa. Examining the celebrity–cause congruence, therefore, would help companies, nonprofit organizations, and public policy makers to create more effective social marketing campaigns.

Future Research on Contemporary Marketing Issues

A majority of the research on celebrity endorsements has been conducted with traditional celebrities like actors and actresses, sports athletes, political figures, and singers. The popularity of social media, however, has led to self-created celebrities called *influencers*. Similar to traditional celebrities, influencers are well-known by large groups of people, and they regularly endorse products on their "private channels" (e.g., Instagram, Facebook, Twitter, blogs) either through paid or unpaid endorsements (Kapitan & Silvera, 2016). Indeed, an experiment conducted by Schouten et al. (2020) showed that influencers can even be more effective than celebrity endorsements in terms of generating positive ad and product attitudes and purchase intentions, as "participants identify more with influencers than celebrities, feel more similar to influencers than celebrities, and trust influencers more than celebrities" (p. 258). Accordingly, it is important to include influencers in celebrity endorsement studies, especially to see if the theories used to understand celebrity endorsement effectiveness in traditional media would apply to influencers or if new, novel theories and methodologies are needed to examine social media celebrities. For instance, most influencers focus on a product category, and not a brand, to promote through their social media accounts (e.g., suggesting products from the fashion industry, not from a specific fashion brand). As discussed earlier, endorsing multiple brands in traditional media has a negative impact on consumer responses (Tripp et al., 1994). Influencers, however, are not seemed to be negatively affected when they endorse multiple brands; on the contrary, they may even be expected to give suggestions on multiple products and brands. Indeed, it is possible that influencers are perceived as opinion leaders, and not celebrity endorsers, by their followers, making endorsing multiple brands acceptable even when they disclose that they are paid for their endorsements. Casaló et al. (2020), for instance, studied, in a comprehensive model, both the antecedents and consequences of celebrity endorsement effectiveness (treated as opinion leadership by the authors) on Instagram. The study, conducted with followers of a fashion Instagram influencer, revealed that perceived originality and uniqueness of the influencer affect the opinion leadership perceptions, which, in turn, affect consumer behavioral intentions (intention to interact with the influencer account, intention to recommend, and intention to follow the advice of the influencer). More research is needed to understand how influencers differ from traditional celebrity endorsers.

Early studies on the effectiveness of these social media, or digital, influencers focused on fashion and beauty products (e.g., Torres et al., 2019), mostly because these influencers promote those types of products more often. More research is needed to understand the effectiveness of influencer endorsements for different product categories (e.g., art supplies, household products), the meanings of congruence between influencers and products (an attractive influencer promoting beauty products vs. a fine art artist promoting art supplies), the difference between disclosed versus disguised endorsements in terms of effectiveness and ethical considerations, and the effectiveness of paid versus unpaid endorsements.

REFERENCES

Aaker, J. L. (1997). Dimensions of brand personality. *Journal of Marketing Research*, 34(3), 347–356. https://doi.org/10.1177/002224379703400304

Agnihotri, A., & Bhattacharya, S. (2018). The market value of celebrity endorsement: Evidence from India reveals factors that can influence stock-market returns. *Journal of Advertising Research*, 58(1), 65–74. https://doi.org/10.2501/JAR2016-021

Agrawal, J., & Kamakura, W. A. (1995). The economic worth of celebrity endorsements: An event study analysis. *Journal of Marketing*, 59(3), 56–62. https://doi.org/10.1177/002224299505900305

Albert, N., Ambroise, L., & Valette-Florence, P. (2017). Consumer, brand, celebrity: Which congruency produces effective celebrity endorsements? *Journal of Business Research*, 81, 96–106. https://doi.org/10.1016/j.jbusres.2017.08.002

Ambroise, L., Pantin-Sohier, G., Valette-Florence, P., & Albert, N. (2014). From endorsement to celebrity co-branding: Personality transfer. *Journal of Brand Management*, 21(4), 273–285. https://doi.org/10.1057/bm.2014.7

Amos, C., Holmes, G., & Strutton, D. (2008). Exploring the relationship between celebrity endorser effects and advertising effectiveness: A quantitative synthesis of effect size. *International Journal of Advertising*, 27(2), 209–234. https://doi.org/10.1080/02650487.2008.11073052

Baker, M. J., & Churchill, G. A., Jr. (1977). The impact of physically attractive models on advertising evaluations. *Journal of Marketing Research*, 14(4), 538–555. https://doi.org/10.1177/002224377701400411

Batra, R., & Homer, P. M. (2004). The situational impact of brand image beliefs. *Journal of Consumer Psychology*, 14(3), 318–330. https://doi.org/10.1207/s15327663jcp1403_12

Bergkvist, L., Hjalmarson, H., & Mägi, A. W. (2016). A new model of how celebrity endorsements work: Attitude toward the endorsement as a mediator of celebrity source and endorsement effects. *International Journal of Advertising*, 35(2), 171–184. https://doi.org/10.1080/02650487.2015.1024384

Biswas, D., Biswas, A., & Das, N. (2006). The differential effects of celebrity and expert endorsements on consumer risk perceptions. *Journal of Advertising*, 35(2), 17–31. https://doi.org/10.1080/00913367.2006.10639231

Boyd, T. C., & Shank, M. D. (2004). Athletes as product endorsers: The effect of gender and product relatedness. *Sport Marketing Quarterly*, 13(2), 82–93.

Caballero, M. J., & Solomon, P. J. (1984). Effects of model attractiveness on sales response. *Journal of Advertising*, 13(1), 17–33. https://doi.org/10.1080/00913367.1984.10672870

Campbell, M. C., & Warren, C. (2012). A risk of meaning transfer: Are negative associations more likely to transfer than positive associations? *Social Influence*, 7(3), 172–192. https://doi.org/10.1080/15534510.2012.663740

Carlson, B. D., & Donavan, T. (2008). Concerning the effect of athlete endorsements on brand and team-related intentions. *Sport Marketing Quarterly*, 17(3), 154–162.

Casaló, L. V., Flavian, C., & Ibanez-Sanchez, S. (2020). Influencers on Instagram: Antecedents and consequences of opinion leadership. *Journal of Business Research*, 117, 510–519. https://doi.org/10.1016/j.jbusres.2018.07.005

Choi, S. M., & Rifon, N. J. (2012). It is a match: The impact of congruence between celebrity image and consumer ideal self on endorsement effectiveness. *Psychology and Marketing*, 29(9), 639–650. https://doi.org/10.1002/mar.20550

Collins, A. M., & Loftus, E. F. (1975). The theory of semantic processing. *Psychological Review*, 82(6), 407–428. https://doi.org/10.1037/0033-295X.82.6.407

Debevec, K., & Iyer, E. (1986). The influence of spokespersons in altering a product's gender image: Implications for advertising effectiveness. *Journal of Advertising*, 15(4), 12–20. https://doi.org/10.1080/00913367.1986.10673033

de los Salmones, M. M. G., Dominguez, R., & Herrero, A. (2013). Communication using celebrities in the non-profit sector: Determinants of its effectiveness. *International Journal of Advertising*, 32(1), 101–119. https://doi.org/10.2501/IJA-32-1-101-119

Dwivedi, A., Johnson, L. W., & McDonald, R. E. (2015). Celebrity endorsement, self-brand connection and consumer-based brand equity. *Journal of Product and Brand Management*, 24(5), 449–461. https://doi.org/10.1108/JPBM-10-2014-0722

Elberse, A., & Verleun, J. (2012). The economic value of celebrity endorsements. *Journal of Advertising Research*, 52(2), 149–165. https://doi.org/10.2501/JAR-52-2-149-165

Feick, L., & Higie, R. A. (1992). The effects of preference heterogeneity and source characteristics on ad processing and judgments about endorsers. *Journal of Advertising, 21*(2), 9–24. https://doi.org/10.1080/00913367.1992.10673364

Fleck, N., Korchia, M., & Le Roy, I. (2012). Celebrities in advertising: Looking for congruence or likability? *Psychology and Marketing, 29*(9), 651–662. https://doi.org/10.1002/mar.20551

Friedman, H. H., & Friedman, L. (1979). Endorser effectiveness by product type. *Journal of Advertising Research, 19*(5), 63–71.

Glover, P. (2009). Celebrity endorsement in tourism advertising: Effects on destination image. *Journal of Hospitality and Tourism Management, 16*(1), 16–23. https://doi.org/10.1375/jhtm.16.1.16

Goldsmith, R. E., Lafferty, B. A., & Newell, S. J. (2000). The impact of corporate credibility and celebrity on consumer reaction to advertisements and brands. *Journal of Advertising, 29*(3), 43–54. https://doi.org/10.1080/00913367.2000.10673616

Gouranga, P., & Brajesh, K. (2011). Celebrity endorsement in FMCGs advertising—A case study in a culturally vibrant society. *Advances in Management, 4*(8), 24–28.

Gupta, S. (2009). How do consumers judge celebrities' irresponsible behavior? An attribution theory perspective. *Journal of Applied Business and Economics, 10*(3), 1–14.

Gurel-Atay, E., & Kahle, L. R. (2009). *Celebrity endorsements and advertising effectiveness: The importance of value congruence* [Paper presentation]. North American Conference of the Association for Consumer Research, Pittsburgh, PA, United States.

Gurel-Atay, Eda (2011). *Celebrity endorsements and advertising effectiveness: The importance of value congruence* [Unpublished doctoral dissertation]. University of Oregon. https://scholarsbank.uoregon.edu/xmlui/bitstream/handle/1794/11566/GurelAtay_Eda_phd2011sp.pdf?sequence=1&isAllowed=y

Halonen-Knight, E., & Hurmerinta, L. (2010). Who endorses whom? Meanings transfer in celebrity endorsement. *Journal of Product and Brand Management, 19*(6), 452–460. https://doi.org/10.1108/10610421011085767

Harris, E., & Ruth, J. A. (2014). Analysis of the value of celebrity affiliation to nonprofit contributions. *Nonprofit and Voluntary Sector Quarterly, 44*(5), 1–23. https://doi.org/10.1177/0899764014546428

Heider, F. (1958). *The psychology of interpersonal relations*. John Wiley and Sons. https://doi.org/10.1037/10628-000

Herrmann, A., & Huber, F. (2000). Value-oriented brand positioning. *International Review of Retail, Distribution and Consumer Research, 10*(1), 95–112. https://doi.org/10.1080/095939600342424

Hock, S. J., & Raithel, S. (2020). Managing negative celebrity endorser publicity: How announcements of firm (non)responses affect stock returns. *Management Science, 66*(3), 1473–1495. https://doi.org/10.1287/mnsc.2018.3243

Hovland, C. I., & Weiss, W. (1951). The influence of source credibility on communication effectiveness. *Public Opinion Quarterly, 15*(4), 635–650. https://doi.org/10.1086/266350

Hung, K. (2014). Why celebrity sells: A dual entertainment path model of brand endorsement. *Journal of Advertising, 43*(2), 155–166. https://doi.org/10.1080/00913367.2013.838720

Ilicic, J., Kulczynski, A., & Baxter, S. (2018). How a smile can make a difference: Enhancing the persuasive appeal of celebrity endorsers boosting consumer perceptions of celebrity genuineness through the use of a "Duchenne smile" in advertising. *Journal of Advertising Research, 58*(1), 51–64. https://doi.org/10.2501/JAR-2016-003

Jain, V., & Roy, S. (2016). Understanding meaning transfer in celebrity endorsements: A qualitative exploration. *Qualitative Market Research, 19*(3), 266–286. https://doi.org/10.1108/QMR-03-2015-0020

Kahle, K. E., & Kahle, L. R. (2006). Sports celebrities' image: A critical evaluation of the utility of Q scores. In L. R. Kahle & C.-H. Kim (Eds.), *Creating images and the psychology of marketing communication* (pp. 227–236). Lawrence Erlbaum Associates. https://doi.org/10.4324/9781410617392-21

Kahle, L. R. (1996). Social values and consumer behavior: Research from the List of Values. In C. Seligman, J. M. Olson, & M. P. Zanna (Eds.), *The psychology of values: The Ontario Symposium* (Vol. 8, pp. 135–152). Lawrence Erlbaum Associates.

Kahle, L. R., & Homer, P. M. (1985). Physical attractiveness of the celebrity endorser: A social adaptation perspective. *Journal of Consumer Research, 11*(4), 954–961. https://doi.org/10.1086/209029

Kahle, L. R., & Timmer, S. G. (1983). A theory and a method for studying values. In R. Lynn (Ed.), *Social values and social change: Adaptation to life in America* (pp. 43–69). Praeger.

Kamins, M. A. (1989). Celebrity and noncelebrity advertising in a two-sided context. *Journal of Advertising Research, 29*(3), 34–42.

Kamins, M. A. (1990). An investigation into the match-up hypothesis in celebrity advertising: When beauty may be only skin deep. *Journal of Advertising, 19*(1), 4–13. https://doi.org/10.1080/00913367.1990.10673175

Kamins, M. A., Brand, M. J., Hoeke, S. A., & Moe, J. C. (1989). Two-sided versus one-sided celebrity endorsements: The impact on advertising effectiveness and credibility. *Journal of Advertising*, 18(2), 4–10. https://doi.org/10.1080/00913367.1989.10673146

Kang, Y. S., & Herr, P. M. (2006). Beauty and the beholder: Toward and integrative model of communication source effects. *Journal of Consumer Research*, 33(1), 123–130. https://doi.org/10.1086/504143

Kapitan, S., & Silvera, D. H. (2016). From digital media influencers to celebrity endorsers: Attributions drive endorser effectiveness. *Marketing Letters*, 27(3), 553–567. https://doi.org/10.1007/s11002-015-9363-0

Kelley, H. H. (1973). The processes of causal attribution. *American Psychologist*, 28(2), 107–128. https://doi.org/10.1037/h0034225

Kelman, H. C. (1961). Processes of opinion change. *Public Opinion Quarterly*, 25(1), 57–78. https://doi.org/10.1086/266996

Knoll, J., & Matthes, J. (2017). The effectiveness of celebrity endorsements: A meta-analysis. *Journal of the Academy of Marketing Science*, 45(1), 55–75. https://doi.org/10.1007/s11747-016-0503-8

Knoll, J., Matthes, J., Munch, A., & Ostermann, M. (2017). How long does celebrity meaning transfer last? Delayed effects and the moderating roles of brand experience, celebrity liking, and age. *International Journal of Advertising*, 36(4), 588–612. https://doi.org/10.1080/02650487.2016.1213062

Knowles, L. L., Mathur, I., & Rangan, N. (1996). The wealth effects associated with a celebrity endorser: The Michael Jordan phenomenon. *Journal of Advertising Research*, 37(3), 67–73.

Lee, J. G., & Thorson, E. (2008). The impact of celebrity-product incongruence on the effectiveness of product endorsement. *Journal of Advertising Research*, 48(3), 433–449. https://doi.org/10.2501/S0021849908080446

Lee, Y., & Koo, J. (2016). Can a celebrity serve as an issue-relevant argument in the elaboration likelihood model? *Psychology and Marketing*, 33(3), 195–208. https://doi.org/10.1002/mar.20865

Liu, M. T., & Brock, J. L. (2011). Selecting a female athlete endorser in China: The effect of attractiveness, match-up, and consumer gender difference. *European Journal of Marketing*, 45(7/8), 1214–1235. https://doi.org/10.1108/03090561111137688

Louie, T. A., Kulik, R. L., & Jacobson, R. (2001). When bad things happen to the endorsers of good products. *Marketing Letters*, 12(1), 13–23. https://doi.org/10.1023/A:1008159717925

Louie, T. A., & Obermiller, C. (2002). Consumer response to a firm's endorser (dis)association decisions. *Journal of Advertising*, 31(4), 41–52. https://doi.org/10.1080/00913367.2002.10673684

Maddux, J. E., & Rogers, R. W. (1980). Effects of source expertness, physical attractiveness, and supporting arguments on persuasion: A case of brains over beauty. *Journal of Personality and Social Psychology*, 39(2), 235–244. https://doi.org/10.1037/0022-3514.39.2.235

Madrigal, R., & Boush, D. M. (2008). Social responsibility as a unique dimension of brand personality and consumers' willingness to reward. *Psychology and Marketing*, 25(6), 538–564. https://doi.org/10.1002/mar.20224

Malik, M. E., Ghafoor, M. M., Iqbal, H. K., Ali, Q., Hunbal, H., Noman, M., & Ahmed, B. (2013). Impact of brand image and advertisement on consumer buying behavior. *World Applied Sciences Journal*, 23(1), 117–122.

McCracken, G. (1989). Who is the celebrity endorser? Cultural foundations of the endorsement process. *Journal of Consumer Research*, 16(3), 310–321. https://doi.org/10.1086/209217

McGuire, W. (1969). The nature of attitudes and attitude change. In G. Lindsey & E. Aronson (Eds.), *The handbook of social psychology* (Vol. 3, pp. 136–314). Addison-Wesley.

Miller, F. M., & Allen, C. (2012). How does celebrity meaning transfer? Investigating the process of meaning transfer with celebrity affiliates and mature brands. *Journal of Consumer Psychology*, 22(3), 443–452. https://doi.org/10.1016/j.jcps.2011.11.001

Mills, C. W. (1956). *The power elite*. Oxford University Press.

Misra, S., & Beatty, S. E. (1990). Celebrity spokesperson and brand congruence: An assessment of recall and affect. *Journal of Business Research*, 21(2), 159–173. https://doi.org/10.1016/0148-2963(90)90050-N

Moore, D. J., Mowen, J. C., & Reardon, R. (1994). Multiple sources in advertising appeals: When product endorsers are paid by the advertising sponsor. *Journal of the Academy of Marketing Science*, 22(3), 234–243. https://doi.org/10.1177/0092070394223004

Mowen, J. C. (1980). On product endorser effectiveness: A balance model approach. *Current Issues and Research in Advertising*, 3(1), 41–57.

Park, S. Y. (2016). Celebrity endorsement for nonprofit organizations: The role of experience-based fit between celebrity and cause. *International Business Research*, 10(1), 8–21. https://doi.org/10.5539/ibr.v10n1p8

Paul, J., & Bhakar, S. (2018). Does celebrity image congruence influences brand attitude and purchase intention? *Journal of Promotion Management*, 24(2), 153–177. https://doi.org/10.1080/10496491.2017.1360826

Percy, L. (1983). A review of the effect of specific advertising elements upon overall communication response. *Current Issues and Research in Advertising 6*(2), 77–118.

Petty, R. E., Cacioppo, J. T., & Schumann, D. (1983). Central and peripheral routes to advertising effectiveness: The moderating role of involvement. *Journal of Consumer Research, 10*(2), 135–146. https://doi.org/10.1086/208954

Rao, A. R., & Ruekert, R. W. (1994). Brand alliances as signals of product quality. *Sloan Management Review, 36*(1), 87–97.

Roy, S., Gammoh, B., & Koh, A. C. (2012). Predicting the effectiveness of celebrity endorsements using the balance theory. *Journal of Customer Behaviour, 11*(1), 33–52. https://doi.org/10.1362/147539212X13286273975238

Schimmelpfennig, C., & Hunt, J. B. (2020). Fifty years of celebrity endorser research: Support for a comprehensive celebrity endorsement strategy framework. *Psychology and Marketing, 37*(3), 488–505. https://doi.org/10.1002/mar.21315

Schouten, A. P., Janssen, L., & Verspaget, M. (2020). Celebrity vs. influencer endorsements in advertising: The role of identification, credibility, and product-endorser fit. *International Journal of Advertising, 39*(2), 258–281. https://doi.org/10.1080/02650487.2019.1634898

Silvera, D. H., & Austad, B. (2004). Factors predicting the effectiveness of celebrity endorsement advertisements. *European Journal of Marketing, 38*(11/12), 1509–1526. https://doi.org/10.1108/03090560410560218

Sirgy, M. J. (1982). Self-concept in consumer behavior: A critical review. *Journal of Consumer Research, 9*(3), 287–300. https://doi.org/10.1086/208924

Snyder, M., & Rothbart, M. (1971). Communicator attractiveness and opinion change. *Canadian Journal of Behavioural Science, 3*(4), 377–387. https://doi.org/10.1037/h0082280

Tajfel, H., & Turner, J. C. (1985). The social identity theory of intergroup behavior. In S. Worchel & W. G. Austin (Eds.), *Psychology of intergroup relations* (Vol. 2, pp. 7–24). Nelson-Hall.

Till, B. D., & Busler, M. (2000). The match-up hypothesis: Physical attractiveness, expertise, and the role of fit on brand attitude, purchase intent, and brand beliefs. *Journal of Advertising, 29*(3), 1–13. https://doi.org/10.1080/00913367.2000.10673613

Till, B. D., & Shimp, T. A. (1998). Endorsers in advertising: The case of negative celebrity information. *Journal of Advertising, 27*(1), 67–82. https://doi.org/10.1080/00913367.1998.10673543

Torres, P., Augusto, M. G., & Matos, M. (2019). Antecedents and outcomes of digital influencer endorsement: An exploratory study. *Psychology and Marketing, 36*(12), 1267–1276. https://doi.org/10.1002/mar.21274

Tripp, C., Jensen, T. J., & Carlson, L. (1994). The effects of multiple product endorsements by celebrities on consumers' attitudes and intentions. *Journal of Consumer Research, 20*(4), 535–547. https://doi.org/10.1086/209368

Um, N. H., & Kim, S. (2016). Determinants for effects of celebrity negative information: When to terminate a relationship with a celebrity endorser in trouble? *Psychology and Marketing, 33*(10), 864–874. https://doi.org/10.1002/mar.20923

Wang, S., & Kim, K. (2019). Consumer response to negative celebrity publicity: The effects of moral reasoning strategies and fan identification. *Journal of Product and Brand Management, 29*(1), 114–123. https://doi.org/10.1108/JPBM-10-2018-2064

Wang, S. W., & Close-Scheinbaum, A. (2018). Enhancing brand credibility via celebrity endorsement: Trustworthiness trumps attractiveness and expertise. *Journal of Advertising Research, 58*(1), 16–32. https://doi.org/10.2501/JAR-2017-042

Wheeler, R. T. (2009). Nonprofit advertising: Impact of celebrity connection, involvement and gender on source credibility and intention to volunteer time or donate money. *Journal of Nonprofit & Public Sector Marketing, 21*(1), 80–107. https://doi.org/10.1080/10495140802111984

White, D., Goddard, L., & Wilbur, N. (2009). The effects of negative information transference in the celebrity endorsement relationship. *International Journal of Retail & Distribution Management, 37*(4), 322–335. https://doi.org/10.1108/09590550910948556

Wright, S. A. (2016). Reinvestigating the endorser by product matchup hypothesis in advertising. *Journal of Advertising, 45*(1), 26–32. https://doi.org/10.1080/00913367.2015.1077360

PART V

CONSUMERS PROCESS COGNITIONS AND AFFECT

CHAPTER 23

OMISSION NEGLECT AND CONSUMER JUDGMENT AND INFERENCE BASED ON LIMITED EVIDENCE

Frank R. Kardes, Steven S. Posavac, and Donald R. Gaffney

What you see is all there is.
—Daniel Kahneman, *Thinking, Fast and Slow*

OMISSION NEGLECT

When Sherlock Holmes asked Inspector Gregory to consider last night's "curious incident," Gregory replied that nothing happened (in Sir Arthur Conan Doyle's "The Silver Blaze"). "That was the curious incident," Holmes replied triumphantly. This clue enabled Holmes to infer that the murderer must have been someone familiar to the victim's dog because the dog did not bark when the murderer appeared. Most people would miss this important clue because most people, like Inspector Gregory, pay little attention to nonoccurrences (L. Ross, 1977).

Nonoccurrences are important in other situations as well. When forming beliefs about cause and effect, people typically focus on cases in which the cause and the effect co-occur. Control group cases involving the absence of the cause tend to be neglected even though such cases are essential for establishing causality (Mill, 1887). Another remarkable illustration of how difficult it is for people to consider the absence of information includes the number zero and its meaning of nothing, or the absence of quantity. It took early mathematicians thousands of years to develop the crucial concept of zero, in part because people are surprisingly insensitive to absences (Ifrah, 1985).

In everyday life, consumers often make consequential decisions based on limited or incomplete information about products and services without considering the implications of unmentioned or unknown pieces of information. This occurs because consumers have become accustomed to using whatever information is readily available to them, and they frequently overestimate the importance of this information (Sanbonmatsu et al., 2003). *Omission neglect*—or insensitivity to missing, unmentioned, or unknown options, attributes, issues, or possibilities—is particularly troublesome due to the nature of the world in which we live. The amount of information used to characterize various options (including politicians, job candidates, products and services, and medical procedures) fluctuates considerably across alternatives and circumstances. All matters, in some way or another, are partially or incompletely described.

Research on omission neglect has shown that people often fail to detect the absence of important missing information, and this leads them to form strong judgments on the basis of weak evidence (Sanbonmatsu et al., 1991, 1992, 1997, 2003). Strong judgments are overly extreme with respect to the judgmental implications of the available evidence and are held with a high degree of confidence. Overly extreme judgments are highly favorable or highly unfavorable when the available evidence is only moderately favorable or moderately unfavorable, respectively. In general, people should form more extreme beliefs when a large amount of relevant information is available than when only a small amount of relevant information is available (the set-size effect; Anderson, 1981). However, when people are insensitive to omissions, they form extreme judgments regardless of how much or how little is known about a target of judgment (Sanbonmatsu et al., 1991, 1992, 1997, 2003). Furthermore, this chapter reviews evidence suggesting that omission neglect occurs at each stage of information processing (attention and perception, learning and memory, judgment, and decision making; e.g., Kardes & Wyer, 2013) and in a wide variety of judgmental tasks. We also review studies showing that when omissions are detected, people attempt to form inferences from several different possible bases to fill gaps in knowledge.

Omission Neglect in Attention and Perception

To newborn babies, the world must seem like a magical place. Objects seem to appear from nowhere and then vanish into thin air. However, at about 9 months, babies begin to recognize that objects still exist even when you cannot sense them. Piaget (1972) referred to this as *object permanence* and argued that this is one of the most important principles of cognitive development. He conducted experiments showing that newborns lost interest in an attractive toy when it was covered by a blanket. At about 9 months, however, they would search for the toy under the blanket because they began to recognize that just because you could not see the attractive toy did not mean that it was not there.

Why is object permanence acquired at such a young age? This principle is crucial for survival. Our ancestors learned that just because you could not see hidden food did not mean it was not there. They learned to search for food hidden underground (e.g., root vegetables) and underwater (e.g., seafood). They also learned that just because you could not see a dangerous predator did not mean it was not lurking behind rocks, bushes, and trees.

Primitive people who did not acquire object permanence did not survive long enough to pass on their genes.

Despite the importance of this principle, adults often find it easier to detect the presence of a feature than the absence of a feature. Treisman and Souther (1985) presented various geometric images to participants and manipulated the presence or absence of a target with an extra feature (e.g., a circle with an extra line or without an extra line). One to 12 distractors were also presented. The distractors were similar to the target except that they lacked the extra feature when the target possessed it or they possessed the extra feature when the target lacked it. Search times (in milliseconds) were faster when the target possessed the extra feature than when the target lacked the extra feature, suggesting that it is easier to detect the presence of a feature than the absence of a feature. Furthermore, search times were fast regardless of the number of distractors that were presented when the target possessed the extra feature. When the target lacked the extra feature, however, search times increased dramatically with the number of distractors that were presented.

Wu (2019) partially replicated these results using a verbal description of a new laptop computer. Participants received a description of a new laptop containing four presented features (e.g., Intel processor, HD graphics, four-cell battery, ultrafast storage) and four missing features. After reading the description, one feature at a time was presented on a computer monitor. Participants were asked to press the "present" button if the feature was present in the description and the "absent" button if the feature was absent from the description. Response times were faster for present features than for absent features, indicating that it is easier to detect present features than absent features.

Omission neglect is not limited to perceptions of geometric objects and to perceptions of consumer goods. Caputo and Dunning (2005) found that omission neglect also occurs in self-perceptions. They asked participants to perform various tasks and asked participants to judge how good they were at these tasks. A wide variety of tasks were used, including a word game (i.e., Boggle; Studies 1 and 5), a visual search task (i.e., find Nina;

Study 2), finding grammatical errors (Study 3), and finding methodological flaws in a research report (Study 4). For each of these tasks, more favorable self-assessments were formed as the number of solutions participants generated (i.e., acts of commission) increased. However, the number of solutions participants missed (i.e., acts of omission) had no influence on self-assessments. Later, when participants were asked to judge the relevance of the missed solutions, they indicated that they were highly relevant, and more moderate self-assessments were formed.

Acts of omission versus commission influence perceptions of others as well as self-perceptions. People judge others' harmful acts of omission less harshly than others' harmful acts of commission. Ritov and Baron (1990, 1999) found that participants were unwilling to administer a vaccine to children against a disease that was expected to kill 10 out of 10,000 children when the vaccine's side effects would kill five out of 10,000 children. Even though not administering the vaccine would kill more children, participants recommended not administering the vaccine. Spranca et al. (1991) created several moral scenarios and asked participants to judge the severity of acts of omission versus commission. For example, in one scenario, a tennis player who was going to play against Ivan Lendl, the best tennis player in the world at the time, had dinner with Lendl prior to the match. The player knew Lendl was allergic to cayenne pepper, and he knew that the house salad dressing contained cayenne pepper. In one version of the scenario, Lendl ordered the salad and the player said nothing (i.e., an act of omission). In the other version, the player recommended the salad to Lendl (i.e., an act of commission). The results showed that acts of omission were judged less harshly than acts of commission. Furthermore, this pattern is observed even when controlling for the intentions of the decision maker (Cushman et al., 2006) and even when controlling for the status quo (Ritov & Baron, 1992).

Omission Neglect in Learning and Memory

People often struggle to see the true relationship between two variables, X and Y, because they are often insensitive to missing information. Focus is normally oriented toward cases in which both variables are present and is typically ignored in cases that entail the absence of either. On the other hand, all four cells of the 2 × 2 contingency table are equally important from a statistical perspective. Nevertheless, most people focus on the X present/Y present cell. This often leads people to conclude that a relationship exists between these variables when the relationship may actually be illusory. For example, if a large number of expensive products are high in quality, many people conclude that high price implies high quality. This conclusion is unwarranted, however, because a large number of expensive products are not high in quality, a large number of inexpensive products are high in quality, and a large number of inexpensive products are low in quality.

While beliefs tend to be more reasonable when people are sensitive to omissions, people regularly neglect omitted information. Research on the feature-positive effect, or the tendency to learn more quickly when a distinguishing feature or symbol (e.g., letter, number, geometric figure) is present versus absent, has shown that people find it very difficult to learn that the absence of a feature is informative (Newman et al., 1980). Even when the presence of a feature (e.g., the presence of a circle) and the absence of a feature (e.g., the absence of a circle) are equally informative, the relationship between the predictive feature and a desired event (e.g., food, water, positive feedback) is learned much more rapidly when the feature is present as opposed to absent. The feature-positive effect is so ubiquitous that it has been observed for humans, pigeons, rats, cats, and monkeys, and most young children and animals never learn that the absence of a feature is informative (Newman et al., 1980).

People often are unmotivated to search for information that is absent. One reason for this is that people often feel that they understand phenomena with greater precision, coherence, and depth than they actually do (Rozenblit & Keil, 2002). Participants were asked to evaluate the amount of knowledge they possessed on zippers. After an initial appraisal of how knowledgeable they were of how zippers worked (Time 1), they were then asked to explain how zippers functioned. After they had given an explanation and realized they had difficulty explaining how zippers function, they then were asked again to rate their amount of knowledge on zippers (Time 2). The Time 1 self-appraisal was significantly higher than the Time 2 self-appraisal of knowledge, suggesting an illusion of explanatory depth.

Similar results were reported by Sanbonmatsu et al. (2012), who found that people overestimate how much they know about celebrities, and this leads to inappropriately extreme evaluations of celebrities. Providing detailed information about the private lives of specific celebrities (Experiment 1) or merely asking people questions about the private lives of specific celebrities (Experiment 2) decreases the illusion of knowledge and leads to more moderate evaluations of celebrities. These procedures also reduce the effectiveness of celebrities as spokespersons.

The illusion of knowledge occurs because familiarity is used as a cue for assessing knowledge and because people often experience difficulty separating their knowledge from the knowledge of others (Sloman & Fernbach, 2018). This illusion has been amplified by the internet, a network that provides an enormous amount of information or knowledge to anyone who has access to a computer (Fisher et al., 2015). However, when we believe we are knowledgeable about items and processes that we do not fully understand, we are often unmotivated to continue to search for information (Fernbach et al., 2012; Wu, 2019). This lack of information search leads to a tendency to neglect information that was not presented. Considered together, access to large amounts of information (via the internet) and the tendency to underestimate the implications of missing information suggest that omission neglect is more important today than ever. One consequence of neglecting omitted information is attitude extremity in politics. For example, Fernbach et al. (2013) found that political extremism is often a result of overconfidence in the information people possess and the neglect of unknown information. Importantly, political attitudes became less extreme when participants were asked to explain these complex policies prior to attitude assessment.

This occurred because the explanation task reduced overconfidence by revealing a lack of understanding (Fernbach et al., 2013).

The tendency to neglect information is often a result of overconfidence (Griffin & Tversky, 1992; Kardes et al., 2006). One such example is the tendency to overweigh attributes or evidence presented while severely underweighing information not presented (Sanbonmatsu et al., 1991, 1992, 1997). As a result of judgments being formed primarily on the implications of the presented information, extreme judgments are often constructed on the basis of incomplete information (Fernbach et al., 2019; Kardes et al., 2006; Sanbonmatsu et al., 2003). In marketing, consumers have been found to discount the importance of the interest rate in their judgment and evaluation of a credit card, when omitted, despite consumers rating this information to be the most important information needed when selecting a credit card (Gaffney et al., 2020).

Recent research using a game theory perspective shows that missing information is neglected regardless of whether it is deliberately or nondeliberately withheld (Sah & Read, 2020). Even when information is deliberately withheld by the marketer, consumers fail to assume the worst possible value for the nondisclosed information. Less favorable inferences are formed when the salience of deliberate nondisclosure is highlighted using forceful language (e.g., "declined" or "refused") or when some marketers disclose and some do not (e.g., a comparative judgment context). Sah and Read (2020) argued that marketers tend to overestimate the influence of nondisclosure on consumers, and consumers tend to underestimate the implications of nondisclosure, and, consequently, both parties are strategically naïve.

Although omission neglect is common in everyday life, debiasing techniques do exist. Procedures that reduce epistemic certainty or overconfidence have been found to be effective in reducing omission neglect. Methods such as a priori ratings of presented and omitted attributes (Kardes et al., 2006), a priori criteria consideration (Kardes et al., 2006), consider-the-unknown technique (Walters et al., 2016), highlighting nonalignable differences in comparative judgment contexts (Sah & Read,

2020; Sanbonmatsu et al., 1997, 2003), the feeling of not knowing it all (Yang et al., 2019), and the distrust mindset (Gaffney et al., 2020) reduce overconfidence and decrease estimates of the strength of the available evidence. Epistemic uncertainty, or uncertainty stemming from a lack of knowledge, is distinct from aleatory uncertainty, or uncertainty stemming from a stochastic or probabilistic environment (Fox & Ülkümen, 2011). When probability distributions are held constant, people often exhibit greater aversion to epistemic uncertainty than to aleatory uncertainty (Heath & Tversky, 1991).

Omission Neglect in Judgment

People are also surprisingly insensitive to omissions when forming judgments, opinions, beliefs, and attitudes. Even though most objects and issues are described incompletely, people often respond as though they have all the information they need to form an informed judgment. Research on omission neglect in judgment suggests that ignoring or underweighting the implications of missing or unknown information is the default response (Kardes & Sanbonmatsu, 1993, 2003; Sanbonmatsu et al., 1991, 1992, 1997, 2003). When omission neglect occurs, people experience low epistemic uncertainty, and this leads to the formation of extreme judgments. The left side of Figure 23.1 shows the default response to omissions.

Figure 23.1 also shows that, under some circumstances, people may detect important omissions, and this leads to high epistemic uncertainty. Omission cuing, or highlighting specific omissions or warning people that important information may be missing, increases the likelihood of omission detection. Omissions are typically nonsalient, and, therefore, manipulations that increase the salience of missing information also increase sensitivity to omissions. Omission detection also increases with objective (but not subjective) prior knowledge about a particular topic and with comparative as opposed to singular information processing (i.e., mode of information processing). In singular judgment, objects are evaluated individually in isolation, and appropriate reference points for how much information is needed and what specific information is needed are often unclear. Finally, presented information can interfere with the ability

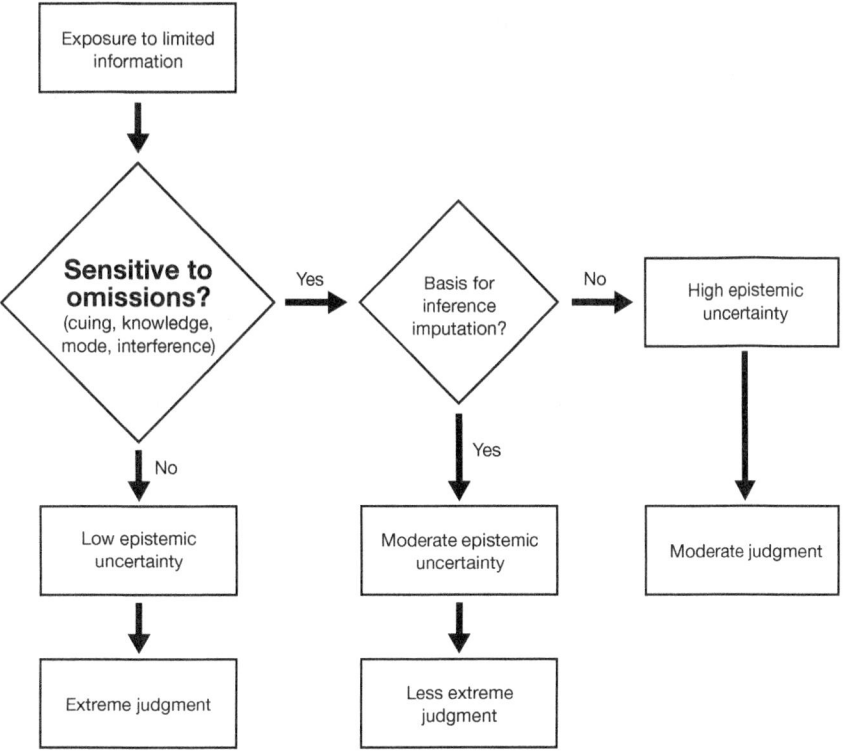

FIGURE 23.1. Omission neglect.

to generate missing or unmentioned attribute dimensions.

If people are unable to identify a basis for inference imputation about the possible values of missing pieces of information, they continue to experience high levels of epistemic uncertainty, and this leads to the formation of moderate judgments. On the other hand, if missing attributes are assumed to be correlated with presented attributes, people may form inferential judgments that fill gaps in knowledge, thereby reducing epistemic uncertainty. Inferences can also be formed on the basis of attitudes or overall evaluations (i.e., the halo effect) or on the basis of categorical or schema-based knowledge. The properties of a category prototype or a typical exemplar of a category are assumed to apply to most members of the category (e.g., most cars have four wheels, even if the number of wheels is not mentioned in a product description). A schema or an organized knowledge structure may also provide a basis for inference imputation. When inferences are formed, epistemic uncertainty decreases, albeit incompletely due to a lack of direct evidence, and this leads to moderate inferences that encourage the formation of less extreme overall judgments. Note, however, that omission detection is an important prerequisite for inference imputation, and an appropriate basis for inference generation and utilization is also needed (Kardes & Sanbonmatsu, 1993).

Several studies suggest that omissions are typically nonsalient. After receiving a relatively brief description of a 10-speed bicycle, participants indicated their overall evaluations of the product and completed a category-specific objective knowledge quiz (Sanbonmatsu et al., 1992). Half of the participants were asked to consider two missing attributes before reporting their evaluations, and half were not. This prompt to consider missing attributes resulted in more moderate evaluations for moderate knowledge participants but not for low- or high-knowledge participants. A follow-up test showed the low-knowledge participants were insufficiently knowledgeable to appreciate the relevance of the missing attributes. However, high-knowledge participants formed moderate evaluations regardless of whether or not they received the prompt, suggesting that they spontaneously detected relevant omissions. In a second experiment, participants blocked into low, moderate, and high camera knowledge conditions received either a relatively large amount of information about a new camera (eight attributes) or one of two small sets of information (four attributes). When participants were unknowledgeable or moderately knowledgeable about cameras, they formed equally favorable evaluations toward the target regardless of how much or how little information was presented. Only the relatively small subset of consumers who were highly knowledgeable exhibited a set-size effect on evaluations.

Similar results are observed in inferential judgments, or judgments that go beyond the information given (Sanbonmatsu et al., 1991). Participants received information concerning a bicycle and were asked to evaluate its durability despite there being no information provided relating to the durability of the bicycle in question. When evaluating the bicycle immediately after its brief description, participants found the lack of information regarding durability evident and formed moderate inferences about durability. However, when participants inferred the durability of the bicycle 1 week after reading the description, highly positive inferences were formed and were held with great certainty. Only highly knowledgeable participants formed moderate inferences after the delay. Unknowledgeable and moderately knowledgeable participants forgot more attribute information over time and formed more extreme and confidently held inferences over time (the remembering-less-and-inferring-more effect).

Beliefs about the strength of the correlation between presented and missing information often contribute to the inferences being made. When presented and omitted information are assumed to be correlated, consumers can make inferences about excluded information based on the implications of the presented information. One such illustration is the relationship many consumers make between the price and quality of a product. This often leads consumers to infer that a high price signals high quality. However, consumers are unlikely to attempt to form an inference about a missing attribute if they fail to notice that information is missing or if they assume that the presented and the missing information are uncorrelated (Kardes & Sanbonmatsu, 1993). Consumers experience little epistemic uncertainty and form extreme judgments when omissions are neglected. In the relatively rare instances in which omissions are detected, however, epistemic uncertainty increases and judgmental extremity decreases. Moderate judgments are appropriate when information is limited (Griffin & Tversky, 1992), are more readily updated as new information becomes available (Cialdini et al., 1973), and are more justifiable to oneself and others (Lerner & Tetlock, 1999; Shafir et al., 1993).

Research using cognitive load manipulations also suggests that omissions are nonsalient and are, therefore, difficult to detect (Sanbonmatsu et al., 1994). Although people frequently form extreme impressions of salient targets (e.g., minorities), more moderate impressions are formed as cognitive load decreases due to reduced time pressure or due to a decrease in the number of targets to be judged.

Singular versus comparative judgment contexts also influence sensitivity to omissions (Sanbonmatsu et al., 1997). In singular judgment contexts, a single product is judged in isolation, whereas in comparative judgment contexts, consumers map the attributes of one product to another. When the two products are described on different attribute dimensions, omissions become more readily apparent. Because a product described by a large set of attributes possesses unique attributes relative to another product described by a small set of attributes, the latter product is evaluated more moderately. When both products are described in terms of unique attributes, however, both products are evaluated more moderately.

Cross-category set-size effects were also observed by Sanbonmatsu et al. (1997). After receiving a large (vs. small) amount of attribute information pertaining to a camera, participants formed more moderate judgments of a bicycle described by a small amount of information. Similarly, after receiving a large (vs. small) amount of attribute information regarding a bicycle, participants formed more moderate judgments of a camera described by a small amount of information. Follow-up studies showed that cross-category set-size effects were found even when the contextual information pertained to soybeans and the target was a camera or a bicycle. Furthermore, this cross-category set-size effect was mediated by judgments of the perceived sufficiency of the evidence presented for a target. Considered together, the results suggest that in comparative processing, same-category set-size effects occur because specific missing attributes are cued. However, cross-category set-size effects occur due to a general sense that something is missing, and no specific omissions are cued.

Sanbonmatsu et al. (2003) conducted several experiments showing that, in singular judgment contexts, participants overestimate the importance of the presented information and underestimate the importance of omitted information, even when the relevance of the missing information is controlled. However, these effects are reduced in comparative judgment contexts. In Study 1, participants received one of two sets of four attributes pertaining to a bicycle. After reading the product description, participants were asked to list the attributes they considered to be the most important for evaluating a bicycle. They were asked to list at least four attributes and not more than eight. The results showed that more presented than nonpresented attributes were listed by low and moderate objective knowledge participants, regardless of the valence of the presented information. Only high knowledge participants recognized the importance of nonpresented attributes. In Study 2, participants listened to a radio ad describing an automobile using one of three sets of three attributes that pretested for importance. More presented than nonpresented attributes were listed as the most important attributes for evaluating an automobile in singular judgment contexts but not in comparative judgment contexts. More extreme and more confidently held evaluations were also formed in singular than in comparative judgment contexts.

In Study 3, participants listened to a radio ad describing an automobile using one of three sets of three attributes that were pretested for importance. Participants were asked to rate the importance of each of nine attributes or rate the importance of each of the three attributes that were included in the description on a 100-point constant sum scale. An all-other attribute category was included in the scale. The results showed that the presented attributes were rated as more important in the partial list condition than in the complete list condition. In addition, the automobile was evaluated more extremely, and the perceived sufficiency or strength of the presented information was higher in the partial list condition than in the complete list condition. Considered together, the results suggest that the criteria used for judgment are often ambiguous, and, as a result, the presented attributes often determine the criteria used for judgment. Furthermore, the results are inconsistent with a conversational norms account suggesting that cooperative communicators present only relevant information and omit only irrelevant information (Schwarz, 1996). Participants were explicitly instructed to consider missing information in all three studies, but they found this task exceedingly difficult in singular judgment contexts.

Additional evidence inconsistent with a conversational inference perspective was reported by Houghton et al. (1998). Participants received attribute information about an automobile ostensibly from a credible (*Consumer Reports*) or noncredible (an ad) source. Participants rated attributions for why information was missing (e.g., the automobile performs poorly on unmentioned attributes; only favorable features were mentioned; there was not enough space to mention other attributes; only the most important information was mentioned) either before or after participants evaluated the automobile. The results showed that source credibility and attributions for omissions influenced evaluations when attributions were measured prior to evaluations but not when evaluations were measured prior to attributions. This pattern of results suggests that consumers do not spontaneously form attributions for omissions, but they can do so when explicitly asked.

Muthukrishnan and Ramaswami (1999) also demonstrated that singular versus comparative judgment contexts influence sensitivity to omissions. Participants evaluated a target product in either a singular or a comparative judgment context. After a delay, participants received an attack or a challenge of the target product in either a singular or a comparative judgment context. When the initial judgment of the target was formed in a singular judgment context, a comparative challenge was more persuasive. However, when the initial judgment of the target was formed in a comparative judgment context, a singular challenge was more effective. Hence, judgment revision depends on the perceived strength of the initial information available about a target and on the perceived strength of the subsequent challenge.

Omissions are typically nonsalient, especially in singular judgment contexts. In addition, some studies suggest that the presented information can interfere with the ability to think about nonpresented information. Simply asking participants to consider their criteria for judgment before exposing them to a product description increases sensitivity to omissions and results in more moderate evaluations (Kardes et al., 2006). However, asking participants to consider their criteria for judgment after exposing them to a product description is ineffective. In this case, their criteria are biased by the description, as observed by Sanbonmatsu et al. (2003). Similarly, asking participants to rate each presented attribute and each of several missing attributes before forming an overall evaluation increases sensitivity to omissions and produces more moderate evaluations. However, asking participants to rate attributes after forming an overall evaluation is ineffective.

Construal levels, or the degrees of abstractness with which information is represented in memory (Trope & Liberman, 2010), also influence the salience of missing information (Pfeiffer et al., 2014). It is easier to miss important specific details when information is represented abstractly rather than concretely. Consequently, sensitivity to omissions increases and more moderate judgments are formed when psychological distance is low due to near-future (vs. distant-future) judgment tasks, due to why (vs. how) behavioral framing, or due to individual differences in concrete (vs. abstract) interpretations of behaviors.

As the perceived diagnosticity of the presented attribute and brand name information increases, sensitivity to omissions decreases for moderately knowledgeable participants (Hernandez et al., 2014). However, this effect was reduced for experts, and when a well-known brand was presented to novices, they were insensitive to omissions regardless of the level of diagnosticity of the attribute information. Wu et al. (2019) showed that the fluency with which the presented information can be processed can also influence sensitivity to omissions. The presented information seemed more diagnostic and produced greater interference with the ability to consider missing information when this information was presented in an easy-to-read font. Furthermore, when font readability decreased, response times for correctly identifying attributes as missing attributes also decreased.

Omission Neglect in Decision Making

Nobel laureate Daniel Kahneman (2010) argued that insensitivity to omissions is one of the most important biases in decision making and referred to this insensitivity as WYSIATA, or What You See Is All There Is. He cited a study showing that participants who received one-sided evidence supporting either the plaintiff or the defendant in a legal scenario overlooked the strength of the evidence supporting the other side (Brenner et al., 1996). As a result, both parties were overconfident that their side would win.

Research on the fault-tree effect also shows that insensitivity to omissions is the norm (Russo & Kolzow, 1994). People using fault trees to troubleshoot focus selectively on the problems listed in the tree and underestimate the likelihood that an unmentioned alternative could be the cause of a problem. This result is observed regardless of how many or how few possibilities are listed (analogous to the finding that extreme beliefs are formed regardless of how many or how few attributes are presented in a product description; Sanbonmatsu et al., 1992).

Missing information is also neglected in the Ellsberg paradox: People prefer to bet on known probabilities rather than on unknown probabilities (Fox & Weber, 2002). When gambling on the likelihood of a red or black marble being drawn, most individuals are indifferent if the jar contains an equal number of each color. When the distribution of red and black marbles is unknown, people still tend to be indifferent in their wagering of which color marble will be drawn. However, when offered the choice, individuals often choose to gamble on the jar with the 50:50 distribution rather than the jar with the unknown distribution. Comparative judgment contexts (e.g., contexts involving multiple choice options) increase sensitivity to missing attributes (e.g., Sanbonmatsu et al., 1997, 2003) and to missing probability distributions (Fox & Weber, 2002).

Alignable differences, or directly comparable differences between products (e.g., Automobile A gets 35 mpg and Automobile B gets 30 mpg), are weighed more heavily in decision making relative to nonalignable differences (e.g., Automobile A gets 35 mpg and Automobile B has smooth handling; Markman & Loewenstein, 2010; Slovic & MacPhillamy, 1974). Consequently, when consumers make pair-wise comparisons of three choice options having different missing attributes, intransitive choices are commonly observed (Kivetz & Simonson, 2000). Because consumers experience difficulty thinking about the implications of missing information, nonalignable differences are ignored or underweighted.

OMISSION DETECTION

Consumer Judgment and Inference

When consumers detect that information about a product or service is missing, they often try to fill in the omissions in what they know based on the information that they do have (Kardes, Posavac, & Cronley, 2004). For example, communications such as what is presented online, in an advertisement, or in a sales pitch often do not provide a complete bundle of information about a product. To develop a fuller perception of a target object described by incomplete information, consumers first must draw inferences about what they do not know. Making such inferences is useful for consumers because they may be more confident when their judgments and decisions are based on information perceived to be more (vs. less) complete. Indeed, consumers are more likely to make versus defer a choice when they fill in an informational gap with an inference (Gunasti & Ross, 2009).

Of course, the nature of the judgments that are rendered and the choices that are made when omissions have been detected will be heavily influenced by the specifics of what consumers infer to fill in the informational blanks. Although we will discuss numerous types of inferences and inferential contexts, the common underlying process is that consumers typically employ implicit theories to make conclusions about what they do not know based on what they do. An *implicit theory* is a belief about the nature of relations between entities (Wyer, 2004) and often takes the form of an if-then linkage. For example, consumers may have an implicit theory that if a product is widely adopted, then it must be a good product because it is popular (Deval et al., 2013). Thus, in the absence of information about the quality of a product, consumers may infer how good or bad it is based on their belief about the implications of product quality for marketplace popularity.

There are four primary types of if–then linkages that govern consumers' inferences when they have detected an omission of information: Inferences may be based on known attributes of a target product or service, overall attitudes toward the product, knowledge of the category to which the product belongs, and schemas relevant to the entity under consideration (e.g., product, firm). The remainder of our chapter considers these different types of inferences.

Inferences Based on Attributes

Consumers have a rich set of implicit theories regarding the relationships between attributes that govern their inferences regarding attributes about which they do not have information. For example, a consumer may believe the higher priced a product is, the higher quality it must be. In much the same vein, the presence of a strong warranty may be taken to signal excellent reliability, whereas a poor or nonexistent warranty may drive an inference that the product will not hold up over time. Researchers have cataloged an impressive set of these implicit theories and their implications for judgment and choice. Generally, if a consumer believes that there is a correlation between multiple attributes and they know the value of at least one of the attributes, they can draw inferences about the attribute values that they do not know (Broniarczyk & Alba, 1994; Dick et al., 1990).

An example of an implicit theory regarding the relationship between two attributes is the belief that food that is healthy is more expensive compared with less healthy food (Haws et al., 2017). Although consumers often believe that the correlation between the health value and the expense of food is higher than it objectively is, the implicit theory of a strong relationship between these attributes has important consequences for inferences when information is missing, as well as for decision making. Specifically, Haws et al. (2017) demonstrated than when information about the healthiness of a food product is missing, consumers infer that it is healthier if it is priced higher. This implicit theory has bidirectional implications; when price of a product is unknown, consumers infer that healthier products are more expensive. Moreover, Haws et al. showed that these inferences of missing information drive consumers' choices. A related implicit theory that has also proved to drive inference is that unhealthy (vs. healthy) food tends to taste better (Raghunathan et al., 2006).

In addition to specific attributes such as the taste and health implications of food discussed in the preceding paragraph, consumers often must draw more general conclusions about product quality before making a purchase decision. Indeed, it is rare for consumers to have a good understanding of the quality of the vast number of options competing to meet their needs. Instead, consumers often must draw summary inferences of the overall quality of options if they are to feel confident in their choices. One of the most ubiquitous inferential cues to product quality is price, such that products that cost more are inferred to be of higher quality (Broniarczyk & Alba, 1994).

Cronley et al. (2005) explored factors that affect how heavily price is used as an inferential basis when judging quality and the implications that price-based quality inferences have for choice. Cronley et al. argued that selective hypothesis testing may underlie the tendency for consumers to overestimate the price–quality relationship, such that consumers' belief that such a correlation exists serves as an operative hypothesis when they consider brands and brand attributes. Because cases consistent with the hypothesis of a strong relationship between price and quality are likely to be overweighted compared with inconsistent cases, which in turn are likely to be neglected, quality inferences based on price are likely to be particularly extreme when selective processing is facilitated in the market context (Kardes, Cronley, et al., 2004; Kardes, Posavac, & Cronley, 2004).

Across five experiments, Cronley et al. (2005) demonstrated that when quality of a brand is not available, consumers tend to make quality inferences heavily dependent on price. This tendency is particularly strong when selective processing is likely in the choice context, specifically, when need for closure is high, information load is high, and when information about other brands on which the expectation of a price–quality relationship is based is presented in rank order versus randomly. Importantly, consistent with the notion that a prime reason why consumers draw inferences when an omission of information has been detected is to facilitate choice, Cronley et al. demonstrated that when context makes selective processing likely, quality inferences are heavily based on price, and consumers spend more of their money in real choices to the extent that they have formed quality inferences based on price.

Individuals' beliefs that two or more variables associated with some target fuel halo effects in inference. The concept of halo effects has a deep history in social psychology and was first discussed in the context of person perception. Participants in Asch's (1946) study were read a list of attributes about another person, and whether the person was described as "warm" or "cold" was embedded and manipulated within the list. When the target other was described as warm versus cold, the target was inferred to be more generous, sociable, and good natured. Dion et al. (1972) first identified the what-is-beautiful-is-good tendency, whereby physically attractive people are inferred to possess multiple additional favorable attributes.

In the consumer domain, such halo effects have been shown to be strong drivers of inferences that both drive choice and have important social implications. For example, Andrews et al. (1998) reported that knowledge of a brand possessing one healthy attribute (no cholesterol) leads consumers to believe that the brand is favorable on other health-relevant attributes about which consumers have no information (low in fat). Thus, there often may be a "health halo" in perceptions of food products.

Halo effects have been demonstrated in multiple contexts in which consumers have to infer missing information about an attribute based on their knowledge of another attribute. Schuldt et al. (2012) demonstrated that knowledge that a target chocolate brand had been produced using "fair trade" practices, or following an ethical code of treatment for workers, led consumers to infer that the chocolate had fewer calories. Moreover, greater consumption of ethically produced chocolate was deemed to be appropriate because it was perceived to have a lower calorie count. Schuldt and Schwarz (2010) reported a similar consumer response when a brand was associated with the attribute of being "organic." Again, knowledge of one favorable attribute was shown to guide inferences of an unknown (and factually unrelated) attribute due to consumers' implicit theory of the relation between a favorable attribute and a health-relevant attribute.

In addition to exploring different interattribute correlation perceptions that drive inference following omission detection, researchers have also considered the nature of inferences drawn based on the distribution of attribute values. One such determinant is how much variability there is in the values of the known attribute. To the extent that the range of possible values that an attribute can take increases, consumers perceive greater variability, which affects the inferences that they draw. Generally, when attribute variability is high, inferences tend to be more moderate. For example, Meyer (1981) considered perceptions of a pizza restaurant and explored how consumers inferred values for information that they did not have based on attribute values that they did know. When perceived attribute variability was high, uncertainty about the possible values of missing attributes increased and less extreme inferences regarding the values of unknown attributes were formed. Janiszewski and

Lichtenstein (1999) reported that attribute variability can also play a role in price perceptions, while Park and Park (2013) showed how variability in online product reviews can drive consumers' product evaluations.

The relationship between attribute variability and inferences of missing information has important implications for marketing strategy. One of the most attractive tools in brand managers' toolkits is extending brands, where an existing brand name is used in the launch of a new product into an existing line or into a new category where the brand has not previously had a presence. Kardes and Allen (1991) explored how variability in quality of existing products in a category as well as in the parent brand (i.e., is the parent brand an umbrella brand characterized by high variability or a niche brand associated with low variability?) affects inferences of the quality of brand extensions. When variability is lower in a category in which an extension will be launched, inferences about the quality of the extension based on the parent brand are more favorable. In contrast, when category variability is high, inferences about a potential extension are more conservative and moderate. This core finding was even more pronounced when the parent brand served as an umbrella for a variety of extant products versus a more focused niche brand.

Sundar and Kardes (2015) explored inferences about nutritional attributes and found, consistent with prior research, that consumers made less favorable inferences about nutrition-relevant attributes when perceived attribute variability was high versus low. This effect was observed in a number of foods, such as potato chips, orange juice, and chocolate with attributes like sugar content, MSG, and calories. Sundar and Kardes also considered the relative potency of attribute variability and the presence of a health halo to drive inferences of missing information. Results showed that the influence of perceived attribute variability becomes diminished when a health halo label such as "organic" or "fair trade" was present. That is, when a health halo signal is associated with a brand, favorable attitudes are formed, which drives subsequent inferences regarding missing information regardless of perceived attribute variability.

Inferences Based on Attitudes

All of the findings we have discussed regarding inferences of missing attribute values based on known attributes are predicated on consumers perceiving a correlation between an unknown attribute and at least one known attribute. But what happens when consumers perceive an omission but do not believe that known attributes are predictive of omissions in attribute values? In this case, as long as a consumer possesses an accessible overall attitude toward the product or brand, the attitude may be used as the basis for inference (Dick et al., 1990). If the attitude is favorable, consumers may infer a favorable value for the unknown attribute, whereas an unfavorable attitude may be taken to imply that the unknown attribute is unfavorable.

If consumers have neither knowledge of attributes that correlate with detected omissions nor an accessible attitude, they are unlikely to form strong inferences regarding missing information but are instead likely to make more moderate judgments that reflect their uncertainty (Kardes & Sanbonmatsu, 1993). Moreover, even if an attitude is accessible but is not diagnostic of the missing information, strong inferences are unlikely, whereas moderate judgments are common.

Interestingly, an attitude that is perceived to be diagnostic of the attributes of a target object may be used to form attribute inferences even if consumers have experience with the object. In a person perception context, Nisbett and Wilson (1977) demonstrated that the global attitudes people form toward others drive inferences of unknown attributes of others' personality. More germane to marketplace phenomena, Beckwith and Lehmann (1975) explored the role of global attitudes on attribute inference in entertainment products and demonstrated that attitudes guide consumers' perceptions of attribute levels even when they have had direct experience with the product. That is, rather than holding a set of independent perceptions of attributes that are aggregated into an overall attitude per assumptions of the multi-attribute model (Nelson, 1999), consumers' overall attitudes both are influenced by and also influence attribute perceptions. This result is particularly interesting because, in theory, participants' direct experience could be sufficient to form attribute beliefs, but nevertheless Beckwith and Lehmann's (1975) respondents relied on global attitudes to draw specific inferences about product attributes.

Given that attitudes are often used as a basis for inferences of missing information, it is important to understand factors that determine when consumers will draw upon their attitudes in this way. Sanbonmatsu et al. (1991) replicated the finding that when consumers are aware that information is limited, they often make inferences that missing attributes have moderate values. However, when consumers are less aware that information is missing, inferences tend to be based on overall attitudes toward products. Even when important information about a product is missing in a communication such as an advertisement, if a consumer considers the product sometime after the communication has been received, they are likely to forget exactly what was and what was not contained in the communication and instead will perceive all of the product's attribute values in line with their overall attitude toward the product. This tendency is less likely for experts, who are more sensitive to missing information during product learning and have more developed mental frameworks that assist in the recall of what is not known. Thus, experts are chronically more sensitive to missing information, more likely to form moderate inferences when information is missing, and less likely to engage in attitude-based inference compared with consumers with lower knowledge.

Dick et al. (1990) also considered when attribute- versus attitude-based inference would occur and reported that attribute-based inference was more likely when attributes could be easily recalled from memory but that attitude-based inference predominated when attributes were more difficult to retrieve. Generally, in the marketplace overall, product attitudes are much more easily recalled than are specific attributes. Thus, inferences of unknown attributes are typically more likely to be based on attitudes than known attributes, but if consumers do know an attribute that is correlated with a missing attribute, then inference will likely be attribute based. Study of when and why consumers make attribute- versus attitude-based inferences has persisted in consumer psychology. Recently, Walters and Hershfield (2020) found that when consumers make inferences about forgotten information, they often use attitude-based inferences. However, when forming inferences about unknown information, consumers form attribute-based inferences.

Inferences Based on Categories

As our chapter has emphasized thus far, when consumers detect omissions in the information they have about a product, they are likely to fill in their gaps in knowledge using an inference. The first two types of inference we discussed, attribute- and attitude-based inference, each require some knowledge about the target product, whether specific information about an attribute or a general attitude. In some cases, though, very little is known about a product that could serve as a basis for inference. For example, when a new product is launched, marketers' main challenge is to provide signals that the product will meet consumers' needs.

One efficient strategy is to leverage category-based inference processes. When consumers are led to perceive a product as belonging to a given category about which they have knowledge, consumers may make inferences about the product based on what they know or believe about the category. That is, they may generalize what they perceive about a product's category to the product itself. For the consumer psychologist, a relevant category is usually defined by a group of brands, products, services, firms, or other marketing entities that consumers perceive to be related in some way (Loken et al., 2008). For example, consumers may believe that products made in Germany will be engineered with precision or that jewelry from Cartier will be of high quality. The critical questions, then, are when will consumers engage in category-based inference, and what inferences are they likely to draw?

One marketplace phenomenon where category-based inferences play a particularly important role is brand extensions. As we referenced earlier, in a brand extension, an existing brand name, as well as some of the brand's elements like visual imagery or a slogan, are attached to a new product being introduced to the marketplace. The hope is that what consumers know about the existing, or parent, brand transfers onto the new product because of the shared name and brand elements. If this occurs, the new product that is launched is more likely to be quickly adopted and achieve market success. A key to whether this process works for a given new product is the fit between the new product and the parent brand category. To the extent that there is a good fit, consumers will infer that the new product shares the features and quality of the parent brand (Loken et al., 2008), and sales are thereby facilitated. For example, when Procter and Gamble wanted to launch an over-the-counter sleep aid, they named it ZzzQuil and packaged it similarly to their cold remedy NyQuil, which is known for helping people sleep. Because ZzzQuil was a logical fit with NyQuil, consumers' recognition and trust of NyQuil were transferred to ZzzQuil via a categorical inference process, which put ZzzQuil in a position of brand strength relative to the category (Kapoor & Heslop, 2009), and ZzzQuil quickly became the market leader.

The country in which a product is made can serve as a powerful reference category for a product about which little is known. If a product is categorized in terms of where it was made, what a consumer knows and believes about its country of origin may be used to infer qualities of the product. Thus, the associations a consumer has with the country of a product's origin may serve as a proxy and fill in unknown information about a product's quality and reliability, as well as specific attributes (Abraham & Patro, 2014). Moreover, in addition to inferences such as quality and reliability that are cognitive in nature, categorical inference based on the country of origin can result in affective inferences as well (Adina et al., 2015). That is, consumers may infer how they should feel about a product based on the affect they experience when considering the country in which the product was made.

Interestingly, categorical inferences based on a product's country of origin may work for the benefit or detriment of the product as a function of the match between the knowledge consumers have regarding the country of origin and the set of inferences that would make the product attractive in the marketplace. The default inferential process will result in a product's being seen through the lens of the country in which it is made; thus, the persuasive impact may be positive if there is congruence between knowledge of the country and marketers' desired positioning of a product or negative if there is a mismatch (Adina et al., 2015).

Hong and Wyer (1990) reported several studies that demonstrate the ubiquity of category-based inference in the country of origin effect context. Hong and Wyer showed that even if attribute information about a target product is available, and accordingly, category-level information is not needed to form an impression of the product, the country of origin effect nevertheless may be observed in product evaluations, interest in the product, and diligence in processing information about the product. A core takeaway from Hong and Wyer's studies is that if a product's country of origin is known well in advance of exposure to the product, the country of origin acts as a perceptual lens that guides subsequent information processing.

Although a product's country of origin will often act as the basis for categorical inferences about the product, Li and Wyer (1994) made the important point that product categories can sometimes act like attributes in the inference process. Li and Wyer demonstrated that when consideration of all information about a product is facilitated by the choice context because decision importance is high and country of origin is presented before other product information, the country of origin serves as an attribute in inference. Consistent with prior research, when there is a paucity of information about a product, and accordingly, there are significant omissions in product knowledge, the product is categorized as a function of its country of origin, which serves as the basis of categorical inference.

Given that consumers can draw inferences from both attributes as well as categories, the question arises as to when each type of inference is likely. Fiske and Pavelchak (1986) focused on the qualities of and information about a target object, such as a product, that affect whether a category will be used as a basis for inference or whether a piecemeal approach will be used in which specific information about an object will be sought to fill in informational gaps. If category membership about a newly encountered object is evident, for example, because it has been made clear in an advertisement or on packaging, and no other information about the object is available, inferences about the object will be made based on the category to which it belongs. If an object is readily categorized and attribute information is available, then categorical inference is likely if the object matches the category well, but specific attribute information is likely to be sought if the fit is weak between the object and the category. Finally, if category membership of a target object is not evident, category-based inference may still occur but only if the object spontaneously cues the category.

In addition to features of a target object, the mindset of the individual judging the object is an important determinant of whether category-based inference is likely. Making inferences about information that one does not know about an object based on a category to which it belongs is a very efficient process, and Brewer (1988) argued that category-based inference is particularly likely when involvement is low, because such inferences will be of more cognitive ease compared with attribute-based judgments. If information about a target object is available and involvement in the judgment or decision is high, individuals are more likely to try to learn the specific attributes of the object to arrive at an overall assessment. Even under conditions of high involvement, though, category-based inference is the fallback when information about a target object is not available.

Sujan (1985) noted a third determinant of the likelihood of category-based inference: individuals' category knowledge. When knowledge of a category is high, individuals can quickly assess whether a target object fits their understanding of the category. If the object is a good match with the category, category-based inference is likely. If the object does not match well with the category, individuals tend toward attribute-based inferences. For individuals without category knowledge, however, category-based inference is always likely because they cannot assess if an object fits or does not fit a category. Consistent with Brewer (1988), in the absence of the ability to engage in attribute-based inference due to limited knowledge, and accordingly, low involvement, inferences tend to be based on the category.

Although the fit between a target object and a category is an important determinant of the extent to which individuals will make inferences of the object based on the category, category membership is a powerful driver of inference of unknown information regardless of how well or poorly the object and category match (Yamauchi & Markman, 2000). Across several studies, Yamauchi and Markman (2000) asked participants to infer the missing features of an item given a category label and other features. Interestingly, results showed that even if an item is dissimilar compared with the category label given to it, category membership nevertheless drives inference. Being a category member is such a potent inferential basis because members of the category, by definition, possess properties that define the category. Accordingly, if individuals accept that an object belongs to a category, they are very likely to infer that the object possesses attribute values common to the category. Moreover, in addition to basing inference on the category to which an object belongs, once categorized, individuals tend to neglect other potential inferential inputs (B. H. Ross & Murphy, 1996).

Yamauchi and Markman's (2000) results have important implications for marketers launching new products. Even if a new product is not a great logical fit with a parent brand category, attributes of the category will nevertheless be used in inference. Thus, although some academic authors and practitioners have wisely cautioned against the risks of pursuing a brand extension strategy if there is not a good logical fit between the parent brand and the extension, it seems that the way consumers use categories in inference when information is unknown provides some latitude for marketers to leverage categorical inference for less than perfect correspondence between a parent brand and a proposed extension. As an example, consider the "Branded House" strategy pursued by Virgin, which affixes its corporate brand to entities as diverse as health care, travel, finance, and hospitality. Although the industries are quite different, the core associations that Virgin has built are used by consumers as they infer the quality of the services they will receive.

We need to close this section with a caveat. Earlier we discussed how an attribute such as organic can drive halo effects in attribute-based inference. It is important to emphasize that some inferential cues can serve multiple roles. As we discussed, "organic" can act as an inferential cue because it is an attribute that is perceived to be correlated with other attributes. However, the line between attribute- and category-based processing gets a little fuzzy here because organic in many consumers' minds is a category that subsumes product types. Thus, if a consumer learns that a product is organic, their beliefs about the organic category, versus what organic means as an attribute for a given product, may drive inference. Conversely, as we discussed earlier, Li and Wyer (1994) demonstrated that what is often a category can serve as an attribute when certain conditions hold. Thus, it is important for the researcher as well as the practitioner to consider what role a given feature will play in inferences of unknown information about a target object.

Inferences Based on Schemas

The concept of schemas has a rich history in social psychology and is used to describe mental structures that help individuals organize their understanding of people, entities, and events (Fiske & Taylor, 2021). Suppose an individual has categorized some entity (defined broadly). If they have an extant schema for that entity, the schema may dictate expectations for attributes about or actions relating to the entity. For example, many individuals share a schema for the action of going to a movie. The schema suggests ideas and occurrences that are true for the typical movie attendance experience. Thus, the ideas that a choice to go to a movie is made in the service of recreation and fun, as well as expected subbehaviors like buying a ticket, going to the concession area, and so on, would be contained in the movie-going schema. If one hears from a friend that they went to a movie, expectations about the experience driven by one's schema may both guide processing and interpretation of incoming stimuli (what one hears from the friend), as well as filling in information missing from the story.

Given the importance of consumption phenomena in individuals' lives, it is unsurprising that consumers may have a host of schemas that may drive their processing of consumption-related entities and events. As an example of a potent schema about business that drives inferential processes, consider the idea of a successful firm. The content of the schema of a successful firm involves the attributes of the firm, its activities, its communications, and its products (Kirmani & Wright, 1989; Posavac et al., 2010).

In a set of experiments, Posavac et al. (2010) demonstrated that whether the "successful firm" schema was activated or not had important downstream implications for inferences consumers drew about a firm's communications and products. Specifically, participants read about various products across experiments such as a prescription drug, a three-dimensional TV, and a cellphone, as well as information about the manufacturing firm. Information that the firm was successful based on profitability was either present or not present in the descriptions of the products. When the successful firm schema was active, participants' inferences of the manufacturing firm were more favorable, advertising was perceived as more credible, and more favorable product inferences were formed, which ultimately led to stronger purchase intentions. In sum, the contents of consumers' schemas for a successful firm powerfully drove their inferences on multiple levels, which in turn affected choice intent.

A related schematic inference process was demonstrated by Kirmani and Wright (1989), who reported that product quality is inferred to be higher when the manufacturing firm engages in heavy advertising. As with Posavac et al.'s (2010) studies, the if-then linkage in this case is based on the schema of successful firms; firms with good products are successful, and firms with good products are sufficiently confident to engage in more advertising of those products. Thus, consumers perceive that if a product is being heavily advertised, then it must be a good product. Going forward, we suggest that there are ample opportunities for researchers to delineate consumption-relevant schemas and explore their inferential implications.

SUMMARY

People find it surprisingly difficult to detect, interpret, evaluate, and integrate omissions in attention, learning, memory, judgment, and decision making. Although omission neglect is the default process, sensitivity to omissions can increase when analytic processing is likely, which can be due to omission cuing, high levels of prior objective knowledge (Sanbonmatsu et al., 1991, 1992, 1997, 2003, 2012), low levels of cognitive load (Sanbonmatsu et al., 1994), or low construal levels (Pfeiffer et al., 2014). Comparative processing can also increase sensitivity to omissions by revealing nonalignable differences between alternatives (Kardes & Sanbonmatsu, 1993; Muthukrishnan & Ramaswami, 1999). Recent research suggests that positive affect can also increase sensitivity to omissions by increasing cognitive flexibility (Mantel et al., 2020). Debiasing techniques, such as a priori ratings of presented and omitted attributes (Kardes et al., 2006), a priori criteria consideration (Kardes et al., 2006), consider-the-unknown technique (Walters et al., 2016), the feeling of not knowing it all (Yang et al., 2019), and the distrust mindset (Gaffney et al., 2020), also improve judgment by increasing sensitivity to omissions. When omissions are detected, consumers attempt to fill gaps in knowledge by forming attribute-based, attitude-based, category-based, or schema-based inferences. Consumers generally form better judgments and decisions when they think about omissions, even though this is surprisingly difficult to do.

REFERENCES

Abraham, A., & Patro, S. (2014). "Country of origin" effect and consumer decision making. *Management and Labour Studies*, *39*(3), 309–318. https://doi.org/10.1177/0258042X15572408

Adina, C., Gabriela, C., & Roxana-Denisa, S. (2015). Country-of-origin effects on perceived brand positioning. *Procedia Economics and Finance*, *23*, 422–427. https://doi.org/10.1016/S2212-5671(15)00383-4

Anderson, N. H. (1981). *Foundations of information integration theory*. Academic Press.

Andrews, J. C., Netemeyer, R. G., & Burton, S. (1998). Consumer generalization of nutrient content claims in advertising. *Journal of Marketing*, *62*(4), 62–75. https://doi.org/10.1177/002224299806200405

Asch, S. E. (1946). Forming impressions of personality. *Journal of Abnormal and Social Psychology*, *41*(3), 258–290. https://doi.org/10.1037/h0055756

Beckwith, N. E., & Lehmann, D. R. (1975). The importance of halo effects in multi-attribute models. *Journal of Marketing Research*, *12*(3), 265–275. https://doi.org/10.1177/002224377501200302

Brenner, L. A., Koehler, D. J., & Tversky, A. (1996). On the evaluation of one-sided evidence. *Journal of Behavioral Decision Making*, *9*(1), 59–70. https://doi.org/10.1002/(SICI)1099-0771(199603)9:1<59::AID-BDM216>3.0.CO;2-V

Brewer, M. (1988). A dual process model of impression formation. In T. K. Srull & R. S. Wyer (Eds.), *Advances in social cognition* (Vol. 1, pp. 1–36). Lawrence Erlbaum Associates, Inc.

Broniarczyk, S. M., & Alba, J. W. (1994). The role of consumers' intuitions in inference making. *Journal of Consumer Research*, *21*(3), 393–407. https://doi.org/10.1086/209406

Caputo, D., & Dunning, D. (2005). What you don't know: The role played by errors of omission in imperfect self-assessments. *Journal of Experimental Social Psychology*, *41*(5), 488–505. https://doi.org/10.1016/j.jesp.2004.09.006

Cialdini, R. B., Levy, A., Herman, C. P., & Evenbeck, S. (1973). Attitudinal politics: The strategy of moderation. *Journal of Personality and Social Psychology*, *25*(1), 100–108. https://doi.org/10.1037/h0034265

Cronley, M. L., Posavac, S. S., Meyer, T., Kardes, F. R., & Kellaris, J. J. (2005). A selective hypothesis testing perspective on price-quality inference and inference-based choice. *Journal of Consumer Psychology*, *15*(2), 159–169. https://doi.org/10.1207/s15327663jcp1502_8

Cushman, F., Young, L., & Hauser, M. (2006). The role of conscious reasoning and intuition in moral judgment: Testing three principles of harm. *Psychological Science*, *17*(12), 1082–1089. https://doi.org/10.1111/j.1467-9280.2006.01834.x

Deval, H., Mantel, S. P., Kardes, F. R., & Posavac, S. S. (2013). How naïve theories drive opposing inferences from the same information. *Journal of Consumer Research*, *39*(6), 1185–1201. https://doi.org/10.1086/668086

Dick, A., Chakravarti, D., & Biehal, G. (1990). Memory-based inferences during consumer choice. *Journal of Consumer Research*, *17*(1), 82–93. https://doi.org/10.1086/208539

Dion, K., Berscheid, E., & Walster, E. (1972). What is beautiful is good. *Journal of Personality and Social Psychology, 24*(3), 285–290. https://doi.org/10.1037/h0033731

Fernbach, P. M., Light, N., Scott, S. E., Inbar, Y., & Rozin, P. (2019). Extreme opponents of genetically modified foods know the least but think they know the most. *Nature Human Behaviour, 3*(3), 251–256. https://doi.org/10.1038/s41562-018-0520-3

Fernbach, P. M., Rogers, T., Fox, C. R., & Sloman, S. A. (2013). Political extremism is supported by an illusion of understanding. *Psychological Science, 24*(6), 939–946. https://doi.org/10.1177/0956797612464058

Fernbach, P. M., Sloman, S. A., Louis, R. S., & Shube, J. N. (2012). Explanation fiends and foes: How mechanistic detail determines understanding and preference. *Journal of Consumer Research, 39*(5), 1115–1131. https://doi.org/10.1086/667782

Fisher, M., Goddu, M. K., & Keil, F. C. (2015). Searching for explanations: How the internet inflates estimates of internal knowledge. *Journal of Experimental Psychology: General, 144*(3), 674–687. https://doi.org/10.1037/xge0000070

Fiske, S. T., & Pavelchak, M. A. (1986). Category-based vs. piecemeal-based affective responses: Developments in schema-triggered affect. In R. M. Sorrentino & E. T. Higgins (Eds.), *Handbook of motivation and cognition* (pp. 167–203). Guilford Press.

Fiske, S. T., & Taylor, S. E. (2021). *Social cognition: From brains to culture* (4th ed.). Sage.

Fox, C. R., & Ülkümen, G. (2011). Distinguishing two dimensions of uncertainty. In W. Brun, G. Keren, G. Kirkebøen, & H. Montgomery (Eds.), *Perspectives on thinking, judging, and decision making* (pp. 21–35). Universitetsforlaget.

Fox, C. R., & Weber, M. (2002). Ambiguity aversion, comparative ignorance, and decision context. *Organizational Behavior and Human Decision Processes, 88*(1), 476–498. https://doi.org/10.1006/obhd.2001.2990

Gaffney, D. R., Neybert, E., Kardes, F. R., & Wyer, R. S., Jr. (2020). *The veil of trust: How trust conceals the truth* [Unpublished manuscript]. University of Cincinnati.

Griffin, D., & Tversky, A. (1992). The weighing of evidence and the determinants of confidence. *Cognitive Psychology, 24*(3), 411–435. https://doi.org/10.1016/0010-0285(92)90013-R

Gunasti, K., & Ross, W. T. (2009). How inferences about missing attributes decrease the tendency to defer choice and increase purchase probability. *Journal of Consumer Research, 35*(5), 823–837. https://doi.org/10.1086/593684

Haws, K. L., Reczek, R. W., & Sample, K. L. (2017). Healthy diets make empty wallets: The healthy = expensive intuition. *Journal of Consumer Research, 43*(6), 992–1007. https://doi.org/10.1093/jcr/ucw078

Heath, C., & Tversky, A. (1991). Preference and belief: Ambiguity and competence in choice under uncertainty. *Journal of Risk and Uncertainty, 4*, 5–28. https://doi.org/10.1007/BF00057884

Hernandez, J. M. C., Han, X., & Kardes, F. R. (2014). Effects of the perceived diagnosticity of presented attribute and brand name information on sensitivity to missing information. *Journal of Business Research, 67*(5), 874–881. https://doi.org/10.1016/j.jbusres.2013.07.006

Hong, S. T., & Wyer, R. S., Jr. (1990). Determinants of product evaluation: Effects of the time interval between knowledge of a product's country of origin and information about its specific attributes. *Journal of Consumer Research, 17*(3), 277–288. https://doi.org/10.1086/208557

Houghton, D. C., Kardes, F. R., Sanbonmatsu, D. M., Ho, E. A., & Posavac, S. S. (1998). The role of conversational norms and sensitivity to omissions in judgment based on limited evidence. In J. W. Alba & J. W. Hutchinson (Eds.), *NA - Advances in consumer research* (Vol. 25, pp. 146–150). Association for Consumer Research.

Ifrah, G. (1985). *From one to zero: A universal history of numbers*. Viking.

Janiszewski, C., & Lichtenstein, D. R. (1999). A range theory account of price perception. *Journal of Consumer Research, 25*(4), 353–368. https://doi.org/10.1086/209544

Kahneman, D. (2010). *Thinking, fast and slow*. Farrar, Straus and Giroux.

Kapoor, H., & Heslop, L. A. (2009). Brand positivity and competitive effects on the evaluation of brand extensions. *International Journal of Research in Marketing, 26*(3), 228–237. https://doi.org/10.1016/j.ijresmar.2009.05.001

Kardes, F. R., & Allen, C. T. (1991). Perceived variability and inferences about brand extensions. In R. H. Holman & M. R. Solomon (Eds.), *NA - Advances in consumer research* (Vol. 18, pp. 392–398). Association for Consumer Research.

Kardes, F. R., Cronley, M. L., Kellaris, J. J., & Posavac, S. S. (2004). The role of selective information processing in price-quality inference. *Journal of Consumer Research, 31*(2), 368–374. https://doi.org/10.1086/422115

Kardes, F. R., Posavac, S. S., & Cronley, M. L. (2004). Consumer inference: A review of processes, bases, and judgment contexts. *Journal of Consumer*

Psychology, 14(3), 230–256. https://doi.org/10.1207/s15327663jcp1403_6

Kardes, F. R., Posavac, S. S., Silvera, D., Cronley, M. L., Sanbonmatsu, D. M., Schertzer, S., Miller, F., Herr, P. M., & Chandrashekaran, M. (2006). Debiasing omission neglect. *Journal of Business Research, 59*(6), 786–792. https://doi.org/10.1016/j.jbusres.2006.01.016

Kardes, F. R., & Sanbonmatsu, D. M. (1993). Direction of comparison, expected feature correlation, and the set-size effect in preference judgment. *Journal of Consumer Psychology, 2*(1), 39–54. https://doi.org/10.1016/S1057-7408(08)80074-5

Kardes, F. R., & Sanbonmatsu, D. M. (2003). Omission neglect: The importance of missing information. *Skeptical Inquirer, 27*(2), 42–46. https://skepticalinquirer.org/2003/03/omission-neglect-the-importance-of-missing-information/

Kardes, F. R., & Wyer, R. S. (2013). Consumer information processing. In D. E. Carlston (Ed.), *The Oxford handbook of social cognition* (pp. 806–828). Oxford University Press.

Kirmani, A., & Wright, P. (1989). Money talks: Perceived advertising expense and expected product quality. *Journal of Consumer Research, 16*(3), 344–353. https://doi.org/10.1086/209220

Kivetz, R., & Simonson, I. (2000). The effects of incomplete information on consumer choice. *Journal of Marketing Research, 37*(4), 427–448. https://doi.org/10.1509/jmkr.37.4.427.18796

Lerner, J. S., & Tetlock, P. E. (1999). Accounting for the effects of accountability. *Psychological Bulletin, 125*(2), 255–275. https://doi.org/10.1037/0033-2909.125.2.255

Li, W. K., & Wyer, R. S. (1994). The role of country of origin is product evaluations: Informational and standard of comparison effects. *Journal of Consumer Psychology, 3*(2), 187–212. https://doi.org/10.1016/S1057-7408(08)80004-6

Loken, B., Barsalou, L. W., & Joiner, C. (2008). Categorization theory and research in consumer psychology: Category representation and category-based inference. In C. P. Haugtvedt, P. M. Herr, & F. R. Kardes (Eds.), *Handbook of consumer psychology* (pp. 133–163). Lawrence Erlbaum Associates.

Mantel, S. P., Montag-Smith, T., & Kardes, F. R. (2020). *Malleable effects of positive affect on cognitive flexibility and omission neglect* [Unpublished manuscript]. University of Cincinnati.

Markman, A. B., & Loewenstein, J. (2010). Structural comparison and consumer choice. *Journal of Consumer Psychology, 20*(2), 126–137. https://doi.org/10.1016/j.jcps.2010.01.002

Meyer, R. J. (1981). A model of multiattribute judgments under attribute uncertainty and informational constraint. *Journal of Marketing Research, 18*(4), 428–441. https://doi.org/10.2307/3151336

Mill, J. S. (1887). *A system of logic.* Harper & Brothers.

Muthukrishnan, A. V., & Ramaswami, S. (1999). Contextual effects on the revision of evaluative judgments: An extension of the omission-detection framework. *Journal of Consumer Research, 26*(1), 70–84. https://doi.org/10.1086/209551

Nelson, P. (1999). Multiattribute utility models. In P. E. Earl & S. Kemp (Eds.), *Consumer research and economic psychology* (pp. 392–400). Elgar.

Newman, J., Wolff, W. T., & Hearst, E. (1980). The feature-positive effect in adult human subjects. *Journal of Experimental Psychology: Human Learning and Memory, 6*(5), 630–650. https://doi.org/10.1037/0278-7393.6.5.630

Nisbett, R. E., & Wilson, T. D. (1977). The halo effect: Evidence for unconscious alteration of judgments. *Journal of Personality and Social Psychology, 35*(4), 250–256. https://doi.org/10.1037/0022-3514.35.4.250

Park, S. B., & Park, D. H. (2013). The effect of low versus high variance in product reviews on product evaluation. *Psychology and Marketing, 30*(7), 543–554. https://doi.org/10.1002/mar.20626

Pfeiffer, B. E., Deval, H., Kardes, F. R., Ewing, D. R., Han, X., & Cronley, M. L. (2014). Effects of construal level on omission detection and multiattribute evaluation. *Psychology and Marketing, 31*(11), 992–1007. https://doi.org/10.1002/mar.20748

Piaget, J. (1972). *The psychology of intelligence.* Littlefield, Adams.

Posavac, S. S., Herzenstein, M., Kardes, F. R., & Sundaram, S. (2010). Profits and halos: The role of firm profitability information in consumer inference. *Journal of Consumer Psychology, 20*(3), 327–337. https://doi.org/10.1016/j.jcps.2010.06.020

Raghunathan, R., Naylor, R. W., & Hoyer, W. D. (2006). The unhealthy = tasty intuition and its effects of taste inferences, enjoyment, and choice of food products. *Journal of Marketing, 70*(4), 170–184. https://doi.org/10.1509/jmkg.70.4.170

Ritov, I., & Baron, J. (1990). Reluctance to vaccinate: Omission bias and ambiguity. *Journal of Behavioral Decision Making, 3*(4), 263–277. https://doi.org/10.1002/bdm.3960030404

Ritov, I., & Baron, J. (1992). Status-quo and omission bias. *Journal of Risk and Uncertainty, 5*(1), 49–61. https://doi.org/10.1007/BF00208786

Ritov, I., & Baron, J. (1999). Protected values and omission bias. *Organizational Behavior and Human Decision Processes, 79*(2), 79–94. https://doi.org/10.1006/obhd.1999.2839

Ross, B. H., & Murphy, G. L. (1996). Category-based predictions: Influence of uncertainty and feature associations. *Journal of Experimental Psychology: Learning, Memory, and Cognition, 22*(3), 736–753. https://doi.org/10.1037/0278-7393.22.3.736

Ross, L. (1977). The intuitive psychologist and his shortcomings: Distortions in the attribution process. *Advances in Experimental Social Psychology, 10*, 174–214. https://doi.org/10.1016/S0065-2601(08)60357-3

Rozenblit, L., & Keil, F. (2002). The misunderstood limits of folk science: An illusion of explanatory depth. *Cognitive Science, 26*(5), 521–562. https://doi.org/10.1016/S0364-0213(02)00078-2

Russo, J. E., & Kolzow, K. J. (1994). Where is the fault in fault trees? *Journal of Experimental Psychology: Human Perception and Performance, 20*(1), 17–32. https://doi.org/10.1037/0096-1523.20.1.17

Sah, S., & Read, D. (2020). Mind the (information) gap: Strategic nondisclosure by marketers and interventions to increase consumer deliberation. *Journal of Experimental Psychology: Applied, 26*(3), 432–452. https://doi.org/10.1037/xap0000260

Sanbonmatsu, D. M., Kardes, F. R., & Herr, P. M. (1992). The role of prior knowledge and missing information in multiattribute evaluation. *Organizational Behavior and Human Decision Processes, 51*(1), 76–91. https://doi.org/10.1016/0749-5978(92)90005-R

Sanbonmatsu, D. M., Kardes, F. R., Houghton, D. C., Ho, E. A., & Posavac, S. S. (2003). Overestimating the importance of the given information in multiattribute consumer judgment. *Journal of Consumer Psychology, 13*(3), 289–300. https://doi.org/10.1207/S15327663JCP1303_10

Sanbonmatsu, D. M., Kardes, F. R., Posavac, S. S., & Houghton, D. C. (1997). Contextual influences on judgment based on limited information. *Organizational Behavior and Human Decision Processes, 69*(3), 251–264. https://doi.org/10.1006/obhd.1997.2686

Sanbonmatsu, D. M., Kardes, F. R., & Sansone, C. (1991). Remembering less and inferring more: Effects of time of judgment on inferences about unknown attributes. *Journal of Personality and Social Psychology, 61*(4), 546–554. https://doi.org/10.1037/0022-3514.61.4.546

Sanbonmatsu, D. M., Mazur, D., Pfeiffer, B. E., Kardes, F. R., & Posavac, S. S. (2012). The less the public knows the better? The effects of increased knowledge on celebrity evaluations. *Basic and Applied Social Psychology, 34*(6), 499–507. https://doi.org/10.1080/01973533.2012.728408

Sanbonmatsu, D. M., Shavitt, S., & Gibson, B. D. (1994). Salience, set size, and illusory correlation: Making moderate assumptions about extreme targets. *Journal of Personality and Social Psychology, 66*(6), 1020–1033. https://doi.org/10.1037/0022-3514.66.6.1020

Schuldt, J. P., Muller, D., & Schwarz, N. (2012). The "fair trade" effect: Health halos from social ethics claims. *Social Psychological & Personality Science, 3*(5), 581–589. https://doi.org/10.1177/1948550611431643

Schuldt, J. P., & Schwarz, N. (2010). The "organic" path to obesity? Organic claims influence calorie judgments and exercise recommendations. *Judgment and Decision Making, 5*(3), 144–150.

Schwarz, N. (1996). *Cognition and communication: Judgmental biases, research methods, and the logic of conversation*. Lawrence Erlbaum Associates, Inc.

Shafir, E., Simonson, I., & Tversky, A. (1993). Reason-based choice. *Cognition, 49*(1–2), 11–36. https://doi.org/10.1016/0010-0277(93)90034-S

Sloman, S., & Fernbach, P. (2018). *The knowledge illusion: Why we never think alone*. Penguin.

Slovic, P., & MacPhillamy, D. (1974). Dimensional commensurability and cue utilization in comparative choice. *Organizational Behavior and Human Performance, 11*(2), 179–194. https://doi.org/10.1016/0030-5073(74)90013-0

Spranca, M., Minsk, E., & Baron, J. (1991). Omission and commission in judgment and choice. *Journal of Experimental Social Psychology, 27*(1), 76–105. https://doi.org/10.1016/0022-1031(91)90011-T

Sujan, M. (1985). Consumer knowledge: Effects on evaluation processes mediating consumer judgments. *Journal of Consumer Research, 12*(1), 31–46. https://doi.org/10.1086/209033

Sundar, A., & Kardes, F. R. (2015). The role of perceived variability and the health halo effect in nutritional inference and consumption. *Psychology and Marketing, 32*(5), 512–521. https://doi.org/10.1002/mar.20796

Treisman, A., & Souther, J. (1985). Search asymmetry: A diagnostic for preattentive processing of separable features. *Journal of Experimental Psychology: General, 114*(3), 285–310. https://doi.org/10.1037/0096-3445.114.3.285

Trope, Y., & Liberman, N. (2010). Construal-level theory of psychological distance. *Psychological Review, 117*(2), 440–463. https://doi.org/10.1037/a0018963

Walters, D. J., Fernbach, P. M., Fox, C. R., & Sloman, S. A. (2016). Known unknowns: A critical determinant of confidence and calibration. *Management Science, 63*(12), 4298–4307. https://doi.org/10.1287/mnsc.2016.2580

Walters, D. J., & Hershfield, H. E. (2020). Consumers make different inferences and choices when product uncertainty is attributed to forgetting rather than ignorance. *Journal of Consumer Research, 47*(1), 56–78. https://doi.org/10.1093/jcr/ucz053

Wu, R. (2019). *Omission neglect: The effects of knowledge and disfluency* [Unpublished dissertation]. University of Cincinnati.

Wu, R., Shah, E. D., & Kardes, F. R. (2019). *Disfluency diminishes omission neglect* [Unpublished manuscript]. University of Cincinnati.

Wyer, R. S., Jr. (2004). *Social comprehension and judgment: The role of situation models, narratives, and implicit theories.* Lawrence Erlbaum Associates, Inc.

Yamauchi, T., & Markman, A. B. (2000). Inference using categories. *Journal of Experimental Psychology: Learning, Memory, and Cognition, 26*(3), 776–795. https://doi.org/10.1037/0278-7393.26.3.776

Yang, H., Carmon, Z., Ariely, D., & Norton, M. I. (2019). The feeling of not knowing it all. *Journal of Consumer Psychology, 29*(3), 455–462. https://doi.org/10.1002/jcpy.1089

CHAPTER 24

THREE MECHANISMS OF MIND–BODY INFLUENCE: FEELINGS, CONCEPTS, AND PROCEDURES

Spike W. S. Lee and Lorenzo Cecutti

In Lewis Carroll's novel *Alice's Adventures in Wonderland*, the Cheshire Cat's body disappears from time to time. It is a convenient feature that we humans do not have. Our body is always with us. Despite its constant companionship, "the philosophical and religious tradition . . . cast the body in an inferior and objectified position relative to the disembodied soul, mind, and consciousness" (Falk, 2001, para. 14), a tendency noted by Nietzsche and challenged by Freud and Merleau-Ponty. Behavioral sciences, including consumer psychology, share this tendency to focus on the mind and leave the body in the dark, as if the latter were irrelevant or insignificant to a full understanding of human behavior.

But the field has taken a turn in the past 15 years. Accumulating evidence indicates that bodily processes exert predictable influence on consumers' feelings, judgments, and behaviors, and vice versa. For example, putting people in a warm environment increases their feelings of physical warmth and belief in global warming (for both liberals and conservatives; Risen & Critcher, 2011). Smelling something fishy, which is metaphorically associated with the concept of suspicion, decreases people's investment in trust-based economic games (S. W. S. Lee & Schwarz, 2012). Beyond sensory experiences, motor procedures such as discarding a piece of paper (Briñol et al., 2013) or enclosing it in an envelope (X. Li et al., 2010) not only physically separate that object from a person's body but also psychologically separate it from their self, such that their attitudes and emotions are less influenced by information on the discarded or enclosed paper.

Inspired by findings of this sort, our chapter seeks to direct the spotlight to various modalities of the body and their tractable interplay with mental processes. In so doing, we address a few broad questions:

- What versions of mind–body influence exist? Which versions are more controversial and which less so? What is their overall theoretical significance?
- What are the major theoretical frameworks that describe and explain mind–body influence? What are their strengths and weaknesses?
- What mechanisms underlie mind–body influence? How do they operate? What are their conditions? What predictions do they make?
- What are some exciting future directions?

We review illustrative work, mostly experimental, that provides causal evidence. While bidirectional causality is generally observed between mental and bodily processes (S. W. S. Lee & Schwarz, 2012), we devote more space to effects of bodily processes on mental ones because they pertain to the more stirring claim that the body influences the mind. The primary goal of this chapter, however, is not to provide a comprehensive review of findings but to offer a theoretical treatment and a multiprocess model. We submit that three proximate mechanisms underlie mind–body influence: feelings, concepts, and procedures. They can interact (e.g., feelings triggered by concepts), but they can also operate in tandem. By unpacking these mechanisms, we hope to facilitate empirical and theoretical advances.

WHAT IS MIND–BODY INFLUENCE, AND WHY DOES IT MATTER?

A proper understanding of mind–body influence requires us to be clear about what we mean by mind and body, what exactly are the kinds of influence that exist between them, and why such influence deserves scientific and philosophical recognition.

Definitions

The *Oxford English Dictionary* (n.d.) defines *body* as "the physical form of a person, animal, or plant." The human physical form affords sensory (e.g., touch, taste, smell, sound, sight), motor (e.g., gesture, posture, locomotion), and interoceptive capacities (e.g., hunger, thirst, muscle tension). These capacities underlie a person's bodily states and action in a present situation ("online experience"); they also support multimodal simulation (i.e., the brain's reenactment) of sensory, motor, and introspective experience acquired in prior situations ("offline experience"; Barsalou, 2008). We refer to this constellation of entities as body. Wherever necessary, we specify which entity is the most relevant to a theory or finding.

Paralleling the multiplicity of meanings of body, the term *mind*, according to the American Psychological Association's *APA Dictionary of Psychology* (n.d.), refers to multiple mental processes and outcomes, from emotion and motivation to perception and memory to knowledge and reasoning. As such, mind–body influence covers a variety of directional links between both sides. Some of these links are widely accepted; others are more controversial. A brief survey of them will provide the intellectual backdrop against which the significance of mind–body influence can be better appreciated.

Different Kinds of Mind–Body Influence

That emotional and motivational processes involve changes in bodily states is obvious and uncontroversial. For example, anger involves heightening of physiological arousal (James, 1890; Russell, 2003) and contraction of certain facial muscles (Ekman et al., 1972). Also mainstream is the converse idea that changes in bodily states influence one's attitude and evaluation (Cacioppo et al., 1993; Centerbar & Clore, 2006) and one's perception and comprehension of emotional information (for reviews, see Niedenthal, 2007; Niedenthal et al., 2005). Such influences have been observed in lab as well as naturalistic conditions. For example, cosmetic use of Botox, which blocks the facial muscles used in frowning, selectively undermines the efficiency of processing sentences that evoke emotions typically expressed by frowning (anger and sadness) without altering the processing of sentences that evoke another emotion typically not expressed by frowning (happiness; Havas et al., 2010).

Unlike emotion and motivation, whose ties to the body seem clear, cognition has traditionally (i.e., since the cognitive revolution in the 1960s) been regarded as phenomena within the brain but not beyond. Sure, thoughts can direct motor action and inform sensory experience, but the latter were ascribed no causal role in cognitive functioning. It is against this intellectual backdrop that the idea of bodily influence on cognition has stirred controversy. This idea, commonly known as *embodied cognition*, is actually not a singular claim but a collection of at least six views that are closely aligned with but conceptually distinguishable from each other (M. Wilson, 2002). Of the six views (see the Appendix at the end of this chapter for a summary), two appear most resonant with consumer and social psychologists' use of the term *embodied cognition*.

One view emphasizes that cognitive processes do not occur in a vacuum but are situated in dynamic, constantly changing real-world contexts. The body's sensorimotor capacities are necessary to perceive and act on these contexts. The constantly changing perceptual inputs and motor outputs are inseparable from and inherent to cognitive functioning (Beer, 2000; Chiel & Beer, 1997).

Another view highlights that offline cognitive processes, like online ones, can be body-based: "Mental structures that originally evolved for perception or action appear to be co-opted and run 'offline,' decoupled from the physical inputs and outputs that were their original purpose, to assist in thinking and knowing" (M. Wilson, 2002, p. 633). For example, we can move our fingers to facilitate counting, but we are also capable of mentally running a sensorimotor simulation of finger movements to attain the same goal. Even more subtly, the motor program responsible for finger movements may be covertly activated in the brain without resulting in any overt movement or conscious simulation, while still facilitating counting. These basic attributes of being offline and body based are observed in a number of fundamental cognitive activities that serve to represent information and draw inferences from it, such as mental imagery (Kosslyn, 1994; Parsons et al., 1995; Reisberg, 1992), working memory (Baddeley & Hitch, 1974), episodic memory, implicit memory (N. J. Cohen et al., 1985; Johnston et al., 1985), reasoning, and problem solving (Glenberg & Robertson, 1999, 2000).

These two views, with their strong focus on the body and sensorimotor simulation, are particularly compatible with consumer and social psychologists' recent wave of interest in a diverse range of phenomena under the label of embodied cognition. The theoretical stance of embodied cognition and the research it has inspired have broad implications for cognitive science and philosophy of mind.

Theoretical Significance of Embodied Cognition

From the perspective of scientific comprehensiveness, researchers' tendency to focus on processes in the head without taking bodily states or cues of the physical environment into account implies that some of the influences on mental processes and outcomes, including those that matter in consumer contexts (e.g., product evaluation, decision making), are not being captured. It limits the comprehensiveness of our description, explanation, and prediction of the mind and our ability to influence it. In fact, from James to Piaget to Bruner, the history of psychology features a rich tradition of analyzing the interplay between mental and bodily processes. Ignoring such interplay runs the risk of satisficing ourselves with contrived models of how the mind works.

From the perspective of philosophy of mind, embodied cognition provides a direct response to the symbol grounding problem (Harnad, 1990). Language is symbolic. The sound, shape, and spelling of a word bear symbolic, abstract relations to its referents in reality. The same referent (e.g., an apple) can be denoted by different symbols in different languages ("apple" in English, "pomme" in French, "ping4 gwo2" in Cantonese). For words in a language to have meaning, they have to ultimately refer to something in reality, be it tangible or intangible. They cannot merely refer to other words, for that would constitute a merry-go-round from one meaningless symbol to another. For words to be meaningful, they have to be grounded in something other than just more meaningless symbols. That is the symbol grounding problem.

How does embodied cognition resolve this problem? It posits that abstract symbols are ultimately grounded in physical reality, which we experience and act upon via our body's sensorimotor modalities. Meanings are acquired through modality-based experiences and actions as well as scaffolded through additional mechanisms such as conceptual metaphors (see Mechanism 2: Concepts). Meanings are thus either directly grounded in bodily experience or indirectly grounded through other symbols that are themselves grounded in bodily experience. Shedding light on how symbols may be grounded, there is neural evidence for the key assumption that mental content can be represented in sensorimotor systems, whereas there is no clear evidence for the existence of an additional layer of mental representation called amodal symbols (Barsalou, 1999). There is also behavioral evidence from social and cognitive experiments for bidirectional influence between motor experience and linguistic processing (M. Chen & Bargh, 1999; Creem & Proffitt, 2001; Glover & Dixon, 2002; Pulvermüller et al., 2005; Tucker & Ellis, 1998; Zwaan & Taylor, 2006). These findings challenge the prevailing assumption of amodal symbols since the cognitive revolution in the 1960s and favor the stance of embodied cognition.

An implication of embodied cognition—one that has particularly drawn researchers' attention—is that bodily processes predictably influence mental ones. A multitude of body-to-mind effects has been observed. Different subsets of them are described and explained by different theories, to which we now turn.

MAJOR THEORETICAL FRAMEWORKS

Several theories are most often invoked by consumer psychologists to motivate and interpret bodily influence on mental processes. The names, basic claims, and relevant bodily processes and mental functions of these theories are summarized in Table 24.1.

Each theory has its strengths and weaknesses. Conceptual metaphors map out a full landscape of specific links between sensorimotor experience in concrete domains (e.g., cleanliness) and conceptual knowledge about and experience of abstract domains (e.g., morality). The former scaffolds the latter. The extensiveness of these links gives the theory tremendous heuristic value, as is evident from the amount of research it has inspired in fields spanning linguistics, philosophy, and psychology. At the same time, these links predict domain-specific effects (e.g., between cleanliness and morality) and cannot account for domain-general effects that are not reflected in metaphorical linguistic expressions (e.g., effects of cleanliness on decision making, risk taking, optimism, and more; S. W. S. Lee & Schwarz, 2016).

The tradition of bodily and facial feedback focuses on the embodiment of affective processes such as emotion, motivation, and attitude. It does not seek to explain nonaffective, basic cognitive operations. The somatic marker hypothesis highlights the causal role of physiological states in higher order cognitive processes such as reasoning and decision making. It does not account for lower order cognitive processes such as memory and knowledge activation. Those are the meat and potatoes of grounded cognition, which covers all aspects of cognitive functioning but tends to focus on mental processing of concrete entities (e.g., chair) rather than abstract ones (e.g., justice). Its all-encompassing nature also prioritizes explanation of general mental processes over specific mental content.

Inspired by the grand perspective of grounded cognition and the specific mappings of conceptual metaphors, the midrange theory of grounded procedures highlights the role of motor action (e.g., physical cleansing) in cognitive functioning (e.g., mental separation), resulting in predictable domain-general effects. While it emphasizes the psychological power of motor action, it does not address that of sensory perception.

All of these theories are compatible with a fundamental organizational principle of the brain called neural reuse (Anderson, 2010). According to this principle, "it is quite common for neural circuits established for one purpose to be exapted (exploited, recycled, redeployed) during evolution or normal development and put to different uses, often without losing their original functions" (Anderson, 2010, p. 245). To be clear, neural reuse is about the brain; it does not explicitly ascribe cognitive functions to the body. But by noting that brain processes recruited for evolutionarily and developmentally older uses in bodily functioning can be exapted for newer, nonbodily uses, the principle of neural reuse is well-aligned with theories of embodied cognition. And through this lens, findings of embodied cognition become less magical and more sensible.

THREE MECHANISMS

To unpack findings of embodied cognition, beyond the general principle of neural reuse, we see the need to identify proximate mental mechanisms. Interest in embodied cognition rose in the mid-2000s. Initial work consisted largely of existence proof of metaphorical effects of bodily states on mental processes. Recognizing this trend, theorists called for attention to underlying mechanisms and boundary conditions (Meier, Schnall, et al., 2012) rather than demonstration after demonstration. Some mechanisms have been discussed in particular areas of interest, such as embodied influence on metaphorical social cognition (Landau et al., 2010), on judgment and decision making

TABLE 24.1

Theories of Bodily Influence on Mental Processes

Theory	Basic claim	Entities (other than the brain) to which the theory ascribes mental functions	Typical mental functions the theory focuses on explaining
Conceptual metaphors, scaffolding (Lakoff & Johnson, 1980, 1999; Landau et al., 2010; Williams et al., 2009)	Concrete bodily experience structures and activates conceptual knowledge about abstract domains and experience of them, as reflected in linguistic metaphors.	Sensory perception, motor action	Knowledge about and experience of abstract domains
Bodily and facial feedback, embodied affect (Cacioppo et al., 1993; Niedenthal et al., 2005; Strack et al., 1988; Wells & Petty, 1980)	Motor states and proprioceptive feedback from them (e.g., gesture, posture, movement, facial expression) are causally involved in the experience/processing of affect typified by the motor states.	Motor states, proprioceptive feedback	Affect, emotion, motivation, attitude
Somatic marker hypothesis (Bechara & Damasio, 2005; Damasio, 1996)	Marker signals arising in bioregulatory processes (e.g., in feelings) are causally involved in reasoning and decision making.	Physiological states	Reasoning, decision making
Grounded cognition (Barsalou, 1999, 2008; Glenberg & Kaschak, 2002)	Bodily states, situated action, and modal simulations implement a fully functional cognitive system (e.g., thought, knowledge, memory, language).	Sensory states, motor action	Knowledge, memory, and language about concrete domains
Grounded procedures (S. W. S. Lee & Schwarz, 2021)	Motor action functions as bodily procedures that structure and activate mental procedures applicable across content domains.	Motor action	Processing of concrete and abstract domains

Note. Different theories highlight different bodily and mental processes. On the bodily side, some theories broadly encompass all sorts of bodily experience or states, or even simulations of these states by sensorimotor modalities in the brain. Other theories focus on more specific aspects, such as motor states and proprioceptive feedback, marker signals, and motor action. On the mental side, work that draws on bodily and facial feedback, embodied affect, and somatic marker hypothesis tends to highlight the embodiment of emotion and motivation (as outlined in Different Kinds of Mind–Body Influence) and the role of feelings (see Mechanism 1). Work derived from grounded cognition tends to highlight the embodiment of cognition. Work inspired by conceptual metaphors, scaffolding, and grounded procedures tends to be broader in that it highlights the embodiment of cognition but its effects extend to experiential aspects such as emotion and motivation, often with direct relevance to social and consumer psychology. In grounded cognition, conceptual metaphors, and scaffolding, the role of concepts (Mechanism 2) is prominent. In grounded procedures, the role of motor action, or procedures (Mechanism 3), is prominent.

(S. W. S. Lee & Schwarz, 2014), and on information processing (Körner et al., 2015). Here we offer three mechanisms that underlie bodily influence on mental processes in general. They include feelings, concepts, and procedures (Figure 24.1, solid lines), with predicted moderators (top-down arrows). Other mechanisms may exist as well (dotted lines).

Each of the proposed mechanisms operates according to well-established principles. Each has received experimental support that covers a

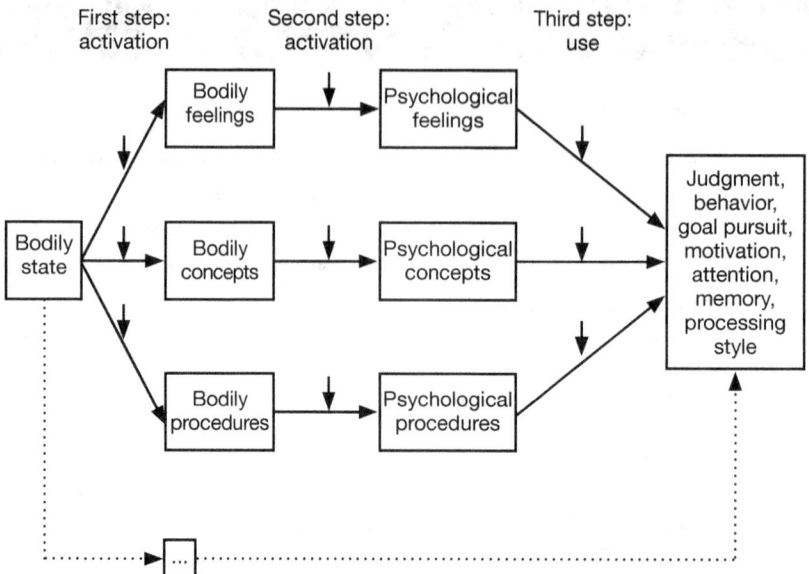

FIGURE 24.1. Examining bodily influence on mental processes through three mechanisms. Examples of bodily state are arousal, posture, facial expression, tactile sensation, and motor action. Examples of psychological feelings are specific emotions like fear, joy, pride, amusement, and anger, as well as processing fluency in motor action and sensorimotor simulation. Examples of psychological concepts are morality, importance, willpower, agreeableness, and suspicion. Examples of psychological procedures are separation and connection.

spectrum of bodily states and mental processes. For each mechanism, we articulate the principles and review relevant experimental evidence. After introducing all three mechanisms, we identify general moderators that determine their likelihood of activation and use.

Mechanism 1: Feelings

Many bodily states (e.g., physiological arousal, full-body posture) involve subjective feelings. Feelings are diverse in kind, ranging from low-level sensations ("bodily feelings" in Figure 24.1) to generic moods to specific emotions to metacognitive experiences ("psychological feelings" in Figure 24.1). All of these can influence judgments and cognitive processes according to the logic of feelings as information (Schwarz, 2012; Schwarz & Clore, 2007). Specifically, feelings can serve as a source of information in judgments. They can also inform people about the nature of their current situation (e.g., task, environment), thereby attuning their cognitive processes to the situational demands.

Feelings can provide valid information when they are elicited by the judgment target or the situation at hand. Feelings generally do not provide valid information when they are elicited by unrelated cues. But because people are often unaware of the source of their feelings, they are susceptible to the influence of even invalid and irrelevant feelings. Yet once attention is drawn and attribution made to the source of their current feeling, people often mentally correct for its influence. To illustrate these dynamics, consider first the psychological influence of physiological arousal.

Physiological arousal. Schachter and Singer's (1962) two-factor theory of emotion posited that many emotions are underlain by a general state of physiological arousal due to excitation of the sympathetic nervous system, which turns into specific emotions when labeled, interpreted, and identified by "a cognition appropriate to this state of arousal" (p. 380) in a given situation. For example, arousal experienced while seeing a person with a gun in a dark alley is labeled as fear; arousal experienced while winning a major award is labeled as joy. Their experimental work showed that extraneous arousal induced by epinephrine injection lent itself to alternative interpretations (anger or euphoria), but such malleability in interpretations was eliminated once participants received clear information about the physiological effects of epinephrine and thus had a clear attribution of their arousal.

Similar effects can result from behavioral, nonmedical inductions of arousal. In general, arousal induced in one behavioral context can be transferred to another context to exert its psychological influence. A few classic examples in social psychology attest to this point. Excitation from watching a film led to increased aggressive behavior (Zillmann, 1971). Standing on a fear-arousing suspension bridge increased men's sexual thoughts on a projective test and their tendency to contact an attractive female interviewer after the experiment, presumably due to transfer of arousal from anxiety to sexual attraction (Dutton & Aron, 1974). Arousal from cognitive dissonance (Festinger, 1957) could be induced by writing essays counter to one's initial attitude (under the condition of free choice; Linder et al., 1967; Waterman & Katkin, 1967), leading to a change in one's subsequent attitude. But once the arousal was attributed to a pill, its influence on subsequent attitude was eliminated (Zanna & Cooper, 1974), consistent with the general principles of feelings as information.

Proprioceptive feedback from posture and facial expression. Proprioceptive feedback from specific full-body postures or facial expressions can activate psychological feelings typically associated with them (Cacioppo et al., 1993), with downstream consequences for judgment and behavior. For example, adopting a slumped (as opposed to an upright) posture increased subsequent helplessness behaviors (Riskind & Gotay, 1982). Adopting an upright (as opposed to a slumped) posture strengthened feelings of pride from performing well on an achievement task (Stepper & Strack, 1993, Experiment 1). Facilitating (as opposed to inhibiting) the facial expression of a smile unobtrusively increased participants' amusement by cartoons (Strack et al., 1988; see Wagenmakers et al., 2016, for failed replications; Noah et al., 2018, for successful replications and boundary conditions).

Disrupting facial or postural feedback can interfere with their corresponding mental processes. For example, when people experience and express negative emotions, they often frown (contracting the corrugator muscle). Cosmetic use of Botox (botulinum toxin-A) paralyzes the corrugator muscle. In so doing, Botox was found to slow down comprehension of sad and angry sentences but not happy sentences (Havas et al., 2010). When people feel angry, they often exhibit approach motivation and want to take action (Carver & Harmon-Jones, 2009). A supine posture makes it difficult to take action. Accordingly, approach-motivation neural responses to anger evocation were weaker in a supine than in an upright posture (Harmon-Jones & Peterson, 2009).

When facial or postural expressions contradict mental states, a sense of incoherence results and triggers incoherence-reduction mental processes such as expansion of category boundaries. For example, category inclusiveness was higher when participants maintained a smiling face during sad recall or a frowning face during happy recall than when they maintained a smiling face during happy recall or a frowning face during sad recall (L. Huang & Galinsky, 2011, Experiments 1–2). Likewise, category inclusiveness was higher when participants maintained an expansive posture in a low-power role or a constrictive posture in a high-power role than when they maintained an expansive posture in a high-power role or a constrictive posture in a low-power role (Experiments 3–4). These experiences of mind–body incoherence are atypical in daily life. Thus, experimental instantiations of them can activate an atypicality mindset that enhances creative association, insight, and generation (L. Huang, 2019).

Even in the absence of incoherence with mental states, however, certain bodily states can generate proprioceptive signals of experiential ease or difficulty in and of themselves. For example, a light smile is typically associated with positive experiences of ease, a furrowed brow with negative experiences of difficulty. Cues of experiential ease tend to sustain or amplify the preexisting influence of recalled information on judgment, whereas cues of experiential difficulty tend to diminish or reverse it (Schwarz et al., 1991; for a review, see Schwarz, 2015). Demonstrating these principles, recall of a few behavioral episodes of high (vs. low) self-assurance led participants to judge themselves as higher on the trait of self-assurance—if they had been maintaining the facial expression of a light smile (contracting the zygomaticus muscle). But if they had been maintaining the facial expression of a furrowed brow (contracting the corrugator muscle), recall of high (vs. low) self-assurance led participants to judge themselves as *lower* on the trait of self-assurance (Stepper & Strack, 1993, Experiment 2).

While certain bodily states can generate signals of ease or difficulty, all motor actions can be performed with varying degrees of fluency, resulting in diverse effects. We turn to these now.

Fluency of motor action, motor simulation, and sensory simulation. People perform motor actions with greater ease and fluency using their dominant than nondominant hand. That means right-handers experience greater fluency in rightward space, left-handers in leftward space. Because experiential fluency generally serves as a positive signal (Schwarz & Clore, 2007), right-handers exhibit a robust tendency to associate positive ideas (e.g., intelligence, attractiveness, happiness) with rightward space and negative ideas with leftward space, whereas left-handers exhibit the opposite associations (Casasanto, 2009). As evidence that these associations are driven by motor fluency, right-handers who had a unilateral stroke that disabled their right hand would associate good with left, but those who had a stroke that disabled their left hand would associate good with right (Casasanto & Chrysikou, 2011, Study 1). Temporarily handicapping right-handers' right hand, which increased relative motor fluency with their left hand, resulted in associations of good with left, whereas temporarily handicapping their left hand resulted in associations of good with right (Study 2). Similar effects also resulted from varying degrees of motor fluency in observed actions by others (de la Fuente et al., 2015) or in imagined actions by oneself (de la Fuente et al., 2017).

The association of valence with laterality (e.g., good with right) is observed not only in explicitly performed, observed, or imagined action but also in implicitly simulated action. Visual ads depicting a product as oriented toward people's dominant (vs. nondominant) hand enhanced the ease of mentally simulating motor action for consuming the product and resulted in stronger purchase intentions (Elder & Krishna, 2012). These effects generalized across various manipulations of orientation in product depiction—a bowl of yogurt or soup with a spoon oriented to the right versus left, a burger held in the right versus left hand, a piece of cake with a fork on the right versus left, and a coffee mug with the handle on the right versus left (Experiments 1–4). Highlighting the causal role of motor simulation, if participants had to hold a clamp in their dominant hand, which occupied the manual modality needed for motor simulation, they showed the opposite effect, with stronger purchase intentions for a product depicted as oriented toward their nondominant hand (Experiment 2). If participants had to hold clamps in both hands, their purchase intention was unaffected by product orientation in its depiction. Further supporting the role of motor simulation, depicting a product as oriented toward the dominant (vs. nondominant) hand increased purchase intentions if it was a positive product, but decreased purchase intentions if it was a negative product (Experiment 3). Conceptually similar effects of motor simulation have been found across products and extended from purchase intention to product evaluation and choice (M. Chen & Lin, 2021; Eelen et al., 2013).

Paralleling the psychological effects of motor action, motor simulation, and their fluency (Körner et al., 2015) are the psychological effects of sensory states, sensory simulation, and their fluency. For example, on days that seemed warmer (as opposed to colder) than usual, participants had stronger belief in global warming, had greater concerns about it, and donated more money to a relevant charity (Y. Li et al., 2011). In contrast, unseasonably cold weather decreased belief in global warming (Schuldt & Roh, 2014). Large-scale correlational effects of local weather predicting belief in global warming have been found, particularly among people with high school education or less and people who lean Republican (Egan & Mullin, 2012). Experimentally, inductions of the sensory state of warmth increased participants' belief in global warming, an effect that was significant among both liberals and conservatives (Risen & Critcher, 2011, Experiments 1–3). It was driven by the fluency and clarity with which participants mentally simulated scenes of global warming (e.g., hot and dry deserts; Experiments 6a–6b). In short, sensory states increased beliefs in corresponding states of the world.

Summary. Across these lines of work, feelings from bodily states exert mental and behavioral influences. Physiological arousal increases psychological feelings that are typically high on arousal (e.g., euphoria, anger, aggression, sexual attraction). Attribution or misattribution of arousal changes its effects. Proprioceptive feedback from postures and facial expressions activates psychological feelings typically associated with them (e.g., helplessness, pride, amusement). Disrupting such feedback interferes with the corresponding mental processes (e.g., emotional comprehension, approach motivation). Some bodily states can generate proprioceptive signals of experiential ease (e.g., smiling) or difficulty (e.g., frowning). These feelings amplify or diminish the influence of recalled information on judgment. Feelings of ease and difficulty, or fluency and disfluency, also drive effects of motor laterality on thought valence (e.g., right-handers' association of right with good) and effects of sensory states on specific beliefs (e.g., global warming).

Mechanism 2: Concepts

A bodily state can activate concepts of directly relevant perceptual experience (sensory, proprioceptive, or introspective) and concepts of other perceptual experience commonly associated with it. For example, being in a hot room can activate the concept "hot," grounded in the sensory experience of temperature. Grasping a mug can activate the concept "grasp," grounded in the proprioceptive experience of manual action. It can activate the concept "thirst," grounded in the introspective experience of physiological need or desire. It can also activate the concepts "hot" and "coffee," which are experiences commonly associated with grasping a mug.

These examples are intuitive enough to the behaviorally and cognitively oriented. How do they operate neurally? From the perspective of grounded cognition (Barsalou, 1999, 2008), during perceptual experience, components of the full analog experience are extracted and stored by neural mechanisms (e.g., association areas in the brain). The componential patterns of neural activation can later be partially reactivated (e.g., by a bottom-up bodily state or a top-down mental goal) to implement symbolic cognitive functions (e.g., categorization, proposition). In this sense, cognitive processes are grounded in perceptual ones. The broad notion of grounding has inspired research in grounded social cognition (see Semin & Smith, 2008, for an edited book) and sensory marketing (Krishna, 2012; see Krishna et al., 2017, for an edited issue), some of which will be reviewed in this section.

Note that the proposed neural processes hinge on the initial extraction of components from perceptual experience. It is relatively easy to imagine how they work for concrete concepts such as "hot," "grasp," "thirst," and "coffee," which have clear perceptual referents in the external world that are experienced through sensorimotor modalities of the body ("bodily concepts" in Figure 24.1). But how about abstract concepts?

Some abstract concepts are associated with specific sensorimotor states, such that putting people in those states can directly activate the corresponding abstract concept (S. W. S. Lee, 2016). For example, head nodding increases agreement (Wells & Petty, 1980). Many abstract concepts, however, lack direct perceptual referents, such as truth, justice, importance, time, trust, and willpower. These are the kind of concepts that consumer and social psychologists care about. More fundamentally, humans' ability to comprehend them, apply them to specific instances, use them to guide thinking, and generate them in the first place is an impressive set of cognitive accomplishments (Bolognesi & Steen, 2018; Borghi et al., 2018; Brown, 1958; Burgoon et al., 2013; Liberman & Trope, 2008) that has to be accounted for in any comprehensive treatment of mental processes.

Grounded cognition accounts for this by assuming that abstract concepts can be represented directly in perceptual symbols (through technical mechanisms such as framing of event sequences, simulating the events, and mapping them onto perceived situations; Barsalou, 1999). These assumptions were met with immediate resistance (see commentary on Barsalou's target article). Of the various alternative perspectives, conceptual metaphor theory has garnered the most attention in consumer and social psychology.

Conceptual metaphor theory (Lakoff & Johnson, 1980, 1999) assumes that abstract concepts about psychological domains (e.g., morality, emotion, time) are structured and comprehended with the aid of concrete experiences in sensorimotor domains (e.g., cleanliness, force, space). Relative to abstract concepts, concrete ones are easier to comprehend and emerge earlier both developmentally and evolutionarily (Williams et al., 2009). Therefore, concrete domains (e.g., experience with physical objects) typically serve as a source of image schemas, motor schemas, and relational structures, which are mapped onto abstract domains (e.g., experience with nonphysical ideas) to scaffold conceptual understanding and inferences about them (e.g., treating ideas as if they were objects that can be given, taken, sold, bought, kept, lost, thrown out, bounced off). These cross-domain mappings are called conceptual metaphors. They are detectable in systematic patterns of linguistic metaphors (e.g., "let me give you a better idea," "he stole my idea," "I lost my train of thought").

The promise of conceptual metaphors is that they are not just "language-deep" (Boroditsky, 2000, p. 6) but "cognition-deep," that is, they are the mechanisms by which people conceptualize and thus experience the world. If that is the case, conceptual metaphors should be able to influence mental and behavioral outcomes even in the absence of linguistic cues. Sensorimotor cues should be able to trigger these outcomes. Indeed, research in the past 15 years has documented an impressive array of psychological consequences of conceptual metaphors. Effective nonlinguistic manipulations span all sensorimotor modalities (e.g., touch, taste, smell, sound, sight).

Touch. Of the multiple human senses, touch is the earliest to develop in a lifetime (Gallace & Spence, 2008). It plays an important role in scaffolding higher order mental content along metaphorical lines. Examples include cleanliness–morality, weight–importance, roughness–difficulty, hardness–stability, and firmness–willpower.

Following recall of one's immoral behavior, wiping one's hands clean (vs. no wiping) reduced one's immoral feelings and compensatory prosocial behavior (Zhong & Liljenquist, 2006, Experiment 4). Likewise, a manipulation of handwashing (vs. no washing) changed participants' moral sense and led them to judge others' transgressions as more wrong (Schnall, Benton, et al., 2008, Experiment 2). While some exact replications found null effects, others found positive effects (S. W. S. Lee & Schwarz, 2021). Integrating evidence from all original experiments, exact replications, and conceptual replications, a comprehensive meta-analysis (S. W. S. Lee, Chen, et al., 2020) of over 200 effects of cleansing-related manipulations (e.g., actual cleansing, simulated cleansing) on morality-related outcomes (e.g., moral judgment, moral emotion, moral behavior) estimated overall effect sizes in the small-to-medium range (J. Cohen, 1988) after taking publication bias into account. Effects were robust across manipulations, measures, and populations.

Turning to other dimensions of tactile experience, weight is metaphorically associated with abstract meanings such as importance and profundity. When participants completed a questionnaire on a heavy (vs. light) clipboard, they judged the information in the questionnaire to be more important and processed it more elaborately (Jostmann et al., 2009). Specifically, they judged foreign currencies to be worth more (Experiment 1). They considered it more important for a university committee to listen to student opinions (Experiment 2). They also showed higher correlation in substantively related judgments (Experiment 3) and greater polarization between judgments of strong versus weak arguments (Experiment 4), indicating more elaborate thinking. As a conceptual replication, shoppers carrying a heavy bag with three bottles of water (vs. empty bottles) assigned greater importance to voicing opinions in public (M. Zhang & Li, 2012, Experiment 2). The weight effect disappeared if participants had been primed with conflicting concepts (by writing down three light objects), but it remained significant if they had been primed with neutral concepts (by writing down three familiar brands). It suggests that the metaphorical effect of weight on importance is at least partly driven by the accessibility of "heavy" concepts, which is why the effect disappears when conflicting "light" concepts are made accessible.

Roughness is metaphorically associated with meanings such as difficulty and harshness. Participants who completed a puzzle with pieces covered in rough sandpaper (vs. uncovered and thus smooth) subsequently perceived an ambiguously valenced social interaction as less well-coordinated (Ackerman et al., 2010, Experiment 3). The same manipulation of roughness also increased compensatory bargaining behavior in the form of making better offers in an ultimatum game to avoid rejection (Experiment 4). Extending the basic idea, other manipulations of roughness have been shown to heighten participants' attention to others' hardship such as pain and need, thereby promoting empathy and helping behavior (C. Wang et al., 2015).

Hardness is metaphorically associated with meanings such as stability, strictness, and toughness. Participants who touched a hard block of wood (vs. a soft piece of blanket) subsequently perceived a target person described in an ambiguous social interaction as having a more rigid and strict personality (Ackerman et al., 2010, Experiment 5). Participants sitting in a hard wooden chair (vs. a soft cushioned chair) were less willing to change their financial offers to a dealer in a hypothetical car purchase situation (Experiment 6). Hardness also activates stereotypically relevant concepts. For example, squeezing a hard (vs. soft) ball and pressing hard (vs. gently) with a pen were found to increase participants' tendency to categorize gender-ambiguous faces as male rather than female (Slepian et al., 2011, Experiments 1–2), faces of politicians as Republican rather than Democrat (Slepian et al., 2012, Experiment 2), and photographs of professors as physicists rather than historians (i.e., hard science rather than soft discipline; Experiment 3).

Closely related to the tactile experience of hardness is the proprioceptive experience of firmness. A variety of muscle firming manipulations have been found to firm one's willpower in self-control situations for long-term goals (I. W. Hung & Labroo, 2011). For example, grasping a pen tightly (vs. holding it naturally) increased participants' likelihood of donation (Experiment 1). Clasping a pen tightly (vs. supporting it freely) increased participants' duration of keeping their other hand immersed in ice-cold water (Experiment 2). Stretching calf muscles (vs. no action) increased participants' consumption of a healthy but awful-tasting vinegar tonic (Experiment 3). Stretching fingers (vs. holding them naturally) increased participants' choices of healthy food at a snack bar (Experiment 4). Contracting biceps (vs. keeping them natural) increased participants' likelihood of choosing an apple over a chocolate bar (Experiment 5). These findings point to the potential utility of firming one's muscles, which can be initiated and attained at will without requiring external tools or stimuli, in self-control situations throughout daily life.

Taste. Turning from the physical sense of touch to the chemical sense of taste, metaphorical effects of sweet, spicy, and bitter tastes have been observed. Sweetness is one metaphorical descriptor of kind people ("Thanks for the gift, you're so sweet"). Supporting this conceptual association, participants perceived targets to have a more agreeable personality if the targets liked sweet food than if the targets liked bitter, salty, sour, or spicy food (Meier, Moeller, et al., 2012, Experiment 1). The effect was specific to agreeableness and did not emerge for the other personality dimensions examined (extraversion and neuroticism). Individual differences in liking for sweet food correlated with prosocial personality, intention, and behavior (Studies 2–3). As causal evidence, experimental manipulations of sweetness by tasting a sweet chocolate (vs. a sour tangerine, a water cracker, or no food) led participants to self-report higher levels of agreeableness and longer durations of volunteering to help another researcher (Experiments 4–5). These effects are mirrored in associations between preferences for sweet foods and agreeableness or prosociality in daily life (Fetterman et al., 2017). Sweetness has also been found to have linguistic, behavioral, emotional, cognitive, or neural associations with other psychological concepts, such as gratitude (Schlosser, 2015), revenge (Hellmann et al., 2013; Sjöström et al., 2018), and romance (Chan et al., 2013; Ren et al., 2015; L. Wang & Chen, 2018; L. Wang et al., 2019; Yang et al., 2019).

Inspired by the diverse metaphorical meanings of spicy, researchers have found a range of psychological effects. For example, tasting spicy (vs. nonspicy) potato chips increased variety-seeking in choosing candy bars after a time delay (Mukherjee et al., 2017, Experiment 1). The effect replicated with another manipulation (spicy vs. nonspicy candy) and paralleled the influence of semantic priming of the linguistic metaphor "variety is the spice of life" (Experiment 2), highlighting the role of metaphorical concepts. Less flattering is the metaphorical association between spicy and aggressive. Individuals who prefer spicy food tend to score higher on trait aggression (Batra et al., 2017, Study 1). Tasting a spicy (vs. nonspicy) tortilla chip or seeing images of spicy (vs. nonspicy) foods activated aggression-related concepts and increased perception of aggressive intent of a target person (Experiments 2–3).

Pitting sweet and spicy against each other in the Israeli cultural context presents a theoretically interesting case (Gilead et al., 2015). Preverbal infants prefer sweet over spicy, that is, sweet is more positive than spicy. But linguistically and metaphorically, for Israelis, sweet indicates inauthenticity, whereas spicy indicates intellectual competence, that is, spicy is more positive than sweet. If metaphorical effects of sensory experience operate through preverbal mechanisms, sweet (vs. spicy) tastes should result in more positive judgments. If they operate through linguistic concepts (cf. S. W. S. Lee & Schwarz, 2012), spicy (vs. sweet) tastes should result in more positive judgments. Empirically, tasting spicy (vs. sweet) snacks led participants to perceive a target person as more intellectually competent, less inauthentic, and more positive overall (Gilead et al., 2015), supporting the role of metaphorical concepts.

Although preverbal valence and metaphorized valence sometimes diverge (as in the case of sweet and spicy for Israelis), typically they do converge. Bitter taste, for example, is aversive. Its metaphorical meanings are also negative, a prominent one of which is disgust. The word "disgust" finds its etymological roots in the Latin *dis-* (expressing reversal) and *gustus* (meaning taste). Research has found that tasting a bitter drink, seeing photographs of contaminants, and being treated unfairly in an economic game all activated the levator labii facial muscles, which are responsible for producing an oral-nasal rejection response (Chapman et al., 2009). Directly tapping into the link between taste and morality, drinking Swedish Bitters (vs. the sweet Minute Maid Berry Punch or plain water) led to harsher judgments of moral violations, especially among political conservatives (Eskine et al., 2011). These results suggest a link between gustatory distaste and moral disgust.

Metaphorical meanings of bitter extend beyond the moral realm though. For example, bitter enemies are characterized by hostility and antipathy. Tasting a bitter (vs. sweet or neutral) drink increased participants' self-reported hostile mood (Sagioglou & Greitemeyer, 2014, Experiment 1), hypothetical aggressive feelings and behavioral intentions (Experiment 2), and hostile evaluation of the experimenter as less competent and less friendly (Experiment 3). Bitter taste is also associated with harsh environments and the corresponding motivation to survive (B.-B. Chen & Chang, 2012). Accordingly, tasting a bitter drink or food (vs. neutral drink or sour or sweet food) sped up participants' responses to survival-related words in a lexical decision task (Experiments 1–2), increased their present focus and thus discounting rate in an intertemporal choice (Experiment 3), and improved their retrieval of survival-related words in a surprise recall task (Experiment 4).

Smell. Like taste, smell is a chemical sense that can be stimulated in both positive and negative valences. On the negative side, metaphorical associations between smell and suspicion are found in at least 18 languages (Ibarretxe-Antuñano, 2019; Soriano & Valenzuela, 2008). Inspired by these linguistic observations, a series of experiments probed the metaphorical association between social suspicion and fishy smells among English speakers (S. W. S. Lee & Schwarz, 2012), as reflected in linguistic expressions like "something smells fishy." Incidental presentation of fishy smells (vs. nonfishy disgusting smells or no smell) decreased participants' trust-based monetary investment in a trust game (Experiment 1) and a public goods game (Experiment 2). Conversely, inductions of social suspicion increased participants' ability to correctly label fishy smells but not other smells (Experiments 3a–3c). An experimental causal-chain approach suggested that such enhancement in correct labeling of fishy smells was driven by the accessibility and applicability of metaphorical concepts: Social suspicion activated suspicion-related concepts (Experiment 4), which activated fishy concepts (Experiment 5), which were applied to the identification of target smells (Experiment 6). The metaphorical effect extends from the conceptual to the perceptual level, as shown in a signal detection paradigm where suspicion induction improved perceptual sensitivity to low concentrations of fishy smells but not other smells (Experiment 7).

Follow-up research generalized the effects of fishy smells to suspicion in nonsocial contexts of information processing and reasoning. For example, consider the simple question "How many animals of each kind did Moses take on the Ark?" The correct answer is not two, but that it was Noah rather than Moses (Erickson & Mattson, 1981). Participants became more likely to identify the semantic distortion in such trick questions if they were exposed to fishy smells (vs. no smell; D. S. Lee et al., 2015, Experiment 1). Incidental exposure to fishy smells (vs. no smell) also increased participants' likelihood of engaging in hypothesis testing that falsified (rather than confirmed) their initial intuitions (Experiment 2), improving their performance in a classic rule discovery task (Wason, 1960).

These effects have been replicated with extensions. For example, incidental exposure to fishy smells (vs. nonfishy disgusting smells or no smell) decreased participants' investment in a public goods game (Sebastian et al., 2017). This effect overrode an otherwise observed correlation between individual differences in distrust and reduced investment in the game. Fishy smells also increased participants' likelihood of falsification hypothesis testing and the amount of time they took to complete the experiment, which suggested more information processing. Consistent with that possibility, another lab used the misinformation paradigm in memory research and found that fishy smells (vs. no smell) enhanced discrepancy detection, thereby eliminating interference by misinformation and reducing suggestibility (Sheaffer et al., 2021). All of these findings indicate that fishy smells elicit suspicion, which can both undermine social cooperation and enhance cognitive processing.

Turning from unpleasant smells to pleasant ones, clean scents exert judgmental and behavioral effects along metaphorical lines. For example, participants reciprocated more money in a trust game if they were in a room sprayed with citrus-scented Windex than in an unscented room (Liljenquist et al., 2010, Experiment 1). Clean scents (vs. no scent) also increased interest in volunteering for a charitable organization and likelihood of donating money (Experiment 2). As a conceptual opposite of clean scents, a disgusting odor (fart spray) intensified condemnation of moral violations (Schnall, Haidt, et al., 2008, Experiment 1). In short, participants behaved in more virtuous ways in the presence of clean scents and judged more harshly in the presence of disgusting smells, consistent with the clean–moral/dirty–immoral metaphorical association.

Sound and sight. The physical senses of sound and sight convey rich information about the spatial environment, often in intertwined ways. Consider sound-distance associations. Back vowels (e.g., "oo") were shown to convey a sense of distance, front vowels (e.g., "ee") a sense of closeness, with consequences for spatial judgment, perception, and action (Rabaglia et al., 2016). Because distance (vs. closeness) typically elicits higher level (vs. lower level) mental construal (Trope & Liberman, 2010), back vowels tended to evoke higher level construals than did front vowels (Maglio et al., 2014), resulting in visual and conceptual imprecision (Experiments 1–2). Accordingly, consumer evaluations of products and services with back-vowel (vs. front-vowel) names tended to be driven by high-level rather than low-level considerations (i.e., desirability rather than feasibility, primary rather than secondary features, long term rather than short term; Experiments 3–5).

Sound–shape associations also exist. The most well-known example is the *bouba-kiki* effect (Ramachandran & Hubbard, 2001), where a soft-sound word like "bouba" is generally chosen to represent a curved shape, and a sharp-sound word like "kiki" is chosen to represent an angular shape (for reviews, see Imai & Kita, 2014; Lockwood & Dingemanse, 2015). The effect occurs across languages (Bremner et al., 2013) and even in children under 3 years of age (Maurer et al., 2006). These sound–shape mappings are driven by phonology and occur automatically prior to conscious awareness of visual shapes (S.-M. Hung et al., 2017).

In addition to the robust sound–sight associations noted earlier, fundamental dimensions of sight, such as location and shape, are rich in psychological associations. Consider a single dimension: verticality, or vertical location in space. Experimental work has found that being high up (vs. down low) in space is not only linguistically but also cognitively, affectively, and behaviorally associated with a variety of abstract concepts, such as status (Dannenmaier & Thumin, 1964; P. R. Wilson, 1968), power (Giessner & Schubert, 2007; Schubert, 2005), positive valence (Meier & Robinson, 2004), freedom and abstraction (Meyers-Levy & Zhu, 2007), morality (H. Li & Cao, 2017; Meier, Sellbom, et al., 2007), divinity (Meier, Hauser, et al., 2007), and rationality (Cian et al., 2015), with consequences for consumer behavior (for a review, see Cian, 2017).

Shapes have been extensively studied as well. Sharp contours conveyed a sense of threat and were less preferred than curved contours (Bar & Neta, 2006). Downward-pointing triangles were perceived as particularly threatening and categorized faster as unpleasant than as neutral or pleasant, whereas upward-pointing triangles or circles did not exhibit such affective associations (Larson et al., 2012). Sharp (vs. round) shapes increased perception of aggression in others and aggressive choices in decision making (Hess et al., 2013). Angular-shaped seating arrangements activated the need for uniqueness and thus led participants to favor self-oriented or minority-endorsing persuasive messages, whereas circular-shaped seating arrangements activated the need to belong and thus led participants to favor family-oriented or majority-endorsing persuasive messages (Zhu & Argo, 2013). Angular-shaped (vs. circular-shaped) brand logos increased perception of company and product attributes such as durability (vs. comfortableness) through visuospatial imagery (Jiang et al., 2016). Finally, square (vs. round) shapes have also been shown in a variety of verbal and reaction-time measures to be associated with competence (vs. warmth; Okamura & Ura, 2018, 2019a), business (vs. dating; Okamura & Ura, 2019b), and male (vs. female; Stroessner et al., 2020).

Summary. Across sensorimotor modalities (touch, taste, smell, sound, sight), diverse psychological consequences have been observed along metaphorical lines (Lakoff & Johnson, 1980, 1999). These dynamics matter for effective advertising (Krishna, 2012) and creative thinking (Zhu & Mehta, 2017). The heuristic value of conceptual metaphors lies in the fact that they are manifest in and thus inferable from linguistic expressions, generating specific predictions that map a sensorimotor domain to a psychological domain. These mappings exert predictable affective, conceptual, judgmental, and behavioral influences (Landau, 2017; S. W. S. Lee & Schwarz, 2014).

Mechanism 3: Procedures

Conceptual mappings underlie many mind–body effects but not all of them. For example, cleanliness is conceptually associated with morality (Lakoff & Johnson, 1999), especially the moral foundation of sanctity/degradation (Haidt & Graham, 2007) and the corresponding emotion of disgust (Rozin et al., 2008). But psychological consequences of cleanliness extend far beyond the realms of morality and disgust (S. W. S. Lee & Schwarz, 2011, 2016). How do we explain these effects?

An emerging perspective conceptualizes bodily actions (e.g., cleansing) as grounded procedures

(S. W. S. Lee & Schwarz, 2021). Drawing on the research tradition of information processing, a *procedure* is defined as "the sequence of steps that can be taken to attain a particular objective" (Wyer et al., 2012, p. 241). Procedures can be operationalized at the mental or physical level, that is, there are "cognitive or motor" procedures (Wyer et al., 2012, p. 239). The interesting thing about procedures is their generalizable application: Activating a procedure to attain a particular objective renders the procedure more likely to be used in a subsequent context, even if the original objective is no longer relevant. In other words, a procedure is applicable across content domains (Janiszewski & Wyer, 2014).

Combining these properties of a procedure with the assumptions of grounded cognition (Barsalou, 1999, 2008) gives rise to the perspective of grounded procedures (S. W. S. Lee & Schwarz, 2021). The core claim here is that physical procedures can ground mental procedures. Representationally, physical procedures can constitute mental procedures. Functionally, engagement of a physical procedure can activate a corresponding mental procedure, and vice versa. Upon activation, a physical or mental procedure becomes more likely to be applied to subsequent tasks and situations, even if they are unrelated to the original procedural objective.

Through this theoretical lens, the bodily action of cleansing can be conceptualized as a grounded procedure of separation. Any act of cleansing involves separating physical entities from each other (e.g., separating dirt from one's hands). Such separative experiences can ground mental procedures of separating psychological entities from each other (e.g., separating past behavior from one's present self). Based on mental inclusion/exclusion principles (Bless & Schwarz, 2010), the psychological influence of the separated entity should be reduced.

This mechanism (grounded procedures) generates a number of process-oriented predictions distinct from predictions derived from other mechanisms (concepts and feelings). For example, the physical action of cleansing should reduce the psychological influence of any separated entity, regardless of the entity's (a) domain and (b) valence. In contrast, conceptual metaphor theory only associates cleansing with the moral domain, the emotion of disgust only captures cleansing effects that involve (physically or morally) disgusting stimuli, and both views predict only positive effects of cleansing as it confers a sense of morality or reduces disgust. In addition to generalizability across psychological domains and valences, another prediction of grounded procedures is generalizability across actions: If separation is the mechanism at work, (c) similar effects should result not only from physical cleansing but also from other physical procedures of separation. We review support for these and other predictions next, starting with the most specific case of cleansing, then broadening to other grounded procedures of separation, and finally to their conceptual opposite (connection). Examples of grounded procedures other than separation and connection also exist but are beyond the scope of this chapter.

Cleansing and separation. Physical cleansing has been shown to produce psychological consequences in nonmoral, nondisgusting contexts. In the context of decision making, for instance, after making a free choice between two similarly attractive options, people often experience postdecisional dissonance ("Did I make the right choice?"; Brehm, 1956; Festinger, 1957). To reduce the aversive state of dissonance, a cognitive process unfolds where attention is directed to positive features of the chosen alternative and to negative features of the rejected alternative. As a result, people tend to evaluate the chosen alternative more favorably after than before choice and evaluate the rejected alternative less favorably after than before choice. This classic effect of postdecisional dissonance was eliminated if participants were prompted to wash their hands using a bottle of hand soap (under the pretense of product evaluation) right after choice and before subsequent evaluation (S. W. S. Lee & Schwarz, 2010b, Experiment 1). Merely examining the hand soap without using it did not eliminate the classic effect. A conceptual replication found the same pattern (Experiment 2): Using an antiseptic wipe right after choosing between similarly attractive fruit jams eliminated postdecisional dissonance, whereas merely examining the wipe did not.

Extended replications found the same phenomenon in a German sample (Marotta & Bohner, 2013) and uncovered individual differences and boundary conditions. Cleansing eliminated postdecisional dissonance for participants who scored low on generalized anxiety, rumination, and intolerance of uncertainty, but not for participants who scored high on these measures (De Los Reyes et al., 2012). Cleansing also did not eliminate postdecisional dissonance if participants received memory cues about their predecisional evaluation during their postdecisional evaluation (Camerer et al., 2018). Integrating all findings into a meta-analysis estimated the overall effect to be $d = 0.204$, $SE = 0.084$, $p = .015$, 95% CI [0.040, 0.349], indicating a small effect of washing away postdecisional dissonance (S. W. S. Lee & Schwarz, 2018).

In addition to reducing the influence of a recent decision on subsequent evaluation, cleansing can also reduce the influence of recent financial luck on subsequent risky choice. After recalling financial good (vs. bad) luck, participants became more risk-seeking (vs. risk-averse) in a vicarious managerial decision, but using an antiseptic wipe reversed this effect (Xu et al., 2012, Experiment 1). Likewise, following a winning (vs. losing) streak in a monetary gambling task, participants were more (vs. less) likely to bet in a final round, but using a hand soap eliminated this effect (Experiment 2).

Cleansing oneself (vs. no cleansing or cleansing an object) has also been found to reduce the influence of an academic failure on subsequent pessimism and compensatory effort (Kaspar, 2013), the influence of successful and failing performance on subsequent optimism (Körner & Strack, 2019), the influence of product endowment on subsequent desire for product exchange (Florack et al., 2014), the influence of effort on subsequent feelings of ownership (A. Lee & Ji, 2015), and the influence of physical and social threats on subsequent affect and physiology (S. W. S. Lee, Millet, et al., 2020). These findings highlight that cleansing effects are observed in a variety of nonmoral, nondisgusting contexts, for both positive and negative entities (e.g., good and bad luck, successful and failing performance, endowment, threat).

Beyond cleansing, various grounded procedures of separation can reduce the influence of the physically separated entity. For example, leading participants to tempt fate by saying they or their friend would never encounter a specific bad situation (e.g., accident, theft) increased their perceived likelihood of encountering the bad situation (Y. Zhang et al., 2014). This effect of tempting fate was reduced by both culturally symbolic actions of separation (knocking on wood, which involves moving one's hand away from one's body; Experiment 1) and nonsymbolic actions of separation (e.g., throwing a ball away; Experiments 2a–2b), due to reduced clarity of mental imagery about the bad situation (Experiment 3). Even pretending to throw a ball away, which engages the motor muscles of actual throwing without distancing the ball from oneself, eliminated the effect of tempting fate (Experiment 5), suggesting that it was the motor procedure that mattered, not the spatial distance.

Furthermore, writing about a regretful experience on a piece of paper elicited negative feelings, but enclosing the piece of paper in an envelope reduced subsequent negative feelings (X. Li et al., 2010, Experiment 1a). The same manipulation reduced the affective impact of writing about an unsatisfied desire (Experiment 1b) and reading about a sad event (Experiment 2). Enclosure can also influence choice satisfaction. Specifically, after a free choice of one out of 24 pieces of chocolate on a tray, if participants were instructed to cover the tray with a transparent lid, it reduced their mental comparison between the chosen and forgone options, thereby increasing their feelings of choice completion and satisfaction (Gu et al., 2013, Experiment 1). Closing a menu after choosing one out of 24 options of tea (Experiment 2) or biscuit (Experiments 3a–3b) produced similar effects.

From cleansing to enclosure, grounded procedures of separation reduced the psychological influence of the physically separated entity. Opposite to separation, grounded procedures of connection also exist and produce conceptually parallel effects.

Connection. Acts that connect physical entities to each other (e.g., connecting a product to one's hands) can ground mental procedures of connecting psychological entities to each other (e.g., connecting an idea to one's self), such that the psychological influence of the connected entity is amplified (in cases of preexisting influence) or created (in cases of no preexisting influence). These patterns have been observed across psychological domains, across their valences, and across operationalizations of physical connection, from spatial continuity to approach movement to actual contact.

Visualizing 4 years of college experience as a spatially continuous journey increased college students' experience of psychological connection between their present and future identities, in turn increasing their academically relevant motivation and performance (Landau et al., 2014). Jotting down thoughts about the Mediterranean diet on a piece of paper and then physically connecting it to oneself (folding and putting it in one's pocket; vs. control conditions that involved no physical connection) increased the psychological influence of the jotted thoughts on subsequent attitudes toward the Mediterranean diet, such that positive thoughts led to even more positive attitudes and negative thoughts led to even more negative attitudes (Briñol et al., 2013, Experiment 2). Actual contact with (vs. mere examination of) a robot increased existing attitudes toward robots, regardless of whether they were positive or negative (Wullenkord et al., 2016).

Actual contact also amplifies contagion effects, which occur for negative as well as positive entities (J. Y. Huang et al., 2017). Objects that had been in contact with disdained individuals were perceived as retaining essences and properties from the individuals and thus disliked (Nemeroff & Rozin, 1994). Products that had been in contact with previous shoppers were evaluated as worse (Argo et al., 2006), but products that had been in contact with attractive opposite-sex others were evaluated as better (Argo et al., 2008). Items that had been in contact with celebrities commanded especially high prices at auctions (Bloom & Gelman, 2008; Newman & Bloom, 2014; Newman et al., 2011). Sporting goods (e.g., golf club, ball) that had been in contact with successful athletes increased participants' athletic self-perception and performance (Kramer & Block, 2014; C. Lee et al., 2011).

In cases of no preexisting influence, connecting otherwise neutral entities to the self tends to create a positive influence because people generally evaluate the self positively (Baumeister, 1999). Even subtle cues of physical connection can produce these effects. For example, company names, person names, and nonsense words beginning with front consonants (e.g., "B," "M") and ending with rear consonants (e.g., "G," "K") were favored over their counterparts (beginning with rear consonants and ending with front consonants) because front-to-rear articulation involves oral approach movement, whereas rear-to-front articulation involves oral avoidance movement (Topolinski, 2017). In another modality, flexing (vs. extending) arm muscles resembles manual approach (vs. avoidance) movement and created favorable evaluation of otherwise neutral stimuli (Cacioppo et al., 1993; Priester et al., 1996).

Grounded procedures of connection have applied consequences in the marketplace. Actual contact or mentally simulated contact with objects confers a sense of ownership among buyers and sellers alike, increasing valuation (Peck et al., 2013; Peck & Shu, 2009). When the same product is available in physical and digital forms, a stronger sense of ownership and higher valuation are ascribed to physical than digital forms (Atasoy & Morewedge, 2018). With digital shopping interfaces, touch-based devices like tablets give consumers a stronger sense of ownership and result in higher valuation than do non-touch-based devices like laptops (Brasel & Gips, 2014).

All in all, physical acts of connection, mental simulation of them, and platforms that facilitate them tend to confer a sense of psychological connection, with downstream consequences for attitude strength, perceived ownership, and monetary valuation.

Across Mechanisms: Predicted Moderators

The three mechanisms predict a range of moderator variables, some of which are mechanism-general and others are mechanism-specific. Together, the predicted moderator variables tap into contextual, individual, cultural, and other group differences. A brief overview of select moderators is provided next (for a full treatment, see S. W. S. Lee & Schwarz, 2020).

With reference to the first step in Figure 24.1, the starting point of all mechanisms is the bodily state, both the modality and processing of which matter. For example, cleanliness can be attained in different bodily modalities such as manual (hands), oral (mouth), and facial (whole face). The relative salience of these modalities moderates metaphorical effects between cleanliness and morality. Participants evaluated mouthwash more favorably after telling a malevolent lie on voicemail (using the mouth) than on email (using the hands) but evaluated hand sanitizer more favorably after telling a malevolent lie on email than on voicemail (S. W. S. Lee & Schwarz, 2010a). Paralleling such situational salience, chronic salience of modality produces similar effects. East Asian cultures are known as *face* cultures (Leung & Cohen, 2011), where one's face metaphorically represents one's public image. Given this cultural background, immoral recall heightened East Asian participants' desire for face-cleaning products, and wiping the face clean (vs. wiping hands or no wiping) was the most effective for reducing their moral guilt (S. W. S. Lee et al., 2015).

Processing of a bodily state involves attributes such as awareness, subjectivity, and simulation. Drawing on principles of social cognition, if participants are highly aware of a bodily state manipulation and its irrelevance to the task at hand, mental correction is likely to occur (Bless & Schwarz, 2010; Greifeneder et al., 2011) to eliminate its otherwise observed influence. Bodily states are subjective to some extent. A 1.5 kg shopping bag felt a little heavy on the arm if participants expected the bag to contain bags of potato chips, but the same objective weight felt a little light if participants expected the bag to contain a dozen cans of Coke, and this subjective experience of heavy (vs. light) increased the metaphorically associated perception of importance (M. Zhang & Li, 2012). Related to subjectivity is the power of mental simulation of a bodily state. Compared with actually experiencing a bodily state, mentally simulating it can produce qualitatively similar (though often quantitatively weaker) metaphorical effects. For example, detailed imagination of being physically clean (vs. dirty) led participants to see themselves as morally cleaner and judge others' transgressions more harshly (Zhong et al., 2010). First-person imagination of holding a cup of iced (vs. hot) coffee also led participants to judge a target person as socially colder (Macrae et al., 2013).

As for the second step in Figure 24.1, moderation is easiest to illustrate with the mechanism of concepts. For bodily activation of psychological concepts to occur, the conceptual association needs to be both available and accessible. Certain associations are available in specific cultures, not in others. For example, in different cultures, the same gesture can have different meanings (e.g., thumbs up indicating approval in North America but insult in the Middle East), and different gestures can have the same meaning (e.g., agreement indicated by nodding in America but head bobbling in India). Some conceptual metaphorical associations seem to have culture-general structures but culture-specific contents. For example, suspicion is metaphorically described as bad smell across languages, but some languages specify a particular bad smell (e.g., fishy in English), other languages specify a different bad smell, and yet other languages leave it unspecified (S. W. S. Lee & Schwarz, 2012). Temporal relations are metaphorically described in spatial terms across cultures, but the specific spatial dimension differs between cultures. The past/future is in the back/front for English speakers ("I look forward to meeting you," "Let's put this behind us"; Boroditsky, 2000) but front/back for Aymara speakers (Núñez & Sweetser, 2006), top/bottom for Mandarin speakers (Boroditsky, 2001), and East/West for Pormpuraawans (a remote Australian aboriginal culture; Boroditsky & Gaby, 2010). Experiments have confirmed these culture-specific conceptual associations, with cognitive and behavioral consequences.

Just because a metaphorical association is available in memory does not mean it is accessible in context; availability is a necessary but not sufficient condition for accessibility (Higgins, 1996). A highly accessible metaphorical association increases the likelihood and strength of bodily activation of psychological feelings, concepts, and procedures. For example, drinking a cup of iced (vs. hot) tea led participants to feel physically cold and increased their liking for romantic movies—but only if they had a highly accessible association of romantic movies with warm feelings (Hong & Sun, 2012). Using the right (vs. left) hand in physical actions activated positive concepts such as "goodness" and "victory" (vs. negative concepts such as "badness" and "loss")—but only if participants were right-handed and thus had a chronically accessible association of right-side with positive valence (Casasanto, 2009, 2011).

Accessible psychological contents (feelings, concepts, or procedures) have to be used or applied to specific outcomes (third step in Figure 24.1). If the accessible psychological contents include multiple domains (e.g., verticality activates both powerfulness and valence), in which domain will an effect be observed? An important determinant is attention, that is, to which domain participants pay attention (for a related view on priming, see Bargh, 2006; on metacognitive experience, see Schwarz, 2010; on metaphor, see Santiago et al., 2011). To illustrate, when a task required participants to judge groups as powerful or powerless, they made more efficient judgments (fewer errors) for powerful (vs. powerless) groups appearing at the top (vs. bottom) of the screen, but the groups' valence had no influence at all (Schubert, 2005, Experiment 5a). When a task required participants to judge groups as good or bad, they made more efficient judgments (shorter response latencies) for good (vs. bad) groups appearing at the top (vs. bottom) of the screen, but the groups' power had no influence at all (Experiment 5b). Whichever domain participants attended to, the metaphorical effect was observed, suggesting a manner in which multiple contents get channeled into specific outcomes.

These patterns of moderation reflect a small subset of the full range of moderators, which will be a fruitful avenue for investigation. Together with the basic operation of the three mechanisms, they open up exciting future directions for theoretical and empirical work.

FUTURE DIRECTIONS

Teasing apart the mechanistic roles of feelings, concepts, and procedures in mind–body influence will be important next steps. The reviewed evidence suggests that a bodily state can activate the three mechanisms in general, but at a given moment does it activate all three mechanisms simultaneously? Or sequentially, that is, one at a time? Our stance is that simultaneous activation is generally plausible (e.g., physical cleansing can confer feelings of purity, prime concepts of cleanliness, and instigate procedures of separation all at once), such that different dependent measures (e.g., self-report feelings, reaction time in lexical decisions, motor movement, behavioral intentions) will capture manifestations of different mechanisms. Meanwhile, different bodily states may activate the three mechanism to different extents. For example, in a state of high physiological arousal, feelings and procedures may be more potent than concepts. Spatial relations may cue temporal relations more strongly than specific feelings or procedures. Such subtlety can be empirically addressed by identifying and testing mechanism-specific moderators.

Much of consumer psychology research on mind–body relations has focused on experimental demonstrations of situational influence (of bodily on mental states and vice versa) over short timespans (e.g., minutes). Long-term effects remain unexplored. Furthermore, individual differences in mind–body relations, their within-person fluctuations, and their chronic influence are less well-understood, even though many constructs in consumer psychology lend themselves to interpretation through the lens of mind–body interplay. Consider dimensions of brand personality (Aaker, 1997) as an example. Drawing on research illustrating metaphorical conceptualizations of human personality, we expect brand sincerity to be associated with warm temperature, brand excitement with physiological arousal, brand competence or reliability with proprioceptive firmness, brand sophistication with high verticality, and brand ruggedness with tactile toughness. As another example, mental accounting involves psychologically separating money into different categories (Thaler, 1985). Are mental accounting effects stronger among individuals high on obsessive–compulsive tendencies and need for order, structure, and closure?

More generally, various domains of consumer behavior involve mind–body relations. As work in sensory marketing has illustrated, subtle and incidental cues of bodily states—whether directly experienced or mentally simulated—can influence consumer judgments and decisions, often without their attention or awareness (Krishna, 2010). The diversity of such influence creates opportunities for marketers to shape consumers' minds and behaviors without requiring conscious focus, which is particularly useful in an era with ever-increasing competition for consumers' limited attentional resources. Technological advances have also led to more sophisticated user interfaces that go beyond the traditional focus on visual modality (e.g., touchscreen devices, voice assistants). There needs to be a better understanding of what psychological consequences result from these modalities (e.g., on affect-laden choices; Shen et al., 2016) and how to leverage their unique affordances to enhance consumer well-being.

Finally, the pervasiveness of bodily influence on mental processes raises a broad theoretical question: What is a good model of the human mind? Evidence reviewed in this chapter indicates that bodily states can influence feelings through physiological arousal, proprioceptive feedback, and metacognitive experience. They can activate concepts that are directly, symbolically, or metaphorically related. They can involve procedures such as separation and connection, with process implications across content domains. Clearly, the body cannot be ignored in a comprehensive model of mental functioning. The model may be stretched even further, as mental functioning in the wild involves dynamic interactions with tools in the environment (e.g., paper, calculator, laptop, smartphone; Cecutti et al., 2021; Clark & Chalmers, 1998) and transactive cognitive processes with other minds (e.g., romantic partner, group members; Wegner, 1987; Wegner et al., 1991). A fully contextualized model of the human mind will require proper delineation of the cognitive loops among mind, body, and external reality.

APPENDIX: A BRIEF SUMMARY OF SIX VIEWS OF EMBODIED COGNITION (M. WILSON, 2002)

Embodied cognition can mean that (1) cognitive processes do not occur in a vacuum but are situated in dynamic, constantly changing real-world contexts. The body's sensorimotor capacities are necessary to perceive and act on these contexts. The constantly changing perceptual inputs and motor outputs are inseparable from and inherent to cognitive functioning (Beer, 2000; Chiel & Beer, 1997). Because of its situatedness in dynamic real-world contexts, (2) cognitive functioning needs to be analyzed under realistic time pressure, through the lens of real-time interactions with the environment, rather than under experimental conditions of unrealistic time pressure or leisure (Brooks, 1991; van Gelder & Port, 1996).

In addition to posing temporal challenges to cognition, (3) the environment can also be recruited to facilitate cognition. Given our limited information-processing capacities (e.g., attentional span, working memory; Baddeley, 1992; Miller, 1956), humans routinely off-load cognitive work to the environment, as when we do complicated math with the aid of paper and pencil, constantly off-loading information onto the paper and accessing it when needed, freeing our working memory for manipulation of information rather than overburdening it with mere storage of information (Clark, 1997). Recognizing the continuous flow of information between the human mind and the environment (and the bodily capacities required for such flow), some theorists go one step further and argue that (4) the environment is part of the cognitive system proper. In other words, cognition needs to be analyzed not as phenomena exclusive to the human mind but as activities distributed across a system that includes mind, body, and environment (Beer, 1995; Clark, 2017; Greeno & Moore, 1993; Thelen & Smith, 1994; Wertsch, 2017). This position, called *extended cognition* (Clark & Chalmers, 1998), is highly controversial in cognitive science (Menary, 2010; Rupert, 2004).

Another facet of embodied cognition focuses on the ultimate functions of cognitive processes: (5) Cognition is for action in context. It is argued, for example, "that memory evolved in service of perception and action in a three-dimensional environment, and that memory is embodied to facilitate interaction with the environment" (Glenberg, 1997, p. 1). Similar claims have been made of lower level cognitive processes: "Vision, like other sensory functions, has its evolutionary rationale rooted in improved motor control" (Churchland et al., 1994, p. 25), compatible with the ecological approach to perception (Gibson, 1966, 1979). From this perspective, the primary goal of cognition is not to create veridical representations of external entities ("what they are") but to conceptualize them in ways that prioritize their functional relevance for us ("what to do with them").

The final aspect of embodied cognition, as noted in the main text, turns the focus from the environment and online cognitive processes of the sort discussed earlier to the body and offline cognition. It highlights that (6) offline cognition can be body-based: "Mental structures that originally evolved for perception or action appear to be co-opted and run 'offline,' decoupled from the physical inputs and outputs that were their original purpose, to assist in thinking and knowing" (M. Wilson, 2002, p. 633).

Not all of the six views have enjoyed similar research attention. The first and last views, with their strong focus on the body and sensorimotor simulation, appear most resonant with consumer and social psychologists' use of the term embodied cognition and their recent wave of interest in phenomena under this label. To minimize risks of confusion and maximize chances of knowledge accumulation, we recommend that researchers be clear about which specific view is espoused in their work or assessment of others' work.

REFERENCES

Aaker, J. L. (1997). Dimensions of brand personality. *Journal of Marketing Research*, 34(3), 347–356. https://doi.org/10.1177/002224379703400304

Ackerman, J. M., Nocera, C. C., & Bargh, J. A. (2010). Incidental haptic sensations influence social judgments and decisions. *Science*, 328(5986), 1712–1715. https://doi.org/10.1126/science.1189993

American Psychological Association. (n.d.). *APA dictionary of psychology*. https://dictionary.apa.org/mind

Anderson, M. L. (2010). Neural reuse: A fundamental organizational principle of the brain. *Behavioral and Brain Sciences*, 33(4), 245–266. https://doi.org/10.1017/S0140525X10000853

Argo, J. J., Dahl, D. W., & Morales, A. C. (2006). Consumer contamination: How consumers react to products touched by others. *Journal of Marketing*, 70(2), 81–94. https://doi.org/10.1509/jmkg.70.2.081

Argo, J. J., Dahl, D. W., & Morales, A. C. (2008). Positive consumer contagion: Responses to attractive others in a retail context. *Journal of Marketing Research*, 45(6), 690–701. https://doi.org/10.1509/jmkr.45.6.690

Atasoy, O., & Morewedge, C. K. (2018). Digital goods are valued less than physical goods. *Journal of Consumer Research*, 44(6), 1343–1357. https://doi.org/10.1093/jcr/ucx102

Baddeley, A. D. (1992). Working memory. *Science*, 255(5044), 556–559. https://doi.org/10.1126/science.1736359

Baddeley, A. D., & Hitch, G. (1974). Working memory. In G. H. Bower (Ed.), *Psychology of learning and motivation* (Vol. 8, pp. 47–89). Elsevier. https://doi.org/10.1016/S0079-7421(08)60452-1

Bar, M., & Neta, M. (2006). Humans prefer curved visual objects. *Psychological Science*, 17(8), 645–648. https://doi.org/10.1111/j.1467-9280.2006.01759.x

Bargh, J. A. (2006). What have we been priming all these years? On the development, mechanisms, and ecology of nonconscious social behavior. *European Journal of Social Psychology*, 36(2), 147–168. https://doi.org/10.1002/ejsp.336

Barsalou, L. W. (1999). Perceptual symbol systems. *Behavioral and Brain Sciences*, 22(4), 577–660. https://doi.org/10.1017/S0140525X99002149

Barsalou, L. W. (2008). Grounded cognition. *Annual Review of Psychology*, 59(1), 617–645. https://doi.org/10.1146/annurev.psych.59.103006.093639

Batra, R. K., Ghoshal, T., & Raghunathan, R. (2017). You are what you eat: An empirical investigation of the relationship between spicy food and aggressive cognition. *Journal of Experimental Social Psychology*, 71, 42–48. https://doi.org/10.1016/j.jesp.2017.01.007

Baumeister, R. F. (Ed.). (1999). *The self in social psychology*. Psychology Press.

Bechara, A., & Damasio, A. R. (2005). The somatic marker hypothesis: A neural theory of economic decision. *Games and Economic Behavior*, 52(2), 336–372. https://doi.org/10.1016/j.geb.2004.06.010

Beer, R. D. (1995). A dynamical systems perspective on agent-environment interaction. *Artificial Intelligence*, 72(1–2), 173–215. https://doi.org/10.1016/0004-3702(94)00005-L

Beer, R. D. (2000). Dynamical approaches to cognitive science. *Trends in Cognitive Sciences*, 4(3), 91–99. https://doi.org/10.1016/S1364-6613(99)01440-0

Bless, H., & Schwarz, N. (2010). Mental construal and the emergence of assimilation and contrast effects: The inclusion/exclusion model. *Advances in Experimental Social Psychology*, 42, 319–373. https://doi.org/10.1016/S0065-2601(10)42006-7

Bloom, P., & Gelman, S. A. (2008). Psychological essentialism in selecting the 14th Dalai Lama. *Trends in Cognitive Sciences*, *12*(7), 243. https://doi.org/10.1016/j.tics.2008.04.004

Bolognesi, M., & Steen, G. (2018). Editors' introduction: Abstract concepts: Structure, processing, and modeling. *Topics in Cognitive Science*, *10*(3), 490–500. https://doi.org/10.1111/tops.12354

Borghi, A. M., Barca, L., Binkofski, F., & Tummolini, L. (2018). Varieties of abstract concepts: Development, use and representation in the brain. *Philosophical Transactions of the Royal Society of London: Series B. Biological Sciences*, *373*(1752), 20170121. https://doi.org/10.1098/rstb.2017.0121

Boroditsky, L. (2000). Metaphoric structuring: Understanding time through spatial metaphors. *Cognition*, *75*(1), 1–28. https://doi.org/10.1016/S0010-0277(99)00073-6

Boroditsky, L. (2001). Does language shape thought? Mandarin and English speakers' conceptions of time. *Cognitive Psychology*, *43*(1), 1–22. https://doi.org/10.1006/cogp.2001.0748

Boroditsky, L., & Gaby, A. (2010). Remembrances of times East: Absolute spatial representations of time in an Australian aboriginal community. *Psychological Science*, *21*(11), 1635–1639. https://doi.org/10.1177/0956797610386621

Brasel, S. A., & Gips, J. (2014). Tablets, touchscreens, and touchpads: How varying touch interfaces trigger psychological ownership and endowment. *Journal of Consumer Psychology*, *24*(2), 226–233. https://doi.org/10.1016/j.jcps.2013.10.003

Brehm, J. W. (1956). Postdecision changes in the desirability of alternatives. *Journal of Abnormal and Social Psychology*, *52*(3), 384–389. https://doi.org/10.1037/h0041006

Bremner, A. J., Caparos, S., Davidoff, J., de Fockert, J., Linnell, K. J., & Spence, C. (2013). "Bouba" and "Kiki" in Namibia? A remote culture make similar shape-sound matches, but different shape-taste matches to Westerners. *Cognition*, *126*(2), 165–172. https://doi.org/10.1016/j.cognition.2012.09.007

Briñol, P., Gascó, M., Petty, R. E., & Horcajo, J. (2013). Treating thoughts as material objects can increase or decrease their impact on evaluation. *Psychological Science*, *24*(1), 41–47. https://doi.org/10.1177/0956797612449176

Brooks, R. A. (1991). New approaches to robotics. *Science*, *253*(5025), 1227–1232. https://doi.org/10.1126/science.253.5025.1227

Brown, R. (1958). How shall a thing be called? *Psychological Review*, *65*(1), 14–21. https://doi.org/10.1037/h0041727

Burgoon, E. M., Henderson, M. D., & Markman, A. B. (2013). There are many ways to see the forest for the trees: A tour guide for abstraction. *Perspectives on Psychological Science*, *8*(5), 501–520. https://doi.org/10.1177/1745691613497964

Cacioppo, J. T., Priester, J. R., & Berntson, G. G. (1993). Rudimentary determinants of attitudes. II: Arm flexion and extension have differential effects on attitudes. *Journal of Personality and Social Psychology*, *65*(1), 5–17. https://doi.org/10.1037/0022-3514.65.1.5

Camerer, C. F., Dreber, A., Holzmeister, F., Ho, T.-H., Huber, J., Johannesson, M., Kirchler, M., Nave, G., Nosek, B. A., Pfeiffer, T., Altmejd, A., Buttrick, N., Chan, T., Chen, Y., Forsell, E., Gampa, A., Heikensten, E., Hummer, L., Imai, T., . . . Wu, H. (2018). Evaluating the replicability of social science experiments in *Nature* and *Science* between 2010 and 2015. *Nature Human Behaviour*, *2*(9), 637–644. https://doi.org/10.1038/s41562-018-0399-z

Carver, C. S., & Harmon-Jones, E. (2009). Anger is an approach-related affect: Evidence and implications. *Psychological Bulletin*, *135*(2), 183–204. https://doi.org/10.1037/a0013965

Casasanto, D. (2009). Embodiment of abstract concepts: Good and bad in right- and left-handers. *Journal of Experimental Psychology: General*, *138*(3), 351–367. https://doi.org/10.1037/a0015854

Casasanto, D. (2011). Different bodies, different minds: The body specificity of language and thought. *Current Directions in Psychological Science*, *20*(6), 378–383. https://doi.org/10.1177/0963721411422058

Casasanto, D., & Chrysikou, E. G. (2011). When left is "right." Motor fluency shapes abstract concepts. *Psychological Science*, *22*(4), 419–422. https://doi.org/10.1177/0956797611401755

Cecutti, L., Chemero, A., & Lee, S. W. S. (2021). Technology may change cognition but not necessarily harm it. *Nature Human Behavior*. https://doi.org/10.1038/s41562-021-01162-0

Centerbar, D. B., & Clore, G. L. (2006). Do approach-avoidance actions create attitudes? *Psychological Science*, *17*(1), 22–29. https://doi.org/10.1111/j.1467-9280.2005.01660.x

Chan, K. Q., Tong, E. M. W., Tan, D. H., & Koh, A. H. Q. (2013). What do love and jealousy taste like? *Emotion*, *13*(6), 1142–1149. https://doi.org/10.1037/a0033758

Chapman, H. A., Kim, D. A., Susskind, J. M., & Anderson, A. K. (2009). In bad taste: Evidence for the oral origins of moral disgust. *Science*, *323*(5918), 1222–1226. https://doi.org/10.1126/science.1165565

Chen, B.-B., & Chang, L. (2012). Bitter struggle for survival: Evolved bitterness embodiment of survival motivation. *Journal of Experimental Social Psychology*,

48(2), 579–582. https://doi.org/10.1016/j.jesp.2011.11.005

Chen, M., & Bargh, J. A. (1999). Consequences of automatic evaluation: Immediate behavioral predispositions to approach or avoid the stimulus. *Personality and Social Psychology Bulletin, 25*(2), 215–224. https://doi.org/10.1177/0146167299025002007

Chen, M., & Lin, C.-H. (2021). What is in your hand influences your purchase intention: Effect of motor fluency on motor simulation. *Current Psychology, 40*, 3226–3234. https://doi.org/10.1007/s12144-019-00261-6

Chiel, H. J., & Beer, R. D. (1997). The brain has a body: Adaptive behavior emerges from interactions of nervous system, body and environment. *Trends in Neurosciences, 20*(12), 553–557. https://doi.org/10.1016/S0166-2236(97)01149-1

Churchland, P. S., Ramachandran, V. S., & Sejnowski, T. J. (1994). A critique of pure vision. In C. Koch & J. L. Davis (Eds.), *Large-scale neuronal theories of the brain* (pp. 23–60). MIT Press.

Cian, L. (2017). Verticality and conceptual metaphors: A systematic review. *Journal of the Association for Consumer Research, 2*(4), 444–459. https://doi.org/10.1086/694082

Cian, L., Krishna, A., & Schwarz, N. (2015). Positioning rationality and emotion: Rationality is up and emotion is down. *Journal of Consumer Research, 42*(4), 632–651. https://doi.org/10.1093/jcr/ucv046

Clark, A. (1997). *Being there: Putting brain, body, and world together again*. MIT Press.

Clark, A. (2017). Embodied, situated, and distributed cognition. In W. Bechtel & G. Graham (Eds.), *A companion to cognitive science* (pp. 506–517). Blackwell Publishing Ltd. https://doi.org/10.1002/9781405164535.ch39

Clark, A., & Chalmers, D. (1998). The extended mind. *Analysis, 58*(1), 7–19. https://doi.org/10.1093/analys/58.1.7

Cohen, J. (1988). *Statistical power analysis for the behavioral sciences* (2nd ed.). Lawrence Erlbaum Associates.

Cohen, N. J., Eichenbaum, H., Deacedo, B. S., & Corkin, S. (1985). Different memory systems underlying acquisition of procedural and declarative knowledge. *Annals of the New York Academy of Sciences, 444*(1), 54–71. https://doi.org/10.1111/j.1749-6632.1985.tb37579.x

Creem, S. H., & Proffitt, D. R. (2001). Grasping objects by their handles: A necessary interaction between cognition and action. *Journal of Experimental Psychology: Human Perception and Performance, 27*(1), 218–228. https://doi.org/10.1037/0096-1523.27.1.218

Damasio, A. R. (1996). The somatic marker hypothesis and the possible functions of the prefrontal cortex. *Philosophical Transactions of the Royal Society of London: Series B. Biological Sciences, 351*(1346), 1413–1420. https://doi.org/10.1098/rstb.1996.0125

Dannenmaier, W. D., & Thumin, F. J. (1964). Authority status as a factor in perceptual distortion of sizes. *Journal of Social Psychology, 63*(2), 361–365. https://doi.org/10.1080/00224545.1964.9922246

de la Fuente, J., Casasanto, D., Martínez-Cascales, J. I., & Santiago, J. (2017). Motor imagery shapes abstract concepts. *Cognitive Science, 41*(5), 1350–1360. https://doi.org/10.1111/cogs.12406

de la Fuente, J., Casasanto, D., & Santiago, J. (2015). Observed actions affect body-specific associations between space and valence. *Acta Psychologica, 156*, 32–36. https://doi.org/10.1016/j.actpsy.2015.01.004

De Los Reyes, A., Aldao, A., Kundey, S. M. A., Lee, B. G., & Molina, S. (2012). Compromised decision making and the effects of manipulating physical states on human judgments. *Journal of Clinical Psychology, 68*(1), 1–7. https://doi.org/10.1002/jclp.20851

Dutton, D. G., & Aron, A. P. (1974). Some evidence for heightened sexual attraction under conditions of high anxiety. *Journal of Personality and Social Psychology, 30*(4), 510–517. https://doi.org/10.1037/h0037031

Eelen, J., Dewitte, S., & Warlop, L. (2013). Situated embodied cognition: Monitoring orientation cues affects product evaluation and choice. *Journal of Consumer Psychology, 23*(4), 424–433. https://doi.org/10.1016/j.jcps.2013.04.004

Egan, P. J., & Mullin, M. (2012). Turning personal experience into political attitudes: The effect of local weather on Americans' perceptions about global warming. *Journal of Politics, 74*(3), 796–809. https://doi.org/10.1017/S0022381612000448

Ekman, P., Friesen, W. V., & Ellsworth, P. (1972). *Emotion in the human face: Guidelines for research and an integration of findings*. Pergamon Press.

Elder, R. S., & Krishna, A. (2012). The "visual depiction effect" in advertising: Facilitating embodied mental simulation through product orientation. *Journal of Consumer Research, 38*(6), 988–1003. https://doi.org/10.1086/661531

Erickson, T. D., & Mattson, M. E. (1981). From words to meaning: A semantic illusion. *Journal of Verbal Learning and Verbal Behavior, 20*(5), 540–551. https://doi.org/10.1016/S0022-5371(81)90165-1

Eskine, K. J., Kacinik, N. A., & Prinz, J. J. (2011). A bad taste in the mouth: Gustatory disgust influences moral judgment. *Psychological Science, 22*(3), 295–299. https://doi.org/10.1177/0956797611398497

Falk, P. (2001). Philosophy and the body. In C. Blakemore & S. Jennett (Eds.), *The Oxford companion to the body*.

Oxford University Press. https://www.encyclopedia.com/medicine/encyclopedias-almanacs-transcripts-and-maps/philosophy-and-body

Festinger, L. (1957). *A theory of cognitive dissonance*. Stanford University Press.

Fetterman, A. K., Meier, B. P., & Robinson, M. D. (2017). Dispositional properties of metaphor: The predictive power of the sweet taste metaphor for trait and daily prosociality. *Journal of Individual Differences, 38*(3), 175–188. https://doi.org/10.1027/1614-0001/a000234

Florack, A., Kleber, J., Busch, R., & Stöhr, D. (2014). Detaching the ties of ownership: The effects of hand washing on the exchange of endowed products. *Journal of Consumer Psychology, 24*(2), 284–289. https://doi.org/10.1016/j.jcps.2013.09.010

Gallace, A., & Spence, C. (2008). The cognitive and neural correlates of "tactile consciousness": A multisensory perspective. *Consciousness and Cognition, 17*(1), 370–407. https://doi.org/10.1016/j.concog.2007.01.005

Gibson, J. J. (1966). *The senses considered as perceptual systems*. Houghton Mifflin.

Gibson, J. J. (1979). *The ecological approach to visual perception*. Houghton, Mifflin and Company.

Giessner, S. R., & Schubert, T. W. (2007). High in the hierarchy: How vertical location and judgments of leaders' power are interrelated. *Organizational Behavior and Human Decision Processes, 104*(1), 30–44. https://doi.org/10.1016/j.obhdp.2006.10.001

Gilead, M., Gal, O., Polak, M., & Cholow, Y. (2015). The role of nature and nurture in conceptual metaphors: The case of gustatory priming. *Social Psychology, 46*(3), 167–173. https://doi.org/10.1027/1864-9335/a000238

Glenberg, A. M. (1997). What memory is for: Creating meaning in the service of action. *Behavioral and Brain Sciences, 20*(1), 41–50. https://doi.org/10.1017/S0140525X97470012

Glenberg, A. M., & Kaschak, M. P. (2002). Grounding language in action. *Psychonomic Bulletin & Review, 9*(3), 558–565. https://doi.org/10.3758/BF03196313

Glenberg, A. M., & Robertson, D. A. (1999). Indexical understanding of instructions. *Discourse Processes, 28*(1), 1–26. https://doi.org/10.1080/01638539909545067

Glenberg, A. M., & Robertson, D. A. (2000). Symbol grounding and meaning: A comparison of high-dimensional and embodied theories of meaning. *Journal of Memory and Language, 43*(3), 379–401. https://doi.org/10.1006/jmla.2000.2714

Glover, S., & Dixon, P. (2002). Semantics affect the planning but not control of grasping. *Experimental Brain Research, 146*(3), 383–387. https://doi.org/10.1007/s00221-002-1222-6

Greeno, J. G., & Moore, J. L. (1993). Situativity and symbols: Response to Vera and Simon. *Cognitive Science, 17*(1), 49–59. https://doi.org/10.1207/s15516709cog1701_3

Greifeneder, R., Bless, H., & Pham, M. T. (2011). When do people rely on affective and cognitive feelings in judgment? A review. *Personality and Social Psychology Review, 15*(2), 107–141. https://doi.org/10.1177/1088868310367640

Gu, Y., Botti, S., & Faro, D. (2013). Turning the page: The impact of choice closure on satisfaction. *Journal of Consumer Research, 40*(2), 268–283. https://doi.org/10.1086/670252

Haidt, J., & Graham, J. (2007). When morality opposes justice: Conservatives have moral intuitions that liberals may not recognize. *Social Justice Research, 20*(1), 98–116. https://doi.org/10.1007/s11211-007-0034-z

Harmon-Jones, E., & Peterson, C. K. (2009). Supine body position reduces neural response to anger evocation. *Psychological Science, 20*(10), 1209–1210. https://doi.org/10.1111/j.1467-9280.2009.02416.x

Harnad, S. (1990). The symbol grounding problem. *Physica D: Nonlinear Phenomena, 42*(1–3), 335–346. https://doi.org/10.1016/0167-2789(90)90087-6

Havas, D. A., Glenberg, A. M., Gutowski, K. A., Lucarelli, M. J., & Davidson, R. J. (2010). Cosmetic use of botulinum toxin-a affects processing of emotional language. *Psychological Science, 21*(7), 895–900. https://doi.org/10.1177/0956797610374742

Hellmann, J. H., Thoben, D. F., & Echterhoff, G. (2013). The sweet taste of revenge: Gustatory experience induces metaphor-consistent judgments of a harmful act. *Social Cognition, 31*(5), 531–542. https://doi.org/10.1521/soco.2013.31.5.531

Hess, U., Gryc, O., & Hareli, S. (2013). How shapes influence social judgments. *Social Cognition, 31*(1), 72–80. https://doi.org/10.1521/soco.2013.31.1.72

Higgins, E. T. (1996). Knowledge activation: Accessibility, applicability, and salience. In E. T. Higgins & A. W. Kruglanski (Eds.), *Social psychology: Handbook of basic principles* (pp. 133–168). Guilford Press.

Hong, J., & Sun, Y. (2012). Warm it up with love: The effect of physical coldness on liking of romance movies. *Journal of Consumer Research, 39*(2), 293–306. https://doi.org/10.1086/662613

Huang, J. Y., Ackerman, J. M., & Newman, G. E. (2017). Catching (up with) magical contagion: A review of contagion effects in consumer contexts. *Journal of the Association for Consumer Research, 2*(4), 430–443. https://doi.org/10.1086/693533

Huang, L. (2019). Mind–body dissonance: A catalyst to creativity. *Personality and Social Psychology Bulletin*,

46(5), 754–768. https://doi.org/10.1177/0146167219875145

Huang, L., & Galinsky, A. D. (2011). Mind–body dissonance: Conflict between the senses expands the mind's horizons. *Social Psychological & Personality Science*, 2(4), 351–359. https://doi.org/10.1177/1948550610391677

Hung, I. W., & Labroo, A. A. (2011). From firm muscles to firm willpower: Understanding the role of embodied cognition in self-regulation. *Journal of Consumer Research*, 37(6), 1046–1064. https://doi.org/10.1086/657240

Hung, S.-M., Styles, S. J., & Hsieh, P.-J. (2017). Can a word sound like a shape before you have seen it? Sound-shape mapping prior to conscious awareness. *Psychological Science*, 28(3), 263–275. https://doi.org/10.1177/0956797616677313

Ibarretxe-Antuñano, I. (2019). Perception metaphors in cognitive linguistics: Scope, motivation, and lexicalisation. In L. J. Speed, C. O'Meara, L. San Roque, & A. Majid (Eds.), *Converging evidence in language and communication research* (Vol. 19, pp. 43–64). John Benjamins Publishing Company. https://doi.org/10.1075/celcr.19.03iba

Imai, M., & Kita, S. (2014). The sound symbolism bootstrapping hypothesis for language acquisition and language evolution. *Philosophical Transactions of the Royal Society of London: Series B. Biological Sciences*, 369(1651), 20130298. https://doi.org/10.1098/rstb.2013.0298

James, W. (1890). *The principles of psychology*. H. Holt. https://books.google.ca/books?id=JLcAAAAAMAAJ

Janiszewski, C., & Wyer, R. S., Jr. (2014). Content and process priming: A review. *Journal of Consumer Psychology*, 24(1), 96–118. https://doi.org/10.1016/j.jcps.2013.05.006

Jiang, Y., Gorn, G. J., Galli, M., & Chattopadhyay, A. (2016). Does your company have the right logo? How and why circular- and angular-logo shapes influence brand attribute judgments. *Journal of Consumer Research*, 42(5), 709–726. https://doi.org/10.1093/jcr/ucv049

Johnston, W. A., Dark, V. J., & Jacoby, L. L. (1985). Perceptual fluency and recognition judgments. *Journal of Experimental Psychology: Learning, Memory, and Cognition*, 11(1), 3–11. https://doi.org/10.1037/0278-7393.11.1.3

Jostmann, N. B., Lakens, D., & Schubert, T. W. (2009). Weight as an embodiment of importance. *Psychological Science*, 20(9), 1169–1174. https://doi.org/10.1111/j.1467-9280.2009.02426.x

Kaspar, K. (2013). Washing one's hands after failure enhances optimism but hampers future performance. *Social Psychological & Personality Science*, 4(1), 69–73. https://doi.org/10.1177/1948550612443267

Körner, A., & Strack, F. (2019). Conditions for the clean slate effect after success or failure. *Journal of Social Psychology*, 159(1), 92–105. https://doi.org/10.1080/00224545.2018.1454881

Körner, A., Topolinski, S., & Strack, F. (2015). Routes to embodiment. *Frontiers in Psychology*, 6, 940. https://doi.org/10.3389/fpsyg.2015.00940

Kosslyn, S. M. (1994). *Image and brain: The resolution of the imagery debate*. MIT Press. https://doi.org/10.7551/mitpress/3653.001.0001

Kramer, T., & Block, L. G. (2014). Like Mike: Ability contagion through touched objects increases confidence and improves performance. *Organizational Behavior and Human Decision Processes*, 124(2), 215–228. https://doi.org/10.1016/j.obhdp.2014.03.009

Krishna, A. (2010). *Sensory marketing: Research on the sensuality of products*. Routledge. https://doi.org/10.1177/1469540512474532b

Krishna, A. (2012). An integrative review of sensory marketing: Engaging the senses to affect perception, judgment and behavior. *Journal of Consumer Psychology*, 22(3), 332–351. https://doi.org/10.1016/j.jcps.2011.08.003

Krishna, A., Lee, S. W. S., Li, X., & Schwarz, N. (2017). Embodied cognition, sensory marketing, and the conceptualization of consumers' judgment and decision processes: Introduction to the issue. *Journal of the Association for Consumer Research*, 2(4), 377–381. https://doi.org/10.1086/694453

Lakoff, G., & Johnson, M. (1980). *Metaphors we live by*. University of Chicago Press.

Lakoff, G., & Johnson, M. (1999). *Philosophy in the flesh: The embodied mind and its challenge to Western thought*. Basic Books.

Landau, M. J. (2017). *Conceptual metaphor in social psychology: The poetics of everyday life*. Routledge, Taylor & Francis Group.

Landau, M. J., Meier, B. P., & Keefer, L. A. (2010). A metaphor-enriched social cognition. *Psychological Bulletin*, 136(6), 1045–1067. https://doi.org/10.1037/a0020970

Landau, M. J., Oyserman, D., Keefer, L. A., & Smith, G. C. (2014). The college journey and academic engagement: How metaphor use enhances identity-based motivation. *Journal of Personality and Social Psychology*, 106(5), 679–698. https://doi.org/10.1037/a0036414

Larson, C. L., Aronoff, J., & Steuer, E. L. (2012). Simple geometric shapes are implicitly associated with affective value. *Motivation and Emotion*, 36(3), 404–413. https://doi.org/10.1007/s11031-011-9249-2

Lee, A., & Ji, L.-J. (2015, February). *Physical cleansing moderates the link between investment of labor and feelings of ownership* [Poster presentation]. Annual meeting of the Society for Personality and Social Psychology, Long Beach, CA, United States.

Lee, C., Linkenauger, S. A., Bakdash, J. Z., Joy-Gaba, J. A., & Profitt, D. R. (2011). Putting like a pro: The role of positive contagion in golf performance and perception. *PLOS ONE*, *6*(10), e26016. https://doi.org/10.1371/journal.pone.0026016

Lee, D. S., Kim, E., & Schwarz, N. (2015). Something smells fishy: Olfactory suspicion cues improve performance on the Moses illusion and Wason rule discovery task. *Journal of Experimental Social Psychology*, *59*, 47–50. https://doi.org/10.1016/j.jesp.2015.03.006

Lee, S. W. S. (2016). Multimodal priming of abstract constructs. *Current Opinion in Psychology*, *12*, 37–44. https://doi.org/10.1016/j.copsyc.2016.04.016

Lee, S. W. S., Chen, K., Ma, C., & Hoang, J. (2020). *Psychological antecedents and consequences of physical cleansing: A meta-analytic review* [Manuscript in preparation].

Lee, S. W. S., Millet, K., Grinstein, A., Pauwels, K., Johnston, P. R., Volkov, A. E., & van der Wal, A. (2020). *Threat and cleaning* [Manuscript in preparation].

Lee, S. W. S., & Schwarz, N. (2010a). Dirty hands and dirty mouths: Embodiment of the moral-purity metaphor is specific to the motor modality involved in moral transgression. *Psychological Science*, *21*(10), 1423–1425. https://doi.org/10.1177/0956797610382788

Lee, S. W. S., & Schwarz, N. (2010b). Washing away postdecisional dissonance. *Science*, *328*(5979), 709. https://doi.org/10.1126/science.1186799

Lee, S. W. S., & Schwarz, N. (2011). Wiping the slate clean: Psychological consequences of physical cleansing. *Current Directions in Psychological Science*, *20*(5), 307–311. https://doi.org/10.1177/0963721411422694

Lee, S. W. S., & Schwarz, N. (2012). Bidirectionality, mediation, and moderation of metaphorical effects: The embodiment of social suspicion and fishy smells. *Journal of Personality and Social Psychology*, *103*(5), 737–749. https://doi.org/10.1037/a0029708

Lee, S. W. S., & Schwarz, N. (2014). Metaphor in judgment and decision making. In M. Landau, M. D. Robinson, & B. P. Meier (Eds.), *The power of metaphor: Examining its influence on social life* (pp. 85–108). American Psychological Association. https://doi.org/10.1037/14278-005

Lee, S. W. S., & Schwarz, N. (2016). Clean-moral effects and clean-slate effects: Physical cleansing as an embodied procedure of psychological separation. In R. Duschinsky, S. Schnall, & D. H. Weiss (Eds.), *Purity and danger now: New perspectives* (pp. 136–161). Routledge.

Lee, S. W. S., & Schwarz, N. (2018). Methodological deviation from the original experiment. *Nature Human Behaviour*, *2*(9), 605. https://doi.org/10.1038/s41562-018-0403-7

Lee, S. W. S., & Schwarz, N. (2020). *A multi-process model of mind–body relations* [Manuscript in preparation].

Lee, S. W. S., & Schwarz, N. (2021). Grounded procedures: A proximate mechanism for the psychology of cleansing and other physical actions. *Behavioral and Brain Sciences*, *44*, e1. https://doi.org/10.1017/S0140525X20000308

Lee, S. W. S., Tang, H., Wan, J., Mai, X., & Liu, C. (2015). A cultural look at moral purity: Wiping the face clean. *Frontiers in Psychology*, *6*, 577. https://doi.org/10.3389/fpsyg.2015.00577

Leung, A. K.-Y., & Cohen, D. (2011). Within- and between-culture variation: Individual differences and the cultural logics of honor, face, and dignity cultures. *Journal of Personality and Social Psychology*, *100*(3), 507–526. https://doi.org/10.1037/a0022151

Li, H., & Cao, Y. (2017). Who's holding the moral higher ground: Religiosity and the vertical conception of morality. *Personality and Individual Differences*, *106*, 178–182. https://doi.org/10.1016/j.paid.2016.11.016

Li, X., Wei, L., & Soman, D. (2010). Sealing the emotions genie: The effects of physical enclosure on psychological closure. *Psychological Science*, *21*(8), 1047–1050. https://doi.org/10.1177/0956797610376653

Li, Y., Johnson, E. J., & Zaval, L. (2011). Local warming: Daily temperature change influences belief in global warming. *Psychological Science*, *22*(4), 454–459. https://doi.org/10.1177/0956797611400913

Liberman, N., & Trope, Y. (2008). The psychology of transcending the here and now. *Science*, *322*(5905), 1201–1205. https://doi.org/10.1126/science.1161958

Liljenquist, K., Zhong, C.-B., & Galinsky, A. D. (2010). The smell of virtue: Clean scents promote reciprocity and charity. *Psychological Science*, *21*(3), 381–383. https://doi.org/10.1177/0956797610361426

Linder, D. E., Cooper, J., & Jones, E. E. (1967). Decision freedom as a determinant of the role of incentive magnitude in attitude change. *Journal of Personality and Social Psychology*, *6*(3), 245–254. https://doi.org/10.1037/h0021220

Lockwood, G., & Dingemanse, M. (2015). Iconicity in the lab: A review of behavioral, developmental, and neuroimaging research into sound-symbolism. *Frontiers in Psychology*, *6*, 1246. https://doi.org/10.3389/fpsyg.2015.01246

Macrae, C. N., Raj, R. S., Best, S. B., Christian, B. M., & Miles, L. K. (2013). Imagined sensory experiences can shape person perception: It's a matter of visual perspective. *Journal of Experimental Social Psychology*, *49*(3), 595–598. https://doi.org/10.1016/j.jesp.2012.10.002

Maglio, S. J., Rabaglia, C. D., Feder, M. A., Krehm, M., & Trope, Y. (2014). Vowel sounds in words affect mental construal and shift preferences for targets. *Journal of Experimental Psychology: General*, *143*(3), 1082–1096. https://doi.org/10.1037/a0035543

Marotta, M., & Bohner, G. (2013, September). *Dissonanz abwaschen, Dissonanz reinreiben: Symbolische Abschwächung vs. Verstärkung von Dissonanz nach Entscheidungen* [Washing dissonance off, rubbing dissonance in: Symbolic attenuation and intensification of postdecisional dissonance]. Tagung der Fachgruppe Sozialpsychologie, Hagen, Germany.

Maurer, D., Pathman, T., & Mondloch, C. J. (2006). The shape of boubas: Sound–shape correspondences in toddlers and adults. *Developmental Science*, *9*(3), 316–322. https://doi.org/10.1111/j.1467-7687.2006.00495.x

Meier, B. P., Hauser, D. J., Robinson, M. D., Friesen, C. K., & Schjeldahl, K. (2007). What's "up" with God? Vertical space as a representation of the divine. *Journal of Personality and Social Psychology*, *93*(5), 699–710. https://doi.org/10.1037/0022-3514.93.5.699

Meier, B. P., Moeller, S. K., Riemer-Peltz, M., & Robinson, M. D. (2012). Sweet taste preferences and experiences predict prosocial inferences, personalities, and behaviors. *Journal of Personality and Social Psychology*, *102*(1), 163–174. https://doi.org/10.1037/a0025253

Meier, B. P., & Robinson, M. D. (2004). Why the sunny side is up: Association between affect and vertical position. *Psychological Science*, *15*(4), 243–247. https://doi.org/10.1111/j.0956-7976.2004.00659.x

Meier, B. P., Schnall, S., Schwarz, N., & Bargh, J. A. (2012). Embodiment in social psychology. *Topics in Cognitive Science*, *4*(4), 705–716. https://doi.org/10.1111/j.1756-8765.2012.01212.x

Meier, B. P., Sellbom, M., & Wygant, D. B. (2007). Failing to take the moral high ground: Psychopathy and the vertical representation of morality. *Personality and Individual Differences*, *43*(4), 757–767. https://doi.org/10.1016/j.paid.2007.02.001

Menary, R. (Ed.). (2010). *The extended mind*. MIT Press. https://doi.org/10.7551/mitpress/9780262014038.001.0001

Meyers-Levy, J., & Zhu, R. (2007). The influence of ceiling height: The effect of priming on the type of processing that people use. *Journal of Consumer Research*, *34*(2), 174–186. https://doi.org/10.1086/519146

Miller, G. A. (1956). The magical number seven plus or minus two: Some limits on our capacity for processing information. *Psychological Review*, *63*(2), 81–97. https://doi.org/10.1037/h0043158

Mukherjee, S., Kramer, T., & Kulow, K. (2017). The effect of spicy gustatory sensations on variety-seeking. *Psychology and Marketing*, *34*(8), 786–794. https://doi.org/10.1002/mar.21022

Nemeroff, C., & Rozin, P. (1994). The contagion concept in adult thinking in the United States: Transmission of germs and of interpersonal influence. *Ethos*, *22*(2), 158–186. https://doi.org/10.1525/eth.1994.22.2.02a00020

Newman, G. E., & Bloom, P. (2014). Physical contact influences how much people pay at celebrity auctions. *Proceedings of the National Academy of Sciences of the United States of America*, *111*(10), 3705–3708. https://doi.org/10.1073/pnas.1313637111

Newman, G. E., Diesendruck, G., & Bloom, P. (2011). Celebrity contagion and the value of objects. *Journal of Consumer Research*, *38*(2), 215–228. https://doi.org/10.1086/658999

Niedenthal, P. M. (2007). Embodying emotion. *Science*, *316*(5827), 1002–1005. https://doi.org/10.1126/science.1136930

Niedenthal, P. M., Barsalou, L. W., Winkielman, P., Krauth-Gruber, S., & Ric, F. (2005). Embodiment in attitudes, social perception, and emotion. *Personality and Social Psychology Review*, *9*(3), 184–211. https://doi.org/10.1207/s15327957pspr0903_1

Noah, T., Schul, Y., & Mayo, R. (2018). When both the original study and its failed replication are correct: Feeling observed eliminates the facial-feedback effect. *Journal of Personality and Social Psychology*, *114*(5), 657–664. https://doi.org/10.1037/pspa0000121

Núñez, R. E., & Sweetser, E. (2006). With the future behind them: Convergent evidence from Aymara language and gesture in the crosslinguistic comparison of spatial construals of time. *Cognitive Science*, *30*(3), 401–450. https://doi.org/10.1207/s15516709cog0000_62

Okamura, Y., & Ura, M. (2018). Draw squares, and you will discover that many competent and rigorous people are around you: Shape priming influences impressions regarding the interpersonal environment. *Psychological Thought*, *11*(2), 106–111. https://doi.org/10.5964/psyct.v11i2.290

Okamura, Y., & Ura, M. (2019a). I am physically and personality-wise warmer when wearing round eyeglasses: Shape priming influences personality judgments and estimated temperature. *Psychological Thought*, *12*(2), 176–184. https://doi.org/10.5964/psyct.v12i2.361

Okamura, Y., & Ura, M. (2019b). Round shapes are for dating, square shapes are for business: Priming the concept of warmth and competence activates the representation of shapes. *Problems of Psychology in the*

21st Century, 13(1), 39–45. https://doi.org/10.33225/ppc/19.13.39

Oxford University Press. (n.d.). *Oxford English dictionary.* https://www.oed.com/

Parsons, L. M., Fox, P. T., Downs, J. H., Glass, T., Hirsch, T. B., Martin, C. C., Jerabek, P. A., & Lancaster, J. L. (1995). Use of implicit motor imagery for visual shape discrimination as revealed by PET. *Nature, 375*(6526), 54–58. https://doi.org/10.1038/375054a0

Peck, J., Barger, V. A., & Webb, A. (2013). In search of a surrogate for touch: The effect of haptic imagery on perceived ownership. *Journal of Consumer Psychology, 23*(2), 189–196. https://doi.org/10.1016/j.jcps.2012.09.001

Peck, J., & Shu, S. B. (2009). The effect of mere touch on perceived ownership. *Journal of Consumer Research, 36*(3), 434–447. https://doi.org/10.1086/598614

Priester, J. R., Cacioppo, J. T., & Petty, R. E. (1996). The influence of motor processes on attitudes toward novel versus familiar semantic stimuli. *Personality and Social Psychology Bulletin, 22*(5), 442–447. https://doi.org/10.1177/0146167296225002

Pulvermüller, F., Shtyrov, Y., & Ilmoniemi, R. (2005). Brain signatures of meaning access in action word recognition. *Journal of Cognitive Neuroscience, 17*(6), 884–892. https://doi.org/10.1162/0898929054021111

Rabaglia, C. D., Maglio, S. J., Krehm, M., Seok, J. H., & Trope, Y. (2016). The sound of distance. *Cognition, 152,* 141–149. https://doi.org/10.1016/j.cognition.2016.04.001

Ramachandran, V., & Hubbard, E. (2001). Synaesthesia—A window into perception, thought and language. *Journal of Consciousness Studies, 8*(12), 3–34.

Reisberg, D. (Ed.). (1992). *Auditory imagery.* Lawrence Erlbaum Associates, Inc.

Ren, D., Tan, K., Arriaga, X. B., & Chan, K. Q. (2015). Sweet love: The effects of sweet taste experience on romantic perceptions. *Journal of Social and Personal Relationships, 32*(7), 905–921. https://doi.org/10.1177/0265407514554512

Risen, J. L., & Critcher, C. R. (2011). Visceral fit: While in a visceral state, associated states of the world seem more likely. *Journal of Personality and Social Psychology, 100*(5), 777–793. https://doi.org/10.1037/a0022460

Riskind, J. H., & Gotay, C. C. (1982). Physical posture: Could it have regulatory or feedback effects on motivation and emotion? *Motivation and Emotion, 6*(3), 273–298. https://doi.org/10.1007/BF00992249

Rozin, P., Haidt, J., & McCauley, C. R. (2008). Disgust. In M. Lewis, J. M. Haviland-Jones, & L. F. Barrett (Eds.), *Handbook of emotions* (3rd ed., pp. 757–776). Guilford Press.

Rupert, R. D. (2004). Challenges to the hypothesis of extended cognition. *Journal of Philosophy, 101*(8), 389–428. https://doi.org/10.5840/jphil2004101826

Russell, J. A. (2003). Core affect and the psychological construction of emotion. *Psychological Review, 110*(1), 145–172. https://doi.org/10.1037/0033-295X.110.1.145

Sagioglou, C., & Greitemeyer, T. (2014). Bitter taste causes hostility. *Personality and Social Psychology Bulletin, 40*(12), 1589–1597. https://doi.org/10.1177/0146167214552792

Santiago, J., Román, A., & Ouellet, M. (2011). Flexible foundations of abstract thought: A review and a theory. In T. W. Schubert & A. Maass (Eds.), *Spatial dimensions of social thought* (pp. 39–108). De Gruyter. https://doi.org/10.1515/9783110254310.39

Schachter, S., & Singer, J. E. (1962). Cognitive, social, and physiological determinants of emotional state. *Psychological Review, 69*(5), 379–399. https://doi.org/10.1037/h0046234

Schlosser, A. E. (2015). The sweet taste of gratitude: Feeling grateful increases choice and consumption of sweets. *Journal of Consumer Psychology, 25*(4), 561–576. https://doi.org/10.1016/j.jcps.2015.02.006

Schnall, S., Benton, J., & Harvey, S. (2008). With a clean conscience: Cleanliness reduces the severity of moral judgments. *Psychological Science, 19*(12), 1219–1222. https://doi.org/10.1111/j.1467-9280.2008.02227.x

Schnall, S., Haidt, J., Clore, G. L., & Jordan, A. H. (2008). Disgust as embodied moral judgment. *Personality and Social Psychology Bulletin, 34*(8), 1096–1109. https://doi.org/10.1177/0146167208317771

Schubert, T. W. (2005). Your highness: Vertical positions as perceptual symbols of power. *Journal of Personality and Social Psychology, 89*(1), 1–21. https://doi.org/10.1037/0022-3514.89.1.1

Schuldt, J. P., & Roh, S. (2014). Of accessibility and applicability: How heat-related cues affect belief in "global warming" versus "climate change." *Social Cognition, 32*(3), 217–238. https://doi.org/10.1521/soco.2014.32.3.217

Schwarz, N. (2010). Meaning in context: Metacognitive experiences. In B. Mesquita, L. F. Barrett, & E. R. Smith (Eds.), *The mind in context* (pp. 105–125). Guilford Press.

Schwarz, N. (2012). Feelings-as-information theory. In P. A. M. Van Lange, A. W. Kruglanski, & E. T. Higgins (Eds.), *Handbook of theories of social psychology* (pp. 289–308). Sage. https://doi.org/10.4135/9781446249215.n15

Schwarz, N. (2015). Metacognition. In M. Mikulincer & P. R. Shaver (Eds.), *APA handbook of personality and social psychology: Vol. 1. Attitudes and social cognition* (pp. 203–229). American Psychological Association.

Schwarz, N., Bless, H., Strack, F., Klumpp, G., & Rittenauer-Schatka, H., & Simons, A. (1991). Ease of retrieval as information: Another look at the availability heuristic. *Journal of Personality and Social Psychology, 61*(2), 195–202. https://doi.org/10.1037/0022-3514.61.2.195

Schwarz, N., & Clore, G. L. (2007). Feelings and phenomenal experiences. In A. W. Kruglanski & E. T. Higgins (Eds.), *Social psychology: Handbook of basic principles* (2nd ed., pp. 385–407). Guilford Press.

Sebastian, P., Kaufmann, L., & de la Piedad Garcia, X. (2017, January). *In the nose, not in the beholder: Embodied cognition effects override individual differences*. Society for Personality and Social Psychology.

Semin, G. R., & Smith, E. R. (Eds.). (2008). *Embodied grounding: Social, cognitive, affective, and neuroscientific approaches*. Cambridge University Press. https://doi.org/10.1017/CBO9780511805837

Sheaffer, R., Gal, R., & Pansky, A. (2021). Resisting misinformation via discrepancy detection: Effects of an unaware suspicion cue. *Memory*. https://doi.org/10.1080/09658211.2021.1917618

Shen, H., Zhang, M., & Krishna, A. (2016). Computer interfaces and the "direct-touch" effect: Can iPads increase the choice of hedonic food? *Journal of Marketing Research, 53*(5), 745–758. https://doi.org/10.1509/jmr.14.0563

Sjöström, A., Magraw-Mickelson, Z., & Gollwitzer, M. (2018). What makes displaced revenge taste sweet: Retributing displaced responsibility or sending a message to the original perpetrator? *European Journal of Social Psychology, 48*(4), 490–506. https://doi.org/10.1002/ejsp.2345

Slepian, M. L., Rule, N. O., & Ambady, N. (2012). Proprioception and person perception: Politicians and professors. *Personality and Social Psychology Bulletin, 38*(12), 1621–1628. https://doi.org/10.1177/0146167212457786

Slepian, M. L., Weisbuch, M., Rule, N. O., & Ambady, N. (2011). Tough and tender: Embodied categorization of gender. *Psychological Science, 22*(1), 26–28. https://doi.org/10.1177/0956797610390388

Soriano, C., & Valenzuela, J. (2008, May 31). *Sensorial perception as a source domain: A cross-linguistic study* [Paper presentation]. Seventh International Conference on Researching and Applying Metaphor (RaAM 7), Cáceres, Spain.

Stepper, S., & Strack, F. (1993). Proprioceptive determinants of emotional and nonemotional feelings. *Journal of Personality and Social Psychology, 64*(2), 211–220. https://doi.org/10.1037/0022-3514.64.2.211

Strack, F., Martin, L. L., & Stepper, S. (1988). Inhibiting and facilitating conditions of the human smile: A nonobtrusive test of the facial feedback hypothesis. *Journal of Personality and Social Psychology, 54*(5), 768–777. https://doi.org/10.1037/0022-3514.54.5.768

Stroessner, S. J., Benitez, J., Perez, M. A., Wyman, A. B., Carpinella, C. M., & Johnson, K. L. (2020). What's in a shape? Evidence of gender category associations with basic forms. *Journal of Experimental Social Psychology, 87*, 103915. https://doi.org/10.1016/j.jesp.2019.103915

Thaler, R. (1985). Mental accounting and consumer choice. *Marketing Science, 4*(3), 199–214. https://doi.org/10.1287/mksc.4.3.199

Thelen, E., & Smith, L. B. (1994). *A dynamic systems approach to the development of cognition and action*. MIT Press.

Topolinski, S. (2017). Articulation patterns in names: A hidden route to consumer preference. *Journal of the Association for Consumer Research, 2*(4), 382–391. https://doi.org/10.1086/692820

Trope, Y., & Liberman, N. (2010). Construal-level theory of psychological distance. *Psychological Review, 117*(2), 440–463. https://doi.org/10.1037/a0018963

Tucker, M., & Ellis, R. (1998). On the relations between seen objects and components of potential actions. *Journal of Experimental Psychology: Human Perception and Performance, 24*(3), 830–846. https://doi.org/10.1037/0096-1523.24.3.830

van Gelder, T., & Port, R. F. (1996). It's about time: An overview of the dynamical approach to cognition. In R. Port & T. van Gelder (Eds.), *Mind as motion: Explorations in the dynamics of cognition* (pp. 1–43). Massachusetts Institute of Technology.

Wagenmakers, E.-J., Beek, T., Dijkhoff, L., Gronau, Q. F., Acosta, A., Adams, R. B., Jr., Albohn, D. N., Allard, E. S., Benning, S. D., Blouin-Hudon, E. M., Bulnes, L. C., Caldwell, T. L., Calin-Jageman, R. J., Capaldi, C. A., Carfagno, N. S., Chasten, K. T., Cleeremans, A., Connell, L., DeCicco, J. M., . . . Zwaan, R. A. (2016). Registered replication report: Strack, Martin, & Stepper (1988). *Perspectives on Psychological Science, 11*(6), 917–928. https://doi.org/10.1177/1745691616674458

Wang, C., Zhu, R. J., & Handy, T. C. (2016). Experiencing haptic roughness promotes empathy. *Journal of Consumer Psychology, 26*(3), 350–362. https://doi.org/10.1016/j.jcps.2015.11.001

Wang, L., & Chen, Q. (2018). Experiencing sweet taste affects romantic semantic processing. *Current Psychology, 38*, 1131–1139. https://doi.org/10.1007/s12144-018-9877-8

Wang, L., Chen, Q., Chen, Y., & Zhong, R. (2019). The effect of sweet taste on romantic semantic processing: An ERP study. *Frontiers in Psychology, 10*, 1573. https://doi.org/10.3389/fpsyg.2019.01573

Wason, P. C. (1960). On the failure to eliminate hypotheses in a conceptual task. *Quarterly Journal of*

Experimental Psychology, 12(3), 129–140. https://doi.org/10.1080/17470216008416717

Waterman, C. K., & Katkin, E. S. (1967). Energizing (dynamogenic) effect of cognitive dissonance on task performance. *Journal of Personality and Social Psychology, 6*(2), 126–131. https://doi.org/10.1037/h0024573

Wegner, D. M. (1987). Transactive memory: A contemporary analysis of the group mind. In B. Mullen & G. R. Goethals (Eds.), *Theories of group behavior* (pp. 185–208). Springer. https://doi.org/10.1007/978-1-4612-4634-3_9

Wegner, D. M., Erber, R., & Raymond, P. (1991). Transactive memory in close relationships. *Journal of Personality and Social Psychology, 61*(6), 923–929. https://doi.org/10.1037/0022-3514.61.6.923

Wells, G. L., & Petty, R. E. (1980). The effects of over head movements on persuasion: Compatibility and incompatibility of responses. *Basic and Applied Social Psychology, 1*(3), 219–230. https://doi.org/10.1207/s15324834basp0103_2

Wertsch, J. V. (2017). Mediated action. In W. Bechtel & G. Graham (Eds.), *A companion to cognitive science* (pp. 518–525). Blackwell Publishing Ltd. https://doi.org/10.1002/9781405164535.ch40

Williams, L. E., Huang, J. Y., & Bargh, J. A. (2009). The scaffolded mind: Higher mental processes are grounded in early experience of the physical world. *European Journal of Social Psychology, 39*(7), 1257–1267. https://doi.org/10.1002/ejsp.665

Wilson, M. (2002). Six views of embodied cognition. *Psychonomic Bulletin & Review, 9*(4), 625–636. https://doi.org/10.3758/BF03196322

Wilson, P. R. (1968). Perceptual distortion of height as a function of ascribed academic status. *Journal of Social Psychology, 74*(1), 97–102. https://doi.org/10.1080/00224545.1968.9919806

Wullenkord, R., Fraune, M. R., Eyssel, F., & Šabanović, S. (2016). Getting in touch: How imagined, actual, and physical contact affect evaluations of robots. *2016 25th IEEE International Symposium on Robot and Human Interactive Communication (RO-MAN)*, 980–985. https://doi.org/10.1109/ROMAN.2016.7745228

Wyer, R. S., Xu, A. J., & Shen, H. (2012). The effects of past behavior on future goal-directed activity. In J. M. Olson & M. P. Zanna (Eds.), *Advances in experimental social psychology* (Vol. 46, pp. 237–283). Academic Press. https://doi.org/10.1016/B978-0-12-394281-4.00014-3

Xu, A. J., Zwick, R., & Schwarz, N. (2012). Washing away your (good or bad) luck: Physical cleansing affects risk-taking behavior. *Journal of Experimental Psychology: General, 141*(1), 26–30. https://doi.org/10.1037/a0023997

Yang, X., Mao, H., Jia, L., & Bublitz, M. G. (2019). A sweet romance: Divergent effects of romantic stimuli on the consumption of sweets. *Journal of Consumer Research, 45*(6), 1213–1229. https://doi.org/10.1093/jcr/ucy044

Zanna, M. P., & Cooper, J. (1974). Dissonance and the pill: An attribution approach to studying the arousal properties of dissonance. *Journal of Personality and Social Psychology, 29*(5), 703–709. https://doi.org/10.1037/h0036651

Zhang, M., & Li, X. (2012). From physical weight to psychological significance: The contribution of semantic activations. *Journal of Consumer Research, 38*(6), 1063–1075. https://doi.org/10.1086/661768

Zhang, Y., Risen, J. L., & Hosey, C. (2014). Reversing one's fortune by pushing away bad luck. *Journal of Experimental Psychology: General, 143*(3), 1171–1184. https://doi.org/10.1037/a0034023

Zhong, C.-B., & Liljenquist, K. (2006). Washing away your sins: Threatened morality and physical cleansing. *Science, 313*(5792), 1451–1452. https://doi.org/10.1126/science.1130726

Zhong, C.-B., Strejcek, B., & Sivanathan, N. (2010). A clean self can render harsh moral judgment. *Journal of Experimental Social Psychology, 46*(5), 859–862. https://doi.org/10.1016/j.jesp.2010.04.003

Zhu, R. J., & Argo, J. J. (2013). Exploring the impact of various shaped seating arrangements on persuasion. *Journal of Consumer Research, 2*(1), 336–349. https://doi.org/10.1086/670392

Zhu, R. J., & Mehta, R. (2017). Sensory experiences and consumer creativity. *Journal of the Association for Consumer Research, 2*(4), 472–484. https://doi.org/10.1086/693161

Zillmann, D. (1971). Excitation transfer in communication-mediated aggressive behavior. *Journal of Experimental Social Psychology, 7*(4), 419–434. https://doi.org/10.1016/0022-1031(71)90075-8

Zwaan, R. A., & Taylor, L. J. (2006). Seeing, acting, understanding: Motor resonance in language comprehension. *Journal of Experimental Psychology: General, 135*(1), 1–11. https://doi.org/10.1037/0096-3445.135.1.1

CHAPTER 25

THE INTERPLAY OF AFFECT AND COGNITION: A REVIEW OF HOW FEELINGS GUIDE CONSUMER BEHAVIOR

Rashmi Adaval and Maria Galli

> Your reason and your passion are the rudder and the sails of your seafaring soul.
>
> If either your sails or your rudder be broken, you can but toss and drift, or else be held at a standstill in mid-seas. For reason, ruling alone, is a force confining; and passion, unattended, is a flame that burns to its own destruction.
>
> —Kahlil Gibran, *The Prophet*

Gibran's quote in *The Prophet* aptly summarizes our perception of the role that feelings and cognitions play in all human experience. Consumer experiences are no exception. Whether one stares longingly at a rich, chocolate cake that invites gluttony in the face of a dietary restraint or whether one wonders about the wisdom of taking out a bigger loan for a bigger, more attractive home, our reasons and our passions might often appear to be in conflict. Yet, consumers navigate these waters by heeding both.

In the last 3 decades, consumer psychologists have investigated how feelings (whether they emerge from the task at hand or from seemingly irrelevant contextual factors) influence the judgments and decisions consumers make. Issues investigated include the impact of moods on tolerance to risk (e.g., Isen & Patrick, 1983) and creativity (e.g., Isen et al., 1985, 1987), the effect of feelings on attitudes (e.g., Batra & Stayman, 1990), the affect transfer from ads to brands (e.g., Allen & Janiszewski, 1989), the use of affect as information about one's reactions to product information (e.g., Pham, 1998), how feelings affect information processing (e.g., Adaval, 2001, 2003), how metacognitive feelings affect judgments and decisions (e.g., A. Y. Lee, 2002; A. Y. Lee & Labroo, 2004), and the impact of specific emotions on judgments and decisions (e.g., Garg et al., 2005). Although the topics covered seem diverse, certain central and core findings as they pertain to the behavior of consumers have become apparent. These are consolidated in the current chapter.

This chapter reviews the effects of both pleasant and unpleasant feelings on consumption behavior, taking into account their interplay with cognitions. The relatively large body of literature on affective experience consists of research on the effects of generalized positive and negative affective (mood) states and emotions (e.g., fear, anger, embarrassment, guilt). In addition, prior research has examined how subjective feelings (e.g., feelings of fluency arising out of processing ease or difficulty) impact judgment and choice and how affective stimuli paired with brands impact how these brands are judged.

https://doi.org/10.1037/0000262-025
APA Handbook of Consumer Psychology, L. R. Kahle (Editor-in-Chief)
Copyright © 2022 by the American Psychological Association. All rights reserved.

To make this rather large body of work tractable, the chapter begins with definitions of terms and a brief historical perspective on how feelings and emotions have been viewed and the specific challenges researchers faced in studying these topics. This is followed by a discussion of the role of cognitive appraisals in the elicitation of feelings and findings from the cognitive neuroscience literature that parallel some of the appraisal stages. Next, after a brief discussion of sources of feelings, key findings from research on moods, specific emotions, and metacognitive feelings are summarized.

DEFINITION AND PERSPECTIVES

Although *affect* typically refers to positively or negatively valenced subjective reactions, the definition of affective terms (e.g., emotions and moods), their constituent parts, and their representation has remained elusive. Initial conceptualizations (Bower, 1981; Forgas, 1995; Isen et al., 1978; Wyer & Srull, 1989) assumed that moods and emotions were concepts in memory, associated with various features and attributes (including the subjective reactions one experiences). For example, a happy mood concept might be associated with things that make one happy, such as ice cream, sunny days, beaches, and so forth. The activation of any of these could cue the retrieval of this happiness concept along with all of its associated concepts and could affect the interpretation of information. However, empirical evidence for the cuing of affect-congruent concepts in memory was weak (Niedenthal & Setterlund, 1994; Niedenthal et al., 1997; see also Wyer et al., 1999), leading to questions about how one should think about various feelings.

Differences in perspectives regarding the definition of affective terms have partly arisen because researchers have focused on different parts of the subjective experience. The following examples help illustrate this. Consider the feelings elicited by two situations. First, imagine you are walking down a dark alley and hear footsteps. A surreptitious glance back reveals a group of four men picking up their pace. The experience of fear consists of different parts, including an evaluative component, such as an appraisal that this might be bad and dangerous; a physiological reaction, such as an increased heart rate, sweating, and elevated blood pressure; the overt, physical manifestation of this reaction through pale skin and quick, darting eyes; a behavioral aspect that urges you to flee; and mental states of alertness and vigilance. All of this can, of course, be experienced as an overall unpleasant reaction. Next, consider a somewhat different situation where you wake up feeling down. As you drag yourself to get some coffee, you try but cannot articulate the reasons why you feel down. Even though the appraisal does not yield any clues about why you feel down, the physiological reactions and their overt expression, as well as the action (or inaction) tendencies that are elicited, are also present in this second situation. Although both experiences feel different subjectively, they share commonalities.

In attempting to arrive at a working definition, researchers have focused on different aspects of the earlier situations, such as how the experience consciously feels, the evaluation of the eliciting stimuli, their motivational properties, or the behavioral responses they elicit, and this has led to varying definitions (Scarantino & de Sousa, 2018). In the current chapter, we focus on the commonalities shared by the two experiences described and adopt the definition of affect proposed by Wyer et al. (1999). Specifically, *affect* is defined as a cluster of physiological reactions that is subjectively experienced and recognized as positive or negative feelings. It arises out of a cognitive appraisal process in which both the stimulus eliciting the feelings and the feelings themselves might be evaluated. Under this broad umbrella term exist other types of affective reactions such emotions and moods.

Emotions are typically elicited in response to cognitions about actions, events, or objects. Different cognitive appraisals of the same situation could lead to different emotions (Ortony et al., 1988). Losing one's job could, for instance, elicit sadness and anxiety, if one focuses on the consequences, or alternately anger, if one focuses on the actions of the company. Other mild states of euphoria or dysphoria are referred to as *moods*. In general, moods are residual effects of emotions where the eliciting cause (or the associated cognitive activity) is no longer salient and the reactions to it have not fully dissipated.

Although a large body of work has focused on moods and emotions, other types of affective reactions exist. These include feelings of ease or difficulty, as well as other epistemic feelings such as feelings of knowing, uncertainty, surprise, and so forth. These fall under the broad umbrella of metacognitive experience. *Metacognitions* are essentially thoughts about thinking, and such thoughts can be applied to certain subjective reactions as well (Carruthers, 2017; Schwarz, 2015). For example, one can realize that a body of text is difficult to read without realizing that this is because the lighting is poor or because the fonts are difficult to process. This metacognitive experience of ease or difficulty thus has an affective response that together with the thoughts about it could impact judgments. We refer to this affective response as *metacognitive feelings*.

To understand the interaction between declarative knowledge (e.g., "I feel afraid") and the various types of affective reactions (e.g., a sinking feeling in one's stomach), it helps to understand the numerous assumptions that have been made in the past. As mentioned earlier, initial conceptualizations of affect (Bower, 1981; Isen et al., 1978; Wyer & Srull, 1989) assumed that it was a concept in memory, which could affect the interpretation of information by cuing the retrieval of associated concepts. However, available evidence was at odds with these initial conceptualizations. In later conceptualizations of affect, Wyer et al. (1999) suggested that affective reactions are responses to concepts and schemata. Thus, one might experience a racing heart at the sight of a tiger. Though a racing heart is not part of the cognitive system itself, one might form concepts about this reaction (e.g., "I feel afraid"), and these concepts can be used in much the same way as other concepts. For instance, they may be used to interpret other stimuli or might trigger response tendencies that generalize to new situations. Distinguishing between the physiological reactions that one experiences in the previous example (i.e., a racing heart) and the awareness of the (subjective) experience as unpleasant allows for the possibility that the latter information can be an input in one's decisions or judgment (Schwarz & Clore, 1983).

That is, concepts about how one feels provide a valid basis for decision making, just as any other relevant concept.

This theoretical development was particularly significant for research on consumption behavior because in this domain, there is a conscious attempt to not only make the consumer feel good (e.g., by playing music in stores) but also to present to them an array of offerings that might themselves elicit positive affect. The recognition of affective experience as a source of information in the judgment process allowed one to consider affect from both sources and sparked considerable research. To summarize, many different kinds of affective experiences are possible, and to understand the diversity of affective experiences and their intimate relationship with cognitions, it is important to understand how they are elicited.

THE ELICITATION OF FEELING

Feelings typically arise as a consequence of appraisals of one's environment. These appraisals can be of different types and might consist of several stages as the individual attempts to assess the extent and seriousness of rewards and threats in the environment. Several cognitive theories of appraisal exist. Rather than summarizing all of them, we focus instead on discussing the sequential nature of these appraisals and draw parallels to recent research in cognitive neuroscience that matches these stages.

Cognitive Appraisal Theories

Magna Arnold (1960) was among the first ones to suggest that individuals typically evaluate things that they encounter as "good," "bad," or "neutral" and that this process happens automatically and immediately upon exposure to the target object. These initial appraisals can result in approach, avoid, or ignore behaviors (Ellsworth & Scherer, 2003). Several theories of appraisal exist (e.g., Frijda, 1986; Lazarus, 1991a, 1991b; Schachter & Singer, 1962; Scherer et al., 2001; Smith & Ellsworth, 1985), and they share some commonalities. They are almost always sequential in their description of the appraisal process. At the outset, they involve the detection of novelty and change as well as the assessment of whether this change is pleasant or unpleasant. Next, relevance is assessed: Is this change conducive to the individual's survival and well-being? Is it consistent with their currently active goals? The final stages consist of an assessment of one's ability to deal with the new situation, an assessment of the possible outcomes, and a consideration of the implications of one's actions in a larger social context.

According to appraisal theorists, the type of emotion that is elicited can be predicted reliably if the nature of the appraisal is known. Thus, for example, a similar feeling could be appraised as either shame or guilt depending on whether it is contextualized relative to the self (shame) or other (guilt). Ellsworth and Scherer (2003) suggested that emotions provide an evolutionarily evolved system of responding because they simply motivate behavior in a manner that can be altered, if needed, after a reappraisal of the situation (Lazarus, 1966). Thus, primary appraisals might be followed by secondary appraisals, and further reappraisals might be initiated to allow the individual to adapt to the situation.

A true test of what the underlying dimensions of these appraisal processes are has proved difficult because these tests typically rely on measured emotions and self-reports. Manipulating emotions and obtaining self-reports of appraisal processes have addressed this criticism to some extent (Ellsworth & Scherer, 2003). However, some researchers have raised questions about this type of circular reasoning. For example, a manipulation that elicits fear and then measures the appraisal dimensions raises the question: Are appraisals the eliciting features of the emotion, or are they the result of the induced emotion (cf. Ellsworth & Scherer, 2003)? More recently, however, findings in cognitive neuroscience suggest intriguing parallels with some of the dimensions outlined by appraisal theorists and might provide support for their existence.

The Cognitive Neuroscience of Affective Experiences

Brain imaging techniques have provided valuable tools to study emotional experience and identify how we react to attractive versus unattractive stimuli, how feelings influence decision making, and the variability in emotional responses between individuals (Damasio, 1994; Davidson, 1995; Deak, 2011; LeDoux, 1996; Panksepp, 1998).

Although several regions of the brain are responsible for appraising and responding to stimuli, there are four that appear germane to the current discussion: the amygdala, the insula, the anterior cingulate cortex, and the orbitofrontal cortex. The amygdala was initially associated with the detection of threat (i.e., fear-eliciting stimuli) and the coding of emotional signals such as facial expressions (LeDoux, 1996). However, more recent research suggests a broader role that encompasses detecting stimuli that are arousing and relevant to the individual (Hermann et al., 2010; Sander, 2009), as well the assessment of valence (Whalen et al., 2001). Thus, its role might be to help regulate information processing and guide the individual's attention to emotionally relevant stimuli. This appears to coincide with the early appraisal dimensions of valence and novelty.

A second region, the insula, is also known to coordinate sensorimotor response to threatening and unexpected stimuli (Szily & Kéri, 2008). That is, the insula appears to sound the alarm bell when a threat is imminent (Reiman et al., 1997). To that end, it has a role to play in bringing emotions to the level of consciousness (Critchley et al., 2004). This interoceptive awareness likely leads to a response, since it might signal a state of reward or threat (Craig, 2002; Reiman et al., 1997).

The insula is also active during the recall or imagination of an emotional event (Phan et al., 2002), suggesting that once the emotion-eliciting stimulus has been experienced, it is retained in memory (Lane et al., 1997). Once again, the parallels to the appraisal dimension of self-relevance and importance to the individual are noteworthy. A related part of the brain, the anterior cingulate cortex, is also involved in emotional monitoring and the regulation of emotion with respect to ongoing goals and priorities so that the appropriate responses can be selected and signals can be sent to the prefrontal cortex in case further behavior modification is desirable (Bush et al., 2000).

Finally, the orbitofrontal cortex appears to be responsible for learning how stimuli might have emotional and motivational value. It shows valence-independent activity and responds to both rewards and punishment. Further, there is some lateral specialization such that the left prefrontal area is connected to approach behaviors and the maintenance of goals, whereas the right regions are associated with avoidance and withdrawal (Davidson, 1992a, 1992b, 1995, 1998). Additionally, the structure of the orbitofrontal cortex allows it not only to integrate sensory information but also to modulate processing and provide input in the elicitation of motor responses (Morris & Dolan, 2004), tying in with the idea that appraisal theorists have often pushed: Appraisals are adaptive and elicit approach and avoidance responses. Thus, evidence from fairly diverse domains using different methodologies provides converging evidence that initial appraisals elicit affective reactions to the object, event, or situation being appraised. This affective reaction, however, can spill over to stimuli that happen to be present in close proximity to it.

SOURCES OF AFFECT

Consider a situation in which a consumer stops at a store to purchase a pair of shoes. The specific models of shoes that are available can elicit affect. Feelings can also be elicited by situations that are unrelated to what the consumer is judging, such as the terrible traffic encountered on the way to the store. How do these various sources of affect combine to influence consumer responses? To understand how the consumer might be influenced, a distinction between the sources of integral and incidental affect is important. *Integral affect* is a label used to describe the affect elicited by the object being evaluated (in the example, the pair of shoes) or the difficulty experienced in making a decision (Loewenstein & Lerner, 2002). *Incidental affect* refers to affect that is extraneous to the judgment situation (in the example, the negative mood the consumer might be in because of the traffic).

Integral affect is important because it helps individuals navigate their environment and determine what they like or dislike (Kahneman et al., 1997). The categorization process is made easy because positive or negative feelings associated with objects and events are linked directly or indirectly to somatic or bodily states (Damasio, 1994). Negative somatic markers typically alert the individual that something is awry, whereas positive ones suggest rewards. Thus, there appears to be a pool of affectively tagged objects or experiences that facilitate decision making (Slovic et al., 2002).

The processes underlying the creation of these integral affective responses are unclear. However, Pham et al. (2001) suggested three mechanisms by which this could happen. The first involves basic, sensorimotor affective responses that are automatic and wired in because they are important for survival (e.g., the avoidance of bitter food). A second type of feeling occurs because the object is deemed to be similar to previously formed schemas that have been associated with an affective response through conditioning. A third type of affective response can be developed through more deliberative appraisal of the pros and cons of the target object. We discuss the second type of response (which is most common in marketing) to show how everyday objects such as brands acquire an affective tag and the feelings they elicit (integral affect) can be confused with feelings arising from extraneous sources (incidental affect).

A great many objects come to be imbued with affect because of the settings and stimuli in which they are encountered. A basic mechanism by which brands and products become imbued with affect is evaluative conditioning (Martin & Levey, 1978). The evaluative conditioning procedure involves repeatedly pairing an originally neutral stimulus, such as an unknown brand name, with another stimulus that elicits an affective reaction that is typically positive (e.g., an attractive model). As a result, the perceiver acquires an attitude toward the brand name similar in valence to the one that it is paired with. A vehicle for evaluative conditioning to occur could be an advertisement, product packaging, event sponsorship, or any other situation that allows for the pairing of neutral brands or products with affective stimuli.

Considerable research has demonstrated the effectiveness of evaluative conditioning in shaping consumers' attitudes toward brands and products (e.g., Allen & Janiszewski, 1989; Allen & Madden, 1985; Bierley et al., 1985; Dempsey & Mitchell,

2010; Gibson, 2008; Gorn, 1982; Hasford et al., 2018; Janiszewski & Warlop, 1993; Kim et al., 1996; Shimp et al., 1991; Stuart et al., 1987; Sweldens et al., 2010). In a seminal study by Gorn (1982), hearing liked or disliked music while being exposed to a product—a neutral pen—directly affected preferences for it in a way that was consistent with the music's valence. That is, after the pairing, the pen elicited positive feelings or negative feelings by itself.

Subsequent research in this area has not only shown that the basic evaluative conditioning effect is robust but also investigated various properties of the processes by which it occurs. For example, pairing a product or brand with an affective stimulus several times leads to greater evaluative conditioning than pairing it only a few times (Stuart et al., 1987). Experiencing the brand or product in other contexts beforehand, particularly when these prior exposures elicit a strong preference for the brand, reduces evaluative conditioning (Gibson, 2008; Hasford et al., 2018; Stuart et al., 1987). Finally, pairing brands with affectively positive stimuli affords them greater attention when they are subsequently seen in a product display (Janiszewski & Warlop, 1993). Thus, not only can consumption objects (brands) acquire an affective tag, they can also impart feelings to other affectively neutral brands (e.g., a brand extension).

Feelings elicited by the target being evaluated (e.g., a brand) might often be confused with incidental affect that emerges from other nondecision related sources. Many types of incidental feelings (e.g., moods, emotions, metacognitive feelings) exist, and they can impact evaluations independently of the integral affect elicited by the consumption object. These various sources of affect can often be confused for each other, and it is possible to misattribute feelings arising from one source to the other. The type of effect these feelings have and the mechanism by which this effect occurs are considered next.

MOOD

Positive and negative affective (mood) states are common, and their implications for consumer behavior have been widely studied. Mood has been shown to have an effect on consumers' judgments of a product (Gorn et al., 1993; Pham, 1998) and on the shopping experience as a whole (Swinyard, 1993).

Many different accounts for the effects of mood on judgment have been proposed. A review of the many studies suggests it might be useful to consider three basic factors in understanding these effects. The first is the use of affect as a direct source of information. The second is the indirect effect of affect via its influence on how information is processed. The third involves the consideration of the motivational aspects of feelings.

Affect as a Direct Source of Information

Positive affect typically makes us see things through rose-colored lenses, and evaluations become more favorable when one is in a good mood. Such effects of affect on judgments presumably occur because people cannot distinguish between feelings elicited by the object being judged (integral affect) and those elicited by extraneous sources (incidental affect or moods). When participants are asked how they feel about the product, they misattribute the feelings they are experiencing for other reasons (i.e., their mood) to the product being judged, and this shifts their evaluations in mood-congruent directions. However, drawing attention to the source of affect removes its biasing effect (Gorn et al., 1993; Pham, 1998). The use of affect as a direct source of information about the product is likely when feelings are relevant to the decision being made, such as when participants evaluate products using hedonic criteria (Adaval, 2001; Yeung & Wyer, 2004), have consummatory motives, or process information in a visual and sensory manner (Pham, 1998).

Some studies have examined additional contingencies in the biasing effects of different mood states. Kramer and Yoon (2007), for instance, showed that although positive affect is used by people regardless of whether they have an approach or avoidance motive, negative affect is more likely to be used by people with an approach motive presumably because it signals a problem.

Other contingencies have been noted as well. Priming uncertainty, for instance, appears to increase reliance on affective bases for judgment. That is, uncertainty amplifies the effects of a host of affective stimuli (e.g., a musical soundtrack, an attractive picture, affective attributes) and states (e.g., mood states and disgust). This is because subjective cues like affect are presumably closer to the self (Faraji-Rad & Pham, 2017; see also Chang & Pham, 2013).

Focusing attention on oneself also leads consumers to rely on their affective feelings when making decisions about affective products (but not utilitarian products), increasing evaluations of products that are affectively superior while decreasing evaluations of those that are inferior (Chang & Hung, 2018). Relying on one's affective feelings (e.g., through consciously monitoring them) when making evaluative judgments toward a target can be beneficial. For instance, it results in evaluations that are quicker (i.e., compared with reason-based judgments of the target), more stable and consistent across individuals, and more predictive of the number and valence of people's thoughts (Pham et al., 2001; see also Avnet et al., 2012). Also, the more one trusts one's feelings, the more accurate one's predictions about future events become (provided one has sufficient background knowledge about the prediction domain; Pham et al., 2012).

Indirect Effects of Affect on Judgments

A large body of research has focused on understanding how moods affect the manner in which people process information about the product and how that processing, in turn, affects product evaluations and choice. The following sections summarize some of the key findings from this research and are organized as (a) effects on information processing and judgment and (b) effects on choice.

Effects on information processing and judgments.
An individual's mood can influence information processing in many ways. For example, mood can influence how information is perceived (i.e., one's initial impression of the product, the interpretation of information provided about it, and how it is weighted when computing a judgment). It can affect how disparate objects might be categorized and how involved people are in processing the information they receive.

Changes in how information is perceived. Affect may alter the manner in which information is perceived and weighted when computing an evaluation. The indirect ways in which affect can influence judgments were conceptualized using components of an information integration model (Adaval, 2003). Such a model consists of an initial impression that consumers form and a consideration of other product information (e.g., attributes, brand name, price). Each of these components has an evaluative good/bad component as well as a relative weight that is given to it in the overall evaluation. A few findings from this research are noteworthy. Consumers typically increase the weight they give to information that is similar in valence to the affect they are experiencing (Adaval 2001). This is because a transitory mood state can confirm or disconfirm their reactions to positive or negative attribute information, leading them to weight it differentially. Thus, attribute information that is congruent in valence with an individual's mood (i.e., positive mood with positive attribute information; negative mood with negative attribute information) is weighted more heavily than attribute information that is incongruent. These effects are, however, apparent only when consumers are using affective criteria as a basis for judgments.

Adaval (2003) also showed that consumers experiencing positive affect tend to rely more on brand information when making judgments—not because they give the brand greater weight (i.e., using it as a heuristic cue) but rather because they perceive the evaluative component (i.e., the scale value) differently. Specifically, when people are feeling good, a brand name with an initial positive evaluation is subjectively perceived as better and a brand name with an initial negative evaluation is perceived as worse. And this is reflected in participants' overall evaluations of the product.

Although Adaval (2003) did not find any effects of mood on the initial impression participants formed, subsequent studies by Yeung and Wyer (2004) showed that this effect is evident when consumers see the product before receiving attribute information. The product's appearance stimulates them to form an affect-based initial impression that they later use as a basis for judgment regardless of what other information they might receive. If, however, they receive verbal information of the product's attributes initially, they judge it in mood-congruent ways, depending on whether they believe that the product should be judged on the basis of hedonic or utilitarian criteria. The fact that a product's visual appearance might be critical was validated by King and Janiszewski (2011), who showed that people in a positive affective state are more sensitive to visual benefits of a product, whereas those experiencing negative affect are more sensitive to tactile benefits.

Changes in tendency to categorize. The mood an individual is in also affects memory for brand names. For instance, participants learned brand names better when they were in a positive mood than when in a neutral mood (A. Y. Lee & Sternthal, 1999). Recall patterns in A. Y. Lee and Sternthal's (1999) studies showed that participants in a positive mood were thinking about brands relationally and, in that process, were classifying brands using category membership. The tendency for people in a positive mood to rely on category membership led to other questions about how brand names might be perceived and categorized.

A brand name is typically considered a categorical knowledge structure that provides a packet of information about a product. It might be associated with a set of attributes and features of a product and other characteristics such as workmanship, types of users, and so forth. Thus, the brand name "Nike" activates significant knowledge about sports shoes, athletic wear, and athletes. Barone et al. (2000) examined how positive mood affected consumers' evaluations of extensions of such a brand name. The brand extensions varied in their similarity to the parent brand. They found that positive mood enhanced evaluations of extensions that were moderately similar, especially if the parent brand was regarded favorably. Extensions that were very similar or dissimilar were unaffected. This finding suggests that when the extension was unambiguously part of the category or not part of it, mood had no effect. However, when the fit between the extension and the parent brand was ambiguous,

a positive mood led to a tendency to include the extension as part of the brand family, and liking for the brand transferred to the extension. This converges with Kahn and Isen's (1993) finding that positive mood increases the tendency to categorize nontypical items as belonging to a predefined category. Interestingly, when the parent brand was unfavorable, mood did not affect how the extensions were evaluated (Barone & Miniard, 2002). It is also worth noting that these effects were evident only when consumer involvement was high. Under low involvement conditions, the effects of mood were more ubiquitous and did not depend on extension similarity (Barone, 2005).

Changes in involvement and extent of processing. Mood can also serve as a signal indicating how the information should be processed. This has implications for a number of domains, such as advertising. A consumer's mood when encountering an advertisement affects the way they process information contained in it and the effect it has. Being in a positive mood facilitates the effect of print advertising on brand attitudes by reducing the amount of total cognitive elaboration, biasing the evaluation of argument quality, and peripherally affecting brand attitudes (Batra & Stayman, 1990). These findings suggest that consumers are being cognitively lazy and processing information superficially.

Other research, however, suggests the opposite. Commercials seen during happy TV programs that tend to induce a positive mood are perceived to be more effective because they prompt additional affectively positive cognitive responses and, to that extent, lead to better ad recall than commercials seen during sad TV programs (Goldberg & Gorn, 1987). Better ad recall suggests that consumers are processing the information more carefully. These contrasting effects suggest that positive mood might lead to different information processing tendencies depending on the availability of other information or the consumer's goals. Indeed, when information about a target is not accessible or unavailable, positive mood serves as a heuristic. When information about a target is available, however, positive mood facilitates relational processing (Bakamitsos, 2006; A. Y. Lee & Sternthal, 1999). Similarly, consumer goals (enjoyment vs. making the best decision) can affect the extent to which they process information (Chen & Wyer, 2015). When they are in a good mood and their goal is to make a good decision, they are more likely to use abstract (desirability-related) criteria for long-term decisions than concrete (feasibility-related) criteria. However, when their goal is to enjoy themselves, then the reverse is true.

The extent to which mood facilitates message processing also depends on the congruence between the mood induction technique and the target. When there is high congruency (e.g., the mood-inducing event was through exposure to a sports ad and the targets being judged are sports shoes and athletic clothes), positive mood facilitates the processing of the ad message. Incongruent conditions, in contrast, lead to more heuristic processing (see also Fedorikhin & Cole, 2004). Finally, positive moods are also known to signal a benign state and consequently foster abstract construals and a focus on abstract future goals. In contrast, negative mood signals danger or the fact that attention must be paid to the immediate environment. This fosters concrete construal and a tendency to move away from the abstract future goals (Labroo & Patrick, 2009; see also Pyone & Isen, 2011).

The arousal dimension of affective states can also influence information processing and judgments in several ways. One way is by polarizing responses. For instance, when a to-be-evaluated ad had a clear affective tone, an incidental high arousal state polarized ad evaluations in the direction of the ad's affective tone, and this was especially the case when evaluations were self-relevant ("I like the ad") compared with object-relevant ("The ad is good"; Gorn et al., 2001). When the to-be-evaluated ad's affective tone was ambiguous, however, only valence had an effect, coloring the evaluation of the ad in a mood-congruent direction. Another way in which arousal influences ad processing is by stimulating the generation of counterarguments, thus facilitating resistance to attitude change (Raju & Unnava, 2006). Finally, arousal can increase heuristic processing, thereby affecting what ad elements influence brand judgments. For instance, a study showed that when arousal was high, brand evaluations were influenced to a greater degree by endorser status (celebrity or noncelebrity) than by argument strength, with the reverse manifesting under moderate arousal (Sanbonmatsu & Kardes, 1988).

Effects on choice. The effects of affect on choice were initially examined by pitting an affect-rich option with less favorable cognitions (e.g., a chocolate cake) against one that had less intense positive affect but more favorable cognitions (e.g., a fruit salad). When choosing between such alternatives, those with limited processing resources chose the affect-rich option, whereas those who had the cognitive resources chose the alternative with favorable cognitions (Shiv & Fedorikhin, 1999).

Although Shiv and Fedorikhin's (1999) studies focused on integral affect, the impact of incidental affect (mood) on comparative judgments yielded a different effect. Qiu and Yeung (2008) found that when more than one alternative was considered, the sequence of exposure mattered. When items were evaluated individually as they were encountered, participants in a good mood, relative to those in a bad mood, preferred the first option they saw. That is, mood affected the choice alternative that was evaluated immediately after it was induced. However, when participants were asked to withhold their evaluations until they had seen all alternatives, participants in a good mood, relative to participants in a bad mood, showed a preference for the last alternative. The difference in effects in these two conditions was presumably because the timing of the evaluation in the second instance led affect to be applied to what was most salient at the time of evaluation.

Qiu and Yeung's (2008) studies focused on choice situations in which participants formed a global evaluation of each alternative and then compared them. Other choice situations that involve an attribute-by-attribute comparison might yield different effects. For example, when the choice task requires such difficult trade-offs, happy consumers are more likely to defer choice relative to control participants (Etkin & Ghosh, 2018).

This research makes clear that the role of affective (mood) states on judgments and behavior is complex. Mood can at times be used as a direct basis for judgment. At other times, it can affect how consumers process the information provided, thus influencing judgments indirectly. Further, the effects on choice appear to depend on how information about the choice options is presented.

Incorporating Motivational Variables: Regulating and Predicting Affect

The effects of mood outlined thus far suggest that the extent to which people engage in information processing depends on the intensity of the feelings they experience. At times, people in positive moods are inclined to use heuristics. At other times, they engage in more elaborate processing. What appears clear is that the nature of the interface between incidental mood states and reactions to the target would be incomplete without a consideration of other motivational tendencies.

Mood maintenance and mood repair. *Mood maintenance* is a tendency to maintain one's current mood state. Individuals who are happy strive to maintain that pleasant state. To do so, they might avoid unpleasant things and tasks. Consumers, for example, often avoid products and decisions that might make them feel bad (Etkin & Ghosh, 2018; Fedorikhin & Patrick, 2010; Meloy, 2000). At times, these products might actually be bad for them. For instance, Fedorikhin and Patrick (2010) showed that positive mood facilitates resistance to temptation in the face of an unhealthy, sinful, and hard-to-resist snack—unless the individual is experiencing elevated arousal. If a person is experiencing a high level of arousal, the cognitive depletion that accompanies it will interfere with the self-regulatory focus of positive mood, hampering resistance to temptation.

Other research shows that individuals have a tendency to avoid information that disconfirms one's preferences (Meloy, 2000). Predecisional distortion (i.e., biased evaluation) of new product information typically occurs prior to decision making in order to support a tentatively preferred brand. A study examining the effects of a good mood on predecisional distortion found that a positive mood doubled the magnitude of this bias, leading individuals to disregard negative information about their preferred alternative (Meloy, 2000).

Thus, the drive to preserve a good mood can be strong enough to override the potential costs associated with a poor choice.

Just as mood maintenance serves the goal of preserving positive mood, mood repair involves reducing the impact of negative moods. This can be done through the consumption of mood-changing products (Andrade, 2005). However, research findings have shown inconsistent results. There are times when sad people prefer aesthetically consistent experiences and do not repair their mood (e.g., they listen to sad songs). C. J. Lee et al. (2013) suggested that this preference for mood-congruent aesthetic experiences might occur because such experiences serve as a surrogate for sharing the experience with a friend.

Whether consumers take action to regulate a current affective state depends on their beliefs about the transience of emotion (Labroo & Mukhopadhyay, 2009). If consumers believe that feelings are short-lived, those feeling happy will engage in affect regulation because they infer that they need to act if their positive feelings are to last. In contrast, if consumers believe that emotion is lasting, it is those feeling unhappy that will engage in affect regulation, as they infer that the negative feelings will persist unless they act to change them.

Predicting and forecasting feelings. Given that the regulation of feelings has an adaptive component, consumers attempt to predict and forecast how much they will like certain activities and the resultant effects these activities will have on their feeling states. However, consumers often fail to correctly predict how an affective experience will feel or how marketing stimuli will influence them, and this can impact their decisions and evaluations in various ways. For instance, people tend to refrain from engaging in public hedonic activities (e.g., bowling) alone, partly because they overestimate how much their enjoyment of the activity actually depends on others being there and partly because they anticipate that others will judge them negatively (i.e., they might infer that their social connections are poor; Ratner & Hamilton, 2015). This is unfortunate because these activities can be perfectly enjoyable on one's own.

People also have beliefs that knowing in advance exactly how long an affective episode will last attenuates the experience. (For example, they might believe that good movies will be experienced as less positive, and bad ones as less negative, if they are long.) However, knowing the duration in advance actually intensifies the affective experience instead; for instance, good movies become better, and bad movies worse (Zhao & Tsai, 2011). It should be noted though that experiences that disconfirm expectations are not always bad in the sense that they lead to negative evaluations; it is only when a consumer's forecast is disconfirmed downward (i.e., the actual experience is worse than predicted) that product evaluations are negatively impacted (Patrick et al., 2007).

Regulating different types of feelings. The type of regulation strategy an individual adopts may depend on the specific type of affect. For instance, anxiety and sadness, both aversive, lead to different strategies; anxiety triggers a preference for options that are safer and provide a sense of control, while sadness triggers a preference for options that are more rewarding and comforting (Raghunathan et al., 2006), such as indulgent consumption (Andrade, 2005; Salerno et al., 2014). This underscores the need to look at specific emotion types and the motivations they trigger (Lerner & Keltner, 2000).

Studies by Labroo and Rucker (2010) underscored the need to look at the motivational aspects of emotions when it comes to affect regulation. For instance, positive approach emotions (e.g., joy, happiness) can regulate negative emotions that also have an approach orientation (e.g., sadness, anger). Similarly, positive avoidance emotions (e.g., calmness) can regulate negative avoidance emotions (e.g., anxiety, embarrassment). To understand the underpinnings of emotion research, the next section provides a perspective on how research in this area has progressed and summarizes work on some key emotion types.

EMOTIONS

Emotional experience can vary along several dimensions. For example, emotions might vary in the extent to which they are consciously or nonconsciously experienced, the extent of cognitive processing involved in their elicitation, the extent to which they provoke strong motivations to act, and the extent to which they have expressive tendencies. The heterogeneity of emotional experience that is possible has led to repeated attempts to classify them. The principal question that researchers were initially concerned with was what evaluative, physiological, phenomenological, expressive, behavioral, and mental components are necessary to distinguish each emotion (Prinz, 2004). What resulted from this classification attempt was a collection of theories that follow three broad traditions (Scarantino & de Sousa, 2018). These include (a) theories that focus on the eliciting conditions, (b) theories that define emotions in terms of their conscious experience, and (c) theories that define them in terms of distinctive motivational states.

Consider, for example, two theoretical perspectives: the basic emotions approach and the core affect approach. The basic emotions approach focuses on a small set of distinct emotions that are critical from an evolutionary perspective and are tied to distinct neural substrates. These basic emotions are believed to have specific expressions associated with them that tend to be consistent across cultures (Ekman, 1992). This theory obviously has its roots in what has elicited the emotion from an evolutionary perspective and focuses on its distinct expressive tendencies. The core affect approach suggests that emotions emerge from the assessment of the two core dimensions of valence (pleasant vs. unpleasant) and arousal (low vs. high) and are a function of autonomic responses, approach/avoidance reactions, and other cognitions such as beliefs and appraisals. This approach denies the existence of any natural kinds of emotions and instead sees different expressions of them along a continuum of emotional experience.

In the current chapter, we organize research on emotions into distinct types for the purposes of aggregation of research. Further, given the range of emotional experiences that exist, we summarize research for only those emotions that have an aggregation of research findings. We do not, however, take a stance on the validity of one theoretical perspective or the other. Instead, we suggest that researchers might find it helpful to conceptualize existing research in terms of its ability to inform on (a) the various appraisals or conditions that might elicit the emotion, (b) the effects the experience of the emotion has on different aspects of information processing, and (c) the motivational tendencies they elicit. We discuss the research on each emotion type using this organizational framework.

Anger

Given the large number of situations in which consumers can get upset with service providers, it is surprising how little research has examined the effect of anger on consumer behavior. Most of the research to date has documented conditions that elicit anger in consumers. For example, individuals are known to react negatively to incivility. Specifically, when they witness incivility between two employees, it elicits anger, which then leads to ruminations about the uncivil incident. These ruminations make customers more likely to make negative generalizations about others who work at the firm or about the firm in general (Porath et al., 2010).

Other triggers that elicit anger and aggression include competition for resources. When consumers were exposed to signs suggesting that a product might be available in limited quantities, it activated aggression that generalized to other situations (Kristofferson et al., 2017). Although in this work consumers were not made angry but rather a desire to compete for scarce goods might have triggered the aggressive behavior, it does raise the possibility that anger and aggression might be elicited by a large number of other similar triggers that appear to restrict or infringe on one's ability to thrive.

Another possibility that has been explored is the relationship between self-control and anger. People are known to exhibit aggression when they are asked to exert self-control (e.g., not eat a doughnut), and this aggression is evident in how they respond to a subsequent insult (DeWall et al., 2007). People on diets also tend to be irritable and aggressive (Polivy, 1996). Gal and Liu (2011) extended this work to examine whether self-control leads to just aggression or whether it extends to other anger-related behaviors. They found that when people exerted self-control, they showed more interest in angry faces, were more likely to get irritated with others who tried to control their behavior, and endorsed anger-themed appeals. Thus, it appears that certain triggers can elicit anger, which can then manifest itself in a range of different behaviors.

In most of the aforementioned studies, researchers have focused on what elicits anger (e.g., scarcity of resources, self-control, incivility). Very few studies have actually manipulated anger and examined the effects it has on behavior. One of the few demonstrations of the effects of anger on choice was provided by Garg et al. (2005). They proposed that anger and sadness differ on the appraisal dimension of certainty, with anger being associated with a higher degree of certainty compared with sadness. Because certainty makes angry individuals process information more heuristically and sad individuals more systematically (Tiedens & Linton, 2001), this difference has implications for the extent to which angry and sad consumers are likely to go with the status quo option. The status quo option is typically chosen when people experience decision difficulty, and it is seen as a simplifying heuristic in a difficult situation (Luce, 1998). However, anger increases certainty and makes people more confident that they are doing the right thing by choosing the status quo option when trade-off difficulty is high. When trade-off difficulty is low, however, then anger reduces the pressure to maintain the status quo.

In another demonstration of the effects of anger, Su et al. (2018) showed that feelings of anger arising out of a response to an international incident led to increased complaints to a restaurant about a problem that customers encountered, relative to control conditions in which such incidental anger was not elicited. As such, despite the relatively scant literature on anger, studies suggest that its role in consumer decision making might be well served if researchers focused not only on the triggers or antecedent conditions that elicit anger but also on the effects of anger on behavior relative to other negative emotions. In fact, the longer term motivational tendencies that are triggered by the experience of anger have barely been studied. For example, although researchers have studied consumer boycotts (Jost et al., 2017; Jung et al., 2017), this research has been from the perspective of system justification theory and ideological differences in satisfaction with existing systems. The experience of anger and the motivations it elicits have typically not been considered as factors that fuel such boycotts over a sustained period.

Pride

Unlike much of the research on anger, which focuses on conditions that elicit anger and not on its effects per se, research on pride focuses primarily on the effects it has on behavior. Pride can be elicited in different ways. When people achieve something or experience success, their emotional reaction is one of pride (Lazarus, 1991b; Tracy & Robins, 2007). However, pride can be felt on behalf of someone else (e.g., a child who has done well) or an organization or brand that one strongly identifies with. Much of the consumer research that has been done is on feelings of pride that are elicited for reasons that are not directly related to the purchase situation. Such incidental feelings of pride can affect consumption decisions in numerous ways. Consider a situation in which one experiences pride because of a demonstrated ability to do something special. This type of authentic pride can actually increase the purchase of luxury goods and products that one can display in public relative to those that are consumed in private (McFerran et al., 2014). However, pride that is experienced because of a sense of superiority relative to others is called hubristic pride and does not lead to increases in demand for luxury products or the purchase of products for public display. Thus, the type of pride one experiences can have different motivational effects on the tendency to display one's success through products.

Ironically, the very act of making or not making an unintended purchase can elicit feelings of pride and guilt (Mukhopadhyay & Johar, 2007). Not buying something suggests restraint and elicits pride, which is then evident in a preference for pride appeals over happy appeals encountered later on. Feelings of pride have also been shown to affect consumer repurchase intentions. Specifically, when pride is accompanied with a strong prevention orientation, it can lead to lower repurchase intent than when it is accompanied with a strong promotion orientation (Louro et al., 2005).

Such motivational effects that appear to restrain the pride-induced exhibitory tendencies were specifically examined in the context of the effects of incidental pride on consumer self-control by Wilcox et al. (2011). They asked the question: When do people celebrate their achievements, and when do they exercise restraint? They found that pride can elicit a sense not only of achievement but also of self-awareness. Achievement is more likely to promote the consumption of indulgence products, whereas self-awareness promotes the consumption of virtuous products. The relative emphasis on achievement versus self-awareness is responsible for the extent to which people will indulge in celebratory products. Further, as Salerno et al. (2015) found, the presence of a self-regulation goal makes individuals focus on personal agency ("This was my achievement, not someone else's achievement") and this increases the tendency to indulge. However, when a self-regulation goal is not present, then the focus is on the locus of control ("I contributed to this achievement; it was not luck"), and this urges self-restraint. Thus, pride can lead to symbolic displays of success through products and celebratory indulgences when it is authentic, accompanied by a promotion orientation and focused on achievement.

A recent set of studies focused on a somewhat different question about an object that elicits pride. For example, how do people who feel pride in a selective or exclusive brand react to "intruders" or new consumers who might potentially dilute the brand's image? Bellezza and Keinan (2014) found that core users of the brand continue to exhibit feelings of pride if the new users are considered "tourists" who do not claim membership in the brand community. Core users are, however, less positive to "brand immigrants" who consider themselves part of the core group. Thus, consumers appear to guard these emotional states of feeling proud and display the same sorts of affect regulation tendencies discussed previously.

To summarize, pride is typically elicited through achievements that might have little to do with the consumption situation. However, its effects on consumption are clear and depend largely on where the focus of the appraisal is. If the focus is on the achievement, then it could have implications for celebratory consumption products. But if the focus is on one's capabilities that led to the achievement, then it could lead to less conspicuous celebrations, fewer indulgences, and increased self-restraint.

Embarrassment

Embarrassment is experienced when people engage in an act that they believe is socially inappropriate or is likely to be disapproved of by others. Embarrassment is, therefore, more about self-presentation to others, and no lasting damage is done to one's sense of self. The act eliciting embarrassment also does not have negative consequences for others. Given the social nature of this emotion, early conceptualizations suggested that a behavior had to be observed before it would be considered embarrassing (Goffman, 1959). Studies in consumer behavior, however, showed that the imagined presence of someone was sufficient to elicit embarrassment. For example, Dahl et al. (2001) examined how consumers reacted to real and imagined social presence when they were acquiring an embarrassing product (e.g., condoms). Embarrassment was elicited in both cases, and this reduced the likelihood of acquiring the product. Familiarity with the purchase act, however, moderated this effect.

More recent conceptualizations of embarrassment have incorporated this idea and recognize that the imagined presence of someone is sufficient to elicit embarrassment (Krishna et al., 2019). This raises a question about the nature of the appraisal. If embarrassment occurs in private (in the absence of others) then this embarrassment could be the result of disapproval by an imagined other or, alternatively, disapproval by oneself (Krishna et al., 2015). Thus, acts such as wetting one's bed at the age of 25 might not be observed, and neither might an imagined other be present. However, an individual might observe themselves and regard this with disapproval, causing embarrassment.

Independent manipulations of embarrassment have yielded avoidance behaviors like those observed by Dahl et al. (2001). For example, people generally try to affiliate with physically attractive service providers. However, when they recall an embarrassing experience prior to this interaction, it decreases how willing they are to spend time with a service provider even though the provider is unaware of the embarrassing experience (Wan & Wyer, 2015).

To cope with embarrassment, consumers often take certain measures, and these might be conscious or nonconscious. For example, when an embarrassing product is in one's shopping basket, consumers might purchase other items to deflect attention from the embarrassing product. However, this strategy might be successful only insofar as the additional products attenuate the identity conveyed by the embarrassing purchase. In some cases, however, it might complement the identity conveyed, and in this case, embarrassment might actually increase (Blair & Roese, 2013). Other nonconscious effects are likely as well. Recalling embarrassing incidents has been shown to lead to a preference for products that help hide one's face (through a preference for dark glasses) or to save it (through a preference for facial moisturizer). These actions are considered symbolic and engaged in nonconsciously (Dong et al., 2013).

Guilt and Shame

Guilt and shame are social emotions (like embarrassment). The importance of appraisal processes in the elicitation of these social emotions was demonstrated by Hung and Mukhopadhyay (2012). Specifically, when participants appraise an event using the perspective of the actor in the event, greater hedonic emotions such as joy, sorrow, and excitement are elicited. However, when participants appraise an event from the perspective of an observer, the focus on the self elicits self-conscious emotions such as guilt and embarrassment.

Although guilt and shame have certain social aspects in common with embarrassment (e.g., the disapproval of others) and might co-occur, they are the result of distinct appraisals (Tangney et al., 1996). People experience shame when they do something that is perceived negatively by others and reflects badly on one's personality. Thus, it is more likely to affect one's self-esteem and self-worth, unlike embarrassment, which does not have lasting effects on the self. Moreover, the experience of shame appears to lead to an inward focus with an emphasis on coping with the emotion being experienced. Guilt, on the other hand, results when one violates certain personal standards that one has set for oneself. It is accompanied by a strong motivation to rectify the negative consequences of one's behavior and typically does not affect one's sense of self-worth. For example, Allard and White (2015) showed that the experience of guilt leads to a greater demand for self-improvement products because it activates a desire to improve oneself and this spills over to other domains. In their experiments, participants were asked to choose between teas that either improved brainpower or mood. Those who felt guilty were more likely to choose the tea that improved brainpower, whereas those who felt ashamed showed no such preference. Interestingly, this effect holds only for personal choices. It is also not evident when the self is seen as fixed. Other emotions such as shame, embarrassment, sadness, or envy do not elicit this self-improvement motive.

Many other self-improvement behaviors have also been observed after the experience of guilt, such as avoiding waste (Kivetz & Keinan, 2006), support of recycling (Chu et al., 2018), and a preference for utilitarian consumption (Levav & McGraw, 2009). Shame, in contrast, does not elicit such self-improvement motivations but, rather, focuses attention on the self.

To show distinctions in information processing between guilt and shame, Han et al. (2014) examined the information processing tendencies of consumers experiencing these emotions. Consumers experiencing guilt appeared to focus more on remedying the consequences of their actions, and a focus on the offending behavior led to lower level construals. Thus, when they were asked to consider going to a concert, they focused more on feasibility (cost of the tickets) than desirability (how good the performers were). In contrast, consumers experiencing shame were more likely to focus on how the entire self might be perceived, and this elicited a more global appraisal and higher level construals (i.e., a focus on desirability over feasibility).

Given the self-improvement tendencies noted earlier, it is not surprising that guilt and shame have often been used as part of advertising appeals to discourage certain behaviors. Duhachek et al. (2012), for example, showed that in the context of responsible drinking behavior, consumers can be made to feel guilty or ashamed. Guilty appeals that use an additional gain frame are found to be more effective than those that use a loss frame. This is because guilt, with its focus on problem solving, is more compatible with a gain frame. In contrast, appeals that use shame are more likely to be more effective with a loss frame. This is because a loss frame elicits emotion-focused coping that is compatible with the motivation elicited by shame. This sort of fit between the frame and the emotion facilitates coping and engenders a sense of fluency, making the message more effective. Specifically, this type of compatibility results in an increase in the amount of time people spend watching alcohol advertising as well as in a reduction in the extent to which they report wanting to drink. An intriguing effect occurs when the aforementioned compatibility is tested on consumers who are actually experiencing guilt and shame for reasons that have little to do with the appeal. In this case, compatibility between the motivation induced by the message and the frame backfires. Messages become less effective because consumers engage in defensive processing to feel less bad (Agrawal & Duhachek, 2010).

Guilt and shame are two emotions that are elicited quite often in the course of consumption. People can feel guilty about consuming things. Sometimes these are indulgent items. At other times, this consumption could be of items that are not sustainable and are harmful to the environment. Consumers can also feel guilty about having too many possessions when they encounter others who have very little. Although guilt is typically seen as a negative emotion, it is also associated with pleasure. The term "guilty pleasures" clearly implies that such an association exists. Goldsmith et al. (2012) found that activating guilt actually increases pleasure with hedonic consumption, unlike other negative emotions. Such increases in pleasure are typically likely when the behavior only has consequences for oneself. Thus, feeling guilty while eating an entire tub of ice cream might yield pleasure because it does not damage anyone else. When the consequences to others are negative, however, guilt obviously affects consumer behavior in other ways. For example, people might experience guilt not purchasing from a friendly salesperson and in this case might purchase more from them or give them more credit for later purchases (Dahl et al., 2005). Guilt, however, can be mitigated if there is a gap between the time when the decision is made to engage in the action and the actual performance of the act (Duke & Amir, 2019). Having a temporal gap between the two stages allows the feelings of guilt to decay.

The research summarized suggests that although guilt and shame are closely related, they differ in where attention is focused. Guilt focuses on the behavior that fell short of one's standards. Consequently, it elicits a desire to remedy the implications of this behavior. Shame on the other hand, is focused on the self and, given its damaging consequences for self-esteem, might lead to different motivations. Past research has not fully examined the consequences of such motivations of shame. Given the importance of the effects of shame on self-esteem and self-worth, this remains an important area that merits research.

Fear and Anxiety

Appraisals of the environment allow consumers to pick up cues that might be threatening, and these cues can elicit anxiety and fear. Cues could pertain to the environment (e.g., lighting and sound), or ads (e.g., ads reminding one of the possibility of getting the flu or an illness; ads for burglar alert systems). Sometimes interaction partners in consumption situations (e.g., financial advisors, salespersons) might elicit anxiety or fear. For example, if the transaction partner is a member of a group that is negatively stereotyped, it can elicit anxiety. In such cases, consumers exhibit anxiety and a reluctance to purchase from such providers. These feelings can be alleviated by environmental cues such as soothing scents (K. Lee et al., 2011).

Several studies have examined situations in which anxiety is elicited. For example, ambient cues such as low-pitched sounds have been found to signal a threat and increase anxiety among consumers (Lowe et al., 2019), leading to choices that are less risky (e.g., foods that are lower in taste uncertainty) as well as a greater desire for safety-oriented products (e.g., greater willingness to pay more for car insurance). Similar findings were noted by Raghunathan et al. (2006), who showed that anxiety elicits a preference for safer products that help consumers regain a sense of control. This is more likely if the source of anxiety is not salient.

In general, fear and anxiety are elicited together, and it is sometimes difficult to separate the effects of one from the other. However, anxiety appears to induce a state of watchfulness over a prolonged period whereas fear typically elicits an immediate reaction. When people experience fear, they cope with it by attempting to affiliate with others to seek safety. Interestingly, when this is not possible, they turn to inanimate objects such as available brands. Past research has shown that brand affiliation and emotional attachment get stronger when people experience fear but not when they experience other feelings such as happiness, sadness, or excitement (Dunn & Hoegg, 2014).

The tendency among fearful consumers to latch onto certain cues that presumably provide assurance was observed during the COVID-19 pandemic (Pena-Marin et al., 2021). An analysis of the S&P 500 stock prices at this time showed a marked preference for high-priced stocks over lower priced ones when the market crashed. Experimental evidence obtained through an independent manipulation of fear (using scary films) and reminders of the pandemic's seriousness yielded similar effects and suggested that when the stock market was declining, people used high prices as a heuristic for safety and stability. Related research on the effects of fear on financial decision making suggests that incidental fear leads participants to sell their stock early if they believe that the stock value is peer-generated and not generated by a computer (C. J. Lee & Andrade, 2011). Thus, fearful investors appear to use cues that signal stability or the lack thereof.

Fear is often elicited through commercials as well. Such fear appeals have been well documented (Sternthal & Craig, 1974), and messages are often used to discourage behavior (e.g., ads against smoking). However, they have often been ineffective. Keller and Block (1996), who examined the effectiveness of ads against smoking, found that low levels of fear were typically not as effective because they did not elicit enough elaboration about the consequences of the destructive behavior. Similarly, high levels of fear were also not effective, but this was because too much elaboration about the consequences of the behavior interfered with the processing of the recommendations provided. Elaboration, however, could be increased in low-level fear conditions using imagery and self-referencing and decreased in high-level fear conditions by focusing on others and objective processing. Fear appeals can also be made more effective when they are combined with other emotions such as guilt and regret (emotions that make the individual self-accountable), and this increases the likelihood of engaging in behaviors such as using sunscreen, eating high-fiber foods, and so forth (Passyn & Sujan, 2006). Interestingly, merely inducing high accountability without the corresponding emotional drive does not produce equivalent effects and suggests that the affective reactions are indispensable in this case.

Mixed Emotions

Mixed emotions are often elicited by ads, films, and life events. Thus, although one might rejoice at finding a new job and feel happy at the prospect of starting anew, one might experience sadness when thinking about leaving friends behind. Advertising often communicates these types of emotions and situations, and consumers can vicariously experience these feelings when they watch these ads. Research examining mixed emotions has partly focused on studying how individual differences determine responses. Mixed emotions can create discomfort for certain kinds of people, leading them to evaluate ads eliciting mixed emotions more negatively than ads with pure positive emotions (Hong & Lee, 2010; Williams & Aaker, 2002). For instance, people with a low propensity to accept duality (e.g., Anglo Americans; younger adults) experience more discomfort upon processing an ad eliciting mixed emotions than people with a higher propensity to accept duality (e.g., Asian Americans; older adults; Williams & Aaker, 2002). This is because the former chronically construe

information at a low, concrete level and the latter construe information at a higher, more abstract level (Hong & Lee, 2010).

Often, mixed emotions can be elicited through consumption experiences. For example, one might sample three different jelly beans and like one, dislike the other, and feel neutral about the third. These mixed feelings can affect how the entire consumption experience is viewed. Lau-Gesk (2005) showed that in a mixed affective episode of the sort described, the degree of similarity between the sources of the different positive and negative bits is an important determinant of whether the episode is evaluated positively or negatively. When the sources of the different feelings experienced during the episode are seen as highly similar, close temporal proximity between negative and positive affect leads to unfavorable evaluations. Thus, in the case where the positive and negative feelings are elicited by the same (or a very similar) source, it would help to temporally separate the events or elements creating such feelings. But when the sources of the different feelings in a mixed affective episode are regarded as dissimilar, individuals prefer to experience the positive and negative affect close together, consistent with a buffering explanation (i.e., the parts of the episode that make me feel good help me cope with the parts that make me feel bad; see also Labroo & Ramanathan, 2007).

While ads are a common source of mixed emotions, certain behaviors can elicit them as well. One such behavior is indulgence. How people feel after indulging is rather complex and typically includes a mixture of positive and negative emotions, with their specific composition depending on how chronically impulsive the person is (Ramanathan & Williams, 2007). More prudent consumers are bothered to a greater degree than less prudent consumers by the emotions felt after indulgence, leading the former to seize opportunities to wash away their negative emotions after an indulgence episode (Ramanathan & Williams, 2007).

Finally, mixed emotions behave differently from unipolar emotions in the accuracy with which they are remembered. Experiences eliciting mixed emotions are recalled less accurately over time than those eliciting unipolar emotions. This is because their intensity is generally underestimated because of their complexity and the conflict they provoke makes memory of them decay (Aaker et al., 2008). Thus, at the end of the day, individuals experiencing mixed emotions might be left with a nebulous feeling of unease.

METACOGNITIVE FEELINGS

Subjective feelings of ease or difficulty can be elicited either when one attempts to retrieve information or in the course of processing information. Such feelings can be misattributed to the behavior one is engaging in or to the target described in the information (Alter & Oppenheimer, 2009; Reber & Schwarz, 1999; Schwarz, 2004; Winkielman et al., 2003; see also Krishna & Schwarz, 2014). Early studies on the ease of retrieval in consumer behavior (Wänke et al., 1997) found that the ease experienced while retrieving information had a positive effect on product evaluations because people had certain thoughts about these feelings. For example, participants who were asked to retrieve either one or 10 reasons for choosing a BMW over a Mercedes found it easier to retrieve one reason than 10. This subjective feeling of ease led BMW to be evaluated more favorably in the former condition than in the latter. This was presumably because people thought that *if* it was easier to generate reasons to prefer BMW over a Mercedes, then they must actually prefer it. Thus, metacognitions about the ease or difficulty experienced while retrieving information can be used as a basis for making judgments and decisions independently of the actual content retrieved. Such metacognitive experiences comprising both cognitions and affective reactions are typically used effortlessly and unconsciously (Menon & Raghubir, 2003).

Although ease of retrieval effects can theoretically be affected by the content of what is retrieved, the impact that this ease has on judgments has been shown to be independent of specific characteristics of the information processed or retrieved. For example, in other studies, these feelings have been elicited by a variety of contextual factors that are objectively irrelevant to the decision. Processing ease has been altered by manipulating the figure-ground contrast (Reber et al., 1998), by varying the difficulty of the font in which information is presented (Novemsky et al., 2007; Pocheptsova et al., 2010; Shen et al., 2010), by making it easier to process information by presenting a matching contour of an object before it is actually seen, and also by varying the frequency of exposure of the target (Reber & Schwarz, 1999; Zajonc, 1968). In general, the easier a target is to process as a result of these manipulations, the more positive its evaluation (for reviews, see Krishna & Schwarz, 2014; Schwarz, 2004; Winkielman et al., 2003).

The effects of such metacognitive feelings have been widely studied in the context of brands and choice. In most of these studies, a target is judged more favorably when the processing is easy because the positive feelings of ease are misattributed to it. When it comes to evaluations of brands, processing ease typically increases the likelihood that a brand will be selected if it is either conceptually or perceptually more fluent. Such fluency could arise because of prior exposure to items or features that enable people to anticipate seeing it (A. Y. Lee, 2002). A. Y. Lee and Labroo (2004), for example, found that when a target came to mind more readily, participants' attitudes toward it were more favorable. This ease of retrieval could occur because it was placed in a context where it was expected or because it was primed by a related construct. This finding has implications for choice. Labroo et al. (2008), for instance, used semantic primes to cue a visual identifier in one of two products (e.g., a bottle of wine with a frog on the label), and the placement of this identifier increased preference for it over an alternative that did not have such an identifier.

It is worth noting that in typical choice situations, more than one alternative is presented and disfluent processing conditions might apply equally to both alternatives. In a set of studies by Novemsky et al. (2007), participants were presented with two alternatives in either a difficult-to-read font or an easy-to-read font and were asked to choose between them. Choice deferral was an option. Participants were less likely to choose an option if they experienced processing disfluency (i.e., the options were in a difficult font) than if they experienced fluency (i.e., the options were in an easy font). This was because disfluency experienced during choice implied lower confidence in the alternatives.

Fluency in processing might not always be beneficial. The manner in which fluency or disfluency is interpreted can depend on consumers' construal levels (Thomas & Tsai, 2012) and can alter the confidence one has in the choice process (Tsai & McGill, 2011). For example, under low levels of construal, processing ease or fluency is interpreted as an indication that the choice process is going smoothly, and this increases confidence in choices. In contrast, at high levels of construal, participants interpret processing ease or fluency as an indication that their effort is not sufficient to attain a desirable outcome, and this lowers their confidence in their choices.

Other findings corroborate the idea that disfluent processing is not always bad and can be interpreted positively. Pocheptsova et al. (2010), for instance, showed that the effects of metacognitive feelings might depend on the consumption domain. When the products are of the sort that consumers use every day, negative feelings arising out of processing disfluency might make them less attractive. However, when the products are special or exclusive, feelings of disfluency might increase the attractiveness of the product because they appear unique and uncommon. Similar positive effects of disfluency are noted when people are pursuing a goal. Goal attainment usually requires adopting some means to attain the goal (e.g., donate to a charity in order to become a kinder person). Disfluency can make the means to attain a goal seem effortful and therefore more desirable. If people are not pursuing a goal, then fluency improves evaluation of the means (Labroo & Kim, 2009).

The effect that processing disfluency has on targets that are judged subsequently is intriguing. The mood literature suggests that affect transfers to objects that are presented subsequently. Thus, if processing is difficult and people experience a feeling of disfluency, this should likely spill over to a neutral target presented subsequently, lowering evaluations of it. However, it is also conceivable that this neutral target might be evaluated more favorably in comparison. Shen et al. (2010) found evidence for both. When processing difficulty or disfluency increases, information about a subsequently encountered product becomes relatively easier to process, leading to more favorable evaluations of it. This occurs because the two experiences are seen as distinct. If, however, the two products are categorized as part of the same overall experience, then the negative feelings elicited by difficulty in processing information about the first product transfer to the second product, leading it to be evaluated more unfavorably.

In a different set of studies by A. Y. Lee and Labroo (2004; see also Avnet & Higgins, 2006), participants were shown sequential ads for two products, one of which served as a prime and the other as a target. When the regulatory goal of the first ad (promotion- or prevention-focused) matched the regulatory goal of the target, a goal fluency effect was observed and participants indicated higher purchase intent and evaluations of the target. Thus, it appears that some sort of binding between two successive experiences is necessary for the fluency effects to have the same effect on a subsequent target.

Other effects of fluency on behavior should be noted. When instructions to perform a novel behavior (e.g., cooking a certain dish) are presented in a hard-to-read font, participants find it difficult to simulate the behavior and are less likely to engage in it (Song & Schwarz, 2008). Similarly, just measuring a person's intention to behave is known to increase the likelihood of their engaging in the behavior. This happens not necessarily because of increased accessibility of the behavior but because the cognitive processes used to generate the response are similar to the cognitive processes used to decide whether to engage in the behavior. This process redundancy creates a sense of fluency that is considered supportive of the behavior (Janiszewski & Chandon, 2007).

CONCLUSION

The research reviewed indicates that feelings can influence the behavior of consumers in myriad ways. This chapter attempted to cover the breadth of emotional experience and in the process identified a variety of different effects. Some of the key conclusions that can be drawn from this body of work include the following. Incidental feelings that are elicited by factors that have little to do with the task at hand can color consumer evaluations and behavior. As the research on evaluative conditioning shows, brief exposure to affective stimuli can affect the evaluations of a brand that by itself is affectively neutral. Further, mild positive mood states that are often experienced for other reasons can have direct effects on judgments through their use as a source of information. Additionally, they can have indirect effects on judgment by altering the manner in which information is processed. The use of feelings is often dependent on the extent to which consumers are aware of the feelings, whether the consumer trusts these feelings, and whether the feelings are considered relevant to the decision at hand. Further, consumers appear to regulate these feelings by forecasting how the task will make them feel.

This review also covered the effects of metacognitive feelings. Their effects appear very similar to those of mood, in that they are used as a source of information. However, they arise because of very subtle changes in contextual factors such as the font in which a product is shown, the background and foreground colors, and so forth. Yet, they affect consumer evaluations and choice processes. In this context, it is worth pointing out that consumers might be aware of their feelings but not the source of their feelings. The inability to identify the source allows feelings (be they mood or metacognitive feelings) to exert an impact on consumers' judgments.

It is worth noting that as the source of the affect becomes salient, appraisals elicit specific emotions that have their unique effects. In attempting to summarize some of this work, we have highlighted differences in the consequences of these emotions. However, given the relatively large body of research that is covered, in some instances research on specific emotions has been omitted. Taken collectively though, the emotion literature shows that the experience of different emotions elicits either strong approach or avoidance tendencies. These tendencies appear to spill over to other consumption domains. In all cases, however, feelings and cognitions appear to move hand in hand, one guiding the other in a symbiotic manner.

REFERENCES

Aaker, J., Drolet, A., & Griffin, D. (2008). Recalling mixed emotions. *Journal of Consumer Research*, 35(2), 268–278. https://doi.org/10.1086/588570

Adaval, R. (2001). Sometimes it just feels right: The differential weighting of affect-consistent and affect-inconsistent product information. *Journal of Consumer Research*, 28(1), 1–17. https://doi.org/10.1086/321944

Adaval, R. (2003). How good gets better and bad gets worse: Understanding the impact of affect on evaluations of known brands. *Journal of Consumer Research*, 30(3), 352–367. https://doi.org/10.1086/378614

Agrawal, N., & Duhachek, A. (2010). Emotional compatibility and the effectiveness of antidrinking messages: A defensive processing perspective on shame and guilt. *Journal of Marketing Research*, 47(2), 263–273. https://doi.org/10.1509/jmkr.47.2.263

Allard, T., & White, K. (2015). Cross-domain effects of guilt on desire for self-improvement products. *Journal of Consumer Research*, 42(3), 401–419. https://doi.org/10.1093/jcr/ucv024

Allen, C. T., & Janiszewski, C. A. (1989). Assessing the role of contingency awareness in attitudinal conditioning with implications for advertising research. *Journal of Marketing Research*, 26(1), 30–43. https://doi.org/10.1177/002224378902600103

Allen, C. T., & Madden, T. J. (1985). A closer look at classical conditioning. *Journal of Consumer Research*, 12(3), 301–315. https://doi.org/10.1086/208517

Alter, A. L., & Oppenheimer, D. M. (2009). Uniting the tribes of fluency to form a metacognitive nation. *Personality and Social Psychology Review*, 13(3), 219–235. https://doi.org/10.1177/1088868309341564

Andrade, E. B. (2005). Behavioral consequences of affect: Combining evaluative and regulatory mechanisms. *Journal of Consumer Research*, 32(3), 355–362. https://doi.org/10.1086/497546

Arnold, M. B. (1960). *Emotion and personality*: Vol. I. *Psychological aspects*. Columbia University Press.

Avnet, T., & Higgins, E. T. (2006). Response to comments on "How regulatory fit affects value in consumer choices and opinions." *Journal of Marketing Research*, 43(1), 24–27. https://doi.org/10.1509/jmkr.43.1.24

Avnet, T., Pham, M. T., & Stephen, A. T. (2012). Consumers' trust in feelings as information. *Journal of Consumer Research*, 39(4), 720–735. https://doi.org/10.1086/664978

Bakamitsos, G. A. (2006). A cue alone or a probe to think? The dual role of affect in product evaluations. *Journal of Consumer Research*, 33(3), 403–412. https://doi.org/10.1086/508525

Barone, M. J. (2005). The interactive effects of mood and involvement on brand extension evaluations. *Journal of Consumer Psychology, 15*(3), 263–270. https://doi.org/10.1207/s15327663jcp1503_11

Barone, M. J., & Miniard, P. W. (2002). Mood and brand extension judgments: Asymmetric effects for desirable versus undesirable brands. *Journal of Consumer Psychology, 12*(4), 283–290. https://doi.org/10.1207/15327660260382324

Barone, M. J., Miniard, P. W., & Romeo, J. B. (2000). The influence of positive mood on brand extension evaluations. *Journal of Consumer Research, 26*(4), 386–400. https://doi.org/10.1086/209570

Batra, R., & Stayman, D. M. (1990). The role of mood in advertising effectiveness. *Journal of Consumer Research, 17*(2), 203–214. https://doi.org/10.1086/208550

Bellezza, S., & Keinan, A. (2014). Brand tourists: How non-core users enhance the brand image by eliciting pride. *Journal of Consumer Research, 41*(2), 397–417. https://doi.org/10.1086/676679

Bierley, C., McSweeney, F. K., & Vannieuwkerk, R. (1985). Classical conditioning of preferences for stimuli. *Journal of Consumer Research, 12*(3), 316–323. https://doi.org/10.1086/208518

Blair, S., & Roese, N. J. (2013). Balancing the basket: The role of shopping basket composition in embarrassment. *Journal of Consumer Research, 40*(4), 676–691. https://doi.org/10.1086/671761

Bower, G. H. (1981). Mood and memory. *American Psychologist, 36*(2), 129–148. https://doi.org/10.1037/0003-066X.36.2.129

Bush, G., Luu, P., & Posner, M. I. (2000). Cognitive and emotional influences in anterior cingulate cortex. *Trends in Cognitive Sciences, 4*(6), 215–222. https://doi.org/10.1016/S1364-6613(00)01483-2

Carruthers, P. (2017). Are epistemic emotions metacognitive? *Philosophical Psychology, 30*(1–2), 58–78. https://doi.org/10.1080/09515089.2016.1262536

Chang, H. H., & Hung, I. W. (2018). Mirror, mirror on the retail wall: Self-focused attention promotes reliance on feelings in consumer decisions. *Journal of Marketing Research, 55*(4), 586–599. https://doi.org/10.1509/jmr.15.0080

Chang, H. H., & Pham, M. T. (2013). Affect as a decision-making system of the present. *Journal of Consumer Research, 40*(1), 42–63. https://doi.org/10.1086/668644

Chen, F., & Wyer, R. S., Jr. (2015). The effects of affect, processing goals and temporal distance on information processing: Qualifications on temporal construal theory. *Journal of Consumer Psychology, 25*(2), 326–332. https://doi.org/10.1016/j.jcps.2014.09.004

Chu, M. Y., Wan, L. C., & Wyer, R. S. (2018). *Do moral emotions make people responsible consumers?* [Unpublished manuscript]. Open University of Hong Kong.

Craig, A. D. (2002). How do you feel? Interoception: The sense of the physiological condition of the body. *Nature Reviews Neuroscience, 3*(8), 655–666. https://doi.org/10.1038/nrn894

Critchley, H. D., Wiens, S., Rotshtein, P., Öhman, A., & Dolan, R. J. (2004). Neural systems supporting interoceptive awareness. *Nature Neuroscience, 7*(2), 189–195. https://doi.org/10.1038/nn1176

Dahl, D. W., Honea, H., & Manchanda, R. V. (2005). Three R's of interpersonal consumer guilt: Relationship, reciprocity, reparation. *Journal of Consumer Psychology, 15*(4), 307–315. https://doi.org/10.1207/s15327663jcp1504_5

Dahl, D. W., Manchanda, R. V., & Argo, J. J. (2001). Embarrassment in consumer purchase: The roles of social presence and purchase familiarity: Table 1. *Journal of Consumer Research, 28*(3), 473–481. https://doi.org/10.1086/323734

Damasio, A. R. (1994). *Descartes' error: Emotion, reason, and the human brain.* Avon.

Davidson, R. J. (1992a). Anterior cerebral asymmetry and the nature of emotions. *Brain & Cognition, 20*(1), 125–151. https://doi.org/10.1016/0278-2626(92)90065-T

Davidson, R. J. (1992b). Emotion and affective style: Hemispheric substrates. *Psychological Science, 3*(1), 39–43. https://doi.org/10.1111/j.1467-9280.1992.tb00254.x

Davidson, R. J. (1995). Cerebral asymmetry, emotion and affective style. In R. J. Davidson & K. Hugdahl (Eds.), *Brain asymmetry* (pp. 361–387). MIT Press.

Davidson, R. J. (1998). Affective style and affective disorders: Perspectives from affective neuroscience. *Cognition and Emotion, 12*(3), 307–330. https://doi.org/10.1080/026999398379628

Deak, A. (2011). Brain and emotion: Cognitive neuroscience of emotions. *Review of Psychology, 18*(2), 71–80. https://hrcak.srce.hr/81460

Dempsey, M. A., & Mitchell, A. A. (2010). The influence of implicit attitudes on choice when consumers are confronted with conflicting attribute information. *Journal of Consumer Research, 37*(4), 614–625. https://doi.org/10.1086/653947

DeWall, N. C., Baumeister, R. F., Stillman, T. F., & Gailliot, M. T. (2007). Violence restrained: Effects of self-regulation and its depletion on aggression. *Journal of Experimental Social Psychology, 43*(1), 62–76. https://doi.org/10.1016/j.jesp.2005.12.005

Dong, P., Huang, X. I., & Wyer, R. S., Jr. (2013). The illusion of saving face: How people symbolically cope with embarrassment. *Psychological Science, 24*(10),

2005–2012. https://doi.org/10.1177/ 0956797613482946

Duhachek, A., Agrawal, N., & Han, D. (2012). Guilt versus shame: Coping, fluency, and framing in the effectiveness of responsible drinking messages. *Journal of Marketing Research*, 49(6), 928–941. https://doi.org/10.1509/jmr.10.0244

Duke, K. E., & Amir, O. (2019). Guilt dynamics: Consequences of temporally separating decisions and actions. *Journal of Consumer Research*, 45(6), 1254–1273. https://doi.org/10.1093/jcr/ucy049

Dunn, L., & Hoegg, J. (2014). The impact of fear on emotional brand attachment. *Journal of Consumer Research*, 41(1), 152–168. https://doi.org/10.1086/675377

Ekman, P. (1992). An argument for basic emotions. *Cognition and Emotion*, 6(3–4), 169–200. https://doi.org/10.1080/02699939208411068

Ellsworth, P. C., & Scherer, K. R. (2003). Appraisal processes in emotion. In R. J. Davidson, K. R. Scherer, & H. H. Goldsmith (Eds.), *Series in affective science* (pp. 572–595). Oxford University Press.

Etkin, J., & Ghosh, A. P. (2018). When being in a positive mood increases choice deferral. *Journal of Consumer Research*, 45(1), 208–225. https://doi.org/10.1093/jcr/ucx121

Faraji-Rad, A., & Pham, M. T. (2017). Uncertainty increases the reliance on affect in decisions. *Journal of Consumer Research*, 44(1), 1–21. https://doi.org/10.1093/jcr/ucw073

Fedorikhin, A., & Cole, C. A. (2004). Mood effects on attitudes, perceived risk and choice: Moderators and mediators. *Journal of Consumer Psychology*, 14(1–2), 2–12. https://doi.org/10.1207/s15327663jcp1401&2_2

Fedorikhin, A., & Patrick, V. M. (2010). Positive mood and resistance to temptation: The interfering influence of elevated arousal. *Journal of Consumer Research*, 37(4), 698–711. https://doi.org/10.1086/655665

Forgas, J. P. (1995). Mood and judgment: The affect infusion model (AIM). *Psychological Bulletin*, 117(1), 39–66. https://doi.org/10.1037/0033-2909.117.1.39

Frijda, N. H. (1986). *The emotions*. Cambridge University Press.

Gal, D., & Liu, W. (2011). Grapes of wrath: The angry effects of self-control. *Journal of Consumer Research*, 38(3), 445–458. https://doi.org/10.1086/659377

Garg, N., Inman, J. J., & Mittal, V. (2005). Incidental and task-related affect: A re-inquiry and extension of the influence of affect on choice. *Journal of Consumer Research*, 32(1), 154–159. https://doi.org/10.1086/426624

Gibson, B. (2008). Can evaluative conditioning change attitudes toward mature brands? New evidence from the implicit association test. *Journal of Consumer Research*, 35(1), 178–188. https://doi.org/10.1086/527341

Goffman, E. (1959). *The presentation of self in everyday life*. Doubleday.

Goldberg, M. E., & Gorn, G. J. (1987). Happy and sad TV programs: How they affect reactions to commercials. *Journal of Consumer Research*, 14(3), 387–403. https://doi.org/10.1086/209122

Goldsmith, K., Kim, E., & Dhar, R. (2012). When guilt begets pleasure: The positive effect of a negative emotion. *Journal of Marketing Research*, 49(6), 872–881. https://doi.org/10.1509/jmr.09.0421

Gorn, G. J. (1982). The effects of music in advertising on choice behavior: A classical conditioning approach. *Journal of Marketing*, 46(1), 94–101. https://doi.org/10.1177/002224298204600109

Gorn, G. J., Goldberg, M. E., & Basu, K. (1993). Mood, awareness, and product evaluation. *Journal of Consumer Psychology*, 2(3), 237–256. https://doi.org/10.1016/S1057-7408(08)80016-2

Gorn, G. J., Pham, M. T., & Sin, L. Y. (2001). When arousal influences ad evaluation and valence does not (and vice versa). *Journal of Consumer Psychology*, 11(1), 43–55. https://doi.org/10.1207/S15327663JCP1101_4

Han, D., Duhachek, A., & Agrawal, N. (2014). Emotions shape decisions through construal level: The case of guilt and shame. *Journal of Consumer Research*, 41(4), 1047–1064. https://doi.org/10.1086/678300

Hasford, J., Kidwell, B., & Hardesty, D. M. (2018). Emotional ability and associative learning: How experiencing and reasoning about emotions impacts evaluative conditioning. *Journal of Consumer Research*, 45(4), 743–760. https://doi.org/10.1093/jcr/ucy026

Hermann, P., Deak, A., Papp, P., Révész, Gy., & Bereczkei, T. (2010, September). *Neuropsychological correlates of processing emotional stimuli: Rethinking the role of amygdala: An fMRI-study* [Poster presentation]. 9th Alps-Adria Psychology Conference, Klagenfurt, Austria.

Hong, J., & Lee, A. Y. (2010). Feeling mixed but not torn: The moderating role of construal level in mixed emotions appeals. *Journal of Consumer Research*, 37(3), 456–472. https://doi.org/10.1086/653492

Hung, I. W., & Mukhopadhyay, A. (2012). Lenses of the heart: How actors' and observers' perspectives influence emotional experiences. *Journal of Consumer Research*, 38(6), 1103–1115. https://doi.org/10.1086/661529

Isen, A. M., Daubman, K. A., & Nowicki, G. P. (1987). Positive affect facilitates creative problem solving. *Journal of Personality and Social Psychology*, 52(6), 1122–1131. https://doi.org/10.1037/0022-3514.52.6.1122

Isen, A. M., Johnson, M. M., Mertz, E., & Robinson, G. F. (1985). The influence of positive affect on the unusualness of word associations. *Journal of Personality and Social Psychology*, 48(6), 1413.

Isen, A. M., & Patrick, R. (1983). The effect of positive feelings on risk taking: When the chips are down. *Organizational Behavior and Human Performance*, 31(2), 194–202. https://doi.org/10.1016/0030-5073(83)90120-4

Isen, A. M., Shalker, T. E., Clark, M., & Karp, L. (1978). Affect, accessibility of material in memory, and behavior: A cognitive loop? *Journal of Personality and Social Psychology*, 36(1), 1–12. https://doi.org/10.1037/0022-3514.36.1.1

Janiszewski, C., & Chandon, E. (2007). Transfer-appropriate processing, response fluency, and the mere measurement effect. *Journal of Marketing Research*, 44(2), 309–323. https://doi.org/10.1509/jmkr.44.2.309

Janiszewski, C., & Warlop, L. (1993). The influence of classical conditioning procedures on subsequent attention to the conditioned brand. *Journal of Consumer Research*, 20(2), 171–189. https://doi.org/10.1086/209342

Jost, J., Langer, M., & Singh, V. (2017). The politics of buying, boycotting, complaining, and disputing: An extension of the research program by Jung, Garbarino, Briley, and Wynhausen. *Journal of Consumer Research*, 44(3), 503–510. https://doi.org/10.1093/jcr/ucx084

Jung, K., Garbarino, E., Briley, D., & Wynhausen, J. (2017). Blue and red voices: Effects of political ideology on consumers' complaining and disputing behavior. *Journal of Consumer Research*, 44(3), 511–518. https://doi.org/10.1093/jcr/ucx037

Kahn, B. E., & Isen, A. M. (1993). The influence of positive affect on variety seeking among safe, enjoyable products. *Journal of Consumer Research*, 20(2), 257–270. https://doi.org/10.1086/209347

Kahneman, D., Wakker, P., & Sarin, R. (1997). Back to Bentham? Explorations of experienced utility. *Quarterly Journal of Economics*, 112(2), 375–406. https://doi.org/10.1162/003355397555235

Keller, P. A., & Block, L. G. (1996). Increasing the persuasiveness of fear appeals: The effect of arousal and elaboration. *Journal of Consumer Research*, 22(4), 448–459. https://doi.org/10.1086/209461

Kim, J., Allen, C. T., & Kardes, F. R. (1996). An investigation of the mediational mechanisms underlying attitudinal conditioning. *Journal of Marketing Research*, 33(3), 318–328. https://doi.org/10.1177/002224379603300306

King, D., & Janiszewski, C. (2011). Affect-gating. *Journal of Consumer Research*, 38(4), 697–711. https://doi.org/10.1086/660811

Kivetz, R., & Keinan, A. (2006). Repenting hyperopia: An analysis of self-control regrets. *Journal of Consumer Research*, 33(2), 273–282. https://doi.org/10.1086/506308

Kramer, T., & Yoon, S. (2007). Approach-avoidance motivation and the use of affect as information. *Journal of Consumer Psychology*, 17(2), 128–138. https://doi.org/10.1016/S1057-7408(07)70019-0

Krishna, A., Herd, K., & Aydinoğlu, N. (2015). Wetting the bed at twenty-one: Embarrassment as a private emotion. *Journal of Consumer Psychology*, 25(3), 473–486. https://doi.org/10.1016/j.jcps.2015.02.005

Krishna, A., Herd, K., & Aydinoğlu, N. (2019). A review of consumer embarrassment as a public and private emotion. *Journal of Consumer Psychology*, 29(3), 492–516. https://doi.org/10.1002/jcpy.1086

Krishna, A., & Schwarz, N. (2014). Sensory marketing, embodiment, and grounded cognition: A review and introduction. *Journal of Consumer Psychology*, 24(2), 159–168. https://doi.org/10.1016/j.jcps.2013.12.006

Kristofferson, K., Mcferran, B., Morales, A. C., & Dahl, D. W. (2017). The dark side of scarcity promotions: How exposure to limited-quantity promotions can induce aggression. *Journal of Consumer Research*, 43(5), 683–706. https://doi.org/10.1093/jcr/ucw056

Labroo, A. A., Dhar, R., & Schwarz, N. (2008). Of frog wines and frowning watches: Semantic priming, perceptual fluency, and brand evaluation. *Journal of Consumer Research*, 34(6), 819–831. https://doi.org/10.1086/523290

Labroo, A. A., & Kim, S. (2009). The "instrumentality" heuristic: Why metacognitive difficulty is desirable during goal pursuit. *Psychological Science*, 20(1), 127–134. https://doi.org/10.1111/j.1467-9280.2008.02264.x

Labroo, A. A., & Mukhopadhyay, A. (2009). Lay theories of emotion transience and the search for happiness: A fresh perspective on affect regulation: Table 1. *Journal of Consumer Research*, 36(2), 242–254. https://doi.org/10.1086/597159

Labroo, A. A., & Patrick, V. M. (2009). Psychological distancing: Why happiness helps you see the big picture. *Journal of Consumer Research*, 35(5), 800–809. https://doi.org/10.1086/593683

Labroo, A. A., & Ramanathan, S. (2007). The influence of experience and sequence of conflicting emotions on ad attitudes. *Journal of Consumer Research*, 33(4), 523–528. https://doi.org/10.1086/510226

Labroo, A. A., & Rucker, D. D. (2010). The orientation-matching hypothesis: An emotion-specificity approach to affect regulation. *Journal of Marketing Research, 47*(5), 955–966. https://doi.org/10.1509/jmkr.47.5.955

Lane, R. D., Reiman, E. M., Bradley, M. M., Lang, P. J., Ahern, G. L., Davidson, R. J., & Schwartz, G. E. (1997). Neuroanatomical correlates of pleasant and unpleasant emotion. *Neuropsychologia, 35*(11), 1437–1444. https://doi.org/10.1016/S0028-3932(97)00070-5

Lau-Gesk, L. (2005). Understanding consumer evaluations of mixed affective experiences. *Journal of Consumer Research, 32*(1), 23–28. https://doi.org/10.1086/429598

Lazarus, R. S. (1966). *Psychological stress and the coping process*. McGraw Hill.

Lazarus, R. S. (1991a). *Emotion and adaptation*. Oxford University Press.

Lazarus, R. S. (1991b). Progress on a cognitive-motivational-relational theory of emotion. *American Psychologist, 46*(8), 819–834. https://doi.org/10.1037/0003-066X.46.8.819

LeDoux, J. E. (1996). *The emotional brain: The mysterious underpinning of emotional life*. Simon and Schuster.

Lee, A. Y. (2002). Effects of implicit memory on memory-based versus stimulus-based brand choice. *Journal of Marketing Research, 39*(4), 440–454. https://doi.org/10.1509/jmkr.39.4.440.19119

Lee, A. Y., & Labroo, A. A. (2004). The effect of conceptual and perceptual fluency on brand evaluation. *Journal of Marketing Research, 41*(2), 151–165. https://doi.org/10.1509/jmkr.41.2.151.28665

Lee, A. Y., & Sternthal, B. (1999). The effects of positive mood on memory. *International Journal of Plant Sciences, 26*(2), 115–127. https://doi.org/10.1086/209554

Lee, C. J., & Andrade, E. B. (2011). Fear, social projection, and financial decision making. *Journal of Marketing Research, 48*(SPL), S121–S129. https://doi.org/10.1509/jmkr.48.spl.s121

Lee, C. J., Andrade, E. B., & Palmer, S. E. (2013). Interpersonal relationships and preferences for mood-congruency in aesthetic experiences. *Journal of Consumer Research, 40*(2), 382–391. https://doi.org/10.1086/670609

Lee, K., Kim, H., & Vohs, K. D. (2011). Stereotype threat in the marketplace: Consumer anxiety and purchase intentions. *Journal of Consumer Research, 38*(2), 343–357. https://doi.org/10.1086/659315

Lerner, J. S., & Keltner, D. (2000). Beyond valence: Toward a model of emotion-specific influences on judgment and choice. *Cognition and Emotion, 14*(4), 473–493. https://doi.org/10.1080/026999300402763

Levav, J., & McGraw, A. P. (2009). Emotional accounting: How feelings about money influence consumer choice. *Journal of Marketing Research, 46*(1), 66–80. https://doi.org/10.1509/jmkr.46.1.66

Loewenstein, G., & Lerner, J. S. (2002). The role of affect in decision making. In R. J. Davidson, H. H. Goldsmith, & K. R. Scherer (Eds.), *The handbook of affective science* (pp. 619–642). Oxford University Press.

Louro, M. J., Pieters, R., & Zeelenberg, M. (2005). Negative returns on positive emotions: The influence of pride and self-regulatory goals on repurchase decisions. *Journal of Consumer Research, 31*(4), 833–840. https://doi.org/10.1086/426619

Lowe, M. L., Loveland, K. E., & Krishna, A. (2019). A quiet disquiet: Anxiety and risk avoidance due to nonconscious auditory priming. *Journal of Consumer Research, 46*(1), 159–179. https://doi.org/10.1093/jcr/ucy068

Luce, M. F. (1998). Choosing to avoid: Coping with negatively emotion-laden consumer decisions. *Journal of Consumer Research, 24*(4), 409–433. https://doi.org/10.1086/209518

Martin, I., & Levey, A. B. (1978). Evaluative conditioning. *Advances in Behaviour Research and Therapy, 1*(2), 57–101. https://doi.org/10.1016/0146-6402(78)90013-9

McFerran, B., Aquino, K., & Tracy, J. L. (2014). Evidence for two facets of pride in consumption: Findings from luxury brands. *Journal of Consumer Psychology, 24*(4), 455–471. https://doi.org/10.1016/j.jcps.2014.03.004

Meloy, M. G. (2000). Mood-driven distortion of product information. *Journal of Consumer Research, 27*(3), 345–359. https://doi.org/10.1086/317589

Menon, G., & Raghubir, P. (2003). Ease-of-retrieval as an automatic input in judgments: A mere-accessibility framework? *Journal of Consumer Research, 30*(2), 230–243. https://doi.org/10.1086/376804

Morris, J., & Dolan, R. (2004). Functional neuroanatomy of human emotion. In K. J. Friston, C. D. Frith, R. Dolan, C. J. Price, S. Zeki, J. Ashburner, & W. Penny (Eds.), *Human brain function* (pp. 365–396). Elsevier.

Mukhopadhyay, A., & Johar, G. V. (2007). Tempted or not? The effect of recent purchase history on responses to affective advertising. *Journal of Consumer Research, 33*(4), 445–453. https://doi.org/10.1086/510218

Niedenthal, P. M., Halberstadt, J. B., & Setterlund, M. B. (1997). Being happy and seeing "happy": Emotional state mediates visual word recognition. *Cognition and Emotion, 11*(4), 403–432. https://doi.org/10.1080/026999397379863

Niedenthal, P. M., & Setterlund, M. B. (1994). Emotion congruence in perception. *Personality and Social Psychology Bulletin, 20*(4), 401–411. https://doi.org/10.1177/0146167294204007

Novemsky, N., Dhar, R., Schwarz, N., & Simonson, I. (2007). Preference fluency in choice. *Journal of Marketing Research, 44*(3), 347–356. https://doi.org/10.1509/jmkr.44.3.347

Ortony, A., Clore, G. L., & Collins, A. (1988). *The cognitive structure of emotions*. Cambridge University Press. https://doi.org/10.1017/CBO9780511571299

Panksepp, J. (1998). *Affective neuroscience: The foundations of human and animal emotions*. Oxford University Press.

Passyn, K., & Sujan, M. (2006). Self-accountability emotions and fear appeals: Motivating behavior. *Journal of Consumer Research, 32*(4), 583–589. https://doi.org/10.1086/500488

Patrick, V. M., Macinnis, D. J., & Park, C. W. (2007). Not as happy as I thought I'd be? Affective misforecasting and product evaluations. *Journal of Consumer Research, 33*(4), 479–489. https://doi.org/10.1086/510221

Pena-Marin, J., Adaval, R., & Shen, L. (2021). Fear in the stock market: How COVID-19 affects preference for high- and low-priced stocks. *Journal of the Association for Consumer Research*. Advance online publication. https://doi.org/10.1086/711930

Pham, M. T. (1998). Representativeness, relevance, and the use of feelings in decision making. *Journal of Consumer Research, 25*(2), 144–159. https://doi.org/10.1086/209532

Pham, M. T., Cohen, J. B., Pracejus, J. W., & Hughes, G. D. (2001). Affect monitoring and the primacy of feelings in judgment. *Journal of Consumer Research, 28*(2), 167–188. https://doi.org/10.1086/322896

Pham, M. T., Lee, L., & Stephen, A. T. (2012). Feeling the future: The emotional oracle effect. *Journal of Consumer Research, 39*(3), 461–477. https://doi.org/10.1086/663823

Phan, K. L., Wager, T., Taylor, S. F., & Liberzon, I. (2002). Functional neuroanatomy of emotion: A meta-analysis of emotion activation studies in PET and fMRI. *NeuroImage, 16*(2), 331–348. https://doi.org/10.1006/nimg.2002.1087

Pocheptsova, A., Labroo, A. A., & Dhar, R. (2010). Making products feel special: When metacognitive difficulty enhances evaluations. *Journal of Marketing Research, 47*(6), 1059–1069. https://doi.org/10.1509/jmkr.47.6.1059

Polivy, J. (1996). Psychological consequences of food restriction. *Journal of the Academy of Nutrition and Dietetics, 96*(6), 589–592. https://doi.org/10.1016/S0002-8223(96)00161-7

Porath, C., Macinnis, D., & Folkes, V. (2010). Witnessing incivility among employees: Effects on consumer anger and negative inferences about companies. *Journal of Consumer Research, 37*(2), 292–303. https://doi.org/10.1086/651565

Prinz, J. (2004). *Gut reactions: A perceptual theory of emotion*. Oxford University Press.

Pyone, J. S., & Isen, A. M. (2011). Positive affect, intertemporal choice, and levels of thinking: Increasing consumers' willingness to wait. *Journal of Marketing Research, 48*(3), 532–543. https://doi.org/10.1509/jmkr.48.3.532

Qiu, C., & Yeung, C. W. M. (2008). Mood and comparative judgment: Does mood influence everything and finally nothing? *Journal of Consumer Research, 34*(5), 657–669. https://doi.org/10.1086/522096

Raghunathan, R., Pham, M. T., & Corfman, K. P. (2006). Informational properties of anxiety and sadness, and displaced coping. *Journal of Consumer Research, 32*(4), 596–601. https://doi.org/10.1086/500491

Raju, S., & Unnava, H. R. (2006). The role of arousal in commitment: An explanation for the number of counterarguments. *Journal of Consumer Research, 33*(2), 173–178. https://doi.org/10.1086/506298

Ramanathan, S., & Williams, P. (2007). Immediate and delayed emotional consequences of indulgence: The moderating influence of personality type on mixed emotions. *Journal of Consumer Research, 34*(2), 212–223. https://doi.org/10.1086/519149

Ratner, R. K., & Hamilton, R. W. (2015). Inhibited from bowling alone. *Journal of Consumer Research, 42*(2), 266–283. https://doi.org/10.1093/jcr/ucv012

Reber, R., & Schwarz, N. (1999). Effects of perceptual fluency on judgments of truth. *Consciousness and Cognition, 8*(3), 338–342. https://doi.org/10.1006/ccog.1999.0386

Reber, R., Winkielman, P., & Schwarz, N. (1998). Effects of perceptual fluency on affective judgments. *Psychological Science, 9*(1), 45–48. https://doi.org/10.1111/1467-9280.00008

Reiman, E. M., Lane, R. D., Ahern, G. L., Schwartz, G. E., Davidson, R. J., Friston, K. J., Yun, L. S., & Chen, K. (1997). Neuroanatomical correlates of externally and internally generated human emotion. *American Journal of Psychiatry, 154*(7), 918–925. https://doi.org/10.1176/ajp.154.7.918

Salerno, A., Laran, J., & Janiszewski, C. (2014). Hedonic eating goals and emotion: When sadness decreases the desire to indulge. *Journal of Consumer Research, 41*(1), 135–151. https://doi.org/10.1086/675299

Salerno, A., Laran, J., & Janiszewski, C. (2015). Pride and regulatory behavior: The influence of appraisal information and self-regulatory goals. *Journal of*

Consumer Research, 42(3), 499–514. https://doi.org/10.1093/jcr/ucv037

Sanbonmatsu, D. M., & Kardes, F. R. (1988). The effects of physiological arousal on information processing and persuasion. *Journal of Consumer Research, 15*(3), 379–385. https://doi.org/10.1086/209175

Sander, D. (2009, August). *What is the function of the human amygdala in emotion?* [Paper presentation]. Conference of International Society of Emotion Researchers, Louvain, Belgium.

Scarantino, A., & de Sousa, R. (2018, Winter). Emotion. In E. N. Zalta (Ed.), *The Stanford encyclopedia of philosophy*. https://plato.stanford.edu/archives/win2018/entries/emotion/

Schachter, S., & Singer, J. E. (1962). Cognitive, social, and physiological determinants of emotional state. *Psychological Review, 69*(5), 379–399. https://doi.org/10.1037/h0046234

Scherer, K. R., Schorr, A., & Johnstone, T. (2001). *Appraisal processes in emotion: Theory, methods, research*. Oxford University Press.

Schwarz, N. (2004). Metacognitive experiences in consumer judgment and decision making. *Journal of Consumer Psychology, 14*(4), 332–348. https://doi.org/10.1207/s15327663jcp1404_2

Schwarz, N. (2015). Metacognition. In M. Mikulincer, P. R. Shaver, E. Borgida, & J. A. Bargh (Eds.), *APA handbook of personality and social psychology: Vol. 1. Attitudes and social cognition* (pp. 203–229). American Psychological Association. https://doi.org/10.1037/14341-006

Schwarz, N., & Clore, G. L. (1983). Mood, misattribution, and judgments of well-being: Informative and directive functions of affective states. *Journal of Personality and Social Psychology, 45*(3), 513–523. https://doi.org/10.1037/0022-3514.45.3.513

Shen, H., Jiang, Y., & Adaval, R. (2010). Contrast and assimilation effects of processing fluency. *Journal of Consumer Research, 36*(5), 876–889. https://doi.org/10.1086/612425

Shimp, T. A., Stuart, E. W., & Engle, R. W. (1991). A program of classical conditioning experiments testing variations in the conditioned stimulus and context. *Journal of Consumer Research, 18*(1), 1–12. https://doi.org/10.1086/209236

Shiv, B., & Fedorikhin, A. (1999). Heart and mind in conflict: The interplay of affect and cognition in consumer decision making. *Journal of Consumer Research, 26*(3), 278–292. https://doi.org/10.1086/209563

Slovic, P., Finucane, M. L., Peters, E., & MacGregor, D. G. (2002). The affect heuristic. In T. Gilovich, D. Griffin, & D. Kahneman (Eds.), *Heuristics and biases: The psychology of intuitive judgment* (pp. 397–420). Cambridge University Press. https://doi.org/10.1017/CBO9780511808098.025

Smith, C. A., & Ellsworth, P. C. (1985). Patterns of cognitive appraisal in emotion. *Journal of Personality and Social Psychology, 48*(4), 813–838. https://doi.org/10.1037/0022-3514.48.4.813

Song, H., & Schwarz, N. (2008). If it's hard to read, it's hard to do: Processing fluency affects effort prediction and motivation. *Psychological Science, 19*(10), 986–988. https://doi.org/10.1111/j.1467-9280.2008.02189.x

Sternthal, B., & Craig, C. S. (1974). Fear appeals: Revisited and revised. *Journal of Consumer Research, 1*(3), 22–34. https://doi.org/10.1086/208597

Stuart, E. W., Shimp, T. A., & Engle, R. W. (1987). Classical conditioning of consumer attitudes: Four experiments in an advertising context. *Journal of Consumer Research, 14*(3), 334–349. https://doi.org/10.1086/209117

Su, L., Wan, L. C., & Wyer, R. S., Jr. (2018). The contrasting influences of incidental anger and fear on responses to a service failure. *Psychology and Marketing, 35*(9), 666–675. https://doi.org/10.1002/mar.21114

Sweldens, S., van Osselaer, S. M. J., & Janiszewski, C. (2010). Evaluative conditioning procedures and the resilience of brand attitudes. *Journal of Consumer Research, 37*(3), 473–489. https://doi.org/10.1086/653656

Swinyard, W. R. (1993). The effects of mood, involvement, and quality of store experience on shopping intentions. *Journal of Consumer Research, 20*(2), 271–280. https://doi.org/10.1086/209348

Szily, E., & Kéri, S. (2008). Emotion-related brain regions. *Ideggyógyászati Szemle [Clinical Neuroscience], 61*(3–4), 77–86.

Tangney, J. P., Miller, R. S., Flicker, L., & Barlow, D. H. (1996). Are shame, guilt, and embarrassment distinct emotions? *Journal of Personality and Social Psychology, 70*(6), 1256–1269. https://doi.org/10.1037/0022-3514.70.6.1256

Thomas, M., & Tsai, C. (2012). Psychological distance and subjective experience: How distancing reduces the feeling of difficulty. *Journal of Consumer Research, 39*(2), 324–340. https://doi.org/10.1086/663772

Tiedens, L. Z., & Linton, S. (2001). Judgment under emotional certainty and uncertainty: The effects of specific emotions on information processing. *Journal of Personality and Social Psychology, 81*(6), 973–988. https://doi.org/10.1037/0022-3514.81.6.973

Tracy, J. L., & Robins, R. W. (2007). The psychological structure of pride: A tale of two facets. *Journal of*

Personality and Social Psychology, 92(3), 506–525. https://doi.org/10.1037/0022-3514.92.3.506

Tsai, C. I., & McGill, A. L. (2011). No pain, no gain? How fluency and construal level affect consumer confidence. *Journal of Consumer Research, 37*(5), 807–821. https://doi.org/10.1086/655855

Wan, L. C., & Wyer, R. S., Jr. (2015). Consumer reactions to attractive service providers: Approach or avoid? *Journal of Consumer Research, 42*(4), 578–595. https://doi.org/10.1093/jcr/ucv044

Wänke, M., Bohner, G., & Jurkowitsch, A. (1997). There are many reasons to drive a BMW: Does imagined ease of argument generation influence attitudes. *Journal of Consumer Research, 24*(2), 170–177. https://doi.org/10.1086/209502

Whalen, P. J., Shin, L. M., McInerney, S. C., Fischer, H., Wright, C. I., & Rauch, S. L. (2001). A functional MRI study of human amygdala responses to facial expressions of fear versus anger. *Emotion, 1*(1), 70–83. https://doi.org/10.1037/1528-3542.1.1.70

Wilcox, K., Kramer, T., & Sen, S. (2011). Indulgence or self-control: A dual process model of the effect of incidental pride on indulgent choice. *Journal of Consumer Research, 38*(1), 151–163. https://doi.org/10.1086/657606

Williams, P., & Aaker, J. L. (2002). Can mixed emotions peacefully coexist? *Journal of Consumer Research, 28*(4), 636–649. https://doi.org/10.1086/338206

Winkielman, P., Schwarz, N., Fazendeiro, T. A., & Reber, R. (2003) The hedonic marking of processing fluency: Implications for evaluative judgment. In J. Musch & K. C. Klauer (Eds.), *The psychology of evaluation: Affective processes in cognition and emotion*. Lawrence Erlbaum Associates.

Wyer, R. S., Jr., Clore, G. L., & Isbell, L. M. (1999). Affect and information processing. *Advances in Experimental Social Psychology, 31*, 1–77. https://doi.org/10.1016/S0065-2601(08)60271-3

Wyer, R. S., Jr., & Srull, T. K. (1989). *Memory and cognition in its social context*. Erlbaum.

Yeung, W. M. C., & Wyer, R. S., Jr. (2004). Affect, appraisal and consumer judgment. *Journal of Consumer Research, 31*(2), 412–424. https://doi.org/10.1086/422119

Zajonc, R. B. (1968). Attitudinal effects of mere exposure. *Journal of Personality and Social Psychology, 9*(2, Pt.2), 1–27. https://doi.org/10.1037/h0025848

Zhao, M., & Tsai, C. I. (2011). The effects of duration knowledge on forecasted versus actual affective experiences. *Journal of Consumer Research, 38*(3), 525–534. https://doi.org/10.1086/660114

CONSUMER INVOLVEMENT AND ENGAGEMENT: FROM INVOLVEMENT'S ELABORATION LIKELIHOOD TO ENGAGEMENT'S INVESTMENT PROPENSITY

Linda D. Hollebeek and Rajendra K. Srivastava

Though the concepts of consumer involvement (CI) and consumer engagement (CE) are discussed extensively in the consumer behavior and broader marketing literature, their respective areas of commonality, divergence, and fit remain surprisingly underilluminated. That is, while a number of authors have identified involvement as an important antecedent of engagement (e.g., Harrigan et al., 2018; Hollebeek et al., 2014), little remains known regarding the applicability or transferability of involvement's theoretical foundations to engagement, as therefore explored through involvement's elaboration likelihood model (ELM) in this chapter (Petty & Cacioppo, 1986, pp. 1–24).

To realize this objective, we review important literature on CI and CE and develop an integrative framework that extends involvement's ELM-based foundations for applicability to CE. We first synthesize literature on CI, which has significantly advanced understanding of consumer behavior since the 1980s. Defined as a consumer's interest or personal relevance in an object or activity (e.g., a brand; Zaichkowsky, 1986, 1988), the CI concept fits within the traditional market-to paradigm, where consumers are viewed as relatively passive recipients of incoming brand-related information (Cretu & Brodie, 2007; Sasser et al., 2014).

However, over time and stimulated by various external factors (e.g., the advent of highly interactive two-way modes of communication, including social media and online brand communities), a paradigmatic shift has occurred toward a market with and among orientation from the late 1990s and onward (Cova & Salle, 2008; see also Chapter 21, this volume). Here, consumers are viewed as proactive contributors to their own brand experience and cocreation of meaning (Bakker et al., 2012; Hollebeek, 2011a, 2011b), which has seen soaring scholarly interest in the last 2 decades. In this paradigm, CE has rapidly gained traction in the last 10 to 15 years (Brodie et al., 2011; Kumar et al., 2019; Patterson et al., 2006).

Our primary purpose is to develop an integrative framework of CI and CE that extends Petty and Cacioppo's ELM across highly versus low-engaged consumers (Cacioppo et al., 1986; Petty & Cacioppo, 1984, 1986, pp. 1–24). We thus revise the ELM for applicability to CE, which culminates in our integrative framework of consumer engagement propensity (CEP). This chapter makes the following contributions. First, we detail key areas of theoretical similarity and discrepancy across CI and CE, thereby advancing insight into these concepts and their interface.

The authors acknowledge Brodie et al. (2016; EMAC) for a discussion on involvement and engagement.
https://doi.org/10.1037/0000262-026
APA Handbook of Consumer Psychology, L. R. Kahle (Editor-in-Chief)
Copyright © 2022 by the American Psychological Association. All rights reserved.

Second, we extend the ELM by developing a framework of CEP that acknowledges the existence of consumer-behavior-based differences across highly and low-engaged consumers, similar to highly/low-involved consumers in the ELM. Given the notable lack of insight into the transferability of the ELM's foundations to engagement, our integrative analyses offer new insight. Through our analyses, we also develop the notions of (highly) active and (highly) inactive CE styles, thus extending Prior and Marcos-Cuevas's (2016) and Hollebeek's (2018) notion of engagement styles, and hypothesize the existence of differences across these consumers. Like the ELM, the CEP offers actionable suggestions for managers in terms of how to best approach, communicate with, or target consumers with highly active (vs. inactive) engagement styles.

Next, we review important literature on CI and CE and discuss their key areas of conceptual similarity and discrepancy. Our observations form the foundation for the development of our framework of CEP in the following section. The chapter concludes with a discussion of theoretical and practical implications that arise from our analyses.

LITERATURE REVIEW

In this section, we review relevant literature on the concepts of CI and CE, and synthesize their respective areas of commonality and divergence.

Consumer Involvement

Since Sherif and Cantril's (1947) introduction of the involvement concept, it has become widely used to explain consumer behavior in sectors ranging from automobiles and computers to blue jeans and wine. Across contexts, CI has been identified to impact a range of behaviors, including product-/service-related decision making and choice, usage (e.g., frequency), response to persuasive messages, depth of advertising processing, and word-of-mouth communication, to name a few (Hollebeek, 2005; Houston & Rothschild, 1978; Laurent and Kapferer, 1985; Zaichkowsky, 1985).

Scrutiny of the literature reveals the existence of multiple related forms of involvement, including product, enduring, ego, purchase, brand-decision, instrumental, audience, and response involvement (Bloch & Richins, 1983; Muncy & Hunt, 1984; Sherif & Cantril, 1947). Of these, product (or brand) involvement is the most commonly used variant, which therefore represents the focus of this chapter. A key benefit of product involvement lies in its relatively stable nature, rendering it suitable as a market segmentation variable. Despite this, it can and will change over time, particularly in the long run (e.g., as one's needs or situation changes). Consequently, any involvement form (including product involvement) contains an important situational component, where differing involvement intensity may ensue across contexts (e.g., those characterized by differing levels of perceived risk/value; Laurent & Kapferer 1985).

Debate also exists regarding its conceptualization (Cohen, 1983; Mittal & Lee, 1989). For example, while Zaichkowsky (1985) defined involvement as "a person's perceived relevance of the object based on inherent needs, values, and interests" (p. 342; see also Celsi & Olson, 1988), Mittal and Lee (1989) viewed it as an internal, motivational state that reflects an individual's level of arousal/interest evoked by a stimulus in a particular context (Park & Mittal, 1985). Despite these differing views, we observe two main areas of agreement across the majority of proposed definitions.

First, involvement reflects the degree of personal relevance or importance of an object or activity to an individual (Engel & Blackwell, 1982; Greenwald & Leavitt, 1984). Second, it represents the perceived value of a goal-object, as manifested through one's level of interest in the object (Hollebeek, Sprott, & Andreassen, 2019; Mittal & Lee, 1989). Therefore, Zaichkowsky's (1985) and Mittal and Lee's (1989) views, while phrased differently, are reconcilable into the common involvement tenet of the individual's interest in an object (e.g., a brand) or the level of personal relevance of the object in their lives.

Involvement's broader theoretical foundations are commonly viewed to reside in the ELM of persuasion, which originated in the psychology literature and was introduced in the field of consumer behavior in the 1980s (Greenwald & Leavitt, 1984;

Petty et al., 1983). In the ELM, highly involved consumers are motivated to undertake elaborate cognitive processing of central cues offered in marketing communications (e.g., in-depth product information; see Chapter 31). On the other hand, low-involved consumers tend to focus on peripheral message cues that require less extensive cognitive processing (e.g., color, packaging), given their limited motivation to process brand-related cues (Petty & Cacioppo, 1986, pp. 1–24). That is, highly involved consumers think more about their product categories or brands, search more widely for product-/brand-related information, process information in greater depth, and spend more time making purchase decisions than their less involved counterparts (Greenwald & Leavitt, 1984; Houston & Rothschild, 1978).

For marketers, the development and nurturing of highly involved customers/consumers represent important strategic goals. That is, owing to their extensive product-/brand-related motivation, these consumers spend more time on their product-related decision making, are more likely to recommend particular products, and tend to exhibit a higher willingness to pay premium prices (see Chapter 30). On the downside, these consumers can have high product-related expectations, rendering them more challenging to satisfy or delight (Zeithaml et al., 1993). They can also be more critical of the product/brand (e.g., as they have meaning wrapped up in it). We next review key literature on CE.

Consumer Engagement

As discussed, academic interest in the CE concept has proliferated in the last 10 to 15 years, reflecting its relative recency vis-à-vis CI's academic legacy. While early writings on CE emerged around the mid-2000s (e.g., Patterson et al., 2006), it wasn't until around 2010 that scholarly works on the topic started to appear in academic marketing journals (e.g., Brodie & Hollebeek, 2011; Hollebeek, 2013; van Doorn et al., 2010; Vivek et al., 2012). Correspondingly, from 2010 onward, the Marketing Science Institute (MSI) has consistently listed CE as an important research priority (e.g., MSI, 2010, 2014, 2018), reflecting the rising academic and managerial interest in CE during this period.

This interest is underpinned by CE's postulated superior contribution to organizational performance relative to existing consumer behavior concepts, including involvement (Brodie et al., 2011; Hollebeek, 2011a). Specifically, owing to its interactive nature, CE is heralded to generate sales increases, heightened positive word of mouth and referrals, and elevated profit margins (Beckers et al., 2018; Bijmolt et al., 2010).

However, debate surrounds CE's conceptualization. For example, while Brodie et al. (2011) defined it as "a psychological state, which occurs by virtue of interactive customer experiences with a focal agent/object within specific service relationships" (p. 252), Hollebeek, Srivastava, and Chen (2019) viewed CE as "a customer's motivationally driven, volitional investment of specific operant and operand resources into brand interactions in service systems" (p. 171). Based on empirical research, Vivek et al. (2014) viewed CE as a (potential) customer's level of interaction and connection with the brand/firm's offerings or activities. Often, these interactions involve connected others (e.g., through brand-, offering-, or activity-based social networks; Hollebeek et al., 2017; Leclercq et al., 2020). Hence unlike Brodie et al.'s (2011) generic in- and extra-role perspective of CE (Hollebeek, 2011b; Hollebeek & Chen, 2014; Keller, 2013; Kumar et al., 2019), Vivek et al. (2012, 2014) limited CE to the customer's beyond-purchase dynamics.

Adopting service-dominant (S-D) logic as their guiding theoretical perspective, Hollebeek, Srivastava, and Chen (2019) viewed customers' operant resource investments in their interactions to be cognitive, emotional, behavioral, or social in nature, which may be supplemented with operand resource investments that collectively constitute CE. Here, operand resources are assets "upon which an act is performed to produce an effect (e.g. raw ingredients being transformed into a final product)" (Hollebeek, 2019, p. 91), while operant resources are "used to act upon operand resources (e.g. skills)" (Hollebeek, 2019, p. 91; Vargo & Lusch, 2016, 2004). For example, a customer using their smartphone to look up bus times is integrating operant (e.g., reading skills) and operand resources (e.g., phone, app) to obtain the desired information, thereby creating value (Hollebeek, 2011a, 2013; Vargo & Lusch, 2008).

CE's interactivity lies at the heart of its theoretical departure from involvement (Brodie et al., 2011; Hollebeek, 2011a, 2011b). That is, though involvement captures the individual's interest in a particular object (e.g., a brand; Mittal & Lee, 1989), it reveals little about the customer's subsequent investment in their interactions with that brand. For instance, while a consumer may be interested (i.e., involved) in Ferrari cars, a shortfall in their financial means (i.e., operand resources) will yield their typically limited brand engagement. For managers, it is pivotal to understand this distinction (e.g., for revenue reasons). Unlike involvement, which is predominantly cognitive/affective in nature (see Chapter 25) and which commences prior to a customer's brand interactions, CE centers on the customer's intra-interaction dynamics (Hollebeek & Rather, 2019). In these interactions, CE extends beyond involvement by encompassing a behavioral and, sometimes, a social dimension (Brodie et al., 2013; Hollebeek, Srivastava, & Chen, 2019). Accordingly, Vivek et al. (2012) and Hollebeek et al. (2014) established involvement as a CE precursor.

As stated, higher CE is traditionally thought to translate into enhanced organizational performance, including through rising sales or profit margins (Brodie et al., 2011). However, Hollebeek and Chen (2014) raised the idea that while engagement can be positive (and yield corresponding results), it may also see negative expressions that can, in fact, harm the brand (e.g., establishment of antibrand communities, negative word of mouth, or other forms of brand sabotage; Bowden et al., 2017). Since then, scholarly interest in negative engagement and its interface with positive engagement and key consumer-behavior-based outcomes has sparked in the literature, though negative engagement's operationalization lags behind to date (Dessart et al., 2016). In this respect, debate also exists: While some authors view positive/negative engagement as opposite anchors of the same continuum, others believe that these represent independent constructs. In the next section, we distill key areas of similarity and departure between CI and CE.

Synthesis of Involvement-/Engagement-Based Commonalities and Divergence

In this section, we outline important areas of theoretical similarity and discrepancy for CI and CE, starting with key commonalities.

Key similarities. First, both involvement and engagement are motivational variables, implying the consumer's internal desire to act toward the brand in some salient manner when they experience some degree of involvement or engagement, respectively (Fan & Williams, 2010; Hollebeek, Sprott, & Andreassen, 2019). This desire may be driven by various reasons: It may reflect the individual's free choice to exhibit an interest in (i.e., for involvement) or interact with the brand (i.e., for engagement), such as by choosing one's holiday destination or clothes (Hollebeek, Srivastava, & Chen, 2019; Kumar et al., 2019).

However, while both concepts include a volitional aspect, they may also be subject to less voluntary factors, including institutions, which Vargo and Lusch (2016) defined as "humanly devised rules, norms, and beliefs that enable and constrain action, and make social life predictable and meaningful" (p. 6). As a result, Hollebeek et al. (2018) denoted engagement a "boundedly volitional" (p. 97) concept, akin to bounded rationality in economics. For example, in monopolistic markets, consumers are presented with limited choice and may consequently do business with a firm they would not choose otherwise.

Second, both concepts reflect the consumer's particular psychological state at a specific point in time (Brodie et al., 2011, Zaichkowsky, 1985). Involvement or engagement's state-based nature can be relatively stable, such as for brand advocates, apostles, or evangelists, which reflects not only these individuals' long-term brand loyalty but also their extensive brand-related referrals and favorable word of mouth. However, owing to this state-based nature, involvement and engagement levels can fluctuate (Hollebeek et al., 2014). As a result, more stable forms of involvement or engagement are particularly desirable to segment customers (e.g., product involvement), as discussed.

On the other hand, more transient involvement states are exemplified by situational (e.g., purchase) involvement or rapidly oscillating engagement within or across interactions. Hollebeek et al. (2014) posited, "Consumer [engagement] with a brand may fluctuate: (i) during (i.e., within) a brand interaction, and (ii) across interactions" (p. 162). To address engagement's potential fluctuations, which render it less suitable to segment customers, the more stable concept of CE styles reflects the consumer's typical or characteristic way of engaging with a brand (Prior & Marcos-Cuevas, 2016).

Key discrepancies. Differences between CI and CE also exist. First, as outlined, involvement reflects a consumer's level of interest in or personal relevance of an object (e.g., a brand; Mittal & Lee, 1989; Zaichkowsky, 1985). Engagement, on the other hand, goes beyond mere interest to denote the consumer's level of resource investment in particular brand interactions (Hollebeek, Srivastava, & Chen, 2019; Kumar et al., 2019). As such, CE reveals the consumer's level of active brand-related participation, enthusiasm, and social interactions (Vivek et al., 2012).

These definitions, however, reveal a close association between involvement and engagement: Without any interest in a brand, consumers are much less likely to invest in their interactions or relationships with particular brands (see Chapter 14). Consequently, involvement is commonly viewed as a major antecedent or driver of engagement (e.g., Harrigan et al., 2018). Vivek (2009) posited that while involvement lacks a behavioral component, CE does contain such behavioral facet, which Hollebeek et al. (2014) designated brand-related activation.

Second, as discussed, while engagement can be positively or negatively valenced (Hollebeek & Chen, 2014), literature-based applications of involvement have predominantly focused on the concept's positive expressions. That is, the notion of interest (as per involvement's definition), by its very nature, centers on positive or favorable brand-related connotations and associations. By contrast, engagement-based resource investments in brand interactions can be made with a positive, ambivalent, or negative intent (Clark et al., 2020). For example, while constructive word of mouth reveals positive engagement, negative referrals can be made with the main or sole intent to harm the brand (e.g., based on spite, envy), thereby damaging the brand.

Third, though debate rages regarding involvement and engagement's dimensionality, the latter in particular has been predominantly viewed as multidimensional. For example, while many authors view engagement to comprise cognitive, emotional, and behavioral dimensions (Harrigan et al., 2018), Hollebeek, Srivastava, and Chen (2019) and Brodie et al. (2013) extended this to incorporate a social facet, as stated earlier. On the other hand, though involvement has been viewed to contain cognitive and emotional aspects, it lacks an explicit behavioral tenet (i.e., its designating interest or personal relevance lack an inherent behavioral trait; Vivek, 2009), thereby further differentiating the two concepts. In the next section, we develop an integrative conceptual framework that integrates involvement's ELM-based foundations and extends these into the realm of CE.

CONCEPTUAL FRAMEWORK

While the ELM is focused on message/communication strategy, our engagement-based extension thereof, the CEP framework (cf. Brodie et al.'s, 2016, engagement *disposition*), covers any brand strategy that is designed to engage consumers (Figure 26.1).

On the framework's left-hand side, we include CE, which we—in accordance with Hollebeek, Srivastava, and Chen (2019, p. 166)—define as a consumer's operant/operand resource investment in their brand interactions (Keller, 2013; Kumar et al., 2019). In the CEP's foundational model of the ELM, involvement is included at a similar position.

In the framework, we focus on more enduring (vs. transient) forms of engagement. When CE is and remains high over time, we refer to this as a (highly) active CE style, as shown in Figure 26.1. Recall that CE styles represent a consumer's typical or characteristic way of interacting with an object (Hollebeek, 2018; Prior & Marcos-Cuevas, 2016).

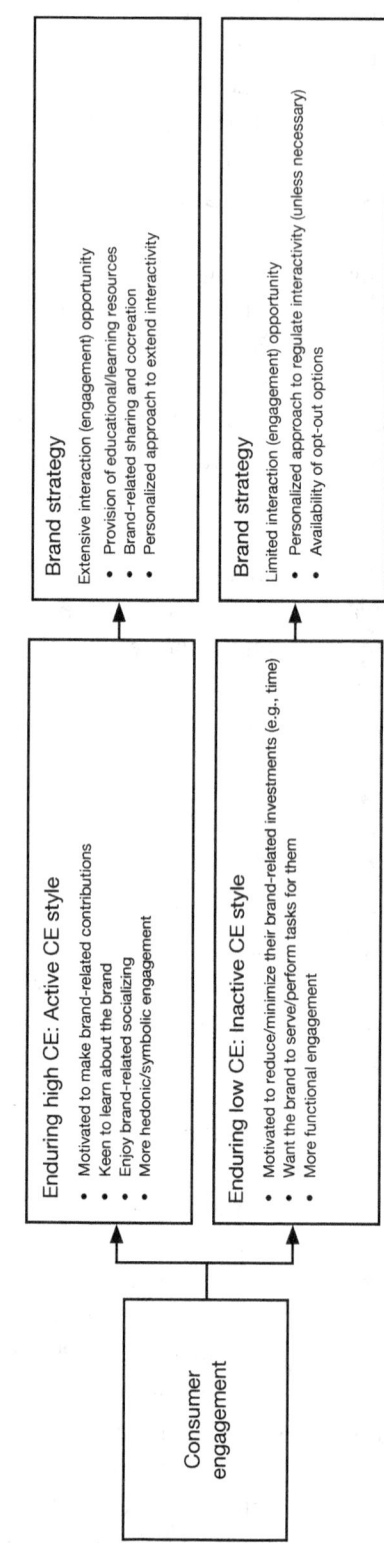

FIGURE 26.1. Consumer engagement (CE) propensity model. Data from Petty and Cacioppo (1981, 1984, 1986).

Highly active CE styles are characterized by the consumer's extensive cognitive, emotional, behavioral, and/or social brand engagement, which manifests through extensive brand-related processing, the individual's enjoyment of making brand-related contributions (e.g., by offering ideas for the brand's new product/service development), a keenness to learn about the brand, and a motivation to socialize around the brand (e.g., in online/offline brand communities), which can reveal consumer citizenship behaviors (van Doorn et al., 2010; Yi et al., 2013). As such, highly active CE styles display the consumer's more hedonic and/or symbolic engagement, though they will expect their more functional brand-related needs to also be met at the same time (Voss et al., 2003).

By contrast, highly inactive CE styles typify those consumers who prefer to reduce or minimize their brand-related interactivity unless it is deemed necessary (e.g., in core service delivery interactions). As such, their brand interactions are more functionally oriented (Hollebeek, 2013). These individuals also desire the brand to perform activities for them, rather than being expected to make extensive brand-related contributions themselves. Consequently, they typically enjoy more extensive levels of service provision and may be willing to pay a premium to receive such service.

Note that while the foregoing discussion centered on the consumer's positive engagement, CE may also be negative for highly active or inactive CE styles. For example, an individual with a highly active CE style may harbor a negative intent (e.g., extensive investments in establishing or developing an antibrand community, disseminating negative brand-related word of mouth; Bowden et al., 2017). We next discuss important implications that arise from this research.

DISCUSSION AND IMPLICATIONS

Implications for Research

In this chapter, we reviewed important literature on CI and CE and distilled their key areas of similarity and discrepancy. From our discussion, we extended involvement's ELM and applied its theoretical principles to CE, thereby culminating in the CEP framework. Extending the ELM, the CEP envisages differences between highly versus low-engaged consumers and suggests effective, actionable communication and targeting strategies for these consumer segments. Relatedly, we develop the notions of highly active versus inactive CE styles, thus complementing the emerging work of Prior and Marcos-Cuevas (2016) and Hollebeek (2018). In contrast to the ELM, which focuses on message/communication persuasiveness across highly/low-involved consumers, the CEP extends to any strategic brand action to engage consumers or customers.

Based on these analyses, we derive the following avenues for further research. First, owing to the purely conceptual nature of our analyses, we encourage the undertaking of further empirical research in this area to verify and validate our findings. For example, what percentage of consumers belongs to each segment? Does a significant neutral or ambivalently engaged segment exist for particular product/service categories? How stable are consumers' highly active versus inactive engagement styles across individuals, product categories, brands, or time? Consequently, how suitable might they be for market segmentation purposes in particular contexts?

Second, we recommend further empirical study on our managerial recommendations, per the framework's right-hand side. That is, to what extent or under which conditions do consumers with a highly active CE style enjoy making brand-related contributions? In which cases may they, too, prefer to sit back and enjoy comprehensive service (e.g., luxury holidays)? How does product/service pricing affect or drive the development of an individual's engagement style with particular offerings or in specific categories (Zaichkowsky, 1988)?

Third, in our review, we identified several involvement and engagement subforms, including product/situational involvement and consumer/audience engagement. From this observation, our focus was on consumers' more enduring product involvement (Zaichkowsky, 1985) coupled with more enduring engagement (Hollebeek et al., 2014). The following question therefore arises: How and to what extent does the CEP pan out for different forms of involvement and their association with differing engagement types? Further scrutiny of various involvement/engagement combinations is therefore warranted. We next discuss important practical implications that ensue from our analyses.

Practical Implications

This chapter also describes a number of practical or managerial implications. First, by advancing the notion of highly active versus inactive CE styles, we derive further insight into engagement's more enduring dynamics and traits. That is, given that CE may fluctuate either within an interaction or across interactions, it is less suitable as a segmentation variable. By reflecting the consumer's characteristic engagement with a brand, Prior and Marcos-Cuevas's (2016) notion of CE styles makes headway in overcoming this issue (Hollebeek, Islam, et al., 2019). We further add to this insight by developing the notions of highly active/inactive CE styles, similar to the ELM's highly/low-involved consumer. In addition, we advance important managerial recommendations for these groups, as shown in Figure 26.1's right-hand side and discussed further next.

First, we broadly view those with highly active CE styles to thrive under the provision of extensive brand-related investment (i.e., engagement) opportunities. For example, brands may offer repositories containing elaborate brand-related learning or educational resources, which consumers may access in their own time (Hollebeek, Srivastava, & Chen, 2019). As consumers learn over time, it is important to develop progressive learning resources so that more skilled consumers are able to maintain their learning at their desired pace. To facilitate continuous learning, new technologies such as applications based on the internet of things or virtual reality can be used (Kannan & Li, 2017). As another example, brands are encouraged to foster brand-related sharing, not only between the brand and particular consumers (e.g., via customized customer profiles) but also on a consumer-to-consumer or peer-to-peer level to further deepen their engagement (Chen et al., 2018; Hollebeek et al., 2017; Lusch & Nambisan, 2015). In sum, brand-related personalization should focus on extending and leveraging consumer interaction opportunities, particularly those that are more hedonic or symbolic in nature, on a voluntary or opt-in basis.

By contrast, consumers with highly inactive CE styles are motivated to reduce or minimize their brand-related investments (e.g., by saving time). For these individuals, we also recommend a personalized approach, though this should be focused on limiting, controlling, regulating, or guarding the consumer's brand-related interactivity. Therefore, for these consumers, interactivity should be restricted to what is absolutely necessary, but in other instances (e.g., where interactivity is noncore), it should be lowered, minimized, or removed altogether. Relatedly, the availability of opt-out options at any stage of an interaction is particularly important for these consumers.

We conclude by raising an important caveat to our analyses. That is, while CE styles were shown to be relatively enduring or stable, consumers can and do shift across segments (e.g., over time, as their needs change). Therefore, managers need to closely monitor any developments in their consumers with highly active/inactive CE styles to ensure the application of the correct targeting and positioning approach to particular individuals.

REFERENCES

Bakker, A. B., Tims, M., & Derks, D. (2012). Proactive personality and job performance: The role of job crafting and work engagement. *Human Relations, 65*(10), 1359–1378. https://doi.org/10.1177/0018726712453471

Beckers, S., van Doorn, J., & Verhoef, P. (2018). Good, better, engaged? The effect of company-initiated customer engagement behavior on shareholder value. *Journal of the Academy of Marketing Science, 46*(3), 366–383. https://doi.org/10.1007/s11747-017-0539-4

Bijmolt, T., Leeflang, P., Block, F., Eisenbeiss, M., Hardie, B., Lemmens, A., & Saffert, P. (2010). Analytics for customer engagement. *Journal of Service Research, 13*(3), 341–356. https://doi.org/10.1177/1094670510375603

Bloch, P., & Richins, M. (1983). A theoretical model for the study of product importance perceptions. *Journal of Marketing, 47*(3), 69–81. https://doi.org/10.1177/002224298304700308

Bowden, J. L. H., Conduit, J., Hollebeek, L., Luoma-Aho, V., & Solen, B. A. (2017). Engagement valence duality and spillover effects in online brand communities. *Journal of Service Theory and Practice, 27*(4), 877–897. https://doi.org/10.1108/JSTP-04-2016-0072

Brodie, R., Fehrer, J., Jaakkola, E., Hollebeek, L., & Conduit, J. (2016, May). *From customer to actor engagement: Extending the conceptual domain* [Paper presentation]. European Marketing Academy Conference, Oslo, Norway.

Brodie, R., & Hollebeek, L. D. (2011). Advancing and consolidating knowledge about customer engagement. *Journal of Service Research, 14*(3), 283–284. https://doi.org/10.1177/1094670511415523

Brodie, R., Hollebeek, L. D., Jurić, B., & Ilić, A. (2011). Customer engagement: Conceptual domain, fundamental propositions, and implications for research in service marketing. *Journal of Service Research, 14*(3), 252–271. https://doi.org/10.1177/1094670511411703

Brodie, R., Ilić, A., Jurić, B., & Hollebeek, L. (2013). Consumer engagement in a virtual brand community: An exploratory analysis. *Journal of Business Research, 66*(1), 105–114. https://doi.org/10.1016/j.jbusres.2011.07.029

Cacioppo, J. & Petty, R. E. (1984). The elaboration likelihood model of persuasion. In T. C. Kinnear (Ed.), *NA - Advances in consumer research* (Vol. 11, pp. 673–675). Association for Consumer Research.

Cacioppo, J., Petty, R. E., Kao, C. F., & Rodriguez, R. (1986). Central and peripheral routes to persuasion: An individual difference perspective. *Journal of Personality and Social Psychology, 51*(5), 1032–1043. https://doi.org/10.1037/0022-3514.51.5.1032

Celsi, R., & Olson, J. (1988). The role of involvement in attention and comprehensive processes. *Journal of Consumer Research, 15*(2), 210–224. https://doi.org/10.1086/209158

Chen, T., Drennan, J., Andrews, L., & Hollebeek, L. (2018). User experience sharing: understanding customer initiation of value co-creation in online communities. *European Journal of Marketing, 52*(5/6), 1154–1184. https://doi.org/10.1108/EJM-05-2016-0298

Clark, M., Lages, C., & Hollebeek, L. (2020). Friend or foe? Customer engagement's value-based effects on fellow customers and the firm. *Journal of Business Research, 121*, 549–556. https://doi.org/10.1016/j.jbusres.2020.03.011

Cohen, J. B. (1983). Involvement and you: 1000 great ideas. In R. P. Bagozzi & A. M. Tybout (Eds.), *NA - Advances in consumer research* (Vol. 10, pp. 325–328). Association for Consumer Research.

Cova, B., & Salle, R. (2008). Marketing solutions in accordance with the SD logic: Co-creating value with customer network actors. *Industrial Marketing Management, 37*(3), 270–277. https://doi.org/10.1016/j.indmarman.2007.07.005

Cretu, A., & Brodie, R. (2007). The influence of brand image and company reputation where manufacturers market to small firms: A customer value perspective. *Industrial Marketing Management, 36*(2), 230–240. https://doi.org/10.1016/j.indmarman.2005.08.013

Dessart, L., Veloutsou, C., & Morgan-Thomas, A. (2016). Capturing consumer engagement: Duality, dimensionality and measurement. *Journal of Marketing Management, 32*(5–6), 399–426. https://doi.org/10.1080/0267257X.2015.1130738

Engel, J., & Blackwell, R. (1982). *Consumer behavior*. Dryden Press.

Fan, W., & Williams, C. (2010). The effects of parental involvement on students' academic self-efficacy, engagement, and intrinsic motivation. *Educational Psychology, 30*(1), 53–74. https://doi.org/10.1080/01443410903353302

Greenwald, A., & Leavitt, C. (1984). Audience involvement in advertising: Four levels. *Journal of Consumer Research, 11*(1), 581–592. https://doi.org/10.1086/208994

Harrigan, P., Evers, U., Miles, M., & Daly, T. (2018). Customer engagement and the relationship between involvement, engagement, self-brand connection and brand usage intent. *Journal of Business Research, 88*, 388–396. https://doi.org/10.1016/j.jbusres.2017.11.046

Hollebeek, L. (2005). *The importance of region of origin, price and price discounts on purchase intentions for white wine: An empirical investigation* [Master's thesis]. University of Auckland. https://catalogue.library.auckland.ac.nz/primo-explore/fulldisplay?docid=uoa_alma21135328680002091&vid=NEWUI&context=L

Hollebeek, L. (2011a). Demystifying customer brand engagement: Exploring the loyalty nexus. *Journal of Marketing Management, 27*(7–8), 785–807. https://doi.org/10.1080/0267257X.2010.500132

Hollebeek, L. (2011b). Exploring customer brand engagement: Definition & themes. *Journal of Strategic Marketing, 19*(7), 555–573. https://doi.org/10.1080/0965254X.2011.599493

Hollebeek, L. (2013). The customer engagement/value interface: An exploratory investigation. *Australasian Marketing Journal, 21*(1), 17–24. https://doi.org/10.1016/j.ausmj.2012.08.006

Hollebeek, L. (2018). Individual-level cultural consumer engagement styles: Conceptualization, propositions, and implications. *International Marketing Review,*

35(1), 42–71. https://doi.org/10.1108/IMR-07-2016-0140

Hollebeek, L. (2019). Developing business customer engagement through social media engagement-platforms: An integrative S-D logic/RBV-informed model. *Industrial Marketing Management, 81*, 89–98. https://doi.org/10.1016/j.indmarman.2017.11.016

Hollebeek, L., Andreassen, T. W., Smith, D. L., Grönquist, D., Karahasanovic, A., & Marquez, A. (2018). Service innovation actor engagement: An integrative model. *Journal of Services Marketing, 32*(1), 95–100. https://doi.org/10.1108/JSM-11-2017-0390

Hollebeek, L., & Chen, T. (2014). Exploring positively- vs. negatively-valenced brand engagement: A conceptual model. *Journal of Product and Brand Management, 23*(1), 62–74. https://doi.org/10.1108/JPBM-06-2013-0332

Hollebeek, L., Glynn, M., & Brodie, R. (2014). Consumer brand engagement in social media: Conceptualization, scale development and validation. *Journal of Interactive Marketing, 28*(2), 149–165. https://doi.org/10.1016/j.intmar.2013.12.002

Hollebeek, L., Islam, J., Macky, K., Taguchi, T., & Costley, C. (2019). Personality-based consumer engagement styles: Conceptualization, research propositions & implications. In L. Hollebeek & D. Sprott (Eds.), *The handbook of research on customer engagement* (pp. 224–244). Edward Elgar. https://doi.org/10.4337/9781788114899.00017

Hollebeek, L., Juric, B., & Tang, W. (2017). Virtual brand community engagement practices: A refined typology and model. *Journal of Services Marketing, 31*(3), 204–217. https://doi.org/10.1108/JSM-01-2016-0006

Hollebeek, L., & Rather, R. (2019). Service innovativeness and tourism customer outcomes. *International Journal of Contemporary Hospitality Management, 31*(11), 4227–4246. https://doi.org/10.1108/IJCHM-03-2018-0256

Hollebeek, L., Sprott, D., & Andreassen, T. (2019). Customer engagement in evolving technological environments. *European Journal of Marketing, 53*(9), 1665–1670. https://doi.org/10.1108/EJM-09-2019-969

Hollebeek, L., Srivastava, R. K., & Chen, T. (2019). S-D logic-informed customer engagement: Integrative framework, revised fundamental propositions, and application to CRM. *Journal of the Academy of Marketing Science, 47*(1), 161–185. https://doi.org/10.1007/s11747-016-0494-5

Houston, M., & Rothschild, M. (1978). Conceptual and methodological perspectives on involvement. In S. C. Jain (Ed.), *Research frontiers in marketing: Dialogues and directions* (pp. 184–187). American Marketing Association.

Kannan, P., & Li, H. A. (2017). Digital marketing: A framework, review and research agenda. *International Journal of Research in Marketing, 34*(1), 22–45. https://doi.org/10.1016/j.ijresmar.2016.11.006

Keller, K. L. (2013). *Strategic brand management* (4th ed.). Pearson Prentice-Hall.

Kumar, V., Rajan, B., Gupta, S., & Dalla Pozza, I. (2019). Customer engagement in service. *Journal of the Academy of Marketing Science, 47*(1), 138–160. https://doi.org/10.1007/s11747-017-0565-2

Laurent, G., & Kapferer, J.-N. (1985). Measuring consumer involvement profiles. *Journal of Marketing Research, 22*(1), 41–53. https://doi.org/10.1177/002224378502200104

Leclercq, T., Poncin, I., Hammedi, W., Kullak, A., & Hollebeek, L. D. (2020). When gamification backfires: The impact of perceived justice on online community contributions. *Journal of Marketing Management, 36*(5–6), 550–577. https://doi.org/10.1080/0267257X.2020.1736604

Lusch, R., & Nambisan, S. (2015). Service innovation: A service-dominant logic perspective. *Management Information Systems Quarterly, 39*(1), 155–175. https://doi.org/10.25300/MISQ/2015/39.1.07

Marketing Science Institute. (2010). *Research priorities 2010–2012*.

Marketing Science Institute. (2014). *Research priorities 2014–2016*.

Marketing Science Institute. (2018). *Research priorities 2018–2020*.

Mittal, B., & Lee, M. (1989). A causal model of consumer involvement. *Journal of Economic Psychology, 10*(3), 363–389. https://doi.org/10.1016/0167-4870(89)90030-5

Muncy, J., & Hunt, S. (1984). Consumer involvement: Definition issues and research directions. In T. C. Kinnear (Ed.), *NA - dvances in consumer research* (Vol. 11, p. 193). Association for Consumer Research.

Park, C. W., & Mittal, B. (1985). A theory of involvement in consumer behavior: Problems and issues. In J. N. Sheth (Ed.), *Research in consumer behavior* (Vol. 1). JAI Press.

Patterson, P., Yu, T., & DeRuyter, K. (2006, December 4–6). *Understanding customer engagement in services, advancing theory, maintaining relevance* [Conference proceedings]. ANZMAC Conference, Brisbane, Australia.

Petty, R., & Cacioppo, J. (1981). *Attitudes and persuasion: Classic and contemporary approaches*. Routledge.

Petty, R., & Cacioppo, J. (1984). Source factors and the elaboration likelihood model of persuasion. In T. Kinnear (Ed.), *NA - Advances in consumer research*

(Vol. 11, pp. 668–672). Association for Consumer Research.

Petty, R., & Cacioppo, J. (1986). *Communication and persuasion*. Springer.

Petty, R., Cacioppo, J., & Schumann, D. (1983). Central and peripheral routes to advertising effectiveness: The moderating role of involvement. *Journal of Consumer Research, 10*(2), 135–146. https://doi.org/10.1086/208954

Prior, D., & Marcos-Cuevas, J. (2016). Value co-destruction in interfirm relationships: The impact of actor engagement styles. *Marketing Theory, 16*(4), 533–552. https://doi.org/10.1177/1470593116649792

Sasser, S., Kilgour, M., & Hollebeek, L. (2014). Marketing in an interactive world: The evolving nature of communication processes using social media. In K. Lertwachera & A. Ayanso (Eds.), *Harnessing the power of social media and web analytics: Techniques, tools, and applications* (pp. 29–52). IGI Global. https://doi.org/10.4018/978-1-4666-5194-4.ch002

Sherif, M., & Cantril, H. (1947). *The psychology of ego involvement*. Wiley.

van Doorn, J., Lemon, K., Mittal, V., Naß, S., Pick, D., Pirner, P., & Verhoef, P. (2010). Customer engagement behavior: Theoretical foundations and research directions. *Journal of Service Research, 13*(3), 253–266. https://doi.org/10.1177/1094670510375599

Vargo, S., & Lusch, R. (2004). Evolving to a new dominant logic for marketing. *Journal of Marketing, 68*(1), 1–17. https://doi.org/10.1509/jmkg.68.1.1.24036

Vargo, S., & Lusch, R. (2008). Service-dominant logic: Continuing the evolution. *Journal of the Academy of Marketing Science, 36*(1), 1–10. https://doi.org/10.1007/s11747-007-0069-6

Vargo, S., & Lusch, R. F. (2016). Institutions and axioms: An extension and update of service-dominant logic. *Journal of the Academy of Marketing Science, 44*(1), 5–23. https://doi.org/10.1007/s11747-015-0456-3

Vivek, S. D. (2009). *A scale of consumer engagement* [Doctoral dissertation, University of Alabama]. https://www.proquest.com/openview/37c28b386791bf7590cf43eb74cb84e8/1?cbl=18750&pq-origsite=gscholar

Vivek, S. D., Beatty, S. E., Dalela, V., & Morgan, R. M. (2014). A generalized multidimensional scale for measuring customer engagement. *Journal of Marketing Theory and Practice, 22*(4), 401–420. https://doi.org/10.2753/MTP1069-6679220404

Vivek, S. D., Beatty, S. E., & Morgan, R. M. (2012). Customer engagement: Exploring customer relationships beyond purchase. *Journal of Marketing Theory and Practice, 20*(2), 122–146. https://doi.org/10.2753/MTP1069-6679200201

Voss, K., Spangenberg, E., & Grohmann, B. (2003). Measuring the utilitarian and hedonic dimensions of consumer attitude. *Journal of Marketing Research, 40*(3), 310–320. https://doi.org/10.1509/jmkr.40.3.310.19238

Yi, Y., Gong, T., & Lee, H. (2013). The impact of other customers on customer citizenship behavior. *Psychology and Marketing, 30*(4), 341–356. https://doi.org/10.1002/mar.20610

Zaichkowsky, J. L. (1985). Measuring the involvement construct. *Journal of Consumer Research, 12*(3), 341–352. https://doi.org/10.1086/208520

Zaichkowsky, J. L. (1986). Conceptualizing involvement. *Journal of Advertising, 15*(2), 4–34. https://doi.org/10.1080/00913367.1986.10672999

Zaichkowsky, J. L. (1988). Involvement and the price cue. In M. J. Houston (Ed.), *NA - Advances in consumer research* (Vol. 15, pp. 323–327). Association for Consumer Research.

Zeithaml, V., Berry, L. L., & Parasuraman, A. (1993). The nature and determinants of customer expectations of service. *Journal of the Academy of Marketing Science, 21*(1), 1–12. https://doi.org/10.1177/0092070393211001

CHAPTER 27

NEURAL BASIS OF CONSUMER DECISION MAKING AND NEUROFORECASTING

Alexander Genevsky and Carolyn Yoon

Neuroscience, in recent years, has contributed significantly to a better understanding of how individuals make decisions and how these decisions are influenced by context, states, and individual traits. The past decade has seen the emergence of consumer neuroscience as an academic field of inquiry that applies tools and theories from neuroscience to better understand consumer behavior. These studies have primarily used functional magnetic resonance imaging (fMRI) and electroencephalography (EEG), although the field extends to a wider range of tools, such as facial coding, eye-tracking, heart rate monitoring, and galvanic skin response.

Investigating meaningful questions with appropriately designed studies that leverage neuroscientific knowledge has allowed researchers to generate useful insights about consumers from both theoretical and practical perspectives. Plassmann et al. (2015) identified five concrete ways in which consumer neuroscience has been applied to improve understanding of consumer behavior. First, it can be used to validate, refine, or extend existing theories by elucidating the underlying mechanisms. It has also suggested empirically testable hypotheses about preferences, judgments, or choices (e.g., Ho & Spence, 2009; Wadhwa et al., 2008) that accord with an understanding of biology. Second, neuroscience techniques have provided information about implicit processes that are difficult to access using other methods (e.g., Plassmann et al., 2008; Yoon et al., 2006). Third, neural measures have been used to test for dissociations between psychological processes. For example, fMRI has been used in studies to examine the extent to which two different kinds of decisions use similar or different neural mechanisms and thus whether they are likely to use similar or different cognitive processes (e.g., decisions under risk and ambiguity; Hsu et al., 2005; I. Levy et al., 2010). Fourth, fMRI studies have tested whether different individuals perform the same decision task in different ways (e.g., using heuristic vs. deliberative decision strategies; Venkatraman et al., 2009). Fifth and finally, studies have incorporated neural measures into models of choice and decision making to improve predictions. Although all five ways are indeed important ways in which consumer neuroscience can contribute to knowledge about consumers, this chapter focuses primarily on reviewing the research related to neural predictions. We choose to do so, in part, because there are already a number of recently published review articles that have described the advantages of neuroscientific methods and their contributions to consumer research more generally (Karmarkar & Plassmann, 2019; Karmarkar & Yoon, 2016; Plassmann et al., 2015; Smidts et al., 2014). However, the main impetus for the present topic is that it is currently garnering much research interest among academic scholars and practitioners alike for holding the promise of expanding our insights about

https://doi.org/10.1037/0000262-027
APA Handbook of Consumer Psychology, L. R. Kahle (Editor-in-Chief)
Copyright © 2022 by the American Psychological Association. All rights reserved.

consumer decision making and improving predictions at the individual as well as aggregate level in real-world settings.

Prior studies have found that neural measures inform predictions of individual responses to social influence (Campbell-Meiklejohn et al., 2010; Klucharev et al., 2009; Zaki et al., 2011), health behavior change (Chua et al., 2009, 2011; Falk et al., 2010, 2011), and consumer decisions (Knutson et al., 2007; I. Levy et al., 2011). Building on this research, more recent investigations have focused on how neural activity of individuals can be used to predict large-scale, out-of-sample outcomes ranging from music album sales (Berns & Moore, 2012) and microfinancing outcomes (Genevsky & Knutson, 2015) to the virality of news articles (Doré et al., 2019).

In this chapter, we first provide a selective review of prior research findings about the neural processes underlying decision making. In so doing, we discuss how the insights about neural processes have served to provide a basis for research incorporating neural measures to improve within-individual predictions of preferences, choice, and decision making in consumer domains. The bulk of the chapter then discusses emerging research findings in neuroforecasting involving the use of neural data to forecast the aggregate behavior of a separate and independent group. We consider how the neuroforecasting findings can advance our understanding of real-world decisions and improve market-level predictions in a variety of choice domains, including consumption, health, and financial decision making. We highlight some notable gaps in knowledge and the challenges associated with conducting neuroforecasting studies. Finally, we discuss some future research opportunities and directions that hold promise for informing the design and selection of better marketing practices, as well as public policies and intervention programs.

NEURAL BASIS OF DECISION MAKING

Consumer researchers have traditionally used self-report and choice measures to predict future behavior despite their well-documented limitations. Prominent among these is the need to rely on participants to honestly and accurately report on the mental processes on which they are often unwilling or unable to accurately reflect. Indeed, we often require participants to respond regarding attitudes and behavior that will occur at some point in the future, an exercise we know people are generally unable to do accurately. In some cases, the very act of asking individuals to reflect on their internal processes fundamentally changes their experiences in a way that makes them incompatible with the real-world phenomena being examined. Use of neural data to capture what is hidden in consumers' brains to make predictions may thus provide a window into decision-making processes that are informative in improving predictions. We review the research efforts from the past decade to understand consumers' neural processes associated with true underlying preferences and implicit processes.

Neuroscientific methods have developed to a point where they can indeed be used by themselves or to complement the traditional approaches to improve predictions of consumer preferences and behavior. Prior studies have incorporated neural measures into decision-making models to improve predictions of consumer-related behavior over and beyond the traditional measures. In particular, fMRI is the most commonly used method in academic consumer neuroscience research, followed by EEG (for a comprehensive discussion of neuroscientific methods, see Shaw et al., 2018). Accordingly, the vast majority of the studies dealing with neural preferences and choices reviewed in this chapter use fMRI.

Although preferences have received a great deal of research attention, the ways in which they are defined are surprisingly broad and diverse. Whereas some have conceptualized preferences as innate and biologically determined traits (e.g., Eysenck, 1990), the more common view is that they are dynamic, flexible, and frequently inconsistent representations of liking for different goods or entities. Consumer researchers have been heavily influenced by the economists' definition of preference, which entails a consistent ordering of choices based on relative utility. However, given that choices often reflect high variability and inconsistency, much of the prior research efforts have been devoted to exploring different models of stochastic preference rather than addressing the complexity around preferences. Understanding how consumer preferences for products or brands are represented in the brain and how they are influenced by contextual factors is an area of inquiry that has recently received more research attention.

Much of the neuroscience research on preferences has been done within the framework of understanding value-based decision making, which entails the idea that decision making is driven by, or reflects, underlying preferences or representations of value. A consensus view to emerge is that parts of the prefrontal cortex, together with the subcortical structures, play key roles in encoding subjective valuations (Kable & Glimcher, 2007). In particular, converging evidence indicates that the critical neural areas for subjective valuation include the orbital frontal cortex (OFC), ventromedial prefrontal cortex (VMPFC), and ventral striatum (VS). Moreover, there is commonality in the processes underlying subjective valuation, which has been termed a "common neural currency" (see D. J. Levy & Glimcher, 2012, for a meta-analysis). According to this view, neural responses in the areas implicated in subjective valuations are domain-general. That is, if one is faced with different types of value (e.g., primary rewards, secondary rewards), the valuation signals in the brain reflect direct comparisons that have been transformed onto a common scale. Increases in amounts of reward or affective value capturing the brain's value system have been found to scale with higher liking or pleasantness ratings, greater willingness to pay, and choice measures.

Converging evidence has suggested that the OFC is associated with the encoding of reward value underlying preferences (Padoa-Schioppa & Assad, 2006). The OFC has been implicated in representations of expected value for stimuli involving sensory processes such as taste (Plassmann et al., 2008; van den Bosch et al., 2014), touch (Rolls, 2004), and smell (Gottfried & Zald, 2005) and encoding of abstract stimuli such as aesthetics (Kawabata & Zeki, 2004), money (Elliott et al., 2000), facial attractiveness (Cloutier et al., 2008), and social stimuli (Rushworth et al., 2007; Spitzer et al., 2007).

Neuroimaging studies have documented a strong link between subjective value and activity in both the VMPFC and OFC. Initial studies examined the neural correlates of hypothetical preferences. In one study, participants viewing pictures of preferred (vs. nonpreferred) soft drinks had greater VMPFC and OFC activations (Paulus & Frank, 2003). In another study, male participants who viewed pictures of preferred (vs. nonpreferred) beer brands and female participants presented with pictures of preferred (vs. nonpreferred) coffee brands showed higher activations in the VMPFC and OFC (Deppe et al., 2005). Plassmann et al. (2007) scanned the brains of hungry participants while they placed bids for the right to eat 50 different snacks in a Becker–DeGroot–Marschak auction (Becker et al., 1964). The participants placed bids on 100 different trials, and on each trial, they were allowed to bid $0, $1, $2, or $3 for an appetizing snack that was visually presented. They found that the willingness-to-pay amounts for the items correlated with activation in the VMPFC and OFC. These studies have been interpreted as supporting evidence for a close correspondence in regional brain activity between the anticipation of rewarding events, the consumption of enjoyable goods, and the willingness to pay for them.

Although the OFC has been discussed as a leading candidate brain region for representing preferences that can predict choice at the time of decision, it does not have direct access to motor output networks supporting choice or action, unlike the cortical and subcortical regions of the brain that have been strongly associated with valuation. Insofar as the computing value is often associated with a decision involving an action or choice, a large body of neuroscientific research on decision making has focused on the VMPFC and VS as correlates of subjective utility that form the core of a valuation system supporting choice and decision making. These regions have consistently shown higher activity for more valuable items. A meta-analysis of 206 published fMRI studies found evidence of reliable correlates of a domain-general signal of subjective value in the VMPFC and anterior VS (Bartra et al., 2013). Positive effects in these regions were seen for both decision subjective value (i.e., when a decision is made) and experienced subjective value (i.e., when an outcome is experienced). As already mentioned, the positive effects in the VMPFC and VS were also evident in response outcomes for both primary (e.g., food) and secondary (e.g., money, social) rewards and serve to provide empirical support for the unitary neural system (i.e., common neural currency), representing different facets of an individual's value perceptions not only across different categories of goods but also features of the goods (Chib et al., 2009; D. J. Levy & Glimcher, 2011).

Prior studies have also examined the role of valuation signal in VMPFC and VS in more complex decision-making settings involving risk and ambiguity, intertemporal discounting, and social decisions (for a review, see Ruff & Fehr, 2014). I. Levy and colleagues found that activity in the VMPFC and VS correlated with predicted value during choice under both risk and ambiguity (I. Levy et al., 2010). In their fMRI study, participants made choices when presented with lotteries varying systematically in the amount of money offered and in the probability of winning the amount or the ambiguity around that probability. They found that activity in the VMPFC and VS correlated with subjective valuation under both conditions of risk and ambiguity. Kable and Glimcher (2007) tracked the participants' choices between immediate and delayed monetary payoffs while undergoing brain scans and found that VMPFC and VS activation varied with the subjectively discounted value of future rewards. In a study of social behavior involving charitable giving, Hare and colleagues (2010) showed that VMPFC correlated with the amount of money donated during free trials and provided evidence that valuation signals in the VMPFC represent an integration of input from neural regions involved in social cognition. In another study involving social situations, participants taking part in a social reward task in which they received positive evaluations of their personalities by others versus a nonsocial monetary gambling task (Izuma et al., 2008) showed activation in the VMPFC and VS. Similar patterns of VMPFC and VS activation have been found when participants are informed that others like (Davey et al., 2010), understand (Morelli et al., 2014), or want to meet them (Cooper et al., 2014).

NEURAL PREDICTORS OF DECISIONS

Some research efforts have focused on incorporating measures of activity in specific brain areas to complement existing psychological measures to predict outcomes within individuals. The idea was tested by Knutson and colleagues (2007), who showed that predecisional activation in relevant brain regions predicted subsequent choice. They distinguished between purchased-item and nonpurchased-item trials and found significant differences in activation in the nucleus accumbens (NAcc) part of the VS during product presentation and both medial prefrontal cortex (MPFC) deactivation and insula activation during processing of excessive prices. They estimated brain activity in these three regions of interest and entered them as covariates in logistic regression along with self-report measures of preference and net value to predict subsequent purchasing decisions. The results indicated that the full model (i.e., including the neural measures) provided significantly better predictive power than a model with only the self-report measures. Importantly, the study provided additional evidence of the representation of subjective value in the VMPFC and VS during the choice process. Even though the advantage of the full model including the neural measures was relatively small in this study, Grosenick et al. (2013), in a subsequent study, used multivariate methods to model the data from the Knutson et al. (2007) study and obtained substantial improvements in predictive validity.

A related question that stems from the evidence that the VMPFC and VS activation represents an integration of various inputs into a common neural currency is the extent to which the integration occurs automatically in response to exposure to stimuli regardless of whether a choice is hypothetical or even when no decision is currently needed. Kang et al. (2011) found that VMPFC activity was associated with the decision value of an item even when the choice was hypothetical. Other findings have suggested that the valuation signals encode information that predicts subsequent behavior when it is implicitly processed and in the absence of a specific judgment or choice.

Lebreton et al. (2009) scanned participants while they rated the pleasantness of faces, houses, and paintings or made judgments about age. Outside of the scanner, they were then presented with pairs of the same images and asked to identify which one was more pleasant. They found greater VS and VMPFC activity for images that were subsequently preferred, suggesting an automatic valuation process even though the participants did not know they would be asked to make a choice before assessing the pleasantness of the images. Tusche and colleagues (2010) used a multivariate decoding approach in a study comparing the neural responses of participants in the high-attention group (i.e., paid attention to different products presented on the screen and rated their attractiveness) to participants in the low-attention group (i.e., attention directed away from the products on the screen). The participants in both groups were then asked to indicate their willingness to buy each product. A comparison of the activation patterns for the two groups during product exposure revealed similar activation patterns in the VMPFC and VS, such that choice could be predicted equally well in both attention groups. Thus, valuation signals corresponded to the subjective value of an item that was implicitly processed.

Building on the studies by Lebreton et al. (2009) and Knutson et al. (2007), I. Levy et al. (2011) investigated the extent to which neural activity in the VS and VMPFC during passive viewing of consumer goods (e.g., CDs, DVDs, books, monetary lotteries) could predict subsequent consumer choices. They found that activation in the valuation areas in the absence of choices was indeed predictive of subsequent decision making. These findings suggest that there are elements of preference that are similarly represented in the brain, regardless of how the target is encountered. Whereas the aforementioned studies focused on within-subject classification or prediction, Smith et al. (2014) sought to predict out-of-sample choices from nonchoice neural activity. They had participants view images of 100 different snack foods while being scanned and did not tell them that they would be asked to make choices among the alternatives outside the scanner. Their findings provided further support for the idea that neural responses to products when participants are not making choice decisions could nonetheless be used to predict choices that people would make, especially in settings where actual choice data are difficult to obtain or do not exist.

While the findings reviewed thus far contribute to foundational knowledge for understanding consumer decision making, they are arguably more informative about the brain than consumer behavior. They are nonetheless important in expanding our understanding of decision processes that allow for productive ways to generate better predictions based on more refined models, assumptions, and hypotheses related to behavioral outcomes and patterns.

NEUROFORECASTING: USING NEURAL DATA TO FORECAST MARKETS

To this point, we have reviewed research in consumer neuroscience focused on understanding and predicting individual preferences and behavior. This body of work suggests that neural measures in specific areas of the brain can track decision attributes or the choice process across time even before a conscious decision is made. It further indicates that neural data may have a unique ability to predict an individual's future pattern of behavior from their own brain activations. This work has laid the foundation for an exciting new body of research focused on scaling predictions beyond the individual to account for aggregate-level behavior at the market and even population level. The term *neuroforecasting* has been used to describe this new direction of neural prediction—in which the focus is on forecasts of aggregate outcomes—and distinguish it from previous work focused on prediction of individual choice (Knutson & Genevsky, 2018).

Many of the most consequential decisions across business, economics, and public policy rely on information collected from a relatively small group of individuals to forecast the behavior of much larger groups. As an example, firms often use survey responses and focus groups to inform large-scale marketing strategies and campaigns.

Advances in brain imaging design and analysis, and the increasing availability of market-level data, have allowed researchers to apply neural analyses to the forecasting of aggregate behavior (for reviews, see Hakim & Levy, 2019; Knutson & Genevsky, 2018). Even relatively small improvements in forecasting accuracy can have significant consequences across many domains. As one example, neural responses to health campaigns could be used to forecast how effective they will be in eliciting real and widespread changes in health behavior (Falk et al., 2010, 2011).

Evidence is mounting that neural measurements of less observable intervening processes responsible for the assessment and evaluation of incoming stimuli may be the most informative for improving forecasts of aggregate behavior. Because neuroforecasting researchers are interested in scaling prediction beyond the individual to account for behavior at the aggregate level, there are important conceptual implications for how experiments are designed and analyzed. Typically, in conventional analysis, the individual is the unit of analysis. Data are collected (both neural and behavioral) in an effort to predict the choices of that individual. On the other hand, in neuroforecasting research, the focus is on prediction at the aggregate level. Data collected from a sample of individuals are used to predict the behavior of much larger groups. As a consequence, the unit of analysis becomes the stimulus itself, whose real-world impact on an outcome of interest is what we seek to predict.

In the next section, we begin by reviewing recent work in neuroforecasting that has shed light on the potential of neural data to improve forecasts of aggregate outcomes and also improve our understanding of how individual decision processes may scale to inform aggregate-level behavior. We then discuss the practical and theoretical contributions of this body of work and place it within the context of existing neural and behavioral marketing research. Finally, we conclude by highlighting some of the biggest questions currently facing neuroforecasting research and the directions the work is likely headed in the foreseeable future. A list of published articles on neuroforecasting is presented in Table 27.1.

fMRI Studies of Market Prediction

The first neuroforecasting study was conducted by Berns and Moore in 2012, though, of course, it was not called such at the time—the term would not be used until 2018. The authors had conducted a study a few years prior on an unrelated topic: the impact of social influence on music preferences. The stimuli they used in that study were songs uploaded by musicians to a popular social media website. Importantly, these bands were not well known at the time, and the songs were unfamiliar to the study participants. The participants listened to the song clips while being scanned in an MRI, and, thus, their neural responses to each unique clip were recorded. Participants also provided self-reported ratings regarding their preference for each of the songs. After a couple of years had passed, some of the songs had enjoyed a measure of commercial success. The authors realized that they could now look back at the original neural responses collected years earlier to see if the participants' responses (neural or behavioral) were at all related to the eventual real-world sales outcomes. They first looked at the subjects' own preference ratings and found that they were not predictive of the songs' market success. However, when they reanalyzed the brain data, they found that neural activity in the NAcc and MPFC, the same regions often associated with reward and valuation in studies of individual decision making, were also significantly associated with the aggregate-level commercial success. In other words, the authors found that a component of an individual's basic neural responses not only predicted their own music preferences but, once averaged across participants, also forecasted real-world aggregate-level outcomes. This first demonstration of neural data from a relatively small sample forecasting aggregate-level behavior signaled the beginning of neuroforecasting.

The work by Berns and Moore was soon followed by a study focused on public health messages conducted by Falk et al. (2012). Departing from traditional consumer behavior metrics (e.g., sales figures, willingness to pay, ad engagement), the authors sought to forecast the relative effectiveness of smoking cessation advertisements. Effectiveness in this context was defined as the number of

TABLE 27.1

Neuroforecasting Studies: Research Using Neural Activity Collected in a Laboratory Sample to Predict Real-World Aggregate-Level Outcomes

Authors	Year of publication	Method	Study stimulus	Aggregate outcome
Berns and Moore	2012	fMRI	Songs	Album sales
Falk et al.	2012	fMRI	Ads	Ad-related calls
Dmochowski et al.	2014	EEG	TV episodes; video ads	Twitter activity; ad ratings
Genevsky and Knutson	2015	fMRI	Microlending requests	Loan funding rates
Venkatraman et al.	2015	fMRI, EEG	Ads	Sales elasticity
Boksem and Smidts	2015	EEG	Movie trailers	Box office sales
Baldo et al.	2015	EEG	Shoe products	Sales
Kuhn at al.	2016	fMRI	Ads	Ad-related sales
Dietz et al.	2016	EEG	Video ads	Online views
Scholz et al.	2017	fMRI	News articles	Online sharing
Genevsky et al.	2017	fMRI	Crowdfunding appeals	Funding success
Barnett and Cerf	2017	EEG	Movies	Box office sales
Guixeres et al.	2017	EEG	Video ads	Online views
Hakim et al.	2018	EEG	Video ads	Online views
Shestyuk et al.	2019	EEG	Television programs	Viewership and Twitter volume
Tong et al.	2020	fMRI	YouTube videos	Online views/duration

Note. EEG = electroencephalography; fMRI = functional magnetic resonance imaging.

individuals in the target markets that subsequently called antismoking hotlines indicated in the advertisements. Participants in the study were presented with advertisements while being scanned in the MRI magnet. Their subjective ad effectiveness ratings were also subsequently collected. The authors found that neural activity in the MPFC while viewing the advertisements was significantly associated with their aggregate volume of calls to the hotline. This relationship held even when controlling for the self-reported effectiveness scores. This study was the first to explicitly advance the brain-as-predictor approach and also represents one of the first examples of directly testing the relative contribution of various neural and behavioral predictors.

In 2015, Genevsky and Knutson continued to build on these early examples, exploring forecasting of real-world prosocial behavior. Their study was set in the context of microlending—small, interest-free loans, typically made by a large number of donors to support people in need across the globe. In this study, the authors used neural activity recorded as participants were presented with real loan request pages scraped from the largest active microloan website on the internet (kiva.org). In response to each loan request, participants were also asked whether they would like to make a real donation using their own money and rated various features of the loan page and recipient. Subsequent analyses demonstrated that not only was the neural data associated with the real-world outcomes for these loans on the internet (i.e., whether they were funded) but they contributed predictive power above and beyond the participants' own lending behavior and subjective ratings. Given the large economic scale of online microlending in which millions of dollars are raised each year, even relatively modest improvements in forecasting represent substantial increases in overall giving.

The results reported by Genevsky and colleagues highlight an important aspect of current neuroforecasting research programs. Beyond demonstrating that neural activity is associated with aggregate-level behavior, researchers must remain mindful of the additional effort and cost associated with these methods and thus place their relative contributions in the context of traditional behavioral methods, such as consumer surveys and focus groups. Venkatraman et al. (2015) did exactly this in a study of advertising effectiveness. In fact, the authors directly contrasted the relative predictive powers of a number of traditional, neural, and physiological measures, including consumer surveys, psychological surveys, eye tracking, biometric measures (e.g., heart rate, respiration, skin response), EEG, and fMRI. While many of these measures, when considered separately, demonstrated an association with real-world advertisement effectiveness, only the fMRI measures were observed to improve forecasts beyond what was possible using traditional pencil-and-paper measures. This work made an important contribution because it demonstrated not only that neuroscientific methods can improve our ability to forecast real-world consumer behavior outside the laboratory but that we must focus on when and why individual methodological approaches might be most optimal.

In another innovative example of neuroforecasting being applied in a marketing-relevant context, Kühn et al. (2016) explored the effectiveness of point-of-sale supermarket advertisements on sales of chocolate. Participants in the study were presented with advertisements and products in the scanner and subsequently made subjective ratings of their liking of the products. After the neural data collection, the purchasing behavior of over 60,000 shoppers in a supermarket was recorded and analyzed. When the authors compared the ability of the laboratory measures to forecast the relative sales of the products, they found neural responses to both the advertisement and the product itself outstripped the predictive power of subjective ratings. Building on previous studies, this work is a useful demonstration of the potential for neuroscience-based forecasts to inform the kind of real-world marketing challenges often faced by firms.

Genevsky et al. (2017) went on to apply neuroforecasting to outcomes of crowdfunding campaigns, another growing market with significant financial implications. In this case, the participants' own funding behavior and an array of survey data, including liking, emotional responses, and estimations of the projects' likelihood of success, were all found not to be associated with the real-world outcomes of projects on the crowdfunding website. In other words, behavioral measures from the laboratory sample were not informative about the larger marketplace's funding behavior. However, neural activity collected while participants viewed the projects in the scanner was found to predict their success or failure months later on the crowdfunding website. Interestingly, while regions associated with both positive affect (NAcc) and value integration (MPFC) were associated with the participants' own individual funding decisions, only the NAcc activity effectively scaled to forecast aggregate-level outcomes. This observation raises the intriguing possibility that not all neural processes associated with individual decision-making processes may be implicated in forecasts of aggregate choice. This insight has led to follow-up work exploring the neural and psychological mechanisms underlying neuroforecasting, as described later in the chapter.

A study by Scholz et al. (2017) further demonstrated the potential of neuroforecasting to make an impact across a large range of market-relevant domains. The ubiquity of online content has made information-sharing behavior an integral element of understanding how consumers interact and engage with firms and their messages. Developing an understanding of why certain messages are shared more often, and even being able to predict which messages will become viral, is an invaluable tool in today's marketing environment. In this study, the authors presented a series of *New York Times* online articles to participants while they were in the scanner. They then attempted to forecast the real-world sharing volume of those same news pieces on the *New York Times* website. As hypothesized, activity in the aforementioned reward-related regions of the brain (i.e., NAcc and MPFC) was predictive of online sharing. In particular, the neural activity improved forecasts above and beyond what was possible using features of the articles themselves or the participants' own self-reported sharing intentions.

To this point, we have primarily described decision contexts in which individuals were making choices regarding financial resources. However, we are steadily moving toward a world in which a new currency is quickly becoming increasingly valuable. Our very attention and engagement, often measured by our allocation of time, increasingly represent the most valuable commodity to firms. This is particularly true in entertainment and online media platforms. Tong et al. (2020) explored whether neuroforecasting can expand beyond traditional decision making to account for real-world engagement in these attention markets. To accomplish this, the authors extracted aggregate measures of engagement from YouTube (e.g., how many people watched a video per day and the average viewing duration of the videos they watched). Participants in the scanner watched the first few seconds of these same videos and then decided whether to continue watching. They also provided self-reported ratings regarding their viewing preferences. The authors found that the participants viewing behavior and their ratings were not significantly associated with the frequency of views on YouTube. However, the neural analyses indicated that activity in affective circuits was significantly associated with these real-world aggregate metrics. Importantly, the neural data could also forecast the aggregate view duration of the videos. This demonstration of a neural predictor of viewer engagement (and disengagement) has important implications for optimizing the design of online content and messaging.

EEG Studies of Market Prediction

The use of EEG has gained popularity in both academia and industry due to its relative affordability and ease of use when compared with fMRI. Indeed, EEG is the primary source of neural data collected in private industry and by commercial neuromarketing firms (Hakim & Levy, 2019). EEG studies have taken a different approach to aggregate prediction. Whereas fMRI studies largely leverage the spatial resolution afforded by functional imaging to localize and extract predictive brain activity, EEG studies generally rely on other types of analyses, including decomposition of frequency bands, symmetry of activity across brain hemispheres, and correlations of neural activity across individuals. In this section, we review the existing EEG studies of aggregate prediction.

One way EEG data can be used is by assessing the extent to which neural activity while experiencing a stimulus is correlated in time across individuals. Rather than imposing predefined models on the data, this intersubject correlation (ISC) analysis uses neural responses derived from a subject to predict responses in other subjects (see Hasson et al., 2004, 2010; Mukamel et al., 2005). Originally applied to fMRI data, ISC analyses are often used in EEG studies involving the reliability and synchronization of neural responses across individuals. In particular, when used in connection with dynamic stimuli (e.g., commercial advertisements, videos), the ISC purports to capture engagement as represented by activity common across viewers. This technique was used by Dmochowski et al. (2014) in their study of viewer engagement with popular media and advertising. First, EEG activity was recorded in a small group of participants while they watched episodes of the popular American television show *The Walking Dead*. Analyses found that the shared neural activity during the viewing period correlated with real-world engagement with those episodes by the viewing public. Specifically, the ISC was associated with the size of the viewership of the episodes and the volume of relevant tweets posted during airing of the episodes. Next, the researchers turned their attention to an exploration of Super Bowl advertisements. There, they found that the correlation of neural activity within a laboratory sample of participants was associated with the real-world ratings of the advertisements. Taken together, these studies suggest that correlated neural activity measured via EEG may represent a common form of engagement that can be informative in predicting market-relevant behavior.

A similar analysis of correlated neural activity across individuals was employed by Barnett and Cerf (2017) in their study of movie trailers. Eschewing the traditional laboratory environment, the researchers took the admirable step of collecting EEG data from individuals as they watched film trailers in a real movie theater. Despite the myriad technical challenges presented by this study, the authors found that the extent to which neural responses were correlated across viewers was associated with the real-world success of the films, as measured by box office sales. Additionally, the researchers compared the strength of this relationship against other more commonly collected types of viewer data, including the participants' own ratings of the movie trailers and their assessments of willingness to pay to view the full film. They found that of these measures, the EEG similarity metric demonstrated the strongest association with box office sales.

Another method utilized frequently in EEG analysis, termed spectral decomposition, separates the various frequencies of neural activity into defined bands, often associated with various psychological processes and states. As an example, Boksem and Smidts (2015) used spectral analysis of participants' neural activity as they watched movie trailers to forecast the real-world success of the films after release. As participants watched promotional trailers for the films, their neural responses were collected and subsequently decomposed into predefined frequency bands. The power of the signal observed in specific frequency bands was found to be positively associated with the real-world revenue of the films. In another example, Guixeres et al. (2017) utilized a variety of EEG analyses including spectral decomposition to forecast engagement with Super Bowl advertisements. Applying machine learning algorithms to a combination of EEG metrics, the authors could predict the number of YouTube views for the advertisements. The authors went on to compare the various measures and found that the asymmetry across brain hemispheres in a particular frequency range, interpreted as a measure of pleasantness, was the single best predictor of YouTube views.

A prime example of the movement of neuroforecasting research beyond simple existence proofs to more sophisticated analysis of the relative contributions of various methods and analysis techniques comes from a study by Hakim et al. (2018). In this work, the authors recorded EEG data from participants as they watched a number of video advertisements for various consumer products. They additionally collected survey data regarding the participants' preferences and intentions of purchasing those same products. While the questionnaire data could forecast the aggregate-level responses to the various products with 64.2% accuracy, adding the EEG measures improved the forecasts, reaching a rate of 68.5%. This relatively modest yet significant improvement in prediction suggests that despite the usefulness of traditional marketing measures, neuroscientific methods can contribute significant additional explanatory power to models attempting to predict behavior beyond the participant sample—a goal often at the forefront of modern-day marketing.

Up until this point, we have discussed academic research, primarily conducted in business schools at universities. However, as mentioned at the beginning of this section, due to the practical and logistical advantages of EEG, it has become the preferred method of neuroscientific research in neuromarketing departments of international firms, as well as a growing number of smaller dedicated neuromarketing firms. While the research published by these private organizations is not as easily interpretable due to proprietary methods and data sources, it remains informative to be aware of the work being done by these firms. In a study of Super Bowl advertisements, Deitz et al. (2016) at Sands Research used a proprietary EEG analysis method to predict advertisement view metrics on YouTube. In another example, Baldo et al. (2015), from Neuromarketing Labs, reported success using proprietary EEG metrics of emotional engagement to forecast shoe sales. These examples point to the growing use of neuroscientific methods in industry. The goals of these studies have shifted from gaining an understanding of consumer motivations to making actionable forecasts of consumer behavior.

Scaling Prediction: From Individual Decisions to Aggregate Behavior

The body of work reviewed leads us to a very important question: How can neural activation recorded in a laboratory sample predict aggregate behavior, at times better than self-report measures or observed behavior? More specifically, what are the mechanisms that support the scaling of prediction from the individual to the aggregate? While few studies have addressed these questions to date, they represent an important direction for continuing research.

One theory put forward by Knutson and Genevsky (2018) suggested that while a number of neural processes are involved in an individual decision-making process, only a subset of these regions may scale to inform forecasts of aggregate behavior. More specifically, basic affective responses indexed by evolutionarily conserved subcortical circuits may represent a more universal, or generalizable, measure of the response to a stimulus. The affect–integration–motivation framework describes a hierarchical model whereby a decision stimulus first elicits an affective reaction. This affective reaction is then integrated by higher order cognitive processes that include idiosyncratic preferences and concerns. This then leads to a motivational state, whether to approach or avoid the stimulus. Finally, the response is manifested as an observable behavior: the end point of the decision-making process.

Knutson and Genevsky (2018) offered an illustrative example of how neuroforecasting may play out. They painted an image of a researcher entering a crowded lecture hall carrying a tray of warm, freshly baked chocolate-chip cookies. As the delicious smell wafts throughout the room, the students likely experience a very similar and strong affective response. If those same researchers then stepped back and recorded the students' behavior (i.e., whether they took a cookie), they would observe a great variety of reactions. Similarly, if they surveyed the students regarding their behavior, the responses would likely include a great deal of idiosyncratic variability reflecting the individual students' dietary and motivational goals. However, if the researchers were able to capture that first affective response as the tray of cookies entered the room, they would have a more universal and generalizable index of the preference for that cookie. To complete the metaphor, the neural response, specifically that recorded in the NAcc, represents this generalizable response. Thus, these basic responses, unadulterated by idiosyncratic differences, offer the best opportunity to improve forecasts of the larger population's behavior.

One consequence of this framework is that it makes specific testable predictions. Forecasts based on generalizable neural activity should be less impacted by the representativeness of the sample to the population than forecasts that rely on less generalizable self-report measures. Recently, Genevsky and colleagues tested this prediction. In their unpublished work, Genevsky et al. (2021) found that while the accuracy of behavioral forecasts based on traditional measures collected from a sample is highly impacted by the representativeness of that sample to the population, neural forecasts demonstrate a much lower impact of representativeness. This finding suggests that compared with observable behavior and self-report measures, neural activity may represent a more generalizable index of preference across individuals.

In this section, we have reviewed a new and growing literature on neuroforecasting. Across methodologies, there are now numerous examples of how neural data collected in the laboratory can make market-relevant predictions about outcomes in the real world. As the field continues forward, it is imperative that researchers continue to move toward studies that address how, when, and why neural forecasts work. This understanding can then be applied to optimize forecasts to achieve maximum prediction accuracy. The work reviewed earlier in the chapter on the neural mechanisms of individual choice has set the stage for neuromarketing to fulfill the potential of consumer neuroscience to make tangible and substantial contributions to the marketing fields in both academia and industry.

CONCLUSION

As the field of consumer neuroscience has continued to grow, there has been increasing interest in leveraging theoretical and practical insights from brain-based studies on decision making to improve within-individual predictions and aggregate-level forecasts. The work described in this chapter covers research advances and significant insights that serve to inform and guide better predictions in a variety of consumer domains. An important caveat to keep in mind is that the extent to which specific processes can be inferred from neural data is limited, and caution is warranted when interpreting brain data. In general, combining multiple complementary methods can offer benefits in terms of the researchers' ability to provide more definitive empirical evidence. We now have a critical mass of findings that we can draw on to reveal a distinct set of brain signals from consumers that can potentially outperform the commonly used behavioral measures. In parallel with advances in academia, practitioners' interest in applying neuroscience methods has been growing as a means for gaining insights into implicit or automatic processes.

Looking forward, neuroscientific studies can provide useful insight about the underlying causes and mechanisms that can be used to perform predictive analytics on problems in the age of big data. Predictive analytics essentially rely on vast amounts of past observations to connect inputs with outputs and typically do not account for underlying mechanisms. This black box approach without a sound understanding of the underlying forces that drive outcomes can lead to inadequate predictive models. The work on the neural basis of consumer decision making can be useful for understanding what actions and interventions are effective and ineffective under specific conditions and why they do or do not work. This work can help practitioners put structure on the question at hand so that unobserved and latent information can be properly accounted for when making inferences. It can ultimately guide practitioners and policy makers to be better at understanding cause-and-effect relationships between input and output variables, identifying real drivers of outcomes, and parsing out spurious patterns. For academic scholars, the work adds value to decision-making research by enhancing the ability to make inferences beyond our usual variables and paradigms, develop more comprehensive theories, and generate hypotheses that are empirically testable. This ultimately puts us in a better position to generalize this knowledge, understand the contextual influences on decision making, and create interventions or influence decisions more effectively. Such process knowledge can be important not just in consumer settings but in other settings such as those involving policy, legal, financial, or health decisions.

REFERENCES

Baek, E. C., Scholz, C., O'Donnell, M. B., & Falk, E. B. (2017). The value of sharing information: A neural account of information transmission. *Psychological Science*, 28(7), 851–861. https://doi.org/10.1177/0956797617695073

Baldo, D., Parikh, H., Piu, Y., & Müller, K. M. (2015). Brain waves predict success of new fashion products: A practical application for the footwear retailing industry. *Journal of Creating Value*, 1(1), 61–71. https://doi.org/10.1177/2394964315569625

Barnett, S. B., & Cerf, M. (2017). A ticket for your thoughts: Method for predicting content recall and sales using neural similarity of moviegoers. *Journal of Consumer Research*, 44(1), 160–181. https://doi.org/10.1093/jcr/ucw083

Bartra, O., McGuire, J. T., & Kable, J. W. (2013). The valuation system: A coordinate-based meta-analysis of BOLD fMRI experiments examining neural correlates of subjective value. *NeuroImage*, 76, 412–427. https://doi.org/10.1016/j.neuroimage.2013.02.063

Becker, G. M., DeGroot, M. H., & Marschak, J. (1964). Measuring utility by a single-response sequential method. *Behavioral Science*, 9(3), 226–232. https://doi.org/10.1002/bs.3830090304

Berns, G. S., & Moore, S. E. (2012). A neural predictor of cultural popularity. *Journal of Consumer Psychology*, 22(1), 154–160. https://doi.org/10.1016/j.jcps.2011.05.001

Boksem, M. A., & Smidts, A. (2015). Brain responses to movie trailers predict individual preferences for movies and their population-wide commercial success. *Journal of Marketing Research*, 52(4), 482–492. https://doi.org/10.1509/jmr.13.0572

Campbell-Meiklejohn, D. K., Bach, D. R., Roepstorff, A., Dolan, R. J., & Frith, C. D. (2010). How the opinion of others affects our valuation of objects. *Current Biology*, 20(13), 1165–1170. https://doi.org/10.1016/j.cub.2010.04.055

Chib, V. S., Rangel, A., Shimojo, S., & O'Doherty, J. P. (2009). Evidence for a common representation of decision values for dissimilar goods in human ventromedial prefrontal cortex. *Journal of Neuroscience*, 29(39), 12315–12320. https://doi.org/10.1523/JNEUROSCI.2575-09.2009

Chua, H. F., Ho, S. S., Jasinska, A. J., Polk, T. A., Welsh, R. C., Liberzon, I., & Strecher, V. J. (2011). Self-related neural response to tailored smoking-cessation messages predicts quitting. *Nature Neuroscience*, 14(4), 426–427. https://doi.org/10.1038/nn.2761

Chua, H. F., Liberzon, I., Welsh, R. C., & Strecher, V. J. (2009). Neural correlates of message tailoring and self-relatedness in smoking cessation programming. *Biological Psychiatry*, 65(2), 165–168. https://doi.org/10.1016/j.biopsych.2008.08.030

Cloutier, J., Heatherton, T. F., Whalen, P. J., & Kelley, W. M. (2008). Are attractive people rewarding? Sex differences in the neural substrates of facial attractiveness. *Journal of Cognitive Neuroscience, 20*(6), 941–951. https://doi.org/10.1162/jocn.2008.20062

Cooper, J. C., Dunne, S., Furey, T., & O'Doherty, J. P. (2014). The role of the posterior temporal and medial prefrontal cortices in mediating learning from romantic interest and rejection. *Cerebral Cortex, 24*(9), 2502–2511. https://doi.org/10.1093/cercor/bht102

Davey, C. G., Allen, N. B., Harrison, B. J., Dwyer, D. B., & Yücel, M. (2010). Being liked activates primary reward and midline self-related brain regions. *Human Brain Mapping, 31*(4), 660–668. https://doi.org/10.1002/hbm.20895

Deitz, G. D., Royne, M. B., Peasley, M. C., & Coleman, J. T. (2016). EEG-based measures versus panel ratings: Predicting social media-based behavioral response to Super Bowl ads. *Journal of Advertising Research, 56*(2), 217–227. https://doi.org/10.2501/JAR-2016-030

Deppe, M., Schwindt, W., Kugel, H., Plassmann, H., & Kenning, P. (2005). Nonlinear responses within the medial prefrontal cortex reveal when specific implicit information influences economic decision making. *Journal of Neuroimaging, 15*(2), 171–182. https://doi.org/10.1111/j.1552-6569.2005.tb00303.x

Dmochowski, J. P., Bezdek, M. A., Abelson, B. P., Johnson, J. S., Schumacher, E. H., & Parra, L. C. (2014). Audience preferences are predicted by temporal reliability of neural processing. *Nature Communications, 5*(1), 1–9. https://doi.org/10.1038/ncomms5567

Doré, B. P., Scholz, C., Baek, E. C., Garcia, J. O., O'Donnell, M. B., Bassett, D. S., Vettel, J. M., & Falk, E. B. (2019). Brain activity tracks population information sharing by capturing consensus judgments of value. *Cerebral Cortex, 29*(7), 3102–3110. https://doi.org/10.1093/cercor/bhy176

Elliott, R., Friston, K. J., & Dolan, R. J. (2000). Dissociable neural responses in human reward systems. *Journal of Neuroscience, 20*(16), 6159–6165. https://doi.org/10.1523/JNEUROSCI.20-16-06159.2000

Eysenck, H. J. (1990). Genetic and environmental contributions to individual differences: The three major dimensions of personality. *Journal of Personality, 58*(1), 245–261. https://doi.org/10.1111/j.1467-6494.1990.tb00915.x

Falk, E. B., Berkman, E. T., & Lieberman, M. D. (2012). From neural responses to population behavior: Neural focus group predicts population-level media effects. *Psychological Science, 23*(5), 439–445. https://doi.org/10.1177/0956797611434964

Falk, E. B., Berkman, E. T., Mann, T., Harrison, B., & Lieberman, M. D. (2010). Predicting persuasion-induced behavior change from the brain. *Journal of Neuroscience, 30*(25), 8421–8424. https://doi.org/10.1523/JNEUROSCI.0063-10.2010

Falk, E. B., Berkman, E. T., Whalen, D., & Lieberman, M. D. (2011). Neural activity during health messaging predicts reductions in smoking above and beyond self-report. *Health Psychology, 30*(2), 177–185. https://doi.org/10.1037/a0022259

Falk, E. B., O'Donnell, M. B., Cascio, C. N., Tinney, F., Kang, Y., Lieberman, M. D., Taylor, S. E., An, L., Resnicow, K., & Strecher, V. J. (2015). Self-affirmation alters the brain's response to health messages and subsequent behavior change. *Proceedings of the National Academy of Sciences, 112*(7), 1977–1982. https://doi.org/10.1073/pnas.1500247112

Genevsky, A., & Knutson, B. (2015). Neural affective mechanisms predict market-level microlending. *Psychological Science, 26*(9), 1411–1422. https://doi.org/10.1177/0956797615588467

Genevsky, A., Tong, L. C., & Knutson, B. (2021). *Generalizability of brain activity in forecasting market choice* [Unpublished manuscript]. Rotterdam School of Management, Erasmus University.

Genevsky, A., Yoon, C., & Knutson, B. (2017). When brain beats behavior: Neuroforecasting crowdfunding outcomes. *Journal of Neuroscience, 37*(36), 8625–8634. https://doi.org/10.1523/JNEUROSCI.1633-16.2017

Gottfried, J. A., & Zald, D. H. (2005). On the scent of human olfactory orbitofrontal cortex: Meta-analysis and comparison to non-human primates. *Brain Research Reviews, 50*(2), 287–304. https://doi.org/10.1016/j.brainresrev.2005.08.004

Grosenick, L., Klingenberg, B., Katovich, K., Knutson, B., Taylor, J. E. (2013). Interpretable whole-brain prediction analysis with GraphNet. *Neuroimage, 72*(2), 304–321. https://doi.org/10.1016/j.neuroimage.2012.12.062

Guixeres, J., Bigné, E., Ausín Azofra, J. M., Alcañiz Raya, M., Colomer Granero, A., Fuentes Hurtado, F., & Naranjo Ornedo, V. (2017). Consumer neuroscience-based metrics predict recall, liking and viewing rates in online advertising. *Frontiers in Psychology, 8*, 1808. https://doi.org/10.3389/fpsyg.2017.01808

Hakim, A., Klorfeld, S., Sela, T., Friedman, D., Shabat-Simon, M., & Levy, D. J. (2018). Pathways to consumers' minds: Using machine learning and multiple EEG metrics to increase preference prediction above and beyond traditional measurements. *bioRxiv*, 317073. https://doi.org/10.1101/317073

Hakim, A., & Levy, D. J. (2019). A gateway to consumers' minds: Achievements, caveats, and prospects of electroencephalography-based prediction in neuromarketing. *Wiley Interdisciplinary Reviews: Cognitive*

Science, 10(2), e1485. https://doi.org/10.1002/wcs.1485

Hare, T. A., Camerer, C. F., Knoepfle, D. T., O'Doherty, J. P., & Rangel, A. (2010). Value computations in ventral medial prefrontal cortex during charitable decision making incorporate input from regions involved in social cognition. *Journal of Neuroscience, 30*(2), 583–590. https://doi.org/10.1523/JNEUROSCI.4089-09.2010

Hasson, U., Malach, R., & Heeger, D. J. (2010). Reliability of cortical activity during natural stimulation. *Trends in Cognitive Sciences, 14*(1), 40–48. https://doi.org/10.1016/j.tics.2009.10.011

Hasson, U., Nir, Y., Levy, I., Fuhrmann, G., & Malach, R. (2004). Intersubject synchronization of cortical activity during natural vision. *Science, 303*(5664), 1634–1640. https://doi.org/10.1126/science.1089506

Ho, C., & Spence, C. (2009). Using peripersonal warning signals to orient a driver's gaze. *Human Factors, 51*(4), 539–556. https://doi.org/10.1177/0018720809341735

Hsu, M., Bhatt, M., Adolphs, R., Tranel, D., & Camerer, C. F. (2005). Neural systems responding to degrees of uncertainty in human decision making. *Science, 310*(5754), 1680–1683. https://doi.org/10.1126/science.1115327

Izuma, K., Saito, D. N., & Sadato, N. (2008). Processing of social and monetary rewards in the human striatum. *Neuron, 58*(2), 284–294. https://doi.org/10.1016/j.neuron.2008.03.020

Kable, J. W., & Glimcher, P. W. (2007). The neural correlates of subjective value during intertemporal choice. *Nature Neuroscience, 10*(12), 1625–1633. https://doi.org/10.1038/nn2007

Kang, M. J., Rangel, A., Camus, M., & Camerer, C. F. (2011). Hypothetical and real choice differentially activate common valuation areas. *Journal of Neuroscience, 31*(2), 461–468. https://doi.org/10.1523/JNEUROSCI.1583-10.2011

Karmarkar, U. R., & Plassmann, H. (2019). Consumer neuroscience: Past, present, and future. *Organizational Research Methods, 22*(1), 174–195. https://doi.org/10.1177/1094428117730598

Karmarkar, U. R., & Yoon, C. (2016). Consumer neuroscience: Advances in understanding consumer psychology. *Current Opinion in Psychology, 10*, 160–165. https://doi.org/10.1016/j.copsyc.2016.01.010

Kawabata, H., & Zeki, S. (2004). Neural correlates of beauty. *Journal of Neurophysiology, 91*(4), 1699–1705. https://doi.org/10.1152/jn.00696.2003

Klucharev, V., Hytönen, K., Rijpkema, M., Smidts, A., & Fernández, G. (2009). Reinforcement learning signal predicts social conformity. *Neuron, 61*(1), 140–151. https://doi.org/10.1016/j.neuron.2008.11.027

Knutson, B., & Genevsky, A. (2018). Neuroforecasting aggregate choice. *Current Directions in Psychological Science, 27*(2), 110–115. https://doi.org/10.1177/0963721417737877

Knutson, B., Rick, S., Wimmer, G. E., Prelec, D., & Loewenstein, G. (2007). Neural predictors of purchases. *Neuron, 53*(1), 147–156. https://doi.org/10.1016/j.neuron.2006.11.010

Kühn, S., Strelow, E., & Gallinat, J. (2016). Multiple "buy buttons" in the brain: Forecasting chocolate sales at point-of-sale based on functional brain activation using fMRI. *NeuroImage, 136*, 122–128. https://doi.org/10.1016/j.neuroimage.2016.05.021

Lebreton, M., Jorge, S., Michel, V., Thirion, B., & Pessiglione, M. (2009). An automatic valuation system in the human brain: Evidence from functional neuroimaging. *Neuron, 64*(3), 431–439. https://doi.org/10.1016/j.neuron.2009.09.040

Levy, D. J., & Glimcher, P. W. (2011). Comparing apples and oranges: Using reward-specific and reward-general subjective value representation in the brain. *Journal of Neuroscience, 31*(41), 14693–14707. https://doi.org/10.1523/JNEUROSCI.2218-11.2011

Levy, D. J., & Glimcher, P. W. (2012). The root of all value: A neural common currency for choice. *Current Opinion in Neurobiology, 22*(6), 1027–1038. https://doi.org/10.1016/j.conb.2012.06.001

Levy, I., Lazzaro, S. C., Rutledge, R. B., & Glimcher, P. W. (2011). Choice from non-choice: Predicting consumer preferences from blood oxygenation level-dependent signals obtained during passive viewing. *Journal of Neuroscience, 31*(1), 118–125. https://doi.org/10.1523/JNEUROSCI.3214-10.2011

Levy, I., Snell, J., Nelson, A. J., Rustichini, A., & Glimcher, P. W. (2010). Neural representation of subjective value under risk and ambiguity. *Journal of Neurophysiology, 103*(2), 1036–1047. https://doi.org/10.1152/jn.00853.2009

Morelli, S. A., Torre, J. B., & Eisenberger, N. I. (2014). The neural bases of feeling understood and not understood. *Social Cognitive and Affective Neuroscience, 9*(12), 1890–1896. https://doi.org/10.1093/scan/nst191

Mukamel, R., Gelbard, H., Arieli, A., Hasson, U., Fried, I., & Malach, R. (2005). Coupling between neuronal firing, field potentials, and fMRI in human auditory cortex. *Science, 309*(5736), 951–954. https://doi.org/10.1126/science.1110913

Padoa-Schioppa, C., & Assad, J. A. (2006). Neurons in the orbitofrontal cortex encode economic value. *Nature, 441*(7090), 223–226. https://doi.org/10.1038/nature04676

Paulus, M. P., & Frank, L. R. (2003). Ventromedial prefrontal cortex activation is critical for preference judgments. *Neuroreport, 14*(10), 1311–1315. https://doi.org/10.1097/01.wnr.0000078543.07662.02

Plassmann, H., O'Doherty, J., & Rangel, A. (2007). Orbitofrontal cortex encodes willingness to pay in everyday economic transactions. *Journal of Neuroscience, 27*(37), 9984–9988. https://doi.org/10.1523/JNEUROSCI.2131-07.2007

Plassmann, H., O'Doherty, J., Shiv, B., & Rangel, A. (2008). Marketing actions can modulate neural representations of experienced pleasantness. *Proceedings of the National Academy of Sciences of the United States of America, 105*(3), 1050–1054. https://doi.org/10.1073/pnas.0706929105

Plassmann, H., Venkatraman, V., Huettel, S., & Yoon, C. (2015). Consumer neuroscience: Applications, challenges, and possible solutions. *Journal of Marketing Research, 52*(4), 427–435. https://doi.org/10.1509/jmr.14.0048

Rolls, E. T. (2004). The functions of the orbitofrontal cortex. *Brain and Cognition, 55*(1), 11–29. https://doi.org/10.1016/S0278-2626(03)00277-X

Ruff, C. C., & Fehr, E. (2014). The neurobiology of rewards and values in social decision making. *Nature Reviews Neuroscience, 15*(8), 549–562. https://doi.org/10.1038/nrn3776

Rushworth, M. F., Behrens, T. E. J., Rudebeck, P. H., & Walton, M. E. (2007). Contrasting roles for cingulate and orbitofrontal cortex in decisions and social behaviour. *Trends in Cognitive Sciences, 11*(4), 168–176. https://doi.org/10.1016/j.tics.2007.01.004

Scholz, C., Baek, E. C., O'Donnell, M. B., Kim, H. S., Cappella, J. N., & Falk, E. B. (2017). A neural model of valuation and information virality. *Proceedings of the National Academy of Sciences of the United States of America, 114*(11), 2881–2886. https://doi.org/10.1073/pnas.1615259114

Shaw, S. D., Acikalin, Y., Shiv, B., & Yoon, C. (2018). Neuroscientific methods and tools in consumer research. In F. R. Kardes, P. P. Herr, & N. Schwarz (Eds.), *Handbook of research methods in consumer psychology* (pp. 293–315). Routledge.

Shestyuk, A. Y., Kasinathan, K., Karapoondinott, V., Knight, R. T., & Gurumoorthy, R. (2019). Individual EEG measures of attention, memory, and motivation predict population level TV viewership and Twitter engagement. *PLOS ONE, 14*(3), e0214507. https://doi.org/10.1371/journal.pone.0214507

Smidts, A., Hsu, M., Sanfey, A. G., Boksem, M. A., Ebstein, R. B., Huettel, S. A., Kable, J. W., Karmarkar, U. R., Kitayama, S., Knutson, B., Liberzon, I., Lohrenz, T., Stallen, M., & Yoon, C. (2014). Advancing consumer neuroscience. *Marketing Letters, 25*(3), 257–267. https://doi.org/10.1007/s11002-014-9306-1

Smith, A., Bernheim, B. D., Camerer, C., & Rangel, A. (2014). Neural activity reveals preferences without choices. *American Economic Journal: Microeconomics, 6*(2), 1–36. https://doi.org/10.1257/mic.6.2.1

Spitzer, M., Fischbacher, U., Herrnberger, B., Grön, G., & Fehr, E. (2007). The neural signature of social norm compliance. *Neuron, 56*(1), 185–196. https://doi.org/10.1016/j.neuron.2007.09.011

Tong, L. C., Acikalin, M. Y., Genevsky, A., Shiv, B., & Knutson, B. (2020). Brain activity forecasts video engagement in an internet attention market. *Proceedings of the National Academy of Sciences of the United States of America, 117*(12), 6936–6941. https://doi.org/10.1073/pnas.1905178117

Tusche, A., Bode, S., & Haynes, J. D. (2010). Neural responses to unattended products predict later consumer choices. *Journal of Neuroscience, 30*(23), 8024–8031. https://doi.org/10.1523/JNEUROSCI.0064-10.2010

van den Bosch, I., Dalenberg, J. R., Renken, R., van Langeveld, A. W. B., Smeets, P. A. M., Griffioen-Roose, S., Ter Horst, G. J., de Graaf, C., & Boesveldt, S. (2014). To like or not to like: Neural substrates of subjective flavor preferences. *Behavioural Brain Research, 269*, 128–137. https://doi.org/10.1016/j.bbr.2014.04.010

Venkatraman, V., Dimoka, A., Pavlou, P. A., Vo, K., Hampton, W., Bollinger, B., Hershfield, H., Ishihara, M., & Winer, R. S. (2015). Predicting advertising success beyond traditional measures: New insights from neurophysiological methods and market response modeling. *Journal of Marketing Research, 52*(4), 436–452. https://doi.org/10.1509/jmr.13.0593

Venkatraman, V., Payne, J. W., Bettman, J. R., Luce, M. F., & Huettel, S. A. (2009). Separate neural mechanisms underlie choices and strategic preferences in risky decision making. *Neuron, 62*(4), 593–602. https://doi.org/10.1016/j.neuron.2009.04.007

Wadhwa, M., Shiv, B., & Nowlis, S. M. (2008). A bite to whet the reward appetite: The influence of sampling on reward-seeking behaviors. *Journal of Marketing Research, 45*(4), 403–413. https://doi.org/10.1509/jmkr.45.4.403

Yoon, C., Gutchess, A. H., Feinberg, F., & Polk, T. A. (2006). A functional magnetic resonance imaging study of neural dissociations between brand and person judgments. *Journal of Consumer Research, 33*(1), 31–40. https://doi.org/10.1086/504132

Zaki, J., Schirmer, J., & Mitchell, J. P. (2011). Social influence modulates the neural computation of value. *Psychological Science, 22*(7), 894–900. https://doi.org/10.1177/0956797611411057

CHAPTER 28

CONSUMING FOR HAPPINESS

Siok Kuan Tambyah and Soo Jiuan Tan

The connection between consumption and happiness is a question that has garnered considerable research interest over the years. Happiness is one aspect of subjective well-being (SWB), which encompasses both affective aspects (e.g., happiness, positive affect, or negative affect) and cognitive aspects (e.g., life satisfaction). In this chapter, we first consider the many facets of SWB before exploring how consumption behaviors can contribute to the well-being of individuals and communities. In the literature review to follow, we highlight the research studies that have suggested how having money and spending it right can help to enhance consumers' well-being. We end with implications for future research.

SUBJECTIVE WELL-BEING

SWB is a multifaceted concept that comprises people's life satisfaction, their evaluation of their life domains, and how they think and feel about these aspects of their lives (Diener & Biswas-Diener, 2008). Researchers have measured an individual's cognitive and affective perceptions of and reactions to their whole life, as well as to specific domains of life (Diener, 1984, 2006; Myers & Diener, 1995). Cognitive well-being (or life satisfaction) is derived from a conscious judgment based on some standard. It reflects the perceived distance between what is experienced and what is expected as a better life or envisioned as an ideal life. Affective well-being refers to feelings or emotional states which reflect spontaneous reactions to events in the individual's immediate experience. For instance, when happiness is used as an indicator of SWB, we usually consider the hedonic level of affect or the pleasantness of hedonic experiences such as feelings, emotions, and moods (Veenhoven, 2012).

These conceptualizations of the cognitive and affective aspects of well-being are aligned with the *hedonism of happiness* approach. Higher levels of life satisfaction and positive emotions are supposed to lead to greater levels of SWB. A complementary approach is that of the *eudaemonism of happiness*, which focuses on the intrinsic meaning of life and the fulfillment of life goals and skills (Seligman, 2012), engagement, and other aspects of psychological flourishing (Diener & Biswas-Diener, 2008). The eudaemonic approach to understanding SWB suggests that meaning and purpose are important contributors to the significance of one's life (Baumeister et al., 2013; Ryan & Deci, 2001; Seligman, 2012). Psychological flourishing "goes beyond an individual's pursuit of her own happiness to include her contributions to society and the happiness of others" (Diener & Biswas-Diener, 2008, p. 241).

MONEY AND HAPPINESS

As suggested by the need-fulfillment theory, absolute income (or actual income) is important because money is an enabling resource for the acquisition of

https://doi.org/10.1037/0000262-028
APA Handbook of Consumer Psychology, L. R. Kahle (Editor-in-Chief)
Copyright © 2022 by the American Psychological Association. All rights reserved.

goods and services that contribute to one's happiness (Diener & Biswas-Diener, 2002). Similarly, the material desires concept proposes that people will be happy to the extent that they can obtain things they desire or work toward fulfilling these desires. Thus, having the means to meet one's needs and wants increases SWB. On average, studies have shown that richer nations tended to be happier than poorer ones (e.g., Deaton, 2013; Diener & Oishi, 2000; Powdthavee et al., 2017). Sengupta et al. (2012) also found that household income had positive logarithmic associations with subjective quality of life and happiness. Income seemed to be linked more strongly to people's evaluations of their life than to their happiness.

In addition, it is important to consider how consumers spend their income and the choices they make regarding the kind of activities and behaviors that could enhance their well-being. Shifting the focus from household income toward everyday spending decisions may provide more "options for consumers in search of happiness" (Aknin et al., 2018, p. 2). This shift in focus also gives rise to a stream of research that looks at people's spending choices, that is, volitional activity or the intentional actions in which one chooses to engage (Lyubomirsky et al., 2005). Drawing on the self-determination theory (Ryan & Deci, 2000), it has been proposed that humans flourish when they fulfill the three basic psychological needs of autonomy, competence, and relatedness. It has been suggested that using one's income to meet these needs would be wise (Aknin et al., 2018).

Dunn et al. (2011) outlined eight principles for "spending money right" that can potentially help consumers be happier. These principles are based on insights drawn from the research on affective forecasting and also consider contextual factors. These principles include (a) buy experiences instead of things, (b) help others instead of yourself, (c) buy many small pleasures instead of few big ones, (d) buy less insurance, (e) pay now and consume later, (f) think about what you are not thinking about, (g) beware of comparison shopping, and (h) follow the herd instead of your head.

In the sections to follow, we review the various considerations around the prescriptive advice of the first two principles of (a) material versus experiential purchases and (b) self-focused spending versus other-focused spending. Due to the space constraints of the book chapter, we have decided to focus on these two theoretically and practically interesting principles; there has been a fair amount of research on them as well.

Material Versus Experiential Purchases

Material purchases are those that lead to an acquired possession, while experiential purchases are designed to provide an experience (Rosenzweig & Gilovich, 2012). Extant literature on spending choices has postulated that consumers are happier when they spend money on experiences than on material possessions (Burroughs & Rindfleisch, 2002; Carter & Gilovich, 2010; Frank, 1985; Gilovich et al., 2015; Nicolao et al., 2009). In particular, Gilovich et al. (2015) did an extensive review of the literature and documented 37 empirical studies that supported the claim that experiential purchases provided greater satisfaction and happiness because of the three core psychological mechanisms of social connection, identity, and comparison (see Gilovich et al., 2015, Table 1). Consumers anticipate and remember experiences more than material purchases. They also consider experiences to be more self-defining, unique, difficult to compare, and likely to be shared with other people (Van Boven & Gilovich, 2003). There is also a slower rate of adaptation to experiential purchases (Nicolao et al., 2009).

Another line of argument follows from the research on materialism and luxury consumption. Although it has been claimed that materialistic people consider the possession of goods as a path to personal happiness (Ahuvia & Wong, 2002; Fournier & Richins, 1991), studies have suggested that people who pursue material goals tend to experience lower SWB (Christopher et al., 2009; Kashdan & Breen, 2007; Miesen, 2009). High materialistic consumers have also been found to experience more negative feelings and are less satisfied with life than less materialistic consumers (Christopher et al., 2009; Kashdan & Breen, 2007). It appears that material purchases do not bring long-lasting happiness compared with experiential purchases.

Are material purchases less capable of meeting the happiness needs of consumers through the psychological mechanisms of social connection, identity, and comparison? Rather than drawing the line squarely between material and experiential purchases, other important factors such as consumer characteristics (e.g., consumer goals) and cultural contexts could be considered. While the momentum for spending on experiences is still going strong, most of the research studies were conducted using Western subjects. Aknin et al. (2018) acknowledged that most of the studies reviewed in their article were "conducted in North America or other Western Educated Industrialized Rich and Democratic countries (Henrich et al., 2010)" (p. 8). They proposed that certain spending suggestions such as self-expression may be less effective in other cultures; hence, more cross-cultural research would be needed. Specifically, research on consumer characteristics (e.g., identity, nature of consumption goals) can shed more light on how experiential or material purchases can fulfill the needs of non-Western consumers and enhance their sense of well-being. For instance, the psychological mechanisms of social connection and identity may work differently in non-Western contexts. Schütte (1998) proposed a modified Maslow's hierarchy of needs to explain the needs and wants of Asian consumers, noting that unlike Western consumers, the three highest levels emphasized social needs. Hence, both material and experiential purchases may be equally capable of promoting social connections and nurturing one's identity for non-Western consumers.

Some researchers have suggested that material purchases can fulfill not only functional but also psychological needs related to happiness depending on the cultural context. Yu et al. (2016) showed that experiential purchases did not necessarily induce more happiness than material purchases, especially for consumers who were high in self-discrepancy (SD). SD is the gap between the actual and the ideal relevant self that motivates people to pursue the ideal self (Higgins, 1987). Yu et al. found that for consumers with high SD, happiness was derived more from material consumption for the sake of status. It is interesting to note that this study was also among the few so far to address non-Western respondents (in this case, of Chinese ethnicity). Face is known to be an important value in collectivistic cultures (Zhou & Belk, 2004), and the pursuit of face significantly affects the consumption behaviors of these consumers (Li & Su, 2007). Hence, Yu et al. (2016) surmised that the consumers in collectivistic cultures may be more concerned with the perceptions and opinions of others around them compared with consumers from individualistic cultures, as the former care more about the extrinsic benefits (e.g., signaling and social benefits) of goods than the intrinsic benefits (e.g., functional and hedonic benefits).

In another study on non-Western respondents, Wang et al. (2019) found supportive evidence for both material and experiential purchases contributing to happiness. The analysis was done on a panel data set of 14,960 households and 33,300 individuals across China, representing about 95% of the Chinese population. Transportation and communication are the primary vehicles through which individuals maintain contact, which lends support to arguments made by Frank (1985) and others that experiential goods, such as "spending time with family and friends, is an important source of happiness" (Wang et al., 2019, p. 133). While maintaining contact, "speaking on one's brand name cell phone or internet via smartphones can also be highly conspicuous reinforcing the conspicuous consumption effect" (Wang et al., 2019, p. 133). In this way, owning a high-status cellphone (a material purchase for the sake of status) also contributes to happiness.

To investigate why consumers continue to pursue material goals despite a possible negative impact on happiness, Hudders and Pandelaere (2012) hypothesized that the short term gain from luxury consumption (termed as a "silver lining" by the authors) may alleviate some of the negative consequences of materialism on SWB, thus trapping consumers into an unending journey in the pursuit of material goals. Using a survey of 584 students in the Flemish part of Belgium, Hudders and Pandelaere (2012) found a negative relationship between materialism and life satisfaction, "indicating that high materialistic consumers are less satisfied with their lives than low materialistic consumers"

(p. 421). Materialism is also found to be positively related to negative affect, indicating that "high materialists experience negative feelings more often than low materialists" (Hudders & Pandelaere, 2012, p. 421). However, they also found a positive relationship between luxury consumption and SWB. The consumption of luxury goods was positively related to life satisfaction and frequency of positive affect, although there was "no evidence that luxury consumption alleviates the frequency of negative affect" (Hudders & Pandelaere, 2012, p. 421). Their results also showed the mediated effect of materialism on satisfaction with life via luxury consumption in that "the more high materialistic consumers consume luxury goods, the more satisfied they are with their lives" (Hudders & Pandelaere, 2012, pp. 425–426). However, there is no such mediating effect of materialism on positive and negative affect for luxury consumption. These results demonstrated that it would be important to consider how consumers in different cultural contexts view money, material goods, and status and how these views influence their consumption choices in the pursuit of happiness.

Self-Focused Spending Versus Other-Focused Spending

There is a growing stream of research that supports the distinction of happiness as self- or other-oriented, which can be achieved by building affect or meaning. People can increase their happiness not by buying things for themselves but by prosocial spending, that is, spending money on others such as donations to charities, gifts for friends and family, and so forth (Aknin et al., 2012, 2013; Dunn et al., 2008; W. Zhang et al., 2018). Spending money and time on activities that are social in nature and involve people who consumers enjoy being with will enhance levels of happiness (Aaker et al., 2011; Dunn et al., 2011).

Another aspect of prosocial spending involves a concern for larger social issues relating to consumption, such as the environment, sustainability, and ethical choices. Studies have focused on specific consumption behaviors like buying fair-trade products (e.g., De Pelsmacker et al., 2005), recycling and closely related behaviors (e.g., Thøgersen & Ölander, 2006), air travel (e.g., Higham et al., 2014), or a whole range of sustainable/ethical consumption behaviors (e.g., Ganglmair-Wooliscroft & Wooliscroft, 2016a, 2016b, 2019; Kaiser et al., 1999; Wooliscroft et al., 2014).

Aknin et al. (2013) found that prosocial spending was associated with greater happiness in 136 countries around the world, in poor and rich countries alike. Their two in-depth studies examining the causality of this relationship found that recalling a past instance of prosocial spending had a causal impact on happiness across countries that differed greatly in terms of wealth (namely, Canada, Uganda, and India), while "participants in both Canada and South Africa reported higher levels of positive affect after choosing a gift for someone else than after choosing something for themselves" (Aknin et al., 2013, p. 646). The relationship between happiness and spending on others seemed to hold up in various cultures (Aknin et al., 2013). Although the research participants from various cultures spent their money in different ways, their reflections on spending on others generated greater feelings of happiness.

Using an online sample of 360 Austrian respondents, Ganglmair-Wooliscroft and Wooliscroft (2019) found that eudaemonic well-being (measured via the Flourishing scale; Diener et al., 2010) correlates significantly with everyday ethical consumption behavior (eECB), measured via a battery of 30 environmental and social behaviors that range from "recycling or choosing local products, to having no car or avoiding mainstream supermarkets" (Ganglmair-Wooliscroft & Wooliscroft, 2019, p. 145). Hedonic well-being (measured via the Pleasure Orientation scale; Peterson et al., 2005) is negatively correlated with eECB.

In line with ethical consumption, another consumption choice could be related to voluntary simplicity (first coined by Gregg, 1936), that is, a way of living that focuses on reducing consumption and its effects on the environment (Breen Pierce, 2000; Elgin, 2010; Elgin & Mitchell, 1977). Various motivations have been identified to explain why people adopt the voluntary simplicity consumption lifestyle, including ecological responsibility, self-sufficiency, reduced materialism, spiritualism and increased control over one's life (Elgin & Mitchell, 1977), personal preference, health, financial savings, and environmental concerns (Alexander & Ussher, 2012). People who experienced higher levels of gratification of three psychological needs (needs for autonomy, competency, and relatedness) also tended to engage in more simplifying behavior (Rich et al., 2017). Research has shown that people who engaged in such simplified lifestyles reported being happier (Alexander & Ussher, 2012; Breen Pierce, 2000) and experiencing higher life satisfaction (Boujbel & d'Astous, 2012; Brown & Kasser, 2005; Rich et al., 2017).

A related stream of research examines happiness activities and their foci (self-focused vs. other-focused). *Happiness activities* refer to specific activities that, when performed on a regular basis, have been empirically shown to increase an individual's level of happiness (Lyubomirsky, 2011; Lyubomirsky et al., 2005). Some examples include expressing gratitude, cultivating optimism, living in the moment, performing acts of kindness, and working on one's goals (Lyubomirsky, 2001). Both self- and other-focused happiness activities raise consumers' levels of happiness as compared with a baseline. However, other-focused activities outperformed self-focused activities and had a greater propensity to build happiness (Sääksjärvi et al., 2017). By classifying happiness activities according to their foci and engaging in a mix of different activities, consumers may be able to better manage their levels of happiness.

It appears that consumers who engage in prosocial spending and other-oriented happiness are often concerned with higher order goals. This includes embracing values that are beyond the self. The "healthy values" perspective suggested that pursuing values that are aligned with growth and self-actualization could help to promote SWB (e.g., Bobowik et al., 2011; Sagiv & Schwartz, 2000). Self-transcendence is a higher order value that could encourage growth and self-actualization with a focus on others and beyond the self. Studies using the Schwartz's Portrait Values Questionnaire have shown that self-transcendence made a significant and positive contribution to psychological flourishing (Howell & Buro, 2015; Tan & Tambyah, 2020).

Sortheix and Lönnqvist (2014) used life satisfaction as their well-being indicator and found that self-transcendence was also positively related to this aspect of well-being.

The findings from research on the positive effects of prosocial spending and other-oriented activities on happiness are very much in line with research on the importance of social networks (e.g., family and friends) as an important pillar for well-being. Easterlin (2006) first documented that income, family relations, job, and health were the four key determinants of overall life satisfaction. Kapteyn et al. (2010) confirmed that satisfaction with life was positively associated with satisfaction within each of these four domains, with the highest weight given to family and social relations, followed by job, health, and income. Studies have found that satisfaction with interpersonal relationships are important for well-being, such as family life and marriage (Campbell, 1976) and friendships (Demir & Ozdemir, 2010). This could be because interpersonal relationships meet an individual's psychological needs and make one feel important to others (Demir et al., 2010).

IMPLICATIONS FOR FUTURE RESEARCH

In this book chapter, the theoretical premise for material versus experiential purchases was challenged through research studies that suggest that buying material possessions (particularly status goods) can also fulfill higher order desires (e.g., resolving SD) similar to buying experiences. Other studies also highlight the need to consider complementary societal and cultural factors to the underlying psychological processes of consuming for happiness. These factors include consumer characteristics (e.g., identity, nature of consumer goals) and cultural contexts (e.g., the importance of money, material goods, and status). These are all areas of research that can potentially be expanded.

Future studies can continue to interrogate additional consumer characteristics, for instance, the importance of specific goals such as consuming for purpose or meaning beyond shorter term gratification. Current studies have tended to focus on the measurable outcomes of life satisfaction and happiness (positive affect and negative affect). As there are multiple facets of well-being, outcomes such as psychological flourishing and the eudaemonic dimensions of purpose and meaning should be explored as well. These outcomes are often desired by consumers who are other-focused and pursue higher order values.

The influence of the cultural context cannot be overstated, as societal attitudes, beliefs, and norms about materialism and status are key influences on how money is spent. Some societies are also more self-focused. Research collaborations across cultural contexts or using respondents from multiple cultural backgrounds within a particular society would help to uncover more pertinent cultural drivers of consumption. For instance, research studies could explore how to evoke an other-focus in consumers, as prosocial spending has been shown to enhance the happiness levels of consumers. This might be especially useful for societies that are more self-focused.

As seen in the literature review, there are many types of consumption behaviors that would contribute to happiness. It is encouraging to note that there are many possible routes and opportunities to enhance happiness. However, there needs to be a strategic fit between happiness-enhancing consumption behaviors and personality, identity (e.g., ideal self), cultural values (e.g., the importance of social ties, materialism), and societal factors (e.g., stress-levels).

The effect of experiential purchases on happiness was smaller or nonexistent for material buyers compared with experiential buyers (J. W. Zhang et al., 2014). In a similar vein, prosocial spending did not help to increase the levels of happiness for consumers whose values did not reflect a concern for others (Hill & Howell, 2014). In terms of aligning one's values with eco-friendly consumption, Furchheim et al. (2020) hypothesized that consumers who conjointly endorsed green and materialistic values would experience stress, which would then be related to diminished satisfaction with life. They found that subjects who had high value conflicts between materialism (measured via Richins's, 2004, Material Value Scale) and green consumption (measured via the Green Consumption Values Scale; Haws et al., 2014) were more likely to experience elevated levels of stress (measured via the stress subscale of the Depression Anxiety Stress Scale; Lovibond & Lovibond, 1995), which in turn led to lowered satisfaction with life (measured via Diener et al.'s, 1985, Satisfaction With Life Scale). Thus, if there is a mismatch of values, there could be unintended and negative consequences for consumer well-being.

Matz et al. (2016) found that consumers who spent on products that better matched their personalities reported higher levels of life satisfaction. This theory of psychological fit can be applied to both material and experiential purchases (goods and services). Introverted consumers were happier with their books (a material purchase) rather than going to a bar (an experiential purchase). One possible marketing implication is that personal recommendation systems can guide consumers toward products that provide a closer fit for their personalities.

The sustainability of happiness-inducing consumption behaviors is also an important area for future research. To what extent would consumers be able to continue enacting and participating in happiness-enhancing consumption behaviors? As pointed out by Sääksjärvi et al. (2017), they had to test and curate a mix of self-focused and other-focused activities that would sustain the interest of their research subjects. These issues would likely be compounded by the rapid advent of digital technologies, which have created significant disruptions to the consumer's consumption experience. Besides empowering consumers to expertly make use of digital tools to easily research and compare products, place orders, and get products delivered to their doorstep, digital technology also helps to transform "users from passive to active consumers who create content about products and consumption experiences" (Duan & Dholakia, 2017, p. 404; see also Hutton, 2012). In a digital world where instant gratification is desired and boredom sets in quickly, how can researchers continue to identify activities that are viable in the long run? How will marketers capitalize on managing and implementing these activities for consumers?

Duan and Dholakia (2017) found that the practice of posting purchases on social media had a positive influence on consumers' happiness through the mediating roles of the perceived impact of these purchases on the self and interpersonal relationships. Consumers' posting of their purchases on social media can be a digital form of conspicuous consumption, and such postings can help consumers achieve goals of expressing self-identity and connecting with others. Future research studies could explore how the many evolving realms of digital, technology-enabled, and highly interactive consumption could possibly be tapped into to increase the happiness and engagement levels of consumers. In terms of harnessing technology, there are currently many apps that help consumers to sustain their happiness-enhancing consumption behaviors. In addition to the conventional apps for diets, exercise, and fitness, there are now more and more apps related to meditation, mindfulness, journaling, practices of kindness and gratitude, and so forth.

On a final note, it would be good to consider some of the ethical issues surrounding the issue of consuming for happiness. Consumption brings people together and can also drive people apart. While the linkages between consumption and happiness are acknowledged, we need to be aware that some consumers may not be able to participate in happiness-enhancing consumption behaviors for various reasons. Certain groups of consumers, including those who are cognitively, emotionally, or materially disadvantaged, may have limited or no access to these resources and opportunities. While consumption can help enhance happiness, socially responsible consumers would be careful to consider their goals as consumers and how their consumption choices influence those around them and the community in which they live.

REFERENCES

Aaker, J. L., Rudd, M., & Mogilner, C. (2011). If money does not make you happy, consider time. *Journal of Consumer Psychology, 21*(2), 126–130. https://doi.org/10.1016/j.jcps.2011.01.004

Ahuvia, A. C., & Wong, N. Y. (2002). Personality and values based materialism: Their relationship and origins. *Journal of Consumer Psychology, 12*(4), 389–402. https://doi.org/10.1207/S15327663JCP1204_10

Aknin, L. B., Barrington-Leigh, C. P., Dunn, E. W., Helliwell, J. F., Burns, J., Biswas-Diener, R., Kemeza, I., Nyende, P., Ashton-James, C. E., & Norton, M. I. (2013). Prosocial spending and well-being: Cross-cultural evidence for a psychological universal. *Journal of Personality and Social Psychology, 104*(4), 635–652. https://doi.org/10.1037/a0031578

Aknin, L. B., Dunn, E. W., & Norton, M. I. (2012). Happiness runs in a circular motion: Evidence for a positive feedback loop between prosocial spending and happiness. *Journal of Happiness Studies, 13*(2), 347–355. https://doi.org/10.1007/s10902-011-9267-5

Aknin, L.B., Wiwad, D., & Hanniball, K.B. (2018). Buying well-being: Spending behavior and happiness. *Social Personal Psychology Compass, 12*(5), 12386. https://doi.org/10.1111/spc3.12386

Alexander, S., & Ussher, S. (2012). The voluntary simplicity movement: A multi-national survey analysis in theoretical context. *Journal of Consumer Culture, 12*(1), 66–86. https://doi.org/10.1177/1469540512444019

Baumeister, R. F., Vohs, K. D., Aaker, J. L., & Garbinsky, E. N. (2013). Some key differences between a happy life and a meaningful life. *Journal of Positive Psychology, 8*(6), 505–516. https://doi.org/10.1080/17439760.2013.830764

Bobowik, M., Basabe, N., Páez, D., Jiménez, A., & Bilbao, M. Á. (2011). Personal values and well-being among Europeans, Spanish natives and immigrants to Spain: Does the culture matter? *Journal of Happiness Studies, 12*(3), 401–419. https://doi.org/10.1007/s10902-010-9202-1

Boujbel, L., & d'Astous, A. (2012). Voluntary simplicity and life satisfaction: Exploring the mediating role of consumption desires. *Journal of Consumer Behaviour, 11*(6), 487–494. https://doi.org/10.1002/cb.1399

Breen Pierce, L. (2000). *Choosing simplicity: Real people finding peace and fulfillment in a complex world*. Gallagher Press.

Brown, K. W., & Kasser, T. (2005). Are psychological and ecological well-being compatible? The role of values, mindfulness, and lifestyle. *Social Indicators Research, 74*(2), 349–368. https://doi.org/10.1007/s11205-004-8207-8

Burroughs, J. E., & Rindfleisch, A. (2002). Materialism and well-being: A conflicting values perspective. *Journal of Consumer Research, 29*(3), 348–370. https://doi.org/10.1086/344429

Campbell, A. (1976). Subjective measures of well-being. *American Psychologist, 31*(2), 117–124. https://doi.org/10.1037/0003-066X.31.2.117

Carter, T. J., & Gilovich, T. (2010). The relative relativity of material and experiential purchases. *Journal of*

Christopher, A. N., Saliba, L., & Deadmarsh, E. J. (2009). Materialism and well-being: The mediating effect of focus of control. *Personality and Individual Differences, 46*(7), 682–686. https://doi.org/10.1016/j.paid.2009.01.003

Deaton, A. (2013). Income, health, and well-being around the world: Evidence from the Gallup World Poll. In B. Frey (Ed.), *Recent developments in the economics of happiness* (pp. 342–361). Edward Elgar Publishing.

Demir, M., & Ozdemir, M. (2010). Friendship, need satisfaction and happiness. *Journal of Happiness Studies, 11*(2), 243–259. https://doi.org/10.1007/s10902-009-9138-5

De Pelsmacker, P., Driesen, L., & Rayp, G. (2005). Do consumers care about ethics? Willingness to pay for fair-trade coffee. *Journal of Consumer Affairs, 39*(2), 363–385. https://doi.org/10.1111/j.1745-6606.2005.00019.x

Diener, E. (1984). Subjective well-being. *Psychological Bulletin, 95*(3), 542–575. https://doi.org/10.1037/0033-2909.95.3.542

Diener, E. (2006). Guidelines for national indicators of subjective well-being and ill-being. *Journal of Happiness Studies, 7*(4), 397–404. https://doi.org/10.1007/s10902-006-9000-y

Diener, E., & Biswas-Diener, R. (2002). Will money increase subjective well-being? A literature review and guide to needed research. *Social Indicators Research, 57*(2), 119–169. https://doi.org/10.1023/A:1014411319119

Diener, E., & Biswas-Diener, R. (2008). *Happiness: Unlocking the mysteries of psychological wealth*. Blackwell Publishing. https://doi.org/10.1002/9781444305159

Diener, E., Emmons, R. A., Larsen, R. J., & Griffin, S. (1985). The satisfaction with life scale. *Journal of Personality Assessment, 49*(1), 71–75. https://doi.org/10.1207/s15327752jpa4901_13

Diener, E., & Oishi, S. (2000). Money and happiness: Income and subjective well-being across nations. In E. Diener (Ed.), *Culture and subjective well-being* (pp. 185–218). MIT Press.

Diener, E., Wirtz, D., Tov, W., Prieto, C. K., Choi, D., Oishi, S., & Biswas-Diener, R. (2010). New well-being measures: Short scales to assess flourishing and positive and negative feelings. *Social Indicators Research, 97*(2), 143–156. https://doi.org/10.1007/s11205-009-9493-y

Duan, J., & Dholakia, R. R. (2017). Posting purchases on social media increases happiness: The mediating roles of purchases' impact on self and interpersonal relationships. *Journal of Consumer Marketing, 34*(5), 404–413. https://doi.org/10.1108/JCM-07-2016-1871

Dunn, E. W., Aknin, L. B., & Norton, M. I. (2008). Spending money on others promotes happiness. *Science, 319*(5870), 1687–1688. https://doi.org/10.1126/science.1150952

Dunn, E. W., Gilbert, D. T., & Wilson, T. D. (2011). If money doesn't make you happy, then you probably aren't spending it right. *Journal of Consumer Psychology, 21*(2), 115–125. https://doi.org/10.1016/j.jcps.2011.02.002

Easterlin, R. A. (2006). Life cycle happiness and its sources: Intersections of psychology, economics, and demography. *Journal of Economic Psychology, 27*(4), 463–482. https://doi.org/10.1016/j.joep.2006.05.002

Elgin, D. (2010). *Voluntary simplicity* (2nd ed.). Harper Collins.

Elgin, D., & Mitchell, A. (1977). Voluntary simplicity. *Planning Review, 5*(6), 13–15. https://doi.org/10.1108/eb053820

Fournier, S., & Richins, M. L. (1991). Some theoretical and popular notions concerning materialism. *Journal of Social Behavior and Personality, 6*(6), 403–414.

Frank, R. H. (1985). The demand for unobservable and other nonpositional goods. *American Economic Review, 75*(1), 101–116. https://www.jstor.org/stable/1812706

Furchheim, P., Martin, C., & Morhart, F. (2020). Being green in a materialistic world: Consequences for subjective well-being. *Psychology and Marketing, 37*(1), 114–130. https://doi.org/10.1002/mar.21285

Ganglmair-Wooliscroft, A., & Wooliscroft, B. (2016a). Diffusion of innovation: The case of ethical tourism behavior. *Journal of Business Research, 69*(8), 2711–2720. https://doi.org/10.1016/j.jbusres.2015.11.006

Ganglmair-Wooliscroft, A., & Wooliscroft, B. (2016b). Ethical holiday behavior, wellbeing and orientations to happiness. *Applied Research in Quality of Life, 11*(1), 83–103. https://doi.org/10.1007/s11482-014-9356-9

Ganglmair-Wooliscroft, A., & Wooliscroft, B. (2019). Well-being and everyday ethical consumption. *Journal of Happiness Studies, 20*(1), 141–163. https://doi.org/10.1007/s10902-017-9944-0

Gilovich, T., Kumer, A., & Jampol, L. (2015). A wonderful life: Experiential consumption and the pursuit of happiness. *Journal of Consumer Psychology, 25*(1), 152–165. https://doi.org/10.1016/j.jcps.2014.08.004

Gregg, R. (1936). *The value of voluntary simplicity* (Pamphlet #3). Pendle Hill.

Haws, K. L., Winterich, K. P., & Naylor, R. W. (2014). Seeing the world through GREEN-tinted glasses: Green consumption values and responses to environmentally friendly products. *Journal of Consumer Psychology*, 24(3), 336–354. https://doi.org/10.1016/j.jcps.2013.11.002

Henrich, J., Heine, S. J., & Norenzayan, A. (2010). Beyond WEIRD: Towards a broad-based behavioral science. *Behavioral and Brain Sciences*, 33(2–3), 111–135. https://doi.org/10.1017/S0140525X10000725

Higgins, E. T. (1987). Self-discrepancy: A theory relating self and affect. *Psychological Review*, 94(3), 319–340. https://doi.org/10.1037/0033-295X.94.3.319

Higham, J. E., Cohen, S. A., & Cavaliere, C. T. (2014). Climate change, discretionary air travel, and the "Flyers' Dilemma." *Journal of Travel Research*, 53(4), 462–475. https://doi.org/10.1177/0047287513500393

Hill, G., & Howell, R. T. (2014). Moderators and mediators of pro-social spending and well-being: The influence of values and psychological need satisfaction. *Personality and Individual Differences*, 69, 69–74. https://doi.org/10.1016/j.paid.2014.05.013

Howell, A. J., & Buro, K. (2015). Measuring and predicting student well-being: Further evidence in support of the flourishing scale and the scale of positive and negative experiences. *Social Indicators Research*, 121(3), 903–915. https://doi.org/10.1007/s11205-014-0663-1

Hudders, L., & Pandelaere, M. (2012). The silver lining of materialism: The impact of luxury consumption on subjective well-being. *Journal of Happiness Studies*, 13(3), 411–437. https://doi.org/10.1007/s10902-011-9271-9

Hutton, G. (2012). *Six major consumer trends in social media*. UM Social Media Communication Agency. https://www.shellypalmer.com/2012/07/six-major-consumer-trends-in-social-media/

Kaiser, F. G., Wölfing, S., & Fuhrer, U. (1999). Environmental attitude and ecological behavior. *Journal of Environmental Psychology*, 19(1), 1–19. https://doi.org/10.1006/jevp.1998.0107

Kapteyn, A., Smith, J. P., & van Soest, A. (2010). Life satisfaction. In E. Diener (Ed.), *International differences in well-being* (pp. 70–104). Oxford University Press. https://doi.org/10.1093/acprof:oso/9780199732739.003.0004

Kashdan, T. B., & Breen, W. E. (2007). Materialism and diminished well-being: Experiential avoidance as a mediating mechanism. *Journal of Social and Clinical Psychology*, 26(5), 521–539. https://doi.org/10.1521/jscp.2007.26.5.521

Li, J. J., & Su, C. (2007). How face influences consumption. *International Journal of Market Research*, 49(2), 237–256. https://doi.org/10.1177/147078530704900207

Lovibond, P. F., & Lovibond, S. H. (1995). The structure of negative emotional states: Comparison of the Depression Anxiety Stress Scale (DASS) with the Beck Depression and Anxiety Inventories. *Behaviour Research and Therapy*, 33(3), 335–343. https://doi.org/10.1016/0005-7967(94)00075-U

Lyubomirsky, S. (2001). Why are some people happier than others? The role of cognitive and motivational processes in well-being. *American Psychologist*, 56(3), 239–249. https://doi.org/10.1037/0003-066X.56.3.239

Lyubomirsky, S. (2011). Hedonic adaptation to positive and negative experiences. In S. Folkman (Ed.), *Oxford handbook of stress, health, and coping* (pp. 200–224). Oxford University Press.

Lyubomirsky, S., Sheldon, K. M., & Schkade, D. (2005). Pursuing happiness: The architecture of sustainable change. *Review of General Psychology*, 9(2), 111–131. https://doi.org/10.1037/1089-2680.9.2.111

Matz, S. C., Gladstone, J. J., & Stillwell, D. (2016). Money buys happiness when spending fits our personality. *Psychological Science*, 27(5), 715–725. https://doi.org/10.1177/0956797616635200

Miesen, H. (2009, June 11–13). *Love is all you need: Social relatedness needs, materialism and subjective well-being* [Paper presentation]. Happiness and Social Relatedness Goods Conference, Venice, Italy.

Myers, D. G., & Diener, E. (1995). Who is happy? *Psychological Science*, 6(1), 10–19. https://doi.org/10.1111/j.1467-9280.1995.tb00298.x

Nicolao, L., Irwin, J. R., & Goodman, J. K. (2009). Happiness for sale: Do experiential purchases make consumers happier than material purchases? *Journal of Consumer Research*, 36(2), 188–198. https://doi.org/10.1086/597049

Peterson, C., Park, N., & Seligman, M. E. (2005). Orientations to happiness and life satisfaction: The full life versus the empty life. *Journal of Happiness Studies*, 6(1), 25–41. https://doi.org/10.1007/s10902-004-1278-z

Powdthavee, N., Burkhauser, R. V., & De Neve, J. (2017). Top incomes and human well-being: Evidence from the Gallup World Poll. *Journal of Economic Psychology*, 62, 246–257. https://doi.org/10.1016/j.joep.2017.07.006

Rich, S. A., Hanna, S., & Wright, B. J. (2017). Simply satisfied: The role of psychological need satisfaction in the life satisfaction of voluntary simplifiers. *Journal of Happiness Studies*, 18(1), 89–105. https://doi.org/10.1007/s10902-016-9718-0

Richins, M. L. (2004). The material values scale: Measurement properties and development of a short form. *Journal of Consumer Research*, 31(1), 209–219. https://doi.org/10.1086/383436

Rosenzweig, E., & Gilovich, T. (2012). Buyer's remorse or missed opportunity? Differential regrets for material and experiential purchases. *Journal of Personality and Social Psychology, 102*(2), 215–223. https://doi.org/10.1037/a0024999

Ryan, R. M., & Deci, E. L. (2000). Self-determination theory and the facilitation of intrinsic motivation, social development, and well-being. *American Psychologist, 55*(1), 68–78. https://doi.org/10.1037/0003-066X.55.1.68

Ryan, R. M., & Deci, E. L. (2001). To be happy or to be self-fulfilled: A review of research on hedonic and eudaimonic well-being. In S. Fiske (Ed.), *Annual review of psychology* (Vol. 52, pp. 141–166). Annual Reviews, Inc.

Sääksjärvi, M., Hellén, K., & Desmet, P. (2017). The "you and I" of happiness: Investigating the long-term impact of self-and other-focused happiness-enhancing activities. *Psychology and Marketing, 34*(6), 623–630. https://doi.org/10.1002/mar.21010

Sagiv, L., & Schwartz, S. H. (2000). Value priorities and subjective well-being: Direct relations and congruity effects. *European Journal of Social Psychology, 30*(2), 177–198. https://doi.org/10.1002/(SICI)1099-0992(200003/04)30:2<177::AID-EJSP982>3.0.CO;2-Z

Schütte, H. (1998). *Consumer behavior in Asia.* NYU Press. https://doi.org/10.1007/978-1-349-14862-2

Seligman, M. (2012). *Flourish: A visionary new understanding of happiness and well-being.* Altraria Book.

Sengupta, N. K., Osborne, D., Houkamau, C. A., Hoverd, W. J., Wilson, M. S., & Halliday, L. M. (2012). How much happiness does money buy? Income and subjective well-being in New Zealand. *New Zealand Journal of Psychology, 41*(2), 21–34.

Sortheix, F. M., & Lönnqvist, J. E. (2014). Personal value priorities and life satisfaction in Europe: The moderating role of socioeconomic development. *Journal of Cross-Cultural Psychology, 45*(2), 282–299. https://doi.org/10.1177/0022022113504621

Tan, S. J., & Tambyah, S. K. (2020). Values and well-being in Singapore. In G. J. Rich, J. L. Jaafar, & D. Barron (Eds.), *Psychology in Southeast Asia: Sociocultural, clinical, and health perspectives* (pp. 102–115). Routledge.

Thøgersen, J., & Olander, F. (2006). To what degree are environmentally beneficial choices reflective of a general conservation stance? *Environment and Behavior, 38*(4), 550–569. https://doi.org/10.1177/0013916505283832

Van Boven, L., & Gilovich, T. (2003). To do or to have? That is the question. *Journal of Personality and Social Psychology, 85*(6), 1193–1202. https://doi.org/10.1037/0022-3514.85.6.1193

Veenhoven, R. (2012). Happiness also known as "life satisfaction" and "subjective well-being." In K. C. Land, A. C. Michalos, & M. J. Sirgy (Eds.), *Handbook of social indicators and quality of life research* (pp. 63–77). Springer.

Wang, H., Cheng, Z., & Smyth, R. (2019). Consumption and happiness. *Journal of Development Studies, 55*(1), 120–136. https://doi.org/10.1080/00220388.2017.1371294

Wooliscroft, B., Ganglmair-Wooliscroft, A., & Noone, A. (2014). The hierarchy of ethical consumption behavior: The case of New Zealand. *Journal of Macromarketing, 34*(1), 57–72. https://doi.org/10.1177/0276146713508560

Yu, Y., Jing, F., Su, C. T., Zhou, N., & Nguyen, B. (2016). Impact of material vs. experiential purchase types on happiness: The moderating role of self-discrepancy. *Journal of Consumer Behaviour, 15*(6), 571–579. https://doi.org/10.1002/cb.1598

Zhang, J. W., Howell, R. T., Caprariello, P. A., & Guevarra, D. A. (2014). Damned if they do, damned if they don't: Material buyers are not happier from material or experiential consumption. *Journal of Research in Personality, 50*, 71–83. https://doi.org/10.1016/j.jrp.2014.03.007

Zhang, W., Chen, M., Xie, Y., & Zhao, Z. (2018). Prosocial spending and subjective well-being: The recipient perspective. *Journal of Happiness Studies, 19*(8), 2267–2281. https://doi.org/10.1007/s10902-017-9918-2

Zhou, N., & Belk, R. W. (2004). Chinese consumer readings of global and local advertising appeals. *Journal of Advertising, 33*(3), 63–76. https://doi.org/10.1080/00913367.2004.10639169

Part VI

Businesses Use Psychology to Carry Out Functions

CHAPTER 29

OMNICHANNEL RETAILING: A CONSUMER PERSPECTIVE

Peter C. Verhoef, Koert van Ittersum, P. K. Kannan, and Jeff Inman

Three decades ago, consumers had limited choices of how to search for and purchase products and services. The local brick-and-mortar store or branch was very dominant, and beyond that some consumers used home-shopping channels, such as catalogues, telephone, and home-shopping television. While home-shopping channels, and especially the catalog business, were significant back in the day, in general, a relatively small share of consumers actually used these channels. For example, Darian (1987) found that housewives, part-time female workers with preschool children, and households in the middle-income groups were most likely to use home-shopping channels. Furthermore, catalog business was typically prevalent in noncity areas, such as the Midwest United States.

While catalogs never vanished, and actually may be making a comeback (Zhang, 2020), with the advent of the internet in the early 1990s, the online channel has entered consumer lives. In the early days, some specific products, such as CDs, books, and software, could be purchased online, but only a small specific segment of consumers had started searching and purchasing online (e.g., Verhoef & Langerak, 2001). Since then, the online channel has become a dominant channel in many markets and consumers have adopted it widely. Consumers nowadays routinely search for and purchase goods and services online. A recent study of Herhausen et al. (2019) showed that 80% of the North American market use a combination of online and offline channels, implying that only about 20% rely solely on offline stores.

As a result, Alphabet and Amazon have become among the most valuable firms in the world. Such development not only occurred in Western markets but in Asia as well, with online retail firms like Alibaba. The explosive growth of the online channel has dictated that multichannel retailing has become the norm rather than the exception from both a firm and customer perspective. Firms that fail to be successful handling multiple channels face grave difficulties. For example, recently one of the oldest travel agency firms, United Kingdom-based Thomas Cook, did not survive the fierce competition from digital players such as Booking.com, Tripadvisor, and Expedia. There will be more firms facing similar problems as digital firms develop aggressive growth strategies that severely affect existing businesses (e.g., Reinartz et al., 2019; Verhoef & Bijmolt, 2019; Verhoef et al., 2021). Consumer behavior is also changing drastically. The context of consumer behavior has moved from single channel to multichannel to omnichannel environments (e.g., Herhausen et al., 2019; Konuş et al., 2008). Omnichannel environments are characterized by a synergetic and complementary set of channels, aimed at optimizing the customer experience across channels

We thank Scott Neslin for providing very thoughtful comments on the first version of this chapter.
https://doi.org/10.1037/0000262-029
APA Handbook of Consumer Psychology, L. R. Kahle (Editor-in-Chief)
Copyright © 2022 by the American Psychological Association. All rights reserved.

and the performance over channels, as opposed to multichannel environments, which are characterized by a more independent set of channels.

In this chapter, we provide a psychological perspective on consumer behavior in an evolving digital environment. Prior work in this area has mainly considered a retailing or customer-management perspective but rarely has taken a consumer perspective with a focus on psychological aspects of this behavior. A recent exception is the study by Lee et al. (2018), which focuses on the shopping journey.

We start this chapter with a short discussion on some definitions and developments to make the reader familiar with specific terms in multichannel and omnichannel retailing. We then introduce a consumer-focused omnichannel model. Next, we address the drivers of channel choice decisions, multichannel and omnichannel segmentation studies, and the consequences of omnichannel behavior. We subsequently focus on the consumers' path to purchase and customer journey and extend the focus with an elaborate discussion on how new digital technologies are shaping the consumers' buying process. We conclude with a brief research agenda for consumer research in this emerging area.

MULTICHANNEL AND OMNICHANNEL RETAILING

Multichannel retailing started to attract attention in the early 2000s after the increasing popularity of online retailing. Not surprisingly, the main question being asked by traditional retail firms was whether they should add an online channel to complement their physical operations or whether online firms should add a retail presence. From a consumer perspective there were many studies on the drivers of online channel preferences and choice (e.g., Ha & Stoel, 2009; Verhoef & Langerak, 2001). The concept of a *multichannel customer* emerged as research investigated differences between multi- and single-channel customers, specifically focusing on purchase outcomes and customer profitability (Kushwaha & Shankar, 2013; Venkatesan et al., 2007; J. Xu et al., 2014).

The conceptual foundations for multichannel retailing are discussed in Neslin et al. (2006). This foundation focuses on customer behavior, with a *channel* as "a customer contact point, or a medium through which the firm and the customer interact" (Neslin et al., 2006, p. 96). In their definition of a channel, Neslin et al. emphasized the two-way exchange between customers and the firm through a channel. Next, they defined *multichannel customer management* as "the design, deployment, coordination, and evaluation of channels to enhance customer value through effective customer acquisition, retention, and development" (p. 96). In this seminal multichannel paper, the authors proposed a customer-focused model including multiple phases in the buying process from search to purchase to after-sales in which customers can use multiple channels. Following this paper, multiple studies have considered how and why customers use these channels in the buying process, how they migrate between channels (e.g., Polo & Sese, 2016; Valentini et al., 2011; Verhoef et al., 2007), and what the effects are on purchase behavior outcomes, such as loyalty (e.g., Ansari et al., 2008). For in-depth discussions on the multichannel literature, we refer to Neslin and Shankar (2009), Verhoef (2012), and Liu et al. (2019).

To allow for a more synergistic approach, the omnichannel perspective has extended the scope of multichannel retailing by considering multiple touchpoints during the customer journey and also focusing more on experiential outcomes (e.g., Herhausen et al., 2015, 2019). Verhoef et al. (2015) defined *omnichannel management* as the "synergetic management of the numerous available channels and customer touchpoints, in such a way that the customer experience across channels and the performance over channels is optimized" (p. 3). They extended multichannel retailing by focusing more on touchpoints, which may also include more one-way directed communication channels impacting the customer in multiple phases in the buying process. They also focused strongly on the customer experience, thereby emphasizing a more seamless experiences across channels and touchpoints in the customer journey (e.g., Baxendale et al., 2015; Homburg et al., 2015; Lemon & Verhoef, 2016). To achieve this, a more integrated way of managing channels is required. In multichannel retailing, channels are frequently managed independently as single channels offered next to each other by a retailer. In contrast, omnichannel retailers manage them in an integrated way, thereby allowing consumers to use a combination of channels and/or a single channel to optimize their experience (Herhausen et al., 2019).

Approaching the customer journey from an omnichannel perspective has encouraged research into the role of specific digital technologies and mobile devices, such as artificial intelligence (AI), dynamic AI pricing tools, augmented and virtual reality (AR and VR), facial recognition tools, and mobile apps. Devices are thus different digital tools to connect with the firms during the buying process that vary on dimensions, such as portability, screen size, and risk. For example, de Haan et al. (2018) considered how moving from a mobile device to a more fixed device (i.e., personal computer) affects purchase behavior. Recently, researchers have also started to investigate how mobile apps affect purchase outcomes and firm value (e.g., Boyd et al., 2019; Gu & Kannan, 2019; van Heerde et al., 2019).

A CONSUMER-FOCUSED OMNICHANNEL ORIENTATION

We adopt a consumer perspective on omnichannel retailing. This implies that we focus on consumer choices and resulting behavior of consumers in their customer journey. Building on the process model of multichannel retailing, Neslin et al. (2006) and Lemon and Verhoef (2016) discussed a customer-experience model in which the customer journey starts with search and ends with after-purchase experiences, consumption, and disposal. The shift to the consumer-oriented omnichannel orientation focuses on ways consumers are affected by brand-owned, partner-owned, customer-owned, and social/external touchpoints.

Contrary to existing multichannel models, which adopt a rather classic and sequential model of consumer behavior, the proposed consumer-focused omnichannel orientation allows consumers to move through different stages in the journey but also to skip phases, such as search, or to move between phases. Moreover, current models tend to ignore the role of touchpoints to stir up the purchase process by triggering consumer demand and uncovering consumer needs. Second, they ignore that within channels and touchpoints, consumers also have a kind of shopper journey (e.g., Lee et al., 2018). Third, these models ignore the role of technologies and mobile devices. Mobile devices, for example, have become extremely important in the customer journey, and consumers can switch between devices in their journey (e.g., de Haan et al., 2018). Moreover, mobile devices can be used within specifically offline channels to digitally search for alternatives, as well as for shopping support and promotion tools (e.g., Fong et al., 2015; Gensler et al., 2017; Rapp et al., 2015).

We present our consumer-focused omnichannel model in Figure 29.1. In our model, we posit that consumers move through multiple phases from need recognition to after-sales. As noted, prior models tend to emphasize the role of channels less in the need recognition phase and immediately start with the search phase (e.g., Lemon & Verhoef, 2016; Neslin et al., 2006). Further, we explicitly acknowledge that marketing activities through these touchpoints may alter consumer behavior. The first aspect we consider is triggering the recognition of unmet needs. Social media channels may be considered relevant in this regard. Firms can inform existing customers about offerings, trigger unmet needs with the promise of immediate social approval, and stimulate potential customers to move to the purchase phase, often skipping the search and shopping phases.

Next, consumers move to a search phase to resolve the need. In this search phase, most consumers can use digital, offline (i.e., store), and social touchpoints. Notably, consumers can switch between these touchpoints in their search behavior and/or use them simultaneously. A simultaneous use would be that within a store, consumers search for information and at the same time use their mobile device to find more information and compare offers (e.g., Rapp et al., 2015).

Importantly, we add an intervening phase where we focus on the shopping (or browsing) behavior within a touchpoint. Within touchpoints,

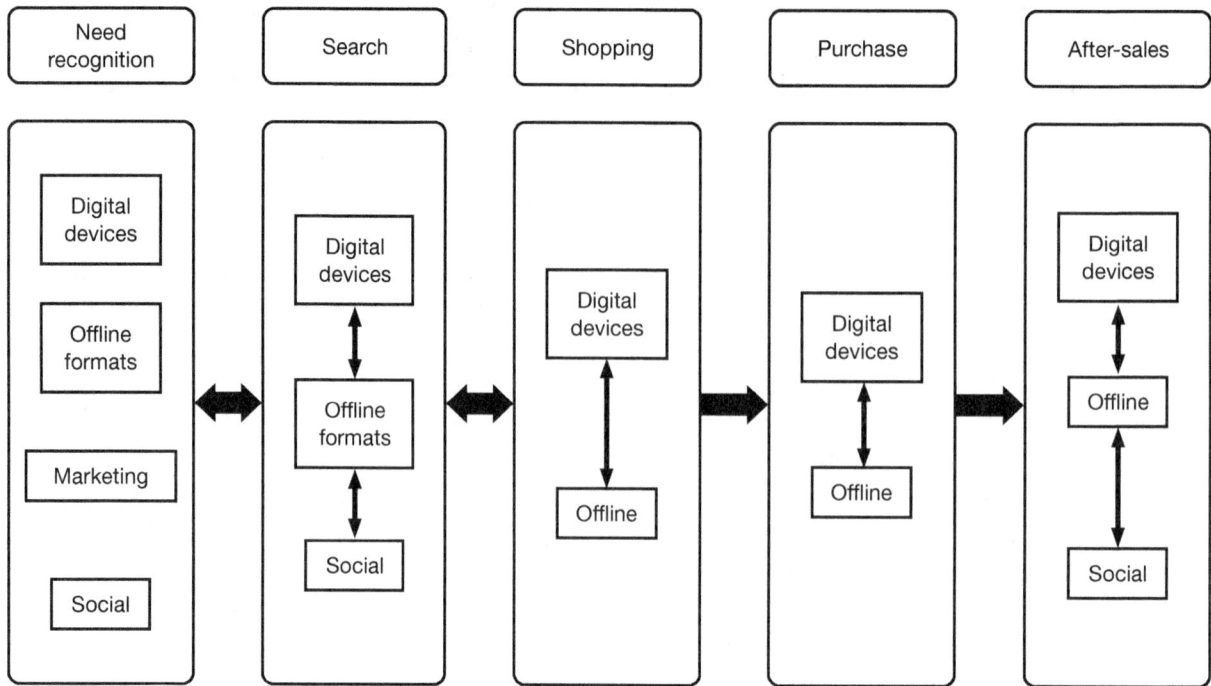

FIGURE 29.1. Consumer-focused omnichannel journey.

consumers also have their journey. One could argue whether this is indeed a next phase or a kind of in-depth treatment of the search phase. In this model, we consider it as a next phase, as consumers enter a specific channel and then start their shopping within a store either online or offline. The shopping phase distinguishes itself from the search and purchase phase in that the prepurchase search for product information has ended and consumers have narrowed their consideration set to a number of alternatives in the channel and move toward the actual purchase. Further, after entering the channel and before actually purchasing a product, the consumer may browse some more, look for promotional opportunities, receive reinforcement from reviews, watch an instruction video, and do some final price, service, shipping, and delivery-condition comparisons across multiple channels and stores, both online and offline, bringing the consumer back into the search phase. A special case in point is in both online and offline grocery shopping, where most of the channel experience depends on the shopping phase. The relevance of the shopping phase is corroborated by the growing literature on the role of digital shopping devices (i.e., mobile devices, smart shopping carts, shop bots) that guide and inform consumers during the shopping phase within a channel and sometimes offer concrete advice or recommendations (e.g., van Ittersum et al., 2013).

Next, consumers move to the purchase phase where they use one or more channels for their transactions. Many early researchers assumed that consumers can use only one channel for purchase (Verhoef et al., 2007). However, nowadays consumers can, for example, buy online and pay and pick up in the store in so-called Click & Collect formats (Gielens & Gijsbrechts, 2018). Also, within a store one can use digital tools to make a purchase.

Finally, the journey concludes with the after-sales phase, where service is provided to consumers if required when consumers are using the product and face problems with using the product. Multiple touchpoints can be used for this stage, and we observe an increasing use of digital tools, such as chatting and automated response forms, as well as social media. AI technology is becoming important here to determine support needs of individual customers. Note that traditional information on packages but also websites can be used in the after-sales phase. Furthermore, customers may be enticed to share their experiences in relevant social media channels (and receive a discount from the firm or the approval of their peers), which in turn may trigger the recognition of unmet needs among potential customers. In all the considered phases, marketing plays a role, which we ignore in this process model, as it focuses on the shopping process and not how it is influenced.

OMNICHANNEL CONSUMER DECISIONS

During the customer journey, as depicted in Figure 29.1, consumers constantly choose which (combination of) channels to use. There has been ample attention in extant research on drivers of channel choices and specifically on the decision to use the online channel. Recently, we see an increasing attention on acceptance and usage of new digital technologies and mobile devices. Moreover, researchers have studied the use of channels and touchpoints across the distinct phases in the omnichannel journey. Therein, the focus has been mainly on the identification of specific consumer groups or segments, as well as understanding specific so-called research-shopping patterns (e.g., Gensler et al., 2017; Verhoef et al., 2007).

Channel Decisions

Based on prior research, we distinguish six factors that can be considered as determinants of channel choices: (a) channel attributes, (b) marketing efforts, (c) social influences, (d) contextual factors, (e) consumer characteristics, and (f) channel experiences.[1]

Studies of online channel choice have addressed the effects of general channel attributes using theoretical models, such as the technology acceptance model and the theory of reasoned action. These studies focus on ease of use, usefulness, enjoyment, risk, and trust as drivers of consumers' channel adoption (e.g., Verhoef & Langerak, 2001; Vijayasarathy, 2004). More recent studies have extended these factors and considered capabilities and functions of (online) channels, including security and privacy (e.g., Ha & Stoel, 2009), service quality (e.g., Kollmann et al., 2012), information quality (e.g., Noble et al., 2005), the speed of purchase and response time (e.g., Verhoef et al., 2007), convenience (e.g., Kollmann et al., 2012), system accessibility (e.g., Lin & Lu, 2000), website design (e.g., Montoya-Weiss et al., 2003), and price (e.g., Teerling & Huizingh, 2005).

Marketing efforts may drive consumers to specific channels (Dholakia et al., 2005; Montaguti et al., 2016). Marketing efforts indeed have an effect on channel choices in such a way that digital efforts induce consumers to move to a digital channel, whereas standard offline methods tend to steer customers to offline channels. For example, Ansari et al. (2008) showed that marketing communication through email accelerates customer migration to online channels, while marketing communication through catalogs promotes customers' use of catalogs. There is also some evidence for what we call cross-channel effects. This implies that digital marketing efforts (i.e., banner ads) may drive customers to the store (e.g., Lobschat et al., 2017), while offline efforts may also have effects on online purchase behavior (e.g., Lesscher et al., 2020).

Customers' channel choices are also affected by their interaction with their social networks (Choi et al., 2010). Bilgicer et al. (2015) showed that a customer's network influences the adoption of a new online channel. This occurs because these customers live in a consumer's proximity, and consumers may imitate their behavior. Social media nowadays may also induce more social-influence effects. Research also suggests that social-influence effects on channel adoption decrease over time (Choi et al., 2010), which is also observed for other adoption decisions (Risselada et al., 2014).

Situational factors cover environmental conditions and temporal issues. Environmental conditions influencing channel choice refer to the environment in which consumers access a specific channel, "together with any complicating factors arising from the intervening technologies" (Nicholson et al., 2002, p. 134). They include weather, mobility, distance, crowdedness, and visible configurations of channels. For example, customers with limited time are more likely to purchase online

---

[1] This section is partially based on an earlier overview written by one of the authors of this chapter: Liu et al. (2018, pp. 16–21).

(Konuş et al., 2008; Melis et al., 2016). Studies also suggest that holidays and event proximity, such as date relative to payday, can affect customers' channel choices (e.g., Nicholson et al., 2002; van Nierop et al., 2011; R. J. H. Wang et al., 2015).

It is important to note that cross-cultural factors that affect both social networks and situational factors can have a significant impact on customers' omnichannel behavior. Nam and Kannan (2020) argued that the perceived switching costs are higher in high-uncertainty-avoidance cultures such as Japan, Western Europe, and Latin American countries and, therefore, customers in such cultures are less likely to switch to different channels (Pick & Eisend, 2016). Focusing on online channels, this reluctance implies that despite the lack of channel lock-in costs for online retailers as compared with offline retailers, the lock-in costs in high-uncertainty-avoidance cultures are higher than in low-uncertainty-avoidance cultures. Additionally, individualist and collectivist cultures influence multichannel shopping behaviors. Customers in collectivist cultures focus more on relationship building, interpersonal communication, and social exchanges, and thus social networks can play a more important role in influencing channel decisions than in individualist cultures. Similarly, in individualist cultures, customers start a relationship when a retailer provides a convenient service but are ready to leave the retailer's channel if it becomes less convenient. In collectivist cultures, however, depth of the social relationship with a retailer enhances word of mouth and customer loyalty (Pick & Eisend, 2016). Consequently, in collectivist cultures, customers are less likely to switch channels during the journey (Nam & Kannan, 2020).

Several psychographic characteristics are very relevant as antecedents of channel choices. Generally innovative consumers tend to explore and use new products and thus also new channels (e.g., Arts et al., 2015). Online self-efficacy, defined as "a consumer's self-assessment of his/her capabilities to shop online" (Vijayasarathy, 2004, p. 751), can improve consumers' preference for online shopping (O'Cass & Fenech, 2003). Bruner and Kumar (2005) showed that consumers who are more predisposed toward a visual model have a higher tendency to adopt online channels, as they tend to process information by mental imagery and are more attracted by visual cues. Price sensitivity is a relevant psychographic variable. Price-sensitive consumers tend to choose online channels more often (Degeratu et al., 2000; Lynch & Ariely, 2000). Goal-oriented consumers are also more likely to use online channels, while experiential-oriented consumers are more likely to use physical stores (Pauwels & Neslin, 2015). Next to psychographics, there is ample evidence that sociodemographics are correlated with online channel use. Generally, there is a negative relationship between age and online channel choice (e.g., De Keyser et al., 2015; Narang & Shankar, 2019; van Nierop et al., 2011; Xue et al., 2011). Some studies report that male customers are more inclined to use new channels than female customers (Li et al., 2016; Narang & Shankar, 2019; Venkatesan et al., 2007). Education and income are also positively related to online channel use (e.g., Kumar & Venkatesan, 2005; van Nierop et al., 2011). Larger families tend to prefer online shopping (Ansari et al., 2008; Kushwaha & Shankar, 2013). Finally, store distance matters. Customers who live far away from the closest physical store are more likely to purchase through digital channels (Melis et al., 2016; Venkatesan et al., 2007; K. Wang & Goldfarb, 2017).

The final factor influencing channel decisions is channel experience. There is ample evidence that consumers tend to use the same channel over time (e.g., Gensler et al., 2012). This is also referred to as state-dependence, and from a psychological perspective this can also be viewed as behavior based on habits (Verplanken & Aarts, 1999), which Cambro-Fierro et al. (2020) referred to as channel habits. A consumer accustomed to a physical supermarket is more likely to continue to shop there if nothing dramatically changes. Interestingly, store closures due to the COVID-19 crisis are forcing consumers to move massively toward shopping online. Whether and which consumers revert back to their pre-COVID-19 shopping patterns are intriguing research questions. We finally acknowledge that the effect and relevance of each of the first five factors will in part be determined by the channel knowledge and experience the customer has. Finally, it is worth noting that channel knowledge and experience are dynamic and evolve over the journey and over time.

Multi- and Omnichannel Segments

Within marketing segmentation, it is of crucial importance to understand markets and to classify consumers in groups that can be targeted differently.[2] In the multichannel literature there has been ample attention to segmentation, based on the multichannel behavior of customers. Konuş et al. (2008) suggested the existence of multiple multichannel segments, where there are two multichannel-oriented segments and a store segment focusing on a single channel. One of these multichannel segments can be considered as a true multichannel segment, preferring multiple channels for search and purchase of products. The other segment has a multichannel orientation but in general does not have a strong preference for multiple channels.

De Keyser et al. (2015) replicated the study of Konuş et al. (2008) and extended it by also including the phone channel and adding the after-sales phase. They identified two multichannel segments that encompass 45% of a firm's customers and three single-channel focused segments (web, store, and phone). These segments mainly vary on loyalty and revenue. The call-center and the store-focus segment are the most loyal, while the multichannel segments have the highest revenue. In a recent study, Herhausen et al. (2019) segmented customers based on the customer journey, thereby including a wide range of touchpoints and also including mobile devices. They identified five distinct segments, analyzing data collected in 2013 and 2016 that strongly differ in the use of the number and type of touchpoints. The first segment consists of heavy-touchpoint users who use, on average, seven touchpoints. Replicating the findings of Konuş et al. (2008) and Montaguti et al. (2020), the second segment consists of consumers who largely eschew online purchasing and prefer to use the store as their major touchpoint or channel. In contrast, a third segment is strongly web focused, searching and purchasing on the web only. Herhausen et al. identified a fourth segment of consumers with lengthy journeys who shop around online and also buy online. Finally, they found a fifth segment of web-rooming consumers who search online and buy offline. Interestingly, Herhausen et al. analyzed data at two points in time, before and after mobile device usage became prevalent. Their findings showed that mobile devices are mainly added to the journey in specific segments (i.e., the heavy-touchpoint user segment).

Research Shopping

Verhoef et al. (2007) were one of the first to discuss research shopping. In their study, research shopping implied that a consumer uses one channel for searching and the other channel for purchase. By defining research shopping this way, they clearly separate the information-gathering phase from the purchase phase. Information gathering is done in a separate channel than where the purchase occurs. The main form of research shopping they identified was from online search to offline purchase. Recently, retail practice distinguishes two forms of research shopping behavior: showrooming and web-rooming. *Showrooming* implies that a consumer searches in-store and purchases online (e.g., Gensler et al., 2017; Rapp et al., 2015). *Web-rooming* implies that a consumer does the opposite, searching online and purchasing offline. Verhoef et al. identified attribute differences, channel lock-in, and cross-channel synergies as three mechanisms that explain research shopping behavior. Some channels, such as the internet, may have an attribute advantage in terms of search (i.e., easy to search) but a disadvantage in terms of purchase (i.e., higher risk), thus leading to internet search and in-store purchase. The lack of lock-in implies that a channel does not have the stickiness to keep customers within the customer journey through both search and purchase. Rapp et al. (2015) and Fassnacht et al. (2019) showed that salespersons within a store are important to create such stickiness within the store channel.

The cross-channel synergy mechanism implies that consumers experience a synergy for using a

---

[2]This part is to some extent based on a recent overview on customer experience by one of the coauthors: Verhoef (2020).

different channel search and purchase because using different channels for search and purchase allows them to get more value. These synergies go beyond attribute differences, as the attribute differences focus on the fact that one channel is better for search (i.e., more convenience), while the other channel is better for purchase (i.e., lower risk). By using two channels for search and purchase, synergies are achieved above these differences by achieving more value through actively benefiting from these differences. For example, consumers are able to negotiate better prices in the store if they search online, or from a psychological point of view they might experience smart-shopper feelings (Schindler, 1998). Moreover, customers might also enjoy shopping across channels during the buying process. Konuş et al. (2008) showed that consumers in the enthusiastic multichannel segment indeed have a higher shopping enjoyment. Flavián et al. (2019) showed that web-rooming consumers experience stronger smart-shopper feelings than showrooming consumers and thus also achieve stronger purchase satisfaction. In a related study, Flavián et al. (2020) showed that web-roomers additionally have greater perceptions of time/effort savings and of making the right purchase. Furthermore, web-rooming leads to higher personal attribution than showrooming, meaning that consumers feel responsible and in control of their purchase outcomes.

Showrooming has also gained strong attention in the recent omnichannel literature. Gensler et al. (2017) studied determinants of showrooming behavior. Not surprisingly, showrooming is more likely when there is a substantially lower price online than offline or if consumers expect higher price dispersion online than offline, which implies more opportunities to find lower prices. Furthermore, expected positive quality gains of buying online also lead to more showrooming. However, the authors also showed that in-store service factors are important. A long waiting time within the store drives consumers to shop online. Gensler et al. found limited evidence for the importance of specific psychographic characteristics, such as shopping mavenism. Interestingly, Schneider and Zielke (2020) recently identified four showrooming segments that differ in retailer loyalty, usage of in-store information, devices used, and place and time of the online purchase. They further showed that loyal versus competitive showroomers differ in psychographic variables, such as price consciousness, desire for social contact, and guilt during showrooming.

One important issue is how retailers can cope with the often-considered destructive behavior of showrooming (Daunt & Harris, 2017). Rapp et al. (2015) and Fassnacht et al. (2019) studied how store sales employees should psychologically deal with this type of behavior, as customers purchasing elsewhere can be seen as a rejection of their service. Mehra et al. (2018) argued that stores can limit showrooming using price matching guarantees or by having an exclusive brands or offerings that are not sold at competing stores. Given the presumed negative consequences for retailer profits of both showrooming and web-rooming, we expect that more studies will focus on how to circumvent these types of behavior.

It would be interesting to observe and investigate whether web-rooming will remain prevalent in the coming years or whether it will vanish as, for example, online retail becomes more dominant and many aspects of offline stores can be found online as well.

Consequences of Multichannel Shopping

Many researchers have found that consumers are shifting from single- to multichannel retailers (e.g., Kumar & Venkatesan, 2005). This is of extreme importance for single-channel firms, especially online-only firms, and explains why so many of them are also establishing an offline presence. Amazon and Whole Foods are major examples, as well as Apple, Google, and Microsoft, with their offline stores. Understanding what multichannel consumers want is of course also critical for retailers who already offer both an online and offline channel. Customers may switch buying behavior across these channels, and firms may also create cross-channels synergies across these channels (e.g., Emrich et al., 2015). In a cross-sectional analysis, Kumar and Venkatesan (2005) reported that multichannel customers are more profitable.

The question is why this occurs. There could be self-selection; multichannel customers are already more loyal, and therefore they express multichannel behavior, as they like shopping using the retailers' multiple offered channels. Marketing could also play a role, as marketing instruments might drive customers to become multichannel and more loyal (Valentini et al., 2011). However, the use of multiple channels could also induce more loyalty and spending because consumers enjoy more convenience and experience greater service levels and the channels serve their specific needs better over time. If the latter occurs, there is a true multichannel effect. Kumar et al. (2019) summarized the available studies on this topic. In their own empirical study, accounting for self-selection effects, they showed that multichannel customers purchase more frequently, have higher spending levels, and also are profitable, though the study used relatively old data from when digital competition was not yet so severe.

A key question, therefore, is whether the relationship is causal—does multichannel behavior increase customer revenues and profits? Valentini et al. (2011) found that marketing can induce multichannel behavior, but in their experimental study they also showed that, when accounting for self-selection, multichannel customers are indeed more profitable. Thus, they concluded that driving consumers to become multichannel can be profitable for retailers offering multiple channels. The consistent conclusion from prior research is that multichannel customers tend to be more profitable. An important question that remains is whether multichannel behavior also leads to more consumer well-being.

UNDERSTANDING CONSUMERS' PATH TO PURCHASE

Understanding how customers respond to marketing stimuli in the different channels they use and how these stimuli impact their use of multiple channels is key to developing effective and efficient marketing investments across channels. We first focus on cross-channel effects and then discuss the important role of attribution.

Understanding Cross-Channel Effects

Cross-channel effects occur when consumers in their path to purchase are influenced by multiple touchpoints affecting their behavior in other channels or touchpoints. Hence, it is important to distinguish between firm-initiated touchpoints and customer-initiated touchpoints (e.g., de Haan et al., 2018). Customers exhibit significant heterogeneity in their behaviors with regard to how they are impacted by various stimuli they encounter on their customer journey, and at the aggregate level these effects determine the carryover and spillover across channels and devices (de Haan et al., 2018; Li & Kannan, 2014). A carryover effect occurs within the same touchpoint when consumers visit the touchpoint or channel (i.e., website) multiple times and finally purchase through that channel. A spillover effect occurs when consumers start with using a channel and then move to other channels and finally make a purchase from the last used channel (e.g., start with search engine, next click on display ad leading to final purchase). Early work focusing on measuring synergies across media and channels has used aggregate data (e.g., Naik & Raman, 2003), while individual user-level and aggregate data have been used to determine cross-channel impacts and customers' channel migration (e.g., Ansari & Mela, 2003; Ansari et al., 2008), focusing on offline and online channels.

Some of the touchpoints in the customer journey are customer-initiated, where customers seek out information through search engines, review sites, or direct visits to websites, while others are firm-initiated, such as display ads and emails. The distribution of such touchpoints in the different stages of the customer stage can provide insights into the baseline propensities for purchase for each customer (Kannan et al., 2016). Of course, these baseline propensities are enhanced or attenuated depending on the types of marketing stimuli customers encounter. For example, Kireyev et al. (2016) showed that customers exposed to display advertisements online show positive spillover effects in the search channel, while Joo et al. (2016) established the positive spillover linkage between offline advertising and online search behavior. Various stimuli can have very different impacts across different stages of the customer journey, thereby affecting the nature of carryover and spillover.

Colicev et al. (2019) showed that user-generated content has a greater impact on consumers at the awareness and postpurchase (satisfaction) stages, while firm-generated content is more effective at the consideration and purchase intent stage. Even within each type of content, their features could also have different impacts on consumers' search and purchase behaviors. This highlights the importance of incorporating the characteristics of the touchpoints in understanding cross-channel effects, including firm- versus customer-initiated touchpoints, duration of display ad exposure, duration of search session, the website where the display ad was shown, and the characteristics of the emails (see, e.g., Zantedeschi et al., 2016).

The Challenge of Assessing Touchpoint Contribution to Consumer Choices

An understanding of how customers react to and get impacted by the various features and stimuli at each touchpoint in the customer journey is necessary for understanding the different ways in which these touchpoints contribute to the outcomes desired by the marketer for each customer journey. For example, some touchpoints could be very effective in starting a fruitful customer journey and some very effective in ending the journey with a purchase event. The so-called attribution problem is to determine the roles and the specific contributions of each feature of each touchpoint (both firm- and customer-initiated; e.g., Li & Kannan, 2014) to the outcome of interest—that is, allocating the credit due to each of the touchpoints for outcome event— be it purchase, customer satisfaction, or customer retention. Such an attribution of credit could be useful to understand the real costs of obtaining the outcome and thereby allocate appropriate budget to each marketing touchpoint. Researchers (e.g., Abhishek et al., 2012; Li & Kannan, 2014; L. Xu et al., 2014) have used different methodologies to allocate credit, looking for associations between touchpoint usage and purchase. Recent research (Berman, 2018; Danaher & van Heerde, 2018) examined the more sophisticated issues in attribution such as gaming behavior of players in the advertisement supply chain and budget allocation for marketing mix. We also observed the use of experiments in which touchpoints are manipulated to infer stronger causal effects (e.g., Lesscher et al., 2020). In comparison with more associational studies, the true effects of typically a limited number of touchpoints can be inferred. Studies building on existing data and the associations between touchpoints and purchase have to infer the effects from the data using sophisticated methodologies but can do so for a larger set of touchpoints.

Cultural and situational factors in omnichannel consumer behavior make this difficult problem of attribution even more difficult. Whereas extant research has viewed this mainly as a decompositional problem—splitting the credit for an outcome into many pieces across marketing devices—a newer approach further divides the outcome into many stages (e.g., creating awareness, increasing the probability of consideration, increasing purchase intent, increasing satisfaction) and tries to assign credit for instruments at each stage. This approach acknowledges that customers use both multichannels and multiple devices in their customer journey. Mapping each stage of the customer journey to a device and understanding the role of devices (e.g., de Haan et al., 2018; K. Xu et al., 2017) in the customer journey could lead to more useful insights for attribution.

Technological advancements continue to push the boundaries of the channels in such a way that they become increasingly seamless. For example, new retail store formats are emerging that allow the use of mobile apps within retail stores for searching for products, scanning products for prices, scanning for purchases, and self-checkouts with auto payments through the apps. Similarly, online and mobile environments are being melded together, for example, with event tickets (e.g., Basu et al., 2020). Newer technologies like VR and AR can complement a web-based interaction as well as mobile-app-based or wearable-device-based interactions. In such cases, omnichannel behavior will be more of a norm than an exception. This will necessitate examining the issues of spillovers and attribution in a new light. This will be a ripe area for future research.

However, despite all these technological changes, offline instruments may still affect both online and offline purchasing behavior. For example, Mark et al. (2019) found that catalogs still have an effect on purchase behavior for multichannel retailers, while Konuş et al. (2014) showed that the elimination of the catalog channel reduces sales but improves profitability. Still, more attention is required to the interplay between online and offline touchpoints on purchase behavior.

NEW DIGITAL TECHNOLOGIES AND CONSUMER OMNICHANNEL EXPERIENCE

The omnichannel approach is generally considered to focus on linking online and in-store shopping experiences. Moreover, there are growing technological opportunities to connect the online with the offline and to offer customers a unique experience. AI can automate and customize the retail experience and be used for market research. Beacons are small, wireless transmitters that use low-energy Bluetooth technology to send signals to other smart devices nearby. Beacons allow location- and time-sensitive in-store marketing activities and self-service checkout systems within a physical store to facilitate the speed and convenience of checking out (Argyros, 2017; Baird, 2017). AR and VR allow for virtually trying on products like clothes and makeup and immersing customers into the product usage experience (Holzwarth et al., 2006; Inman & Nikolova, 2017; van Ittersum et al., 2013). However, we argue that the development of new digital technologies, mobile devices, and apps on these devices allows for more than merely linking the online with the offline. It allows for a full integration and expansion of both channels. Based on a search in the popular media, we created Table 29.1, with the most prominent new digital technologies and mobile devices (without claiming to be exhaustive; see also Shankar et al., 2011). Next, we discuss some of these via a structured discussion of the five stages of the customer journey. We focus on how the technology and mobile devices influence the shopping experience, potential pitfalls, and directions for future research.

The following discussion describes the potential of these new technologies on consumer behavior. In many cases, whether this potential is realized will depend on consumer adoption of the technology. Inman and Nikolova (2017) introduced a framework describing the factors that drive the success of shopper-facing retail technology. They applied equity theory in arguing that consumers assess the value of the technology to them compared with what the retailer receives. In a study of six different retailing technologies, they found that retail technologies that provide value without (a) requiring a big investment in time or money by the shopper or (b) treading on their privacy were valued the most highly by consumers. In the next sections, we discuss how technology can help with the stages of the consumer purchase journey.

Need Recognition

New digital technological advances and devices enable marketers to approach customers with ideas and suggestions that increase the salience of specific unmet needs or wants consumers may have. For example, smart beacons allow retailers to identify when customers are in the neighborhood or, for example, where they are inside the store. Customers may not recognize they have a need to visit the store or move toward a specific part of the store, However, a message from the store may trigger an unmet need or want that next entices customers to follow through. For example, Hui et al. (2013) presented evidence that targeted mobile promotions aimed at increasing in-store path length can increase unplanned spending. They showed that a coupon requiring consumers to travel farther from their planned path through the store increases exposure to in-store cues (e.g., signs, physical displays), thereby increasing the likelihood of in-store need recognition compared with a coupon for a category near the planned path.

New digital technological advances also offer the ability to track the consumers and the environmental circumstances and identify whether a specific need is growing. An example is the ability to keep track of a consumers' stock of products in a refrigerator. With this knowledge, specific replacement orders can be made automatically. Or, building on a recent study

TABLE 29.1

New Technologies and Consumer Omnichannel Process

		Potential relevance of technology in different phases						
		Need recognition	Search	Shopping	Purchase	After-sales	Need for active customer	Privacy concerns
Technological developments								
Artificial intelligence (AI)	Automation and customizing/ personalization of retail experience (automated stores)	√	√	√	√	√		√
Voice activation AI (Alexa, Siri)	Searching, ordering, service complaints, medical help, service chatbots	√	√	√	√	√	√	√
Augmented reality	Virtually trying clothes, makeup, or new furniture		√	√			√	
Virtual reality (VR)	In-store VR experience of a product (e.g., Audi)	√	√	√			√	
New devices								
Mobile devices	Mobile devices may carry apps that allow for mobile-armed sales staff, mobile-enhanced product reviews, mobile-responsive websites, discount on demand, and automated stores		√	√	√	√	√	√
Mobile wallets	Easy and quick payment				√			√
Smart beacons	Used near or inside store to interact with customers while shopping (e.g., personal discounts) and also great to test effectiveness		√	√				√
Facial recognition tools	Used to track where customers gravitate within a store and determine customer demographics			√	√			√
Cloud services	Used for inventory tracking, stock availability, shipping details, and orders, reducing costs and offering real-time information			√	√	√		√
QR codes	Used inside store to offer more product information to customers (e.g., harvest dates, sourcing information)	√	√	√	√	√	√	

		Potential relevance of technology in different phases					
		Need recognition	Search	Shopping	Purchase	After-sales	Need for active customer	Privacy concerns
New devices								
Robots	Used to support and service customers throughout the entire or parts of the shopping trip		√	√	√		√	√
Smart shopping carts	Shopping carts that offer real-time information on products customers consider to purchase (and on potential alternatives)			√	√		√	√
Autonomous shopping carts	Shopping carts that follow customers around the store (instead of having to be pushed), keeping the customers hands-free			√	√			
Imaging software	Produces 3D model of a customer's face, analyzes it, and selects glasses that best suit the person's face shape, gender, and age (reducing search process)		√	√			√	√
Digital pricing	Used for digital prices and nutritional information, reducing energy costs and allowing for dynamic pricing			√	√			√
Telemedicine	Health-related services and information via electronic information and communication technologies	√	√	√			√	√

by Sheehan and van Ittersum (2018) that demonstrated that the price sensitivity of shoppers varies depending on the total spending amount, retailers can offer price promotions depending on how much money a shopper already spent. The growing penetration of digital pricing tools (i.e., tools and tags that allow for presenting digital prices in the store), combined with AI technologies, allows for refined dynamic pricing schemes that benefit from identifying consumer needs as a function of shopping trip characteristics. Another example would be that when a retailer can track that consumers buy pancake mix or put it in their shopping basket, the retailer can then offer deals on syrup and lead them to attractive other deals.

While intriguing, these approaches may be subject to consumer backlash over privacy and implicit discrimination concerns. For example, Ali et al. (2019) found that Facebook ads for employment and housing were significantly skewed along gender and racial lines despite inclusive targeting parameters set by the advertisers. We discuss challenges associated with privacy in a separate section later on.

Search

New digital technological advances and devices increase accessibility to a vast amount of information during the customer journey. Multiple studies have considered the adoption of mobile devices for shopping purposes. For example, Hubert et al. (2017) found that usefulness and ease of use mediate the effects of perceived risk and perceived benefits on mobile shopping intentions. Mobile devices have particular characteristics that differentiate them from fixed devices. These characteristics of mobile devices, including location specificity, portability, screen size, and wireless features, make them ideal for search purposes. Consumers, for example, use their mobile device to find online reviews and determine the lowest price offering in the market. Retailers may also provide in-store QR codes that consumers may scan to acquire additional product information, such where products are produced, from where the raw materials are sourced, and so forth. In many ways, the marketplace has become more transparent. One could argue that this may result in information overload. However, new technologies such as AI enable firms to customize the information in real time and offer complex information in a more accessible and understandable manner.

One can, for instance, think of advanced visualization tools that may offer customized visualizations of complex information that would otherwise be ignored by consumers. For example, it could be interesting to study whether and how the offering of customized visualizations of nutrition information (kcal, protein, fat, saturated fat, carbohydrate, sugar, and sodium [a component of salt] in the food) simplifies the search process for consumers interested in purchasing healthier groceries. Research suggests that front-of-package labels—which provide a simplified visualization of nutrition information—may contribute to healthier shopping baskets. Similarly, Nikolova and Inman (2015) showed that the introduction of simplified nutritional information by a retailer leads to healthier choices. Smart shopping carts mounted with a scanner and a digital screen can offer real-time information on products consumers consider purchasing. The visualization may be customized and presented in real time while shopping. Consumers showing an interest in buying a less salty product can be informed by the amount of salt in the product that they intend to purchase and about other less salty products available in the store. This information can potentially be more easily provided when consumers are shopping for food products online, but this rarely happens.

Interestingly, our understanding of the acceptance and effects of real-time feedback on the shopping experience, purchase behavior, and consumer knowledge levels remains limited. Moreover, one could argue that with the growing availability of these kinds of technologies and devices, the autonomous search for information before or during shopping trips becomes obsolete and this search of information is integrated in the purchase phase. Consumer dependence on the provider of the information increases, which may influence the acceptance of the information. Consumers may also resist the threat to their autonomy in the purchase process; they may exhibit reactance. In psychology *reactance* is generally considered as a kind of unpleasant motivational arousal that emerges when people experience a threat to or loss of their free behaviors (Brehm & Brehm, 1981). Research does suggest that certain consumers exhibit reactance, for example toward marketing loyalty programs (Wendlandt & Schrader, 2007). More research on consumer reactance in the context of omnichannels is called for. Also, how does the provision of product information by retailers affect the general knowledge level of consumers? It would be interesting to research whether and how knowledge level develops among shoppers who receive this kind of real-time feedback on a regular basis versus consumers who more autonomously have to search for information on the products they prefer to purchase.

Shopping

As noted in our section on the process model, we distinguish between the search and shopping phase. We also note that the distinction between search and shopping is not always clear, and consumers may move in a kind of fluent way from searching to shopping. The distinction in a shopping phase is especially relevant as new digital technological advances and devices may offer opportunities to guide the shopping process in real time. Consumer surveys indicate that 72% of shoppers would welcome radio-frequency identification tags on products to help them better track their in-store spending (https://www.infosys.

com), and 85% of leading retailers rate self-service customer-facing technologies, such as smart shopping carts, as one of the three top opportunities for increasing consumer satisfaction and revenue (Rosenblum, 2007). In addition to enabling shoppers to track their in-store spending (Nelson, 2008), smart shopping carts may help improve customer satisfaction by offering customized and timely promotions, recommending complementary products, sharing nutritional information and recipes, and even allowing customers to skip the checkout lane (e.g., Hui et al., 2013; Osborne, 2012; Quaid, 2005).

Retailers can use mobile devices and apps to inform shoppers about desirable deals and engage shoppers at any point in their shopping trip depending on, for example, their in-store location or the contents of their shopping baskets (Clifford & Hardy, 2013; Hui et al., 2013). More specifically, retailers can use such technologies to offer shoppers promotions at any moment before they reach the actual point of purchase, where promotional material has been traditionally displayed. This raises new questions, such as whether separating the moment shoppers encounter a promotion from when they encounter the promoted product on the shelf influences a consumer's response to promotions. For instance, consider a grocery shopper who is going to purchase frozen pizza. Would encountering a price promotion for a specific premium brand of frozen pizza before arriving to the product on the shelf (i.e., separate promotion) produce a different response than encountering that same promotion with the product on the shelf (i.e., joint promotion)? Sheehan and van Ittersum (2021) demonstrated in three studies that isolated promotions—promotions shoppers encounter while shopping independently from the point-of-purchase for the promoted product—for premium brands are more effective than traditional shelf promotions in persuading consumers to purchase the promoted brand, as these promotions alter how consumers evaluate and justify purchasing the promoted brands. Specifically, isolated promotions lead consumers to focus relatively less on the price of the promoted brand compared with its quality. This reduced focus on price assuages the negative effect of guilt associated with purchasing a more expensive, premium brand.

Building on the examples from the previous sections, next to offering information about the products consumers intend to purchase, a smart shopping cart may offer customized alternatives based on the product that a consumer intends to purchase and show their location in the store. If a consumer wants healthier choices, a smart cart may offer one or more healthier alternatives. Similarly, the retailer can draw from the consumer's past purchase history and use predictive AI tools to generate suggested purchases based on projected household inventory levels. Little is known about whether this kind of real-time feedback and recommendation is effective in the short or in the long term. Furthermore, the acceptance of these kinds of recommendations may also vary among consumers. More generally, the acceptance of algorithms that offer guidance and recommendations deserves scientific attention. Besides concerns about their privacy, consumers may feel a sense of loss of autonomy.

Purchase

New digital technological advances and devices may offer opportunities to impact the purchase process. However, that impact can also be negative if, as discussed earlier, the additional use of a mobile device might increase the risk and effort associated with the purchase (de Haan et al., 2018; Fritz et al., 2017). Similar to K. Xu et al. (2017), de Haan et al. (2018) and Fritz et al. (2017) showed that consumers are more likely to purchase on desktop computers when they first searched on a mobile device where they could also see the product. The likelihood of purchasing on desktop computers increases with the risk associated with the purchase (i.e., higher priced products, less experience). Thus, we believe that the risk of buying on a mobile device induces consumers to mainly use a mobile device for searching information and less for purchasing.

Retailers and other service providers aim to overcome this risk issue with the use of mobile store apps next to the use of mobile websites. Mobile store apps create a more secure environment, and consumers may consider it as less risky. Moreover, mobile apps create a more personalized environment and can create a stronger lock-in. Indeed, Liu et al. (2018) supported the notion that apps are less risky than mobile websites. They showed that when consumers move from a mobile website to an app, their purchase frequency increases and that this specifically occurs in riskier purchase situations (i.e., for higher priced products). Multiple studies have also looked at the impact of app adoption on purchase frequency and loyalty. The main conclusion was that app adopters indeed tend to buy more frequently and buy more (e.g., van Heerde et al., 2019; R. J. H. Wang et al., 2015, 2018). However, these effects might differ between consumers. For example, van Heerde et al. (2019) found that apps generate more incremental sales among distant customers compared with near customers and more incremental sales among offline-only customers compared with online customers. Gu and Kannan (2019) showed that not all firms reap the benefits of the app.

New technologies and devices can improve the purchase process, specifically the payment and pickup process. Smart shopping carts, mobile wallets, and automated stores minimize or even eliminate the payment process. While these technologies and devices may improve the shopping experience, for example by reducing the pain of paying experienced, they may also increase the risk of running up debts among low-income consumers. Research has demonstrated that shoppers spend up to 100% more when using their credit card to pay instead of cash (Prelec & Simester, 2001), due to a reduction in the experience of pain of paying. That is, by using seamless payment system, a decoupling of the product acquired or the consumption experience associated with the product and the payment for that product occurs (Prelec & Loewenstein, 1998). Seamless payment systems and devices are prone to similar effects, putting low-income households at a potential risk.

While we argued that new digital technological advances and devices allow for an integration of the off- and online world, there may also be a growing decoupling of specific phases and experiences in the customer journey. For example, by decoupling the purchase and payment process from the actual acquisition of the purchased goods and service, a temporal distance arises that may influence the outcomes of the purchase and payment process. For example, Milkman et al. (2010) studied whether decisions made for tomorrow or 2 days in the future differ from decisions made for several days in the future. They report that as the delay between order completion and delivery increases, grocery customers spend less, order a higher percentage of "should" items (e.g., vegetables), and order a lower percentage of "want" items (e.g., ice cream), controlling for customer fixed effects. Thus, while sales in stores may increase such impulse purchases, a move to more than 2-day delivery to homes may result in fewer impulse purchases.

After-Sales

Research on the path to purchase mainly focuses on the single outcome of the path to purchase: transaction or purchase (e.g., Kannan et al., 2016). McKinsey consultants suggested the existence of a loyalty loop, where the purchase journey should result in repeat purchases (Edelman & Singer, 2015). For example, van Ittersum et al. (2013) demonstrated how real-time spending feedback while shopping for groceries using smart shopping carts reduces the spending uncertainty of budget shoppers, improves their shopping experience, and increases their repatronage intentions. This meshes well with the interest on long-term purchase outcomes and metrics (i.e., customer lifetime value), which has been advocated in the customer relationship management literature (Kumar & Reinartz, 2016). Within multichannel research, there has been attention for these loyalty effects as discussed earlier in the section of consequences of multichannel behavior. However, studies on customer journey and the path to purchase mainly focus on how touchpoints affect the purchase. Herhausen et al. (2019) is one of the few studies considering loyalty as an outcome variable. They studied the impact of product satisfaction, journey satisfaction, and customer inspiration on customer loyalty for their identified customer segments and identified differences between customers segments. For example, for the segment exposed to many touchpoints, both customer journey satisfaction and customer inspiration are related to customer loyalty, while product satisfaction is not related. However, for two online-oriented segments, product satisfaction is most strongly related to customer loyalty. Beyond that, studies on app adoption have considered purchase frequency as an outcome variable. However, there is still a lack of studies considering the long-term consequences of touchpoints and other marketing instruments. Firms like Amazon are using new marketing tactics, such as their loyalty program Prime and AI with their use of Alexa, to create more loyalty (Verhoef, 2020).

As mentioned earlier, it would also be valuable to understand the impact of customers who share their experiences with other potential customers using social media channels. First, it may be an effective way to trigger the relevant unmet need among potential customers. Second, potential customers may be more open to experienced input from actual customers than receiving the same information from the firm. The so-called message source effect on the persuasion of potential customers is an important topic that has received considerable attention in consumer behavior and related fields such as marketing communications (Wilson & Sherrell, 1993). Finally, the firm may benefit from social influences, whereby the mere fact that a peer of the potential customers posts their experience may be sufficient for the potential customer to respond (Dahl, 2013).

Privacy Considerations

The use of many specifically data-driven technologies raises issues surrounding consumer privacy and data security. There is some evidence that consumers make a cost-benefit trade-off when deciding on whether to share data with firms. However, one should be aware that many of these decisions are executed unconsciously and that there is a so-called privacy paradox (Beke et al., 2018). Consumers are aware of privacy issues, but they still decide to share data and adopt data-based services. From a consumer psychology perspective, regulatory focus theory can potentially be used to explain why consumers may want to share data (Higgins, 1997). Prevention-focused consumers are potentially less

likely to share data, while promotion-focused consumers tend to focus on the immediate benefits of data sharing. In an international study, Schumacher et al. (2020) linked regular focus theory to national culture variables and showed that data sharing is less present in cultures with a higher long-term orientation, as they might have a stronger prevention focus. Omnichannel retailers also should be aware that using personal data during the customer journey has adverse effects, as it may create customer reactance and disloyalty (van Doorn & Hoekstra, 2013). Much more can be discussed about privacy, but given the focus of this chapter on multi- and omnichannel retail, we refer the interested reader to overview studies (e.g., Beke et al., 2018).

CONCLUSION AND RESEARCH GAPS

We have reviewed the growing research on omnichannel retailing with a focus on the consumer perspective. In this final section, we outline several important gaps in the literature in the hope that researchers will endeavor to fill these gaps. We frame them as research questions and briefly sketch out the domain and context for each one.

Consumer Acceptance of AI and Bots

What role will AI play in helping consumers make better decisions and take on the burden of day-to-day repurchase decisions? Current research suggests that today's consumers are somewhat leery of AI technology (e.g., Longoni et al., 2020), but just as Gen Z consumers are digitally native, so may the next generation be "AI native." Research is needed on consumers' specific concerns and how to address them. Moreover, does the attractiveness of AI differ within customers over time, that is, when Gen Z grows up, will they be less receptive to AI? Or will they be permanently attracted to AI?[3]

Consumer Adoption of Retail Technology

Similar to the aforementioned, how can retailers overcome consumer objections to some of the new retail technologies? Are some technologies, such as

---

[3] We thank Scott Neslin for this suggestion.

proximity marketing, inherently doomed to fail due to privacy concerns and the creepiness factor (e.g., Beke et al., 2018; Inman & Nikolova, 2017)?

Showrooming and Web-Rooming

Are showrooming and web-rooming always a bad thing for customer satisfaction and retailer profitability? Perhaps not. This may be the greatest benefit of omnichannel retailing. We posit that the easier retailers make it to switch seamlessly between in-store and online, the more likely the shopper may be to purchase from the retailer's site. Additional research is needed for testing these kind of assumptions and in general on this important and growing phenomenon.

Unplanned Purchase Behavior

What are the consequences of online shopping for consumers' unplanned purchase behavior? Such purchases are less likely online since consumers are not incidentally exposed to as many product categories compared with a physical store (Inman et al., 2009). If consumers then have to place multiple online orders due to less efficient trips, the added shipping incurred will either decrease firm surplus or consumer surplus, depending upon who bears this cost.

Omnichannel Versus Multichannel

Is omnichannel more effective than multichannel? In this chapter, we have highlighted many of the benefits of omnichannel retailing. However, making the consumer experience seamless across online and offline channels with multiple touchpoints in an integrated way comes at a cost. Is it worth the investment, or is a multichannel approach sufficient? A sufficient number of retailers have transitioned from multichannel to omnichannel to conduct an empirical investigation into the net effect and address this critical question.

Loyalty Loop

How does omnichannel affect consumers who are in the loyalty loop? Many of the steps discussed in this chapter are bypassed once the consumer has identified a satisfactory product and has begun to engage in routinized decision making (e.g., Howard & Sheth, 1969). It is unclear if or how omnichannel influences such consumers. If omnichannel is only effective for big ticket product categories such as durables and on consumers who engage in active search, its value may be mitigated.

REFERENCES

Abhishek, V., Fader, P., & Hosanagar, K. (2012). Media exposure through the funnel: A model of multi-stage attribution. *Social Science Research Network*, 1–47. https://doi.org/10.2139/ssrn.2158421

Ali, M., Sapiezynski, P., Bogen, M., Korolova, A., Mislove, A., & Rieke, A. (2019). Discrimination through optimization: How Facebook's ad delivery can lead to biased outcomes. *Proceedings of the ACM Conference on Human-Computer Interaction*, 3, 1–30. https://arxiv.org/pdf/1904.02095.pdf

Ansari, A., & Mela, C. F. (2003). E-customization. *Journal of Marketing Research*, 40(2), 131–145. https://doi.org/10.1509/jmkr.40.2.131.19224

Ansari, A., Mela, C. F., & Neslin, S. A. (2008). Customer channel migration. *Journal of Marketing Research*, 45(1), 60–76. https://doi.org/10.1509/jmkr.45.1.60

Argyros, T. (2017, July 21). How artificial intelligence is helping retailers bridge the gap between online and offline data. *Forbes*. https://www.forbes.com/sites/forbestechcouncil/2017/07/21/how-artificial-intelligence-is-helping-retailers-bridge-the-gap-between-online-and-offline-data/#182ee4fa8717

Arts, K., van der Wal, R., & Adams, W. M. (2015). Digital technology and the conservation of nature. *Ambio*, 44(4), 661–673. https://doi.org/10.1007/s13280-015-0705-1

Baird, N. (2017, April 30). Three ways artificial intelligence will transform online shopping. *Forbes*. https://www.forbes.com/sites/nikkibaird/2017/04/30/three-ways-artificial-intelligence-will-transform-online-shopping/?sh=701ebcb3adb6

Basu, M., Inman, J. J., & Wakefield, K. (2020). *The impact of device used in digital paths on deadline-driven purchase decisions* [Working paper]. University of Pittsburgh.

Baxendale, S., Macdonald, E. K., & Wilson, H. N. (2015). The impact of different touchpoints on brand consideration. *Journal of Retailing*, 91(2), 235–253. https://doi.org/10.1016/j.jretai.2014.12.008

Beke, F. T., Eggers, F., & Verhoef, P. C. (2018). Consumer informational privacy: Current knowledge and research directions. *Foundations & Trends in Marketing*, 11(1), 1–71. https://doi.org/10.1561/1700000057

Berman, R. (2018). Beyond the last touch: Attribution in online advertising. *Marketing Science, 37*(5), 771–792. https://doi.org/10.1287/mksc.2018.1104

Bilgicer, T., Jedidi, K., Lehmann, D. R., & Neslin, S. A. (2015). Social contagion and customer adoption of new sales channels. *Journal of Retailing, 91*(2), 254–271. https://doi.org/10.1016/j.jretai.2014.12.006

Boyd, D. E., Kannan, P. K., & Slotegraaf, R. J. (2019). Branded apps and their impact on firm value: A design perspective. *Journal of Marketing Research, 56*(1), 76–88. https://doi.org/10.1177/0022243718820588

Brehm, S. S., & Brehm, J. W. (1981). *Psychological reactance: A theory of freedom and control.* Academic Press.

Bruner, G. C., II, & Kumar, A. (2005). Explaining consumer acceptance of handheld internet devices. *Journal of Business Research, 58*(5), 553–558. https://doi.org/10.1016/j.jbusres.2003.08.002

Cambro-Fierro, J., Melero-Polo I., Patricio, L. & Sese, J. (2020). Channel habits and the development of successful customer-firm relationships in services. *Journal of Service Research, 23*(4), 456–475. https://doi.org/10.1177/1094670520916791

Choi, J., Hui, S. K., & Bell, D. R. (2010). Spatiotemporal analysis of imitation behavior across new buyers at an online grocery retailer. *Journal of Marketing Research, 47*(1), 75–89. https://doi.org/10.1509/jmkr.47.1.75

Clifford, S., & Hardy, Q. (2013, July 14). Attention, shoppers: Store is tracking your cell. *New York Times.*

Colicev, A., Kumar, A., & O'Connor, P. (2019). Modeling the relationship between firm and user generated content and the stages of the marketing funnel. *International Journal of Research in Marketing, 36*(1), 100–116. https://doi.org/10.1016/j.ijresmar.2018.09.005

Dahl, D. (2013). Social influence and consumer behavior. *Journal of Consumer Research, 40*(2), iii–v. https://doi.org/10.1086/670170

Danaher, P. J., & van Heerde, H. J. (2018). Delusion in attribution: Caveats in using attribution for media budget allocation. *Journal of Marketing Research, 55*(5), 667–685. https://doi.org/10.1177/0022243718802845

Darian, J. C. (1987). In-home shopping: Are there consumer segments? *Journal of Retailing, 63*(2), 163–186.

Daunt, K. L., & Harris, L. C. (2017). Consumer showrooming: Value co-destruction. *Journal of Retailing and Consumer Services, 38*, 166–176. https://doi.org/10.1016/j.jretconser.2017.05.013

Degeratu, A. M., Rangaswamy, A., & Wu, J. (2000). Consumer choice behavior in online and traditional supermarkets: The effects of brand name, price, and other search attributes. *International Journal of Research in Marketing, 17*(1), 55–78. https://doi.org/10.1016/S0167-8116(00)00005-7

de Haan, E., Kannan, P. K., Verhoef, P. C., & Wiesel, T. (2018). Device switching in online purchasing: Examining the strategic contingencies. *Journal of Marketing, 82*(5), 1–19. https://doi.org/10.1509/jm.17.0113

De Keyser, A., Schepers, J., & Konuş, U. (2015). Multichannel customer segmentation: Does the after-sales channel matter? A replication and extension. *International Journal of Research in Marketing, 32*(4), 453–456. https://doi.org/10.1016/j.ijresmar.2015.09.005

Dholakia, R. R., Zhao, M., & Dholakia, N. (2005). Multichannel retailing: A case study of early experiences. *Journal of Interactive Marketing, 19*(2), 63–74. https://doi.org/10.1002/dir.20035

Edelman, D. C., & Singer, M. (2015). Competing on customer journeys. *Harvard Business Review, 93*(11), 88–100.

Emrich, O., Paul, M., & Rudolph, T. (2015). Shopping benefits of multichannel assortment integration and the moderating role of retailer type. *Journal of Retailing, 91*(2), 326–342. https://doi.org/10.1016/j.jretai.2014.12.003

Fassnacht, M., Beatty, S. E., & Szajna, M. (2019). Combating the negative effects of showrooming: Successful salesperson tactics for converting showroomers into buyers. *Journal of Business Research, 102*, 131–139. https://doi.org/10.1016/j.jbusres.2019.05.020

Flavián, C., Gurrea, R., & Orús, C. (2019). Feeling confident and smart with webrooming: Understanding the consumer's path to satisfaction. *Journal of Interactive Marketing, 47*, 1–15. https://doi.org/10.1016/j.intmar.2019.02.002

Flavián, C., Gurrea, R., & Orús, C. (2020). Combining channels to make smart purchases: The role of webrooming and showrooming. *Journal of Retailing and Consumer Services, 52*, 101923. https://doi.org/10.1016/j.jretconser.2019.101923

Fong, N. M., Fang, Z., & Luo, X. (2015). Geo-conquesting: Competitive locational targeting of mobile promotions. *Journal of Marketing Research, 52*(5), 726–735. https://doi.org/10.1509/jmr.14.0229

Fritz, W., Sohn, S., & Seegebarth, B. (2017). Broadening the perspective on mobile marketing: An introduction. *Psychology and Marketing, 34*(2), 113–118. https://doi.org/10.1002/mar.20978

Gensler, S., Neslin, S. A., & Verhoef, P. C. (2017). The showrooming phenomenon: It's more than just about price. *Journal of Interactive Marketing, 38*, 29–43. https://doi.org/10.1016/j.intmar.2017.01.003

Gensler, S., Verhoef, P. C., & Böhm, M. (2012). Understanding consumers' multichannel choices across the different stages of the buying process. *Marketing Letters*, 23(4), 987–1003. https://doi.org/10.1007/s11002-012-9199-9

Gielens, K., & Gijsbrechts, E. (Eds.). (2018). *Handbook of research on retailing*. Edward Elgar Publishing. https://doi.org/10.4337/9781786430281

Gu, X., & Kannan, P. K. (2019). *The dark side of mobile app adoption: The impact on consumers' multichannel purchase* [Working paper]. The Robert H Smith School of Business, University of Maryland.

Ha, S., & Stoel, L. (2009). Consumer e-shopping acceptance: Antecedents in a technology acceptance model. *Journal of Business Research*, 62(5), 565–571. https://doi.org/10.1016/j.jbusres.2008.06.016

Herhausen, D., Binder, J., Schoegel, M., & Herrmann, A. (2015). Integrating bricks with clicks: Retailer-level and channel-level outcomes of online–offline channel integration. *Journal of Retailing*, 91(2), 309–325. https://doi.org/10.1016/j.jretai.2014.12.009

Herhausen, D., Kleinlercher, K., Verhoef, P. C., Emrich, O., & Rudolph, T. (2019). Loyalty formation for different customer journey segments. *Journal of Retailing*, 95(3), 9–29. https://doi.org/10.1016/j.jretai.2019.05.001

Higgins, E. T. (1997). Beyond pleasure and pain. *American Psychologist*, 52(12), 1280–1300. https://doi.org/10.1037/0003-066X.52.12.1280

Holzwarth, M., Janiszewski, C., & Neumann, M. M. (2006). The influence of avatars on online consumer shopping behavior. *Journal of Marketing*, 70(4), 19–36. https://doi.org/10.1509/jmkg.70.4.019

Homburg, C., Vomberg, A., Enke, M., & Grimm, P. H. (2015). The loss of the marketing department's influence: Is it really happening? And why worry? *Journal of the Academy of Marketing Science*, 43(1), 1–13. https://doi.org/10.1007/s11747-014-0416-3

Howard, J. A., & Sheth, J. N. (1969). *The theory of buyer behavior*. John Wiley and Sons.

Hubert, M., Blut, M., Brock, C., Backhaus, C., & Eberhardt, T. (2017). Acceptance of smartphone-based mobile shopping: Mobile benefits, customer characteristics, perceived risks, and the impact of application context. *Psychology and Marketing*, 34(2), 175–194. https://doi.org/10.1002/mar.20982

Hui, S. K., Inman, J. J., Huang, Y., & Suher, J. (2013). The effect of in-store travel distance on unplanned spending: Applications to mobile promotion strategies. *Journal of Marketing*, 77(2), 1–16. https://doi.org/10.1509/jm.11.0436

Inman, J. J., & Nikolova, H. (2017). Shopper-facing retail technology: A retailer adoption decision framework incorporating shopper attitudes and privacy concerns. *Journal of Retailing*, 93(1), 7–28. https://doi.org/10.1016/j.jretai.2016.12.006

Inman, J. J., Winer, R. S., & Ferraro, R. (2009). The interplay among category characteristics, customer characteristics, and customer activities on in-store decision making. *Journal of Marketing*, 73(5), 19–29. https://doi.org/10.1509/jmkg.73.5.19

Joo, M., Wilbur, K. C., & Zhu, Y. (2016). Effects of TV advertising on keyword search. *International Journal of Research in Marketing*, 33(3), 508–523. https://doi.org/10.1016/j.ijresmar.2014.12.005

Kannan, P. K., Reinartz, W., & Verhoef, P. C. (2016). The path to purchase and attribution modeling: Introduction to special section. *International Journal of Research in Marketing*, 33(3), 449–456. https://doi.org/10.1016/j.ijresmar.2016.07.001

Kireyev, P., Pauwels, K., & Gupta, S. (2016). Do display ads influence search? Attribution and dynamics in online advertising. *International Journal of Research in Marketing*, 33(3), 475–490. https://doi.org/10.1016/j.ijresmar.2015.09.007

Kollmann, T., Kuckertz, A., & Kayser, I. (2012). Cannibalization or synergy? Consumers' channel selection in online–offline multichannel systems. *Journal of Retailing and Consumer Services*, 19(2), 186–194. https://doi.org/10.1016/j.jretconser.2011.11.008

Konuş, U., Neslin, S. A., & Verhoef, P. C. (2014). The effect of search channel elimination on purchase incidence, order size and channel choice. *International Journal of Research in Marketing*, 31(1), 49–64. https://doi.org/10.1016/j.ijresmar.2013.07.008

Konuş, U., Verhoef, P. C., & Neslin, S. A. (2008). Multichannel shopper segments and their covariates. *Journal of Retailing*, 84(4), 398–413. https://doi.org/10.1016/j.jretai.2008.09.002

Kumar, V., Nim, N., & Sharma, A. (2019). Driving growth of Mwallets in emerging markets: A retailer's perspective. *Journal of the Academy of Marketing Science*, 47(4), 770. https://doi.org/10.1007/s11747-018-00623-9

Kumar, V., & Reinartz, W. (2016). Creating enduring customer value. *Journal of Marketing*, 80(6), 36–68. https://doi.org/10.1509/jm.15.0414

Kumar, V., & Venkatesan, R. (2005). Who are the multichannel shoppers and how do they perform? Correlates of multichannel shopping behavior. *Journal of Interactive Marketing*, 19(2), 44–62. https://doi.org/10.1002/dir.20034

Kushwaha, T., & Shankar, V. (2013). Are multichannel customers really more valuable? The moderating role of product category characteristics. *Journal of Marketing*, 77(4), 67–85. https://doi.org/10.1509/jm.11.0297

Lee, L., Inman, J., Argo, J. J., Böttger, T., Dholakia, U., Gilbride, T., van Ittersum, K., Kahn, B., Kalra, A., Lehmann, D. R., McAlister, L. M., Shankar, V., & Tsai, C. I. (2018). From browsing to buying and beyond: The needs-based shopper journey model. *Journal of the Association for Consumer Research*, *3*(3), 277–293. https://doi.org/10.1086/698414

Lemon, K. N., & Verhoef, P. C. (2016). Understanding customer experience throughout the customer journey. *Journal of Marketing*, *80*(6), 69–96. https://doi.org/10.1509/jm.15.0420

Lesscher, L., Lobschat, L., & Verhoef, P. C. (2020). *Do offline and online go hand in hand? Cross-channel and synergy effects of direct mailing and display advertising* [Working paper]. University of Groningen.

Li, H. A., & Kannan, P. K. (2014). Attributing conversions in a multichannel online marketing environment: An empirical model and a field experiment. *Journal of Marketing Research*, *51*(1), 40–56. https://doi.org/10.1509/jmr.13.0050

Li, H. A., Kannan, P. K., Viswanathan, S., & Pani, A. (2016). Attribution strategies and return on keyword investment in paid search advertising. *Marketing Science*, *35*(6), 831–848. https://doi.org/10.1287/mksc.2016.0987

Lin, J. C. C., & Lu, H. (2000). Towards an understanding of the behavioural intention to use a web site. *International Journal of Information Management*, *20*(3), 197–208. https://doi.org/10.1016/S0268-4012(00)00005-0

Liu, H., Lobschat, L., & Verhoef, P. C. (2018). Multichannel retailing: A review and research agenda. *Foundations and Trends in Marketing*, *12*(1), 1–79. https://doi.org/10.1561/1700000059

Liu, H., Lobschat, L., Verhoef, P. C., & Zhao, H. (2019). App adoption: The effect on purchasing of customers who have used a mobile website previously. *Journal of Interactive Marketing*, *47*, 16–34. https://doi.org/10.1016/j.intmar.2018.12.001

Lobschat, L., Osinga, E. C., & Reinartz, W. J. (2017). What happens online stays online? Segment-specific online and offline effects of banner advertisements. *Journal of Marketing Research*, *54*(6), 901–913. https://doi.org/10.1509/jmr.14.0625

Longoni, C., Bonezzi, A., & Morewedge, C. K. (2020). Resistance to medical artificial intelligence. *Journal of Consumer Research*, *46*(4), 629–650. https://doi.org/10.1093/jcr/ucz013

Lynch, J. G., Jr., & Ariely, D. (2000). Wine online: Search costs affect competition on price, quality, and distribution. *Marketing Science*, *19*(1), 83–103. https://doi.org/10.1287/mksc.19.1.83.15183

Mark, T., Bulla, J., Nirai, R., Bulla, I., & Scharwäller, W. (2019). Catalogue as a tool for reinforcing habits: Empirical evidence from a multichannel retailer. *International Journal of Research in Marketing*, *36*(4), 528–541. https://doi.org/10.1016/j.ijresmar.2019.01.009

Mehra, A., Kumar, S., & Raju, J. S. (2018). Competitive strategies for brick-and-mortar stores to counter "showrooming." *Management Science*, *64*(7), 3076–3090. https://doi.org/10.1287/mnsc.2017.2764

Melis, K., Campo, K., Lamey, L., & Breugelmans, E. (2016). A bigger slice of the multichannel grocery pie: When does consumers' online channel use expand retailers' share of wallet? *Journal of Retailing*, *92*(3), 268–286. https://doi.org/10.1016/j.jretai.2016.05.001

Milkman, K. L., Rogers, T., & Bazerman, M. H. (2010). I'll have the ice cream soon and the vegetables later: A study of online grocery purchases and order lead time. *Marketing Letters*, *21*(1), 17–35. https://doi.org/10.1007/s11002-009-9087-0

Montaguti, E., Neslin, S. A., & Valentini, S. (2016). Can marketing campaigns induce multichannel buying and more profitable customers? A field experiment. *Marketing Science*, *35*(2), 201–217. https://doi.org/10.1287/mksc.2015.0923

Montaguti, E., Neslin, S. A., & Valentini, S. (2020). Identifying omnichannel deal prone segments, their antecedents, and their consequences. *Journal of Retailing*, *96*(3), 310–327. https://doi.org/10.1016/j.jretai.2020.01.003

Montoya-Weiss, M. M., Voss, G. B., & Grewal, D. (2003). Determinants of online channel use and overall satisfaction with a relational, multichannel service provider. *Journal of the Academy of Marketing Science*, *31*(4), 448–458. https://doi.org/10.1177/0092070303254408

Naik, P. A., & Raman, K. (2003). Understanding the impact of synergy in multimedia communications. *Journal of Marketing Research*, *40*(4), 375–388. https://doi.org/10.1509/jmkr.40.4.375.19385

Nam, H., & Kannan, P. K. (2020). Digital environment in global markets: Cross-cultural implications for evolving customer journeys. *Journal of International Marketing*, *28*(1), 28–47. https://doi.org/10.1177/1069031X19898767

Narang, U., & Shankar, V. (2019). Mobile app introduction and online and offline purchases and product returns. *Marketing Science*, *38*(5), 756–772. https://doi.org/10.1287/mksc.2019.1169

Nelson, S. (2008). Attention shoppers: Smart carts . . . aisle 6. *Daily Herald*. https://prev.dailyherald.com/story/?id=180936

Neslin, S. A., Grewal, D., Leghorn, R., Shankar, V., Teerling, M. L., Thomas, J. S., & Verhoef, P. C. (2006). Challenges and opportunities in multichannel customer management. *Journal of Service Research*, *9*(2), 95–112. https://doi.org/10.1177/1094670506293559

Neslin, S. A., & Shankar, V. (2009). Key issues in multichannel customer management: Current knowledge and future directions. *Journal of Interactive Marketing, 23*(1), 70–81. https://doi.org/10.1016/j.intmar.2008.10.005

Nicholson, M., Clarke, I., & Blakemore, M. (2002). "One brand, three ways to shop": Situational variables and multichannel consumer behaviour. *International Review of Retail, Distribution and Consumer Research, 12*(2), 131–148. https://doi.org/10.1080/09593960210127691

Nikolova, H. D., & Inman, J. J. (2015). Healthy choice: The effect of simplified POS nutritional information on consumer food choice behavior. *Journal of Marketing Research, 52*(6), 817–835. https://doi.org/10.1509/jmr.13.0270

Noble, S. M., Griffith, D. A., & Weinberger, M. G. (2005). Consumer derived utilitarian value and channel utilization in a multi-channel retail context. *Journal of Business Research, 58*(12), 1643–1651. https://doi.org/10.1016/j.jbusres.2004.10.005

O'Cass, A., & Fenech, T. (2003). Web retailing adoption: Exploring the nature of internet users web retailing behaviour. *Journal of Retailing and Consumer Services, 10*(2), 81–94. https://doi.org/10.1016/S0969-6989(02)00004-8

Osborne, C. (2012). Smart cart follows you when grocery shopping. *Smartplanet.com*. https://www.zdnet.com/article/smart-cart-follows-you-when-grocery-shopping/

Pauwels, K., & Neslin, S. A. (2015). Building with bricks and mortar: The revenue impact of opening physical stores in a multichannel environment. *Journal of Retailing, 91*(2), 182–197. https://doi.org/10.1016/j.jretai.2015.02.001

Pick, D., & Eisend, M. (2016). Customer responses to switching costs: A meta-analytic investigation of the moderating influence of culture. *Journal of International Marketing, 24*(4), 39–60. https://doi.org/10.1509/jim.15.0139

Polo, Y., & Sese, F. J. (2016). Does the nature of the interaction matter? Understanding customer channel choice for purchases and communications. *Journal of Service Research, 19*(3), 276–290. https://doi.org/10.1177/1094670516645189

Prelec, D., & Loewenstein, G. (1998). The red and the black: Mental accounting of savings and debt. *Marketing Science, 17*(1), 4–28. https://doi.org/10.1287/mksc.17.1.4

Prelec, D., & Simester, D. (2001). Always leave home without it: A further investigation of the credit-card effect on willingness to pay. *Marketing Letters, 12*(1), 5–12. https://doi.org/10.1023/A:1008196717017

Quaid, L. (2005, May 9). New computers make grocery carts smarter. *Rutland Herald*. https://www.rutlandherald.com/news/new-computers-make-grocery-carts-smarter/article_35af3844-1824-5725-866e-e145aa9e837b.html

Rapp, A., Baker, T. L., Bachrach, D. G., Ogilvie, J., & Beitelspacher, L. S. (2015). Perceived customer showrooming behavior and the effect on retail salesperson self-efficacy and performance. *Journal of Retailing, 91*(2), 358–369. https://doi.org/10.1016/j.jretai.2014.12.007

Reinartz, W., Wiegand, N., & Imschloss, M. (2019). The impact of digital transformation on the retailing value chain. *International Journal of Research in Marketing, 36*(3), 350–366. https://doi.org/10.1016/j.ijresmar.2018.12.002

Risselada, H., Verhoef, P. C., & Bijmolt, T. H. (2014). Dynamic effects of social influence and direct marketing on the adoption of high-technology products. *Journal of Marketing, 78*(2), 52–68. https://doi.org/10.1509/jm.11.0592

Rosenblum, P. (2007, March). *Technology-enabled customer centricity in the store* [Benchmark report]. Retail Systems Research. https://www.rsrresearch.com/research/technology-enabled-customer-centricity-in-the-store

Schindler, R. M. (1998). Consequence of perceiving oneself as responsible for obtaining a discount: Evidence for smart-shopper feelings. *Journal of Consumer Psychology, 7*(4), 371–392. https://doi.org/10.1207/s15327663jcp0704_04

Schneider, P. J., & Zielke, S. (2020). Searching offline and buying online—An analysis of showrooming forms and segments. *Journal of Retailing and Consumer Services, 52*, 101919. https://doi.org/10.1016/j.jretconser.2019.101919

Schumacher, C., Eggers, F., Verhoef, P. C., & Maas, P. (2020). *The effect of cultural differences on consumers' willingness to share personal information* [Working paper]. University of St. Gallen.

Shankar, V., Inman, J. J., Mantrala, M., Kelley, E., & Rizley, R. (2011). Innovations in shopper marketing: Current insights and future research issues. *Journal of Retailing, 87*(Suppl. 1), S29–S42. https://doi.org/10.1016/j.jretai.2011.04.007

Sheehan, D., & van Ittersum, K. (2018). In-store spending dynamics: How budgets invert relative-spending patterns. *Journal of Consumer Research, 45*(1), 49–67. https://doi.org/10.1093/jcr/ucx125

Sheehan, D., & van Ittersum, K. (2021). Isolating price promotions: The influence of promotional timing on promotion redemption. *Journal of the Association for Consumer Research, 6*(1), 81–90. https://doi.org/10.1086/710247

Teerling, M. L., & Huizingh, E. K. (2005). *The complementarity between online and offline consumer attitudes and behavior* [Working paper]. University of Groningen, the Netherlands.

Valentini, S., Montaguti, E., & Neslin, S. A. (2011). Decision process evolution in customer channel choice. *Journal of Marketing*, 75(6), 72–86. https://doi.org/10.1509/jm.09.0362

van Doorn, J., & Hoekstra, J. C. (2013). Customization of online advertising: The role of intrusiveness. *Marketing Letters*, 24(4), 339–351. https://doi.org/10.1007/s11002-012-9222-1

van Heerde, H. J., Dinner, I. M., & Neslin, S. A. (2019). Engaging the unengaged customer: The value of a retailer mobile app. *International Journal of Research in Marketing*, 36(3), 420–438. https://doi.org/10.1016/j.ijresmar.2019.03.003

van Ittersum, K., Wansink, B., Pennings, J. M., & Sheehan, D. (2013). Smart shopping carts: How real-time feedback influences spending. *Journal of Marketing*, 77(6), 21–36. https://doi.org/10.1509/jm.12.0060

van Nierop, J. E., Leeflang, P. S., Teerling, M. L., & Huizingh, K. E. (2011). The impact of the introduction and use of an informational website on offline customer buying behavior. *International Journal of Research in Marketing*, 28(2), 155–165. https://doi.org/10.1016/j.ijresmar.2011.02.002

Venkatesan, R., Kumar, V., & Ravishanker, N. (2007). Multichannel shopping: Causes and consequences. *Journal of Marketing*, 71(2), 114–132. https://doi.org/10.1509/jmkg.71.2.114

Verhoef, P. C. (2012). Multichannel customer management strategy. In V. Shankar & G. Carpenter (Eds.), *Handbook of marketing strategy* (pp. 135–150). Edward Elgar Publishing Limited. https://doi.org/10.4337/9781781005224.00017

Verhoef, P. C. (2020). Customer experience creation in today's digital world. In B. Schlegelmilch & R. Winer (Eds.), *The Routledge companion to strategic marketing* (pp. 107–122). Routledge.

Verhoef, P. C., & Bijmolt, T. H. (2019). Marketing perspectives on digital business models: A framework and overview of the special issue. *International Journal of Research in Marketing*, 36(3), 341–349. https://doi.org/10.1016/j.ijresmar.2019.08.001

Verhoef, P. C., Broekhuizen, T., Bart, Y., Bhattacharya, A., Dong, J. Q., Fabian, N., & Haenlein, M. (2021). Digital transformation: A multidisciplinary reflection and research agenda. *Journal of Business Research*, 122, 889–901. https://doi.org/10.1016/j.jbusres.2019.09.022

Verhoef, P. C., Kannan, P. K., & Inman, J. J. (2015). From multi-channel retailing to omni-channel retailing: Introduction to the special issue on multi-channel retailing. *Journal of Retailing*, 91(2), 174–181. https://doi.org/10.1016/j.jretai.2015.02.005

Verhoef, P. C., & Langerak, F. (2001). Possible determinants of consumers' adoption of electronic grocery shopping in the Netherlands. *Journal of Retailing and Consumer Services*, 8(5), 275–285. https://doi.org/10.1016/S0969-6989(00)00033-3

Verhoef, P. C., Neslin, S. A., & Vroomen, B. (2007). Multichannel customer management: Understanding the research-shopper phenomenon. *International Journal of Research in Marketing*, 24(2), 129–148. https://doi.org/10.1016/j.ijresmar.2006.11.002

Verplanken, B., & Aarts, K. (1999). Habit, attitude, and planned behaviour: Is habit an empty construct or an interesting case of goal-directed automaticity? *European Review of Social Psychology*, 10(1), 101–134. https://doi.org/10.1080/14792779943000035

Vijayasarathy, L. R. (2004). Predicting consumer intentions to use on-line shopping: The case for an augmented technology acceptance model. *Information & Management*, 41(6), 747–762. https://doi.org/10.1016/j.im.2003.08.011

Wang, K., & Goldfarb, A. (2017). Can offline stores drive online sales? *Journal of Marketing Research*, 54(5), 706–719. https://doi.org/10.1509/jmr.14.0518

Wang, R. J. H., Krishnamurthi, L., & Malthouse, E. C. (2018). When reward convenience meets a mobile app: Increasing customer participation in a coalition loyalty program. *Journal of the Association for Consumer Research*, 3(3), 314–329. https://doi.org/10.1086/698331

Wang, R. J. H., Malthouse, E. C., & Krishnamurthi, L. (2015). On the go: How mobile shopping affects customer purchase behavior. *Journal of Retailing*, 91(2), 217–234. https://doi.org/10.1016/j.jretai.2015.01.002

Wendlandt, M., & Schrader, U. (2007). Consumer reactance against loyalty programs. *Journal of Consumer Marketing*, 24(5), 293–304. https://doi.org/10.1108/07363760710773111

Wilson, E. J., & Sherrell, D. L. (1993). Source effects in communication and persuasion research: A meta-analysis of effect size. *Journal of the Academy of Marketing Science*, 21(2), 101–112. https://doi.org/10.1007/BF02894421

Xu, J., Forman, C., Kim, J. B., & Van Ittersum, K. (2014). News media channels: Complements or substitutes? Evidence from mobile phone usage. *Journal of Marketing*, 78(4), 97–112. https://doi.org/10.1509/jm.13.0198

Xu, K., Chan, J., Ghose, A., & Han, S. P. (2017). Battle of the channels: The impact of tablets on digital commerce. *Management Science*, 63(5), 1469–1492. https://doi.org/10.1287/mnsc.2015.2406

Xu, L., Duan, J. A., & Whinston, A. B. (2014, June). Path to purchase: A mutually exciting point process model for online advertising and conversion. *Management Science, 60*(6), 1392–1412. https://doi.org/10.1287/mnsc.2014.1952

Xue, M., Hitt, L. M., & Chen, P. Y. (2011). Determinants and outcomes of internet banking adoption. *Management Science, 57*(2), 291–307. https://doi.org/10.1287/mnsc.1100.1187

Zantedeschi, D., Feit, E. M. D., & Bradlow, E. T. (2016). Measuring multi-channel advertising effectiveness using consumer-level advertising response data. *Management Science, 63*(8), 2706–2728. https://doi.org/10.1287/mnsc.2016.2451

Zhang, J. Z. (2020, February 11). Why catalogs are making a comeback. *Harvard Business Review.* https://hbr.org/2020/02/why-catalogs-are-making-a-comeback

CHAPTER 30

PERCEIVED PRICE DIFFERENCES AND CONSUMER BEHAVIOR

Kent B. Monroe

Prices are an important aspect of people's lives. Studying how people respond to price information is an important aspect of understanding consumer psychology. Behavioral characteristics unique to each individual influence these responses. Consumers neither have perfect information about the market nor perceive prices or form value judgments similarly. They react to prices and sellers' pricing tactics in multiple ways, some of which they may not even be aware. Over the past 4 centuries, an important issue for researchers, scholars, and managers has been to understand how people perceive, remember, process, and use price information.

Some philosophers in the 1700s wrote essays pondering this issue. In the 1800s, psychophysics researchers conducted experiments on how people discriminated between different magnitudes of physical stimuli. While Marshall (1890) recognized the subjectivity of money, he nevertheless dropped this idea in later versions of his neoclassical economic theory of how price information influences buyer behavior. This theoretical perspective dominated thought on this issue until recently. Today, behavioral price researchers contend that demand for products and services depends on people's perceptions of differences in prices that vary across individuals and context. Leavitt (1954) experimentally showed people likely would choose a higher priced product when (a) they perceived price differences between choices were relatively large and (b) they believed there were quality differences between choices. In the next two sections, a historical perspective about early consumer price research and some important behavioral price concepts are briefly summarized.

An important recent development has been psychological and neural research helping us understand the human brain. Of interest for pricing research is the area of numerical cognition, or how humans perceive and process numerical information. The third section of this chapter summarizes concepts from numerical cognition relevant for understanding how people perceive and respond to price differences. Given the widespread use of price promotions to enhance demand, the fourth section expands on the premise that people's price judgments are comparative in nature by examining some examples of recent price promotions and providing practical prescriptions for developing effective price communications. A brief summary concludes this chapter.

PRICE PERCEPTION AND BEHAVIORAL PRICE CONCEPTS

We begin with the premise that a price, similar to other physical stimuli such as light or sound, is a stimulus of consumer behavior. In 1738, Daniel Bernoulli (1738/1954) suggested each equal increment of a monetary gain yields an advantage inversely proportional to current wealth:

$$dy = b(dx/x),$$

where dy is a person's perceived increase in utility resulting from a monetary gain dx, x is the monetary amount of goods previously owned, and b is a constant.

Later, Weber (1834/1965), using a logarithmic function, showed that the perceived utility of an amount of money gained is less than the perceived utility of the same amount of money lost from the same reference level of wealth. We can derive two key points from these observations: (a) The perceived value of money differs depending on whether it is perceived as a gain or a loss, and (b) the amount of this perceived change in value is relative to a person's previous position. This previous position is a person's reference point. Weber argued people discriminate between two similar stimuli based on *"relative differences"* between them rather than an absolute difference (Herrnstein & Boring, 1965, p. 64, emphasis added). Moreover, for an increase in a stimulus level to become just noticeably different (*jnd*), a constant percentage must be added. This *jnd* for a stimulus is given by the following:

$$\Delta I/I = K_w,$$

where I is the magnitude of the current stimulus, ΔI is the extra amount needed for a similar stimulus to be perceived as *jnd*, and K_w is Weber's Fraction.

Weber's law applies to *perceived differences* between two intensities of a stimulus, that is, small, equally perceptible changes in a response correspond to proportional changes in the stimulus. This ratio expresses a person's sensitivity to changes or differences in a stimulus. It helps us understand people's responses to price information and the way people encode numbers in their brain: "The neural representation of number is comparable to a logarithmic scale we learned years ago" (Dehaene, 2003, p. 147). Fechner (1860/1965) showed the magnitude of sensation experienced (y) is related logarithmically to the magnitude of the stimulus (x): $y = \log x$. He also introduced the concept of a lower stimulus threshold where sensation begins and an upper threshold where sensation ends. These concepts and ideas help us understand how people perceive and respond to price information and how to present price information to people.

Considering price as a stimulus means exposure to price information induces sensory signals in the brain of each individual. Our senses provide a connection to both our nonconscious and conscious mental processes. *Sensation* is the process of receiving these sense impressions in our mind. Whatever influences brain function affects perception: our emotion state, previous experiences, expectations, motivational state, cultural conditioning, and personality (Lobel, 2014).

Processing Price Information

Number processing is the mental ability of people to manipulate a sequence of words or symbols according to specific rules (Dehaene, 1992). Such processing occurs when people calculate or estimate a numerical difference between two prices; add the amounts for tax, shipping, and handling to determine the total cost of a purchase; calculate the effect of an advertised percentage discount; or calculate the unit price of an offering.

Processing price information begins with initial exposure to price information, followed by price encoding (bringing price information into mind), representing and storing price information in memory, processing the information, and responding (or not) to this information (Cheng & Monroe, 2013). The way price information is presented to people influences their reactions, inducing sensations. Our brain makes inferences about these inputs and decides where to send the sensory signals. *Attention* is necessary for perception to occur. Even so, there is still some mental processing for all incoming sensory information. Attention allows us to allocate our finite mental resources. Our perceptual systems learn as we gain experience. *Perceptual learning* occurs nonconsciously.

Internal Reference Price

Knowing how people perceive and respond to price information is useful when setting and managing prices. An underlying premise for these behavioral responses is that people judge prices comparatively. Unique to each individual and situation, an *internal reference price* (P_{ref}) anchors price judgments. "*It is a **dynamic, internal** price to which **an individual*** *compares another price consciously or nonconsciously*" (Cheng & Monroe, 2013, p. 108, bold and italics in original). A person's reference price is unobservable and is specific to each person, product category, sales environment, and point in time. A reference price may be influenced by other prices or numerical stimuli at the time of price comparison (Adaval & Monroe, 2002; Nunes & Boatwright, 2004).[1]

In a business-to-business context, customers who paid a price higher (lower) than their reference price purchased smaller (larger) quantities than would be expected if they only considered the actual price. They responded to the perceived difference between their reference price and the actual price ($P_{ref} - P_{actual}$). Business customers were more sensitive to price increases than to price decreases, and salespersons had their own reference prices influencing the transaction price (Bruno et al., 2012; Faranda, 2011; Moosmayer et al., 2012). When people evaluate options as price differences from a reference price, their brain uses the same type of decision making as it does during hearing, seeing, and other sensory processes. Relying on a comparative reference price is a simple but efficient tool for people.

A purchase occurs when a buyer acquires (gains) a product but gives up (loses) what is paid to obtain it. Whether people expect a transaction to be satisfactory or not depends partly on their perceptions of an offer as well as the acquisition itself. Paying a price perceived to be less than an internal reference price ($P_{ref} > P_{selling}$) would induce a favorable evaluation. People may be dissatisfied if they perceive a selling price is more than their reference price for an acquisition ($P_{ref} < P_{selling}$). If so, the extra amount they would pay relative to their reference price would be perceived negatively (i.e., loss). For a perceived price difference of ΔP from a reference price reflecting a price increase (loss), the decline in perceived value will be perceptually larger than if the ΔP reflects a price reduction or increase in perceived value.

Differential Price Thresholds

Price elasticity of demand is a measure of the sensitivity of a group of buyers to a price change (or difference). There are two issues concerning when people would (a) perceive a price differs from their past exposure or expectation (differential perceptual price threshold) and (b) respond to the perceived price difference with a change in their buying behavior (differential response price threshold). The first issue stems from Weber's law, specifying a relationship between a specific stimulus level (price) and the amount that needs to be added to that level for people to perceive there is a difference. Perception of a price difference depends on the magnitude of the price difference relative to a reference price:

$$\Delta P/P_{ref} = K,$$

where ΔP is the minimum change (or difference) in price to induce a change in perception (*jnd*), P_{ref} is an individual's reference price, and K is a constant.

This ΔP is a differential price threshold, the minimum difference in price between a price in question and a person's reference price necessary to induce a perception of a price difference. People's sensitivity to price differences is not only individual but also product and market dependent. When a price is changed, it cannot be assumed consumers will perceive a price difference. There are two important questions: (a) Do consumers perceive the prices differ? (b) If yes, do they change their purchase behavior? Just because a person perceives a change in price does not mean the difference will induce a change in purchasing behavior. The first question of whether a person perceives a price difference is an issue of whether a differential perceptual threshold has been reached. Whether a person changes their buying behavior is an issue of a differential response threshold.

Latitude of Price Indifference

Small actual differences in selling price from a consumer's internal reference price (positive or negative) are unlikely to induce any perceived price differences (*latitude of price indifference*; Cheng & Monroe, 2013). Although people may notice there is a numerical difference between their reference and a selling price, the two prices may not be perceived to differ relative to a degree of expensiveness. If this occurs, the perceived price difference is

---

[1] Some scholars have dichotomized the reference price concept as either external (i.e., in an individual's external environment) or internal (i.e., in an individual's mind). However, since all reference prices are in the brains of individuals, they must be internal, regardless of the initial source of the stimulus (Cheng & Monroe, 2013).

unlikely to induce a change in purchase behavior. When a consumer does perceive such a difference in price and relative expensiveness, a differential perceptual price threshold has been reached.

Figure 30.1 illustrates these differential price threshold concepts. On the horizontal axis are ± percentages of price differences relative to an internal reference price, with the midpoint representing no perceived price difference. On the vertical axis are ± percentage changes in buy response induced by perceived price differences. The latitude of price indifference is a flat area to the left and right of the reference price (RP), bounded on the left by PT_l, the low differential perceptual price threshold, and on the right by PT_h, the high differential perceptual price threshold. To the left of PT_l and the right of PT_h are areas indicating increasing sensitivity to price differences. Initially these areas may induce little or no change in purchase behavior as the ± percentage price differences increase. Some people may perceive a price difference, judge there has been a change in relative expensiveness, but not immediately change purchase behavior. However, other buyers may have yet to perceive there is a price difference. As the percentage price difference increases in either direction, more people will perceive and respond to the difference. RT_l and RT_h indicate the low and high differential response thresholds, respectively. Perceived price differences to the right of RT_h and to the left of RT_l indicate the percentage price differences have led to prices increasingly unacceptable to potential buyers.[2]

An underlying premise is that buyers respond to perceived price differences relative to their internal reference price ($P_{ref} - P_{actual}$). The P_{actual} may be a price of an item being considered by a consumer, a price on promotion, another price in the firm's product line, a competitor's price for a similar

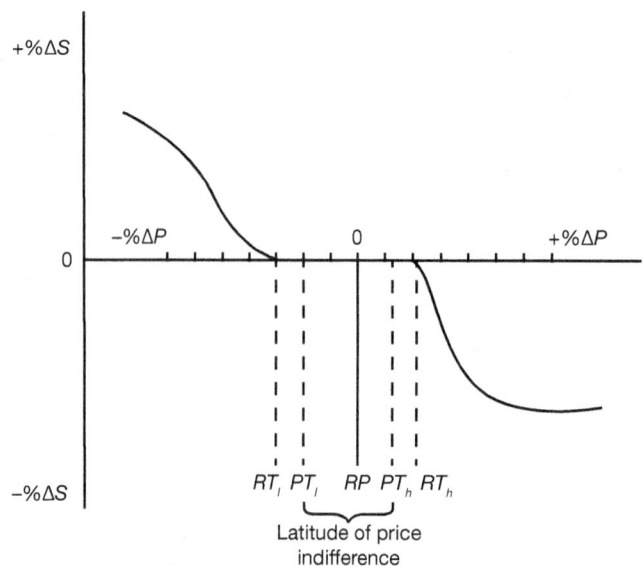

RP = internal reference price
PT_l and PT_h = differential price perceptual thresholds low and high
RT_l and RT_h = differential price response thresholds low and high
%ΔP = perceived percentage change (difference) in price
%ΔS = percentage change in sales

FIGURE 30.1. Change in sales and latitude of price indifference.

---

[2]These differential thresholds are relatively small distances along the percentage price difference axis, depicting changes in sensitivity to price differences.

compares another price consciously or nonconsciously" (Cheng & Monroe, 2013, p. 108, bold and italics in original). A person's reference price is unobservable and is specific to each person, product category, sales environment, and point in time. A reference price may be influenced by other prices or numerical stimuli at the time of price comparison (Adaval & Monroe, 2002; Nunes & Boatwright, 2004).[1]

In a business-to-business context, customers who paid a price higher (lower) than their reference price purchased smaller (larger) quantities than would be expected if they only considered the actual price. They responded to the perceived difference between their reference price and the actual price ($P_{ref} - P_{actual}$). Business customers were more sensitive to price increases than to price decreases, and salespersons had their own reference prices influencing the transaction price (Bruno et al., 2012; Faranda, 2011; Moosmayer et al., 2012). When people evaluate options as price differences from a reference price, their brain uses the same type of decision making as it does during hearing, seeing, and other sensory processes. Relying on a comparative reference price is a simple but efficient tool for people.

A purchase occurs when a buyer acquires (gains) a product but gives up (loses) what is paid to obtain it. Whether people expect a transaction to be satisfactory or not depends partly on their perceptions of an offer as well as the acquisition itself. Paying a price perceived to be less than an internal reference price ($P_{ref} > P_{selling}$) would induce a favorable evaluation. People may be dissatisfied if they perceive a selling price is more than their reference price for an acquisition ($P_{ref} < P_{selling}$). If so, the extra amount they would pay relative to their reference price would be perceived negatively (i.e., loss). For a perceived price difference of ΔP from a reference price reflecting a price increase (loss), the decline in perceived value will be perceptually larger than if the ΔP reflects a price reduction or increase in perceived value.

Differential Price Thresholds

Price elasticity of demand is a measure of the sensitivity of a group of buyers to a price change (or difference). There are two issues concerning when people would (a) perceive a price differs from their past exposure or expectation (differential perceptual price threshold) and (b) respond to the perceived price difference with a change in their buying behavior (differential response price threshold). The first issue stems from Weber's law, specifying a relationship between a specific stimulus level (price) and the amount that needs to be added to that level for people to perceive there is a difference. Perception of a price difference depends on the magnitude of the price difference relative to a reference price:

$$\Delta P/P_{ref} = K,$$

where ΔP is the minimum change (or difference) in price to induce a change in perception (*jnd*), P_{ref} is an individual's reference price, and K is a constant.

This ΔP is a differential price threshold, the minimum difference in price between a price in question and a person's reference price necessary to induce a perception of a price difference. People's sensitivity to price differences is not only individual but also product and market dependent. When a price is changed, it cannot be assumed consumers will perceive a price difference. There are two important questions: (a) Do consumers perceive the prices differ? (b) If yes, do they change their purchase behavior? Just because a person perceives a change in price does not mean the difference will induce a change in purchasing behavior. The first question of whether a person perceives a price difference is an issue of whether a differential perceptual threshold has been reached. Whether a person changes their buying behavior is an issue of a differential response threshold.

Latitude of Price Indifference

Small actual differences in selling price from a consumer's internal reference price (positive or negative) are unlikely to induce any perceived price differences (*latitude of price indifference*; Cheng & Monroe, 2013). Although people may notice there is a numerical difference between their reference and a selling price, the two prices may not be perceived to differ relative to a degree of expensiveness. If this occurs, the perceived price difference is

---

[1] Some scholars have dichotomized the reference price concept as either external (i.e., in an individual's external environment) or internal (i.e., in an individual's mind). However, since all reference prices are in the brains of individuals, they must be internal, regardless of the initial source of the stimulus (Cheng & Monroe, 2013).

unlikely to induce a change in purchase behavior. When a consumer does perceive such a difference in price and relative expensiveness, a differential perceptual price threshold has been reached.

Figure 30.1 illustrates these differential price threshold concepts. On the horizontal axis are ± percentages of price differences relative to an internal reference price, with the midpoint representing no perceived price difference. On the vertical axis are ± percentage changes in buy response induced by perceived price differences. The latitude of price indifference is a flat area to the left and right of the reference price (RP), bounded on the left by PT_l, the low differential perceptual price threshold, and on the right by PT_h, the high differential perceptual price threshold. To the left of PT_l and the right of PT_h are areas indicating increasing sensitivity to price differences. Initially these areas may induce little or no change in purchase behavior as the ± percentage price differences increase. Some people may perceive a price difference, judge there has been a change in relative expensiveness, but not immediately change purchase behavior. However, other buyers may have yet to perceive there is a price difference. As the percentage price difference increases in either direction, more people will perceive and respond to the difference. RT_l and RT_h indicate the low and high differential response thresholds, respectively. Perceived price differences to the right of RT_h and to the left of RT_l indicate the percentage price differences have led to prices increasingly unacceptable to potential buyers.[2]

An underlying premise is that buyers respond to perceived price differences relative to their internal reference price ($P_{ref} - P_{actual}$). The P_{actual} may be a price of an item being considered by a consumer, a price on promotion, another price in the firm's product line, a competitor's price for a similar

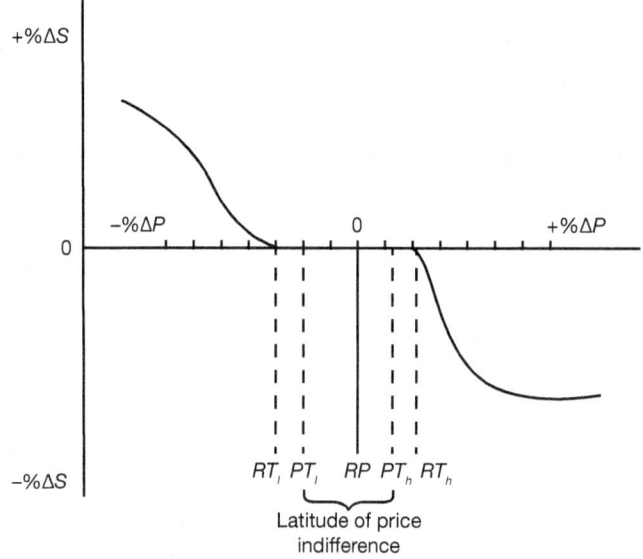

RP = internal reference price
PT_l and PT_h = differential price perceptual thresholds low and high
RT_l and RT_h = differential price response thresholds low and high
%ΔP = perceived percentage change (difference) in price
%ΔS = percentage change in sales

FIGURE 30.1. Change in sales and latitude of price indifference.

---

[2]These differential thresholds are relatively small distances along the percentage price difference axis, depicting changes in sensitivity to price differences.

item, or the price another customer has paid. Since people generally prefer gains to losses, a negative response to a perceived price increase occurs sooner than a positive response to a perceived price reduction of the same magnitude from the same reference price. The shape of the response curve to the left of RT_l is expected to be reverse S-shaped or concave. The general shape of the response curve to the right of the RT_h is expected to be convex.

In a study of three brands of a household product, price sensitivity varied with brands and the amount of a percentage price change. In 1 year, the 30 different versions of these brands had 54 price increases and 28 price decreases. Price changes of about ±2% had little effect on the share of any brand. For price changes greater than 2%, price sensitivity differed relative to each brand's price position in the market, the direction of the price change, and the amount of the change (George et al., 1996; see also Han et al., 2001; Terui & Dahana, 2006). Other research on food items showed short-term price discounts of 5% to 10% were necessary to produce significant sales responses (Van Heerde et al., 2001).

The width of the latitude of price indifference is important for both the amount of a price reduction necessary to stimulate positive consumer response as well as the magnitude of a price increase permissible before there might be significant negative buyer response. Estimates of the width of the latitude of price indifference have varied from ±2% to ±10% or more from an individual's reference price (Della Bitta et al., 1981; Gupta & Cooper, 1992; Kalyanaram & Little, 1994; Xia & Monroe, 2009). How large must a price discount be to induce an increase in sales volume overcoming the unit margin sacrificed by a price reduction? How much can a price be increased before buyers perceive a decrease in value and change purchase behaviors? An important implication is that the extent unit product sales are sensitive to price differences varies relative to the perceived distance a price is from a buyer's internal reference price ($P_{ref} - P_{actual}$). These differential price thresholds indicate how consumers may respond to price changes, short-term price promotions, relative changes in the price structure of a product line, and competitive changes of any of these factors. For the same magnitude of price change, ΔP, the latitude of price indifference for a perceived price increase would be narrower than the latitude of price indifference for a perceived price reduction. The perceived distance between P_{ref} and PT_h would be less than the perceived distance between P_{ref} and PT_l when relative to the same reference price.

The existence of price thresholds and reference prices suggests consumers may not notice a price promotion unless a price reduction exceeds a minimum threshold (Raman & Bass, 2002). An internal reference price is unobservable and not the same as the last price paid for an item being considered. An internal reference price is not dependent on a person remembering or recalling specific numerical prices. The width of the latitude of price indifference will be influenced by several factors summarized next.

The latitude of price indifference for brand-loyal buyers likely will be wider than for nonbrand buyers, due primarily to their tolerance for price increases (Anderson, 1996). Brand-loyal consumers are likely to be satisfied with the benefits they believe they gain and therefore focus more on the benefits of the brand than on its price. A positive relationship between customer satisfaction and willingness to tolerate price increases suggests the distance between P_{ref} and both PT_h and RT_h will be positively associated with customer satisfaction and be wider for loyal buyers.

Price knowledge is not stored in the mind as exact knowledge but involves an approximate element related to market price characteristics and the way people store numerical quantities such as price in their minds (Marques & Dehaene, 2004; Vanhuele & Drèze, 2002). People's knowledge about the distribution and variation of prices for items in a product category is related to their frequency of purchases in the category. More accurate price knowledge of items in a category increases the likelihood consumers will perceive when prices differ from their reference prices. The relationship between people's price knowledge and price acceptability exhibits an inverted-U relationship for most people. People with moderate price knowledge have wider ranges of price acceptance than either low- or high-knowledge buyers.

The frequency of price promotions negatively influences consumers' perceptions and responses to price information. Frequent price promotions may reduce their reference price for a product. Consumers' reference prices adapt to lower promoted prices and do not readily return to previous levels. People learn to wait for the next promotion and tend not to purchase at a nondeal price. Waiting for the next deal may reduce the frequency of purchases and the proportion of sales made at regular prices: "Managers may not appreciate the implied deal-to-deal buying behavior because products are decreasingly sold at full margin, but a possible way to avoid this effect is to reduce the frequency of price promotions" (Bijmolt et al., 2005, p. 153).

When consumers focus on the next deal, they become less concerned about product benefits. As their reference price falls to a lower deal price, the prior regular price may be perceived negatively as it becomes higher than their reference price. The reduction in the attractiveness of future promotions leads to increases in the magnitude of advertised discounts. The pervasive discounting along with increasing amounts of discounts off the regular price has also whet buyers' appetite for discounts, a form of addiction similar to heroin. Relatively large discounts increase customer disbelief they are valid or belief that the original list prices were inflated. Frequent price promotions wherein prices fluctuate between so-called regular and promotional levels induce customers to become suspicious of what is the real regular price. When "no one pays full price," a regular or list price loses its integrity.[3]

PSYCHOLOGICAL THEORIES UNDERLYING BEHAVIORAL PRICING

This section very briefly identifies four theories that have been used to explain people's responses to prices. *Adaptation-level theory* assumes people judge stimuli relative to internal norms representing the effects of present and past experiences. All judgments are influenced by a person's existing, but constantly changing, adaptation level (AL; Helson, 1964). The judgment of any stimulus depends on the ratio of the value of that stimulus relative to a person's current AL. AL is the value of the stimulus judged neutral and is hypothesized to be a weighted geometric mean of the past stimuli a person has encountered previously. If a stimulus is perceived greater than the current AL, it is judged higher than the standard. Every new price encountered by an individual tends to move an internal reference price (AL) in its own direction (*anchoring effect*). New prices near a consumer's original reference price will have little effect in changing the AL and may be judged to be neutral or medium. Prices outside this neutral range, whether above or below the reference price, would not only move the AL level in their direction but may also change a person's perception of other prices in a category (*contrast effect*).

People maintain a representation in their minds of price for a product (AL or internal reference price). They also compare external market prices (sale prices, suggested list prices) with this reference price when judging the acceptability of these external prices. Over time their brains develop separate product–price categories that help them judge specific prices in the categories.

Price acceptability judgments depend partly on the specific product–price category used as an exemplar. A person evaluating a new car price might judge it to be too high if the AL used is for a domestic compact car. If the person evaluates that price relative to a midsize car, the price might be judged high but acceptable. This person previously has formed separate internal product–price categories for cars with a reference price and acceptable price range for each category.

Early research on the acceptable price concept was based on *assimilation-contrast theory* (M. Sherif & Hovland, 1961). This theory posits new stimuli encountered by a person are compared against a background of previous experiences within that category. Prior experiences form a person's reference standard that changes when new stimuli are added or the range of stimuli values shifts. The reference standard is the basis for an individual to compare and evaluate other subsequently encountered

---

[3]The increase of class action lawsuits alleging retailers use fictitious regular or original prices in their price promotions attests to this possibility. See Streitfeld (2016).

stimuli of the same category. An individual may encounter a new price that serves as an anchor and moves the reference price in the direction of this new price. Whether this change of the reference price induces assimilation or a contrast effect depends on how other prices in the category are judged after the person observes the new price. If a new price is higher than the reference price, the reference price would move toward the new price.

After this shift, prices previously lower than the old reference price perceptually become further away from the reference price. If judgments of these previously perceived low prices do not change thereafter, an *assimilation effect* has occurred. If a new price displaced the reference price sufficiently far in its direction, the previous lower prices would be perceived as lower than before and a *contrast effect* would have occurred.

People sorted a set of price slips for a product (winter coat, dress shoes, sport coat) into different groups of prices perceived to be similar or to belong together. Participants labeled the groups of prices as acceptable or unacceptable and gave reasons for their judgments. A low unacceptable price threshold implies there are prices greater than zero that are not acceptable to pay. A person may be suspicious of a product's quality below such a low price. There is also a high absolute acceptable price threshold above which a person would be unwilling or unable to pay for the item. Prices between a person's highest and lowest acceptable prices form an *acceptable price range* for that product and occasion. In this research, the center of their acceptable price range was within their most acceptable prices category. There were also other acceptable prices below as well as above the most acceptable prices category. In the sport coat and dress shoes conditions, the low-price limit in the most acceptable prices category for both products was 30% below the scale center, whereas the most acceptable high-price limits were 8% and 2%, respectively, above the scale center (Monroe, 1971; C. W. Sherif, 1963).

Range-frequency theory concerns how the range of prices (the difference between the lowest and highest prices) in an evaluation set affects consumers' assessment of the relative expensiveness of the product, that is, whether a price is low (too low), just right (acceptable), or high (too high). When there is a set or distribution or array of prices, the lowest and highest prices (price range) in the set influence people's price judgments (Parducci, 1965; see Cheng & Monroe, 2013, for a brief review of price range research on consumers' purchase behavior). The spacing between these prices and the frequency of the prices also influence price judgments.

Prospect theory draws on the principles of perception and judgment from psychophysics and adaptation-level theory (Kahneman & Tversky, 1979). Prices or outcomes are compared with a reference point. Perceptions of value depend on the current reference point and the magnitude of difference, positive or negative, from the reference point. From this reference price, outcomes are judged as gains or losses. The value of an economic exchange can be decomposed into the perceived value of the economic good itself and the perceived value of the offer or deal. If a price is less than a person's reference price ($P_{ref} > P_{actual}$), there will be positive perceived offer value enhancing the perceived value of the good itself (Grewal et al., 1998; Thaler, 1985).[4] Prices numerically equidistant from the reference price are perceived to be closer to that reference point if they are more than the reference price than if they are less. If the reference price is $80, then $90 will be perceived to be closer to $80 than would $70, even though the price difference is $10 in each comparison (Dehaene, 1989, 1997, 2011).

RELEVANT NUMERICAL COGNITION CONCEPTS

Processing price information begins with exposure to price information, followed by price encoding, representation of price information in memory, the cognitive tasks of processing the information, and responses to this information. These situations occur when people calculate or estimate the numerical difference between two prices; add additional

---

[4] A comparison with a reference is represented as a subtractive function. The comparative is presented first in the expressions.

amounts for shipping, handling, and tax to determine the total cost of a purchase; or calculate the effect of an advertised discount. "Tasks such as measurement, comparison of prices, or approximate calculations solicit an 'approximation mode' in which we access and manipulate a mental model of approximate quantities similar to a mental 'number line'" (Dehaene, 1992, p. 20). Approximation is the process of converting Arabic or verbal numerals into an internal magnitude representation of the quantity depicted. Typically, our brain tends to ignore the input mode and scale, (e.g., $, £, ¥, €, oz), and the numeral quantities are represented and processed in the intraparietal sulcus (IPS) similar to other magnitudes such as size, distance, or weight. This encoding is automatic, fast, and independent of the number (Tzelgov et al., 1992).[5]

Encoding and Internal Representation of Price Information

How are prices represented in our minds? Whenever a number is used to denote an amount, such as price, age, or weight, the magnitude of the number is meaningful. A price may be encoded nominally in that the exact number is stored in memory. Memory price awareness research implicitly assumes nominal representation by asking people to reproduce exactly a price previously paid. Or people may encode a price as a magnitude in that either the exact numerical price or an approximation of it is encoded and stored in memory. If the item is a cashmere sweater, $40 may be represented as inexpensive. Yet if the item is a typical paperback novel, it might be represented as expensive.

An approximation or an exact number may be encoded and stored in memory. To influence purchase decisions, people must encode a price as a magnitude rather than the exact numerals. Although people may not intend to encode price information as magnitudes, such encoding may proceed automatically, effortlessly, and nonconsciously (Tzelgov et al., 1992). Consumers must deal with numerals at the level of meaning by relying on a form of semantic representation (i.e., what the price means to them: high, low . . . expensive).

Regardless of how prices are presented, the visual, auditory, and analog representations in our brains are connected neurologically. Perceived price magnitude is a function of (a) the actual digits in a price, (b) the number of specific digits, and (c) the sequence of the digits. Working memory for written text depends on the phonological length of the words and is approximately equal to the number of words a person can read aloud in 1.5 to 2 seconds (about 13 syllables for English). Children learn to associate (map in their brain) numerical magnitude with the syllabic length of a number because of the time it takes to process the number. Processing is slower for large numbers (more syllables) than small numbers. People nonconsciously tend to perceive greater numerical magnitude with prices requiring longer processing time (Coulter et al., 2012).

Several transformations are involved in the encoding process between the presentation of prices and the internal representation of price information in our brain. Numbers are semantically represented and activated on an ordered continuum. The psychological meaning of a price is determined by mentally mapping the number (or symbol) to a magnitude representation in our minds. In one context, 15 may be perceived to be high, but in another situation, it might be judged low.

People initially recode and compare numbers as quantities. Numerical quantity refers to the question "how many?" The IPS region of the prefrontal cortex of our brain is activated whenever humans compare or calculate with Arabic numerals. The IPS region can be activated also by spelled-out or spoken number words. When presenting numbers in a price message, individually or in combination, it is important to make it easy for people to process the numerical information. When price information is processed consciously, a person pays attention to the price and judges the product using information from the external environment and/or retrieved from memory. The magnitude representation of a price and its evaluation may be transferred from working memory into long-term memory, making it likely a person will remember the price. Or the evaluative judgment of a price may be

---

[5]This apparent ignoring of the denominator of the price equation during price judgments has been labeled the *unit effect* (see Burson et al., 2009; Monga & Bagchi, 2012; Pandelaere et al., 2011).

encoded into long-term memory. If so, a consumer may not remember that price later but may observe the product is either "expensive" or "reasonably priced."

Forms of Price Presentations

Prices may be presented verbally (thirty-six dollars) or in Arabic numerals ($36). The Arabic notation has the same meaning as the verbal notation, using arbitrary symbols with visual appearance unrelated to the meaning or pronunciation of the numerals. The primary meaning of a number is its magnitude information. Price magnitude is a person's perception of the "size" of a price relative to an internal reference price for a product. Elements such as font size, spatial distance between prices, or location within a message influence perceptions of price magnitude. In practice, a price promotion may present both a regular price and a sale price in vertical or horizontal order, close together, or apart. The higher price may be presented before the lower sale price. Other times, a reverse order may occur.

The horizontal physical distance between the regular and sale prices influences perceptions of discount magnitude. When these two prices are presented close together a discount is underestimated, but a discount is overestimated when they are about 5 inches apart (Coulter & Norberg, 2009). When the IPS area of our brain is involved, both physical distance and prices are processed as magnitudes.[6] If prices are placed physically close horizontally, a perception of a narrow distance interferes with the perception of the discount, leading to an underestimation. If prices are presented further apart horizontally, however, perception of a wide physical distance exaggerates the perception of the discount, and overestimation may occur.

We often encounter numbers arrayed in ascending order. Convention has rulers or other forms of linear distance increasing in order of magnitude from left to right. In one study, people estimated a higher price for products shown on the right of a display than those shown on the left. These effects were reversed when participants processed a printed page from right to left (Cai et al., 2012).

Processing Effects

It takes people longer to decide 8 is larger than 6 than to decide 8 is larger than 2. This *distance effect* indicates that the time people take to compare two numbers is inversely related to the numerical distance between the numbers. Initially, our brain nonconsciously encodes the digits 1, 2, 3, or 4 as "small," while 6, 7, 8, or 9 are encoded as "large." For equal numerical distance between two digits, the *magnitude effect* indicates it is easier to differentiate between two small numbers (e.g., 1 compared with 2) than two large numbers (e.g., 8 compared with 9). When discriminating between two prices, our brain automatically encodes each price nonconsciously and classifies the prices as small or large. Judging which number in a pair of numbers is larger, the task is easier when both numbers are perceived as large than when both numbers are perceived as small (judging which of two small numbers is larger is more difficult). The opposite effect occurs when people judge which of two large numbers is smaller.

The *size congruity effect* occurs when people are judging which of two prices is larger. It is easier if the larger of the compared prices is displayed in a larger font size. A similar result occurs when people are judging which of two numbers is smaller (e.g., searching for a low price or evaluating a price promotion) and the lower price is in a smaller font size. People may not only perceive and encode the numerical values of the prices they compare (e.g., an item is priced higher than another item); they may also evaluate (e.g., it is expensive). When prices are processed nonconsciously, a consumer may not focus on the prices. Nonetheless, an inference about the value of the product and a purchase decision may occur. The individual may not remember the product's price at a later time but may still be able to indicate the product is reasonably priced.

---

[6]The IPS is a long crevice located in the parietal lobe of the human brain. The IPS is activated whenever we think about a number, independently of the type of the task being performed. This activation occurs even with a quantitative reference, such as "some more," "many," or "bigger than the other one" (Dastjerdi et al., 2013; Dehaene, 2011).

Consumers' Purchase Goals and Motivation to Process Price Information

Consumers' purchase goals influence how they process price messages. Some people may seek to save money and minimize losses, whereas others may seek to acquire things and gain benefits. "Pay less" may induce people to be concerned about the sacrifice aspect of a purchase, while "save more" or "save now" may induce them to focus on a potential gain from the message. Messages framed as gains (e.g., "$x off"; "save") prime people to make positive inferences. Messages framed to minimize perceived losses (e.g., "pay less") prime people to reduce negative inferences (Ramanathan & Dhar 2010). People planning to purchase a specific product are more responsive to messages for that product framed as reduction of a loss. Customers without a prepurchase goal respond more to messages framed as additional gains. These effects emerge without intentional learning by consumers, occur nonconsciously, and may transfer to other products in the buying situation (J. Choi et al., 2012; Xia & Monroe, 2009).

Processing price information depends on buyers' motivation to process information and whether they have the mental resources for this processing. If not motivated or unable to process the information, they are more likely to use heuristics. When buyers process price information, they may focus on price's sacrifice dimension. When they are constrained by either mental resources or time to decide, they may process price information heuristically. To evaluate a price message, people have to encode the information and perhaps perform calculations to determine the amount to pay. Such calculations require using working memory, a limited-capacity system for temporary storage, and manipulation of information in the prefrontal cortex of the brain (Suri et al., 2013).

Round (Even) Versus Sharp (Odd) Prices

"Certain numerals, called 'round numbers,' can refer to an approximate quantity, while all other numerals necessarily have a sharp and precise meaning" (Dehaene, 2011, p. 95). Round numbers, such as 10 or 20, are used more frequently, better liked, and facilitate number processing. Round prices induce evaluation by feelings, whereas sharp prices induce evaluation by cognition (the *rounded price effect*; Wadhwa & Zhang, 2015). People process round numbers more easily, while nonround prices are perceived to be precise and derived from calculations, the *price precision effect* (Coulter & Roggeveen, 2014; Thomas et al., 2010). A majority of prices paid in pay-what-you-want outlets were round. Over 80% of tips left in a restaurant were a whole-dollar or a half-dollar amount. A majority of over 1,300 self-pumped gasoline purchases were a round amount (Lynn et al., 2013; Riener & Traxler, 2012). In England, six automobile parts and accessories stores continued using 9-ending prices for 10 products while six other stores posted 0-ending prices. Over a 12-week period, sales of nine of these 10 products increased significantly in the 0-ending price stores (Bray & Harris, 2006).

DESIGNING PRICE MESSAGES

Price promotions and deals have become endemic in many selling situations. In this section, we present recent consumer price research that offers insights about ways to develop and present effective price messages. There are multiple combinations of four pieces of information that may be presented in a price message. Some messages provide only the selling price along with a semantic cue such as "Regular," "Original," or "Sale." The formats of most other price messages may require buyers to calculate or estimate the price to pay when assessing a seller's offer. Although the actual price consumers would pay may not vary for a given message, their perceptions and responses may differ.

Multiple factors influence people's perceptions of and responses to a price message:

- a perceived price difference ($P_{ref} - P_{selling}$) is a stimulus
- the consumers themselves
- the numbers in the message
- the relationships between these numbers
- the comparison other (a competitor, another consumer, or the seller itself)
- the individual's manner of assessing the message

Consumers' assessments of a price message depend on (a) their perceptions of the numbers, (b) a perceived price difference, (c) the layout of the message, and (d) their processing of the words (semantic cues) and pictures in the message. These cues activate related representations in mind, making them more accessible, and this activation can spread to related constructs. Consumers' motivation to process and the ease of processing the information affect these responses. Processing fluency influences the perceived attractiveness of the message and purchase intentions (Coulter & Roggeveen, 2014). Comparing a former or competitors' prices with a lower current selling price provides buyers with a frame of reference. Price messages offering a deal might induce people to infer a gain or positive outcome might occur. Others might perceive that message as a way to reduce an outlay.

Price messages typically contain a combination of different pieces of numerical information (regular price, sale price, absolute [monetary] discount, relative [percentage] discount). Price information is accompanied with various semantic cues (e.g., "save," "sale") to facilitate consumers processing a message. People process most information in a price message nonconsciously, yet the message still influences their responses. As illustrated in this chapter, color, font and font size, spatial location of the regular price and sale prices, and numerical differences between the regular and sale prices influence people's perceptions of the message. Also, relationships between numbers in a message can influence how people perceive price messages, assign meaning, and retrieve the numerical information.

Choosing the Numbers

A price message may contain a price or a combination of multiple prices along with other relevant textual and numerical information. When these prices and numbers in a message, in combination, are perceived to belong together, such as multiples of two or 10, they are processed faster and more easily. In one study, people evaluated advertised offers and indicated their purchase intentions. One ad offered three medium pizzas with up to eight toppings for $24 while an alternate ad offered the pizzas with unlimited toppings also for $24 (3 × 8 = 24). A second ad offered four small pizzas with up to six toppings for $24 while its counterpart ad offered four small pizzas with unlimited toppings for $24 (4 × 6 = 24). An offer for unlimited toppings in either situation is a better deal, yet the alternate limited number of toppings choice was preferred. The combination of numbers in the limited toppings choices was related to a common arithmetic fact, facilitating processing (King & Janiszewski, 2011).

A second promotion offered 50% off on women's coats originally priced at $400 on sale for $200. Round prices were used and were presented in a high to low sequence. The higher original price, $400, was prior to and above the lower, $200, sale price. The numbers 400, 200, and 50 are multiples of 50. In contrast, a third promotion headlined savings of $801 for a sofa sale priced at $1,599, original price of $2,400. The sequence of prices was low to high: 801, 1,599, 2,400. By changing the sale price to $1,600 and sequencing the prices to 2,400, 1,600, 800, the message would be more easily processed. Using a high to low price sequence with number multiples of 800 would be easier to process. See Suk et al. (2012) and Della Bitta and Monroe (1974) for evidence and rationale for the superior effect of presenting multiple prices in a descending in contrast to an ascending order. Also, in the original promotion, the smallest number, 801, was presented in a larger font size than the original 2,400 price, creating perceptual incongruity: a lower price presented in a larger font (King & Janiszewski, 2011).

Enhancing processing ease when presenting price information will induce positive feelings in recipients of a price message. Effectively presenting prices to others requires understanding how our brain represents the corresponding quantities the symbols or words indicate.

Location of Price Information

Where should prices be placed in a message such that people perceive an offer as intended? Comparative prices may be presented vertically or horizontally, close together, or apart. The higher original price may appear before the lower sale price. However, as the above coat promotion illustrates, the reverse order often occurs. The lower selling price may be in a larger font size than the higher original price. As previously illustrated, spatial separation of prices influences perceptions of the magnitude of a difference between a seller's pre- and postchange prices or between the seller's and competitors' prices. Separating these prices spatially in a message affects people's ability to integrate the information when evaluating a price difference. The greater the horizontal distance between two prices in a message, the greater the perceived amount of a difference. As presented earlier, a discount was underestimated when regular and sale prices were 1.8 inches apart in an advertisement but overestimated when they were placed 4.2 inches apart. If prices are placed close horizontally, a perception of a narrow distance interferes with a perception of the discount amount, inducing an underestimation of the difference. When prices are farther apart, a perceived wide distance exaggerates the difference and overestimation occurs.

When two prices are presented physically close, vertically, and in the same metric, it is easier to process the prices. If people perceive estimating a price difference is relatively easy, they may evaluate the price message positively. When a lower sale price is presented either to the right of or below a higher original price, consistent with the subtraction principle from elementary arithmetic, people are more likely to evaluate an offer favorably (Biswas et al., 2013).

When a lower selling price is presented in a font size larger than the former higher price, perceptual incongruity (lower selling price in a larger font size) interferes with processing the message. This incongruity increases the difficulty for people to estimate and assess the price difference. Presenting a price difference as a percentage involves multiple metrics (percentage and monetary), increasing processing difficulty. Prices shown on the right side of a message may be perceived to be higher than when shown on the left. This effect may be due to a general left to right orientation of people's logarithmic mental number line (Cai et al., 2012; P. Choi & Coulter, 2012; DelVecchio et al., 2009; Valenzuela & Raghubir, 2015).

Items positioned up or high in a message may be perceived positively ("thumbs up"), while items positioned down or low may be perceived negatively ("thumbs down"). An explanation for this relationship between affect and vertical position depends on how children's cognition develops based on their sensorimotor experiences. Children learn from their sensations as they experience things in their environment. They learn to think and reason abstractly from these experiences and learn to associate "up" positively and "down" negatively. People automatically evaluate items positioned high and in their right visual field positively, but people tend to judge items positioned low and in their left visual space negatively (Giuliani et al., 2017; Meier & Robinson, 2004; see also Valenzuela & Raghubir, 2015). To induce a positive incentive to buy, information priming a gain should be placed in the upper right visual space of a message. Placing price information in the lower visual space reinforces a low price message.

Ease of Computing Price Differences

When the IPS area of the brain is involved, perceived numerical differences between prices, perceived spatial distance between prices, and perceived differences in font sizes will be processed in our brain as magnitudes. Presenting two prices vertically makes it easier to compute the numerical difference between them (Barone et al., 2015). An ease of processing effect is more likely to occur if the higher (original) price is presented above the lower (sale) price. Positioning a lower sale price vertically above or before a higher regular price increases computational difficulty. In one study, easier to compute price differences were perceived to be larger than actual, while more difficult to compute price differences were perceived to be less than actual for price discounts or differences in prices (Thomas & Morwitz, 2009). In practice, messages often place a lower sale price before a higher regular price and often in a larger font size. Such incongruities between perceptions of price differences, and between font sizes, induce a size incongruity effect.

Left Digit Effect and Right Digit Price Endings

Our brain tends to divide digits less than 10 into two groups, above and below 5: The digits 1 to 4 are encoded as "low or small," and digits 6 to 9 are encoded as "high or large" (Tzelgov, et al., 1992). The digit 5 has a "neutral" status between these two groups of digits. This encoding carries over to the left digit of larger numbers, including prices. A study for a bank of people's willingness to pay interest rates found the acceptability of interest rates declined as they were increased steadily. However, when the interest rate increased above 10%, acceptability of an interest rate increased initially rather than continuing to decline. One possible explanation for this puzzling result is the left digit "1" was encoded by some respondents' brains as "low," not as "10." If so, for these people, an interest rate a little higher than 10.0% may not have been interpreted as "high" or "too high."

Typically, sale prices are presented with ending digits less than whole round numbers, such as xx.99 or xx.95. If people focus on the ending digits 99 or 95, the price could nonconsciously be encoded as large because a "9" is encoded as "large." Contrary to this practice, sale prices with small right digit endings (e.g., xx.22) were perceived to have larger discounts than sale prices with large right digit endings (e.g., xx.99). The prices with perceived small right digits actually had smaller percentage discounts! The perceived discount was larger with small right ending digits compared with a similar promotion with large right ending digits (Coulter & Coulter, 2007).

Communicating Price Differences

The attractiveness (or not) of a price difference depends not only on the amount of the monetary difference but also on the magnitude of the comparative (reference) price. People might perceive a $40 reduction on either a $200 jacket or an $800 television similarly if they process the $40 savings absolutely. If the offers are processed relatively, a $40 (20%) savings on the $200 jacket is more attractive than a 5% savings on the television. A $40 increase on the $200 jacket would be perceived more unfavorably than if on the $800 television. In general, previous research has shown percentage-off promotions are perceived more favorably for low-price products, while money-off promotions are more attractive for high-price products. A percentage surcharge on an item priced less than (more than) 100 was evaluated less (more) favorably than if presented as a monetary amount (S.-F. S. Chen et al., 1998; González et al., 2015; Weathers et al., 2012; Weisstein et al., 2013).

When people's internal reference price (or external price anchor) is less than 100,

- a percentage price decrease will be perceived more favorably than an equivalent monetary reduction;
- a percentage price increase (or surcharge) will be perceived less favorably (i.e., more unfavorably) than an equivalent monetary increase (or surcharge).

When people's internal reference price (or external price anchor) is more than 100,

- a percentage price decrease will be perceived less favorably than an equivalent monetary reduction;
- a percentage price increase (or surcharge) will be perceived less favorably (i.e., more unfavorably) than an equivalent monetary increase or surcharge (see Berger, 2013, pp. 170–171, "The Rule of 100").

Price Differences and Information Processing

Sellers may offer gifts, bonus packs, cash gift cards, or a discount for a product when full price is paid for another product. A bonus pack could be "XX brand toothpaste, 50% more free, 7.5 oz at the 5.0 oz price." These formats may be difficult to process as both monetary and nonmonetary metrics are used. When moderate discounts are offered, people may process information more completely. A perceived small discount would not stimulate much processing. The amount of savings for a perceived large discount is less uncertain, and extensive information processing would be less necessary. This prediction was supported for a dress shirt and three discount amounts (small: $5; moderate: $10; and large: $15; Grewal et al., 1996). Separately, price differentials based on prices intermediately above market prices were more acceptable than price differentials based on prices either slightly or highly above market prices.

When might people prefer receiving monetary discounts compared with additional quantity (bonus packs), or money-off versus percentage-off promotions? Discounts for toothpaste were presented separately as either "SAVE $0.26, $.65, or $1.29." A bonus pack offered "x% MORE FREE, y.y oz [5.7, 6.5, or 7.8] at the 5.2 oz price." The SAVE $1.29 offer was preferred over the bonus pack (50% MORE FREE) at the high level. People were indifferent between receiving price discounts or bonus packs at other levels (Hardesty & Bearden, 2003).

Over a 16-week period, using hand lotion priced at $13.50 per bottle, a store offered on alternate weeks either a 35% off price discount or a "50% more free bonus pack." The store sold more bottles using the 50% more bonus pack compared with the 35% price discount, enjoying a positive effect on revenue for the product. Promotions with the larger percentage free (50%) were more attractive than offers with a smaller price off (35%) though the offers were economically equivalent. Other studies compared preferences for a bonus pack of coffee versus a percentage off price promotion. Considering price increases and decreases, people favored receiving 50% more coffee to paying 33% less money in a price decrease condition. In contrast, they favored receiving 33% less coffee to paying 50% more money in a price increase condition (H. Chen et al., 2012).

SUMMARY

Although we can trace research on how people respond to prices back several centuries, we are still learning about how prices affect consumers' perceptions of alternative offers and how these perceptions influence their purchase decisions. A key question lies in learning what influences the different sensitivities people exhibit when evaluating prices in a product category. Differences in price sensitivities cause the variances in the width of both differential price thresholds as well as the latitude of price indifference and, therefore, how readily consumers are able to distinguish changes or differences in prices. People respond more favorably to items of familiarity, numbers notwithstanding. As shown by the multiple research studies cited here, people might also process and interpret price information differently than intended by sellers or prescribed by previous theoretical thought.

Current knowledge on how people perceive and process price information indicates it is more complex than commonly assumed. "The apparent ease with which we use numbers hides the fact that very complex cognitive processes are required to recognize numerical stimuli and to make basic numerical comparisons or calculations" (Monroe, 2003, p. 109). Research studying numerical comparative judgments, whether against a standard or between numbers, indicates numerical quantities are not compared at a symbolic level but are initially recoded and compared as quantities. When prices are processed as magnitudes, they may not be encoded or stored in memory, even if consumers actively evaluate the alternatives and consciously process the price information. As developed in this chapter, it is important to understand that the way prices are initially presented to people influences their reactions inducing their sensations and, consequently, their perceptions.

Central to studying human price information processing is understanding how people encode and represent price and price-related information in their minds. People may encode and represent price information in memory as approximations (e.g., less than $100) or as evaluations (e.g., not expensive). People compare prices, make calculations and estimates when evaluating options, and make choices. They may not always handle these tasks effortlessly or accurately. We have presented theoretical and empirical evidence indicating people process numbers, and prices, in ways not previously understood by researchers, public policy makers, consultants, or pricing managers. We are still learning about how our brain processes numbers and prices. What we do know now suggests many current pricing practices need to be reexamined both as to their presumed effects and their actual effects on consumers' purchase behaviors.

REFERENCES

Adaval, R., & Monroe, K. B. (2002). Automatic construction and use of contextual information for product and price evaluations. *Journal of Consumer Research*, 28(4), 572–588. https://doi.org/10.1086/338212

Anderson, E. W. (1996). Customer satisfaction and price tolerance. *Marketing Letters*, 7(3), 265–274. https://doi.org/10.1007/BF00435742

Barone, M. J., Lyle, K. B., & Winterich, K. P. (2015). When deal depth doesn't matter: How handedness consistency influences consumer response to horizontal versus vertical price comparisons. *Marketing Letters*, 26(2), 213–223. https://doi.org/10.1007/s11002-013-9276-8

Berger, J. (2013). *Contagious: Why things catch on*. Simon and Schuster Paperbacks.

Bernoulli, D. (1954). Exposition of a new theory on the measurement of risk (L. Sommer, Trans.). *Econometrica*, 22(1), 23–36. https://doi.org/10.2307/1909829 (Original work published 1738)

Bijmolt, T. H. A., van Heerde, H. J., & Pieters, R. G. M. (2005). New empirical generalizations on the determinants of price elasticity. *Journal of Marketing Research*, 42(2), 141–156. https://doi.org/10.1509/jmkr.42.2.141.62296

Biswas, A., Bhowmick, S., Guha, A., & Grewal, D. (2013). Consumer evaluations of sale prices: Role of the subtraction principle. *Journal of Marketing*, 77(4), 49–66. https://doi.org/10.1509/jm.12.0052

Bray, J. P., & Harris, C. (2006). The effect of 9-ending prices on retail sales: A quantitative UK based field study. *Journal of Marketing Management*, 22(5–6), 601–617. https://doi.org/10.1362/026725706777978631

Bruno, H. A., Che, H., & Dutta, S. (2012). Role of reference price on price and quantity: Insights from business-to-business markets. *Journal of Marketing Research*, 49(5), 640–654. https://doi.org/10.1509/jmr.09.0334

Burson, K. A., Larrick, R. P., & Lynch, J. G., Jr. (2009). Six of one, half dozen of the other: Expanding and contracting numerical dimensions produces preference reversals. *Psychological Science*, 20(9), 1074–1078. https://doi.org/10.1111/j.1467-9280.2009.02394.x

Cai, F., Shen, H., & Hui, M. (2012). The effect of location on price estimation: Understanding number-location and number-order associations. *Journal of Marketing Research*, 49(5), 718–724. https://doi.org/10.1509/jmr.11.0203

Chen, H., Marmorstein, H., Tsiros, M., & Rao, A. R. (2012). When more is less: The impact of base value neglect on consumer preferences for bonus packs over price discounts. *Journal of Marketing*, 76(4), 64–77. https://doi.org/10.1509/jm.10.0443

Chen, S.-F. S., Monroe, K. B., & Lou, Y.-C. (1998). The effects of framing price promotion messages on consumers' perceptions and purchase intentions. *Journal of Retailing*, 74(3), 353–372. https://doi.org/10.1016/S0022-4359(99)80100-6

Cheng, L. L., & Monroe, K. B. (2013). An appraisal of behavioral price research (Part 1): Price as a physical stimulus. *AMS Review*, 3(3), 103–129. https://doi.org/10.1007/s13162-013-0041-1

Choi, J., Lee, K., & Ji, Y.-Y. (2012). What type of framing message is more appropriate with nine-ending pricing? *Marketing Letters*, 23(3), 603–614. https://doi.org/10.1007/s11002-012-9164-7

Choi, P., & Coulter, K. S. (2012). It's not all relative: The effects of mental and physical positioning of comparative prices on absolute versus relative discount assessment. *Journal of Retailing*, 88(4), 512–527. https://doi.org/10.1016/j.jretai.2012.04.001

Coulter, K. S., Choi, P., & Monroe, K. B. (2012). Comma n' cents in pricing: The effects of auditory representation encoding on price magnitude perceptions. *Journal of Consumer Psychology*, 22(3), 395–407. https://doi.org/10.1016/j.jcps.2011.11.005

Coulter, K. S., & Coulter, R. A. (2007). Distortion of price discount perceptions: The right digit effect. *Journal of Consumer Research*, 34(2), 162–173. https://doi.org/10.1086/518526

Coulter, K. S., & Norberg, P. A. (2009). The effects of physical distance between regular and sale prices on numerical difference perceptions. *Journal of Consumer Psychology*, 19(2), 144–157. https://doi.org/10.1016/j.jcps.2009.02.008

Coulter, K. S., & Roggeveen, A. L. (2014). Price number relationships and deal processing fluency: The effects of approximation sequences and number multiples. *Journal of Marketing Research*, 51(1), 69–82. https://doi.org/10.1509/jmr.12.0438

Dastjerdi, M., Ozker, M., Foster, B. L., Rangarajan, V. & Parvizi, J. (2013). Numerical processing in the human parietal cortex during experimental and natural conditions. *Nature Communications*, 4, 2528. https://doi.org/10.1038/ncomms3528

Dehaene, S. (1989). The psychophysics of numerical comparison: A reexamination of apparently incompatible data. *Perception & Psychophysics*, 45(6), 557–566. https://doi.org/10.3758/BF03208063

Dehaene, S. (1992). Varieties of numerical abilities. In S. Dehaene (Ed.), *Numerical cognition* (pp. 1–42). Blackwell.

Dehaene, S. (1997). *The number sense: How the mind creates mathematics*. Oxford University Press.

Dehaene, S. (2003). The neural basis of the Weber-Fechner law: A logarithmic mental number line. *Trends in Cognitive Sciences*, 7(4), 145–147. https://doi.org/10.1016/S1364-6613(03)00055-X

Dehaene, S. (2011). *The number sense: How the mind creates mathematics* (Rev. ed.). Oxford University Press.

Della Bitta, A. J., & Monroe, K. B. (1974). The influence of adaptation levels on subjective price perceptions. In S. Ward & P. Wright (Eds.), *NA - Advances in consumer research* (Vol. 1, pp. 359–369). Association for Consumer Research.

Della Bitta, A. J., Monroe, K. B., & McGinnis, J. M. (1981). Consumer perceptions of comparative price advertisements. *Journal of Marketing Research, 18*(4), 416–427. https://doi.org/10.1177/002224378101800402

DelVecchio, D., Lakshmanan, A., & Krishnan, H. S. (2009). The effects of discount location and frame on consumers' price estimates. *Journal of Retailing, 85*(3), 336–346. https://doi.org/10.1016/j.jretai.2009.05.010

Faranda, W. T. (2011). The impact of service deregulation on buyers' reliance of a market-based reference price: A test in a B2B insurance context. *Services Marketing Quarterly, 32*(2), 129–145. https://doi.org/10.1080/15332969.2011.557605

Fechner, G. T. (1965). Elemente der psychophysik [Elements of psychophysics]. In R. J. Herrnstein & E. G. Boring (Eds.), *A source book in the history of psychology* (pp. 562–572). Harvard University Press. (Original work published 1860)

George, J., Mercer, A., & Wilson, H. (1996). Variations in price elasticities. *European Journal of Operational Research, 88*(1), 13–22. https://doi.org/10.1016/0377-2217(95)00203-0

Giuliani, F., D'Anselmo, Tommas, L., Brancucci, A. & Pietroni, D. (2017). Hemispheric asymmetries in price estimation: Do brain hemispheres attribute different monetary values? *Frontiers in Psychology, 8*, 2042. https://doi.org/10.3389/fpsyg.2017.02042

González, E. M., Esteva, E., Roggeveen, A. L., & Grewal, D. (2016). Amount off versus percentage off—When does it matter? *Journal of Business Research, 69*(3), 1022–1027. https://doi.org/10.1016/j.jbusres.2015.08.014

Grewal, D., Marmorstein, H. & Sharma, A. (1996). Communicating price information through semantic cues: The moderating effects of situation and discount size. *Journal of Consumer Research, 23*, 148–155.

Grewal, D., Monroe, K. B., & Krishnan, R. (1998). The effects of price-comparison advertising on buyers' perceptions of acquisition value, transaction value, and behavioral intentions. *Journal of Marketing, 62*(2), 46–59. https://doi.org/10.2307/1252160

Gupta, S., & Cooper, L. G. (1992). The discounting of discounts and promotion thresholds. *Journal of Consumer Research, 19*(3), 401–411. https://doi.org/10.1086/209310

Han, S., Gupta, S., & Lehmann, D. R. (2001). Consumer price sensitivity and price thresholds. *Journal of Retailing, 77*(4), 435–456. https://doi.org/10.1016/S0022-4359(01)00057-4

Hardesty, D. M. & Bearden, W. O. (2003). Consumer evaluations of different promotion types and price presentation: The moderating role of promotional benefit level. *Journal of Retailing, 79*, 17–25.

Helson, H. (1964). *Adaptation-level theory*. Harper & Row.

Kahneman, D., & Tversky, A. (1979). Prospect theory: An analysis of decision under risk. *Econometrica, 47*(2), 263–291. https://doi.org/10.2307/1914185

Kalyanaram, G., & Little, J. D. C. (1994). An empirical analysis of latitude of price acceptance in consumer package goods. *Journal of Consumer Research, 21*(3), 408–418. https://doi.org/10.1086/209407

King, D., & Janiszewski, C. (2011). The sources and consequences of the fluent processing of numbers. *Journal of Marketing Research, 48*(2), 327–341. https://doi.org/10.1509/jmkr.48.2.327

Leavitt, H. J. (1954). A note on some experimental findings about the meanings of price. *Journal of Business, 27*(3), 205–210. https://doi.org/10.1086/294039

Lobel, T. (2014). *Sensation: The new science of physical intelligence*. Atria Books.

Lynn, M., Flynn, S. M., & Helion, C. (2013). Do consumers prefer round prices? Evidence from pay-what-you-want decisions and self-pump gasoline purchases. *Journal of Economic Psychology, 36*, 96–102. https://doi.org/10.1016/j.joep.2013.01.010

Marques, J. F., & Dehaene, S. (2004). Developing intuition for prices in euros: Rescaling or relearning prices? *Journal of Experimental Psychology: Applied, 10*(3), 148–155. https://doi.org/10.1037/1076-898X.10.3.148

Marshall, A. (1890). *Principles of economics*. Macmillan.

Meier, B. P., & Robinson, M. D. (2004). Why the sunny side is up: Association between affect and vertical position. *Psychological Science, 15*(4), 243–247. https://doi.org/10.1111/j.0956-7976.2004.00659.x

Monga, A., & Bagchi, R. (2012). Years, months, and days versus 1, 12, and 365: The influence of units versus numbers. *Journal of Consumer Research, 39*(1), 185–198. https://doi.org/10.1086/662039

Monroe, K. B. (1971). Measuring price thresholds by psychophysics and latitudes of acceptance. *Journal of Marketing Research, 8*(4), 460–464. https://doi.org/10.1177/002224377100800409

Monroe, K. B. (2003). *Pricing: Making profitable decisions* (3rd ed.). McGraw-Hill Book Co.

Moosmayer, D. C., Schuppar, B., & Siems, F. U. (2012). Reference prices as determinants of business-to-business price negotiation outcomes: An empirical perspective from the chemical industry. *Journal of Supply Chain Management, 48*(1), 92–106. https://doi.org/10.1111/j.1745-493X.2011.03254.x

Nunes, J. C., & Boatwright, P. (2004). Incidental prices and their effect on willingness to pay. *Journal of Marketing Research*, 41(4), 457–466. https://doi.org/10.1509/jmkr.41.4.457.47014

Pandelaere, M., Briers, B., & Lembregts, C. (2011). How to make a 29% increase look bigger: The unit effect in option comparisons. *Journal of Consumer Research*, 38(2), 308–322. https://doi.org/10.1086/659000

Parducci, A. (1965). Category judgment: A range-frequency model. *Psychological Review*, 72(6), 407–418. https://doi.org/10.1037/h0022602

Raman, K., & Bass, F. M. (2002). A general test of reference price theory in the presence of threshold effects. *Tijdschrift Voor Economie en Management*, 57(2), 205–226.

Ramanathan, S. & Dhar, S. K. (2010). The effect of sales promotions on the size and composition of the shopping basket: Regulatory compatibility from framing and temporal restrictions. *Journal of Marketing Research*, 47(3), 542–552. https://doi.org/10.1509/jmkr.47.3.542

Riener, G., & Traxler, C. (2012). Norms, moods, and free lunch: Longitudinal evidence on payments from a pay-what-you-want restaurant. *Journal of Socio-Economics*, 41(4), 476–483. https://doi.org/10.1016/j.socec.2011.07.003

Sherif, C. W. (1963). Social categorization as a function of latitude of acceptance and series range. *Journal of Abnormal and Social Psychology*, 67(2), 148–156. https://doi.org/10.1037/h0043022

Sherif, M., & Hovland, C. I. (1961). *Social judgment*. Yale University Press.

Streitfeld, D. (2016, March 6). It's discounted, but is it a deal? How list prices lost their meaning. *New York Times*. https://www.nytimes.com/2016/03/06/technology/its-discounted-but-is-it-a-deal-how-list-prices-lost-their-meaning.html

Suk, K., Lee, J., & Lichtenstein, D. R. (2012). The influence of price presentation order on consumer choice. *Journal of Marketing Research*, 49(5), 708–717. https://doi.org/10.1509/jmr.11.0309

Suri, R., Monroe, K. B., & Koc, U. (2013). Math anxiety and its effects on consumers' preference for price promotion formats. *Journal of the Academy of Marketing Science*, 41(3), 271–282. https://doi.org/10.1007/s11747-012-0313-6

Terui, N., & Dahana, W. D. (2006). Price customization using price thresholds estimated from scanner panel data. *Journal of Interactive Marketing*, 20(3–4), 58–70. https://doi.org/10.1002/dir.20067

Thaler, R. (1985). Mental accounting and consumer choice. *Marketing Science*, 4(3), 199–214. https://doi.org/10.1287/mksc.4.3.199

Thomas, M., & Morwitz, V. (2009). The ease of computation effect: The interplay of metacognitive experiences and naïve theories in judgments of price differences. *Journal of Marketing Research*, 46(1), 81–91. https://doi.org/10.1509/jmkr.46.1.81

Thomas, M., Simon, D. H., & Kadiyali, V. (2010). The price precision effect: Evidence from laboratory and market data. *Marketing Science*, 29(1), 175–190. https://doi.org/10.1287/mksc.1090.0512

Tzelgov, J., Meyer, J., & Henik, A. (1992). Automatic and intentional processing of numerical information. *Journal of Experimental Psychology: Learning, Memory, and Cognition*, 18(1), 166–179. https://doi.org/10.1037/0278-7393.18.1.166

Valenzuela, A., & Raghubir, P. (2015). Are consumers aware of top–bottom but not of left–right inferences? Implications for shelf space positions. *Journal of Experimental Psychology: Applied*, 21(3), 224–241. https://doi.org/10.1037/xap0000055

Van Heerde, H. J., Leeflang, P. S. H., & Wittink, D. R. (2001). Semiparametric analysis to estimate the deal effect curve. *Journal of Marketing Research*, 38(2), 197–215. https://doi.org/10.1509/jmkr.38.2.197.18842

Vanhuele, M., & Drèze, X. (2002). Measuring the price knowledge shoppers bring to the store. *Journal of Marketing*, 66(4), 72–85. https://doi.org/10.1509/jmkg.66.4.72.18516

Wadhwa, M., & Zhang, K. (2015). This number just feels right: The impact of roundness of price numbers on product evaluations. *Journal of Consumer Research*, 41(5), 1172–1185. https://doi.org/10.1086/678484

Weathers, D., Swain, S. D., & Carlson, J. P. (2012). Why consumers respond differently to absolute versus percentage descriptions of quantities. *Marketing Letters*, 23(4), 943–957. https://doi.org/10.1007/s11002-012-9189-y

Weber, E. H. (1965). De pulsu, resorptione, auditu et tactu: Annotationes anatomicae et physiologicae [Concerning pulse, respiration, hearing, and touch: Anatomical and physiological notes]. In R. J. Herrnstein & E. G. Boring (Eds.), *A source book in the history of psychology* (pp. 172–175). Harvard University Press. (Original work published 1834)

Weisstein, F. L., Monroe, K. B., & Kukar-Kinney, M. (2013). Effects of price framing on consumers' perceptions of online dynamic pricing practices. *Journal of the Academy of Marketing Science*, 41(5), 501–514. https://doi.org/10.1007/s11747-013-0330-0

Xia, L., & Monroe, K. B. (2009). The influence of pre-purchase goals on consumer perceptions. *International Journal of Retail & Distribution Management*, 37(8), 680–694. https://doi.org/10.1108/09590550910966187

CHAPTER 31

THE BRAND PROPERTY STRENGTH FRAMEWORK: INTEGRATING THEORY AND RESEARCH ON BRAND CONSUMER PSYCHOLOGY

Joseph R. Priester, Monique A. Fleming, Leigh Anne Novak Donovan, and Chaumanix Dutton

What makes a brand successful? Consider one of the world's most valuable brands, Apple (Duffin, 2020). Customers are willing to wait for new Apple products rather than purchase other brands, eagerly adopt new Apple products, are willing to pay a price premium, and form communities based upon their interest in Apple (e.g., The Villages Apple User Group; https://www.tvaug.org). A natural question arises upon consideration of Apple: What are the properties or characteristics that Apple, and other brands, possess that lead to their success with customers?

The goal of this chapter is to provide insight into this question. To do so, we review the brand literature in consumer psychology. Note, however, that this consumer psychology perspective is but one of many by which to consider the function, role, and influence of brands. For example, the influence of brands on firms and their financial performance has been a thriving area of research (e.g., D. A. Aaker & Jacobson, 2001; Golder & Tellis, 1993; Lane & Jacobson, 1995; Rust, Ambler, et al., 2004; Rust, Lemon, & Zeithaml, 2004; Srivastava et al., 1998).

From an entirely different perspective, brands have also been of interest to historical scholarship (e.g., Flandreau & Flores, 2009), revealing, for example, that brands were used to discriminate between different product alternatives as early as ancient Greece and Egypt (e.g., Riley, 1984; Twede, 2002).

THE CONSUMER PSYCHOLOGY BRAND LITERATURE: A REVIEW

Consumer psychology research on brands is vibrant and vast. This research has produced an abundance of findings and models that have provided insight into the role of brands and the psychological processes underlying their effects. With such an abundance, however, come challenges beyond the daunting size and volume.[1] Perhaps the most important challenge is a lack of coherence across findings and models. By lack of coherence, we do not imply contradiction. Rather, we mean the extent to which theories do (or do not) reference and relate to one another. Developing an understanding of the ways in which different findings and models

---

[1] The Web of Science lists well over 25,000 academic papers and chapters published in business and psychology that touch upon brands. This research has especially flourished in the most recent decade, during which 20,000 of the 25,000 papers and chapters were published.

https://doi.org/10.1037/0000262-031
APA Handbook of Consumer Psychology, L. R. Kahle (Editor-in-Chief)
Copyright © 2022 by the American Psychological Association. All rights reserved.

are related to one another provides the potential to develop a broader and more unified theoretical understanding of brands and to uncover psychological processes that span across disparate findings and models. Such is the goal of this chapter.

THE BRAND PROPERTY STRENGTH FRAMEWORK: HOW DIFFERENT FINDINGS AND MODELS RELATE

To begin the process of overcoming this lack of coherence, we offer the brand property strength framework as a tool by which to meaningfully organize the consumer psychology brand literature. It is intended to describe the state of the field as it currently exists, in a way that facilitates further integration across findings and models. The framework proposes that psychological brand properties (consumers' thoughts, feelings, or emotions about or in response to a brand) are the key constructs to an understanding of the consumer psychology of brands. Further, the framework is based on two dimensions: (a) the causal sequence of constructs and (b) the hierarchy of brand property strength. We describe the three aspects of the framework in turn.

Brand Properties

The brand property strength framework arose from a broad reading of the consumer psychology brand literature, which suggested that consumer perceptions of and psychological reactions to brands have been, perhaps not surprisingly, the focus of the substantial majority of research and theorizing in this area. We conceptualize these consumer perceptions of and psychological reactions to brands as "psychological brand properties" and refer to them as *brand properties* for brevity. Thus, psychological brand properties are consumers' perceptions of a brand (or aspects of a brand), their psychological reactions to a brand, or their mental conceptualizations of brands. For example, brand properties include the associations that come to mind when encountering a brand (Keller, 1993), brand attitudes (Nedungadi, 1990), and the perception of a brand as a relationship partner (Fournier, 1998).

From our broad reading, seven such brand properties appear to cohere and to have been the focus of research. After deciding upon these seven properties, the 75 most cited brand papers were then reviewed in order to examine whether any additional brand properties were needed in order to categorize the brand properties across the set of 75 papers.[2] From this analysis, we discerned that no additional properties were needed; all could be categorized according to one of the seven properties.

Consideration of the consequences associated with each of these brand properties suggested a hierarchical ordering. We propose that the brand properties in order of strength (from weakest to strongest) are brand associations, brand attitudes, customer-based brand equity, brand meaning, brand personality, brand relationships, and brand community. Once these brand properties were established, additional papers within each property were identified and included in order to provide a more comprehensive review. In our view, these are the psychological brand properties that have been the focus of theory and research to date. We return in the discussion to the question of which brand properties we think should be ones of particular interest going forward for purposes of further integration and theory building.

Causal Sequence of Constructs

To better explicate the psychological processes underlying brand properties, it is helpful to elucidate what leads or gives rise to them (i.e., the antecedents of brand properties) and what are their effects (i.e., the consequences of brand properties). Thus, the *causal sequence of constructs* distinguishes three sequential and causally connected constructs: antecedents of brand properties, brand properties, and consequences of brand properties. Of the three constructs, brand property is of the greatest interest, in that it is this construct that addresses the critical

---

[2] A search of the Web of Science was used to create the list of top-cited papers. The search included those papers with the term "brand" in the topic and that were published in the *Journal of Consumer Research*, the *Journal of Marketing*, the *Journal of Marketing Research*, or the *Journal of Consumer Psychology*. Fourteen papers fell outside of the scope of the present review (three examined market performance, six firm strategy, and five non-brand entities). The 61 remaining papers are identified in the references by asterisks. The coding of these papers is available from the authors.

question: "Through what psychological processes are brands more or less successful with customers?" Thus, this causal sequence of constructs is organized for each brand property separately. Figure 31.1 presents the causal sequence of constructs dimension of the framework.

Brand properties include measures and conceptualizations of that particular property (e.g., in the case of brand attitude, liking for the brand). Antecedents of a particular brand property are those constructs that precede, influence, and create that particular brand property. Some antecedents are variables that are separate from brand properties, such as management actions (e.g., advertising and offering promotions) and characteristics of the consumer that predate encountering the brand (e.g., having a predisposition to form attitudes; Jarvis & Petty, 1996). And as will be seen, in several instances, one particular brand property has been found to be an antecedent of another brand property, as when a consumer's positive brand association in turn contributes to forming a positive brand attitude. Both types of antecedent variables are included because they have been shown to influence a particular brand property, again as a way to foster and draw attention to connections across disparate theories and findings. Consequences of a brand property, on the other hand, are those constructs that are the result of a particular brand property. As with antecedents, some consequences are separate from psychological brand properties, and these tend to be behavioral (e.g., purchase) or involve new products and other brands (e.g., evaluation of other brands). Thus, for example, brand attitudes have been found to have consequences for purchase and evaluation of other brands.

Thus, papers were also coded with regard to (a) which brand property or properties were being examined; (b) what antecedents to brand property were examined, if any; and (c) what consequences of brand property were examined, if any. Indeed, though a small number of papers examined only the nature of a brand property (e.g., brand personality; J. L. Aaker, 1997), the overwhelming majority of papers (and thus theory and research) examined either a brand property and its antecedent(s), a brand property and its consequence(s), or all three: a brand property and both its antecedents and consequences.

Hierarchy of Brand Property Strength

Finally, the *hierarchy of brand property strength* posits that different brand properties differentially influence consequences. Specifically, the hierarchy of brand property strength advances a continuum of brand property strength, such that a brand's influence can range from relatively weak and transient to relatively strong and enduring. Note that such continua have been proposed within some of the brand properties (e.g., attitude strength). Our proposition differs in that we focus on how such a continuum may span brand properties, such that some brand properties possess greater strength than others. As will become clear, it appears that through its history, the literature on the consumer psychology of brands has generally examined stronger and stronger brand properties.

A REVIEW OF BRAND PROPERTIES: HIERARCHY, ANTECEDENTS, AND CONSEQUENCES

We structure the review as follows: Each of the seven brand properties is described in order of its hypothesized strength, from weakest to strongest. In addition, the antecedents and consequences are explored for each of the brand properties.

Brand Associations

The first empirical research on the consumer psychology of brands examined simply brand name, with the question of whether it had a measurable effect. Brand name is the label or identifier of a brand and is often the key distinguishing feature

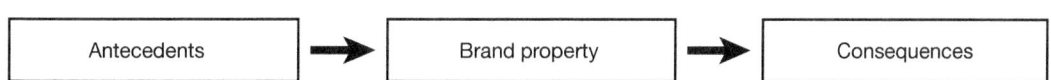

FIGURE 31.1. The causal sequence of constructs.

of a brand. Indeed, one of the first academic brand papers considered brand name to be the key "weapon in the competitive struggle" between competitors (Wilcox, 1934, p. 80). Research has demonstrated the important consequences brand name can have. Brand name influences perceived product quality (Rao & Monroe, 1989) when the actual product experienced is the same (e.g., a taste test of a product with a national brand vs. store-brand label; Richardson et al., 1994; see also Allison & Uhl, 1964), and brand name has a greater effect on perceived product quality than product price, product physical appearance, and retailer reputation (Dawar & Parker, 1994; see also Dodds et al., 1991). Furthermore, brand name leads to a greater willingness to purchase (Richardson et al., 1994). In recognition of the importance of brand names, Keller (1993) postulated that the correct choice of a brand name is a critical step in creating brand equity (discussed later).

But the question arises: What is it about the brand name that influences consumers so? In order for a brand name to have consequence, there must be some association of that brand name with another attribute, information, or knowledge. Such associations have been the focus of research. Indeed, the notion of brand associations underlying, at least in part, the power of brands to influence consequences is fundamental to many conceptualizations of brand consumer psychology (e.g., Keller, 1993, 2003). These associations can range from abstract concepts (e.g., brands can have brand-unique abstract meanings, such as high status, that compose the brand's concept; C. W. Park et al., 1991; see also Han et al., 2010) to specific attributes with which a brand is associated (e.g., a toothpaste associated with dental protection vs. fresh breath; Broniarczyk & Alba, 1994).

Brand associations can form from general knowledge, stereotypes, or experiences about product categories or types of brands (e.g., national brands tending to be of higher quality than store brands) as well as past brand purchase and advertising (Winer, 1986). And brand associations can be diluted when, for example, the attributes of a brand extension are inconsistent with the family brand attributes (Loken & John, 1993). However, the extent to which such associations are evaluated positively is also important. For example, a brand association that has been examined is country of origin. When consumers have animosity toward the country signaled by a brand, willingness to buy can be decreased even above and beyond judgments about the quality of products from that country (Klein et al., 1998). In contrast, when consumers want to socially identify with the country signaled by a brand, they may prefer it to local brands above and beyond the influence of brand quality (Batra et al., 2000).

Brand Attitudes

In the consumer behavior literature, brand attitudes are most often conceptualized as basic evaluative reactions and measured by items such as the extent to which a brand is liked or disliked. Other attitudinal constructs have been advanced, such as different bases of attitudes (e.g., hedonic/utilitarian; Voss et al., 2003), the accessibility of a brand attitude (i.e., the speed with which an evaluation comes to mind; Fazio et al., 1986, 1989; Nedungadi, 1990), and the nature of the attitudinal measure (e.g., implicit vs. explicit; Gibson, 2008; Maison et al., 2004). Importantly, particularly for practitioners, well-designed single-item brand attitude measures can be as predictive as multiple-item measures (Bergkvist & Rossiter, 2007).

The antecedents of brand attitudes include many antecedents studied in both classic (Hovland et al., 1953) and contemporary (e.g., Albarracin & Johnson, 2018) attitude and persuasion research. Examples of classically studied antecedents include source characteristics such as credibility and attractiveness (Dholakia & Sternthal, 1977; Goldsmith et al., 2000; Kahle & Homer, 1985; Till & Busler, 2000) and classical conditioning (Stuart et al., 1987; Sweldens et al., 2010). An example of contemporarily studied antecedents is fluency, which is the experience of the ease with which information about a brand is retrieved: If positive information is experienced as easy to retrieve, a more positive attitude is formed than if positive information is experienced as difficult to retrieve (e.g., Lee & Labroo, 2004; Novemsky et al., 2007). Given the nature of consumer behavior, research has also included antecedents unique to marketing. Of particular interest are consumers' feelings and attitudes toward an advertisement (e.g., Batra & Ray, 1986a; Mitchell, 1986). A meta-analysis of this research revealed that advertisement cognitions influence attitude toward the advertisement, which influences both brand cognitions and brand attitudes (S. P. Brown & Stayman, 1992; see also Bergkvist & Rossiter, 2007; Mitchell & Olson, 1981). Rather than detail the list of antecedents of brand attitudes, it is more useful to consider the different models by which brand attitudes have been studied.

One of the earliest theoretical approaches to brand attitudes is *expectancy-value models*. As illustrated in the previous section, the extent to which brand associations are evaluated positively is critical. This evaluative component of brand associations constitutes the "value" component in expectancy-value models (Fishbein, 1963; Rosenberg, 1956). Expectancy-value models assess two brand dimensions: (a) the perceived likelihood that an attribute is associated with the brand (i.e., the association) and (b) the evaluation of the attribute potentially associated with a brand (i.e., the extent to which that attribute is liked or disliked). Consumer behavior researchers explored and built upon this model in order to conceptualize and measure overall brand attitudes (for a review, see Wilkie & Pessemier, 1973; see also Bass, 1972; Bass & Talarzyk, 1972; Cohen et al., 1972; Sheth, 1972). One benefit of this approach is that it provides insight into possible mechanisms by which to change brand attitudes. For example, changing the perceived likelihood that a brand possesses an attribute is likely to lead to greater brand attitude change than attempting to change the evaluation of that attribute (Lutz, 1975).

Cognitive response models explore the influence of self-generated thoughts on brand attitudes. These models grew in reaction to the repeated observation that the associations between attitudes and memory for the information provided to a consumer about the attitude object are often quite low (Greenwald & Albert, 1968). In contrast, the associations between an attitude and the valence of a consumer's thoughts about the attitude-relevant information (i.e., cognitive responses) are stronger (Petty et al., 1981). As such, using the cognitive response approach provided potentially greater insight into not only attitudes but also attitude change within the context of marketing (Sternthal et al., 1978; Wright, 1973, 1980).

Motivational models of brand attitudes have been, and continue to be, a powerful theoretical lens by which to understand the psychological processes underlying consumer brand behavior (e.g., Batra & Ray, 1986b; Beatty et al., 1988; MacInnis et al., 1991; MacKenzie & Spreng, 1992). These models are based upon the consistent finding that motivation influences both the processes underlying and the consequent strength of brand attitudes (e.g., Petty et al., 1983). When motivated (and able), a consumer's cognitive responses underlie brand attitudes. This cognitive response process is relatively effortful. When not motivated (or able), a consumer's brand attitude is instead the result of relatively nonthoughtful processes such as classical conditioning and easily used heuristics. These motivational models help resolve the problem of lack of consistent attitude consequences and provide deeper insight into the processes underlying brand attitudes. The brand attitudes that result from the more thoughtful processes are more consequential than attitudes that result from the less thoughtful processes. As such, these motivational models explicate a hierarchy of strength, albeit within the brand attitude property.

A number of consequences of brand attitudes have been examined, the most common of which are consideration and choice (Nedungadi, 1990; Priester et al., 2004; Vakratsas & Ambler, 1999) and purchase intent and behavior (e.g., S. P. Brown & Stayman, 1992; Mitchell & Olson, 1981; Voss et al., 2003). Other brand attitude consequences include the influence of brand attitudes on evaluations of brand extensions (Boush & Loken, 1991), resistance to counterpersuasion attempts (Ahluwalia et al., 2000), and new product evaluations (T. J. Brown & Dacin, 1997).

Customer-Based Brand Equity

Customer-based brand equity is another important construct that has been advanced in order to provide an understanding of the consumer psychology of brands. Distinct from brand equity, which is the value of the brand for a corporation, customer-based brand equity is the value of the brand to the consumer. In the most comprehensive theoretical and empirical treatment (Keller, 1993, 2003), customer-based brand equity is conceptualized and operationalized as brand knowledge, which is composed of brand awareness (brand recall and brand recognition) and brand image (brand association type, attitude, strength, and uniqueness).

Of note is that customer-based brand equity theoretically could encompass any brand property and is more akin to an umbrella construct. Thus, it is unclear whether customer-based brand equity should be conceptualized as a brand property.[3] We include it for completeness because a large and influential portion of theory and research on the consumer psychology of brands has used the term and so that readers can come to their own conclusions. Further, we situate it here near the middle of the hierarchy of brand properties because of the types of consequences the vast majority of customer-based brand equity work has examined and because of where in the literature the term appeared and came into favor in the development of ideas about consumer brand psychology. We return to these issues in the discussion of future work.

Since its introduction, brand equity has been operationalized and defined in many different ways. Brand equity has been conceptualized and/or operationalized as being composed of brand attitude and brand familiarity (Lane & Jacobson, 1995), brand meaning and awareness (Berry et al., 2002), positive past experiences with a brand (Tax et al., 1998), and value above and beyond the value of a product's specific attributes (C. S. Park & Srinivasan, 1994), including brand quality (e.g., Dawar & Pillutla, 2000) and even brand relationships (Keller, 2003), to name just a few examples. Chaudhuri and Holbrook (2001) succinctly summarized the brand equity literature:

> Almost all conceptualizations of brand equity agree that the phenomenon involves the value added to an offering by consumers' perceptions of and associations with a particular brand name ([D. A.] Aaker 1996; Baldinger 1990; Baldinger and Rubinson 1996; Bello and Holbrook 1995; Dyson, Farr, and Hollis 1996; Holbrook 1992; Keller 1993; [C. S.] Park and Srinivasan 1994; Winters 1991). (p. 90)

In the brand equity model (Keller, 1993), antecedents of brand equity are hypothesized to be the choice of brand identities (e.g., brand name, logo, or symbol) and the integration of the brand entities into the supporting marketing program. Keller (2003) further proposed that the critical antecedent of brand equity is the connection (link) of brands to other (positively viewed) entities such as another person, place, thing, or brand. Research supports these proposals. A brand's advertising and promotion activity more broadly (Ailawadi et al., 2003), event sponsorship (Gwinner & Eaton, 1999), and associations with a positive brand ally (Rao et al., 1999) have all been shown to be antecedents of brand equity (e.g., see Keller, 1993, 2003, for reviews).

The defining consequence of brand equity is that consumers respond more favorably to an element of the marketing mix when that element is attributed to a brand than to a fictitiously named or unnamed version of the product or service (Keller, 1993). The work reviewed on brand name contains demonstrations of this consequence, and variation in brand equity influences a wide range of consumer behaviors. For example, brand equity influences brand satisfaction and loyalty (e.g., price insensitivity; Ailawadi et al., 2003), leads to greater market share and equity of a brand extension and supports price premiums (C. S. Park & Srinivasan, 1994), and provides a buffer when poor service occurs (e.g., Tax et al., 1998). Once a brand has achieved high equity, subsequent marketing mix variables further improve responses to the extent that the variables are congruent with the brand associations already established. For example, for high-equity brands, sales promotions are most effective when they provide benefits congruent with the products being promoted (e.g., money for high-equity brands seen as utilitarian,

---
[3]We thank Keven Keller for this important suggestion.

nonmonetary promotions for high-equity brands seen as hedonic; Chandon et al., 2000).

Brand Meaning

Another interesting brand property that has been examined is the meaning of a brand to consumers. Though some research has incorporated meaning into conceptualizations of brand equity, in a manner akin to associations (e.g., Berry et al., 2002), more recent work has adopted richer, deeper notions of the construct. At the simplest level, brands can represent a set of core values that are reflected in the meanings attributed to the brand (Schouten & McAlexander, 1995). And at the broadest level, retro brand meaning has been shown to consist of allegory (the brand story), aura (the brand essence), arcadia (the idealized community), and antinomy (the brand paradox; S. P. Brown et al., 2003). Thus, like brand equity, brand meaning could theoretically encompass any brand property, and we include it and situate it here in the hierarchy using the same criteria as with brand equity.

Regarding antecedents, as children age, their knowledge of brands becomes more nuanced, as evidenced by increased brand awareness and recall, preference, and understanding of the symbolic meaning of brands (John, 1999; see also Braun-LaTour et al., 2007). As will be seen later, meaning creation has been found to be both an antecedent and consequence of brand relationships and brand communities, in addition to influencing more traditional consequences such as evaluations of brand extensions (e.g., C. W. Park et al., 1991). Research on brand meaning has particularly benefited from diverse methodologies, including netnography (S. P. Brown et al., 2003) and hermeneutical analysis of consumer's consumption stories (Thompson, 1997). This diversity has allowed researchers to go beyond preconceived and potentially limited notions of the meanings brands can have for consumers.

Brand Personality

Perhaps surprisingly, research has found that consumers can perceive brands to possess different personalities, in a manner akin to how they perceive humans to have personalities. Brand personality can be understood as an instantiation of the tendency for consumers to anthropomorphize brands (MacInnis & Folkes, 2017): Consumers are able to perceive brands in human terms, and this anthropomorphism can lead to greater brand liking (Aggarwal & McGill, 2007, 2012; see also Puzakova et al., 2013). Analogous to human personality, brand personality has also been shown to consist of five facets, though different from the five facets of human personality. These brand personality facets are sincere (e.g., honest, down to earth), exciting (e.g., trendy, cool), competent (e.g., intelligent, hardworking), sophisticated (e.g., good looking, glamorous), and rugged (e.g., tough, masculine; J. L. Aaker, 1997).

Several antecedents of brand personality have been found, and it has been shown to have various downstream consequences. For example, physical aspects of the brand, such as package design, influence perceptions of brand personality (Orth & Malkewitz, 2008). Further, consumers who believe personalities and traits are fixed (entity theorists) are more likely to perceive brands as having a personality than consumers who believe personalities and traits are flexible (incremental theorists; J. K. Park & John, 2010). Brand experiences that are sensory, affective, intellectual, and/or behavioral can be an antecedent of perceived brand personality, and experiences influence customer satisfaction and loyalty both directly and through their effect on perceived brand personality (Brakus et al., 2009).

Interestingly, entity consumers incorporate the positive brand personality traits into their own self-perception, such that they believe themselves to be more glamorous after using a Victoria's Secret bag and more intelligent after using an MIT pen (J. K. Park & John, 2010). Congruence between a brand's personality and a consumer's salient self-construct leads to more positive brand attitudes (J. L. Aaker, 1999). Similarly, congruence between a brand's personality and a consumer's actual (rather than ideal) self-construct increases emotional brand attachment (Malär et al., 2011). And brand personality (sincere vs. exciting) has been shown to affect perceived brand partner quality (i.e., the extent to which the brand can be counted on), which in turn affects the strength of a consumer's relationship with a brand

(J. L. Aaker et al., 2004). Specifically, sincere brands increase in brand relationship strength over time, whereas exciting brands decrease in brand relationship strength over time. However, following transgression, sincere brands decrease in brand strength (due to lower perceptions of brand partner quality), whereas exciting brands do not.

Brand Relationship

Consumers not only perceive brands in human terms but can come to develop relationships with brands. Indeed, research on brand relationships has burgeoned since the introduction of this important brand property by Fournier in 1998. Before we review this research, however, it is helpful to consider what it means for a consumer to have a relationship with a brand. Is the construct of brand relationship a metaphor by which to understand how consumers feel and behave toward a brand? Or does the construct of brand relationship imply that the psychological processes underlying consumer brand relationships correspond to the psychological processes underlying interpersonal relationships? Research exists that supports the latter. On a neurological level, brands to which consumers feel close activate similar neurological substrates as those associated with interpersonal love (the insula; Reimann et al., 2012). On a psychological level, consumers demonstrate remarkably similar behavior toward brands as they do people. For example, it is well known that when fearful, people affiliate with others (Schachter, 1959). Revealingly, in the absence of people, fearful consumers affiliate with available brands, and this affiliation fosters deeper feelings of attachment for the brand (Dunn & Hoegg, 2014). Together, these two findings make a compelling case that consumers treat brands as they treat people and that similar psychological processes underlie both brand and interpersonal relationships.

What, then, is known of brand relationships? Brand relationships that have been studied have ranged in intensity, from self–brand connection (Escalas & Bettman, 2003, 2005) to brand relationship strength (J. L. Aaker et al., 2004), brand emotional attachment (e.g., Malär et al., 2011; Thomson et al., 2005), brand attachment–aversion (e.g., C. W. Park et al., 2013), brand relationship quality (Fournier, 1998), and even brand love (Batra et al., 2012). The construct of brand relationship quality was first proposed and validated in in-depth interviews by Fournier (1998), which suggested it is composed of self-connection, commitment, interdependence, intimacy, brand partner quality, and love/passion. Subsequent research has explored brand relationships using one or more of these components, and some research streams have expanded upon these facets, as with, for example, brand attachment–aversion (based upon self–brand connection/distance and the extent to which thoughts about a brand come naturally and automatically to mind; C. W. Park et al., 2013) and brand love (based upon seven components; Batra et al., 2012).

Antecedents of brand relationships also appear to range in intensity, with more intense antecedents being associated with more intense forms of brand relationships. Merely affiliating a brand with a specific reference group (i.e., an ingroup) increases self–brand connection when the consumer belongs or wishes to belong to that group (Escalas & Bettman, 2003). This effect is magnified when the brand image matches that of the valued reference group (Escalas & Bettman, 2005). As mentioned, brand personality, perhaps a more potent antecedent, can influence perceptions of brand partner quality (self-connection, satisfaction, commitment, and intimacy; J. L. Aaker et al., 2004) and emotional attachment (affection, connection, and passion; Malär et al., 2011). The attachment–aversion model of consumer behavior (C. W. Park et al., 2013) reveals three key antecedents (the 3 Es): the extent to which brands (a) provide hedonically and/or aesthetically pleasing experiences (enticing the self), (b) create a sense of an efficacious and capable self (enabling the self), and/or (c) create the opportunity for self-identity and self-expression (enriching the self).[4] The most extensive processes, consisting of meaning creation, elaboration, and reinforcement, all of which are the result of interplay between brand and consumer behaviors, lead

---

[4] The attachment–aversion model of consumer behavior builds upon the brand attachment model (C. W. Park et al., 2010), extending it in a number of ways, most relevantly, by articulating antecedents to the brand relationship.

to brand relationship quality (which includes love/passion; Fournier, 1998).⁵ Finally, there even exist individual differences in the propensity of consumers to form relationships with brands, such that some consumers are chronically predisposed to form relationships with brands to a greater extent than others (e.g., those that agree with statements such as "I often feel a personal connection between me and my brands"; Sprott et al., 2009).

The consequences stemming from brand relationships include relatively traditional brand-related measures. For example, brand action that conforms with rather than violates a relationship norm (communal vs. exchange) leads to more positive brand attitudes and behaviors (Aggarwal, 2004), as does self–brand connection (Escalas, 2004). Similarly, brand love (along with its antecedent product quality) influences brand loyalty, word of mouth, and resistance to negative information (Batra et al., 2012; see also C. W. Park et al., 2013; Thomson et al., 2005).

Brand relationship consequences go beyond these relatively traditional measures and include consequences strikingly similar to those studied in the interpersonal relationship literature. A critical dynamic underlying successful interpersonal relationships is motivated reasoning (e.g., Finkel et al., 2002; Murray et al., 1996; Rusbult et al., 1991). The essence of motivated reasoning is that one's wish, desire, or preference for an outcome can bias cognitive processes such that one's understanding of a person, event, or object are consistent with one's desire (Kunda, 1990). For example, people use motivated reasoning to maintain desired relationships even after relationship transgressions (Donovan & Priester, 2017, 2020; see also Finkel et al., 2002). So too do consumers use motivated reasoning within brand relationships. In order to maintain relationship stability and durability, consumers use a variety of motivated reasoning tools such as positively biased brand-partner perceptions, devaluation of alternatives, attribution biases, accommodation, tolerance, and even forgiveness (Fournier, 1998).

Consumers can even come to feel a sense of loss and mourning when a brand relationship ends (e.g., because the brand is discontinued; Russell & Schau, 2014). Finally, brand relationships can also have consequences beyond those within the dyadic consumer–brand relationship, such that brand relationship quality increases brand community identification (Algesheimer et al., 2005).

Brand Community

As the previous finding suggests, brands can also provide the basis for individuals to form communities with other consumers of the brand. One influential conceptualization of brand community is as a triad that is composed of the brand, consumer, and community. The bases of this conceptualization are legitimacy (really knowing the brand), oppositional brand loyalty (counterarguing other brands), and consciousness of kind (a stronger connection to other community members than to the brand; Muñiz & O'Guinn, 2001). Note the incorporation of an important potential consequence—loyalty—into the very meaning of brand community (cf. McAlexander et al., 2002). Other conceptualizations have emphasized a sense of membership and identity (Schau et al., 2009) or four dimensions of community (the relationship between the consumer and product, the consumer and brand, the consumer and company, and the consumer and other consumers, McAlexander et al., 2002).

Several antecedents to brand community have been found. Experiential marketing events designed to facilitate interaction with the brand, product, company, and other customers have been shown to strengthen brand communities (McAlexander et al., 2002). As mentioned, brand relationship quality increases brand community identification (Algesheimer et al., 2005). Bagozzi and Dholakia (2006) found that desire to become part of a brand community is driven by five factors: brand attitude, positive anticipated emotions, lack of negative anticipated emotions, subjective norms, and social identity. Not all brands, however, are necessarily able

---

⁵A possible exception to this pattern of more intense antecedents resulting in more intense brand relationships is the finding that product quality (e.g., well-made, functional, and practical) leads to brand love (Batra et al., 2012). However, it seems plausible that extremely high levels of product quality, in which a consumer's needs are understood, responded to, and even anticipated (e.g., as described in an early review of the Apple iPhone; Heisler, 2014), could lead to intense forms of brand relationship such as brand love.

to build brand communities. For example, Zipcar (an access-based brand) has been unable to develop such a community despite the firm's efforts to create one, perhaps due to the lack of product ownership or avoidance of a negative group image of customers being cheap (Bardhi & Eckhardt, 2012).

Meaning creation is an important antecedent to, and consequence of, brand communities. For example, brand meaning is cocreated with the community's input, such that they are reciprocal influences on each other: Brand meaning leads to the formation of a brand community, and brand community, in turn, revises and expands upon the brand meaning, which then further sustains and strengthens the community, and so on (S. P. Brown et al., 2003). Other consequences examined are also quite extensive and involved. Brand community has been found to lead to shared consciousness, fostering rituals and traditions such as celebrating the history of the brand, sharing brand stories, and even creating a sense of moral responsibility to the community and its individual members (Muñiz & O'Guinn, 2001). Further, brand communities have been shown to foster community engagement (composed of documenting, badging, marking milestones, and staking), brand use (composed of customizing, grooming, and commoditizing), social networking (composed of welcoming, empathizing, and governing), and impression management (composed of evangelizing and justifying). Brand communities can even strengthen after discontinuation of a brand (e.g., the Apple Newton; Muñiz & Schau, 2005). Reflecting upon the wealth of brand consequences, it is not surprising that brand communities can even lead to a sense of transformation of self (Schouten & McAlexander, 1995).

THE BRAND PROPERTY STRENGTH FRAMEWORK: ANTECEDENTS AND CONSEQUENCES ACROSS BRAND PROPERTIES

For the purposes of developing a broader understanding of consumer brand behavior that spans brand properties, it is helpful to compare antecedents and consequences across brand properties. To do so, we distilled the antecedents and consequences for each brand property in order to more easily make this comparison. Specifically, we summarized the findings and models from both (a) the literature review of the 75 most-cited brand papers and (b) the additional literature reviewed to more fully capture the different brand properties. These results are presented in Figure 31.2. Inspection of Figure 31.2 reveals that at one end of the continuum, the influence of brand properties on consumers is relatively narrow and transient. At the other end of the continuum, the influence is relatively broad and enduring. The review of the literature suggests that antecedents, as well as consequences, fall along a hierarchy of strength continuum similar to that of brand properties.

Hierarchy of Antecedents: Involvement, Interaction, and Experience

Antecedents to brand properties range from prior brand purchase and advertising forming initial associations on one end of the continuum to experiential marketing events, brand relationship quality, and social identity fostering brand communities on the other. We propose that increasing successful *involvement*, *interaction*, and *experience* of the consumer with the brand can parsimoniously describe the hierarchy of antecedents across brand properties. Note that each has been used to explain aspects of consumer brand behavior within brand properties. Greater involvement with a brand (and the information associated with that brand, e.g., advertising) leads to stronger brand attitudes (e.g., MacInnis et al., 1991), and (though not focal) involvement influences brand equity (i.e., brand awareness and image; Keller, 1993). Interaction between consumer and brand is fundamental to brand relationships (Fournier, 1998). Depth of experience is critical to understanding brand communities (McAlexander et al., 2002; Schmitt, 2013; Schmitt et al., 2015). We propose that involvement, interaction, and experience form the basis for the hierarchy of antecedents spanning across all brand properties. This is a testable hypothesis. It is possible that involvement, interaction, and experience may affect one another reciprocally in an upward spiral in which an increase in one leads

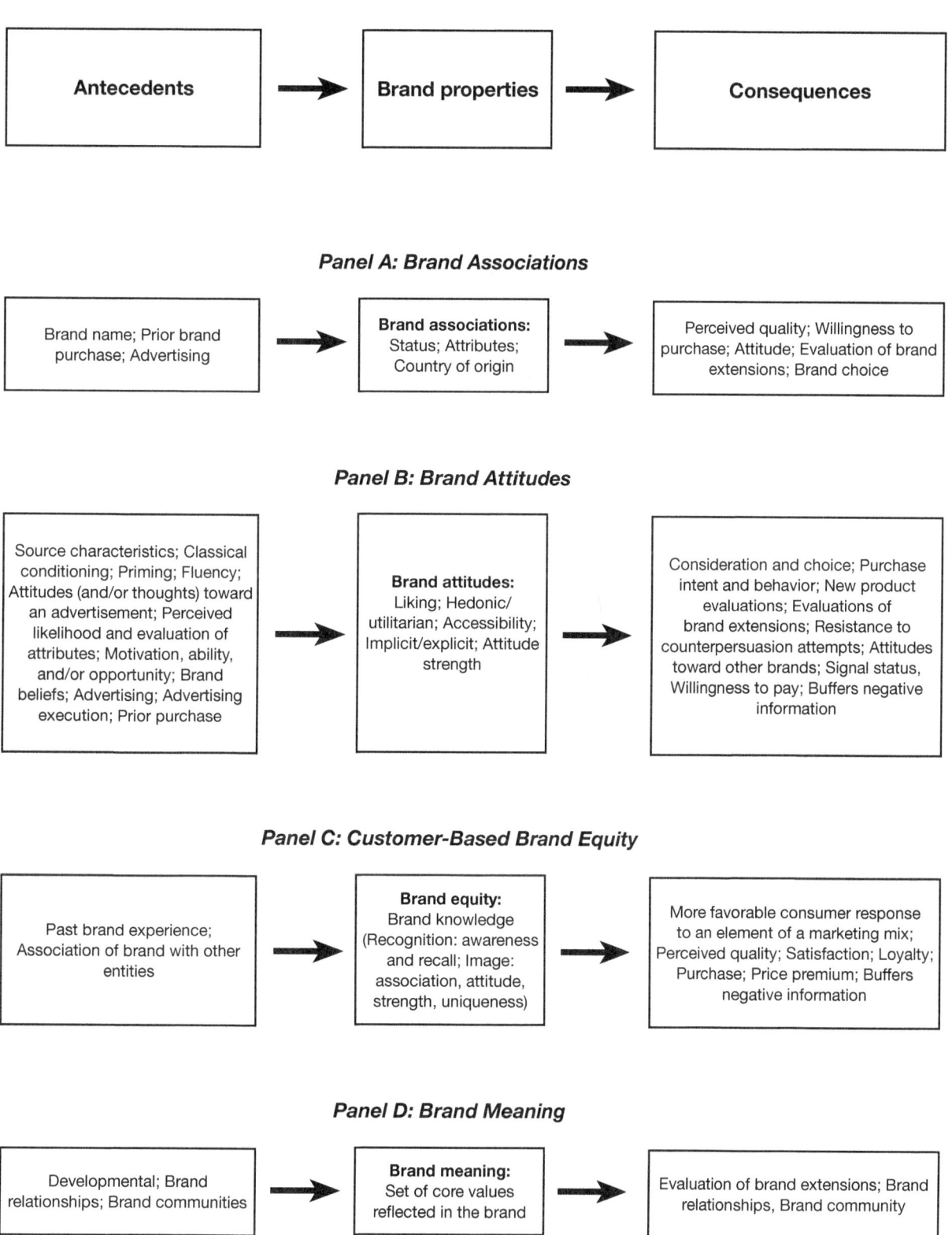

FIGURE 31.2. The causal sequence of constructs for each brand property. (*Continues*)

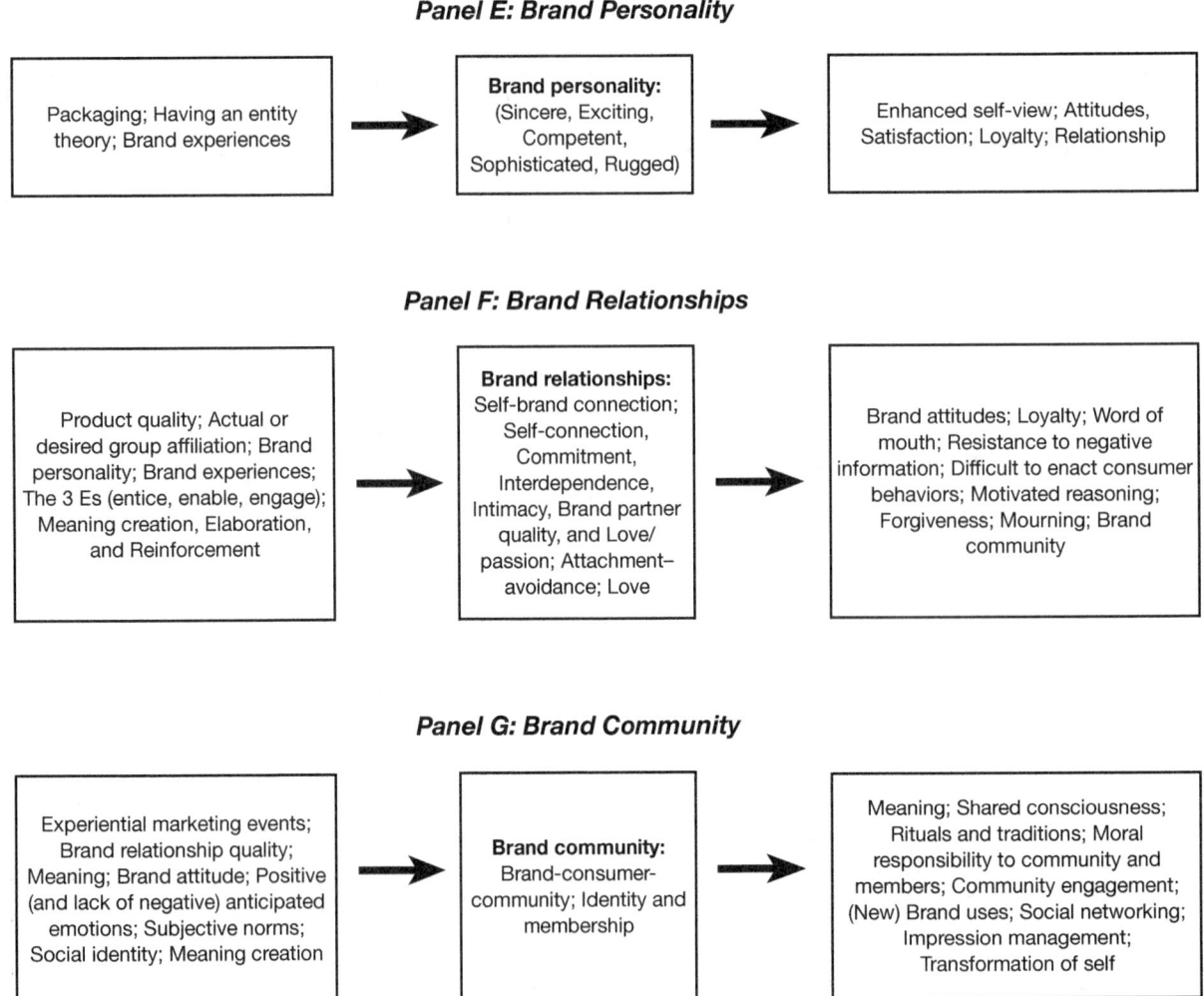

FIGURE 31.2. *(Continued)* The causal sequence of constructs for each brand property.

to an increase in another and so on. For example, experience may play an especially critical role, in that it may provide the means by which to increase both brand involvement and interaction. Low levels of all three may lead to weaker brand properties, and higher levels of all three may produce stronger brand properties. Alternatively, it is also possible that involvement may uniquely predict brand associations and (strong) brand attitudes, interaction may uniquely predict brand personality and brand relationship, and experience may uniquely predict the strongest brand property and brand community. Indeed, one of the first academic brand papers proposed that brand strength "is entirely a matter of a person's past experience" (Geissler, 1917, p. 277).

Hierarchy of Consequences: Self–Brand Integration

What is remarkable about the hierarchy of consequences is the extent to which it goes beyond the mere strength of a property to influence a specific outcome. In addition to mere strength, the hierarchy of consequences reveals a brand's potential influence on a staggering breadth of different types of thoughts, feelings, and behaviors. That is, it is not simply that stronger brand properties have a greater influence on the same consequences, such as stronger brand attitudes leading to greater purchase intent than weaker brand associations (though this is true; Petty et al., 1983). And it is not just that stronger brand properties, such as brand attachment, lead consumers to engage in more difficult brand-related behaviors than weaker brand properties, such as brand attitudes (though this is also true; C. W. Park et al., 2010, 2013). Rather, as the brand properties grow in strength, they come to influence an ever-expanding array of outcomes, spanning from perceptions of brand quality and brand usage all the way to feelings of mourning, shared consciousness, rituals, traditions, and transformation of self.

Such consequences are beyond the wildest dreams of early brand research and support the observation that conceptualizations, and perhaps lay experiences, of important brand properties have shifted from an emphasis on brand image as defined by advertisers and the firm (the 1950s modern approach) to consumer-led ideas of brand community and brand meaning, in which consumers use brands to volitionally construct their ideal self (the 1960s to today postmodern approach; Holt, 2002). Put another way, consequences appear to range from mere awareness of a brand being out there, separate from the self, and as a good or service to potentially obtain or use but not at all reflective of the self to total inclusion of the other (i.e., a brand) in the self, use or ownership thereof being an important way to define and express the self, connect and identify with others, and organize one's social world.

How best to account for the differences in consequences across brand properties? We propose that the psychological process underlying the hierarchy of brand consequences is the extent to which the self is integrated with the brand. Note that this is slightly, but importantly, different from how close one feels to a brand or even how much one loves a brand, though both of these are steps in the self-integration process. As the brand consequences increase in strength, they can be understood from the perspective of consumer–brand integration. The weaker brand consequences, such as perception of brand quality and purchase intent, are consistent with a lack, or very low level, of self–brand integration. The strongest brand consequences, such as self-identification, meaning, and transformation, are consistent with the highest levels of self–brand integration.

THE CONSUMER PSYCHOLOGY BRAND LITERATURE: INTEGRATED MODEL AND FUTURE RESEARCH

Recall that the goal of this chapter, and the brand property strength framework, is to develop a broader and more unified theoretical understanding of brands, an understanding that provides insight into the psychological processes that span across disparate findings and models. We organized the findings and models according to the brand property strength framework (Figure 31.2), and thus this chapter presents one such solution. The many findings and models on consumer brand psychology can be understood from the constructs proposed to account for the psychological processes underlying the influence of antecedents on brand properties and the influence of brand properties on brand consequences. The greater the extent to which consumers are involved, interact, and have experience with a brand, the more likely the brand property is to be stronger. And the greater the brand property strength, the more likely a brand is to have consequences that flow from self–brand integration. As such, the brand property strength framework provides a guide to understanding and organizing the many findings and models regarding the consumer psychology of brands.

We consider this framework a preliminary organization of the consumer psychology brand literature that describes the state of the field as it currently stands—its important findings, constructs, and theoretical perspectives to date. From this point, further theoretical and empirical work is needed to clarify a number of important remaining questions toward the goal of developing a broader, unifying theory of consumer brand psychology.

Which Brand Properties Are Empirically Distinguishable?

First, it will be helpful to examine whether any of the brand properties are best combined. Importantly, further investigation of these constructs individually will still be useful. The following are suggestions for possible reconceptualizations and empirical examinations of brand properties toward the goal of a broader, unifying theory of consumer brand psychology. Both the brand property strength framework and alternatives proposed next constitute testable hypotheses.

As mentioned, customer-based brand equity theoretically could encompass any brand property and thus may more accurately be conceptualized as an umbrella construct. Similarly, brand meaning may also be better understood as an umbrella construct. For a consumer, a brand can mean anything from a simple association to one's definition of self and one's community or social identity. In testing these notions empirically, it will be important to incorporate operationalizations of particularly useful and distinct aspects of definitions of brand equity and brand meaning, to examine if they cohere into the remaining more specific brand properties. For example, the brand equity model (Keller, 1993, 2003) outlines several useful aspects of associations not highlighted elsewhere, such as association type and uniqueness. Similarly, brand meaning scholarship describes associations that are especially elaborate, such as the brand story, and elusive, such as the brand essence. The broad range of methodologies used in these literatures can be usefully applied to all brand properties to more fully and accurately capture their nature, antecedents, and consequences.

After considering customer-based brand equity and brand meaning, five properties remain: brand associations, brand attitudes, brand personality, brand relationship, and brand community. Brand personality could be conceptualized as and found to be a more specific form of associations, perhaps relatively more developed and organized.[6] Further, recall that knowing the extent to which such associations are evaluated positively is crucial, particularly for understanding downstream consequences. Thus, associations could be found to be subsumed under attitudes, as in the expectancy-value approaches. The value (or meaning) of associations, including brand personality types, could vary by person and situation (e.g., a customer especially values dental protection, a transgression has occurred). Thus, brand attitude, relationship, and community may be revealed to be the most important and empirically distinct properties (subsuming the others).[7]

Alternatively, it could be the case that perceiving a brand to have a personality is a mechanism by which a strong positive attitude leads to development of a strong brand relationship. Anthropomorphism seems a necessary step in forming a brand relationship—perceiving a brand as an entity with which to have a relationship—and entails perceiving a nonhuman entity as having human traits (personality?) and qualities (associations?). This view would predict that brand attitudes, personality, relationship, and community would be revealed to be the most important and empirically distinct properties.

Is There a Hierarchy of Antecedents and Consequences of Brand Properties, and Thus Do Brand Properties Vary in Strength?

The notion of a hierarchy of brand property strength appears to have reasonable support given the evidence organized in Figure 31.2. However, there are very few investigations that have simultaneously examined more than one brand property and compared their ability to predict consequences. Examples using such an approach are provided by C. W. Park et al. (2010, 2013), wherein the ability of brand attachment (attachment–avoidance) to predict an array of behaviors is compared with that of brand attitudes. And there are no investigations of which we are aware that have examined multiple antecedents and compared their ability to predict multiple brand properties. Thus, the critical questions remain: Which antecedents are necessary and sufficient for which brand properties, and which brand properties are necessary and sufficient for which consequences? For example, brand attitudes have been shown to be insufficient in predicting more difficult brand behaviors, and brand relationships have been shown to be sufficient (C. W. Park et al., 2013). However, it remains unclear whether brand relationships are necessary or merely one of several properties that can predict more difficult

---

[6] We thank Keven Keller for this very helpful suggestion.

[7] We thank C. W. Park for this very intriguing, and testable, hypothesis.

brand behaviors (e.g., might brand communities do so as well?). It remains to be seen whether, for example, brand relationships are necessary and sufficient to predict the formation of brand communities.

All are testable models that can be validated, refined, or invalidated by data, moving the field forward. To test between the brand property strength framework and other models (e.g., see Footnotes 6 and 7), research is needed that simultaneously examines and operationalizes all seven properties, the variables proposed to explain the hierarchy of antecedents (involvement, interaction, and experience), and consequences spanning the full range of brand self-integration (from willingness to purchase to shared consciousness/rituals and traditions/self-transformation) and compares how each model, and any others proposed, fits and explains the data. Given the increasing branding of social movements such as #BlackLivesMatter and #MeToo and the success of such strategies in sustaining activism toward social change, understanding what leads to the formation of strong brands and the consequences of brand strength takes on increased importance. We eagerly look forward to this and other work that facilitates an integrated understanding of the consumer psychology of brands.

REFERENCES

Aaker, D. A. (1996). Measuring brand equity across products and markets. *California Management Review*, 38(3), 102–120. https://doi.org/10.2307/41165845

Aaker, D. A., & Jacobson, R. (2001). The value relevance of brand attitude in high-technology markets. *Journal of Marketing Research*, 38(4), 485–493. https://doi.org/10.1509/jmkr.38.4.485.18905

*Aaker, D. A., & Keller, K. L. (1990). Consumer evaluations of brand extensions. *Journal of Marketing*, 54(1), 27–41. https://doi.org/10.1177/002224299005400102

*Aaker, J. L. (1997). Dimensions of brand personality. *Journal of Marketing Research*, 34(3), 347–356. https://doi.org/10.1177/002224379703400304

*Aaker, J. L. (1999). The malleable self: The role of self-expression in persuasion. *Journal of Marketing Research*, 36(1), 45–57. https://doi.org/10.1177/002224379903600104

*Aaker, J. L., Fournier, S., & Brasel, S. A. (2004). When good brands do bad. *Journal of Consumer Research*, 31(1), 1–16. https://doi.org/10.1086/383419

Aggarwal, P. (2004). The effects of brand relationship norms on consumer attitudes and behavior. *Journal of Consumer Research*, 31(1), 87–101. https://doi.org/10.1086/383426

Aggarwal, P., & McGill, A. L. (2007). Is that car smiling at me? Schema congruity as a basis for evaluating anthropomorphized products. *Journal of Consumer Research*, 34(4), 468–479. https://doi.org/10.1086/518544

Aggarwal, P., & McGill, A. L. (2012). When brands seem human, do humans act like brands? Automatic behavioral priming effects of brand anthropomorphism. *Journal of Consumer Research*, 39(2), 307–323. https://doi.org/10.1086/662614

*Ahluwalia, R., Burnkrant, R. E., & Unnava, H. R. (2000). Consumer response to negative publicity: The moderating role of commitment. *Journal of Marketing Research*, 37(2), 203–214. https://doi.org/10.1509/jmkr.37.2.203.18734

Ailawadi, K. L., Lehmann, D. R., & Neslin, S. A. (2003). Revenue premium as an outcome measure of brand equity. *Journal of Marketing*, 67(4), 1–17. https://doi.org/10.1509/jmkg.67.4.1.18688

*Ailawadi, K. L., Neslin, S. A., & Gedenk, K. (2001). Pursuing the value-conscious consumer: Store brands versus national brand promotions. *Journal of Marketing*, 65(1), 71–89. https://doi.org/10.1509/jmkg.65.1.71.18132

*Alba, J., Lynch, J., Weitz, B., Janiszewski, C., Lutz, R., Sawyer, A., & Wood, S. (1997). Interactive home shopping: Consumer, retailer, and manufacturer incentives to participate in electronic marketplaces. *Journal of Marketing*, 61(3), 38–53. https://doi.org/10.1177/002224299706100303

Albarracin, D., & Johnson, B. T. (Eds.). (2018). *Handbook of attitudes*. Routledge.

*Algesheimer, R., Dholakia, U. M., & Herrmann, A. (2005). The social influence of brand community: Evidence from European car clubs. *Journal of Marketing*, 69(3), 19–34. https://doi.org/10.1509/jmkg.69.3.19.66363

Allison, R. I., & Uhl, K. P. (1964). Influence of beer brand identification on taste perception. *Journal of Marketing Research*, 1(3), 36–39. https://doi.org/10.1177/002224376400100305

Bagozzi, R. P., & Dholakia, U. M. (2006). Antecedents and purchase consequences of customer participation in small group brand communities. *International Journal of Research in Marketing*, 23(1), 45–61. https://doi.org/10.1016/j.ijresmar.2006.01.005

References marked with an asterisk indicate studies included in the meta-analysis.

Baldinger, A. L. (1990). Defining and applying the brand equity concept: Why. *Journal of Advertising Research*, *30*(3), RC-2.

Baldinger, A. L., & Rubinson, J. (1996). Brand loyalty: The link between attitude and behavior. *Journal of Advertising Research*, *36*(6), 22–35.

*Bardhi, F., & Eckhardt, G. M. (2012). Access-based consumption: The case of car sharing. *Journal of Consumer Research*, *39*(4), 881–898. https://doi.org/10.1086/666376

*Bart, Y., Shankar, V., Sultan, F., & Urban, G. L. (2005). Are the drivers and role of online trust the same for all web sites and consumers? A large-scale exploratory empirical study. *Journal of Marketing*, *69*(4), 133–152. https://doi.org/10.1509/jmkg.2005.69.4.133

Bass, F. M. (1972). Fishbein and brand preference: A reply. *Journal of Marketing Research*, *9*(4), 461. https://doi.org/10.1177/002224377200900421

Bass, F. M., & Talarzyk, W. W. (1972). An attitude model for the study of brand preference. *Journal of Marketing Research*, *9*(1), 93–96. https://doi.org/10.1177/002224377200900121

*Batra, R., Ahuvia, A., & Bagozzi, R. P. (2012). Brand love. *Journal of Marketing*, *76*(2), 1–16. https://doi.org/10.1509/jm.09.0339

*Batra, R., Ramaswamy, V., Alden, D. L., Steenkamp, J. B. E., & Ramachander, S. (2000). Effects of brand local and nonlocal origin on consumer attitudes in developing countries. *Journal of Consumer Psychology*, *9*(2), 83–95. https://doi.org/10.1207/S15327663JCP0902_3

Batra, R., & Ray, M. L. (1986a). Affective responses mediating acceptance of advertising. *Journal of Consumer Research*, *13*(2), 234–249. https://doi.org/10.1086/209063

Batra, R., & Ray, M. L. (1986b). Situational effects of advertising repetition: The moderating influence of motivation, ability, and opportunity to respond. *Journal of Consumer Research*, *12*(4), 432–445. https://doi.org/10.1086/208528

*Bearden, W. O., & Etzel, M. J. (1982). Reference group influence on product and brand purchase decisions. *Journal of Consumer Research*, *9*(2), 183–194. https://doi.org/10.1086/208911

Beatty, S. E., Homer, P., & Kahle, L. R. (1988). The involvement—commitment model: Theory and implications. *Journal of Business Research*, *16*(2), 149–167. https://doi.org/10.1016/0148-2963(88)90039-2

Bello, D. C., & Holbrook, M. B. (1995). Does an absence of brand equity generalize across product classes? *Journal of Business Research*, *34*(2), 125–131. https://doi.org/10.1016/0148-2963(95)00008-G

*Bergkvist, L., & Rossiter, J. R. (2007). The predictive validity of multiple-item versus single-item measures of the same constructs. *Journal of Marketing Research*, *44*(2), 175–184. https://doi.org/10.1509/jmkr.44.2.175

*Berry, L. L., Seiders, K., & Grewal, D. (2002). Understanding service convenience. *Journal of Marketing*, *66*(3), 1–17. https://doi.org/10.1509/jmkg.66.3.1.18505

*Boush, D. M., & Loken, B. (1991). A process-tracing study of brand extension evaluation. *Journal of Marketing Research*, *28*(1), 16–28. https://doi.org/10.1177/002224379102800102

*Brakus, J. J., Schmitt, B. H., & Zarantonello, L. (2009). Brand experience: What is it? How is it measured? Does it affect loyalty? *Journal of Marketing*, *73*(3), 52–68. https://doi.org/10.1509/jmkg.73.3.052

Braun-LaTour, K. A., LaTour, M. S., & Zinkhan, G. M. (2007). Using childhood memories to gain insight into brand meaning. *Journal of Marketing*, *71*(2), 45–60. https://doi.org/10.1509/jmkg.71.2.045

*Broniarczyk, S. M., & Alba, J. W. (1994). The importance of the brand in brand extension. *Journal of Marketing Research*, *31*(2), 214–228. https://doi.org/10.1177/002224379403100206

*Brown, S. P., Kozinets, R. V., & Sherry, J. F., Jr. (2003). Teaching old brands new tricks: Retro branding and the revival of brand meaning. *Journal of Marketing*, *67*(3), 19–33. https://doi.org/10.1509/jmkg.67.3.19.18657

*Brown, S. P., & Stayman, D. M. (1992). Antecedents and consequences of attitude toward the ad: A meta-analysis. *Journal of Consumer Research*, *19*(1), 34–51. https://doi.org/10.1086/209284

*Brown, T. J., & Dacin, P. A. (1997). The company and the product: Corporate associations and consumer product responses. *Journal of Marketing*, *61*(1), 68–84. https://doi.org/10.1177/002224299706100106

*Chandon, P., Wansink, B., & Laurent, G. (2000). A benefit congruency framework of sales promotion effectiveness. *Journal of Marketing*, *64*(4), 65–81. https://doi.org/10.1509/jmkg.64.4.65.18071

*Chaudhuri, A., & Holbrook, M. B. (2001). The chain of effects from brand trust and brand affect to brand performance: The role of brand loyalty. *Journal of Marketing*, *65*(2), 81–93. https://doi.org/10.1509/jmkg.65.2.81.18255

Cohen, J. B., Fishbein, M., & Ahtola, O. T. (1972). The nature and uses of expectancy-value models in consumer attitude research. *Journal of Marketing Research*, *9*(4), 456–460. https://doi.org/10.1177/002224377200900420

*Dawar, N., & Parker, P. (1994). Marketing universals: Consumers' use of brand name, price, physical

appearance, and retailer reputation as signals of product quality. *Journal of Marketing, 58*(2), 81–95. https://doi.org/10.2307/1252271

Dawar, N., & Pillutla, M. M. (2000). Impact of product-harm crises on brand equity: The moderating role of consumer expectations. *Journal of Marketing Research, 37*(2), 215–226. https://doi.org/10.1509/jmkr.37.2.215.18729

Dholakia, R., & Sternthal, B. (1977). Highly credible sources: Persuasive facilitators or persuasive liabilities? *Journal of Consumer Research, 3*(4), 223–232. https://doi.org/10.1086/208671

*Dodds, W. B., Monroe, K. B., & Grewal, D. (1991). Effects of price, brand, and store information on buyers' product evaluations. *Journal of Marketing Research, 28*(3), 307–319.

Donovan, L. A. N., & Priester, J. R. (2017). Exploring the psychological processes underlying interpersonal forgiveness: The superiority of motivated reasoning over empathy. *Journal of Experimental Social Psychology, 71*, 16–30. https://doi.org/10.1016/j.jesp.2017.02.005

Donovan, L. A. N., & Priester, J. R. (2020). Exploring the psychological processes that underlie interpersonal forgiveness: Replication and extension of the model of motivated interpersonal forgiveness. *Frontiers in Psychology, 11*, 2107. https://doi.org/10.3389/fpsyg.2020.02107

Duffin, E. (2020, November 9). Biggest companies in the world by market capitalization 2020. *Statista*. https://www.statista.com/statistics/263264/top-companies-in-the-world-by-market-capitalization/

*Duncan, T., & Moriarty, S. E. (1998). A communication-based marketing model for managing relationships. *Journal of Marketing, 62*(2), 1–13. https://doi.org/10.1177/002224299806200201

Dunn, L., & Hoegg, J. (2014). The impact of fear on emotional brand attachment. *Journal of Consumer Research, 41*(1), 152–168. https://doi.org/10.1086/675377

Dyson, P., Farr, A., & Hollis, N. S. (1996). Understanding, measuring, and using brand equity. *Journal of Advertising Research, 36*(6), 9–22.

*Escalas, J. E. (2004). Narrative processing: Building consumer connections to brands. *Journal of Consumer Psychology, 14*(1–2), 168–180. https://doi.org/10.1207/s15327663jcp1401&2_19

*Escalas, J. E., & Bettman, J. R. (2003). You are what they eat: The influence of reference groups on consumers' connections to brands. *Journal of Consumer Psychology, 13*(3), 339–348. https://doi.org/10.1207/S15327663JCP1303_14

*Escalas, J. E., & Bettman, J. R. (2005). Self-construal, reference groups, and brand meaning. *Journal of Consumer Research, 32*(3), 378–389. https://doi.org/10.1086/497549

Fazio, R. H., Powell, M. C., & Williams, C. J. (1989). The role of attitude accessibility in the attitude-to-behavior process. *Journal of Consumer Research, 16*(3), 280–288. https://doi.org/10.1086/209214

Fazio, R. H., Sanbonmatsu, D. M., Powell, M. C., & Kardes, F. R. (1986). On the automatic activation of attitudes. *Journal of Personality and Social Psychology, 50*(2), 229–238. https://doi.org/10.1037/0022-3514.50.2.229

Finkel, E. J., Rusbult, C. E., Kumashiro, M., & Hannon, P. A. (2002). Dealing with betrayal in close relationships: Does commitment promote forgiveness? *Journal of Personality and Social Psychology, 82*(6), 956–974. https://doi.org/10.1037/0022-3514.82.6.956

Fishbein, M. (1963). An investigation of the relationships between beliefs about an object and the attitude toward that object. *Human Relations, 16*(3), 233–239. https://doi.org/10.1177/001872676301600302

Flandreau, M., & Flores, J. H. (2009). Bonds and brands: Foundations of sovereign debt markets, 1820–1830. *Journal of Economic History, 69*(3), 646–684. https://doi.org/10.1017/S0022050709001089

*Fournier, S. (1998). Consumers and their brands: Developing relationship theory in consumer research. *Journal of Consumer Research, 24*(4), 343–373. https://doi.org/10.1086/209515

*Ganesh, J., Arnold, M. J., & Reynolds, K. E. (2000). Understanding the customer base of service providers: An examination of the differences between switchers and stayers. *Journal of Marketing, 64*(3), 65–87. https://doi.org/10.1509/jmkg.64.3.65.18028

Geissler, L. R. (1917). Association-reactions applied to ideas of commercial brands of familiar articles. *Journal of Applied Psychology, 1*(3), 275–290. https://doi.org/10.1037/h0074861

Gibson, B. (2008). Can evaluative conditioning change attitudes toward mature brands? New evidence from the Implicit Association Test. *Journal of Consumer Research, 35*(1), 178–188. https://doi.org/10.1086/527341

Golder, P. N., & Tellis, G. J. (1993). Pioneer advantage: Marketing logic or marketing legend? *Journal of Marketing Research, 30*(2), 158–170. https://doi.org/10.1177/002224379303000203

Goldsmith, R. E., Lafferty, B. A., & Newell, S. J. (2000). The impact of corporate credibility and celebrity credibility on consumer reaction to advertisements and brands. *Journal of Advertising, 29*(3), 43–54. https://doi.org/10.1080/00913367.2000.10673616

Greenwald, A. G., & Albert, R. D. (1968). Acceptance and recall of improvised arguments. *Journal of*

Personality and Social Psychology, 8(1, Pt. 1), 31–34. https://doi.org/10.1037/h0021237

Gwinner, K. P., & Eaton, J. (1999). Building brand image through event sponsorship: The role of image transfer. *Journal of Advertising*, 28(4), 47–57. https://doi.org/10.1080/00913367.1999.10673595

*Han, Y. J., Nunes, J. C., & Drèze, X. (2010). Signaling status with luxury goods: The role of brand prominence. *Journal of Marketing*, 74(4), 15–30. https://doi.org/10.1509/jmkg.74.4.015

Heisler, Y. (2014, January 21). An incredible 2001 iPod review accurately predicted the iPod's impact on computing. *Engadget*. https://www.engadget.com/2014/01/21/an-incredible-2001-ipod-review-accurately-predicted-the-ipods-i/

Holbrook, M. B. (1992). Product quality, attributes, and brand name as determinants of price: The case of consumer electronics. *Marketing Letters*, 3(1), 71–83. https://doi.org/10.1007/BF00994082

*Holt, D. B. (2002). Why do brands cause trouble? A dialectical theory of consumer culture and branding. *Journal of Consumer Research*, 29(1), 70–90. https://doi.org/10.1086/339922

Hovland, C. I., Janis, I. L., & Kelley, H. H. (1953). *Communication and persuasion: Psychological studies of opinion change*. Yale University Press.

*Jacoby, J., & Kyner, D. B. (1973). Brand loyalty vs. repeat purchasing behavior. *Journal of Marketing Research*, 10(1), 1–9. https://doi.org/10.1177/002224377301000101

Jarvis, W. B. G., & Petty, R. E. (1996). The need to evaluate. *Journal of Personality and Social Psychology*, 70(1), 172–194. https://doi.org/10.1037/0022-3514.70.1.172

*John, D. R. (1999). Consumer socialization of children: A retrospective look at twenty-five years of research. *Journal of Consumer Research*, 26(3), 183–213. https://doi.org/10.1086/209559

Kahle, L. R., & Homer, P. M. (1985). Physical attractiveness of the celebrity endorser: A social adaptation perspective. *Journal of Consumer Research*, 11(4), 954–961. https://doi.org/10.1086/209029

*Keller, K. L. (1993). Conceptualizing, measuring, and managing customer-based brand equity. *Journal of Marketing*, 57(1), 1–22. https://doi.org/10.1177/002224299305700101

*Keller, K. L. (2003). Brand synthesis: The multidimensionality of brand knowledge. *Journal of Consumer Research*, 29(4), 595–600. https://doi.org/10.1086/346254

*Keller, K. L., & Aaker, D. A. (1992). The effects of sequential introduction of brand extensions. *Journal of Marketing Research*, 29(1), 35–50. https://doi.org/10.1177/002224379202900104

*Klein, J. G., Ettenson, R., & Morris, M. D. (1998). The animosity model of foreign product purchase: An empirical test in the People's Republic of China. *Journal of Marketing*, 62(1), 89–100. https://doi.org/10.1177/002224299806200108

*Kozinets, R. V., De Valck, K., Wojnicki, A. C., & Wilner, S. J. (2010). Networked narratives: Understanding word-of-mouth marketing in online communities. *Journal of Marketing*, 74(2), 71–89. https://doi.org/10.1509/jm.74.2.71

Kunda, Z. (1990). The case for motivated reasoning. *Psychological Bulletin*, 108(3), 480–498. https://doi.org/10.1037/0033-2909.108.3.480

Lane, V., & Jacobson, R. (1995). Stock market reactions to brand extension announcements: The effects of brand attitude and familiarity. *Journal of Marketing*, 59(1), 63–77. https://doi.org/10.1177/002224299505900106

Lee, A. Y., & Labroo, A. A. (2004). The effect of conceptual and perceptual fluency on brand evaluation. *Journal of Marketing Research*, 41(2), 151–165. https://doi.org/10.1509/jmkr.41.2.151.28665

Loken, B., & John, D. R. (1993). Diluting brand beliefs: When do brand extensions have a negative impact? *Journal of Marketing*, 57(3), 71–84. https://doi.org/10.1177/002224299305700305

Lutz, R. J. (1975). Changing brand attitudes through modification of cognitive structure. *Journal of Consumer Research*, 1(4), 49–59. https://doi.org/10.1086/208607

MacInnis, D. J., & Folkes, V. S. (2017). Humanizing brands: When brands seem to be like me, part of me, and in a relationship with me. *Journal of Consumer Psychology*, 27(3), 355–374. https://doi.org/10.1016/j.jcps.2016.12.003

*MacInnis, D. J., Moorman, C., & Jaworski, B. J. (1991). Enhancing and measuring consumers' motivation, opportunity, and ability to process brand information from ads. *Journal of Marketing*, 55(4), 32–53. https://doi.org/10.1177/002224299105500403

MacKenzie, S. B., & Spreng, R. A. (1992). How does motivation moderate the impact of central and peripheral processing on brand attitudes and intentions? *Journal of Consumer Research*, 18(4), 519–529. https://doi.org/10.1086/209278

Maison, D., Greenwald, A. G., & Bruin, R. H. (2004). Predictive validity of the Implicit Association Test in studies of brands, consumer attitudes, and behavior. *Journal of Consumer Psychology*, 14(4), 405–415. https://doi.org/10.1207/s15327663jcp1404_9

*Malär, L., Krohmer, H., Hoyer, W. D., & Nyffenegger, B. (2011). Emotional brand attachment and brand personality: The relative importance of the actual and the ideal self. *Journal of Marketing*, 75(4), 35–52. https://doi.org/10.1509/jmkg.75.4.35

*McAlexander, J. H., Schouten, J. W., & Koenig, H. F. (2002). Building brand community. *Journal of Marketing, 66*(1), 38–54. https://doi.org/10.1509/jmkg.66.1.38.18451

Mitchell, A. A. (1986). The effect of verbal and visual components of advertisements on brand attitudes and attitude toward the advertisement. *Journal of Consumer Research, 13*(1), 12–24. https://doi.org/10.1086/209044

*Mitchell, A. A., & Olson, J. C. (1981). Are product attribute beliefs the only mediator of advertising effects on brand attitude? *Journal of Marketing Research, 18*(3), 318–332. https://doi.org/10.1177/002224378101800306

*Muñiz, A. M., Jr., & O'Guinn, T. C. (2001). Brand community. *Journal of Consumer Research, 27*(4), 412–432. https://doi.org/10.1086/319618

*Muñiz, A. M., Jr., & Schau, H. J. (2005). Religiosity in the abandoned Apple Newton brand community. *Journal of Consumer Research, 31*(4), 737–747. https://doi.org/10.1086/426607

Murray, S. L., Holmes, J. G., & Griffin, D. W. (1996). The benefits of positive illusions: Idealization and the construction of satisfaction in close relationships. *Journal of Personality and Social Psychology, 70*(1), 79–98. https://doi.org/10.1037/0022-3514.70.1.79

*Nedungadi, P. (1990). Recall and consumer consideration sets: Influencing choice without altering brand evaluations. *Journal of Consumer Research, 17*(3), 263–276. https://doi.org/10.1086/208556

Novemsky, N., Dhar, R., Schwarz, N., & Simonson, I. (2007). Preference fluency in choice. *Journal of Marketing Research, 44*(3), 347–356. https://doi.org/10.1509/jmkr.44.3.347

Orth, U. R., & Malkewitz, K. (2008). Holistic package design and consumer brand impressions. *Journal of Marketing, 72*(3), 64–81. https://doi.org/10.1509/JMKG.72.3.064

Park, C. S., & Srinivasan, V. (1994). A survey-based method for measuring and understanding brand equity and its extendibility. *Journal of Marketing Research, 31*(2), 271–288. https://doi.org/10.1177/002224379403100210

Park, C. W., Eisingerich, A. B., & Park, J. W. (2013). Attachment–aversion (AA) model of customer–brand relationships. *Journal of Consumer Psychology, 23*(2), 229–248. https://doi.org/10.1016/j.jcps.2013.01.002

*Park, C. W., MacInnis, D. J., Priester, J., Eisingerich, A. B., & Iacobucci, D. (2010). Brand attachment and brand attitude strength: Conceptual and empirical differentiation of two critical brand equity drivers. *Journal of Marketing, 74*(6), 1–17. https://doi.org/10.1509/jmkg.74.6.1

*Park, C. W., Milberg, S., & Lawson, R. (1991). Evaluation of brand extensions: The role of product feature similarity and brand concept consistency. *Journal of Consumer Research, 18*(2), 185–193. https://doi.org/10.1086/209251

Park, J. K., & John, D. R. (2010). Got to get you into my life: Do brand personalities rub off on consumers? *Journal of Consumer Research, 37*(4), 655–669. https://doi.org/10.1086/655807

Petty, R. E., Cacioppo, J. T., & Schumann, D. (1983). Central and peripheral routes to advertising effectiveness: The moderating role of involvement. *Journal of Consumer Research, 10*(2), 135–146. https://doi.org/10.1086/208954

Petty, R. E., Ostrom, T. M., & Brock, T. C. (1981). *Cognitive responses in persuasion*. Erlbaum.

Priester, J. R., Nayakankuppam, D., Fleming, M. A., & Godek, J. (2004). The A2SC2 model: The influence of attitudes and attitude strength on consideration and choice. *Journal of Consumer Research, 30*(4), 574–587. https://doi.org/10.1086/380290

Puzakova, M., Kwak, H., & Rocereto, J. F. (2013). When humanizing brands goes wrong: The detrimental effect of brand anthropomorphization amid product wrongdoings. *Journal of Marketing, 77*(3), 81–100. https://doi.org/10.1509/jm.11.0510

*Rao, A. R., & Monroe, K. B. (1989). The effect of price, brand name, and store name on buyers' perceptions of product quality: An integrative review. *Journal of Marketing Research, 26*(3), 351–357. https://doi.org/10.1177/002224378902600309

*Rao, A. R., Qu, L., & Ruekert, R. W. (1999). Signaling unobservable product quality through a brand ally. *Journal of Marketing Research, 36*(2), 258–268. https://doi.org/10.1177/002224379903600209

Reimann, M., Castaño, R., Zaichkowsky, J., & Bechara, A. (2012). How we relate to brands: Psychological and neurophysiological insights into consumer–brand relationships. *Journal of Consumer Psychology, 22*(1), 128–142. https://doi.org/10.1016/j.jcps.2011.11.003

*Richardson, P. S., Dick, A. S., & Jain, A. K. (1994). Extrinsic and intrinsic cue effects on perceptions of store brand quality. *Journal of Marketing, 58*(4), 28–36. https://doi.org/10.1177/002224299405800403

Riley, J. A. (1984). Pottery analysis and the reconstruction of ancient exchange systems. In S. E. van der Leeuw & A. C. Pritchard (Eds.), *The many dimensions of pottery: Ceramics in archaeology and anthropology* (pp. 55–74). University of Amsterdam Press.

Rosenberg, M. J. (1956). Cognitive structure and attitudinal affect. *Journal of Abnormal and Social Psychology, 53*(3), 367–372. https://doi.org/10.1037/h0044579

Rusbult, C. E., Verette, J., Whitney, G. A., Slovik, L. F., & Lipkus, I. (1991). Accommodation processes in close relationships: Theory and preliminary empirical evidence. *Journal of Personality and Social Psychology, 60*(1), 53–78. https://doi.org/10.1037/0022-3514.60.1.53

Russell, C. A., & Schau, H. J. (2014). When narrative brands end: The impact of narrative closure and consumption sociality on loss accommodation. *Journal of Consumer Research, 40*(6), 1039–1062. https://doi.org/10.1086/673959

Rust, R. T., Ambler, T., Carpenter, G. S., Kumar, V., & Srivastava, R. K. (2004). Measuring marketing productivity: Current knowledge and future directions. *Journal of Marketing, 68*(4), 76–89. https://doi.org/10.1509/jmkg.68.4.76.42721

Rust, R. T., Lemon, K. N., & Zeithaml, V. A. (2004). Return on marketing: Using customer equity to focus marketing strategy. *Journal of Marketing, 68*(1), 109–127. https://doi.org/10.1509/jmkg.68.1.109.24030

Schachter, S. (1959). *The psychology of affiliation*. Stanford University Press.

*Schau, H. J., Muñiz, A. M., Jr., & Arnould, E. J. (2009). How brand community practices create value. *Journal of Marketing, 73*(5), 30–51. https://doi.org/10.1509/jmkg.73.5.30

Schmitt, B. (2013). The consumer psychology of customer–brand relationships: Extending the AA Relationship model. *Journal of Consumer Psychology, 23*(2), 249–252. https://doi.org/10.1016/j.jcps.2013.01.003

Schmitt, B., Brakus, J. J., & Zarantonello, L. (2015). From experiential psychology to consumer experience. *Journal of Consumer Psychology, 25*(1), 166–171. https://doi.org/10.1016/j.jcps.2014.09.001

*Schouten, J. W., & McAlexander, J. H. (1995). Subcultures of consumption: An ethnography of the new bikers. *Journal of Consumer Research, 22*(1), 43–61. https://doi.org/10.1086/209434

Sheth, J. N. (1972). Reply to comments on the nature and uses of expectancy-value models in consumer attitude research. *Journal of Marketing Research, 9*(4), 462–465. https://doi.org/10.1177/002224377200900422

*Simonin, B. L., & Ruth, J. A. (1998). Is a company known by the company it keeps? Assessing the spillover effects of brand alliances on consumer brand attitudes. *Journal of Marketing Research, 35*(1), 30–42. https://doi.org/10.1177/002224379803500105

Sprott, D., Czellar, S., & Spangenberg, E. (2009). The importance of a general measure of brand engagement on market behavior: Development and validation of a scale. *Journal of Marketing Research, 46*(1), 92–104. https://doi.org/10.1509/jmkr.46.1.92

Srivastava, R. K., Shervani, T. A., & Fahey, L. (1998). Market-based assets and shareholder value: A framework for analysis. *Journal of Marketing, 62*(1), 2–18. https://doi.org/10.1177/002224299806200102

Sternthal, B., Dholakia, R., & Leavitt, C. (1978). The persuasive effect of source credibility: Tests of cognitive response. *Journal of Consumer Research, 4*(4), 252–260. https://doi.org/10.1086/208704

Stuart, E. W., Shimp, T. A., & Engle, R. W. (1987). Classical conditioning of consumer attitudes: Four experiments in an advertising context. *Journal of Consumer Research, 14*(3), 334–349. https://doi.org/10.1086/209117

Sweldens, S., van Osselaer, S. M., & Janiszewski, C. (2010). Evaluative conditioning procedures and the resilience of conditioned brand attitudes. *Journal of Consumer Research, 37*(3), 473–489. https://doi.org/10.1086/653656

*Tax, S. S., Brown, S. W., & Chandrashekaran, M. (1998). Customer evaluations of service complaint experiences: Implications for relationship marketing. *Journal of Marketing, 62*(2), 60–76. https://doi.org/10.1177/002224299806200205

*Thompson, C. J. (1997). Interpreting consumers: A hermeneutical framework for deriving marketing insights from the texts of consumers' consumption stories. *Journal of Marketing Research, 34*(4), 438–455. https://doi.org/10.1177/002224379703400403

*Thomson, M., MacInnis, D. J., & Park, C. W. (2005). The ties that bind: Measuring the strength of consumers' emotional attachments to brands. *Journal of Consumer Psychology, 15*(1), 77–91. https://doi.org/10.1207/s15327663jcp1501_10

Till, B. D., & Busler, M. (2000). The match-up hypothesis: Physical attractiveness, expertise, and the role of fit on brand attitude, purchase intent and brand beliefs. *Journal of Advertising, 29*(3), 1–13. https://doi.org/10.1080/00913367.2000.10673613

Twede, D. (2002). Commercial amphoras: The earliest consumer packages? *Journal of Macromarketing, 22*(1), 98–108. https://doi.org/10.1177/027467022001009

*Vakratsas, D., & Ambler, T. (1999). How advertising works: What do we really know? *Journal of Marketing, 63*(1), 26–43. https://doi.org/10.1177/002224299906300103

*Voss, K. E., Spangenberg, E. R., & Grohmann, B. (2003). Measuring the hedonic and utilitarian dimensions of consumer attitude. *Journal of Marketing Research, 40*(3), 310–320. https://doi.org/10.1509/jmkr.40.3.310.19238

Wilcox, C. (1934). Brand names, quality, and price. *Annals of the American Academy of Political and Social*

Science, 173(1), 80–85. https://doi.org/10.1177/000271623417300111

Wilkie, W. L., & Pessemier, E. A. (1973). Issues in marketing's use of multi-attribute attitude models. *Journal of Marketing Research*, 10(4), 428–441. https://doi.org/10.1177/002224377301000411

*Winer, R. S. (1986). A reference price model of brand choice for frequently purchased products. *Journal of Consumer Research*, 13(2), 250–256. https://doi.org/10.1086/209064

Winters, L. C. (1991). Brand equity measures: Some recent advances. *Marketing Research*, 3(4), 70.

Wright, P. L. (1973). The cognitive processes mediating acceptance of advertising. *Journal of Marketing Research*, 10(1), 53–62. https://doi.org/10.1177/002224377301000108

Wright, P. L. (1980). Message-evoked thoughts: Persuasion research using thought verbalizations. *Journal of Consumer Research*, 7(2), 151–175. https://doi.org/10.1086/208804

CHAPTER 32

INNOVATION AND PRODUCT DEVELOPMENT

Doug Hall

> One is born with a natural inclination to learn. Learning is a source of innovation. One inherits a right to enjoy his work. Good management helps us to nurture and preserve these positive innate attributes of people.
>
> —Dr. W. Edwards Deming, *The New Economics for Industry, Government, Education*

American statistician Dr. W. Edwards Deming pioneered the use of system thinking as a method for improving business success. His work in Japan following World War II and in the Western world in the 1980s was initially focused on innovations in manufacturing. Instead of inspecting for quality, quality was built into the system of manufacturing by reducing variation in materials and methods. Deming advocated creating a culture where every employee learned and applied system thinking as opposed to having a few experts.

Deming's work was applied to manufacturing, as quality and efficiency were the greatest business needs at the time. However, Deming saw the factory as only 3% of the opportunity for realizing company improvement from system thinking. He felt that 97% of the opportunity lay in applying system thinking to strategy, innovation, and how people work together (Deming, 1994). The first of his 14 points for management focused on the need for never-ending, continuous innovation (Deming, 1986).

In his later years, Deming organized his teachings into four principles that he named the "system of profound knowledge" (Deming, 1994). Among the four principles was psychology. Deming (1994) wrote in *The New Economics*, "Psychology helps us to understand people, interaction between people and circumstances, interaction between customer and supplier, interaction between teacher and pupil, interaction between a manager and his people and any system of management" (p. 73).

Deming had found it easy to create innovation and change in manufacturing methods in Japan, as the leaders of companies were desperate to improve their quality. In the Western world, improving quality was important but not nearly as urgent as it had been in Japan. Claire Crawford-Mason, producer of the NBC White Paper documentary *If Japan Can, Why Can't We,* which featured Deming, told me in an interview in April 2014 that after over 10 years of frustration with Western companies, Deming told her that if he were to do it all over again, he would have spent more time learning about psychology.

This chapter outlines learning from a unique academic and industry collaboration known as the Innovation Engineering. It has been created with the support of the Deming Institute to apply Deming's work to strategy, innovation, and how we work together.

https://doi.org/10.1037/0000262-032
APA Handbook of Consumer Psychology, L. R. Kahle (Editor-in-Chief)
Copyright © 2022 by the American Psychological Association. All rights reserved.

Innovation Engineering is supported by a combination of academic literature, an overwhelming amount of proprietary industry data, and thousands of "Plan, Do, Study, Act" cycles of learning on over $19,000,000,000 in real-world innovations. The support of industry is a blessing and a curse. Industry is so hungry for knowledge on how to create a culture that supports system-driven innovation they are conducting experiments and sharing learnings openly. The Innovation Engineering Institute has been established to facilitate academic data access—at no cost—to what is arguably the world's largest data set on innovation people, processes, and products.

WHY IS INNOVATION NEEDED?

Innovation has become a universal solution for all organizations. Innovation promises to transform profitability, grow sales, and neutralize competitive threats. The classic application of innovation is in the creation of new or improved products or services. The most common application of innovation is in ideas for improving work systems.

To leadership, innovation offers hope for the company's future. A company's innovation pipeline is leadership's plan for generating profitable growth in a fast-changing global marketplace.

To employees, innovation creates hope for company growth leading to opportunities for advancement. Innovation also offers opportunities for bringing greater meaningfulness to their work when they are part of the process of creating, developing, and commercializing new ideas.

To shareholders, innovation creates hope for increasing the value of the company through sales and profit growth plus the creation of intellectual capital through patented discoveries.

WHAT IS INNOVATION?

The simplest definition of innovation is the creation of something new. The new thing can be new-to-the-world products and services. It can be ideas for improvements to existing products and services. The new thing can also be an idea for how to "work smarter" on a particular task you or others face.

The challenge with the simple definition is that it comes with risk. A new idea can be new in a good way or can be new in a bad way. Figure 32.1 (Hall, 2001) shows the distribution of customer perceptions of "purchase intent" and "new and different" for a broad collection of new product ideas. As ideas become more innovative and unique, customer reaction increases in variability from very high to very low.

This high variance in customer reaction and, consequently, the actual success of the new idea is one of the primary reasons for the fear common among adults toward innovation. A survey by the Innovation Engineering Institute of 12,272 executives found that 80% felt their organization was fearful of taking action on new ideas (Hall, 2019).

A survey by the management consulting firm McKinsey found that more than 70% of senior executives feel that innovation will be one of the top three drivers of growth for their company in the next 3 to 5 years. However, 65% of the senior executives they surveyed were not highly confident about the decisions they make on innovation (Barsh et al., 2008).

This finding aligns with the fundamental challenge of risk aversion. Adults are motivated more by prevention of a negative than by the promise of a positive outcome (Cox & Cox, 2001; Keller & Block, 1996; Meyerowitz & Chaiken, 1987). The result is that it is common for executives who are facing business challenges to avoid innovation until all other options, such as cost cutting, reorganization, and/or firing of managers, have been exhausted.

A more specific definition of innovation is an idea that offers meaningful uniqueness to someone. "Meaningful" implies that the idea has significant value. "Unique" implies that it cannot be realized easily through other offerings or options. Research has found that a blended weighting of purchase intent with customer perception of uniqueness was more effective in predicting actual behavior than purchase intent alone (Kahle et al., 1997). A study by the Innovation Engineering Institute found that a weighting of 60% for purchase intent and 40% for newness had the highest correlation with marketplace results (Hall, 2010).

Meaningful uniqueness is a simple metric that can be quantified by asking potential customers—

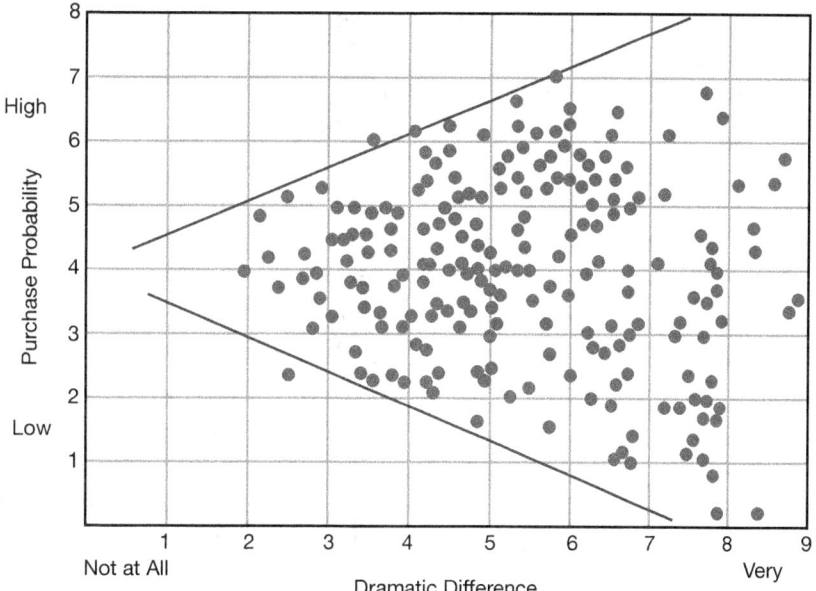

FIGURE 32.1. Relationship between purchase intent and new and different perceptions of customers toward new product ideas. From *Jump Start Your Business Brain*, p. 139, by D. B. Hall, 2001, Clerisy Press. Copyright 2001 by Eureka! Institute. Reprinted with permission.

be they external customers for a new product/service or internal customers for a new work system—to give their perceptions of meaningfulness and uniqueness toward the idea.

Other common definitions of innovation used by industry include a customer's willingness to pay more money for the innovation. Customers will only pay more than the classic market price if they perceive they are getting something that has value to them that cannot be realized any other way. Another definition of innovation is the ability to acquire a patent on the product, process, or method that makes the innovation possible. Patents are a government-supported monopoly that helps organizations realize commercial gain from their innovations by providing a barrier to copying. For an innovation to be patentable, it must be nonobvious to someone with ordinary skill in the art (U.S. Patent Office, n.d.).

HOW ARE INNOVATIONS CREATED?

The simple explanation for how ideas are created is that ideas are feats of association (Debono, 1999; Hall, 1995; Herrmann & Herrmann-Nehdi, 2015; Osborn, 1963). Two or more unrelated ideas (also known as stimuli) come together in the innovator's mind, and a new idea is inspired. In effect it is a 1 + 1 = 3 phenomena. This process can be accelerated when a group of diverse people gather to collaboratively work on creating ideas. Each person sees the stimuli in a different way, creating an exponential increase in ideas (Hall, 2010).

The process is constrained by fear of failure, as discussed later, and is high within the individual or individuals who are creating ideas. In part, this result is because the fear acts as a gate on the free-association process. Instead of allowing each idea to build on the one before, the idea stream is stopped by psychological fears.

Fun appears to be fundamental to reducing psychological fears of looking foolish in front of others. When people are laughing, they appear to have a greater openness to more innovative solutions to problems they face (Isen et al., 1987).

HOW DO ORGANIZATIONS MANAGE PRODUCT DEVELOPMENT?

Innovation can be reactive or proactive. *Reactive* innovation is when an organization is forced to pursue new ideas because of a perceived competitive or marketplace threat to sales, profitability, or survival. *Proactive* innovation is when leadership or employees are creating new ideas without the pressure of market forces.

A proactive mindset requires a willingness to confront the reality of your existing situation. This comes together with the potential for failure to create high fear within leadership. When fear is great, leaders often use avoidance as a means for reducing their fear. They use avoidance through methods such as the following.

Outsourcing Innovation

Leaders remove themselves from personal engagement in innovation. Instead of being involved in creating, developing, or deciding on innovations, they outsource the work. They bring in outside experts, create teams separate from the day-to-day business, or use crowdsourcing to handle innovation. By removing themselves from the actual project, they reduce their fear of failure. They now have someone or some process to blame if the innovation does not work out as planned.

In practice, this often causes significant delays and lack of confidence in the innovation because, without hands-on involvement during the process of innovation, the leader does not have the confidence in the ideas that those who are closer to the work have.

Innovation by Gates and Metrics

Leadership removes the perception of emotional engagement with innovations by managing through numeric standards for sales, profits, and return on investment. The most common approach to this strategy is known by the trademarked name Stage-Gate, developed and commercialized by Cooper (2001). Stage-Gate sets up a series of decision gates with criteria for approval. The company reports that over 80% of large companies in the United States use a version of Stage-Gate to manage their innovations (Edgett, 2018).

Breaking innovation decisions into a series of smaller decisions gives leadership the ability to command and control the release of time, energy, and money on the idea. In addition, by having leadership review an idea multiple times during development, a habituation develops that makes it easier for leadership to become comfortable with the risk.

Challenges to Stage-Gate include the potential for continuing to say yes to an idea because of the sunk cost from previous decisions. As ideas move toward the marketplace, they often are compromised on their efficacy and price/value. A leadership team that has become comfortable with an idea may not be willing to say "Stop!" when a compromise occurs that dramatically increases risk of failure.

Another challenge with the Stage-Gate approach is that the metrics assigned at each stage have high variance for the sales and success for an idea in the future. And, although market research methods can provide forecasts of potential for an idea in a static marketplace, innovations are not static. When a company introduces a new idea, it sets off a chain reaction among customers and competitors. If a competitor risks losing sales, it might increase advertising or promotion support to blunt the success of the new idea. In addition, estimates of costs and manufacturing efficiencies are hypothetical estimates until a factory is up and running on a continuing basis.

Fast Follower

Another use of innovation avoidance is to choose to be a follower of the innovations of competitors instead of being a pioneer. Research finds that, on average, brands that are second to market generate 71% of the sales of the pioneer. Those that are third generate 58%, and those that are fourth, 51%. Basic economics also advises that profitability will decline as the number of competitors increases (Kalyanaram et al., 1995; Robinson, 1988; Robinson & Fornell, 1985; Urban et al., 1986).

THE FEAR OF INNOVATION

The desirability of bringing new news to the marketplace is well understood. It is also well understood that many, if not most, innovation projects are not judged by their organizations as successful financial investments. The rate of failure for innovations is debated among scholars (Castellion & Markham, 2013). An explanation for the reason for debating failure rate is the boundaries put on when a project is considered to be a real project. For example, if we consider innovations on which an organization has made a meaningful investment of time, energy, and money to develop, then the rate of failure is high—in the 85% to 95% range (Castellion & Markham, 2013). However, if our boundaries are pushed later in the development process, when ideas are actually introduced to a broad market, then the rate of failure is likely 35% to 50% (Castellion & Markham, 2013). The variance in numbers within corporations is due in part to what they consider to be a meaningful investment. In spite of these failure rates, leaders have no choice but to innovate because change is inevitable.

The tension between the need to innovate and the fear of failure with new ideas is the fundamental psychological challenge when it comes to igniting innovation within organizations. There are many methods being utilized to address this fear.

Mission-Driven Innovation Gives Power Over Fear

Fear of failure, especially with new ideas, is real. Avoidance does not reduce that failure; it only removes it from daily stresses. An alternative approach is to transform innovation from a tactical asset to a mission-driven one. When an innovation is mission driven, there is a deep clarity among all involved regarding the importance of being successful with the innovation challenge at hand. This clarity of goals creates a sense of purpose among employees and leadership. It provides a sense of belonging to a purpose that is greater than your work, department, or job tasks.

The innovation mission can be written in any manner of formats. Many military organizations around the world have moved to a method commonly called "Commander's Intent" (Hall, 2019). Its goal is to provide a clear articulation of the purpose and boundaries of the mission and in particular the "why" behind the mission. When troops understand why a mission matters, there is a deeper level of intrinsic engagement. Understanding the larger context versus simply giving tasks to complete engages the minds of troops or employees. When they know "what" and "why," they are more enrolled in the challenge at hand.

To the leader, mission-driven innovation transforms the management of innovation from a debate on ideas to accomplishment of a higher order business purpose. This change reduces fears by igniting a positive moment toward the development and delivery of the new idea.

System-Driven Innovation Gives Power Over Fear

System-driven innovation approaches new ideas as a system of interconnected parts that accomplish an innovation mission. This approach is the same mindset taught by Dr. W. Edwards Deming to Japanese manufacturing leaders after World War II and to manufacturing leaders in the Western world in the 1980s (Hall, 2019). In the case of manufacturing, Deming taught leaders to think about production as a set of interrelated tasks that work together to create high-quality product at a low cost.

Innovations require that leaders also see the execution of ideas as a set of interrelated tasks across areas such as sales, marketing, manufacturing, and finance that work together to create a profitable innovation success. Meaningful innovations result in a different result for customers. Different results require that one or more of the stakeholders must change how they work. Changes to how work is done often have an adverse effect on a department's efficiency or effectiveness. When the organization has an appreciation for the system nature of innovations, then they are more supportive of the disruptions caused by the innovation and are supportive of one another, resulting in less organizational fear of failure.

Rapid Research Learning Cycles Give Power Over Fear

The ability of managers to debate when faced with the unknowns associated with a new innovation is infinite. In many cases, debates on innovations are driven by a passive-aggressive mindset that verbalizes fears, uncertainties, and doubts. Research finds that 75% of business leaders self-identify as what is called a "left brain logical" thinking style as opposed to a "right brain visionary" thinking style (Hall, 2005). Research, and in particular quantitative research, is one of the most powerful ways to reduce fear for left brain thinkers.

With research, there are two fundamental approaches.

The *judge and jury* approach uses research at the end of development to support a "go or no go" decision to proceed to the next stage of development or launch. This approach is historically popular. A primary driver of the judge and jury approach is the high cost and time required to conduct quantitative research. An outcome of having a high-consequence assessment at the end of a development stage is that teams invest time and energy optimizing their idea without meaningful feedback. This tactic can result in significant delays. Importantly, there is no evidence that this additional work actually improves the odds of success for the innovation.

The *cycles of learning* approach uses rapid research learning cycles to provide a quantitative feedback loop to those who are developing the innovation. Data on consumer perceptions of the marketing concept and/or the product performance are used to guide improvement of the idea. This type of data is particularly helpful when, during the development process, issues such as product performance, cost of goods, or consumer reaction to pricing result in a need to adapt the overall idea. When teams can get quantitative data in 1 to 2 hours at 2% to 10% of the cost of judge & jury research, they are able to make changes and validate the correct path very quickly.

A positive consequence of cycles of learning is that the team's confidence builds with each round of research. A negative consequence is that if leadership has either not adopted the cycle of learning mindset or does not stay up to date with learning, they can lose confidence in the team as a result of seemingly never-ending changes.

BARRIERS TO INCREASED PRODUCT DEVELOPMENT SPEED AND SUCCESS

The consulting firm of McKinsey & Co. found that 98% of executives viewed speed to market as important (Hunter et al., 2018). The following are areas that industry practitioners have found negatively impact product development speed and success.

Low Engagement by Leadership

The creation of something new offers unique challenges versus the execution of a known set of tasks. And, while it is possible to manage the work with established tasks, innovations that offer something new require leadership engagement to enable organizational courage in the face of high uncertainty and the need for hundreds of tradeoff decisions. When leadership is not engaged in innovations, especially disruptive innovations, then it is inevitable that decisions to invest in development, capital equipment, or marketing will be slowed as leadership does not have internal confidence in the proposition.

Extrinsic Versus Intrinsic Motivation

The literature (Deming, 1994; Hall, 2019) and industry practice have found that when employees are intrinsically motivated, they are more willing to take what they perceive as a risk with new ideas and innovations. Intrinsic motivation with innovations is driven by a sense of purpose or meaningfulness that results from achieving the outcome of the innovation. Conversely, extrinsic motivation is driven by financial rewards and recognition. Extrinsic motivation can be motivating in the short term. However, it is rarely enough to drive the continuing cycles of experimentation and change required to turn an innovation challenge into reality. Intrinsic motivation sparks an energy to keep going in the face of adversity. Extrinsic motivation sets off a balance-sheet mindset of "risk versus reward" in employee minds. With each obstacle or failure during product development, the employee weighs in their mind "Is it worth it?" to continue with the innovation. An answer of "Yes" results in continuing cycles of learning with the potential for success. An answer of "No" results in stopping the project, resulting in a lost opportunity for the organization. In practice, a third option beyond a yes or no is a compromise. In this case, the employee decides to compromise on the promise of the innovation by reducing success standards, compromising on quality, or changing the pricing model. A Fortune 50 company found that, on average, compromises during product development resulted in innovations losing half of their projected market value

(Hall, 2019). A small base study of innovation leaders across corporations in a range of industries found similar results.

No System for Innovation

Organizations have systems for accounting, distribution, purchasing, and even hiring and firing of employees. However, it is rare that they have a documented system for innovation. Rather, it is left up to employees to find their own way to create ideas, problem solve, and manage their innovation projects through the organizational maze. In the place of a system for innovation with documented best practices and training, there is often installed a system of success metrics that are required to be met for an innovation to gain the investment of time, energy, and money required to turn it from idea to reality. Without a method to accomplish the metrics, employees end up wasting time, energy, and money. It is like a coach telling a football team the score they need to achieve to win without giving them a game plan for how to win against their opponent. Without a method for how to innovate, the employee's risk is increased. Not only can they be blamed for their idea failing; they can also be blamed for the method they used to create or problem solve their idea. Conversely, when there is a clear set of documented methods for how to create, communicate, and commercialize innovations, then employee risk is reduced, as they are following the organization's system of best innovation practices.

Focus on the "Front End" of Innovation

Another barrier to product development speed is when an organization focuses most if its energy on what is known as the front end of innovation: the discovery of the idea itself. This approach is also known as the "big idea hunt." It is a batch process where a collection of ideas is discovered and screened with customers and/or internal feasibility experts all at one time. The intent is to find the best idea of the set. With the big idea defined, it is thought that it will be a simple matter to have the various departmental groups develop the idea into a profitable business opportunity. Yet, as mentioned previously, it is in development that ideas become compromised, losing as much as 50% of their value. An alternative to the front-end focus within the innovation and product development community is a focus on the development system itself. The thinking is that any idea can be made better through iterative cycles of learning. This approach is built on the Deming theory of knowledge known as "Plan, Do, Study, Act" (PDSA; Deming, 1994). It is an interactive, continuous flow process of learning cycles involving setting the success destination (Plan); running an experiment (Do); studying why it worked or did not work (Study); and then either declaring success, doing another cycle, or abandoning the mission (Act). Psychologically, the PDSA approach is more motivating to employees and leadership. With PDSA, ideas improve over time versus the front-end approach, where ideas tend to decline in value. Industry tracking studies of $19,000,000,000 in innovations show that with the PDSA approach to development, ideas grow in value during development by about 28% versus declining by about 50%, as stated earlier (Hall, 2019).

Lack of Rapid Feedback System to Guide Development Tradeoffs

At the front end of innovation, much time is spent sorting and selecting the right projects to pursue. This work is often guided by quantitative research on potential customers' perceptions of each possible new product. Having defined the innovation, work then begins on developing the actual product itself. Inevitably, during the process of sourcing, engineering, designing, and building the innovation, the development team will face feasibility or financial challenges with the project. These challenges require changes to the product design and business proposition. With most companies, these changes are made on judgment. The result can be many starts and stops as the judgments made are debated as projects move through the gates of approval with leadership and across departments. The use of rapid research systems to gather quantitative data on customer perceptions on topics such as design changes, appeal, cost/value, or performance reduces debates, thus increasing speed to market.

To be specific, in the new world, rapid research is being able to get quantitative data from statistically reliable samples in 1 to 2 hours instead of 2 to 3 months (Hall, 2019).

Project Management Rigidity

Industry experience finds that most project management systems are designed around a "conformance to requirements." Tasks with success requirements are defined in a static database system. Meetings are held to determine when and if employees have completed the tasks. This checklist approach is valuable when the tasks have low variance in what is required to complete them. This approach is effective when something is being done that has been done many times before. For example, at Procter & Gamble, the installation and start-up of the 50th Pampers diaper production line has a relatively low variance, as it has been done many times before. With innovations that are meaningfully unique, there are often high levels of variance with tasks, as the innovation is being brought to life for the first time. The rigidity of classic project management creates emotional stress on those charged with completing tasks on meaningfully unique innovations. They are required to set delivery dates on tasks that have a high uncertainty about them because they are new. This specificity can be stressful because employees have a risk of not delivering the completion of the task on time.

A new approach being developed is to design project management systems that are comfortable working through uncertainties. At least two companies are providing project management systems that include the option to incorporate PDSA cycles of learning when working on tasks with high uncertainty. With this approach, employee and organizational stress is reduced, as there is visibility that there are challenges that will require innovative thinking to be resolved. By having clarity on the existence of uncertainty, the collective team can plan resources appropriately, thereby reducing waste, frustration, and rework.

Project Profit and Loss Rigidity

Innovations by definition have uncertainty. This observation is especially true when it comes to innovation project profit and loss statements. As with project management, when innovation projects are locked down with sales and profit targets, a chain reaction of negative behaviors can be sparked that results in wasted time and energy. Teams waste time justifying variances versus budget when in truth the first budget had variance even if not disclosed.

Time and energy can be conserved if financial statements associated with innovations are presented with clarity on potential variance. When variance and reasons for variance are clear and transparent across the organization, then needless justification sessions and worrying about justification are reduced. In effect, when uncertainty in an innovation is expressed in numbers that represent the numeric uncertainty, leadership and teams have a better understanding of the true opportunity the innovation offers.

Variance documentation can be as simple as identifying each number that makes up a profit and loss with a color coding: green = low potential for variance, yellow = some potential for variance, red = high potential for variance.

Variance documentation can be taken to more sophisticated levels by documenting each number, plus a standard deviation and an articulation of the rationale for the variance (past experiences, measurements, or rationale). With each number identified with variance, then a Monte Carlo probability simulation is utilized to execute the innovation 10,000 times, creating 10,000 financial outcomes. The financial calculations are then rank ordered with results reported for median case, worst case (80% odds that the finances will be better than this number), and best case (20% odds that the finances will be above this number).

Big Bang Versus Learning Labs

The speed of today's marketplace encourages leadership to feel a need to introduce innovations quickly and in the broadest possible marketplace. There is a fear that they will miss out if they do not take advantage of a trend or an idea quickly. They are correct in the fact that the pioneer in a product or service area can achieve significantly higher reward (Kalyanaram et al., 1995; Robinson, 1988;

Robinson & Fornell, 1985; Urban et al., 1986). A challenge with the big bang strategy of rapid expansion is that the scale up from low to high volume in sourcing, production, distribution, marketing, and sales often generates executional challenges that cost time and money. Another challenge with the big bang approach is that it puts stress on employees, who have to be perfect the first time they execute as there is only one broad scale implementation. This pressure can cause rework, uncertainty, and time delays even with "go big" strategies.

The alternative approach is the learning lab or test market approach to innovation. The innovation is first experimented with in a small region or small number of customers. Learnings from this experiment are then applied to the idea as the idea is introduced into additional markets. When there is sufficient confidence in the systems for production and selling, then the innovation is scaled broadly. Although this approach may take longer to get to broad scale distribution, it is certain to reduce odds of failure, as improvements can be made along the way that increase sales and profitability.

The learning lab approach uses proprietary intellectual property to reduce the risk of being quickly copied by a competitor and thus losing the first-to-market advantage. Intellectual property protections that can create delays for competitors include patents, trade secrets, difficult production systems, and raw material sourcing challenges.

OTHER PSYCHOLOGICAL CHALLENGES WITH INNOVATION AND PRODUCT DEVELOPMENT

There are many personal and social dynamics with innovation that become a barrier to success. Here are a few that have been observed.

Creation of "We/They" Innovation Elitism

Many organizations set up small teams of innovators that work to incubate ideas separate from the mainstream organization. These teams are usually provided specialized training, tools, and work systems to accelerate their success. One Fortune 20 CEO told me in 2015 that he was investing in small teams because he did not have the time and energy to train everyone. The World Economic Forum found in their research that the need for retraining employees is very high. They forecasted, "By 2022, no less than 54% of all employees will require significant re- and upskilling" (Leopold et al., 2018, p. ix). The report went on to say,

> Proficiency in new technologies is only one part of the 2022 skills equation, however, as "human" skills such as creativity, originality and initiative, critical thinking, persuasion and negotiation will likewise retain or increase their value, as will attention to detail, resilience, flexibility and complex problem-solving. (Leopold et al., 2018, p. ix)

Being separated from the mainstream culture—and provided specialized training, tools, and objectives—the small innovation team creates their own innovation/entrepreneurial culture separate from the balance of the organization. The result can be high conflict when ideas are transitioned from the incubation team to the mainstream organization. Senior executives are beginning to realize the need for engaging everyone in innovation—as Deming did with quality. Some 94% of executives feel that people and corporate culture are the most important drivers of innovation (Barsh et al., 2008). What is needed is a reliable and efficient system for retraining existing employees across the organization as companies such as Toyota do with their Toyota Way of Manufacturing.

Avoidance of Major Death Threats

When confronted with the creation of a new idea, there is always a collection of challenges or, in the words of innovators, death threats to the success of the project. Some of these are minor issues, such as regulatory forms, sourcing standard raw materials, or finding time to schedule product testing. Some of them are major death threats, such as will the technology work, will customers pay the price we will need to charge, or can we protect the innovation with a patent? The prevailing behavior of most adults is to avoid the major death threats and work the smaller challenges because of the sense of reward they get from task completion. They convince themselves it is valuable because they are "getting small challenges out of the way" in order to be able to focus on the major death threats. In truth, the result is they spend 6 months on small challenges only to see the project die 6 months later when they start work on the major death threats and find that these issues truly do kill the potential for this idea. The result is a major waste of time and money.

Alternatively, when the biggest death threats are worked on first, less time is wasted if the project ends up having to be stopped or archived. Leadership can encourage this mindset by establishing that a "smart kill" is as important of a victory as a successful project. The prevention of wasted time and money enables focusing on ideas that have greater potential.

Fear of the Unknown

By its nature, the development of innovative ideas involves doing something that has never been done before. This goal requires a comfort with uncertainty. With the uncertainty there is a probability of success and of failure. Given the high odds of innovation failure (Edgett, 2018), it is not surprising that some 84% of the population, according to E. M. Rogers's (2003) theory of diffusion of innovation, are reluctant to be first movers on a new idea.

Fear of the unknown can be addressed by focusing on the 16% who are, in Rogers's (2003) terms, "innovators and early adopters." Within an organization, however, where the help of people is required to move an innovation from idea to reality, this standard can be a limiting function. The application of success standards for approval to move to the next phase of development is a method to give confidence to those who are scared of taking action. Additionally, the connection of innovation ideas to a bigger and broader strategic mission provides a sense of purpose to the idea that is bigger than the idea itself.

Leadership Insecurity With Innovation

Most leaders of organizations achieve their position through successfully managing the business. They organize the people, develop strategies and plans, and execute them. The work involves levels of uncertainty. However, the level of uncertainty is a fraction of what it is when leading the organization into the unknown of innovative ideas. To use one of the patent office's standards for patentability as stated earlier, to be patentable an idea must be nonobvious to someone with ordinary skill in the field (U.S. Patent Office, n.d.). The consequence of this standard is inherently more risk variance with innovations.

Leaders without experience managing this kind of risk will fall back on reducing the risk factor by compromising on the idea's breadth or impact. To reduce their fears, employees will make the idea look and feel as close to what they are used to doing as possible. The impact of this approach is a reduction in the odds of success for the innovation.

Employee Fear of the Unknown and Fear of Failure

Employees' fears are multiplied with meaningfully unique innovation as they feel less control over their destiny. For most organizations, it is perceived that if you fail you are wrong and that not failing is more valuable than succeeding. Employees can also feel that with a failure, there will need to be someone to blame, and thus if it is their idea or project, they will be blamed.

Confronting employee fear of failure and the unknown is best done by the leadership reframing failure. When failure is framed as a step in the learning process, fear is reduced. When failure is done fast and inexpensively, as in through an experiment, then fear is reduced. When fear is seen as a stepping stone toward a strategic mission of great importance, then fear is reduced.

OPPORTUNITIES FOR FUTURE RESEARCH

The transition from innovation as a specialized expertise that only few have to a reliable system enabled by all employees is a new approach with many opportunities for research. Areas that are of interest to the Innovation Engineering community for learning include the following.

Impact of Cross-Training of Engineers and Marketing Managers

The integration of technology assets (product, production, engineering) with customer needs (problems, promises, pricing) often generates conflict and inefficiencies. It has been proposed that cross-training of engineers in customer understanding and marketing managers in technology can facilitate bigger ideas happening faster, as there is more collaboration and less conflict. Another method for accomplishing this goal is for employee rotation across departments.

Methods to Enable Forensic Research as a Tool for Guiding Systemic Change

The analysis of past successes and failures should offer great opportunities for identifying opportunities for improving an organization's systems for creating, communicating, evaluating, and going to market with new ideas. In practice, this investigation has proven nearly impossible, as there is often missing data and those involved are reluctant to share the data and wisdom they have for fear of being blamed. What is needed is a new approach to confronting the psychological barriers to using the past actions to improve the future.

The Use of Patents as Creative Tools

Patents offer enabling disclosures of innovations that at the time of their invention are nonobvious to those with ordinary skill in the art. Given that patents expire after 20 years, most patents that have been filed are today in the public domain, and it would seem that examination of patents could be useful as stimulus to spark new ideas. However, in practice this tactic is extremely difficult to find support. Research on why this situation exists and theories on how to address it would be useful.

Fear of Doing the Math on Economics Early in the Process

The use of math early in the development process can have a profound impact on the direction of an innovation project. It can provide guidance on engineering and marketing tradeoffs. It can also identify when a project has low odds of commercial success and should either be radically changed or archived. Sadly, even with training in methods for estimating unknown numbers (e.g., order of magnitude estimating, Monte Carlo simulation, high/low bounding), very few innovators are willing to do the math early. Research to understand why this is and that offers possible solutions would be invaluable to industry.

CONCLUSION

Innovation offers hope for the future. It enables us to create and activate ideas for working smarter, living healthier, selling more, and even making the world around us a better place. To paraphrase Dr. W. Edwards Deming's quote at the start of this chapter, everyone is born with a natural inclination to innovate. Innovation is not a matter of luck or something that is available only to a few geniuses. Reliable systems for innovation can and should be discovered and validated scientifically so as to enable everyone to think smarter, faster, and more innovatively.

REFERENCES

Barsh, J., Capozzi, M. M., & Davidson, J. (2008, January 1). *Leadership and innovation.* McKinsey & Company. https://www.mckinsey.com/business-functions/strategy-and-corporate-finance/our-insights/leadership-and-innovation

Castellion, G., & Markham, S. K. (2013, September). Perspective: New product failures rates: Influence of argumentum ad populum and self-interest. *Journal of Product Innovation Management, 30*(5), 976–979. https://doi.org/10.1111/j.1540-5885.2012.01009.x

Cooper, R. G. (2001). *Winning at new products, accelerating the process from idea to launch.* Perseus Publishing.

Cox, D., & Cox, A. D. (2001, July). Communicating the consequences of early detection: The role of evidence and framing. *Journal of Marketing, 65*(3), 91–103. https://doi.org/10.1509/jmkg.65.3.91.18336

Debono, E. D. (1999). *Six thinking hats* (Rev. ed.). Back Bay Books.

Deming, W. E. (1986). *Out of the crisis* (2nd ed.). MIT Press.

Deming, W. E. (1994). *The new economics for industry, government, education* (2nd ed.). MIT Press.

Edgett, S. J. (June, 2018). *The Stage-Gate® model: An overview.* Stage-Gate International. https://www.

stage-gate.com/wp-content/uploads/2018/06/wp10english.pdf

Hall, D. (1995). *Jump start your brain*. Warner Books.

Hall, D. (2001). *Jump start your business brain*. Clerisy Press.

Hall, D. (2005). *Jump start your marketing brain* (4th ed.). Clerisy Press.

Hall, D. (2010, February). *The new art and science of leading innovation*. League of Innovation in Community Colleges Innovations Conference, New York City, NY, United States.

Hall, D. (2019). *Driving Eureka!* Clerisy Press.

Herrmann, N., & Herrmann-Nehdi, A. (2015). *The whole brain business book* (2nd ed.). McGraw-Hill Education.

Hunter, E., Marchessou, S., & Schmidt, J. (2018, March 14). *The need for speed: Capturing today's fashion consumer*. McKinsey & Company. https://www.mckinsey.com/industries/retail/our-insights/the-need-for-speed-capturing-todays-fashion-consumer

Isen, A. M., Daubman, K. A., & Nowicki, G. P. (1987). Positive affect facilitates creative problem solving. *Journal of Personality and Social Psychology*, 52(6), 1122–1131. https://doi.org/10.1037/0022-3514.52.6.1122

Kahle, L. R., Hall, D. B., & Kosinski, M. J. (1997). The real-time response survey in new product research: It's about time. *Journal of Consumer Marketing*, 14(3), 234–248. https://doi.org/10.1108/07363769710166819

Kalyanaram, G., Robinson, W. T. & Urban, G. L. (1995). Order of market entry: Established empirical generalizations, emerging empirical generalizations, and future research. *Marketing Science*, 14(3 Suppl.), G212–G221. https://doi.org/10.1287/mksc.14.3.G212

Keller, P. A., & Block, L. G. (1996, March). Increasing the persuasiveness of fear appeals: The effect of arousal and elaboration. *Journal of Consumer Research*, 22(4), 448–459. https://doi.org/10.1086/209461

Leopold, T. A., Ratcheva, V., & Zahidi, S. (2018). *The future of jobs report*. World Economic Forum. https://www3.weforum.org/docs/WEF_Future_of_Jobs_2018.pdf

Meyerowitz, B. E., & Chaiken, S. (1987). The effect of message framing on breast self-examination attitudes, intentions, and behavior. *Journal of Personality and Social Psychology*, 52(3), 500–510. https://doi.org/10.1037/0022-3514.52.3.500

Osborn, A. F. (1963). *Applied imagination, principles and procedures of creative problem-solving* (3rd ed.). Charles Scribner's Sons.

Robinson, W. T. (1988, February). Sources of market pioneer advantages: The case of industrial goods industries. *Journal of Marketing Research*, 25(1), 87–94. https://doi.org/10.1177/002224378802500109

Robinson, W. T., & Fornell, C. (1985, August). Sources of market pioneer advantages in consumer goods industries. *Journal of Marketing Research*, 22(3), 305–317. https://doi.org/10.1177/002224378502200306

Rogers, E. M. (2003). *Diffusion of innovations* (5th ed.). Free Press.

Urban, G. L., Carter, T., Gaskin, S., & Mucha, Z. (1986, June). Market share rewards to pioneering brands: An empirical analysis and strategic implications. *Management Science*, 32(6), 645–659. https://doi.org/10.1287/mnsc.32.6.645

U.S. Patent Office 35 U.S.C. 103 (n.d.). Conditions for patentability; non-obvious subject matter. https://www.uspto.gov/web/offices/pac/mpep/s2141.html

CHAPTER 33

HUMAN FACTORS RESEARCH AND USER-CENTERED DESIGN

Robert W. Proctor, Leon Zeng, and Kim-Phuong L. Vu

The field of human factors and ergonomics (HFE) encompasses disciplines including engineering psychology, human cognition and performance, and user-centered design, among others. HFE has its roots in military psychology, as a consequence of the new technologies being introduced in aircraft, submarines, and other tools and equipment used by the military in World War II (Roscoe, 1997). The human interactions with machines highlighted the needs for psychologists to be involved in the design of equipment and the training of users to operate the equipment. The need for research led to the founding of research laboratories and professional societies, with Division 21 of the American Psychological Association (APA; then Society of Engineering Psychologists, now Applied Experimental and Engineering Psychology) and the Human Factors Society (now Human Factors and Ergonomics Society [HFES]) both established in 1957 (Alluisi, 1994). In the succeeding decades, research in HFE has grown to encompass essentially all interactions of humans with simple and complex systems (Proctor & Van Zandt, 2018).

APPLYING THE HUMAN FACTORS FRAMEWORK TO CONSUMER PSYCHOLOGY

Several fundamental doctrines underlie HFE. One is that an interdisciplinary approach to applied problems is needed. The two main disciplines that contribute to HFE are psychology and industrial engineering. Given that HFE is interdisciplinary, many fields are involved as well, including computer science, heath care, visual and industrial design, data analytics, and robotics. The HFES has 24 technical groups that specialize in distinct topic areas. Many are relevant to consumer psychology, but we mention only two. The first is the Product Design Technical Group, whose members are concerned with developing consumer products that are not only desirable but also safe and usable. The second is the Usability and System Evaluation Technical Group, whose members use a multimethod approach to evaluate products for their usability and effectiveness. As evident in the title of this technical group, the systems engineering concept is essential in HFE.

The basic idea behind systems engineering is that the human and nonhuman components in the operation of a system or use of a product are treated as a human–machine system (Proctor & Van Zandt, 2018). This means that the human users must be taken into account within the context of the overall system design. The focus is on the characteristics and performance of the overall system with respect to the system goals. Consideration of human factors late in the design process is not typically sufficient for meeting the needs and capabilities of the users; the user aspects need to be considered throughout

https://doi.org/10.1037/0000262-033
APA Handbook of Consumer Psychology, L. R. Kahle (Editor-in-Chief)
Copyright © 2022 by the American Psychological Association. All rights reserved.

the design process, from the beginning. This consideration is especially important for consumer psychology because the emphasis is placed on developing products for consumer uptake. If the targeted user group is not considered early in the design process, it is likely that the resulting product will not address their needs. As a result, consumers may not purchase the product initially or may discontinue its use and switch to a competing product.

Another essential component of HFE is application of the scientific approach (Proctor & Van Zandt, 2018). Emphasis is placed on data collected under conditions that are controlled as much as possible so that causal relations can be isolated. However, because HFE is an applied science, a range of methods including naturalistic observation, surveys, and interviews must necessarily be used in addition to more controlled studies. Regardless of the method used, a distinguishing feature of HFE is to approach all problems with scientific thinking, making design decisions on sound empirical data and evaluations.

USER-CENTERED DESIGN

User-centered design is an approach to product design that takes into consideration the users at every step in the design process (Lowdermilk, 2013). In the conceptualization of the product, targeted user groups are defined. Personas, profiles of specific users, can be generated for each user group through focus groups and interviews with representative users. These personas are then used during the design process to guide the designers' conceptualization of the users' interactions with the product. In addition, the designers can take a participatory approach where they bring in users as members of the design team. These end users can provide insight as to how the product will be used, and they remind designers that the users need to be taken into account at every step of the design process.

Alternative design concepts are considered and evaluated based on compatibility with the user goals and objectives, as well as correspondence with guidelines and principles based in scientific evidence (Vu et al., 2012). Once a wire-frame or working prototype is available, heuristic analyses (the extent of conformance with design guidelines) and cognitive walkthroughs (evaluations based on actions that users are likely to perform when interacting with the product) are conducted by usability specialists to ensure that the product does not violate known design principles and standards. Formal usability testing can be conducted to systematically evaluate user performance and preferences under more controlled conditions in which users interact with the product to perform specific tasks.

It is essential to take into consideration individual differences within the entire target population of users and potential consumers (Szalma, 2009). Because of the diversity of the user groups, oftentimes there has to be some flexibility in the design that allows for a range of users to be able to interact with the product effectively. These user variations can be physical differences in their weight, size, and height, as accommodated by the seating settings that are available in automobiles and ergonomic chairs. The interface can also be customized to accommodate cognitive differences in knowledge, skills, and abilities, as in designing a product for users with different levels of expertise. Although a solution for individual differences is to allow for self-customization (Townsend et al., 2015), it should be noted that what users select for preferred attributes of a product may not be most beneficial in terms of performance (Vu et al., 2019). One reason for this disparity is that users tend to select attributes based on preferences that are not related to performance. For example, when customizing the foreground and background colors of a display, users may select their favorite colors rather than colors that maximize contrast and benefit accuracy and comfort of visual perception.

HUMAN INFORMATION PROCESSING

Contemporary cognitive psychology relies on the human information-processing approach, according to which task performance can be analyzed by articulating processes within a cognitive architecture (Proctor & Vu, 2016). Many aspects of human information processing need to be taken into account in product design. Among these aspects are perception, attention, and memory, as well as decision making and action selection.

Perception, Attention, and Memory

The term *perception* is used to refer to an early stage of human information processing that is affected primarily by stimulus attributes, which, for consumer psychology, would be those provided by the product and the environment in which it is placed. The term is also often used to refer more generally to the conscious experience of a person, which may include much beyond what the sensory systems provide. An example is the concept of risk perception, which involves assessment of the personal or societal risks associated with performing an action.

One relevant area of research for consumer psychology is that of visual search, which has been studied for many years in basic and applied settings. Visual search is particularly important for locating a product among others (e.g., finding a vehicle in a parking lot or seeing a particular product among competitors on a supermarket shelf). A salient object that can be distinguished by a single feature will "pop out" of a display relatively automatically (Treisman, 1982). Even when pop out does not occur, visual search can be guided to subsets of possible objects. This ability for search to be more efficient is due to attentional mechanisms that are influenced by several factors (Wolfe & Horowitz, 2017). One of these, stimulus-driven guidance, is where a salient visual property, such as a distinctive color, shared by several possible targets allows search to be restricted to the possible targets rather than having to consider all elements in the search field.

Another factor, user-given guidance, is "top-down" in the sense that the person utilizes knowledge about known features to restrict the search set. For example, in searching for an application icon that the user knows to be a global shape, the user can quickly search through only those icons that have a similar global shape (Rauschenberger et al., 2009). In natural scenes, physical relations and semantic relations based on knowledge of the scene direct attention to regions in which there is likely to be a target (Biederman et al., 1982). For example, if looking for ice cream in a supermarket, consumers are guided to the frozen food section. Search is also modulated by the perceived value of items, for example, by differential rewards for items of one color than for those of another color (Anderson et al., 2011).

Memory is what information can be recalled about a perceptual event once the original stimulus is removed. Memory is involved in essentially all activities and is an important cognitive process because people can base decisions and actions on what readily comes to mind (i.e., recalled in working memory). There are two types of memory systems. The first is one based on experience, called *implicit memory*. Implicit memory can be procedural memories developed in acquisition of a skill (e.g., how to ride a bike) or primed memories (i.e., exposure to an item can bring highly associated items to mind; Schacter et al., 1993). The associated information that is activated is often outside of awareness; individuals are typically unable to verbalize this information, but it can influence decisions and actions. *Explicit memory* is within awareness, and these items can be verbalized by individuals (i.e., specific experience using a product or the major brands of a type of product; Surprenant & Neath, 2013). Retrieval of explicit memories can be effortful, incomplete, and inaccurate, especially as time passes. In performing everyday tasks, human behavior is influenced by both memory systems. Later in the chapter, the section on behavioral finance will refer to activation of implicit memories as part of "System 1" processing and recall of explicit memories as "System 2" processing.

One area of memory that is relevant to consumer psychology is *sponsorship memory*, which is the memory of the relationship between a sponsor and an event (Cornwell & Humphreys, 2013). Sponsors typically contribute a lot of money to an event, with the goal of being positively associated with that event. This positive association should increase consumers' uptake of the sponsor's products. Early work on sponsorship memory showed that limited exposure to brand fragments (e.g., sponsor's logo or headlines) can trigger brand associations. Specifically, Pham and Vanhuele (1997) found that the brand association could be activated by only two exposures of the brand's name if the exposures were focal (e.g., program endorsements), and only four exposures were needed if they were nonfocal (e.g., on a billboard in view). However, later work showed that memory does not necessarily influence the consumer's attitude about the brand or their intentions to purchase, especially in the case of unhealthy products (e.g., tobacco and fast food ads; McDaniel & Heald, 2000).

More important from a brand marketing perspective is the fact that consumers can and will confuse competitors for the sponsor (Cornwell & Humphreys, 2013). The confusion is likely due to consumers not being able to explicitly recall the sponsor's name, but the implicit associations with product category prime the competitor brand. The good news is that this confusion does not seem to result in long-term damage to the sponsor (Cornwell & Humphreys, 2013). Thus, the design of marketing material to highlight sponsorship (i.e., use of explicit messaging) can establish relational links between the sponsor and the event, but this link may not always result in more favorable attitudes or intentions from consumers.

Decision Making and Action

How humans make judgments and decisions has received considerable interest in recent decades because these processes are involved not only in purchasing decisions but also in a variety of other contexts. Models of optimal decision making have been developed, but people have been shown to deviate from optimal decision-making strategies (Tversky, 1975), in part because of the limited capacity to process information. Often, explicitly or implicitly, people will rely on heuristics (i.e., mental shortcuts) that yield satisfactory outcomes, though not necessarily optimal ones (Tversky & Kahneman, 1974). A good example is purchasing a smartphone, for which the market is saturated with options. An ideal decision maker will take into account all of their wants and needs with respect to the features and capabilities of each phone. This obviously can be an effortful and time-consuming process in which most consumers simply will not engage. Consumers may use an elimination by aspects heuristic (Tversky, 1972), in which initial reductions of alternatives are made on the basis of significant features (e.g., brand, operating system, mobile carrier). Moreover, consumers may simplify their decision making even more by purchasing the latest model of the product they are currently using, under the assumption that it will satisfy their needs. We discuss heuristics further in the section on behavioral finance to illustrate factors that influence consumers' decision making.

Another factor that influences consumer decision making of which marketers take advantage is the framing of costs versus benefits. Framing effects take advantage of the fact that people are averse to loss, and thus, perceived loss is given more emphasis in decision making than perceived gains. For example, Kahneman et al. (1990) had participants play the role of a buyer or seller of a mug. When asked how much the buyer was willing to pay for the mug and how much the seller was willing to take to give up the mug, the sellers indicated a median price to sell to be 2 to 3 times higher than the willing price to buy. The reason for the seller valuing the mug at a higher price can be attributed to the perceived loss of giving up the product being more than the perceived gain by the buyer from purchasing the product. Use of loss aversion (i.e., "surcharge" for one type of payment versus "savings" for another type) in the framing of messages can then influence consumers' decisions about the payment type.

Framing can also influence consumer decision making by activating associations related to qualities of a product (Burton & Babin, 1989). If the message is framed in terms of benefits, positive attributes of the product are given more consideration. In contrast, if the message is framed in terms of costs, negative attributes of the product are given more consideration. For example, Levin et al. (1985) had participants perform a consumer judgment task in which they had to indicate their satisfaction with purchasing meat at different prices based on the quality of the meat. The quality of the meat was framed positively (% lean meat) or negatively (% fat). For conditions in which the meat quality was identical (e.g., positive frame = 75% lean meat; negative frame = 25% fat), the mean consumer satisfaction was rated higher for the positive frame than negative frame.

In addition to directing people's attention to specific attributes of a product or task, framing can also influence the implicit goals that motivate consumers. Cui and Wiggins (2017) had cookie trays placed in different levels of a college building. Each tray was accompanied by a cardboard box asking consumers to "pay what you want," "pay what you can," or "pay what you think it's worth." They found that college students were willing to pay almost twice as much with the "worth" framing than the "want" framing. In a second study, Cui and Wiggins presented the different messages during an intermission at a jazz club when contributions were being collected. They found that the "worth" framing resulted in about 40% more money contributed by the attendees compared to the "want" framing. The "can" framing yielded an intermediate amount for the cookies and close to the "worth" framing amount for the jazz club. Thus, the research on framing effects shows that consumer decisions can be influenced by the salience of stimuli provided in its messaging.

Another factor that takes advantage of environmental cues to influence people's actions is population stereotypes. For example, when approaching a door, people will tend to rotate a knob, push a handlebar, and pull a handle (Vu & Sun, 2019). These natural response tendencies are a result of spatial relationships made salient by the product. *Population stereotypes* are learned responses based on everyday interactions navigating a spatial environment or through cultural teachings (Proctor & Vu, 2010). For products that require compatible visual-motor movements (e.g., direction of rotatable knobs is made in the direction of compatible wrist rotations), similar responses are provided by people regardless of their demographic or cultural background. This consistency in expected relationships occurs because the physical environment imposes the same constraints for all individuals. For products that are not constrained by the physical environment, expected responses may vary based on cultural norms (e.g., whether the natural response tendency to flip a switch up or down to turn on a light differs depending upon the country in which you live).

For products that result in interactions that are not constrained by the physical environment, designers can use multiple stereotypes to nudge an individual into generating the intended response.

For example, there are many established population stereotypes regarding direction-of-motion responses to displays controlled by a knob (Chan & Hoffman, 2015). These stereotypes include, among others, (a) clockwise to up, (b) clockwise to increase, and (c) Warrick's principle (the pointer will move in the same direction as the side of the knob closest to the display). When the display and control is arranged in a manner that results in consistent predictions by all of the stereotypes, individuals tend to make the same, expected response regardless of their demographic and country of origin (Vu & Sun, 2019). In contrast, if the display-control arrangement only complies with predictions made by a subset of stereotypes, then the responses are dependent on the unique experiences of the users.

BEHAVIORAL FINANCE AND ITS APPLICATIONS TO INFLUENCE DECISION MAKING AND BEHAVIOR

Behavioral finance (also known as behavioral economics) is a recent field that applies psychological theories and knowledge to financial decisions (Ackert & Deaves, 2010). In this section, we use it as an example case to illustrate how research in cognitive psychology and human factors can play a significant role in helping organizations to predict and influence consumer decisions. Companies are often surprised by the fact that consumers are not optimizers when it comes to decision making but are influenced by heuristics and emotional factors. However, behavioral finance techniques can allow them to acquire new clients more effectively, better engage existing clients, and ultimately create more value for their customers, the business, and society as a whole (Van Praet, 2012).

As alien as it may sound to psychologists, behavioral finance techniques actually employ a lot of research findings known to cognitive psychologists. Behavioral finance essentially is about practical applications of psychology (especially cognitive psychology and consumer psychology) to understand and thus more effectively influence human decision making and behavior with regard to economic and financial activities. Broadly speaking, consumers' purchasing decisions and subsequent consumption behaviors can be viewed as a type of economic/financial activity. Behavioral finance attempts to understand those underlying reasoning patterns of consumers, including the influence of emotional processes on decision making (Ricciardi & Simon, 2000).

WHY CONSUMERS FREQUENTLY MAKE DECISIONS THAT SEEM IRRATIONAL

Classic economics, likely without consulting the field of psychology, made a set of fundamental assumptions that served as the bedrock for the construction of a series of economics theories and models. When applied descriptively to human decision making, these assumptions essentially viewed humans as optimizers who are emotionless and analytical and can efficiently compute the optimal path to maximize personal gains. This type of rational cognition is described as explicit, or System 2 thinking, by theorists (Kahneman, 2011). This is contrasted with System 1 thinking, which is guided by more implicit associations (see Figure 33.1). System 2 thinking is based on classic theories of decision making that depict human decision makers as utility maximizers who can (a) list the possible decision paths and subsequent outcomes, (b) estimate accurate probabilities for all of the paths, and (c) efficiently calculate which decision path will yield the maximal utility (Lehto & Nah, 2006; Tversky, 1975). When applied descriptively, these assumptions and associated theories essentially portray humans as rational decision makers who follow normative rules (Kahneman, 2011; Thaler & Sunstein, 2009).

These assumptions are unrealistic when applied to people making decisions in everyday life. Though reluctantly, economists in general have come to acknowledge that many classic economic theories and models do not accurately capture human decision making and conflict with actual human behavior. Theories established in the field of behavioral finance, which apply System 1 thinking, not only can better explain real-world behavior but also have substantiated those fundamental understandings in cognitive psychology about limitations in human cognition and the resulting bounded rationality (Proctor & Van Zandt, 2018). In other words, consumers are humans with limited attention, cognitive, and reasoning abilities. These limitations make consumers rely on other factors such as heuristics, biases, and affective reactions in everyday decision making, including low-stakes everyday consumptions to high-stakes investment and financial decisions. People often are satisfied with workable yet less than optimal solutions yielded from processes that require low effort. As Herbert Simon (1956) put it, humans are "satisficers" and not "optimizers." Because many of these cognitive processes are implicit and not verbalizable, they are often a consequence of the faster, less effortful, and more

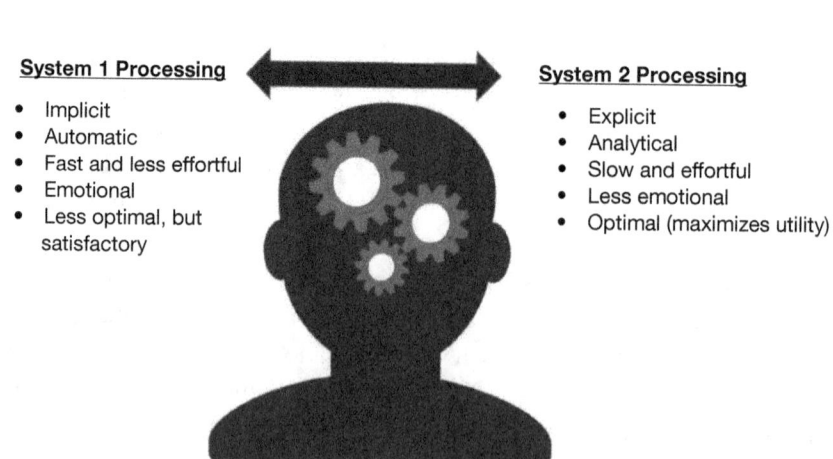

FIGURE 33.1. Comparison between System 1 and System 2 processing for decision making.

emotional System 1 thinking (Kahneman, 2011; Thaler & Sunstein, 2009).

As noted earlier, behavioral finance takes advantage of System 1 processes to predict and influence consumer decision making. Before we describe a practical approach of using behavioral finance, we list a set of heuristics and cognitive biases that often impact consumer decisions (see Exhibit 33.1). Though not comprehensive, this list should be a good starting point for psychologists who want to consult the behavioral finance literature to get more in-depth information of how each listed heuristic/bias influences consumers' decisions.

A PRACTICAL BEHAVIORAL FINANCE APPROACH TO DRIVE IMPACT

After discussing the "why" (i.e., why behavioral finance) and the "what" (i.e., what heuristics/biases could be impactful), we address the critical "how" part. Many practitioners are baffled by the tricky nature of behavioral finance and have difficulty applying behavioral finance theories and techniques to create meaningful, long-lasting impact. Built upon business consulting and management experience of the second author, we provide a viable business process/framework that can be used to drive effective behavioral changes and deliver values to both the consumer and the organization (see Figure 33.2).

Many business challenges faced by organizations are behavioral in nature. For example, utility companies would like to promote residents' economical energy consumption behaviors, firms in the consumer packaged-goods sector desire to help people form heathy eating habits, banks want to nudge customers to save more, and asset management firms encourage investors to invest smartly and build wealth in a sustainable way. All of these business goals are (a) behavioral in nature; (b) well-intended to create win-wins for the consumer, the organization, and the larger society; and (c) nontrivial requests that could be challenging to address.

Faced with such business opportunities/behavioral challenges, many organizations have mainly resorted to traditional System-2-driven market research and marketing approaches to (a) understand consumer decision making and (b) influence customer behaviors, respectively. Though most intuitive for business practitioners to apply, System-2-driven market research and marketing approaches have fundamental drawbacks. The typical market research tools (e.g., focus groups, in-depth individual customer interviews, and surveys) require explicit recall of cognitive processes built upon those unwarranted classic economics assumptions that consumers can reliably recall the purchase decision made and explain why such a decision was made. Consumers are typically asked questions such as "Why did you purchase X instead of Y?" "Why did you do this and didn't do that?" and "What prompted you to make this decision?" Based on what is known in cognitive and consumer psychology, practitioners should realize that it is quite challenging to get valid and reliable business insights from System-2-driven market research. Consumers often have difficulty accurately recalling

EXHIBIT 33.1

List of Impactful Heuristics and Cognitive Biases in Consumer Decision Making

Anchoring bias	Aspirational thinking
Representative bias	Loss aversion
Availability bias	Confirmation bias
Default effect	Endowment effect
Consistency/status quo bias	Power of free
Primacy and recency biases	Positive versus negative reciprocity
Positive versus negative social proof	Compromise effect and decoy effect
Least effort/path of least resistance	Instant gratification/hyperbolic discounting

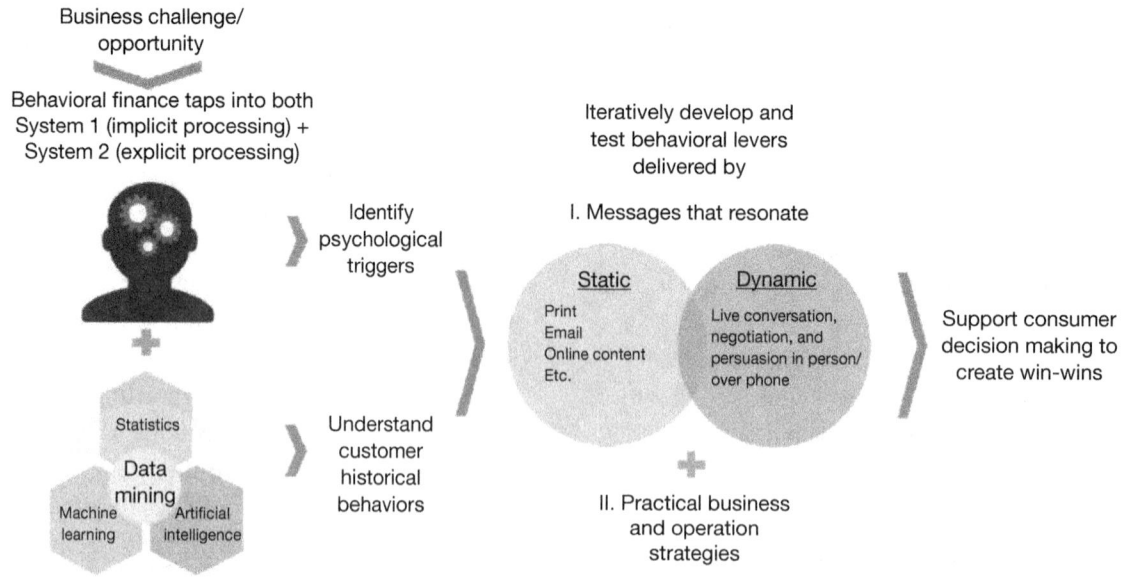

FIGURE 33.2. A practical behavioral finance approach to drive impact.

in what specific context a purchase decision was made, not to mention what contextual cues, environmental factors, and heuristics may have affected the decision. Many consumers try to rationalize why a purchase decision was made, even though such a decision was largely made using System 1 processing, which is implicit. Because participants are engaging in a paid survey or focus group, they may feel obligated to provide the market researcher with a plausible reason, even if it is not the one that was actually used. Therefore, market researchers need to realize that consumers make a lot of decisions every day (possibly including trivial purchase decisions and nontrivial financial decisions), and due to limited mental capacity they most likely do not pay much attention to the stimuli from various organizations in a recallable manner. To be effective business practitioners, one should accept the fact that consumers often do not take into account what businesses and organizations present to them about the product at a given time, and thus they probably cannot recall why they made certain decisions.

Ironically, some companies even ask consumers about their unrealized unmet needs and what new features would make the company's products/services more competitive in the market. If consumers could accurately articulate their unmet needs and what new features the company should provide to gain an edge in the market, then all cell phone producers would have developed identical models with the same features. As such, Apple's products would not be regarded as more innovative and revolutionary than others. As Steve Jobs's famous quote goes, "A lot of times, people don't know what they want until you show it to them" (Valentino-DeVries, 2011). Though this quote is a bit of an exaggeration, it is a caution to practitioners who believe that directly translating consumer voices to actual products will necessarily help the organization acquire sustainable competitive advantages.

Explicit marketing approaches, on the other hand, also have considerable limitations. Many firms primarily create explicit messages (e.g., "apply now," "learn more," and "best offer") without realizing that (a) explicit messaging would naturally trigger System 2 critical thinking and would likely make consumers more cautious of the marketing claims made and that (b) the effectiveness of explicit messaging fades away quickly (i.e., the so-called fatigue effect) and thus it typically entails fine segmentation and rapid-cycle evolution to keep explicit messaging effective across market segments.

Recognizing the fundamental drawbacks of marketing research and marketing approaches driven by System 2, the behavioral finance approach also provides values from System 1 to help practitioners drive meaningful long-term impact. The approach not only leverages traditional market research tools to gain anecdotal firsthand consumer feedback, but most critically, it also conducts in-depth psychological analyses to identify underlying triggers that drive certain consumer behaviors of interest. In-depth psychological analyses will often yield two sets of triggers: (a) psychological drivers that act in favor of the consumer and the organization to promote certain behaviors of interest and (b) psychological obstacles that act against the consumer and the business to suppress the desired behavioral motivation.

For example, in the aforementioned case where banks could use heuristics like those listed in Exhibit 33.1 to encourage customers to save more, one psychological driver could be social proof, where individuals see their friends, relatives, or neighbors who have saved more and would like to catch up. On the other hand, a typical psychological barrier could be procrastination/decision paralysis, caused by an overwhelming number of savings accounts available from various banks as well as the complexity of financial terms and jargon. Another psychological obstacle could be instant gratification/hyperbolic discounting, when individuals feel that even though saving is important, it is more desirable to just spend the money now to treat themselves and save later.

In addition to conducting psychological analyses to hypothesize potential behavioral triggers that drive certain consumer behaviors of interest, it can be instrumental for the organization to develop critical business insights from mining its own data. Nowadays, it is common for organizations to have large databases that record how prospective clients reacted to their marketing stimuli and how existing clients interacted with their products/services. Consumer historical behavioral data are often more accurate than consumers' reports. As compared to System 2 market research as discussed earlier, business insights derived from mining consumer historical behavioral data through advanced analytics and machine learning techniques may help organizations better understand consumer historical behaviors and even identify key consumer demographic/behavior attributes that can predict behaviors of interest.

Integrating insights from both psychological analyses and data mining, business practitioners will have a much better chance to develop meaningful behavioral hypotheses and identify the most promising behavioral levers to influence consumer decision making and subsequent behaviors. In business applications, such levers are typically delivered by a combination of explicit and implicit messaging through static and/or dynamic channels (see Figure 33.2). Static messaging channels include those one-way noninteractive channels such as print, email, direct mail, and online banner advertisements. Dynamic messaging channels, on the other hand, are interactive in nature and encompass live conversation, negotiation, and persuasion with consumers in person/over the phone. To be most effective, such messaging should be supported by underlying business and operation strategies.

It should be noted that implicit messaging, as compared to explicit messaging, is less subject to the fatigue effect and more effective because humans are essentially wired in the same way and people with different cultural and ethnic backgrounds are subject to the same set of heuristics and biases when making decisions (Kahneman, 2011; Thaler & Sunstein, 2009; Van Praet, 2012). Additionally, implicit messaging can support a one-size-fits-all marketing approach if the deployed cues in a parsimoniously selected set can effectively point consumers toward a single choice that would benefit the organization. For example, if implicit nudge A (e.g., social proof) is not effective for a certain segment of individuals, but nudge B (e.g., loss aversion) is effective for that segment, then the two nudges delivered in the same marketing platform would influence both groups of individuals. Thus, practitioners do not have to worry about which nudge technique is more effective to which specific segment/individual. Furthermore, the deployment of multiple implicit nudging techniques in a marketing platform should not just render additive effects but often have a synergistic effect (i.e., $1 + 1 > 2$), where different techniques interact to further enhance the overall nudging power. Because implicit messaging is often more subtle, it can be more effective than explicit messaging.

Finally, to have a meaningful, long-lasting impact, business practitioners should refine their hypotheses iteratively and test evolving behavioral techniques to maximize the values created for consumers, the organization, and ideally the larger society. A feedback loop formed from iterative testing can help the organization pursue continuous improvement of their products, become more effective over time, and drive sustainable, long-term behavioral changes.

BEHAVIORAL FINANCE APPLICATIONS IN INDUSTRY: EXAMPLE CASE STUDIES

Even after a thorough discussion of the behavioral finance approach in the preceding subsection, how to practically apply this framework may still seem unclear to readers. We hereby present a number of applications by leading organizations across various industry sectors to demonstrate how those organizations leveraged behavioral finance to implicitly support better consumer decision making, enhance customer experience, and create win-wins for all stakeholders.

The first application is about how to enable aspirational thinking to let consumers feel the benefits/values of the product/service provided. According to consumer psychology, people purchase products/services not based on features or even advantages of those features but ultimately based on benefits brought by those features and advantages. Essentially, consumers need to justify the purchase decision based on the belief that the product/service acquired will better their life (de Rose, 1991; Mowen & Minor, 2000; Terho et al., 2012). This notion is commonly known as a marketing best practice termed "sell on value" or "value selling." Rather than explicitly making a value proposition claim of the product/service, an often more effective approach to getting the value proposition across is to enable aspirational thinking and let consumers feel the benefits. An ingenious application is Apple's "Silhouettes" campaign to market its iPod MP3 player. In October 2003, Apple launched a nation-wide mass media campaign across TV and print channels, featuring dark gray or black silhouettes of a diversified group of consumers in sharp contrast to white iPods and vivid, colorful backgrounds. Another characteristic, different from the traditional explicit, System 2 marketing messaging approach, is the stark conciseness of this implicit messaging design—without description of even one single feature or advantage of iPod in the advertisement. Those dark diversified silhouetted figures enable prospective buyers of different ages, shapes, and forms to see themselves listening and dancing to their favorite music. Perhaps their current life is sort of boring or bland, as primed by those dark consumer figures, yet by using iPod their life would become so much more colorful and enjoyable. All of these subtle nudges are rendered through this implicit messaging campaign, which tripled analysts' estimated sales of iPod in the first quarter of 2005 and helped Apple take over nearly 90% of the category market share (Van Praet, 2012).

The approach of enabling aspirational thinking is also widely deployed in the sports and nutrition industry, where contrasting images of the same consumer were shown to demonstrate the stark pre- versus postdifference of taking the nutrition package or using the workout equipment advertised. Similar ads are also seen in the cosmetic industry and even recently in the financial industry to demonstrate how relevant products/services (e.g., makeup, installment loans, insurance policies) can better someone's life.

In a similar vein of value selling applications, Michelin tires also tried to convey the value proposition of its high-quality products in an implicit and emotional way. Rather than making an explicit claim about its high-quality tires by listing supporting features (e.g., are very reliable, endure harsh conditions, last for a long time), Michelin launched an implicit ad campaign featuring a baby sitting by its tire with the headline "Michelin. Because so much is riding on your tires." The motivation behind this ad campaign is perhaps Michelin's realization that emotional resonance, once established, can help win customers' hearts in a faster and more effective way then explicit messaging about product features.

Besides value selling, leading businesses have also realized the importance of humanizing the seemingly impersonal service process resulting from an increasingly wide application of computer and artificial intelligence technologies (Lupton, 1995). One interesting application is by Priceline.com. Consumers who have searched for travel packages on Google and Priceline most likely have experienced very different treatments from these two search engines. Unlike Google, which presents the search results immediately after a consumer's specified detailed travel preferences (e.g., dates, location, services needed), Priceline did not present the final search results right away. Instead, it presented a transitioning popup page featuring the famed Priceline negotiator William Shatner conveying messages along the lines of "Priceline negotiator is searching for the best travel package for you" and then after several seconds presenting "Priceline negotiator is now negotiating your travel package . . ." and then after several seconds saying "Priceline negotiator is now finalizing your travel package . . ." and then after several seconds finally displaying the search results. If consumers were surveyed whether they would like to see the search results immediately, the most likely answer would be "yes." Of course, nowadays' computer technology can enable immediate provision of the search results. However, by counterintuitively and artificially slowing down the travel package search process and showing consumers what major steps the system was taking to get them what they wanted, Priceline appealed to consumers' emotions. By humanizing its service process to implicitly demonstrate that due diligence and effort were provided to give consumers the best service from the site, Priceline was able to win business from consumers.

In addition to value selling and humanizing the service process to gain trust from consumers, fundamental behavioral finance concepts such as "social proof" have also been widely applied by organizations to influence consumer decision making and behaviors. One interesting application is by ComEd, where the utility provider tried to encourage customers to save electricity during peak utility using time. Once a customer signed up for its "Peak Time Savings Program," ComEd would notify the customer of the predicted peak utility period (likely hot summer days). If the customer made an effort to curb electricity consumption during the specified period and saved more electricity than an average home, then the customer would receive an email from ComEd featuring an explicit pat-on-the-back message (e.g., "good job") as well as a bar chart showing that the energy saving was better than average homes but not as good as the most efficient homes. It is this bar chart that provided the implicit nudge for the consumer to continue to save even more energy going forward.

An even more interesting point is that besides all of the aforementioned cases where the business successfully applied behavioral finance to promote desired consumer behaviors and create win-wins, there are also cases where explicit messaging created with good intentions backfired because the underlying implicit message was ignored and not done correctly. One famous example is theft mitigation at the Petrified Forest National Park in Arizona. To discourage tourists from sneakily stealing valuable petrified wood fossils in the park, staff put up signage across the park displaying a well-intended explicit message: "Your heritage is being vandalized everyday by theft losses of petrified wood of 14 tons a year, mostly a small piece at a time." However, instead of curbing the theft rate, this message ended up provoking even more stealing of petrified wood (Cialdini, 2003). This backfire is likely due to consumers receiving a different implicit message of "Stealing petrified wood is rampant in the park, and if you are not getting a piece for yourself, you are missing out." In behavioral finance this effect is called negative social proof, and when practitioners are not paying attention to it, it can often backfire and undermine the positive behavioral impact sought by the organization.

In conclusion, behavioral finance concepts/ theories and the proposed behavioral finance deployment approach, when applied appropriately, can help practitioners drive meaningful long-term impact and create values for the consumer, the organization, and ideally the society at large. However, ignoring implicit messaging or not using it correctly can not only limit the effectiveness of the overall messaging campaign but sometimes even drive undesired outcomes.

IT IS ALL ABOUT ETHICS AND DRIVING FOR A GOOD CAUSE

The last but perhaps most critical topic we would like to discuss is that of ethical applications of behavioral finance. Just like knowledge in many fields, behavioral finance theories/concepts can be a double-edged sword—whether they are applied to create value or harm depends on the ethical standards to which practitioners adhere. Social proof, a concept discussed in the preceding subsection, can be applied by ComEd to promote energy saving and create values for the consumer, the company, and the society as a whole, but the exact same concept can also potentially be used to sell more cigarettes/alcohol to minors. In the real world, some luxury brands even artificially force a waiting line outside of their stores (perhaps to demonstrate the popularity of the brand to passers-by through social proof), even though there may not be many patrons inside the stores.

There is thus an urgent need to address the ethics of applying behavioral finance. Even though there could be many controversial areas where it is challenging to judge what is absolutely ethical from different shareholders' perspectives, we hereby propose a high-level and hopefully widely applicable ethical standard to practitioners: An ethical application of behavioral finance should support informed consumer decision making to drive desired consumer behaviors for the good of the consumer, the organization, and the society at large.

To help adhere to this standard, we propose three more detailed guiding principles:

1. Focus on driving behaviors that the majority of people desire for their long-term well-being. When it is challenging to determine if the behavior an organization intends to drive is ethical or not, it could be helpful to evaluate whether such behavior and its impact are desired by the majority of consumers to achieve their long-term goals.
2. Ensure that the business goals are aligned with clients' goals. Such alignment should help the business thrive in the long run.
3. Always have clients' best interests in mind—a fiduciary mentality. The fiduciary mentality is a popular concept in the financial industry, where the client's interests are put first before the interests of the organization and the practitioner. Such a mentality should help win consumers' trust and enable long-term business success.

CONCLUSION

It should be evident from this chapter that consumer behavior is influenced by many factors. In this chapter we focused on how fundamental characteristics of human information processing affect the decisions and actions of individuals. We also showed how organizations can use knowledge of human factors to design products and messaging to drive desired behaviors and yield benefits to both the consumer and the company. Because of the potential misuse of this power, it is incumbent on research psychologists and practitioners to uphold the highest ethical standards when applying human factors and decision-making principles to create true values and long-lasting benefits for the consumer, the organization, and the society at large. In the end, it is all about striving for a good cause. Ethics should be viewed as essential to promote continuous development and resulting prosperity in both the science and practice of human factors in general and behavioral finance in particular.

REFERENCES

Ackert, L. F., & Deaves, R. (2010). *Behavioral finance: Psychology, decision-making, and markets.* South-Western, Cengage Learning.

Alluisi, E. A. (1994). APA Division 21: Roots and rooters. In H. L. Taylor (Ed.), *Division 21 members who made distinguished contributions to engineering psychology* (pp. 4–22). American Psychological Association.

Anderson, B. A., Laurent, P. A., & Yantis, S. (2011). Value-driven attentional capture. *Proceedings of the National Academy of Sciences of the United States of America, 108*(25), 10367–10371. https://doi.org/10.1073/pnas.1104047108

Biederman, I., Mezzanotte, R. J., & Rabinowitz, J. C. (1982). Scene perception: Detecting and judging objects undergoing relational violations. *Cognitive*

Psychology, *14*(2), 143–177. https://doi.org/10.1016/0010-0285(82)90007-X

Burton, S., & Babin, L. A. (1989). Decision-framing helps make the sale. *Journal of Consumer Marketing, 6*(2), 15–24. https://doi.org/10.1108/EUM0000000002543

Chan, A. H., & Hoffmann, E. R. (2015). Effect of display location on control-display stereotype strength for translational and rotational controls with linear displays. *Ergonomics, 58*(12), 1996–2015. https://doi.org/10.1080/00140139.2015.1051593

Cialdini, R. B. (2003). Crafting normative messages to protect the environment. *Current Directions in Psychological Science, 12*(4), 105–109. https://doi.org/10.1111/1467-8721.01242

Cornwell, T. B., & Humphreys, M. S. (2013). Memory for sponsorship relationships: A critical juncture in thinking. *Psychology and Marketing, 30*(5), 394–407. https://doi.org/10.1002/mar.20614

Cui, A. P., & Wiggins, J. (2017). What you ask changes what I pay: Framing effects in pay what you want pricing. *Journal of Marketing Theory and Practice, 25*(4), 323–339. https://doi.org/10.1080/10696679.2017.1345281

de Rose, L. J. (1991). Meet today's buying influences with value selling. *Industrial Marketing Management, 20*(2), 87–90. https://doi.org/10.1016/0019-8501(91)90026-C

Kahneman, D. (2011). *Thinking, fast and slow*. Farrar, Straus and Giroux.

Kahneman, D., Knetsch, J. L., & Thaler, R. H. (1990). Experimental tests of the endowment effect and the Coase theorem. *Journal of Political Economy, 98*(6), 1325–1348. https://doi.org/10.1086/261737

Lehto, M. R., & Nah, F. (2006). Decision-making models and decision support. In G. Salvendy (Ed.), *Handbook of human factors and ergonomics* (3rd ed., pp. 191–242). Wiley. https://doi.org/10.1002/0470048204.ch8

Levin, I. P., Johnson, R. D., Russo, C. P., & Deldin, P. J. (1985). Framing effects in judgment tasks with varying amounts of information. *Organizational Behavior and Human Decision Processes, 36*(3), 362–377. https://doi.org/10.1016/0749-5978(85)90005-6

Lowdermilk, T. (2013). *User-centered design: A developer's guide to building user-friendly applications*. O'Reilly Media.

Lupton, D. (1995). The embodied computer/user. *Body & Society, 1*(3–4), 97–112. https://doi.org/10.1177/1357034X95001003006

McDaniel, S. R., & Heald, G. R. (2000). Young consumers' responses to event sponsorship advertisements of unhealthy products: Implications of schema-triggered affect theory. *Sport Management Review, 3*(2), 163–184. https://doi.org/10.1016/S1441-3523(00)70084-2

Mowen, J. C., & Minor, M. (2000). *Consumer behavior: A framework*. Prentice Hall.

Pham, M. T., & Vanhuele, M. (1997). Analyzing the memory impact of advertising fragments. *Marketing Letters, 8*(4), 407–417. https://doi.org/10.1023/A:1007995112055

Proctor, R. W., & Van Zandt, T. (2018). *Human factors in simple and complex systems* (3rd ed.). CRC Press.

Proctor, R. W., & Vu, K.-P. L. (2010). Universal and culture-specific effects of display-control compatibility. *American Journal of Psychology, 123*(4), 425–435. https://doi.org/10.5406/amerjpsyc.123.4.0425

Proctor, R. W., & Vu, K.-P. L. (2016). Principles for designing interfaces compatible with human information processing. *International Journal of Human-Computer Interaction, 32*(1), 2–22. https://doi.org/10.1080/10447318.2016.1105009

Rauschenberger, R., Lin, J. J.-W., Zheng, X. S., & Lafleur, C. (2009). Subset search for icons of different spatial frequencies. *Proceedings of the Human Factors and Ergonomics Society Annual Meeting, 53*(17), 1101–1105. https://doi.org/10.1177/154193120905301712

Ricciardi, V., & Simon, H. K. (2000). What is behavioral finance? *Business, Education & Technology Journal, 2*(2), 1–9. https://ssrn.com/abstract=256754

Roscoe, S. N. (1997). *The adolescence of engineering psychology*. The Human Factors and Ergonomics Society. https://doi.org/10.1037/e721682011-001

Schacter, D. L., Chiu, C. Y. P., & Ochsner, K. N. (1993). Implicit memory: A selective review. *Annual Review of Neuroscience, 16*(1), 159–182. https://doi.org/10.1146/annurev.ne.16.030193.001111

Simon, H. A. (1956). Rational choice and the structure of the environment. *Psychological Review, 63*(2), 129–138. https://doi.org/10.1037/h0042769

Surprenant, A. M., & Neath, I. (2013). *Principles of memory*. Psychology Press. https://doi.org/10.4324/9780203848760

Szalma, J. L. (2009). Individual differences in human–technology interaction: Incorporating variation in human characteristics into human factors and ergonomics research and design. *Theoretical Issues in Ergonomics Science, 10*(5), 381–397. https://doi.org/10.1080/14639220902893613

Terho, H., Haas, A., Eggert, A., & Ulaga, W. (2012). "It's almost like taking the sales out of selling"—Towards a conceptualization of value-based selling in business markets. *Industrial Marketing Management, 41*(1), 174–185. https://doi.org/10.1016/j.indmarman.2011.11.011

Thaler, R. H., & Sunstein, C. R. (2009). *Nudge: Improving decisions about health, wealth, and happiness*. Penguin.

Townsend, C., Kaiser, U., & Schreier, M. (2015). User design through self-customization. In M. I. Norton, D. Rucker, & C. Lamberton (Eds.), *The Cambridge handbook of consumer psychology* (pp. 233–254). Cambridge University Press. https://doi.org/10.1017/CBO9781107706552.009

Treisman, A. (1982). Perceptual grouping and attention in visual search for features and for objects. *Journal of Experimental Psychology: Human Perception and Performance*, 8(2), 194–214. https://doi.org/10.1037/0096-1523.8.2.194

Tversky, A. (1972). Elimination by aspects: A theory of choice. *Psychological Review*, 79(4), 281–299. https://doi.org/10.1037/h0032955

Tversky, A. (1975). A critique of expected utility theory: Descriptive and normative considerations. *Erkenntnis*, 9(2), 163–173.

Tversky, A., & Kahneman, D. (1974). Judgment under uncertainty: Heuristics and biases. *Science*, 185(4157), 1124–1131. https://doi.org/10.1126/science.185.4157.1124

Valentino-DeVries, J. (2011, August 24). Steve Jobs's best quotes. *Wall Street Journal*. https://blogs.wsj.com/digits/2011/08/24/steve-jobss-best-quotes/

Van Praet, D. (2012). *Unconscious branding: How neuroscience can empower (and inspire) marketing*. St. Martin's Press.

Vu, K.-P. L., Latham, A., Diep, T., Van Luven, J., Fritz, R., & Dick, W. E. (2019). Use of customized text can be beneficial to students who read online materials under constrained visual conditions. In S. Yamamoto & H. Mori (Eds.), *Human interface and the management of information: Visual information and knowledge management* (pp. 137–150). Springer. https://doi.org/10.1007/978-3-030-22660-2_10

Vu, K.-P. L., Proctor, R. W., & Garcia, F. G. (2012). Website design and evaluation. In G. Salvendy (Ed.), *Handbook of human factors and ergonomics* (4th ed., pp. 1323–1353). John Wiley. https://doi.org/10.1002/9781118131350.ch48

Vu, K.-P. L., & Sun, Y. (2019). Population stereotypes for objects and representations: Response tendencies for interacting with everyday objects and interfaces. *Human Factors*, 61(6), 953–975. https://doi.org/10.1177/0018720818823570

Wolfe, J. M., & Horowitz, T. S. (2017). Five factors that guide attention in visual search. *Nature Human Behaviour*, 1(3), 1–8. https://doi.org/10.1038/s41562-017-0058

Index

ABA (American Bar Association), 9
Abilities. *See also* Conscious cognitive abilities; Mental abilities; Nonconscious cognitive abilities
   bias and deception detection and, 187
   of children, 193
   deficits in, 30
   system of, 228
Aboutness, 83–85
Abstracta, 86. *See also* Beliefs; Desires
Abstraction. *See also* Means-end theory
   hierarchy, 254
   levels of, 57, 251
Acceptability threshold for reliabilities, 119
Accessibility
   cognitive-affective units of, 227
   degree of, 227
   goods and services and, 172
   implications of, 21
   increase of, 20
   knowledge and effect on beliefs, 54
   lack of, 167, 169
   levels of chronic, 227
   likelihood of purchasing and, 21
   marketplace and, 167
   perceptions of, 170
   restrictions in, 166
   routes of consumer markets and lifestyles, 280
Accommodations, 5
Accountability, 311, 597
Accuracy paradox, 430–431, 434–435, 446. *See also* Media, economics and
   individual expectations, 431–432
   "representative agent" model, 432
   single national comparative standard, 433
Achievement
   measures of, 253
   pride and, 593
ACR (Association for Consumer Research). *See* Association for Consumer Research (ACR)
Actions, 97
   behavior and, 105
   bodily movement and, 105
   coordination of, 309
   definition of, 105
   function of desires and beliefs and, 82
   impulsive, 230
   individual vs. group, 310
   intentions and, 109
   involvement of, 105
   norms in, 310
   reasoned, 251
   reasons for, 83, 131
   tendencies of, 125
Activation
   brand-related, 613
   levels of, 227
   linkages and, 227
   patterns of, 227
   processes of, 56
   recency of, 52
Activities. *See also* Activities, interests, and opinions (AIO)
   context of, 272
   control of, 95
   effortful cognitive, 221
   examination of, 271
   marketing, xxiv
   metacognitive, 335
   neuroscience, 108
   purchase and consumption, xxiii
   types of, 271
Activities, interests, and opinions (AIO), 269–270. *See also* Activities; Interests; Opinions
   adaptations of, 272
   approach, 271–273
   clusters, 273
   framework, 271
   inventories, 270, 272
   marketing, xxiv
Acts of kindness, 641
Adaptation rate, 638
ADHD (attention deficit/hyperactivity disorder), 230
Adolescents, 197
Advertisers. *See also* Advertising
   motivation of, 187
   professionals as cultural intermediaries, 207
   tactics of, 188, 191
Advertising, xxiv. *See also* Advertisers
   accommodation of, 252
   acquiescent responses to, 478
   advertorials, 475
   alerting in, 477
   analysis of, 252, 275, 312
   appeals in, 4, 65, 311
   assimilation of, 252
   attention to, 481
   attitudes toward, 252, 475
   attributes for, 480
   avoidance of, 475–476
   barriers to, 477

Advertising (continued)
  beliefs about the truthfulness of, 187
  bias in, 187
  brand affect and, 25
  campaigns in, 480
  children and, 10–11, 185, 189, 191
  cigarettes and, 197
  code barriers in, 10
  code-switching in, 461
  cognitive defenses against, 186, 191
  comparative, 9, 12
  compensation, 473
  concerns in, 188
  conformity vs. individuality in, 312
  consumer behavior and, 3
  corrective, 9
  creation of, 274
  critique of, 204, 207
  deception in, 9, 12, 187, 188
  depictions of violence in, 207
  disclosures in, 188
  disguised, 475, 480
  editorial content and, 475
  effectiveness of, 3, 251–252, 262, 478, 627–628
  entertainment and, 187
  expenditures in, 473
  exposure to, 188, 473
  familiarity of, 481
  features of, 478, 479
  feelings and, 24
  forced viewings of, 479
  forms of processing, 477
  gender and, 207, 210
  goals of, 15, 187, 189
  guidance in, 477
  high value congruence of, 252
  individuality and, 312
  information and, 187
  input breakthroughs in, 478
  internet and, 473
  intersection of gender, media, and, 205
  interventions in, 197
  knowledge of, 186, 191
  loose cultures in, 311
  low value congruence of, 252
  mainstream imagery in, 208
  memory for, 480–481
  men and masculinity in, 207
  mixed emotions, 597
  narrative, 479
  nature of, 186
  negative effects of, 199
  neural activity and, 629
  originality of, 481
  overstatements in, 188
  persuasion and, 475
  practitioner theory in, 478
  predictors of, 481
  premiums and, 188, 189
  priming statements in, 252
  principles of, 3
  process, 3
  product placement in, 475
  protections against, 8
  psychologists working in, 4
  psychology of, 473
  public relations and, 480
  recall of, 3, 252, 588
  research on, 3, 9, 191, 471
  responses to, 12, 23, 478, 482
  sexual appeal in, 208
  shifts in, 4
  society and, 475
  substantiation and, 9
  surrealistic, 252
  tactics in, 191
  targeted to ingroups, 313
  television spending on, 473
  tight cultures and, 311
  variety of, 312
  video, 630
Advocacy, 335–342. See also Advocacy research
Advocacy research. See also Advocacy
  audience factors in, 340
  message variables in, 339
Affect. See also Emotions
  biasing effect in, 586
  choices and, 589–590
  conceptualizations of, 583
  congruency and, 25
  definition of, 582
  direct vs. indirect effect of, 586–587
  elicitation of, 583
  evaluative conditioning of, 585
  framework with integration and motivation, 631
  hedonic level of, 637
  incidental, 585–586, 589
  influence of, 25, 62, 585
  information hypothesis, 63
  integral, 585–586, 589
  judgments and, 586
  length of experience, 591
  lower order, 230
  motivational variables, 590–591
  negative, 586
  neuroforecasting and, 628
  positive, 586–587, 640
  product pairing and, 586
  regulation of, 25, 590
  reliance on, 587
  sources of, 62, 585–587
Affective. See also Affective reactions; Affective responses; Affective states
  experiences, 583
  feelings, 587
  forecasting, 638
  influences on economic expectations, 441–445
  well-being, 637
Affective reactions, 62–63
  declarative knowledge, 583
  metacognitive experiences, 598
  responses as, 583
  types of, 583
Affective responses
  metacognitive experiences and, 583
  types of, 585
Affective states, 171. See also Mood
  mixed, 597
  uncertainty in, 587
Affirmation
  disclosure, 10
  seeking of, 172
Age, xxiv
  differences in children, 187, 193
  differences in materialism, 195
  traits and, 220
  trends, 187
Aggregate-level expectations, 433–434. See also Accuracy paradox; Accurate time series predictions; Expectations
Aggregate Marketing System (AGMS), 6
Aggression, 592
AIO (activities, interests, and opinions). See Activities, interests, and opinions (AIO)
Alcohol advertising, 595
Alliances, 309
Allocation, 174
Alternatives
  evaluation of, 171
  to purchase process, 13

Ambiguity
    acceptance of, 222
    subjective valuation and, 624
American Bar Association (ABA), 9
American Council on Consumer Interests, 8
American Psychological Association (APA), xxiii
    Consumer Psychology Division (Division 23), 5
    Dictionary of Psychology, 552
Analyses
    advertisements and, 275
    clusters and, 220
    content and, 312
    domains of, 79
    factors and, 220
    levels of, 210
    lifestyles and, 274
    means-end chain, 277
    posteriori, 270, 272
    purchases and, 272
    Q factor, 273
Analysis of variance (ANOVA), 103, 104, 115, 127
    limitations in, 116
    traditional design of, 132
Analytics, 632
Anchoring, 418
Anger, 65, 592–593
    choices and, 592
Annual percentage rates (APRs), 28
Annual Review of Psychology, 103
    attributions, 80
ANOVA (analysis of variance). *See* Analysis of variance (ANOVA)
Antecedents, 179
Anthropology, 13
Antibrand communities, 612
Antimedia, 274. *See also* Media
Anxiety, 596–597
APA (American Psychological Association). *See* American Psychological Association (APA)
Appeals
    attitudes and, 324
    collectivistic themes with, 312
    of fear, 4
    to human desires, 4
    individualized, 267
    psychological, 4
Appearance, 588

Apple, 691
    "Silhouettes" campaign, 734
    unmet needs and, 732
Appraisals
    cognitive theories of, 583
    early dimensions of, 584
    emotions and, 584, 591
    upon exposure, 583
    nature of, 585
    processes of, 584, 594
    reappraisals and, 584
    self-relevance and, 584
    situation-specific, 64
Apprehension, 65
Approaches. *See also* List of Values (LOV)
    to activities, interests, and opinions (AIO), 271–273
    analyses of purchase in, 272
    to attitudes and activities, 269, 271
    complementary, 136
    lifestyle, 270
    principal, 276
    theory-driven, 128
    values, 270–271
    values and life style (VALS), 271, 272
APRs (annual percentage rates), 28
Arguments
    counterattitudinal, 340
    efficacy of, 336
    incongruent with values, 342
    strength of, 329, 331, 332
    validity of, 305
Arousal, 589, 591
Asian consumers, 639
Assimilation, 21
Association for Consumer Research (ACR), 180
    fellow recognitions, 6
    original goals of, 5
Associations
    network model of, 49
    positive, 21
    self-object, 303
    strength of, 21
Assumptions
    about consumer psychology, xxiv
    economic, 12
    rationality and, 81
    scientific, 81
    unexamined, 104
Attacks, persuasive, 332
Attention, 629, 674, 727–728

advertisements and, 481
attentional adhesion, 236
behavior and, 236
definition of, 481
disengagement bias, 236
engagement and, 481
impact of, 481
impulsive vs. nonimpulsive individuals and, 237
independent networks, 236
indexing, 481
maintenance bias, 236
patterns of, 236
systems, 236
temptations and, 239
valuation and, 625
Attention deficit/hyperactivity disorder (ADHD), 230
Attention, Interest, Desire, and Action (AIDA) model, 4
Attitude certainty. *See also* Attitudes
    advocacy and, 336, 338, 341
    argumentation efficacy, 336
    attitude strength and, 337
    attitudinal advocacy and, 337
    audience effects on, 333
    boosts in, 333
    building of, 334
    consensus feedback and, 332
    definition of, 330
    effects and influences on, 332, 334
    implications for, 338
    message processing and, 334
    message strength and, 332–333
    persuasion intentions and, 336
    predictions from, 336
    production of, 331
    reductions in, 332, 334
    reports of, 332
    shifts in, 330
    source effects and, 330, 331, 335
    strength of, 330
    types of, 336
    valence and, 332
Attitude change, 323
    compliance vs., 326
    foundation of, 328
    research on, 327
Attitudes, 14, 80, 83. *See also* Attitude certainty; Persuasion
    accessibility of, 21, 324
    advertising and, 252, 475, 481
    affect and, 24, 324, 338
    ambivalent, 305, 324

Attitudes (*continued*)
  appeals and, 324
  approaches to, 271
  aspects of, 324
  basis of, 324, 338
  behaviors and, 20, 323, 324, 331
  bolstering of, 476
  brands and, 252, 323
  of children, 189
  class of products and, 270
  cognitions and, 286, 324, 338
  confidence about, 330
  consensus effects, 332
  of consumers, 7, 262
  defense of, 331
  definition of, 128, 323
  delayed change, 332
  durability of, 324
  about entities, 323
  evaluative conditioning and, 585–586
  examination of, 271
  explicit, 325
  expression of, 335
  extremity of, 324
  familiarity of objects and, 334
  formation of, 254, 323, 329, 335
  identity congruent, 313
  implicit, 208, 324, 338
  importance of, 324
  influences on, 24, 131, 261
  initial, 332, 334
  inputs of, 336
  kinds of, 134
  measures of, 324
  metacognitive effects in, 333
  money and, 250
  multidimensional, 128
  nature of, 338
  objects, 334
  origin of, 324
  perceptions of, 324, 333, 336, 338
  persuasion and, 342
  polarization of, 341, 342
  positive vs. negative, 323
  prediction of, 314, 481
  toward products, 323
  reflections on, 335
  relevant information, 333
  research on, 13, 323
  resultant, 333
  role of, 278, 323
  salient, 335
  shaping of, 334
  shifts in, 324, 340, 341
  social expression of, 310
  stability of, 338, 341
  statement of, 335
  supporting existing, 326
  target entities and, 323
  theories about, 338
  thought confidence and, 330
  tripartite theory of, 324
  uncertainty of, 332, 337
  understanding of, 323
  valence of, 324
  validity of, 330, 332
  values and, 261, 270
  variation of, 323
Attitude strength
  attitude certainty and, 337
  certainty and, 335
  dimensions of, 337
  increase in, 324
  markers of, 324
  properties of, 332
Attractors. *See also* Traits
  conceptualization of, 235–236
  state of, 229, 237
  strength of, 228, 238
Attributes
  abstract, 254
  advertising and, 480
  beliefs, 23
  of brands, 312
  of children, 192
  comparison, 589
  concrete, 251, 254
  connection of, 306
  consistency of, 475
  cultural significance, 312
  descriptions of, 53
  desirability and, 22, 23
  determination of, 250
  information, 192
  intangible, 22
  intrinsic and extrinsic, 22
  linkage with consequences, 250, 254
  perceptual, 192
  preferences for, 192
  relevant, 192
  of sources, 325
  theories about, 503–504, 513, 515, 520
Audiences
  characteristics of, 340
  demographics of, 327
  effects, 333, 336
  emotional state of, 327
  factors of, 325, 327
  habits and values of, 274
  motivation of, 327
  physical behavior of, 327
  psychographics of, 327
  shifts of, 340
  varied media, 274
Auditory blasts, 95
Automatic information processing and learning, 439–440, 444. *See also* Conscious cognitive abilities; Nonconscious cognitive abilities; Nonconscious learning
Automaticity, 18
Automatic processes, 632
Autonomy, 638, 641
Average variance extracted (AVE), 120
Avoidance behavior, 65
Awareness, 15, 47, 69

Back-to-back strategy, 423
BAS (behavioral activation system), 233
Basic emotions approach, 591
BAS Reward Responsiveness Scale, 228, 239
Becker-DeGroot-Marschak auction, 623
Behavioral activation system (BAS), 233
Behavioral economics, 7
Behavioral finance
  behavioral levers and, 733
  benefits of, 729, 734
  business process/framework and, 731
  data mining and, 733
  definition of, 729
  dynamic messaging channels and, 733
  ethics and, 736
  explicit marketing approaches and, 732
  explicit messaging and, 733–734
  feedback loop and, 734
  fiduciary mentality and, 736
  guiding principles of, 736
  heuristics and, 733
  implicit messaging and, 733–734
  instant gratification/hyperbolic discounting and, 733
  memory recall and, 731

misuse of, 736
procrastination/decision paralysis and, 733
purpose of, 730
social proof and, 736
static messaging channels and, 733
System 1 thinking and, 730, 732
System 2 thinking and, 731–732
triggers and, 733
unmet needs and, 732
Behavioral finance case studies, 734–735. *See also* Apple
Behavioral inhibition system (BIS), 233
Behavioral perspective model (BPM), 90, 98
Behavioral responses, 105
consequences as, 172
premise for, 674
self-destructive, 172
Behaviorism. *See also* Three-term contingency
bounds of, 89, 93
intentional, 86, 88, 89, 91
positivist application of, 80
SEMs and, 105
sources of limitation in, 91
verbal behavior and, 94
Behaviors, xxiii, 21
accounts of, 81, 93
action and, 105
advocacy, 337
aggregate-level, 625, 626, 628, 630
analysis of, 13, 89, 90, 91, 105
aspects of, 268
attention and, 236
attitudes and, 20, 323, 324, 331
autonomy of, 222
avoidance, 594
capacities for, 81
of children, 198
closeness and, 355
cognitive science and, 88
commitment of, 12, 29
competence-signaling, 308
compulsive shopping, 226
computation of, 133
consequences of, 171
consistency in, 13, 235
consumer citizenship, 615
consumer goals and, 250, 355
consumption, xxiii, 640, 642

continuity and discontinuity of, 91
contrasting consumer, 302
contribution, 131, 133
control of, 92
corporations and, 113
cultural differences in, 310
decisions and, 47, 62
defensive vs. nondefensive, 170
definition of, 105
Dennett's approach to, 81
determination of, 254
deviant, 310–311
dispositions of, 58
drivers of, 88, 129, 220, 310, 355
economic, xxiii
engagement and, 610, 613
environment and, 90
equilibrium in, 235
factors of, 17
of fans, 278
folk-psychological account of, 83
forms of, 231
giving, 176
goal-directed, 69, 131, 250
guide to future, 252
ideas and, 12
identical individual, 270
imitation of, 67
impulsive, 230
incidental emotion and, 64
inductions on, 64
inferences in, 233
information-sharing, 628
interindividual differences, 225
justification for, 311, 475
language and, 91, 460
law of, 105
levels of, 220
links with, 82
listener and, 95
manipulations of, 107
mediators of, 19
mental events and, 80
mindsets on, 57
motivations of, 230, 249, 250, 584
movement toward, 3
norms and, 310
observed, 104, 594
patterns of, 105, 220
perceived, 131
personal level of exposition, 91
power holders and, 307
precursors of, 14

previous experiences and, 47
price information and, 673
processes of, 55, 81
pro-environmental, 12
prorelationship, 356
prosocial, 174
purchasing, 232, 251, 628
reasoning and, 82
recycling of, 251
research on, 89, 249
resultant, 227
saving, 168
sciences and, 82
self-improvement, 595
self-regulation of, 137
self-reports of, 80
sets of, 226
shaping of, 219
shifts in, 19, 220, 254, 315
socioeconomic, 269
spectrum of, 95
sponsor, 285
tendencies in, 231
terms of intentionality, 86
theories about, xxiv, 251
traits and, 219
type generalization, 272
underlying processes in, 233
variability in, 219–220
warmth-signaling, 308
warnings on, 226
within-person variation in, 226
Belief/desire model, 83
Beliefs, 16, 80, 82
associated with advertising practitioner theory, 478
attitudes and, 324
attitudinal, 128
basis for, 55
doubt of, 339
emotions and, 591
impact of, 93
influences on, 54
information and, 475
justification of, 475
model of organization of, 55
about power distance, 308
practitioner, 478, 481
shopping based on, 393
types of, 17
Belonging tensions, 177
Benefits
extrinsic vs. intrinsic, 639
utilitarian vs. informational, 90

Index

Bias
　in abilities, 187
　in advertising, 187
　affect and, 586
　in attention, 236
　of children, 187
　cognitive processes and, 14
　confirmation, 474
　conscious cognitive abilities and, 433
　cross-sex, 208
　evaluations with, 590
　expectations and, 438, 444
　method, 132–133
　monomethod, 121
　orientations and, 236
　in reasoning, 474
　recognition of, 187
　source of, 125
Biconditionals, 95
Bicultural identity integration (BII), 314
Big data, 632
Big Five. *See* Personality's Big Five
Big ideas, 127–130
BII (bicultural identity integration), 314
Bilingualism
　psycholinguistic approach to, 461–462
　sociolinguistic approach to, 460–461
BIS (behavioral inhibition system), 233
#BlackLivesMatter, 705
Body
　grounded cognition and, 554–555, 559–560
　influence on mental processes, 554–555
　movements, 63, 334
　processes and psychology, 551
　responses of, 48
　satisfaction, 207
　thought confidence and, 335
Boycotts, 593
BPM (behavioral perspective model), 90, 98
　BPM-E (extensional model of consumer choice), 90–91, 95, 99
　BPM-I (intentional model of consumer choice), 93, 95
Brain
　association with, 109
　components of, 441

　development of, 474
　encoding numbers in the, 674
　hemisphere asymmetry, 630
　imaging, 626
　limbic system, 442
　regions, 584–585, 623
　sensory signals in the, 674
　states, 109
Brain-as-predictor approach, 627
Brand associations, 693–694, 704
　product design and, 727
Brand community, 125, 704
　antecedents of, 699
　antibrand, 612
　brand relationships and, 699
　conceptualization of, 699
　consequences of, 700
　social media and, 495–496
Brand equity, 696
　model of, 704
Brand extensions, 13
　downward vs. upward, 308
　success of, 22
Brand loyalty, 128
　of children, 185
　cross-cultural differences in, 311
　effect of, 52
　social media and, 504
Brand names, 693–694
　accessibility, 20
　children's awareness of, 190
　prototypic, 314
　rhymes in, 453
　sounds associated with, 453
　spelling of, 454
　value of, 22
Brand property strength framework
　antecedent variables, 693
　brand property consequences, 693
　brand property construct, 692
　causal sequence of constructs, 692–693
　dimensions of, 692
　future research and, 703, 705
　goal of, 703
　hierarchy of brand property strength, 693
　management actions, 693
Brand relationships. *See also* Brands; Relationships
　antecedents of, 698
　anthropomorphism and, 704
　attachment–aversion model and, 698

　brand community and, 699
　brand image and, 698
　consequences of, 699
　of heterosexual men, 205
　motivated reasoning and, 699
　necessity of, 705
　quality of, 698–699
　research on, 698
Brands. *See also* Brand loyalty; Brand names; Brand property strength framework; Brand relationships
　advocates of, 612
　affect of, 25, 585, 586
　affiliation of, 596
　allegiance to, 279
　associations of, 15
　attachment to, 704
　attitudes about, 252, 323, 694–695, 704
　attributes of, 312
　awareness, 15
　awareness of, 696
　bonds with, 313
　categories in, 190
　coolness of, 129
　as cultural icons, 313
　culture and, 307, 312–313
　elicited feelings from, 585
　emotional attachment to, 311
　evaluation of, 20, 305
　expressive and symbolic significance of, 13
　extension of, 306, 586, 588
　familiarity of, 312
　family of, 588
　hatred of, 125, 130
　iconic, 313
　image development of, 282
　image management of, 13
　image of, 307, 696
　insights on, 13
　interactions with, 615
　investment, 616
　judgment of, 25
　learning, 312, 616
　legitimacy of, 206
　love of, 128
　meaning of, 692, 697, 704
　membership of, 593
　metacognitive feelings and, 598
　metaphors and, 454
　mood and, 25
　name of, 453
　national vs. private-label, 308

negative engagement, 612
paradox, 697
parent, 588
perceptions of, 303, 306
performance of, 17
personality of, 697–698, 704
personal vs. relational characteristics of, 303
persuasion of, 251
preferences for, 16
product category of, 190
properties of, 693, 703–704
prosocial, 307
psychological underpinning of, 103
quality, 128
recognition and recall of, 14
retrieval of, 20
self-concepts and, 195
sex-role concept with, 203
sexual appeal and, 208
social aspects of, 190
social causes and, 23
social identity and, 23
social involvement from, 393
social meaning of, 195
sounds associated with, 453
spelling of, 454
sponsorships and, 279, 283, 285
sports marketing and, 285
status of, 308
stereotypes and, 207
strength, 22
valuation of, 313
values and, 307
Brands and social media
authenticity, 504
backlash, 495
baiting, 495
brand communities, 495–496
cultural discourses, 494–495
goals, 505
network stability, 495
owned vs. paid vs. earned social media, 494
reactance, 495
receptivity, 495
social presence, 494
Brief Self-Control Scale (BSCS), 231–232
Bureau of Labor Statistics, 432
Business community, 11

CAPS (cognitive affective process system). *See* Cognitive affective process system (CAPS)

Casual path differences, 131
Categories
of brands, 190
core concepts of, 190
defining features of, 16
exemplars of, 16
membership of, 588
separation of product-price, 678
Categorization
changes to, 588
by children, 190
issues of, 16
thinking styles and, 306
Causality, 529, 551
factors of, 176
issues of, 82, 136, 137
mental states and, 137
processes of, 137
relations of, 110–111
Caveat emptor, 8
CE (consumer engagement). *See* Consumer engagement (CE)
Celebrities. *See also* Celebrity endorsement
persuasive influence of, 325
values of, 252
Celebrity endorsement, 252. *See also* Celebrities
associative learning theory and, 518
attractiveness model and, 518
attribution theory and, 515
benefits of, 519–520
cognitive resources and, 518
congruence and, 517, 520, 521
contemporary marketing and, 522–523
effectiveness of, 515–516
elaboration likelihood model (ELM) and, 518
expectancy and, 518
identification and, 518, 521
long-term impact of, 519
match-up hypothesis and, 516–518
meaning transfer model and, 515–516
multiple product endorsements and, 520
network models and, 520
overuse of, 520
positive effects of, 515, 519
prescriptive framework and, 519
profitability of, 519

recall and, 518
risks of, 520–521
social adaptation theory and, 517
social identity theory and, 518
source credibility model and, 519
traditional marketing and, 521–522
CEP (Consumer Engagement Propensity). *See* Consumer Engagement Propensity (CEP)
Certainty
advocacy and, 336, 337
appraisals and, 333
attitude strength and, 335
audience effects on, 333
bodily movements and, 334
cognitive states and, 333
conviction and, 338
degree of, 132
emotions and, 333, 335
feelings of, 331, 334, 338
induction of, 335
levels of, 338, 339
lowering of, 333
mental content and, 335
metacognitive, 330
moderate, 338
thoughtfulness and, 334
timing and, 334
CFA (confirmatory factor analysis), 116
CFA model, 128–129
Changes
in responses vs. stimuli, 674
sensitivity to, 674
stability vs., 220
understanding of, 254
Children
advertising influence on, 189
advertising knowledge of, 191, 192
age differences in, 187, 193
age progression in, 187
aspects of knowledge in, 189
attitudes of, 189
attribute information of, 192
awareness of brand names, 190
beliefs approaching adolescence, 187
brand loyalty of, 185
categorization of items by, 190
concerns about well-being of, 195
consumer attitude of, 189
consumer behavior of, 185
consumer goals for, 194

Children (*continued*)
    consumer knowledge of, 185, 190
    consumer socialization of, 194
    consumption behavior of, 185
    consumption constellations of, 195
    decision-making strategies of, 192, 193
    development of abilities in, 193
    development of knowledge in, 189
    development of materialism in, 194
    development of strategies in, 193
    eating behaviors of, 198
    effects of marketing on, 186
    experience of, 191
    expression of self-concepts in, 195
    identification of content by, 187
    increase of preference in, 188
    inferences by, 190
    influence of, 185, 193
    information gathering in, 193
    levels of materialism in, 196
    material goods and, 195
    measures to assess understanding by, 187
    media engagement of, 199
    obesity in, 198
    parental influence on, 193
    parental social support to, 196
    peer influence on, 196
    performance of, 191
    preferences and choices of, 185
    premium advertising and, 189
    product evaluation by, 192
    product recognition by, 189
    purchase requests of, 193
    recognition of bias and deception by, 187
    recognition of consumption symbolism by, 190
    recognition of intent by, 187
    research on, 185, 189
    response to advertising by, 191
    self-esteem of, 196
    socialization of, 185, 189
    television advertising and, 185
    understanding of advertising by, 186, 191
    vulnerability of, 189
    well-being of, 185, 194
Choices
    affect and, 589–590
    anger and, 592
    culture and, 312
    deferral of, 598
    drivers of, 303
    internal reactions and, 303
    moderation in, 309
    neural activation and, 625
    neural measures and, 621
    strategy of, 58
    values in, 251
CI (consumer involvement). *See* Consumer involvement (CI)
CIS (consumer impulsiveness scale). *See* Consumer impulsiveness scale (CIS)
Classifications
    based on relational or symbolic connections, 305
    constructs, 240
    impulsive vs. nonimpulsive, 224
Cleansing and separation, 565–566
Clinical techniques, 4
Closeness
    attachment style, 352
    behavior and, 355
    competitiveness and, 360
    decision making and, 357
    definition of, 352, 353, 355
    everyday favors and, 358
    familiarity and, 358
    feelings of, 353
    gift giving and, 358
    goal pursuit and, 356
    interdependence, 352
    interpersonal, 353
    perceived, 358
    persuasion and, 456
    in relationships, 352
    self-concepts and, 355
CNDS (competing neurobehavioral decision systems model), 96
Cobb-Douglas utility function analysis, 91
Cognition, 82
    appraisal, 227, 228
    attitudes based on, 286, 324, 338
    effortful activities, 221
    hot, 230, 234
    knowledge, 227, 228
    metacognitive experiences and, 598
    need for, 219, 221, 327, 328
    numerical, 673
    in persuasion, 327
    reinforcement of, 229
    sets of, 226
    situation-specific, 64
    social, 251
    units of, 227
    variables in, 92
Cognitive
    closure, 327
    defenses against advertising, 186
    deliberation, 57
    elaboration, 588
    engagement, 13
    goal representation, 57
    load, 68
    processing, 611, 631
    psychology paradigm, 82
    resources, 14
    response to products, 14
    revolution, 81
    skills, 50, 66
    states, 333
    structures, 80
    systems, 476
    well-being, 637
Cognitive abilities, 434. *See also* Conscious cognitive abilities; Nonconscious cognitive abilities
Cognitive affective process system (CAPS), 226–228, 230, 233, 235
Cognitive explanation
    of consumer behavior, 82
    definition of, 82
    inaccuracies in, 80
    nature of, 81
    perspectives on, 81
    philosophical demands of, 97
Cognitive processes, 48, 451, 553
    ad evaluations and, 208
    biased, 14
    linguistic factors on, 452
    narrative building, 459
Collective intentionality, 97
Collectivism, 131
Collectivistic cultures, 639
Commercials. *See also* Advertising
    effects of, 54
    fear appeals of, 596
    intent of, 187
    sugary foods and, 188
Commitment contract, 29
Common neural currency, 623, 624
Communications, 639
    in business, 455
    consumer-related, 455
    emotional or noncognitive, 432
    families, 193, 194

marketer-to-consumer, 456
persuasive, 456
phases of, xxiv
promotional, xxiv
social, 432, 455
strategies on, 251
Communities. *See also* Brand community
antibrand, 612
contribution to, 131
LGBTQ+, 206
Comparative judgment mindsets, 58
Comparisons
conscious vs. nonconscious, 675
cross-cultural differences, 302
of prices, 675
shopping with, 638
standards of, 53
Competency, 638, 641
Competing neurobehavioral decision systems model (CNDS), 96
Competitiveness
closeness and, 360
concerns in, 361
cooperation and, 353
decision making and, 361
definition of, 352
envy and, 361
experiences with, 360, 361
factors increasing, 360
individual vs. situational factors of, 360
interpersonal, 359
in the marketplace, 361
motivation and, 359–360
orientation style, 353
in relationships, 359
research on, 360
role in goal orientations, 360
settings of, 361
uniqueness, 361
Completion principle, 50
Composite reliability, 119–120
Comprehension, 47
basis for, 48
knowledge activation and, 51
Compromise option, 418
Concepts
abstract, 559–560
concrete, 560
grounded cognition and, 559–560, 565
perceptual experience and, 559
sensorimotor cues, 560

sensory marketing and, 559, 564
statements, 128
Conceptualization, 48, 115
domains of, 79
framework of, 81, 179
implications of, 63, 67
Conceptual metaphor theory, 455, 560, 565
Conceptual schemes, 128
Conditioning, 105
Conferences, 5
Gender, Marketing, and Consumer (GENMAC), 205
Marketing and Public Policy Conference (MPPC), 11
Confidence, 58
degrees of, 80, 330
interval, 120
manipulations of, 339
Confirmatory factor analysis (CFA), 116
Conformity, 59, 65
advertisements focusing on, 312
to group values, 310
tendency toward, 312
Congruence, 589
affect and, 25
of celebrity endorsements, 517, 520, 521
high vs. low value, 252
of values, 252, 340
Connections
activation of, 227
models, 48
between personality processes, 227
procedures, 566–567
signaling of, 358
Conscientiousness, 231
Conscious awareness, 14
Conscious cognitive abilities, 436, 444. *See also* Nonconscious cognitive abilities
deductive logic, 438
deliberative decisions, 437
instant conscious awareness, 439
limitations of, 437–438
nonconscious cognitive abilities vs., 439
processes of, 438
Consciousness, 107
Consequences
absence of, 222
actions and, 251
of behavior, 171

behavioral responses as, 172
in brand communities, 700
in brand equity, 696–697
of brand properties, 693
in brand relationships, 698
for consumer behavior, 314
consumer identification of, 250
current situations and, 251
decisions and, 61
desired vs. undesired, 128, 250
functional, 251
in goal activation, 57
hierarchy of, 702–703
linkage with attributes, 250, 254
of means-end chain (MEC) model, 254
in messages, 335
perceived deficits and, 179
in products, 277
psychological, 166
of social media, 489
values and, 254
of vulnerability, 170
Consideration
of circumstances, 170
in decision-making, 171
set, 16
Conspicuous consumption effect, 639, 643
Construal levels, 60, 226, 599
Constructs
boundary conditions of, 131
components of, 126
focal, 112
measurement of, 122
multidimensionality of, 120
representation of, 103
Construct validity, 103, 121
convergent validity, 122
discriminant validity, 122
tests of, 123
Consumer attitudes
on the business climate, 7
about personal finances, 7
shaping of, 262
Consumer behavior, 137
aggregate, 6
approaches to, 270
assumptions of, 81
attempts to explain, 82
books on, 5
children and, 185
cognitive explanation of, 82
comparisons of, 302
consequences for, 314

Consumer behavior (*continued*)
   consistency and, 81
   consumer-situation and, 94
   context of, 173, 335
   contributions to the standard of life, 5
   cultural factors affecting, 315
   economics of, 91
   explanations of, 80, 111
   extensional model of, 88
   five-factor model of personality and, 221
   groups in, 352
   impact of, 6
   implications of, 79
   importance of the self to, 203
   impoverished, 169, 175
   impulsivity and, 230
   incidental fear and, 65
   influences on, 14, 58
   instrumental activity and, 88
   items related to, 253
   links to societal development, 6
   mainsprings of, 82
   management of, 14
   nature of, 80
   nuances of, 6
   paradigms in, 171
   parental influence in, 194
   personality traits and, 221
   perspective, 179
   pragmatic understanding of, 82–83
   precursor of, 90
   predictors of, 251
   processes and outcomes of, 179
   realities of, 79
   reductive physicalism, 107
   relationships affecting, 353
   research on, 3, 8, 12, 31, 221
   role in marketing curriculum, 5
   role in the economy, 5
   role of advertising in, 3
   role of personality in, 221
   setting, 90
   society and, 306
   stimuli of, 673
   subjective experience and, 62
   values and, 252, 253
   variables in, 268
   variation in, 269
Consumer behavior settings, 33
   components of, 95
   effect of, 98
   outcomes of, 91
   scope of, 91
   social communication interactions in, 455
   stimuli composing, 91
   structural characteristics of, 94
Consumer Bill of Rights, 8
Consumer choice, 20
   accounts of, 82
   extensional model (BPM-E) of, 86, 90–91, 95, 99
   factors of, 170
   situational influences on, 80
   understanding of, 81
Consumer culture, 173
   contemporary, 209
   theory, 204
Consumer engagement (CE), 609. *See also* Engagement
   conceptualization of, 611
   endurance of, 616
   fluctuations, 613
   interactivity, 612, 615
   involvement vs., 612, 612–613
   literature review, 611–612
   research on, 615–616
   styles of, 615
Consumer Engagement Propensity (CEP), 613–615
   elaboration likelihood model (ELM) revision, 609
   model, 614
Consumer evaluations
   code-switching in, 461
   effects on, 453
Consumer expectations
   mismatches in, 457
   nature of, 8
   role of, 8
Consumer Financial Protection Bureau, 12
Consumer impulsiveness scale (CIS), 231, 232, 234
Consumer Information Task Force, 10
Consumer involvement (CI), 609. *See also* Involvement
   conceptualization of, 610
   engagement vs., 612–613
   literature review, 610–611
   research, 615–616
Consumerism, 8
Consumerist groups, 9
Consumer knowledge
   of children, 185, 190
   development of, 185
   generation of, 80
Consumer messages
   attributes of, 479
   avoidance of, 472
   contact with, 471
   digital world and, 472
   mediated, 473
   narratives, 479
   responses to, 471
   stimulus attributes of, 479
Consumer phenomena
   cultural factors and, 301
   impact of power distance on, 308
Consumer price index (CPI), 431, 433, 435–436
Consumer psychologists, 165
   emphasis of, 136
   goals of, 119
   impact of, 174, 180
Consumer psychology, xxiii
   approaches to, 104
   assumptions in, xxiv
   attention to, xxiv
   behavioral sciences and, 82
   brands and, 691–692
   construct validity in, 122
   consumer theory-driven (CT), 32, 33
   contemporary, 105
   cross-cultural differences, 301
   definition of, 31
   development of, 5
   digital media and, 472
   disciplines and approaches of, 31
   domains of, 301, 315
   explanations in, 80
   factors within, 4
   focus on individuals in, 6
   goals in, 33
   growth of knowledge in, 82
   institutional infrastructure of, 5
   interpersonal power and, 362
   issues involved in, 80
   marketing and, xxiv
   marketplace-driven (MD), 31
   neglect of economic and societal issues in, 5
   paradigmatic, 127
   phenomena in, 130
   philosophy and, 80
   principles of, 112
   psychological theory-driven (PT), 32
   public policy and, 6
   research on, 3
   relevance of, 472

SEMs and, 103
topics of consideration in, 180
traditional media and, 472
value of, 472
value theories in, 249
Consumer research, 3
basis for, 80
classifications in, 303
contributions in, 4
discussions in, 210
evolution of, 4
gender and, 203
grants, 180
intervention-focused, 20
legitimization of, 8
level of needs and, 250
measures in, 103
methods in, 103, 166
scholarship, 210
self-awareness in, 111
utility in, 109
validity of, 112
values in, 249
Consumer response
cultural factors of, 301
differences in, 221
logical structure of, 3
to reference prices, 306
to stereotypes, 207
Consumers
activists and, 11, 186
adaptation of, 175
advertising responses of, 208
advocates of, 8
age of, 473
anxiety of, 27
assertiveness of, 223
bicultural, 314
bilingual, 459
bodily movement of, 105
brand-loyal, 677
categorization of, 13
characteristics of, 105, 251
children as, 185
choice of and intentional model (BPM-I) for, 93, 95
citizenship of, 615
collectivistic vs. individualistic, 310
communication of, 455
decisions of, 622
differences in, xxiv
disadvantaged, 165
dynamics between, 209
efforts of, 30
endowment effect of, 303
experiences of, 8, 209
exploitation of, 176
focus of, xxiv
goals of, 355, 639
grouped based on values, 253
guidance of, 30
happiness of, xxiv
idealized system treatment of, 89, 95
identification of consequences by, 250
impacts on, 171
impoverished, 168
impressions of, 62
impulsiveness of, 232
independent self-construals in, 302
independent vs. interdependent, 303–304
individual differences across, xxv
influences on, 305
information of, 10
interactions with marketplace, 351, 611
interdependent self-construals in, 302
interests of, 8
involvement of, 588
issues of, xxiii, 3, 10
knowledge of, xxiii
learning history of, 90
lifestyles of, 174
material deficits of, 178
meeting needs of, xxiv
memory of, 94
migrant, 174
motivations of, 301
negative perceptions of, 207
options of, 306
outcomes of, 8
perceptions of, 13
as performers, 206
personal characteristics of, 190
pitfall susceptibility of, 170
policy issues and, 12
profiles of, 273
protection of, 11
psyches of, 4
psychological constructs for, 168
reception among, 208
rights of, 8
rituals of, 205
scarcity contexts and, 171
segmentation of, 276
segments of, 273
self-image of, 13
sexual orientation of, 208
skills of, 167
spending of, 6
sponsorship and, 282
status of, 168
target view of, 8
technology anxiety of, 27
terminal values of, 254
typologies of, 272, 277
values of, 274
welfare policies of, 63
well-being of, 168
Consumer-situation
in consumer behavior setting, 90
extensional vs. intentional, 95
Consumer socialization
aspects of, 192
children and, 189
materialism and, 195
research in, 189–190
studies of, 195
Consumer traits
assertiveness, 223
deal proneness, 222
dispositional innovativeness, 219, 221
exploratory tendencies, 221–222
impulsiveness, 219, 220, 222, 223
individual difference measures, 224
mavenism, 219, 223
need for cognition, 219, 221, 327, 328
need for uniqueness, 222, 332
prevention focus, 222
price-consciousness, 219
prosociality, 223
regulatory focus, 222
self-control, 222
stability in, 220
susceptibility to normative influence, 219, 223
Consumer vulnerability
contingencies of, 170
definition of, 170–171
reasons for, 172
Consumption, xxiii, 25
advertising, 205
aspects of, 177
bilingual, 460
characterization of, 169
collective narratives in, 206

Consumption (*continued*)
　conspicuous, 639, 643
　constellations, 195
　consumer interactions in, 351
　contexts for, 171, 210, 460
　cultural drivers of, 642
　cultural effects in, 311
　decisions, 311, 358
　displacement, 273
　dynamics, 210
　effects of culture on, 311
　environment and, 172, 174, 640
　ethical, 393, 640, 642, 643
　evolutionary markers of, 273
　experience, 94, 459
　gender and, 205
　history, 90, 92
　indulgent, 351
　influence on identity, 23
　intersection of men, masculinity, and, 205
　lifestyles and modes of, 273
　masculinity and, 206
　methods of, 272
　modern vs. traditional, 273
　opportunities, 166
　patriarchal bargain and, 206
　patterns of, 274
　psychological consequences of, 166
　recognition of, 273
　restriction and, 171, 273
　role of, 209
　shifts in, 209
　social media, 205
　social value of, 190
　sports, 278
　study of, 5
　styles of, 272, 273
　subcultural, 206
　sustainability and, 640
　symbolism of, 190, 195
　trade-offs in, 471
　varied, 273
Consumption adequacy, 168
　aspects of, 179
　governmental role in, 175
　as a guide, 179
　impoverishment and, 172
　threshold, 178
Consumption behavior. *See also* Behaviors
　of children, 185
　shifts in, 361

Contagion
　of goals, 355
　procedures, 567
　social, 458
Contamination, 114
Contemporary young mainstream female achievers (CYMFAs), 206
Content
　competing, 478
　creation of, 471
　delivery of, 471
　price of, 471
　streaming, 473
　surrounding, 478
Contexts
　for activities, 272
　bilingual, 460
　choosing-for-others, 358
　for consumer behavior, 173, 335
　for consumption, 171, 210
　cultural, 173, 639, 640, 642
　for decision making, 629
　of a disaster event, 171
　economic theories and, 436
　effects of, 336, 481
　factors of, 328
　of gender, 205, 206
　of happiness, 639, 641–642
　of media, 209, 471
　of persuasion, 328, 334
　pillars of persuasion, 325, 327–328
　power in, 362
　products in, 305
　for research, 122
　scarcity, 171
　social relationships in, 361–362
　source credibility and, 329
　of traits, 225
Contingency-representations, 93, 94
Control
　of activities, 95
　of behavior, 92
　locus of, 253
　over outcomes, 361, 362
　power and, 361
　of prices, 7
　of resources, 170
　restoration route of, 170
　stimuli and, 92
　top-down processes of, 231
Conventional economic theory. *See* Orthodox economic theories

Convergent validity, 122, 123
Coping
　new normal and, 174
　practices of women, 210
　strategies, 174
Copy tests, 14
Core affect approach, 591
Corporations, 113
　violations by, 114
Counterfactual thinking, 59
COVID-19 pandemic, 596
CPI (consumer price index). *See* Consumer price index (CPI)
Credibility, 14
　assumptions about, 329
　conditions of, 331
　messages and, 330
　persuasion and, 331
　of sources, 329
Criteria
　abstract vs. concrete, 589, 597
　for segmentation, 273
　sociopsychological, 269
　types of, 112
CRM (customer relationship management), 19
Cross-cultural research, 302, 639, 642
Cross-linguistic differences, 459
CT (consumer theory-driven) consumer psychology, 32, 33
Cues
　central vs. peripheral, 611
　perceptual, 190
　sensory, 198
　target, 190
　time as a currency and, 418
　underlying, 190
Cultural capital, 206
Cultural contexts
　material environment and, 173
　material vs. experiential purchases, 639
　prosocial spending, 640
　research, 642
Cultural dimensions
　incorporation of, 315
　looseness (L), 310
　power distance, 308
　tightness (T), 310
Cultural diversity, 309
Cultural group, 313

Cultural identity
  bicultural identity integration (BII), 314
  commitment to, 313
  connections to, 313
  mindset and, 61
  monocultural, 314
  multicultural, 314
  needs of, 313
Cultural meaning systems, 302–303
Cultural orientations
  brands and, 307
  horizontal collectivism (HC), 307, 309
  horizontal individualism (HI), 307, 308
  information processing and, 309
  power and, 307, 308
  reflections of, 311
  vertical collectivism (VC), 307, 308, 310
  vertical individualism (VI), 307, 309
Cultures
  adaptive response, 309
  borders among, 262
  boundaries of, 314
  collectivist, 302, 639
  comprehensive understanding of, 309
  conceptions about, 309
  conflict between, 313
  consumer psychology and, 301
  definition of, 301–302, 313
  differences across, 250
  differences in self–brand connection, 303
  elements of contrastive, 313
  exposure to, 302, 315
  factors of, 301
  frame-switching of, 302, 314
  frameworks of, 302, 313
  heterogeneous, 311
  homogeneous, 311
  horizontal vs. vertical, 307
  ideals of, 313
  identity and, 302
  individualistic, 302, 639
  influence of, 312
  integration of, 314
  interactions of, 313
  manifestation of, 311
  marketing communications across, 262
  material representations of, 311–312
  meaning systems and, 302
  mixing of, 313–314
  national, 307
  norms of, 310
  operationalizations of, 302, 303
  paradigms of, 309
  perceived differences between, 314
  poverty and, 173
  processes of, 451
  representations of, 314
  schemes of, 314
  self-presentations in, 304
  sensitivity regarding, 461
  socialization into, 306
  symbols of, 313
  values of, 262
Customer-based brand equity, 695–697, 704
  antecedents of, 696
  brand equity model and, 696
  brand property and, 696
  consequences of, 696–697
  definition of, 696
  literature review of, 696
  marketing and, 696–697
Customer relationship management (CRM), 19
Customer satisfaction, 457
CYMFAs (contemporary young mainstream female achievers), 206

Danger evaluations, 477
Data, 127
  analysis, 7
  behavioral, 626
  collection, 7, 166
  neural, 626
  representative collection of, 263
  rise of big, 268
Davidson, Donald, 109
Deadlines
  consumption time windows, 422
  time scarcity and, 423
Deception in advertising, 9, 12, 187, 188
Decision making, 47
  action and, 728–729
  adaptive, 193
  affective feelings and, 587
  basis for, 583
  closeness and, 357
  cohesion of, 271
  competitiveness and, 361
  contexts, 629
  developing skills for, 192
  ethical, 393
  expectations and, 429
  explanation of, 109
  feelings and, 584
  framing effects and, 728–729
  heuristics and, 728, 730
  implicit goals and, 728
  impulsivity and, 233
  irrational, 730–731
  loss aversion and, 728
  neural basis of, 622–624, 631, 632
  neural measures and, 621
  options to improve, 8
  political, 175
  population stereotypes and, 729
  power and, 362
  self-report and, 622
  valuation signal in, 624
  value-based, 623
Decisions, xxiii. See also Decision making
  accountability for, 311
  consequences of, 61
  fatigue of, 359
  identity-consistent, 313
  joint, 351
  joint-consumption, 359
  joint consumption and, 362
  low-involvement, 18
  for oneself vs. others vs. jointly made, 352
  overt behavior and, 66
  process of making, 351
  purchase, 351
  restructuring of, 27
Declarative knowledge, 47–48
  activation, 69
  affective reactions and, 583
  memory and, 50
  types of, 56
Deficits
  consequences of perceived, 179
  in desirability, 26
  material, 178
  needs, 250
  resource, 176
  structural, 176
  subgroups with, 175
  values of, 253
Delayed gratification, 233
Deliberative processes, 58

Deliberative system, 66
Demands
　characteristics, 125
　price elasticity of, 675
　price promotions and, 673
Deming, Edwards W., 713, 717. *See also* Innovation Engineering; System of profound knowledge "Plan, Do, Study, Act" (PDSA) theory, 719
Demographics, 325, 327
Dennett, Daniel, 81
　criticism of, 87
Department of Agriculture Division of Program Survey, 7
Depression Anxiety Stress Scale, 642
Deprivation, 175, 176
Desirability, 19
　activities and, 68
　attributes and, 23
　deficits in, 26
　deliberating in, 58
　feelings and, 24
　judgments of, 24
　performance attributes and, 22
　sense of, 305
　social identity and, 23
　sources of, 22, 24
Desires, 80, 82
　amplitudes in, 240
　autonomy, 476
　choice and, 93
　global, 168
　influences on, 131
　innate human, 476
　stickiness in, 239
　toward temptations, 222
　variability and, 228
Determinants
　behavioral, 250
　cognitive, 47
　motivational, 47
Development opportunities, 175
Dialectical examination, xxvi
Diets, 643
Diffusion of innovation theory, 722
Digital tools, 642
Dimensions
　measuring, 120
　observations of, 128
　relationships and, 352
　of self, 125
Directionality, 104
Disadvantage, sources of, 174, 176
Disclosure, 480

Discounts
　effect of, 674
　magnitude of advertised, 678
Discretionary purchasing, 7
Discriminant validity, 120–123
Discrimination. *See also* Racial discrimination
　implicit, 661
　price, 401
　refugees and, 174
　social stigmas and, 172–173
　systemic, 173
Disfluency, 314, 599
Dispositions, 224
Domains
　audience, 274
　compatibility of, 271
　consumer, 220
　consumer psychology, 301, 315
　general effects, 554
　individual differences in, 219
　life, 278, 637
　motivational, 271, 275
　opposing, 271
　specific effects, 554
　substantive, 301
Dualism, 111, 597
Dubious ontology, 82

Ecolabeling, 26
Ecological responsibility, 640
Economic expectations. *See also* Expectations
　assumptions of, 432–433
　consumer sentiment surveys and, 430
　costs and benefits, 444
　economic boom and, 442
　nonconscious cognitive processes and, 430
　optimism vs. pessimism and, 442, 445
　rational expectations hypothesis, 429, 446
Economics
　assumptions of, 432, 436
　behavior science and, 8
　deflationary psychology, 444
　downturns, 173
　emotion and, 441
　expectations and, 429–430, 436, 438
　growth, 7
　inflation and, 432, 444
　information and, 12

　insurance model and, 436
　qualitative data and, 432
　quantitative data and, 432
　rationality, 14
　theories of, 10, 82, 432
　trends and, 435
eECB (everyday ethical consumption behavior), 640
EEG (electroencephalography). *See* Electroencephalography (EEG)
Effects
　contingent, 132
　cross-language, 451
　goal-activated vs. production-activated, 69
　moderation of, 332
　mutation of, 478
　priming, 47
Efficiency planning, 423
Elaboration, 25, 597
Elaboration likelihood model (ELM), 609, 611
　celebrity endorsement and, 518
　consumer engagement propensity (CEP) and, 609
Electroencephalography (EEG), 621, 622, 627
　fMRI vs., 629
　intersubject correlation analysis, 629
　market prediction studies, 629–630
Eliminativism, 107, 108, 111
ELM (elaboration likelihood model), *See* Elaboration likelihood model (ELM)
Embarrassment, 65, 594
Embodied cognition, 63
　amodal symbols and, 553
　concepts and, 559–560
　feelings and, 556–559
　future questions on, 569
　initial work of, 554
　meanings and, 553
　mechanisms of, 554–556
　moderators of, 568–569
　procedures of, 564–567
　symbol grounding problem and, 553
Emoticons, 457
Emotions, 591–598. *See also* Affect; Feelings; Mood
　advertising-related, 481
　anticipated, 133

appraisal of, 64, 582, 584
categories of, 481–482, 591
causes for, 225
certainty and, 333, 335
coding signals in, 584
conceptualization of, 582
conscious experience of, 584, 591
definition of, 582
dimensional systems and, 482
effects of, 64, 600
elicitation of, 584, 591
goals and, 584
information processing and, 592
judgment-based, 131
manipulations of, 584
mixed, 597–598
motivations and, 591, 592
nature of, 235
negative approach vs. avoidance, 591, 600
persuasion and, 340
positive approach vs. avoidance, 591, 600
reactions and, 171
recall of, 584
regulation of, 584
relevance of, 481
research on, 179, 584
as responses, 582
social, 594
stimuli, 584
subjectivity in, 582
transience of, 590
variability in, 584
Empathy, 109
Empirical concerns, 118
Empirical meaning
  ambiguity in, 119
  obscured, 116
  ways of appraising, 119
Empirical research, 91–92
  generated data in, 81
  methodology, 79
  variables in, 81
Enclosure, 566
Encodings, 226
Endorsements. *See also* Celebrity endorsements
  expert, 514, 517
  by gender, 260
  motive for, 253
  peer, 312
  status of, 589
  stereotypes and, 260
  value, 260, 314

Engagement, 609. *See also* Consumer engagement (CE)
  audience, 615
  brand, 612
  definition of, 283
  disposition, 613
  issues in, 283
  marketing, 283
  market-level predictions and, 629
  measurement of, 283
  multidimensional, 613
  negative, 612, 615
  neural activity and, 629
  resource investment and, 613, 616
  sponsorship and, 283
  state-based nature, 612
  styles of, 283, 610
Enterprise social media (ESM), 490
Entities
  attitudes about, 323
  default positivity of, 332
  examination of, 251
  products vs., 251
  theorists, 697
Environments
  adaptation to, 251
  consumption, 172, 174
  cues for anxiety and fear in, 596
  inputs of, 21
  marketplace, 172
  situational features in, 226
  stimuli behavior of, 82
Epiphenomena, 109
Episodic memory, 553
Equifinality, 64
Errors
  confirmation bias, 474
  correcting for, 136
  examination of random, 104
  examination of systematic, 104
ESM (enterprise social media), 490
Ethical consumption, 393, 640–641
Ethics
  of behavioral finance, 736
  code of, 393
  of representation, 209
Ethnicity, 210
Eudaemonism, 637, 640
Evaluations
  biased, 590
  brand name, 587
  categories of, 18
  conditioning, 585–586
  disfluency and, 599

feelings and, 586
hedonic criteria in, 586
information, 587
life domains, 637
metacognitive feelings and, 598
numerical expressions in, 28
self-relevant vs. object-relevant, 589
timing of, 589, 597
Events
  physical states of, 110
  promotional, 274
Everyday Ethical Consumption Behavior (eECB), 640
Everyday spending, 638
Evoked set, 16
Evolutionary purpose of expectations, 437–439, 445–446
Evolutionary theory, 472
Examination
  of activities, 271
  of attitudes, 271
  of entities, 251
  of indexes, 120
  of personality, 220
  of posited effects, 104
  of random error, 104
  of systematic error, 104
Excitation, 49
Exemplars, full-scale, 130
Exercise, 643
Existences
  end-states of, 271
  realities of subsistence, 168
Expectations, 7. *See also* Economic expectations
  accuracy and, 430
  affective influences on, 441–445
  beliefs and, 444
  bias and, 438, 444
  bounded rationality hypothesis, 429–430
  dopamine and, 439
  evolutionary purpose of, 437–439, 445–446
  of highly-involved consumers, 611
  purpose of, 437, 444
  social networking and, 443–444
  stereotype-based, 55
Experiences
  accumulation of, 191
  awareness of, 583
  changes in, 254
  children's acquisition of, 191

Experiences (*continued*)
  of emasculation, 206
  generalizations about, 191
  implications of, 335
  of impoverished consumers, 174
  instantiation of, 229
  interactions and, 252
  lived, 175, 177
  marketing based on, 24
  measured, 129
  metacognitive, 583
  openness and, 221, 314
  representation of, 105
  of sensation, 674
  understanding of changes in, 252
Experiential purchases, 638–640
  research, 641
  types of buyers, 642
Experimentation, 133
Expert endorsement, 514, 517
Explanations
  accounts in, 82
  characteristic mode of, 98
  desires and beliefs in, 82
  extensional vs. intentional, 94
  personal vs. subpersonal levels of, 85
Explanatory modes, 80
Exposition, personal level of, 87, 92
Exposure, 15
  differences in time of, 237
  evaluations upon, 583
  sequence of, 589
Expression, modes of, 86
Extensionality
  brands and, 588
  existential inference, 84
  intensionality vs., 84
  language of, 86
  sciences of, 87
  tests of, 84
Extensional model of consumer choice (BPM-E), 90–91, 95, 99
Externalist program, 87
Extraversion, 231
Extrinsic benefits, 639

Face, 639
Facebook, 490
  algorithm of, 501
  fake accounts and, 491
  memory-keeping, 502
  misinformation and, 506
  norms of, 498
  social presence and, 493

Facilitating conditions, 27
Factors
  correlations among, 123
  distinctiveness of, 120
  emotions and, 125
  empirical measures and, 122
  exploratory analysis, 128
  first-order, 125
  higher-order, 125
  individual vs. situational, 360
  intercorrelated, 125
  loadings of, 131
  second-order, 125
  self, 125
  structure, 131
  variances, 131
Fair-trade products, 640
Familiarity
  closeness and, 358
  ease of, 453
  judgments and, 453
Families
  communication patterns of, 193, 194
  consumption of, 210
  materialism in, 196
  resemblance of, 16
  role of, 194
  types of, 193–194
Fate, tempting, 566
Fatherhood, 209
  sustainability and, 205
Favorability, 21–22
Fear
  appeals, 596–597
  effects of, 65
Feasibility, 19
  complexity and conflict of, 27
  deficits in, 26, 28
  issues of, 27
  judgments of, 29
  obstacles, 26
  perceived, 27
  support systems enhancing, 30
Federal Trade Commission (FTC), 6. *See also* Project MAC
  1974 proposed guideline, 189
  1978 Staff Report, 188
  budget, 11
  Consumer Information Task Force, 10
  guidelines for, 10
  Joe Camel case, 11
  needs of, 9
  projects, 9

proposals of, 186
Section 5 of FTC Act, 11
Feedback
  consensus, 332
  loops, 734
  proprioceptive, 62–63
  sensorimotor, 63
  systems of, 719–720
Feelings, 14, 18. *See also* Emotions; Metacognitive feelings; Mood
  attitudes and, 324
  aversive, 591
  consumer judgments and, 24
  consumption behavior and, 581–586
  depletion and, 334
  embodied cognition and, 556–559
  forecasting, 590–591, 600
  incidental, 586, 600
  information processing and, 590
  metacognitive, 598–599
  power and, 334, 362
  predictions and, 587, 590–591
  regulation of, 591
  subjective, 598
Femininity. *See also* Women
  in advertising, 207
  masquerade of, 209
Feminism, 204
Figure-ground contrast, 598
Financial decisions, 20
Flourishing scale, 640
Fluency, 595, 598, 599
fMRI (functional magnetic resonance imaging). *See* Functional magnetic resonance imaging (fMRI)
Focal objects, 305
Folk psychology, 86, 87, 97, 111
Font, 598, 599
Forecasting behavior, 625, 631. *See also* Neuroforecasting
Formative indicators, 117–118
Formative models, 117–118
4Ps (product, price, place, and promotion) paradigm, 19, 20
Frame of reference, 23
Frameworks, 130, 451
Frequency
  bands, 630
  effect of, 52
  voice pitch and, 454
FTC (Federal Trade Commission). *See* Federal Trade Commission (FTC)

Functionalism, 105
	experimental examples for, 107
	mental states and, 109
	reductive physicalism vs., 109
	states under, 109
Functional magnetic resonance imaging (fMRI), 108, 621, 622
	EEG vs., 629
	market prediction studies, 626–629
	valuation studies, 623

Gain frame, 595
GDP (gross domestic product), 6, 431
Gender, xxiv
	advertising and, 207
	aspects of, 210
	binaries, 203, 204
	conceptualizations of, 204, 206, 209
	consumption and, 205
	contested notions of, 206
	differences, 203
	discourses of, 207
	effectiveness of portrayals, 207
	endorsement by, 260
	ethnicity and, 210
	everyday context of, 206
	fashion and, 205–206
	fluidity, 204, 209
	gendered imagery, 207
	hierarchical relations of, 203
	ideals, 209
	identities, 206
	implications for, 207
	inequality, 210
	inequities in society, 204–205
	intersectionality and, 210
	intersection of advertising, media, and, 205
	issues, 209, 211
	justice, 210
	lenses of, 206
	literature on, 204, 210
	malleability of identities, 206
	marketing and, 203
	masculinity vs. femininity, 203
	in media, 209
	men and masculinity, 205, 209
	models of, 210
	multiplicity in identities, 206
	navigation of, 209
	neglection of, 206
	performances of, 209
	performativity, 206
	portrayals, 207
	relations, 207
	representations of, 209
	research on, 203, 204–205, 211
	in ritualized contexts, 205
	scholarship, 203
	self and, 203
	sex-role concept, 203
	sex vs. identity, 203, 204
	shopping and, 210
	socializing force of, 209
	sociological roots of, 205
	stereotypes, 204, 207
	studies of, 208–209, 211
	theories of, 205, 210
	traditional roles, 206
	undoing of, 210
	as a variable, 204
	video games and, 209
	violence, 206
	vulnerability and, 207
	work associated with, 208
Gender, Marketing, and Consumers (GENMAC), 204
	Behavior Conference, 205
Generality, 130
Generalizable response, 631
GENMAC (Gender, Marketing, and Consumers), 204
Globalization, 60, 262, 313
Goal-object, 610
Goals
	abstraction and, 228
	accessibility of, 234
	accomplishment of, 302
	of ACR (Association for Consumer Research), 5
	activation of, 57, 68
	adoption of, 362
	in advertising, 15
	of advertising, 187, 189
	agentic, 304
	attainment, 304
	behavior and, 250, 355
	brands and, 505
	chronic hedonic, 236
	closeness and pursuit of, 356
	competitiveness and, 360
	consumption decisions and, 352
	contagion of, 355
	disfluency and, 599
	emotions and, 584
	individually held vs. jointly held, 352
	interpersonal closeness and, 355
	maintaining social position and, 309
	maintenance of, 304
	in marketplace, 8
	nature of, 233
	observation of, 270
	organizing principles of, 270
	parallelization of, 355, 356
	partner-oriented, 355
	potential sabotage, 360
	power and, 362
	predicting, 304
	priming of, 57
	pursuit of, 29, 355
	recycling, 251
	regulatory focus and, 356, 599
	satiation of, 355
	self-oriented, 355, 356, 360
	self-presentations and, 304
	self-regulatory processes and, 304
	self-worth from, 302
	setting of, 355
	sharing of, 355
	system-oriented, 355
	transactive goal dynamics (TGD), 355
	value-related, 261
	web of, 355
Goods
	affordability of, 168
	monetary amount of, 674
	necessary for existence, 168
	services and, 272
	situation-specific understanding of, 177
	study of consumption of, 270
	trial probability of, 219
Governmental programs, 175
Government regulation, 10, 186
Grants, 180
Granularity, 225
Gratification, 96, 233
Gratitude, 641
Gray areas, 79
Great Recession, 431
Green Consumption Values Scale, 642
Green marketing, 19
Gross domestic product (GDP), 6, 431
Groups
	as agents, 310
	conformity to values of, 311
	consumer behavior of, 352
	identities in, 13

Growth
  needs for, 250
  opportunities for, 167, 175
  self-actualization and, 641
Guilt
  embarrassment and, 594
  pleasure and, 595
  pride and, 593
  self-worth and, 595
  shame vs., 596

Habits, 107
  choices of, 80
  purchases due to, 18
  system, 503
Handbook of Marketing Scales, 219
Happiness, xxiv. *See also* Subjective well-being (SWB)
  as a consumer characteristic, 639, 641–642
  consumption behaviors and, 642
  cultural contexts of, 639, 641–642
  eudaemonism of, 637
  experiential vs. material purchases, 638–639
  hedonism of, 637
  limited access and, 643
  money and, 637–640
  prosocial spending and, 640
  research on, 641–643
  self- vs. other-focused activities, 641–642
HC (horizontal collectivism), 307
Health risks, 197–198
Hedonism, 640
  activities of, 590, 595
  criteria of, 54
  of happiness, 637
  measurement of, 253
  products of, 417
Helplessness, culture of, 179
Hermeneutics, 81
Heuristics
  anger and, 592
  behavioral finance and, 733
  decision making and, 728, 730
  numerosity, 415
  positive mood and, 588, 590
  processing, 589
  products and, 308
Heuristic-systematic model (HSM), 328, 329
Hierarchy
  of antecedents, 700–702
  of consequences, 702–703
  differences in the acceptance of, 308
  of effects, 16–17
  in interpersonal relations, 307
  levels of, 250
  of needs, 249, 253
  of power, 498
  principles for, 225
  scales to measure, 250
Higher order value (HOV), 641–642
HI (horizontal individualism), 307
Historical periods, 185
Homelessness, 172
Horizontal collectivism (HC), 307
Horizontal individualism (HI), 307
Hostility, 56
Household savings, 8
HOV (higher order value), 641–642
HSM (heuristic-systematic model). *See* Heuristic-systematic model (HSM)
Hubristic pride, 593
Human
  behavior, 104
  information processing, 472, 726
  tragedy, 172
Human factors and ergonomics (HFE), 725–726
Hybrid models, 49
Hypotheses
  of bounded rationality, 433
  development of, 116
  factors in, 117
  formation of, 115
  joint, 433
  measurement of, 104
  of rational expectations, 433
  Sapir-Whorf, 460
  substantive, 121
  testing of, 130

IBRS (Intentional Behaviorist Research Strategy), 88–89
Iconic brands, 313
ICS (Index of Consumer Sentiment), 7
Idealism, 107
Ideal self, 639
Ideas
  contributing to consumer psychology, xxiii
  defense of, 336
  receptivity to, 222
Identification with others, 260
Identities, 638
  aspects of, 23
  consumption and, 23
  decisions consistent with, 313
  development of, 307
  embarrassment and, 594
  ethnic, 176, 313
  formation of, 493–494
  integration of, 314
  intersection of, 210
  longevity of, 502
  management of spoiled, 173
  markers of, 210
  masculine, 207
  navigation of, 209
  related judgments, 24
  salience of, 313
  social media and, 493–494, 502
  theories on, 108, 109
Indicators, formative vs. reflective, 117–118
Illata, 86, 87, 95
Imagery
  analysis of, 209
  fear conditions and, 597
  implicit vs. explicit, 208
  mainstream, 208
  types of homosexual, 208
Immigration, 174
Impact, 340
  of attention, 481
  of celebrity endorsement, 519
  on consumer behavior, 6
  of consumer psychologists, 174, 180
  on consumers, 171
  of impoverishment, 165
  of poverty, 168
  of power distance, 308
  of Project MAC, 11
  on quality of life, 175, 179
  of research, 79
  of risks, 196
  of schemas, 50
  of sources, 332
  of values, 262, 276
Implementation
  intentions in, 107
  mindset for, 58
  prevention, 107
Implicational molecules, 50
Implicit learning, 440–441
Implicit memory, 553
Implicit processes, 621, 622, 632
Implicit theories, 50, 538

Importance
    hierarchy of, 250
    theoretical, 59
    of values, 260
Impoverishment
    consumer behavior in, 165, 169, 172, 179
    designations of, 175
    impact of, 165
    life satisfaction and, 168
    likelihood of, 175
    local vs. global manifestations of, 167
    quality of life and, 165
    racial discrimination and, 165, 167, 173
    reasons for, 172
    research on, 166, 172
    restrictions in, 171
    solutions for, 176
    subpopulations in, 167
Impression formation task, 52
Impulses
    overriding of, 304
    purchasing and, 26, 28
Impulsive behavior
    facets of, 231
    tendencies in, 233
Impulsivity, 303, 597
    across domains, 232
    antecedents of, 230, 231, 234
    attentional, 231
    Barratt Impulsiveness Scale, 231
    behavioral activation system (BAS), 233
    behavioral inhibition system (BIS), 233
    Brief Self-Control Scale, 231
    characterization of, 234
    Consumer Impulsiveness Scale (CIS), 231
    cultural differences in, 304
    decision making and, 233
    dimensions of, 230
    domain-specific, 232
    dynamic model of, 235
    models of personality and, 230
    motivational systems of, 233
    motor impulsiveness, 231
    nonplanning impulsiveness, 231
    PersDyn model and, 239
    prudence vs., 235
    related factors of, 231
    in relationships, 232
    responsiveness and, 234
    self-control and, 232
    self-reported measures of, 233
    stability vs. variability of, 235
    structural model of, 232
    systems of, 28, 66
    temptation and, 235
    trait models of, 233–234
    UPPS scale (urgency, premeditation, perseverance, and sensation seeking), 231
Incidental emotions, 64
Incivility, 592
Income
    absolute, 637
    definition of, 7
    disparities, 177
    distribution, 177
Incongruity intolerance, 306
Incremental theorists, 697
Indeterminacy, 119
Index of Consumer Sentiment (ICS), 7
Index of Leading Indicators, 430
Individualism, 174
Individualism–collectivism, 131
    distinction, 307
Individualistic cultures, 639
Individuals
    adaptation of, 251
    change vs. consistency among, 226
    classification of, 273
    desires vs. resistance in, 231
    dispositional features of, 221
    external response by, 269
    feminist understanding of, 204
    gendered, 205
    identical behaviors in, 270
    independent action of, 310
    interaction of, 309
    profile groups of, 272
    representation of, 277
    role of lifestyles in, 268
Indulgence, 235, 597
Inequities, 165
Inferences, 47, 51
    based on attitudes, 540–541
    based on attributes, 538–540
    based on categories, 542–544
    making of, 105
Influences
    automatic and conscious, 21
    of cognitive and affective states, 236
    conscious vs. nonconscious, xxv
    decision making and, 352
    degree of, 193
    of desires, 131
    domains of, 352
    emotional, 131
    of family communication patterns, 193
    goals and, 352
    on hypotheses, 112
    informational, 131
    literature on, 352
    of metaphors, 455
    mutual, 104, 353
    of predictors, 126
    of peers, 196
    phenomena, 104
    resisting, 361
    social, 131, 269
    susceptibility to, 219
    tactics of, 362
Information
    acceptance of, 474
    access to, 330
    accommodation of, 252
    adaptive, 251, 252
    assimilation of, 252
    attitude-relevant, 333
    attributes of, 192
    availability of, 25
    awareness of sources of, 192
    beliefs and, 475
    changes in perception of, 587–588
    comprehension of, 53
    consistency of, 333, 474
    from daily life, 254
    effectiveness of, 51
    encoding of, 53
    familiarity of, 54
    goal-relevant, 49
    improvement of format, 27
    as input, 583
    integration of, 254, 587
    interpretation of, 52, 583
    latent, 632
    loss of, 133
    mood and perception of, 587
    objective accuracy of, 333
    positive vs. negative, 332
    presentation of, 28
    proattitudinal vs. counterattitudinal, 326, 332
    recall of, 309
    responses to, 14
    retention of, 189

Information (*continued*)
  retrieval, 598
  sharing of, 458, 628
  single-faceted gathering of, 270
  stereotyping, 309
  trends in, 54
  valence of, 332
  validity of, 330
Information processing
  bodily sensation and, 63
  concept mapping, 455
  costs of, 10
  cultural orientations and, 309
  demands, 10
  effects on, 587–589
  emotions and, 595
  of humans, 472, 726
  iconic brands and, 313
  involvement and, 611
  linguistic factors and, 455
  manners of, 326, 586
  mechanisms of, 10
  metacognitions and, 598
  mood and, 587
  power concepts in, 309
  product evaluations and, 587
  regulation of, 584
  stages of, 15, 47
  theory on, 10
Ingroups
  defense of, 309
  standing of, 307
Innovation, 714–722. *See also* Product development
Innovation Engineering, 713–714, 722
Inputs, 674
  of attitudes, 336
  breakthroughs, 478
  environmental, 21
  information as, 583
Inquiry, 137
Institutional review boards (IRBs), 166, 169
Institutional theory, 209, 210
Institutions, 612
Instrumentalism, 112, 119
Insula, 624
Insurance, 638
Integrated marketing communication (IMC), 480
Intellectual cooperation, 79
Intellectual progress, 81
Intellectual property, 721

Intensionality
  criterion, 87
  definition of, 84
  explanation of, 87
  extensionality vs., 84
  fluency of, 88
  intentionality vs., 83, 84
Intent, 187
Intentional behaviorism, 80–81
  models for, 86
  philosophy of, 100
  separation of levels of exposition and, 87
Intentional Behaviorist Research Strategy (IBRS), 88–89
Intentional consumer-situation, 93, 94
Intentional expressions, 83
Intentional interpretation
  consistency of, 98
  development of, 92
  formation of, 93
  verification of, 95
Intentionality, 81
  aboutness and, 83, 85
  collective vs. individual, 97
  conscious experience and, 85
  definition of, 83–84
  Dennett's conception of, 86
  derived vs. underived, 85
  explanation of, 82
  imperatives of, 93
  intensionality vs., 83, 84
  internalist conception of, 88
  predictability and, 84
  reconstructing, 94
  requirements of, 86
  systems of, 84
  tests for, 88
Intentional model of consumer choice (BPM-I), 93, 95
Intentional objects, 93
Intentional psychology, 82
  folk psychology, 86, 87, 97, 111
  intentional systems theory (IST), 86–88, 95, 97
  subpersonal cognitive psychology (SPCP), 86, 88, 95, 97
Intentional reasoning, 87
Intentional stance, 81, 84, 86
Intentions, 80
  interventions affecting, 337
  predicting actions in terms of, 83
  sharing of, 336

Interactions
  anonymous or nonpersonal, 361
  brand-related, 616
  consumer engagement, 612
  consumption and lifestyle, 273
  declarative knowledge and affective reactions, 583
  effects of, 131
  elemental traits with culturally driven processes, 225
  with environment, 226, 254
  experiences and, 252
  peer-to-peer, 312
  personal values, attitudes, activities, and consumption, 270
  representation of, 134
  traits with context, 225
Interests
  centers of, 271
  hidden motives of, 4
  involvement and, 610
  observation of, 270
  satisfaction of, 271
  structures for, 271
Interindividual differences, 219–220
Intermittent scheduling, 423
International Society for Research on Impulsivity, 230
Internet, 473. *See also* Online; Social media; Websites
Interpersonal mentalizing, 107
Interpersonal perception and social media, 496–497
Interpersonal relationships, 641, 643
Interpretations
  development of, 80
  of validity, 123
Intersectionality, 174
  discussions of, 210
  gender and, 210
  of income and race, 176
  in politics, 210
  problems of, 176
  in research, 210
  transformative, 211
Intersubject correlation (ISC) analysis, 629
Interventions, 19, 26
Intra-individual systems, 226
Intrapersonal cognition, 82
Intrinsic benefits, 639
Involvement, xxiv, 15, 609. *See also* Consumer involvement (CI)
  aspects of, 613

from brands, 393
forms of, 610
practical implications, 616
product, 610, 615
situational component of, 610, 615
social and political, 393
state-based nature, 612
IRBs (institutional review boards). *See* Institutional review boards (IRBs)
Irritability, 592
Issues
in causality, 82, 136, 137
in categorization, 16
consideration of, 333
for consumer, xxiii, 3, 10
in consumer psychology, 80
economic, 5
of engagement, 283
feasibility, 27
foundational, 133
gendered, 209, 211
of judgment, 138
legal, 10
LGBTQ+, 206
marketing to children, 186
in marketplace, 169, 176
nonconsumption, 175
nonpersonal, 173
nonreductive physicalism, 110
philosophical, 82
policy and information processing, 10
psychological, xxvi
public policy, 186
societal, 5, 12
strategies for, xxiv
tensions as, 176
in traditional marketing, 521

JCA (Journal of Consumer Affairs), 8
JCP (Journal of Consumer Psychology). *See Journal of Consumer Psychology (JCP)*
JCR (Journal of Consumer Research). *See Journal of Consumer Research (JCR)*
Jealousy, 65
Joint decisions, 351
Journal of Advertising Research, 5
Journal of Consumer Affairs (JCA), 8
Journal of Consumer Psychology (JCP), 5, 165, 185

Journal of Consumer Research (JCR), 5, 12, 165, 180, 185
Journal of Economic Psychology, 12
Journal of Marketing, 5, 185
Journal of Public Policy and Marketing, 10–11
Journal of the Association for Consumer Research, 211
Judgments
basis for, 47, 51, 587
determinants of, 47
dialectical, 305
effect of mood on, 586, 589–590, 600
familiarity and, 453
formation of, 333
if-then linkage, 538, 544
implicit theory and, 538
importance of, 54
issues with, 138
justification for, 311
metaphoric association and, 455
of novelty, 453
omission neglect in, 529–537, 545
overt behavior and, 66
of price acceptability, 678
of risk, 453
shifting of, 315
societal, 172
stereotypes and, 308
subsets in, 53
tasks in, 530
thinking styles and, 305
types of, 62
use of inferences and, 537
values and, 249
voice pitch in, 454
Juvenile delinquency, 172

Kahneman, Daniel, 537
KAPA (knowledge-and-appraisal model of personality architecture). *See* Knowledge-and-appraisal model of personality architecture (KAPA)
Katona, George, 6–8
Kiva, 627
Knowledge. *See also* Consumer Knowledge; Declarative knowledge; Knowledge accessibility; Knowledge activation
of advertising, 186, 191
alternative routes to, 80
analysis of, 79

availability of, 79
categorical structure, 588
of children, 185, 189, 190–192, 194
cognition and, 227, 228
confidence in, 80
in consumer psychology, 82
criteria for the establishment of, 82
decisions and, 50
deficits in, 26
of generated behavior, 94
ideals of, 273
lack of, 29
limitations in, 69
in memory, 48
metatheoretical implications of, 80
nonverbal, 48
personality and, 227
philosophy of, 80
poverty and, 167
of prices, 191, 677–678
procedural, 48, 50, 191
of product categories, 190
proposals for gaining, 82
representations of, 48
retrieval of, 55
scientific, xxvi
self-knowledge, 234
semantic, 47, 62
social media and, 489
storing of, 48, 81
structure of, 14, 190
subset of, 47
summary of, 111
system of profound knowledge, 713
tentativeness of, 100
theoretical, 115
traditional conceptualizations of, 62
transformation of, 50–51
trust of, 80
types of, 47, 50
units of, 48
Knowledge accessibility, 54
conceptualizations of, 66
effects of, 47, 51, 55
traditional theories of, 63
Knowledge activation
comprehension and, 51
conceptualizations of, 49
effects of, 47

Knowledge-and-appraisal model of personality architecture (KAPA), 226–228, 235

Languages
- advertising and, 460
- assertive, 457, 458
- behavior and, 460
- code-switching, 461
- cognitive processes and, 451–452
- consensus, 458
- consumer psychology and, 455–457
- conventions of, 459
- cultural sensitivity and, 461
- development of, 474
- differences across, 459
- emoticons in, 457
- explaining, 459
- figurative vs. literal, 458–459
- hypotheses about, 451
- imperative style of, 476
- influences of, 451, 459
- literature on, 451
- native (minority), 460
- nonverbal cues and, 457
- perceptions and, 451
- proficiency in, 461
- psychological processes of, 104, 451
- schemas in, 460–461
- textual paralanguage, 457
- tone of, 457

Larger-later (LL) reward, 414
Leadership insecurity, 722
Learning
- associative, 519
- automatic information processing and, 439–440, 444
- brands and, 312, 616
- concepts, 16
- histories, 90
- implicit, 440–441
- messages and, 14
- needs, 225
- nonconscious, 440–441
- observation, 196
- omission neglect in, 531–533, 545
- perceptual, 674
- resources, 616
- tensions, 177
- theories about, 518

Leisure, 272
Lenses, 220

Levels
- first-order, 125
- personal and subpersonal, 96

LGBTQ+
- communities, 206
- imagery in advertising, 208
- issues, 206
- representation of individuals, 208
- scholarship, 206

Life satisfaction, 637
- four domains of, 641
- impact of poverty, 168
- materialism and, 639
- voluntary simplicity and, 641

Lifestyle marketing. *See also* Marketing; Sports marketing
- emulation and, 267
- sports marketing vs., 267, 286

Lifestyle research
- analysis and, 274
- applications of, 267
- data and, 268
- distribution models in, 273
- programs of, 273
- uses of, 267

Lifestyles, 267–274, 278–279, 286
Liking, 15, 18
Linguistic factors
- cognitive processes and, 452
- effectiveness of, 451, 455
- information processing and, 455
- metaphor, 452
- phonetic symbolism, 452
- unusual spelling, 452

Linguistic relativity, 451, 460
Linkages
- activation of, 227
- attributes–consequences–values, 251
- attributes–values, 251

List of Values (LOV), 271, 273, 275
Living conditions
- of refugees, 174
- subpar, 171

LL (larger-later) reward, 414
Long-range interest (LRI), 96
Loss
- framework, 595
- of social capital, 171

LOV (List of Values). *See* List of Values (LOV)
LRI (Long-range interest), 96
Luxury consumption, 638
- positive and negative affect, 640
- short term gain, 639

Macrocognitive psychology, 97
Macromarketing, 8
Managerial recommendations, 615
MANCOVA (Multivariate analysis of covariance), 137
Manipulation, 15
- checks in, 133
- of emotions, 584
- of words or symbols, 674

Many-to-many structures, 497
Many-to-one structures, 497
Marketing. *See also* Lifestyle marketing; Sports marketing
- academics and, 8, 204
- activity, xxiv
- backgrounds in, 5
- boundaries for, 9
- communications, 176
- concept of, xxiv, 9
- conceptualization of, xxiv
- consumer psychology and, xxiv
- cross-cultural, 278
- curriculum, 5
- effects on children, 186
- engagement, 283
- environment, 8
- facets of, 5
- fast food and obesity, 12
- feminism and, 204
- gender distinctions in, 203
- globalization of, 315
- job opportunities, 5
- lifestyles in, 267
- literature, 173
- modern, 269
- negative effects of, 199
- neuroforecasting and, 628
- omnichannel, xxvi
- rejection of, 204
- relationship, 278
- of risky products, 196
- strategies and tactics, 8, 250, 286
- tactics and, 168
- teenagers and, 185
- tools and, 19
- traditional topics, 13
- understanding of, 204
- values and, 274
- variables and, 91

Marketing and Public Policy Conference (MPPC), 11
Marketing Science Institute (MSI), 10, 611

Marketplace
  access of, 167, 170
  acquirement of goods in, 170
  behavior, 18
  choices, 80
  conditions, 175
  consumers interactions in, 351
  dislodging, 174
  environments, 172
  feminist understanding of, 204
  goals of, 8
  issues in, 169, 176
  masculinity and, 205
  navigation of, 175
  outcome emphasis, 19
  performance, 206
  predictions, 626–630
  procedural knowledge and, 48
  rejection of, 204
  representations, 206
  restrictions in, 172
  shifting of ideologies in, 209
  stigma, 180
  sustainability and, 11
  types of, 167
  underground, 175
Market segmentation, 4, 12
  identification of, 219
Market-to paradigm, 609
Market-with and among orientation, 609
Masculinity, 205–207
Maslow's hierarchy of needs, 639
Match-up hypothesis, 513. See also Social adaptation theory (SAT)
  attractiveness, 516
  balance theory and, 519
  brand attitudes and, 517
  congruence, 517, 520
Materialism, 185, 194–196, 638–641
Material purchases, 638–640
  functional vs. psychological needs, 639
  research, 641
Material self, 130
  facets of, 125
  scale, 120
Material Value Scale, 642
Material well-being, 179
MD (marketplace-driven) consumer psychology, 31
Meaning, 637
  empirical, 112–113
  of goods and services, 179
  mental, 129
  relationships of, 115
  spurious, 112, 114
  theoretical, 112–113
  types of, 115
Meaning transfer model (MTM), 513
  associative learning and, 519
  conditions for, 516
  effectiveness of, 516
  stages of, 515–516
Means-end chain (MEC) model, 249
  consequences of, 254
  critique of, 251
  elements of, 251
  research on, 251
Measurement
  of achievement, 253
  of brain activation, 108
  correlation, 122
  development of techniques in, 194
  error, 105, 120, 123, 133
  estimation of specificity, 115
  generalizability, 130–131
  of hedonism, 253
  of factors, 128
  physical, 105
  procedures, 117
  requirements in, 116
  of social values, 254
  specificity, 115
  standardized scales of, 250
  theory and, 104
  unobservables, 105
  of values, 252
  variants, 117
Measures
  attractor strength, 228
  correspondence between, 109
  of impulsivity, 231
  of individual differences, 224
  of lifestyles, 270
  in a monomethod design, 121
  of social desirability, 125
MEC (means-end chain) model. See Means-end chain (MEC) model
Media. See also Social media; Traditional media
  capabilities of, 279
  context of, 209, 471
  daily use of, 473
  developments in, 279
  digitally-based, 472
  economics and, 431–432, 436
  effect of medium in, 480
  emotional communication and, 442
  evaluation of, 274
  gender in, 209
  innovation, 473
  interaction between, 479
  intersection of advertising, gender, and, 205, 209
  male gaze in, 207
  as a platform, 471
  richness in social media, 491–492, 499–501
  shifts in, 472
  synergy in, 480
  as text, 209
  time spent with, 473
  types of, 209
Medial prefrontal cortex (MPFC), 624
  neuroforecasting, 626
  value integration, 628
Mediation, 473
  of variables, 128
Meditation, 643
Memory, 727–728
  accessibility in, 60
  of advertising, 480–481
  associations in, 20
  in behavioral finance, 731
  concepts in, 582, 583
  consumers and, 94
  cultural, 502
  declarative knowledge, 50
  definition of, 727
  distribution of, 49
  episodic, 553
  explicit, 727
  Facebook, 502
  implicit, 553, 727
  inferences based on, 20
  judgments and, 48
  malleability of, 502
  mixed emotions and, 597–598
  modalities in, 49
  mood effects on, 588
  omission neglect in, 531–533, 545
  priming of, 727
  retrieval of, 47, 727
  salient attribute information in, 20
  social media and, 502
  in women, 50
  working, 553

Mental events, 105. *See also* Attitudes; Intentions
　interaction of, 107
　postulation of, 109
Mental imagery, 553
Mentalities of corporate entities, 173
Mental meanings, 129
Mental phenomena, 83
　aspects of, 108
　dimensionality of, 127–128
　meaning of, 110–111
Mental processes, 674
Mental representation theories, 49, 63
Mental schema, 252. *See also* Schemas
Mental state, 105, 126
　casual relations of, 110
　existence of, 108
　interaction of, 110
　interpretation of, 109
　realization of, 111
　as variables, 112
Mental structure, 129
Mental variables, 82
Mereological consistency, 97
Mereological fallacy, 86, 87
Mesocognitive psychology, 96
Messages
　advocacy and, 339
　antecedents and consequences of, 335
　appeals in, 311, 312
　arguments and, 14
　assertive cues in, 476
　attitude certainty and strength of, 332
　avoidance of, 479
　categories of, 478
　characteristics, 274
　consistency, 333
　construction of persuasive, 339
　content of, 326, 327
　counterarguments to, 326, 331, 332, 340, 475
　creativity of, 478
　credibility of, 330
　delivery and, 15
　effects, 332, 336
　emotional states and, 333
　factors in, 326–327
　framed as gains, 222
　generation of, 340
　implementation of, 478
　implications of, 334
　independent effects of, 325
　learning and, 14
　neutral, 326
　number of arguments in, 326
　one-sided, 326
　persuasiveness of, 324, 325, 327, 331, 615
　playback/recall and, 14
　position of, 326, 332
　positive responses to, 222
　power and, 339
　predicting effectiveness of, 308
　proattitudinal, 326, 332
　processing of, 328, 334, 472, 589
　reactions against, 479
　receptiveness to, 326
　rejection of, 472, 479
　related thought, 334
　repetition of, 326
　resistance to, 332
　scrutiny of, 329
　self-generated, 340
　source of, 475
　strength of, 332
　strong vs. weak arguments in, 326
　structure of, 475
　target preferences of, 340
　two-sided, 326
　valence of, 332
　warmth of, 339
Metacognition
　activity in, 335
　affective responses and, 583
　certainty, 330
　definition of, 583
　effects of, 333
　experiences of, 25
　factors in persuasion, 329
　feelings of, 583
　psychological certainty, 329
　reasoning, 334
　systems of, 95
　variables in, 329
Metacognitive feelings, 600
　disfluency, 599
　fluency, 598
　information processing and, 598
Metatheoretical frameworks, 79
Metatheoretic Model of Motivation and Personality (3M), 225
Method bias, 132–133
Methodologies
　alternatives in, 81
　evaluation of, 81
　of investigation, 82
　problematic, 479
#MeToo, 705
Microcognitive psychology, 96
Microlending, 627
Migrants, 174
Migration, 174
Military psychology, 725
MIMIC (multiple indicator multiple cause) model, 119
Mimicry, 67
Mind, 104
Mind–body influence, 552–553, 569–570
Mind–body theories, 104, 105
　concerns in, 136
　dualist, 107, 111
　monist, 107
　physicalist, 107
Mindfulness, 643
Mindsets
　acquisition, 60–61
　action, 59
　activation of, 59
　application of, 59–60
　behavioral influence of, 61
　bolstering, 59
　chronic, 60
　collectivistic, 309
　conformity, 59
　counterarguing, 59
　culturally distinct, 309
　culture-related, 61
　individualistic, 310
　individuating, 309
　influences of, 58
　prevention-focused, 356
　promotion-focused, 356
　stereotyping, 309
　types of, 57, iv
　uncertainty-avoidance, 58
　visual processing, 60
　which-to-choose, 58
Mirror neurons, 432
Missions, 176
Modality, 48
Models
　benefit of, 125
　categorization, 16
　causal, 276
　concept learning, 16
　constraints of, 472
　covariance structure analysis, 276
　elaboration likelihood, 13
　of gender, 210
　health belief model, 30
　hierarchy of effects, 4

hierarchy of personality, 225
of judgment, 13
means–end chain (MEC), 249, 250
Metatheoretic Model of Motivation and Personality (3M), 225
modified, 251
multi-attribute, 13, 22
multifactored, 125
multiprocess, 329
of personality, 225
of persuasion, 327
of planned behavior, 27
procession of, 251
psychological continuum, 279
self-regulatory, 170
specification of, 133
validity, 122
Models of personality
dynamic, 220
five-factor, 220, 221
guiding principles behind, 226
impulsivity and, 230
PersDyn, 228, 235, 239
six-factor, 221
structural, 228
Models of persuasion
elaboration likelihood model (ELM), 328, 329
heuristic-systematic model (HSM), 328, 329
Moderators, 131
Modern behaviorism, 81
Money, 637
experiential purchases, 638–640
happiness and, 637–640
material purchases, 638–640
perceived value of, 674
subjectivity of, 673
Monism, 107, 109
Monomethod biases, 121
Mood. *See also* Emotions
aesthetic experiences and, 590
appraisal of, 582
brand attitudes and, 25
conceptualization of, 582
consumer judgment and, 586
definition of, 582
implications of, 586
impressions and, 587–588
information processing and, 587, 588
judgments and, 589–590
maintenance, 590
perception and, 587

persuasion and, 327
processing disfluency and, 599
repair, 590
sources of, 25
subjectivity in, 582
transitory state, 587
Mood-based behavior, 25
Mood-congruent recall, 25
Mood-influenced purchasing, 21
Mood repair
conceptualizations of, 64
motivation and, 65
Mood states, 250
Morality
advocacy and, 337
approaches to, 114
behavior, 137
conviction, 337
Motivation, 98, 336
of audience, 327
of behaviors, 250
compensatory, 338
competitiveness and, 359
domains of, 271, 275
emotional, 275
evolutionary perspective of, 474
factors of, 4
fans, 278
fluctuation of, 360
implications for, 360
levels of, 335
mood repair and, 65
power and, 362
to process messages, 328
pull of, 228
rational, 275
research on, 4
role of, 341
self-reports of, 80
source credibility and, 329
state of, 631
strengthening of, 30
theory of, 250
values and, 275, 277
variables of, 610, 612
Movies
affect and, 591
trailers, 629
MPFC (medial prefrontal cortex).
See Medial prefrontal cortex (MPFC)
MPPC (Marketing and Public Policy Conference), 11

MSI (Marketing Science Institute).
See Marketing Science Institute (MSI)
MTM (meaning transfer model).
See Meaning transfer model (MTM)
MTMM (multitrait-multimethod) matrix, 123
Multicollinearity, 125–126
Multidimensional constructs, 120
Multifinality, 57
Multimethod design, 133
Multiple indicator multiple cause (MIMIC) model, 119
Multiple realizability, 110
Multiple regression, 127, 132
Multiplicity, 170
Multivariate analysis of covariance (MANCOVA), 137

NAcc (nucleus accumbens).
See Nucleus accumbens (NAcc)
Natural catastrophes, 174
Needs. *See also* Values
for activity, 225
for arousal, 225
belongingness, 250
for cognition, 219, 221, 327, 328
consumer research and, 250
of consumers, xxiv
cultural identities and, 313
deficit, 250
for esteem, 250
of Federal Trade Commission (FTC), 9
fulfillment of, 175, 637
functional vs. psychological, 639
for growth, 250
hierarchy of, 249, 253
higher order, 250
for learning, 225
levels of, 250
for love, 250
material, 225
physical/bodily, 225
physiological, 250
for safety, 250
satisfaction of, 250
self-actualization, 250
social, 639
for uniqueness, 222, 332
unmet, 732
wants and, 638
Negative emotions, 64
Network, 236

Neural activity
  frequency bands, 629
  generalizable, 631
  predicting outcomes, 622, 628
  reward and valuation, 626
Neural measures, 621–622, 624
Neural mechanisms, 621, 631
Neural predictors, 621, 624–625
Neural reuse principle, 554
Neurocognitive behavior systems, 96
Neuroforecasting, 621, 625–632. *See also* Predictions
  aggregate behavior, 626
  crowdfunding, 628
  effort and cost, 628
  fMRI studies, 626–629
  generalizable response, 631
  microlending, 627
  movie trailers, 630
  online content, 628
  outside the laboratory environment, 629–630
  point-of-sale advertisements, 628
  research on, 622, 627, 631
Neuroimaging studies, 623
Neuromarketing, 630
Neuroscience
  caveats, 631
  research, 630
  testable hypotheses, 621, 632
  underlying mechanisms, 621
Neuroticism
  emotional stability and, 232
  impulsivity and, 231
Nomological generalizability, 131
Nomological validity, 125, 128
Nonchoice neural activity, 625
Nonconscious cognitive abilities, 436–439, 444. *See also* Conscious cognitive abilities
  benefits of, 446
  "black box", 438–439
  concerns of, 438
  processes of, 437, 439
  rationalizations and, 438
  revision of expectations and, 437
Nonconscious learning, 440–441
Nonoccurrences, 529
Nonpersonal issues, 173
Nonprofit organizations, 175–176
Nonreductive physicalism, 109
  definition of, 111
  issues for, 110
  popularity of, 111

Nonreductive realization physicalism (NRP), 110–111
Non-Western consumers, 639
Norms
  accountability of, 311
  action and, 310
  beauty, 310
  challenges to, 209
  in collectivistic vs. individualistic cultures, 309
  compliance with, 309, 310
  definition of, 310
  deviations from, 310, 311
  as drivers of behavior, 310
  enforcement of, 311
  heteronormative, 206
  of intended audience, 311
  looseness (L) of, 310
  monitoring of, 311
  reinforcement of, 301
  system of, 309
  tightness (T) of, 310
  variation in, 309
Nostalgia, 66
NRP (Nonreductive realization physicalism), 110–111
Nucleus accumbens (NAcc), 624
  generalizable response, 631
  neuroforcasting, 626
  positive affect, 628
Number processing, 674
  "mental number line" and, 440
  numerical differences, 28
  numerosity heuristic, 415
Nutritional education programs, 176

Object categorization, 305
Objectives, 271
Object permanence, 530
Observable phenomena, 105
Observation, 81
Observation learning, 196
OFC (orbital frontal cortex), 623
Olfactory stimulation, 64
Omission detection, 537–545
Omission neglect
  acts of commission and, 531
  acts of omission and, 531
  alignable differences and, 537
  consumers and, 529
  decision making and, 537
  definition of, 529
  Ellsberg paradox and, 537
  fault-tree effect and, 537
  gambling and, 537

  information processing and, 530
  in judgments, 529–537, 545
  in learning, 531–533, 545
  in memory, 531–533, 545
  omission insensitivity, 537
  perception and, 530, 531
  research on, 529
  self-perceptions and, 530–531
  sensitivity to, 545
"One look" campaigns, 480
One-to-many structures, 497
One-to-one structures, 497
Online. *See also* Internet; Social media
  content, 628
  media platforms, 629
  sharing, 628
Ontological meaning, 129
Operand resources, 611, 613
Operant resources, 611, 613
Opinions
  expressions of, 337
  on respective environments, 271
Opportunities
  for growth, 167
  for personal advancement, 168
Opportunity cost, 417
Optimism, 641
Orbital frontal cortex (OFC), 623
Organizational performance, 612
Organizations
  hybrid of, 176
  nonprofit, 175
Orientations. *See also* Cultural orientations
  associated cultural values, 307
  bias and, 236
  chronic vs. situational, 61
  horizontal, 307
  inductions of, 61
  promotion and prevention, 61
  sociosexual, 236
  vertical, 307
Orthodox economic theories
  context and, 436
  costs and benefits, 444
  failure of, 438
  federal statistical agencies and, 436
Other-focused spending, 640–641
Outcomes
  avoidance of negative, 222
  control over, 361, 362
Output generation, 47
Overconsumption, 227

Overt behavior
　causes of, 80
　generation of, 66
　transformation into, 67

Parental socialization types, 194
Parent brand, 56
Partial least squares (PLS), 138
Patterns
　emergence of, 236
　equilibrium of, 309
　granularity in, 226
　of healthy eating, 198
　of information processing, 309
　materialism, 196
　of media consumption, 274, 472
　predicting purchase, 278
　of recurrence, 229, 238
　repetition of, 227
　of variation, 312
PDB (power distance beliefs), 308
PDSA ("Plan, Do, Study, Act") theory, 719–720
Perceived ability, 28
Perception-behavior link, 21, 67
Perceptions, 13, 21, 727–728
　of advocacy, 338
　affecting, 251
　of attitudes, 324, 333, 336, 338
　brain function and, 674
　conflict vs. harmony, 314
　definition of, 727
　distance vs. overlap, 314
　implications of, 55
　languages and, 451
　about products, 453
　of risks, 727
　satisfaction and, 307
　sound-symbolic, 453
　of source credibility, 330
　of status, 308
　thinking styles and, 305
　of validity, 330
　voice pitch and, 454
Perceptual cues, 187
Perceptual symbol systems, 63
Performances
　gendered, 206
　predicting, 479
Performativity, gender, 206
Performing, 176
Peripheral message aspects, 15
Permanence in social media, 492, 502–503, 505
Personal capacities, 172

Personal choice, 98
Personal criteria, 131
Personality. *See also* Personality's Big Five
　baseline for, 228
　categories of, 220
　characterization of, 220, 221, 222, 235
　deviation from, 228
　dimension of, 231
　disorders, 230
　dynamic models of, 220
　elements of, 220
　examination of, 220
　facets of, 221, 230
　guides to, 226
　hierarchy models of, 224–225
　identifications in, 219
　impulsivity in, 231
　inferred differences in, 233
　interindividual differences of, 220
　items, 219
　knowledge and, 227
　pattern of changes in, 228
　PersDyn model, 228
　processes and, 226, 227
　psychology and, 219
　representations of, 220
　research on, 219, 221, 269
　role in consumer behavior, 221
　six-factor model of, 221
　stability of, 220
　stereotypes of, 260
　structural approach to, 220, 226, 232
　theories on, 219, 225, 231
　traits, 221, 338
　underpinnings of, 219
　variables, 220, 227, 269
　views of, 230
　vocabulary of, 221
Personality's Big Five, 224–225, 232
　agreeableness, 221, 223
　conscientiousness, 221
　extraversion, 221, 223
　neuroticism, 221, 223, 224
　openness, 221
Personalization, 616
Personal significance, 129
Personal status, 307
Perspectives
　adjustment of, 174
　advocacy, 323, 335
　binary, 206
　classic, 323, 335

　on cognitive explanations, 81
　complementary, 82
　consumer behavior, 179, 285
　of dynamic systems, 220
　evolutionary, 309
　of fan, 285
　of healthy values, 641
　individual, 271
　influences on, 81
　interindividual, 231
　metacognitive, 323, 335
　societal, 271
Persuasion, 13, 14. *See also* Pillars of persuasion; Reactance; Resistance
　advertising and, 475
　assertive language and, 457
　attacks of, 332
　attempts at, 472, 474
　attention to, 323
　attitude certainty and, 324, 329, 330, 342
　avoidance of, 475
　backfire effect of, 331
　barriers to, 478, 480
　certainty emotions and, 333
　closeness and, 456
　code-switching in, 461
　cognition in, 327
　consumer-mediated, 474
　contestation of, 475
　context of, 328, 334
　credibility and, 325, 331
　developments in, 325
　distractions and, 327
　early views on, 323
　ease in, 333
　effects of, 324, 325, 332, 475
　efforts in, 335, 476
　elaboration likelihood model (ELM), 328–329
　emotion and, 340
　evolutionary perspective on, 474
　facilitation of, 331
　heuristic-systematic model (HSM), 328–329
　hindering of, 331
　implications for, 333
　integration of, 480
　intelligence and, 327
　intentions, 336, 339
　interpersonal attempts at, 477
　literature on, 325
　mediated attempts of, 474
　message repetition and, 326

Persuasion (*continued*)
   metacognition and, 329, 333
   moods and, 327
   numerical status on, 332
   objectives in, 479
   outcomes of, 323, 334
   persuasion knowledge model (PKM), 475, 476, 477
   persuasive messages, 324
   process of, 327, 335
   production of, 325
   product presentation and, 326
   protection from, 478
   quality of arguments for, 326
   reduction of, 327
   reflections about, 329
   responses to, 472, 474
   self-validation hypothesis on, 330
   situations of, 335
   source credibility and, 329, 331
   speech rates and, 454
   stimulated cues of, 475
   tactics, 327
   target selection in, 340
   thinking conditions and, 328
   third-person effect, 476
   thought confidence in, 329
   understanding of, 15
   variables in, 325, 328
   voice pitch and, 454
   word of mouth and, 458
Persuasion knowledge model (PKM), 475, 476, 477
Persuasion research
   classic perspectives in, 325
   developments in, 328
   subareas of, 330
Persuasive processes, 14
PFC (prefrontal cortex). *See* Prefrontal cortex (PFC)
Phenomena
   meaning of, 110
   mental vs. physical, 105, 110
Philosophy
   contributions to, 86
   intentionality and, 83
   issues in, 82
   of knowledge, 80
   literature on, 111
   of intentional behaviorism, 100
   perspectives in, 119
   psychology and, 79
   of research, 80
   of science, 81
Phonetic symbolism, 452–453

Physical phenomena, 105
Physical stance, 86
Physiological reactions, 62, 582
Picoeconomics, 96
Pillars of persuasion, 328, 329, 336. *See also* Persuasion
   audience, 325, 327
   context, 325, 327–328
   message, 325, 326
   source, 325
PKM (persuasion knowledge model). *See* Persuasion knowledge model (PKM)
Plan activation, 67
"Plan, Do, Study, Act" (PDSA) theory, 719–720. *See also* Deming, Edwards W.; Product development barriers
Planning, 80
Platforms. *See also* Social media platforms
   elements of, 279
   firms, 471
   media and, 471
   reach, 279
Pleasure, 482
PLS (partial least squares), 138
Political science, 429
Population surveys, 433
Positions, 177
Positive emotions, 66
Possessions
   meanings of, 167
   self and, 203, 303
Postpurchase, 18
Poverty. *See also* Impoverishment
   alleviation goals in, 173
   children living in, 196
   complexities of, 175
   conferences on, 210
   consumer vulnerability and, 172
   cultural reasons for, 173
   decreases in, 176
   dimensions of, 179
   as a factor, 167
   governmental focus in, 175
   holisitic approach to, 177
   intergenerational conditions of, 168
   levels of, 168
   measures of, 175
   methods of dealing with, 170
   problems associated with, 174
   rate, 165
   reality of, 177

   responses to, 175
   studies of, 171, 180
   subcultural reasons for, 173
   theories on, 171
   thresholds, 165, 175
   understanding of, 179
   vulnerability and, 169
   ways to resolve, 175–176
Power, 352
   abuse of, 307
   baseline vs. salient, 307
   conceptualization of, 308, 309
   control and, 361
   cues, 308
   cultural orientation and, 307, 308
   decision making and, 362
   definition of, 352
   distance, 308
   dynamics of, 362
   effects of, 339, 362
   feelings and, 334, 362
   goal pursuit and, 362
   hierarchies of, 498–499
   high vs. low partners, 362
   holders of, 307
   interpersonal, 361, 362
   literature on, 362
   messages and, 339
   motivation and, 362
   of narratives, 479
   nature of, 362
   positions of, 362
   powerlessness vs., 362
   predictive, 277
   psychological, 308
   relationships and, 352, 361, 362
   relative, 362
   responsibility and, 307, 352, 361
   self-regulation and, 362
   in social contexts, 362
   of sources, 326
   status and, 307, 309
   values of, 313
Power distance beliefs (PDB), 308
Predecisional distortion, 590
Predictability, 84
Predictions, 621. *See also* Neuroforecasting
   aggregate, 629, 630
   analytics of, 632
   feelings and, 587
   generalizability of, 131
   market-level, 622, 625, 626–630, 631
   predecisional activation, 624

predictors, 126
scaling, 630–631
success of, 17
traditional vs. neural measures, 628, 630
types of, 18
Preferences, 630
   definition of, 622
   hypothetical, 623
   increase of, 66
   learned vs. innate, 270
   music, 626
   neural processes of, 622
   reflection of, 359
   research on, 623
Prefrontal cortex (PFC), 96, 434, 442, 623
Prepurchase, 18
Prevention orientation, 61
Price control, 7
Price information
   buyer behavior, 673
   exposure to, 674, 679
   presentation of, 674, 679
   processing, 674, 682
Price-matching, 13
Prices, 50
   acceptability of, 678–679
   actual vs. reference, 675
   alliterative vs. nonalliterative promotions, 453
   anchoring effect on, 678
   attractiveness of differences in, 685
   checking of, 351
   comparative judgments of, 673–675
   of content, 471
   contrast effect on, 678
   demand and, 673
   differential thresholds of, 675, 676, 677
   distribution of, 677
   elasticity of, 675
   encoding of, 674, 679
   external market, 678
   fluctuation of, 678
   increases and decreases in, 675
   inflation and, 7–8
   influences to, 675
   integrity of, 678
   internal reference price, 674, 676, 677
   knowledge of, 191, 677–678
   latitude of price indifference, 675, 677
   magnitude of, 677, 681
   mental representation of, 678
   numerical differences between, 674
   perceived changes in, 673, 675, 677
   percentage changes of, 677
   premise of, 673
   presentation of, 681
   promotions, 673, 677, 682
   reduction amount, 677
   reference, 677
   relative expensiveness and, 676
   representation of, 680
   responses to, 91, 676
   sensitivity to, 675, 677
   setting and managing of, 674
   as stimuli, 674
   thresholds of, 677
   unacceptable, 676
   variation of, 677
Pride, 66, 97, 593–594
Primes, semantic, 598
Priming
   duration of effects, 52
   tasks, 52
   unconscious effects, 53
Priori attitude, 58
Priorities, 260
Priority planning, 423
Privacy, 12
Problem solving, 553
Procedural knowledge
   marketplace and, 48
   representation of, 50
   shopping and, 191
Procedures
   definition of, 565
   of embodied cognition, 564
   estimation, 134
   methodological, 112
   multiple regression, 125
Processes
   of activation, 56
   of advertising, 3
   of categorization, 585
   of consumer behavior, 18
   culturally driven, 225
   decision-making, 250, 351
   explanation, 80
   linear hierarchical response, 4
   mediation of, 227
   of mental comparison, 92
   motivational and goal-directed, 13
   of personality, 227
   postpurchase psychological, 18
   redundancy, 599
   satisfaction of, 30
   shopping, 191
   socialization, 190
   variably motivated decision, 14
Processing
   alternative modes of, 15
   changes to, 588
   deliberative goal-directed, 66
   disfluent, 599
   ease of, 453
   effects of, 68
   fluency, 453
   forms of, 477
   resources, 589
   stages of, 51
   types of, 68
Product development, 251. See also Innovation
   big bang strategy and, 720
   development system and, 719
   extrinsic vs. intrinsic motivation and, 718
   "front end" of innovation and, 719
   intellectual property protections and, 721
   learning lab strategy and, 721
   market value and, 718
   "Plan, Do, Study, Act" theory, 719–720
   psychological challenges, 721–722
   rapid feedback system and, 719–720
   risk vs. reward and, 718
   sales and profit targets and, 720
   static database system and, 720
   variance and, 720
   waste and, 720, 722
Production
   conceptualization, 68
   construct, 67
   meaning of, 128
   preconditions of, 68
Production-activated behavior, 68
Production-governed behavior, 67
Productivity loop, 180
Products
   access to, 8
   adaptation to, 274
   analysis of, 189, 267, 587
   appearance-enhancing, 310
   attitude metaphors of, 455

Products (continued)
    attraction, xxiv
    attribute levels of, 10, 306
    availability of, 166
    awareness potential, 277
    branding of, xxiv
    categorization of, 272, 305
    characteristics, 21, 61, 251
    children and, 189
    choice of, 251, 269, 273
    class, 23, 92, 270
    consequences of, 277
    constellation of, 179
    in context, 305
    cultural frames and, 314
    cultural meanings in, 313
    decisions and, 310
    desirability of, 305
    development, xxiv
    distribution of, xxiv
    entities vs., 251
    evaluation questionnaire, 68
    favorability of, 17
    fit of, 314
    functional considerations of, 62
    hedonic, 251
    heuristics, 308
    intentions to buy, 252
    involvement, 610
    likelihood to try, 221
    offerings of, 313
    perceptions about, 305, 453
    placement of, 306
    positioning, 251
    preferences, 64
    presentation of, 326
    prices and, 306
    prototype, xxiv
    purchase risk of, 311
    qualifiers, 269
    recommendations of, 252
    role of, 272
    sex-role concept with, 203
    social aspects of, 190
    status-oriented, 362
    stereotypes of, 56
    strength of support for, 326
    as symbols, 24
    utilitarian, 251
    values and, 54, 277
    warning labels on, 197
Profiles
    groups of, 272
    if-then, 227
    lifestyles and, 273, 274
    situation-behavior, 226
    by Theophrastus, 268
    types of, 274
Project MAC, 6
    development of, 9
    end of, 12
    impact of, 11
    impetus for, 9
    legacy, 11
Promotions
    attractiveness of, 678
    messages, 677, 682
    mindset, 356
    orientation, 61
    self-regulation and, 304
Proprietary psychometric tests, 79
Prosocial behavior, 176, 627
Prosocial spending, 640
Prosperity, 179
PRT (psychological reactance theory), 474, 476
PSAs (public service announcements), 188
Psychographics, 325, 327
Psychological behaviorism, 105
Psychological brand properties, 692
Psychological challenges
    in product development, 721–722
    in scarcity contexts, 171
Psychological discourse, 104
Psychological distance, 30
Psychological explanation, 93
Psychological flourishing, 637, 640, 641, 642
Psychological identity theory, 107, 109
Psychological processes, 14
    assimilation, 21
    contrast, 21
    differences in, 168
    dissociations, 621
    influence of language in, 451
    inhibition of, 165
    types of, 451
Psychological reactance theory (PRT), 474, 476
Psychological theory-driven (PT) consumer psychology, 32, 33
Psychology, 13. See also Consumer psychology; Social psychology
    Adlerian, 269
    of advertising, 473
    approaches in, 105
    child, 190
    contributions to, 82
    deflationary, 444
    differential, 219
    discursive, 251
    diversity of, 31
    expectations and, 429
    folk, 86, 87, 97, 111
    inflationary, 444
    intentional, 82
    macrocognitive, 97
    mesocognitive, 96
    microcognitive, 96
    military, 725
    mindsets in, 128
    paradigms in, 82
    philosophy and, 79
    of processing advertisements, 478
    relationships and, 352
    self in, 203
    social and cognitive, 5
Psychoticism, 231
PT (psychological theory-driven) consumer psychology, 32, 33
Public policy, 9–10
Public service announcements (PSAs), 188
Purchase behavior
    changes in, 357, 675, 676
    influence of children, 185
    influences on, 13, 24
    intentions, 30, 630
    joint decision and, 351
    metaphors and, 455
    predictions of, 251
    process, 13
    proclivity, 7, 15
    steps prior to, 4
Purchases
    alternatives, 10
    analysis of, 272
    family, 193
    hypotheses of, 272
    material vs. experiential, 638–640
    measures close to, 15
    motivations for, 275
    observation of, 270, 272
    psychological fit, 642
    volume, 303
Purchase sequence, 15
Pure theory, 115
Purpose, 637

Qualia, 108–109, 137
Quality of life, 638
    equity and, 180
    impacts on, 175, 179
    indicators of, 179

Quasi-experiments, 131. *See also* Experiments

Racial discrimination, 165, 167, 173
Radical behaviorism
   deployment of, 89
   explanation of behavior, 94
   extensional explanation of, 88
Random error, 104, 115
Rates
   of adaptation, 638
   of poverty, 165
   of recurrence, 237
   of speech, 454
Rationality, 13
Raw empiricism, 115
Reactance
   attitude bolstering, 476
   avoidance, 474–475
   barriers in, 478
   biased processing, 475
   contesting, 475
   empowerment, 476
   measures of, 479
   optimism bias, 475
   to persuasion, 474
   reducing, 475
   strategies of, 474–476
Reactions. *See also* Affect; Affective reactions
   concepts about, 583
   emotions and, 171
   internal, 303
   against messages, 479
   physiological, 62, 582
   subjective, 583
Reasoning, 553
   assumptions of, 475
   biases in, 474
   circularity of, 224
   cognitive approaches based on, 114
   function of, 474
Recall, 53, 69, 309
   of advertisements, 252, 588
   of brands, 14
   embarrassment and, 65
   endorsements and, 518
   mood-congruent, 25
Reciprocity, 285
Recognition, 15
Recurrences, 229, 237–239
Recycling, 640
Reductive physicalism, 109
Redundancy, 51

Reference prices, 306
Reference system, 28
Referent, 49, 53
Reflective indicators
   factors of, 119
   models of, 117
Reflective system, 66
Refugees, 174
Regulatory fit, 107
Regulatory focus, 107, 304
Regulatory orientation, 107
Reification, 224
Reinforcement
   contingencies of, 97
   origins of, 97
   utilitarian and informational, 94
Relatedness, 638, 641
Relationship psychology, 352
Relationships. *See also* Brand relationships; Social relationships
   between actions and consequences, 251
   with advertised objects, 274
   between attitudes, behavior, and values, 276
   with authority figures, 352
   behavior and, 82
   building, 312
   cause-and-effect, 632
   certainty–advocacy, 336, 337
   complementary, 274
   between constructs and indicators, 121
   consumer behavior and, 94, 351, 353
   between consumer messages and traditional media, 471
   between consumers and brands, 23, 458
   continuity of, 304
   customer–service provider, 457
   dependence, 111
   determination of quality, 284
   directionality of, 116
   egalitarian, 307
   exchange, 179
   hierarchy in, 307
   human, 284
   identification of connections and, 305
   impulsivity in, 232
   between intelligence and persuasion, 327
   interactive, 460

   interpersonal competitiveness in, 359–360
   interpersonal power in, 361
   interrelated dimensions in, 352
   between lack of access and coping styles, 170
   literature on, 221
   malleable, 334
   between mental states, 109
   nonestablished, 352
   of mind to behavior and action, 104
   perceived time in, 359
   perceptions of, 359
   power dynamics within, 362
   between price knowledge and price acceptance, 677
   prototypical definitions of, 353
   reciprocity, 284
   relative power in, 362
   reminders of, 351
   retaining, 282
   satisfaction in, 356
   self–brand, 313
   between sellers and buyers, 19
   sports/brands, 279
   between stimulus and response, 105
   symmetry in, 104
   theoretical dimensions in, 352
   theory-to-measurement, 104
   between traits and behavior, 219
   types of close, 356
   between value consciousness and conscientiousness, 222
   between variables, 116
Relative prosperity, 179
Relevance, 610
Reliability
   computation of, 118
   definition of, 121
   differences in, 131
   incorporation of, 112
   measures of, 119
   of scales, 253
Replication in social media, 492, 503–504
Representation
   commonalities in, 221
   enduring, 227
   lower level, 128
   style vs., 268
Repurchase, 593
Reputation, 305

Research. *See also* Lifestyle research
  on attitude strength, 324
  on brand meaning, 697
  capacity for, 79
  categories of, 33
  on children, 185
  competing priorities in, 5
  context, 122
  discipline-focused, 12
  evaluation of, 31
  experimental-based, 116
  experimental vs. quasi-experimental, 135
  exploratory, 79
  facets of, 104
  in gaming, 209
  impact of, 79
  merging of, 8
  methodologies, 79, 254
  multimethod, 131
  necessities in, 82
  orientations, 3, 31
  paradigms in, 90
  on personality, 269
  on persuasion, 325
  philosophy of, 80
  on physical appearance, 208
  process-oriented, 3
  psychological theory-driven, 33
  regression-based, 115
  scarcity, 169
  on sexual content, 208
  shifts in, 190
  stages of, 82, 97
  strategies, 99
  survey methods in, 190
  system for conducting, 115
  on television advertising effects, 188
  theoretical bodies of, 115
  transdiciplinary, 179
  transformative service, 210
  use of, 136
Resistance
  attenuation of, 238
  fear of deception and, 477
  motives for, 476–477
  suspicion and, 477
  threats to freedom and, 476
  trajectory for, 240
Resources. *See also* Scarcity
  access to, 170
  control over, 170
  deficits, 170, 176
  interventions, 29

  levels, 176
  operant and operand, 611, 613
  reduction of, 477
Responses
  acquiescent, 478
  affective, 229, 583, 585
  behavioral characteristics and, 673
  cognitive, 229
  conditioned, 327
  context effects on, 481
  culture and, 309
  emotions of, 582
  excitation transfer in, 481
  to external environment, 269
  integral affective, 585
  to narratives, 479
  negative, 478
  to price, 673, 677
  psychological, 478
  sensorimotor, 584
  to service failure, 311
  to sex stimuli, 208
  to social coordination, 309
  structure of, 128
  surveying, 478
  tendencies in, 583
Response theories
  adaptation-level, 678
  range-frequency, 679
Responsibility, 207
Restrictions
  focus on, 171
  levels of, 169
  in marketplace, 172
  as norm, 172
  on refugees, 174
  situations of, 173
Retrieval, 598
  cue models, 49
  cues, 49
  ease of, 335
Retrieval effect, 333
Revenue, 471
Rewards
  BAS Reward Responsiveness Scale, 228, 239
  functional, 95
  neuroforecasting and, 626
  primary and secondary, 624
  sensitivity, 92
  sources of, 97
  utilitarian vs. informational, 91–92
  value, 623

Risks
  adolescents and, 196
  alcohol, 197
  cigarettes, 196–197
  consumption, 185, 194, 196
  deterrents to, 194
  endorsements and, 520–521
  health, 197–198
  impact of, 196
  of innovation, 714, 716, 722
  judgments of, 453
  perception of, 727
  pronunciation and, 453
  purchase, 311
  subjective valuation and, 624
Roles
  of advertising, 3
  of attitudes, 323
  of competitiveness, 360
  of consumer behavior, 5
  of consumer expectations, 8
  of consumption, 209
  of family, 194
  gender, 206–207
  of government, 175
  of lifestyles, 268
  of motivation, 341
  mutual understanding of, 309
  of personality, 221
  of products, 272
  sex-role concept, 203
  of sponsorship, 279, 281, 282
  traditional, 206
Routledge International Handbook of Consumer Psychology, *xxiii*
Ruminations, 592

Sadness, 64
Safety, 596
Safety nets, 168, 173
Salespersons, 477, 596
Sapir-Whorf hypothesis, 460
Satiation, 503
Satisfaction
  of interests, 271
  of lower needs, 250
  meaning of, 251
  measures of, 179
  perception and, 307
  of physiological needs, 250
  predictor of, 250
  theory, 251
Satisfaction With Life Scale, 642

SAT (social adaptation theory).
    See Social adaptation theory
    (SAT)
Saving behaviors, 168–169
Scales
    BAS/BIS, 233
    hedonic vs. prudent, 231
    interval-level, 254
    ordinal level, 253
Scarcity, 592
    context for consumers, 171
    definition of, 171–172
    psychological challenges, 171
    reduction route, 170
    research on, 170–171
    situations of, 173
    strategies in, 170
Scene framing, 274
Schemas, 64, 560
    activation of, 50
    alignment with, 252
    consumers and, 544
    experiments on, 544
    impact of, 50
    plan-goal, 57
    theories, 50
Schwartz's Portrait Values Questionnaire, 641
Scientific falsification, 100
Scientific inquiry, 81, 112
Scientific instruments, 79
Scientists
    philosophers and, 86
    private vs. public, 79
SD (self-discrepancy), 639
S-D (service-dominant) logic, 611
Search behavior, 13
Segmentation, 249
    criteria, 273
    geographic/psychographic systems, 272
    global customer, 262
    importance of, 262
    lifestyle, 262
    responses to, 274
    variables, 616
Self, 301
    advocacy and, 338, 340
    agency of, 302
    aspects of the, 203, 227
    consumer behavior and, 203
    consumer research on the, 203
    cultural understanding of, 302, 304
    definition of, 302
    development of, 306

differences in view of, 303
discrepancy theory, 203
emotions relative to, 584
extended, 203
factors, 125
gender and, 203
impulses, 303
independent view of, 302–303, 310
interdependent view of, 302–303, 310
judgments of, 227
looking glass, 203
multidimensional, 203
notion of, 137
personal possessions and, 303
qualities of, 302
sense of, 337
separation of the, 203
situations and, 220
socialization and, 302
in society, 306
Self-actualization, 641
Self-affirmation, 341
Self-awareness, 111
Self-brand connections
    basis for, 195
    cultural differences in, 303
    development of, 195
    between sports fans and sports brands, 279
Self-concepts, 14
    actual, 203
    brands and, 195
    children and, 195
    closeness and, 355
    consistency of, 203
    expression of, 195
    ideal, 203
    possessions and, 203
    psychology of, 203
Self-consciousness, 137
Self-construal, 306
Self-control
    anger and, 592
    facets of, 231
    impulsivity and, 231
    indicators of reduced, 356
    measures of, 232
    pride and, 593
    scales of, 232
    Spending Self-Control scale, 232
Self-determination
    effects of, 168
    theory of, 638

Self-discrepancy (SD), 639
Self-efficacy, 27, 30
Self-enhancement, 458
Self-esteem, 97, 172
    in childhood, 196
    materialism and, 196
    reduction in, 476
    self-perception and, 207
Self-expression, 639
Self-focused spending, 640–641
Self-image, 207
Self-knowledge, 234
Self-organization
    examples of, 236
    systems of, 240
Self-perceptions
    body perception and, 207
    consumer vulnerability and, 170
Self-persuasion, 340–341
Self-presentations, 304
Self-referent emotions, 65
Self-regulation
    focus, 590–593
    mechanisms, 226
    power and, 362
    prevention focus, 304
    processes, 304
    promotion focus, 304
Self-relevance
    appraisals and, 584
    fear and, 597
Self-reliance, 307
Self-reports
    of behavior, 133
    consumer research and, 622
    effectiveness of, 478
    of preferences, 624
    problems in, 80
    ratings and, 629
    reliance on, 631
    surveys and, 478
Self-sufficiency, 640
Self-transcendence, 641
Self-uncertainty, 337
Self-validation hypothesis, 329
Semantic knowledge, 47, 62
SEMs (structural equation models).
    See Structural equation models (SEMs)
Sense modalities, 48
Sensitivity, 675
Sensorimotor
    feedback, 63
    stimulation, 63
    system, 553–554, 560

Sensory experiences, 64
Sentiment Index, 434–435
Service delivery, 176
Service-dominant (S-D) logic, 611
SET (social exchange theory), 284, 285
Sex appeals, 208
Shame, 97, 594–596
Shopping
  belief-based, 393
  momentum, 58
  motives for, 221
  procedural knowledge for, 191
  process, 191
  scripts, 191
  transformation from experiences to scripts, 191
Shortages, 169
Short-range interest (SRI), 96
Sight, 563–564
Situational factors, 47
  influence of, 61
  self and, 220
  types of productions in, 68
Situation-trait interaction, 98
Sleeper effect, 54
Smaller-sooner reward (SS), 414
Smart agents, 30
Smell, 562–563
Snapchat, 490
  memory malleability, 502
  psychological reward, 503
Sociability, 307
Social
  adaptation, 275
  behaviors, 310, 624
  causes, 19
  communications, 455
  connections, 271, 590, 638
  contagion, 458
  coordination, 301–308
  desirability, 125
  diffusion, 92
  entrepreneurship, 176
  influence, 478, 622, 626
  marketing, 9, 26, 210
  movements, 211
  needs, 639
  networks, 641
  patterns, 309
  presence, 491–494
  processes, xxiv, 451
  reality, 54
  resources, 26
  reward, 624

stigmas, 172
support, 196
understanding of, 176
Social adaptation theory (SAT)
  attractiveness and, 517
  cognition and, 286
  description of, 251
  formation of values and, 254
  match-up hypothesis and, 516–518
  values and, 252
Social and cognitive psychology, 5
Social exchange theory (SET), 284
Social identity
  aspects of, 126
  components of, 125
  concepts of, 13
  desirability and, 23
  theory, 498
Social interactions
  coordination of, 310
  evolution of, 474
Social intuitionist model, 114
Socialization
  efforts in, 194
  self and, 302
  sports and, 278
Social media, xxiv
  application of empirical models via, 277–278
  brands and, 493
  collective memory and, 502
  consequences and, 489
  crowdsourcing platforms and, 497
  cultural memory and, 502
  definition of, 489, 490–491
  ephemerality and, 502
  goals and, 491, 494, 505
  governments and, 491
  habits and, 503
  happiness and, 642
  identity formation and, 493–494, 502
  interpersonal perception and, 493
  irony and, 497
  knowledge development and, 489
  monetization within, 209
  narcissism and, 493
  negative effects of, 504
  online communities and, 490
  permanence in, 492, 502–503, 505
  "phantom" users, 491
  polarization and, 501, 505–506
  political implications of, 505–506

portrait, 267
privacy and, 505
psychological reward, 503
psychology development and, 505
replication in, 309, 492, 503–504
research within, 204, 209
richness, 491–492, 499–501
rise of, 268
routinization and, 491
social presence in, 493–496
social proof and, 491
social structures in, 493–494, 497–499
stereotypes and, 504
surveillance and, 278, 505
temporal structures in, 491–492, 497–499
traditional media vs., 471
usage patterns, 490–491
use of, 262, 282, 490–491
virality and, 497
well-being and, 504–505
Social media platforms. *See also* Facebook; Snapchat; YouTube
  LinkedIn, 490, 498
  Pinterest, 490
  Sina Weibo, 490
  Slack, 490
  TikTok, 490, 498
  Twitter, 490, 498–499
  WeChat, 490
Social networking, 443–445
Social psychology
  concepts in, 13
  conformity, 286
  interpersonal effects in, 352
  recent advances, xxv
  relational factors in, 353
Social relationships. *See also* Relationships
  with consumers, 455
  context of, 361–362
  interpersonal, 641, 643
  pronouns in, 456
Social sciences, 12
Social Security Administration (SSA), 175
Social values
  changes in, 254
  definition of, 261
  expression of, 261
  global, 262
  in marketing, 262
  measurement of, 254
  trends in, 252, 254, 262

Societal distinctions, 307
Societal recognition, 172
Societal standing, 307
Societies, 301
   advancement within, 179
   advertising and, 475
   coordination problems in, 309
   dichotomy between portions of, 172
   evolution of, 254
   expectations of, 306
   fit of self in, 306, 309
   gender inequities in, 204–205
   impoverished consumers in, 180
   multicultural, 314
   position in, 309
   power distance in, 308
   shifting of, 261
   social hierarchy, 306
   structural inequities within, 172
Socioeconomic groups, 174
Socioeconomic status, 13
Sociologists, 13
Sociology, 13
   expectations and, 429
Somatic states, 585
Sounds
   brand performance and, 453
   concepts associated with, 452
   embodied cognition and, 563–564
   repetition of, 453
   speech rates, 454
   voice pitch, 454
Source credibility
   attitude certainty and, 331, 335
   context and, 329
   motivation and, 329
   perceptions about, 330
   persuasion and, 331
   on thought confidence, 330–331, 335
Sources
   ability of, 325
   attractability of, 325, 514–515
   attributes of, 325, 514
   celebrity, 325
   credibility of, 325, 329, 514, 519, 520
   effects of, 330, 336
   familiarity, 514
   impact of, 332
   likability of, 325, 514
   majority vs. minority, 332
   numerical status of, 331, 332, 335
   of persuasion, 325
   power of, 326
   similarity of, 325, 514
Spaces
   domestic, 206
   feminized, 209
Spectral decomposition, 630
Spending
   decisions, 638
   other-focused, 640–641
   prosocial, 640
   research, 639
   self-focused, 640–641
Spending Self-Control scale, 232
Sponsorships
   activation, 283
   as an activity, 281
   as brand image development, 282
   brands and, 279, 283, 285
   capabilities of, 280
   consumer response to, 285
   corporate, 279
   current industry, 280
   definitions of, 279
   development of, 280, 282
   effectiveness of, 282
   engagement and, 283
   examples of, 281
   expenditure, 280
   global market of, 280
   goodwill generation, 283–285
   perceptions of, 279
   as a platform, 279
   as pseudo-advertising, 282
   as publicity, 282
   relationships, 282, 284
   research on, 281, 282
   role of, 279, 281, 282
   scale of, 280
   sports marketing and, 279
   structures, 280
   television and, 280
   types of interactions, 280–281
   understanding of, 282
   undisclosed, 477
   value of, 279
Sports, 278, 286
Sports brands, 278–279
Sports fans, 278
Sports marketing, 278–279
   brands and, 285
   emulation and, 267
   lifestyle marketing vs., 267, 286
   sponsorship and, 279
Spurious meaning, 119
SRI (short-range interest), 96
SSA (Social Security Administration), 175
SS (smaller-sooner reward), 414
Stability, 220
Stakeholders, 177
Stakeholder theory, 177
Starch, Daniel, 3
Statistical Procedures, 103, 116
Status, 639
   of brands, 308
   of consumers, 168
   differences, 173
   of endorsements, 589
   as an icon, 313
   numerical, 331, 332, 335
   perceptions of, 308
   personal, 307
   power and, 307, 309
   products and, 362
   socioeconomic, 13
Status quo, 592
Stereotypes, 308
   activation of, 55, 67
   brand attitudes and, 207
   of brands, 56
   consumer responses to, 207
   country-of-origin, 56
   decision making and, 729
   defense, 475
   depiction of, 207
   effects of, 55
   endorsement and, 260
   expectations based on, 55
   of gender, 204, 207
   information congruent with, 309
   information incongruent with, 309
   judgment and, 308
   mindsets for, 309
   personality and, 260
   of products, 56
   social media and, 504
Stigmas, 173
Stimulation, 478
Stimuli, 22
   abstract, 623
   adaptation level of, 678
   affective, 587, 600
   antecedent, 105
   attractive vs. unattractive, 584
   buying, 230
   changes in, 674
   conditioned responses with, 327

Stimuli (*continued*)
   configurations of, 50
   consumer behavior as, 137
   in consumer behavior setting, 91
   consumption history and, 90
   detection of, 236, 584
   dimensions of, 478
   discriminative, 94, 673
   dynamic, 629
   emotionally relevant, 584
   environmental, 82
   information, 51
   intensities of, 674
   judgment of, 60
   lack of, 92
   magnitudes of, 673
   manipulation of, 109
   mental states vs. physical, 83
   nonverbal, 48
   perceived differences of, 674
   prices as, 674
   priming of, 455
   relative differences of, 674
   representations of, 50
   responses to, 64
   reward vs. punishment and, 90, 585
   salient, 47
   selective attention to, 236
   sensory processes, 623
   sexual, 208
   sources of control and reward, 92
   valence-independent activity of, 585
   value of, 68, 584–585
   verbal discriminatory, 95
Stock market, 596
Stories, 4
Strategies
   acquisition, 179
   adaptive use of, 193
   advertising, 252
   of communication, 251
   for coping, 170, 172, 174
   decision-making, 192
   discursive, 207
   effectiveness of, 262
   emergence of, 192
   evaluation of, 58
   of global brands, 301
   for issues, xxiv
   marketing, 250, 301
   positioning, 251, 252
   self-help, 174
   survival, 172
   switching, 193

Stress, 642
Structural equation models (SEMs)
   advantages of, 133
   applications of, 130
   behaviorism, 105
   benefits of, 135
   courses for, 138
   elements in, 112
   experiments with, 112
   features of, 110, 133
   group analyses by, 133
   implementation of, 132
   lens, 105
   multicollinearity and, 126
   opportunities to use, 103
   principles in, 130
   problems with, 103, 133, 138
   procedures in, 116
   programs, 138
   research on, 107, 110
   traditional methods vs., 103
   use of, 131, 132, 133, 137, 138
Structures
   organization of, 128
   in social media, 493–494, 497–499
   traditional family, 206
Studies. *See also* Research
   cross-cultural, 276
   development of, 270
   empirical, 271
   motivational, 268
Style-of-processing scale, 60
Subcortical structures, 623, 631
Subgoal concepts, 67
Subjective experiences, 62, 63
Subjective valuation, 623
Subjective well-being (SWB). *See also* Happiness
   affective vs. cognitive aspects, 637
   cross-cultural research, 639
   healthy values and, 641
   luxury consumption and, 640
   materialism, 638
   research, 641–643
Sugared products, 188
Super Bowl advertisements, 629, 630
Supervenience, 111
Survey research
   advances in, 7
   methods, 7
   representative sampling, 7
   SEMs and, 135
   uses for, 4, 7, 136
Survey Research Center, 7

Sustainability
   consumption and, 640
   fatherhood and, 205
   in the marketplace, 11
Sustained behavior, 12
SWB (subjective well-being). *See* Subjective well-being (SWB)
Symbolic symbol systems, 49
Symbols, verbal vs. nonverbal, 309
Sympathetic nervous system, 556
Synchronous behavior, 59
Systematic error, 104, 115, 116
Systems
   automatic reflexive, 229
   aversive vs. appetitive, 233
   cultural meaning, 302
   dynamic, 236
   engineering of, 725
   in which consumers operate, 6
   of norms, 309
   perceptual, 674
   of profound knowledge, 713

Tailored expectations, 434–437, 445–446
Target brands, 306
Target cues, 190
Target marketing, 262
Target product, 51
Taste, 561–562
TCR (Transformation Consumer Research Movement). *See* Transformative Consumer Research Movement (TCR)
Technology, 642
Teenagers, homeless, 176
Television, 629
   commercials vs. programs, 186, 187, 588
   definition of, 473
   intent of, 186
   maintenance of, 473
   streaming and, 473
Television advertising
   banning of, 186
   to children, 185, 188
   concerns about, 188, 189
   effects of, 185, 186
   exposure to, 189
   fairness of, 185
   impact vs. health-related messages, 188
   limitations on amount of, 188
   persuasion of, 186
   targets of, 186

Temporal framing, 20, 29
Temporal structures, 491–492, 497–499
   descriptive vs. injunctive norms, 498
   network theory, 499
   power hierarchies, 498–499
   prosumers, 491
   sentiment-grain, 499
   social identity theory, 498
Temptation, 590
Tendencies
   compulsive buying, 232
   in interpersonal relationships, 232
   situation-specific, 224
Tensions, 177
Tests
   of correlation, 120
   of differences, 130
   of factor distinctiveness, 121
   goodness-of-fit, 117
   of mediation, 133
   of reliability, 122
   of substantive hypotheses, 121
TGD (transactive goal dynamics), 355
TGJF (transformative gender justice framework), 210
Theophrastus, 268
Theoretical development, 180
Theoretical minimalism, 99
Theoretical predictions, 131
Theories. *See also* Mind–body theories; Orthodox economic theories; Social adaptation theory (SAT)
   application of, 177
   approaches driven by, 128
   about associative learning, 518
   attitude-intention-behavior causation, 83
   of attitudes, 338
   about attributes, 503–504, 513, 515, 520
   about balance, 519
   of behaviors, xxiv, 251
   from child psychology, 190
   of cognitive appraisal, 105, 583, 584
   from cognitive psychology, 190
   conceptual metaphor, 455, 560, 565
   construal level, 416
   construction, 112
   on consumer culture, 204
   from decision making, 190
   development of, 253
   diffusion of, 722
   dynamical systems, 228
   economic, 10, 82, 432
   evolutionary, 472
   explanatory, 131
   five-factor, 220, 221
   of gender, 205, 210
   on identity, 108–109
   implicit, 50
   incorporation of, 194
   on information processing, 10
   institutional, 209–210
   intentional systems theory (IST), 86–88, 95, 97
   intercommunication of, 79
   of knowledge activation, 63
   measurement and, 104
   of mental representation, 49, 63
   method and, 128
   mind–body, 104, 105
   of mind response, 109
   of motivations, 250
   about networks, 499
   of personality, 219, 225, 231
   "Plan, Do, Study, Act" (PDSA), 719
   about poverty, 171
   practitioner, 478
   psychological identity, 107, 109
   psychological reactance theory (PRT), 474, 476
   pure, 115
   queer, 205, 209
   reader-response, 205
   of reasoned action, 251
   regulatory focus, 251
   of response, 678–679
   of satisfaction, 251
   of schemas, 50
   self-construal, 251
   about self-determination, 638
   self-discrepancy, 203
   social exchange theory (SET), 284
   about social identity, 498, 518
   stakeholder, 177
   testing of, 253
   tripartite, 96, 324
   of trying, 133
   value, 249
   of variability, 220
Theory–Measurement Distinction, 104
"Think, Feel, Do" process, 15
Thinking
   analytic, 305, 306
   categorization, 306
   conditions, 335
   demands of, 335
   extent of, 335
   holistic, 305
   incongruent, 306
   reasoning, 306
Thought confidence. *See also* Confidence
   attitudes and, 330
   audience effects on, 333
   bodily movements and, 334, 335
   certainty emotions and, 333
   feelings of, 334, 341
   message effects on, 332
   numerical status on, 331
   in persuasion, 329
   reduction of, 342
   source effects and, 330, 330–331, 335
Thoughtfulness, 334
Thoughts
   autonomy of, 222
   effects of, 342
   generation of, 341
   message-relevant, 331, 334
   number and valence of, 587
   salient, 335
   validity of, 330
Threats, 476
3M (Metatheoretic Model of Motivation and Personality), 225
Three-stage model, 88
Three-term contingency, 85, 95
Time
   allocation of, 629
   arbitrary cues and, 418
   construal level theory and, 416
   as currency, 416–419
   deficit of, 417
   definition of, 413
   as distance, 414–416
   economic value and, 416–417, 419, 421
   emotions and, 419
   events and, 415–416
   happiness and, 419
   others' time, 420–421
   patience and, 421
   perspectives of, 413
   product attributes and, 417–418
   psychophysics of, 414
   as quantity, 419–423

Time (*continued*)
  risk and, 418
  scarcity and, 419–420, 422–423
  spatial orientation and, 416
  surplus of, 417
  well-being and, 422
Time-series predictions, 432–434, 446
  education and, 433
  "representative agent" model, 432
  single national comparative standard, 433
Timing
  as a factor, 334
  moderation by, 335
  time as a currency and, 417
Tolerance of deviant behavior, 310
Touch, 560–562
Trade rule regulation, 186
Traditional marketing
  background in, 5
  brand personality studies, 521–522
  celebrity endorser and consumer dynamics, 521
  concepts of, 13
  congruence, 521–522
  experience-based vs. symbolic-based fit, 522
  issues in, 521
  measures of, 630
  relationships in, 281
Traditional media
  abandonment of, 472
  alternatives to, 471
  business of, 471
  consumer age in, 473
  consumption of, 472
  development of, 471, 473
  integration of, 480
  message processing in, 471, 472, 474, 479
  motivations in, 472
  natural advertising in, 478
  persuasion processes in, 472
  platform business structure of, 472
  processing advertising in, 472, 478
  social media vs., 471
  study of, 473
  technological change and, 473
  types of, 471
Trait-method-error model, 123

Traits
  age and, 220
  behaviors and, 219, 228
  cardinal, 224, 225
  central, 224, 225
  characterizations of, 220
  compound, 225
  concepts of, 47, 53
  conscientiousness, 222
  in context, 225
  development of, 227
  elemental, 225
  as elliptical explanations, 224
  emergence of, 227
  evolution of, 220
  extraversion, 222–223
  factors of, 123
  global measures of, 220
  identification of, 219
  impulsiveness, 230, 231, 234
  influence of, 219
  interplay of, 235
  linking behaviors to, 221
  lower level, 225
  manifestation of, 219
  mapping of, 221
  measurement of, 219, 221
  motivational antecedents of, 233
  multidimensionality of, 232
  openness to experience, 221, 222
  self-control, 231
  situational, 225, 232
  stability in, 220
  sublevels of, 220
  surface, 224, 225, 232
  theorists, 219
  unreliability, 224
  value, 123
Transactive goal dynamics (TGD), 355
Transdisciplinary research
  advantages of, 179
  domains, 180
  models in, 180
Transformative Consumer Research Movement (TCR), 12, 176, 204
  conferences, 210
  efforts, 180
  gender, 211
  perspectives, 205
  tradition, 210
Transformative gender justice framework (TGJF), 210
Transitory mood state, 587

Transportation, 639
Trial purchases, 18
Tripartite theory, 96, 324
Truthfulness, 83, 453

Uncertainty
  avoidance and, 58
  in priming, 587
Unemployment rate, 432–434
Uniqueness model, 123
Units of cognition, 227
Urgency, Premeditation, Perseverance, and Sensation Seeking (UPPS) scale, 231
Utilitarian products, 417
Utility, subjective, 623

Valence, 15, 591
  assessment of, 584
  shifts across, 340
Validity
  analysis of, 123
  of attitudes, 332
  convergent, 122, 123
  establishment of, 123
  of experiments, 136
  feelings of, 330
  of information, 330
  of measurements, 122, 130
  of scales, 253
  sense of, 329
  of tests, 121
  tests for, 120
  threats to, 112, 133
VALS approach, 271–272
Valuation
  automatic process of, 625
  brain regions associated with, 623–624
  choice and, 625
  neuroforecasting and, 626
  subjective, 623
Value measurements. *See also* Values
  alternatives to, 254
  laddering method, 249, 254
  List of Values (LOV), 249, 253, 254
  reliability of, 253
  Rokeach Value Survey (RVS), 249, 252, 253, 254
  Schwartz Value Scale (SVS), 249, 253, 254
  validity of, 253
Values. *See also* Needs; Social values; Value measurements; Value systems

adaptation value (AL), 678
adhesion to, 269
adoption of, 272
American-defining, 261
applications of, 274
approaches to, 271
attitudes and, 270
behavior and, 249, 252
categorization of, 275
celebrity, 252
chains, 261
changes in, 254, 260–263, 275, 674, 677
cognitions of, 286
common elements of, 249
compatibility of, 253
conformity of, 310
congruence, 252, 340
connections between, 277
consciousness, 222
consequences and, 254
conservation of, 313
consumer segmentation and, 253, 276
of consumption, 190
contemporary, 271
culture and, 260, 261, 276, 312
decision making and, 623
decline of, 260
deficit of, 253
definitions of, 249
deliberation and, 313
differentiation of, 254, 276
dimensions of, 253
endorsement of, 252, 314
end-states and, 250
excess, 253
external vs. internal, 253
focus on, 267
formation of, 176, 251–254, 262, 270, 274
fulfillment of, 251
fun-enjoyment-excitement, 260
global, 275, 276
goals and, 261
hierarchical structure of, 250, 270
impact of, 262, 276
importance of, 249, 251, 260
incongruent with arguments, 342
individual-level, 272
influence of, 276
influencing attitudes, 261
instrumental, 251–252, 252
integration of, 628

interdisciplinary application of, 271
internal excess, 260
internally focused vs. externally focused, 261
interpersonal, 253
inventory of, 271
judgments and, 249, 673
linking of, 275, 277
marketing to, 274, 276
materialistic, 196
measurement of, 276
mental schemas and, 252
meta-attitude vs., 270
motivations and, 275, 277
objectives and, 271
organization of, 253, 276
orientation of, 275
personal, 267
predictive power of, 277
probabilities of, 277
of products, 252
profiles of, 276
ranking of, 252
relevance of, 254
research into, 249, 252–253, 270, 275–276
respect, 260
scales of, 263
security, 261
segments of, 277
self-actualizing, 261
self-direction, 314
self-enhancement, 313
self-fulfillment, 260
self-respect, 254, 261
sense of accomplishment, 260
sense of belonging, 260, 272
shared, 262
similar, 253
social affiliation, 261
sports and, 278
stimulation, 314
system of, 270
terminal, 252, 275
theories of, 249
treatment of, 270
types of, 623
use of, 249, 253, 261
warm relationships, 260–261
well-being and, 642
women's, 260
Value systems
assessment of, 271

Rokeach Value Survey (RVS), 271, 275, 276
Schwartz Value Survey (SVS), 275
Variability
desire and, 228
interindividual, 226
intra-individual, 225, 234
patterns of, 312
in personality, 227
situational vs. temporal, 227
sources of, 220
theories of, 220
Variables
affecting persuasion, 328
antecedents, 693
cognitive, 92
of consumer behavior, 268
correspondence of, 132
dependent, 106, 120
empirical, 116
endogenous, 118
errors in, 116
factors and, 125, 126
gender as, 204
groups of, 269
high-thinking conditions, 328
independent, 120
indicators and, 117
individual difference, 114
intentional, 97
latent, 115
limited choice of, 268
low-thinking conditions, 328
mapping of, 227
of marketing, 91
measurement of, 131
mediation of, 128
mental, 82
mental state, 112
messages as, 339
metacognitive, 329
as moderators, 131–132
in motivation, 610, 612
of motivational affect, 590–591
multicollinearity and, 127
with multiple dimensions, 120
nonmanipulable vs. manipulable, 136
of personality, 220, 227, 269
predictability of, 104
proposed measures of, 117
regression of, 126
relationship of, 116
in research, 81
scales for, 132

Variables (*continued*)
  of segmentation, 616
  separation of, 131
  theoretical, 116
  unobservable hypothetical, 104, 109
Variance
  common, 117
  error, 116
  shared, 120
  sources of, 123
VC (vertical collectivism), 307
Ventral striatum (VS), 623
  automatic valuation process, 625
  predicted value correlation, 624
Ventromedial prefrontal cortex (VMPFC), 623
  automatic valuation process, 625
  predicted value correlation, 624
Venturesomeness, 231
Verbal behavior, 95
Verbal descriptions, 61
Verbal processors, 61
Vertical collectivism (VC), 307
Vertical–horizontal distinction, 307
Vertical individualism (VI), 307
Virtual reality (VR), 616
Visual information processors, 61
VI (vertical individualism), 307
VMPFC (ventromedial prefrontal cortex). *See* Ventromedial prefrontal cortex (VMPFC)
Volitional concepts, 612
Voluntary simplicity, 250, 640
VR (virtual reality), 616

VS (ventral striatum). *See* Ventral striatum (VS)
Vulnerability, 12, 169
  of children, 186
  consequences of, 170
  dimensions of, 170
  gender and, 207
  research on, 170

Warrick's principle, 729
Watchfulness, 596
Wealth, 674
Weber's law, 440–441
Websites, 628. *See also* Internet; Online
Well-being. *See also* Subjective well-being (SWB)
  affective, 637
  child and adolescent, 185, 194
  cognitive, 637
  concerns about, 195
  of consumers, 168
  eudaemonic, 640
  factors related to, 194
  hedonic, 640
  material, 179
  self-transcendence and, 641
  social networks and, 641
  spending decisions and, 638
  values and, 642
Western consumers, 639
We/They elitism, 721
What You See Is All There Is (WYSIATA), 537
Willingness to pay, 7, 623, 630

Willpower, 137
Women. *See also* Femininity
  body satisfaction of, 207
  coping practices of, 210
  female empowerment and, 209
  growth of, 260
  inequity experienced by, 210
  memory of, 50
  representations of, 209
  rise of, 260
  self-perceptions of, 207
  sense of belonging for, 260
  standards of beauty for, 209
  thin-ideal and, 207–208
  values of, 260
  in video games, 209
  violence against, 206
Word of mouth, 613
  explanations, 459
  functions of, 458
  modes of, 458
  negative, 612, 615
Work
  interests and attitudes toward, 272
  workmanship, 588
Working memory, 553
WYSIATA (What You See Is All There Is), 537

Youth outreach programs, 176
YouTube, 490, 629–630

Zeigarnik effect, 57